CHURCH AND SOCIETY

Church and Society

Catholic Social and Political Thought

and Movements

1789-1950

Edited by **Joseph N. Moody** *in collaboration with:*

Edgar Alexander
Carlos E. Castaneda
Francis Downing
Henry Haag
Carlos D. Hamilton
Christopher Hollis
William Juhasz
Charles Micaud
Zbiegniew Ossowski
Jaroslav Pechacek
Paul Vignaux
Adam Zoltowski

Arts, Inc. - New York

BR N5. 56
M 81

Library of Congress Catalog Card Number: 53-10712

The text of this book is set in Linotype Baskerville
at the Polyglot Press, New York City.

Printed in the United States of America

TO

FRANCIS CARDINAL SPELLMAN

Archbishop of New York

TABLE OF CONTENTS

DOCUMENTS

Man is older than the State. And prior to the formation of any State he holds by nature the right to provide for the life of his body!

Leo XIII, *Rerum Novarum*

The Church does not regard it as one of its duties to decide which form of government is the best or what are to be the institutions appropriate to the government of a Christian Policy. The Church rejects none of the various forms of State, provided only that religion and morality are protected!

Leo XIII, *Sapientiae Christianae*

Men are not created for the sake of the Church; the Church exists for the sake of Man: *propter nos homines et propter nostram salutem!*

Pius XI, *Allocution, February 28, 1927*

INTRODUCTION

by

JOSEPH N. MOODY

INTRODUCTION

The outstanding fact in European history in the four centuries since the Reformation has been its secularization. Accepting this term to mean the diminution of religious influence in political and social life, it is safe to say that the process is characteristic of the centuries called modern. It is still going on, despite some evidence of religious revival among certain groups and in certain countries. One cannot speak very optimistically of spiritual resurrection when millions of Christians are still descending into the tomb-like silence of Bolshevist tyranny. Even the claim that compensating gains have been made in the new lands opened by exploration is less valid today when large areas are being closed to Christian missionary effort.

The Catholic Church has suffered acutely from this process which has introduced sharp tension into the modern history of all religious bodies. She has lost a large proportion of her adherents and much of her influence in the ancient strongholds of her faith. These members have been lost in a variety of ways: many, from Luther till today, have left her of their own choice; many others, from the peasants of northern Europe in the sixteenth century to the continental industrial workers of the nineteenth, have drifted away imperceptibly under the impact of adverse conditions; still others were torn from her by violence. It is important to recognize that not all the victories of secularism have been won peacefully. Reforming princes in the sixteenth and Russian Czars in the nineteenth century used force to change the religious affiliation of their subjects. So, Jacobin proconsuls and Kremlin agents applied violence to win recruits to new secular creeds. Even more common has been the use of State power to exert pressure against the free exercise of Catholicism. The restrained letter of the Archbishop of Malines, asking for a minimum of liberty in the practice of the Catholic faith,[1] is an interesting instance because it was a success and because it illustrates the dimensions of the problem. But it was unusual. In most cases protests were of no avail. Nearly every continental European country in the nineteenth century affords examples of legislative discrimination against Catholicism.

Were this the whole story, we would have a simple record of persecution. But it is not. Catholics in the modern centuries have not merely suffered violence at the hands of the political powers. They have also used it for their purposes. There is truth, as well as paradox, in Lamennais' lament[2] that the time is long past when Catholics should sever the connection between their faith and the denial of liberty. Nothing has been more damaging to the long-range interests of Catholicism than the use of State coercion in religious matters. The men of the Enlightenment were able to filch the title of Rationalism from the heirs of Aquinas; they were successful in appropriating the mantle of science from the descendants of Albertus Magnus and Copernicus; but their greatest triumph was the taking of the banner of liberty from those who had inherited the tradition of Ambrose and Suarez.

The last point invites elucidation. Christianity is founded on the strict monotheistic concept of its Judaic antecedents. Since God is one, the human race is a natural unit, deriving from a single ancestor and possessing a common nature. Since man is a spiritual as well as material being, he is the highest product of creation: he has been made in the image of God. His nature is both rational and free, and it is these capacities which constitute human dignity.

It was to protect this human dignity that the Christian ethical system, germinal in the Gospels, was elaborated, with the emphasis on the correlative functioning of rights and duties, and with its double focus on relationships to God and to fellow man. This Christian moral code was a projection of the Mosaic, with important additions drawn from the Gospels. In its roots, as in its flowering, it had as its primary purpose the defense of the human person, who was inviolable because of his spiritual heritage. It is this emphasis which has ever protected Christians from the appeal of fatalism and materialism which would have linked man's destiny to the stars or to the earth.

But Christianity not merely included in its teaching the religious personalism of the Old and New Testaments. It also, at least in the West, reinforced its philosophical teaching by the natural law personalism of the Stoics. The latter had introduced into Western thought the concept of the personal autonomy of the concrete human being. On this premise, they proclaimed man's liberty and the idea of a universal natural order from which they derived their doctrine of the natural law. Cicero, Seneca, and Marcus Aurelius gave wide circulation to these ideas in the Roman world, and through them they passed into the heritage of Latin Christianity. Four great fathers of the

West—Tertullian, Cyprian, Ambrose and Augustine[3]—all concentrate their attention on the living human person. They distinguished sharply between res profanae (worldly affairs) and res sacrae (religious affairs), and thus rejected Caesaro-Papism and oriental despotism. The Church was to be independent of the political and administrative powers; hence there could be no all-embracing political collectivism. They also distinguished between res publicae and res privatae, which is the crux of any defense against totalitarianism. And they defended the maxim, "Grace perfects nature," by which they meant that the divine action sanctifies man by operating in his natural equipment—a view that was the magna carta of human dignity.

This last point suggests the importance of two central doctrines of Christianity—the Incarnation and the Redemption—in reinforcing the Christian view of the value of man. All religions aim to make man aware of God. But only Christianity dared affirm that God so loved man that He accepted our human condition and became one with us. The purpose of this identification was human salvation, which was nothing less than the capacity of man to share God's life while he lived on earth so that he might enjoy perfect union with God after death. This salvation was not to be confined to a favored few in Catholic Christianity. It was open to all men, for all were the objects of a momentous divine intervention and all were to be one in Christ.

Christianity, like all religions, was acutely aware of the latent possibilities of evil in man. It had no illusions as to the destructive potentialities of man's freedom and intelligence when they were harnassed for malicious ends. Yet no creed has ever etched more glorious possibilities for human nature, which was declared capable of exalted development since it had once held captive the Godhead Itself. This implied not merely the divinization of a few exceptional men like the heroes of the ancient myths whose qualities seemed too exceptional to be encased in the weak flesh which bound their fellows. For the Christian, all men could be saved and united with God.

These beliefs were set forth in one of the earliest defenses of the faith to come from the primitive Church, the Epistle to Diognetus:

"For God loved mankind for whose sake He made the world, to whom He subjected all things which are in the earth, to whom He gave reason, to whom He gave mind, on whom alone He enjoined that they should look upward to Him, whom He made in His own image, to whom He

sent His only begotten Son, to whom He promised the
Kingdom in heaven,—and He will give it to them who
love Him. And when you have this full knowledge, with
what joy do you think that you will be filled, or how
greatly will you love Him who thus first loved you? But
by your love you will imitate the example of His goodness.
And do not wonder that it is possible for man to be the
imitator of God; it is possible when he will. For happiness
consists not in the domination over neighbors, nor in
wishing to have more than the weak, nor in the wealth and
power to compel those who are poorer, nor can anyone be
an imitator of God in doing these things, but these things
are outside His majesty. But whoever takes up the burden
of his neighbor, and wishes to help another, who is worse
off in that in which he is stronger, and by ministering to
those in need the things which he has received and holds
from God becomes a god to those who receive them,—
this man is an imitator of God. . . ." [4]

These beliefs were not intended to be cherished as abstractions; they were intended for application to concrete living. The
purpose of Christianity is social—to establish the Kingdom of
God on earth, to build a universal society in which the world
and humanity would be transformed and without which man
would find it impossible to realize his spiritual destiny.

Hence, those who held these religious beliefs logically attempted to apply them to political thought. In this task the
early Christians were assisted by their struggle for survival in
the pagan Roman Empire. In the Imperial Age, religion was
associated with loyalty to the State. Great latitude was permitted the citizens of the Empire in the worship of their local gods
provided this was not considered detrimental to the public
order. But reverence was demanded toward the imperial deities
as a symbol of patriotism. It was the Christians rejection of this
official cult which led to their persecution.

The pages of the early Christian Fathers are filled with protests against this constraint. Minucius Felix, Tertullian, and
Arnobius attacked the legal enactments and official acts in the
name of liberty of conscience. The essence of their argument
can be seen in these sentences from Lactantius:

"There is no point in recourse to violence and injustice,
because religion cannot be forced, (religio cogi non potest).
Words, and not physical means, can alone act on the human will . . . . We do not draw anyone against his inclina-

tion. Only God can bring faith and piety to non-believers. We defend religion, not by killing, but by dying, not by cruelty, but by patience. One does not defend religion by blood and torture; one defiles it thereby. For there is nothing so free as religious assent. . . .The pagans themselves destroy their gods by the distrust of their power: they are impious rather than atheistic. . . .There is no true sacrifice when it is extorted by force; if it is not spontaneous and sincere, it becomes a sacrilege. . . .For our God, we do not seek a forced adoration, and in case of refusal we are not irritated: we have too much confidence in His power." [5]

This persistent demand for religious liberty was finally written by Constantine into the Edict of Milan (313) in almost the exact terms in which generations of Christians had phrased it: "We have decided to grant to Christians and to all others the right to practice the religion of their choice. . . .It has appeared to us very just and reasonable not to deny to any of our subjects either Christian or otherwise, the right to practice the religion that appeals to them." It was not because he felt the State was incompetent in theology that Constantine granted toleration. There was an element of utility—religious liberty would aid pacification—and greater emphasis on the new Emporer's unwillingness to offend any deity. But the cardinal idea was the acceptance of the oft-repeated Christian claim that religion must be free: "It is necessary that the Supreme Being, whose cult we practice with free minds (*cujus religioni liberis mentibus obsequimur*), will in all things grant us his favor and benevolence." [6] It is, of course, a matter of historical record that when the Christians had gained toleration and an increasingly dominant position in the Empire, they invoked the secular authority against those who had recently been their persecutors!

This illustrates a simple truth: the transference of theological principle to the domain of political fact was made by fallible men who were seriously conditioned by the general historical currents of their age and by the realities of their own position. Thus, a wide variety of political concepts have been justified by Christians in the course of their history. But in this maze of conflicting political opinions held by professed Christians a few general points of agreement are revealed:

1. A Christian cannot logically accept the divinization of the State. An omnipotent State clearly violates the words of the Gospel.

2. The realization of justice can be the only true end and objective of the State. When a political power acts contrary to a rationally determined justice, it becomes a "great robber." [7]

3. Though human freedom may be diminished on the basis of other demands, the fundamental truth of man's free nature remains a central doctrine of Catholic Christianity and finds at least some reflection in its political thought.

In this volume, there are citations from Suarez[8] which maintain as Catholic political theory: that an unjust law does not require obedience; that political power resides in the community as a whole and cannot be transferred to specific individuals without common consent; that unjust rulers can be eliminated under certain conditions; that it is morally wrong to coerce unbelievers into the Catholic faith; and that unbelievers should be allowed to practice their own religion, provided its ceremonies are not contrary to the natural law, i.e., not involving infanticide, incest, polygamy, etc. This Spanish Jesuit of the early seventeenth century, like every other Christian political thinker, was unquestionably influenced by the special currents of his time. In his case, the effects of Spain's dramatic expansion into the New World and the widening knowledge of the variations of human culture attendant upon it, certainly affected his thought. Yet he claimed a consistent tradition for each of the points mentioned above and carefully cited numerous authorities from the Bible to St. Thomas to support his positions.

But while Suarez was reaffirming and expanding traditional political positions, new historical forces were reshaping Western Europe and making themselves felt in the political thinking of Catholics. During the Middle Ages, Europe had made an effort to build it social and political life on the basis of a unity of theological faith.[9] The attempt was relatively successful for several centuries, but new currents in the fifteenth weakened it, while the Reformation created a schism in the body of Europe which turned out to be permanent. Yet so powerful was the concept of a united Christendom that men were reluctant to surrender it in the face of new realities. Catholics struggled to restore universal religious unity. Protestants were determined to insure the religious homogeneity of particular states, national or regional. This reluctance to accept the reality of religious division contributed to the "religious wars," during which the hostile camps attempted to reestablish unity by battle. The effort led to exhaustion and the tardy abandonment of the concept of political unity founded on religion. Ultimately, men were obliged to seek a new basis for political agreement; but their indisposition to do so is still apparent in the laymen who drew up the Civil Constitution of the Clergy in the initial phase of the French Revolution.[10]

The weakening of the idea that political society should rest on religious community of opinion led men to seek a substitute foundation in "Reason" or "Humanity." They proposed that a common set of principles could be readily discovered by the observation of nature and that these could be welded into a "scientific" creed to which all would give assent.[11] In the pursuit of this objective, they developed an indifference to or hostility toward religion. The more adventurous maintained that the task of reconstructing human unity would be facilitated if all superstition, i.e., religion, were suppressed. Thus, the claims of competing creeds would be ignored and common ground discovered in the self-evident principles, clearly perceptible in the visible world.

At the opening of the period covered by this volume, there existed two competing ideologies which advanced different principles for the organization of human society. The more recent was the non-religious, or "secularist," which maintained that religion was a private affair that had no place in public life and that its standards had no relevance to politics or economics. This radical innovation in thought, which had been gathering force for several centuries, would in itself have represented a challenge to the existing religious authorities. But the challenge was more direct since the supporters of the new viewpoint often professed an immense scorn toward religious values and an hostility toward religious institutions. The nineteenth century would witness the conflict between these divergent conceptions.

But if two opinions on the relations of religion and politics had crystallized by 1789, the realities were still on the side of the "established church," a religious body granted favor and support by the State for the fulfillment of its mission. In England, this establishment did not prevent a certain amount of liberty to certain classes of dissenters. In the federal constitution of the emergent American Republic, religious diversity had prompted an attitude of benevolent neutrality by the State towards all creeds.[12] But these were exceptions to the general pattern in Catholic and Protestant areas alike.

The gradual accumulation of centralized state power in the centuries before 1789 had altered the relations of Church and government in the states of the Old Regime. Support generally implied various degrees of control over the ecclesiatical establishment, which control was justified by the theories known variously as regalism, Febronianism, and Gallicanism. This power over the religious bodies made the ruling powers of these states as unwilling to accept the thesis that religion was a private affair, as were most religious bodies, both Catholic and Protestant, to surrender the tangible advantages that flowed from state support.

It is the purpose of this volume to trace some of the tangled relations of *sacerdorium* and *imperium,* or Church and State, in the last century and a half, and to outline the varying reactions of Catholics to those movements which proclaimed human liberty as their slogan.

A certain pattern will be seen to emerge in the regional studies which form the substance of this volume. In a certain number of modern states, Catholics had never experienced the phenomenon of the "established church", with the financial support and preferential position accorded to Catholicism in return for wide state control over the national Church in the appointment of bishops, etc. This was the case in the United States, Great Britain and Ireland, Canada, Australia, New Zealand, South Africa, the British Empire, Belgium, the Netherlands, the North German States (and the German Empire after 1871), Scandinavia, and generally speaking in Switzerland and Poland. In these areas, Catholics found little difficulty in adjusting to the new political conditions of the nineteenth century: to the trend toward the Liberal and later to the democratic state with its emphasis on civil rights, toleration to all religious groups, and no special privilege to Catholicism. Not only did these Catholics adjust readily as De Tocqueville noted in respect to American Catholics, but they found it hard to appreciate the difficulties of their co-religionists who had a different historical experience.

In a second area, in the Iberian Peninsula, Latin America, France, the Italian States, and the area of the Austrian-Hungarian Empire, Catholics had known the established church, with its tangible advantages and its less evident disadvantages. That Catholics found it difficult to disentangle themselves from this experience and accept the new political conditions, is the second major fact in this survey. This dichotomy in the historical experience of modern Catholics in their relations to the modern State is the cause of considerable confusion. We hope this study will clarify this basic factor.

There is a second field of interest within the compass of this study. For several centuries before 1789, Europe had been developing a complex commercial civilization which had profoundly affected its class structure and its views toward the acquisition of wealth.[13] This economic and social transformation was to be enormously intensified (in the period embraced in this volume) by the utilization of new sources of energy. The tempo of change would be greatly accelerated. This volume will survey the attitude of Catholics to this "social question" as magnified by the expanding industrialism.

Theoretically, Catholics should not have found it difficult to reject the doctrines of Economic Liberalism, or *Laissez-faire*, which was the entelechy of the long effort by men of business to assert their autonomy against any restraining influences. A rooted assumption of Christianity had always been that the moral law extends to all human activity. In no field had Christians been more explicit in stating the claims of morality than in the economic.

Basing their views on the Gospel, Christians from the beginning expressed a profound concern for the poor. The poor were *blessed* because they were in the same material status as Christ. They needed only to keep themselves worthy of that status; the rich must struggle to attain it, by detaching themselves from riches—by becoming poor in spirit—and by loving, honoring, and aiding the actual poor.[14] The wealthy must remember that they have the same human nature as the poor and must base their relationships on the recognition of this fact.[15] The rich must give their surplus goods to the poor as *gifts*; for they are brothers in Christ and must always be treated as friends.[16] Nor have the rich any title to these goods when others are in want since they are not absolute owners of property but only stewards and dispensers:

> "Those who neither make after others' goods nor bestow their own are to be admonished to take it to heart that the earth they come from is common to all and brings forth nurture for all alike. Idly then do men hold themselves innocent when they monopolize for themselves the common gift of God. In not giving what they have received, they work their neighbors' death; every day they destroy all the starving poor whose means to relief they store at home. When we furnish the destitute with any necessity, we render them what is theirs, not bestow on them what is ours; we pay the debt of justice rather than perform the works of mercy. . . ."[17]

This did not imply a Manichean attitude that material things are evil in themselves; they become evil only when unlawfully acquired or used. The ideal remained a freely accepted poverty; but destitution, or the absence of the basic necessities, was declared to be an evil that was an obstacle to spiritual progress. A

poverty that had sufficiency of worldly goods was more conducive to virtue than were riches since it freed one from pride and
the anxieties which accompany wealth.[18]

Nowhere is this classic Christian position on the social question more vigorously expressed than in Ambrose. In both his
political and economic thinking, this Latin Father was indebted
to non-Christian authors, particularly the Stoics; and his teaching entered the common body of Western Christian tradition
both through his own influence and that of his pupil, Augustine. In *De Nabuthae*,[19] he sets forth his premise: "For all has
the world been created, which you few rich men are trying to
keep for yourselves."[20] Hence, "not from your own do you bestow upon the poor man, but you make return from what is his.
*For what has been given as common for the use of all, you ap-
propriate to yourself alone. The earth belongs to all, not to the
Rich*; but fewer are those who do not use what belongs to all
than those who do. Therefore you are paying a debt, you are
not bestowing what is not due." [21]

Yet the rich ignore their obligations and criminally oppress
their brethren. They even use religion as a cloak:

> "You may see them at such times coming to church, duti-
> ful, humble, and assiduous, in order that they may deserve
> to obtain the accomplishment of their wickedness."[22] " . . .
> Do you hear, O rich man, what the Lord God says. You
> too come to church, not to bestow anything on a poor man
> but to take away. You fast, not that the cost of your ban-
> quet may profit the needy, but that you might obtain spoil
> from those in want. . ." [23]

But "Mercy is sown on earth, germinates in heaven, is trans-
planted in the poor man, and grows with God."[24]

One of the strongest elements in this tradition is the prohibition against usury—taking advantage of a brother's need by
lending him money at interest. Generations of Popes, councils
and fathers inveigh against this practice, citing evidence from
the Old Testament as proof of its inherent immorality. Ambrose's tract, *De Tobia*,[25] cites the principle: "Lending by
which usury is sought is evil," [26] and then proceeds with the
indictment:

> "For what is more vile than the man who puts out money
> at interest today and requires it tomorrow. Such a man
> is hateful, Scripture says. For bland is the giving, but cruel
> the exaction. . . .One sum is given by the usurers, and how

many are exacted from the debtors! How many terms have they made for themselves! Money is given, it is called a loan; it is termed money at interest, it is designated capital; it is written down as debt; this huge monster of many heads (capitum) causes frequent exactions. . . ."[27]

"This feeding on another's hunger" is explicitly condemned, says Ambrose. After citing several Old Testament texts, he concludes: "This decision of God has excluded in general all increase of capital."[28] Rather than being concerned with expanding his capital, the rich man should be primarily interested in the welfare of his employees:

"And whence do you know that you may not defraud some just man of his hire—this is worse if he be infirm, for 'woe to him that shall scandalize one of these little ones.' How do you know whether there be an angel in him? For we ought not to doubt that there can be an angel in the hired servant, since Christ can be, who is accustomed to be in the least. Give the hired servant his reward therefore and do not defraud him of the price of his labor, because you too are a hired servant of Christ. . . .Do not therefore injure the servant working in truth, nor the hired servant giving his life; do not despise the needy man who spends his life at his labor and maintains it by his hire. For this is to kill a man, to deny him the succor required for his life. You too are a hired servant on this earth; give his reward to the hired servant. . . ."[29]

This ancient attitude toward wealth and interest, so rooted in the Christian tradition, was subjected to increasing strain as the commercial revolution transformed European social life in the later Medieval and early modern period. "The spirit of Capitalism", in Tawney's phrase, came to be the prevailing attitude. The old exhortations and prohibitions continued to be made, but with less emphasis and certainly with less effect. By the date that marks the beginning of this volume, the older religious and moral restrictions had been completely repudiated by the social class most directly involved. The man of business explicitly declared that he was confined by no bonds other than the laws of the market and the operation of his self-interest. Only by the working of these "natural laws" would the social welfare be achieved. Ethical considerations were irrelevant.

The second area of investigation in this volume is an attempt to see how Catholics reacted to this changed economic climate and to the social problems arising from the new techniques of production.

To assay the attitudes of Catholics in these two fields, a few generalizations must be attempted. To use Wilfrid Ward's phrase Catholicism in the modern centuries has been in a "state of siege." The shattering of religious unity in the Reformation, and the attacks on the foundations of religion which followed, left an enduring impression on the Catholic mind. Catholics tended to consider themselves as perpetually on the defensive. As a consequence, they inclined rather to concentrate on preserving positions from assault than on exploring new implications of their heritage. The vigorous application of religious principles to new situations, so characteristic of a figure like Aquinas, was a quality rare among Catholics in the nineteenth century.

Besides, the general intellectual climate of that century was intensely unfavorable to the religious values which Catholics professed. The dominant economic philosophy was basically hostile to Christianity and irreconcilable with it. Economic Liberalism was, in a sense, a rival faith, founded on the worship of technique as its central *mystique*, on science viewed as religion, and on a boundless faith in human reason, narrowly understood. Its utilitarian ethics ignored all values that did not immediately contribute to man's economic needs. Religion was banished from the market place, and in its niche was enshrined the goddess of unrestrained freedom in the pursuit of economic satisfaction. Equally in politics, the claim of religion to be heard in public affairs was denied. Churches were regarded as merely voluntary associations with which the State should concern itself only as they affected public order. More fundamentally, the unlimited optimism of the age led to the rejection of the basic Christian doctrine of original sin and the Redemption.

Catholics entered this critical period with certain predispositions drawn from their immediate past. All peoples are the product of their historical experience. In the centuries immediately preceding the nineteenth, Catholics had lived in the stuffy atmosphere of the Old Regime. The fact conditioned their attitude to the new forces and modes of thought. Since these had implicitly or directly declared themselves hostile to the principles of Christianity, adjustment would be painful and delayed. Actually, there was a point of contact in the concept of the dignity of the human person, which was professed by believers and non-believers. But time was needed on both sides to reveal the possibility of some common elements. It was only when contemporary catastrophes and the threat of totalitarian-

ism had shattered the complacency of the non-religious, and
when Catholics had re-explored the roots of their tradition,
that a more favorable climate began to exist in our time.

The scope of this volume, then is strictly limited. It is not a
history of Catholicism since the French Revolution. The
Catholic Church is essentially a religious body,[30] and its spiritual doctrines and interests are its primary concern. But they lie
outside the purview of this volume. This is no effort to trace
the religious life of the Church, to examine its formulations
of theology or canon law, to sketch the lives of its saints or the
work of its religious orders, or to consider the remarkable vitality of its missions. All of these considerations are formally pre-
cinded from; they may be touched upon where they are deemed
necessary adjuncts to the major theme. That theme is the relation of Catholics to the major secular forces of the period
1789-1950.   ,

Such a point of view determines the judgements that are
reached in these pages. One would obviously render a different
verdict if he treated Gregory XVI as the Pope who revitalized
the foreign missons, or if he confined his attention to the Pope's
efforts to maintain his political position in Central Italy. Likewise, one would portray French Catholics differently were he to
treat of the Curé of Ars, Bernadette of Lourdes, and Thérèse
of Lisieux instead of the blatant political errors of French
Catholics as a citizenry. The sole concern of this volume is the
social and political activity of Catholics, and their efforts to
erect a theoretical structure that would satisfy the demands of
their tradition amid the pressures of the age.

Roughly speaking, Catholic opinion in this period tended to
divide itself along these lines:

1. The authoritarian, which exalted order over liberty and
aimed at the preservation of those political and political-
ecclesiastical arrangements which were characteristic of the Old
Regime. After a century of rear-guard action that ended in
frustration, certain strands of this tendency blended with dynamic movements of non-Christian inspiration, such as *Action
française* or Italian Fascism. In the social field, the authoritarians desired to retain the older hierarchical structure of secular society, yet often made genuinely sympathetic gestures
toward the growing industrial proletariat.

2. The "Liberal," which sought to relate Catholicism to the
Constitutional State, to freedom of thought and expression, to
bourgeois domination of politics and culture, and to the prevailing economic theories which justified this domination.

Hence these Catholics tended to be accommodating toward political change but resistant to movements which expressed the discontent of the working class.

3. The Christian Democratic which supported the widest possible extension of political rights and at the same time favored movements and doctrines that emphasized the social welfare of the working classes, both urban and rural. This group generally labored under many handicaps, but were gradually strengthened, particularly after the appearance of the modern Encyclicals.

In order to see these trends in their concrete historical relationship, it is necessary to break down this study on a regional or national basis. This should aid the reader to concentrate on actual conditions rather than on abstractions. It should also reveal how impossible it is to generalize in regard to a Catholic position on politics and social matters, without taking careful account of the diverse factors which have shaped the thinking of Catholics in different geographical and historical settings.

To encourage the reader to pass his own judgment on the intellectual efforts of Catholics in the fields under discussion, there has been appended to each section some selections by Catholic authors on political and social questions. The efforts has been to make these citations as representative as possible of the major trends of Catholic thought.

This is intended as an exploratory study. It does not attempt to prove a thesis. The effort has been made to avoid thinking in formulae or in terms of single casuality. The volume contains a number of parallel "case histories," built around a common theme, but exhibiting wide diversity. It is hoped that a study of these will throw some light on a number of questions to which too facile answers have often been given:

1. Has Catholicism a preconceived doctrinal attitude that prevented it from accepting Liberalism and democracy, as the anticlerical thesis of Quinet and Michelet contends?

Does its concentration on its mission of salvation give it a natural propensity toward theocracy?

Or, to what degree is the position of Catholics on temporal matters influenced by external conditions, favorable or unfavorable to the Church, inclining them to act in a particular way in response to those conditions?

To what extent have social forces influenced the position of Catholics, and, dialectically, in what respect have these positions reacted on the social conditions? Here the geographical-historical extension of the study should be of value, for the reaction of

Catholics to new forces has obviously been different in the English-speaking world, in France, in Latin Europe, in Germany, and in the Slav States. But how different and why? Are there further significant differences within the national boundaries as between the Basques and the rest of Spain, between the Rhineland and the South Germans, the North and North-east and the rest of France?

2. Is the Church necessarily conservative because of its institutional character—institutional in the broad sense, not merely including property and economic interests but also its religious interest in saving souls?

Does this ecclesiastical aspect of the Church incline it to resist change?

Yet, granted that Catholics must adjust themselves to new secular forces to survive, does the *tempo* of change affect their disposition to accept new historical forces?

Specifically, do they find it easier to fit into new regimes that develop as a result of gradualism and peaceful evolution, as in England and the United States, than into those that come into being by way of revolution, as in France?

Again, is the reactionary position of some Catholics in certain circumstances due in part to the apparent instability of new revolutionary regimes, giving rise to the hope that the "good old days" may yet return?

Finally, after an upheaval, may not Catholics come to reflect one side for historical reasons, thereby making it difficult for them to reach a rapprochement with the forces of change?

3. To what extent does the minority position of Catholics in a particular country incline them to the liberal position?

Is this to be explained on the anticlerical assumption that they are liberal or democratic only when they have to be, or, are there other considerations present?

4. To what extent is the attitude of Catholics in any area determined by the social group to which most of them belong, e.g., the aristocratic-peasant in Spain as against the immigrant in the United States?

To what extent does the social basis of the clergy affect Catholic thinking?

5. How has the position of the Church been affected by nationalism?

What is the result of Catholicism's becoming the cement of nationalist forces against foreign oppression as in Ireland and Poland, or, of its becoming the link with imperial interests against nationalist aspirations as in the old Austro-Hungarian Empire?

6. To what extent does the Pope's international position affect the thinking of Catholics on political issues?

7. What happens when a regime, such as the First or Second French Empire, uses the Church to win popular support or even to suppress political opposition?

8. To what extent has historical accident shaped the views of Catholics?

9. To what extent does the absence of anticlericalism, as in England and in the United States, assist adjustment?

We are not rash enough to propose that one short study of this type can give definite answers to these and related questions. But it may start thinking along these lines and thus curtail the effect of those generalizations which are proposed all too frequently in this area. What has been aimed at is a survey of the general political and psychological atmosphere of the period, with the local variations that influenced particular regions. Only on this basis can we explain why the new secular forces which made their appearance in the nineteenth century appeared potentially or actually dangerous to some Catholics, while to others they appeared neutral or favorable. While these relationships may not be subject to exact analysis, their consideration may open fields for further study. A study of Catholic Social theories as a companion piece to this volume is already projected.

J. N. Moody.

NOTES

1 Cited below, pp. 319-322.

2 Text, see pp. 229; 232; 319.

3 Augustine incorporated all these positions in the first great Christian synthesis. Cf. Edgar Alexander, *Christianity and the Middle East;* chapt. I, *Rome and Western Christianity.* Cornell Univ. Press, Ithaca, 1953.

4 Greek and English text in Loeb Classical Library, *The Apostolic Fathers,* Vol. II, chap. X, pp. 371-372. The precise date of this epistle is unknown, but it is commonly ascribed to the second century.

5 *Dictionnaire d'archeologie chrétienne et de liturgie,* Paris, Letouzey et Ane, 1930, Tome IX, p. 546.

6 *Idem,* pp. 545-546.

7 Augustine, *City of God,* Bk. IV, ch. 4; Bk. XIX, ch. 21

8 Cf. below, pp. 786-789.

9 Jacques Maritain in *Man and the State,* Chicago Univ. Press, 1951, pp. 108 sq., uses the striking adjective *sacral* to describe the Medieval ideal, in contrast with the *secular* or temporal approach of contemporary thought. It is strongly recommended that readers of this volume acquaint themselves with M. Maritain's most recent work, which is a convenient synthesis of his mature political thought. It is an outstanding example of present-day Catholic thinking on political questions and is an essential companion-piece to this study.

10 Cf. below, pp. 110-1.

11 If some did not, then force would have to be applied; cf. the observations of Rousseau on Civil Religion in the *Social Contract*, Bk. IV, ch. 8, pp. 106-115, in the Carlton House edition.

12 Four of the state constitutions retained an established church.

13 For the effect of social change on the intellectual patterns of the period, cf. Harold J. Laski, *The Rise of European Liberalism*, 2nd ed., London, George Allen and Unwin, 1947, particularly pp. 161-237.

14 St. Leo the Great, *Sermon* 95, 2.

15 Augustine, *Enarrationes in Psalmos,* 72, No. 26.

16 Gregory of Nazienzen, *Verses against the Rich*, Migne, *Patrologia Graeca*, Vol. XXXVII, pp. 856-884.

17 Pope Gregory the Great, *Regulae Pastoralis Liber*, III, 21.

18 Jerome, *Epistola ad Rusticum, 125, 20;* Thomas, *Summa Theologica*, II, II, 3 ad 3; 188, 7, c. A convenient summary of patristic selections on this theme will be found in Walter Shewring, *Rich and Poor in Christian Tradition*, London, Burns, Oates and Washbourne, 1948.

19 The most convenient text and commentary by Martin R. P. McGuire, Patristic Studies XV, Washington, Catholic Univ. Press, 1927.

20 *Idem*, p. 53.

21 *Idem*, p. 83.

22 *Idem*, p. 75.

23 *Idem*, p. 77

24 *Idem*, p. 83.

25 Good text and commentary by Lois Miles Zucker in Patristic Studies XXXV, Washington, Catholic Univ. Press, 1933.

26 *Idem*, p. 27.

27 *Idem*, p. 57.

28 *Idem*, p. 67.

29 *Idem*, p. 103.

30 Cf. the essay on Germany in this volume, chap. I, *The Sociological Problematic of Catholicism.*

PART I:

THE PAPACY

*The Church and the New Forces
in Western Europe and Italy*

by

JOSEPH N. MOODY

THE NEW FORCES AND THE PAPACY

1. *The Time of Resistance* (1789-1878)

In the eighteenth century, the Papacy exercised little influence in Europe's public life.[1] Its spiritual position as head of Catholic Christendom was recognized by Catholics, but its direct control over the various segments of the Church was checked by the secular powers. Considerable concessions in ecclesiastical government had been gained by the monarchs and princes of Catholic Europe. The prevailing regalist doctrine reinforced the tendency of the civil power to dispose of, according to its own interest, those affairs of the Church which the State considered to be within its jurisdiction. The Regalists had proclaimed the subordination of the Church to the State and had justified the right of the latter to use its coercive power to enforce its claims against the Church. In their view, only the constant supervision by government would insure the Church's proper discharge of its duties. They, therefore, demanded that the State control the calling of all synods, maintain the right to veto the promulgation of all bulls, pass judgment on appeals against clerical "abuses," regulate the use of Church property, and confiscate that property if it were not used in conformity with the terms of its donation or with the interests of the State. Behind these specific points was the general proposition that the State was supreme in its territories and that any compromise of its "sacred freedom" in its dealings with the Church would lead to its enslavement.[2]

This prevailing interpretation of Church-State relationships did not remain academic. It was the driving force behind much of the ecclesiastical policy of Louis XV, Joseph II, Pombal, and many other eighteenth century men of affairs. Such a political doctrine was rarely pushed to its utmost conclusion, but its net effect was to deprive the Papacy of the effective direction of many matters of primary concern for the spiritual welfare of the Church.

Papal resistance to these concepts was only feebly persistent. The Popes of the eighteenth century were uniformly upright men—pious, vigilant, and apostolic—but only one, Benedict XIV (1740-1758), had the strength or perception to oppose adequately the prevailing currents unfavorable to the cause of religion. He alone grasped the significance of that great movement of ideas, the Enlightenment, and attempted positive steps to counteract its influence by establishing societies for higher ecclesiastical studies. Generally, the intellectual defense of the Church remained weak in the face of the most serious attack it had yet sustained.

Pius VI (1775-1799), a typically pious pope of the Old Regime, was called upon to face a momentous crisis. Having delayed eight months before condemning the Civil Constitution,[3] he finally declared it contrary to the constitution of the Church and motivated by a false concept of religious liberty. His symapthies were fully on the side of the harrassed Louis XVI. His initial distaste for the course of events in France deepened proportionately to the anti-religious activities of Revolutionary governments. By 1795, France had secured possession of Belgium and the Left Bank of the Rhine,[4] and was vigorously applying her anti-clerical policy in the conquered provinces. The defeat of the First Coalition in the same year freed the Revolutionary armies for a descent upon Italy and brought the Revolution and the Papacy into dramatic confrontation.

The consequences of that conflict were to affect the history of the Church for more than a century. The struggle with Napoleon was but one phase of the Papacy's long effort to check the consequences of 1789. Since we know the final verdict, it is easy for us to pass judgment on the defenders of a lost cause. For one thing, however, it is doubtfully valid to base an analysis solely on the long-range results of a policy; by such standards, many otherwise noble human decisions could be censured. The precise historical conditions in which decisions are made and the limiting factors of tradition must also be considered. Our current situation should incline us to moderation in judgment: today, we are acutely aware of the difficulty men face in appraising, and adapting themselves to, a new complex of political realities. Hesitation in the face of the sudden and the threatening is not a characteristic limited to nineteenth century clerics.

In meeting the Revolution and its impact on Italy in the period under review (1789-1878), the Papacy had to contend with the following factors:

1. The new political force had exploded in Europe with revolutionary intensity. As such, it had caused considerable

damage to the material interests and moral influence of the
Catholic Church. Side by side with the Revolution marched
Secularism, often enough attended by the grim specter of persecution. To the Popes of the period, the new political forces
must have appeared as threatening as the Soviet menace to the
West of today. Once this impression was fixed, it was not easily
exorcised. Pacca notes that the fear that a general revolution
would politically destroy the Church was one of the principal
causes for Gregory XVI's decision to condemn *L'Avenir*.[5]

2. Many of the revolutionaries were avowedly anti-clerical
and made no effort to hide their intention of destroying the
Papacy as an obstacle to progress. This was the attitude of
Barras and two of his fellow members of the Directory as the
French moved into Lombardy in 1796. It was the view of many
other champions of the Liberal creed. Such opinions precluded
a proper estimate of the programs for change. The intransigence
of Pius IX can be explained largely as his reaction to the
anti-clerical nature of the Piedmontese regime.

3. Even under the best conditions, it would have required
considerable skill to detach the Church from the practices of
the Old Regime. While these practices had been only accidentally or historically connected with Catholicism, centuries
of habit had interwoven them in a sort of inter-locking tapestry.
New conditions demanded the kind of modification which
would call for a peaceful evolutionary situation in which both
sides could exercise moderation and tact. This never took
place.

4. Had the first onslaught of the Revolution brought complete triumph to the new political principles, the Papacy would
have been compelled to make its peace. But the victory was
only partial. In Britain, after an initial conflict in which Catholics were reduced to an impotent minority, the interests of
religion were not directly affected in an adverse manner, once
the movement became evolutionary. In France, the impact
truly had been severe, but the full success of the Revolution
was checked under the Restoration. Elsewhere, in Central,
Southern and Eastern Europe, the new ideas had been resisted
and ultimately defeated. In most of the European states after
1815, the defenders of the old order were in control. The fact
that Metternich could preside as the dominant figure on the
Continent for a third of a century indicates that the issue was
far from settled. The victorious powers set down at Vienna a
policy of containment and opposition. They had restored the
Papal States in the name of Legitimacy. They were closer to
the center of papal activity and could more readily exert pres-

sure. Nor did they scruple to do so, as Metternich's interventions indicate. While it would be a mistake, then, to conclude that the Popes of the early nineteenth century were coerced into an anti-Liberal position—they, indeed, freely chose their course—it would be equally a mistake to charge them exclusively with narrow obstinacy. They were painfully conscious of the forces that would be set in motion were they to adopt the alternative policy.

5. Specifically, the papal attitude was fashioned with pointed effect by the situation in Italy. The impact of Liberalism and Nationalism on the Papal States was of utmost importance in determining Papal policy. A more detailed treatment is in order.

Curiously, the initial effect of the French occupation of Northern Italy was an effort at compromise that nearly succeeded. The armistice signed at Bologna, 21 June 1796, did not suppress the Papal States. Pius VI accepted a suggestion to send a legate to Paris with the Brief, *Pastoralis Sollicitudo*,[6] which favored conciliation and warned against dissension among Catholics in France. But, like all such efforts under the Directory, the move failed when Gregoire succeeded in convincing the dominant group in Paris that it must reject the offer unless the Pope would withdraw his condemnation of the Civil Constitution— a step the latter would not take though he remained willing to compromise. The opportunity was gone once persecution broke out again in France and General Berthier marched on Rome.[7] The eighty-one year old Pontiff was taken into captivity, where he died a prisoner in Valence, 29 August 1799. So low were the fortunes of the Papacy at this juncture that it was confidently predicted no successor could be elected.

The choice of Cardinal Chiaramonti as Pius VII at Venice (14 March 1800) marked an important change in the destinies of the Papacy. Elected at the age of fifty-eight, he appeared too young to many accustomed to aged men in the chair of Peter. Were one to accept the too facile division of Popes into religious and political, one would definitely place Pius in the former category, for this Benedictine was completely dedicated to spiritual interests. Moreover, he was cultured, enlightened, and receptive to the ideas of his time. While he was bishop of Imola, his see city was taken by the French. He addressed his flock: "The form of democratic government, adopted for us, is not at all repugnant to the Gospel; on the contrary, it demands all the sublime virtues which are learned only in the school of Jesus Christ." And he concluded: "Be good Christians and you will be a good democrats." Bonaparte remarked that he preached like a Jacobin!

Pius's intention to move with events was evident in his first pontifical act, the nomination of Cardinal Consalvi as Secretary of State. The Pope and the Secretary made an excellent combination and worked in full confidence. Together, they carried to completion the restoration of relations with France.[9] They also negotiated a much more favorable concordat for the Church in Italy (16 September 1803) though it, too, was compromised by the unilateral addition of the Melzi decrees.[10] But the agreements could not blot out the basic differences. The new Charlemagne expected obedience; Pius VII refused to accept dictation. When the Pope declined to surrender the English in Rome and to act as a political ally, Napoleon ordered the invasion of the Papal States and their inclusion in his Empire. The Pope was taken prisoner and carried across the Alps where he remained a thorn in the imperial flesh until the waning days of the regime.

This conflict between Napoleon and the Papacy underlines the genuine dilemma that lay behind the question of the Temporal Power. Had the Pope been merely a territorial prince, the ruler of a "paltry Duchy," as Napoleon sneeringly called him, he could have acted as did many of his princely contemporaries: he could have bowed before the storm and submitted provisionally until "better days" returned. But as spiritual leader of the Church, he could not have identified himself with any particular state. As head of an international spiritual organization, he had to preserve a strict neutrality in temporal issues and to reject any attempt to force him into a "system." Subjection to a sovereign, especially one like Napoleon, would have injured irreparably his spiritual position. Bonaparte, engaged in a death struggle with a foreign coalition, his autocratic temperament intensified by success, had no inclination to make nice distinctions. Pius VII felt that any threat to the Church's spiritual independence must be resisted to the end.

This spiritual independence had become identified with the papal position as political ruler. Obviously, the Temporal Power was not an essential condition of the Papacy. Its acquisition had been historical and accidental; and even Pius IX, its most resolute defender, carefully removed it from the realm of dogma. But at the beginning of the nineteenth century, having endured for more than a millenium, it was the most venerable political institution in Europe. At first, the temporal possessions of the Popes were merely properties bequeathed to the

Holy See. The collapse of civil authority in Italy had thrust
political functions upon the Papacy, and practical needs gave
popular support to papal rule. Besides, the ideas and conditions
of the feudal world blended nicely with the concept of the
Bishop of Rome as sovereign of central Italy.

Curiously, the rise of national states, each claiming the fulness
of sovereign power, appeared to make more imperative the
retention of the Temporal Power. The existence of the latter
was tangible evidence that the Papacy was not subject to any
worldly power and was, consequently, free to act in spiritual
matters. Hence, while nationalism was to become the greatest
threat to its continued existence, nationalism appeared, at first,
its most profound justification. If the Papacy was to be heard
in the Council of Nations, it seemed necessary to recognize it
as a temporal sovereign. The coming of the Reformation made
this need more pressing. Several of the growing nations were
unwilling to accept the spiritual claims of the Papacy, but were
quite satisfied to deal with the Popes as sovereigns of some
Italian territory. Prevailing attitudes in England, for example,
made it impossible for her statesmen to do anything that might
seem to recognize the spiritual jurisdiction of Rome; but there
was no prejudice against Rome's interest in Italian political
affairs. It was as political rulers that the Popes were able to
negotiate in the interests of His Majesty's Catholic subjects.

Thus, the venerable age of the Temporal Power had blurred
somewhat the vital distinction between the spiritual and temporal concerns of the Roman Pontiffs. A more fundamental
reason seemed to demand the maintenance of the Papal States.
A nineteenth century defender of the Temporal Power might
have stated it thus: the Church is universal and supranational,
and its head cannot be subject to an earthly power. The Pope
must be independent and sovereign. Were he to recognize any
temporal ruler, he would immediately be challenged in the
spiritual realm. The independence of the Vatican must not
only be recognized by Catholics, but, in a nationalistic world,
must also be respected by governments. Since nineteenth century governments required some territorial extension before
sovereignty would be admitted, the Pope must rule over some
territory.

The bitterness of the quarrel over the Temporal Power
can never be understood unless this argument is grasped.
Nineteenth century Popes might be inclined to fight for the
retention of their territories because of tradition and sentiment,
because of prestige, or because such territory provided a framework for the activities of the Papal Court. But their essential

reason was the fear that the loss of their temporal possessions
would mean the end of spiritual independence. Pius IX's remark that he would not become a chaplain to the House of
Savoy neatly summed up the papal position. To him, and
others, the loss of his territory would mean the identification
of the Papacy with a single national state and the end of its
supranational position. The very intensity of nationalist feeling
in the nineteenth century seemed to lend substance to their
fears.

It is clear that those who held this position did not foresee
the future course of events: that the loss of the Temporal
Power would free the Papacy from concern with political rule
and greatly enhance its moral prestige and spiritual power. But
if adherents to the Temporal Power did not envisage this
possibility, neither did many of its opponents. The prevailing
opinion on both sides was that the loss of territories would
have serious consequences.

Yet, the existence of the Temporal Power was a genuine
dilemma. Though no solution to it seemed likely, circumstances
were making its continuance impossible. Under favorable Medieval conditions, the Temporal Power had still carried with
it grave disadvantages. During the Reformation, the involvement of the Papacy in petty Italian disputes was one of its
most serious handicaps. Finally, the rise of modern nationalism,
appearing to make the preservation of the Papal States more
necessary, ultimately worked toward their dissolution. The
Napoleonic experience of the Papacy argued for temporal sovereignty as an essential safeguard of spiritual independence; but
it also showed that the militarily weak Papal States could be
defended under modern power conditions only through the
protection of a strong nation and that this protection would
inevitably involve the Papacy in power struggles. In a world
of nation states, it was both undesirable and impossible that
the Papacy become one itself. It must either remain a substantial territorial state, too weak to protect itself and thus
dependent upon other states, or be stripped of territorial possessions while relying on moral prestige for its defense. The
latter seemed too hazardous a consideration during much of
the nineteenth century. Today, in fact, it has proved to be the
solution, at least up to the present. Whether it would remain
so under the further spread of totalitarianism is, of course,
speculative. Final solutions, in this as in most sizable human
problems, are impossible to discover.

A great deal of polemic has surrounded the internal administration of the Papal States during the final century of their

existence. The complaints of the Papacy's nineteenth century nationalist opponents, re-examined recently in the context of present events, are thought to be inflated. Generally speaking, papal rule was benevolent and sentimentally satisfactory to many of its subjects, though not to the point where they would defend it with arms or lament its passing. It did not concede religious freedom though the coercive imposition of religious uniformity was sporadic and never ruthless; a good deal of practical tolerance was granted, and the territory was a favored spot for exiles of every sort. Unquestionably, papal rule was inefficient. Popes were usually elected at an advanced age; their reigns were short; their preoccupations, many. These circumstances precluded the possibility of basic reform. At the time of Napoleon's invasion, the administration was a hodge-podge of local arrangements, even less uniform and systematized than the average state of the Old Regime. Consalvi's reforms were a notable advance, but they were largely canceled by his successors. Pius IX had the sincere intention of making his domain a model state and did succeed in transferring a majority of the posts to laymen; unfortunately, the troubles of '48 and the loss of the more prosperous areas in the north limited the extent and value of the changes, which were probably too late in any event.

No matter how the balance sheet be drawn, one point seem clear: in the conditions of the nineteenth century, the Papal States were an anachronism. The lackadaisical government, the parade-soldiers, the complicated financial structure (almost always heavily in debt), the clerical administrators (until the advent of Pius IX), the juridical system depending on canon law, the inflexibility of the whole political structure in the face of changing conditions—all these combined to show the intrinsic weakness in the structure of the Papal States and to render obsolete and ineffectual their resistance to the political and economic tides that were sweeping in to alter the entire face of Europe. Granted that detractors often exaggerated the blunders of the Pope's temporal administrators, the net effect most surely was to weaken the international and moral esteem in which the Papacy had been held.

The dilemma, then, was this: in both internal administration and its relation to the state structure of Europe, the Temporal Power was an anachronism; but, while not essential to the Papacy (it had not existed in the early centuries), it was considered necessary as the one means to assure spiritual independence. Wherefore, nineteenth century Popes made strong efforts to preserve it. Its retention became a major concern, the objective of much of their policy and of many of their formal statements. Committed to the defense of the Temporal Power, they correctly saw Nationalism and Liberalism as its major foes. Absorbed in a struggle to preserve the Papal States, their vision of foreign movements was influenced by their analysis of Italian conditions. In the words of the best contemporary Catholic scholar on the subject:

"The secular interests of their kingdom sometimes drove the Popes into courses of action which undoubtedly conflicted with the interests of the universal Church, making them take sides against their own spiritual subjects in other lands. Worse still, after the States of the Church had been restored in the name of the principle of 'legitimacy' at the Congress of Vinna, their ruler was bound to the chariot of political reaction in Europe, and *thus was intiated the tragic and largely unnecessary conflict between the Church and the rising forces of democracy in traditionally Catholic lands.* The general attitude of the Curia towards 'Liberalism' of all kinds was far too deeply coloured by local preoccupations in the Papal States." [11]

It is in this context that the historian must view Consalvi's great diplomatic triumph at the Congress of Vienna. His handicaps were enormous: Avignon and the Comtat Venaissin having already been lost by the Treaty of Paris, Austria was in a favorable position for claims on the Legations; Murat was a threat in the South; and moral appeals had little weight in the cynical atmosphere of Vienna. Though Consalvi had to wait until the last day of the Congress for the verdict (9 June 1815), he achieved nearly complete success. The Pope was to recover immediately all his territories in Italy except a small strip north of the Po. The reconstructed Papal States were to enjoy a privileged status in international law. Nor did the gains require explicit commitments: the Pope was not obliged to joint Metternich's system; he refused to adhere to an Italian combination to combat Jacobinism; he was not bound to become a member of the Holy Alliance. The coveted freedom of action had apparently been regained.

The recession of the Napoleonic tide had left few territorial changes in the map of Italy, but the French occupation had profoundly altered Italian destiny. The instinct to hail the Corsican as one of the founders of United Italy is sound. Negatively speaking he had shaken the peninsula from its somnolence and had introduced wide social and legal changes that could be modified but not erased. More important was his positive contribution. Though he left behind a memory and

a body of ideas that at first appealed to only a few, the ultimate
response was to broaden with time as these ideas swept aside
the patient work of reconstruction so laboriously engineered
by the statesmen of Vienna.

Consalvi was less successful in his second aim—to remodel the
internal administration of the Papal States. His efforts at reform
were aided by the fact that many of the local obstacles had
been removed during the French occupation. But Consalvi's
plans, which he knew to be essential for survival, were opposed
by the *Zealanti*.[12] Thus, while he effected substantial improvements, his work was incomplete. Nor could the modest changes
win the support of the population: the Carbonari became increasingly active in the Papal States after 1817. Mounting
tension was evidenced in sporadic lawlessness and insurrection
that were to build up to the explosion of 1848.

The death of Pius VII removed from the Chair of Peter a
Pontiff who had shared Consalvi's reforming views and had
given him full support. His successor, the sickly Leo XII
(1823-1829), a pious man sincerely interested in improving
religious conditions, held a political policy that was essentially
retrogressive. He dismissed Consalvi and appointed the conservative Somaglia as Secretary of State.[13] His attempt to rule
the Papal States by authoritarian measures merely intensified
the discontent, and rebellion broadened as Consalvi's reforms
were brusquely annulled.

The conspicuous failure of Leo XII in both internal and
international affairs contributed to the election of Cardinal
Castiglioni as Pius VIII.[14] He had been preferred by Pius VII
as his successor and belonged to the school of Consalvi. In the
delicate political situation of 1830, he followed a policy of
wisdom and moderation. Impressed by Lamennais's warnings,
he advised the clergy against identifying themselves with any
political cause and refused to admit into his territories the
monarchist bishops who had fled France at the collapse of the
Bourbons.[15]

Pius VIII died (November, 1830) before his policy could
bear fruit. The conclave met in an atmosphere of dread that
the Revolution in France might spread to Central Italy. The
new Pope, Gregory XVI (chosen 2 February 1831), was phys-
ically vigorous, ascetic, and zealous. But his rigorous life as a
Camaldolite had not prepared him for the delicate problems he
had to face. Considerably successful in spiritual matters, he
approached political questions with an intransigence heightened
by an uncompromising manner. Almost immediately upon his
accession, he faced a serious revolt in his domain, a rebellion

supported by most of the papal troops. When his promises
and threats were equally unavailing, he was forced to call upon
Austria. Metternich was more than willing to be of service.
The subsequent French occupation of Ancona created a tense
situation as long as the two armies remained on papal soil.[16]
Meanwhile, a conference of the ambassadors of the Great
Powers, meeting on the issue, demanded extensive reforms in
papal government. The Pope acceded in every respect but the
constitutional; however, the changes were too limited to appease
the dissident. Nor did suppression bring happier results. At
the time of Gregory's death in 1846, the States of the Church
were in turmoil.

During this Pontificate, Italian nationalism became a major
issue for the Papacy. Fundamentally, it was not inevitable that
the two should clash. Until 1848, a federalist solution that
would have preserved the Temporal Power was a very possible
solution. But foreign repression and papal reluctance to compromise were giving encouragement to the republican propaganda of Mazzini's *Young Italy*.[17] This romantic movement
was broadening its appeal to include all classes. It was uncompromising in its flat declaration that without Rome as the
capital of a unified Italy there could be no freedom. To the
extent that it gained adherents, Italian nationalism was becoming actively anti-clerical.

It is clear that the *Risorgimento*, or the process of Italian
national unification, had a special characteristic that set it apart
from similar movements in the nineteenth century. In other
areas, the proponents of a national state had to overcome the
particularism and apathy of their fellow nationals. Generally,
they had to face the interested opposition of foreign powers or
imperial possessors. In Italy, circumstances forced the partisans
of unification to face the additional religious problem. The
Papal States lay in the heart of the peninsula, and the Papacy
considered them vital for the exercise of its spiritual jurisdiction. It is this fact which gave the *Risorgimento* its dramatic
character and made it a thorny question in international
politics.

The lines were not clearly drawn until 1848. In the first half
of the century, three parallel movements can be distinguished.
There was the desire for independence from foreign control,
which meant the expulsion of Austria from the peninsula. This
was particularly strong in Lombardy, where Hapsburg rule
had brought economic advantages offset by stringent political
repression. There was the movement for unification, which
found expression in three clasic solutions: the neo-Guelf of

Gioberti,[18] a federal Italy under the presidency of the Pope; the Mazzinian, a republican unitary Italy; the Piedmontese, a monarchist Italy under the House of Savoy. Finally, there was the Liberal movement, which sought political and social change in line with British and French developments. Until 1848, there was considerable fluidity in these varied currents along with some conflict among them. All, however, had a common base in the numerically small bourgeoisie, who alone made public opinion. After 1848, events and the genius of Cavour were to solidify the groupings in a common effort.

The leaders of the *Risorgimento* faced the religious issue with considerable reluctance. A considerable proportion of the early patriots were staunch Catholics of the stamp of Alessandro Manzoni. Others were unbelievers, who preferred to retain religion for the masses; their view point was partly inspired by British influence. Mazzini and some of his associates were sincere religious idealists who rejected Catholicism. A concluding and important segment was fundamentally anti-religious. Events made the unification of Italy appear a triumph for the anti-religious element and a sharp defeat for the Catholic Church.

Even though the unification came to be so regarded, the men involved accepted the reality of conflict with the Church with varying degrees of reluctance. Cavour was fundamentally a Catholic. Though in his early career he associated himself with an anti-clerical position, after 1859 he sought a conciliatory solution with the Papacy. He would not accept a concordat, which he felt would be harmful to both parties; yet, he definitely rejected sectarian anti-clericalism. His death in 1861 was undoubtedly a great tragedy, for there was no one who could execute his rather delicate policy of balance and moderation. His successor, Ricasoli, attempted to maintain a similar approach but failed to gain concrete results. Until 1870, only one of the Piedmontese leaders, Ratazzi, deviated from a conciliatory handling of the thorny issue.[19]

The *Risorgimento* caused complications in Italy. However, so did the quest for institutional change. The movement known as Liberalism defies exact definition. It has meant different things to different people and to different popes. Generally, it may be described as the eighteenth and nineteenth century attempt to modify the political and social structures of Europe in order to give expression to new demands for representative government, civil rights, and unrestrained economic activity; and to diminish the public influence of religion. It was a complex movement and touched many spheres of human activ-

ity: it involved a re-evaluation of intellectual and moral positions and principles; it embraced a number of political changes;
it was a response to new economic conditions; it implied a shift
of power to an emerging social class; it elaborated an economic
doctrine which was thought to be founded on natural law;
and, over all, it took a neutral, sometimes hostile, attitude
toward religion. Only custom, really, can justify assembling
these many aspects under a single heading.

Complicating the matter further is the fact that not all these
phases were found in any individual representative, nor were
they all resident in equal strength among the varied groups
to which the label has been given. This variety of concrete
manifestatitions leads us to such qualifying designations as Economic Liberals, Constitutional Liberals, Catholic Liberals, etc.
Besides, Liberalism was in evolution, as are all historical movements, and it cannot be considered apart from its temporal context. Moreover, it diverged considerably in different geographical areas. Again, its development varied according to its relation with Nationalism. While Liberalism and Nationalism appealed to the same groups, partcularly to the educated middle
class, priority given to the one or the other in any chosen area
depended on the answer to pertinent questions. Did a national
state already exist or must it be fought for? If so, how strong
was the internal and external opposition to its creation? What
was the strength of the groups seeking the change? What had
been the character of the resistance to past social modifications?
Consequently, Liberalism underwent wide variations in the
different countries.

In England, where a national state had developed early, subsequent social changes occurred with relatively less violence.
In France, where the national state had been secured, the desire for internal changes, nevertheless, provoked a profound
revolution. In Germany, the thwarted desire for a national
state overshadowed other demands.

In Italy, at least after 1848, Liberalism and Nationalism becoming associated, both assumed an anti-clerical hue. Even before that date, contemporaries had difficulty in making distinctions among the varied aspects of a complex process. Certainly,
Gregory XVI did not make them. Engaged in a frustrating
effort to prevent anarchy in his domains, he did not hesitate
to make a sweeping condemnation of "Liberalism" in his
Mirari Vos. His attention fixed upon Italy, he placed the issue
on doctrinal grounds, but the application of the principle to
other areas caused manifold difficulties. His Catholic subjects
in Belgium, Poland, and Ireland were invoking "liberty" to

gain religious and national independence, and in the first two countries the struggle was being waged against absolutist governments. In England, a liberal government had granted religious freedom to its Catholic population. In the United States, a rapidly evolving and progressive form of the same type was treating its Catholic minority generously. Elsewhere, as in Spain, Portugal, and Switzerland, it was the enemies of the Church who were invoking "liberal" concepts. Faced with these complications, the Pope attempted to salvage the principle while submitting to the practice. The Bull *Solicitudo Ecclesiarum*, 7 August 1831, implied the famous distinction between thesis and hypothesis, that is, maintenance of the principle as the "ideal" along with recognition of the necessity of accepting actual conditions. However, in his own States, the Pope remained committed to the full implementation of the doctrine.

Even this distinction did not dissipate all the problems. The Belgian Catholics were not condemned for their liberal associations,[20] but relations with the Vatican were somewhat strained. Gregory XVI was very sympathetic toward the Poles, yet called upon them to submit to the Czar in their revolution of 1831.[21] Toward the English and Irish Catholics, Gregory remained reserved.

While the Pope struggled hard against these forces, it was a rearguard action with few favorable results. Politically, Gregory was a failure. Far from arresting the currents of his age, he succeeded merely in canalizing their energy against the Church or intensifying their hostility. In relgious matters, he made considerable contributions to the well-being of the church.[22]

So patent was the failure of Gregory XVI that it took only the unusually short time of two days for the conclave of 1846 to elect a man who seemed to embody the very tendencies which his predecessor had combatted. Cardinal Mastai Ferretti, who became Pius IX, was known as a nationalist and a liberal— a patriotic Italian who believed in far-reaching reform. Liberals everywhere greeted his election with intense enthusiasm, and Italian nationalists rejoiced that an active sympathizer now occupied the Papal Throne.

Only to a limited extent was this expectancy justified. The new Pope was an earnest partisan of Italian independence.[23] He had read the leading literature of the *Risorgimento*. He was critical of the past administration of the Papal States and was determined to grant the concessions most loudly demanded by public opinion. But there were two limiting factors which were to have important bearing on his reactions to the events of 1848:

1. The Pope, deeply relgious, was very conscious of his pastoral obligations to all Catholics. Though opposed to Austrian rule in the peninsula, he had no intention of leading a holy war against his other Catholic subjects in Austria for the sake of Italian independence.

2. Though critical of all regimes which would not make concessions, he had no intention of surrendering his Temporal Power, which he sincerely believed was essential for the spiritual interests of the Church. His reforms would be extensive but would not affect his sovereignty.[34] Actually, they were not to go beyond the demands of the representatives of the Great Powers of 21 May 1831. Nor did he accept the neo-Guelf thesis: he had no desire to enlarge the Temporal Power.

It is these limitations which explain his action in the decisive year, 1848. His allocution of the 29th of April came as a shock to the nationalists, who could not appreciate his refusal to join the war against Austria. The Pope maintained that he was the Vicar of a Christ Who was the Author of peace and charity and that he was thus bound to embrace all nations with the same paternal love. *This decision, correct though it was, was the key to all the Pontiff's future troubles.* That it was correct is clear: in a Europe of mounting nationalism, no tragedy would be greater than for the Papacy to become a national institution. In March, the Pope had granted a parliamentary Constitution to his subjects. In mid-September he appointed the liberal, Pellegrino Rossi, as his chief minister. Rossi, laboring energetically to make the new constitution work, was assassinated on the 15th of November in disorders that threatened the safety of Pius himself.[25] The Pope, despairing of achieving any result by reform, fled in disguise to Gaëta in the Kingdom of Naples. On the 4th of December, he appealed to the Christian Powers, invoking the international guarantees of the Congress of Vienna. The reforming phase of Pope Pius's pontificate was concluded, and the Temporal Power had become an international issue.

From Gaëta, Pius IX watched the Constituent Assembly at Rome declare the end of the Temporal Power and the establishment of a Republic for all Italy. He was now convinced that liberal reforms were incompatible with papal rule and would only lead to further disturbance. The European Powers were agreed on a resoration, but Austrian-French rivalry and British suspicions of French intentions made a solution difficult. Pius would have preferred Austrian intervention on the model of 1831. The issue became critical when a French expeditionary force landed at Civitavecchia on 24 April, 1849. The Pope was not well disposed to a restoration by the cynically irreligious and nationalistic President of the French, nor were the other Powers gratified by the dominant role France was assuming in Italian affairs. But all bowed before the *fait accompli*. Pius was back in his capital on 12 April 1850. It was evident at once that he was no longer the bold political innovator of 1846.. He resented the suggestions that a modified constitutional government be re-established, on the ground that such a government would impede his spiritual freedom.

From 1849 until 1870, the question of the Temporal Power retained the twofold feature of the Gaëta interlude. First, it remained an international issue, dependent for its solution on the action of the Powers. Thus, the Austrian defeat in 1859 prepared the way for the loss of all the papal territories save those around Rome; and even these latter in turn had to be surrendered when the withdrawal of the French sealed their doom in 1870. Second, the Pope remained adamant against all substantial concessions both to his subjects and to the encroaching power of Italian nationalism, now incarnate in the House of Savoy. His interpretation of the Piedmontese legislation of 1855 made him even more unyielding, and he saw each advance of the House of Savoy as an extension of godlessness in Italy.[26] Indeed, the fundamental dilemma lay unresolved: for the Italian nationalist, there could be no Italy without Rome; for the Vatican, there could be no Catholicism without the territorial independence of the Papacy. On this latter assumption, Pius remained irreconcilable until the end. A more politically minded Pope might have sought an arrangement; Pius actually went to his death believing that the fate of the Church was linked to this issue.

After 1870, the Roman Question entered a new phase, with the Pope accepting voluntary imprisonment in the Vatican. He cut off all official ties with the Italian State. He rejected the Law of Guarantees, which was in fact a tissue of compromises that contained concessions to the Italian Left. To Pius IX, it was totally unacceptable because it was a unilateral grant that could be amended or abrogated by any subsequent Italian government To him it seemed the most fragile sort of protection for papal independence. In 1876, the formation of the actively anti-clerical Depretis government ended for the time the possibility of compromise.

Two points in the *Dissidio* need to be noted:

1. The King of United Italy, Victor Emmanuel II, was sincerely Catholic, as were most of his ministers. It is ironic that "the Roman Question was created by a government of Catholics and settled by a government largely composed of agnostics."[27]

2. A serious division existed among Italian Catholics on the wisdom of the *Dissidio*. The considerable body of Catholic opinion that supported the nationalist cause provided an important bridge between the Vatican and the government. Earlier, the neo-Guelfs had made it possible to reconcile the Catholic cause with nationalist feeling; now, clerical and episcopal dissent from the official papal position diminished the danger of serious popular repercussions. In the North and in the South, most Catholics were friendly to a united Italy. The bishops, generally, remained silent out of respect for the Pope, but many were known to be sysmpathetic to the nationalist position. This internal division helps to explain why Italian anti-clericalism never attained the success achieved by the French. No one can deny the seriousness of the anti-Catholic feeling of the convinced opponents of the Church.[28] But they never won the masses, and in rural Italy were almost without influence. As a consequence, the Church-State conflict in Italy had some of the atmosphere of those scenes in Verdi's operas where the singing soldiers shout defiance to the accompaniment of the drums and the brandishing of wooden spears, only to retire into the wings to chat amiably till the next entrance.

These divisions among Catholics saddened the Pope, but they did not dissuade him. His pontificate was a prolonged personal tragedy. The longest since Peter, it spanned one of the most decisive periods of European history. It witnessed the forging of an industrial society, the triumph of the principle of nationalism, the creation of a new balance of power in Europe with the unification of Bismarck's Germany, the elaboration of the social theory of Marx, and the emergence of a new intellectual mood that has been summarized under the title, *A Generation of Materialism*. Distracted by his Italian troubles, Pius IX watched these aforementioned changes with deep anxiety. Personally, he was refined, affable, spiritual, and anxious for popular approval; yet, in Italy and in Europe generally, he was driven by his convictions into an intractable position that he maintained without reference to consequences.

Politically, his pontificate was an almost unrelieved record of failure.[29] Before the unification of Germany, he was involved in disputes with several German states; after 1871, he sustained the shock of Bismarck's Kulturkampf. Relations with Switzerland were generally unhappy. He managed to negotiate a Russian concordat, but it was not put into effect; and the Catholic subjects of the Czar, especially the Poles, continued to suffer persecution. His concordat with Austria was subsequently abrogated. There were conflicts with governments in the Iberian peninsula and in several Latin American countries. At his death, only four states continued to send representatives to the Holy See, and the international position of the Papacy reached its nadir. His pronouncements on contemporary issues, especially *Quanta Cura* and the *Syllabus of Errors,* created intense antipathy among non-Catholics and considerable uneasiness among many Catholics.

The clear antithesis between his political views before and after 1848 suggests that they were influenced by the collapse of his hopes for moderate reform in the Papal States. Before the murder of Rossi, he had criticized regimes "which attempted to rule by force instead of charity." [30] Thereafter, his optimism vanished. He was not impressed by the arguments for the separation of Church and State. The contention that they could be divorced, or, in the words of T. S. Eliot, that the "public affairs of this world and those of the next have nothing to do with each other. . . . ," and that "in a perfect world those who like golf could play golf and those who liked religion could go to Church," appeared to him as nonsense. Either a regime would be benevolent, in which case it would publicly proclaim its protection of religion, or it would be hostile. The neutrality of the state in religious or economic matters, which so appealed to his contemporaries, was for him a myth.

Nor was he impressed by claims to complete liberty of opinion and worship. Total liberty, he felt, was a mirage. No state would permit dissent were its existence threatened, nor would any civilized nation carry religious tolerance to the point where it would recognize a creed which proclaimed human sacrifice or polygamy. Hence, professions of full liberty were hypocritical. He invoked the principle: error may not claim the same rights as truth.

These objections were vigorously presented. But when one examines the many declarations of this Pontiff, one is struck by their predominantly negative character. Certainly his pontificate was a "Time of Resistance." He condemned many contemporary movements of thought and action, but he did not provide well-constructed alternatives. This was particularly true in regard to the social question, which had become acute in Europe during his time in the Vatican. He did denounce Socialism and Communism in terms which many in our time would accept. But there was no examination of the new social conditions and no positive proposals. The most profound of modern movements was scarcely reflected in papal declarations up until 1878.

II. *The Time of Constructive Achievement* (1878-1950)

The election of Leo XIII represents a watershed in the history of the modern Papacy. Most of his immediate predecessors had engaged in a struggle with new forces that were the expression of changes occurring in the social structure of modern Europe. Generally speaking, it had been for the Papacy a time of resistance, an attitude of rejection. While the Popes had made some telling points in the domain of principle, as in their reprobation of exaggerated nationalism, theirs had been largely a losing battle ending in isolation. Negative and inflexible, they had been unable to stem the political forces which they had opposed partly because they may not have adequately understood them. The significance of the economic factors remaking European life seems to have escaped them. On the whole, they did not offer constructive solutions to the challenge presented by political and social changes. Ultimately, the losses to the Faith in the old Catholic areas of Europe were immense.[31]

Leo XIII's pontificate marked a decisive change. There was no sharp doctrinal reversal: in all essentials, the principles were maintained. Still, the difference in policy was profound enough to be considered revolutionary. Primarily, it was a change of attitude:

1. A softening of the tactic of denunciation conjoined with a search among the traditions of the Church for positive solutions to contemporary questions.

2. An understanding of the character and complexity of modern problems consequent upon a real knowledge of the issues involved, including the social problems lying at the root of modern politics. As an historian, philosopher, and diplomat, Leo was well equipped for his role.

3. A true sympathy was extended modern man in his dilemma.

4. A sense of the practical was applied to politics "as the art of the possible," involving a willingness to meet actual conditions. Leo always kept his feet on the actual terrain.

In sum, Leo XIII was eminently intelligent. Austere and religious, he was also cultured and urbane. Appointed Nuncio to Brussels in 1843, he had had an opportunity to study the remarkable Catholic movements in Belgium as well as to visit London, Paris, and the Rhineland. Made Archbishop of Perugia, he administered his See for thirty-two years, including the difficult period when Umbria was annexed to the Kingdom of Italy. Such a background, not too noticeably different from that of many Popes, nevertheless served to develop in him a wide understanding of the problems he was to face in his pontificate.

Since Leo XIII inaugurated a new direction in Vatican policy that was followed in greater or less degree by his successors, it may prove clearer to adopt a topical division of the political and social activity of the modern Popes.

A. *The Roman Question*

While in nearly every other field Leo introduced practical innovations, his handling of the Roman Question did not differ substantially from that of his predecessor. In fact, it was largely his prestige that kept it in the foreground of international affairs during the quarter-century of his pontificate. He exercised the *non expedit* against Catholic participation in Italian national elections; he maintained an official aloofness from Italian politics; he issued sixty-two formal protests against past or contemporary actions of the government. In a sense, relations worsened during his time, as several of the more prominent Italian ministers, notably Crispi, were frankly anti-Christian. But though the strains persisted, neither side carried its official stand to its logical conclusion. Informal contacts between the Quirinal and the Vatican were maintained through intermediaries. The Pope rejected several attempts by prominent ecclesiastics to achieve a reconciliation though on two occasions he himself explored the possibilities of a settlement. In general, the Italian genius for practical solutions is evident in the indisposition of both parties to the dispute to engage in total war. Along with theoretical intransigence, there remained the facility for *combinazione*.

Proof of this is seen in the fate of anti-clerical legislation during the pontificate of Leo XIII and that of his successor. Throughout most of this period, the Italian government was directed by convinced anti-clericals who were responsible for introducing into the Parliament many proposals unfavorable to the Church, some of which were passed. But the five major efforts in which these hostile forces engaged never fully fructified despite vigorous campaigns in the country and in the legislature:

1. Abrogation of the Law of Guarantees. Although this legislation was never accepted by the Papacy,[32] it was attacked by the anti-clerical Left as a symbol of excessive moderation. Anti-Catholics objected that it placed the Papacy in a privileged position which could be used to damage the nation. All attacks on the Law of Guarantees were fruitless. It was not amended

to suit the demands of the Vatican, nor was it revoked to please the anti-clericals.

2. Punishment for the neglect of civil marriage. The Code of 1865 made the civil ceremony obligatory, but complaints against laxity in enforcement were constant. Opponents of religion consistently failed to pass legislation that would impose severe sanctions for non-compliance.

3. The introduction of civil divorce. This was a major objective of all anti-clerical activity, but it failed completely in the face of determined opposition by the overwhelming majority of Italians.

4. The status of religion orders. They had been suppressed in the new Kingdom before 1870, and the ban was extended to Rome and its environs in 1873. The law caused severe hardships: many religious activities were suspended and important properties were seized by the government. But the fact that the courts were not consistent in applying the decree made local authorities complacent. After the initial setback, the religious orders increased both in personnel and influence. Enraged enemies made every effort to check the revival; but, because the country as a whole was sympathetic to the prohibited congregations, they continued to grow.

5. The status of the teaching of religious knowledge in elementary schools. The Casati Law of 1859 made it obligatory except where parents objected in writing. It was to be given by the ordinary teachers without supervision by the ecclesiastical authorities, beyond a yearly oral examination of the children by the parish priest. When, however, the "interpretation" of the Higher Council of Education, 29 September 1870, reversed the conditions, it made written requests by the parents a necessary pre-condition for the instruction. This was a severe check. In addition, the examination by the parish priest was gradually discouraged. The Lex Coppino (1877) and the Lex Credaro (1911) occasioned further unfavorable consequences to the teaching of religious knowledge. Yet, efforts to exclude the subject entirely from the public schools failed; the principle that parents had the right to determine the formation of their children remained a basic formulation of Italian law.

Considerable successes against Catholicism were achieved. The Church and her representatives were subject to constant abuse in a segment of the press. Religion was eliminated from higher education and from welfare institutions. Sporadic incidents increased the bitterness.[33] Besides, the legal position of the Church was completely unsatisfactory. Deprived of the pro-

tection formerly accorded by establishment, it was still subject
to the regalism inherited from the past. Ecclesiastics could not
take over their posts without governmental approval, and the
administration of the Church was far from that freedom which
Cavour proclaimed as the ideal. Despite these handicaps, a
working compromise was evolved in Italy after 1878, and it
operated more smoothly as time passed.

With Pius X (1903-1914),[34] the Roman Question entered a
new phase. "A rural pastor on the papal throne," Pius was a
man of unusual simplicity and sanctity, with no interest in or
understanding of political matters. He was not favorable to the
revival of the Temporal Power; with him, the Roman Question
ceased to be a major problem in Italian and world politics.
Friendly contacts with the government increased. A fear of rising radicalism prompted the Pope to remove the *non expedit* in
those dioceses where the bishops deemed it opportune.

Pius so distrusted political solutions that he repelled all efforts of Catholics to form political parties. His ideal was Catholic Action on a diocesan basis under strict episcopal control,
with the bishops instructing their flocks in the use of the ballot
where religious issues were at stake. His views were set forth
in the Encyclical, *Il Fermo Proposito*,[35] which enumerated the
following points:

1. Catholics should not confine their concern to religious
questions but push efforts to relieve economic needs.

2. Methods should be adapted to actual conditions.

3. Catholics should employ the techniques developed by
the social and economic sciences.

4. They should not be shackled by a blind reliance on ancient methods.

5. They should employ all the rights of citizenship in order
to prove themselves worthy of the liberty offered by the modern
state and to strengthen the civil and material well-being of the
people.

6. They should not form political or quasi-political associations but merely accept recommendations by the bishops.

Although the wisdom of most of these directives was unquestioned, the basic proposal on political action led to disastrous
results when applied to Italian politics. The Pope himself,
realizing its ineffectiveness, sanctioned the transference of the
task of approving pro-Catholic candidates to committees composed principally of laymen. He did not for a moment relax his
antipathy to political parties. When a dispute arose over the direction of the federation of Catholic societies[36] in the early
days of his pontificate, he dissolved the organization. The

nascent Christian Democratic movement under Father Murri refused to accept the decision; when the Pope suppressed the movement, most of its leaders left the Church. This opposition of the Pope was sufficient to quash the beginnings of an Italian development that might have moved along the same lines as in France.[37]

Benedict XV (1914-1922) was a true follower of Leo and Rampolla in his approach to political problems, but he deviated from his models in dealing with the Roman Question. He removed the *non expedit* completely (1919), as well as the ban on Catholic rulers visiting the Quirinal.[38] Relations with the Italian government noticeably improved during and after the war, even though the latter succeeded in excluding the Vatican from the Peace Conference.[39]

The appearance of a vigorous Christian Democratic party on 18 January 1919 found Benedict XV benevolently neutral. This was the only attitude desired by Dom Sturzo, who wished to avoid the handicaps of a truly confessional party.[40] The *Popolari* was radically democratic and progressive, with a political program based on the protection of the individual against a centralized state of any kind and on full liberty in the civil and religious spheres. It demanded electoral reform; protection for the family, commune, and province; and full support of the League of Nations. In the social area, it favored workers' and peasants' associations, cooperatives, land reform, extension of the welfare services, and an elimination of all monopolies. Its phenomenal expansion assured the Church of a friendly political force for the first time in modern Italy. It also provided the firmest support of Constitutional government against the threat of the Radical Left and the growing challenge of Fascism.

The year 1922 marked a decisive change in Church-State relationships in Italy. January saw the election of Pius XI, who, after his elevation, took the unprecedented step of blessing the faithful from the outer balcony of St. Peter's. The significance was not lost on the vast crowd in the square, for the obvious interpretation was that the new Pope was determined to solve the Roman Question. Relations with the Italian government had improved steadily; Pius XI recognized the change by indicating that he was departing from the "voluntary prisoner" attitude established by Pius IX. It is important to note that Pius XI had manifested this intention before the collapse of Parliamentary government in Italy.

October of the same year witnessed the March on Rome and the advent of Fascism. This caused great uneasiness in Vatican circles inasmuch as Mussolini had been a violent anti-clerical [41] and the original Fascist program had had anti-religious overtones. In the violence that had marked the Fascist ascent to power, clerics and religious activities had frequently been the target of the *squadristi*. Most of the leading personalities in the movement had no religious sympathies; many were clearly antireligious.

The fear of Fascist persecution proved unfounded. On the eve of his triumph, the Duce himself had assured the Church that it had no cause for concern. This most opportunistic of modern dictators, personally without religious faith, had concluded that Catholicism was too deeply imbedded in Italian tradition for an outright war against it. His ultimate purpose was to harness the Church for his own purposes in the Napoleonic manner; his immediate aim was to crush the *Popolari*, the firmest obstacle to his unquestioned rule. This was achieved by a variety of methods: frontal attack, enticement of the Right Wing by ostentatiously favoring religion, and vigorous persecution of rebellious elements. Sturzo and several of the leaders were forced into exile, and the others were cowed into submission. This lamentable suppression, marking the extinction of democratic rights in Italy, drew no protest from the Vatican. Pius XI, sharing the prejudice of Pius X against Catholic political parties, had proclaimed it the duty of Catholics to remain "above parties." [42]

The consolidation of Fascist power made the settlement of the Roman Question imperative. The official favoring of religion masked a fundamentally hostile political philosophy and evinced a lack of scruples concerning the means which such a philosophy might employ. It might well have led to serious conflict. Nonetheless, the evidence of Fascist "friendliness" provided a favorable atmosphere for negotiations, granted that the improvement had long antedated its advent. But the Fascist doctrine that the State includes all values and permeates the whole life of a people created the danger that reconciliation with such a totalitarian power would identify the Church with a regime that preached aggressive nationalism and that was intolerant of all autonomy. The character of the negotiations and the nature of the settlement reveal that Pius XI, while conscious of the risks, was convinced that the existing situation was intolerable and that a settlement was long overdue.

The Lateran Pacts of 1929 had a twofold character: [43] a Treaty which formally ended the claims of the Papacy to its ancient states, yet preserved its territorial sovereignty by the recognition of Vatican City; [44] and a concordat which regulated the status of the Catholic Church in Italy, recognizing it as the official religion and detailing its relation to the State. The Pope had insisted that the two aspects be handled together. In the settlement, both sides made concessions: the State promised full liberty to all religious activities but gained a practical veto over appointments to ecclesiastical office.

Although the Pacts were not an ideal arrangement—nor could there be any such as long as papal territory was an enclave in a state such as Mussolini's Italy—they were certainly the best obtainable under the circumstances. The immense joy with which it was received in Italy and the general approval in the outside world testified to the common belief that the regularization of the status of the Vatican was considered a distinct improvement.

The Church and the Italian State, then, had successfully composed their surface differences; they had not, however, resolved the basic contradiction. A regime declaring that "no human or spiritual values can exist outside the State" could hardly live at peace with a Church maintaining the primacy of the spiritual and proclaiming itself the divinely appointed custodian of Truth. The settlement had been possible only because the Duce, who took no doctrine seriously, quite appreciated the practical advantages of removing a cancer from Italian public life. But he had no intention of compromising what he considered the essentials of power. Nor was he impressed by arguments drawn from the Gospels.

One source of conflict had been removed in that the Church had disavowed the *Popolari* and had written into the Concordat a prohibition against Catholic organizations in politics. The deeper issues remained unsolved.[45] The training of youth was a particularly thorny question. Before 1929, the successful Catholic Scouts had been eliminated, and Fascist disapproval had been directed to other religious youth organizations. Such groups had been granted general protection through the Concordat; still the government continued to stifle any competition against its own *Balilla*. Mussolini's attack soon broadened to include all Catholic Action,[46] for every phase of the latter embodied a threat to Fascist monopoly. The climax of this struggle was reached in 1931 with the usual accompaniment of violence. During this period, the Pope had waged relentless war on the regime. Deprived, by governmental control, of an effective press, he now employed the *Osservatore Romano*, printed in Vatican territory; frequently, it was confiscated as soon as it reached Italian soil. More effective was his use of audiences to appeal to the conscience of Italy and the world.[47]

On 29 June 1931, Pius XI forged his most formidable weapon in his Encyclical, *Non abbiamo bisogno,* which was flown by an American prelate to Paris for publication.[48] It was a vigorous condemnation of the basic premises of Fascism, contrary as they were to Catholic teaching, and featured a particular rejection of the claims of the State on the minds of youth. It added, moreover, a detailed refutation of the charges against Catholic Action. It succeeded in rallying world opinion and disposed the regime to a compromise after a decent interval of defiance. The September Agreement brought a truce which permitted Catholic Action to remain, though in a highly restricted form.[49]

Thereafter, Church-State relations remained relatively calm until the introduction of the Nazi racialist laws into Italy. These laws represented a philosophy of life that struck at the roots of Christianity, and the aged Pope rose to their challenge. He had already condemned the persecution of Jews in other lands; now his declarations were to evoke the charge of "philo-Semitic" in the Fascist press. On 25 March 1938, the Holy Office decreed:

> "The Church, just as it reproves all rancors and conflicts between peoples, particularly condemns hatred of the people once chosen by God, the hatred that commonly goes by the name of Anti-Semitism." [50]

The Pope was equally emphatic:

> "If there is anything worse than the various theories of racialism and nationalism, it is the spirit that dictates them. There is something peculiarly loathesome about this spirit of separatism and exaggerated nationalism which, precisely because it is unchristian and irreligious, ends by being inhuman." [51]

The strongest gesture came on the occasion of Hitler's visit to Rome: the Pope ostentatiously left the city for his summer villa before the Nazi's arrival even though the visit occurred at a time of the year when he normally remained in Rome.

The regime countered with vicious press attacks and renewed violence against Catholic associations. There was no relaxation until the death of Pius XI.[52] With the election of his successor, the acerbity of the struggle lessened somewhat, without fundamental change of position on either side. The coming of war diverted attention from internal issues. The democratic governments of Italy since the war have accepted the general terms of the settlement of 1929 despite Communist opposition. A common antagonism to the new totalitarian threat has assured cordial relations between reviving Italy and the Vatican.

The intermittent conflict between Italian Fascism and the Papacy produced a notable advantage in removing the danger that the Church would be identified with a totalitarian regime. The staunch papal assertion of primary positions was particularly necessary in view of the enthusiasm of many Italian Catholics, clerical and lay, for the regime which both protected and policed religion.

Any fear that the Vatican would be swayed in international questions by its proximity to the Fascist regime was dissipated by events. Pius XI, in maintaining most cordial relations with France, with the United States, and generally with Great Britain, did much to offset the Italian Fascists' dislike for all three countries. Even as he took every occasion to show marks of favor toward the democracies, Vatican relations with Nazi Germany, strained almost from the beginning, steadily grew worse. The Pope deplored attacks upon Austria and opposed the *Anschluss.* He condemned the foundations of the Nazi regime in *Mit Brennender Sorge.*[53] As relations between Italy and Germany became closer after 1935, those between Italy and the Holy See cooled. Pius XI showed great sympathy for the Czechs,[54] and Pius XII attempted to save the Poles. On the whole, the papal record was one of uncompromising opposition to totalitarianism and aggression,[55] and, concomitantly, of firm suport for basic human rights. The settlement of the Roman Question had not solved all questions inherent in the geographical and historical position of the Papacy. But, obviously, neither had it led to a surrender of its spiritual independence.

B. *The Social Question*

The pontificate of Leo XIII marked the beginning of an official effort to restate the traditional social teaching of the Catholic Church in the context of modern industrialism. The social encyclicals did not initiate the movement. In large part they were the consequence of pioneering by social-minded lay and clerical Catholics in many of the countries affected by the new conditions. But with Leo's reign, the movement "captured" the Papacy in the way that the eleventh century Reform had "captured" Leo IX or the Reform of the sixteenth century had Paul III.[56] In 1878, the See of Peter was occupied by a man who was familiar with the broad social currents of the age and who was personally sympathetic to the needs of the industrial proletariat. From this time on, social issues were to receive major papal attention.

The materials for a Catholic social doctrine were already at hand. The Gospels inherently contained the outlines of a program, for Christ had given the religious and ethical foundations of human relations. The early Church Fathers, conscious of their social environment, had applied Christian principles, often with startling vigor, against the social abuses of their age. The Scholastic philosophers had systematized this teaching in the light of Medieval economic conditions. What was needed was not a search for principles but a new or fresh application of these principles to the radically different conditions of the nineteenth century.

As Archbishop of Perugia, Leo had been interested in the material well-being of his flock. In his pastoral letter of 1877, he had written of the "colossal abuses perpetrated against the poor and the weak" and had called for legislation to correct the "inhuman traffic" of children in factories.[57] Upon becoming Pope, he took a special interest in the international meetings of social Catholics at Fribourg under the chairmanship of Msgr. Mermillod.[58] Leo encouraged their investigations and, in his encyclicals, drew heavily on their conclusions.

To evaluate the work of Leo and his successors in this field, the following points must be considered:

1. The Popes have sought merely to formulate the moral directives that should govern economic life. They have claimed no competence in the purely technical aspects of production and distribution. But they have argued that religious authorities are justified in intervening in economic matters, not only because these matters profoundly affect human beings and are therefore subject to moral law but also because the objectives of economics are themselves matters of moral concern. For instance, whereas no Pope would deem it within his competence or prerogative to write a text on military tactics, he would feel perfectly justified in writing or speaking on the ends for which a war might be fought, on the conditions of a just war, and on the treatment to be accorded prisoners and civilians.[59]

2. The Popes have spoken for a world-wide audience; hence, they have confined themselves to general directives, leaving it to their followers in each country to apply the ethical norms to precise conditions.

3. The encyclicals carefully avoid the extreme positions of outright individualism or outright collectivism. Such an intermediate position is necessarily less amenable to exact formulation than the absolute asseverations of the simplifiers.

The social encyclicals build their ethical structure upon these basic assumptions:

1. Man is necessarily a social being. He is not sufficient unto himself but needs his fellowmen in order to realize fully his powers and aspirations. This need to live in society adds a new dimension to man's rights and duties as an individual. Since man's social need is rooted in his nature, it must be attributed to the will of his Creator.[60]

2. Man is the center of the universe, the greatest act of God's creation. Because he is a creature of God, possessed of a spiritual nature with reason and free will, destined for eternal life with God, every man has a sublime innate dignity that raises him above all creation. Thus, it is man who is, who must be the measure of all economic activity. No social arrangement is valid which denies man's essential worth. "The origin and the primary scope of social life is the conservation, development, and perfection of the human person. . . ."[61] The major objective of all economic life is to provide a proper atmosphere for the fulfillment of man's capabilities.

3. Since man is sacred, he radically possesses "God-granted" rights. These are not conferred by society, nor are they the consequence of law and custom. They do not depend on the state or on the will of the community. They do not flow from expediency and social utility though these may strengthen man's claim to their possession. Human rights are inherent, inalienable. But they do not exist apart from duties, for duties and rights are correlative: each right implies a corresponding duty to recognize a right in others.

Human rights are not all on the same level: the primary ones are those most intimately connected with man's nature. Pius XI listed these in *Divini Redemptoris*:

> "In consequence, man has been endowed by God with many and varied prerogatives: the right to life, to bodily integrity, to the necessary means of existence; the right to tend toward his ultimate goal in the path marked out for him by God; the right of association and the right to possess and use property . . . "[62]

Of these, the most sacred of all is the right to life. It necessarily implies the right to the possession of economic goods. This is not satisfied by mere subsistence that would not give title to a truly human condition of life. Human dignity demands opportunity for leisure in order that man may develop his intellectual and spiritual faculties. Also, man has a right to a family, for without family life his fundamental needs could not be satisfied.

4. The primary objective of a social order is justice, which may be defined as a recognition of such rights and duties of the human person as will result in each receiving his due. The

concept of justice is essentially moral, and it can be secured only where moral values are recognized. Inherent in the idea of justice is the acceptance of the fundamental equality of the human person.

On the basis of these ethical principles, the Popes proceed to reject two common approaches to the social problem:

1. That of extreme individualism, as formulated by the Economic Liberals. They declare it inadequate because it ignores the moral factor in human relations. Nor can its principle of competition be accepted as the sole regulator of the economic system. Competition has its place and is "certainly useful provided it is kept within certain limits, but it clearly cannot direct economic life—a truth which the outcome of the application in practice of the tenets of this evil individualistic spirit has more than sufficiently demonstrated."[63] Among the undesirable consequences of unbridled competition are the failure to recognize man's need for security, the neglect of his human personality, waste, duplication, and the artificial stimulation of wants. Perhaps most serious is its final consequence: the consolidation of economic power in the hands of a few.

"This concentration of power and might, the characteristic mark, as it were, of contemporary economic life, is the fruit that the unlimited freedom of struggle among competitors has of its own nature produced, and which lets only the strongest survive; and this is often the same as saying, those who fight the most violently, those who give least heed to their conscience.

"This accumulation of might and power generates in turn three kinds of conflict: first, there is the struggle for economic supremacy itself; then, there is the bitter fight to gain supremacy over the state in order to use in economic struggles its resources and authority; finally, there is the conflict between states themselves, not only because countries employ their power and shape their policies to promote every economic advantage of their citizens, but also because they seek to decide political controversies that arise among nations through the use of their economic supremacy and strength."[64]

2. That of collectivism. Leo XIII censured materialistic Socialism as unjust and dangerous to the freedom of the human person.[65] Pius XI, reaffirming the condemnation,[66] notes that Socialism has split into two bitterly hostile sections. One of these, Communism, "has undergone almost the same change as the capitalistic economic system." It preaches class war, aims at violent revolution, and is absolutely indifferent to human rights. Its entire philosophy is repugnant to Christian teaching.[67]

"The other section, which has kept the name Socialism, is surely more moderate. It not only professes the rejection of violence, but modifies and tempers to some degree, if it does not reject entirely, the class struggle and the abolition of private ownership. One might say that, terrified by its own principles and by the conclusions drawn therefrom by Communism, Socialism inclines toward, and in a certain measure approaches, the truth which Christian tradition has always held sacred; for it cannot be denied that its demands at times come very near those that Christian reformers of society justly insist upon . . . it can even come to the point that imperceptibly these ideas of the more moderate Socialism will no longer differ from the desires and demands of those who are striving to remould human society on the basis of Christian principles." [68]

But in so far as it has retained its initial materialistic philosophy, it is still in error.

Having rejected these alternatives, the Popes set forth these constructive points as guides to the solution of the social question:

I. *Reform of morals.* Since the social question is not merely economic, it cannot be improved without moral reform.[69] Men will be self-centered or God-centered. Only if they discover a principle outside themselves will they recognize the objectives of justice and charity. If men are to live together, they must practice virtue: they must cultivate moderation and benevolence, and restrain excessive desire for wealth, insatiable greed, and a thirst for pleasure. Many have lost all sense of conscience in the grim battle for economic advantage.[70] Individualism encourages greed, and corruption is inevitable. As a consequence, men are often wretched amid abundance. Happiness does not depend solely on material possessions.

Catholics are not exempted from these strictures. Some "are almost completely unmindful of that sublime law of justice and charity that binds us not only to render to everyone what is his but to succor brothers in need as Christ, the Lord Himself; and, what is worse, out of greed for gain do not scruple to exploit the workers. Even more, there are men who abuse religion itself, and under its name try to hide their unjust exactions in order to protect themselves from the manifestly just demands of the workers. The conduct of such We shall never cease to censure gravely." [71]

True religion is still a necessary ingredient of the social order. Man's freedom rests on an assertion of his spirituality; so do his rights and his dignity. Man cannot recapture the necessary reverence for work without religious motivation. Nor is there any truth in the charge that Christians are so preoccupied with the next world that they have no concern for this. On the contrary, everything material takes on a new importance, for it is by use of the material that man gains eternal life. "A convinced Christian witnesses the needs and miseries of his brothers." [72]

II. *Self-help through organization.* A constant theme in the social encyclicals is the right of labor to organize to protect its interests and to fulfill its needs. Leo XIII called this "a right of nature" which the state cannot deny. As a consequence of the right to associate freely, workers have the right "to adopt the organization and the rules which they judge most appropriate to achieve their purpose." [73] Only through organization can the individual worker protect himself from entrenched power—and he has the greatest need of this protection.[74]

The basis of this prerogative is the principle that the worker has the right to those things consonant with his human dignity. By individual effort, he cannot present his views effectively or marshal power to win attention. Even though his material interests be secure, he still needs his union as a coordinating and representative body; indeed, if the class-war mentality is to be replaced by cooperation, workers must have organization.

Certain conclusions follow from the oft-repeated affirmation of the natural right of workers to organize. On the principle that all rights have correlative duties, it is clear that employers must recognize duly constituted labor unions. Moreover, it is equally evident that these unions have the right to strike for valid ends and with lawful means. As the Australian Hierarchy declared:

> "Under modern conditions, the right to organize in trade unions and the right to strike, under certain defined conditions, are inseparable. It would be futile to urge the formation of trade unions if the Church did not realize this recognition of the right to strike, as a last resort, and when other measures of achieving social justice have failed." [75]

Finally, it may be argued that workers have an obligation to organize. Without this first step, there can be no further institutional reform; just conditions in an industrial unit do not depend entirely on the good will of an individual employer but on the ensemble of economic conditions in the industry, which conditions cannot be assured without industry-wide labor organization.[76]

Not only has the industrial worker the right to organize, but, according to the papal encyclicals, all other groups are equally urged to do so. Employers, farmers, clerical and civil service personnel, even professional people have need of organization. Only if all classes have their appropriate social units will it be possible to proceed to that radical transformation of society the Popes propose.

The encyclicals recognize the reality of class conflict. Pius XI terms it "the deadly internal struggle that is rending the family of mankind" and "a conflict between hostile classes." [77] But such a condition is not desirable. The State and every good citizen should work to the abatement of the class struggle. Harmonious cooperation must be developed among various social groups. This is not Utopian: industrial production has been a unifying as well as a divisive force, and the modern urbanized community is much more closely integrated than the pre-industrial agricultural societies. Besides, basic social improvement depends on higher levels of production, and these cannot be achieved in an atmosphere of conflict.

As one can see, the Popes sketch the ideal toward which industrial society must move:

"The time has come to repudiate empty phrases, and to attempt to organize the forces of the people on a new basis; to raise them above the distinction between employers and would-be workers, and to realize that higher unity which is a bond between all those who cooperate in production, formed by their solidarity in the duty of working together for the common good and filling together the needs of the community. If this solidarity is extended to all branches of production, if it becomes the foundation for a better economic system, it will lead the working classes to obtain honestly their share of responsibility in the direction of the national economy . . . " [78]

The realization of this ideal demands the acceptance of the Industrial Council Plan.[79] This is neither a rigid blueprint nor a magic nostrum but an institutional reform that would encourage a new attitude in industrial relations and promote the intelligent cooperation of capital and labor. The basis of the Plan is the association of trade unions and managerial bodies on all levels: plant, industry, the whole economy; local, regional, national, and international. These bodies of employers and employees would determine wages and industrial conditions; control prices and profits; plan the quality, quantity, and distribution of the product; fix the qualifications for workers; arrange pensions, insurance plans, and other social benefits; associate the workers in production in order that their experience might be utilized to improve methods; and, on the highest levels, discuss general policy for the development of industry, technological changes, and access to raw materials.

In presenting this Plan as the ultimate objective of social reform, the Popes are anxious to avoid two misconceptions:

1. That the organization of industry would eliminate competition. Obviously, this factor would no longer be supreme, as it certainly is not in fact in our contemporary society; but it would not disappear. Cooperation in fixing the rules of the game does not destroy competition in sports; nor would it in business.

2. More importantly, that the Plan would be tantamount to governmental direction of the economy. Precisely because of the perversions of Fascism, Pius XI, when discussing the Plan in *Quadragesimo Anno,* used the word "free" five times in a single paragraph.[80] The very purpose of this free association of autonomous groupings would be to protect them from giant power, either political or economic, and to encourage free activity without dependence on the impersonal State. These groups are not to be *organs of the State,* nor are their representatives to be chosen by the political power. The essence of the Plan is its voluntary character. Hence, the Popes expect it to be achieved only by evolution. The State would have only the general, regulatory power that it exercises over all private and semi-private associations.

III. *Wider ownership of productive property.* The encyclicals approach this broad question from the viewpoint of the dignity of human labor. They explicitly reject the Liberal Economists' definition of labor as a commodity.[81] "No one should be ashamed because he makes his living by toil,"[82] for labor has been sanctified by the example of Christ and is an important contributor to virtuous living. These ends, however, cannot be secured if workers are subjected to conditions which belie their human dignity.[83] Workers must not be treated as slaves or regarded as engaged in shameful activity.

> "It is inhuman to use men as things of gain and to put no more value on them than they are worth in muscle or energy . . . Likewise, more work is not to be imposed than strength can endure, nor that kind of work which is unsuited to a worker's age or sex." [84]

Since men are morally equal and intrinsically valuable, they shall not be prevented, because of exhausting hours of work and inhuman conditions, from making their just contribution to society.[85] And in justice they must be granted a living wage.

Leo XIII struck a fundamental and often casually ignored truth when he wrote:

" . . . *it is incontestable that the wealth of nations arises from no other source than from the labor of workers*. Equity therefore commands that public authority show proper concern for the worker so that from what he contributes to the common good, he may receive what may enable him. . . to live his life without hardship."[86]

All wage contracts that take advantage of a worker's need by paying him less than is sufficient for his decent support are immoral.[87] To be sure, mere payment of a subsistence wage is not enough. Since man has the right to family life, he must receive a wage adequate for the support of wife and children in decent comfort.[88] Finally, he cannot be denied the opportunity to acquire a modest fortune and "so make suitable provision through public or private insurance for old age, and for periods of illness and unemployment."[89]

Certain consequences follow from this principle of the living wage:

1. It justifies the workers' right to unions and collective bargaining.[90]

2. It implies that women should get equal pay for equal work, both in justice and by way of preventing the depression of wage standards.

3. Payment of a living wage is due "in strict justice"; consequently, employers who are able to pay it and do not are bound to restitution.

4. The standard of a living wage is not absolute but relative to the resources and economic situation in a given country; still, it can never fall below a basic minimum.

5. Because most industrial workers depend on their wage, work is a right to which man is justly entitled. Property owners have a duty to provide work and, where they cannot, the State must intervene.[91]

6. Failure to provide a living, family wage often ends, deplorably enough, in the practice of engaging child and female labor in industrial establishments.

"To abuse the years of childhood and the limited strength of women is grossly wrong. Mothers, concentrating on household duties, should work primarily in the home or in its immediate vicinity. It is an intolerable abuse, to be abolished at all costs, for mothers, on account of the fathers' low wage, to be forced to engage in gainful occupations outside the home to the neglect of their proper cares and duties, especially the training of children. Every effort must therefore be made that fathers of families receive a wage large enough to meet ordinary family needs adequately. . ." [92]

7. A just wage, for all of that, is not the final goal of the workers' participation in the fruits of industry.

"We consider it more advisable, however, in the present condition of modern society that, as far as is possible, the work contract, be somewhat modified by a partnership contract, as is already being done in various ways and with no small advantage to owners and workers. *Workers and other employees thus became sharers in ownership and management or participate in some fashion* in the profits received." [93]

8. Work, like ownership, has a social as well as individual character, which can never be ignored. [94]

These considerations on the dignity of labor and the right to a just wage are necessary to appreciate the doctrine of property that appears in the social encyclicals. In large part, the doctrine is based on St. Thomas: [95] property is desirable and natural to man in the present order of human society, and is productive of the best social results. His arguments for private property are largely utilitarian, laying particular emphasis on its value as a preservative of human freedom. But as regards its use: "Man ought to possess external things, not as his own, but as common, so that, to wit, he is ready to communicate to them in need."

This distinction of St. Thomas between the individual and social aspects of private property is preserved in the encyclicals. [96] The popes assert the right of private property in order that "individuals may provide for themselves and their families," [97] but stress also the social obligations that are inherent in its possession. [98]

Private property is not an absolute right, but is a "right circumscribed by the necessities of social living." [99] While abuses do not destroy the right, they have led men to question it, for some "so interpret and use the relationships of private property that they succeed—even better than their adversaries—in overturning this very institution, so natural and indispensable to human life, and especially to the family." [100]

The ownership of private property involves duties. [101] Men are only the stewards of the goods which God has given. Property is a trust, and superfluous wealth must be devoted to charity or used to promote new opportunities for employment.

The social aspects of property become more prominent when there is question of productive property. All property, especially the latter type, must be regulated in the interest of the common good though not to the point of collectivization. The owners of property have also resspsonibilities toward the State, and taxation should be imposed progressively according to ability to pay.

The Popes always insist that property be extended to include the largest possible number as owners. The aim, therefore, should

". . . not [be] to abolish private property, which is the foundation of family stability, but to work for its extension as the reward of the conscientious toil of every working man and woman. . ." [102]

"The Church is opposed to the accumulation of these goods in the hands of a relatively small and exceeding rich group, while vast masses of people are condemned to a pauperism and an economic condition unworthy of human beings." [103]

"The immense multitude of non-owning workers on the one hand, and the enormous riches of certain very wealthy men on the other, establish an unanswerable argument that the riches which are so abundantly produced in our age of 'industrialism,' as it is called, are not rightly distributed and equitably made available to the various classes of people. Therefore, with all our strength and effort we must strive that at least in the future, the abundant fruits of production will accrue equitably to those who are rich and will be distributed in ample sufficiency among the workers. . .that they may increase their property by thrift. . . and have assurance that, when their lives are ended, they will provide in some measure for those they leave after them." [104]

IV. *Sound social legislation.* The welfare concept, so much a matter of present controversy, is advocated in the papal encyclicals. The philosophical basis, again, is the value of the human person. The State has the right and duty to interfere in the economic process when the welfare of the whole society is at stake or where the rights of an individual or of a group are threatened. Especially must legislation "prevent the worker, who is or will be a father of a family, from being condemned to an economic dependence and slavery which is irreconcilable with his rights as a person." [105]

Quadragesimo Anno praised the progress that had been made in this field of social legislation during the forty years before it. It reiterated the position of Leo XIII that

"government must not be a mere guardian of law and good

order, but rather must put forth every effort that 'through the entire scheme of laws and institutions. . .both public and individual well-being may develop spontaneously out of the very structure and administration of the State.' Just freedom of action must, of course, be left both to individuals and to families, yet only on condition that the common good be preserved and wrong to any individual be abolished. The function of the rulers of the State, moreover, is to watch over the community and its parts; but in protecting private individuals in their rights *chief consideration ought to be given to the weak and the poor.*" [106]

The State must regulate private property in the common interest; it thus furnishes a service to owners and strengthens property rights by preventing intolerable evils.[107] It should not succumb to the evil of individualism[108] but recall that one of its primary functions is to benefit the condition of the workers.[109] On this basis, the Popes approve a wide range of welfare legislation.[110]

One caution is introduced: the State ought to allow subordinate groups to handle matters of lesser importance and should confine itself to "directing, watching, urging, restraining, as occasion requires and necessity demands." This is the principle of "subsidiarity," so frequently referred to in papal documents. "The State should be the coordinator and supreme guardian, encouraging private groups where possible and intervening only where necessary to correct abuses."[111]

This principle is applied to the problem of nationalization. Complete nationalization is unequivocally condemned. But where there is danger of excessive individual concentration of economic power, nationalization is approved:

> "For certain kinds of property, it is rightly contended, ought to be reserved to the State, since they carry with them a dominating power so great that cannot without danger to the general welfare be entrusted to private individuals." [112]

But in general, public control is preferable to public ownership; likewise, limited public ownership on the model of the TVA is more desirable than the absorption by the State of a whole segment of the economy.

V. *Organization of international economic life.* The economic relations among nations should aim at such a harmony and cooperation as should be the goal of the classes within the national economy. Nations are historic facts, but they should not ignore the larger truth that

> "the human race is bound together by reciprocal ties, moral and juridical, into a great commonwealth directed to the good

of all nations and ruled by special laws which protect its unity and promote its prosperity. Now no one can fail to see how the claim to absolute autonomy for the State stands in open opposition to this natural law that is inherent in man—nay, denies it utterly—and, therefore, leaves the stability of international relations at the mercy of the will of rulers, while it destroys the possibility of true union and fruitful collaboration directed to the general good." [113]

As leaders of a supranational religious community, the Popes had little tolerance of the economic nationalism that played such a large role in the history of this century. They consistently pleaded that "all nations have a right to live and seek prosperity." They opposed "the egoism which tends to hoard economic resources and materials destined for the use of all, to such an extent that the nations less favored by nature are not permitted access to them." [114] Evidences of a disposition on the part of possessing nations to share their riches were warmly praised. But much remains to be done:

"In international trade relations, let all means be sedulously employed for the removal of those artificial barriers to economic life which are the effects of distrust and hatred. All must remember that the peoples of the earth form one family in God." [115]

Barriers to emigration are equally deplored. The favorable distribution of men over the surface of the earth "which God created and prepared for the use of all" is both a human and economic boon. Emigration will be a real asset to the recipient country if it will give the newcomers a plot of land. Thus,

"the thickly inhabited areas will be relieved and their peoples will receive new friends in foreign countries; and the states which receive the emigrants will acquire industrious citizens. In this way, the nations which give and those which receive will both contribute to the increased welfare of man and the progress of human culture." [116]

In all international matters the principle is the same:

"Since the various nations largely depend on one another in economic matters and need one another's help, they should strive with a united purpose and effort to promote by wisely conceived pacts and institutions a prosperous and happy international cooperation in economic life." [117]

* * * * *

The social encyclicals concentrate on the moral aspects of

the social problem. As the summary given above indicates, the term "moral" stresses the human factors in economics. Religion is necessarily involved. Men must be human beings before they can be Christians, and it is difficult to preach virtue if the foundations of human living are destroyed.

The Popes, while stressing the importance of moral and religious remedies, do not claim that these are sufficient. We might compare their analysis to the distinction that should be made today between Soviet imperialism and Communism. The former can be met primarily by military means although the moral factor is an element in military strength. The latter cannot be repelled by arms but must be fought by intellectual and spiritual weapons, as well as by social reform. In economic questions, problems of unemployment and production are largely technical; but the overall purpose of economic activity and of factors such as distribution have important moral aspects. It is to these that the Popes have directed their attention.

Finally, the Popes do not intend the encyclicals to remain essays in ethical elucidation. The documents are studded with demands that Catholics translate these principles into concrete action. The clergy are particularly urged to interest themselves in social matters, to study them scientifically, and to work for the economic betterment of their flocks. To them was addressed the command: "Go to the workingman, especially where he is poor; and, in general, go to the poor."[118]

> "If you truly love the laborer (and you must love him because his conditions of life approach nearer to those of the Divine Master), you must assist him materially and religiously: materially, bringing about in his favor the practice not only of commutative justice but also of social justice, that is, all those provisions which aim at relieving the condition of the proletarian; and then religiously, giving him again the religious comforts without which he will struggle in a materialism that brutalizes him and degrades him." [119]

The laity too must engage: "The first and immediate apostles to the workers ought to be workers; the apostles to those who follow industry and trade ought to be from among themselves."[120] A constant theme is that Catholic Action must be a social apostolate and work for the betterment of economic conditions. In this effort, the Catholic press can play a prominent role.[112]

C. Modern State

The social and intellectual movements that have been

sketched in the essay on France[122] profoundly altered the political arrangements of Continental Europe in the course of the
nineteenth century. The absolutist states of the Old Regime
no longer were in accord with the social realities of an evolving
world. Gradually they were replaced by new political forms
that may be designated as Constitutional or Liberal. These
new states possessed three general characteristics which had
been foreshadowed in the principles of 1789:

1. They affirmed basic civil rights of the individual, which
were ordinarily enshrined in a written Constitution. These
rights, variously enumerated, added up to "liberty, property,
security, and resistance to oppression." Founded on the concept
of the inviolability of the human person, these rights were at
first rooted in the notions of the Natural Law; but as the
century progressed, the tendency was to abandon the principles
of Natural Law in favor of a contractual law that was considered
more suitable to a commercial society. In stating these rights,
the new states emphasized, above all, the untrammeled communication of free speech and of a free press. They considered
property a sacred and inalienable right, regarding any restrictions upon it as violations of fundamental law. Economic
freedom was to them, of course, a logical corollary. Finally,
they permitted certain citizens to choose an elected Parliament
that was the source of legislative power.

2. The Liberal States declared themselves secular, in the
sense that they were indifferent to religion. They treated all
religions equally but thought none of them necessary to public
life. Theoretically, at least, they neither supported nor suppressed any particular creed.

3. These states claimed competence over wider areas of human life. They maintained that the nation-state was the source
of all sovereignty, with full power to determine its law without
interference from any other authority or body of principles.
They declared themselves solely competent to deal with marriage, education, and welfare activities. These claims were
strengthened by the development of an emotional identification
of the individual with the nation-state—a consciousness that his
well-being was firmly linked with its security and prosperity.
This growing nationalism found itself in conflict with an older
mood that had grown out of the struggle with absolutism: a
feeling that political power was always dangerous; that it should
be hemmed in by the sternest restrictions; that the State should
not interfere with a citizen unless he directly injured another.
Because of these two divergent tendencies of nationalism and
individualism, the Constitutional regimes betray a certain ambi-

valence: the right of association was ordinarily denied, at least to workers; individual preferences were ignored in favor of State demands in matters such as conscription and compulsory education.[123]

These Liberal States proved to be transitory phenomena that soon faced new pressures from the growing political consciousness of the masses. Previously, peasants, town workers, craftsmen, and the lower bourgeoisie had been generally passive in politics. In times of stress or of particular hardship, they may have risen in revolt; but, generally, their uprisings lacked direction and subsided in defeat.[124] Even the French Revolution brought them no permanent *political* gains although it had left a memory that could not be entirely erased.

The nineteenth century witnessed decisive changes that were to awaken the political ambitions of the "little men" of Western Europe. The most striking of these derived from the growing industrialism and affected the class created by machine production. The factory concentrated the industrial worker, giving him a common bond and a common grievance. It also provided a disciplined strength that he had not known before. The spread of popular education and the development of new popular media of communication offered opportunity to diffuse discontent and to establish organizations and programs. The catalytic force was the vision of progress, which gradually seeped down from the confident ranks of the upper bourgeoisie and professional classes. In these groups, the great dream of an earthly Paradise was a comforting phantasy that could justify existing relationships, offering new vistas that would be realized when the last remnants of the past would be swept away. But as this vision of universal peace and plenty filtered down to lower economic levels, it awakened a most bitter discontent with the prevailing low standards. It was idle for statisticians to provide graphs showing a rising standard in all classes of the population. The bitterness derived from relative, not absolute, criteria—the disparity between the promises and the reality, between the Utopia of the romantics and the grinding poverty of the slums. *In the nineteenth century, it was man's expectations that were defeated.* He may have been lengthening his life span and increasing his consumption, but the slow process mocked the soaring flight of his fancy. Life was still hard and uncertain despite the promise of the machine.

The average man of nineteenth century Europe was being given the means to become an active citizen at the very time when his mind was awakened to new horizons. Actually, the factory worker was not the first to be stirred by the new possibilities; more frequently, it was the discontented intellectual, the small tradesman, the skilled worker or craftsman who showed him the way. Once the movement gained momentum, it was not confined to the urban areas but ultimately made itself felt in the rural populations. The net effect was a great surge of popular political activity that has given all political movements of the twentieth century a common character that we designate with the label "mass."

These popular stirrings found different degrees of satisfaction according to the political and social background of the various areas. In the egalitarian atmosphere of the United States, they found relatively rapid response in the expansion of the franchise and in the activity of political parties.[125] In England, the evolutionary tradition, which had made possible the peaceful translation of power to the bourgeoisie, proved flexible enough to meet the new demands though only after a struggle that has left its imprint on British political life. Several of the smaller states of Western Europe were also able to canalize these demands into mass democratic parties.

But many of the political structures of the Continent, still in a transitional stage toward Liberal national states, proved less responsive to new challenges coming from below, which became more clamorous when denied an outlet. It is in this atmosphere that one can explain the enormous appeal of Marxism, which was able to attract a considerable number of the politically awakened European masses. Marx's contribution consisted of a vision of history as a great drama in which the most suffering class of modern society redeems the whole of mankind through that victory over the powers of darkness known as the proletarian revolution. This vision was capable of a variety of interpretations, reformist or revolutionary. In a vulgarized form, it could also be merged into cruder interpretations of the prevailing nationalism so as to give rise to strange hybrids like Italian Fascism.[126]

These new political movements, democratic, Marxist, and Fascist, vary widely in aim and method. All, however, have a common base: they are mass movements which aim to satisfy new aspirations born of modern man's political awareness. To understand the period we are surveying, it is important to bear in mind one primary political fact: the "common man," who had been mute throughout most of human history, was in the process of demanding an active voice in the direction of public affairs. The method by which that demand was fulfilled or frustrated makes the political history of our time.

* * * * *

Leo XIII ascended the pontifical throne at a time when this ground swell was still in an incipient stage throughout most of Europe. But, by 1878, the Constitutional or Liberal state had established itself in the western half of the Continent. It was with this that he was principally concerned. His objective was to clarify the Catholic position toward the Liberal State and to minimize the area of conflict without denying substantial points of difference. He did not aim to elaborate a new political philosophy. His approach was exclusively moral. He concerned himself with the institutional only where he felt it touched the spiritual destiny of man. To him, political institutions were accidental, historical, and transitory. It is their philosophical basis that he considered important.

Because of the complexity of the subject, this survey will be confined to five major points in the politico-moral teaching of the modern Papacy. In each category, the views of Leo XIII will be sketched, following which there will be a brief notation of signicant contributions by his successors. It must be borne in mind always that the rapid political evolution suggested above required the Popes of the twentieth century to face drastically new political situations.

I. *The Origin of the State.* The starting point of Leo's political thinking is the premise that all civil authority comes from God. This is the most frequently repeated text in the encyclicals, and it is the criterion by which political philosophies are judged. ". . . Catholics trace the right to rule back to God as its natural and necessary source."[127] The reason is found in man's social nature. Man must live in society to develop his personality, but society cannot hold together unless there is a ruling authority.[128]

This emphasis on the divine basis of civil authority is open to misconstruction. Leo was concerned because many not only denied the dependence of the political upon God but also rejected the proposition that authority originates in the divine order. He refused to accept the doctrine that government derives exclusively from the arbitarary will of men. But his refusal stemmed from the failure of government to see the ultimate source of authority in God. The holders of political power, he maintained, can be freely elected by the people; but an election can only designate those who shall rule. It does not confer the right itself.[129] Thus, the Pope did not condemn popular sovereignty as a political principle of constitutional law; what he did was to reject the philosophical justification that society is but as an accidental association of citizens who temporarily surrender their rights in a covenant.[130]

Fundamentally, Leo was trying to answer Rousseau's great query in the *Social Contract:* why should one man obey another?[131] He says that fear is not an adequate motive: "....for those who are brought under control by fear will revolt all the more readily, once an opportunity offers itself of doing so unpunished . . ." Fear is the mother of rebellion. Obedience must be secured by motives of a higher order. No man has in himself the right to restrict the free will of others by binding commands; nor will men accept such commands unless they find an adequate reason. Such a motive can be found only in the proposition that, because God ordains men to live in civil society, He also commands them to obey duly constituted authority. Obedience to lawful civil authority, therefore, is part of the general obligation of religion. "It is God alone who can commit to a man power over his fellow man." Nor does man surrender his self-respect by civil obedience; rather, he is fulfilling the divine plan etched in his human nature.[132]

The constant repetition of this principle in papal documents may cause wonder. But Leo XIII considered it essential not merely to explain the citizen's obligation of obedience but also to avoid all forms of statism which would place the political organization above the divine law. Limitation of the State's power rests on the doctrine that it is not *sui juris* but a delegation from God. That power cannot be exercised merely for the profit of the rulers or in a way that perverts justice and the dignity of man.[133] The State cannot impose arbitrary or capricious commands on its subjects.[134] Those whose exercise authority in the State must pattern their conduct on the divine concern for the human race.[135]

Another consequence of the divine origin of the State's authority is that the State must make public acknowledgment of the link that binds it to God. This duty of the State is fulfilled "by the public profession of religion." Men must not only worship God as individuals; they must also recognize Him collectively in their political community. "Society, no less than individuals, owes gratitude to God, who gave it being and maintains it, and whose ever-bounteous goodness enriches it with countless blessings."[136]

It is this principle that is the starting-point for the Pope's criticism of the Liberal State. He insists that the Church has always been the defender of human liberty because its doctrine rests on the belief that man is a spiritual, as well as material being, who has the faculties of reason and free will. Never has the Church countenanced fatalism or determinism. Human liberty has its limitations: man can freely choose evil. It needs the enlightenment that is provided by law, for freedom cannot exempt from law. Freedom is the guide that assists man to a right choice, and it rests upon the Natural Law that God "has implanted in rational creatures, which inclines them to their right action and end."[137]

The major objections to the Liberal State are:

1. It denies that God is the source of authority and thereby rejects the sovereignty of His Law. By this denial, the State becomes "absolute and omnipotent"; though it extols liberty, the road has been open to tyranny.[138] This does not mean that Catholics should begin a crusade against the Liberals:

> "If. . .a remedy is desired, let it be sought for in a restoration of sound doctrine, from which alone the preservation of order and, as a consequence the defense of true liberty, can be confidently expected." [139]

2. In the name of liberty, the State permits the exploitation of the poorer members of society and does not give adequate protection to the working class.[140] The State has the obligation to seek the common good and to direct the resources of the community so that they promote the maximum general welfare. The Liberal claim that the State is neutral in these matters is specious inasmuch as social groups tend to capture and use it for their own purposes.

While Leo placed major emphasis on the divine origin of civil society, he did not ignore the historical roots of the State. How the State actually came into being, though a theoretical question, has important practical consequences.[141] The Pope considered the State as a development of the family and as a consequence of free human action and initiative: "Diverse families, without abandoning the rights and duties of the domestic society, unite under the inspiration of nature in order to constitute themselves as members of another greater family, the civic society." Their purpose in so doing

> ". . .is not only to find therein the means of providing for their material welfare, but, above all, to draw thence the boon of moral improvement. Otherwise, society would rise but little above the level of an aggregation of beings devoid of reason, whose whole life would consist in satisfaction of sensual instincts. Moreover, without this moral improvement it would be difficult to demonstrate that civil society was an advantage, rather than a detriment to man, as man." [142]

The following points are to be noted in this significant passage:

1. Men constitute the State as free rational beings—a position roughly similar to the legal fiction of the Social Contract Theory.

2. They do so as a consequence of their social nature, both biological and rational. The contract, then, is not formal, as in seventeenth and eighteenth century political theory. It need not be specific. Nor does it constitute a transfer of individual natural rights. But the Pope demands as morally necessary some form of convenant or consent.[143]

3. The condition of man in political society is an improvement because of the moral opportunities it gives him. Only in political life may man fully realize the possibilities of his nature. This returns us to the original proposition that, since man must live in a State to fulfill the Natural Law, civil authority is a necessary consequence of the divine plan for man.

II. *The Form of the State.* The second basic assumption of Leo's political teaching is that there is no one form of government which alone satisfies the requirements of morality. The organization of the State is the result of historical processes, and there is no absolute in this area. The primary interest of the Church is in the working operation of government:

> "Of the various forms of government, the Church does not reject any that are fitted to procure the welfare of the subjects; she wishes only—and this nature herself requires—that they should be constituted without involving wrong to anyone, and especially without violating the rights of the Church." [144]

Naturally, difference of opinion on the question of the best form of government is permissible; and no one should be condemned as failing in the Faith who prefers any type, including the democratic.[145]

Leo's statement that the democratic form of government is permissible for Catholics may sound strange to contemporary Americans. The Pope does not canonize the representative type of government, but he insists that it is comfortable to Christian moral teaching. It is important to recall the historical context in which this letter was written.[146] Its significance lies in the repudiation of the oft-repeated claim that monarchy alone fitted into the framework of Catholic theology and that the hierarchical constitution of the Church demanded a similar form in civil society. Leo strongly condemned this pseudo-theological reasoning: the papal monarchy is not to be considered a model for political constitutions. By removing this obstacle, Leo paved the way for the acceptance of democratic government in theory, as he did in practice, by his conciliatory approach to the Third French Republic.[147]

A more positive approach to democratic government can be seen in the encyclicals of later Popes, particularly in Pius XII's *Christmas Message* of 1944.[148] Written on the sixth Christmas of the Second World War, Pius entitled his discourse *Democracy and Peace*. In th midst of carnage, he finds material for hope:

> "While armies are still spending themselves in mortal conflict and using more and more cruel methods of warfare, we see statesmen, responsible representatives of their respective nations, meeting together for conferences and conversations, to determine the fundamental rights and duties which are to provide the basis of a reconstituted community of nations, and to trace out the path that shall lead to a better future, a future more secure and more worthy of humanity."[149]

Citizens "are becoming more and more resentful of the exclusive claims of a dictatorial authority which allows of no control or discussion, and are demanding a system of government more consistent with the dignity and liberty of the citizen."[150] They feel that "had it been in their power to control or direct the action of the authorities, the world would not have been drawn into the disastrous maelstrom of the war, and that to avoid the recurrence of a similar catastrophe, effective guarantees must be created within the people itself." Thus, democracy gains favor among those who demand an effective share in government. The Church leaves to each people the right to choose its form of government, being primarily interested in man, *"who, far from being a merely material and passive element in social life, is and must always be an active sharer in it,* the ground upon which it is built, and the end for which it exists."[151] The dignity of man is the first and chief consideration, a dignity most strikingly confirmed by the Birth of the Son of God among men.

> "So far-reaching and decisive has the activity of the State become in modern times that a democratic form of government is considered by many today to be a natural postulate of reason itself. Therefore, the demand for 'more and better democracy' can only mean the demand that the citizens shall be increasingly in a position to hold his own personal opinion, express it, and to give effect to it in a manner consistent with the common good."[152]

The Pope contrasts the concept of the "inert mass" and that of a true people,

"exuberant with a life that diffuses itself throughout the State
and all its organs, instilling into them with constantly renewed
vigor the consciousness of their responsibility and a true appreciation of the common good."

"In a people worthy of the name, the citizen is conscious of
being a person with his own duties and rights; while he is conscious of his own freedom, he respects the liberty and dignity
of his fellows." [153]

There are no obstacles to "a genuine spirit of common fellowship and brotherhood." There is true civic equality because
"every man has the right honorably to live his own personal
life . . ."[154]

Because democracy rests upon moral values, it must give
proper place to God. More than any other form, it needs
religious foundations because it makes the greatest demands on
electors and elected. A healthy democracy, resting on principles
of natural law and revealed truth, will resist the false doctrine
of State absolutism. It will also recognize the "unity of the
human race and of the family of nations," which unity is the
sole guarantee of peace. And it will heed the Church's message
on the dignity of man and on his vocation to be a son of God.
This is the meaning of Christmas and the only firm base for
democracy.

The whole spirit of this message, one of the most important
political statements of the modern Papacy, provides a moral
foundation for a synthesis of democracy and Christianity. While
the attitude of neutrality to the various forms of government
still stands, there is evident a pronounced papal benevolence
toward the active participation of all citizens in government
and a strong rejection of absolutism in all its forms.

III. *Limitations of the State.* The condemnation of the
absolute State is one of the most fundamental points in the
papal political doctrine. Leo emphasized the distinction between the State and the community.[155] Society is broader than
the State. The former includes families and social groups whose
rights the State cannot invade. Civil society is supreme in its
sphere, but its main function is to promote the common good
in the material and cultural areas. Although it is supreme,
it is not all-absorbing. It cannot destroy the rights of the
individual, the family, or the Church.

The political philosophy of Leo is pluralistic. It affirms the
right of the family and of vocational, professional, educational,
and religious institutions to exist and to pursue their own
specific ends. They may be interwoven into the public order
by the State, but they have their own inviolable rights and

functions. The role of the State is to protect and to preserve these bodies, not to incorporate them. Civil society can provide their external form, but their inner content is independent of its control. Papal doctrine emphatically rejects the monistic State, which would destroy the autonomous groups grounded in the rights of the human person.

The basic concept, then, is that there is an element of the sacred in human life, which may not be dominated by the secular power of the State. Included in this area of the sacred are the following relationships:

1. Husband-wife relationship. Marriage is subject to both civil and canon law. The State has the power to determine its civil effects, such as property relationships and financial support.[156] But marriage is essentially a spiritual bond. It has been established by God and raised by Christ to the dignity of a Sacrament: it is the holiest human association.[157] According to divine command, marriage is monogamous and indissoluble, and the divorce of sacramentally married couples is contrary to God's law. Human marriage will bring good results only as long as it is recognized as a holy union that must endure for life.[158] Because it is holy, Christ has placed the sacramental aspects of marriage in the care of His Church. She alone has competence in the valid marriage of baptized persons. Among the rights she claims for her children is the freedom to enter marriage or not, as they choose.[159]

2. Parent-child relationship. The child is a citizen of two worlds: he is a member of the Church, destined for salvation in it; he is a member of a State which must assure his temporal needs. The latter cannot absorb the entire role of education. Parents have a natural right to educate their children; all other agencies, including the State, are auxiliary. Parents have a duty to see that the education of their children does not harm their Faith, which is a precious gift of God, and that their education is permeated with the spirit of Christian piety. The ideal in education is the Christian school, in which the whole instruction takes into account the place of God in human society.[160]

As the struggle for the soul of youth became more intense in the present century, subsequent Popes gave greater emphasis to the subject of education. It is a major theme in Pius XI's protest against Italian Fascism,[161] and an even more important item in his indictment of German National Socialism.[162] Against the totalitarian claim to complete control over the formation of youth, the Pope reaffirmed the principle that parents had a primary and original right to the education of the children given them by God. Governmental regulations that disregard the parental rights guaranteed by the Natural Law, or threats and violence which nullify these rights, are essentially immoral:

"The Church of Christ cannot wait until her altars have been overthrown, until sacrilegious hands have set the houses of God on fire, before she begins to mourn and lament. When the attempt is made to desecrate the tabernacle of a child's soul sanctified in baptism, by an education that is hostile to Christ; when from this living temple of God the eternal lamp of belief in Christ is cast out and in its place is brought the false light of a substitute faith that has nothing in common with the faith of the Cross, then the time of spiritual profanation is at hand, then it is the duty of every professing Christian to separate clearly his responsibility from that of the other side, to keep his conscience clear of any culpable co-operation in such dreadful work and corruption. . .

"Meanwhile do not forget this: from the bond of responsibility established by God that binds you to your children, no earthly power can loose you. No one of those who today are oppressing you in the exercise of your rights in education and pretend to free you from your duty in this matter will be able to answer for you to the Eternal Judge when He asks you the question: 'Where are those I have given you?' " [163]

While the modern dictatorships have pressed the State's claim to exclusive control over education to its logical completeness, other governments have moved somewhat in the same direction. Accordingly, Pius XI surveyed the whole field of education in *Divini Illius Magistri*.[164] Education must equip man for more than the acquisition of material skills; it must prepare him for the ultimate purpose of his existence, which is God. Education must certainly be religious if it is to achieve the maximum of well-being for human society; in truth, only religious education aims at the Supreme Good.

Education is the responsibility of three distinct societies:

a. The Church, which, given the right to teach by Jesus Christ, has the task of forming her children in the way of truth and virtue. The Church has evidenced such interest from the beginning, and the great universities of Europe are eloquent testimony of the fulfillment of her mission.

b. The family, whose rights are founded in its role of generating life. The rights of the family come before the rights of the State. They cannot be violated by the State; they endure along with the parents' duty to care for the child. The common sense of mankind agrees that human life comes, not from the State, but from the parent. It is through the family in which

they are born that children become a part of the State. These
rights of parents extend to the whole field of education though
they are not despotic or absolute.

    c. The State, whose rights in education also come from
God, in her capacity as promoter of the general temporal
welfare. Its function is to "protect and foster . . . the family
and the individual," to respect their prior rights and also the
supernatural position of the Church. The State must "protect
the rights of the child himself" against neglectful parents and
assist them with means for educating their children. The State
also has the right to take measures to ensure that all its citizens
are sufficiently educated to carry out their civic and political
duties and that they have adequate physical training. But "any
State monopoly which forces families to use government schools
contrary to the dictates of their Christian conscience—or even
against their legitimate preferences—is unjust and unlawful." [165]
Nor should the State abuse its prerogative by inculcating excessive nationalism or militarism. Essentially, the State's role is
to assist the initiative of the family and of the Church in the
fulfillment of their duties to the child.

    3. *Ruler-citizen relationship.* In all its legislation, the State
must take cognizance of the Natural Law, which is the supreme
standard of human conduct. Every human authority is subject
to it; citizens cannot be forced to act against it. This Natural
Law is the moral guarantee of liberty. Its denial would destroy
the freedom of the human person. All basic human rights are
founded upon it; the State cannot violate these individual
rights; without acting against the fundamental principles implanted by the Creator.

    The State, then, has a legitimate competence. As long as it
remains in this field, the citizen has a duty to obey.[166] But when
it oversteps its rightful boundaries, especially when it commands
violations of justice or of divine law, then "resistance becomes
a positive duty, obedience a crime." However, Catholics should
be cautious in resorting to violence in defense of their rights.[167]
Never should they use their religious associations for political
purposes.[168] Restoring Christianity effectually in the face of
unjust regimes demands, most of all, the holiness of the clergy
and the willingness of the laity to cooperate in apostolic work.[169]
This spirit, joined to an active interest in social problems and
to an adequate intellectual formation, is the best antidote
against the campaigns of the godless.[170]

    IV. *Relations of Church and State.* The Popes maintain that
there is no necessary conflict between man's duties as a citizen
and as a Catholic. Church and State are equally sovereign in

their respective spheres. Any real clash between them is impossible if each observes the limits that God has marked out for it.[171] The State is founded to secure the "tranquillity of public life." Its aim should be to provide an amosphere in which the citizen can secure his material needs in peace, and in which he can serve God by practicing virtue. The Church, founded by Christ, participates in His twofold nature: it is divine in its origin and in the Life it has from God; it is human in its composition. Its constitution stems from its Founder, Who made it a free society with competence over all that pertains to salvation or the worship of God.

Conflict will arise when the State trenches on the domain of the spiritual; when the Church is prevented from fulfilling her mission, from preaching the Gospel, or from educating her children. In such cases, she has the duty to protest and to resist. Even where this invasion does not exist, there will always be some practical difficulties because the same human beings are the subjects of a twofold authority. Yet, God has provided the Church and the State with the capability of enjoying mutual harmony by defining the nature of the powers committed to each.[172] Their double jurisdiction might be compared to two concentric circles, each possessing an area of rights proper to itself, both possessing a common segment which will widen or narrow according to historical circumstances and to the proportion of Catholics in the State. Total absorption by either is fatal since each has its proper sphere of independent action.[173]

It is not enough that there two centers of authority avoid conflict. The political community, bound to recognize God as its Father and Creator, owes Him reverence and public worship. It cannot discharge these positive obligations to God while declaring itself indifferent to religion. Leo had written a letter to the bishops of Brazil, praising them for their share in the abolition of Negro slavery.[174] He followed it by one to the Emperor, in which he protested against the philosophical principle of agnosticism, which declares the State neutral in regard to religion, not because it reveres conscience, but because it believes that there is no possibility of truth in these matters. This attitude, says the Pope, violates the prerogatives of the divinely instituted Church.[175]

Therefore, maintained Leo, the Church does not hold as an ideal the separation of Church and State. The problem did not appear until the shattering of religious unity inclined the State to withdraw from all religious questions. It became neutral or secular. Man as a citizen became divorced from man as a religious being and member of the Church. No religious group

benefited from privileges. The Church was organized according
to the ordinary rules of civil law; legal relations between
Church and State were reduced to a minimum.

The Pontiff wrote that this was theoretically not desirable
although in certain historical circumstances, e.g., in the absence
of religious unity, it might be the best arrangement. In such a
case, union of Church and State might lead to greater evils
like compulsion and deceit. Thus, he says in his Encyclical on
Catholicity in the United States:

> "Thanks are due to the equity of the laws which obtain in
> America and to the customs of the well-ordered Republic. For
> the Church amongst you, unopposed by the Constitution and
> government of your nation, fettered by no hostile legislation,
> protected against violence by the impartiality of the tribunals, is
> free to live and act without hindrance." [176]

These happy conditions in the United States do not justify
a universal principle. Leo distinguished between two kinds of
separation:

1. A radically hostile one, which is introduced not out of
concern for a diversity of sects but out of a desire to emphasize
the rejection of supernatural religion. By such a separation,
the State aims to destroy the Christian faith of its citizens. It
controls education, emptying it of all religious content. It
restricts the activity of the Church and curtails her ownership
of property. Such action denies to Catholics their basic human
rights and their protection by law. While all separation denies
by implication the complete public honor due God, this type
is a fundamental and sinister denial of liberty.

2. The benevolent type, as practiced in the United States.
A man's choice of religion being purely his own, the Church
may deal only with those who freely accept her direction. Where
she is not recognized as a divine society, however, she should
still be free to operate within the framework of the civil law.
Governmental neutrality toward religion, in a nation of many
religious sects, may be a practical necessity.

Finally, Leo XIII denies that "man has an unlimited right to
say and to print what he likes." No State could or does grant
such a freedom. It is true that

> "in all matters of opinion which God leaves to man's free dis-
> cussion, full liberty of thought and speech is naturally within
> the right of every man; for such liberty never leads men to
> suppress the truth, but often to discover it and to make it
> known."

But this does not mean the privilege to circulate lies or to publish deceitful statements.[177]

V. *Relations among States.* The problem of international relations has become a major preoccupation of the Papacy in the twentieth century. The collapse of the Concert of Europe in the late nineteenth century and the heightening intensity of national feeling made the search for an international society the major question of our time. Papal attention to the issue of war and peace grew as the crisis deepened. Whereas the subject was treated in broad outline in the writings of Leo XIII, it became a matter of primary concern for his successors.

Leo belonged to the international tradition characteristic of Vatican diplomacy. For him the rising nationalism of his period was a cause of deep concern. He watched the jealousy and mistrust of European nations, the quest for self-sufficiency, and the tendency to rely on material force. These manifestations of the nationalistic spirit occasioned melancholy reflections. He discerned their root in the weakening of the concept of the brotherhood of man and felt that their cure lay in the strengthening of the idea that the human race is one great family.[178]

One expression of this dangerous spirit of national rivalry was the growth in armaments. The Pope insisted that military preparations do not prevent war, as is commonly alleged, but rather prove

"a threat more likely to increase jealousy and suspicion than to allay them. These armaments trouble the minds of all with anxious forebodings of what is to come, and there is this special misfortune about them that they lay such burdens on the population that often, seemingly, war itself might be more bearable." [179]

Since an armed peace is intolerable, it is imperative that nations arrive at contractual limitation of armaments. To do this, they must renounce exaggerated nationalism. Conscription, also, ought to be abolished in order to release men's energies for peaceful work.

Leo was vitally interested in the Hague Conferences. Their objective, he felt, should be to make the arbitration of international disputes compulsory. He accepted enthusiastically when asked to act as arbiter in the Caroline Islands dispute between Germany and Spain. Nothing was more important, he wrote, than to ward off the danger of war, for it always brings immense disaster, especially on account of the growing power of destructive weapons. Those who work for peace make a major contribution to public safety.[180]

Benedict XV (1914-1922) devoted most of his energies to the

question of war and peace. The major lines of his thought can
be found in his celebrated Peace Appeal of 1 August 1917, cited
below.[181] No avenue for restoring peace was left unexplored
and every effort was made to alleviate war's horrors. The Pope's
neutrality, reaffirmed so frequently, was misunderstood and
misapplied in the passionate amosphere of the period; but his
work for peace and his interest in all the victims of war added
immeasurably to the popular prestige of the Papacy.

The immensity of war's destruction convinced Benedict of
the need for an international organization. On May 1920,
surveying the work of the Conference of Paris, he appealed to
all nations to unite in a league that would act as a family of
nations to safeguard the order of human society. Only through
such an organization could the danger of war be lessened and
the burden of military expenditures be reduced. The Pope
promised the full aid of the Church in the establishing of such
an international society. The Church, perfect type of an international socity that she is, yearns to promote the material as
well as the spiritual well-being of the world. The ideal of a
world order is not impossible. Was there not once a Christendom in which all peoples accepted an international authority.[182]

Tragedy stained the years of Pius XI's pontificate (1922-1939).
Efforts to re-establish an international equilibrium after the
war were generally unsuccessful. Some encouragement to mankind's hopes for a world of peace and freedom was given during
the 20's, but the resentments that had been stimulated by the
conflict continued to smolder. Intensified nationalism blocked
constructive measures for peace. The older patterns of international trade were not restored. The economic collapse of
the 30's flamed all the latent political and social tensions. The
totalitarian menace revealed itself in all its primitive fright-
fulness. As nations lapsed into barbarism, the menace of a new
war loomed unmistakably.

Pius XI attempted to mobilize the forces of reason and
religion to meet the threat. At the beginning of his pontificate,
he took as his motto, "The Peace of Christ in the Reign of
Christ." He called the attention of the Reparations Conference
at Genoa to the "beautiful device of the Red Cross—*Inter arma
caritas*—" and warned: "It should not be forgotten that the
best guarantee of peace is not a forest of bayonets, but mutual
confidence and friendship."[183] He continued to urge his theme:
"Peace is the first and indispensable condition of all social
reconstruction."[184] It was because he saw the totalitarian regimes as a threat to international order as well as unchristian

violators of natural rights that he reserved to them his severe condemnation.[185]

Pius XII was elected on 2 March 1939.[186] On the very next day, he addressed the world by radio in an appeal for peace, "the fairest of God's gifts." As the shadows lengthened, his voice became more urgent until it was drowned out by a fresh resound of arms.[187]

On the first Christmas Eve of World War II, Pius XII delivered the first of his major addresses on an international theme. Entitled *In Questo Giorno,* it became well known because it first enunciated the Five Points for Peace that were widely discussed during the war. It began with a catalogue of crimes deserving condemnation:

"a calculated act of aggression against a small, industrious, and and peaceful nation, on the pretext of a threat that was neither real nor intended nor even possible; atrocities; the unlawful use of destructive weapons against non-combatants and refugees, against old men and women and children; a disregard for the life and liberty of man. . ." [188]

"To break down the gigantic walls of hatred and hostility that have been built up," the Pope set forth his major aims:

1. To alleviate the terrible misfortunes of war as it affects individuals by reawakening among men the spirit of charity.

2. To plan for necessary social and economic reconstruction after the war since to care for man's spiritual needs will not be enough.

3. "To define clearly the fundamental points of a just and honorable peace," in pursuit of which aim, he offered his Five Points which all men of good will can support:

    a. The right of every nation, small or great, to an independence guaranteed "according to the rules of justice and reciprocal equity."

    b. Progressive and mutually agreed-upon disarmament, that will be spiritual as well as material.

    c. The erection of "some juridical institution which shall guarantee the loyal and faithful fufillment of the conditions agreed upon, and which shall, in case of recognized need, revise and correct them."

    d. The protection of racial minorities and the peaceful solution of disputed allegiances.

    e. The creation of the spirit of justice and of universal love, which is enshrined in the Christian ideal.

Pius XII returned to the same theme in his Christmas Message of 1941, in which he detected the following as root causes of the conflict:[189]

1. The idea of force has shocked and perverted the rule of law.

2. The demand for material progress has become man's major incentive. States have responded to this demand by emphasizing the impulse toward expansion.

3. "Private property has become, for some, a power directed to the enjoyment of the work of others, and for other people it has begotten jealousy, impatience, and hate."[190]

4. An atheistic or anti-Christian concept of the State has robbed the individual of independence, even in his private life.

The result of these is a tension, both domestic and international, that will destroy the human race. The war but intensifies all these trends. The heart of the evil is not the machine or technology, but the neglect of religious and moral principles. Without doubt, there can be no lasting peace until there are assured:

1. The incontestable right of the small state to freedom, neutrality, and economic development.

2. The right of national minorities to cultural and economic freedom.

3. The right of all nations to share the word's natural resources, canceling any monopoly of these sources of life that were intended for all.

4. A limitation of armaments and a fidelity to treaties that will prevent the scourge of World War III from overwhelming humanity. This requires an international institution to guarantee the sincere fulfillment of treaties and the necessity of revisions.

5. Freedom of religion, to provide the moral strength with which the world may begin anew on the basis of love and of the brotherhood of men.[119]

Early in the War, the Pope warned that victory would not solve the basic problem. Underlying all contemporary political questions is the international chaos deriving from the fact that each national state demands unlimited powers. This concept of unlimited sovereignty makes orderly international relations impossible; it simply drains international law of its vigor and prevents peaceful solutions of disputes. The State that seeks absolute powers has lost its sense of responsibility. Bonds among nations are at the mercy of a capricious despotism under which mutual confidence is impossible. There must be reform.

"Those who hold the fate of kingdoms in their hands assure us that, once the bloodthirsty discords of the present moment have been laid aside, they will introduce a new order of things, based on a foundation of justice and economic settlement. But is it really to be different, is it really to be (what is more important) a better and happier age? At the end of this war there will be fresh pacts, fresh arrangements of international relations. Will they be conceived in a spirit of justice and fairness all round, in a spirit of reconstruction and peace, or will they disastrously repeat our old and our recent failures? Experience shows that it is but an empty dream to expect a real settlement to emerge at the moment when the conflagration of war has died down. The day on which victory dawns may bring triumph to him who has won it, but there is danger to him in that moment: a new conflict has begun, this time between the angel of justice and the devil of coercion. The heart of the victor is often hardened; calm views and long views are mistaken for weakness and indecision. The heady sympathies of the crowd, excited by all the losses and miseries they have endured, often have a stupefying effect on those who are responsible for the conduct of affairs. They are asked to shut their ears to the voice of clemency and justice, which is lost and drowned in the terrible cry of '*Vae Victis.*' If this is the atmosphere in which plans are made and quarrels are judged, it may well be that nothing results but injustice, with a thin coat of justification to disguise it.

". . .It is not from the sword that deliverance comes to nations! The sword cannot breed peace, it can only impose terms of peace. The forces, the influences, that are to renew the face of the earth, must spring from men's hearts."

No new order in international relations can arise after the war unless it is firmly based on the Natural Law.[192] It must begin with the notion of the human person and must be directed toward his development and perfection, taking into full account the religious values which the Creator has assigned to every man and to the human race as a whole.[193]

This concern of Pius XII with the creation of an organized international community was most emphatically stated in an audience with delegates to the Fourth Congress of the World Movement for World Federal Government, 6 April 1951.[193]

". . .The maintenance or the re-establishment of peace has always been and increasingly will be the object of our constant solicitude. And if, too often, the results have fallen far short of what our efforts and our acts aimed at, lack of success will never discourage us, so long as peace does not reign in the world. Faithful to the spirit of Christ, the Church is striving and working for peace with all her strength; she does this by her precepts and her exhortations, by her incessant activities and her ceaseless prayers.

"The Church is indeed a power for peace, at least wherever are respected and appreciated at their true value the independence and the mission which the Church holds from God, wherever men do not seek to make her the docile servant of a political egoism, wherever she is not treated as an enemy. The Church longs for peace, she strives incessantly for peace, and her heart is ever with those who, like her, desire peace and devote themselves to it. She knows also, and this is her duty, how to distinguish between the true and the false friends of peace.

"The Church desires peace, and therefore applies herself to the promotion of everything which, within the framework of the divine order, both natural and supernatural, contributes to the assurance of peace. Your movement dedicates itself to realizing an effective political organization of the world. *Nothing is more in conformity with the traditional doctrine of the Church, nor better adapted to her teaching concerning legitimate and illegitimate war,* especially in the present circumstances.[195]

"It is necessary therefore to arrive at an organization of this kind, if for no other reason than to put a stop to the armament race in which, for decades past, the peoples have been ruining themselves and draining their resources to no effect. You are of the opinion that this world political organization, in order to be effective, must be federal in form. If by this you understand that it should not be enmeshed in a mechanical unitarism, again you are in harmony with the principles of political and social life so firmly founded and sustained by the Church. . .

"Therein lies a vast field of work, study and action. You have understood this and looked it squarely in the face. You have the courage to spend yourselves for this cause. We congratulate you. We express to you our wishes for your good success, and with all our heart We pray to God to grant you His light and help in the performance of your task."

With this prayer for world government, the Papacy faces the future. In the past, its political views have given rise to dispute. But all men of good will can support its present efforts for peace, and most would be happy to accept the general framework of its plan for an organized international society.

J. N. MOODY

NOTES

1 The best account in English of the problems facing the Papacy in this century is Ludwig von Pastor's *The History of the Popes from the Close of of the Middle Ages,* Vols. XXXIII-XXXIV, Ernest Graf, editor, St. Louis, B. Herder, 1941; Vols. XXXV and XXXVI, E. F. Peeler, editor, London, Routledge and Kegan Paul, 1949-1950. These cover the years from 1700-1769.

2 Cf. Pietro Giannone, *Dell'istoria civile del regno di Napoli,* Napoli, Nella

Stamperia di G. Gravier, 1770. Variations of this doctrine were found everywhere in Catholic Europe.

3 *Quod Aliquantum,* 10 March 1791. Cf. below p. 111

4 Confirmed by the Treaty of Basle, 1795.

5 Letter of Cardinal Pacca to Lamennais in P. Didon's *Lamennais et le Saint-Siège,* Paris, 1911, pp. 400-403.

6 Dated 8 June 1796.

7 He entered the city 10 February 1798.

8 Quotations in L. Seche, *Les Origines du Concordat,* 2 vols., Paris, 1894, Vol. II, p. 14.

9 For the Concordat of 1801, Cf. below, p. 117.

10 Compare the Organic Articles. The Melzi decrees diverged even more sharply from the text of the agreement and in a few sections were clearly contrary to it.

11 D. A. Binchy, *Church and State in Fascist Italy,* London, Oxford University Press, 1941, p. 12. Italics mine.

12 Members of the Curia who resisted all change of French inspiration.

13 Leo might be excused for having no personal affection for the great Secretary. When he was sent as legate to Paris in 1814, he was instructed by Consalvi to make all speed so that papal claims could be presented to the Allies. He was overtaken en route by Consalvi, who reprimanded him most vigorously for his tardiness. But the cause of the Secretary's removal was more immediate: it was Consalvi's policy that had been the issue at the papal election. The choice of Cardinal della Genga as Leo XII implied a *Zealanti* program.

14 The admonition of Chateaubriand, the French ambassador, to the Conclave, may have helped: "One of the conditions of the permanence that has been promised it [the Papacy] is that it would always belong to the age in which it lived." Cf. Artaud de Montori, *Histoire du pape Pie VIII,* Paris, 1844, p. 53.

15 *Idem,* pp. 289 and 256.

16 Both withdrew in 1838.

17 Cf. G. F. and J. J. Berkeley, *Italy in the Making,* 3 vols., Cambridge Univ. Press, 1932-40, for a good account of the *Risorgimento* until 1848. For Mazzini, Cf. Vol. I, pp. 9-24; also, Bolton King, *A History of Italian Unity, 1814-1871,* 2 Vols., London, J. Nisbet and Co., 1934 (4th ed. revised).

18 Berkeley, *idem,* Vol. I, pp. 154-173.

19 However, the Italian government probably acted in bad faith when Louis Napoleon withdrew his regular French troops in compliance with the Steptember Convention of 1865. Winking at violations of the agreement, it permitted Garibaldi to gather volunteers and to attack Rome once again. The city was saved with the return of the French and the defeat of the Italians at Mentana.

20 Unless *Mirari Vos* is interpreted as an oblique condemnation. Cf. H. Haag, *Les Origines du Catholicisme liberal en Belgique, 1789-1839,* Louvain, E. Nauwelaerts, 1950, pp. 132-8; 163-180.

21 Cf. the Brief *Impensa Caritas,* 9 February 1831; and the stronger *Superiori anno,* 9 June 1832.

22 He was extremely active in the reorganization of the foreign missions, reformed many religious orders, tightened Church discipline, etc. He had said that he intended to be custodian of souls, first, and prince, second, Cf. F. Engel-Janosi, *Jugendzeit des Grafen Prokesch-Osten,* Innsbruck, 1938, p. 150.

23 Note the distinction above, pp. 32-33. It was quite possible to be anti-Austrian without seeking a unified national Italy; many prominent Italians shared this position at this time.

24 For the background of these reforms, Cf. Berkeley, *op. cit., Vol. II, pp.* 12-140.

25 The outbreak in Rome occurred after the summer defeat of the Piedmontese forces ended hopes of driving the Austrians out of Italy. By November, too, the tide of reaction had already set in Central Europe.

26 The Siccardi Laws of 1855 limited the position of the Church in Piedmont They were extended to the new territories as these were incorporated. While they do not deserve the appellation "persecution," at least by current standards they did diminish the position of the clergy. They were anti-clerical in inspiration, and they contributed to that atmosphere of mistrust that characerized the relations of the Papacy and Savoy.

27 Binchy, *op. ci.,* p. 24.

28 Garibaldi called the Pope "a cubic meter of dung," and meant it. The intellectuals who opposed Catholicism would have enjoyed erasing it from Italian life. These opponents had a strong weapon of political and social pressure in Freemasonry. But they remained a minority though they did preempt a predominant position in the administration. Cf. George M. Trevelyan, *Garibaldi and the Making of Italy,* N. Y., Longmans Green, 1911.

29 For a convenient summary of the international relations of the Papacy during the latter part of Pius IX's pontificate, Cf. Lillian P. Wallace, *The Papacy and European Diplomacy, 1869-1878,* Chapel Hill, Univ. of North Carolina Press, 1948. The author has a certain sympathy for Pius's problems. He is described as a redoubtable foe of the modern state; its development in the direction of totalitarianism is said to go far in justifying his fears (p. 4). "Could either one [Cavour or the King] have foreseen how the whole power of the modern national state was to become so overgrown as to absorb spiritual, as well as economic and intellectual functions, perhaps they would have been more charitably disposed to a papal policy which seemed in their day stubborn or, perhaps, avaricious and self-seeking" (p.7) .

30 This was his verdict on the February Revolution that ended the July Monarchy. Cf. Duc de Broglie, *Memoires, 1825-1871,* in *Revue des Deux Mondes,* 1921, No. XXVII, p. 420.

31 Pius XI declared, in a private audience with Canon Cardijn in 1925, that "the scandal of the nineteenth century was that the Church lost the working class." He added, in praise of the founder of the Jocists, 'Finally, someone speaks to me about masses." Quotations verified by the Secretariat International of the YCW, 78 Boulevard Poincaré, Brussels.

32 The Papacy continued to object to this law on the ground that the State had fixed the extent of papal liberty and could change it at will. Certain currents in Italian political life convinced the Vatican that it was the purpose of the law to cut the Vatican off from all international poliical contacts. Both sides were suspiious of each other. For background, Cf. the excellent study of S. William Halperin, *Italy and the Vatican at War,* Chicago Univ. Press, 1939. The same author's *The Separation of Church and State in Italian Thought from Cavour to Mussolini,* Chicago Univ. Press, 1937, and Mario Falco's *The Legal Position of the Holy See before and after the Lateran Agreements,* Oxford Univ. Press, 1935, are very useful.

33 E. g., the erection of the statue of Giordano Bruno near St. Peter's, of that of Garibaldi on the Janiculum overlooking the Vatican, and the disturbances on the occasion of the translation of the remains of Pius IX.

34 This election saw the last use of the Veto against a papal candidate by a national government. It was invoked by Austria against Cardinal Rampolla,

Leo XIII's choice, who would have followed his policies. Pius X prohibited its future use, under the strictest penalties.

35 12 June 1905. Text in Koenig, *op. cit.*, pp. 113-116. For attempt to apply to France, Cf. below, p. 163. It must be kept in mind that Catholics do not consider an encyclical to be covered by papal infallibility. It might contain an infallible statement, for example, that Christ was truly divine, but the bulk of the material is not considered as protected from error. The term used in their regard is authentic, which implies that they are the teaching of the highest authority in the Church at a precise moment in history, and are thus official in a given set of circumstances.

36 *L'Opera dei Congressi e dei Comitati.*

37 Cf. below, p. 167 sq. Pius X was also hostile to Sillon. Italy was not to have a serious Christian Democratic movement until the spectacular rise of the *Populari*. The speed with which Dom Sturzo's movement grew indicates that some sentiment for this solution existed in Italy and might have developed earlier had Leo XIII's conciliatory approach been followed. The earlier abortive attempts also provided some of the leadership for *Popolari*.

38 *Pacem Dei Munus Pulcherrimum,* 23 June 1920, Keonig, *op. cit.*, pp. 289-290.

39 Contained in Article 5 of the Treaty of London. For text, Cf. Humphrey Johnson, *The Papacy and the Kingdom of Italy,* Sheed and Ward, London, 1926, p. 130. Benedict generously let it be known that he had no desire to send a representative to Paris.

40 For the political views of the founder, Cf. *Italy and Fascism,* Harcourt Brace, N. Y., 1927; *Politics and Morality,* Burns Oates and Washbourne, London, 1938; *Church and State,* Longmans Green, N. Y., 1939; *Nationalism and Internationalism,* Roy, N. Y., 1946.

41 Cf. G. Megaro, *Mussolini in the Making,* Houghton, Mifflin, N. Y., 1938. The Fascist program of 1919 called for the confiscation of all religious property.

42 Binchy, *op. cit.*, pp. 147-164, details the motives for papal disapproval and the Catholic reaction to the disappearance of this valuable ally, the Popolari.

43 It need not be emphasized that a treaty or a concordat is no sign of official favor or sympathy. In the interest of its mission, the Church has always sought friendly contacts with governments of all types.

44 The Vatican City is the "Franciscan minimum," as Pius XI called it. It compromises 108.7 acres around St. Peter's, plus an extra-territorial status for thirteen other buildings. Its population is rigidly restricted to ecclesiastics and employees in the Vatican City, in all normally less than a thousand. It has all the external aspects of sovereignty. For Pius's attitude during the negotiations, Cf. Philip Hughes, *Pope Pius XI,* N. Y., Sheed and Word, 1937, pp. 195-257.

45 Almost immediately after the signing of the Pacts, the Pope had found it necessary to object to Mussolini's speeches on the supremacy of the State. Cf. Letter to Cardinal Garparri, 30 May 1929; text in *Documentation Catholique,* 15-22 June 1929, No. 1504-1510. The Pope, after affirming the sovereignty and independence of the Church and the validity of her educational mission, makes the following criticisms of the regime's interpretation of the Concordat:

1 The State claims a preventive veto on ecclesiastical appointments, but the text of the Concordat indicates that this is not justified.

2 The State claims the right to confer juridical personality on ecclesiastical bodies, but the text does not say "confers"; it says "recognizes." (This difference in language is important and was insisted upon in the negotiations.)

3 The marriage sections of the Concordat are satisfactory. Now, however, it is claimed that "no one can be restrained to a religious marriage." But the

Church can restrain by *spiritual* means, by excluding from membership in the Church all Catholics who do not seek a religious marriage.

4 The retroactive character of Article V is now denied, but the whole spirit of the settlement shows that it was so considered.

These observaions directly contravened remarks in Mussolini's address.

46 A generic term to include organizations of lay Catholics for religious or social purposes.

47 E. g., talk to the students of the College of Mondragone, 14 May 1929, Koenig, *op. cit.*, p. 388.

48 Msgr. Francis J. Spellman, now Cardinal Spellman of New York, was the papal messenger. Text, in Koenig, *idem*, pp. 446-448.

49 E. g., lay leadership was practically eliminated; national organization was replaced by diocesan groupings; non-religious activity, defined in the narrowest terms was banned. This eliminated all sporting events, etc.

50 Cf. T. Lincoln Bouscaren, *Canon Law Digest, 1917-1933*, Bruce, Milwaukee, 1934, pp. 616-617.

51 Address to Chaplains of Catholic Youth Organizations, 21 July 1938, in *Civilta Cattolica*, 1938, Vol. III, p. 271. Cf., also, Address to the Students of the Collegio de Propaganda Fide, 21 August 1938, Koenig, *op. cit.*, p. 545; Allocution, *Con Grande*, to the College of Cardinals, 24 December 1938, Koenig, *idem.*, pp. 549-551; Allocution, *Il Santo Padre Ha Incominciato*, to the College of Cardinals, 24 December 1937, Koenig, *idem*, pp. 539-540.

52 10 February 1939. He died just two days before he had scheduled a speech to the assembled bishops of Italy that had been forecast as his strongest denunciation of totalitarianism.

53 14 March 1937, Koenig, *idem*, pp. 498-510.

54 The author was present at a general audience in the summer of 1937 in which the ailing Pope addressed a delegation of Czech school teachers. He was patently ill, but as he talked his frame shook with emotion. His theme was a condemnation of aggression and of the violation of international agreements.

55 For a possible exception, one might cite the complex question of the attitude of the Vatican to the Abyssinian war. Cf. the objective discussion in Binchy, *op. cit.*, pp. 637-651.

56 The reform movements which from time to time had revitalized the Church applied Christian doctrine and practice to new conditions. Until the time of Leo XIII, the industrial backwardness of Central Italy and the papal concentration on the importance of the Temporal Power had only served to obscure the social problem.

57 Eduardo Soderini, *The Pontificate of Leo XIII*, trans. by Barbara Barclay Carter, London, Burns Oates and Washbourne, 1934, Vol. I, p. 112.

58 The first of these met in 1885. The most prominent Italian representative, Guiseppe Toniolo (1845-1918), Professor of Law at Pisa, founded a study group at Bologna in 1888 for the elaboration of Catholic social teaching.

59 The papal claim to speak on the ethical aspects of the social question set forth by Pius XII in *La Solennitá della Pentecoste*, on the fiftieth anniversary of *Rerum Novarum*. Cf. Koenig, *op. cit.*, pp. 720-721.

60 Leo XIII, *Immortale Dei*, 1 November 1885, No. 2, Koenig, *op. cit.*, p. 25.

61 Pius XII, *Christmas Broadcast*, 24 December 1937, Koenig, *op. cit.*, p. 792. Cf. Pius XI, *Divini Redemptoris*, 19 March 1937, Koenig, *op. cit.*, p. 520: "Society is made for man and must subserve the human person."

62 Koenig, *op. cit.*, p. 520. Pius XII made the most systematic examination of the rights of man in his *Christmas Broadcast* of 1942. Cf. *Selected Letters and Addresses of Pius XII*, London, Catholic Truth Society, 1949, pp. 275-298. He

adds the following to the above list: the right to maintain and develop physical moral, and spiritual life, and in particular, the right to a religious training and education; the right to worship God both in private and public, including the right to engage in religious works of charity; the right, in principle, to marriage and to the attainment of the purpose of marriage, the right to wedded society and home life;*the right to work as an indispensable means for the maintenance of family life;* the right to the free choice of a state of life and, therefore, of the priestly and religion state; the right to the use of material goods, subject to its duties and its limitations, p. 290.

63 Pius XI, *Quadragesimo Anno,* 15 May 1931, No. 88, Koenig, *op. cit.,* p. 425.

64 *Quadragesimo Anno,* No. 107-108, *idem,* pp. 429-430.

65 *Rerum Novarum,* 15 May 1891, No. 7-9, *idem,* pp. 53-54.

66 *Quadragesimo Anno,* No. 112-120, *idem,* pp. 431-434.

67 *Divini Redemptoris* explains the basis of the condemnation in greater detail; *idem,* pp. 510-535.

68 *Quadrangesimo Anno,* No. 113-114, *idem,* p. 432.

69 *Rerum Novarum, idem,* pp. 60-65. *Quadragesimo Anno,* No. 98, *idem,* p. 428: "The first and most necessary remedy is a reform of morals." Cf. Pius XII, *Summi Pontificatus,* 20 October 1939, *idem,* p. 439.

70 *Quadragesimo Anno,* No. 132, *idem,* p. 439.

71 *Quadragesimo Anno, idem,* p. 436.

72 Pius XII, *Christmas Message,* 1948. The same Pope saw no opposition between Christian law and "the postulates of a genuine brotherly humanitarianism." *Summi Pontificatus,* 20 October 1939, Koenig, *op. cit.,* p. 610.

73 *Rerum Novarum,* No. 72, *idem,* p. 76; No. 76, *idem,* p. 78-79.

74 *Rerum Novarum, idem,* p. 74. Workers' duties are variously stated: conscientious work; respect for employer's property; cooperative attitude.

75 *Peace in Industry,* in John F. Cronin, *Catholic Social Principles,* Milwaukee, Bruce, 1950, p. 407.

76 The present author has delineated this argument in *Trade Union Membership—A Duty?,* in *Commonweal,* 13 September 1940, pp. 420-422, and 8 November 1940, pp. 70-73.

77 *Quadragesimo Anno,* No. 39, Koenig, *op. cit.,* p. 409; No. 81, *idem,* p. 423.

78 Pius XII, *Address to Italian Workers,* Cronin, *op. cit.,* p. 204.

79 This has been called the heart of the papal social program. It has been variously termed "Vocational Groups," "Organized Professions," "Industrial Democracy."

80 No. 87, Koenig, *op. cit.,* pp. 424-425. In the same paragraph, the adverb "freely" and the noun "freedom" also appear.

81 *Quadragesimo Anno, idem,* p. 423; *Rerum Novarum, idem,* p. 59.

82 *Rerum Novarum,* No. 37, *idem,* p. 62.

83 *Quadragesimo Anno,* No. 101, *idem,* p. 428.

84 *Rerum Novarum,* No. 31, *idem,* p. 59.

85 *Rerum Novarum, idem,* pp. 69-71.

86 *Rerum Novarum* No. 51, *idem,* p. 73, Italics Supplied.

87 *Rerum Novarum, idem,* p. 73.

88 *Divini Redemptoris,* No. 52, *idem,* p. 528.

89 *Divini Redemptoris,* No. 52, *idem,* p. 528.

90 *Divini Redemptoris,* No. 52, *idem,* p. 528.

91 *Quadragesimo Anno,* No. 74, *idem,* p. 421.

92 *Quadragesimo Anno,* No. 71, *idem,* pp. 419-420.

93 *Quadragesimo Anno,* No. 65, *idem,* p. 418. Italics supplied.

94 *Quadragesimo Anno, idem,* p. 419.

[95] *Summa Theologica*, II, II, 66, 2. The paragraph above contains a summary of the Thomistic doctrine, Cf. Hans Meyer, *The Philosophy of St. Thomas Aquinas*, St. Louis, B. Herder, 1945, pp. 475-479.

[96] *Quadragesimo Anno*, No. 4, Koenig, *op. cit.*, p. 411.

[97] *Quadragesimo Anno*, No. 45, *idem*, p. 411.

[98] Pius XII, *La Solennità della Pentecoste, idem*, pp. 723-724. Cf., also, *Divini Redemptoris*, No. 50, p. 527: "Is it not deplorable that the right of private property, defended by the Church, should so often have been used as a weapon to defraud the workingman of his just salary and his social rights. . .?"

[99] *Quadragesimo Anno*, No. 48, *idem*, p. 412.

[100] Pius XII, *Address to the Congress of International Exchange*, 7 March 1948, Cronin, *op. cit.*, p. 530.

[101] *Rerum Novarum*, No. 36, Koenig, *op. cit.*, pp. 61-62.

[102] Pius XII, *Discourse to Italian Workers*, 13 June 1943, Cronin, *op. cit.*, p. 459.

[103] Pius XII, *Discourse to Catholic Action Men*, 7 September 1947, *idem*, p. 470.

[104] *Quadragesimo Anno*, No. 60-61, Koenig, *op. cit.*, p. 417. Cf. also Pius XII, *Christmas Broadcast* of 1942, *idem*, p. 798: "If possible, then, the ownership of private property must be granted to all."

[105] *Quadragesimo Anno*, No. 61, *idem*, p. 417.

[106] *Quadragesimo Anno*, No. 25, *idem*, p. 404. Italics supplied.

[107] *Quadragesimo Anno*, No. 49, *idem*, pp. 412-413.

[108] *Quadragesimo Anno*, No. 78, *idem*, p. 422.

[109] *Rerum Novarum*, *idem*, p. 66.

[110] *Quadragesimo Anno*, No. 28, *idem*, p. 405.

[111] *Quadragesimo Anno*, *idem*, pp. 422-423.

[112] *Quadragesimo Anno*, No. 114, *idem*, p. 432. The Australian Hierarchy (1948) lists these as: banking and insurance; the manufacture of steel and heavy chemicals; rail, sea, and air transport; public utility services (electricity, gas, tramways) ; armaments. Cf. *Socialization, Social Justice Statement, 1948*, Melbourne, A.N.S.C.A., 1948, pp. 12-17; *Studies in Australian Social Problems*, Melbourne, Catholic Education Office, 1950, pp. 32-37; Gerard Heffey, *Christendom and Nationalism*, in *Twentieth Century*, Vol. III, No. 2, December, 1948. For background material on the progressive views of the Australian Hierarchy, Cf. *Studies in Catholic Action*, Melbourne, A.N.S.C.A., 1948; James G. Murtagh, *Australia, The Catholic Chapter, N. Y.*, Sheed and Ward, 1946.

[113] Pius XII, *Summi Pontificatus*, 20 October 1939, Koenig, *op. cit.*, pp. 604-605.

[114] Pius XII, *Nell' Alba*, 24 December 1941, *idem*, pp. 757-758. Cf. also *Christmas Broadcast* of 1942, *idem*, pp. 801-802, where the success of the social reforms within each nation is said to depend on the sharing of resources between the strong and the weak. The principle of the Marshall and Schuman Plans was approved before the event.

[115] *Divini Redemptoris*, No. 76, *idem*, p. 534.

[116] Pius XII, *La Solennità della Pentecoste, idem*, p. 728.

[117] *Quadragesimo Anno*, No. 89, *idem* p. 426. Italics supplied.

[118] *Divini Redemptoris*, No. 61, *idem*, p. 530.

[119] Pius XI, Encyclical *Firmissiman Constantiam*, on the religious situation in Mexico, 28 March 1937, Cronin, *op. cit.*, p. 568.

[120] *Quadragesimo Anno*, No. 141, Koenig, *op. cit.*, p. 444.

[121] *Divini Redemptoris*, No. 56, *idem*, p. 529.

[122] Cf. below, p. 95 sq. It is important to reemphasize the difference between

the experience of the Church with continental political movements and with those in English-speaking lands. For instance, the evolution toward democracy in the United States rested on *two* basic concepts: the sovereignty of the people and the idea of inalienable human rights. The latter idea, enshrined in our first Ten Amendments, was supported by a whole body of precedents arising from the Common Law, and represented an effective check on the principle of popular sovereignty. To put it succinctly: in the Anglo-American world, Rousseau was balanced by Locke. While the same concepts were proclaimed in emerging continental Liberalism, the idea of natural rights lacked strong traditional support and wide popular acceptance. Accordingly, in political crises such as the French Revolution, Jacobin absolutism could ignore human rights in practice. So Rousseau, in his chapter on Civic Religion in the *Social Contract,* could find justification for unrestricted state pressure on individuals. It was the impact of this experience with the practical consequences of the Doctrine of Popular Sovereignty that made rapprochement between the Church and the new political forces so difficult.

..123 The classic example of this conflict was the Revolutionary *Loi Chapelier* of 1791 denying the right of association; it was not effectively removed for French trade unions until 1884. Also, national danger justified the suspension of all civil rights under the Terror.

124 There had been exceptions in the Medieval communes, particularly in Italy, where guild organization gave town workers and craftsmen an effective voice in politics for longer or shorter periods. These popular rights were ultimately lost to centralizing tendencies and to the growing power of the upper bourgoisie.

125 Many factors, of course, facilitated the political success here: greater economic resources; the continuing flow of immigrants with initially lesser expectations; the existence of slavery and, later, of socially oppressed Negro labor; the "frontier," etc.

126 It is not being suggested that Italian Fascism was a balanced blend of denatured Marxism and exaggerated nationalism. It was far too opportunistic and personalized for such classification. Besides, it contained bits of Sorel and Hegel, without ever having a consistent ideology. But, in a sense, Marx and Mazzini did meet in Mussolini, even though the prototypes would have been abashed at their progeny. The radical Socialist turned Nationalist trimmed his sails to many winds, but he never lost sight of the need for mass appeal. His borrowings from Socialism and Nationalism may have made a strange brew but the draught had the planned, intoxicting effect. Other twentieth century dictators have varied the formula considerably in response o historical circumstances. But all have directed their efforts to capture the masses.

127 *Diuturnum Illud,* Hughes, *op. cit.,* p. 54.

128 *Immortale Dei, idem,* p. 62.

129 *Diuturnum, idem,* p. 54.

130 *Idem,* p. 55

131 This is the major theme of *Libertas Praestantissimum,* Koenig, *op. cit.,* pp. 40-45.

132 *Sapientiae Christianae,* Hughes, *op. cit.,* p. 88.

133 *Diuturnum Illud, idem,* p. 56.

134 *Libertas Praestantissimum, idem,* p. 79.

135 *Immortale Dei, idem,* p. 63.

136 *Immortale Dei, idem,* p. 63.

137 *Libertas Praestantissimum,* Koenig, *op. cit.,* pp. 40.42. As an example of

the use of the Natural Law principle to condemn totalitarianism. Cf. *Mit Brennender Sorge,* Hughes, *op. cit.,* p. 112.

[138] *Libertas Praestantissimum, idem,* p. 83.

[139] *Idem,* p. 83.

[140] Cf. above, p 51; also, *Rerum Novarum,* Keonig, *op. cit.,* pp. 65-67.

[141] The classic example was the use of the Contract Theory.

[142] *Au Milieu des sollicitudes,* Koenig, *op. cit.,* p. 82.

[143] *Diuturnum Illud,* Hughes, *op. cit.,* p. 55.

[144] *Libertas Praestantissimum,* in *Great Encyclical Letters, op. cit.,* p. 162.

[145] *Immortale Dei, idem,* pp. 126-127.

[146] For the political views of the majority of French Catholics of this period Cf. below, p. 150 sq. The date of this document is 1 November 1885.

[147] *Au Milieu des sollicitudes,* Koenig, *op. cit.,* pp. 81-85. Cf. his praise of the United States government in *Longinqua Oceani,* 16 January 1895, in *Great Encyclical Letters, op. cit.,* p. 323.

[148] Text in *Selected Letters and Addresses of Pius XII,* London, Catholic Truth Society, 1949, pp. 301-318.

[149] *Idem,* p. 302.

[150] *Idem,* p. 303.

[151] *Idem,* p. 304. Italics supplied.

[152] *Idem,* p. 305.

[153] *Idem,* p. 306.

[154] *Idem,* p. 306.

[155] *Rerum Novarum,* Koenig, *op. cit.,* pp. 75-77.

[156] *Arcanum,* 10 February 1880, Hughes, *op. cit.,* p. 121.

[157] *Idem,* pp. 117-118.

[158] *Idem,* p. 120.

[159] *Idem,* p. 119. Pius XI develops the same themes in *Casti Connubii,* Hughes *op. cit.,* pp. 122-135.

[160] Leo XIII, *Affari Vos,* 8 December 1897, to the Bishops of Canada *Acta Sanctae Sedis,* Vol. XXX, pp. 356-362.

[161] Koenig, *op. cit.,* pp. 446-448.

[162] *Idem,* pp. 498-510.

[163] *Mit Brennender Sorge,* Hughes, *op. cit.,* pp. 114-115. For a condemnation of the Soviet attitude toward education, Cf. *Divini Redemptoris, idem,* pp. 43-44.

[164] 31 December 1931, *idem,* pp. 136-244. What follows is a summary of the argument of this encyclical. For further treatment of the relation between the state and the family, Cf. Pius XII, *Summi Pontificatus,* in *Selected Letters, op. cit.,* pp. 22-27.

[165] *Idem,* p. 139.

[166] Leo XIII, *Sapientiae Christianae,* Hughes, *idem,* p. 88.

[167] Cf. Leo's cautions to the Archbishop of Dublin, 3 January 1881, *Acta Sanctae Sedis,* Vol. XIII, pp. 248-250, Encyclical to the Irish Bishops, 1 August 1882, *Acta Sanctae Sedis,* Vol. XV, pp. 97-98.

[168] Pius XI, *Acerba Animi,* to the Catholics of Mexico, 29 September 1932, Hughes, *op. cit.,* p. 98.

[169] Pius XI, *Nos es Muy,* to the Bishops of Mexico, 29 March 1937, *idem,* p. 100.

[170] Yet, as a last resort, the right to revolt against tyranny remains. *Idem,* p. 102.

[171] Leo XII, *Sapientiae Christianae, idem,* p. 92.

[172] *Immortale Dei, idem,* p. 65.

[173] *Sapientiae Christianae, idem,* p. 91.

[174] *In Plurimis,* 5 May 1888, Koenig, *op. cit.,* pp. 38-39.

[175] Cf., also, *Immortale Dei,* Hughes, *opc. cit.,* pp. 66-67. In this whole area, it must be remembered that the Popes declare that their major interest is to refute the principles of theological Indifferentism and philosophical Relativism. On the practical issue of the treatment of minorities, it is well to note the Bull of Gregory IX (6 April 1233) to the Bishops of France concerning the protection of Jews: the Jews are to be shown that benignity which the Christians living in pagan countries wish to experience for themselves.

Leo XIII defined "separation of Church and State" as equivalent to the separation of human legislation from Christian and divine legislation" (*Au Milieu des sollicitudes,* 16 February 1892, in *Great Encyclical Letters, op. cit.,* pp. 261-262). Hence, the essence of separation lies in a policy, not in a specific form. "Union of Church and State" does not imply any particular form of politico-ecclesiastical organizational relationship; it means that the State takes into account the legislation of the Church in making its laws.

[176] *Longinque Oceani,* 6 January 1895, in *Great Encyclical Letters, op. cit.,* p. 323.

[177] *Libertas Praestantissimum,* Hughes, *op. cit.,* p. 82.

[178] *Pervenuti,* 19 March 1902, *idem,* p. 186.

[179] *Acta Apostolicae Sedis,* Vol. XXVI (1894), No. 714; also, Vol. XXI (1889), No. 387.

[180] *Nostis Errorem,* 11 February 1889, Hughes, *op. cit.,* pp. 183-85.

[181] Cf. above, p. Koenig, *op. cit.,* gives the partial or complete text of a wide variety of documents authored by Benedict XV and his Secretary of State, Cardinal Gasparri: 83 on the general question of war and peace; 33 on the treatment of civilians and victims of war; 13 on the care of prisoners and wounded; 8 on the Peace Conference; 4 against the bombing of undefended cities; 2 against the deportation of laborers into Germany; single letters in praise of the Red Cross, on the need of rebuilding Louvain Library, on respect for international law, on generous treatment toward Jewish sufferers, on universal suppression of conscription, in praise of the Washington Arms Conference; and an appeal to Lenin in behalf of the persecuted Orthodox Christians. This is but a sample of the efforts of the Vatican during and immediately after the war.

[182] *Pacem Dei Munus Pulcherrimum,* Koenig, *op. cit.,* pp. 290-291.

[183] *Con Vivo Piacere,* 7 April 1922, *idem,* p. 320.

[184] *Très Opportunément,* 24 May 1922, *idem,* p. 324.

[184] *Très Opportunément,* 24 May 1922, *idem,* p. 324.

[185] Cf. above, pp. 70-1. No pope has spoken so vigorously against extreme nationalism. Cf. Hughes, *op. cit.,* p. 203.

[186] On the first day of the conclave, which was the shortest since 1623. It was thought that he would continue the forceful policies of Pius XI, with whom he had been so closely associated.

[187] *Dum Gravissimum,* 3 March 1939, Koenig, *op. cit.,* pp. 554-555. For his last minute appeal to the heads of European Governments, 31 August 1939, Cf. *idem,* p. 86.

[188] Text in Hughes, *op. cit.,* pp. 206-210. The reference to the Nazi aggression on Poland is unmistakable.

[189] *Nell' Alba,* 24 December 1941, *idem,* pp. 210-216.

[190] *Idem,* p. 212.

[191] This point is further emphasized in *Summi Pontificatus,* 20 October 1939, in *Selected Letters of Pius XII, op. cit.,* pp. 16-21.

[192] *Idem,* pp. 28-31.

[193] *The Rights of Man,* Christmas, 1942, *idem,* p. 281. Catholics are urged to take their part in the reconstruction of international society on these foundations. Cf. *Ancora Una Volta,* 1 June 1946, *idem,* p. 340.

[194] French original and English translation in *Pope Pius XII on World Federal Government,* Association for Education in World Government, N. Y., 1951.

[195] Italics supplied.

PART II:

CATHOLICISM and SOCIETY
in
FRANCE

Catholic Social and Political Movements
1789 - 1950

by

JOSEPH N. MOODY - CHARLES A. MICAUD
PAUL VIGNAUX

CHAPTER I

FROM OLD REGIME TO DEMOCRATIC SOCIETY

The Gathering Storm

Dr. Trevelyan in his *English Social History* defines his subject as "history with politics left out." This is a strange definition for it implies that politics is not a social activity and that it is not related intimately to the economic and cultural activities of men. But the influence of social forces on politics and institutions cannot easily be exorcised by a formula. Political power in a modern community depends on a number of factors; the ideological framework, the institutional setting, and the development of the historical process.[1] But it is certainly tremendously affected by economic groupings and by the influence such groups are able to exert on public policy.

It is from this point of view that the author has chosen to sketch the reactions of French Catholics to the problems posed since the Revolution of 1789. Sociologically, the history of modern Europe is the successive emergence of two social groups, the bourgeoisie and the industrial workers. While neither of these groups can be precisely delimited and while neither has worked with conscious unity toward definite objectives, they are historical realities, and the general characteristics of their thought and action are legitimate subjects for the historian. Social classes can be described as algebraic symbols which the historiographer uses to clarify the complex phenomena of man's past. If it is understood that there are wide differences of attitude within these groups and that conclusions drawn from their activities are only generally true, they can provide valuable insights into the stream of historical change.

French Catholics, as well as all men, were forced to take cognizance of these new social forces as their role in modern European history unfolded. In a human sense, the Catholic Church depends for its survival, as an organization, on its capacity to adjust itself to new historical conditions. Adaptability is the necessary characteristic of every institution that endures. But the process is difficult for any organism or organization. To exert influence in any period, an institution must satisfy human needs and address itself to man's immediate concrete problems. Hence, it must enmesh itself in any given cultural complex. But human needs and problems are forever in flux. If an institution is to avoid eclipse and retain its vitality, it must adjust itself to new situations, reapply its fundamental concepts, and modify its organizational techniques.[2]

Historically, the amazing survival power of the Catholic Church is evidence that it has possessed this ability.[3] Born in a provincial background with a predominantly Jewish cultural heritage, it moved successfully into the wider arena of the imperial world. Mediterranean in its early associations, it was translated to northern Europe and to wide areas of Asia. Adjusted to Roman stability, it lasted when that central authority disappeared in the West, and it was an important factor in reconstituting the fragments of Western society in the empirical arrangement we know as feudalism. The dynamic changes of the Medieval period were met without serious loss, at least in Western Europe. Only with the Reformation did this capacity appear to be diminished. As a consequence, the Church was forced to face modern problems with its social unity shattered and its self-confidence impaired.

One of the most serious of these challenges was the change in the structure of society that had been in process for centuries. The stabilization of Western Europe by the eleventh century, with the consequent relative peace and immunity from external attack, encouraged the revival of trade. The role of the merchant assumed new importance. Town life revived to offer him a center for his activities and a base for the handicraft production that was essential for his operations. By the thirteenth century, France was dotted with communes, and their inhabitants were in the process of gaining the security, freedom of movement, and independence from the surrounding feudal system that were necessary for their growth.

Such freedom was not won without a struggle. Occasionally the burghers were forced to fight the lay feudal lords; but, as the interest of the latter was predominantly on the land and as they continually needed the money and services of the town-dwellers, the opposition was sporadic and victory usually rested with the communes. More serious struggles occurred with the bishops, whose sees were located in the urban centers. In addition to the occasional necessity of freeing themselves from the temporal jurisdiction of the bishops, the new social class came into conflict with the Church on larger issues. Their spirit of acquisitiveness, their financial operations, and, above all, their need to lend money at interest clashed with the accepted ethical standards of the Medieval Church. While they gradually escaped or evaded the ecclesiastical prohibitions against usury, the stigma attaching to their activities was slow to disappear.. This explains recurrent evidences of bourgeois anti-clericalism and their receptiveness to certain Medieval heresies.[4] Yet, on the whole, the French middle class in the Medieval period remained profoundly Christian in spirit and provided the Church with an increasing proportion of its leadership.

Within the towns, social cleavage appeared in the later Middle Ages. Thirteenth century trade was fundamentally non-capitalistic. The guilds preserved a rough equality among their members, and the differences in the material conditions of the urban populations were relatively slight. But expanding operations widened the gap between the larger traders and the artisans and workers. Growing concentration of capital modified the methods of production and offered new opportunities for wealth. Discrepancies in income and status created social conflict, especially when the richer elements attempted to seize political power and to exclude the poor from public affairs. In the later Medieval period, French towns often saw bloody strife. In Flanders, where class conflicts were most serious, aristocrats and clergy sometimes formed coalitions with the common people against the wealthier elements.

In their quest for power and in their social conflicts, the bourgeoisie found a natural ally in the national monarch. By the time of Philip the Fair, the terms of this alliance were clear. The major political preoccupations of the rising class were control of the judiciary and finance. By royal favor they won the control of the administration of justice from the seigneurial lords through venality of offices and diminished the power of the Church courts. They served the King well, providing him with lawyers and administrators, and advanced their own interests by their elaboration of the Roman law concept of private property, their possession of state offices, and their acquisition of seigneurial lands. The connection was further cemented under Louis XI. By that time, the French bourgeoisie had developed their tendency to look to the central power for the defense of their interests. The same monarch initiated the program of mercantilism, which at this stage was highly profitable for the bourgeoisie, and he aided in transforming the guilds into hereditary corporations on a caste basis.

France was definitely a modern state by the time of Louis XI. Feudal enclaves had been greatly reduced. Monarchy had gained in prestige as the restorer of order after the English and Burgundian wars. The tendency toward the expansion of the national frontiers consolidated monarchical power, and the classical revival offered ideological justification for absolute rule. The religious wars, which were also political conflicts, endangered royal authority, but it was restored under Henry IV. A strong monarchy appeared as the only cure for internal divisions, and the first of the Bourbons used this favorable climate to solidify his personal rule, reduce the liberties of towns and Provincial Estates, and eliminate the Estates General. Parliaments were humored but kept in check; hereditary possessions of judicial office was confirmed by *La Paulette* and protests against the sale of these positions lost all efficacy. The contributions of Richelieu and Louis XIV to this development are too well known to require comment. Richelieu was opposed to this venality, but could do nothing about it.

During this expansion of royal power, the bourgeoisie remained firm supporters of monarchical claims. The Reformation, appearing in France in its Calvinist form, offered them a considerable temptation. The Huguenot defense of wealth and its exaltation of the bourgeois virtues of thrift and industry, made their appeal, and the ranks of French Protestantism had a fair proportion of well-to-do traders and townsfolk. But the ensemble of the French bourgeoisie rejected the new doctrine, partly because of the religious conflicts that attended its spread. The restoration of order under Henry IV renewed their allegiance to the throne, and the first half of the reign of Louis XIV marks the apogee of the alliance between monarchy and the upper middle class. Saint-Simon's well-known quip on the influence of the "vile bourgeoisie" in this reign is verifiable.

This period from the accession of Henry IV through the minority of Louis XIV was also the period of the greatest flowering of French Catholicism in modern times.[5] It was an age of intense religious activity, and the bourgeoisie participated fully in the charitable, intellectual, and spiritual works of this fruitful period of Francis de Sales and Vincent de Paul. But the rigid ethical concepts of Jansenism appealed to many of the elite and the bitter strife that followed its introduction contributed to the alienation of the bourgeoisie from the Church.

The continued progress of commerce and the expansion of finance, mining, and industry, which had been continuing for centuries and had been furthered by the opening of the new worlds, were accelerated in the course of the eighteenth century. Speculation offered new opportunities for the rapid acquisition of wealth. Despite disastrous foreign wars, the economic development of France continued in all fields. The principal beneficiaries of this increased prosperity were the bourgeoisie, especially their more aggressive and enterprising members. The inequality of the division of this increased wealth is evident from the accepted estimate that the real wages of the workers were lower in the eighteenth century than they had been at the end of the fifteenth and from the heavy burdens upon the peasantry.[6] It was these classes which bore the brunt of the inflation that characterized the age.

These social tensions of the eighteenth century threatened the stability of the Old Regime. The slow march of monarchy to absolute power represented a revolution in the Western political tradition. The theories of divine right which had been advanced to support royal absolutism conflicted with deeply embedded traditions. The notion of the dignity of the human person, and the associated ideas of natural law, human rights and human liberty had been asserted by some of the Greek and Roman philosophers and by the religious authors of the Old Testament. These ideas were reinforced and universalized in the Christian teaching and struggled for institutional expression during the Middle Ages. Thomas Acquinas gave them their accepted theoretical formulation. The implementation of these concepts was hindered by a variety of obstacles but was fostered by the absence of a monopolistic focus of power. Medieval society, while religious, was not theocratic. Normally power was divided between a political authority and a religious authority, the latter generally regarded as independent and usually acting as a check upon the political. Theoretically, this balance was expressed in the Doctrine of the Two Swords, which remained dominant despite the appearance of views of imperial primacy and *plenitudo potestatis*.

The existence of this double *foci* of political power was made possible by the political fragmentation of the Middle Ages. As this was altered in favor of centralization under the national monarchs, not only were independent or quasi-independent bodies such as free communes, Provincial Diets, and local autonomy modified, but the builders of the modern state became strong enough to eliminate the independent status of the Church. This was done directly in the lands where the Reformation established national or territorial churches, or indirectly in the Catholic areas via the Concordat. Thus, in early modern centuries there appears in Western Europe, for the first time since the classic age, a truly monopolistic political power, claiming absolutism by divine right.

The French bourgeoisie were closely associated with this

development and up through the first half of the reign of Louis
XIV had given it active support. But in the closing decades
of the seventeenth and throughout the course of the eighteenth
century, an important section of bourgeois opinion concluded
that the French political structure no longer reflected the social
realities and that their power entitled them to a more unhampered direction of public affairs. Fundamentally their analysis was justified. The Old Regime showed itself impotent to
complete its work of centralization and rationalization which it
had pursued for centuries. Its administrative techniques were
not readapted adequately to meet new demands. It continued
to favor the older aristocarcy at court, in the army and in
the high positions in the Church. Most seriously, it revealed
its incompetence in the handling of the public treasury; it
fought wars for dynastic reasons or for prestige, it lavished funds
on favorites, it built extravagant monuments. True, it was the
financiers and speculators who profited by the state's inability
to raise revenue to meet its needs and to rationalize its collection of taxation; true, too, the wealthier *rentiers* derived substantial income from loans to the state. But the point was
reached where the incompetence of the regime seemed to
threaten the stability of the public treasury and of the class
most directly involved.

In part, the eighteenth century monarchy failed to make
necessary changes because of Parliament, the most bourgeois of
all institutions, which posed as champion of the people but
resisted all reform that touched its own extensive privileges.
But it was also due to the inability of the Old Regime to deal
with other pressure groups with entrenched positions or to
infuse into French society a sense of common purpose. During
its final decades, it almost ceased to try and ultimately resorted
to a policy of drift.

It was the bourgeoisie who were most conscious of this
failure. They felt confident of their own strength and of their
ability to solve the specific problems facing the nation. Though
they had won extensive privileges, they resented the more
generous exemptions of the old nobility and the clergy. Though
they had favored mercantilist policy, they came to consider it
a handicap and wished to free themselves from all state regulation. They hungered for direct control of state finances, which
had always escaped them. The good sense of the bourgeoisie
revolted against a political order that was inept. While positive
solutions caused wide disagreement and there were fundamental differences in the proposals for change, there was practical
unanimity among informed opinion on the unsuitability of the

existing regime. This discontent was further stimulated by the successful challenge of the British trading classes and the more rational political order which appeared to have emerged beyond the Channel from the great Compromise of 1688.

The last century of the Old Regime saw a twofold divorce that was to affect profoundly the future course of French History. The first was this break in the relations of the monarchy and the bourgeoisie. The second was the cleavage between an important section of the bourgeoisie and the Catholic Church. Since the sixteenth century, there had been an undercurrent of religious skepticism in France, but it did not become pronounced until the end of the seventeenth. The civil wars stemming from the Reformation and the virtual civil war within the Church that was consequent on Jansenism weakened the hold of religious belief in many and prevented believers from giving adequate attention to new problems. The efforts of the central power to crush religious dissent, an effort enthusiastically encouraged by a majority of the clergy, weakened the moral prestige of Catholicism. The failure to accept the reality of a divided Christendom by both Church and State, and the growing inability to impose religious uniformity combined to create the demand for tolerance and free thought that was characteristic of eighteenth century criticism.[7]

The loss of the Church's unique position in European society was matched by a weakening within the fabric of the French Church itself. The *élan* that marked the greater part of the seventeenth century was noticeably absent in the century that followed. While ordinary tasks were done and while the bulk of the teaching and social work was still the task of the clergy,[8] there was an evident decline in the quality of religious writing and religious life. Male religious orders deteriorated both in numbers and in zeal,[9] and the disappearance of the Jesuits left an unfilled gap in the Church's activity and defense. It is no longer customary to dismiss the eighteenth century apologists of Catholicism as benighted bigots,[10] but when due allowance has been made for their skill and sincerity, it is still true that they failed to impress their contemporaries and at times appear not to have profoundly convinced themselves.

The general relaxing of spiritual energy is witnessed by the rarity of figures of extaordinary sanctity. There was not wholesale abuse but considerable mediocre performance. The female religious continued to serve selflessly. The bulk of the lower clergy did their work conscientiously, often heroically under difficult circumstances, and they enjoyed the confidence of the people. In a sense, the Revolution was a judgment on the weakness of the Church under the Old Regime. By this demanding test, the rank and file of the secular clergy did remarkably well. Besides, they were better equipped and trained for their role than most of their successors of the nineteenth century.

Part of the slow paralysis that seems characteristic of the eighteenth century French Church was due to the ever tightening control of the monarchy. The roots of the Church's dependence on the royal power lay in the later Middle Ages, when regalism was advocated by Parliament and the King's bourgeois legalists. It received formal expression in the Concordat of 1516,[11] which gave the King the right to appoint the chief ecclesiastical officials. This power was further extended in the course of the seventeenth century. Regalism was sometimes a source of good, particularly in the early part of this century, but its final effects were highly unfavorable. Royal favorites were increasingly rewarded with Church benefices. By the eighteenth century, the bishops and major Church officers were exclusively of aristocratic birth. While the system produced only a few Talleyrands or Briennes, there were widespread episcopal absenteeism and neglect of spiritual duties. A study of the history of Cluny, Saint Benoit-Sur-Loire, or any of the great monastic foundations will reveal the unhappy consequences of commendatory appointments of abbots. Further, since the disposal of the higher ecclesiastical positions was in royal hands, the King could use the immense fortune of the Gallican Church for his own purposes. Church appointments came to be, in effect, the King's *Civil List,* and he rewarded artists, authors, soldiers, and aged officials with Church benefices. As a result, the great wealth of the Church became a millstone about her neck; she was blamed for its possession and held accountable for its use, but its actual determination lay in royal hands as the price of her survival.

The rigid control of the Church tied it to the fate of the monarchy and robbed it of that independence of spirit essential to its spiritual functioning. While the great preachers of the seventeenth century often used the pulpit to decry abuse in high places, the general atmosphere of the eighteenth century was one of acceptance and reliance on the power of the crown for support. Privileged and wealthy, the Church lost her role as the conscience of the community.

Ecclesiastical acceptance of monarchical control was not a product of the last stages of the Old Regime, nor was it imposed upon unwilling subjects. The term given to the preference for royal national control of the Church, in distinction to papal supra-national direction, is Gallicanism. Gallicanism found its formal expression in the declaration of the French bishops known as the Four Articles (1682). Politically, these affirmed the independence of the French crown in its relations with the Papacy. The Pope could not depose the French King, nor release his subjects from their oath of loyalty, nor exercise any restraint on the temporal powers of rulers. Ecclesiastically, they limited papal power by emphasizing the prerogatives of the bishops and affirming the superiority of a General Council over the Pope in cases of conflict.

Gallicanism does not admit of simple definition. It was an attitude rather than a set of propositions; it meant different things to different groups and it varied with circumstances. Thus the magistrates of Parliament interpreted it to mean that they could supervise relations between the French clergy and Rome. They argued for and won the power to prevent publication of any Apostolic document in France without prior approbation of the sovereign.[12] By an extension of their interpretation of "abuse," they were declaring (in the eighteenth century) their competence to deal with purely spiritual matters, for example, the refusal of the Sacraments. The French bishops rejected these constructions, and their Gallicanism was considerably more modest. They did not deny the unity of the Church, and in the doctrinal conflicts with the Jansenists they sought and accepted Papal decisions. What they would have preferred would have been a kind of balance between the Crown and the Vatican. Among the lower clergy, Gallicanism was often simple national feeling and was found together with resentment against the bishops.[13] It is undoubtedly an exaggeration to say, as is common, that for the clergy of the Old Regime "the liberties of the Gallican Church" were merely liberties against Rome, masking servility to the national monarch. The crisis of the Revolution would prove otherwise. But it is unquestionable that the Gallican spirit made the royal power over the Church more palatable. The bishops would still protest against the King in certain circumstances and retain wide autonomy in administration, but their frame of mind and their social background hardly made them vigilant opponents of growing royal power.

Behind Gallicanism lay a fundamental fact: the national state had come to play a dominant role in the life of Western man, at least in such developed states as France. The time had passed when the supreme loyalty was directed to the universal Church, with only local ties as competition. By the eighteenth century, the national state loomed as the rightful source of supreme authority and was increasingly regarded as competent over a wide area of human affairs. Only the Revolution and subsequent history would reveal all the implications contained in this changed relationship of nation and Church.

The regalistic Catholic monarchs of the Old Regime were not content to win control over the Church in their own domains. They influenced the election of Popes through their appointees, the national Cardinals. Most of the Popes chosen in the eighteenth century were aged men who were considered "safe." The general suppression of the Jesuits is the clearest example of the intrusion of royal power into the central direction of the Church, but the pressure was constant throughout this period.

The eclipse of the Church as an independent body was paralleled by a lessening of her position as a cultural force. Christian Europe had professed a faith that history led to eternity and that in the course of this life clearly defined spiritual duties had to be discharged faithfully and without regard to immediate consequences. It is easy to exaggerate the supernatural orientation of the Middle Ages. Obviously it did not affect all, nor did it uniformly lead to concrete action. But it was the prevailing temper of thought and it did influence the status of religion in society. The growing interest in secular objectives, expanding wealth and acquisitiveness, the quickened interest in classical learning and the exact sciences, all tended to modify the importance of religious belief. The impact of these preoccupations was not felt at once. All classes of early seventeenth century French society were profoundly interested in religious questions. The bourgeoisie, who were most receptive to these new influences, were insulated against certain of their consequences by their sober and industrious lives, which inclined them to a strict Jansenistic morality rather than to a denial of religious values. It was only in the eighteenth century that they began to be converted to secular optimism and that religion was relegated to one of many of man's experiences and endeavors, only a part of his knowledge and a fragment of his interest.

With this change in the intellectual currents, interest in the physical sciences began to take the place which an earlier age had accorded to theology. Thomas Aquinas had succeeded in his attempt to base an entire world view on the science of Aristotle. But Aristotelian physics had been discredited by further discoveries, and a considerable intellectual restatement was necessary to relate Catholicism to the new knowledge. In philosophy, in biblical interpretation, and in popular devotion, a considerable amount of debris would have to be cleared away if the essential doctrines were to be cogently reaffirmed. The atmosphere of insecurity in the Post-Reformation Church was not conducive to this effort, and on the whole it was not successfully accomplished. A major attempt in this direction was made by Descartes, but his sincere purpose did not prevent his thought from acting as a solvent of religious belief and as an incentive to philosophical scepticism.

It was the bourgeoisie who became most attached to the new science. The advance of mathematics had been of material assistance in the conduct of their affairs. Even such a simple mechanical contrivance as the clock had proved useful in rationalizing the working habits of their employees. The world as then revealed by science appeared a well-regulated mechanism that satisfied their sense of order. The abandonment of Christianity in favor of Deism seemed to them justified in light of the interpretations given the growing knowledge of the physical world.

Another source of alienation lay in the accepted view of the nature of man. The Reformation had revived profoundly pessimistic concepts of man and his capabilities. The crux of Protestant theology was its doctrine of justification. Both Lutheranism and Calvinism took an extremely negative position on the possibility of man's contributing anything to assist the process of salvation. The belief that man is saved by faith alone and that his own spiritual works are of no avail, the denial of free will and the doctrine of predestination were sharp deviations from the moderate optimism maintained by the Scholastics. While Catholic Christianity categorically rejected these pessimistic views, it was not unaffected by them. The clearest instance is Jansenism whose attitude on "nature corrupted" was very close to that of Calvin.[41] Pascal's pessimism led him to a denial of the possibility of establishing justice in human societies and to a demand for submission to the order established by force.[15]

Although Jansenism was vigorously condemned by the Popes, it spread widely among the elite of French society and led to bitter controversies. The intervention of the monarchy in these religious disputes weakened its authority and diminished respect for the Church. Jansenism gained strength from the absence of normal channels of political opposition in a complex society, and in its later stages was partly a protest against the restrictive policies of Louis XIV. It also gained force from the general atmosphere of seventeenth century Catholicism. While the earlier masters of the Catholic Revival, the generations of Francis de Sales and Vincent de Paul, retained the flavor of the Scholastic tradition, there was a definite tendency in the later leaders toward a "late Augustinianism" which emphasized the majesty of God and the weakness and sinfulness of man.[16] With the exception of the Jesuits and their followers, the bulk of French Catholics in the second half of the seventeenth century were moving toward a more dismal view of man than had been traditional in Catholic thought. Thus, the abundant religious literature of this period contains scant reference to human rights, liberty, or dignity. This tendency not only produced the worst terrain for resistance to absolute government; it also prepared the way for scepticism, which is the end result of all pessimistic theory. To borrow Newman's dictum—here too, heresy was the penalty for neglected truth.

It was the bourgeoisie in the seventeenth century which felt the strongest attraction to Jansenism.[17] The Jansenists appealed to their middle class contemporaries by their defiance of royal interference in matters of conscience, by their emphasis on lay rather than ecclesiastical authority, and particularly by their strict morality which justified the *honnête homme* who performed his daily tasks with the consciousness that he was pursuing moral ends and doing God's work on earth. But Jansenist rigidity had its limitations. Material and social conditions favored the growth of bourgeois self-confidence. A general climate of optimism became apparent toward the close of the seventeenth century and its effects are clearly seen in French literature. The conquest of physical nature seemed assured. All could now possess knowledge that was denied to the wise men of the past. Man could now dominate his history and by the use of reason eliminate the evils bred by ignorance. Only time and energy were needed to create a perfect world; and, as spirits soared, the task appeared both easier and nearer to fulfillment. The full flowering of this attitude was the doctrine of inevitable progress; its roots lie in that great surge of secular faith that distinguishes the eighteenth century.[18]

Again, it was the upper classes who felt the full impact of this new *élan*. They possessed the wealth and education that would make them responsive to such appealing vistas. They came to identify Jansenism and certain strands of contemporary Catholic thought with orthodoxy and rejected it as incompatible with the spirit of the age and the upward march of mankind. It has been wisely remarked that efficacious ideas, which exercise the most lasting and evident influence on human events, are often confused ideas, for it is their very confusion that permits them to invade the semi-rational and form general attitudes. The air of confident expectancy in the eighteenth century, especially among the upper bourgeoisie, may defy analysis, but its historical importance is beyond question. Equally obvious is the fact that this utopianism could not be adjusted to the experience or the doctrines of the Catholic Church.

To give substance to the new outlook, there was need of a philosophy that would express the ensemble of aspirations and convictions that were spreading in eighteenth century France. The bourgeoisie were the directing class in the elaboration of ideas as in all else. Descartes paved the way for the philosophy of the Enlightenment by his view that only through reason could man gain knowledge. The bourgeois love of precise notions was attracted by the theory of "clear ideas," which were immediately perceptible, while his *tabula rasa* encouraged them to rid themselves of customs that antedated their emergence. While learning from Cartesianism to reject all that could not be easily formulated, they developed the moral idea of the honest man whose foresight removes the unknown from life and leaves little place for mystery.

Descartes' contribution to the evolution of the Enlightenment lay largely in his critical methodology. D'Alembert, in his introductory essay for the Encyclopedia (1751), shows how the seventeenth century philosopher was both repudiated and sustained: his metaphysics had been demolished by Locke and his physics by Newton; yet he praises him for proposing a method which destroyed Scholasticism. Descartes' conception that the thinker must retire from life in order to learn made no impression on merchants and men of the world, who were more intrigued by the economic and political activities of Locke, whom they admired for his good sense. It was this influence from beyond the Channel which gave positive content to the structure of eighteenth century French thought.

The suitability of the Enlightenment as a vehicle for French bourgeois attitudes is evident in the doctrine of earthly happiness, achieved by calculation and skill, and consisting in the avoidance of unpleasant sensations and the cultivation of pleasurable ones; in the concept of natural, self-regulating laws, observable by reason, not requiring divine intervention, and applicable to society; and in the idea of the natural goodness of man, who if allowed to develop his potencies, would avoid error and do good. This doctrine was framed to meet middle class needs as they appeared in eighteenth century France. Even the predominance of prose reflected the sober tastes of the aspiring group.

Voltaire is almost the perfect type of the bourgeois intellectual. A successful business man and speculator who amassed a fortune, he despised the masses and reproached Rousseau, whom he detested, as the son of a cobbler. Distinguished by good sense and by one of the sharpest pens in literary history, he presented problems in their simplest form, without any of the nuances and complexities which he felt were unnecessary for the understanding of reality. Hating the Church and rejecting Christianity, he retained his belief in God and the moral virtues, and felt that religion served a useful purpose by modifying the discontent of the lower classes. He regularly attended Mass in the village church near his estate at Ferney lest a profession of his scepticism incite his tenants to revolutionary ideas.

The Philosophers disagreed on many fundamental points, but they did succeed in convincing an important section of effective opinion of the insuitability of absolute monarchy and a unitary church, and they did present an alternative in general terms of Reason, Liberty, and Justice. Elaborated principally by bourgeois thinkers and appealing primarily to the upper circles of this class, this doctrine had the advantage of being couched in universal language and related to the general welfare. No program which was narrowly drawn in terms of class interest would have aroused the enthusiasm of so many. The Philosophers made no such error: they denounced concrete abuses; they protested against real injustices; they criticized obvious inadequacies; they championed reforms and causes which won wide approval. Above all they appealed to those general sentiments and abstractions which are so deeply buried in the traditions of the West. But interwoven into the pattern are clearly discernible special objectives. These show forth on all critical questions: property, the corporations, workingman's associations, trade, wages, the electorate. They are observable in the major stream of the Enlightenment and in the speeches, legislation, and constitutions of the great drama of the Revolution. Other currents were there, but it is correct to say with Marx that the movement as a whole was overwhelmingly middle class and that the bourgeoisie were the principal beneficiaries.

While critical of existing political institutions, the Philosophers reserved their severest blows for the Church. Christianity was for them the enemy of happiness, defined in bourgeois terms as tranquility or the end of uncertainty; it violated reason and human nature because it professed to be supernatural; and it did not provide an adequate interpretation of history, for the human story is not the result of a divine plan but of an immanent historical process.

Revolution and Its Religious Consequences (1789-1815)

It is essential to avoid a false perspective that would result from a concentration on the literary content of the Enlightenment. Four generalizations must be added to give a balanced picture of the religious position on the eve of the Revolution:

1. While anti-clerical and anti-religious attitudes were widespread in the upper bourgeoisie and in the court nobility and had begun to seep down through the social scale with the flood of pamphlets and popular songs in the last decade of the Old Regime, the bulk of Frenchmen were still deeply attached to the Catholic faith. France was overwhelmingly agrarian, and the countryside was practically untouched by currents of philosophical thought. Among the masses of petty bourgeoisie, artisans, and laborers in the towns, there were individuals who had been affected by the Philosophers, but the vast majority still practiced and accepted the traditional faith, which was firmly rooted in popular culture. This is reflected in the *cahiers* of the III Estate, which though they set forth grievances, with few exceptions demanded that the Church retain her political and social position. It is also seen in the men who came to Versailles in 1789, for "the members of the Constituent Assembly, far from being unbelievers and thorough-going innovators or grudge-bearing Jansenists, were in the great majority sincere Catholics. Only a very restricted minority was hostile and its proposals did go beyond vigorous reforms." [19] Far from having an unchanging religious policy, there was a steady deterioration from the happy accord of the first months to the open hostility of late 1791.

2. While the Church was privileged everywhere in the Catholic area of Europe, she was faced with growing problems, particularly with the intrusion of royal power into spiritual affairs. Later nineteenth century Rightists were to idealize the situation, but contemporary observers, such as the Papal Nuncio Pacca, took a most gloomy view of her actual condition.[20]

3. French Catholics were not opposed to the Revolution from its inception. It was the lower clergy who swung the balance to the bourgeoisie in the critical early days of the Revolution, and clerical deputies played a decisive role in the fall of the Old Regime.[21]

4. The inheritance of the Old Regime was a major handicap in the early stages: all assumed the Gallican position that it was within the competence of the public authority to make fundamental religious changes. It is significant that not a single *cahier* mentioned papal intervention for the reform of the Church.

It was the financial crisis that led to the first definite break. Some of the *cahiers* of the II and III Estates had suggested that the burdens of the treasury would be met by a reduction of the religious orders. The debates on the renunciation of privileges (August 4) hinted that ecclesiastical property belonged to the nation. Pamphlets appeared during the summer to show that this resource would practically suffice for the deficit. These suggestions were not revolutionary, and the authors cited precedents from the Old Regime.[22] Talleyrand made the argument palatable in his famous speech which carefully indicated not only that nationalization of Church lands was just and beneficial but that *it in no wise threatened the sacred principle of private property*. Behind the decisions was a growing popular excitement, the beginning of the tendency to identify the interests of the monarchy and the Church and the first expansion of anti-clericalism. But the basic factor was expediency and the regalistic theory of the unitary state. The nationalization decree was passed on 2 November 1789, 510 votes to 346.

As a consequence, there occurred the great transfer of property that was to influence the entire course of the Revolution. The lands were bought often for speculation by moneyed groups, bourgeoisie, nobles, even émigré bishops. It had the effect of binding the possessors to the new order, and it destroyed the economic power of the Church as the renunciation of privileges had weakened its social power.

Popular anti-clericalism continued to grow and the flood of pamphlets and journals included the clergy in the hated term "aristocrats," a designation which had partial justification in the social origin of the bishops and higher officials. But this merely provided additional pressure in the drafting of the Civil Constitution of the Clergy (12 July 1790), which marks the definitive divorce of the Revolution and Catholicism. Its major aim was to establish institutions "on the sacred bond of religion," as Martineau, its *rapporteur* put it; religion was to be the tie which bound men to the state so that it could demand obedience as a sacred duty. Far from being an expression of separation of Church and State in the modern sense, it was intended as a recognition of the importance of a *state-controlled religion* in maintaining national unity. What is surprising from our perspective is the willingness of its authors to concede everything to the state and the absence of any fear that such a policy might be dangerous.

The Civil Constitution deprived the Catholic Church in France of its religious autonomy and set up a national Church dependent on the civil power. It rearranged dioceses on a de-

partmental basis. Bishops were to be elected by those who had
the franchise in each department; they were to receive canonical
institution from archbishops, who were forbidden to seek confirmation from Rome, but were permitted to notify the Pope
of their election. *Curés* were appointed by bishops but were
autonomous in their parishes. Canons and other categories of
ecclesiastics were abolished. All clerics were salaried. No French
citizen could be the religious subject of a foreign bishop or
pastor. The Assembly burned its bridges by requiring all the
clergy to take an oath to support the Civil Constitution (27
November 1790).

This drastic innovation in Church discipline failed of its
purpose, for it divided both the Church and France and
endangered the new order instead of strengthening it. Debidour
calls it "a capital error" [23] and Mathiez is even more specific:[24]
"The result was that a great number of priests, up till then
supporters of the Revolution, were conscientiously obligated to
a conflict which they neither desired nor foresaw. As a consequence, the aristocratic party was strengthened by a formidable increase and instead of instituting a national church,
the Assembly had only established the Church of a party, the
party in power, with the ancient Church becoming the Church
of the party temporarily vanquished." Faithfulness to Rome
meant hostility to a movement which many had approved.
Thus, the association of Catholicism and monarchism became
strengthened.

The French bishops rejected the Civil Constitution, but their
remonstrance was weakened by the fact that most had emigrated
by the time of its passage. Pope Pius VI disapproved strongly;
but fearful of schism and not anxious to worsen the position
of Louis XVI, he delayed for eight months. Then in the brief
Quod Aliquantum of 10 March 1791 he condemned not only
the Civil Constitution, but the principles of the Revolution as
well, thus placing papal approval on the identification of the
Revolution with anti-religion. The clergy divided, with a slight
majority refusing the oath.[25] The minority which accepted did
so in order not to appear unpatriotic, because they approved
of its objectives, because of their unwillingness to abandon
their flocks and for the variety of personal motives of security
which affect men in crises. Many sincerely hoped to preserve
religion in France and to reconcile the Church with the new
conditions.

The division of the Church and country into two camps was
not foreseen and certainly not sought. For a time the non-jurors
were treated moderately, but events did not favor moderation.

The flight of the King, foreign war, the growing hostility of Rome to the new regime, and the continued growth of popular anti-clericalism, all encouraged stern measures of repression. The royalists quickly saw the profit they could draw from the religious quarrel. Their actions, both in France and abroad, contributed to the conviction of the basic incompatibility of the Church and the Revolution. The war identified the Church with the enemies of the nation, and non-jurors were regarded as Fifth Columnists at the time when nationalist feeling was greatly stimulated. Political and religious opposition to the regime was hard to separate when in many persons they were found together. Not all the non-jurors were Counter-Revolutionaries, but the efforts of conciliatory clerics such M. Emery, who tried to disentangle the Church from partisan strife and find a *modus vivendi* between religion and civic duty, were ignored.

As a consequence, there unfolded the melancholy story of the Terror and the de-Christianization. The causes of the extreme persecution of religion under the Convention are complex and highly controverted.[26] Certainly, the shedding of blood had opened an unbridgeable gulf, and the Revolution originally not hostile to Catholism, had, during the crisis of the Terror, developed conceptions that were irreconcilable with it. Originally claiming competence in the field of discipline, it was now invading the domain of dogma, Ultimately, it adopted a policy of complete repression. This policy struck heavily at the Constitutional Church for the non-jurors had previously been forced into hiding and had become accustomed to clandestine operations.[27] True the supporters of this extremist policy were still in a minority, and local studies show that whenever there was a lull in the pressure, there was an immediate return to religious practice. Robespierre's opposition to persecution, like Bonaparte's later, was simply a recognition of fact.

The Thermidorians, leaders in the Terror and de-Christianization, were the last to desire a return to moderation. But when opinion interpreted their *coup d'état* as a restoration of normalcy, as opportunists they accepted the myth. The removal of the external threat also favored a relaxation of persecution. Besides, religion was less dead than they had thought, and the nation had resisted the suppression of Christianity and the imposition of new cults. A spontaneous revival occurred in the latter half of 1794. When the revolutionary generals accepted the surrender of the Vendeans on the guarantee of religious liberty (February 1795), it became difficult to deny it elsewhere in the face of popular demand. The pacification of the West also permitted Republicans to distinguish between royalism and religion, for the rebels had accepted the Republican regime in return for liberty of worship. The law of 3 Ventose III (21 February 1795), the first law of separation of Church and State, extended toleration to the nation though it hemmed in religious practice by many restrictions.

The effect of this grant of toleration varied. The Church had survived the crisis somewhat as the French nation withstood the occupation of 1940-5; its members had sought survival along different paths. The Constitutionals under Gregoire made a heroic effort to benefit from the new opportunity, but they had been fatally weakened by persecution and by a steady stream of deserters to Rome. Separation meant the ultimate withering of an organization that had been created by official political act.

The non-jurors faced an equally serious problem. By the decree of 11 Prairial III (30 May 1795), use of Church buildings was permitted only to those who would take a new oath "to submit to the laws of the Republic." The reaction of Catholics to this oath of 1795 reveals the basic cleavage which the Revolution had created in the French Church, and which was to cast its shadow over the whole of its nineteenth century history.

There were two basic responses. The party of reason and accommodation, led by M. Emery and the bishops who had remained in France, argued that this oath was completely consistent with Catholic principles. They recognized that profound changes had occurred in thought and conditions. They knew that the old order had gone forever and they proposed to come to terms with the new wherever possible. When principles permitted, they supported the *de facto* government and sought to avoid all political entanglements. In dealing with Constitutionals and apostates, they favored "the method of Paris"— understanding and conciliation.

The second group comprised the Intransigents. They rejected the oath, preferring secret worship and the reorganization of religion by the preaching of missions. They kept in close contact with the émigré bishops, who, like all refugees, had lost touch with conditions in France. Basically fearful of and hostile to the Republic as a consequence of their experience, the Intransigents raised their preference to a rigid formula that placed their political views above all considerations, including the welfare of the Church itself. They were devoted to the monarchy, and their political usefulness was appreciated by the sceptic and Voltarian Louis XVIII who confided his hopes in a letter to his brother.[28] They approached the *"lapsi"* according to the method of Lyons with a rigorous demand for humiliating retractions and long penances.

The subsequent history of the Catholic Church in France could be written in terms of the fluctuations in the strength of these two groups, who maintained their basic positions in all the changing circumstances. The tragedy of French Catholicism was that the second group was usually dominant, especially from 1850 to 1914. The net effect of their policy was to lose the bulk of the nation, attached as it was both to the changes introduced by the Revolution and to the ancestral faith. The stake in this long contest was nothing less than the soul of France. The Intransigents dominated the play and the game was lost.

Since this division was so profound and so lasting, it may be well to explore its roots. The eighteenth century movement of change was not exclusively social; it was accompanied by a great intellectual ferment. Man is complex, and in different ages and cultures he gives prominence to disparate expectations. In varied historical circumstances, he can emphasize certain claims of his nature, seek specific realizations, move toward some possible goals, and lose interest in others. The sum of these expectations creates what it is fashionable to call the intellectual climate of an age. And the totality of man's hopes in a given environment produces an atmosphere which every institution must take into account.

Christianity clearly recognizes that man is capable of wide variations of conduct; he can scale the heights or plumb the depths. What he will do in fact will depend on the degree of his submission to the law of God. Man cannot develop his potentialities here or gain eternal life unless he cooperates positively with the Divine. All Christians would agree that the supernatural is essential for human happiness, here and hereafter. This fundamental notion is capable of nuances in interpretation. It can be given an optimistic emphasis as with the Scholastics or Jesuits, or a pessimistic turn as with the Jansenists. The prevailing view in the French Church in the eighteenth century was veering toward the latter, which sharpened the conflict with the Philosophers.

The Philosophers rejected the foundations of Christian thinking. They limited man in time by denying his supernatural destiny; they enlarged him in space by declaring that he could readily reach human happiness by the free use of his natural faculties and solve all the problems of life and death by his own rational activity.

The response of Catholics to this challenge would depend on the answer to a further question: was the intellectual world of the time permanently lost to Catholicism? Those who answered negatively were faced with an intellectual problem; to search the roots of their own thinking to see if the current expression of belief accurately reflected its fundamentals; and to examine the thought of the age to discover a basis of contact. The search would be enlivened by the conviction that not all the sons of the Revolution were equally committed to extreme naturalism and that time and reality would dampen the more extravagant optimism. This would be the approach of Emery's group. It would later be that of Lamennais, of the Liberal Catholics, and of the men of the Catholic Revival, who demonstrated that Christianity and rationality could be shown compatible. All these would be confident of the power of Christian truth; hence they would be inclined to grant liberty of thought to dissenters or at least to affirm toleration as the lesser evil in a divided society.

The Intransigents answered the basic question affirmatively. Hence their solution was not primarily intellectual but political: to confine the enemy so that he could do the least harm and to insulate the good from contamination. They were correct in their assertion that, whatever the original intention of the Revolution, it had ultimately used all its power to separate the French Church from its international foundation; and that when this attempt proved unsatisfactory, it had turned on the Church with fury and used every effort to destroy it. From this fact, the Intransigents drew a simple conclusion: there could be no compromise with the Revolution or with the philosophy which had "created" it. The only hope for them was to rebuild the entire structure that the Revolution had demolished and so to recover for the Church the eminent position it had lost. That both this analysis and conclusion were invalid is evident from nineteenth century French history. The tragic consequences of this over-simplified position will be seen as the story unfolds. But it would be completely misleading to conclude that the Intransigent position was an automatic reaction that bore a necessary relation to the nature of Catholicism. The responses of men amid the political conflicts of our time indicate that this two-fold division is a normal human reaction to a profound challenge.[29]

The position of the Intransigents was strengthened by the religious policy of the Directory. This would have been an ideal time for reconciliation, for a separation of the religious and political questions. But the Directory was fundamentally hostile to Catholicism and frightened by the religious revival. In this, they were supported by the irreducible core of opponents of religion, who were impervious to any spirit of compromise. This group had been enlarged by events since 1789 when the vague anti-religious ideas of many had been solidified by conflict. The ranks of the hostile had been swelled by functionaries of the revolutionary governments, purchasers or speculators in Church property, workers (especially in Paris), who had been stirred by the vision of democracy, and by the bulk of the intellectuals. The failure of this anti-clerical group to make concessions hardened clerical opposition and made future reconciliation more difficult since both sides clung to maximum demands. One can be excused from speculating on what would have been the consequences had there triumphed the spirit of Emery and of Carnot, the one member of the Directory who was somewhat liberal. Instead, religious peace came from the hand of the Corsican.

The failure to reconcile Church and Republic under the Directory represents a definite break between Catholicism and the French bourgeoisie. Certainly, the majority of this class would have been content with the political—ecclesiastical arrangements of the Constituent Assembly, but those arrangements were essentially unworkable and events moved forward regardless of original intentions. The Directory, which was socially very conservative, was equally opposed to royalist reaction and popular "extremism." Essentially, it represented a stabilization of bourgeois control of the state. While fear of radical disturbances caused some of them to feel that the real enemy was no longer the Church, those who ruled were still swayed by the passions of the Terror. The new persecution of Fructidor, 1797, inflamed old wounds and ended all hope of reconciliation.

In part, the Church was saved by its own efforts—by the stubborn refusal of many of its adherents to bow before persecution. It was a recognition of this perseverance under attack that was the major factor in Napoleon's religious policy. In part too, the Church was rescued by an outside agency, and the conditions of her rescue were to affect her subsequent history. Napoleon was completely realistic in his approach to religion. He was without any personal belief,[30] but he had been impressed by the heroic defense in the Vendee and was convinced that France was fundamentally Catholic. He believed religion indispensable to the state in guaranteeing order and property and in preaching respect for authority—an approach that inevitably led to fatal consequences for the Church. Religion was to be used, but the civil power was to be supreme; and it must discipline and control the Church.

In this spirit Napoleon concluded the Concordat of 1801.[31] Pope Pius VII and his magnificent Secretary of State, Consalvi, were also realists and were prepared to make concessions to the Revolution. They were willing to ignore the violent protests of Louis XVIII, who realized that an accord would deprive him of the support of religion. They had hoped to preserve the independence of the French Church. In this they were disappointed for they were forced to make extensive concessions in the state nomination of bishops and in the police control of external worship. But they gained inestimable advantages: worship was reestablished throughout France; the Constitutional schism was ended; the position of the Papacy was recognized along with its right to institute and depose bishops; and the fact that the Pope was to demand the resignation of all existing French bishops, both Roman and Constitutional, was a death-blow to Gallican theory. Even with the Gallican Organic Articles which Napoleon appended unilaterally, the Concordat of 1801 was more satisfactory from the Papal point of view than the arrangement under the Old Regime.

Napoleon treated the clergy as functionaries and as spiritual auxiliaries of his temporal regime. He favored a much stronger control of the lower clergy by the bishops, and the loss of the independent position of the *curés* is one of the salient features of the Concordatory Church. But he broke the aristocratic monopoly of the episcopate and drew on all classes for Church leaders. His bishops were generally good men, of higher caliber than those of the eighteenth century. Secure in its position, the Church of France made remarkable strides in reconstruction after 1801.

But some of the damage was not easily repaired:[32]

1. *Material:* while bishops and priests received salaries from the government, which deprived them of their independence, many of the important works of the Church, e.g., Seminaries, were not provided for in the Concordat. The loss of her material possessions forced the Church to struggle with poverty, which handicapped her functions. Though the great landed wealth of the Church had created one set of problems in the Old Regime, its absence produced another. It seems clear that the poverty of the nineteenth century French Church contributed to her dependence first on the aristocracy, and later on the bourgeoisie. Behind the splendid facade, the indigence of the Concordatory Church was real, and only the heroism of the simple *curés* and religious made its work possible.

2. *Psychological:* the fear of renewed violence and strict government control made for a timid and submissive clergy.

3. *Human:* the great loss of personnel during the Revolution, coupled with the Church's poverty, made the recruitment of an adequate and trained clergy difficult. Poor Seminary facilities led to a very evident decline in the intellectual level of the French clergy, from which the Church was to suffer for a long time.

4. *Educational*: handicapped by lack of funds and trained leaders, the Church found it impossible to regain the elite which she had lost during the Old Regime. A further obstacle arose in the state monopoly, the University, set up by Napoleon in 1808. While it granted certain latitude on the primary level, Napoleon carefully reserved to the state the education of the bourgeoisie, who furnished the leadership of his administration and army. The amosphere of the schools remained irreligious, despite the provision for chaplaincies.

5. *Geographical*: the recovery of the French Church was not equal in all areas. From the beginning of the nineteenth century we find the distinction between the districts of strong religious practice as in the West, and the regions of relative indifference, as in the Paris area and the South-West. These spots of relative tepidity were to expand during the nineteenth century.

Had Napoleon been able to modify his ambitions, he might have succeeded in his aim to heal the internal wounds opened during the Revolution. While there was no conspicuous *rapprochement* between the bourgeoisie and the Church during his regime, at least both sides lived in peace under his watchful eye, and an eventual drawing together might have occurred. But religious peace was shattered by his conflict with the Papacy. Pius VII was taken prisoner on 6 July 1809 and followed the footsteps of his predecessor into exile in France. The Emperor continued to receive the support of the vast majority of the borgeoisie, a support which he richly rewarded in the Civil Code and administration until his military adventures finally alienated them in the last years of his reign. By the time of his defeat, both groups he had tried to win, clergy and bourgeoisie, had gone into opposition—although not for the same reasons or into the same camp.

Official Favor and Partial Recovery (1815-1830)

Not into the same camp. In that phrase is concentrated the religious history of the Restoration.[33] The divisons that had marked the clerical response to the oath of 1795 remained though the relative strength of the two groups was altered. The moderates, led by M. Emery, had represented a large sector of Catholic opinion under the Directory. But after 1815 certain factors contributed to the growing trend toward political conservatism.

1. Monarchy and the Church had been the twin victims of the Revolution, and it was natural that resentment toward its policies would draw the two together. The memory of the Terror blurred the religious realities of the Old Regime and led Catholics to regard the latter as the best of all possible worlds. This was already apparent under Napoleon. He was at first appreciated as the architect of a new religious situation, and the conventional phrases of respect were wafted in his direction. However, he never won the loyalty of the bulk of the clergy, and they turned positively hostile when the Emperor came into conflict with the Pope. Here again is tragedy: the man who attempted to reconcile religion and the Revolution was himself a despot, and his policies ultimately widened the breach. Thus, there was great clerical rejoicing at the first return of the Bourbons in 1814. It was a bit premature and proved embarrassing during the Hundred Days: the canons of Notre Dame had enthusiastically destroyed the relics of Napoleon's coronation and were abashed when the Emperor wryly demanded them on his return.

2. The support of the clergy for the Restoration was heightened by a continued sense of insecurity. Napoleon had contained anti-clericalism, but it had not been diminished, and it manifested itself vigorously during the Hundred Days. French clerics felt that only a strong, friendly state could safeguard the interests of the Church. Their apprehension was not without foundation since precedents indicated that their opponents would appeal to the state power where possible. But fear distorts perspective, and prevents a balanced judgment. Frightened by the prospect of a renewal of persecution, most of the French clergy unfortunately saw salvation only in the regime. It was a further misfortune that the regime was born of French military defeat and imposed by foreign will and so could never evoke popular enthusiasm.

3. The Bourbons followed a calculated policy of using religion to bolster their position. While firmly Gallican and insisting on the dependence of the Church, they did give it official favors. Some of these were of doubtful value: heavy penalties for sacrilege and laws for Sunday observance. Some appeared to hold real promise, e.g., episcopal control of the

University.[34] All ultimately aroused bitterness and failed of their purpose.[35] Far from winning the élite back to the Church, these favors widened the gap and had the fatal consequence of binding Catholicism to a cause that was doomed.

4. The émigré nobles, who had been generally sceptical under the Old Regime, returned in large numbers to the Church as a result of their experiences.[36] While many of these conversions, as that of Chateaubriand, were genuine, they were undoubtedly associated with the feeling that the Church could bolster the aristocratic position. In avowing their devotion to the Church, the nobility were hungry for the recovery of their privileges and possessions,[37] desires that did not fail to disturb other social groups. This was not the last time that the French Church succeeded in attracting a threatened social group, with consequent identification of interests.[38] But if the aristocrats returned, the bourgeoisie remained Voltarian.[39]

The intellectual religious revival did not succeed in regaining these lost loyalties. Actually, there was an intellectual renaissance, closely connected with romanticism. It was peculiar in that the clergy played little role therein, as their training was still very inadequate.[40] But while a good deal of the romantic literature extolled religion, it did little to repair the intellectual foundations of Catholicism, which had been so badly neglected. Here, as in the political field, there was a rescue, but for doubtful motives and with doubtful results.

The principal tangible effect of this literary flowering was a strengthening of the position of the Intransigents. Two of the best-known Catholic writers were De Maistre and De Bonald. Their major effort was to forge a philosophical justification for the union of throne and altar. Their basic assumption was the fundamental weakness of human nature. Though it is fashionable today to recognize their criticism of the facile optimism of their contemporaries, their pessimistic reaction was highly exaggerated and obviously unpalatable in the prevailing mood.

To De Maistre and De Bonald, the Enlightenment was the source of all evil and its natural consequence was the Revolution. Only by a return to the twin pillars of religion and absolutism could society be saved, for stability was impossible without Christianity and the divine plan could not be realized without legitimate monarchy. God and religion were invoked to bless the Old Regime, and change was denounced as impiety.[41]

Such writings served to reinforce the reactionary trends within the Church; it did little to win dissident opinion and it further alienated the bourgeoisie. The same may be said of more popular efforts to revive the faith. The most successful attempt to re-enkindle religious enthusiasm was the missions, a series of popular sermons by itinerant preachers. In the majority of these, royalism was presented as a necessary safe-guard of Catholicism. While religion may have profited from the zeal of the missionaries, their intemperate political opinions often aroused hostility. The *Congregation,* an important Catholic organization of the period, was directed by staunch royalists.[42] Indeed the bond between Church and monarchy was nearly complete; to the enforced submission demanded by the Concordat was added the voluntary and unqualified adhesion of the greatest part of Catholic leadership, both Catholic and lay.

Only a minority resisted. Royer-Collard,[43] the leader of the Constitutional Monarchists, was an outstanding Catholic who tried to find a middle ground between the Ultras and the Liberals. His pleas for compromise had little effect in an atmosphere fouled with mutual suspicion. The Baron d'Eckstein[44] in his writings and in his journal, *Catholique,* attacked the myth of a nation entirely Catholic. He deplored coercion in religious matters and the artificial linking of royalism and Catholicism. He praised liberty as the sole congenial framework for religion and saw the Revolution as a just verdict on the Old Regime.

The most effective of the Catholic opponents to the pre-vailing currents was the Abbé Félicité Lamennais. This fiery Breton was a product of the abnormal religious conditions of his time. His father, a merchant of Saint Malo, had sheltered a priest during the Terror, and the heroism of the refugee had appealed to the young man. He was also receptive to revolu-tionary ideas and for a time neglected religion. The ordination of his brother Jean-Marie (1804) was a decisive factor in his formation, and soon both were dedicated to the defense of the Church. Though his education had been haphazard and largely self-directed, Lamennais's early writings indicate great power of mind and pen. The first volume of his *Essai sur l'indifférence en matière de religion* (1817), published shortly after his ordi-nation, marked him as the first successful apologist for Cath-licism since the Enlightenment and the leading personality among the French Clergy.

Originally an intransigent royalist, Lamennais only slowly evolved liberal political ideas. Their genesis lay in his hatred of Gallicanism, which led him to substitute "Pope and People" for "Pope and King." To him, "servitude is the burden of

every national church and the first condition of its existence."[45]
Only if religion were freed from the burden of State control
could it fulfill its mission. The throne was crushing the altar
in its embrace, and unless this grip were broken religion could
not escape destruction. This demand for separation of Church
and State was the basic innovation of Lamennais' thinking. It
required two changes in the existing condition: a strengthening
of the Papacy and a break with the Bourbons.

Lamennais's approach, like Marx's, was essentially sociological; new conditions demanded new relations of the Church
with government and society. The state power did not benefit
religion; opinion was basically divided, and only liberty of
belief and expression were practical.[46] When society became
Catholic again, the pressure of opinion would force government
to be Catholic. But the work of reconversion must be entirely
voluntary.

In the latter years of the Restoration, Lamennais occupied
himself with a defense of the Church against unbelief and with
an attempt to reconcile the two basic needs of liberty and order.
He surrounded himself with an enthusiastic group of young
clergy and founded the "Congregation of Saint Peter" for missionary and educational work. His impact upon youth, especially in clerical circles, was immense.

Like most prophets with a burning sense of mission, Lamennais created vigorous opposition. Vehement and personal in
his denunciation of his opponents, he found himself involved
not only with the regime but with a majority of the Gallican-
minded bishops and influential Royalist Catholics. Archbishop
Quelen of Paris condemned him in a pastoral, to which the
Abbé replied with two open letters unreservedly critical of his
superior. Rome refused appeals to silence him. Leo XII thought
of making him a Cardinal after his visit to Rome in 1824, and
Pius VIII was well-disposed.

Read today, the genius of Lamennais is still apparent. His
talent lay in his power to analyze existing conditions. Few have
interpreted their age more accurately. Prophecy is the most
hazardous of occupations; yet the forecasts of this Breton priest
were verified in most major respects. He correctly explained
the growing apostasy from Catholicism in France and the unhappy consequences of the link between monarchism and the
Church. The religious aspects of the Revolution of 1830 could
be constructed from his prophecies. In addition to his perception, he attracts as a man of courage and personal integrity,
and charms with his skill in expression. But Lamennais, like
most men, had the defects of his talents. To be successful in

his task of accommodating Catholicism to the prevailing Liberal doctrines, he needed other qualities, and these were lacking. His intemperate language, understandable in the face of intransigent opposition, weakened his appeal. More seriously, the deficiences of his early training deprived him of theological, philosophical and historical knowledge adequate for his role. Like many of his contemporaries, he reacted against the eighteenth century's emphasis on reason. His whole system was constructed on the premise that the individual reason could not reach truth, which he felt could only be attained by the universal consent of mankind. While he used this principle to justify Christianity, it contradicted the basic Catholic tenet that the human mind can discover the rational foundations of belief.

Checks and Balances (1830-1848)

The Charter of 1815 had given adequate protection to the bourgeoisie. It embodied the principles of laissez-faire, made property inviolable, prohibited associations of workingmen, and by a narrow franchise delivered the lower house to bourgeois control. But the French upper middle class distrusted the aims of the aristocrats. When Charles X's actions gave substance to these fears, they prepared for revolt. The July Revolution had several characteristics of its great predecessor: its leadership was bourgeois; it was aimed at the older ruling groups; it was marked by considerable anti-clericalism; and it represented a temporary coalition of the bourgeoisie and the masses, with the substantial benefits going to the former. The July Monarchy was so obviously bourgeois that this adjective by itself can identify it.[47]

Lamennais followed these events with mixed feelings. He rejoiced at the passing of the Bourbons though he would have preferred to see them replaced by a democratic republic. He sadly observed the outbusts of anti-clericalism which he had predicted. He determined to force the new ruling group to abide by its own liberal principles in all that concerned religion, especially in the field of education. For this purpose, he and his disciples[48] founded L'Avenir (16 October 1830). Like many French journalistic ventures, it soon gave birth to a movement, L'Agence pour la défense de la liberté religieuse (18 December 1830), to protect religion against the arbitarary action of the State.

L'Avenir, which carried on its masthead the provocative God and Liberty, applied the principles which had been elaborated by Lamennais and his group. Its theme was the

regeneration of the world. This demanded a two-fold liberation: of the Church from the control of government—all Concordats must be abolished for they had outlived their usefulness
under changed conditions; and there must be a liberation of
the people: they must be given the franchise and protected by
liberty of the press, education, association, and assembly. Regional freedom must be preserved by decentralization, and
oppressed peoples like Irish, Poles, Belgians, and Italians be
allowed to choose their own governments. Workers must be
protected against exploitation.[49] It is evident that the program
did not stop at the current boundaries of Liberalism; it was
emphatically democratic, the first Christian Democratic movement in French history.

Obviously, such a platform angered Louis Phillipe's government. It also caused uneasiness in other European capitals. It
particularly aroused the French legitimists, smarting from defeat and already hostile to Lamennais's opinions. Nor would
bishops who were having difficulties in meeting the needs of
their dioceses and who had reasons to suspect the generosity
of their flocks be particularly moved by ardent appeals to
disavow the budget for religious worship and trust to the
goodness of the people. All this opposition was stimulated by
the tart observations on opposing principles and personalities
which spiced the pages of *l'Avenir*. The popularity of the journal among the young clergy and seminarians heightened the
alarm. Episcopal warnings, and ultimately prohibitions, multiplied.

Pressure from all these sources mobilized at Rome. The
governments of France, England, and Austria lodged protests,
and clerical opponents demanded action. Under Pius VIII,
these had little effect; but he died in November 1830, and his
successor was of a different mentality. Faced with this growing
opposition and with the loss of revenue it entailed, *L'Avenir*
suspended on 15 November 1831 after twenty months of publication, and Lamennais decided to appeal personally to Rome.

This visit of the "Pilgrims of Liberty" was a grave tactical
error. It revealed a total misconception of the climate of opinion at the Vatican and had the added disadvantage of forcing
Rome to act. In the circumstances, it failure was foreordained[50]
and its consequence was *Mirari Vos*. This papal document
was phrased in the traditional form of the new Pope's first
Encyclical; it referred to many other matters and did not
mention *L'Avenir*. Yet it was an obvious reprobation of the
major tenets advanced by the French Liberal Catholics. Lamennais's associates accepted the condemnation loyally and their

leader declared his adhesion. But he felt that the Encyclical undermined his whole philosophy of *raison générale;* after a period of wavering he publicly announced his revolt in *Les Paroles d'un croyant* (April, 1834). Until his death in 1854, Lamennais remained an enemy of the Church. He continued to write, but except for a brief period in 1848, he played a relatively unimportant role in French life.

The condemnation of *L'Avenir* was a personal tragedy which involved the most promising figure in French Catholicism. Had Lamennais adjusted himself to the papal condemnation, as his friends had urged, he could have continued as they did, to exercise an important influence in moulding Catholic thought in the direction of an acceptance of the new conditions. It is probably an exaggeration to say that the shadow of Lamennais hung over the entire history of French Catholicism in the nineteenth century; careful examination does not reveal that his example acted as a *conscious* restraint upon other pioneers. But his condemnation and revolt not only cost the Church a brilliant leader, the most authentic genius in French Catholicism in the century, but it strengthened the hands of reaction and acted as a brake on the enthusiasm of the younger clergy. To some degree, the tragedy of Lamennais explains the timidity of so many of them in their handling of contemporary problems. The condemnation had the added effect of alienating several of the literary romantics who had been attracted to Catholicism by sentiment. They now sadly withdrew, convinced that the Church leadership was deaf to the aspirations of the age. Most importantly, it indicated that the Church would not react to the shock of the Revolution, as it had to that of the Reformation, by a sudden and intense vitality. The ties to the Old Regime would pass, but only after an agonizing delay. Many of Lamennais' ideas would triumph, but painfully and after further loss. Something, indeed, was saved from the wreckage. The disciples, who had been sparked by his genius and who had remained faithful, went on to lead the French Church to its most fruitful decades in its nineteenth century history.

Initially, the Bourgeois Monarchy was unfriendly to Catholicism, and its early years were marked by anti-clerical measures. The reason is obvious: it depended for support on the upper bourgeoisie who were solidly Voltarian. As time passed, this attitude of hostility diminished. This was partly due to the absence of overt Catholic opposition to the Orleanist regime. Pius VIII, in a brief of 29 September 1830, gave the clue when he asked French Catholics to acquiesce in the new political situation. Generally, this sage advice to bury the past was followed. On the other side, the collapse of the Restoration and of the artificial structure it supported removed bourgeois fear of clerical influence and aristocratic ambition. In its place, there appeared a growing apprehension of the demands of the industrial workers. Strikes for higher wages in the years 1831-36 were ruthlessly suppressed by the government, but the threat remained and there was no inclination to compromise in this direction. Therefore it was natural that the older Voltarian tenet of the social utility of religion should reappear. Guizot frankly urged it when he sponsored the Law of 1833 which gave the clergy supervision of primary teaching.[51] It is significant that not until the III Republic gave an effective franchise to the masses did the educational struggle extend to the elementary field.

Menaced in its privileges, the Liberal bourgeoisie moved perceptibly to rapprochement with the Church. It was not difficult. The majority, like Louis Philippe himself, were "too sceptical to be persecutors." Actually it never went the full distance because of conflict in the field of secondary education. The Charter of 1830 had formally promised liberty of teaching, and Montalembert rallied Catholics to demand their rights. The issue was the domination of the young bourgeoisie, recognized by all as the future leaders and as the source of political power under the existing franchise.

The school question united all Catholics behind the popular banner of Liberty. It was the single instance since 1789 when French Catholic opinion was practically unanimous. But it was a specious unity that hid grave divisions in method. The moderates, such as Arbishop Affre of Paris and Dupanloup, were shocked by the intemperate language of their confreres. The Intransigents found a new leader in the rising star of Louis Veuillot, the brilliant editor of *Univers*. Converted on a visit to Rome,[52] he plunged into controversy without any special doctrinal preparation and soon showed himself the most able polemicist of the century. Devoted to the Church, exemplary in his private life, Veuillot lacked all capacity for moderation and strove, as Ozanam declared, not to win opponents but to inflame partisan passions. Under his direction, *Univers* was to become the "scandal of Catholicism."

Despite efforts on both sides, no solution was found for the question of religious secondary education. As a result, any close tie between the regime and the Church was impossible. During the July Monarchy, Catholics apparently succeeded in detaching themselves from the old absolutism without becoming again involved. They lost the support of the government, but were beginning to regain popular following. Their continual appeals for liberty on the school question made a deep impression; probably not even they realized that their devotion was accidental rather than profound. Yet herein lies the key to the events of 1848. For the moment, none had doubts. When the "liberal" Pius IX was elected Pope (17 June 1846), France and Liberals everywhere hailed with enthusiasm the adjustment of the Church to the modern regime of freedom.

Temporarily cut off from political ties, the Church devoted herself to her mission with increasing success. All observers noted the renewed vitality. Heine, who had spoken of her as a corpse in 1830, referred to this new life and the alert de Tocqueville confirmed his observation. The regime assisted by appointing, generally from the intellectual bourgeoisie,[53] rather able bishops who were superior to the nominees of the Restoration. It also winked at the reappearance of the unauthorized congregations: the challenge of Lacordaire's white habit in the pulpit of Notre Dame went unanswered.[54]

Even more important activities came from within the Catholic body. There was growth in the quantity and quality of the personnel of the religious orders. There was a liturgical revival associated with Dom Guéranger, one of Lamennais's group. Lacordaire's conference at Notre Dame introduced new apologetic methods that created an interest in religious problems among the elite for the first time since Jansenism. At the same time, there was a revival in ecclesiastical scholarship: Migne's *Patrology*, Montalembert's *Monks of the West* and Ozanam's lectures at the Sorbonne were signs of an intellectual stirring. Most promising was the establishment by Mgr. Affre of *des Carmes,* a school for higher ecclesiastical studies since "theology must not be apart from other knowledge and must meet new problems." Thus, the 1840's marked a quickening of Catholic intellectual activity after a long decadence. Much was accomplished, but a long time would be required to repair the damage. Tragically enough, the time allotted was short before poltical questions would again intrude.

Until 1830, the major problem facing French Catholics was adjustment to a new world dominated by the bourgeoisie and by Liberal political and economic thinking. But the years of the July Monarchy witnessed the transformation of the agrarian and commercial society in which the Revolution of 1789 had occurred into an industrial economy that saw the creation of a new working class. While the process was relatively slow in France and not confined to the period under review, the change

guided by Buchez, who retained their own independent spirit
and point of view. More authentically than any of the others,
the companions of *L'Atelier* were the precursors of later Christian democracy.

The ensemble of these movements won the sympathy of the
people for the clergy and for religion. The socialism of the
period, with some exceptions, was not anti-religious and often
had a strong evangelical undertone. Unique in French history,
the Revolution of 1848 was not anti-clerical. The armed workers acclaimed Christ, the priests, and Pius IX. Pictures of Christ
appeared on the barricades along with revolutionary slogans;
clerics were respected and religious symbols honored. All
pointed to the wisdom of Ozanam's dictum, "Avoid politics
and concentrate on the social question." By 1848, the Church
in France appeared to have made its peace with the political
regime of liberty and to have sided with the workers' demands
for social justice. But again appearances were deceptive.

The Years of Decision (1848-1850)

"Everyone has the right to complain against the Republic,
but Religion." So wrote the Legitimist and Social Catholic,
the Vicomte de Melun.[57] Yet before the Republic had reached
its first birthday, the preponderance of Catholics had allied
themselves with the party of bourgeois order, (personified by
the Voltarian Thiers), had rallied to Louis Napoleon, renewed
the alliance between the throne and altar, and socially had
rejected any amelioration in the condition of the industrial
workers. The ultimate consequences of these actions was the
permanent estrangement of the Church from the masses of the
French people. It was not the Great Revolution of 1789 which
permanently divorced the Church from the main currents of
French life, though it certainly had prepared the way. 1848
was the year of decision for the Catholic Church in France.

It is difficult at first glance to explain the great sundering of
Catholics and Republicans. Almost unanimously, Catholics had
hailed the end of the July Monarchy and the formation of the
Second Republic. It is not surprising to find staunch Republican sentiments in the newly established *L'Ère nouvelle,* the
democratic newspaper of Lacordaire, Ozanam and Meret. Even
Univers seemed almost as enthusiastic, and Veuillot saw common ground between Catholicism and Republicanism since
both placed the divine right of peoples above that of monarchs.
The bishops universally called upon their subjects to rally to
the new government, and some declared that it reflected the

principles of the Gospel which consecrated liberty, equality and fraternity.[58] Throughout the country, the clergy solemnly blessed trees of liberty and performed elaborate rites for the fallen heroes of the barricades.

The accord could have hardly been more complete. But if all Catholics seemed to be Republicans on the morrow of the Revolution, they were not all so for the same reason or to the same degree. Three basic views soon reappeared, corresponding roughly to the divisions which mark French Catholicism throughout the century. Only the general satisfaction at the fall of the July Monarchy makes it difficult to distinguish the groups in the first weeks of the Republic's history:

1. The sincerely democratic, who saw the new regime as the work of God in history and as the final flowering of the Gospel. So *L'Atelier* and *L'Ère nouvelle;* although on the editorial board of the latter, Lacordaire maintained some reserve both on the political and social questions. *L'Ère nouvelle* for a short time had 20,000 subscribers; it enjoyed the firm support of Archbishop Affre and it reached a large proportion of the French clergy. Both journals aimed to reconcile Catholicism with democracy and with the demands of social justice.

2. The "Liberal" view of Montalembert, who was hesitant in his support and who would have preferred a modified form of the fallen regime with an extension of clerical rights in education. Initially this group saw the Republic as an improvement upon its predecessor.

3. The Legitimists, whose most intelligent spokesman was Falloux[59], accepted the Republic as a necessity to which they must submit.

The events of 1848 shifted both these latter groups to the Right. Even before the crisis of May-June, the outlines of an anti-Republican coalition of Liberals and Legitimists began to appear. The plain speaking of *L'Ère nouvelle* in favor of political and social change challenged the temporizers and revealed the purely negative character of Catholic unity. The doctrines of Economic Liberalism, practically universal among the bourgeoisie, were naturally shared by many Catholics of education and means, and the memory of *L'Avenir* convinced others that the language of the Christian Democrats was extravagant.

The decisive cleavage between Catholics and the Republic arose on the social issue. As Ozanam saw then, and as all know now, the Revolution of 1848 in France was both political and social. More accurately, it was a rejection of the Orleanist regime, with undertones of democracy and socialism. It had occurred in a serious economic depression that had intensified social misery, and economic conditions worsened noticeably as revolutionary outbreaks engulfed most of the continent. The presence of Louis Blanc in the Provisional Government, along with the schemes for the nationalization of certain enterprises such as the railroads and the existence of the Commission of the Luxembourg Palace,[60] had caused alarm among bourgeois Republicans like Lamartine. By early May, France was in the grip of a financial crisis; government loans were insecure and banks were refusing to make payments. A general collapse of the economic structure was feared. Property owners were dismayed and began to distrust the intentions of the government. Not that the Provisional Government had done anything radical; Tocqueville sagely remarked that the Revolutionaries of 1848 matched the boldness of their words by the timidity of their actions.[61] But in France, Revolution had an ominous connotation to those who had gained extensive economic privileges. By the end of April, bourgeois organs were hinting that only strong action could remove uncertainty. The stern repression of a strike at Rouen was hailed in the Liberal press and seemed to point the way to a solution.

This bourgeois uneasiness was developing parallel to more acute suffering among the workers, on whom the business panic fell heaviest in the form of mounting unemployment. The tax policy of the Provisional Government favored the bourgeoisie and burdened the consumer. The workers, seeing no concrete advantages coming from the Republic, felt they had again made a Revolution, only to be cheated of its friuts. When the election for the Constituent Assembly tapped rural sentiment and produced an overwhelmingly conservative body, a mood of frustration gripped the workers of Paris. They were drifting to the Left at the same time that the possessing classes were moving swiftly to the Right.

The crisis matured on the fifteenth of May when a popular demonstration in favor of Poland invaded the undefended Palais Bourbon and threatened the newly assembled deputies. The consequence was the agglomeration of Conservatives, Liberals and Catholics. The latter were prominent in the Assembly because they alone had the equivalent of an electoral organization in the countryside. Their leaders reacted speedily. Montalembert grieved over the twenty wasted years of attempting to reconcile Catholicism and modern society. Falloux introduced a proposal to disband the National Workshops.[62] The conservative borgeoisie hailed it as magnificent and it was passed on June 19. The immediate consequence was the explosion of the June Days. Mgr. Affre, determined to halt the bloodshed, went to the barricades where he was welcomed by the insurgents, but during the parley he was fatally wounded by a stray bullet. The workers repudiated the act and made every provision for the victim. But the Archbishop died on June 27 with a final request for peace and mercy. His death removed an important check on Catholic intransigents. It also had the effect he wished to avoid: it convinced most Catholics of the impossibility of compromise. Montalembert put it neatly: between Catholicism and Socialism there is no middle ground.

The June Days marked the virtual end of the II Republic. It also marked the definite formation of the Party of Order, that strange coalition of Voltarian bourgeoisie and Catholics, each shorn of its staunch Republican elements. This great conservative bloc united great and small bourgeoisie and peasants against the workers. It had a single fear, Revolution, and a single solution, Order. As often in crises, the Center disappeared, moderation appeared unthinkable, and the decision was left to force. In 1848, the Party of Order had the bigger battalions.

There is doubt of the reality of the fear which fused this grouping, although there was little to justify the apprehension. The bourgeoisie had been shaken by the rumblings which had found stern expression in the Communist Manifesto. They firmly believed the consoling doctrine of freedom of economic action and saw the demands of the workers both as a threat to their own position and as a violation of natural economic law. Catholics on their side had the memory of 1793 to bolster their fear of material loss. Mutual fright drew the two together and ended hope of reasonable social reform. Panic banished any conception that the workers had a reasonable basis for their grievances or that the community had an obligation to the victims of economic crisis. The savage repression of the June Days was a measure of the prevailing fear.

Not all Catholics joined the reaction. Ozanam, in a brilliant series of articles in L'Ère nouvelle, decried bourgeois vengeance and declared that while revolt was put down, the great enemy, poverty, remained. He accused the wealthy of deliberately provoking the uprising by closing their factories and denying the means of subsistence to their employees. The aristocratic Melun still pleaded for social reform. But these were isolated voices. The Catholic majority did not bear the primary responsibility for the social conditions that were the crux of the issue. But they committed a great wrong in throwing their *moral* influ-

ence to the side that was unwilling to make necessary concessions. By this action, they poisoned the action of the Church
in France for nearly a century.

Montalembert and Veuillot were not content to draw the
mantle of religion over the cancerous sores of injustice with
pious declarations that poverty was willed by God. They went
further, and, publicly repudiating democracy, threw the whole
weight of *Univers* into the rally on behalf of Louis Napoleon.
In this, they were encouraged by events in the Papal States.
French Catholics witnessed with great emotion the Roman
Revolution in November, which saw the assassination of the
Papal Minister Rossi and the flight of the Pontiff to Gaëta.
Pius IX, who shed his liberalism as he abandoned his capital,[64]
called on European states to honor the treaties of 1815 against
his own subjects. To most French Catholics this was added
evidence of the dangers of democracy. It direcly affected the
Presidential election campaign then in progress. Cavaignac was
sufficiently Republican to balk at promising to restore Pius to
his domains. Montalembert persuaded Louis Napoleon to make
an equivocal statement that the Catholic leader interpreted in
the sense desired. As added bait, the Prince extended a guarantee of liberty of teaching. Once more, Catholics found themselves united with the Orleanist bourgeoisie in the electoral
campaign. Undoubtedly, Napoleon would have won without
the vigorous support of conservative Catholics for the tide was
running strong. But the rally to Bonaparte opened Catholics
to the accusation that they were the architects of authoritarianism and the betrayers of democracy. It was a charge that was
to bear heavy weight in the future.

Again, Ozanam and the perceptive minority predicted catastrophe: loss of popular support and recurrence of anti-religious
revolution. They saw that henceforth both republicanism and
the working class movement would be strongly anti-catholic.
They deplored the social coalition of Catholics and bourgeoisie
that equated property with religion,—a coalition was now bearing political fruit. Montalembert, who lived to see and regret
these consequences, was later inclined to minimize the role he
had played in the tragic year of 1848.

The future would exact the price for this strange alliance,
strange in that it had no religious foundations. The attitude
of the Orleanist borgeoisie was perfectly expressed by Thiers,
that barometer of nineteenth century politics. He begged his
anti-clerical friends to hasten to support the Church, on the
grounds that it alone could teach resignation to the poor with
the promise of eternal salvation. No longer should the bour-

geoisie speak of "superstition" or recall bygone struggles. He had declared his willingness to make concrete concessions: "In regard to liberty of education, I have changed, not from *a revolution in my convictions,* but from a revolution in social conditions."[65] The Loi Falloux (1850), which gave Catholics freedom in secondary and university education, was a measure of bourgeois social security. It sealed the pact between Catholics and bourgeoisie, justifying the aphorism: "The sons of Voltaire became the sons of the Church." But the phrase "sons of the Church," must be understood in the political and social sense—not in the religious.

The Deepening Chasm (1851-1870)

The Party of Order remained intact throughout the *coup d'ètat* and the creation of the II Empire. It approved the repression of the Republican opposition and encouraged the massive affirmative vote in the plebiscite. These events served to bind the fate of the Church to the new regime and to dry up the promising beginnings of Social Catholicism.

The announced aims of the new government was to heal the divisions which had rent France since the Great Revolution by rallying all Frenchmen behind the banner of nationalism and to abolish the political parties which were the reflection of these divisions.[66] The formula for this unification was to be *le juste milieu:* politically, the principles of 1789 were to be maintained, with Jacobinism and Legitimism eliminated; socially, industry and trade were to be encouraged, but the worker protected; religiously wounds were to be healed by avoiding anti-Catholicism and clericalism.

The effort failed in all essentials. The Republicans were not placated but grew in influence throughout the period. Legitimism appeared entirely vanquished as an active movement but in its more authoritarian form continued to influence a small circle.[67] Socially, the regime made certain paternalistic gestures toward the industrial workers but denied them substantial benefits, which were reserved for the financial and industrial classes. As this was a time of considerable industrialization, this policy brought considerable enrichment to the bourgeoisie but only minor relief to wage earners.

The announced religious policy of the II Empire corresponded to the personal views of Louis Napoleon. He was a man without relgious faith, romantically inclined toward Republicanism and suspicious of the "men in black." His early advisers were generally opportunists without convictions or prejudices. But contrary to his inclinations, he did in fact establish a clerical regime which used religion as a spiritual police force—"the coalition of guardroom and sacristy," as the quickly disillusined Montalembert was to phrase it. The regime gave generously to the Church in the form of official favor, increases in the religious budget, protection of foreign missionaries, suppression of the anti-religious press, and a dismissal of anti-clericals from teaching posts. Catholicism appeared to flourish; there was a notable increase in the clergy and in teaching communities, many churches were built, and the free schools grew so rapidly that by 1870 there were almost as many in the Catholic secondary institutions as there were in the state schools.

Not all Catholics repaid this largess with active support. There were the dwindling group of Liberal Catholics who were prominent in Parisian society and in the Academy but who were politically weak. Abandoned by the bulk of the lower clergy, definitely out of favor at Rome, finding little support among the bishops who were generally friendly to the regime, their protests and qualifications went unheard. Among them were Montalembert, Berryer, Dupanloup and Falloux, all members of the Academy, Archbishop Sibour of Paris and Lacordaire, whose daring sermon in the pulpit of Notre Dame led to his silencing by the government. They used *Ami de la religion* as their organ and revived *Le Correspondant in* 1865.[68]

Most Catholics followed Veuillot's brawling support of Napoleon on the simple basis that the Emperor served the Church's interest. The explanation of *Univers's* amazing control of Catholic opinion was its editor's appeal to the country clergy. A plebeian like themselves, he understood their attitudes and tailored his languaged accordingly. With this backing, Veuillot felt strong enough to defy Bishop Dupanloup's ban on his journal, and his lash fell on all opponents regardless of ecclesiastical rank. His major enemy was the Liberal Catholics, whom he castigated mercilessly with the secret approval of Pius IX.[69]

The II Empire was a period of deepening cleavage within the Church as well as between the Church and French society. The internal division, which we have noted as existent in 1795, appeared again in intensified form after the relative unity of the years before 1848. The full effect of this inner conflict would not be apparent until the crisis of the late 70's when it became evident that the Intransigents had overplayed their hand and that, while the majority of Frenchmen were still loyal to the ancestral faith, only a minority were willing to follow the interpretations of the Intransigent leaders.

Behind the division were two divergent concepts of the role of the Church in society. The Liberal Catholics maintained that the Church must adapt itself to the age which was one of religious disunity, and that liberty was a right belonging to all. The Intransigents started with the fiction that France was still unanimously Catholic. They argued that liberty was the privilege of truth and it is inconceivable to permit free rein to error. Behind this philosophical position was an obsessive fear that had gripped many Catholics since 1789. Moderation and toleration among men are possible only when both sides feel that, if the opposition be victorious, it will not completely destroy them. This assurance was lacking in the heated atmosphere of much of nineteenth century French politics. Granted that their own intransigence generated a great deal of this heat, they still feared destruction as the price of defeat. When the anti-clericals, who professed opposite principles, gained power after 1879, they were not notably more tolerant.

The roots of Veuillot's disastrous sway over the rural clergy is to be found in the continuing low level of seminary instruction in France during the nineteenth century. Priests were draw almost exclusively from the families of peasants and artisans—and their education did little to remove the natural limitations of their background. In the seminaries they received a strict moral training that produced virtuous and holy men. But their intellectual formation was woefully deficient. No vital intellectual movement provided stimulation and leadership. Courses in philosophy and theology were taught from antiquated manuals. Critical history was unknown.[70] The study of the Scriptures was confined to pious commentaries without textual examination. Renan, who was a product of this training, has not been unjust in his evaluation of its defects and its merits.[71] The clergy who came from these seminaries were morally earnest, zealous men who had neither the knowledge nor the flexibility to deal with the problems of their age. For them Christianity had become a moral system, colored by Jansenism, demanding little comprehension of the doctrine that was its foundation and its spirit.[72]

Along the deepening divisions among Catholics was a widening of the gap between Catholics and three dynamic forces in French society: Republicans, the working class movement, and the intellectual currents of the age. The reconciliation with Republicanism which had marked the February Revolution had been ruptured by the events of 1848--1852. It was hardened into final schism by the French expedition to restore Pope Pius IX to his capital. Republicans were convinced that the Church was firmly on the side of oppression and repaid her with lasting hatred and distrust. Throughout the II Empire, with some exceptions, anti-Catholic and Republican were synonymous terms.[73] Michelet's new preface to his *Histoire de la Révolution* advanced the thesis that Christianity and justice were incompatible. Quinet adovcated an alliance of Republicans with non-Catholic Christians who were hostile to the Church.[74] These opinions rested on the conviction that the Church was the great enemy. When the Republican press regained some of its liberty in the 60's, it immediately launched attacks upon Catholicism; its circulation shows how strong anti-clerical feeling had become. This predominance of anti-religious views among Republicans was not exclusively the product of events from 1848-1870. But Catholic reaction turned a tendency into a universal condition and cannot escape major responsibility for the retribution that was to come.

Equally abrupt was the break between the working class movement and the Church. Catholic social teaching went into eclipse at the time of its greatest need. *L'Atelier* expired with a final protest against the paternalism of the regime and of the bourgeoisie, "who wished the working class to resign themselves to their position as inferior class."[75] In the years after the *coup d'état,* there developed a new popular anti-clericalism which sought support from materialist thinkers.[76] During the 60's, the working class élite, strongly influenced by Proudhon's intensified anti-Catholicism,[77] aligned themselves with Free Masonry and the Ligue de l'Enseignement.[78] Their journals argued for the rejection of religion in education because it is hostile to the idea of liberty and unqualifiedly ascribed the origin of this idea to the free thinkers. A meeting of labor leaders at Belleville in 1868 demanded "an education entirely outside the religious conception." The attitude of the Commune is clearly forecast in these lines, and they show the distance traveled by working class opinion in a single generation.[79]

The final cleavage appeared in the realm of ideas. The II Empire was marked by the triumph of Positivism, which challenged Christianity more profoundly than any previous philosophy. A new type of irreligion developed, founded on the attempt of science to explain reality without reference to spiritual factors. Comparative Religion and Biblical Criticism were regarded as having dissolved the bases of Christianity. The intellectual atmosphere we term Romanticism was being replaced by Realism,[80] which represented an immense change in mental attitudes. The generation of anti-clericals who were raised under the II Empire (Littré, Ferry, Gambetta, Clemenceau), shocked their older confreres by the completeness of their denial of the spiritual. Despite divergencies, all could agree with Peyrat: "Clericalism is the enemy." [81]

The great expansion of scientific knowledge into new fields would have been a challenge to religion under any circumstances, but again, as in the eigheenth century, circumstances made it more acute. Catholics were involved in internal conflicts. The triumph of the Intransigents put the Church in the most unfavorable light before informed opinion. Veuillot and his ilk exasperated without convincing and carried on a vigorous apologetic without appreciation of the problems involved. The publication of *Quanta Cura* and the *Syllabus*[82] (1864) seemed an official rejection of all accommodation to prevailing thought. The increasing intellectual criticism of the regime, with which the Church was identified, played its part. During the II Empire, the educated youth of the nation were partially lost to Positivism at a time when the official position of the Church never seemed so secure.[83]

The meeting ground of all these currents was the Masonic Lodges, the only centers of free discussion permitted under Napoleon. Freemasonry, which had vegetated since the turn of the century, enjoyed a great renaissance and became the principal focus for Republican and anti-clerical opposition. While appealing only to the élite, it maintained contact with the working class through the *Ligue de l'Enseignement*.

All the materials for a violent anti-religious movement were present: a philosophical foundation, a program and a determined leadership. The pattern is not too different from that at the end of the Old Regime. However, certain variations from 1789 are noteworthy:

1. The upper bourgeoisie were not solidly in the anti-clerical camp. Some indeed, had moved from the Party of Order during the II Empire, but an important group remained political supporters of the Church.

2. The industrial working class, non-existent during the Great Revolution, were uniformly in the anti-clerical ranks.

3. The peasants remained generally contented and generally Catholic. But they had grown to accept existing institutions, and their loyalty would be shaken were the more extravagant demands of the Intransigents to take concrete form.

Throughout the 50's, the alliance between the Catholic majority and the regime remained intact. The state, laic in principle, was clerical in fact for opportunistic reasons. But the crisis of the Italian War was to reveal the divergent concepts that lay beneath the alliance. The most evident fact of nine-

teenth century French religious history was the growth of
Ultramontanism. Awakened among the lower clergy by the
sufferings of Pius VI and Pius VII, it had become the rallying
point of the Liberal Catholics in their conflict with Gallican
Legitimism.[84] The attack upon the Temporal Power and the
sympathy awakened by the precarious position of Pius IX both
intensified the trend and created a significant change of direction. Liberal Catholics became more reticent in their support
of papal claims; the Intransigents appeared as the most belligerent defenders of the political independence of the Papacy.
The consistent thread was the attitude of the rural clergy, and
one clue to their acceptance of Veuillot's leadership was the
strong pro-papal position of *Univers's* flaming editor. As a
consequence of Ultramontanism, Pius IX was more effectively
the head of the Church in France than any pontiff since the
thirteenth century.

The sympathy for the Pope led the majority of the French
clergy to see the attack upon the Temporal Power as a plot
of the Church's enemies to destroy the spiritual independence
of the Papacy. To the cry of Italian patriots, "No Italy without
Rome," they responded with "No Catholicism without the
Temporal Power." When Louis Napoleon upset the delicate
balance in Italy with his war against Austria, he set in motion
currents that were to prove disastrous both to himself and to
French Catholicism. Faced with the loss of his territories, Pius
IX secretly sent an encyclical to Veuillot, which was promptly
published in *Univers,* appealing to the bishops to arouse the
faithful to defend the integrity of the Patrimony of St. Peter.
The majority responded, and for the first time under the
II Empire there was serious opposition in Parliament.[85] Anti-
Bonapartist sentiment was intense, but it was largely confined
to the Catholic leaders. The mass could not believe that a
regime so obviously friendly had turned against the Church,
and the administration, expert in such matters, prevented the
effective circulation of anti-government material from Catholic sources.

Louis Napoleon reacted against the Catholic opposition in a
twofold direction:

1. Foreshadowing the technique of Ferry and Combes, he
began to apply existing legislation against unauthorized congregations, diminished the influence of the Church in education, and permitted greater latitude to anti-Catholic Republican
journals.

2. While rejecting claims for the integrity of the Papal States

and allowing the annexation by Savoy of a large segment of Pius' territory, he balked Italian efforts to take Rome by maintaining the French expeditionary forces in the Papal capital.

The Roman Question was the central issue in French politics from 1859 to 1863 and it importantly affected French foreign relations. It did not cease to be an irritant until 1869, since the regime's new ecclesiastical policy was maintained in its essentials until that date. The *Quanta Cura* and *Syllabus* were aimed not only at Liberal Catholics and Republicans but also at the basic principles of the II Empire, and the conciliatory interpretation of Dupanloup, accepted by nearly all the French bishops, did not hide the deep disagreement. Pius IX refused to accept the provisions of the Concordat, which allowed the government to nominate bishops and cardinals whenever its nominees displeased him; and in his convocation of the Vatican Council, he did not invite the Catholic Governments to send representatives.

The Roman Question also widened the gulf between Liberal Catholics and Intransigents and between the Catholic majority and anti-clericals. Thus, divisions of French opinion on religious matters, which Louis Napoleon tried to make peripheral, returned as a principal issue in French political life. It was the bad luck of the Emperor that, unable to identfy himself with either party, he ended by offending both.

When the Catholics found themselves embroiled with the Emperor, the Republicans refused to take sides and continued to oppose both Church and government. Unable to find an alliance on the left, Napoleon's deepening difficulties led him to a reconciliation with the majority of Catholics. In January 1870, he called the Third Party[86] into the government. As a result the Emperor ended where the Prince President began. The issue was now clearly drawn between the clerical Party of Order and the anti-clerical Republicans and time was on the Republican side. The elections of 1869 indicated that the clergy no longer commanded a majority in the country but that their strong minority position made their support essential for a Conservative victory and that this victory could only be secured by electoral manipulation. The implications of this revelation would be unfolded during the next decade.

The Regrouping of Forces (1870-1878)

The defeat of Sedan had three important consequences:

1. It ended the II Empire and, after a period of indecision, led to the creation of the III Republic.

2. French troops withdrew from Italy to meet the Prussian menace, thus bringing about the fall of Rome and completing the unification of Italy.

3. A new balance of power was established in Europe, unfavorable to France.

The interaction of these three factors redefined the status of religion in France.

Catholics distinguished themselves for their patriotism during the war and continued to give evidence of their loyalty to the Government of National Defense. This provisional body, formed at Paris (4 September 1870), was intended to conduct the national resistance until the country could be consulted. Strong anti-clerical manifestations occurred in Paris and provincial cities soon after the defeat. The Government of National Defense, Republican in composition but with a Catholic, General Trochu, at its head, gave no support to these spontaneous demonstrations.

Elections for a National Assembly were held on 8 February 1871, within a fortnight after an armistice had ended the desperate resistance of Paris and the country. Of the 650 deputies chosen, 500 were conservative Royalists, divided among themselves, but united against a Republic and extensive social change. The overwhelming majority being Catholics, either by conviction or politics, this was the most Catholic Assembly in France since 1789. But this majority was hopelessly split on the political issue and showed that familiar division between Intransigents and Liberals, with the latter being stronger in the Assembly than they were in the country.

On March, the Assembly decided to sit at Versailles, thus indicating its fear of the Paris population that was both anti-monarchist and anti-clerical. Within a week, resentment exploded into Revolution. The Commune was a spontaneous and complex movement, partly a nationalist reaction against the humiliation of siege and defeat, partly impatience with the conservative and monarchist assembly, partly an expression of social discontent. Though it lacked any single inspiration or direction, it had a common quality in anti-clericalism. This hostility was evidenced in the decree separating Church and State, in instances of pillage of ecclesiastical properties, and in the conversion of 14 Paris churches for secular uses.[87] As the national forces fought their way into the Capital, they inaugurated the practice of killing all prisoners. In reprisal, the Jacobins and Blanquists executed 74 hostages, including the Archbishop of Paris and 23 priests.

This revelation of profound anti-clericalism, confirmed by events in provincial cities brought before French Catholics another critical decision. Experience should have indicated the wisdom of a temperate policy to avoid irritating moderate opinion and to prevent cleavage in their own ranks. As in 1795, they had the alternative of proceeding with the slow work of removing anti-religious prejudices (Cardinal Ferrata's advice) or of seeking a political solution that would restore the traditional position of the Church in French society. Led by Veuillot, the majority chose the latter—a path that led directly to the ruin of the Catholic Church in France.

Not that Catholics did not try to revive religious sentiment. The period of the formation of the III Republic marked a great outpouring of emotional piety. Pilgrimages to the national shrines assumed immense proportions; miraculous incidents were reported in several areas; and a large national subscription was undertaken to build Sacre Coeur in Montmartre as an expiation for the "martyrs of 1871." These activities produced a climate favorable to Monarchism and the Temopral Power. But they did not touch the core of the problem nor did they reach the de-Christianized. In fact, they served to widen the gulf by repelling the intellectuals.

To comprehend the dimensions of the decision taken by the Catholic majority, two questions must be posed. The first is: why did the leaders swing to integral Monarchism after 1871? In part it was due to the habit, strengthened under the II Empire, of seeking support from the State. The clergy and the majority of the episcopate in the 70's were not aristocrats; they came from very humble homes. But they had been conditioned by two decades of Imperial protection, and nothing in their seminary training inclined them to question its desirability. Frightened by the anti-religious flood, they saw no means of containing it except by the authority of the state. They hoped for a miracle to restore religious practice, a wish that could only be realized through a return to the "good old days."

These illusions narrowed their choice. Nothing could be hoped from the Republicans who were unrelentingly hostile and waiting for vengeance. Bonapartism was not entirely dead in the country, but it had slight prospects and Catholics felt no loyalty toward it after the struggle of the 60's. There remained only Monarchism. It had undergone an evolution in the direction of extremism, and the pretender, the Comte de Chambord, had embraced its most absolute formulation. To him and to his cause, the majority of Catholics gave their support. The dwindling popular appeal of Liberal Catholicism made the transition easier.

The swing would not have been so complete had it not been for the Roman Question. The triumph of Ultramontanism at the Vatican Council occurred almost simultaneously with the final destruction of the Temporal Power. Pius IX resolutely refused to accept the verdict of force and appealed to the European Powers and to the Catholic faithful to restore him to his ancient capital. The issue posed a delicate problem for French Catholics: Should they ask a defeated France, partly occupied by the Germans, to risk war against Italy to revive the Temporal Power? To state the question indicates the folly of answering affirmatively. Liberal Catholics and some Intransigents agreed with Thiers that all that could be hoped for was a guarantee of the spiritual independence of the Papacy. But was the Law of Guarantees adequate? To the bulk of the lower clergy it was not. Ten archbishops and bishops asked for direct intervention. *Univers* busied itself gathering petitions and calling for a crusade. Its lay editor did not hesitate to ask for war if necessary[88]—and it would have been. He denounced Catholics who did not take his extreme position; he even extracted an implied promise from Chambord, thus convincing his readers that the two causes were one.

The second question is equally fundamental: Why did the Catholic leaders fail to swing the mass of their followers with them into the monarchist camp? That they did not is abundantly clear. The overwhelming Catholic electoral victory in 1871 was not a true reflection of natonal opinion, for it was partly a repudiation of Gamberta's "war to the finish." But it did show powerful Catholic sentiment. Yet beginning with the partial elections of 2 July 1871 and continuing through the by-elections to the crushing tirumph in 1876, the Republicans won continuous victories. By 1876, the Royalists were an impotent faction in the Chamber, and in 1879 they lost the Senate and the Presidency, the latter by the resignation of MacMahon. The Republic of the Republicans had begun. Never again, not even to avert severe anti-clerical measures, could the Catholics muster a winning combination. Other evidence supports the election returns: there was a mass drift from Catholicism during these decades that was most apparent in the countryside, the ancient stronghold of the faith.[89]

The basic reason for the defection was that Integral Monarchism, which the Intransigents made the touchstone of loyalty to the faith,[90] was entirely out of line with the France of the

1870's. In the fundamentally changed conditions the doctrine was absurd. Chambord, an archaic replica of Charles X, refused to become "The Legitimist King of the Revolution" and stood for a total rejection of the principles of 1789 and of the whole of the Revolutionary tradition. Frenchman sensed the significance of the "white Flag" issue, which seems trivial but goes to the roots of the issue. France had evolved enormously since the beginning of the century, and a serious attempt to revive Divine Right Monarchy was preposterous.

Nor would it have been institutionally possible. The notion of popular sovereignty had struck deeply into French consciousness. No regime since 1789 had dared to disregard it, despite the imposition of practical obstacles. Even the II Empire kept the facade of universal suffrage and a national assembly, and in its final days it permitted considerable vigor to Parliamentary institutions. The proclamation of the Republic in 1870 was greeted in Paris and provinces with mystical acclaim. The idea of popular participation had become instinctive and no appeal to a forgotten *fleur de lys* could reverse the tide.

The implications in the Catholic position of an adventurous foreign policy turned away many who otherwise might have accepted. The face of Europe had been profoundly changed by the events of 1870-71. Two strong national states had appeared in areas where France had exercised influence because of political disunity. Centuries of French diplomatic effort had been nullified now that a united Germany stood on her eastern frontier. Bismarck had committed himself to keeping France friendless and was adroitly using the Roman Question to cement his relations with the new Italy. Prince Frederick Charles announced at Rome that Italy could count on German support. With the national interest demanding every effort to prevent a Rome-Berlin axis, Catholics were asking a weakened France to war with Italy. When Bismarck began the Kulturkampf, he too became the target. It is not hard to see the propaganda appeal of the Republican cry, "Do you want to have your son killed to put the Pope back on his throne?" The agitation gained nothing for the Pope and effectively armed the anticlericals. Even Pius IX and Mgr. Pie had ultimately to urge moderation.[91]

Even had Frenchmen not seen these points clearly, they were effectively brought to their attention. Republican propaganda sharpened every issue, exploited every blunder, exposed every genuine weakness in the Catholic position.[92] Gambetta was particularly successful. He saw what the liberals had never grasped, that though the peasants were conservative, they could be made into republicans. The net effect of fact and propaganda was a sharp move of French opinion toward the left, which isolated the Catholic leaders. And since Catholicism had identified itself with Monarchism, and Republicanism had been firmly anchored in anti-clericalism, a shift in politics mean a decline in religious practice.

It was not only convinced Republicans who saw the trend of events. Again, Thiers acted as a barometer. He correctly interpreted the election of 2 July 1871, and by August he was seeking a formula for a conservative Republic, satisfied that the clergy could no longer be depended upon.[93] The bourgeois elements in the old Party of Order had been frightened by Chambord's abtuseness and by his vague references to social oppression. By 1873, Parisian financial and business circles were willing to follow Thiers's lead. There seemed little danger from the Republican side; in fact Gambetta had declared at Le Havre (18 April 1872), "There is no social question"; and at Romans (18 September 1878), "The social peril is Catholicism." Thus important groups of peasants and bourgeoisie joined with the Republicans to create a new regime that was politically progressive and socially conservative. The conservative Republic suited the great majority—in Thiers's phrase, "It divided least"—and many of the old middle class supporters of order took their place in the Chamber after 1875 as Center-Right and Center-Left, united in a single social policy and divided only by their attitude to religion.

In the social sense, there was little Left in the early decades of the III Republic, except the remnant of the Socialists and a minority of the Republicans. But a new socially conscious group was in the process of formation during the 70's and it derived from Catholic Monarchism. Catholic social thinking was in eclipse under the II Empire, though LePlay expounded a social doctrine in Counter-Revolutionary terms. In the atmosphere of remorse following the Commune, Albert de Mun founded the Committee of Catholic Clubs (23 December 1871). He based his program on the obligation of the privileged classes to aid their working class brothers.[94] Motivated by the highest idealism and absorbing major Catholic energies for several decades, this renascent social movement was doomed to sterility. A true child of the dominant Catholic thinking of the period, it looked back to a hierarchical secular society based on faith. It imagined a working class hostile to the Revolution and missed totally the workers' psychology. Thus it made only a limited appeal in relation to the effort expended. But if its direct influence was small, it developed effective criticism of

Economic Liberalism and fought for the Law of Association and other remedial legislation; in fact, it was one of the first sponsors of the welfare principle in French politics. It did train some leaders and diffuse social consciousness in Catholic circles. Some of its ideas found concrete expression in Leon Harmel's factories and influenced the Papal Encyclicals.[95] But it was too paternalistic and too deeply rooted in Monarchism and Medievalism to meet the needs of the French working class, which was attracted by movements of quite different inspiration.

During this critical period therefore, the Church failed to reach the workers. It was losing the peasants, except in certain regions. It was totally alienated from the professional *milieu*. It retained the loyalty of the politically impotent aristocracy. The attitude of the bourgeoisie, especially its upper sections, reveal a certain ambivalence. While most of this group made its peace with the Republic, the bonds that had linked them with the Church in the years after 1848 were not entirely sundered. Their adhesion to the Church was originally opportunistic, but a subtle change occurred among some in the hundred years from 1850-1950. The tendency to send their children, especially the girls, to Catholic schools and the desire to imitate the attitudes of the aristocracy gradually stimulated some conversions among a segment of this powerful social group. In short, two parallel movements can be detected in the history of the III Republic: the de-Christianization of the masses and a re-Christianization of a part of the bourgeoisie. Nor were the two entirely unrelated. It was from the ranks of this reconverted middle class that most of the leaders of the Catholic Revival were to appear. While ultimately beneficial to the Church, the immediate result was to separate further the religious attitudes of the French on class lines.

Early in 1878, occurred an incident that was to have considerable influence on this "Regrouping of Forces." Death ended the long reign of Pius IX, and Leo XIII assumed the tiara (20 February). It was ironic that the Pope of Conciliation appeared at the height of Catholic reactionary sentiment in France and almost at the moment when militant anti-clericalism triumphed.

Partial Reconliliation and Total Defeat. (1878-1907)

The religious history of the last two decades of the nineteenth century was compounded of three major elements: a conciliatory papal policy, the continued intransigence of French Catholics, and the anti-clericalism of the victorious Republicans. Like recurring motifs in a Wagnerian overtue, the three are always present, with one rising above the rest and then becoming muted while another grows more audible. Since they were human forces and not musical notations, there was bound to be interaction among the three until the final climax of the exclusion of the Church from the public life of France.

The election of Leo XIII marks the turning point in the modern history of the Papacy.[96] It was not his doctrine that was basically different, but his approach. The weakness of Pius IX's policy was its negativism: to the sweeping tendencies of his age he had offered stubborn resistance, but little in the way of constructive alternatives. To him, only the reestablishment of the old order could safeguard the interests of the Church. Leo approached the problems from a fresh viewpoint: he saw that democracy met the general desire of the people of his time and therefore could be expected to survive. Hence, he was concerned to find common ground, to eliminate past misunderstandings, to forget old wounds. Since he was particularly well-disposed to France, he was anxious to discover a means of *rapprochement* with the Republic. He knew that religious peace could be established only if he could break the disastrous association of Catholicism with monarchy and thus remove the major justification for the anti-Catholic policy of the government.

This was a difficult program to effectuate in France. He could count on the support of a handful of bishops such as Guilbert and Lavigerie.[97] and an even smaller group of lay leaders such as Etienne Lamy. The rest would offer varying degress of resistance to the papal policy of conciliation. Still in bondage to the false assumption that France was overwhelmingly Catholic, they ascribed their defeats to the machinations of the Masons and awaited salvation from a monarchical restoration. This was the attitude of most of the popular Catholic press.[98] After 1879, the strident voice of Louis Veuillot was hushed by ill-helath. But a new crusading journal *La Croix,*[99] made its appearance in 1880; it followed the general course which had made *Univers* popular.

The Intransigents were hardened in their attitude by the anti-clerical legislation of the 80's. The passage of these Laic Laws presented a genuine dilemma to sincere Catholics. Were not the Republicans instituting an all-out attack upon the Church that was designed to reduce its piece-meal? Would it not be better to resist now than stand idly by while the demolition continued? Could anything be hoped for from a governmen which had so unmistakenly revealed its intentions? Because these arguments had a certain plausibility, they were generally accepted. In this way, the lines of conflict tightened and the struggle over education prolonged the bitterness that had so long poisoned the soul of France.

The Intransigents were correct in their claim that the elimination of the Church from education and from public life generally was the intention of the Radical Republicans.[100] It was also true that the program was devised in the Masonic Lodges and in allied organizations such as the *Ligue de l'Enseignement*. What they failed to see was that the anti-clericals could be successful only if they could persuade a majority of Frenchmen. The Laic Laws were passed only because France was no longer Catholic; in a sense the educational policy of the III Republic was a factual recognition of the de-Christianization of the nation. Further, the Republic had brought peace and prosperity, and, as sentiment crystalized in its favor, more Frenchmen resented the Intransigent Catholic attempt to change the form of Government and embark on foreign adventures. The key to the success of the laws against the Church was not to be found in the attitude of convinced Catholics or anti-clericals; their position was known in advance. The fate of the Church hung on the opinion of the growing millions who were more or less religiously indifferent. They disliked the clergy's use of their official position to advance the cause of one party. They would approve some diminution of the Church's influence, but fundamentally they were moderates. The length to which they would go would depend on events. Leo correctly analyzed this situation; most French Catholics did not.

Another consideration added solidarity to the anti-clerical ranks. The electoral victory of 1879 was both Republican and Conservative. The majority of the deputies were in favor of the social *status quo*. Gambetta and Ferry were very anxious to retain this conservative support and to disassociate Republicanism from its radical connotations.[101] They strove to assure all that the regime could be profitable and did not object to the use of political position to enhance private fortunes. To keep conservative support and to win further adherents from Legitimism, they knew they must postpone any far-reaching social reform. But how satisfy at the same time the genuine Left? There was always *clericalism,* the issue which divided them least. As Jules Simon saw at the time, anti-clerical legislation was a substitute for social reform; in fact, few important

social improvements were made until after the Separation.
This is a partial explanation of the obvious French lag in
dealing with the more flagrant abuses of industrialism.

The major attack in the 80's was directed against the
Church's position in education.[102] The Ferry Laws had a three-
fold purpose: to make primary education free, compulsory and
lay. A law of 1881 declared that the Communes would henceforth provide only the buildings for elementary education; the
central authority would pay salaries and control both personnel
and content. A law of 1882, often ignored in practice, made
primary education compulsory for children from 8 to 13. Both
these provisions were in keeping with general nineteenth century trends and should have won Catholic support. But the
major feature of the educational legislation was its laic character; it was to be education without specific religious content.[103]
A law of 1881 revoked a privilege of the *Loi Falloux* allowing
religious to teach without a state certificate; one of 1882 forbade
priests to enter communal schools to teach religion; one of
1886 restrained religious from teaching in communal schools.[104]
In addition, text-books and courses were revised to exclude
concrete references to religion.[105] A retroactive provision that
only the state could grant degrees inflicted great personal loss
to religious school graduates. Ecclesiastics were excluded from
educational councils. Faculties of Catholic Theology, though
not of Protestant, were abolished. Catholic schools could not
use the title "university."

The campaign against the religious orders was part of the
same program. Their status in the Concordat and Organic
Articles was ambiguous: some were explicitly authorized; the
rest claimed immunity from the prohibition against associations
on the basis of common law principles and the Penal Code.
When the famous Article 7 of the Law of 1879, aimed at the
non-authorized religious orders, failed in the Senate, the government moved against them by decree. In 1880, the Jesuits were
forcibly expelled, and the other male orders were instructed
to apply for approval. After passionate debate, the majority
of these decided to refuse on the basis of the illegality of the
demand. The government acted and about 10,000 were driven
from their houses, occasionally amid public excitement and
often with a touch of comedy.[106] The houses allowed to remain
open were subject to double taxation.

The ensemble of these measures stimulated fierce Catholic
resistance. The religious press thundered and individuals called
for active opposition. The Papal Nuncio, Czaki, did his best
to moderate the tone of the Catholic spokesmen. The Vatican

protested against the measures, but strove to find ground for understanding. Even as the male religious orders were facing the problem of whether to seek governmental approval, Cardinal Lavigerie, with the encouragement of the Holy See, arranged a compromise with the government whereby the orders would be merely required to make a simple statement disavowing hostility to existing institutions. Leo intervened directly to gain the congregations' assent to this course. Though the plan failed because of the deliberately premature publication of a Royalist newspaper, the Pope had clearly shown his conciliatory policy. To prevent any doubt of his intentions, he followed with several letters and Encyclicals in which he maintained that the Church is always in favor of liberty and is indifferent to the precise form of government.[107] The road to the *Ralliement* was open.

The central aim of the Pontificate of Leo XIII was this effort to win religious peace in France. The Laic Laws and the intense Catholic reaction caused delays, but the Pope never swerved. The Royalists had found keen delight in the conflict between Church and Republic, and did everything possible to magnify the issues. Throughout these stormy years, the wise diplomacy of the Vatican kept some check on Catholic extremists, counselled the bishops, and won several concessions from the government. None of the more extreme measures against the Church, including Separation, got beyond the discussion stage. Nor were the new laws always vigorously enforced. The members of the male religious orders who were so ostentatiously kicked out the door began to climb back through the windows; and the provocative scenes of expulsion were usually followed by quiet return.

The death of the Pretender, the Comte de Chambord (1883), ended the Bourbon dynasty. While the Legitimists regrouped around the Orleanist Comte de Paris, some of the old fire was gone. More dismal was the recognition that France was accustoming herself to Republican institutions and that hopes for a restoration were fading. But to them the most threatening aspect of all was the Papal attitude of friendship toward the Republic. Monarchists, not over-perceptive, still knew that if Catholic support were withdrawn, they would sink to an insignificant sect. Only the most desperate measures seemed capable of preserving the Monarchist bloc which faced dissolution from Vatican action.

Two such last straws appear in the latter half of the 80's.[108] Drumont's *France Juivre*, written in 1886, did not achieve its full impact until the next decade. But the affair of General

Boulanger precipitated a full crisis in 1889. It is a fantastic story: this Radical Republican became the darling of the Monarchists; the anti-clerical *débauchée,* the hope of the Catholics! Because he had some mass following, Boulanger came close to the threshold of power before his nerve failed. His collapse was a crushing blow to the Monarchist cause. That they were led to such extremes must be seen as a consequence of the inflamed debates and dwindling hopes that marked this decisive decade.

Boulangism had revealed the Right in a new and dangerous guise—as the exponent of nationalism and the advocate of *revanche.* Although it clearly showed that Catholics and Monarchists were still hostile to the Republic, it led to no anti-clerical reprisals, partly because the Republicans had a new confidence in the stability of the regime; partly because the bourgeois supporters of the regime showed a growing concern with the "social peril." The advance of militant Socialism and the appearance of a revolutionary Trade Unionism after the law of 1884, caused Ferry and many of his associates to find the real danger on the Left.

The clear evidence of Monarchist futility persuaded Leo XIII to intervene directly in French religious affairs. The establishment of religious peace in the Republic had been his consistent aim since the beginning of his Pontificate. His policy was based on the need of accommodating religion to the forces of the age. France was central in his thinking, both because of his personal preferences and because of his estimate of the international importance of the nation. He had correctly evaluated the internal situation; he knew that monarchist hopes were illusions, that the Church was being used as a tool by a disgruntled political faction,[109] that the majority of Frenchmen accepted the Republic and had shown themselves indifferent to the expulsion of the religious orders,[110] that all forces of the age favored the extension of democracy.[111] The Pope, consequently, was anxious to minimize the reaction against the anti-clerical laws and to integrate Catholics into the democratic regime.

In October 1890, Cardinal Lavigerie had a long conversation with the Pope on the necessity of weaning French Catholics from Monarchists affiliations. Returning to his diocese of Algiers, the Cardinal entertained the officers of the French fleet and prominent military and civil officials in his palace (12 November.) To the amazement of his auditors, he toasted the Republic and called upon all Catholics to support it loyally.

To add flavor to his words, the band of the White Fathers struck up the *Marseillaise.*

Such a unqualified declaration by a prelate known to be in the papal confidence cause wide repercussions. Extreme anti-clericals were alarmed and declared it a Jesuit trick.[112] Mon-archists were outraged, and tried to discredit it as a private statement lacking Vatican approval. When this position proved untenable, they tried to form a "Union of French Christians" which would apparently conform to the papal design but which would be solidly managed by royalists.[113] The varied interpretations, made more acute by an unhappy incident involving French pilgrims in Rome, indicated the need of a direct statement from the Vatican. Leo made it in his Encyclical *Au milieu des solicitudes,* 16 February 1892,[114] putting the full weight of papal approval behind the *Ralliement.*[115]

The Roman initiative to end the association of Catholicism and Monarchism in France faced formidable obstacles. The most vocal of French Catholics still adhered to royalist ideas to the point of emotionalized fixation that neither reason nor authority could lessen. The action of the Holy See caused a neo-Gallicanism in France that was to reach its climax in the *Action française.* This rebellion of the Extreme Right clearly demonstrated that Catholicism had been used as a means to gain political ends and unmasked the religious pretensions of the more violent royalists. The mouthpieces of this opposition were the newspapers *Verité française, Autorité, Gazette de France* and the anti-Semitic *Libre Parole.* This faction received support from such bishops as Fava of Grenoble, Freppel of Angers and Tregaro of Séez; from the heads of certain religious orders such as Dom Couturier of Solesmes and Père Le Doré of the Eudists. It received silent approval from many bishops and clergy who felt that the aged pope would soon die and that his policy would be reversed by his successor.

The majority of the bishops, Legitimists at heart, faced embarrassment in their desire to adjust to the will of the Pope and the fear of reprisals from royalists, who were often their best financial supporters. They saw their confreres who had obeyed the papal injunction vilified in the Rightest press. That threats from the Right to withhold contributions were not idle gestures was evident in the decline of aid for Lavigerie's While Fathers. Furthermore, it was hard to break the pattern of habit, particularly when anti-clericals showed no disposition to welcome the *Ralliés.* By declaring that the Republic must be accepted *en bloc,* the Left Extremists tried to blur the papal distinction between the constitutionality of the regime and the injustice of the anti-clerical legislation.

The leaders of the *Ralliement* were either bishops who had been friendly to the Republic or who were objective enough to see the wisdom of the papal position. At their head stood Cardinal Lavigerie. His motives were unassailable for as a Cardinal he could expect nothing further from the government or the Vatican. On the Minister of Worship's secret list, he was rated "B" (fair in reliability) so that he could not be accused of pliability. He was a man of common sense who understood his age and who was anxious not to dissipate the Church's strength in irrelevant quarrels. As early as 1866, he had seen that the Roman Question was closed and that Pius IX's opposition was placing French Catholics in an unfavorable position. He had taken a dim view of the *Syllabus*. Paul Cambon, Governor General of Algeria, relates in his correspondence that, in a long talk with the Cardinal, the latter confided that "the Good God has seen fit to afflict the Church with the long reign of Pius IX." This able man, the chief target of the opposition, was also the chief spokesman of Leo's policy in France.

Supporting Lavigerie were Cardinals Guilbert and Meignan, and Bishops like Fuzet of Beauvais and the staunch Republican, Billot des Minières of Poitiers. Reports of the prefects show that these ecclesiastics were generally able to keep the majority of clergy in line with papal policy. They received enthusiastic support from the Christian Democratic abbés who had already been encouraged by the appearance of *Rerum Novarum* in 1891. A considerable body of prominent Catholic laymen, led by De Mun, abandoned their Monarchist sentiments and with some internal reluctance, took up the cause of conciliation. Actually, the greatest potential supporters of *Ralliement* were the millions of nominal Catholics, the vast majority of the population, who no longer practiced their faith regularly but who observed the traditional ceremonies on special feasts. These, overwhelmingly Republican, were favorably impressed by the Pope's effort at religious peace.

Interesting cases were presented by two prominent Catholic journals. After the death of Louis Veuillot, the "evil genius" who did so much to discredit Catholicism in France, *Univers* had continued with the same intransigence and with nearly equal success. When Leo's intentions became unmistakably clear, Eugene, Louis' brother, together with Louis's two sons, accepted the Papal order and supported the Republic. Shorn of much of its popular support, the journal evolved in the direction of Liberal Catholicism. Even when it became anti-Dreyfusard, it maintained some reserve and did not try to use the case against the Republic. But two of Louis' trusted lieutenants, encouraged by his sister, left the paper in 1893, and, with the help of Northern industrialists, founded *Vérité* (later *Vérité française*), a journal most violently opposed to the Pope. The tremendously influential *Croix* half-heartedly supported the Pope until 1895 when the *loi d'abonnement* sent it into opposition.

In its early years, the *Ralliement* might be termed a partial success. It gained the support of an influential minority of active Catholics; the opposition, verging on the intense, of an even more influential minority; and the passive acceptance of the relatively indifferent. Most important of all, while it did not affect the core of the anti-clericals, it mollified the moderates and definitely reduced religious tension. The sum of these effects was the *esprit nouveau,* a conciliatory policy followed by the government until the turn of the century. The question remained: Would this limited success become a real victory?

This period of relative religious peace marked the revival of Christian Democracy. The Social Catholics had amazed French opinion by their strenuous campaign for social legislation and had made some contribution to the development of official Catholic social doctrine expounded in *Rerum Novarum*. But their idealization of the Middle Ages, which happily prompted them to reject Economic Liberalism, unhappily mantled their zeal with the cloak of an aristocratic paternalism, that was repugnant to the sturdy independence of French workers. Devoted and idealistic as were the Social Catholics, they were not effectual. A much more promising tendency was appearing in several regions of France in the years just prior to 1890.[116] The early Christian Democrats were generally young priests, whose contact with actual conditions had convinced them that the Church must accept political democracy and promote social reforms; these men welcomed both *Rerum Novarum* and the *Ralliement*. They were not reluctant *Ralliés*. For them, democracy was the form of government best suited to Christianity. They were sharply critical of existing social conditions and of their conservative coreligionists. They showed considerable talent for popular journalism and advanced their cause by a number of short-lived newspapers as well as by conferences and pamphlets. Their praise of the American clergy and their high regard for American political institutions led to the curious conservative reaction known as the Americanism controversy.[117]

Christian Democracy showed great promise as a counter-weight to the Monarchism and Conservatism of French Catholics. It made a powerful appeal to the younger clergy, conscious as they were of the losses suffered by the Church because of the political and social views of its more prominent members. An enthusiastic gathering of about one thousand priests met in Rheims in August, 1896, to hear the Abbé Lemire and others attack capitalism and demand the intervention of the State for the protection of the weaker members of society. At the first national congress of the movement in Lyons in November, 1896, 8,000 attended its largest session, with about 700 priests as delegates or auditors.

This encouraging movement, buttressed in its fundamentals by papal approval,[118] failed lamentably and was in complete collapse by the turn of the century. This disappointing sequel cannot, however, be attributed to the Conservatives, who angrily opposed the Christian Democrats as traitors to the cause. The basic defects were internal. Beginning as a spontaneous movement in various parts of France and led by vigorous personalities who differed in methods, Christian Democracy never achieved an effective national organization. Nor did it elaborate an adequate program. The seeds of a positive doctrine were to be found in the papal encyclicals, but it would have taken time and study to translate these generalities into a concrete body of proposals capable of attracting mass support. The political ambitions of some of the leaders, who dreamed of a Catholic party on the model of the German Center, dragged the movement into the vortex of French politics before it had matured. However, the basic cause of its disintegration was the anti-Semitism of most of its leaders. Fundamentally, it was the Dreyfus Affair which destroyed the Christian democracy of the 90's.

These priests had been led to anti-Semitism by a variety of motives. Some shared the rather common Socialist feeling that the Jews were responsible for capitalism. Others became anti-Semitic as a consequence of their participation in the anti-Masonic campaign of the 80's. But the major factor was the influence of Drumont, who was posing as a champion of social justice and who wove his hatred of the Jews into his criticism of French Society. The decisive moment in the history of French Christian democracy was the invitation of Drumont and his followers to the Lyons Congress. As a consequence, instead of developing along positive lines, the movement fell prey to its more violently anti-Semitic elements and discredited itself completely.

Less spectacular, but more enduring, were the origins of

Christian Trade Unionism. The class-war mentality of the newly legalized labor organizations posed a problem for conscientious Catholics. French efforts to organize workers into confessional trade unions extend back to the 80's, and some progress was made among the white collar class. By the 90's these small groupings had emancipated themselves from the "mixed union" concept[119] and had dropped religious practice as a condition of membership. They kept themselves free from the contamination of employer-sponsored "Yellow Unions." Studying the realities of the industrial order, they were evolving concepts of Trade Unionism and social welfare that were to fructify in the post-war period.

Finally, the period of relative religious peace in the 90's marked the beginnings of the revival of Catholic clerical scholarship. Throughout the nineteenth century, the French clergy had been generally outside the great expansion of scientific thought. By the 90's, ecclesiastical studies of a serious nature were under way: Duchesne and Baudrillart were making important contributions in the field of history; Loisy was pursuing unaccustomed paths in the study of Scripture; Branly, the inventor of wireless, was interesting his students in science. All these were working in the Catholic Institute of Paris. Theology was enjoying a renaissance in several centers, notably Lyons, and philosophy had been stimulated by the publication of Pope Leo's *Aeterni Patris* (4 August 1879.) [102] All this made for a Apologetic that conformed to real needs and was competent to defend Christian concepts on a sound intellectual basis. But as the Dreyfus case proved, this movement of ideas had not yet affected the rank and file of the clergy. And it had yet to survive the serious crisis of Modernism.

The papal effort to win Catholics to the support of the Republic was only partially successful. In effect, it merely emphasized the basic divisions in French Catholicism which had been apparent as early as 1795. These divisions were accentuated, rather than removed, by the papal initative. Besides the cleavage among Catholics, the Pope had to face the prejudice against the clergy in politics, which was shared by all segments of French opinion. The Ralliés, called sarcastically "Papal Republicans," were open to the charge of the Left that they had embraced the Republic only to destroy it. With M. Bourgeois, the Radicals would ask the embarrassing question, "Do you, then, accept the Revolution?," advancing the questionable thesis that the anti-clerical legislation was an integral part of the Republican formula.

The turning point in the Raliement was the *loi d'abonne-*

ment (1895), which taxed the property of the religious orders. The Extreme Right had never relaxed its opposition: Monarchists had voted for anti-clericals in the elections of 1893 rather than support Catholic Republicans; and Drumont had become openly insulting to the Pope.[121] The proposal of 1895 was an excellent opportunity for these groups to renew their attack on the whole basis of the *Ralliement*. The new tax was an actual improvement on existing legislation, but it still placed the congregations under heavier burdens than favored business corporations and so provided a chance for an attack on the Republic. Despite Rome's plea for acceptance, two-thirds of the communities refused to pay the tax and had to be legally coerced. In the resulting bitterness, *Croix* abandoned the papal policy and *Libre Parole* reached new depths of invective.[122]

If the *Ralliement* floundered on the *loi d'abonnement,* it was sunk as a consequence of the Dreyfus case. Had the problem of revision not arisen, it is possible that the papal policy might have succeeded despite the crystallization of views on the law of 1895. But Catholic opposition to the reversal of the verdict on Captain Dreyfus ruined both the *Ralliement* and the Catholic structure in France.

The famous affair began with a military tribunal's unjust condemnation of the Jewish Staff Officer on the charge of treason (1894). At the time, practically all Frenchmen, including Jaurès and Clemenceau, believed in his guilt. Behind the condemnation was a decade of virulent anti-Semitism which had affected many segments of French opinion. The army, where low pay and monarchist sentiment combined to create anti-Republican feeling among the officers, were particularly responsive.

For the Monarchists the condemnation seemed a heaven-sent opportunity. The circumstances of the case made it possible to mobilize both nationalism and anti-Semitism against their inveterate foe, the Republic. Here was a winning combination that would shake the regime. Since opinion had been prepared by the Panama scandals, all could be staked on the Dreyfus case.

It is clear that the issue was the Republic, not the Jews.[123] It was its political implications that made the Affair an *intellectual* crisis, which divided educated Frenchmen more clearly into two camps than at any period of the III Republic's history. Also it was largely a by-product of *Ralliement*. Driven to desperation by the loss of papal support and frustrated in their hopes for Restoration, the Monarchists seized an issue which seemed to offer promise. The fact that the case involved the Army, the final bastion of their influence, merely added to the emotional involvement. As so frequently happens, the Jews were the scapegoat.

By the close of 1897, evidence of Dreyfus's innocence was accumulating and revision was in full progress. The underyling issue was still the form of government, but the immediate question was shifted to respect for the dignity of the human person; should an innocent man suffer injustice to preserve the reputation of the General Staff? On this basis, most Liberals, Radicals, and Socialists, who had previously been generally indifferent or hostile to Dreyfus, swung to his support. The Monarchists clung to their position.

Tragically, French Catholics, who should have responded to this basic human issue, generally did not. The mass of French Catholics, including the bishops, remained silent—a silence that was hard to justify in light of the moral issue involved. True, a valiant core actively supported Dreyfus.[124] But most of the names prominently associated with Catholic activity in France and practically all of the Catholic press were strongly anti-Dreyfusard. Blinded by political passion, these leaders not only betrayed justice; they hopelessly compromised the Church and brought upon her swift retribution.

The Dreyfus Affair created a new rally, the rally for the Defense of the Republic, and a new mood of violent anti-clericalism. After a few preliminaries aimed chiefly at the Assumptionists, the government of Waldeck-Rousseau[125] passed the Law of Association (July, 1901) which banned all religious orders who would not gain governmental approval; it was "the most decisive and vigorous act of anti-religious policy since 1870."[126] The Pope protested but favored submission. The population, as in the 80's, remained generally indifferent when the expulsions got under way. When the elections of 1902 confirmed the anti-clerical majority, Combes succeeded Waldeck-Rousseau and immediately undertook a systematic destruction of the works of the congregations. After refusing authorization to those which appealed,[127] he turned on the authorized communities, closing many of their schools and prohibiting the recruiting of new members. The sale of the seized properties brought immense gains to favored speculators: those of the monks of Charteuse, named "liquor dealers" in the decree, which were valued at nearly 11 million francs, were sold to Cusenier for 629,000. Choice school sites passed into private hands at equal bargains.

At the height of the excitement caused by the expulsion of

the orders, Leo XIII died (20 July 1903). He had initiated a policy that would have integrated French Catholics into the national life. At his death, his work appeared to be a complete failure.

More was to come. Ever since 1876, a growing minority of anti-clericals had favored Separation of Church and State though the majority had wished to retain the Concordat as an instrument of control. Rome and the majority of French bishops opposed Separation on the ground that the Concordat protected religion from more serious assaults, but individual French Catholics had come to favor it. Actually, Separation was the logical outcome of a century of secularizaton, and the political relations of Church and State no longer corresponded to the realities of French life. As Thomson says justly:[128] "Carried through in different circumstances, the Separation would have had a healing effect—like a skillful amputation. But the amputation was not skillful. Combes and his disciples carried out the Association Law of 1901 with more rigor than had been intended. . . . And after the diplomatic breach with the Vatican in 1904, Separation included ruthless measures of expropriation of Church buildings and property of lay bodies. Church and State were torn apart, not neatly separated; and political bitterness was fed with new fuel."

The Law of Separation, promulgated 11 December 1905, contained two distinct provisions. One was basically negative: all state support of religion was suppressed, except for chaplaincies at state institutions, and religious liberty was granted to all, "consistent with the public order." The second was positive: all Church properties were to belong to the State but were to be assigned to religious associations who would administer them and pay for their upkeep. It was this that was destined to cause greater difficulty for, like the Civil Constitution of the Clergy, it was open to the criticism that it violated the traditional hierarchic structure of the Church and that it would make Church administration impossible by fomenting local schisms.[129]

The Departmental elections of 1905, waged in the atmosphere of Separation, revealed the indifference of the majority of Frenchmen to this profound change in relations of Church and State.[130] It was not the hostility of some or the loyalty of others that is significant, but the apathy of the vast majority— an unconcern that was the end result of the ensemble of nineteenth century French history. This was undoubtedly the best justification for Separation. France was not a Catholic country in 1905. Nor did she react as did the Catholic minority

in Germany during the Kulturkampf or the Catholic majority
in Belgium during the school controversy. The Church in
France no longer enjoyed the loyalty of the masses.

The reaction of Catholics varied, as always. The bishops
were mainly conciliatory and wished to proceed with the
establishment of the Associations. The Christian Democrats
welcomed the change. The Intransigents preached resistance.
On 11 February, Pope Pius X, in his encyclical *Vehementer,*
attacked the law as an invasion of the constitution of the
Church. Since the letter contained no sanctions, the division
persisted, and the Assembly of Bishops, meeting in Paris in
May, approved a *modus vivendi* by a large majority. Again
Rome spoke. The Encyclical *Gravissimus* (10 August) condemned all accommodations to the new law on the ground
that the government had acted in a matter affecting the constitution of the Church without prior consultation with the
Holy See. Despite Briand's efforts to find some arrangement,
the date for the functioning of the Associations arrived without
any agreement. Irritated, the government struck hard with a
new series of anti-clerical decrees. But the conflict had reached
its limit. With the threatening international situation, the
government lost its zeal for the full implementation of the law.

The success of anti-clericalism from 1901-1905 had been
made possible by the fusion of the entire Left and Center by
the emotion rising from the Dreyfus Affair,—an alliance that
would necessarily be corroded by urgent social problems. The
churches remained in the practical possession of the curés, but
their title was precarious and extra-legal. After more than a
century of intermittent struggle, there was no real accord.
And the cleavage, caused by this central issue of French
nineteenth cetury politics, remained as an irritant in French
public life.

The Seeds of Recovery (1907-1945)

The Revolution of 1789 had produced a set of principles
that may be summed up in the famous trinity: Liberty, Equality and Fraternity. Theoretically, these ideals could have been
accommodated to Catholic doctrine. They were derived in
large part from Christian principles and had evolved within
a civilization in which Christianity had played the decisive
role. But the Revolution had also declared the autonomy of
the secular by divorcing public life from its traditional association with religion. This presented the great difficulty. The
Church had played an enormous role in the history of France

and national institutions were inextricably bound to the religious. Even this severance might have proceeded amicably, (for "secularism" had been gradually manifesting itself for centuries in Western history and in some areas an adjustment was found without open conflicts),[131] had not the Revolution asserted its right to full control over the structure of the Church within the national boundaries. The violence which this position encouraged, posed the political problem in religious terms; and conversely translated the religious problem into political terms.

Hence there emerged two questions:

First, the intellectual problem: How accommodate the new political and social conceptions with the religious ideals of Christianity?

Second, the political question: To what degree should the previously existing relations between Church and State be maintained?

These two problems—one theoretical, the other practical—dominated a large part of nineteenth century French history. Their solution was made difficult by the memory of the violence which accompanied the initial attempt at reformulation. Other studies in this volume will suggest that where this heritage of Revolution was absent, the problem, though severe, was not insoluble. But in France it was complicated by the interaction of the intellectual and political aspects of the issue: practical conflicts on the pace or extent of the Separation made a theoretical solution incomparably more onerous. The religious history of France from 1789-1907 is a melancholy record of human reactions to this involved issue.

As early as 1795, we can define two Catholic positions: one of opposition, the other of accommodation. The former was reinforced by the nearly universal Catholic fear of a return of the Terror, a fear so widespread that even the wise, moderate, and "liberal" Bishop Dupanloup did not escape its influence as late as the 1870's. It was further strengthened by the first decisive check to the proponents of accommodation, the *Mirari Vos* of 1830. This papal intervention did not end the effort to find a path of adjustment, but the Revolution of 1848 did, and the first phase of the Catholic struggle for compromise was stifled in the tainted atmosphere of the Second Empire.

The second effort, begun under the III Republic, was weaker in that the opposition had gained a greatly intensified emotional and administrative hold over the French Church; but it was stronger because it had the approval of the Papacy in the person of Leo XIII. The latter was not enough; for time was needed for papal influence to calm accumulated passions. But as so often happens in French history, both religious and secular, the necessary time was not accorded. The Dreyfus Affair presented the Right with an issue which they were determined to exploit as a counter-weight to papal defection. An issue favorable to their purpose, it struck their opponents, the Christian Democrats, at their most vulnerable point. The latter, too, would have needed peace, time, and tolerance for their adequate development, and they were given none. So, too, the second effort ended in failure. The Law of 1905 was both an index of that failure and the triumph of a principle implicit in the Revolution. Catholics were still fighting the issues they had lost in 1789, but they were fighting a losing defensive engagement, because they had evolved no constructive alternative.

The Law of 1905 deprived the Church of the prestige of State support; the public authority now declared itself completely neutral and uninterested in religion. The Church had also lost its material aid and thereupon descended into that poverty from which it still suffers. But Separation represented an important moral gain for the clergy recovered its freedom of action, shedding its attitude of subservience to government. The State renounced extensive powers over the Church, which it had exercised for 400 years, except for the interval of 1795-1801. No longer could it threaten recalcitrant clergymen by cutting their salaries; no longer had it the dominant voice in appointing bishops and indirect control over all Church administration. Questions in dispute were shifted from the political bureaus to the judiciary, which was impartial and even friendly. It was largely due to the consistent success of the Church in the French courts that the worst consequences feared from the Law of 1905 never eventuated.

Rome had seen from the first the weakness of the Law of Separation and the difficulties in the application of its provisions regarding Church property. It was confident that the day would come when the French Government would repent and seek its collaboration. Hence, it did not approve even a provisional organization for the French Church. This helped to keep the issue alive, despite the government's desire to come to terms in the face of the danger of war and internal social conflict. The position of the Church remained insecure until the outbreak of the war, at which time no effective steps had been taken to find a *modus vivendi*. Nor did Pius X's substitute for the *Ralliement,* a design for "the grand party of God, the party above all parties," succeed. In the few dioceses where it was attempted, it gained few adherents because of the unalterable fact that the religious question was not the primary factor in the electoral choice of most French voters.

Separation intensified many problems of the French Church. Recruitment of the clergy continued to fall alarmingly—a tendency which was only partially arrested in some dioceses in the 30's and which continues to disturb the French Church today.[132] Religious practice steadily declined as the cumulative effect of the problems examined took their toll.

But there were compensations. Those who remained Catholics after the Separation were inclined to strengthen their spiritual life and their grasp of Christian teaching. The evangelical poverty of the curés, who were living poorly in ill-equipped rectories, removed one source of anti-clerical feeling, And the sight of the Church, weakened and deprived of all political power, removed the fear of her threat to Republican institutions and made it more difficult to present her to the masses as the great national problem. Finally, Separation released a great spiritual energy that was destined to extend into every Catholic activity. The III Republic, which had witnessed the precipitous decline of the French Church, was also to see the beginning of her regeneration.

This regeneration was first evident in the field of thought and literature. The pessimism and materialism of the *fin du siècle* had created a climate more radically unfavorable to religion than the romanticism and positivism of eariler periods. But it was an atmosphere equally unsatisfactory to the human spirit, and caused a sharp reaction. New religious inspirations in poetry can perhaps be found in Baudelaire. Certainly, with Verlaine, the current of Catholic literature was clearly renewed. Within a short period centering around the turn of the century, Huysmans, Coppée, Bourget, Jammes, Péguy, Psichari and Claudel had turned from religious indifference or unbelief and had inaugurated a period of spiritual renaissance in French letters. Nor was the stream to dry up; Mauriac and Bernanos linked the first generation with the promising young writers of today.

This revival owes much to the widespread influence of Bergson, who rejected the pessimism and science worship of his contemporaries and developed a new basis for an optimistic philosophy of action. Péguy testifies to his enthusiastic reaction to Bergson's lectures at the École Normale Supérieure in 1894.[133] Molded by Bergson's thinking, Péguy went on to offer a synthesis of rationalism and nationalism on a Christian moral basis that was to make considerable impact on Republican thinking. The evidence of his moral integrity in his defense of Dreyfus and his romantic death in battle in 1914 gave added stature to this flaming neo-protagonist of the spiritual interpretation of human life.

The interrelation of these personalities who were to supply a new intellectual trend to France and the world is interesting. Péguy induced Raïssa and Jacques Maritain to attend Bergson's lectures at the Collège de France; the Maritains were subsequently converted to the faith through Léon Bloy.[134] Bloy, ignored by the general public, was a scandal to the bourgeois Catholics whom he pilloried; but his intense Catholicism had a profound influence on intellectuals.[135] Through Bloy French Catholic literature broadened and deepened in content and impact.

The first decade of the twentieth century was also the time for a flowering of the religious scholarship which had been slowly maturing in the previous period. The movement was stimulated by Leo's call to go to the people with a mind open to all new currents; and it was made more necessary by reason of the new concepts which were attacking the foundations of human liberty and personality. The deficiencies of Catholic nineteenth century apologetics were followed by a great fermentation. But the penalty of the delayed awakening was evident in the desire to catch up with the course of events; there appeared a too abrupt repudiation of the past, a fear of being classed with reactionaries and a striving to be "up-to-date," to become "incarnate" in the movements of the age. The motives were most sincere; to reclaim both the élite and the masses by removing obstacles to belief. In some, this led to a willingness to sacrifice the essentials of Christianity. The consequence was the crisis of Modernism, which was vigorously condemned by the Encyclical *Pascendi,* 16 September 1907.[136]

Behind the doctrinal controversy lay the political passions that had been aroused by anti- clericalism and the difficulties experienced by Catholics in having their views accepted in an academic world that had long been hostile. That Modernism was a real problem for the Church can be seen in the career of the Abbé Alfred Loisy. In the revival of Catholic thought, the major issue had been the supernatural element in Christianity, and its crux was the interpretation of the Scriptures which had been under rationalist attack for a century. Catholic Scripture scholars like Loisy had been applying rationalist methods in their Biblical commentaries. They had been warned by Leo's Encyclical *Providentissimus Deus,* [137] but the religious authorities had generally forborne with their efforts. Loisy enjoyed the support of Mgr. d'Hulst, the Rector of the Catholic

Institute of Paris, but he had been frequently admonished to moderate his views and refrain from publications which threatened the entire foundations of Christianity. In 1908, the Abbé made an open break with the Church and was excommunicated. For the next 32 years of his life, he continued to teach and to write. His publications since 1908 may be regarded as a sustained effort on his part to demonstrate that the course taken by Rome was the only alternative open to it. His last volume,[138] which appeared in Paris in 1936 and which sums up his mature views, not only asserts the exclusively human nature of Christ, but maintains hypotheses on the late origins of the Gospels that have been repudiated by most critics.

The intellectual revival of French Catholicism was momentarily handicapped by the condemnation of Modernism. The Intransigents used the crisis to attack all their old enemies. Clerical education was menaced by unfair denunciations forwarded to Rome against all who had made efforts, however orthodox, to apply Catholic apologetics to modern problems. The check, serious though it was, was only temporary. After the war the task was continued with new intensity and with considerable success. In the past three decades, French Catholics, reinforced by the return of the religious orders, have made remarkable contributions to religious thought. Scientific Biblical studies of great value have been produced in encouraging profusion. The Fathers have been carefully examined, and scholars like Gilson and Vignaux have developed the historical interpretation of Medieval philosophy. Thomistic thought has been renewed through the work of Sertillanges, Garrigou-Lagrange, Maritain, Guitton, Thibon and Mgr. Calvet. Gabriel Marcel has explored new paths through his profoundly religious philosophy of existence. Spurred by the conviction that too great dependence on the Western tradition has handicapped the Church in its missionary activities in the Near and Far East, scholars have been producing learned studies of oriental religions. Erudite reviews, like *Études* of the Jesuits, *La vie intellectuelle* and *La vie spirituelle* of the Dominicans and the celebrated *Esprit* of the late Emmanuel Mounier, have provided channels of intellectual worth, while specialized publications in every field are championing the religious position. Some of this activity, like that of the Catholic *Progressistes*, who are seeking to accommodate Christianity and Marxism, was highly adventurous, but most proceeded from firm doctrinal positions.

All these activities have had a noticeable effect on French learned circles. Today in *milieux* that were once hostile to religion, practising Catholics hold positions of importance without any need of apologizing for their convictions. In the universities, in the school system and in the literary world, there has been a conspicuous decline of anti-clericalism and a tendency to consider religious claims seriously on an intellectual basis. Catholic students are extremely active. Their *Centre Richelieu,* near the main entrance of the Sarbonne, is not only an intense center of liturgical and sacramental life, but also a forum for the discussion of Catholic thought in its most controversial aspects.[139] The divorce between Catholicism and France began in the domain of the intellect; and it is in this same area that a *rapprochement* has been pursued most earnestly.

Catholic social movements have also expanded remarkably since the Separation. In the decade before World War I the major effort in this field came from the Social Catholics.[140] *Action populaire,* founded at Rheims in 1903, became a central bureau of information and propaganda. It published reviews, brochures, and serious volumes on all aspects of the social question. The *Semaines Sociales,* an annual national congress of those interested in social problems, acted as a migratory popular university for the dissemination of Catholic social teaching. The Catholic Association of French Youth, (ACJF), founded by Albert de Mun, continued its activities, as did the rather unsuccessful Workers Clubs and related activities. Emanating from these was the Popular Liberal Party (*Action Liberale*) which attempted to win electoral support on a program of social legislataion and moral reform.[141] While most of these movements retained the rather conservative flavor of the earlier Social Catholics, the *Semaines Sociales* were open to all points of view, and there was some development of doctrine as a result of research carried on by *Action populaire.*[142]

The thread of Christian Democracy was not entirely broken by Dreyfus Affair. Some of the older leaders, like the Abbés Naudet and Dabry, continued to edit journals and inspire a small following. In addition to their enthusiastic defense of democracy, they favored a definitely class approach to the social question and called on labor to defend its own interests. The two best known of these journals, *Justice sociale* and *Vie catholique,* became involved with the doctrinal Modernists, whom they supported even after *Pascendi,* and were ordered to suspend by Rome.

The most promising of the Christian Democratic groups was Sillon. Begun as an apostolic movement in 1894 by a group of students who met in the crypt of the *Collège Stanislaus,*

it expanded rapidly under the organizing genius of Marc Sangnier. It published a newspaper and a review,[143] instituted popular educational courses that associated intellectuals and workers in genuine harmony, and sponsored open meetings where
speakers accepted the challenges of all opponents.[144] The movement spread to the provinces and from 1902 held national
congresses that won increasing attention. Sillon released a
genuine moral and spiritual revival, and was the most hopeful
apostolic movement since the Revolution.

Its phenomenal success brought high praise from ecclesiastical authorities. Leo XIII decorated Sangnier with the Order
of Gregory the Great; Cardinal Rampolla and most of the
French bishops praised his movement publicly; Pius X received the Catholic leader with great affection. When the
movement was first assailed by conservatives in 1905, not only
did Cardinal Merry del Val, the Secretary of State, reprove the
attack in a commendatory letter that contained a special
blessing from the Pope, but 400 letters in its defense from
cardinals, bishops and other important ecclesiastics were received.

In addition to its religious and social teaching, Sillon had
advocated the close connection of Christianity and democracy,
which it maintained were mutually compatible and necessary
for each other's full development. By 1905 it was defending the
French Revolution and urging that Rousseau and the leading
personalities of 1789 were substantially Christian. It praised the
Russian Revolution of that year, and condemned conservatives
as enemies from within the Catholic body. In 1906 Sangnier
became involved in a stiff quarrel with the Bishop of Quimper.
When it seemed that he would not accept episcopal direction,
he began to lose some of his high ecclesiastical support. In 1906,
Sillon opened its ranks to all believers in democracy and
dreamed of a *Plus grand Sillon* that would unite all in a common brotherhood.

Such views did not go unchallenged. In the heated atmosphere of the Modernist controversy, denunciations flooded into
Rome. On 25 August 1910, Pius X sent a *Letter to the French
Bishops on Sillon,* which praised its good intentions and excellent early work, but pointed out certain doctrinal and practical errors. It asked the directors to reform the movement on
a diocesan basis under the direction of the bishops and to pursue their work under the designation "Catholic."

The condemnation of Sillon is still one of the thorniest questions within the purview of this essay. When the leading con-

temporary Catholic democratic journal, *Témoignage chrétien,* dedicated its issue of 9 June 1950 to the subject on the occasion of Sangnier's death, it declared that the word "condemnation" was unjustified, since while the papal letter was admittedly a call to reform, it chiefly sought a clear distinction between religious and political action.[145] It is certain that the action against Sillon was strongly influenced by Italian conditions. As early as 1900, the refusal of Father Murri and the Italian Christian Democrats to merge with the Catholic Committee and their general attitude of independence to the Papacy had occasioned the *Graves de Communi* of Leo XIII. Their subsequent rebellion and the excommunication of Father Murri and other leaders had hardened Pius X's attitude towards such movements. His preference for diocesan groupings of Catholic Action, and the interconfessional character of the later Sillon also played a role. The Modernist crisis gave *Action française* and conservative groups their most favorable opportunity to attack their most successful enemy.

The Sillonists immediately accepted the papal decision and dissolved their many enterprises. A minority followed the papal suggestion and put themselves under the bishops. Most followed Sangnier's lead in forming political association without religious connections. With a new journal, *La jeune République,* they maintained their vigorous activity until the fall of the III Republic. They became the major Catholic critics of the Rightist social and political policy after World War I, and remained in the forefront of all democratic causes. Though the movement never regained the flaming success of its early days, it helped form an intelligent Catholic Left that distinguished itself in the Resistance.

World War I acted as a solvent of religious bitterness on both sides. Catholics forgot their prejudices against the Republic, and the government seemed anxious to forget its quarrels with the Church.[146] The anti-clerical laws had assured that able-bodied ecclesiastics would serve in the ranks. Ultimately, of the 32,700 of the French clergy who were mobilized for active duty, 4,618 were killed and 10,414 decorated. War proved the value of the excellent moral training of the French curés, who were strong enough to comfort others. Five years of common anguish broke down the barriers that had separated priests and people, and destroyed the cruder prejudices. The clergy of the occupied territories won popular approval for their heroism before the invader, and laymen and clerics distinguished themselves in all sorts of war work. The most striking

example was afforded by the exiled religious, who abandoned
their mission posts or adopted countries to return as volunteers to fight for France.

To the post-war generation, preoccupied with immediate
problems and disillusioned by the failure of the dreams on
which much anti-religious sentiment was based, anti-clericalism
seemed dated and archaic. In 1921, diplomatic relations were
restored with the Holy See.[147] The first fruit of this new understanding was the achievement of a legal basis for the
Church in France. On January 18, 1924 Pius XI, in the Encyclical *Maximam,* accepted the basic provisions of the Law of
1905 by granting permission for the formation of diocesan committees of worship that would be in accord with Canon Law.
The triumph of the *Bloc des Gauches* in the election of 1924
created a brief flurry of anti-clerical activity: but it subsided
quickly before public apathy. The old rallying cry no longer
charmed.

Did Catholics now accept the Republic? Certainly Rome and
a majority of the French bishops did, as did an increasing proportion of Catholics. But the Intransigents remained. *Croix*
was only a thinly-disguised anti-Republican journal in the
early 20's. The real center of abdurate Royalism, however, was
the *Action française.* Begun in 1899 during the Dreyfus Affair,
it had been directed by Charles Maurras, a militant agnostic.
Notwithstadning the positivism of several of its leaders and the
unsavory reputation of a few others, *Action française* had become the mouthpiece of those Royalist Catholics who still
sought a radical rejection of all liberal doctrines coming from
the Revolution. It professed "integral Nationalism," basing its
ultra-nationalist views on pagan racist theories of society and
justifying them by "scientific" arguments. In the 20's it was
violently opposed to the League and to all moderation in
dealing with defeated Germany.

Action française had consistently opposed all papal efforts to
improve relations with the French government. As early as
1913, it had been condemned by several bishops. In 1914, the
Congregation of the Index had moved against the seven principal writings of Maurras, but the publication of the condemnation was delayed by Pius X and the war postponed the
issue.

When it became apparent after the war that the *Action française* was growing in influence among Catholic youth, Pius XI
decided to act. He inspired Cardinal Andrieu of Bordeaux to
write a letter in his diocesan journal condemning the newspaper on religious grounds.[148] The Pope followed with a per-

sonal condemnation in his Consistorial Allocation of 20 December 1926, forbidding Catholics "to support, favor, or read" the newspapers of the movement. Finally, he published the decree of the Index of 1914 (5 January 1927), extending it to cover all issues of the journal. Two bishops who refused full assent were forced to resign, and Cardinal Billot, who had shown himself so energetic in extending the papal directives in the Modernist controversy, was deprived of his red hat because of his failure to obey on this issue.

For the first time in the history of the III Republic, a Rightist movement had caused a crisis, not between Church and government but within the Church itself. Instead of being hailed by the Church as a rampart against irreligion, the *Action française* was now denounced as a pernicious agent of de-Christianization. When it retaliated with violent attacks on the Papacy and the French bishops, the tie between "throne and altar" was effectively broken. The conflict revealed that those who had loudly proclaimed their devotion to the Church were the first to attack her when their cherished political ideas were threatened. It was this revelation that secured the final victory of *Ralliement*. All but the hopelessly sectarian finally saw the point.

The condemnation of *Action française* released considerable pent-up energy of French Catholics. Francisque Gay and many of the present leaders of the MRP first came into prominence as champions of the papal position. Jacques Maritain, who had been partially favorable to the condemned journal, now swung to Christian Democracy, bringing to it his considerable prestige. The dispute also served to divide the Catholic Association of French Youth into specialized branches along class lines. The *Jeunesse oeuvrière catholique* (JOC) was introduced into France and began a remarkable apostolate among young industrial workers, so largely demoralized by industrial conditions. Other specialized groups were formed for students, sailors, and farmers. The Scouts of France, sporting Federations and other agencies completed the appeal to a wide diversity of interests. All of these were united into a national body called Catholic Action, which had its central offices and annual congresses.

Another aspect of the reintegration of Catholicism with democratic France was the growth of the Christian Trade Union movement. The embryonic units of the pre-war period had already rejected the paternalism of the employers and the totalitarianism of the state, and had declared emphatically for the liberty of autonomous workers' groups. These principles were incorporated into the charter of the national confederation (CFTC), which was formed in November, 1919, with some 90,000 members.[149] The program demanded full independence for the trade union movement, which was to enjoy maximum autonomy consistent with the sovereignty of the State. It must be granted the right to strike, to bargain collectively, and to defend freely signed contracts. The program called for an eight hour day, social security, and action by the State in encouraging production and in assuring the best human conditions for its operation. The essential note was the preservation of human dignity and the liberty of the individual. Since many of the leaders were trained in the Christian Democratic movement, the charter was heavily accented in that direction.

The CFTC grew slowly but persistently during the 20's. It participated in strikes for union recognition and gradually won respect as a *bona fide* labor organization. It was reinforced by the appearance of the Jocists, who provided a philosophy of working class solidarity. It was aided by its rapport with Catholic intellectuals, especially with its own Federation of Teachers. Research and study added depth and precision to its program.

By the time of the Popular Front, the CFTC numbered a half million. It did not join the former movement but associated itself with the objectives of this long-delayed social reform. In the strikes of the 30's, the dominant CGT discovered that it was supported by militant trade unionists from the Catholic federation. Some ideological disagreement between the two confederations persisted; still a sense of solidarity was beginning to appear that was to reach fulfillment in the *Manifesto of the Twelve* (15 November 1940), a vigorous defense of free trade unionism and the democratic way of life that provided the intellectual foundation for working class Resistance.[150]

All these various movements needed time to mature peacefully, but again this element was lacking. The 30's were a period of crisis and confusion. The riots of 6 February 1934, raised the specter of a Fascist coup. Thanks to the condemnation of *Action française*, Catholics could no longer be identified with the cause of reaction. Individual Catholics still supported Rightist parties, but others rallied to the defense of the Republic, no longer entrusted exclusively to anti-clericals.[151] When Hitler initiated his persecution of the Jews, one of the first to protest in the name of the French bishops was Cardinal Verdier. The civil war in Spain found Catholics divided, but influential groups opposed the Franco regime. Finally, the realignment of social forces within France[152] caused by the menace of Hitler and the fear of internal revolution, found Frenchmen seriously divided on class and ideological lines, with the religious issue not a decisive factor. When the III Republic was voted out of existence by a panic-stricken Parliament, six Christian Democrats lined up with the handful of deputies in opposition.[153]

The fall of France in 1940 was essentially a military defeat inflicted by an enemy with overwhelmingly greater industrial and military strength who used his superiority with supreme skill and with a consciousness of the value of new tactics. Faced with the reality of defeat, France needed two things for national survival: the salvation of her soul by continued defiance of the enemy—De Gaulle; and the preservation of her body—Vichy. The latter defies easy generalization and judgment. Actually it was not a simple phenomenon, but a highly complex one that underwent basic changes in its brief history. Initially, it received the passive support of most of the French, whose first thought was of survival. It also received the active, though conditioned loyalty of those who considered the war over and the fall of Britain imminent, and the enthusiastic favor of old authoritarian movements like *Action française,* various heterogenous groups of the Right, who had long hated the Republic, and the new Fascist organizations of the ex-Communist Doriot and the neo-Socialist Déat. The absence of cohesion among these disparate elements is seen in their inability to formulate an organic instrument of government and in the shift of the balance within Vichy with each new change in the fortunes of war. "All the passions of the body politic during the preceding 70 years paraded for the last time, in due sequence, down the corridors of Vichy." [156]

The Church was somewhat compromised by this regime. Though Marshal Petain was not a practising Catholic, he made strenuous efforts to capture Catholic support by subsidies to Catholic schools and by gestures like the return of the crucifix to public buildings. The majority of bishops, apparently convinced that the war had definitely been lost and that the people must be protected against greater evils, made their peace with Vichy.[155] Yet the collapse of Vichy which discredited so many pre-war groups, did not seriously impair the prestige of the Church. In part, this was because the bishops, though acquiescent to Vichy, were generally not tainted by collaboration and remained firm when basic human rights were involved, as in the case of the anti-Semitic legislation. In part, too, it was because the curés, who, as always, remained at their post of duty with their people, shared their sufferings at home and in foreign concentration camps, often in the vanguard of Resistance, and sometimes volunteered as forced laborers in order to minister to their flocks; finally it was the contribution of all those groups who had labored to disassociate the Church from its ancient ties and restore its missionary function—the Catholic trade unionists, overwhelmingly anti-Vichy from the first; the Catholic intellectuals, students and youth who played a vital role in Resistance; the Christian Democrats of every class who retained their faith both in Christianity and democracy. It was on these that the Church and France depended in their hour of testing. It is on these also that both must depend in a greater agony that may lie ahead.

J. N. MOODY

NOTES

[1] Cf stimulating study of Franz L. Neumann, *Approaches to the Study of Political Power,* in *Political Science Quarterly,* Vol LXV, No. 2, June 1950, pp 161-180.

[2] The classic presentation of this problem from the Catholic point of view is John Henry Newman's, *An Essay on the Development of Christian Doctrine,* Longmans Green & Co., N. Y., 1927.

[3] Among many others, M. J. Bonn, in *The Crumbling of Empire,* London George Allen and Unwin, 1938, stresses this characteristic.

[4] Bernhard Groethuysen, *Origines de l'esprit bourgeois en France,* Paris, Gallimard, 1927, Vol. 1. Parliament in the following passages is *Parlement,* the corporate body of judges and court personnel.

[5] For the fecund expression of this religious renaissance, cf. Henry Bremond, *A Literary History of Religious Thought in France,* trans. by K. L. Montgomery, Vols I-III, London, S. P. C. K., 1938.

[6] For the transformation of the social classes in the Old Regime, of Philippe Sagnac, *La formation de la société française moderne,* 2 vols., Presses Universitaires de France, 1945, esp. Vol. II, pp 39-77; 148-193.

[7] For an analysis of the trends of the thought of the Enlightenment cf Paul Hazard, *La Pensée européenne au XVIIIème siècle,* 2 vols., Paris, Boivin et Cie, 1946.

[8] Sagnac, *op. cit.,* gives a generally unfavorable picture of the cultural influence of the Church in the eighteenth century; but he pays high tribute "to the ecclesiastics, and particularly the Brothers of the Christian Schools for their complete devotion" to the work of elementary teaching, Vol. 11, p. 138. Figures on the numbers enrolled is impressive, and it was not until well into the second quarter of the nineteenth century, that France had so many pupils in its primary and secondary schools as it did on the eve of the Revolution.

[9] For figures and analysis, cf Jean Leflon, *La Crise révolutionaire,* 1789-1846, Paris, Bloud and Gay, 1949 pp 24-27; and Andre Latreille, *L'Église catholique et la révolution française,* Paris, Hachette, 1946, Vol I, pp. 10 & 24.

[10] Robert R. Palmer's *Catholics and Unbelievers in Eighteenth Century France,* Princeton University Press, 1939, gives this summary of the Catholic defense; "The best of the orthdox writers had some qualities of mind commonly esteemed in discussion, if not very useful in violent dispute. They sometimes had a sense of humor and irony; they ranted less than their opponents; and they often expressed themselves with the grace, force and precision of classic French. And, on the whole, they were less fiercely intolerant. The faith of the philosophers was new and burning; it was their own, their personal creation

and discovery; it sprang from recent and contemporary history; it was offered as a program to cure the specific ills of the age. The faith of Catholicism had none of this timeliness or this urgency; it was more casually held, as an hereditary possession; it was further removed from immediate issues of the day. The philosophers could hardly approach any question without their whole paraphernalia of argument; nature, humanity, the enlightenment of the age, the prejudice of their opponents, the bearing of the particular question on the general perfectability and ultimate happiness of man. The orthodox in the age of reason, on the other hand, were in truth often reasonable—perhaps stodgily reasonable. Their dogmas, even when firmly believed in, were not forever obtruding into consciousness. When they approached a particular question they could deal with it concretely without bringing in the whole apparatus of Christianity. So far as religion was only a special part of their thought, held in one corner of their minds, they were free to discuss other issues in a matter-of-fact way", pp 21-22.

11 The Pragmatic Sanction, an earlier expression of royal control over the Church (1438), had begun to fall into disuse by the fifteenth century. Francis I was anxious to placate the Pope because of his Italian policy and Leo X realized that his threatened abrogation of the Pragmatic Sanction would lead to schism. Both sides were inclined to compromise and the Concordat was the result. That it presented a departure from extreme Gallican views is evident from the *Parlement's* refusal to record it till 1528, and it continued to try cases according to Pragmatic Law until 1527. While the Concordat contributed heavily toward keeping the French monarchy on the Catholic side during the Reformation, it represented an enormous surrender of papal rights to secular control. It may be called the cancer at the heart of the Church of the Old Regime.

12 Thus the important decrees of the Council of Trent were never formally received in France under the Old Regime although the bishops informally obeyed many of their provisions, e.g., on seminaries.

13 Known in the eighteenth century as *Richerism*. Its connection with the exclusively aristocratic recruitment of the episcopacy will be mentioned below.

14 For a discussion of the different interpretations of human nature and the effect of original sin in Saint Thomas and Pascal, cf Jacques Maritan, *Réflexions sur l'intelligence,* Ième ed., Paris, Nouvelle librairie nationale, 1926, p. 334 sq.

15 The practical consequences of the attitude toward nature and original sin are intelligently discussed in Yves Simon *Par dela l'espérence du désespoir,* Montreal, Perizeu et Co. 1945, pp 141-220. The author makes the point that romantic over-evaluations of man lead to despair and that the only preservative from pessimism is an acceptance of original sin, interpreted in terms of moderate optimism.

16 Nigel Abercrombie, *The Origins of Jansenism,* Oxford, Clarendon Press, 1936. Also Bremond, *op. cit.,* vol. III, pp. 309-358.

17 Groethuysen, *op. cit.*

18 Political Jansenism survived through the eighteenth century and helped to prepare the way for the Revolution. The astute d'Argenson went further and said it was *Unigenitus* rather than English philosophy that was the cause of the revolutionary temper. There is similar exaggeration in the contemporary statement that the Jesuits were the first victim of the Jansenists and the monarchy the second.

Until the death of Louis XIV (1715) Jansenism was confined to the élite. Thereafter, it began to affect the popular *milieux* where it served as a vehicle for opposition to the abuses of authority and resentment against deprival of rights. While the upper classes became detached from religious questions, the populace was crowding into the cemetery of St. Medard for miracles at the tomb of one of the sectaries, and the refusal of sacraments to dying Jansenists caused general excitement. In the eighteenth century, Jansenism was no longer in harmony with the values of the upper bourgeoisie, but still fitted the views of small shopkeepers and artisans.

Groethuysen makes the interesting point that the Jesuits in their optimism were much closer to their opponents of the Enlightenment than were the Jansenists.

19 A. Mathiez, *Rome et le clergé français sous la Constituante,* Paris, A. Colin, 1907. p. 7.

20 cf. *Nonciature de Portugal,* in *Oeuvres Complètes,* II, 356-370.

21 Of the clerical deputies, 437 were bishops, 208 curés, mostly from rural areas. While the extent of the accord can be exaggerated (the vote on the merger with the III Estate was 148 for and 136 against), it is clearly in the records of the first six months.

22 Louis XIV had claimed the right; Louis XV had limited the acquisitions of the Church in 1745 and had disposed of the properties of the suppressed orders in 1763 and 1768.

23 A Debidour, *Histoire des rapports de l'Église et de l'État en France de 1789 a 1870,* 2 vols., Paris, Felix Alcan, 1898, Vol I, p. 68.

24 A. Matheiz, *Rome et la clergé français sous la Constituante,* Al. Colin, Paris, p. 205.

25 Only seven bishops, four of them ordinaries, took the oath. P. Sagnac, *Études Statisque sur le clergé constitutional et le clergé refractaire en 1791,* Revue Hist. Moderne et Contemporaine, Vol VIII, 1906, p. 97-115, gives the figure of the jurors at 57.6%. J. Leon, *La Crise révolutionnaire,* Paris, Bloud et Gay 1949, criticizes this figure, pp 71-74. His points seem well taken and are adopted above.

26 Barruel (*Histoire du clergé pendent la Révolution, London, 1893*) sees all as a plot, hatched in the Lodges and progressively realized; Aulard (*Christianity and the French Revolution,* London, Ernest Benn, 1927) as an expedient of national defense against a religion that was the heart of the coalition against the country; Mathiez (*op. cit.* et al.) as a conflict between two irreconcilable ideologies, Catholicism and revolutionary patriotism, each a *mystique* and a universal ideal; Daniel Guérin, the most judicious of the recent Marxist interpretors (*La lutte de classes sous la première République.* Paris, Gallimard, 1946, 2 Vols, Vol I pp 250-305 et passim), dismisses the revolutionary cult as a myth and sees de-Christianization not as a consequence of a philosophy but as a political manoeuvre of vulgar diversion; the essentially bourgeois Convention, disturbed by the demands of the proletariat, turned the masses against the curés so that they would not seek their share of the property spoils. Clearly, none of these is satisfying by itself. For further interpretations, see Paul Farmer, *France Reviews its Revolutionary Origins,* N. Y., Columbia University Press, 1944.

27 Charles Ledre, '*Le Culte caché sous la Révolution,* Paris, Bonne Presse n.d., pp. 23-36. For the whole problem cf. J. Leflon, *Monsieur Emery,* 2 vols., Paris, Bonne Presse, 1945 2ème ed., Vol I pp. 247-286.

28 Cited by E. Daudet, *L'émigration pendent la Révolution,* Paris Vol. II p. 56

29 It would be tempting to develop the reaction of Americans or contemporary Frenchmen to Soviet Communism along these lines. It must also be remembered that the experience of persecution leaves bitter memoiries and emotional responses: The Israeli government continues to ban the singing of German

lyrics by Mozart and songs by Schubert and Brahms, for it cannot "forget that German is the language of the people who, a few years ago, brought disaster to one-third of the Jewish nation," N. Y. Times, 2 January 1951, p. 4.

30 cf. Louis Madelin, *Histoire du Consulat et de l'Empire*, Paris, Hachette, 1937-46, Vol. IV, p. 99. Napoleon's attitude is best summarized in one of his letters to Thibeaudeau: "They pretend that I am a papist, but I am not in any way; I was a Mohammedan in Egypt; I will be a Catholic here for the good of the people. I do not believe in religions but in the idea of God."

31 Henry H. Walsh, *The Concordat of 1801*, N. Y. Columbia Univ. Press, 1933 pp 11-60.

32 cf. A. Latreille, *op. cit.*, Vol II, pp 121-143.

33 The religious history of this period lacks the abundance of monographic studies which are available for the preceeding decades. For a general account, cf. Adrien Dansette, *Histoire religieuse de la France contemporaine*, Paris, Flammarion, 1948, Vol I, pp. 233-284; A Debidour, *Histoire des rapports de l'Église et de l'État en France*, Paris, Felix Alcan ,vol I; Frederick B. Artz, *Reaction and Revolution 1814-1832*, N. Y. Harper Bros., 1945, pp. 49-110 and 263-295; P. de la Gorce, *La Restauration*, Paris, 1926-8, 2 vols., E. de Guichen, *La France morale et religeuse sous le Restauration*, Paris, 1911, 2 vols.

34 Two bishops, Frayssinous and Feutrier, headed the University (the governmental monopoly of education) under the Restoration. Under Mgr. Frayssinous' direction, 20 of the 25 rectors were clerics, enemies of the Church were deprived of teaching positions, and three-quarters of the teachers of philosophy were priests.

35 The Constitutional Bishop Gregoire wrote: "In Paris, more than in the rest of France, it is worship that was reestablished but little religion" (*Mémoires,,* Paris, 1857, Vol II, p. 423). All evidence points to a great drift from religion. Lacordaire estimated that only 7 or 8% of the students of philosophy and literature made their Easter duty in the Paris colleges, and only 1% preserved their faith after leaving school. Only one-tenth of the graduates of Saint-Acheul, the best Jesuit College, practised the faith after graduation.

36 Baldenspenger, *Le mouvement des idées dans l'émigration Française*, Paris, 1924, Vol II p. 13

37 The nobles filled the upper house and gained many administrative posts in government. They were especially successful in having themselves appointed to high positions in the Church: 70 out of the 90 bishops chosen under the Restoration were of noble origin. The Duc de Rohan, who entered the priesthood after the death of his wife, became an archbishop within six years of ordination. Their efforts to recover their lands were generally unsuccessful.

38 After 1848 a similar, though less general, movement of the bourgeoisie, took place, cf. infra, p. 147.

39 *The Mémorial catholique* reported that 2,159,500 copies of the works of Voltaire and Rousseau were sold from 1814-1825. Cf. Artz, *op. cit*, p. 164.

40 For evidence, cf, de Brugerette, *Le prêtre et la societé contemporaine*, Paris, 1935, P. Lethielleux, Vol I, pp 29-51. The moral training of the clergy was generally excellent, but the intellectual formation terribly poor. Lamennais' remark was not entirely unwarranted: "Never has the clergy, taken in the mass, been more ignorant than today, and never is real knowledge more necessary for them." As a consequence, there was a great deal of sound religious work done; the members of clergy and religous increased; and despite the dispersal of personnel and property during the Revolution, one-third of the students in secondary schools were taught by religious. But apologetics remained poor; history was almost neglected; and theology, philosophy and scripture were stagnant.

Weakness in clerical education remained as one of the major difficulties of the French Church.

41 Charlotte T. Muret, *French Royalist Doctrines since the Revolution*, N.Y., Columbia Univ. Press, 1933, pp. 10-34. De Maistre placed great emphasis on the authority of the Papacy. His *Du Pape* was an exception to the prevailing Gallicanism of the Ultras.

42 For royalist sentiment in this *"Catholic Action"* group, cf R. P. de Bertier de Sauvigny, *F. de Bertier et l'énigme de la Conrégation*, Paris, 1949. The same tendencies prevailed in the lay *Chevaliers de la Foi*, which had purely political ends.

43 Muret, *op. cit.*, pp. 48-67.

44 Nicholas Burtin, *Un Semeur d'idèes au temps de la Restauration: le Baron Eckstein*, Paris, de Boccard, 1931.

45 *De la réligion considéré dans ses rapports avec l'ordre politique et civil* lème édition, Paris 1826, p. 233. Christian Marechal, *Lamennais, au drapeau blanc*, Paris, H. Champion, 1946, dates Lamennais' conversion to liberal Catholicism from 1823.

46 *Des progès de la Rèvolution et de la guerre contre l'Église*, in *Oeuvres complètes*, Paris, 1836-7, Vol IX, pp. 67-8. The issues raised by Lamennais are still subjects of discussion. For a modern Catholic view, somewhat reminiscent of Lamennais, cf John C. Murray, in *Theological Studies*, Vol X, no. 2, June 1949, pp. 177-234, and no. 3, September 1949 pp. 409-432. For thorough treatment, cf Heinrich A. Rommen, *The State in Catholic Thought*, St. Louis, B. Herder, 1945, pp. 586-605.

47 cf Alexis de Tocqueville, *Souvenirs*, Gallimard, 1944, Paris pp. 5-6 where he declares that 1830 delivered all political power to a single class, the upper bourgeoisie.

48 The most active on *L'Avenir* were Lacordaire who specialized on relations of Church and State, De Coux, who wrote on social questions, and Montalembert, who joined shortly after publication had started and who wrote on foreign questions. Lamennais set general policy. Other members of Lamennais' circle at La Chênaie, as Gerbet, Rohrbacher, and Gueranger, helped with articles.

49 Though Lamennais later avowed a vague Socialism, at this time he was not directly concerned with the social question. De Coux wrote the articles in this field. Though he did not call for governmental intervention, he condemned abuses and urged the workers' right to organize, cf *Ce que sera le Catholicisme dans la Sociètè Nouvelle, L'Avenir*, 30 June 1831, in *Oeuvres complétes*, ed. Doubrée et Cailleux, Paris 186-7, Vol. X, pp. 348-50 for an example of Lamennais' treatment of the social issues.

50 The Roman background of *Mirari Vos* is discussed below. Gregory XVI's brusque treatment of the sensitive Lamennais was a strong factor in the latter's resentment. For an excellent analysis of Lamennais' influence in Belgium and the effect of Mirari Vos. cf H. Haag, *Les Origines du catholicisme libéral en Belgique*, 1789-1829, E. Nauwelaerts, Louvain, 1950, pp 163-198. For the problems involved, cf. George Weill, *Histoire du catholicisme libéral en France, 1828-1908* (Paris, Felix Alcan, 1909) ; C. Constantine, *Liberalisme catholique*, in *Dictionnaire de théologie catholique*, Vacont et Magenot editors (Paris, Letouzey et ane, 1926) , Vol VII, Col. 507; Fernand Mourret, *Le mouvement catholique en France de 1820 à 1850* (Paris, Blond et Gay, 1917).

51 *Mémoires.* (Paris, 1858-1867), Vol III, pp 70-1, 85.

52 One might defend the view that this conversion was an unmitigated disaster for French Catholicism. In this controversy, however, *Univers* was still highly regarded as an outspoken defender of the Catholic cause.

53 Only 12 of the 72 appointed by the July Monarchy were nobles.

54 In addition to the Dominicans, Benedictines, Trappists and Jesuits reappeared to add considerably to the strength of the Catholic effort. The schools and novitiates of the last were closed by the government in 1845 to allay hostile feeling, but the fathers remained. "The order was dissolved, but not the Jesuits' ". For Lacordaire's views, cf. R.P.H. Lacordaire, *Political and Social Philosophy*, ed. by Rev. D. O'Mahoney, (London, Kegan Paul, Trench, Trauber & Co. 1924) ; *Considérations sur le système philosophique de M. de la Mennais, suivies de la lettre sur le saint siège et d'un mémoire pour le rétablissement en France de l'ordre des frères prechêurs*, (Louvain, C. J. Fonteyn, 1847).

55 A. Cuvillier, *P. J. B. Buchez et les origines du socialisme chrétien*, Presses Universitaries de France, 1948, Paris, pp. 38-52. The best single volume on the origins of Social Catholicism is: J. B. Duroselle, *Les Debuts du catholicisme social, 1822-1870*, Paris Presses Universitaires, 1951. For Buchez and his school pages 80-113; De Coux pp. 40-57; Villeneuve—Bargemont pp. 59-71; *Atelier* 113-20. His conclusion in regard to the last named is: "It is the sole example we know of an effort to create a working class movement of Christian inspiration. But with its aggresiveness, its preference for class conflict, and the relative indifference of its principal editors to dogma, it cannot be included without reservation in the new-born Catholic Social Movement." Duroselle also notes the parallel development and slow *rapprochement* between Socialists and Social Catholics up till 1848.

56 G. Goyau, *Ozanam*, Paris, Payot, 1925.

57 *Letter to Madame Swetchine*, 24 Oct 1848.

58 cf. J. Leflon, *L'Église de France et la Révolution de 1848* Bloud et Gay, Paris, 1948 Archibishop Donnet of Bourdeaux saw French Catholics now enjoying the liberty which was such a boon to their brothers in the U.S. Not all Catholics, of course, were equally enthusiastic.

59 C. B. Pitman (ed), *Mémoirs of the Count de Falloux*, II vols, London, Chapman and Hall, 1888. His views may be profftably compared with a sincere exponent of Christian democracy who remained consistent throughout the crisis: cf. Abbé A. Bazin, *Vie de Mgr. Maret*, III vols, Paris, Berche et Tralin, 1891. The crisis of '48 was to show that genuine Republicans were a minority not only among Catholics, but in the country as a whole, cf. F. A. Simpson, *Louis Napoleon and the Recovery of France*, London, Longmans, Green, 1951, 3rd ed., pp. 17-43.

60 A Commission of inquiry into the conditions of workers. For the small scale of French industry in 1848 with its consequences on the working class, cf J. H. Clapham, *The Economic Development of France and Germany*, 4th ed., Cambridge Univ. Press, 1948, pp. 75-81.

61 *Op. cit.*, p. 145. Cf. Ross W. Collins, *Catholicism and the Second French Republic*, Col. Univ. Press, 1923.

62 They were a highly diluted version of Louis Blanc's associations of producers' cooperatives. In effect, they were nothing more than relief projects on the WPA model. By June, 103,500 jobless had enrolled, and many distressed provincials had wandered into the city to take advantage of the dole. Falloux's provisions to cushion the shock of the dissolution were dropped in the final drafting of the legislation.

63 The revolt of the poor of Paris on June 23. The net effect of these events was that the Conservative Social Catholics lost faith in the workers and tended more definitely toward paternalism. The June Days also caused a further rupture among the various groups of Social Catholics: The Liberals, who might

have acted as a center between the Conservatives and the Democratic and so-cialistically-minded Catholics practically disappeared. Christian democracy, in turn, was almost completely destroyed by the coup d'état of Louis Napoleon. Duroselle, *op. cit.*, p. 293.

[64] cf above, p. 37.

[65] Quoted by H. Guillemin, *Histoire des catholiques français au XIXe siècle* Milieu du Monde, Paris 1947, p. 180 (Italics supplied). Duroselle sees an element of class interest in the negative attitude of Catholics toward the social problem especially after 1848. But he finds the major cause in a total lack of understanding of the new condition introduced by industrialism, an ignorance fostered by the absence of industrial workers in Catholic activities, *op. cit.,* p. 701.

[66] Note the similarity to the program of De Gaulle.

[67] As usual when the outlook for a cause appears gloomy, the more moderate varieties of Legitimists declined. Men like Blanc de St. Bonnet kept alive the more extreme versions of De Maistre and De Bonald, with its strong emphasis on Catholicism, its attachment to Medieval conceptions, and its idealization of the past, of Muret, *op. cit.,* pp. 142-165. Royalism revived somewhat with the quarrels between Catholics and Louis Napoleon in the 60's.

[68] There was also a Legitimist faction in opposition, identified with men such as Mgr. Pie.

[69] When Bishop Dupanloup protested to Pius IX against the intemperate personal attacks of Veuillot, the Pope refused to take sides. But he consistently showed the popular journalist every mark of favor.

The term "Liberal Catholics" is used in the historic sense: Those who wished to live in harmony with the new political and social forces. Obviously they had no common program, although the conferences at Malines showed wide areas of agreement among many of the leaders.

[70] The currently used *Histoire de l'Église* by Abbé Darras was wretchedly mediocre and represented a triumph for the Intransigent interpretation.

[71] cf J. Brugerette, *Le prêtre français et la société contemporaine*, Paris, 1935, P. Letheilleux, 3 vols: passim; esp. Vol III, pp. 47-57.

[72] cf J. Leflon, *op. cit.*, p. 46.

[73] G. Weill, *Histoire du Catholicisme libéral* Paris, F. Alcan, 1909, p. 200.

[74] Several leading Republicans did incline toward liberal Protestantism. George Sand had her two grand-children baptized by a Protestant pastor as a gesture of defiance toward Catholicism. The movement bore fruit in the second decade of the III Republc when several of Ferry's aides and supporters were Pro-testants.

[75] Last issue, 31 July, 1850.

[76] G. Duveau, *La pensée oeuvrière sur l'éducation pendant la second Repub-lique et le second Empire,* Paris, Domat, 1947.

[77] His growing hostility a good barometer, cf H. de Lubac, *The Un-Marxian Socialist*, N. Y., Sheed and Ward, 1948, pp. 73-101.

[78] A society to expand lay public education, founded in 1866 by Jean Mace with the help of three worker allies, cf Dubeau, op. cit,—314.

[79] J. Coornaert, the *Témoignage Chrétien*, 28 May 1948.

[80] cf Robert C. Binkley, *Realism and Nationalism 1852-1871,* N. Y. Harper and Brothers, 1935, pp. 1-71; Carleton J. H., Hayes, *A Generation of Material-ism*, 1871-1900, N. Y., Harper and Brothers, 1941. A good example of the trend in Renan's *Life of Jesus* which combined Positivism, biblical criticism, and a sentimental attachment to the human aspects of the Gospel. It sold 100,000 copies in two years and episcopal condemnation only gave it publicity. Nothing of comparable merit appeared from the Catholic ranks.

81 "Clericalism" came into common use during the II Empire to denote the political utilization of religion.

82 cf above p. 40.

83 While the general intellectual currents were unfavorable to Catholicism, the first seeds of the later Catholic renaissance can be descerned in this period.

84 The authoritarian De Maistre was an exception among the Legitimists. His *Du Pape* was thoroughly Ultramontanist.

85 In the vote of March 1861, 61 voted against the government in the Senate with 79 for, and 91 against and 158 for in the Corps Legislative. For significance of this issue, of Jean Maurain, *La politique ecclésiastique du Second Empire de 1852 a 1869*, Paris, Felix Alcan, 1930, p. 624 and passim.

86 Substantially, the Party of Order of 1848.

87 On the other hand, 55 out of the 69 church buildings remained open throughout the Commune and some priests went about unmolested. Anticlerical sentiment was general, but violent attacks were limited to extreme groups. These had great opportunity as defeat loomed, a fact which explains the execution of the hostages. Earlier, the Commune had tried to exchange Archibishop Darboy and the priests for Blanqui, but Thiers refused despite the pleas of the Papal Nuncio.

88 *Univers*, 13 July 1871

89 F. Boulard, A. Achard and H-J. Emerard, *Problèmes missionaires de la France rurale*, 2 vols, Paris, Cerf 1935 gives the facts and explores the causes, esp. I, pp. 148-185. Aside from the political factor, there was the breaking down of rural isolation through railroads, press, conscription, etc.

90 Veuillot made it a matter of conscience, cf *Univers*, 7 January 1877. Of course there were exceptions: there was Catholic Republicans in Assembly like Dufaure and Lamy; Bishop Guilbert of Gap made public protests against the identification of Catholicism and monarchism; the Catholic Liberals continued their opposition under the astute direction of Bishop Dupanloup. But the conservative majority offered no program but a return to the past.

91 It is interesting to note that the issue which led President MacMahon to dismiss the Simon ministry and dissolve the Chamber (The Seize Mai, 1877) — a prime blunder that played into Republican hands—was a debate on the Roman Question.

92 Some of the propaganda was fictitious, e.g., the rumor spread in the country districts with the help of the Republicans that a Monarchist victory would mean a return of the tithe.

93 Cf. G. Bouniols, *Thiers au pouvoir. 1871-1873*, Paris, 1921. pp. 62-86 where his letters reveal how clearly Thiers saw the Republic as a safeguard against social disorder. For a good summary of middle class attitudes, cf David Thomson, *Democracy in France*, Oxford Univ. Press, 1946, pp. 53-71.

94 The attitude became fashionable in monarchist circles, cf P. Lacanuet, *La fin du Pontificat de Pie IX, 1870-1878 Paris*, F. Alcan p. 398. For an excellent criticism of this influence cf Paul Vignaux, *Traditionalisme et syndicalisme*, Editions de la Maison Francaise, N. Y., 1943, pp. 29-85. For the teaching of those Social Catholicism cf. R. Kothen, *La Pensée et l'action sociales des Catholiques, 1789-1944* Louvain, E. Warny, 1945, pp. 213-240; G. Hoog, *Histoire du Catholicisme social en France*, 1871-1931 Domat, Paris, 1946, pp. 14-39; H. Rollet, *L'Action sociale des Catholiques en France*, 1871-1901, Paris, Boivin et cie, pp. 14-327. Moon, Parker T., *The Labor Problem and the Social Catholic Movement in France*, New York Macmillan, 1921, pp. 77-113.

95 Harmel, though a "Social Catholic," was very slightly paternalistic, and

his policies were nearer to the ideals of the Christian Democrats than to those of De Mun.

96 cf above, p. 41.

97 R. P. Lecanuet, *La vie de l'Égline sous Leon XIII* Felix Alcan, Paris, 1930 pp. 1-119, gives sharp pen pictures of these two archibishops, as well as sketches and views of the rest of the heirachy.

98 cf Lecanuet, *op. cit.*, pp. 208-257. *Le Monde*, founded in 1872, was an exception.

99 *La Croix* was founded by P. Bailly of the Assumptionists, a journalistic genius. Well-written and ably promoted, it grew to be the most widely circulated Catholic daily of the period and a competitor of the secular press. While it had a developed social policy for employees and many innovations, it consistently took an extreme position on all the issues that arose during its heyday. For its part in the Dreyfus Affair, cf Robert F. Byrnes, *Anti-Semitism in Modern France*, Rutgers Univ. Press, New Brunswick, 1950, Vol I, pp. 194-8 et passim.

100 cf Evelyn M. Acomb, *The French Laic Laws*, Columbia Univ. Press., N. Y., 1941, pp. 367-8 Arthur Ranc, a close friend of Gambetta, spoke of "breaking bonds one by one." Deputies in the Chamber spoke of "necessary preparatory measures." Such hints were bound to disturb.

101 Acomb, *op. cit.* gives considerable evidence on this point, cf., pp. 62-83. For the attitudes of the various parties, cf. J. Leon, *Les partis politiques sous la Troisième République*, Paris, 1912, p. 163, Roger Soltau, *French Political Thought in the Nineteenth Century* New Haven, Yale Univ. Press, 1931.

102 Anti-clerical legislation in other fields: loss by members of male religious orders and seminarians of exemption from military duty; reestablishment of divorce; secularization of cemeteries and encouragement of civil funerals; secularization of the Pantheon; legalization of labor on Sunday (a social loss); loss of clerical voice in hospitals and charities, etc. For figures on education, cf G. Hanotaux, *Histoire de la France contemporaine, 1871-1900*. Paris, Combet et Cie, 1903-1908, Vol II, pp. 653-4.

103 A. Debidour, *L'Église catholique et l'état sous la troisième Republique 1870-1906*, 2 vols, Paris, Felix Alcan, 1906-9, Vol I, p. 276.

104 3403 brothers and 14,958 nuns taught in state schools at this time.

105 The new syllabus included a course in moral and civic virtues which emphasized respect for private property. Thompson, *op. cit.*, p. 146: "This blend of Christian ethics without Christian religion or faith, nationalist principles and middle-class virtues, was the creed inculcated by one of the most highly centralized educational machines in the modern world."

106 Sick and infirm members who had locked themselves in their cells were carried out on stretchers; one convent was surrounded and besieged by a formidable contingent of troops although no resistance was offered.

107 *Immortale Dei, The Christian Constitution of States*, 1 Nov 1885, in *Great Encyclical Letters of Leo XIII*, Benziger Bros., N. Y., 1903, pp. 128-9.

108 A more moderate effort, that of De Mun in 1885, to form a Catholic party to fight anti-clericalism, died without result. The Monarchists were indignant: "We are the Catholic Party." For the circumstances and reasons for Papal disapproval, cf H. Rollet, *Albert de Mun et le parti Catholique*, Boivin et Cie, Paris, 1947, pp. 98-109.

109 Leo's Encyclical, *Sapientiae Christianae*, 10 January 1890, protested against the abuse of attaching the Church to a political party making it a mere auxiliary in a constitutional struggle. Text, *op. cit.*, pp. 180-207.

110 When the prefects were asked in 1880 how the expulsions would be

received in their departments, the majority answered that, apart from sympathy toward certain charitable orders of women, the public would receive the order with equanimity. Their forecast proved generally correct, and there was no effective campaign against the Republic as a result of the expulsions.

111 Leo also feared that the situation would lead to a denunciation of the Concordat. While he accepted Separation in non-Catholic countries, he felt that in France it would be the signal for a new attack on religion and that the loss of governmental support would weaken the Church's activity. In his opinion, the success of Separation in the U. S. depended on the benevolent neutrality of the government, a condition absent in France.

112 *Don Quichotte,* a humorous anti-clerical publication with pornographic tendencies, carried a cartoon showing Leo and Bishop Freppel, an extreme monarchist, laughing at the trick that had been perpetrated through Lavigerie.

113 Cardinal Rampolla, Secretary of State, in a letter to the Archbishop of Paris, warned that the *Union* must not be an occult weapon against the Republic and defined the papal intention that the Republic must be accepted "without mental reservations and with the perfect loyalty that befits Christians." The *Union* was disolved.

114 Text, *op. cit.,* pp. 249-263.

115 No satisfactory study of the *Ralliement* exists. The standard treatments of Debidour (anti-clerical) and Lecanuet (Liberal Catholic) are both outdated. A new study based on archival sources is being prepared by John Woodall, an American scholar. The author of this essay is grateful to Dr. Woodall for access to the provocative material he has unearthed.

116 G. Weill, *Histoire du movement social en France,* 1852-1924, Paris F. Alcan, 1924, pp. 415-424; Byrnes, *op. cit.,* pp. 205-224.

117 An intense campaign against the Christian Democrats, particularly the Abbé Klein, for their adulation of American political instieal institutions cf Abbé F. Klein *La route du petit Morvandiau* 7 vols. Paris, Procure generale du clergè and Plon, 1946-49, Vol IV, pp. 5-437. These Memoirs of an active Liberal Catholic contain many interesting insights into the major issues around the turn of the century.

118 While in *Graves de Communi,* 18 Jan 1901, *op. cit.,* pp. 479-94, Leo rejected the Christian Democratic position that only one political form could fulfill the requirements of the Gospel, he continued to show them favor until his death, cf Lecanuet, *op. cit.,* p. 635.

119 The view of the Social Catholics that unions should include both employers and employees as in Medieval guilds. This failure to recognize the fundamental difference between handicraft conditions and industrialism had been a basic cause of the sterility of Social Catholicism. Fortunately the Christian unions did not repeat the mistake, cf. Paul Vignaux, *Traditionalisme et Syndicalisme* N. Y., Editions de la maison française, 1942, pp. 31-47; J. Zirnheld, *Cinquante années de Syndicalisme Chrétien,* Paris, Spes, n. d. pp. 13-96.

The development of Marxist and Revolutionary Syndicalist thought and action had an important influence on French opinion. It tended to moderate the anti-clericalism of the bourgeois Republicans. It forced Social Catholics to re-examine their positions. The evolution toward the Left in the Christian Trade Unions also appears to be a reaction to socialist and syndicalist stimulation.

120 *op. cit.,* pp. 34-57.

121 cf *Libre Parole* 24 August 1898.

122 For example, the issue of 16 April 1895.

[123] There were some 70-80,000 Jews in France. While many held responsible positions and some had been outstanding in the anti-clerical campaigns, anti-Semitic propaganda had completely distorted their attitudes and influence. There were 300 Jewish officers in the French army. The appointment of Captain Dreyfus to the General Staff had caused widespread dissatisfaction among his colleagues. cf Byrnes, *op. cit.*, passim.

[124] *La Comité catholique pour le défense du droit,* founded February 1897 by Paul Viollet, enlisted about 200, including many prominent scholars. A certain number of Catholic Dreyfusard tracts were published, e.g., Abbé Pichot's *La conscience chrétienne et l'affaire* (1898); a number of well-known priests, including the Abbés Fremont and Klein, appealed to their coreligionists in favor of revision. The Pope regretted the blindness of his French subjects and in 1899 ordered Père Bailly, the editor of *Croix,* to moderate his views; in the next year he took the journal from the control of the Assumptionists and had it entrusted to laymen. Many foreign bishops, like Vaughan of England and Ireland of the U. S. and most of the Catholic press outside France, supported Dreyfus. Yet Abbé Klein, who was in the forefront of all these struggles and who is still living in a suburb of Paris (1950), declared to the author of this essay that the Dreyfus Case was still the most deplorable and damaging fact in French Catholic history.

[125] His government was a cabinet of contradiction with the ministers disagreeing on all major issues, except anti-clericalism. cf. Moon, *op. cit.,* pp. 216-220.

[126] Debidour, *op. cit.,* Vol II, p. 314.

[127] Only five communities of men were granted authorization under the terms of the Law of 1901. The rest either went into exile or were secularized and continued as lay teachers. 3,040 in the preaching orders and 15,964 in the teaching communities were dispersed and their properties liquidated. Since many of these had taken no part in the Dreyfus Affair, the innocents were suffering with the guilty. To Combes it was a grand opportunity to settle old scores.

[128] *op. cit.,* p. 143.

[129] For the pertinent documents, cf *La Séparation de l'Église et de l'État en France, Exposé et documents,* (Rome Typograpie Vaticane, 1905), esp. pp. 226-240.

[130] 18 Departmental Councils declared themselves in favor of the law; 17 were against. The rest were silent on the issue. Adrien Dansette, in *De l'Affaire Dreyfus á la Question Scolaire, La vie intellectuelle* October 1951 puts it thus: Throughout the history of the III Republic, French Catholics were under the illusion that they represented the immense majority of their countrymen. In fact, in addition to the two Frances, religious and anti-religious, which are commonly recognized, there had grown a third during the past hundred years —the France of religious indifference—which was more numerous than either of the classic two, which remained minorities. The France of indifference accepted the cultural fact of Catholic traditions, but refused to submit themelvess to eclesiastical influences. For fuller treatment see, *Histoire religieuse de la France contemporaine, Tome II, Sous la IIe République,* Flammarion, Paris 1951, by the same author.

[131] For a discussion of this problem in broad terms, cf. J. V. Ducattillon, *La Guerre, cette révolution,* N. Y., Editions de la Maison Francaise, 1941, esp. pp. 61-89.

[132] F. Boulard, *Problèmes missionaires de la France rurale,* Paris, Editions du Cerf, 1945, Vol II, pp. 72-76. This excellent study cites incidents where in

the prestige of the clergy was further undermined by the withdrawal of State support. For more complete statistics, cf. *Guide de la France chrétiènne et missionaire 1948-1949*, Paris, Centre catholique international de documentations et statistiques pp. 229-438. e. g. Dijon had 506 priests in 1880; 250 today, with half over 60 years of age. For urban centers, cf. H. Godin et Y. Daniel, *La France, Pays de Mission?* Paris, Editions de L'abbaille, 1943, pp. 131-136; F. Boulard, Essor *au déclin du clergè française?* Paris, Editions du Cerf, 1950, esp. pp. 97-292.

133 A. Henry, *Bergson, Maître de Péguy*, Elzinir, Paris, 1948 p. 12 et passim.

134 Raissa Maritain, *We have been Friends Together*, N. Y. Longmans, 1942, pp. 79-140.

135 Bloy, too, gained stature by his repudiation of Drumont and anti-Semiticism, though some of his writing on this subject would cause resentment, cf *Le Salut par les Juifs*, Paris, Demey, 1892.

136 For some of the problems raised by the Modernist controversy, cf. B. A. Binchy, *The Modernist Movement*, Cambridge Journal, January 1948, Vol I, pp. 220-232.

137 *Op cit.*, pp. 271-302. For the role of an important figure in this controversy, cf. Mgr. A. Baudrillart, *Vie de Mgr. D'Hulst*, 2 vols, Paris, J. de Gigord, 1925, IIIème edition, Vol I, 449-492; Vol II, pp. 131-183. For the political views of the same important ecclesiastic, cf. Vol II., pp. 219-444.

138 *The Origins of the New Testament*, trans. by L. P. Jacks, London, Allen and Unwin, 1950.

139 Students in the universities sign invitations to their fellows to join in a corporate Easter Communion. In the *École Polytechnique* 4 signed in 1913, 61 in 1918, 139 in 1919, 5666 in 1925, 13,000 in 1930, and 18,642 in 1936, cf Brugerette, *op. cit.*, Vol III p. 24.

140 cf above pp. 146-7.

141 Debidour is critical of the Rallié mentality of these movements which appealed only to "pious aristocrats and well-intentioned bourgeoisie", *op. cit.*, Vol II, p. 331-2. Parker T. Moon, in *The Labor Problem and the Social Catholic Movement in France*, makes a spirited defense on the constructive nature of their programs. While too enthusiastic, it is true that they were in advance of realities and of the general bourgeois opinion of the time, but not radical enough to make any appeal to the working class. "All that the traffic would bear" might be a fair characterization.

142 Its leader, Abbé Desbuquois, rejected de Mun's utopian "mixed unions" and defended autonomous workers' associations. Majority opinion in the Semaines Sociales continued to favor the older view despite evidence of its unworkability. Marc Sangier and other Christian Democratic groups vigorously propounded the minority position at these annual meetings. For a discussion of Christian Democracy cf, *Christian Democracy in Italy and France*, by Mario Einaudi and François Goguel, University of Notre Dame Press, 1952.

143 Its name derived from the title of its review.

144 Sangnier was a masterful orator, with a great popular appeal; but he also was a fair controversalist. When the ex-Abbé Charbonnel, who had inspired attacks on Parisian churches, appeared before an open meeting on 23 May 1903, the crowd, overwhelmingly Sillonist, made a hostile demonstration. Sangnier calmed the audience with a moving appeal and the debate proceeded, cf Brugerette, *op cit.*, Vol III, p. 227.

145 There is some degree of truth in this claim, but it is doubtful if it will stand examination in light of the text: for the major points in the condemna-

tion, cf Hoog, *op. cit.*, pp. 179-190. Binchy, *op. cit.*, p. 225, puts the major emphasis on Modernism.

146 In the latter years of the war, it gave support to the *Comité de propagande catholique.*

147 Since that date, the Papacy has consulted the French government before the appointment of bishops.

148 19 August 1926. Andrieu was selected because he was known to be a sympathizer with the movement.

149 Full text of program in *Documentation catholique,* 19 June 1920, No. 72. It was adopted in the second national congress at Paris, 23-24 May 1924. For the procedings of the first congress, cf *idem,* 6 December 1919, No. 44.

150 9 CGT and 3 CFTC leaders signed this decree. It led directly to the dissolution of the CFTC by the Vichy government. For a sketch of the CFTC in the Popular Front period, cf Henry W. Ehrmann, *French Labor from Popular Front to Liberation,* N. Y., Oxford Univ. Press, 1947, pp. 126-138.

151 e.g., *"For the Common Good,"* a manifesto signed by 52 Catholic writers.

152 Brilliantly described by Charles A. Micaud, *The French Right and Nazi Germany,* 1933-1939, Duke Univ. Press, 1943.

153 569 voted for provisional plenary powers for Marshall Petain; 80, against.

154 Thomson, *op. cit.*, p. 223.

155 For a detailed and official, though not completely convincing, defense of the bishops' position, cf Mgr. Guerry, *L'Église catholique en France sous l'occupation,* Paris, Flammarion, 1947.

THE POLITICS OF FRENCH CATHOLICS
IN THE IV REPUBLIC

The broad variety of political views held by French Catholics indicates that the Church is either unable or unwilling to give the believers more than general directives. Even these can be interpreted in a variety of ways. Right-wingers and left-wingers have always been able to find quotations from the Encyclicals to justify the concepts of authority or of freedom, of hierarchy or of equality, of capitalism or of socialism, of cooperativism or of trade unionism.

The French hierarchy has also been cautious in recommending a specific course of political action. If most bishops supported the Vichy regime, they easily rallied to the liberal democratic MRP after the liberation. Since then some of them have shown their sympathy for the new RPF of General de Gaulle. They express their views as individuals and with prudence. There is no direct influence of the Church on French politics; the intervention of the clergy would be resented and would weaken rather than strengthen the position of the Church. The daily *La Croix* which some consider the unofficial mouthpiece of the archbishop of Paris, is cautiously apolitical in its conservatism and objective in its presentation of news. The only outwardly political Catholic daily was *l'Aube,* the organ of the MRP; it was careful to stress its independence from the hierarchy. Among Catholic periodicals all political views are expressed from the conservatism of *La France Catholique* to the progressive views of *Témoignage Chretien* and the radicalism of *L'Esprit.* It is also difficult to find a direct influence of the clergy in the many lay organizations such as the *Action Catholique,* the *Action Catholique de la Jeunesse française* and its many branches JOC, JAC, JEC, etc. The same applies, of course, to the MRP and the CFTC. The only organization where the clergy and lay Catholics work openly together is *les Semaines sociales,* a sort of itinerant university where professors, writers, labor leaders, and prelates meet once a year to study economic and social conditions and elaborate a Catholic position.

This non-committal position of the Church is in line with its traditional concern to avoid identification with a particular socio-political system; its primordial duty is to save souls and its spiritual mission demands the reaching of a *modus vivendi* with any regime as well as a certain detachment toward the various forms of political organization. This indifference toward political matters is balanced by an active concern with the guidance of believers in matters of faith and morals which in practice leads often to the handling of political directives as when general principles are being restated, deviations corrected, and errors denounced. But the framework of directives remains broad and the condemnation of non-conformists relatively rare and limited to extreme positions. Even then there is room for interpretation. Thus the recent decree of the Vatican forbidding Catholics to give support to the Communist Party was interpreted more generously by the leftist periodical *Esprit* and by the *Chrétiens progressistes* than it was by the organs of the majority.

This dilemma of the Church hesitating between indifference to political matters and intervention is reflected in the conflict between "intégrisme" and "modernisme," between a continued detachment in non-spiritual matters and the desire to adapt to secular pressures. Cardinal Suhard, Archbishop of Paris, attempted to define the position of the Church as half way between the two poles: it must integrate in a Christian perspective secular needs and values, modern techniques, and new forms of society and government, without sacrificing its spiritual mission and its lofty position well above the changing patterns of social organization.

The absence of a specific Catholic political ideology may be partly explained by the varied clientele of the Church and by its need to find an acceptable common denominator. The political outlook of believers is strongly influenced by economic and social factors; bourgeois, peasants, and workers vote less as Catholics than as members of their respective social groups. Similarly the different social origins of the higher and lower clergy is reflected in different social and political views.

Studies of electoral geography, such as those of André Siegfried and Gabriel le Bras have shown the complexity of the problem of Catholic political behavior. In the first place who is a Catholic? Objective criteria such as habitual or frequent attendance at Sunday mass are not easy to establish nor entirely reliable. If it is true that the regions of France where religion is still a strong factor have generally offered greater resistance to the penetration of the Marxist parties, it remains that some non-Catholic areas are more conservative than others where Church attendance is general. To explain the conservatism of the Western provinces Siegfried considered besides the continued influence of the clergy, such factors as the presence of large estates, the wide distribution of dwellings, and the relative lack of transportation.

In the past the anti-clerical issue was a major bloc to the reintegration of Catholics in the Republican fold as well as to their expression of left-wing political views. This obstacle has now largely vanished, thanks in part to the activity of many Catholics in the Resistance. After the liberation an historical accident gave the leadership of a large Catholic party to men with liberal democratic and socially progressive views who could profit by the discredit of former Rightist leaders and keep their hold on a heterogeneous rank and file. Later on the need to resist Communism and to a lesser extent neo-Gaullism brought the MRP and the Socialist Party into a close partnership that has further consolidated the status of the Catholic party as a true champion of democracy and has helped in keeping the ticklish problem of Church schools in the background.

The MRP could also convince many Catholics of the need for social reforms at a time when the weakened economic position of the middle classes made them more receptive to the need for social security and planned and controlled economy. But if this trend to the left is spectacular, it is also somewhat misleading. Two-thirds of the MRP voters abandoned their leaders for the RPF of General de Gaulle at the municipal elections of 1947. Perhaps this indicates that a majority of French Catholics, particularly among the older generations, are still traditionalist and conservative and ready to follow the strong man who promises order and security.

The following division of the political outlooks of French Catholics between a Right, a Center, and Left is somewhat arbitrary and oversimplified. It has the advantage, however, of corresponding to the three main ideological currents, authoritarian, liberal, and socialist, that have divided French Catholics for more than a century. The first trend, strong at the time of Vichy and unorganized after the liberation has now merged into Gaullism. The second and third currents have combined into the MRP and are difficult to distinguish within the party. Nor can the left-wing Catholics, led mainly by *Esprit*, be clearly separated from the MRP, except by their opposition to the concept of a Third Force and their reluctance to join the anti-Communist camp.

The Right

Although not organized in a political movement or in a philosophical school the authoritarian trend of French Catholicism has not entirely disappeared. A large number of French Catholics followed Marshall Pétain and his "National Revolution"; they have now found a new saviour in General de Gaulle whom they detested as the leader of the Resistance. The success of his RPF since 1947 is due largely to the defection of millions of the followers of the MRP who obviously had accepted its democratic leadership *faute de mieux*. A number of books have appeared in the last few years that attempt to whitewash the Vichy regime and its leaders; others are openly critical of parliamentary democracy and eagerly seek a paternalistic strong state on the cooperative pattern.

A few years after the overthrow of a hated authoritarian regime, it is not without significance to see a Catholic author restate the traditionalist theses of de Maistre, Veuillot, and Maurras with such commending frankness. In his *Histoire de la démocratie Chrétienne,* Robert Havard de la Montagne draws an impassioned prosecution of Christian democracy from Lamennais to the MRP.[1] According to him there is an irreconcilable opposition between the Catholic tradition and the French Republican tradition. All Catholics should be hostile to the Republican ideology and those who become Republican can no longer be good Catholics: "ils sont plus démocrates que chrétiens." The democratic tradition is anchored on an optimistic concept of man to which the author contrasts the realistic outlook of the Church. Democracy would be possible only if all men were good and equal in intellect and in virtue. Its false assumptions lead it inevitably to demagoguery and the irresponsible rule of the collective being; it is a source of disorder, immorality, and social disintegration.

In France, continues the author, the Republican tradition is anti-clerical and anti-Catholic. It makes for a secular religion in open and daily opposition to the Church. To accept the Republic is then to prepare the dechristianization of France. If, some seventy years ago, the Pope asked the believers to rally to the Republican regime, he was not asking them to accept the doctrines of the Republic but only the Republican form of government. The goal was to create a united front of all Catholics in order to put sufficient pressure to improve existing institutions for the advantage of the Church. Christian Democrats and even many liberal Catholics misinterpreted his intention and accepted the Republican doctrine. Thus the *Ral-*

liement became a source of weakness instead of strength for the Church; the Republic could consolidate itself and with the help of Catholics pursue its program of dechristianization. When in 1919 the Catholics controlled the Chamber of Deputies through the victory of the *Bloc national,* they did not even attempt to revise the unjust laws about Church schools; the secular poison had been absorbed by many Catholics and had led them to believe that "laïcité" was legitimate and necessary for the maintenance of liberty. A century ago Catholic liberals like Montalembert and Dupanloup had started this fatal evolution by demanding a "free church in a free state." Their mistake was to believe in freedom, as if liberty could be granted to both truth and error, to goodness and to evil, or if man did not need to be protected against falsehood and sin. It is only within a system of rigid rules that man can really be free. Liberty is a revolution against authority and the door is open to doubt, irresponsibility, and anarchy.

More guilty than the liberal Catholics were the Christian Democrats of the tradition of Lamennnais, of the "petits abbés democrates," and of the *Sillon* of Marc Sangnier. The author recalls the repeated denunciations of this democratic trend by the Vatican. He quotes Pius X condemnation of the *Sillon* as a false doctrine seeking to place all authority in the people and to aim at a levelling of classes, a doctrine that drew a blasphemous parallel between the Gospel and the Revolution; for Christ did not intend to instill in humble people a sense of independent dignity and of rebellion. This false doctrine continued to inspire *l'Aube,* the organ of Catholic democrats between the wars. It led it to advocate a militant *Briandisme* in its defense of collective security, to glorify the anti-clerical Republic, and even to flirt with the Communists during the period of the Popular Front. Now the MRP follows this tradition; it is a usurper and owes its electoral successes to the enforced absence of the legitimate leaders of French Catholics. It is partly responsible for the terror waged against the supporters of Pétain. It has openly adopted the doctrine of the Revolution and has dared to collaborate with the Marxist parties in the government. "Ils ont fait le Mal."

Such a book is indicative of an almost pathological fear of democracy viewed as the mother of revolutions. One can readily believe that the anti-clerical issue reviewed by the author is merely a rationalization of a deeper fear and of a passionate longing for an authoritarian order in a frozen hierarchial society.

Perhaps we have in Havard de la Montagne the representative of a dying political outlook. The younger generation seems to have lost all respect for the traditionalist and authoritarian doctrine preached by Maurras before the war. But in France, of all countries, political traditions are solidly entrenched. The more modern and semi-democratic outlook of the RPF presents the same appeal as the older and openly anti-democratic political creeds, namely the appeal of order and authority, to insecure people who lack the self-confidence required for democratic leadership.

The Center: Mouvement Républican Populaire

The greatest surprise of the general elections of October, 1945, was the spectacular success of a new party, the *Mouvement Républicain Populaire*. For the first time France had a large and disciplined non-Maxist party and for the first time Catholics had voted *en masse* for a party that was not identified with the Right.

The intellectual origins of the new party born in November, 1944, go back to the two currents in the 19th century which opposed the dominant authoritarian trend within the Church: liberal Catholicism, behind Montalembert, Dupanloup, and later Jacques Piou and some of the *Ralliés;* and the democratic and social movement behind Lamennais and later *Le Sillon* of Marc Sangnier. More recently it stemmed from the *Parti démocrate populaire* and the smaller and more genuinely pro-labor *Jeune République*. Both of these parties stressed their loyalty to the III Republic and their desire to bring about social reforms along the lines of the Papal encyclicals *De Rerum Novarum* and *Quadragesimo Anno* which condemned the abuses of capitalism as well as the atheistic materialism of Socialism. The first party was rather vague in its advocacy of social justice; it looked for a solution to class struggle outside capitalism and Marxism in some form of corporativism that would keep "free Trade Unions within the organized profession." The second was more explicit and favored a nationalized and a cooperative sector of the economy, besides the private one. In addition to these two small parties there existed a Catholic Trade Union movement, the CFTC., grouping mainly white-collar workers in addition to industrial workers in predominantly Catholic areas; its democratic and socialist left wing was making steady progress over the corporativist and paternalistic outlook of the right wing. These organizations, as well as various Catholic movements for the study of social conditions, such as the *Semaines sociales* and youth organizations such has JOC, JAC, and JEC, under the influence of the *Action Catholique*, prepared the ground for the coming success of the MRP.

If the Vichy regime had had the support of most of the Church hierarchy, many Catholics played an important role in the Resistance. Georges Bidault, former college professor and editorialist of *l'Aube,* had become the president of the National Council of the Resistance and other prominent leaders of the MRP such as de Menthon, Teitgen, Max André, Robert Lecourt, Albert Gortais had had a brilliant record. Clandestinity brought together men who formerly were divided by their political outlook; the anti-clericalism of many Socialists and the anti-Marxism of many Catholics melted away in the common struggle. Catholics and Socialists often found themselves in agreement over the purposes of the new *Socialisme humaniste,* its attempts at reconciling freedom and social justice and allowing maximum self-realization of individual capabilities against the double threat of capitalism and totalitarianism. Both could agree on the new "Charter of the Resistance," prepared in cooperation by the National Council of the Resistance; it asked for true political and social democracy, structural reforms of the economy, an expansion of social services, and the participation of workers in the management of industry.

The first Congress of the MRP stressed its goal of political, economic and social democracy, the conjunction between Christian values and the desire for liberation and renovation born of the Resistance. Each successive Congress continued to emphasize the double aim of democratic freedom and social justice. At the Congress of 1950, Teitgen, one of the MRP leaders, told the delegates that he refused for the party the destiny of a "grand parti conservateur intelligent" and Georges Bidault, its new president, used the formula "gouverner au centre avec des moyens de droite pour atteindre des buts de gauche." Despite the invitation of the *Modérés* to abandon the Socialists and lead a coalition of the Center and the Right, the MRP has steadily adhered to its alliance with the SFIO. It has also been consistent in its opposition to neo-Gaullism which Teitgen accused of aiming at a "République des notables."

The political philosophy of the MRP as outlined by Jacques Maritain, Etienne Gilson, Albert Gortais and others is in many ways the Catholic version of the Fabian attempt to build a free and just society. Freedom is a value transcending time and space; it stems from the very nature of man, his ability to know, hence to choose and to assume responsibility for his acts. It is the expression of the dignity of the human person and the condition for its growth. It demands the unconditional respect

for the rights of man guaranteed by laws as well as the unhampered practice of political democracy. The MRP emphasizes its basic optimism concerning the ability of man to govern himself and its irreconcilable opposition to the pessimistic
premises of the authoritarians. "Our affirmation of democracy,"
wrote Gilson, "expresses the certitude that those who despise
the people are responsible for the state in which they keep it
so as to have the right to despise it. To trust the people is only
a practical way of affirming our reasoned faith that forces us to
want a government by the whole people, the control of which
can never be given up to a party, or a class, or a man."

Freedom is not absence of restraints. Its counterpart is responsibility. For man is a social being with definite duties towards the community. The extreme individualism taught by
classical liberalism is anti-social and immoral. It must be replaced by a sense of civic duty without which the democratic
state is bound to collapse and to give place to a regime based on
force. "Liberty," said Armand Colin, the general secretary of
the party, "is not only an opportunity, but a responsibility.
One loses the opportunity if one escapes the responsibility."
The citizen must be made to understand the problems facing
his society and to accept sacrifices for the good of the whole
community. He must be made to participate actively in the
conduct of public affairs at the local and national levels. It is
not enough for him to vote once every few years and to feel
that he has discharged his responsibilities toward the state; such
an attitude invites opportunism and cynicism and has contributed to the discredit of parliamentary institutions in the III Republic. It also invites dictatorship. The MRP sees in the attraction of Gaullism an "escape from freedom," an attempt at
unburdening one's own responsibilities into the strong hands
of a saviour who is to be followed blindly. This betrays escapism and "a spirit of *demission* which is the death of democracy."
De Gaulle's offer of constitutional salvation is superficial and
misleading and can only leave unsolved the problems facing
France.

To protect freedom, increase the sense of civic duty, and
prevent the state from dictating its will to the community, the
MRP advocates a pluralistic society in which the natural social
structures—family, town, church, profession, trade unions, etc.
—ought to be protected against centralizing tendencies. The
role of the state would be to promote and coordinate their respective activities and not to replace them by its omnicom-
petence. Hence the MRP's attempt to create a direct representation of these social structures in a second Chamber in order to

complement the representation of individuals in the classical manner of parliamentary democracy.

If democracy requires responsibility on the part of the citizens, its survival is also dependent upon their efforts to bring about a more just society. Justice does not mean absolute equality of all; it means preventing social inequalities from being added to the natural inequalities of men. The MRP holds the bourgeoisie responsible for having established a social order based on the inequality of classes and lack of opportunity for the underprivileged, while at the same time proclaiming the formal equality of all before the law. The problem is to allow the many to fulfill their potentialities even if it means the curtailment of the freedom of the few. "Une égalité democratique des personnes amènerait le plein development de la petitesse de petits comme de la grandeur des grands."

Nothing short of social justice can answer the challenge of Communism. "Communism," wrote Albert Gortais, assistant secretary of the party, "is the mortal sin of the modern world. It is born of the bad conscience of a society that has not known how to improve the human condition of its members. In some quarters many would be glad to get rid of the menace without having at the same time to cleanse their own conscience." Since Communism is born of the misery and alienation of the workers the only effective way of fighting it is the erection of a just social order. Social justice becomes an element of national defense; it is no use condemning the "séparatistes" so long as conditions are not created that will give the workers a real stake in the defense of their country, so long as an end is not put to the exploitation of man by man.

On the other hand the materialistic philosophy of Marxism which ignores the autonomy of the spirit as well as the methods used by the Communists condemns their revolution as destructive of the highest human values. If man must be liberated from the abuses of capitalism he cannot be given the alternative of enslavement by the totalitarian state. The only fruitful Revolution—one that is both lasting and respectful of the dignity and freedom of man—is the "Revolution by the law." Reforms are more effective as a method of change than violence.

The program of reforms of the MRP follows the main lines of the encyclicals of Lee XIII and Pius XI, reinterpreted to fit new conditions. Private property must be open to all as the best safeguard of individual freedom and the best means of allowing the full development of the human person. But property is not a privilege, it is a function. When it comes to the ownership of the means of production the state is justified in

creating a nationalized sector of the economy in order to transform a private monopoly into a public one for the interest of
the whole nation. The state must also control competition and
limit its abuses. It is its duty to develop a broad system of
social security. The best alternative to *laissez-faire* capitalism
is not, however, state collectivism, but the association of capital
and labor through the participation of workers in the management and profits of industry. As a step in this direction the
MRP has helped to create the shop committees (comités d'entre-
prise) that prepare workers to assume future responsibilities.
Only through "associations" can they be reintegrated in the
national community and feel co-partners of management instead of its victims. In the meanwhile trade unions must remain
strong and independent. For the goal is not corporatism of the
fascist type, but according to the formula of Paul Vignaux
"les syndicates libres dans la profession organisée."

The originality of the MRP rests less with its political and
social philosophy than with its attempts at finding empirical
answers to problems facing France and at educating the public
in understanding those problems and accepting necessary sacrifices. The emphasis in the party is less on abstract principles
than on finding solutions to concrete and immediate problems.
The party prides itself on its realistic approach to such problems
as prices and wages, housing, taxation, administrative reforms,
which are studied and discussed by local groups as well as by
national congresses. It contrasts its empirical approach to that
of other parties which subordinate action to the discussion of
principles. The zeal of the MRP is to secure a large basis of
agreement among Frenchmen for the solution of concrete
problems rather than add to fruitless ideological controversies.
With this in mind the party has organized study groups and
published pamphlets that spread information concerning administrative, economic and social matters. It has teams of
"militants" whose goal is to help educate the public and
make it accept its responsibilities.

The party prides itself on not having escaped its own responsibilities. It feels that it was its duty to participate in the
government alongside Socialists and even Communists under
most difficult conditions and in spite of the electoral risks
involved. It justifies its collaboration with the left on two
accounts: the need to participate in a common effort for
economic reconstruction and the need to prevent the creation
of a purely leftist coalition under Communist leadership. It
proved its democratic convictions by refusing to follow General
de Gaulle when he made his spectacular exit in January, 1946,

and a year later by becoming one of the pillars of the Third Force.

Yet for the two years following the liberation the MRP had prided itself on its loyalty to the General: it was "le parti de la fidélité." To this identification it owed part of its early electoral successes, as the party closest to the heart of the great liberator. Its main appeal perhaps came from the belief on the part of many that it presented the best protection against Communism, at a time when the Rightist parties had been discredited, the SFIO was unreliable, and the small parties of the Center without sufficient strength and dynamism. The new party appealed not only to the Catholic progressives but to the traditionally conservative masses, particularly of the Western and Eastern Provinces; it was supported by the clergy, either out of conviction or of necessity. It appealed also to many non-Catholic elements who saw in the strengthening of the Church a necessary element of order and discipline in a troubled world. To some it appeared as the Left wing of the Right, to others as the Right wing of the Left. Even the Communist campaign against the MRP—"une machine à rassembler les Pétainistes"—was an asset. So was the new electoral law and the *reflex* of *voter utile*.

By the time of the municipal elections of the Fall of 1947, the party had lost its major electoral assets; it was no longer de Gaulle's party, it no longer appeared effective in the struggle against Communism, and it had become identified with the failures and shortcomings of the past governments. Some two-thirds of its electors abandoned it for the new RPF of General de Gaulle. In Paris it had lost four-fifths of its following. In spite of grave electoral risks, the party had remained in the government in January, 1946, along with Socialists and Communists after the departure of the general, had accepted a constitution of leftist inspiration, and had continued to be friendly to the Socialists, much to the scandal of the "bien-pensants." The second referendum in June, 1946, made clear that the latter had not followed the party advice to vote for the new constitution.

Yet, despite successive "crises de conscience" and an electoral disaster, party discipline was maintained: only a handful of MRP deputies followed the RPF, most local organizations remained loyal. The party membership acquired new homogeneity and strength. At the cantonal elections of the Spring of 1950 the MRP regained some lost ground and the following congress met in an atmosphere of optimism.

One reason for this success in keeping discipline is the

organization of the party; another, the character of the membership and leadership. The formal organization resembles that
of the Socialist SFIO: it provides for a national Congress and
Council, an Executive Committee, as well as local sections and
federations. The basic difference is that the Executive Committee is made up of a majority of Parliamentarians and of a
minority of representatives of party members elected by regional councils. This provides for effective control of the party
by the Parliamentary leadership, which allows for continuity
of policy and greater elasticity of tactics since the leaders are
not at the mercy of a change of directives by the militants. It
may be added that the Executive Committee has more effective
control over the party candidates than the *Comité Directeur*
of the SFIO, another advantage in maintaining discipline. This
advantage may partly explain that attachment of the MRP for
the present electoral system: a return to the single member
district would weaken the party both electorally and organically.

Another factor that explains the continued cohesion of the
party is the homogeneity of its membership which contrasts
with the heterogeneity of the electorate. The MRP has recruited its militants largely among practicing Catholics, most
of whom have a common political and social outlook anchored
on common religious convictions. Added to this binding force
is the fact that this is a young party that unlike the SFIO has
had no time yet to develop competing sects. Its young men and
women are eager for service and trained to respect their leaders
and doctrines. They have formed teams, "équipes ouvrières,"
"équipes rurales," that effectively reach various occupational
groups and take their educational role very seriously. Perhaps
the religious background of the militants, often trained in
Catholic-sponsored J.O.C., J.A.C., J.E.C., explains their willingness to accept discipline and group action, as well as the
earnestness of their efforts. In this sense the MRP has a greater
pool of human resources to draw upon than any other party,
except the Communists: the qualities of faith, devotion to a
cause, and willingly accepted discipline are present in both
parties.

As in the Communist party, emphasis is put on giving
workers—generally white-collar workers and artisans—priority
over "bourgeois" in positions of responsibility. The party has
also a larger percentage of women both in Parliament and in
party organization than any other except the Communists.
Although not a "confessional" party under the direct influence
of the clergy, the MRP is essentially a party of Catholics; it
must be identified with a faith rather than with a class. It

recruits among all occupational groups, particularly among the lower middle classes.

It has often been observed that the MRP lacks the "stars" of the SFIO or Radicals, brilliant leaders who have their own ideas and following. Perhaps this is due to the youth of the party and the absence of leaders trained in the parliamentary arena of the Third Republic. More likely it is the result of the "cultural pattern"of the Catholic membership: high valuation is put on hard work, earnestness, solidity, reliability, and team work. The ideal leader is Robert Schuman, serious and hard-working rather than brilliant. It is perhaps characteristic that the more magnetic and nervous Maurice Schumann, "the voice of London" and the first president of the party soon disappeared from the party firmament. Besides the new president Georges Bidault, and M. Teitgen, a vigorous and outspoken foe of the Communists, there are few outstanding personalities, although a large number of competent men.

In spite of frequent rumors about dissension within the party, the threatened split has never occurred. Probably the differences of outlook among the leaders of the Right and Left wings are not major ones and the party discipline, as well as its empirical approach, have continued to be binding forces.

The party has suffered from its continued participation in the government and from the basic handicap of having to fight on two fronts for the defense of the regime. It has lost many of its conservative supporters to de Gaulle and has been discredited in the eyes of Catholic left-wingers who criticize the impotence of the Third Force governments and even question the sincerity of the party's aspirations toward social justice.

The Left

There are a number of periodicals representing the positions of Catholics at the left of the MRP. The most widely read is *Témoignage Chrétien* with a circulation of about 100,000. Born during the Resistance it has succeeded in giving its large audience a multi-sided and non-conformist interpretation of the domestic and international scene by a brilliant group of writers. It has championed such varied causes as a socialistic Europe independent of East and West, cooperative experiments and the independence of Viet Nam. It is not systematically opposed to the concepts and methods of the Third Force and its position represents the views of many left-wing supporters of the MRP. Another periodical *Temps Présent*, born at the liberation, became the heir of *Sept*, a progressive Catholic

weekly before the war; financial difficulties forced it to fold
up after a promising start. More recently a group of young
Catholics have produced a monthly with the youthfully defiant
title of *Les Mal Pensants,* while the pro-Communist *Chrétiens
Progressistes* publish their own monthly *Positions.* On a more
technical level mention should be made of *Économie et Humanisme* whose study groups attempt to find concrete solutions
to economic and social problems along the line of a "socialisme
humaniste."

The most important of all left-wing Catholic publications
is *Esprit.* Under the leadership of a brilliant young publisher,
Emmanuel Mounier, who died in 1949, *Esprit* has represented
the most significant attempt at filling the void between the
Third Force and Communism. It opposes what it considers
the hopeless and somewhat hypocritical reformist policy of the
MRP and stands for radical changes in economic and social
structure.

The success of *Esprit* (even among non-Catholic intellectuals)
is due partly to the forcefulness, competence, and integrity
with which Mounier and his teammates have presented to their
readers some of the most important and controversial problems
facing France. Special issues of the revue have dealt courageously with such delicate issues as the rebirth of Fascism
under de Gaulle, France's mishandling of her colonial problems, the Frenchman's lack of civic responsibility, etc.

Another reason for the influence of *Esprit* is the fact that
it represents a complete philosophy as well as a method of
political action; to some extent it plays among non-Communist
left wingers the role that *Action Française* played among the
Rightist intellectuals before the war. Its intellectual and spiritual foundation is the doctrine of *Personnalisme,* a Christian
and progressive interpretation of man and history. It is not
original since its themes are borrowed from those of *le Sillon*
as well as the theses of Charles Renouvier and R. P. Laberthonière. If it is somewhat confused, the fault may be found
with the very nature of the synthesis that it seeks in this
particular historical setting.

Akin to "socialisme humaniste" it has overtones of existentialism and a strong injection of Marxism. Catholicism
furnishes an integrated system that justifies and explains the
supreme values of freedom, responsibility, and love in a community of Christian brotherhood. The influence of existentialism is apparent in the concept of the tragic existence of man
and his need to commit himself and to accept the risks of his
"engagement," Mounier sees in both existentialism and personal-

ism "a reaction of the philosophy of man against the philosophy of ideas and the philosophy of things." His reaction against spiritualism and his desire to see man merge into the concrete world has led Mounier to accept a number of Marxist propositions, such as the essential role played by economic structures on social, cultural and political developments, the reality of class struggle and the need for bringing about collective ownership of the means of production through revolutionary action. Above all he admires in Marxism the most effective instrument for social transformation and the most vigorous call to revolt. The efforts of the Third Force, he dismisses as necessarily sterile because of the class context of the parties in the center coalition. It is only through the active support of the working class that reforms can be made.

This conviction has dictated his attitude toward Communism. Although critical of it before the war as a philosophy that gives no place to spiritual reality and the values of freedom and love, he came after the liberation to share a widely held illusion. The Resistance, he explained, had given a unique chance to reintegrate the Communist party in the national community and to allow it to become a truly French socialist party. It was imperative for all the generous forces of the country to ally themselves with the Communists who had become largely identified with the working classes since nothing revolutionary could be done without their vigor and determination. The good society would come about from the creative shock between a dynamic Revolutionary movement and a rejuvenated Church liberated from its medieval and bourgeois ties. If a synthesis of Marxism and Catholicism was not Mounier's main concern, he affirmed that the two were not irreconcilable enemies. Some day the Church might even bless a new Communism freed from its narrow and doctrinaire materialism, just as it had come to accept democracy. Another reason for keeping an alliance with the Communists was the grave danger of Fascism that remained the main enemy.

Not until 1949 did Mounier admit the impossibility of an alliance with the Communist party since it had proved its complete disregard for truth and human dignity, its blind admiration for the Soviet Union and total subordination to its interests, its complete lack of morality, and its refusal to respect the autonomy of allied groups. Yet *Esprit* continued to refuse to join the anti-Communist camp. For an all-out war against the party would be at the expense of the working class. *Esprit* would continue to side with the Communists whenever necessary to protect the values of material security and social dignity, against them when necessary to protect intellectual honesty, spiritual freedom and civic responsibility. It was still considered necessary to offer a revolutionary alternative to Communism, to keep in close touch with the workers and to try to help reestablish their freedom of inspiration and of action.

Thus Mounier delivered a double "non possumus": for the sake of higher human values he rejected a close alliance with the Communists and for the sake of revolutionary change he refused the solution of the Third Force. He wanted to combine the importance of the individual and the efficacy of Revolution, and not sacrifice one value to the other. Although this position is justified on the theoretical plane, it is perhaps unrealistic. So far the non-Communist left has been unable to present a united front capable of effective action. The many sects and coteries remain intellectual gatherings out of touch with the rank and file of the proletariat. Can the revolutionary ideal be recaptured from the Communists by men who, being vitally concerned with intellectual honesty and moral integrity, cannot offer an effective weapon for the overthrow of the present order? Given this basic handicap a reformist outlook appears to be the only alternative to a revolutionary goal that is unrealizable except under Communist leadership and with Communist methods. The values of freedom and justice so courageously defended by *Esprit* could be served more effectively if its followers acted within the existing political organizations and gave them the impetus necessary for reforms. In the context of a bipolar world, it becomes dangerous to weaken the forces that stand for freedom by refusing to support them for an assumed lack of efficacy which this refusal contributes to create. The resentment of left-wing supporters of MRP at the attack of *Esprit* is somewhat justified.

One must admire, however, its stubborn refusal to sacrifice principles, its vigor, and its absolute integrity. On the long run Mounier's faith in the virtue of "Témoignage," of standing up for the defense of truth and justice against any quarters may have to be justified from the political as well as from the moral standpoint.

From this brief outline of the political attitudes of French Catholics, few generalizations can be made. The politics of French Catholics are not substantially different from the politics of other Frenchmen; they are characterized by the same weakness for abstract principles and logical construction of the mind, by an intellectual propensity combined with an emotional fervor, the ingredients for a political ideology. The

pragmatic outlook of the MRP represents an effort at swim-
ming against the current.

In spite of this diversity of political views, the postwar trend
is characterized by a vigorous reassertion of the rights of the
human person that takes the shape of a defense of political
and social democracy. As a consequence French Catholics have
been largely reintegrated into the Republican family and have
shown a surprising eagerness at accepting the theme of social
reforms. This trend toward the left has however slowed down
under the general distaste for administrative red tape and the
inefficiency and high costs of some of the nationalized enterprises and of social security. It is now being challenegd by the
powerful right swing of the RPF and undermined by a general
apathy and demoralization in the face of the threat of both
Communism and the Soviet Union.

The prospects for the growth of Christian democracy must
be viewed in a French, European, and world perspective. The
domestic situation is far from bright; the Communist party has
succeeded in identifying itself with the fate of the working
classes. It has capitalized on the shortcomings, mistakes and
apathy of the government and has presented itself as the only
party genuinely interested in the well-being of the workers.
It has also succeeded in launching a counter-revolutionary
movement under de Gaulle that has vitally handicapped the
center parties. Whether the Third Force will maintain its
position in the coming elections is dubious; a process of polarization around the two extremes is not unlikely.

In the European and world perspective this process of polarization has already taken place. Fear of war and of the subsequent occupation of western Europe has led to several forms
of escapism, whether the negative one of neutralism or the
positive one of European federation. Catholics have been active
in both. The growing movement for European Federation is
perhaps most significant. It represents a new sense of solidarity
between Catholic parties in the various Western European
countries as well as a growing realization that the nation-state
is outdated and that a larger unit of defense and welfare is
necessary. To some extent it represents a desire to escape from
domestic responsibilities. At the Strasbourg assembly of the
Council of Europe in 1950, most Catholic delegates favored the
concept of European federation. The refusal of Great Britain
and Scandinavia to tie their hands led to a split in the French
delegation; George Bidault and his friends were unwilling to
risk a breach with those Socialists who opposed the creation
of a "Vatican Europe." As a result the motion of A. Philip

favoring Western European unity was defeated by a large
majority. This is perhaps significant of the genuine desire of
the MRP to maintain its close alliance with the Socialists and
to avoid any ground for suspecting the existence of a "Black
International." It is also indicative of the difficulties of launching a new "idée-force" capable of competing with the appeal
of the Communist millennium. Yet it is perhaps in the direction
of European unity that rest the best chances of effective resistance to Communism, demoralization, and panic. In concert
with the Socialist and Liberal parties, Christian democracy can
play a vital role in the realization of the dream of European
unity.

CHARLES A. MICAUD

CHAPTER III

CHRISTIAN TRADE UNIONISM
SINCE WORLD WAR II

The French Experience

At the last elections for workers' representatives on the Administrative Councils of the Social Security Boards (8 June 1950), the candidates offered by the *Confédération Française des Travailleurs chrétiens* (CFTC) obtained 1,172,612 votes against 2,392,067 for those of the *Confédération Générale du Travail* (CGT), and 832,934 for those of the *Confédération Générale du Travail-Force Ouvière* (CGT-FO). The CGT, the "old home" of French labor, fell under Communist control after the Liberation. The non-Communist elements who seceded in December, 1947, make up the CGT-FO. The CFTC is the central organization of the Christian Trade Unions. Since 1933 when the German Christian union movement disappeared—it has not been reconstituted after World War II—the CFTC is the most important Christian workers' movement in the world. Hence we propose a brief analysis of contemporary problems of Christian trade unionism in Europe on the basis of the French experience.

I

To follow recent developments and to grasp their significance, it is important to recall certain general conditions in the historical development of the European working class.

Christian trade unionism was the product of continental European conditions, and is not exclusively French. When a Catholic from the United States or the British Commonwealth asks one of his French, Belgian or Dutch co-religionists, "Why Christian trade unions?" it is not an adequate answer to point to the social doctrine of the Church which inspires these organizations. Beyond this fact lies the deeper one that continental Catholics have not been free to promote this social doctrine in the workers' organizations which have existed in their respective countries. Roughly similar conditions in their national areas induced them to establish similar organizations. At the end of World War I, these coalesced into the *Confédération Internationale des Syndicats Chrétiens*. Up till that time, the French Christian workers had no central organization. In 1919 they federated in the CFTC in order to join the Christian International.

Trade Unionism of Christian inspiration, then, is framed in an international grouping of similar European organizations which provides it support. Today there is still a relationship between the CFTC and the *Confédération Internationale des Syndicats Libres*. These bonds with Belgium and Holland, with Germany before Hitler and Italy before Mussolini, have not prevented deep divergencies among the various Christian groups, of which one must be noted: the Christian Trade Unions of the above-mentioned countries are completely committed to non-political or purely economic unionism; yet they could count upon the political support of at least a section of a powerful political party, Catholic or Christian Democrat, which frequently held posts in the government. It was only after much effort and at a relatively late date that a political party of this character made its appearance in French democracy. Its formation provided a note of novelty to the problem of the relation between the CFTC and the MRP, which arose after the Liberation.

The relations between the trade unions and the parties developed differently in France and in its European neighbors. At the dawn of the twentieth century, the CGT had affirmed its independence of all political parties. This was a distinctive characteristic which made it different from the other European labor confederatons, which were generally strictly bound to the Socialist parties. The old CGT, before the Stalinist penetration, was not "socialist by party, but by doctrine," to borrow a phrase of Léon Jouhaux. Its leaders used the word "socialism" in the sense of "revolutionary syndicalism" before World War I; after that war, they equated it with "the syndicalism of reconstruction." This syndicalism, frequently hostile to political personalities, was never narrowly isolated. It did not hesitate to intervene in political life, partcularly when it considered that democracy was imperiled.

In the nineteenth century, the French working class movement had been closely associated with republicanism, and through it with anti-clericalism. It was "lay," and even irreligious. This attitude was not primarily shaped by Marxist influence. Before falling under Communist control, the CGT was not too rigid in Marxian orthodoxy, as the Social Democratic workers' organizations in the neighboring countries could be. It is the totality of this situation, and particularly the anti-clericalism of the CGT leadership, which must be grasped in order to understand in what sense the founders of the French

Christian trade union movement could reject the CGT and share the *anti-Socialist* position that we find at the root of Catholic trade unionism. In France, this *anti-Socialism* must be conceived, not in the strict doctrinal sense, but in all the characteristics of the early CGT, especially its anti-clericalism.[1]

When the first Christian trade unions were formed in the Belgian textile mills at Ghent or in the mines of the Ruhr, their founders were workers dissatisfied with the recently established ascendency of the Socialists over ancient working class organizations. Before they established a Christian trade unionism, these workers had tried to maintain a religiously neutral organizaton alongsde the Soicalist trade unions. This had been their experience before *Rerum Novarum*. It was also before that encyclical that the *Syndicat des Employés du Commerce et de l'Industrie* was founded in Paris (1887). It was inspired by a Brother of the Christian Schools and enlisted some members of a religious association who wished to unite the Catholic white collar workers of Paris.

When one reviews the history of the different countries of Europe or of the different regions of France, it is not exactly correct to say with André Philip that Christian trade unionism "was not born of a workers' revolt, but from a systematic effort to realize a social doctrine."[2] One would be nearer the facts if one said that the movement stemmed from the need of a trade union organization among those wage-earners who, because of their religious convictions, did not feel themselves at home in the continental trade union movement as it had developed in the last quarter of the nineteenth century.

At their beginning, the Christian trade union members did not gain the support of the Social Catholics, who were still wedded to the concept of the "mixed union" which would gather employers and employees into one organization as in the Old Regime. It was only later, and by slow steps, that the Christian trade unions, which were autonomous organizations of wage-earners, could appeal to a Catholic social doctrine, elaborated after *Rerum Novarum* by the *Semaines Sociales* of France.[3] The atmosphere became more and more understanding of a working class movement to the degree that Catholics in France accepted political democracy with greater conviction.

Certain characteristics of the CFTC, strongly marked up till 1936, can be traced to the circumstances of its origin and early development: a tendency to organize groups which were explicitly Catholic—a condition rather rare in the French industrial world; the preponderant influence of the white collar workers, organized in the most powerful of its federations; the necessity for constant reference to Catholic social doctrine to justify itself against the charge of trade union pluralism from the "socialist" organizations and to defend itself against the criticisms, either violent or false, of the "Catholics of the Right" who were sympathetic with the employers. It is also important to recall the politico-religious struggles which, practically up till 1919 at least, had kept Catholics on the margin of the life of the Third Republic. This fact exercised a decisive influence on several generations, and notably on that which had founded the CFTC.

I have explained elsewhere [4] how the Christian trade union movement developed from its beginnings through the inter-war period and up till the winter of 1941. In this evolution, the social crisis of 1936 assuredly marked an important test: the CFTC succeeded in increasing its effectives sufficiently to avoid being submerged (it was only a trade union minority) in the enormous increase in membership of the CGT, which had just been rejoined by the CGTU.[5] This combined and augmented movement had adhered to the Popular Front, which was victorious in the elections of 1936. In the same year, the Christian trade union organizations managed to assert themselves vigorously in the widespread strikes; to maintain the right to join a minority union in the factories and mines; to recruit in several weeks thousands of new members in their places of work— members who were not necessarily practising Catholics; finally, to give a truly national scope to their confederation which till then had been a cluster of regional forces.

The successful meeting of this test placed the CFTC in a national and international context which must be understood to comprehend further developments, Among the national factors of growth, there must be noted the first influx of young militants trained in the *Jeunesse Ouvrière Chrétienne* (JOC). These young people had acquired in the JOC a most vivid sense of the autonomy, unity and collective destiny of the working class. In addition, there was the revival of the trade union structure by a group of university-trained youth who were alert to all the most recent efforts of Catholic thought and of social research. Finally, the CFTC benefited by the methodical analysis of the French social crisis, 1936-1938, of the United States New Deal, and of the conflict between free trade unionism and the corporate states of the Fascist type. Hence the ideology of the CFTC distinguished radically between its proposals and the corporativism which intrigued the Catholics of the Right and which prepared the social concepts of the Vichy regime. This intellectual growth in France was tied to two foreign experiences: the destruction of Christian trade unionism in Italy by Mussolini and in Germany by Hitler; the establishment by the Austrian Chancellor Dollfuss of state-controlled trade unions and the struggle between the forces of Franco and the Basque Catholic trade unions. In a Europe where only the western fringe retained a free labor movement, Socialists and "Christians," despite their old opposition, had to face the same problems. Thus the conditions were prepared for a democratic working class resistance to the further expansion of Fascism.

It is not necessary here to analyze the circumstances and forms of the Christian trade union participation in the Resistance (1940-1944), but merely to sketch the results of this participation in its subsequent development. In refusing the *Charte du Travail* of Vichy, which was partly an imitation of the pseudo-trade unionism of the Fascists and partly an expression of archaic paternalism, Christian trade unionists did not merely reaffirm their irreducible opposition to every totalitarian regime. They equally divorced themselves from the traditionalism which still remained in certain Catholic social circles. This traditionalism included the ideology or sentiment of Counter-Revolution which could entertain a depth of hostility to free trade unionism and political liberty that is hard to imagine in English-speaking democracies. In taking its position against the *Charter*, the Christian trade unionists showed their independence of action toward the greater part of the episcopate. This was an important fact in a country where the majority, politically anti-clerical, traditionally wonders whether the loyalty of Catholics to democracy is not a pose of pure opportunism to be modified with the appearance of an authoritarian regime, apparently favorable to religion. By their opposition to the internal policy of Vichy, as well as their other work in Resistance, the Christian trade unionists forged new ties with those of other beliefs. At the Liberation, Christian trade unionism was accepted, without a trace of dissent, as one of the three currents of the French working class movement, the other two being the Socialist-syndicalist of Léon Jouhaux and his friends, and the Communist. Events had encouraged a considerable expansion of the last-named.

One of the founders of the CFTC and its Secretary General since its inception, Gaston Tessier, was a member of the National Council of Resistance. This was the clearest expression of the moral position acquired by the movement, a position that would help it surmount all the difficulties which appeared on the morrow of Liberation.

II

These difficulties did not fail to make themselves felt in the second half of 1944-1945. Units that were scattered by the war had to be reconstituted from the bottom. There was the need for implanting Christian trade unionism in areas previously impervious to its influence in the face of the formidable pressure of the CGT, now controlled in the key industries and the principal working class centers by its Communist directors. Perhaps the most remarkable success was achieved by the federation recreated in the nationalized Gas and Electricity industry by a young militant of exceptional ability, Fernand Hennebicq. In this field, the older majority union was led by a Communist who had been in charge of nationalization and who was Minister of Production. Hennebicq, who died before his thirtieth birthday in 1950, was only the most remarkable example in the CFTC of a new militant generation who could speak a common language with all trade unionists—a language so different from the traditional Catholic social idiom—and who could interpret the demands of French labor in a way that could compete progressively with the veteran Communist leadership.

These young men gave a new power to the CFTC. In the meantime, the current of trade union unity, which was less defined in France, led Italian and German Catholics to abandon plans to reconstruct their separate trade unions, which were once so powerful. This reduced Christian trade unionism to a phenomenon almost uniquely French, Belgian and Dutch. But the character of the French organization diverged more and more from the confessional type in vogue in the Low Countries and Flanders. On one point, however, a resemblance developed with these countries: a powerful Christian democratic party, the MRP, appeared and presented itself as the party of legal revolution (*révolution par la loi*). It was an attempt at a synthesis of the revolutionary aspirations of the Resistance and the juridical and moral tradition of the Social Catholics.

In the *Congress of Liberation* (September 1945), the young militants of the CFTC, unknown in the pre-war days and coming up from the Resistance and the JOC, took a minority position on two principal problems in an atmosphere of public debate, itself something new in the CFTC. These were the issue of the vigorous affirmation of the independence of trade unions with regard to political parties, and of the modification of the trade union organizational structure that would set up industrial unions to unite the white collar workers and technicians in metallurgy, the chemical industry, etc. with the manual workers in the same branches. Obviously the Federation of Clerical Workers, Technicians and Foremen, who were a powerful factor in the politics and thinking of the CFTC, opposed this reform.

The struggle for strict political independence, led by Fernand Hennebicq, was successful in the Congress of June 1946. Here it was decided that members of the secretariat and of the Confederal Bureau of CFTC could not unite their position "with the exercise of the office of deputy or councillor general, or with any function in the national or departmental leadership of a political party." This resolution was adopted by 4,006 votes to 1,255 for a less rigorous resolution proposed by the Federation of Railroad Workers.[6] The same resolution had been defeated in the Congress of September 1945 by 2,112 votes to 1,341. The overthrow of the majority had evidently been the result of profound reasons since the electoral victory of the MRP did not at all deter the supporters of an absolutely clear distinction between trade union and political activity. Political and trade union leaders might have common ties of origin, but their responsibilities were different, and hence they must be sharply distinguished. The CFTC wuld not allow itself to be considered an organization under the thumb of the MRP. As a result, the Christian unions were unshaken when, in the years 1949-1950, there arose a profound discontent in the ranks of non-Communist labor over the policy of the governments of the Third Force, and even of the attitude of the MRP.

Two other debates stirred the Congress of 1946. The first, carried over from the preceding year, concerned trade union structure. Thanks to its old-established influence, the Federation of white-collar workers gained its point by 3,357 votes to 1,700. The minority in favor of industrial unionism had gained in one year from 21% of the votes to 33%. The debate was not resumed in the succeeding Congresses. Industrial unionism apparently must be realized by a spontaneous evolution, under the pressure of technical needs, and in keeping with the attitude of the diverse groups. Yet in every way, the influence of the factory workers and their combative approach has more and more marked the general policy of the CFTC.

The second of the great debates, unrolled at the Congress of 1946, which turned on the revision of the Confederation's Constitution, was curtailed, but the organization of public school teachers, (Syndicat Générale de l'Education Nationale), presented a resolution, which was unanimously adopted, to the effect that   ,

"limiting its action strictly to the representation and defense

of the general interests of labor, the CFTC will decide its course
with full responsibility and in full independence of all outside
groups, either political or religious."

Thus trade unionism affirmed the exclusive trade union character of its activity, and clearly distinguished itself from Catholic Action by its objectives and its independence in regard to
the ecclesiastical hierarchy.

A year later, the Congress of 1947 modified with near unanimity the declaration of principles of the CFTC, which had remained unchanged since 1919. These modifications, which
accorded accurately with the views of the *Syndicat Général de
l'Education Nationale,* of a good number of the manual workers' organizations, and of all the young militants desirous of
eliminating every reference to religious doctrine or practice that
might keep non-Catholic workers or non-practicising Catholics
from their organizations, or who were simply anxious that a
trade union should not make dogmatic declarations as though it
were a branch of the Church, but merely elaborate, on its own
responsibility, some technical solutions to material problems.

The new declaration of principles set forth the fidelity of the
CFTC to its origin in its opening formula:

"The Confederation professes and is inspired in its activity by
the principles of Christian social morality."

The movement then declares in precisely stated terms that it
seeks a social transformation

"not by the systematic development of class antagonism, but by
an economic organization conceived in such a manner that
the dignity and independence of workers and their groupings
would be integrally respected."

No one could any longer confuse with an authoritarian corporatism the "democratic organization" of economic life which
the CFTC advocates. A note of independence is struck on the
question of trade unionism and politics:

"for the good order of public life, the trade union organizations
must distinguish their responsibilities from those of political
parties." The Confederation "intends to preserve a complete
independence in its activity in regard to the State, the executive
bodies, and the parties."

The formula of independence adopted by the preceding Congress is found again in the last passage of the declaration of
principles, a document which placed Christian trade unionism
in the tradition of the French working class movement, without injuring the continuity of development of the CFTC.

It is equally in the name of a traditional concept of French
trade unionism, that of "federalism," that the "minority," composed ever since of the university leaders with the young direc-

tors of the manual workers' unions, tried to change some of the confederal statutes at this time of revision. It proposed to reduce the governing powers of the Confederal Bureau, and enlarge those of the National Committee. The latter is the assembly of delegates of all the industrial or professional federations and of all the departmental unions,[7] with the latter traditionally enjoying in French trade unionism a position equal to that of the federations. This radical reform was not successful, but the margin between the majority and the minority was reduced to 2,610 votes against 2,017. This figure will appear remarkable to those who know with how much tenacity established situations and traditional positions are held in a trade union movement.

Let us continue to seek in the annual assemblies of the CFTC for signs of its development. The atmosphere of the Congress of 1948 would have been particularly strained, if there had not been added to the general report, an item proposed by a special commission called *The Twenty-One*. This text guaranteed trade union democracy and the rights of the minority in more precise terms, in an organization where previously basic problems could be settled nearly without debate, by an appeal to the feelings of unanimous fidelity, or by a simple reference to traditional formulas. Although this resolution had been attached to the general report, the latter could not be adopted by a show of hands as was customary. 35% of the delegates either abstained or voted in the negative, indicating by this act a new freedom of discussion.

In the course of this Congress, the Secretary General of the Federation of Metal Workers defined the essential position of the "minority":

"With the Liberation, there has been an increase of young people in posts of responsibility in the CFTC. These new elements have been trained in JOC or Resistance. We injure no one when we say that these young people bring with them the ideas of their generation, a generation that has indeed been trained in study clubs, but also has been initiated into new methods and conditions of action, and toward whom any patronizing attitude is no longer tolerable."

After having recounted the reforming activity of his friends, the young leader of the Metal Workers concluded in these terms:

"We affirm again that *for us trade union pluralism is not an end in itself, but a fact,* which permits, in this present moment in the history of the working class movement in France, the freest

expression and the better organization of the different tendencies, which is the instrument of that expression. *We believe
that we must work for the realization of that desire for unity
which all workers have within them.* Will it be possible one day?
When? Neither you nor I can answer. But we feel that we must
work in that direction. Already there is a means: unity in action
and unity of action. With regard to the *Force Ouvrière,* we do
not forget that its members were with us in the strikes of November-December, that their schism was the manisfestation of their
will to remove politics from trade unionism. This will animates
us as well. It appears that among the different trade union organizations, in so far as the F.O. has fought for that independence, the F.O. is nearer to us."

It is true that in the strikes of November-December 1947, the
non-Communist minority of the CGT was separated from the
Communist directed majority and formed the CGT-FO. This
was the French reflection of the great crisis which, occasioned
by the problem of American aid to Europe, separated the free
trade unionists from the Communist groups with whom they
had grown close in the great current of working class unity
which characterized the war and after-war periods. The CFTC
and the CGT-FO had adopted similar attitudes toward the
Marshall Plan and the subordination of the trade union movement to the Communist Party. Many observers, chiefly foreigners, hoped to see in France the rapid realization of organic
unity among the free trade unions.[8] That is why the position
taken by the CFTC in regard to the FO provoked so much
comment in the months after the schism. Certainly the dominant conviction in the CFTC was that of the permanent and
real value of Christian trade unionism, which had maintained
its continuity throughout the many crises of the French working
class movement. But many leaders of the CFTC, belonging to
the "minority," had welcomed with an evident and publicly
expressed sympathy the foundation of the newly organized FO.
Further, a *cartel interconfédéral* brought them only partial
satisfaction. Such a pact had been concluded by the CFTC
with the FO and a third organization.[10] Its purpose was to force
a lowering of prices by the government of the Third Force
on the supposition that this decline would be more valuable
than another rise in nominal wages. With the political drift
to the Right and the employers' reaction which accompanied
it, the Christian leadership in certain industries, notably that
of Gas-Electricity and Metallurgy, felt itself obliged to defend
the working class by concerted action with the corresponding
federations of the CGT.[11] This move surprised their colleagues

of the FO, who found it difficult to attempt common action with those organizations from which they had recently withdrawn. The unions of the CFTC, which had always maintained their own personality, risked less by such a move. Thus, despite all the clarifications that could be given them, the leaders of the FO determinedly abstained from this "unity of action" with the CGT, which the CFTC limited strictly to immediate economic demands, which prevented all political exploitation of the strikes by the Communists. Thus there developed, in quite a number of working class circles, a situation which had not been foreseen: the Christian labor leaders appeared more combative, and more unyielding to the employers, the political parties, and the inaction of government than their colleagues of the FO.

The Congress of June 1949 opened in this atmosphere, preceded, accompanied and followed by a widespread press campaing against the "unity of action" between the CGT and the CFTC. The campaign was directed particularly against the "minority" of the CFTC, its "left wing," falsely confused with the *Christian Progressives*[12] by a large body of intellectuals who did not belong to the Christian trade unions. To the applause of the Congress, the three leaders who were considered the prime movers of the "left wing" presented a declaration of principles which rejected any possible overtures of the "Christian Progresives":

"We are absolutely apart from this group in doctrine and in its practice of relationships between Christianity and Communism. We reject its historical interpretation, its conception of the role of the Communist parties in public life, and of the role of the USSR in international politics. We have always been, and we remain, unalterably opposed to any totalitarian deviation or utilization of the working class movement. And if we seem to have its method of approach to economic problems, this method has nothing to do with Stalinist Marxism."

One of the curious characteristics of the intellectual situation in post-war France is the attraction of Marxism, and even Stalinism, at least as regards methodology, even on certain Catholics.[13] In opposition to this tendency, the leaders of the "minority" of the CFTC have published a series of studies which go beyond immediate trade union needs.[14] In these they have sought the minimum means, indispensible for active trade unionists at grips with economic problems, in the elaborate analyses prepared by Anglo-American economists on the national income and on full employment. They have stated their purpose as follows:

"In this approach to economic questions, we have found a double advantage. We can direct the attention of the French working class to the factual aspects of the situation, to the heart of the national economy, with its overall problems, its community of interests, and its internal antagonisms. And we can place all this in a current of economic thought, opposed to the old 'Liberalism' of the employers, but compatible, according to the gravity of the problems, with proposals for the simple control of the flunctuations of a capitalist economy, or of the planning or nationalization of the economy, more or less advanced."

In the development of this work of research and education, the "Reconstruction" group has had many opportunities to acquaint the young French leaders with the economic and political activity of the American trade unions and of British Labor. Thus they have consciously demonstrated the achievements of the Western working class movement to workers who are under the constant ideological pressure of Stalinism, which dominates the whole atmosphere of their working environment. This effort has never been interrupted, even when, as in the strikes of the spring of 1950 some Christian unions fought alongside of organizations affiliated with the CGT. At that very moment, *Reconstruction* unsparingly denounced the Communist "campaign for peace" in a study prepared by a Christian leader classified as belonging to the "left wing." He wrote:

"We are not able to add our voice to that of the CGT, because the peace that we seek is not that which comes from the CGT."

The "left wing" of the CFTC is not in any sense a Communist-inclined group. This was clear in the autumn of 1949 and in the spring of 1950 and 1951, with the debates which preceded and followed the foundation of the *Confédération Internationale des Syndicats Libres*.[15] The leaders who had wrongly been labeled "Communist-minded" worked hard for the adhesion of the CFTC to this new International, which all Communists and their sympathizers denounced violently as an "imperialist tool."[16]

All know that, after the conditions imposed by the Congress of London, (November-December 1949), adherence to the CISL would have implied the renunciation of a specifically Christian International, the *Confédération Internationale des Syndicats*

Chrétiens, in which the CFTC was tightly bound to the strictly confessional organizations of Belgium and Holland. Implicit in the problem is the frequently-noted intention of many in the CFTC to escape gradually from the isolation of the Christian trade unions which resulted from the original conditions of their development.

In the judgment of the press, April 1950 saw the National Committee of the CFTC divided, with "all the forces of the 'left wing' " in favor of the CFTG joining the CISL, while the majority, grouped around Gaston Tessier, President both of the CFTC and of the *Confédération International des Syndicats Chrétiens,* were determined to maintain a separate Christian International. The minority obtained about 37% of the votes. The appeal to "fidelity," issued by the most recent Congress of 1951, paradoxically supported by the suspicion of a part of the delegates toward the "Anglo-Saxon bloc," reduced to approximately 32% the minority in favor of the CISL. The debate, in the presence of the Secretary of the Christian International, was significant for those observers who knew of the current attempts to reconstruct the Christian trade unions of Germany or to give a confessional character to the free trade unions of Italy. The position of the "minority" was clearly defined in the following resolution:

> "Since the CFTC has the duty to defend on the international level the interests of the French workers, the Congress should pronounce for the adherence of the CFTC to the *Confédération Internationale des Syndicats Libres.*
> "Conscious at once of the global character of the problems and of the diversity of national situations, the Congress should declare that, while it preserves intact the personality of the CFTC, it choses adhesion as a gesture of solidarity with all the trade union movements which seek social transformation together with the maintenance of international peace and respect for the trade union, political and spiritual liberties.
> "In this spirit, the Congress should give specific support to the British working class effort for a collective economy in a democracy; to the fight of the American trade unions against uncontrolled capitalism; to the struggle of the German workers for co-management; and *to the re-awakening of the working class movement in Spain.*"

As each one in the Congress realized, this resolution affected the entire orientation of the Christian unions. *La Vie intellectuelle* commented in June, 1951,[17] that the problem of the International revealed the opposition of two conceptions of Christian unionism:

"One affirms the *idea* of Christian trade unionism, desiring the maintenance of an International, even on the reduced base of several national bodies, but with the more or less precise hope of reconquest in Germany and Italy, of expansion in overseas territories, particularly in South America; the other conception begins with the *fact* that if the Christian trade union organizations have responded and do respond to the needs of workers in certain countries, in a certain historical situation, they have not been necessary in other situations and in other countries, even for Catholic workers—for instance in the English-speaking countries; in this case, why not accept the formula of the CISL: international unity with respect to trade union, political, and spiritual liberties; recognition of continued pluralism in national centers as it has developed from their complex and variable trade union history?"

Contact after the Liberation with the English-speaking world of labor, principally the American, had convinced the minority favorable to the CISL that trade union organizations explicitly "Christian" were not the only method for the effective participation of Catholics in the working class movement. The post-war conditions which revealed to them a world different from the traditional European formulas, also created for Christian unionism a major role in France as the "largest free trade union organization." Consequently they wished—without objection from the FO—to take their place in the free international trade union body as a representative of the French working class, confident that the influence of the English-speaking countries would assure respect for religious convictions.

This debate at the Congress of 1951 is connected with all the developments which we have traced since 1944. We can agree with *La Vie intelletuelle:*

"If the circumstances emphasize the quarrel over the International, the discussion is obviously more profound. In a body such as Christian trade unionism, even more than in a movement like 'Social Catholicism,' the Christian inspiration is realized in an historical atmosphere, strictly determined in its ingredients and its thinking, to which belong a good part of the apparently doctrinal formulations which derive from tradition. As the situation is modified, the relativity becomes apparent: a certain number of white collar and civil service personnel and specially trained workers will accept the traditional formulas without difficulty and even with a feeling of security; but this will not be the case with others, particularly factory workers and university people, whose origins, training, and experience have posed altogether different problems than those of the popular

religious study circles that were the principal source of the CFTC. That is why the traditionalist leaders manifest periodically that nostalgia for an atmosphere specifically Catholic, protected from the storms of our time, and in which, in their opinion, the CFTC should still find its most solid base for recruitment. But the entire history of the nation and of French Catholicism for the past twenty years at least has altered the conditions of trade union activity of Christian inspiration and has brought to the fore, in thought if not in deed, a good number of leaders who are certainly not of the faith, the doctrine, or the morality of their trade union brothers, but who share a common 'social doctrine'. It is on the basis of the existing problems of French trade unions in general, and of the hope of resolving them, that the 'minority' leaders operate in the CFTC, which for them is specifically a non-spiritual movement which should surrender the religious tasks to the Social Secretariat and to Catholic Action designed for the working class. Which approach can be most efficacious in handling the "Communist problem", in the struggle against social reaction, and in the indispensible renewal of trade union thought in France? This is the essential question that is posed."
(July, 1951).

This is the question that will undoubtedly suggest itself to the readers of this essay. Is it possible for them to respond objectively?

There is no adequate answer in the legitimate satisfaction which the old leaders of the CFTC can feel today as they reflect on the present condition of their organization in comparison with the one of their youth. The generation of founders and the young ones who follow their thinking have been dominated by the problems of *ralliement*. The political work which the *Ralliés* have not been able to accomplish, and which they have pursued through the Chamber of the *Bloc National*, the Popular Democratic Party, and the MRP, the CFTC has achieved on the social level. It has placed and safely installed Catholics in French democratic institutions and thus it has borne witness to Catholicism in public life. From this point of view, the CFTC has succeeded. It has maintained itself as a representative organization in the crises of 1936 and 1944; its leaders form part of the working class representation on international labor organizations; the elections to the administrative boards of Social Security, the *Conseils d'Enterprise*, and the *Délégués du Personnel* have established the principle of proportional representation which the CFTC has always supported, and they have brought it an increasing number of votes. It has an established position, a place among the prevailing institutions. These are advantages which a body such as the Social Catholics, so long exiled from public life and legal influence, would naturally appreciate. It is from the same institutional point of view that French Christian trade unionism feels itself strong in the support of similar movements in Belgium and Holland, and is disturbed by the unity of the free trade unions of Germany and Italy. It glories in the bond of the *Confédération Internationale des Syndicats Chrétiens*, its memberships on international boards, and its possibilities for influence on the European Assembly at Strassbourg where the Christian democratic parties are massively represented. This apparent restoration of Christian social Europe with an anti-Socialist flavor, of which the German Christian labor leader, Adam Stegerwald, dreamed in 1920, this influence and this witnessing in institutions cannot obscure the profound crisis in French labor, which is apparent both to the younger leaders and to analysts who can raise themselves above institutional loyalty.

Is it not this crisis, the weakening of Socialism and traditional trade unionism together with the Communist upsurge, rather than its own effort, which has made the CFTC of 1950 the second largest labor Confederation and the first of the non-Communist organizations? One cannot avoid the question to which there is only one reply which the future will reveal: the mass of French workers no longer give their full support to the CGT, though they still back it with their votes. Hence we must pose the question this way: will it be possible to accomplish through the CFTC what was not realized through the FO: to offer to French labor in all its manifestations a free trade union leadership both on the factory level as well as on the national and international scale? In part, this would require a renewal of tradition, the tradition of old French trade unionism before the Stalinist seizure; in part, it would require an honest confrontation of the problems of the second half of the twentieth century in a nation which is having considerable difficulty in orientating itself in a new world which it has not made, and where it no longer feels itself playing a major role with heavy and exciting responsibilities.

To the statistics we have cited at the beginning of this essay might be appended others from the same elections which illustrate the trends in working class loyalties in the principal metallurgical centers: *Maubege,* CGT: 21,397; CFTC: 8,128; FO: 5,503; *Longwy:* CGT: 16,876; CFTC: 4,440; FO: 3,128 *Montbéliard:* CGT: 10,453; CFTC: 5,793; FO: 3,002; *Saint-Nazaire:* CGT: 8,158; CFTC: 7,410; FO: 5,611; *Saint-Étienne:*

CGT: 38,656; CFTC: 21,343; FO: 8,741: Confirming these figures of June, 1950, in the majority of cases the elections to factory boards seem to have given the second place to Christian trade unionism in the key industries of metallurgy, construction, chemicals, Gas-Electricity, railroads, etc.

At the conclusion of the development which we have traced, we can find at least a few Catholic leaders at all levels of French labor. Today they are the leaders of a substantial and growing minority which the Communist CGT must take into account and which the working class regards with curiosity, and even with a new sympathy. This is adequate as a witness to Catholicism; it is still insufficient to decide the orientation of the mass of French labor, which is a capital factor in the future of Europe. This is the deliberately restrained conclusion of this historical analysis, which must not alter the personal hopes of the author.

PAUL VIGNAUX

NOTES

1 Paul Vignaux, *Introduction à l'Etude historique du Mouvement Syndical Chrétien*, International Review for Social History, Amsterdam, II (1937), pp. 28-49.

2 *Trade Unionisme et Syndicalisme*, Paris, Ambier, 1936.

3 These *Social Weeks* were annual congresses of Catholics and Catholic organizations interested in social questions. Held in a different French city each year since the early part of the century, they have been called "travelling universities of Catholic social thought."

4 *Traditionalisme et Syndicalisme—Essai d'Histoire Sociale, 1884-1941*, New York, la Maison Française, 1942. This volume contains an account of the relations of the Christian trade unions and the Social Catholics.

5 *Confédération Generale du Travail Unitaire*, formed in 1921 by a Communist schism from the CGT.

6 Before the passage of this resolution, many of the officers of the CFTC, in their enthusiasm for the program of the new Christian democratic party, accepted positions in its ranks and had been elected to office.

7 French trade unions are organized vertically into federations on an industrial or craft basis, and horizontally into departmental "unions", or organizations of all members of the confederation working in a single department.

8 In this connection, and subsequently in this essay, "free" means a trade union movement not dominated by Communist or other dictatorial powers.

9 A working agreement for common objectives among various national trade unions without sacrifice of individuality.

10 *Confédération Générale des Cadres*, the organization of superintendants, engineers, and foremen.

11 Autumn of 1948 and beginning of 1949. Copies of the text can be secured from *Fédération des Syndicats de la Metallurgie*, CFTC, 26, rue de Montholon, Paris, IX.

12 A group of young Catholics with Communist tendencies.

13 I have examined some aspects of this attraction in an article in *La Vie intellectuelle*, November 1950.

14 *Reconstruction,* founded in 1946. This excellent analysis appears monthly, and can be obtained from its editor, Ch. Savouillan, 59 rue Condorcet, Paris IX

15 Known in the English-speaking world as the *International Federation of Free Trade Unions,* (IFFTU), established to counteract the Communist-controlled WFTU.

16 Cf. Paul Vignaux, *Une nouvelle fédération mondiale de syndicats, La Vie intellectuelle,* January 1950, and the documents published in the same review in the issue of July, 1951.

17 *Une nouvelle minorité syndicale.*

18 See the figures at the beginning of this essay.

FRENCH AND PAPAL DOCUMENTS

FRENCH AND PAPAL DOCUMENTS

The Challenge: *The Civil Constitution of the Clergy*[155]

Section I: *Ecclesiastical Offices*:

Art. I—Each department will form a single diocese, and each diocese will have the same extent and the same limits as the department.

Art. II— . . . All bishops of the 83 departments of the kingdom who are not named in the present article are and remain suppressed.

Art. IV—It is forbidden for any French church or parish or for any French citizen to recognize in any case and under any pretext whatsoever, the authority of any bishop or metropolitan whose see shall be established under the control of a foreign power, nor shall they recognize the authority of his delegates whether resident in France or elsewhere; all this without prejudice to the unity of faith and of the communion which will be established with the visible Head of the universal Church, which will be set forth below.

Art. VIII—The episcopal parish will not have any other direct pastor except the bishop; all priests resident there will be vicars and will perform their functions.

Art. IX—There will be 16 vicars of the cathedral church in towns of more than 10,000 souls, and 12 in those of less than 10,000.

Art. XIV—The vicars of cathedral churches, the vicar superior and the vicar directors of the seminary will form the permanent council of the bishop, who cannot perform any act of jurisdiction which concerns the government of the diocese or the seminary without having consulted with them . . .

Art. XV—In towns and villages of 6,000 souls and less, there will only be a single parish; the other parishes will be suppressed and joined with the principal church.

Art. XX—All titles and offices, other than those mentioned in the present constitution . . . from the day of the publication of this decree will be suppressed and can never be reestablished in similar form.

Section II: *Nomination to benefices*:

Art. I—From the day of the publication of this decree, the only way bishops and pastors shall achieve their office is by means of elections.

Art. II—All elections shall be by means of ballot, with an absolute plurality of the votes required.

Art. III—The elections of bishops will be held under the same form and with the same electors indicated in the decree of the 22 December 1789 for the selection of the members of the assembly of the department.

Art. XVI—In the month following his election, he who was chosen for bishop shall present himself in person at his metropolitan see, or if he was chosen as metropolitan, to the oldest bishop of his *arrondissement* with the official act of his election and proclamation; and he shall ask that he be accorded canonical confirmation.

Art. XIX—The new bishop cannot appeal to the Pope to obtain any confirmation; but he will write to the visible Head of the universal Church in testimony of the unity of faith and of communion which he should have with him.

Art. XXI—Before the beginning of the ceremony of consecration, the elected shall, in the presence of the municipal officials, the clergy and people, take a solemn oath to watch carefully over the faithful of the diocese assigned to him, to be faithful to the Nation, the law and the King, and to maintain with all his power this constitution decreed by the National Assembly and accepted by the King.

Art. XXV—The election of pastors will take place with the same form and with the electors indicated in the decree of 22 December 1789 for the selection of the administrative assembly of the district.

Art. XXXVIII—Pastors elected and confirmed shall take the same oath as bishops. It shall be taken in their parish church on Sunday before the parochial mass in the presence of the municipal officials of the place, the clergy and people; until then they shall not perform any parochial function.

Section III: Salaries of Ministers of Religion:

Art. I—Ministers of religion exercise the first and most important functions of society, and since they are obliged to reside permanently in the place of service to which the confidence of the people have called them, they shall be paid by the Nation.

The Ultra-Conservative Response: Joseph de Maistre

Essay on the Generative Principle of Political Constitutions[156]

IX—"The more we examine the influence of human agency in the formation of political constitutions, the greater will be our conviction that it enters there only in a manner infinitely subordinate, or as a simple instrument; and I do not believe that there remains the least doubt of the incontestable truth of the following propositions:

1. That the fundamental principles of political constitutions exist before all written law.

2. That a constitutional law is, and can only be, the development or sanction of an unwritten pre-existing right.
3. That which is most essential, most intrinsically constitutional, and most fundamental, is never written, and could
not be, without endangering the state.
4. That the weakness and fragility of a constitution are actually in direct proportion to the multiplicity of written constitutional articles."

X—"We are deceived on this point by a sophism so natural
that it entirely escapes our attention. Because man acts, he thinks
that he acts alone; and because he has the consciousness of his liberty, he forgets his dependence. In the physical order, he listens to
reason; for although he can, for example, plant an acorn, water it,
etc., he is convinced that he does not make the oaks, because he
witnesses their growth and perfection without the aid of human
power; and, moreover, that he does not make the acorn; but in the
social order, where he is present and acts, he fully believes that
he is the sole author of all that is done by himself. This is, in a
sense, as if the trowel should believe himself the architect. Man is a
free, intelligent and noble being; but he is not less an *instrument
of God . . .*"

XVIII—"I have spoken of Christianity as a system of belief; I
will now consider it as a sovereignty, in its most numerous association. There it is monarchical, as all the world knows; and this is
as it should be, since monarchy becomes by the very nature of
things the more necessary, in proportion as the association becomes
more numerous. We do not forget that an observation from an
impure mouth has met with approval in our day, affirming that
France was geographically monarchical. It would be difficult indeed
to express this incontestable truth in a manner more happy . . ."

LXI—"There have always been some forms of religion in the
world, and there have been wicked men who have opposed them;
impiety also has always been regarded as a crime; for as there
cannot be a false religion without some mixture of the true, so
there cannot be any impiety which does not oppose some divine
truth more or less disfigured; *but real impiety can only exist in
the bosom of the true religion;* and, by a necessary consequence,
impiety has never produced in past times, the evils which it has committed in our day; for its guilt is always in proportion to the light
by which it is surrounded. It is by this rule that we must judge
the eighteenth century; for it is under this point of view that it is
unlike any other . . . Now, though impious men have always existed,
there never was, before the eighteenth century, in the heart of
Christianity, *an insurrection against God;* never especially had there
been seen, before this, a sacrilegious conspiracy of all the faculties
against their Author: now, this has been witnessed in our day. The
vaudeville has blasphemed as well as the tragedy, and romance
as well as history and natural philosophy. Men of this age have

prostituted genius to irreligion, and according to the admirable expression of the dying St. Louis, THEY HAVE WAGED WAR AGAINST GOD WITH HIS GIFTS . . ."

LXIV—"Then that character of impiety which belongs only to the eighteenth century, manifests itself for the first time. It is no longer the cold tone of indifference, or at most the malignant irony of scepticism; it is a mortal hatred; it is a tone of anger, and often of rage. The writers of that period, at least the most distinguished of them, no longer treat Christianity as an immaterial human error; they pursue it as a capital enemy; they oppose it to the last extreme; it is a war to the death: and, what would seem incredible, if we did not sad proofs of it before our eyes, is, that many of those men, who call themselves *philosophers,* advanced from hatred of Christianity to personal hatred of its Divine Author . . ."

The Awakening of a Christian Social Conscience:

Villeneuve-Bargemont

Christian Political Economy[157]

. . . We believe that a law should impose on the management of factories who employ more than fifty people the following obligations:

1. To make their factories perfectly healthful and to be open to governmental inspection to insure such conditions;[158]
2. To establish schools in their factories for adult workers;
3. Not to employ in their factories any worker below 14 years of age[159] nor to hire anyone who has not first been certified by a qualified person as able to work without danger to his health or his physical development;
4. Not to hire any worker who cannot read, write and calculate;
5. To separate consistently the sexes and to give sufficient respect for religion and good morals;
6. To provide for their workers savings banks and social insurance, where they can deposit with progressive premiums the part of their wages which are in excess of the needs of themselves and their families. . . .[160]

"The end of society is not only the production of wealth but the greatest possible diffusion of sufficiency, economic well-being and morality among men. The theories of the English school do not lead to this end: hence, they must be modified or replaced by better doctrines."[161]

". . . to return to the question of profits and wages, we agree with the political economists that the speculator who risks his captital in business and who gives it his time, talents and his experience often dearly gained, should rightly receive a large return for his efforts and his intelligent direction; but we demand that he find the greatest part of his return in the widespread consumption of the products; that he does not speculate with the strength, needs or feelings of the workers; that he concern himself with their health, their morals and their education, and that he does not alone enrich himself from their sweat and misery. . ."[162]

The Voice of the Future: L'Avenir

The Moral Conditions of Europe[163]

"Today the fight is no longer that of the Middle Ages: Catholicism is at grips with the aristocracy of wealth, as it once was with the feudal aristocracy.

"In the Middle Ages it broke the latter by appealing to the people, the true people, the immense majority of the tillers of the soil in the name of civil liberty; today it will break the aristocracy of wealth in the same manner by freeing the proletariat from the monopoly which capitalists exert over them by buying their labor to resell it. The token of the victory can be read in all the advanced indications of the ruin of the industrial system. Other relations between master and worker will succeed those which now exist; religion will preside at their birth, and its ministers, become the natural defenders of the poor, will recover the most beautiful, the most imperishable of their earthly powers, that of reconstructing the world . . .

"The democratic tendency of Catholicism in the countries where the poor are menaced by imminent misery is certainly the most remarkable of the phenomena of our time. In England, who are the most ardent partisans of universal suffrage? In Belgium, who wants to reduce the qualifications for voting to 25 florins? In France, who advocates the complete removal of financial restrictions on the ballot? The Catholics. Who opposes everywhere the political liberation of the masses? The great barons of industry, these men who fix wages at their whim and who try to substitute for the restraints of religious beliefs the menace of a famine which would strike the workers immediately they were expelled from the factories. Are either deceived in regard to their true interests? No, certainly, but the world has gone forward. Everywhere the industrial system produces its most bitter fruits; everywhere a frightening distress has followed the well-being which it had at first given to the people. The people no longer have any refuge but in religion; an invincible inclination brings them back to it, for the time of rejoicing is past. They need its consolations today, and their sovereignty will work from now on to the advantage of Catholicism."

The Voice of the Past: Mirari Vos.

"We now turn to the second very fruitful cause of the evils, which to Our great sorrow afflict the Church in Our times, namely indifferentism. This is the perverse belief which has taken hold everywhere through the sophistry of unprincipled men and which proclaims that eternal salvation can be gained by any manner of profession of faith, provided only that men's actions follow the norm of what is right and honorable . . . From this poisonous spring of indifferentism has also flowed the senseless and erroneous idea, better still, absurdity, that freedom of conscience is to be claimed and defended for all men.

"Entrance for this noxious error into the minds of men is paved by the complete and unrestrained freedom of opinion which is spreading everywhere to the harm of both the Church and the State and which many maintain with supreme insolence is advantageous to religion. But in the words of St. Augustine, 'What is a worse death for the soul than the freedom of error?' Assuredly, when every restraint which holds men in the pathways of truth has been removed, our already disordered nature plunges headlong to disaster and We can truly say that the pit of the abyss has been opened from which John (Apoc. 9, 3) saw smoke rising and obscuring the sun, and locusts swarming forth and laying waste the earth . . .

"We find it impossible to foresee happier results for religion and for government from the realization of the wishes of those men who are so eager for the separation of Church and State and for the disruption of the mutual harmony that now exists between State officials and priesthood. It is in fact altogether clear to Us that those who worship this shameless liberty do so because they are so deeply afraid of the harmony which has always had such happy and saving effects for both Church and State.

"Embracing with special paternal affection those who have dedicated themselves to sacred studies and to philosophical inquiry, urge and lead them not to depend on their purely human powers of intellect lest they imprudently turn aside from the straight path of truth and become lost in the by-ways of the ungodly. They should ever remember that *God is the guide of wisdom and the director of the wise* (Wisdom 6, 15), and that it is not possible for men to learn of God without the help of Him Who teaches men to know Him through His Word. We can only describe as proud, or rather as foolish, men who weigh the mysteries of faith, 'which surpass all understanding,' in the scales of human reasons and trust to the reasoning powers of the human mind alone, powers which are, in the present state of our human nature, weak and infirm . . ."[164]

A Further Condemnation: Singulari Nos

"It is a matter of profound grief to Us that the absurdities of human reason have brought men to the point where all, in their eagerness for what is new, strive against the warning of the Apostle, 'to be more wise than they should be' (cf. Rom. 12, 3), and, over-confident in their own powers, think that truth is to be found elsewhere than in the Catholic Church where alone it exists without an admixture of error and which on this account is called and truly is "the pillar and the ground of the truth" (1 Tim. 3, 15). You well realize, Venerable Brothers, that We are here also speaking of that false and altogether deplorable philosophical system, but so recently introduced, which, out of a reckless and unbridled passion for novelties, does not seek truth where it is sure to be discovered but rejects the sacred teachings handed down from the Apostles and accepts different doctrines which are empty, worthless, untrustworthy and not approved by the Church and by which men filled with vanity wrongly hope to support and sustain truth . . ."[165]

The Christian Socialist: Buchez

The Role of the State in the Relief of the Worker[166]

"The means for guaranteeing the basic needs (of the workers) are of two kinds: temporary ones which are immediately realizable; definite reforms which can only be achieved in a future more or less distant.

The temporary reforms are: 1) The establishment of a minimum wage for workers. Thus, for example, in each district of France and in each type of work, an impartial board shall determine the wage necessary for an adequate life. This would become the minimum below which no one could either offer or accept.[167] One could offer and accept more, but not less. 2) An organization should be set up to which poor citizens could appeal in clearly defined circumstances for the necessities of life; but the agency would have the power to use their labor during this period, to change their habitat and to place them in barracks, in a word to employ them as industrial soldiers either as colonizers or in any other form of work.[168] There would be between the voluntary enlistee and the agency a precisely specified temporary contract, which would be equally obligatory for both contracting parties. 3) A development of public assistance to the point where help would everywhere be found where a poor person was in need."

(Buchez then goes on to detail the long-range solution, which was workers' cooperatives of production).

The Pilgrim of Liberty: Montalembert.

Disavowals and Errors[169]

"I am then for liberty of conscience without qualification or hesitation, in the interest of Catholicism. I accept all its consequences which public morality does not forbid and which justice demands. This leads me to a delicate but essential question. I will deal with it without detour for in all these discussions I have recognized the need of getting to the heart of the uncertainty which is very natural and often very sincere in the opponents of liberty for Catholics. Can one today demand liberty for the truth (that is to say for himself, for each one, if he is in good faith, believes he has the truth) and refuse it to error, that is to those who do not think as ourselves?

"I answer clearly: No . . . I confess that I feel an unspeakble horror for the punishments, exiles, deportations and for all the violences against humanity made in the name of religion under the pretext of serving and defending it. The stakes lighted by the Catholic hand cause me as much pain as the scaffolds where the Protestants have immolated so many martyrs. The gag forced into the mouth of anyone who with a pure heart speaks to preach his faith, I feel as though it were between my own lips and I quiver with sorrow. When I am moved by the memory of the glorious martyrs of the liberty of Catholic conscience; when I think of Thomas More and the other victims of the founder of Anglicanism; of all those pious Jesuits who with a modest and unconquerable heroism have reddened cruel England with their blood; of the Franciscans of Gorcum; of the innumerable priests who have mounted the steps of the guillotine or rotted in the prison-ships of Rochefort; of ravaged Vendée, of Ireland conquered, robbed and famished, of Poland in agony, I do not wish that the happy privilege, the holy joy of being able to admire and invoke these martyrs be ever troubled or tarnished by the necessity of approving or excusing other punishments and other crimes, even though they be buried in the bloody night of the past. The Spanish Inquisitor saying to the heretic, *Truth or Death,* is as odious to me as the French Terrorist who said to my grand-father, *Liberty, Fraternity or Death.* The human conscience has the right to demand that no one pose these hideous alternatives."

The Guardian of the Gates: Pius IX.

The Syllabus of Errors[170]

1. "There exists no supreme, most wise, and most provident divine being distinct from the universe, and God is none other than nature, and is therefore subject to change. In effect, God is produced in man and in the world, and all things are God, and have

the very substance of God. God is therefore one and the same with
the world, and thence spirit is the same as matter, necessity with
liberty, true with false, good with evil, justice with injustice.

"Allocution *Maxima quidem,* 9 June 1862.[171]

3. "Human reason, without any regard to God, is the sole arbiter
of truth and falsehood, of good and evil; it is its own law to itself,
and suffices by its natural force to secure the welfare of men and
nations.

"Allocution *Maxima quidem,* 9 June 1862.

15. "Every man is free to embrace and profess the religion he
shall believe true, guided by the light of reason.

"Apostolic Letter *Multiplices inter,* 10 June 1851.
"Allocution *Maxima quidem,* 9 June 1862.

19. "The Church is not a true, and perfect, and entirely free
society, nor does she enjoy peculiar and perpetual rights conferred
upon her by her Divine Founder, but it appertains to the civil
power to define what are the rights and limits with which the
Church may exercise authority.

"Allocution *Singulari quadam,* 9 December 1854.
"Allocution *Multis gravibusque,* 17 December 1860.
"*Allocution Maxima quidem,* 9 June 1862.

27. "The ministers of the Church, and the Roman Pontiff, ought
to be absolutely excluded from all charge and dominion over
temporal affairs.
"Allocution *Maxima quidem,* 9 June 1862.

44. "The civil authority may interfere in matters relating to religion, morality, and spiritual government. Hence it has control
over the instructions for the guidance of consciences issued, con-
formably with their mission, by the pastors of the Church. Further
it possesses the power to decree, in the matter of the administering
of the divine sacraments, as to the dispositions necessary for their
reception.

"*Allocution In Consistoriali,* 1 November 1850.
"Allocution *Maxima quidem,* 9 June 1862.

55. The Church *ought to be separated* from the State, and the
State from the Church.

"Allocution *Acerbissimum,* 27 September 1852.

67. "By the law of nature, the marriage tie is not indissoluble,
and in many cases divorce, properly so called, may be pronounced
by civil authority.

"Apostolic Letter *Ad apostolicae* 22 August 1851.
"Allocution *Acerbissimum,* 27 September 1852.

76. "The abolition of the temporal power, of which the Holy See is possessed, would contribute in the greatest degree to the liberty and prosperity of the Church."

"Allocution *Quibus quantisque,* 20 April 1849.

77. "In the present day, it is no longer expedient that the Catholic religion shall be held as the only religion of the State, to the exclusion of all other modes of worship.

"Allocution *Nemo Vestrum,* 26 July 1855.

78. "Whence it has been wisely provided by law, in some countries called Catholic, that persons coming to reside therein shall enjoy the public exercise of their own worship.

"Allocution *Acerbissimum,* 27 September 1852.

80. "The Roman Pontiff can and ought to reconcile himself to, and agree with, progress, liberalism and civilzation as lately introducted.
"Allocution *Jamdudum cernimus,* 18 March 1861.

The Decree of Infallibility[172]

"Since in Our times, in which the saving efficacy of the Apostolic Office is so badly needed, not a few are to be found who disparage and deny the authority of this Office, We deem it altogether necessary to assert solemnly the prerogative which the Only-Begotten Son of God has designed to attach to the supreme pastoral office.
"Wherefore do We, faithfully adhering to the tradition handed down from the beginning of Our faith, unto the glory of God our Savior, the exaltation of the Catholic Religion, and the salvation of Christian peoples, with the approbation of this sacred Council, teach and define as a divinely revealed dogma that: the Roman Pontiff, when speaking ex cathedra,—that is, when, in the discharge of His Office as pastor and teacher of all Christians, he defines, in virtue of His Supreme Apostolic Authority, a doctrine on faith or on morals, to be held by the whole Church—enjoys, by reason of the Divine assistance promised to him in the person of St. Peter, that infallibility with which the Divine Redeemer wished His Church to be endowed in defining doctrines on faith or morals; and consequently that such definitions of the Roman Pontiff are of themselves and apart from the consent of the Church. irreformable."

The Pope of Conciliation: Leo XIII.

Appeal for Allegiance to the Republic[173]

... "Now We deem it opportune, nay, even necessary, once again to raise Our voice entreating still more earnestly, We shall not say Catholics only, but all upright and intelligent Frenchmen, utterly to disregard all germs of political strife in order to devote their efforts solely to the pacification of their country. All understand the value of this pacification; all continue to desire it more and more. And We who crave it more than anyone, since We represent on earth the God of peace, urge by these present Letters all righteous souls, all generous hearts, to assist Us in making it stable and fruitful ...

"To attain this (the glory of God), We have already remarked that a great union is necessary, and if it is to be realized, it is indispensable that all preoccupation capable of diminishing its strength and efficacy must be abandoned. Here we intend to allude principally to the political differences among the French in regard to the actual republic—a question We would treat with the clearness which the gravity of the subject demands, beginning with the principles and descending thence to practical results.

"Various political governments have succeeded one another in France during the last century, each having its own distinctive form: the Empire, the Monarchy, and the Republic. By giving oneself up to abstractions; one could at length conclude which is the best of these forms, considered in themselves; and in all truth it may be affirmed that each of them is good, provided it lead straight to its end—that is to say, to the common good for which social authority is constituted; and finally, it may be added that, from a relative point of view, such and such a form of government may be preferable because of being better adapted to the character and customs of such or such a nation. In this order of speculative ideas, Catholics, like all other citizens, are free to prefer one form of government to another precisely because no one of these forms is, in itself, opposed to the principles of sound reason nor to the maxims of Christian doctrine. What amply justifies the wisdom of the Church is that in her relations with political powers she makes abstraction of the forms which differentiates them and treats with them concerning the great religious interests of nations, knowing that hers is the duty to undertake their tutelage above all other interests. Our preceeding Encyclicals have already exposed these principles, but it was nevertheless necessary to recall them for the development of the subject which occupies Us to-day.

"In descending from the domain of abstractions to that of facts, we must beware of denying the principles just established: they remain fixed. However, becoming incarnated in facts, they are clothed with a contingent character, determined by the center in which their application is produced. Otherwise said, if every political form is good in itself and may be applied to the government of nations, the fact still remains that political power is not found in all nations under the same form; each has its own. This form springs from a combination of historical or national, though always human, circumstances which, in a nation, give rise to its traditional and even fundamental laws, and by these is determined the particular form of government, the basis of transmission of supreme power . . .

"Thus the wisdom of the Church reveals itself in the maintenance of her relations with the numerous governments which have succeeded one another in France in less than a century, each causing violent shocks. Such a line of conduct would be the surest and most salutary for all Frenchmen in their civil relations with the republic, which is the actual government of their nation. Far be it from them to encourage the political dissentions which divide them; all their efforts should be combined to preserve and elevate the moral greatness of their native land .

"But a difficulty presents itself. 'This Republic,' it is said, 'is animated by such anti-Christian sentiments that honest men, Catholics particularly, could not conscientiously accept it.' This more than anything else has given rise to dissentions, and in fact aggravated them . . . These regrettable differences would have been avoided if the very considerable distinction between *constituted power* and *legislation* had been carefully kept in view. In so much does legislation differ from political power and its form, that under a system of government most excellent in form legislation could be detestable; while quite the opposite under a regime most imperfect in form, might be found excellent legislation. It were an easy task to prove this truth, history in hand, but what would be its use? All are convinced of it. And, who, better than the Church, is in a position to know it—she who has striven to maintain habitual relations with all political governments. Assuredly she, better than any other power, could tell the consolation or sorrow occasioned her by the laws of the various governments by which nations have been ruled from the Roman Empire down to the present . . .

"That several years ago different important acts of legislation in France proceded from a tendency hostile to religion, and therefore to the interests of the nation, is admitted by all, and unfortunately confirmed by the evidence of facts. We Ourselves, in obedience to a sacred duty, made earnest appeals to him who was then at the head of the republic, but these tendencies continued to exist . . .

A French Response: Comte Albert de Mun.

The Civil Action of Catholics[174]

"After the death of the Count of Chambord, I had tried to organize a Catholic Party, a dream of my earlier years. Léo XIII stopped me with a firm hand. It was a hard blow; contrary to my feelings seven years later at the time of the Ralliement, this time I had some difficulty in obeying and achieving mental submission. Later experience and thought clarified for me the thought of Leo XIII. I understood, and I believe it firmly today, that he had a true knowledge of our political and social condition.

"Actually a Catholic Party which would necessarily have to engage in electoral battles, which are so frequent in France, presupposes primarily as in Belgium, Bavaria or Westphalia, a people overwhelmingly Catholic who knows its faith and has confidence in its priests. Except in certain regions such as the one which I have the honor to represent (Pontivy), we must clearly recognize that this condition does not exist in our country. The intervention of the clergy in elections, or even in public affairs, is here nearly everywhere impossible. It is only on the social plane that they can operate profitably, and under the Separation, it will be there that they will find more and more the true field of influence by means of a direct apostolate."

The Papal Social Doctrine: Leo XIII

The Condition of Labor[175]

a. The diagnosis.[176]

"In any event, We see clearly, and all are agreed that the poor must be speedily and fittingly cared for, since the great majority of them live undeservedly in miserable and wretched conditions. After the old trade guilds had been destroyed in the last century, and no protection was substituted in their place, and when public institutions and legislation had cast off traditional religious teaching, it gradually came about that the present age handed over the workers, each alone and defenseless, to the inhumanity of employers and the unbridled greed of competitors. A devouring usury, although often condemned by the Church, but practiced nevertheless under another form by avaricious and grasping men, has increased the evil; and in addition the whole process of production as well as trade in every kind of goods has been brought almost entirely under the power of a few, so that a very few and exceedingly rich men have laid a yoke almost of slavery on the unnumbered masses of non-owning workers."

b. A false solution: Socialism.[177]

"Clearly the essential reason why those who engage in any gainful occupation undertake labor, and at the same time the end to which workers immediately look, is to procure property for themselves and to retain it by individual right as theirs and as their very own. When the worker places his energy and his labor at the disposal of another, he does so for the purpose of getting the means necessary for livelihood. He seeks in return for the work done, accordingly, a true and full right not only to demand his wage but to dispose of it as he sees fit. Therefore, if he saves something by restricting expenditures and invests his savings in a piece of land in order to keep the fruit of his thrift more safe, a holding of this kind is certainly nothing else than his wage under a different form; and on this account land which the worker thus buys is necessarily under his full control as much as the wage which he earned by his labor. But, as is obvious, it is clearly in this that the ownership of movable and immovable goods consists. Therefore, inasmuch as the Socialists seek to transfer the goods of private persons to the community at large, they make the lot of all wage earners worse, because in abolishing the freedom to dispose of wages they take away from them by this very act the hope and the opportunity of increasing their property and of securing advantages for themselves.

But, what is of more vital concern, they propose a remedy openly in conflict with justice, inasmuch as nature confers on man the right to possess things privately as his own . . . "

c. *The role of religion.*[178]

"And first and foremost, the entire body of religious teaching and practice, of which the Church is the interpreter and guardian, can pre-eminently bring together and unite the rich and the poor by recalling these two classes of society to their mutual duties, and in particular to those duties which derive from justice. Among these duties the following concern the poor and the workers: To perform entirely and conscientiously whatever work has been voluntarily and equitably agreed upon; not in any way to injure the property or to harm the person of employers; in protecting their own interests, to refrain from violence and never to engage in rioting; not to associate with vicious men who craftily hold out exaggerated hopes and make huge promises, a course usually ending in vain regrets and in the destruction of wealth. The following duties, on the other hand, concern rich men and employers: workers are not to be treated as slaves; justice demands that the dignity of human personality be respected in them, ennobled as it has been through what we call the Christian character. If we hearken to natural reason and to Christian philosophy, gainful occupations are not a mark of shame to man, but rather of respect, as they provide him with an honorable means of supporting life. It is shameful and inhuman, however, to use men as things for gain and to put no more value on them than what they are worth in muscle and energy. Likewise, it is enjoined that the religious interests and the spiritual well-being of the workers receive proper consideration. Wherefore, it is the duty of employers to see that the worker is free for adequate periods to attend to his religious obligations; not to expose anyone to corrupting influences or the enticements of sin; and in no way to alienate him from care for his family and the practice of thrift. Likewise, more work is not to be imposed than strength can endure, nor that kind of work which is unsuited to a worker's age or sex. Among the most important duties of employers the principal one is to give every worker what is justly due him. Assuredly, to establish a rule of pay in accord with justice, many factors must be taken into account. But, in general, the rich and employers should remember that no laws, either human or divine, permit them for their own profit to oppresss the needy and the wretched or to seek gain from another's want. To defraud anyone of the wage due him is a great crime that calls down avenging wrath from heaven. Finally, the rich must religiously avoid harming in any way the savings of the workers either by coercion, or by fraud, or by the arts of usury; and the more for this reason, that the workers are not sufficiently protected against injustices and violence, and their property, being so meagre, ought to be regarded as all the more sacred."

d. *The dignity of Labor.*[179]

"Those who lack fortune's goods are taught by the Church that, before God as Judge; poverty is no disgrace, and that no one should be ashamed because he makes his living by toil. And Jesus Christ has confirmed this by fact and by deed, Who for the salvation of men, being rich, became poor; and although He was the Son of God and God Himself, yet He willed to seem and to be thought the son of a carpenter; nay, He even did not disdain to spend a great part of His life at the work of a carpenter. Is not this the carpenter, the Son of Mary? Those who contemplate this Divine example will more easily understand these truths: true dignity and excellence in men resides in moral living, that is, in virtue; virtue is the common inheritance of man, attainable equally by the humblest and the mightiest, by the rich and the poor; and the reward of eternal happiness will follow upon virtue and merit alone, regardless of the person in whom they may be found."

e. *The function of the State.*[180]

. . . "Therefore, those governing the State ought primarily to devote themselves to the service of individual groups and of the whole comonwealth, and through the entire scheme of laws and institutions to cause both public and individual well-being to develop spontaneously out of the very structure and administration of the State[180] . . ."

". . . If, therefore, any injury has been done to or threatens either the common good or the interest of individual groups, which injury cannot in any other way be repaired or prevented, it is necessary for public authority to intervene." [181]

"Rights indeed, by whomsoever possessed, must be religiously protected; and public authority, in warding off injuries and punishing wrongs, ought to see to it that individuals may have and hold what belongs to them. In protecting the rights of private individuals, however, special consideration must be given to the weak and the poor. For the nation, as it were, of the rich is guarded by its own defenses and is in less need of governmental protection, whereas the suffering multitude, without the means to protect itself, relies especially on the protection of the State. Wherefore, since wage workers are numbered among the great mass of the needy, the State must include them under its special care and foresight." [182]

f. *The just wage.*

"Let it be granted then, that worker and employer may enter freely into agreements and, in particular, concerning the amount of the wage; yet there is always underlying such agreements an element of natural justice, and one greater and more ancient than the free consent of contracting parties; namely, that the wage shall not be less than enough to support a worker who is thrifty and upright. If, compelled by necessity or moved by fear of a worse evil, a worker accepts a harder condition, which although against his will he must accept because the employer or contractor imposes it, he certainly submits to force, against which justice cries out in protest.[183]

"If a worker receives a wage sufficiently large to enable him to provide comfortably for himself, his wife and his children, he will, if prudent, gladly strive to practice thrift; and the result will be, as nature itself seems to counsel, that after expenditures are deducted there will remain something over and above through which he can come into the possession of a little wealth. We have seen, in fact, that the whole question under consideration cannot be settled effectually unless it is assumed and established as a principle, that the right of private property must be regarded as sacred. Wherefore, the law ought to favor this right and, so far as it can, see that the largest possible number among the masses of the population prefer to own property." [184]

g. *Trade Unions.*

"Finally, employers and workers themselves can accomplish much in this matter, manifestly through those institutions by the help of which the poor are opportunely assisted and the two classes of society are brought closer to each other . . . But associations of workers occupy first place, and they include within their circle nearly all the rest . . . In our present age of greater culture, with its new customs and ways of living, and with the increased number of things required by daily life, it is most clearly necessary that workers' associations be adapted to meet the present need. It is most gratifying that societies of this kind, composed either of workers alone or of workers and employers together, are being formed everywhere, and it is truly to be desired that they grow in number and in active vigor. Although We have spoken of them more than once, it seems well to show in this place that they are highly opportune and are formed by their own right, and, likewise, to show how they should be organized, and what they should do." [185]

"Although private societies (such as Workingmens' Associations) exist within the State and are, as it were, so many parts of it, still it is not within the authority of the State universally and *per se* to forbid them to exist as such. For man is permitted by a right of nature to form private societies; the State, on the other hand, has been instituted to protect and not to destroy natural right, and if it should forbid its citizens to enter into associations, it would clearly do something contradictory to itself because both the State itself and private associations are begotten of one and the same principle: namely that men are by nature inclined to associate." [186]

"In summary, let this be laid down as a general and constant law: workers' associations ought to be so constituted and governed as to furnish the most suitable and most convenient means to attain the object proposed, which consists in this, that the individual members of the association secure, as far as possible, an increase in the goods of body, of soul and of property." [187]

Some French Repercussions

The Social Catholics: Albert de Mun.[188]

"Occupational organization, for which we demand the widest liberty, will assure the public representation of labor in the elected assemblies of the nation. These organizations will determine in each agricultural and industrial occupation, the scale of a just wage, will guarantee indemnities to victims of accidents, to the sick, and unemployed; will create places of retreat for the aged; will prevent conflicts by the establishment of permanent councils of arbitration; will organized corporatively relief for the poor; and finally will give to workers some collectve property along with private property and without prejudice to the latter.

"Legislation will protect the home and the life of the family by regulation of the labor of children and women, the prevention of night work, the limitation of hours of work and the provision for obligatory Sunday rest; in rural regions legislation will prohibit alienation of the house, land, tools and animals of the farmer.

"Legislation will ease the life of the worker and farmer by decreasing and reforming their taxes, especially those which affect their subsistence.

"It will favor participation in profits and the formation of co-operatives of production; in the country it will assist the association of landless farmers.

"Finally, it will protect the national wealth, popular saving and public morality by laws on stock-jobbing, on speculation and the operations of the Stock Exchange, on the functioning of corporations, on the exclusion of foreigners from the exploitation and direction of the great public services, on the prohibition of governmental employees, elected officials and political agents from participating in financial speculation. These are the principal articles of the social program which I advise Catholics to adopt. They are nothing else than the application of the principles contained in the Encyclical on *The Condition of Labor*.

"(The State) . . . should see that the workers are effectively protected against the evils inherent in the human condition and those peculiar to their state . . . (for) . . . thousands of citizens are exposed without sufficient protection to all the vicissitudes of a precarious existence . . . In France, the soldier, magistrate and governmental employee has the right to a pension after 30 years of service. Why not the worker after 30 years of work? . . . During illness, the workers will receive free of charge the services of a doctor, medicines and other needs which are in keeping with his state. Besides, he will be alloted by the insurance fund a daily compensation not less than one-half of his wage . . . "[189]

The Christian Democrats: Abbé Naudet[190]

"What is property? Some say it is a right; others a function. It seems to me that the two opinions can be conciliated by saying that property confers rights to the degree that it imposes duties. The notion of property which is resurrected in our day is utterly alien to this idea, and for that reason we consider it profoundly unjust and destructive of the social order, recalling the famous *jus quiritum* which at Rome was the key to all power and the source of all goods and which the Senate would grant in small lots to peoples and individuals which it wished to attach to itself.

"The right to use it is a legitimate right; the right to use at one's whim without any regard for the needs of the social organism, the right to use to the exclusion of every other person. . . that is an injustice, an unnatural and anti-Christian thing which is born of a pagan concept directly contrary to Catholic doctrine. For in the widest extension of the term property, there is no such things as an absolute right; Saint Thomas taught formally and explicitly that private property becomes common for a man who is dying of hunger . . ." (Naudet goes on to criticize the existing notions of property, and to conclude that all the goods of the earth belong to God, man can only use it without wasting its substance, and even in this use is restrained by the order established by God).

". . . (They say): Capital alone runs risks in founding enterprises, and thence has a right to a privileged position; it is unfair to place it on the same plane with Labor, for Labor does not risk anything, having always received its daily wage no matter how the business goes.

"Without going into the famous question of participation of profits, without enumerating, alongside of the risks of Capital, all the risks of Labor—accidents, occupational sickness, the lowering of the span of life, etc.—we are content to take the question as posed and ask: Is it true? (Naudet argues that it is not, and that Labor has the same legal right as Capital to be considered as a risk-taker, that the worker identifies himself with the enterprise and hence cannot be exposed to perpetual concern for the future nor be cast aside when the business ceases to make profit).[192]

Don Luigi Sturzo: The Birth and Death of a Party.[191]

"To understand the rapid, uncontested success of the Italian Popular Party we must recall that the Catholic social movement, whether or not it was called Christian Democracy, had developed uninterruptedly during the crisis years and the war. Thus, at the beginning of 1919, barely two months after the armistice there were in Italy in the hands of social Catholics more than four thousand co-operatives, some one thousand workers' mutual aid societies, about three hundred popular banks, many professional unions (which had been confederated together in September, 1918) reaching within a short time a membership of almost eight hundred thousand (and in 1920 a million, two hundred thousand). Moreover, many of the students of the secondary schools and universities had been educated for a long time in Catholic Youth Clubs. They had given during the war a magnificent example of military courage and Christian virtues. They came spontaneously into the Popular Party, becoming its intellectual and moral lever, just as the working masses of the Catholic Unions, leagues and Peasants' Co-operatives were its most convinced and disciplined recruits. Finally, the co-operation of the middle and intellectual classes, doctors, lawyers, professors, engineers, and technicians, revealed themselves to be of an importance and breadth never before seen in a young party of a conspicuously social nature. It is strange that American writers and journalists designate the Popular Party nominally as a Peasants' Party belonging largely to southern Italy. The fact is that the Party's strongest contingent came from northern Italy and the large cities where Catholics were better organized and had more schools, more social programs, and study clubs.

"Besides the rapid success of the Italian Popular Party . . . the interesting fact to be noted is its profoundly democratic spirit and program. Among the parties of all countries this one holds the record for truly democratic internal organization. From the local nuclei (the Municipal Sections) to the Provincial Committees, up to the National Congress, the party was formed on the basis of the members' will, with the majority elections and minority representations renewed every year. Thus, the interest of each member of the Party could be represented in the proceedings of the Party . . . This was an internal democracy which not only served to create among the members the spiritual understanding of real democracy, but also caused individual values to emerge in public life as a sense of personal responsibility within a collective dynamism.

"It has been said and written, even in America, by critics who are unacquainted with the true facts of the Popular Party that it was the *longa manus* of the Vatican. This has become one of those uncontrolled reports, which by dint of much repition become axiomatic truths. What may have caused some superficial observers to fall in error is the fact that the author of this book, before founding the party at the end of 1918, went to the Secretary of State, Cardinal Gasparri, to request from the Pope the abolishment of the *non expedit* then in force . . . To have obtained this request ten years before the Lateran Treaty . . . was an advantage for the nascent Popular Party and a unilateral, sympathetic gesture made by Pope Benedict XV toward Italy.

"The political battles engaged in by the Popular Party in its seven years of life can be remembered with honor. The principle one was Agrarian Reform, both for amelioration of agrarian pacts among proprietors and tenants of the farms, and for the salaried peasants. The Party sought the colonization of the *latifundia* of central and southern Italy and Sicily where roads are lacking and the condition of the farm workers is very primitive . . . The proposal of the Populars was approved by the Chamber of Deputies in July, 1922, but with the arrival of the Fascists it was withdrawn from the Senate, where it had gone for a definite approval, by the will of the Duce.

"Another political campaign of the Populars was for the legal recognition of labor unions, their direct and proportional representation in the Superior Labor Council, and the introduction of a system of *workers' shares* which meant that a part of the annual income of factories must be converted into shares for the workers, thus giving them a voice in the shareholders' meetings. These measures were presented to the Chamber of Deputies but were opposed by the Socialists and

Liberals; by the former because they saw their monopolistic position in labor representation compromised; by the latter, because they feared that freedom of enterprise might be shackled.

"The Socialists and Liberals also opposed the effort of the Popular Party to grant the vote to women . . .

"The history of the years between 1920-22 is full of struggles between Populars, Liberals and Socialists in a period when the Fascist peril was rising to power and no one saw it as imminent. When the danger was understood, the Liberals, instead of forming a solid front with the Populars and Socialists, attempted to come to an understanding with the Fascists, in the municipal elections of 1920 and 1921 as well as in the political election of 1921 and in the successive phases of the struggle.

"The author attempted several times to obtain a common front among Social Democrats, Socialists and Populars, and the formation of the government in which the Socialists would participate. But after various discussions, the Socialist leaders preferred to stay out, and at the end they gave their support to the general strike of July-August 1922. The Italian bourgeoisie was alarmed by it and decided for Fascism. The March on Rome took place in October, 1922 . . ."

The Papal Social Doctrine: Pius XI.

Quadrasgesimo Anno[193]

a. Self-help by organization.

"Finally, the wise Pontiff showed that 'employers and workers themselves can accomplish much in this matter, manifestly through those institutions by the help of which the poor are opportunely assisted and the two classes of society are brought closer to each other.' First place among these institutions, he declares, must be assigned to associations that embrace either workers alone or workers and employers together. He goes into considerable detail in explaining and commending these associations and expounded with a truly wonderful wisdom their nature, purpose, timeliness, rights, duties and regulations.

"These teachings were issued indeed most opportunely. For at that time, in many nations, those at the helm of State, plainly imbued with Liberalism, were showing little favor to workers' associations of this type; nay, they rather openly opposed them, and while going out of their way to recognize similar organizations of other classes and show favor to them, they were, with criminal injustice, denying the natural right to form associations to those who needed them most to defend themselves from ill-treatment at the hands of the powerful. There were even some Catholics who looked askance at the efforts of workers to form associations of this type as if they smacked of a socialistic or revolutionary spirit." [194]

"This second method has especially been adopted where either the laws of a country, or certain special economic institutions, or that deplorable dissension of minds and hearts, so widespread in contemporary society, and an urgent necessity of combating with united purpose and strength the massed ranks of revolutionists, have prevented Catholics from founding purely Catholic labor unions. Under these conditions, Catholics seem almost forced to join secular labor unions. These unions, however, should always profess justice and equity and give Catholic members full freedom to care for their own conscience and obey the laws of the Church. It is clearly the office of bishops, when they know that these associations are, on account of circumstances, necessary and are not dangerous to religion, to approve of Catholic workers joining them, keeping before their eyes, however, the principles and precautions laid down by Our Predecessor, Pius X of holy memory. Among these precautions the first and chief is this: side by side with these unions there should always be associations zealously engaged in imbuing and forming their members in the teaching of religion and morality so that they in turn may be able to permeate the unions with that good spirit which should direct them in all their activity. As a result, the religious associations will bear good fruit even beyond the circle of their own membership.

"To the Encyclical of Leo, therefore, must be given this credit, that these associations of workers have so flourished everywhere that while, alas, still surpassed in numbers by Socialist and Communist organizations, they already embrace a vast multitude of workers and are able, within the confines of each nation, as well as in wider assemblies, to maintain vigorously the rights and legitimate demands of Catholic workers and insist also on the salutary Christian principles of society." [195]

"First and foremost, the State and every good citizen ought to look to and strive toward this end: that the conflict between the hostile classes be abolished and an harmonious co-operation of the industries and professions be encouraged and promoted. The social policy of the State, therefore, must devote itself to the re-establishment of the industries and professions. In actual fact, human society now, for the reason that it is founded on classes with divergent aims, and, hence, opposed to one another and, therefore, inclined to enmity and strife, continues to be in a violent condition and is unstable and uncertain.

"Labor, as Our Predecessor explained well in his Encyclical, is not a mere commodity. On the contrary, the worker's human dignity must be recognized. It, therefore, cannot be bought and sold like a commodity. Nevertheless, as the situation now stands, hiring and offering for hire in the so-called labor market separate men into two divisions, as into battle lines, and the contest between these divisions turns the labor market itself almost into a battle-field where face to face the opposing lines struggle bitterly. Everyone understands that this grave evil which is plunging all human society to destruction must be remedied as soon as possible. But complete cure will not come until this opposition has been abolished and well-ordered members of the social body—industries and professions—are constituted in which men may have their place, not according to the position each has in the labor market but according to the respective social functions which each performs." [196]

b. *Sound Social Legislation.*

"With regard to civil authority, Leo XIII, boldly breaking through the confines imposed by Liberalism, fearlessly taught that government must not be thought a mere guardian of law and of good order, but rather must put forth every effort so that 'through the entire scheme of laws and institutions . . . both public and individual well-being may develop spontaneously out of the very structure and administration of the State.' Just freedom of action must, of course, be left both to individual citizens and to families, yet only on condition that the common good be preserved and wrong to any individual be abolished. The function of the rulers of the State, moreover, is to watch over the community and its parts; but in protecting private individuals in their rights, chief consideration ought to be given to the weak and the poor." [197]

"A new branch of law, wholly unknown to the earlier time, has arisen from this continuous and unwearied labor to protect vigorously the sacred rights of the workers that flow from their dignity as men and as Christians. These laws undertake the protection of life, health, strength, family, homes, workshops, wages and labor hazards, in fine, everything which pertains to the condition of wage workers, with special concern for women and children. Even though these laws do not conform exactly, everywhere and in all respects, to Leo's recommendations, still it is undeniable that much in them savors of the Encyclical *On the Condition of Workers* to which great credit must be given for whatever improvement has been achieved in the workers' condition."[198]

"As history abundantly proves it is true that on account of changed conditions many things which were done by small associations in former times cannot be done now save by large associations. Still, that most weighty principle, which cannot be set aside or changed, remains fixed and unshaken in social philosophy: just as it is gravely wrong to take from individuals what they can accomplish by their own initiative and industry and give it to the community, so also it is an injustice and at the same time a grave evil and disturbance of right order to assign to a greater and higher association what lesser and subordinate organizations can do. For every social activity ought of its very nature to furnish help to the members of the body social, and never destroy and absorb them.

"The supreme authority of the State ought, therefore, to let subordinate groups handle matters and concerns of lesser importance, which would otherwise dissipate its efforts greatly. Thereby it will more freely, powerfully and effectively do all those things that belong to it alone because it alone can do them: directing, watching, urging, restraining, as occasion requires and necessity demands. Therefore, those in power should be sure that the more perfectly a graduated order is kept among the various associations, in observance of the principle of 'subsidiary function,' the stronger social authority and effectiveness will be and the happier and more prosperous the condition of the State." [199]

c. Wider Distribution of Private Property

"Therefore, with all our strength and effort we must strive that at least in the future the abundant fruits of production will accrue equitably to those who are rich and will be distributed in ample sufficiency among the workers—not that these may become remiss in work, for man is born to labor as the bird to fly—but that they may increase their property by thrift; that they may bear, by wise management of this increase in property, the burdens of family life with greater ease and security and, emerging from that insecure lot in life in whose uncertainties non-owning workers are cast, they may be able not only to endure the vicissitudes of earthly existence but have also assurance that when their lives are ended they will provide, in some measure, for those they leave after them." [200]

"As We have already indicated, following in the footsteps of Our Predecessor, it will be impossible to put these principles into practice unless the non-owning workers, through industry and thrift, advance to the state of possessing some little property. But except from pay for work, from what source can a man, who has nothing else but work from which to obtain food and the necessaries of life, set anything aside for himself through practicing frugality?" [201]

"In the first place, the worker must be paid a wage sufficient to support him and his family. That the rest of the family should also contribute to the common support, according to the capacity of each, is certainly right, as can be observed especially in the families of farmers, but also in the families of many craftsmen and small shopkeepers. But to abuse the years of childhood and the limited strength of women is grossly wrong. Mothers, concentrating on household duties, should work primarily in the home or in its immediate vicinity. It is an intolerable abuse, and to be abolished at all cost, for mothers, on account of the father's low wage, to be forced to engage in gainful occupations outside the home to the neglect of their proper cares and duties, especially the training of children. Every effort must, therefore, be made that fathers of families receive a wage large enough to meet ordinary family needs adequately. But if this cannot always be done under existing circumstances, social justice demands that changes be introduced as soon as possible whereby such a wage will be assured to every adult workingman. It will not be out of place here to render merited praise to all, who with a wise and useful purpose, have tried and tested various ways of adjusting the pay for work to family burdens in such a way that, as these increase, the former may be raised and indeed, if the contingency arises, there may be enough to meet extraordinary needs." [202]

"We consider it more advisable, however, in the present condition of human society that, so far as is possible, the work-contract be somewhat modified by a partnership-contract, as is already being done in various ways and with no small advantage to workers and owners. Workers and other employees thus become sharers in ownership or management or participate in some fashion in the profits received." [203]

"Lastly, the amount of the pay must be adjusted to the public economic good. We have shown above how much it helps the common good for workers and other employees, by setting aside some part of their income which remains after necessary expenditures, to attain gradually to the possession of a moderate amount of wealth. But another point, scarcely less important, and especially vital in our times, must not be overlooked: namely, that the opportunity to work be provided to those who are able and willing to work. This opportunity depends largely on the wage and salary rate, which can help as long as it is kept within proper limits, but which can be, on the other hand, an obstacle if it exceeds these limits. For everyone knows that an excessive lowering of wages, or their increase beyond due measure, causes unemployment." [204]

d. Moral Reform.

"'Wherefore,' to use the words of Our Predecessor, 'if human society is to be healed, only a return to Christian life and institutions will heal it.' For this alone can provide effective remedy for that excessive care for passing things that is the origin of all vices; and this alone can draw away men's eyes, fascinated by and wholly fixed on the changing things of the world, and raise them toward heaven. Who would deny that human society is in most urgent need of this cure now?" [205]

e. Double Danger.

"Accordingly, twin rocks of shipwreck must be carefully avoided. For, as one is wrecked upon, or comes close to, what is known as 'individualism' by denying or minimizing the social and public character of the right of property, so by rejecting or minimizing the private and individual character of this same right, one inevitably runs into 'collectivism' or at least closely approaches its tenets." [206]

The Papacy and International Affairs.

An Appeal to Cease Fire: Benedict XV. [207]

"Since the beginning of Our Pontificate, amid the horrors of the terrible war let loose on Europe, We have kept in mind three things above all: to maintain perfect impartiality towards all the belligerents, as becomes him who is the common father and who loves with equal affection all his children; to strive constantly to do to all the greatest possible good, without exception of persons, without distinction of nationality or religion, as is enjoined upon Us both by the Universal Law of charity and by the supreme spiritual charge confided to Us by Christ; finally, as Our pacifying mission equally requires, to omit nothing, as far as might be in Our power, that could help to hasten the end of this calamity, by essaying to bring the people and their Leaders to more elaborate counsels and to the serene deliberations of peace—a peace 'just and lasting.'

"Whoever has followed Our work during the three sad years just elapsed has been able easily to recognize that, if We have been ever-faithful to Our resolve of absolute impartiality and to Our beneficent action, We have never ceased to exhort the belligerent peoples and Governments to become brothers once more, even though all that We have done to achieve this most noble aim has not been made public.

"Towards the end of the first year of war We addressed to the nations in conflict the liveliest exhortations, and pointed out, moreover, the path by following which a peace, stable and honourable for all, might be attained. Unfortunately Our appeal was not heeded; and the war went on desperately, with all its horrors, for another two years; it became still more cruel, and spread, on land, on sea—nay, in the very air; upon defenceless cities, quiet villages, and their innocent inhabitants, desolation and death were seen to fall. And now none can imagine how the sufferings of all would be increased and intensified were yet other months, or, still worse, other years, added to this bloody triennium. Shall, then, the civilized world be nought but a field of death? And shall Europe, so glorious and flourishing, rush, as though driven by universal madness, towards the abyss, and lend her hand to her own suicide?

"In a situation so fraught with anguish, in the presence of so grave a peril, We, who have no special political aim, who heed neither the suggestions nor the interests of either of the belligerent parties, but are impelled solely by the feeling of Our supreme duty as the common father of the peoples, by the prayers of Our children, who implore from us intervention, and Our word of peace, by the very voice of humanity and of reason, We raise again a cry for peace, and renew a pressing appeal to those in whose hands lie the destinies of nations. But in order no longer to confine Ourselves to general terms, such as were counselled by circumstances in the past, We desire now to come down to more concrete and practical proposals, and to invite the Governments of the belligerent peoples to bring themselves to agree upon the following points, which seem as though they ought to be the bases of a just and lasting peace, leaving to their charge the completion and the more precise definition of those points.

Seven Suggested Bases for Negotiation

"First, the fundamental point should be that the moral force of right should replace the material force of arms.

2) Whence a just agreement between all for the simultaneous and reciprocal diminution of armaments, according to rules and guarantees to be established, to the extent necessary and sufficient for the maintenance of public order in each State; then 3) in the place of armies, the establishment of arbitration with its exalted pacifying functions, on lines to be concerted and with sanctions to be settled against any State that should refuse either to submit international questions to arbitration or to accept its awards.

4) The supremacy of right once established in this way, let every obstacle be removed from the channels of communication between peoples, by ensuring, under rules likewise to be laid down, the true freedom and common enjoyment of the seas. This would, on the one hand, remove manifold causes of conflict, and would open, on the other, fresh sources of prosperity and progress to all.

5) As to the reparation of damage and to the costs of war, We see no way to solve the question save by laying down as a general principle, complete and reciprocal condonation, which would, moreover, be justified by the immense benefits that would accrue from disarmament; all the more, since the continuation of such carnage solely for economic reasons would be incomprehensible. If, in certain cases, there exist, nevertheless, special reasons that tell in a contrary sense, let these be weighed with justice and equity.

6) But these pacific agreements, with the immense advantages they entail, are impossible without the reciprocal restitution of territories now occupied; consequently on the part of Germany the complete evacuation of Belgium, with a guarantee of her full political, military, and economic independence as regards all Powers whatsoever; likewise the evacuation of French territory. On the part of the other belligerent parties, a similar restitution of the German colonies.

7) With regard to territorial questions, as for examples those at issue between Italy and Austria, and between Germany and France,

there is room to hope that in consideration of the immense advantages of a lasting peace with disarmament, the parties in conflict will be glad to examine them in a conciliatory spirit, taking account, in the measure of what is just and possible, in the way We have mentioned on other occasions, of the aspirations of the peoples and, as opportunity offers, co-ordinating particular interests with the general weal of the great human society.

"The same spirit of equity and justice ought to direct the study of the other territorial and political questions, notably those relating to Armenia, the Balkan States, and to the territories forming part of the ancient Kingdom of Poland, to which, in particular, its noble historical traditions and the sufferings endured, especially during the present war, ought justly to assure the sympathies of the nations.

"Such are the principal bases upon which We believe the future reorganization of peoples should be founded. They are of such a nature as to render impossible the return of similar conflicts, and such as to prepare the solution of the economic question, so important for the future and the material welfare of all the belligerent States. Therefore, in laying them before you, who guide at this tragic hour the destinies of the belligerent nations, We are inspired by the pleasing hope of seeing them accepted, and thus of seeing ended at the earliest moment the terrible struggle that appears increasingly a useless massacre. Everyone recognizes, moreover, that, on the one side and on the other, the honour of arms is safe. Lend, therefore, your ear to Our prayer, accept the fatherly invitation that We address to you in the name of the Divine Redeemer, the Prince of Peace. Think of your very heavy responsibility before God and men; upon your resolves depend the repose and the joy of innumerable families, the lives of thousands of young men, in a word, the happiness of the peoples to whom it is your absolute duty to assure these boons. May the Lord inspire in you decisions in accord with His most holy will. May Heaven grant that, in deserving the plaudits of your contemporaries, you will gain also for yourselves the name of peace-makers among future generations."

For a League of Nations: Benedict XV[208]

The pope finally speaks about one of the most actual topics of the day, the idea of a League of Nations; an idea to which concrete form had been given in the recently signed Treaty of Versailles. 'It is certainly to be desired,' he says, 'that all states, putting aside suspicion, should unite in one league, or rather in a sort of family of peoples, designed both to maintain their own independence and to safeguard the order of human society.' One reason above all should induce states to join in such a league, namely, 'the generally recognized need of making every effort to abolish or reduce the enormous burden of the military expenditure which states can no longer bear, so that such disastrous wars may no longer be possible (or the danger of them be removed as far as possible) and so that every nation's territorial integrity may be preserved within the boundary of just frontiers, and with this its independence.'

But the pope will not base such hopes on any mere perfection of the League's executive machinery. He prefaces his commendation of the idea of such a league by a presupposition about the world in which it is to function. 'All things being restored in this way, therefore' (the pope has been speaking of forgiveness and reconciliation and his own concession just described), 'the system of justice and charity set up anew, with all the nations reconciled each with the other, it is certainly to be desired that all states . . . should unite in one league . . .''

On Reparations: Pius XI [209]

"If then, the debtor, with the intention of making good the immense damage suffered by once prosperous and flourishing peoples and countries, gives proof of a real will to assent to an arrangement which is equitable and defined; if he asks for an impartial decision as to the limits of his own solvency, and pledges himself to allow the experts every means of exercising a check that is true and exact; then justice and social charity—to say nothing of the creditor's own interests, and the interest of all the nations worn out by the wars and longing for peace—seem to demand that the debtor is not asked to pay so much that he cannot find it without entirely exhausting his own resources and his own productive capacity. Were this to be asked of him, the irreparable mischief would follow—for him and for his creditors alike—of social disturbances that would finally ruin Europe itself, and of hates that would foster new threats of yet further disaster and destruction."

On Nationalism: Pius XI [210]

"It is yet more difficult, not to say impossible, that peace can last between peoples and states, if instead of a true genuine patriotism they are dominated and perverted by a harsh and selfish nationalism; by hatred and envy, that is to say, instead of brotherly trustfulness; by competition and strife, instead of harmonious co-operation; by ambitious desires of domination, instead of respect for rights and a will to protect the rights of all and especially of the weak."

"Now if this too great love of self and of one's own, abusing the lawful love of fatherland, and extolling beyond what is right the sentiment of fitting love for one's own nation . . . creeps into the mutual relations and treaties between the different peoples, there will be no crime so great that it may not appear to be blameless; so much so that crimes which, if perpetrated by private citizens, would be reprobated by all, will be thought good actions, and worthy of praise, if done from motives of patriotism.

"Thence it naturally comes about that hatred, ruinous to all, takes the place of the divine law of loving brotherhood which bound all nations and all races in a single family under the one Father who is in heaven."

On The Ethiopian War: Pius XI [211]

'The mere thought of war,' the pope has been saying, must make us all shudder. 'Already,' he goes on to say, 'we notice, they are speaking abroad of a war of conquest, an offensive war.' "This is a supposition upon which We will not allow Our thoughts to linger. It is a supposition that fills us with consternation. A war that was merely a war of conquest would obviously be an unjust war. That is a thing which is beyond all imagination, a thing indescribably sad and horrible."

"It is, however, true, (and We cannot prevent Ourselves from reflecting on this) that, if there is this need for expansion, if also there exists the need to assure the safety of the frontiers through defense, We cannot but desire that all these difficulties may come to be solved by some other means than war. By what means? Obviously, it is not easy to say; but We do not believe it to be impossible. This possibility ought to be studied."

A Last Appeal: Pius XII [212]

". . . Today, notwithstanding Our repeated exhortations and our very particular interest, the fear of bloody international conflict becomes more excruciating. Today when the tension of minds seems to have arrived at such a pass as to make an outbreak of the awful scourge of war appear imminent, We direct, with paternal feeling, a new and more heartfelt appeal to those in power and to their peoples—to the former that, laying aside accusations, threats and causes of mutual distrust, they may attempt to resolve their present differences with the sole means suitable thereunto, namely by reciprocal and trusting agreements; to the latter that, in calm tranquillity, without disordered agitation, they may encourage the peaceful efforts of those who govern them.

"It is by force of reason, and not by force of arms, that justice makes progress, and empires which are not founded on justice are not blessed by God. Statesmanship emancipated from morality betrays those very ones who would have it so. The danger is imminent, but yet there is time. *Nothing is lost with peace; all may be lost with war . . .*"

Toward a United Nations: Pius XII.[213]

"The idea which credits the State with unlimited authority is not simply an error harmful to the internal life of nations, to their prosperity, and to the larger and well-ordered increase in their well-being, but likewise it injures the relations between peoples, for it breaks the unity of supra-national society, robs the law of nations of its foundation and vigor, leads to a violation of others' rights and impedes agreement and peaceful intercourse. A disposition, in fact, of the divinely-sanctioned natural order divides the human race into social groups, nations or States, which are mutually independent in organization and in the direction of their internal life. But for all that, the human race is bound together with reciprocal ties, moral and juridical, into a great commonwealth, directed to the good of all nations and ruled by special laws which protect the unity and promote its prosperity. Now no one can fail to see how the claim to absolute autonomy for the State stands in open opposition to this natural law that is inherent in man—nay, denies it utterly—and, therefore, leaves the stability of international relations at the mercy of the will of rulers, while it destroys the possibility of true union and fruitful collaboration directed to the common good."

". . . the absolute order of beings and purposes . . . comprises also, as a moral necessity and the crowning of social development, the unity of mankind and of the family of peoples . . ." ". . . an essential point in any future international arrangement would be the formation of an organ for the maintenance of peace, of an organ invested by common consent with supreme power to whose office it would also pertain to smother in its germinal state any threat of isolated or collective aggression." [214]

"The calamity of a world war . . . cannot be permitted to envelop the human race for a third time." [215]

The Eleventh Hour: Pius XII.[216]

"Unfortunately, in these past weeks the cleavage which in the external world divides the entire international community into opposite camps grows constantly deeper, placing in jeopardy the peace of the world. Never has the history of mankind known a dissension of greater magnitude. It reaches to the very ends of the earth. If a regrettable conflict should occur today, weapons would prove so destructive as to make the earth 'void and empty' (Gen. 1.2), a desolate chaos, like to a desert over which the sun is not rising, but setting. All nations would be convulsed, and among the citizens of the same country, the conflict would have manifold repercussions. It would place in extreme peril all its civil institutions and spiritual values, seeing that the conflict now embraces all the most difficult issues which normally would be discussed separately.

"The grim and threatening danger imperiously demands, by reason of its gravity, that we make the most of every opportune circumstance to bring about the triumph of wisdom and justice under the standards of concord and peace. Let it be used to revive sentiments of goodness and compassion towards all peoples whose one sincere aspiration is to live in peace and tranquillity. Let mutual trust, which presupposes sincere intentions and honest discussions, return to rule over international organizations. Away with the barriers! Break down the barbed wire fences! Let each people be free to know the life of other peoples, let that segregation of some countries from the rest of the civilized world, so dangerous to the cause of peace, be abolished.

"How earnestly the Church desires to smooth the way for these friendly relations among peoples! For her East and West do not represent opposite ideals, but share a common heritage, to which both have generously contributed, and to which both are called to contribute in the future also. By virtue of her Divine Mission she is Mother to all peoples, and a faithful ally and wise guide to all who seek peace.

"Nevertheless there are some, and they are well known, who accuse Us quite unjustly of wanting war and of collaborating to this end with 'imperialistic' powers, who, they say, place their hopes rather in the power of destructive weapons of war than in the practice of justice.

"What else can We answer to this bitter calumny except: sift the troubled twelve years of Our Pontificate; weigh every word that Our lips have uttered, every sentence Our pen has written; you will find in them only appeals for peace.

"Recall especially the historic month of August 1939. At a time when the prospect of a disastrous world war was growing ever more terrible, from the banks of Lake Albano We raised Our voice, entreating, in the Name of God, governments and peoples to settle their disputes by mutual and sincere agreements. 'Nothing is lost by peace,' we claimed,' everything can be lost by war.' "

Rejecting the Totalitarian State: Pius XI.[217]

Communism: Divini Redemptoris

"Ours is an age 'when unusual poverty, has resulted from the unfair distribution of the goods of this world.' It is not hard, in such an age, to attract a crowd of followers to any theory which speaks of justice and equality, and brotherhood in work, and which has about it something of a religious enthusiasm. Nevertheless the Communist ideal is only a pseudo-ideal; nor has it been, in Russia, for example, the fruitful ideal that Communists claim. What progress has been made in Russia since the Communists ruled it, can be explained by forces that have nothing to do with Communism, e. g. an intensification of industrialism, new exploitation of immense resources (and the methods used have been inhuman), an extraordinary and brutal pressure on multitudes of workers. (The Pope goes on to condemn Communism for its denial of human liberty, its proclamation of class war, its doctrine of man, its concept of the family and its ideal of society.)

Italian Fascism: Non Abbiamo Bisogno.[218]

"There is, in fact, no possible doubt of the Italian State's determination to monopolize completely the young, from their tenderest years up to manhood and womanhood, for the exclusive advantage of a party and of a regime which are based on a system of thought that clearly amounts to nothing else than a true, real, pagan worship of the State."

"But it is not true that the State is a person, an independent person speaking in its own name . . . Thus when one speaks of the soul of the State, it is a way of speaking that has its foundation in reality, but which is really an abstraction. And the State can exercise no personal function except through the individuals who compose it. That is the evidence, but in our day it is no longer recognized in many places. It is said almost everywhere in one way or another—everyone is used to hearing it—that everything belongs to the State, nothing to the individual. Oh! dear sons, what an error lies in this expression! In the first place, it is against the facts, for if the individual is really dependent upon society in some way, society without the individuals would be nothing but a pure abstraction. But there is something very grave behind this; those who say that all belongs to the State also say that the State is something divine." [219]

German National Socialism: Mit Brennender Sorge.[220]

The pope first explains how he came to sign the Concordat with Germany in 1933. The offer was made by the Nazi Government, and Pius XI, 'in spite of many serious misgivings at the time, forced' himself to consent. He was anxious not to lose even the least opportunity of safeguarding the Church's existing rights in Germany, and especially its guaranteed freedom of ministry to souls. He was no less anxious to spare the Catholics of Germany any anxiety and suffering that would have come to them had the pope refused to treat with the new Nazi Government. Finally he felt bound to show that to no one offering peace will the Church ever refuse co-operation. He could not allow it ever to be said that there would be religious peace in Germany had it not been for the pope's fault in refusing the State's proffered friendship. The Pope goes on to detail the German violations of the Concordat and condemns:

a. Those who take the race, the people, the State or the form of government, the active rulers, and deify them with idolatrous worship. He defines this "aggressive neo-paganism:" "Only superficial minds can lapse into the heresy of speaking of a national God, of a national religion, or make the mad attempt of trying to confine within the boundaries of a single people, within the narrow bloodstream of a single race, God the creator of the world . . ."

b. Those who refuse to accept the Old Testament.

c. Those who try to sever, from true belief in God and His revealed commandments, the Natural Law which is the foundation of law and jurisprudence.

d. Those who deny that God-given rights which each individual possesses are inalienable and who assert that they can be disregarded by the state or suppressed.

e. Those who threaten international life with a perpetual state of war, and whose doctrines menace the very existence of the community.

Il Santo Padre.[221]

"We shall call things by their real names. In Germany there is indeed a real religious persecution. It is said, and it has been said for some time past, that this is not true. We know, on the contrary, that there is a terrible persecution; only a few times previously has there been a persecution so terrible, so fearful, so grievous and so lamentable in its far-reaching consequences. This is a persecution in which neither brutality, nor violence, nor the deceits of cunning and falsehood have been lacking . . ."

Racism.[222]

"Professors, too, must apply themselves with all their resources to borrow from biology, history, philosophy, apologetics, and the juridical and moral sciences, arguments to refute solidly and competently the following indefensible assertions:

1. The human races, by their natural and unchangeable characteristics, are so different that the lowest of them is farther removed from the highest race of man than from the highest species of animal.
2. The vigor of the race and the purity of the blood must be preserved by every possible means; whatever conduces to this end is *ipso facto* honorable and licit.
3. From the blood, seat of racial characteristics, all the intellectual and moral qualities of man derive as from their principal sources.
4. The essential purpose of education is to develop the characteristics of the race and to inflame souls with a burning love for their own race as for the supreme good.
5. Religion is subject to the law of race and must be adapted to it.

6. The primary source and supreme rule of all juridical order is the racial instinct.

7. Each man exists only by the State and for the State. Whatever he has in the way of rights derives solely from a concession by the State.

"To these abominable propositions, others may easily be added. . . ."

Anti-Semitism.[223]

(The Pope accepted the missal presented by the pilgrims, read the prayer "Supra quae propitio" from the Canon of the Mass. Then with a voice "progressively heightened with emotion," he said:)

"We say this prayer at the most majestic moment of the Mass when the Divine Victim is solemnly offered. 'Sacrifice of Abel, Sacrifice of Abraham, Sacrifice of Melchisedech.' In these three strokes, three lines, three steps, is the entire religious history of humanity. Sacrifice of Abel: the age of Adam; Sacrifice of Abraham: the epoch of the religion and the stupendous history of Israel; Sacrifice of Melchisedech: announcing the Christian age and religion.

"It is a grand text. Each time We read it, We are moved by strong emotion.

" 'Sacrifice of Our Father Abraham.' Note that Abraham is called our Father, our ancestor.

"Anti-Semitism is not compatible with the thought and sublime reality which is expressed in this text. It is a repugnant movement in which we Christians cannot take any part . . . By Christ and in Christ we are the spiritual descendants of Abraham.

"No, it is not possible for Christians to take part in anti-Semitism. We recognize that each one has the right to defend himself, to protect himself against all that threatens his legitimate interests. But anti-Semitism is unthinkable. We are all spiritually Semites."

The Church and Freedom

Statement signed by the Austrian Hierarchy for the Katholikentag, May 1952:

"The Church fights for freedom, not just for herself, but for all human beings, regardless of their social, party-political or religious divisions.

Freedom of the Church means:

"No return to the 'State Church' conception of past centuries, to a conception which degraded religion to a sort of ideological superstructure for patriotism and good citizenship, and resulted in many generations of priests being brought up in the mentality of rather inactive state officials.

"No return to the erstwhile alliance between 'the throne and the altar', an alliance which put the conscience of the faithful to sleep, and blinded them to the danger of losing the essence of their religion, while maintaining an outer facade of religious manifestations.

"No return to the days when the Church 'enjoyed' the protection of some political party—a situation which, at that time, may have been necessary but which led to the estrangement of untold thousands from the Church.

"No return to those more or less violent attempts to realize Christian principles merely by means of secular laws and organizations.

"Freedom of the Church means that the Church must be free to develop, to fulfill her missionary obligations, to bestow Sacraments, to establish schools, without being hampered or impeded, in her very own sphere—as is the case today as a result of secular marriage and school laws—by state regulations.

"Freedom of the Church also means a Church of wide open doors and wide open arms, a Church prepared to cooperate with the state in all questions of common concern, such as, primarily, marriage, family, and all sections of opinion, for the common good; prepared to cooperate with all religious groups and denominations on the basis of a common belief in God, and with all schools of thought and with all men, whoever they are and wherever they may be, who are prepared to fight with the Church for true humanism, for freedom and the dignity of man. . . . .

"The Church today is the standard bearer of freedom, and if freedom and the dignity of man survive the tempests of our time, it will be chiefly thanks to the Church.

"In this most human of all causes the Church is speaking for all human beings, regardless of their social, party-political or religious divisions. What she demands, she is not demanding for herself only, but for humanity as a whole. She insists on her right to freedom, but she equally stands up for the freedom of all who are willing to cooperate with her in the defense of the basic liberties and the dignity of man. . . . ."

NCWC NEWS SERVICE release, May 1952

Albert Gortais: The Political Significance of the Congress of Toulouse[224]

The author, a leading intellectual in the M.R.P., is attempting an analysis of the Movement as evidenced in the Fourth National Congress which met in Toulouse in the spring of 1948. He declares that the MRP, like any human group, has differences of opinion, but has discovered a firm foundation in its "devotion to spiritual values which give meaning to life and which alone can contribute a human dignity to a civilization" and in its consciousness of service to a cause higher than itself—the cause of human justice and liberty against totalitarian slavery. But the Congress was unique because it concentrated its attention on the actual problems facing the nation, rather then spending its forces on abstract questions. It defined its policy on the elimination of economic evils, on the raising of the standard of living, and on the development of a new relationship with French territories overseas. On this level, the delegates were able to reach substantial agreement. This concentration on immediate and pressing problems is advanced as a possible solution for the conflicts in French political life.

Some cure must be found, for party strife, as it now exists in France, involves the risk not merely of defeating one's political opponents, but of destroying Parliamentary institutions themselves. Liberty is essential, but it must create durable government. "Liberty is not only an opportunity, but a responsibility. One loses the opportunity, if he flees from the responsibility." Then he continues.

"The MRP was early forced to understand this dictum. As soon as it was founded, it took part in the exercise of governmental power. It has not relinquished this responsibility in the four years that have passed. Its attitude cannot be accurately understood unless one keeps in mind certain decisive events which have taken place in this interval. The general political debate which occured on 8 May 1948 at the Congress of Toulouse was the occasion to recall them to the public and to the members of the movement.

"On three occasions the MRP was obliged to take positions which exerted a definite influence on its final evolution: on 20 January 1946, when General de Gaulle abruptly left the government; on 29 September 1946 when, despite the General's speech at Epinal, it decided to approve the second draft of the Constitution; finally, from 23 November 1947 to 4 January 1948, the first phase of the ministry of Robert Schuman, during which the fate of the country was decided on the twofold issue of public order and financial stability.

"Of these three events, the first is the most important. Because it chiefly explains what happened afterwards, it is fitting to recall here the political circumstances.

"One Sunday in January 1946, Charles de Gaulle, during a short meeting, announced to his dumbfounded ministers that he was giving up his office as president of the government. The MRP found itself faced with a formidable alternative. It could follow de Gaulle and lead a grand coalition of anti-Marxists, reinforced by the personal prestige of the leader of the French Resistance; or at the risk of being misunderstood, it could remain in the government in order to save the country from an adventure the consequences of which could have been fatal. The directing Committee of the Movement met the same evening, and for forty-eight hours examined the problem from all points of view—political, economic, social, international. The eighty leaders who participated will never forget the anguished gravity of that debate which placed crushing responsibilities on their shoulders. The decision was to remain. We know well today what would have happened if the other course were taken. The Socialists were then bound to the Communist Party by a 'unity of action.' The two parties formed a constitutional majority. A Marxist government under Communist leadership, in law or in fact, would have exercised power. The example of Budapest, Bucharest and Prague proves that France would have known a regime of 'popular democracy' before Hungary, Rumania and Czechosolavkia. The position of the MRP was not understood at the time. It was attacked, and a certain number of its early supporters abandoned it because of its association with the two Marxist parties. The risk, however, was worth taking to save the essential fact of French independence and of free government. On that day, the MRP, which two months earlier had made every effort to have Charles de Gaulle elected president of the government, was obliged to choose between two attitudes: loyalty to the man or loyalty to the cause. It was on that day, and not at the time of its foundation, that the issue was raised. As long as the personal policies of General de Gaulle had coincided more or less with the aims of the MRP, the latter could not fail to support as the head of the government the man whose vast prestige gave to the common action its maximum appeal. But from the moment when their respective positions clashed on fundamentals, the MRP was bound to remain loyal to the claims of public safety, of service to the nation and to the recovered liberties, no matter what the cost to itself.

"General de Gaulle has never given a clear reason for his departure, despite the potentially grave consequences which might have followed. Nor has he ever explained the reason for his silence before the referendum of May 5, when the MRP, alone of the big parties, fought to preserve the nation from an organization of the Assembly that would have led directly to Party dictatorship. Nor has he explained his personal political position, except in his speeches at Bayeux and Epinal, where he opposed the second draft of the Constitution.

"The purpose of the MRP, evident from its very foundation, was the organization of a movement of opinion based on its own conceptions, and the spread of these ideas in a constitutional manner. General de Gaulle has as much, and even more right than anyone else to have his opinions on the mode of state organization, as on all other matters. He has the right to express them, and to create around them a political party. The MRP only claims the right to its own opinion and to serve the common good as it sees its duty to serve it. It is important to recall that the MRP has never evaded responsibility, even at its own risk and peril. It must be remembered that if, during the first legislative elections of October 1945,

the MRP undoubtedly benefited in public opinion from
practical alliance with de Gaulle, it has not ceased to be attacked since then by all who, rightly or wrongly, claim his
patronage. Since the electorate has had the opportunity since
to express itself four times, the charge that the MRP did not
fulfil its so-called electoral debts shrinks to quite modest proportions. Unless one wishes to pretend that confidence, if not
pure and simple obedience to a man, is the only valid criterion
of a political position, there is no case here against the Movement. Such a concept may well be imagined, but not within
the framework of a Republican regime, which de Gaulle, with
the other forces of the Resistance, intended to establish at the
Liberation.

"The only loyalty of the MRP is the one which it owes to
the human ideal, democratic and patriotic, which it served
during the time of trial. It is that which led it to approve in
October 1946 a Constitution that was imperfect but perfect-
ible, the framework of which permitted the organization without further delay of the economic and social reconstruction of a
bruised country, that could wait no longer.

"Once the Constitution was approved, the work of reconstruction alone dictates the policies of the Movement. It is on
the level of concrete and daily tasks that this effort involves,
that a rapprochement, effected between the MRP and the
Socialist Party, forced in May 1947 the departure of the
Communists from the government without the necessity of
civil war. And it is because, during the last November and
December, the government headed by Robert Schuman could
not be suspected, neither from the republican point of view
nor from the point of view of unselfish service in the interest of the nation, that, in the face of a revolutionary in-
surrectional manoeuvre, the whole working class aligned itself
on the side of the Government in order to protect our institutions."

The author challenges the Gaullist RPF on its opposition to the
financial measures necessary to bring about recovery. The evident
purpose of the Right is to break the nation in two and to risk civil
war over matters that could be settled by compromise. Their vague
program, scarcely constitutional, hardly accords with their announced desire to unite all Frenchmen, since union can only be
effected on practical measures to meet the national crisis. Nor have
the Gaullists specified their charges against the Constitution. They
merely attempt to paralyse its operation in parliamentary alliance
with the Communists. In the meanwhile, the grave issues facing the
country are allowed to drift. Then:

"It cannot be seriously maintained that the modification of
a few texts would stop inflation, lower prices, bring the USSR

to Canossa, and change the American position on the German problem. We agree that the Constitution is imperfect. But greater stability cannot be demanded except by those who do not try to destroy the stability already existing. Even a perfect Constitution, if there were one, would not of itself change the financial, economic, social, and international difficulties, the urgency of which is entirely manifest.

"This hierarchy of needs appeared quite clearly to the MRP and shaped all its actions. This was the only way evident to harmonize the opinions of Frenchmen, better their condition and attach them to the task of recovering the greatness of France.

"The three objectives cannot be separated. They demand something more than political agitation, the only result of which would be to encourage the sabotage for which the Communist Party is always ready and to strengthen its hold on the socially discontented classes who have already suffered most seriously.

"This is the real danger in the political situation. It is an optical illusion to speak of a 'battle on two fronts.' The qualifications of the RPF do not put it on the same level with the dogmatic totalitarianism of the Stalinists. But if the RPF continues on its present course it can only aggravate the threat of Communism against the country."

To call the Communist Party "separatist" is true, but it solves nothing. The real problem is not the Party militants who subscribe to all the Stalinist dogmas. It is the five million Frenchmen who see in the Party their sole hope of improvement. Stalinism is dangerous only in the measure in which it succeeds in holding the bulk of the working class and exploiting their poverty. It has been successful because it epitomizes the bad conscience of a society which has not improved the human life of its members.

The working class will not be detached from the Communists by the De Gaullist cry of "separatism." It will not be seduced by a nationalist appeal because it knows that this has been used for three generations to justify social abuse. It will not be intimidated by an anti-Communist bloc nor convinced by an apologia for economic Liberalism. Class struggles are not mitigated by denying liberty to one and giving full freedom to the other.

"Public order must be protected against any factious undertaking of the Communist Party. It is, and the proof exists. But this does not associate the citizens with the service of the nation. The Movement is an instrument to attract men to daily interest in politics through the activity of teams of active militants in their cities, villages and places of work. This is a great and pretentious ambition that no one expects to be fully realized. But the objective is clearly perceptible and the effort in this direction is more evident as time passes.

"The organization aims at having each local 'grass-roots' section consider all the problems of interest to the population, —the food supply, housing, hygiene, working conditions, education, transportation, sports, etc. By such discussion, they come to know the problems, study them and contribute to their solution, either by working on the government or by organizing public opinion or by direct action.

"Thus the Movement as a whole tends to become a center of inquiry and initiative, as well as an instrument of civic education in the full meaning of the word. The action of those who direct the Movement and its parliamentary groups are more and more in direct contact with the realities of national life, with the concrete problems which interest the French people in their daily existence, with everything that provokes their anxieties and their hopes. Politics lose their abstract and purely tactical character, which dries them up and separates them from the people. They regain their true significance: the service of the Republic. The daily service of the people is inseparable from the spirit of the Movement."

Hence, behind the debates at Toulouse, were four months of discussion in all parts of the country on concrete issues. Local feeling in all its variety was reflected in the National Congress. Hence the latter gave the appearance of being real, constructive, and spirited. Above all, it was animated by a sincere desire to contribute to national reconstruction.

"Basically such a result could not be obtained were it not for a certain conception of life, of man and of society. A Marxist-Leninist disciple does not place himself on this terrain, nor does a more or less conscious follower of Maurras. Our program presupposes man's self-respect, the determined will to assure the best conditions for man's moral, physical and spiritual progress within the social framework, the desire to help man fulfil his destiny. This destiny is not to suffer in society, but to build it and transform it by his own efforts, thus contributing to his own development. Man is not a means, but an end. And for each man, other men must be the object of the service of mutual help and brotherly love. We find here again those fundamental choices from which politics cannot escape in modern time, the choice between spiritualism and materialism under its various forms, for materialism can be individualistic in the style of the Liberals, collectivistic after the fashion of the Marxists, purely political in the thinkng of the followers of Maurras.

"The MRP has not taken the title 'Christian' because a political organization is always capable of error and Christian truth must not run the risk of being officially connected with poltical questions. But it is clear that all its efforts are inspired by the Gospel concern for man. Communism is born from the wretchedness and anxiety of the workers. In order to check it definitely, it is necessary to fight against poverty and to work for justice so that the workers will have a valid hope of improving their condition.

"The MRP has dedicated itself to this end. It aims to explore, express and begin the realization of social objectives. We speak of 'beginning,' for it would be a peculiar blindness not to see the immensity of a task which involves nothing less than the rebuilding of modern society.

"The MRP wants to unite with all those who understand this problem. It cannot surrender to slander. Nor can it take a complacent attitude toward social injustice that would not hide for long the dreadful national and social bankruptcy.

"In its general political report, the Toulouse Congress declared: 'This Congress proclaims that the realization of social and economic justice, which demands the indispensable participation of the free forces of French trade unionism and the active intervention of the popular masses, is the most certain guarantee of the national independence and of the democratic freedoms which are threatened by all totalitarianism.'

"In 1948, French patriotism requires a singular effort to rise above that conservatism which has previously claimed a monopoly on that splendid term 'national.' The protection of the national independence presupposes the unity of the nation itself and internal peace; it involves economic development and the continuous work of all the forces of the population. Hence the future of the country and the social problem are one. The threat of 'separatism' is not only a political problem, but is the whole sum of questions, political, economic and social. There is no Right, Left or Center here; there is only fact, only a pressing reality. There is a close relationship between the minimum standard of living of the French citizens, and firm diplomacy and the security of our frontiers. The greatness of France, today and tomorrow, needs more than a good foreign policy and an adequate national defense; it is equally bound with economic welfare and with the organization of social relationships.

"This point of view is something more than a tactical question for the MRP. The struggle for social justice is an end in itself, not a simple break against Communism. Whether there is Communism or not, this strugle must be fought in the name of respect for man, and for his dignity and freedom. The loyalty of the Movement to its origins is adequate reason why it should dedicate the best of its efforts to this cause. Since this loyalty leads it to the only battleground where Communism can be permanently defeated, it follows that in the difficult circumstances of the present moment, the principle should be again emphasized. It is necessary to pursue the

> social good and thus bring about the unity of all Republicans, without asking first if it be effected at the expense of this party or that faction. France, the Republic, and the service of the people are sufficient reasons for French unity."

These objectives will not be achieved if citizens limit their participation in politics to casting a vote every two or three years. Democracy demands more than voting, and certainly encompasses more than party strife. To the majority, politics seems a remote and mysterious game, divorced from daily life. Yet Democracy demands that the citizen conceive politics as permanent service to the public good. This is the responsibility of all, and the existence of an executive and of a legislative assembly do not dispense the electors from their responsiblity. All current questions—production, strikes, prices,—require the active participation of all.

> "The purposes determined or made more precise at Toulouse in the form of a general policy and in connection with the Communist problem were inspired by the dominant preoccupation of adapting the action of the MRP to the concrete problems arising in the national life. The objective was to avoid separating the service of the State from the service of the people. Such, basically, is the *raison d'etre* of the Movement, to which all its interior organization and its permanent activities are consecrated, according as methods are clarified or events develop.

While nothing is gained by a mere denunciation of parties, in the Gaullist formula, there is certainly a need for a broader understanding of the relation of the citizen to the party and to the State:

> "The insufficiency of the conception of the traditional parties had impressed the majority of the founders of the MRP, and from 1944 they were anxious to create a new form of political activity. The original aspect of the Movement deviated too drastically from established habits to be at once understood by public opinion. Its first great successes were due essentially to its dynamism, to its youth, to the sympathy it inspired in the period of Resistance, to the deep spirit of which animated the founders. It was not its methods which attracted attention, for only time would reveal these. The successive electoral campaigns of 1945, 1946, and 1947, in which it had to take part almost at its birth, obliged it to adopt the appearance of a party before it had a chance to reveal itself in any other way. These repeated elections—one was barely over before it was necessary to prepare for the next —so preoccupied it that it could not organize itself in the direction that its name implied. The party seemed to have killed the Movement at its inception."

Such a transformation was made necessary by events. But the Congress of Toulouse was aware of deeper needs.

"After all, there is not one way of being a citizen in public life and another way of being a man in every day life. It is all the same. The foundation of Democracy is in the conscience of its citizens. The citizens, individually or collectively, are the craftsmen of the salvation or the perdition of a nation. And the nation is composed of those who live today and of the generations of the future. The extent of their knowledge of this fact and the extent in which they act according to its responsibilities determine the human greatness of the democracies.

"The conception of the political action that the MRP wishes to effect comes from this fundamental assertion. The problem is to adapt the Christian message, interpreted according to the exigencies of our times. The fact that there are nonbelievers in its ranks does not detract from this fact. Nonbelievers find themselves welcome in the MRP, because the Christian origin of the Movement makes it emphasize more directly the total human reality, since it stresses respect for the liberty and dignity of man, as well as his elevation towards a genuine fraternity in action. The numerous Christian members are less anxious to compromise their religion in politics in direct proportion to the vigor of their Christian convictions."

If the MRP is successful in renewing the political and party life of France, it will be the result of these fundamental principles. They determine its ends and its methods. But they will succeed only if the Movement achieves its purpose of engaging men actively in the pursuit of the public good. If it does, and if it can communicate its enthusiasm for man's liberty and dignity, it may give a new character to Democracy itself.

Etienne Gilson: *Democracy as We Conceive it.*[2]

". . . Our adversaries of the Right and the Left are more alike than they realize, at least in their conception of man as merely an individual among other individuals. On our Right, there is the Liberalism of Laissez-Faire. It is complacent if the abnormal aggrandizement of certain individuals blocks the free development of others. If this occurs, so much the worse for the others; yes, even so much the better, for they cannot read too often the words of Renan: 'The Politics that mantains that the people must suffer in order to be good, is not, unfortunately, entirely incorrect.' On the Left, there are the Communists who have a similar position, though with an entirely different intention. They speak only of the 'masses' and of the 'activity of the masses.' This expresses their thought exactly, for they believe that the only way that Marxism can avoid having a minority of individuals enslave the majority is to encompass them all in a single 'mass' where each is indistinct and counts only for one.

"The democracy of the MRP regards the word 'mass,' where applied to men, as both harmful and repugnant. If man be a noble creature, no number of them will ever make a 'mass,' because for us, man is not only an individual but a person. We say 'for us,' not because we think that this truth is a question of party politics, but because our party is founded on the unconscious recognition of this principle and because it is our basic proposition. Cut stones in certain positions could be said to form a 'mass;' trees have individuality, but they make a forest; so have animals, who are grouped into flocks. Man is an individual like these. But he is something more—he is a human person, that is, an individual endowed with reason. Capable of knowledge and free to choose, he can give a reason for his actions and assume responsibility. To man alone, among all known creatures, does the application of the pronouns 'I' and 'You' make sense. That is why no group of men form a mass that is measurable in extension nor a flock calculable by the number of heads which compose it. With man it is not number of heads which count, but what is inside. That is why the term 'people' has precise meaning—a grouping of human persons united for the acquisition of the common good which they pursue according to the light of reason.

"Here is the fundamental fact upon which rests our conception of political action considered in its end, as well as in its means. The human being is an end; the State is only there to permit him to attain the fullest development of which he is capable. If human beings form groups, it is because one of them alone, without the help of others, could not attain to all the perfection of which he is capable. The political regime of peoples must, therefore, be a democracy, because it is inconceivable that all human beings who compose a community do not have the capacity to contribute something to their own government, and because the State should contribute to the full development of all human beings who compose it.

"We therefore have the right to retrieve for our use the three great words of the French Revolution, giving them the meaning which they had long before 1789, and which the Revolution itself, for its misfortune and ours, has partially lost.

"*Equality*—because we wish to assure to all Frenchmen, and to other peoples who are welcome to join us in a similar effort, all material and moral conditions required for their full development. We do not believe with Renan that it is good for a certain élite to be happy, and for the people to suffer. We doubt that the élite could really be happy if about them, and perhaps through them, the people suffer, especially if the élite were conscious of its culpability. Are men happy in the possession of continuously precarious privileges which are so bitterly disputed? Are they truly an élite, if the culture for which they pride themselves is paid for by abusive economic inequalities and injustice that no moral law could justify? No political construction can have as its aim the suppression of the natural inequalities of peoples, and still less of their personal difference; but it is possible to hope that *social* inequalities are not added to *natural* inequalities. It is especially possible to wish that social privileges do not place natural inferiorities in a position to command and natural superiorities in a position to obey. A democratic equality of people would assure full development to the smallness of the small as well as of the greatness of the great. Who would then complain, if each knew that he was in his proper place? Social equality does not consist in treating geninuses as laborers, or laborers as geniuses, but of trying to have fewer geniuses lost for the greater good of all.

"*Liberty*—because man does not fulfill himself except in the exercise of his will according to the dictates of reason. To be free, according to the old definition of the jurists, is first to elevate oneself in body,—and this is economic freedom; then in soul,—and this is political freedom. Both are the expression and the guarantee of the inviolability of the human being. These two freedoms are inseparable, because if one possesses his soul without possessing his body, one must be more than a man,—a hero or a saint.

"*Fraternity*—precisely because the Republic we wish will not be the economic hive of Marxism, where the yield is sufficiently assured by the discipline which the State imposes on its subjects. We want the free collaboration of persons who follow the conclusions of reason and of the love which it radiates. Our intention is not to perpetuate a regime of injustice and physical violence to save the culture of some élite or self-styled élite, nor merely to ameliorate such a regime, as the aging Renan came to believe possible. It would be better to suppress such a culture. There is one policy which consists in using man; this is not ours. There is another which aims to serve him. This is the one we propose. And to serve man, one must begin by loving him."

The author goes on to deny that the MRP can be classified merely as a median party, a little to the Right of the Marxists and to the Left of the Liberals.

"We are a political movement animated by the double conviction that the purpose of society is the perfection of the human person, but that this perfection is possible only in, and through, society. We do not admit that society is a debased people, which needs an élite. We feel that such an élite would itself be evil, and that either all should be good and contented together or all should fail. That is why the notion of person and that of community, far from excluding each other, are inseparable. This is not a paradox, but a fact.

"From birth to death, each man is engaged in a plurality of natural social structures, outside of which he could not live or attain his complete development. Each one of these social groups has its own organic unity. While it owes its existence to its members, they participate in the many advantages which this common life assures them. We acknowledge all such groups. All know that the family, the primary social cell, is the center of the natural growth of the child to such a degree that if the State finds itself charged with the upbringing of a child, it must create an artificial social group to replace the family. It is the same with the community. In his excellent essay on communal reform, Leon Harmel quotes from Royer-Collard: 'The community, like the family, exists before the State. Political law discovers it, it does not create it.' This is evident, but what brings into being political law? The latter has not created the school, the college, the university, works of mercy, industrial or commercial enterprises, trade union organization, political parties, national groupings or churches. The State has been able to define, adapt, act as arbiter, direct and coordinate all these groups; yet it has not given birth to any of them, and every effort to substitute its initiatives for theirs only ends with replacing the natural with the artificial, the organic with the organizational, the living with the mechanistic.

"Each one of these groups owes its unity to the particular end for which it was established. . . The MRP merely acts in conformity with political realism when it rejects the pseudo-Liberalism which recognizes the individual and even that collective unity, the social class, as possessing the right to group life, without contributing anything to it. Such an attitude is immoral because it is irrational and unrealistic. The parasite ends by exhausting its host and dying with it. Because the individual cannot be perfected except in groups, our democracy is 'social' by definition.

"But for the same reason it cannot be 'socialistic' in the precise sense of the term. In his classic volume on the *Socialist State,* Anton Menger argues continually from the correct premise that the 'end of the State is the conservation and development of the individual existence,' (we would rather call it 'personal'), to the erroneous conclusion that 'the rights which make the realization of these ends possible must be in the hands of the collectivity' (p. 32). The rights of persons belong to persons, and it is unnatural to take them from persons in order to make their bestowal more certain. To the degree that it implies this 'Statism,' 'Socialism' becomes indistinguishable from Communism. Our democracy is completely hostile to every type of statism, and to avoid it, it supports persons in their social groupings which are their natural environment. . . The authority of the natural groups, coordinated in view of the common good, is the sole efficacious guarantee of personal liberties against the spontaneous totalitarianism of the State. It is the reason why, when Marxism takes power, it begins to monopolize these natural groups.

"In our opinion, the political role of the State is to be the protector and regulator of these natural social groups, which alone permit the free development of human persons in their own interest and in that of the community.

"The MRP is in favor of a resolute intervention by the State in the life of these groups and so in the lives of its citizens. . . But if we believe the action of the State indispensable to assure the coordination and direction of the groups which compose the nation, we do not wish to see the State replace these natural structures. It intervenes only in order that they may attain their own proper ends. Parents desire to see their children receive the best possible education. This does not mean either that the State must control the education of children or that it must abstain from all intervention in order to respect the freedom of families. Rather it must place at the disposal of families the services of social well-being and public education, so that they can educate their children *as they desire that they be educated.* So with property. It should neither be absorbed by the State or left to the arbitrary control of individuals. We want an ordering of private property that would not destroy the right of many for the profit of a few, but would rather assure its exercise to all. The right of private property belongs to persons; the State can and must intervene so that all can enjoy it, not to deprive all by confiscating it for its own profit.

"This is not a matter of abstractions, but of principles that can determine immediately our political activity in its most current manifestations. The natural social groups are positive realities, resistant and efficacious, on which political action can be supported and which will in turn support that party or movement which makes itself the champion of their legitimate interests. Clearly conceived and formulated, such a program will satisfy the many who wish to reconcile the demands of personal liberty with those of social justice. These we can mobilize against the two deadly enemies of liberty: the arbitrary action of the individual and the arbitrary action of the State. It is because they wish to avoid the former that many Frenchmen are willing to succumb to the latter. We must show that both are avoidable, and that out Movement knows the way to avoid them."

The author sums up the program of the MRP as revolution, but *revolution by law*—the only kind that brings enduring results. The method is to eliminate evil by suppressing the cause, e.g., violent action against Communism is not a political program, for a program is always "for," not "against." Hence effective action against Communism must erect a social order that will remove its justification. To do so the State must serve all the liberties of citizens, so that by their own efforts they can reach their proper ends.

Emmanuel Mounier: *Fidelity.*[226]

In this leading article Mounier argues that it was worth making the effort to collaborate with the French Communists, as long as they were contributing to French social awakening. The basis of his argument is that they represent the greatest segment of the French proletariat and that their cause has become the sole hope of the industrial worker. He and his associates had had confidence that the Communist Party would be willing to deal realistically with the problems facing the French and would respect the values of the French people. However, the Party has fallen more and more under the influence of the Soviet, which it has made the touch-stone of its own orthodoxy. But even this fact, which may be a passing illness or an incurable cancer, does not justify a civil war against a party, which is in effect the party of the proletariat. Against this Party, Mounier will use only the weapons of the truth. He will follow two primary rules:

"First, to defend without hesitation all which concerns the value of man; precisely all which concerns his material security; his social dignity (here we will join with the Communists wherever it is necessary) ; his human respect; and whatever involves civic and democratic courage, intellectual honesty, and spiritual freedom. These we will defend in every case, with anyone who will defend them without qualification; and we will oppose those of any stripe who compromise them. We will not base our decisions on 'pro' and 'anti,' but on a vigorous discernment.

"The second task derives from the sad and bloody experience of the Socialist peoples of Europe: to seek every dusty carrier of the germs of inhumanity, either in the doctrines, in the techniques, or in the circumstances of their revolutions. We cannot be blind to the fact that in the course of the pre-Marxist, Marxian and Leninist Socialism, methods have been adopted which have proved successful in the short run. But we must consider the price and the consequences. The problem today for Socialists and others is. has not modern conditions of technology and conflict made progress by killing too dangerous? . . . .

"These two duties do not prevent a third: to avoid with robust impatience and disinterested intelligence any rupture between Communism and the nation. . . .

We have seen the failure of all splinter movements of the Left since the Resistance. The non-Communist Left (with which the author identifies himself) cannot proceed negatively, but must capture the great French revolutionary tradition by positive action. We must remove the barriers which separate the proletariat from the nation, and not add to them by confusing the real issues with "anti-Communism." We will not make our group a refuge for irresolute exiles from the Communist Party. We find it hard to join anti-Communist campaigns, because while conscious of the faults and crimes of the Communists, we are equally aware of the defects which have disfigured the outward appearance of Christianity, the somnolence of Socialism and the patriotic illusions of a once great nation. We will not succomb to extremes: against pessimism we are protected by our Faith; against optimism, by the sting of injustice.

"Oh, injustice! Millions of honest people ignore it in all tranquility, and use their indignation against Communism as a salve for their own remorse and its severe judgment. We shall haunt their nights, and our own, with injustice's raucous voice. When the Socialist revolution deviates, it is all too convenient to pass judgment, and then to turn aside and do nothing. But more than ever we must take up again the revolt and strivings of our youth. A Christian does not abandon the poor; a Socialist does not abandon the proletarian. If they do, they are not worthy of their names. The authorities need not fear that we shall commit this perjury."

NOTES

* 12, July 1790. These minute regulations for the Church contravened Canon Law and were passed without prior consultation with the Pope.

156 English text in *Introduction to Contemporary Civilization in the West*, Vol. II, Columbia Univ. Press, N. Y., 1946, pp. 92-105. French text, *Essai sur le principe générateur des constitutions politiques.*

157 *l'Economie politique chrétienne ou recherches sur la nature et les causes du paupérisme en France et en Europe et sur les moyens de le soulager et de le prévenir*, Paris, Paulin, 1834, 3 vols.

158 The first law to protect the health and security of the worker was passed on 12 June 1893!

159 The age for the employment of children in industrial and commercial establishments was not fixed by law at 14 years until 1936.

160 *op. cit.*, Vol. III, p. 168.

161 *Idem,* Vol. I, p. 82.

162 *Idem,* Vol. I. p. 287.

163 Charles de Coux, *De l'etat moral de l'Europe*, in *L'Avenir*, 21 April 1831.

164 Gregory XVI, "Mirari vos arbitramur," August 15, 1832. Latin text in H. Denziger, *Enchiridon Symbolorum,* Friburg, Herder, 1937, No. 1613-1616, pp. 447-8.

165 Gregory XVI, "Singulari nos affecerant gaudio" to the Bishops of France, June 25, 1834. Latin text in *idem,* No. 1617, p. 448-9.

166 *Traite de politique et de science sociale,* Paris, Amyot, 1866, Vol. I, p. 306

167 The minimum wage concept was late in appearing in French legislation: the decrees of Miller and of 1899 applied it only to those companies which worked on government contracts or furnished materials to the State; the law of 10 July 1915 applied it to some workers in the clothing industry; it was generalized in industry and commerce only by the extension of collective bargaining agreements in the aftermath of the Popular Front electoral victory; for agriculture local committees have fixed minimum wages for each department since 1945.

168 The unemployment law of 1940 follows some of the suggestions of Buchez.

169 Second lecture delivered at the general assembly of Catholics held at Malines in Belgium 18-22 August 1863. Text in *Le Correspondent,* 22 August 1863.

170 Latin text in Denziger, *op. cit.,* No. 1701-1780, pp. 464-473; The accompanying Encyclical, *Quanta Cura,* idem, No. 1688-1699, pp. 459-464.

171 Each proposition is in the form of a short statement of the rejected doctrine, with a reference to the Papal document where a fuller treatment can be found. The full meaning cannot be discovered without exploration of the references. Most of the 80 propositions are on purely religious questions, as the

above. In the selection here given the most controversial have been chosen.

[172] From the Vatican Council. Latin text in Denziger, *op. cit.*, No. 1838-9, pp. 507-8.

[173] *Au Milieu des sollicitudes,* 16 February 1892. English text in *The Great Encyclical Letters of Leo XIII,* Benziger Bros., N. Y., 1903, pp. 249-263. Reprinted from the *Great Encyclical Letters of Leo XIII* with the permission of Benziger Brothers publishers and copyright owners.

[174] *Combats d'hier et d'aujourd'hui, 1902-1910,* Paris, Lethielleux, 1910, Vol. V, p. 169.

[175] *Rerum novarum,* 15 May 1891. English text, *Principles for Peace,* Harry C. Koenig, ed., N.C.W.C. Washington, 1943. It is possible to find papal precedents for nearly all the·social legislation of the New Deal, cf. *The Labor Leader,* Vol. VIII, No. 7, 18 April 1945.

[176] *Idem,* p. 53.

[177] *Idem,* p. 54.

[178] *Idem,* p. 59-60.

[179] *Idem,* p. 62.

[180] *Idem,* p. 65-66.

[181] *Idem,* p. 68.

[182] *Idem,* p. 69.

[183] *Idem,* p. 72-3.

[184] *Idem,* p. 73.

[185] *Idem,* p. 74-5

[186] *Idem,* p. 76.

[187] *Idem,* p. 79.

[188] *Programme Social* from Discours de Saint-Etienne, 18 December 1892, in *Discours et ecrits divers (1871-1902),* Paris, Poussielgue, 1902, 7 'vols. Vol. 5, p. 263. The occasion of the speech was a gathering to establish an organization to spread Catholic social teaching. This speech became celebrated when it recevied an official approbation from Leo XIII in a letter of 7 January 1893. The social doctrine of the speech is very advanced, but it must be recalled that de Mun still clung to his concept of mixed unions.

[189] Proposal for a Law on Social Security. Text in *l'Association Catholique,* 1900, p. 319 sq.

[190] *Premiers principes de Sociologie catholique,* 1899, Bloud et Barral, Paris, 2nd. ed. 1901, p. 30.

[191] *Nationalism and Internationalism,* N. Y., Roy, 1946, pp. 111-116.

[192] Koenig, *op. cit.,* pp. 23-24.

[193] *Forty Years After,* so-called because issued on the fortieth anniversary of *Rerum Novarum,* 15 May 1931. English text *idem.,* pp. 397-446.

[194] *Idem,* pp. 405-6.

[195] *Idem.* pp. 407-8.

[196] *Idem,* p. 423.

[197] *Idem,* p. 404.

[198] *Idem,* p. 405.

[199] *Idem,* pp. 422-3.

[200] *Idem,* pp. 417-8.

[201] *Idem,* p. 418.

[202] *Idem,* pp. 419-420.

[203] *Idem,* p. 418.

[204] *Idem,* pp. 420-1.

[205] *Idem,* p. 437.

[206] *Idem,* p. 411.

207 Appeals for international peace are found scattered throughout all the papal documents of the nineteenth century and have become a major theme in the twentieth. This, known as *Dès le dèbut,* was selected from the seventeen peace pronouncements of Benedict XIV, for it was a diplomatic note addressed directly to the warring powers, 1 August 1917. While it was rejected by the governments, it became the inspiration of the peace resolution passed by the German Reichstag. In addition the Pope made diplomatic proposals for relief of prisoners of war, and against aerial bombing of open towns and the deportation of labor from occupied countries. His Prisoner of War Bureau, set up in December 1914, served as an agency of relief and communication, and was broadened to serve as a general relief organization in Russia and Central Europe after the war. Text in Philip Hughes, *The Pope's New Order,* London, Burns Oates, 1942, pp. 187-190. Permission to quote granted by the Macmillian Co., N. Y.

208 For reasons of space, the above is in the summarized form found in *Idem,* p. 198. For text cf, Keonig, *op. cit.,* pp. 284-292. The Encyclical, known as *Pacem Dei Munus, On Peace and Christian Reconciliation,* 23 May 1920, is an interesting critique on the lacunae of the Pacts of Paris. His anxiety had not been stilled by the signing of the Treaty of Versailles.

209 *Idem,* pp. 201-2, from letter *Quando nel principio,* 24 June 1923. It was written as a commentary on the Rhur invasion and explores the moral principles regarding reparations.

210 *Idem,* pp. 203-5. The first is from an Address to the College of Cardinals, *Benedetto il natale,* 24 December 1930; the second from the Encyclical *Caritate Christi Compulsi,* 3 May 1932, which is a commentary on the Depression. Warnings against exaggerated nationalism are common in nineteenth and twentieth century papal utterances, e.g. *Immortale Dei* of Leo XIII, 1 November 1885.

211 *Idem,* pp. 205-206. *Address to the International Congress of Catholic Nurses,* 27 August 1935, on the eve of the Italian conquest of Ethiopia. The fact that this was delivered at a time when the entire Fascist propaganda apparatus was extolling the need of this war has considerable significance.

212 Keonig, *op. cit.,* pp. 584-5. A radio plea *Un'ora Grave,* addressed to all governments and peoples on 24 August 1939.

213 Encyclical *Summi Pontificatus,* 20 October 1939. Text in Keonig, *op. cit.,* pp. 592-615.

214 Christmas Message, 24 December 1944: full text in *Catholic Mind,* America Press, N. Y., Vol. XLIII, No. 986, February 1945, pp. 65-77; The Pope "hails with joy" the published intentions to create an international organization and calls for a "War on War." The document makes interesting reading in the light of subsequent developments.

215 *Nell'Alba,* 2 December 1941, a radio message to the world which contains the five fundamental conditions essential for an international order which will guarantee a just and lasting peace for all peoples: integrity of small states; protection of minorities; equal access to natural resources; disarmament; freedom of religion. Its importance justifies a reading of the whole text in Keonig, *op. cit.,* pp. 750-62.

216 *The Catholic News,* N. Y., 30 December 1950, p. 6.

217 March 19, 1937. Quoted from schematic summary in Hughes, *op. cit.,* pp. 42-3. Text in Keonig, *op. cit.,* pp. 510-535. Most of this encyclical is concerned with constructive measures to be taken to avoid Communism and hence may be classed with the more important of the Social Encyclicals. Pius IX had condemned Communism in 1846 and 1864, and Leo XIII's *Quod Apostolici Muneris,* 28 December 1878 dealt with the subject in some detail.

[218] 29 June 1931, Hughes, *op. cit.*, p. 106. The Pope calls the Fascist concepts a "Sham of religion."

[219] Keonig, *op. cit.*, p. 547. The passage is from an address, *Violà une audience,* delivered to a pilgrimage of the French Christian Workers' Unions, 18 September 1938. It is interesting in that the condemnation of the doctrine contains the words of Mussolini's description of the Fascist State.

[220] 14 March 1937. Text in Hughes, *op. cit.*, pp. 109-110.

[221] Keonig, *op. cit.*, p. 539, 24 December 1937.

[222] Decree of Sacred Congregation of Seminaries and Universities, under the Presidency of the Pope, 13 April 1938. Text in T. L. Buscaren, *The Canon Law Digest, 1933-1942,* Bruce, Milwaukee, 1943, Vol. II, 395-6.

[223] Address to the pilgrims of the Belgium Catholic Radio Association. Text in *Documentation Catholique,* Vol. 39, no. 885, p. 1461, 5 December 1938. The accompanying account declares the Pope wept as he quoted St. Paul on the spiritual mission of Israel.

[224] In *Politique,* t. V, No. 36, July - August 1948, pp. 612-627.

PART III:

THE CATHOLIC MOVEMENT
in
BELGIUM

1789 - 1950

by

HENRY HAAG - JOSEPH N. MOODY

CHAPTER I

THE POLITICAL IDEAS OF BELGIAN CATHOLICS
(1789-1914)

The Belgian Catholics constitute a characteristic group in the nation. The link that unites them is not material interests; in fact, there are broad differences among Catholic aristocrats, bourgoisie and proletarians. Their distinguishing mark is their acceptance of the leadership of the Roman Catholic Church.

The political thought of the Belgian Catholics reflects both the unity and the differences of their group. They have a fundamental political doctrine that is common to all, and may be defined as "untramontane traditionalism." But its interpretation differs somewhat among the components of the group, and Catholic aristocrats, bourgoisie and proletarians attach varied importance to the different points of the same doctrine.

Belgians are more successful in practical politics than in the formulation of political theory. Their genius for compromise is historically evident in their creation of Unionism, later known as Liberal Catholicism. They were the progentiors of this movement, at least on the continent of Europe. Their efforts in this direction were made more difficult by the condemnations of the modern freedoms by Gregory XVI and Pius IX. But Unionism was protected by their bishops and tolerated by Rome. It is unquestionable that it has rendered, and continues to render, great service to the Belgian Church.

Social Catholicism did not, as some people imagine, oppose "liberal Catholicism," or even ultramontane traditionalism. It contented itself in insisting on the importance of the social problems, which had been too much neglected by the "liberal Catholics" after their condemnation in *l'Avenir*. But even in the social field, the Belgians did not make any conspicuous theoretical contribution.

This essay revolves around four points: 1) ultramontane traditionalism; 2) Liberal Catholicism; 3) the condemnation of Liberal Cotholicism; 4) social Catholicism.

I

Before 1789, Catholic intelligence in Belgium had been benumbered by the long possession of power, by a contented sense of well-being and by a patriarchal life. The triple shock of the Revolution, the invasion, and the French occupation was necessary to wake Catholic Belgians from their sleep. Accordingly, they were not aroused by the unselfish love of truth, but by stern necessity. The presence of the Revolutionary troops forced Catholics to concern themselves with the new ideology. Only then did they try to answer the "Philosophers" and to build an intellectual defense. Similar stimuli initiated a tremendous effort throughout Europe by a pleiad of thinkers: Bonald, De Maistre, Eckstein, Savigny, Görres, and many others. All these were concerned to justify their political position, to spread gradually their ideas, and ultimately to recover the control of government. Belgium did not have any writer capable of vying with these French and German Conservatives, but it did provide many disciples: Feller, Foere, Baepsaet, Robiano, Merode, etc., who tried to resolve their special problems, occasionally with original ideas, but more commonly with borrowed arguments.

Their philosophy had two equally important foundations: traditionalism and ultramontanism. The first aimed at the reorganization of society according to nature and history, or at least what the Conservatives imagined as such; the second set down the relation of Church and State. We will consider each in turn.

The Revolutionaries had proposed to reconstruct society on a clear, thoughtful, logical plan, in order to make it more just, more comfortable and more satisfied. The Conservatives, on the other hand, claimed that they respected spontaneous sociological creations. They wished to bring human arrangements into conformity with the "natural" social order. No arbitrary intervention or fixed ideology must shackle the growth of institutions. Only if permitted to develop naturally would these institutions represent faithfully the customs, the needs and the historical condition of a people; only in this case would they be durable and solid. The Philosophers were fond of citing England as an example. To the Traditionalists, she was not free because of the Magna Carta, the Bill of Rights and Habeas Corpus. She possessed her rights, not because of legal instruments, but because she enjoyed the spirit of freedom. The Traditionalists argued that if the love for liberty was to weaken in the English, the above mentioned documents would lose their vitality; they would fall into disuse, no matter how many signatures and seals they bore. The ruler who suppresses or modifies arbitrarily existing instiutions wounds deeply the people for whose happiness he pretends to strive. The latter, sooner or later, will reject his reforms, just as a healthy organism rejects a medicine which is not suitable to it.

The Traditionalists also advocated the free development and the hierarchical subordination of the various natural communities: family, community, business enterprise, etc. They declared that human life can be visualized without the State, but not without the natural communities. These are the real primitive and fundamental cells of society. They are older than the States, and they have the right to manage their own interests under leaders of their choice and according to the methods they desire. The State's role, accordingly, is reduced to a minimum, and Traditionalism does not at all deserve the designation of absolutism or Caesarism. It is the exact opposite, since it divides power, and erects a multitude of barriers between the individual and the central government. Absolutism, on the contrary, weakens and destroys the intermediate bodies and aristocracies, thus reinforcing the central power so strongly that the individual does not have any recourse against it. Even the possession of theoretical rights, often delusive, does not protect the individual in such a situation. Traditionalism further limits the authority of the rulers of the State by granting privileges, veritable bilateral contracts, which state precisely the rights and duties of masters and subjects. If the ruler violates the agreement concluded with the nation, the subjects are absolved of their obedience to him. In these conditions, they owe him neither service nor help. In certain extreme circumstances, the population is justified in revolting.

Finally, Traditionalism had a certain flexibility. Despite opinion to the contrary, the Conservatives did not wish to preserve an exact copy of the past. The Belgian Conservatives were perfectly conscious of the need for adjustment. They argued that whatever comes from life corresponds to an imperious need; whatever is opposed to it in the name of arbitrary ideas, or even crusted tradition, is futile. The true Constitution evolves slowly, but constantly, affected by time, events and by the contributions of successive generations. It grows with the people and it dies with them.

In order to remedy certain consequences of Traditionalism—among others, the weakness of the central power,—the Conservatives invoked a second concept to complement the first: ultamontism. They imputed to the Church the solution of the problems which they were not able to solve themselves. They reasoned that the Church will maintain order and peace by introducing into society the notion of the *sacred,* an idea that generates both respect and fear. Once the authority of the ruler is covered with the sign of legitimacy, a number of difficulties will be resolved and a number of revolts pacified, including even the rebellion of conscience. Besides, the Church would be empowered to check those in authority who violated their promises, and who did not respect the acquired and sacred rights of their subjects. The Church could take action even in violations of simple equity and could apply certain sanctions, going even so far as absolving the subjects from their oath of loyalty.

The Church, therefore, would subordinate to its supreme authority all communities, all rulers, all States. Would this be theocracy? The Ultramontanists would not be frightened by the term. They insisted that the essential point was that this arrangement was in favor of the people as well as of the kings, of justice as well as of order. And that this sword of justice might be strong and respected, the Conservatives considered necessary that the Church be strong, united, rich, free, and disciplined under a supreme pontiff, the infallible pope. Without him, they believed, society would be dangerously shaken; with him, it would be firmly based. Lamennais later summed up this position in a striking series: "No pope, no Church; no Church, no Christianity; no Christianity, no religion, at least for all peoples who had been Christians; no religion, no society."

The Gallicans and Febronians dismissed all this as empty rationalization. They appealed to documents, texts and traditions which opposed such an expansion of the powers of the pope. They argued that history and experience should warn us against papal ambition. Powerful popes tend to become corrupt, to abuse their authority and to involve the Church and society in their fall, rather than acting as agents of social salvation.

The Conservatives, following Joseph de Maistre, agreed that in the early centuries the bishops had more influence and the pope less authority than today. But should this be a reason for condemning an historical evolution that was required by the very expansion of the Church? Must she remain fixed in a stony immobility? Undoubtedly, the monarchical supremacy of the Sovereign Pontiff was not operative in the beginning and became so only after a few centuries of Christian history; "but it is exactly in this that the Church appears divine; because everything that exists legitimately and over a long period, exists first in embryo and develops gradually." The Church is life. It does not escape, it cannot escape the universal laws of change and evolution.

The Papacy, countered its detractors, has blood on its hands. She has been corrupted with gold and she has corrupted in turn; she has allied herself with the powerful against the weak; she has sought the domination of the world, not the establishment of the Kingdom of God. Exaggerations, answered de Maistre. The Popes have always been satisfied with a very modest temporal state and if, in the Middle Ages, their power was great, it was because it was necessary at the time and no substitute could be found for papal power. Besides, the papacy, in the temporal order, is a monarchy like any other. "And what evils do not result from the best constituted monarchy?" The princes mentioned in history are for the most part unmitigated rascals. If an ordinary man were to commit one-tenth of their crimes he would be put to death forthwith. And yet men have tolerated their rulers; even in retrospect, they support them, since every one realizes that the absence of authority brings disorders infinitely greater than its passing abuses. What is true for the State, is also true for the Church, with this difference, that the pope is "always old, celibate and a priest, facts which exclude ninety percent of the errors and passions that afflict the States."

Is this logic more brilliant than true? Perhaps. The ultramontane traditionalist conception—assuredly debatable—has a certain attraction, and in our way of thinking, historians have not insisted sufficiently on the depth and vigor of the intellectual reaction of the Conservatives. In order to regain the mastery of minds and the reality of power, the Church and the aristocracy opposed syllogism to syllogism, and concept to concept. This effort produced those remarkable works, *The Theory of Power*, *The Papacy, Religion*, and many others, veritable arsenals from which the Belgian Catholics have drawn both justifications and slogans.

II

Political thories, no matter how ingenious, do not of themselves bring victory. To gain power, they must be butressed by skillful tactics. In this respect, the Belgian Catholics found themselves on extremely unfavorable ground. They had experienced first the dictatorship of the "sans culotte," the Terror and persecution; then the police-regime of Napoleon, hostile to all manifestations of free thought; and finally after the allied victory of 1814, the union with Holland under a government just a little less tyrannical than those which had preceeded.

In this government, the Catholics constituted the Opposition. Without being actually persecuted, they were none the less bullied. Febronians were in charge of the ministry which directed religious affairs; the Jesuits and other orders were forbidden; the government interfered in the nomination of bishops and three out of the five sees were vacant; episcopal influence in education was increasingly diminished; negotiations for a Concordat were dragging; the ultramontane and traditionalist nobility were excluded from high position. Catholics were very anxious to change this painful situation. But how escape from a difficult position? The King was obstinate, and the Catholic deputies were in a minority.

The weakness of the Conservative party seemed irreparable when an important change took place. Its significance was not immediately apparent. In 1824-1825 a group of young liberals, gathered around *Mathieu Laensbergh,* a newspaper of Liège, began to preach a new political theory. The older Liberals had feared the clericals and had sacrificed their principles to the advantage of the tyrannical government. But the new generation was sure of its power and no longer was frightened by the Conservatives. They were more deeply disturbed by an "absolutist" government and so they demanded, without fear of consequences, complete liberty for all and the end of governmental despotism.

In an ingenious speech the Baron de Gerlache, the political leader of the Catholics, took advantage of the situation and addressed himself to the young Liberals as follows: "You ask for freedom of industry and of the press. You seek a jury system and an efficient parliamentary control. Very well. But do not forget the freedoms demanded by the Catholics, especially the freedom of education. This is the price of our support. If you recognize our title to liberty, we will unite our forces with yours and the government will be forced to listen."

Thus to embarrass William I, Gerlache aimed to separate some of the Liberals from the government bloc. But would not this entirely new line cause serious embarassment to the Catholics? The Church had not, in principle, approved full freedom of opinion. It could not concede that truth and error should be placed on the same footing. In 1815, Monsignor de Broglie, the bishop of Ghent, had condemned the fundamental law which permitted such a freedom. But why had de Broglie published this judgment? Because he was hoping for a Constitution which would grant to the Church the privileges which she had enjoyed in the Old Regime. He had failed, and everything pointed to the same fate for all similar attempts. Obviously, one could not hope for a policy of the greater good, but must be content with one of the lesser evil. Time was pressing, for the government was moving toward the control of Catholic education. Hence the Church must take advantage of all means of defense at her disposal.

The "doctrinaire" Liberals, although interested in the proposition of Gerlache, would not initially accept it. They believed that it had some merit, but they did not trust the sincerity of its promoter. Two years later, however, they reconsidered their position, and they themselves proposed to the Catholics, through the writings of P. Devaux, a union against the government. They had come to the conclusion that the greater he number of the followers of freedom, the greater were the chances of speedily achieving some concrete results.

In Liège, two newspapers, the *Courrier de la Meuse* (Catholic) and the Mathieu Laensburgh (Liberal), followed henceforth a parallel political line. Their aim was not to overthrow the monarchy of William or the kingdom of the Netherlands, but to establish a truly representative government. Tacit agreements, similiar to the one which linked the *Mathieu* and the *Courrier de la Meuse* were concluded in various other areas. The union expanded during the first months of 1828 to the *Journal du Limbourg* and the *Catholique des Pays-Bas* of Ghent. In October and November of 1828 the *Courrier des Pays-Bas* also embraced Unionism. Thus by the end of this year the union between the various factions of Belgian thought had become a reality: old and new Liberals on the one hand, and Conservatives on the other, had reached an accord. The first petitions, supported secretly by the clergy, had begun to circulate in the vicinity of Roulers. The States-General resounded with vigorous speeches. The general offensive against despotism had begun, and the government was in retreat.

The Catholic-Liberal Union, later called Liberal Catholicism had been born. It is necessary now to define it with precision.

The Liberals no longer regarded William I as their defender; he had become an obstacle to their program. They believed that a free government would bring triumph to their cause, permit them to vanquish the Catholics legally and to govern the country. This was the origin of their desire to establish a Parliamentary regime on a restricted suffrage. They had no intention of surrendering their views on rationalism, individualism or laicism. The *Mathieu* declared it expressly: "The free examination of political matters leads to the free discussion of religious questions."

For the Catholics, William I was another Joseph II. They believed that he would never right their grievances. On the contrary, the Liberals, at least the theoretical Liberals, manifested a more conciliatory dispostition. They advocated general freedom. The Catholics felt that they must take advantage of this opportunity, establish with their help a parliamentary regime, decree the freedom of education and of the press, and then within the new framework, attempt to gain a peaceful preponderance.

The Union did not settle all problems. After, as before the establishment of the parliamentary regime, there would be conflict. But before there was war to the end, with both parties using material violence when they had the opportunity: police, tribunals, censorship, etc. After the expulsion of the Dutch, it became an intellectual war, "with theories attacking theories, with each side defending itself with reasoning and with the triumph going to logic and truth." Instead of wishing as before, and with the use of every means, the exclusive victory of Catholicism and the enslavement of free thought, or on the other hand, the reign of Reason and the persecution of faith, the antagonists had agreed to fight and to win solely by weapons of the spirit.

Unionism, at least in its inception, is therefore nothing else but the acceptance of the freedoms and institutions necessary for the peaceful battle of ideas and parties. Both Catholics and Liberals hoped to gain the maximum advantages from such tactics. There is no question of the surrender of principle. Both retain their own philosophy. Between their respective opinions there is no amalgamation or fusion. There is no abandonment by Catholics of traditionalism and ultramontism. The term "Liberal Catholicism," as used today, does not define its aim properly. Besides, it was almost unknown in 1830 when Union and Unionism were burning issues.

Indeed, if Unionism were a theory and not a simple political method conceived under the pressure of events, it would have previously have developed its theoreticians. But the Catholic intellectuals did not play any important role in its genesis. It was the product of men of action: the Keestens, the Gerlaches, etc. The Abbè de Lamennais, whom some people see as its promoter, actually had no part in it. His book, *Des Progrés de la Révolution*, appeared long after the conclusion of the Liberal-Catholic alliance.

Far from having influenced the Union, Lamennais was influenced by it. It is not our opinion that the author of *Des Progrès* was a simple imitator of the Belgians. We do believe however, with the Abbè Duine, that Lamennais found in Unionism "a decisive argument in favor of his convictions on the value of liberty in the formation of a new society." The Union seemed to him an experience certainly limited in space, but universally valid. He saw its success or failure determining the success or failure of a method which went far beyond the narrow limits of its birth-place. Belgium, during those years 1829 and 1830, was for him the testing-ground, or as George Goyau put it, "the soil of victorious experimentation" of Liberal Catholicism. That is why Lamennais viewed the first efforts of the new politics with such interest. That is also why he proclaimed them to the world and made Unionism the hall-mark of Catholicism in the nineteenth century.

III

The Revolution of September 1830, the complete separation of the northern and southern provinces of the Netherlands and the birth of the Belgian State were not at all included in the first intentions of the Unionist leaders. The victory of the insurgents had unexpectedly far-reaching consequences: it facilitated the realization of their program and led to the adoption of the Constitution.

Lay Catholics considered this new Charter as a reaction against the centralism of William I and consequently as a triumph, at least partial, of their traditionalist theories. If the local powers, especially the provinces, no longer exerted as much influence as under the Old Regime, at least regional tendencies remained strong and very characteristic. The natural communities, with the exception of the province and municipality, found their safeguard in Article XX: "Belgians have the right to assemble; this right is not to be subjected to any preventive measure." The powers of the King, of the government and of the two Houses of Parliament were strictly delimited and counter-balanced. Arbitrary government appeared impossible in the light of these restrictions. Other provisions, no less important, assured Belgians of the maximum guarantees against the abuses of power: the independence of the magistracy, the equality of citizens before the law, the inviolability of the home, freedom of assembly, the right to petition, the privacy of letters, etc. Certainly the whole ground lost by Catholics since 1794 was not recovered,—far from it,—but they had gained considerable improvement. Their triumph might portend other successes, since an honest struggle was now possible with the Liberals. Thus, an air of hope, confidence and pride encouraged the Conservatives. Practically everyone had the conviction that he had remained faithful to his spiritual heritage. It is possible that a great part of this optimism was illusion. But the sentiment was real.

If the Constitution fulfilled the expectations of the Catholic laymen, the clergy appeared equally satisfied. The Prince de Méan, Archibshop of Malines, having been advised by the vicar-general Sterckx and Bishop Van Bommel of Liège, had asked the National Congress in a public letter:

1. That the observance of the Catholic religion should never be prohibited or restrained.

2. That it should be perfectly free and independent in its government, especially in the nomination and installation of its clergy and in its correspondence with the Holy See.

3. That education and association be unrestricted.

4. That the State provide the salaries of clergymen and the expenses of worship.

The wishes of the Archbishop were generally well-received. In spite of the opposition of certain Liberals, the majority sided with the Prince de Méan. Strictly speaking, there would no longer be separation between the religious and civil authorities, but only reciprocal independence. The Church would retain the advantages of protection and of subsidies, but would be relieved of its inconveniences in the form of governmental supervision. Should not the Church be satisfied? The Constitution had adopted almost the entire program which had been presented in 1829 to William I by the Bishop of Liège. The two central themes of this program had been freedom and protection of worship—a freedom that did not exclude protection and a protection that would not destroy freedom.

The Belgian clergy, accordingly, approved Unionism and the Constitution. But the sentiments of Rome differed considerably. In 1832 Gregory XVI published *Mirari Vos*. In this document there was condemned freedom of conscience, freedom of books, the Revolutions, the separation of Church and State, the Union between Catholics and Liberals. However, the Belgian Constitution, which had actualized all these, was not condemned in the Encyclical, both because it had been voted and promulgated before the Encyclical, and because it was a legal and official text, a positive law, not a declaration of principles. Rome felt obliged to respect it. Besides, the vicar-general Sterckx had not hidden his opinions. In agreement with Bishop Van Bommel, he had sent to Rome a very clever report which was extremely favorable to the new Charter. Gregory XVI appreciated certain articles in the Constitution, and Monsignor Capaccini, who had responsibility in the Vatican for Belgian affairs, encouraged the Pope in his favorable attitude. Thus in spite of the continuous intrigues of the Belgian ultra-Conservatives and of several influential Roman prelates, notably Lambruschini, the Constitution was not censured either directly or indirectly, although it was certainly exposed to danger.

The Constitution, then, had excaped the displeasure of Rome. But Unionism, which was the parent of the Constitution, was certainly condemned. Hence the embarassment, anxiety and confusion of the Belgian Catholics was extreme.

A minority among them, the uncompromising Intransigents, sincerely repudiated the Unionist policy. Catholics, wrote Louis de Robiano, have the duty "not to consider as good either freedom of opinion, or of conscience or of the press; not to place their hopes on them, nor to try to establish them where they do not exist, nor to wish to keep them where the Catholic social system could be re-established; and to get together either by conviction or authority and use wisely their means and their faculties (sic) in order to discredit every opinion which deviates from the judgment of Rome."

The vast majority, however, did not pay serious attention to the Encyclical. Unionism, or Liberal Catholicism, was not condemned in Belgium, nor could it be, they argued, because its results were so favorable to the Church. "The Pope," wrote the *Journal des Flandres,* "would not prefer the philosophical College to the Catholic University, the institutions of the atheists to the numerous colleges organized according to the tenets of Catholicism, the closing of the seminaries to the actual prosperity of these clerical nurseries. To tolerate errors is not, after all, to recognize them as truths. Because our Constitution declares that no one may be forced to observe the Sabbath, does it follow that this observance is not obligatory for a Catholic?" The bishops, by not publishing *Mirari Vos,* and according the same treatment later to *Singulari Vos,* gave a semblance of justification to this point of view.

The agitation created by *Mirari Vos* had just subsided, when a second peril appeared: Leopold I determined to increase his powers, and to that end he desired a docile episcopate and clergy. In order to bend them to his wishes, he sought the support of the Nuncio, whom he considered as a sort of natural head of the episcopate. And in order to win over the Nuncio, he counted on the influence in Rome of Prince Metternich.

In reality, the King was laboring under an illusion. Above all else, the Belgian clergy dreaded submission to the civil power. A very powerful King was not at all to their liking. It can be accepted as a general rule that the power of the Church is diminished in the exact ratio as the power of the State is increased. And the Belgian Church was not thinking in terms of limiting its forces, but of increasing them. If the King and his followers succeeded, Unionism would be shelved. Consequently, the Archbishop and several bishops opposed vigorously, although secretly, the royal policies. Instead of condemning those Catholics who opposed the King, as Leopold would have wished, the episcopate showed themselves friendly towards them. They were thus able to frustrate the plans of the government, without involving themselves. In addition, the Nuncio, His Grace Monsignor Gizzi, probably at the instigation of Monsignor Capaccini, the friend of Mgr. Sterkx, no longer supported the royal policy.

Leopold I, vexed by this failure, did not hide his disappointment. He sought the aid of Metternich, who in turn pressured the Holy See by the first available messenger. Gregory XVI immediately asked Mgr. Sterckx for an explanation. The Bishop of Ghent, who had opposed the grant of further powers to the King, was forced to resign. His successor, Mgr. Delebecque used rather harsh means to bring the Flemish clergy back to opinions more in conformity with the Encyclical. The reading of the two Catholic newspapers, the *Journal des Flandres* and the *Vaderlander*, was forbidden to the clergy. Mgr. Gizzi was replaced by Mgr. Fornari, who was completely devoted to the King. A veritable rivalry soon broke out between the new Nuncio and Cardinal Sterckx, who yielded reluctantly to the Nuncio's directives and control. The King, supported by Mgr. Fornari, by Metternich and perhaps by the Jesuits, several times imposed his will on the Cardinal, who appeared deeply wounded. The relations between Fornari and Sterckx became so bad that the Nuncio was recalled. Mgr. Pecci, the future Leo XIII, who replaced him, took the side of the episcopate. Leopold protested. After three years, Mgr. Pecci was also forced to leave Belgium.

It must not be thought from these incidents that Cardinal Sterckx refused to come to an understanding with the State. He deeply desired an agreement, and he succeeded in many instances, notably in matters involving education. But he would not surrender his independence under orders of the government and the King. He intended at all cost to keep his authority, his independence and his power intact—to preserve the advantages which Unionism had brought him. With them he could hold his own victoriously against the State, and even occasionally control it.

From 1839 to 1850 the controversy between the intransigent Catholics and the so-called Liberal Catholics somewhat subsided. It began again a little later under the influence of *L'Univers* of Louis Veuillot and of its Belgian counterpart, the *Bien Public*. The speech of Montalembert at the Congress of Malines (August, 1863) brought to a head the tensions between the two groups. The Belgian organizers of the Congress had not desired a quarrel. But Montalembert was determined to pronounce publically his "political testament." His speech is well-known, particularly his famous formula, "A free Church in a free State." Cardinal Sterckx congratulated the orator who had spoken he said, like a "true theologian." Many in Belgium and in Rome did not share this opnion and were not loath to disclose their views. Various intrigues were set in motion at the Vatican, the details of which need not here detain us.

Cardinal Sterckx, alarmed by these agitations and fearing for Unionism, decided once more to take the lead. Without consulting either the Nuncio or Rome, he wrote two public letters, later published in a brochure entitled, *The Belgian Constitution and the Encyclical of Gregory XVI*. It must be insisted that the Cardinal did not have any intention of starting a theological discussion. He wished merely to save his work, and with it the unity of the Catholics and the Constitution. "My letters," he wrote, "speak neither of the *thesis* nor the *hypothesis*. They have no other aims than to justify our Constitution and the Congress of 1830 which formed it." The author asserted that Gregory XVI had not condemned the Constitution. Nor did the Constitution establish the separation of Church and State, but had merely recognized the distinction between them. Nor did it tolerate the modern errors, except in the civil forum.

The letters created a considerable impression both in Belgium and abroad. The Liberal Catholics applauded. Cardinal Antonelli, on the contrary, was displeased, and it was necessary for Sterckx to justify himself. He succeeded, but not without effort. Montalembert,, meanwhile, had been personally blamed by Pius IX. In December, 1864, there appeared the *Syllabus* and the Encyclical *Quanta Cura*. Even though the speech at Malines was the occasion for these documents, neither Montalembert nor Cardinal Sterckx nor the Belgian Constitution was mentioned. In short, the *status quo* was restored. The Constitution again escaped any censure, but "modern liberties" were once more condemned.

The Belgian Catholics did not understand any better than in 1832 this distinction between the Constitution and Unionism. "If the constitutional liberties are the biggest scourge," declared the *Vaderlander* as early as 1839, "the most natural conclusion is that they must be abolished; and, when they are abolished,

what will remain of the Constitution of 1830? We are curious
to know the answer." The controversy continued. The pamphlet, *Catholique et politique,* which violently attacked the Constitution, created a loud reverberation. In order to reassure
public opinion, the government inserted in a speech from the
throne a passage which mentioned the devotion of the country
to the constitutional liberties. The Catholic Party, torn by
internal struggles, lost the election of 1878.

The death of Pius IX in the same year and the election of
Leo XIII to the pontifical throne radically changed the situation. The new Pope, former Nuncio in Brussels, was well-
acquainted with the Constitution and the Unionism which
established it. His opinion on these matters was much more
delicately shaded than that of his predecessor. His first declaration to the Belgians included the following: "It would be
going against the views of the Holy See to attack or censure
your Constitution. Catholics must obey it without mental reservations. I hope that this question is definitely resolved and
that no Catholic will stir it up again." Further, this distinction
between *thesis* and *hypothesis,* which was factually applied
from the start by most of the Belgian Catholics and which was
later stated explicitly by Mgr. Dupanloup, now received formal
approval. R. P. Dechamps, later Cardinal archbishop of Malines, had especially well defined it: "Freedom of evil is not the
normal system towards which human society should tend; this
is the thesis. But in countries of divided faith or opinions the
government which approves this freedom at the same time that
it approves the freedom of the good, is adapting itself to the
situation; and when this is sanctified by a Constitution which
has all the characteristics of a solemn agreement, it is the duty
of Catholics to remain loyal; this is the hypothesis." The encyclicals of Leo XIII on liberalism gave final satisfaction to consciences, at least in Belgium.

IV

Social Catholicism and Liberal Catholicism are not so opposed to each other as they have often pretended to be. There
is no real antagonism between them. Both accept in theory
untramontane traditionalism, and in practice, the modern
liberties. Taking into consideration the natural evolution of
events and of minds, there is no essential difference between
the opnions of a Henry de Merode and a Godefoid Kurth, of
a François Vergauen and an Arthur Verhaegen. The Liberal
Catholics of 1830, at least the intellectuals among them, wished

to establish society on a solid basis, in conformity with the natural order, or what they considered the natural order to be. They were not committed to any doctrinaire individualism following the rationalist pattern. *L'Avenir* under the signature of de Coux, later professor at the University of Louvain, devoted many articles to the condition of the working classes. In Belgium, Beauffort, Merode, Robiano, not to mention the Catholic democrats such as Bartels, proposed an equitable solution for the social problem. Louis de Robiano, speaking of England,—and the condition was not very different on the Continent—wrote as follows: "The aristocracy, especially the industrial and commercial aristocracy, actually crush the people under their domination. Their arrogance can only be measured by the humiliation of the lower classes; but the latter are ready to emerge from their strange apathy." It must be insisted that the later Social Catholics were not reacting against their liberal Catholic forebears. On the contrary, they were inspired by their predessors' writings and would follow their policy.

With this established, it cannot be denied that there exists in the intellectual domain a hiatus between the first years of Liberal Catholicism, up till about 1839, and the first years of Social Catholicism (about 1870-1890). There is no doubt that Liberal Catholicism did not bear its expected fruit in the social area. To what is this due? Certainly *Mirari Vos* was a factor. In condemning Lamennais, it halted the intellectual Catholic movement. The majority of Catholic Belgian writers, journalists and philosophers approved of Lamennais. After *Mirari Vos* they either kept silence or appeared timid, hesitant, and fearful. The hope and enthusiasm necessary for great intellectual constructions was destroyed. Besides, the Catholic bourgeoisie were finding too many advantages in the economic and liberal social system not to wish its continuation. There followed, at least in practice, a veritable Liberalism of the Catholics. Professor Perin of Louvain appeared as its timid defender. But this development does not warrant accusations of social indifference against men like de Merode and Lamennais. If the "Liberal Catholics" really became liberal in the social sense, this did not occur at the beginning of their movement, but at its end. It was not because they remained faithful to the initial program, but because they misunderstood it.

We perceive the first traces of what shall be called the later Social Catholicism in the general assemblies of Catholics at Malines in 1863, 1864 and 1867. The Secretary General of the Congress, Ed. Ducpétiaux, had engineered a discussion on the organization of modern industry. Besides, he filed a series of resolutions which demanded that "the minimum age for admission to factories be fixed by law; that work be limited to twelve hours per day; that women be prevented by law from working underground; that the hygienic conditions of workshops be regulated by the State; that working conditions be under administrative inspection; that international agreements be concluded for the unification of social legislation." The plan bore no results.

In 1871, another Catholic, G. de Jaer, published in *L'Economie chrétienne* a series of very remarkable articles. He particularly advocated the Sunday rest, the Christian organization of the work of women, respect for apprenticeship in school and factory, the reduction of the daily working hours to a reasonable limit, the payment of wages in cash, the organization of consultive labor committees, the elimination of the worker's compulsory registration card and the abolition of Article 1781 from the Civil Code. M. de Jaer had even less success than Ducpétiaux and was obliged to interrupt his series of articles.

It was the example of the German Catholics which made the greatest impression on the Belgians. After 1873 the program of Bishop Ketteler was adopted by the Catholics beyond the Rhine. Social legislation to protect labor, as well as old age and sickness insurance, had been passed by the Reichstag. Purely liberal ideas were gradually going down to defeat.

These changes influenced the Belgians. But they were even more impressed by events in their own nation. The terrible strikes of 1886, the riots and arsons, the repressions under the direction of General Van der Smissen, and the increasing power of the Socialist Party did more to reveal the existence of the social question and the urgent need for reform than all the theories in the world. Prime Minister Beernaert, a Catholic, applied himself to the problem. In a speech from the throne he said: "The condition of the working classes is a matter of first importance and it will be the duty of the legislature to try with extreme zeal to improve it. Justice demands that the law particularly protect the weak and the suffering. It is especially praiseworthy to encourage the free formation of new bonds between the leaders of industry and the workers which will take the form of councils of arbitration and conciliation. Laws must regulate the work of women and children, must repress abuses existing in the payment of wages, facilitate the construction of suitable housing for the workers, and aid in the development of institutions of assistance, insurance and pensions, and to try to combat the ravage of drunkenness and immorality."

In Liège, Mgr. Doutreloux organized international social congresses (1886, 1887, and 1890) which were very successful. The social program of the Belgian Catholics was summed up by Charles Woeste: regulation of the work of children; obligatory insurance; recognition and organization of trade unions. On the latter point a long and familiar controversy broke out between the proponents of the mixed unions of employers and workers and the advocates of the true trade union. The latter won in 1891 after the publication of the Encyclical *Rerum Novarum*. This same year saw the birth of the Belgian Democratic League, which set out immediately to form trades unions. The League was under the direction of G. Helleputte, A. Verhaegen, L. Mabille, G. Kurth, and the Abbé Pottier. Continuous and painful controversies marked its debut. The employers were generally hostile. A Flemish clergyman with advanced ideas, the Abbé Daens, was barred from the movement in 1897.

The Catholic trade unions never equalled the importance of the Socialist unions. But in the rural areas, the Catholic organizations were far in the lead. With the help of F. Schollaert and the Abbé Mallaerts, Helleputte created the *Boerenbond*, a federation of the rural guilds which applied the cooperative formula to common purchases, insurance, sales of agricultural products, the establishment of creameries, etc. The wealth and power of this organization grew gradually with the years.

The Catholic trade unions contributed to the development of social legislation. They also helped to preserve the religious beliefs and the traditional loyalties of a large part of the population, especially in the Flemish region. The contribution of Belgian Social Catholicism to political thought was, however, quite small. The great Belgian contribution was still Unionism, a spontaneous and general movement which achieved rapid success and which served as an example and encouragement to other European Catholics. Social Catholicism in Belgium remained indebted to other countries, particularly Germany. It progressed slowly, and became a really great factor only in the rural regions.

Traditionalism and ultramontanism, Liberal Catholicism and Social Catholicism can be readily explained and comprehended if one starts with the assumption that in the Belgian nation there was a Catholic group with its own life and interests. As long as it enjoyed these, as under the Old Regime, where it had an uncontested supremacy, it did not produce a political theory or practice, nor did it develop any particular intellectual effort of importance. When adverse pressure was experienced, necessity gave birth to the theories and methods that were essential for the group's conservation and expansion. Liberal Catholicism gained a faster and easier success because it did not concern itself with any material interest; Social Catholicism's progress was slower because it attacked certain privileges of the commercial and industrial bourgeoisie. But both, in the final analysis, stem from the same vital need of the group to adapt to new conditions and so to live.

Henri Haag.

CHAPTER II

CONTEMPORARY CATHOLIC SOCIAL ACTION IN BELGIUM[1]

The Christian Labor Movement in Belgium (C. L. M.) starts with the assumption that employers will grant very little to their workers from conscience or benevolence. Accordingly, it is imperative that workers organize and effect a constant pressure to win just conditions of work and to gain wages that will be in keeping with their legitimate needs and with the fluctuating and developing possibilities of the economy. But workers' organizations must go beyond the satisfaction of these basic needs. They must aim at a structural reform of the economic and social system which has brought bitterness and revolt into the lives of the proletariat, and which has been condemned by the Church.

The fundamental reasons for the Catholic opposition to the existing system may be summarized as follows:

1. Unjust distribution of wealth, which allows some to live in luxury while condemning the majority to conditions that threaten their dignity, security, and freedom, and which robs them of the means for their material and spiritual development.

2. The denial of property rights to workers. Though they labor a lifetime in an industry, they remain simple wage-earners without any share or voice in management.

3. The social and political power of financial and industrial leaders, who use their power to increase profits and deny justice to their employees.

For these reasons, the C. L. M. must have powerful trade unions, political organizations, and social and economic institutions such as mutual insurance companies. All these must be inspired by Christian sociological principles and must enjoy the benefit of unity in a common cause.

The modern industrial worker feels that he has a right to a decent human and Christian life. But he finds himself in the grip of social and psychological conditions which make his hopes illusory. He is the victim of a variety of factors which have depersonalized and de-Christianized him. The moral basis of his life has been destroyed and this has led to a distortion of his fundamental human values:

1. The atmosphere of his work and his home have deprived him of his sense of personal dignity.

2. He has become prey to acute class consciousness, compounded from the conflicting attitudes of class inferiority and class power. This generates a strong distrust of all decisions taken by the "bourgeoisie" and of all alliances with the middle class. It also leads to a presumption in favor of those who propose revolutionary solutions of existing problems.

3. His quest for material means has diminished the influence of moral and spiritual values. To some degree, he has sought pleasure and comfort, resented the obligations of children and married love, lost interest in religion and culture, and diminished his respect for authority.

4. His family ties have weakened because of the pressure of his environment, the atmosphere of the factory, and the weakening of his sense of moral discipline.

5. He has lost his joy in his work which offers him no scope for his personality. His labor has become standardized, monotonous, and over-specialized.

The C. L. M. cannot allow the worker to struggle unaided against these adverse forces. It must reestablish his human and Christian personality. Its primary role is to eliminate the social factors which have dehumanized the workingman. But it must also labor unceasingly for the education, training, and reconversion of the workers, so that they will recapture the meaning of life and recover Christian values. Without this effort to reestablish the ideals of personality, humanity, and Christianity, success in the economic and social field can lead only to disappointment. The real goal is to give back to the worker his full human dignity and worth as a Christian.

The future orientation of the world will depend on the outcome of this struggle for the soul of the industrial worker. He is in a dilemma: he is torn between the forces of atheist and totalitarian Communism and of its less virulent relative, secular state-socialism on the one hand, and social Christianity on the other. The entire human community depends on the choice that is made. Accordingly, Social Christianity must work vigorously for constructive solutions that will include far-reaching social reforms. It must concern itself with the entire life of man, for his life is one and indivisible, with the social and economic closely bound with the spiritual. Its program must be integral Christian humanism; its aim a new social order, based on the true conceptions of man, society, and economics; its activity as broad as the problem itself. Since the world of labor involves the factory, the home, and the family, housing, recreation, culture and ideas, the C. L. M. must encompass them all. Since these conditions affect both sexes, and both adult and young, all must be included in a broad effort. But while all must be gathered into a great unity, there must be specialization within the general framework, so that each sex and age group can find self-expression and a solution for its particular problems.

Most importantly, this movement must remain *in* and *of* the working class, and must not rest on generous spirits who desire to do something *for* the workers. "By the workers, for the workers, among the workers" is the only true formula. The assistance of non-workers is welcome, and may even be necessary. But it must never reduce the role of the worker or his consciousness that this is his movement. The reasons are obvious:

1. The fact of class consciousness. The working class feels that it has come of age and it intends to be its own master. To ignore this reality is to fail. The bourgeoisie must realize that the workers were not born to be silent servants, but are determined to work out their destiny with the dignity and liberty which are the right of every man. We must trust the workers with responsibility for their own movement.

2. The human personality of the worker cannot be restored unless he is entrusted with the task. He must be given a chance to develop his own natural leadership, even though, in the beginning, he may need some help from the outside. A healthy democracy will not function without this conscious and responsible initiative from each social group.

3. There can be no depth or extension of the work among the masses, and no hope of re-conversion, unless authentic workers make it their own cause and push it as their activity. Priests should beware of giving an atmosphere of clericalism, and bourgeois laymen an appearance of paternalism to the movement.

Such an analysis demands that the C. L. M. be organized in a series of activities with a three-fold aim:

1. *Totality*: to deal with the whole man, and to organize the total effort of the working class toward a more equitable world and a more truly human and Christian life. Thus it must deal with:

    a) The worker's whole personality.
    b) Working class life as a whole.
    c) The worker's entire family.
    d) All the wants of labor.
    e) The entire working class.

Hence the worker should find everything he needs in the organization; and it should aim to win over the entire working class. Accordingly, though Christian in principle, it is open to

all workers, and requires for membership no declaration of
faith and no proof of religious practice.

2. *Complexity*. The worker needs:

a) Protection of his professional interests; representation
on commissions and boards; a place in the organic integration of a vocational community—hence, Trade
Unions: *Confédération des Syndicats Chretiens, C.S.C.*

b) Security—mutual insurance companies: *Alliance Nationale des Mutualités 'Chrétiennes.*

c) Economic aid—cooperatives, savings banks, insurance
plans: *Fédération Nationale des Coopératives Chrétie-
nes.*

d) Means to promote social reform on the state level:
political groupings.

e) Agencies for formation, propaganda and the apostolate
which would be specialized according to the needs of
men (KWB: *Katholieke Werkliedenbond; Equipes
populaires*) , women (KAV: Katholieke arbeidersvrou-
*wengilden; LOFC: Ligues Ouvrières Féminines Chré-
tiennes*, young workemen (KAJ: *Katholieke Arbeidersjeugd;* JOC: *Jeunesse Ouvrière Chrétienne*) and
young workwomen (VKAJ: *Vrouwelijke Katholieke
Arbeidersjeugd;* JOCF: *Jeunesse Ouvrière Chrétienne
Féminine*) .

All these organizations are too diverse to be put under the
direct control of one general headquarters. Because each has its
special task and special competence, each should enjoy a large
measure of autonomy in everything that concerns its own special
field. Accordingly, each has its own management, membership,
leaders, and financial resources, although all share the same
secretariat building. This allows each its necessary freedom. Besides, several (the trade unions, mutual insurance companies,
and women's leagues) were in existence before the general
movement was founded in 1921, and had acquired an independent viewpoint. Finally, trade unions and mutual insurance companies, which must be represented on boards beyond the confines of the labor movement, must be free to act with perfect
freedom in their own domain. And the Young Christian Workers (JOC and JOCF), begun in 1925, are a Catholic Action
movement, and thus have a closer tie with the regular ecclesiastical organization.

3. *Unity*: all these are not isolated efforts without organic
relationship, because:

a) The problems of all are interrelated.

b) The organizations need mutual support.

c) Friction and competition among them must be avoided.

d) All deal with the same human material.

Actually, all are mutually complementary. Each is a fraction of a total effort. There must be unity of will and spirit, there must be coordination of attitudes and efforts. There must be a solid front that can become a powerful bulwark in the national life, for only large organizations of the masses are effective in modern democracies.

The present form of the Christian Labor Movement of Belgium was adopted in 1921. It was not a sudden inspiration, but the result of hard historical lessons. Before that date, there had been only unrelated social services and a Catholic Party which included some representatives of Christian social thought. These had expended considerable energies. In a working class that was increasingly suspicious of things Catholic, they had registered only indifferent results. By 1918, the situation had grown critical, and by 1920, the Socialist trade unions had 718,000 members, while the Christian unions numbered 65,000.

It was this growing weakness that forced a reevaluation of the whole movement. The Abbé Rutten had founded the Secretariat of Christian Trade Unions in 1901. Even before that, Christian mutual insurance companies for sickness and old age insurance had been founded in many places. In the same period workers' study circles were being formed. While these social movements were appearing, the Belgian working class was still very faithfully attached to the Christian tradition; the clergy possessed great social influence; Catholic schools, Sunday schools and clubs were to be found everywhere; the Catholic press was well-organized; Saint Vincent de Paul societies for the relief of the poor were numerous, and homogeneous Catholic ministries had held governmental power uninterruptedly from 1883 till 1914.

The Socialists, on the other hand, had begun with a few adherents, mostly ex-Liberals. At first they found it difficult to win supporters in the Catholic parishes. Their press and financial means were very limited. Their representation in Parliament was as yet negligible. Their hostility to the Church faced the opposition of the ancient Catholic tradition of the working class. As assets, they had a program that was bold and revolutionary in tone, a dynamic will to serve the people, and the miserable condition of the urban proletarians.

With these assets, they made steady progress. An analysis led the Social Christians to the following conclusions:

1. The Christian social organizations lacked the distinctly

labor character that was needed to gain the confidence of the workers. For fear of the class warfare preached by the Socialists, the Catholics did not dare to establish purely labor organizations led by workers themselves. This was particularly true in the trade unions, the essential weapon in the struggle for improved working conditions. Generally the Christian social services were financed and managed by well-meaning persons who were anxious to preserve the religious faith of the workers and who were sympathetic with their poverty and discontent. But they were fatally handicapped because they did not belong to the working class. Theirs was social action *for* the worker, but in an atmosphere of bourgeois and clerical paternalism. Their intentions were good, and one can understand their fears. But they lacked confidence and daring, and made a fundamental psychological mistake. On the contrary, the workers felt among themselves with the Socialists. Here there was no bourgeois custody and restraint. Socialism meant self-assertion, while Catholicism appeared as cautious control.

2. The Christian social organizations lacked a positive, constructive, and progressive program. Too often they seemed a mere defense mechanism against Socialism. Their main concern was anti-Socialism, and that is no program. They emphasized its anti-religious and revolutionary character, but used milder words to condemn inhuman social abuses. There was little stressing of, or enthusiasm for, a constructive approach. The leaders were vigorously committed to religious preservation, but only mildly concerned with a thorough and speedy economic reform. The Conservatives, who were numerous and influential in the Catholic Party, viewed the Social Catholics with misgivings and even hostility. They were willing to engage in a fight against Socialism, but would not tolerate any modification of social situations that were favorable to themselves.

The result was that although some Social Christians were vigorous and progressive, they faced formidable obstacles in the Catholic body. This extended to certain influential clergymen. It was this internal opposition that further discredited the social movement in the eyes of the workers.

The Socialists experienced no such curb. They attacked abuses boldly, proposed revolutionary slogans, and emphasized the real poverty of the workers. The latter were quick to sense on which side lay the real will to reform. To them, the Socialists appeared as daring leaders who would achieve their goals despite bourgeois opposition. The workers appeared to be faced with a choice between their religious faith and material improvement. It was a grave error to present them with such an apparent dilemma. The temptation proved too great for most, and they opted for economic liberation.

3. The Christian social institutions did not appear strong enough to inspire confidence. They lacked cohesion, and seemed a mosaic of tiny local and regional efforts. They had no organic bonds and no coordination. The manifold Christian activities had to become a living whole before they could carry through their program against the opposition on the Right and Left.

On such premises, the C. L. M. was overhauled and reorganized in 1921. Since then there has been a continuous effort to apply the lessons learned from historical experience. Results were not quickly achieved; coordination of activities required patient perserverence. New organizations were needed to fill the gaps: the YCW was founded by Canon Cardyn in 1925; adult education became a reality in 1931; the Catholic Workers' Leagues were created in 1941.

The following statistics indicate that the initial assumptions were correct:

A. *Trade Unions.*

Years	Soclialist T.Us.	Christian T.Us.
1898	13,727	----
1901	21,125	11,000
1910	68,984	49,478
1913	126,745	102,177
1920	718,410	65,000
1922	618,871	209,311
1930	537,379	209,311
1933	629,532	300,713
1939	550,000	350,000
1945	511,851	342,500
1947	500,000	420,022
1949	----	500,239

B. *Mutual Insurance Companies.*

Years	Socialist M.I.	Christian M.I.
1913	109,461	188,690
1920	318,947	132,617
1924	419,268	235,164
1930	500,842	376,024
1937	584,827	502,701

after 1946: *compulsory* insurance:

1947	793,747	773,274
1948	803,391	794,712

It must be noted that the younger generation is proportionally much better represented in the Christian Trade Unions and Mutual Insurance Companies than in the comparable Socialist organiaztions. The rising generation is moving toward the C.L.M.

C. *Workingwomen's social organizations.*

Years	Femmes prévoyantes (Soc.)	KAV and LOFC
1922	—————	76,000
1928	100,000	114,138
1935	160,000	220,325
1938	179,000	254,000
1946	135,000	281,000
1948	216,576	345,050

D. *Youth Organizations.*

Years	Jeunes Gardes Socialistes, political, and Fédération d'Education Physique, cultural	JOC and JOCF
1920	13,560	—————
1923	36,791	—————
1924	29,059	—————
1927	23,028	23,700
1930	21,624	70,000
1939	?	80,000
1948	20,000	80,000

E. *Adult Worker Education.*

Years	Socialist	KWB (Equipes populaires omitted)
1941		16,299
1943		26,045
1946	nil.	34,344
1949		50,522

The Educational and Apostolic Effort.

The Encyclicals insist that economic reforms alone will not restore a healthy social life in our industrialized society. The basic Christian values in regard to man and his purposes must be recovered and re-interpreted in terms that will be meaningful in our mechanized world. While the primary agent in this effort will remain the parish priest, the Encyclicals have indicated that the apostles to the world of labor must be workers themselves. Accordingly, the C.L.M. of Belgium insisted that it must widen its vision and include in its activity a positive educational and apostolic program which will be adapted to the mentality of the industrial worker. It must bring him Christian social teaching and convince him that it aims at his liberation and at the complete transformation of his life. It must free him from the tyranny of the mass-mind, restore his sense of personality, his capacity for rational and personal convictions; and it must free him from the pressures of standardized amusements and of mass propaganda. It must teach him to use his gains constructively. It must develop his potentialities so that he can raise the level of his personal and family life. Higher wages must be spent to increase the happiness of the home and to gain access to the ownership of property. It must be realized that leisure without proper education can become a means of moral decay as well as a step toward more wholesome living. Economic gains do not work automatically for progress; all depends on the spirit in which they are used. So, worker education should be one of the major aims of a modern labor movement, and this education should be coordinated with apostolic Christian objectives.

These efforts cannot usefully be performed outside of, or apart from, the general labor movement that is responsible for the defense and economic objectives of the workers. Its success depends on its connection with the leadership of a great labor movement. Only with this relationship can the prejudice against the apostolic action of the Church be mitigated. Besides, the labor movement offers the necessary points of contact, the financial means, and the actual opportunities for extensive educational work. Finally, rivalry between competing organizations is avoided when active collaboration is established.

In Belgium, the educational and apostolic action of the Young Christian Workers (JOC and JOCF) and of the Workingmen's and Women's Leagues constitutes a section of the general labor movement. Their precise contribution is to provide leadership and to infuse spiritual concepts into the whole structure. But these educational organizations remain distinct from the economic and social bodies. They work independently in their own field. They can also establish useful contacts outside the labor movement. But they act within its framework, so that each completes the other and enjoys the benefit of mutual support.

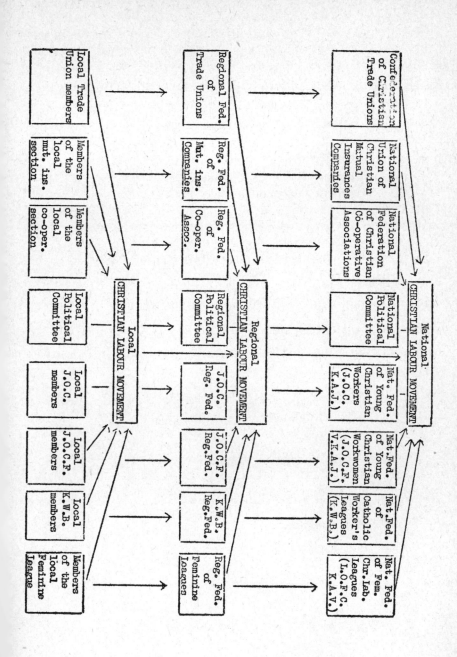

THE ORGANIZATION OF THE LABOR MOVEMENT
IN BELGIUM
at the National Level

Christian Labor Movement:

Algemeen Christelijk Workersverbond—A.C.W.
Movement Ouvrier Chretien—M.O.C.

I. *Economic and Social Organizations*
   (The same organizations for Flanders and Wallonia)

affiliated members

Confederation of Christian Trade Unions (C.S.C.) . . . 500,239

National Union of Christian Mutual Insurance Companies 794,712

National Federation of Christian Co-op Associations . . 250,000

II. *Social and Cultural Organizations*
   (District in Flanders and Wallonia)

affiliated members

Young Christian Workers and Young Christian
Workwomen 80,000

Feminine Christian Labor Leagues 345,050

K.W.B. Equipes populaires 50,522

The Components of the Christian Labor Movement.

A. *Trade Unions.* On 1 January 1949, the Christian trade unions had 500,239 members, as against an estimated 500,000 in the Socialist unions, and 25,000 in the Liberal unions. Their primary function is the protection and advancement of the workers' economic interest. They represent him on public and semi-public boards, act as an agency for the payment of the State unemployment insurance, provide legal assistance, and study the major economic trends with a view toward implementing Christian social principles. They publish the monthly C.S.C., and trade union studies and information.

For the achievement of their objectives, they are organized on an interprofessional basis (with workers of all trades) :

1. On a national level, for the unified management of the entire Christian trade union movement. This national office also provides the major services of study and information, and cares for foreign workers and those who cross the border to work in Belgium.

2. On a regional level: to provide services of regional interest.

3. On a local level: for mutual support and information.

There is also a professional grouping according to particular industry and trade. There are twenty of these, with national, regional and local divisions.

On the international level, the CSC has organized white and Negro unions in the Congo. Membership in these has reached 25,000. While this is only a fraction of the estimated 850,000 Negro workers in the area, it represents a significant advance among a primitive people. Its necessity is obvious. In this field, the CSC has outstripped its Socialist rival. The CSC also belongs to the International of Christian Trade Unions, which in 1948 had 2,406,700 members in eight countries.

The CSC has gained the following results:

1. They have contributed to a fairer distribution of the national income; thus they have aided in the elimination of some of the more flagrant abuses in the social field. This primary work has also contributed to the worker's self-respect and has started him on his ascent to the status of a property-owner.

2. They have helped improve the environmental conditions of the worker.

3. They have introduced many workers to the social objectives of the Encyclicals, particularly the dignity of the human personality and the importance of the human family.

4. They have diminished the attraction of the secular social-ist state.

B. *Mutual Insurance Companies.* Before 1945, illness and disability insurance was purely optional in Belgium. The Christian Mutual Insurance Companies had members of all classes, without distinction. A law of 1945 introduced compulsory insurance for all wage earners. With the principle of "freedom in obligation," it respected the various already existing *national* companies, provided they observed its rules in regard to contributions, risks, and payments. As a consequence of the Act, there is a distinction between the area of compulsory insurance for those subject to the law; and one of voluntary insurance for farmers and the middle class, and for workers who wish insurance beyond the provisions of the law.

The companies maintain local offices for payments and disbursements, and for medical and drug service. Regional offices provide special services (e.g., ambulance), while the national office is legally responsible for the entire work. It also provides sanatoria, special services for tuberculosis and cancer, preventative medical assistance, aid in marriage funds, etc. Aside from the material advantages, the companies have preserved high ethical standards in the treatment of disease. They have encouraged personal initiative rather than state control in the social services. Their visiting nurse's service also acts as an apostolate. The companies also acquaint their members with other agencies in the Christian labor movement.

C. *Cooperatives.* They also have the familiar three-fold division: the local associations have their stores, savings-bank, insurance agent, etc.; the Regional Cooperative Federation groups the local branches, explores the possibility of extension, and engages in education and propaganda. At the apex is the National Federation of Christian Cooperative Associations of Belgium. This accumulates capital for, and manages the following enterprises:

1. *Le Bien-Etre:* general wholesale service for the 807 (1948) local stores, with over 318 million francs yearly trade. Main office: Merxem-Antwerp.

2. C.O.B.—Workers Savings Banks, with 920 local offices, 95,180 members, and 385 million francs invested.

3. *Les Assurances populaires* (Workers' Insurance) with 498 brokers, 36,058 policies and over 24 million francs capital.

The national office also studies economic problems, organizes nation-wide publicity, and represents the group on the national and international level.

A non-affiliated Christian cooperative in Namur and Luxembourg provinces, *Economie populaire,* has 260 stores, with 215 million francs in trade and 409 savings books. There are also a chain of cooperative bakeries with more than a million francs in yearly trade.

These organizations:

1. Save money for the working-class family.
2. Encourage thrift and ownership.
3. Assist financially the other organizations of C.L.M.

D. *Political Activities.* In the 1946 elections, the four political parties polled the following percentage of the votes: Social Christian 42.39%; Socialist 31.59% Communist 12.68%; Liberal 8.92%. The last three are avowedly anti-clerical in program and practice. Accordingly, the Bishops have constantly urged Catholic unity in political matters. The C.L.M. also realizes that it cannot attain many of its objectives (wages and prices, insurance, housing, structural reforms, etc.) without political action. Therefore it must enter some relation with the Catholic Party.

The C.L.M. is not itself a political party, nor does it belong to any party, nor form a wing of any party. Yet since the Catholic Party is both Christian and social in its program, the C.L.M. supports it and hopes that it will implement its announced policies. To assure this, the C.L.M. has established a liaison committee with the Party on the national, regional and local levels. The purpose of this committee is to study economic and social questions in their political implications, to make recommendations to the Party, and then to attempt to attain action. It also scrutinizes candidates of the Party on the score of their acceptability to labor. The Social Christian Party listens to the recommendations, and then acts on its own authority and responsibility. The C.L.M. thus attempts to influence politics without leaving its own proper sphere.

E. *Cultural and Apostolic Organizations.* These emphasize "activity," and attempt to retain the spontaneity, adaptability, and dynamism of a movement, rather than establishing a rigid organization. The account is always on the *personal:* personal observation to learn conditions; personal judgment to decide issues; personal action to get results.

The members attempt to offer a renovated and living representation of Christianity, concretized in the many-sided realities of the world of labor. They are animated by sympathy for their fellow-man and a desire to serve. They have developed considerable self-confidence in their methods and their message.

While their primary aim is the re-Christianization of the workers, they realize that this can only be achieved through service. This service must be performed by men and women from the ranks of labor, who remain in their own environment. Because conditions, language and problems in the Flemish and Waloon sections vary considerably, each of these cultural groups are divided regionally.

I. *The Young Christian Workers* conceives itself as a school for the moral, religious, social and cultural education of its members. An elaborate training program exists for leaders, beginning with monthly meetings of local leaders, and extending to a monthly retreat and an annual week of study on the Regional level and an even more ambitious program on a national basis. This formal study is only part of the plan: the Jocist believes that "practice makes perfect," and that the best training school is daily action in the family, neighborhood, and in places of work and leisure.

Members are trained in monthly meetings and in various ideas for an improved spending of leisure time. They are expected to influence their associates by example, occasional campaigns, distribution of literature, leaflets, and periodicals, and by open meetings.

Since their fellow-workers are to be influenced by service, the Jocists have established a wide variety of social activities: savings-banks, youth hostels, physical training, pre-marital training, vocational advice, service for the sick, soldiers and special groups, etc.

The Jocists represent the workers on official national bodies, in the C.L.M. and in Catholic Action, of which they form a specialized branch.

They are financed by dues, the sale of literature and services, subsidies from the CSC and other bodies.

They are the chief agency for the recovery of an increasingly large section of Belgian youth to religious ideals, and have provided the dynamic yeadership for most of the other social organizations. Their greatest contribution is the formation of splendid types of young men and women, who live a Christian life in a new and more active form.

II. *The Christian Workingwomen's Organizations* have the parish as their basic cell, but build up to regional and national bodies. The formation of leaders follows the pattern of the Youth, but on a more restricted scale due to the heavier obligations of adult women.

Their primary aim is educational: to inspire an ideal of feminine life, to develop practical talents, and to encourage a feeling of community and a desire for progress. Meetings, demonstrations, exhibitions, and entertainments are the ordin-

ary means. To radiate this influence, members are encouraged
to participate in all popular celebrations with the purpose of
animating them with a Christian spirit. Special educational
courses (twelve thirty-hour courses) are offered to married
women in family and domestic training. Other specialized education is given to groups with particular interests. A monthly
review, pamphlets and books, and home visits, complete the
educational effort.

No subject of interest to working women escape the organization. They represent working women on many State-controlled
bodies, on executive committees of the C. L. M. and in other
Catholic bodies. They provide health service for mothers and
children, information, aid and assistance to families, special insurance, pre-matrimonial savings plans, and vocational services.

They have 345,000 members in 1455 sections. Finances are
obtained in much the same way as the Youth groups, plus occasional charity sales, etc. They have performed an inestimable
service in maintaining and expanding the Christian ideals of the
family, and have proved an important instrument of the
apostolate.

III. *The Christian Workingmen's Organization*: Before 1941,
the C. L. M. had organized an educational service to train
workers to assume the direction of trade unions and other
activities. But their primary objective was not to influence the
de-Christianized masses. In 1941 it was determined to broaden
the scope of this effort in the Flemish region to include the
formation of a lay apostolate. The KWB is open to all workers,
without reference to religious affiliation or precise trade union
membership. Its organization, training, and methods is closely
patterned on the Youth organizations from which it has drawn
both inspiration and personnel. Its monthly, *Raak*, reaches 51,-
000 subscribers. The KWB has acted as a vitalizing agency in
the C. L. M., infusing new spiritual energy and idealism. Its
enthusiasm should help the larger organization from hardening
into bureaucratic rigidity.

In the Waloon part of the country, a similiar effort, *Equipes
populaires,* has been undertaken since 1946, but it has not yet
reached the status of an autonomous movement. It also has
the problem of duplication of effort with the *Mouvement Populaire des Familles* which operates among the working class,
though distinct from the C. L. M.

The C. L. M. attempts to bring all these agencies into a common unity of ideas and action. Its national Congress sets the
general policy and coordinates activities. It settles jurisdictional

disputes and sets up employment policies for permanent staff
personnel. The C. L. M. also allocates office space; provides for
the exchange of information and funds. It supports social
schools and organizes national gatherings. It maintains relations
with other national and international bodies.

Its publications are important: the weekly *De Volksmacht*
(338,470) and *En marche* (120,000) ; the daily *Het Volk* (140,-
000) ; the monthly study reviews *De gids op Maatschappelijk*
and *Les Dossiers de l'Action sociale Catholique;* and the docu-
mentary report (2425) .

The supreme authority of the C. L. M., the National Congress, meets every two years. It sets up a Central Council, meeting four times a year, and an Executive Committee with more
limited functions. A Secretariat carries out detailed duties.
These bodies are reproduced on the regional and local levels.
All are formed by delegates from geographical and organizational divisions to keep the balance between unity and autonomy. The different organizations ordinarily share the same
premises, and often have a social center which is used in common. In this, as in all else, the motto is "cordination", with full
freedom for specific purposes.

The hierarchy has provided trained chaplains, whose sole
duty is to assist the various units of C. L. M. These meet
regularly for study and discussion. But in most instances, laymen have assumed full responsibility for the management of
the work, with the clergy merely fulfilling their proper role of
advising and inspiring.

A permanent staff of approximately 2500 are required to
direct the various activities. Every effort is made to prevent
them from falling into bureaucratic routine by periodic retreats and study meetings that are designed to stimulate their
spiritual zeal and cooperative spirit.

In 1921, the Superior School of Louvain[2] was established to
train leaders and executives of C. L. M. Most of the present day
officials have been formed in this institution where they have
the advantage of all the facilities of the University plus special
professors chosen by the Movement. The school offers a two-
year course. It is subsidized by the State and enjoys the financial
support of the C. L. M. Thirty to thirty-five new students are
enrolled each year, some of which go into other organizations
or governmental service. In addition there is a Woman's Social
School[3] to train social workers.

J. N. Moody,

NOTES

1 Prepared by the editor from material provided by Canon A. Brys, General Chaplain of the Christian Labor Movement of Belgium, rue de la loi, 127-129, Brussels.

2 Chaussée de Namur 14, Heverlee-Louvain.

3 rue de la Poste, 111, Brussels.

TABLE OF CONTENTS

Documents

DOCUMENTS

Prince-Archbishop of Malines.

Unionism.

"The Belgians at present are giving a great example to the world, and to France in particular. In the condition in which the governments of Europe have fallen, men can no longer, and must no longer, cling to the theory of a truly Christian society, for, unfortunately, there is no longer anything Christian in the administration or the laws. Everyone observes only a widespread and stubborn war against order and truth. In order to survive, Christianity must break its fetters. Caught between the double oppression of despotic governments and godless revolutionaries, it can resist both only by writing on its mast-head the word "liberty." Was it not this liberty that the early Christians hoped for? Did they not, though conquered by other means, save the world by its assistance? Today it alone can save religion from all its enemies, for no matter under what form revolution presents itself, it is always a violation of this vital liberty. Besides, is it not time, and even past time, to disabuse those who think that the spirit of Catholicism is the spirit of slavery, and to establish a *Union* with all those in the various political parties who are not entirely hostile? Agreement will not be reached on all points. But I believe that today we must avoid above all those things which lead to divisions which are fatal to the common cause, and we must do it without sacrificing any of the principles for which Christians contend."

II. Letter of 13 December 1830 to the National Congress by the Prince-Archbishop of Malines.

"Sirs:

I believe I would fail in one of the most essential duties of my ministry if, at the time when you are about to draw up the Constitution that will govern our worthy country, I did not address myself to you in order to prompt you to guarantee that full and complete liberty to the Catholic religion which alone can assure its peace and prosperity.

"The different plans for the Constitution which have been published to date are far from satisfying the demand for an adequate liberty. The experience of a half century has taught the Belgians that it is not enough to give them a general assurance that they can worship freely. In effect, such an assurance was given them in the old Constitution of Brabant, in the Concordat of 1801, and in the basic law of 1815. Yet religious practice suffered all sorts of fetters, and Catholics were subjected to a variety of vexations under the different governments which ruled during this period.

"I have full confidence that the Congress, which represents a

I have in your intelligence and in the purity of your intentions gives me firm hope that you will adopt them unanimously. You would, thereby, grant me a consolation which I have long been denied; you would fill all hearts with joy; you would acquire unquestioned title to the eternal thanks of your fellow-citizens; and you will have the satisfaction of fulfilling the chief mandate that has been entrusted to you, because you will have consolidated the liberty to which they attach the highest price, namely, the free practice of the religion of their ancestors."

"Assuring you, Sirs . . ."

François-Antoine,
Prince de Méan, archevêque de Malines.

III. The Belgian Constitution.

Art. XIV. Freedom of worship and of the public exercise of religion is guaranteed. So also is the freedom of religion to express its opinions on all questions. The only exception is where crimes are committed during the exercise of these liberties.

Art. XV. No one can be constrained in any manner whatsoever from taking part in the acts and ceremonies of a religion nor from observing its holydays.

Art. XVI. The State has not the right to intervene either in the nomination or the installation of the clergy of any religion; nor to prevent these from corresponding with their superiors, nor from publishing the acts of these superiors, though in the last case, the ordinary responsibility regarding press and publications holds.

Civil marriage must always preceed the nuptial blessing, except for cases established by law, if there are any.

Art. XVII. Education is free; every restrictive measure is forbidden; punishment of crimes is regulated only by law.

Public education, given at the expense of the State, is equally regulated by law.

Art. XVIII. The press is free; censorship will never be established; surety-bonds will not be demanded from writers, editors, or publishers. When the author is known and lives in Belgium, the editor, printer, or distributor cannot be punished.

Art. XX. Belgians have the right to associate; this right shall not be limited by any preventative measure.

IX. Inaugural article in the Catholic-Democratic journal, Het Volk (Le Peuple), 1890.

"Het Volk enters the lists to support and aid in the defense of the material and moral interests of the workers and petty bourgeoisie.

"The worker and the petty bourgeois, in our opinion, are the two victims of the actual organization of society. It is true that the words Liberty, Equality, and Fraternity are written in letters of gold on the pediment of modern civilization.

"But the beautiful promises which these words have proclaimed since 1789 have remained a dead letter for the man who works and does not possess capital.

"Although placed by law on a footing of equality with the upper classes, the worker of today is crushed and oppressed.

"Only the holders of capital can completely enjoy the liberty conceded to all. It must be recognized that they can draw from it privileges which make them the masters and lords of their brothers, the slaves of the machine and the victims of competition.

"What must be done to better this situation? Is it necessary, as the Socialists propose, to suppress private capital. That would be folly, for it would replace one oppression with another.

"What is necessary is to reduce the unlimited power of capital, a liberty that knows no boundaries. It is necessary to protect efficaciously the workers and the petty bourgeoisie from the oppression of wealth, to consider capital and the machine as instruments placed at the disposition of man by the Creator, not to transform the majority of men into the slaves of a small number, but rather to bring help and aid to the popular masses and to assist them to attain the prosperity which is possible here below."

V. Manifesto of the Belgian Democratic League, 1891.

"Our purpose is to improve the social situation of the workers, to bring peace to the world of labor, to induce respect for the rights of all, both employers and employees.

"The Special Congress of Liège, and especially the recent and brilliant Encyclical of Pope Leo XIII on *The Condition of the Workers,* has defined our practical program.

"We propose that the worker be treated, not as an insensible machine, valued only by the work he can perform, but as a free being endowed with an immortal soul, our brother and our equal.

"We propose that neither the worker's strength nor that of his children be drained away by excessive work. We wish that his right to Sunday rest be recognized and that the Lord's Day be also the day of the worker.

"We propose that when sickness, accident or old-age overwhelms him, he be not visited with the added sorrow of seeing poverty enter his dwelling and the suffering of his family added to his own.

"We propose that his wage, in the words of the Pope, 'be sufficient for his sober and respectable subsistence.'

"Finally we propose that workers' associations be fully recognized by the State and receive juridical personality. Founded for the common good, by what right do they refuse them the advantages accorded to so many other associations which have no other purpose but profit and the enrichment of their members?

"It is primarily by the action of these autonomous workers' associations, strongly established, united in a powerful League, that we hope to realize our program.

"We demand secondarily the help of the public authority to obtain the reforms which belong to its own domain, reforms which the labor associations would be powerless to realize and which are necessary for social peace.

"Strong today in the number of our adherents, which now excedes 60,000, the Belgian Democratic League intends to march straight to its goal, without compromise or flinching. It will soon become invincible if it rallies all those who have the courage to love God, the People, and the Nation."

H. Haag

PART IV:

CHURCH and SOCIETY in GERMANY

Social and Political Movements and Ideas
in
German and Austrian Catholicism
1789 - 1950

by

EDGAR ALEXANDER

translated
by
TONI STOLPER

TABLE OF CONTENTS

DOCUMENTS

INTRODUCTION

Ever since the days of Pope Leo XIII Catholic Sociology quite generally followed the principle that a special theological doctrine of social and economic life does not exist, and that accordingly "only natural truths and logical reasoning will be used to derive and establish the Pope's teaching on human society and its members. Therefore the Pope does not intend to build a second, supernatural social order on top of natural society, which might only lead to inconsistencies and great inconveniences" [1] This principle leads on to the further insight "that the concrete forms of human society are at all times tied in with natural and historical conditions (facta contingentia) and are therefore liable to change with these conditions." [2]

In following the historico-ideological developments, Part I of this study (chapt. I-III) expounds the objective justification of this insight. In this process we explore the tragic background of the fact that modern German Catholicism was unable to draw upon indigenous traditions when developing the programs for its social and political actions, in both theory and practice. We also show why in Germany more than anywhere else, Social and Political Catholicism was so deeply influenced by the general political and social conditions that prevailed in this country. In Part II this is explained in detail for the "Social Movement and Social Policies" (chapt. IV) and for "Political Catholicism in Action" (chapt. V), matters which can only be understood as parts of the general picture of German developments from about 1848 until today. Although the ideas which dominated the social and the political spheres respectively often cross or even condition one another, it was thought advisable, principally for systematic reasons, to separate these spheres as much as possible for a parallel treatment. Since in Germany the theoretical exposition of political doctrine and theories of society were late in coming (around 1890), as was intellectual progress in German Catholicism in general, it seemed the correct procedure to treat this also in a separate way (Chap. VI), although the interconnection between theory and practice in Social and Political Catholicism was strong between 1890 and 1933. This seems all the more justified since the theoretical achievements of German Catholic political and social doctrine are of such fundamental significance that they survive, even after the ephemeral organizations of Social and Political Catholicism have succumbed in the recent German catastrophe.

These exemplary achievements of German Catholic Sociology are of incalculable value for the reconstruction of a new Germany and a new Europe in the spirit of the Christian social order, a spirit which strives in deepest earnest to establish practicable political freedom and social justice. The same may be said for America, especially since the United States has become the home and the place of action for a goodly number of former German representatives of Catholic Sociology, among them G. Briefs (Georgetown), F. Mueller and H. Rommen (St. Paul, Minnesota), W. Gurian and F. A. Hermens (Notre Dame, Indiana) and D. von Hildebrand (Fordham, N. Y.).

The Appendix of sources makes no pretense of completeness; it only adds a limited documentation to the text. Because of the special requirements of this international symposium, the entire theme had to be treated with great brevity. I hope before long to offer a fuller treatment of the same subject.

My special thanks are due Dr. Toni Stolper who put her great abilities in the service of the translation and gave my work her constant sympathetic assistance.

E. A.

New York City
Feast of St. Augustine
August 1952

CHAPTER I

THE SOCIOLOGICAL PROBLEM OF CATHOLICISM

1. *The Sociological Problem of Catholicism.*

Social and political developments in modern German Catholicism (1789-1950) deserve the special interest of students of history and sociology, even from the mere angle of sociological methodology (1). It will be made clear how imperative it is to keep oneself free of the current slogans referring to "Catholicism,"and to beware of the meaningless sociological generalizations derived from these slogans (2). Unless this is achieved, it is impossible to form a fair judgment of the actual historical and politcal realities in the relationship between the Catholic Church and society in the various countries. It will prove necessary in this effort to observe three essential conditions:

First, the concept of the "Church" as a sociological reality within society must be correctly analyzed. We should insist from the very beginning on the strictest possible sociological distinction between a) the Church as a *society and organization,* in contrast to b) the religious existence of *the Church as a community and organism* with all its primarily theological categories and religious -apologetic functions. Secondly, Catholicism must be seen essentially as a reality belonging to the realm of historical and cultural phenomena. In this historical aspect, the ethics of the Catholic religion always take a concrete shape, are brought into being by the activities of concrete *i.e.,* living persons, and therefore always refer to situations that are entirely concrete and well-defined in space and time within the ephemeral historic reality. From such insight naturally follows, thirdly, that the development of the *Church as society* and of *Catholicism as a phenomenon of civilization* (specifically, as "political" and "social" Catholicism) must always be judged and understood as being subjected to the laws of historical evolution with all contingencies and limitations this implies, primarily under the aspect of the emergence and the historical destiny of nation-states and peoples' civilizations.

We can achieve a true understanding of the entire complex

of sociological problems arising from Catholicism only if the preceding rules are given their proper methodological weight. The main point is to realize that the eternally unalterable religious essence of the "Church as community and organism" manifests itself in the widely variable and divergent formations of the "Church as society and organization," in the manifold shapes of the several national popular civilizations, as in German, French, English, American Catholicism. We propose to show that more than anywhere else it is necessary to observe our three postulates to gain a true insight into both the achievements and the failures of German Catholicism in particular.

From these basic points of view we arrive at a three-fold picture of the sociological implications of Catholicism:

1. We shall understand that every community, and this very specially includes the Church as a religious community, is fundamentally *personal* in its essence. The theological and religious existence of the *church within man* will be recognized as expressing the personal experience and action of each individual personality when he feels driven toward forming a community. Every religious experience is a deeply personal event. Likewise, every true community can have its origin only in personal relationships and derives its existence from the personal I-Thou relation and the I-Thou involvement from which the We-community arises and endures. In this aspect, the religious existence of the Church, being the primary and most deeply rooted motive force at the birth of the community, merits the utmost attention when the essence of community life is to be examined by sociological methods.

2. We shall understand that every society, and this includes the Church as society, is fundamentally *social* in its essence. All that anyone experiences in a society, has primarily social features. The problem is therefore to understand the manifestations of the historical and social existence of the *Church through man*. Every society has its origin in social relationships and, expressing man's social nature, organizes itself into the various social groupings, in the hierarchical orders in which it finds a durable constitution. Thus, the social existence of the Church as an independent, society-forming agent merits the sociologists' full attention when they study the essence of society.

3. We shall understand that every true community, whether its origin is ontological or personal, must, by its nature, grow beyond the personalistic sphere of the I-Thou-We community, to form a natural society, directed toward factual aims. The same holds true conversely: every naturally formed society must

contain a more or less strong, but genuine nucleus of communal life which represents the quasi-organic essence and self-existence of all forms of society. The significant fact emerges that both the personal and the social nature of man exert influences that are essentially mutual. Man, organically tied to his community and at the same time organizationally tied to his society, expresses the cross-influences in the values and forces alive in a community and thereby exercises his creative cultural powers. It is in these relationships that we discover the innermost essence of Catholicism. Now we comprehend Catholicism as the gathering into one whole of all these manifestations of personal, social, national, and finally universal civilization which, in the mutual cross-influences between the community-forming religious life and the society-forming social existence of the Church, on the one hand, and all the community forms and values and the society forms and values of the material realm of civilization on the other hand, creates the over-all "civilization" characteristic of each historical epoch. Having won this insight, we may now approach the sociological problem of *Catholicism as a manifestation of civilization,* in all the various aspects and relationships in the several national forms of life in society, such as German, English, French, American Catholicism, or in the different material pursuits in society, such as "social Catholicism" or "political Catholicism."

2. *The Church as a Community and Organism.*

It is not easy for the non-theologian, and even less for the non-Catholic, to form a true concept of the theological meaning of the Church in its religious existence, as a sacramental "community" in the sense of the *communio sanctorum,* and as a religious-metaphysical "organism" in the sense of the supranatural articulation of the *corpus Christi mysticum* and the community of the children of God in the Augustinian *civitas Dei.*[3] But it is also very difficult for many theologians, especially the integralists, to give due weight to the socioligical concept of the Church in its historical existence—as an organized "society" in the sense of a natural order of human life and as a social "organization" in the sense of being autonomous under natural law in the various material fields of civilzation. These difficulties are further enhanced by the fact that precisely the universal essence of the "catholic" church concept, the all-embracing (*catholon*) essence of Catholicism, produces a special desire to see both spheres merged, that is, the supra-natural organism with the natural organization, or in other words, the sacramental community with the merely temporal society, in the vital "catholic" unity that encompasses the divine and the worldly, the eternal and the temporal, spirit and nature, soul and body.[4]

In thus striving toward the unity of sacrament and life, of grace and reality (expressed theologically), and also of community and society, of organism and organization (expressed sociologically), the Catholic ethos is just as strongly predicated on the temporal manifestations of life in history, as on life's religious depth and spiritual aims through which all the activities of a Catholic person receive an impetus toward the supranatural and eternal. Because this twofold orientation of the Church can be realized only within a concrete personality, the Catholic existence fulfills itself in both spheres and in that area where they interpenetrate each other and diverge from one another.

Thus, the Church only lives *in* man and *through* man, by virtue of man's natural-supranatural double nature, which makes him a mystical limb of the *Corpus Christi,* indeed the continuation of Christ's own life, and at the same time and just as naturally a member of the human community and society. Insofar as the Church as an objective sacramental institution of grace does its work within a living person and thereby widens the human existence to embrace the supernatural community of all living persons, the Church is liberated from the "laws of this world" and thereby from the voluntaristic and "human" element in man. For here the objective, sacramental values and orders of the Church serve man in the sense of *"gratia supponit naturam"* (grace builds upon nature), and this truth is expressed in the beautiful dictum of Pope Pius XI: "Men are not created for the sake of the Church, the Church exists for the sake of men: *propter nos homines et propter nostram salutem!"* [5] This shows clearly that the "church within man," that is, the religious existence of the Church as community and organism, cannot in any manner at any time be impaired in its orders and values by man himself. Man has only the choice either to open his soul and to devote himself of his own free will to the supranatural divine dispensation and treasure of salvation offered by this Church and thus to partake of its sacramental community, the *communio sanctorum;* or to renounce this "service" and strive to live his life *"extra ecclesiam"* (outside the church). The Church itself, however, as it is here understood as a supranatural community and organism, is not aggrieved by such repudiation. This implies that the Church in its purely theological existence is neither subjected to the human and worldly laws of cause and effect, nor to social and organizational functions, and therefore does not lend itself to a sociological discussion.

However—to state this here in advance—this also implies that whatever criticism is directed against the "church through man," which means, against any achievement or failure of the Church in its sociological existence as "society and organization," can never touch the objective essence of the "church within man" in its religious existence, or diminish its dispensations of grace.[6]

3. The Church as Society and Organization

From the preceding it has become clear that the essence of the Church as society and organization can best be understood if we distinguish its essentially natural, sociological categories from the theological and metaphysical categories of the theological and religious church concept.

The Church as community and organism affects the divine nature and religious existence of man; its character is essentially theological and metaphysical. The Church as society and organization affects the social nature and society of man; its character is therefore essentially sociological and historical. Proceding from this basic insight, it is possible, first purely methodologically, to develop the sequence of all the mutually correlated categories within the scale of values of total human existence in their hierarchical orders and to place them into an analogous relationship respectively to the Church as "community" and as "society." We can see this analogy and this correlation in other concepts: community as compared to society, organism to organization, metaphysics to history, theology to teleology, sin to crime, service to work, love to charity, the personal to the social.

An analogous relationship also exists between man as a person and a Christian versus man as a social being (*politikon zoon*). It is predicated on metaphysical relations based on the ethical concepts underlying the religious principles which give society its forms and values. In other words, every moral attitude (which means, every attitude directed toward concrete life) and activity of men within society has an underlying ethical principle, a "creed" (Gesinnung) which gives the community its philosophical directives. This establishes the truth that at all times the metaphysics and ethics of a community are decisive for the morals and social behavior of that society.

Applied to Catholicism, this signifiies: (1) that the theology of the church-as-community determines first of all the basic ethical principles of the Catholic individual and his personal attitude versus the community; (2) that these ethics of the church-as-community then determine the moral precepts of the church-as-society, thereby forming the "ethos of the Catholic person," or simply the Catholic ethos, as expressed in the social attitudes and activities of these persons within the society of their specific era. In this process the principles of Catholic moral theology and community ethics become effective as orders of Catholic moral philosophy and social doctrine and finally take shape as practical rules of behavior in a Catholic moral code for life in society.[7]

We can now form a sociological concept of Catholicism as being the actual historical manifestation of Catholic ethics through the more or less time-bound materializations in Catholic morals. Or, in other words, Catholicism as a sociological movement and phenomenon represents the attempt to realize the Catholic social ethics and political ethics in the process of bringing to life the Catholic doctrine of state and society. Wherever this attempt is made, Catholicism as a feature of the temporal historical and social reality must be studied as one among several movements in the theory and practice of statecraft and social civilization, and—where this is specially required by the actual conditions of the era—Catholicism must form itself into active political and social organizations. Consequently, a historical and sociological point of view must be taken in the effort to understand and to justify the various Catholic theories of the state and society, as well as the movements of "social Catholicism" and "political Catholicism."

4. *Catholicism and Catholic Movements*

It should not be too difficult to discover that "Catholicism," with its time-bound developments and performances, both in the doctrines of state and society and in practical politics and economics, follows its own laws relative to the universal, religious community forms of the Church. This cultural and social autonomy of Catholicism, the motley forms of its manifestations and interests, enables it to take shape as German, French, English and American Catholicism, and also as social and political Catholicism, with specific historical ties to democratic or conservative forms of society and with monarchical or republican constitutions. The theoretical and organizational multiformity of these national and social variations of Catholicism does not by any means impair the comprehensive, *i.e.,* "catholic" unity of the religious community of the Church and the universal whole and insoluble spiritual unison of all the Church's members. On the other hand, the social and political autonomy and the many variations of Catholicism inside the separate national civilizations demand in practice a variety of applications and adaptations of the principles of Catholic political and social doctrine within the historical and social developments of the various peoples and states.

The differences between the political and social variations of Catholicism in the various countries are of such significance that even a non-Catholic social study will have to see in them objective historical facts without the knowledge of which it would be impossible to arrive at impartial judgments on the merits of the historical achievements and failures of the social organizations of Catholicism in the various countries. Likewise the non-Catholic sociology as well as that of certain circles of integralists and clerical "maximalists" within Catholicism will have to acknowledge two features that concern the essence and value of the Catholic political doctrine and social doctrine, features confirmed by the official Church doctrine in their absolute validity, and more than ever before since the days of the glorious Pope Leo XIII:

1. The principles of the Catholic political doctrine, being true "principles," are directed only toward establishing for the state and society in general their foundations in Natural Law. Every Catholic therefore enjoys unrestricted moral and practical freedom in applying and realizing these principles; he has indeed the moral duty to exercise such freedom, because of his personal social and historical allegiance to a specific national and political group. In practical life this means that, for instance, the allegiance to a democratic constitution may be as much of a right, or even a duty for the American Catholic, as is the allegiance to an anti-capitalist form of society and economic life for the British Catholic, or the allegiance to the monarchy for a Dutch Catholic, or as it is the absolute right and the moral and national duty for a Portuguese Catholic to adhere to the conservative form of his state. Precisely because they are universal and supranational principles, the principles of the Catholic political doctrine are opposed to all absolutes of a partial, practical nature in the shape of any of the concrete sets of principles on state or society. This wise rule is in no way modified by the regrettable fact that it has not always been adhered to, even in the history of Catholicism itself, and that unfortunately as late as in the 20th century certain politicians have been tempted by basic misunderstandings to abuse these principles flagrantly. It may suffice to recall how

they were abandoned in the abortive Austrian attempt to form a so-called "Christian corporate state," or in Franco Spain.

2. The principles of the Catholic doctrine of society and economic life do not require that their application be absolutely valid once and for all. This remains true even when objective ideological and historical facts become shrouded more or less cleverly in the neo-romantic fantasies of an *"oeconomia perennis"* or so-called "Universalism" or in dogmatic absolutes concerning the "true state." These Catholic principles imply by their very nature that their realization will necessarily be modified according to the historically given situation in a given country, in pursuit of the absolute duty to seek to establish a practical order of society and economy that will enhance the general welfare. For "you cannot read a certain economic system into the Christian gospel itself. It is on the contrary up to economic science to construct economic systems. Economic programs framed to suit the conditions, the needs and the possibilities of a specific era can only be expected to originate with the experts in practical economic and political policies." [8]

Neither do the social teachings of the Church or the social encyclicals of the popes establish a dogmatic creed and doctrine. They merely give basic directives and pointers for the activities of Catholic men as citizens and as cooperating members of a concrete order of society, in their efforts to establish its general welfare. Here, likewise, the individual Catholic person as well as the various Catholic social groupings retain their liberty in selecting ways and means in the pursuit of this goal. On the other hand, these basic principles would be vitiated if such political and social ways, means and aims were set up as absolutes, as it happens in the extreme positions of nationalism and socialism.[9] Consequently, a correct interpretation of the Catholic state and society doctrine is just as much opposed to the infusion of clericalism and theology into politics and society as to the intrusion of politics into theology; and on the other hand, this doctrine precludes a total secularization of politics, or absolute worldliness in the social and economic realms of society.[10] Thus, by way of the contemporary media of the political and social movements within Catholicism, the Catholic principles will always tend to re-create a sound, because natural, political "center" position founded on Natural Law, as against all extremes to the "left" and to the "right." "Catholicism binds and looses at the same time; it unties us from all temporal social forms, and it ties us to each temporal society. As against any kind of anarchism, Catholicism will be the strongest conservative force

in safeguarding the basic principles; as against any kind of conformism, it will be the most thorough revolutionist force." "Catholicism protects us against ever becoming slaves to our own
acts of service. For it places the real ties inside man."[11]

All this shows that the Catholic movements, and especially
those concerned with social and political Catholicism, do not
by any means represent the true church-as-community-and-
organism. On the contrary, social and political Catholicism,
both in its theories and its concrete organizational forms, is
only shaped by fortuitous historical necessites through the special constructs and variations of the church-as-society-and-organ-
ization. In other words, political Catholicism is a product of the
activities of the church-as-society within society in general; it is
"Catholicism in action" within the concrete social and political
activities of a certain country or cultural group. The achievements and failures of these variations of Catholicism in action
are therefore on principle tied to and practically dependent on
the concrete social and political structure of a certain society at a
certain time. The Church itself cannot be made responsible for
a temporal failure of "Catholicism" in its defense and practical
enforcement of the Catholic social principles. For instance, the
historically founded absence of social and governmental conscience or its weakness among the Catholics of one country may
simply be an aspect of the general state of development of the
social and governmental conscience in this country as a whole.
Thus, if in many countries we can find hardly any specifically
Catholic movements and no developed doctrines of the state
and society prior to the 19th century, the main reason lies in
the lack of concrete political and social movements in these
countries. When the 19th century finally brought forth and
richly developed the Catholic social doctrines and social and
political movements, this was in consequence of the fact that
this century was in general fundamentally the "century of the
social and political awakening and of social and political movements." It is therefore just as senseless to speak in this context
about "the Church being in default" as, on the other hand, it
would be unjust to absolve the specifically social and organizational church institutions in the various countries from these
responsibilities. But because these duties—especially those of
sociological criticism and evaluation—always emerged and continue to emerge from the concrete and specific states and the
concrete social life of the Catholics in the various countries, the
achievements and shortcomings of social and political Catholicism will not be attributable to the Church as such, but merely
to the historical realities of Catholicism in the respective coun-

tries. Therefore, the development of the social and political ideas of Catholicism in France, for instance, are the responsibility of the French Catholics only, not, as it so often falsely contended, of the "Catholic Church." The same evidently holds true of the development of Catholic theories and policies in other countries, and more than anywhere else of those in Germany because here this development was predicated on historical and political circumstances which differ basically from those prevailing in other countries.[12]

These introductory remarks on the sociological problems connected with Catholicism in general were necessary in order to establish the essential methological and ideological preconditions for a real understanding and fair judgment of the specific problems of German Catholicism, precisely because its social and political ideas and policies have evolved under such ab normal historical circumstances.

CHAPTER II

GERMAN CATHOLICISM IN THE 18TH CENTURY

1. *The Church and the Political Anachronism of the Empire.*

To explain the fundamental divergencies in the development of the Catholic Church in the various countries and under changing historical circumstances, one has to strive for an understanding of the general sociological problems posed by Catholicism.[13] This leads us to our special theme, which is to view the developments in German Catholicism against the background of the general political and social developments in German history. For a firmly based understanding of German Catholicism we need to be thoroughly acquainted with the fundamental characteristics that distinguish German history, and especially German domestic affairs, from the history of all other countries under Western civilization. This basic difference has its origin in the millennial existence of the "Holy Roman Empire of German Nation," and specifically in the fact that the political unity and centralized governmental power of this Empire began its process of territorial disintegration as early as the middle of the 13th century, a disintegration which at the outbreak of the French Revolution had resulted in the peculiarly German "Vielstaaterei" (multiplicity of states). By that time the Empire consisted of 314 territories under the immediate overlordship of the Empire, and in addition comprised 1475 "Staende" (Estates) and "Reichsritter" (knights directly under the Emperor), a total of 1789 autonomous political authorities. "Thus was drawn this map of the Old German Reich, a carnival coat stitched together from innumerable patches, in which among the many Reich knightships, Reich municipalities and Reich villages the princely territorial states were scattered helter-skelter, themselves in fragments and continual flux."[14] (Schmabel)

This is not the place for a detailed account of how and why the Old Empire became such a historical anachronism. It remains however the central fact of German history, responsible for the political and confessional particularism and separatism and in general for the cultural and political mentality peculiar to the various German tribes and regions, estates and Lander, a mentality which all through the centuries the non-German world at large was quite unable to fathom. It is therefore impossible to put too much stress on the intimate knowledge of these tragic developments if one wishes to gain a balanced view of the extraordinary complexities manifested in all epochs of German history, from the outbreak of the French Revolution to the founding of the New Reich in 1871, then passing through the Weimar Republic (1918 to 1933) and the Third Reich (1933 to 1945) and even surviving after 1945 in today's dualism of the two republics of West and East Germany.[15] And such intimate knowledge is needed most of all for a fuller understanding of German Catholicism, both in its ecclesiastical and its social policies. For in German Catholicism, to an infintely larger degree than in that of any other country of Western civilization, the affairs of the Church itself, as also the religious-cultural and the social-organizational developments were influenced by the specific political conditions in each of the German territories, primarily in their relationship to the Empire. All this makes the writing of an objective German church history an even more arduous task than of a political history. This is probably the reason why up to date no such attempt in the sense of modern historical criticism has been undertaken by Catholic scholars. With the praiseworthy exceptions of Joseph Lortz and Franz Schnabel,[16] almost all interpreters of German history were more or less swayed by ideological imponderables, such as a mystical romantic "Reich" concept, or the particularistic viewpoints either of the "smaller German" (Prussian) or "greater German" (to include Austria) concepts of German history, with all the confessional idiosyncracies and prejudices connected with these slanted aspects.

These regrettable circumstances proved fateful obstacles to an understanding of modern German history. In Germany itself no one could form an objective historical picture that would stand up to criticism, a failure which became largely responsible for the tragic growth of tendentious philosophies of history, such as Pan-Germanism and National Socialism. Thus a precondition to sound political judgment, civic self-respect and social conscience—a mature understanding of history—was frustrated among the Germans. And for the other nations of Western civilization it became almost impossible to gather objective knowledge and to form a fair judgment of both the great achievements and the shortcomings in German history and thus to draw a just balance for the motives and consequences of German political action in its unavoidable international repercussions. And what goes for Germany in general has even greater validity for German Catholicism in particular. This same tragic development forced German Catholics, whenever they tried to form an objective picture of the German past, into the methodical and ideological confines of German particularism, even more so than the rest of the Germans. Especially in 19th century Germany, this gave rise to all the tragic phenomena of romanticism and confessionalism, of inferiority complexes, of inactivity in the sciences, and of the methodological backwardness prevalent among Catholic historiographers. This same fact also made it impossible for the non-Catholic Germans to gather intimate knowledge and form a fair judgment of the political and social values and traditions alive in German Catholicism. And the same is true in reverse, through the failure of the German Catholics to grasp the non-Catholic values and traditions in the various fields of public activities. To top it all, non-German Catholicism, even up to the highest authorities in Rome, became unable to know the specific characteristics of German Catholicism in its peculiar achievements and shortcomings, and to judge it objectively.

Though only in rough outline, this characterizes the extraordinary difficulties which non-Germans encounter in their attempts to follow the tragic course of German history. The same difficulties confront those who wish to expound in a somewhat understandable fashion to the non-German world the history of German political and social ideas. Under these handicaps the present attempt at explaining the developments in German Catholicism is being undertaken and will have to be judged. In establishing these tragic facts of German history as the correct starting point, primarily as a matter of method, we have to lay down several basic theses which unfortunately were almost entirely neglected in all previous attempts.[17]

(1) From the early middle ages to the Reformation—and for the ecclesiastical territories even up to the French Revolution—the relations of Church and state in Germany developed in strict contrast to contemporary trends in all other Western countries. In the non-German states, especially in France, Spain and England, the establishment of a centralized monarchy had the result that the secular functions were progressively withdrawn from the Church and turned over to the secular state power. In this process the bishops were more and more deprived of their former secular functions and restored to the concerns of their spiritual office. This led to a sort of state-church system in which, especially in France and Spain, the spiritual power of the Church was subordinated to the secular power

of the state, often to a larger degree than was desirable for
the fulfillment of the Church's spiritual duties. Through the
Reformation even the spiritual power of the Church was further
curtailed in the Protestant countries when the absolutistic
state-church on the Lutheran pattern was instituted, in which
the secular sovereign assumed the additional role of *summus
episcopus*. Although in a somewhat blurred or modified form
the same relationship existed in the other secular territories
of the German Empire, as for instance in Electoral Brandenburg, Electoral Saxony, Electoral Palatinate, Bavaria, Swabia,
Austria. As against this, some developments in the Empire
took the opposite course. To begin with, when in the early
middle ages the power of the Emperor destroyed the tribal
duchies, it set a definite limit to the possibilities that several
secular kingdoms could arise in Germany and expand organically. On the other hand, the foundations for a powerful
ascendency and expansion of the secular dominion of the
Church were laid by the ecclesiastical princes and estates. When
the Emperor's authority faded and no strongly centralized
imperial power remained, at a very early stage the bishops and
ecclesiastical estates—in the first place the mighty ecclesiastical
Electors and Archbishops of Cologne, Trier and Mainz and
the Archbishop of Salzburg—also acquired the unlimited secular
sovereignty over their territories. Thus it came about that
in the ecclesiastical territories of the Empire a sort of absolutistic church-state was set up against which the formal authority of the Empire and the Emperor had not the power to
prevail. The consummation of this first first phase in the fateful
trend came in the Capitulations of Emperor Frederic II, 1220,
1231 and 1235, through which he divested himself of the most
essential regal rights, such as the levying of customs and taxes,
the coinage, and even the judiciary, all of which fell to the
ecclesiastical and secular territorial princes of the Empire. In
the famous "Golden Bull", Emperor Charles IV yielded
to the princes all the remaining supreme judiciary powers of
the Empire. By this act, the Catholic Church also became an
absolute secular power in Germany, and it often exercized its
prerogatives against the interests of the Empire and against
the interests of its true spiritual function.

(2) The establishment of the secular power of the Church
had the consequences that the social institutions of Catholicism
in Germany were secularized and drawn into the sphere of
politics, especially in the territories of the powerful archbishops
of Cologne, Trier, Mainz and Salzburg. It had the further
consequence that the spiritual authority of the Church was

misused to serve the interests of the secular political power. This process has never really been duplicated in any of the other countries of Catholic faith, not even in the Popes' Pontifical State in the worst times of their ambitions in power politics. This tragic fact also gives the fundamental explanation for the advent and success of the Reformation in Germany, and it gives specifically the historical and political causes of the Lutheran Reformation. In utter disregard of the lessons for the real interests of the Church that should have been learned from the events of the Reformation and the reformatory spirit of the Council of Trent, the political absolutism of the Catholic church-state system in Germany found its ultimate implementation in the clauses of the Peace of Westphalia, 1648. In the articles referring to the territorial princes of the Reich, including the ecclesiastical princes, they were given the absolute *superioritas territorialis,* that is, the *libertas* of the imperial princes versus the Emperor, which implied even the right of concluding treaties with non-German governments. As it turned out eventually, the ecclesiastical princes, in the first place the Rhenish archbishops and electors, exercised this *libertas* to the detriment of the Empire.

(3) The extreme involvement of the medieval Church in imperial politics also explains why the religious impulses of the Reformation later found their strongest expression in political action which brought about the definitive cleavage within the Empire along confessional-political lines. The unity of the Church was torn asunder in that fateful dualism of the Catholic and the Protestant confessions, and at the same time the Empire was permanently divided into the *corpus catholicorum* and the *corpus evangelicorum* of the Catholic and Protestant Empire estates—according to the principle of *cujus regio, ejus religio* proclaimed by the Religious Peace of Augsburg 1555. This gave final sanction to a disastrous weakening of the Catholic Church, both in respect to its territory and to its role in power politics. The mighty bishoprics east of the Weser were almost all lost, equally the ecclesiastical abbeys with the exception of the ones situated in the Rhineland, in North Western and in Southern Germany. Of the secular territories only Austria, Bavaria and the tiny Julich-Berg remained faithful to Catholicism, and of the larger Imperial cities only Cologne. The Counter-Reformation gave the Church but little respite in this process of territorial and political retrenchment which continued to the very end of the Old Empire. These losses are the main cause for the painful insulation of the Catholic Church in its aloofness from all new movements which

originated largely under Protestant initiative—in national political and civic thought, in the economic developments of
capitalism, in social progress, and finally from the spiritual
movement of German Enlightenment. These are the historic
reasons for the striking intellectual backwardness of post-
Reformation German Catholicism which was widely discussed
as a spiritual failure, as political inferiority, as a lack of political
conscience and of economic and social initiative in German
Catholic society from the Reformation until far into the 19th
century. Without an intimate knowledge of all these circumstances it is impossible to report and evaluate adequately the
enormous progress which was then achieved by modern German Catholicism in its social and political thinking, and especially the amazing successes in its political organizations and
its progressive social and political doctrines during the last
eighty years.

(4) An objective account of the causes, the course and the
consequences of the religious schism in Germany will have to
state above all that the real cause for the division of the Empire
into a multitude of small principalities and also for its political
impotence was not the Reformation, and that it was not even
the real cause for the territorial losses and the disruption of
the organic unity of the Catholic Church. All these phenomena
were only aggravated by the Reformation. The religious, or
rather the communal confessionalism characteristic of the time
defintely stunted all hopes of a political trend toward centralization in the Empire. At the same time, the pre-Reformation
organizational church community in German Catholicism was
disrupted. And the spirit of unity which had joined together
the German Catholics with those of all other Western countries
also continously disintegrated, while the movement in German
Catholicism away from the authority of the Pope became dangerously active in so-called "Febronianism."

(5) The political causes and consequences of the Reformation in their intimate connection resulted in a fateful
mixture of religious motives with political objectives, expressed both in the church schism and in the political particularism between the tribes and Lander as component parts
of the Empire structure. This placed developments in Germany
into such a marked contrast with those in all other Western
countries. Politically the most dangerous phenomenon was
the antagonism already noticeable in the old Empire between
Prussia on the one hand as the protagonist of the Reformation,
and the Catholic principalities as the leaders in the Counter-
Reformation. This antagonism found its political manifesta-

tion in the *complexio oppositorum* of the "three Germanies" of the Old Empire, *i.e.*, Prussia—Austria—Reich estates, the last group being further divided by the confessional schism between the Protestant and Catholic territories. As the influence of Austria on the reduced body of the Old Empire continued to wane while the Prussian influence grew and the influence of Catholic Electoral Bavaria remained weak, it was only natural that during the 17th and 18th centuries these antagonisms became strongly focused in the religious, political and social estrangements and divisions between Prussia and the ecclesiastical territories.

(6) The resulting situation has received much too little attention. The post-Reformation history of Prussia, its powerful ascendency throughout the 18th century to the Congress of Vienna, became the decisive factor in the subsequent historical developments of 19th century Germany. For the post-French Revolution developments in German Catholicism, the decisive factors were the history and traditions of the ecclesiastical territories, primarily of Cologne, Trier and Mainz, and of the north-western and southern bishoprics, abbeys and monasteries.

(7) In the course of the 19th century, the majority of the ecclesiastical territories became integrated with Prussia. Their history is therefore of special significance for a deep insight into the theme of this study, which is to analyse the developments of political and social thought in modern German Catholicism. It is thus necessary to outline the history of modern Prussian Catholicism from the beginning of the secularization in 1803 to its climax in the Congress of Vienna, 1814-15. With this the history of Southern Germany, especially Bavarian Catholicism, is intimately connected Bavaria having been the chief inheritor of the Southern German ecclesiastical territories. For historical reasons, we have to add the developments of German Austrian Catholicism after the Congress of Vienna, because of its close connection with Southern German Catholicism and its traditions, particularly after the Archbishopric of Salzburg, which had been exceedingly powerful in the Old Empire, was annexed to Austria.

(8) One added consideration will clarify what is the fundamental significance of the complex historical background of the peculiar political and social characteristics of German Catholicism. We here wish to point to the marked contrast between the realism and the democratic principles in the state concept and social doctrine of Prussian Catholicism and the romanticism and conservatism of Southern German Catholicism and the so-called "Vienna movement." [18]

2. *The Heritage of the Ecclesiastical Territories.*

The political and social conditions which prevailed in the ecclesiastical territories in the 18th century had decisive consequences for the developments in modern German Catholicism. This is particularly true of the tragic heritage bequeathed by the electorates of Cologne, Trier and Mainz in their extensive territories. If Catholicism ever was called to prove its extraordinary vitality as a Church in the fundamental, life-giving spiritual functions of a sacramental community, this was the case in 18th century German Catholicism. Despite the flagrant abuses to which the feudal aristocratic hierarchies of this epoch put the traditions and institutions of the Church in pursuit of their political ends, the broad masses of the people kept alive a straightforward popular religion and sensual-aesthetic folk culture of amazing intensity. Otherwise, the dire poverty and social backwardness in which the plain church people were forced to live because of the political and social irresponsibility of most of the ecclesiastical princes might very well have thrown the German Catholics into that same depth of religious despair and estrangement from the Church which later found its lasting expression in the negativistic spirit of the French Revolution. Only through this deeply rooted simple religiosity did modern German Catholicism succeed, once this unfortunate secular reign of its bishops was liquidated, in making a new start on the weary path toward progressive rejuvenation of the ecclesiastical institutions and toward expanded civic responsibilities based securely on the religious convictions of the broad masses of the church folk. Unless this fateful heritage thrust on the German Catholics at the end of the 18th century by the conditions in the ecclesiastical territories is carefully evaluated, it is impossible to size up correctly the enormous difficulties with which German Catholicism, more than that of any other country, had to cope.

It is all the more to be regretted that German Catholic historiography has given such scant attention to these conditions. No satisfactory history of the ecclesiastical territories has yet been written, and for the history of the Rhenish electorates only inadequate monographs exist.[19] German secular historiography, too, has devoted much too little interest to this complex for which we still have to refer only to a long forgotten valuable work by Ludwig Haeusser.[20] This neglect mainly accounts for the lack of a comprehensive, systematic history of the social and political trends in modern German Catholicism, a task which can be tackled only if proper regard is given to the heritage of the 18th century. Without such spadework it is also impossible to account for the tremendous repercussions the French Revolution had on German Catholicism, or to follow the controversial issues of the interrelations between Catholicism and political Romanticism in Germany.[21]

This makes it unavoidable to preface the present sketch of a history of German Catholicism by characterizing briefly the role of the 18th century ecclesiastical states.[22] For our present purpose we can confine ourselves to the three large ecclesiastical electorates because more or less the same conditions prevailed in all the larger or medium-sized ecclesiastical territories as also in the majority of the other bishoprics, church foundations and larger monasteries whose growth was determined by the identical general influences. The three large electorates were of paramount importance because of the fact that their political sovereignty and ecclesiastical jurisdiction reached far beyond their confines. This had most serious consequences in that the bishops' ecclesiastical office and jurisdiction entailed automatically unlimited political power, with all princely functions over the entire territory belonging to the bishopric or the ecclesiastical state. As an example we refer to the Wittelsbach Prince Clemens August, 1700 to 1761, who was not only archbishop and secular sovereign of the electorate of Cologne but, thanks to the system of nepotism, also united in his person the offices and dignities of a bishop of Munster, Paderborn, Osnabrueck and Hildesheim, and in addition was Grand Master of the German Order. This plenitude of power came to Clemens August primarily through the political influence of his father, the Elector Max Emanuel of Bavaria, 1662 to 1726, who besides secured for his second son, Cardinal Johan Theodore of Bavaria, the powers and dignities of the bishoprics of Liège, Regensburg and Freising. This one example may suffice to show how the most venerable bishoprics of the Catholic Church in the 18th century were defenseless against the intrigues of power politics and the worldly designs of princely nepotism and absolutism.

Simony and vicious nepotism rampant in this era were totally alien to the ancient venerable traditions of the Church, but they also ran counter to the stringent reformatory resolutions of the Council of Trent. These abuses could hold such an extraordinarily large sway in Germany only because, after the Peace of Westphalia, all higher offices and dignities of the Catholic hierarchy were handed out exclusively to members of the Catholic princely and aristocratic families. The cathedral chapters were composed solely of the scions of the Catholic

Empire and Lander aristocracy and the ruling princely dynasties with their numerous lateral branches. Catholic feudalism, partly divested of its power by the Reformation, thus found many coveted sinecures in the ecclesiastical benefices of the cathedral chapters. The Catholic Empire aristocracy, which survived in the smaller domains often enclosed within the larger boundaries of the ecclesiastical territories, was made more amenable to the reprehensible political objectives and the service of the ecclestiastical princes by the grants to their sons of sinecures in the cathedral chapters. As a consequence of this system, only few, if any, members of the various cathedral chapters were natives of that part of the country where the bishop had his seat. When these chapters voted on the succession to a vacant bishopric, it was entirely within their power to elect one of the non-residents among their members or even a candidate completely alien to themselves and to the diocese. Again we quote only one example, that of the Elector Clemens August of Cologne whose election as coadjutor in Berchtesgaden and Regensburg in 1715 was managed by his father. "Burdened" with these offices and prebends, he then went to Rome for four years of studies, to be afterwards elected on two successive days to the offices of Prince Bishop of Paderborn and of Muenster. In 1722 he became coadjutor to his uncle, the Elector Joseph Clemens of Cologne after whose death in the following year he was elected Archbishop of Cologne. Nor is this all. In 1724 he became Bishop of Hildesheim and in 1728 Bishop of Osnabrueck. His simultaneous efforts to obtain the bishopric of Liège miscarried, but he was at least able to secure it for his brother, Johan Theodore. Finally in 1732 he took possession of the dignities and copious benefices of the office of Grand Master of the German Order. How little burdened this peculiar *servus servorum Dei* felt by this scandalous accumulation of the ecclesiastical duties pertaining to his many bishoprics can be easily gleaned from the documented fact that in his lifetime he was in Osnabrueck only a couple of times and in his bishopric of Hildesheim only once, and that only "for a few hours, without spending the night." This same "bishop" did not show the slightest interest for the erection of churches in his numerous dioceses, although he is famed for being one of the greatest builders of the 18th century. Among the magnificent buildings on which he lavished the income from his bishoprics there was not one church that owed its existence to his own initiative or endowment.[23] He also manifested distaste rather than interested devotion for the ecclesiastical and secular sciences. Characteristically, the Cologne university was particularly poor in quality and this was only one among many symptoms of the catastrophic deterioration this old Reich city suffered in his reign. This problematical man of God indulged instead in excesses of wordly dissipations, a luxurious hunting and court life, extravagant expenditures for the fine arts and for his political intrigues, hardly surpassed by that extreme example of "rococo" philosophy, the *roi soleil*. To what extent this ecclesiastical territorial sovereign, probably the most unworthy of all the worthless church dignitaries of the 18th century who "suffered the bishop to be submerged by the prince," [24] mismanaged his ecclesiastical and secular duties can be appreciated by the size of his bequests in luxurious art collections and treasures of jewelry, amassed by extortion from his needy subjects, the flock entrusted to his spiritual care.[25]

This one disgraceful example of the Elector of Cologne could be amplified by others among his predecessors and successors, as also his contemporaries in the bishoprics of Trier, Mainz and Salzburg. To be sure, many of these worldly archbishops did not abuse their ecclesiastical prerogatives quite as shamelessly as did Clemens August in Cologne, or Johan Philip (1756 to 1768) and Clemens Wenceslaus (1768 to 1802) in Trier, or Emmerich Joseph (1763 to 1774) in Mainz. With very few exceptions all ecclesiastical princes of the 18th century have in common a strong leaning toward secularization and politization of their ecclesiastical offices and a marked disregard for the spiritual progress and social circumstancess of their subjects. A praiseworthy exception was Franz Ludwig von Erthal who reigned over the two Franconian High Abbeys (Hochstifte) of Wuerzburg und Bamberg from 1779 to 1795. Thanks to him the university of Wuerzburg was the only ecclesiastical academy in the 18th century which could compete honorably with the Protestant universities of the time. The extensive building activities undertaken by almost all ecclesiastical princes and also the large abbeys and monasteries devoured immense sums which it was impossible to raise fully from the people even though there was high taxation and enormous ecclesiastical tithes. The income of the Elector of Mainz was 1,440,000 florins annually, and the incomes of the twenty-four aristocratic members of the cathedral chapter were in the aggregate 380,000 florins. The ecclesiastical princes, primarily the Rhenish electors, had large additional incomes from subsidies which they received time and again from France for petty political services detrimental to the interests of the Empire. Because of these shady political deals among the Rhenish electors, the Rhenish population was interminably harassed by warlike disputes over their territories, and in the 17th and 18th centuries were continually impoverished by the rapacious soldiery from all parts of Europe, especially from France and Spain.

Moreover, at an early stage the antagonisms between the ecclesiastical princes and the Protestant states induced the former to shut themselves off rigidly from spiritual progress and all political and social movements, primarily in the economic sphere which was proscribed as subject to the "Protestant threat." The consequences for the eccelesiastical territories of this insulation from all progressive achievements of the 18th century proved simply catastrophic. We have here the primary cause for the political and social backwardness and spiritual inferiority of German Catholicism in the 19th century. This deplorable situation can be summarized under four aspects.

(1) *Political Backwardness.* Fundamentally, the prevalent system in the ecclesiastical territories was social and corporative rather than *étatiste* and political, in the technical sense of these terms. The ecclesiastical princes took little interest in the education of their subjects in state politics, since they themselves left the business of governing mostly to their cathedral chapters, a practice that had its brighter side in affording some protection against the establishment of personal absolutistic regimes. The peculiar paternalistic family structure of the ecclesiastical and elective monarchies also prevented dynastic traditions from taking root and local bureaucracies or military aristocracies from crystallizing. Up to the French Revolution there existed "under the rule of the crozier" a political and governmental system of fully secularized church-states. The subjects owed obedience primarily to the ecclesiastical authority of their bishop and his spiritual ministers. The secular authority of the territorial sovereign and of his "officials," in the sense of a genuine state bureaucracy, had for them only little, if any, meaning. A student not thoroughly initiated into the secrets of the historical anachronism of these ecclesiastical domains may perhaps form an idea from a description of the state structure and administration of the Electorate of Mainz as it appeared shortly before its downfall.

"In this archiepiscopate, which at that time together with Eichsfeld and Erfurt was estimated at a maximum of 320,000 inhabitants, 2,928 persons belonged to the clergy and another 2,200 were officials, not including soldiers, officers and schoolteachers. Thus approximately 5,100 persons served the 318,000 inhabitants of the state—by taking care of the jurisdiction, cashing in the monies, teaching and protecting, by wearing grey, black or white coats, by cropping their heads or attaching a key to their belts—with the result that every 62nd man was a salaried person, every 106th a cleric." [26] In the other territories conditions were sometimes even worse, and it is thus easy to imagine the political ignorance and the complete lack of political responsibility in a people in which always one clergyman and two clerical officials were in charge of the welfare of about one hundred persons. It proved all the more difficult in the time after the secularization to integrate this politically illiterate population in a civilly productive manner into the rigidly bureaucratic state structure of the secular successor states to the ecclesiastical territories, especially in Protesttant Prussia.

(2) *Economic and Social Backwardness.* To the very end, the economic and social structure of the ecclesiastical territories was characterized by autarchical agriculture and small handicrafts which had shut themselves off hermetically from all progressive economic and commercial developments in the Protestant states and the Imperial cities.

"Everywhere we find the proofs of how little the ecclesiastical aristocrats contributed to the welfare of a territory in which they were not born, in which they often not even lived, content with drawing on its resources. Here, in contrast to the secular states, there was no necessity to take thought of the dynasty and posterity and in their interest to husband the resources of the country with care, to alleviate the burdens of the people, to soften the pressure exerted by the aristocracy and the feudal lords, to increase the strength of townspeople and farmers, and to manage an orderly and thrifty state household. On the contrary, there were in the prevalent structure of the governing classes automatic motives which tended to perpetuate the aristocratic abuses and to carry on the old confusion."

"Here a thriftless and debauched ecclesiastical aristocracy and a wasteful officialdom confronted a depressed peasantry and a bourgeoisie without nerve and impetus. Here hardly anything had been done to elicit vigorous independent action on the part of the country and the people. The physiognomy of the people in the ecclesiastical territories was therefore entirely different from that of the people in the secular regions under abler governments. The rich revenues which a bountiful nature yielded in the ecclesiastical territories were thoughtlessly enjoyed, without too much sacrifice and toil. It was not human devotion that conquered nature, it was lavish nature that gave leave for indolent slothfulness. Nothing in the policies of the Church was intended to free labor from traditional shackles and to induce laborers to utmost exertion. The people were taught to consume what was accorded them and to keep on moving in the habitual grooves. The very aspect of the many idling clerics did not encourage people to apply themselves to their tasks. Everyone took it for granted that numerous persons were supported either through prebends and sinecures or through alms and charitable institutions. Distress and extreme need were thus rarely in evidence, but there was great poverty. The ecclesiastical territories were a paradise for contemplative spiritual inaction and highly aristocratic idleness, the true habitat for protection, sinecures, patronage and large and small scale mendicancy." [27]

This excellent characterization of the social structure, based on contemporary sources and archives, is amplified by Haeusser's equally fine description of the reasons for this economic backwardness.

"Because of all this, the ecclesiastical territories kept themselves shut off from all contact with outside influences. With sure instinct they shunned as much as they could even the smallest influx of Protestant elements, in striving to preserve the old monastic ways of school instruction. While in the larger secular territories men became more tolerant for 'reasons of state,' it still happened in the 18th century in one of the archbishoprics that Protestant communities were quite ruthlessly condemned to utter misery.[28] While in other regions refugees were welcomed, new branches of craftsmanship and industry were cultivated even at the cost of sacrifice, in the ecclesiastical territories careful thought was given only to the protection from such dangerous elements. While everywhere efforts were directed to putting available resources to the best possible use, thereby improving agriculture, industry and commerce, here the rich produce of the land was consumed as voluptuary income, partly outside of the country, and thus withdrawn uselessly from the working population. Statecraft of this sort did not bring about gradually rising standards for a thrifty, laborious, well-to-do population. It did result in feeding fifty clerics and 260 beggars for each one thousand inhabitants on every square mile of these ecclesiastical territories." [29]

Such are the main causes for the economic and social backwardness which continued to afflict most of the Catholic regions all through the 19th century, even after they had been integrated with the economically more progressive secular states, especially with Prussia. Here are also to be found the sources for the failure to develop any social initiative which proved such a severe handicap to the people in the Catholic regions as compared with their Protestant co-nationals. We cannot therefore point out with too much emphasis, as a precondition of real insight into the social and political problems confronting modern German Catholicism, how basically important it is to take into consideration the historical reasons for the social and economic backwardness of German Catholicism, as described in paragraphs 1 and 2.

(3) *Intellectual Inferiority.* It is easy to imagine that under such conditions the development of intellectual culture and spiritual life ran into the most potent obstacles. Combined with the extreme confessional narrowness that prevailed in the ecclesiastical territories, these circumstances led to an almost complete intellectual stagnation in German post-Reformation Catholicism, and at the same time to the atrophy of Catholicism's great pre-Reformation traditions. The decline of the once flowering Catholic universities which in the 17th and 18th centuries degenerated into absolute spiritual and educational incompetence is such a widely known fact of German intellectual history that it may suffice in the present context to point to it. While the Protestant princes made exemplary efforts to foster the sciences and to support the universities, the Catholic territorial princes neglected these duties in a truly criminal manner and thereby condemned their countries to a sort of spiritual blackout for which the contemporary cultural history knows no parellel. It would however not be just to regard these conditions as a necessary concomitant of the inter-European schism between Protestantism and Catholicism, between secular and church-bound ways of life and thought, with all the problems this division engendered. We can make it absolutely clear that this is not so, that on the contrary an unqualified indictment must be pronounced against the aristocratic-feudalistic hierarchy of German Catholicism. We need only compare the developments in Catholic thought in the 17th and 18th centuries in France with parallel "developments" in Germany. Even the activities of the learned Catholic orders, primarily of the Benedictines and the Jesuits, show the same discrepancy between the progressive spirit in France and the reactionary adherence to a pseudo-scholastic barren school routine in Germany.[30] The glorious line of episcopal thinkers and eminent statesmen in French Catholicism—from Richelieu and Mazarin to Fénelon and Bossuet, not to speak of all the embattled spirits implicated in the Jansenist-Jesuit controversy, and on to the precursors of the Revolution, the Abbé Siéyès and the other revolutionary abbés—had not one single opposite figure in German Catholicism. This alone suffices to

show how enormously difficult it was for German Catholicism in the 19th century to recapture and develop an independent political and social intellectual life, in the absence of all the great political and social traditions on which French Catholicism could draw so copiously.[31]

The secularization deprived German Catholicism of eighteen universities. In objective historical perspective this must surely be deplored as a loss of institutional opportunities which might have become useful to German Catholicism in its 19th century struggle to overcome its cultural inferiority. However, in regard to spiritual substance this loss was quite negligible, for—if we disregard the modest legacies of Ingolstadt, Dillingen, Wuerzburg and Mainz—German cultural history can note no important intellectual heritage as coming from these eighteen century universities. Without direct contact with the traditions of the outstanding Protestant universities, primarily with German Enlightenment and German Idealism, it proved immeasurably difficult for 19th century German Catholicism to revive an independent body of thought, especially for the doctrines of the state and society.

(4) *The Ecclesiastical Territories and Rome.* By its extravagant abuse of the social institutions of the Church, the aristocratic, feudalistic hierarchy in Germany was driven with intrinsic historical logic toward a conflict witht the Papacy dedicated to the Tridentine reforms. When the ecclesiastical princes tried to add the sanctions of theory and church law to their actual governmental and ecclesiastical absolutism and thereby to achieve total independence from Rome, this could not but lead them to an open struggle with the Papal See. In this attempt they received some theoretical stimulus and practical encouragement from the movement of Gallicanism in France, which however arose from entirely different motives, and from the reform activities of Joseph II of Austria. The German attempt to cut loose from the hierarchical ties with Rome was given its theoretical formulation by the movement of "Febronianism." It received its practical formulation in the declarations of the three ecclesiastical Electors and the Archbishop of Salzburg, which these imperfect stewards of the most venerable German bishoprics laid down in the Congresses of Coblenz and Ems. In entire church history, no other attempt against the unity of the Church has ever been made to compare with this one, in the utter cynicism of its theoretical reasoning and the boldness of the plans for its practical implementation.

Febronianism was the system of a maximalistic state-church law which would free the Catholic Church in Germany entirely from all legal and hierarchical ties with the Papal See. The foremost objective was to establish the legal autonomy of the German archbishops versus Rome, and at the same time to subordinate all other bishops and prelates to their own jurisdiction. While Gallicanism assumed in exceptional cases that the episcopal synods wielded emergency jurisdiction over individual bishops, Febronianism eliminated such synodal processes, setting up in their stead the arbitrary powers of the archbishop as metropolitan. In practice, this would have enabled the archbishop-electors to enforce their ecclesiastical maximalism just as successfully in secular matters against the diocesan bishops and lower prelates whose secular power was inferior to theirs. In usurping the Papal jurisdiction over all the bishops and prelates of the German Church they wished to reinforce the absolutism of their secular government within their own territories by the ecclesiastical absolutism over all clerical dignitaries in their metropolitan districts—which often were very much wider than their secular domains. While the Gallican system granted each bishop protection against the Papal See or against his archbishop by way of its synodal constitution, Febronianism sought to deprive the bishops of such safeguards by placing the archbishop-electors directly in the seat of both the Pope and the Emperor. Finally, Febronianism also sought to establish the right of all secular Catholic princes to interfere in every dispute which might arise between the Pope and any bishop in the course of this fight of the German archbishop-princes to enforce their principles of anti-Papal church maximalism.[32]

It cannot therefore be regarded as accidental that the true originator of these principles was a trusted disciple and friend of Johan Philipp and Clemens Wenceslaus, the Electors of Trier. He was Johan Nicolaus of Hontheim, suffragan bishop and professor of ecclesiastical law in Trier, who under the pseudonym of Justinius Febronius published in 1763 his momentous thesis *De statu ecclesiae et legitima potestate Romani Pontificis*. Neither was it an accident that, despite a Papal interdict and a formal retraction by Hontheim, these theories of Febronianism were taught until the French Revolution precisely at the electoral universities of Trier, Bonn, Mainz and Salzburg as a main subject in the disciplines of ecclesiastical law.[33]

Strengthened by the theories of Febronianism, the Electors of Trier, Cologne and Mainz launched their first attack on Rome at the Congress of Coblenz, 1769, through their "31 desiderata." For their second attack they chose the occasion of the

"Munich nunciature controversy" of 1786 to publish their "Gravamina against the Apostolic See" with incriminations and demands that by far surpassed even the famous *Gravamina* of the German Reformation. After this, they felt it safe to undertake their main attack with the support of the Archbishop of Salzburg, in the notorious 23 articles of the "Emser Punctations" of August 25, 1786.[34] The claims they pressed in these articles were so exorbitant and are in such flagrant contrast to all legal and historical traditions of Catholicism that even a partial realization would necessarily have led to a total separation of the German Catholic Church from Rome. For what tragic consequences this struggle was heading became clear in the very same year when a conflict arose between the Archbishops of Cologne and Mainz and the Roman See, in which the archbishops claimed "all powers of dispensation without Papal power of attorney, in their own right." Shortly thereafter the outbreak of the French Revolution intervened, which not only set an end to this conflict but quite generally removed the acute threat of this "second German reformation," the potential consequences of which for German Catholicism and for the unity of the Church it is almost impossible to imagine.

3. *The Secularization*

The French Revolution caused incisive changes in German political conditions, perhaps even more fundamental ones than in France itself.[35] There was a considerable territorial transformation in the structure of the Old Reich in the short period between 1793 and 1815. In the course of these events the relations between the Catholic Church and the government were completely altered, and this new order had profound significance for the shaping of modern German Catholicism. This great historical drama—possibly the most radical and consequential revolution in church policies and church law in the entire history of Catholicism—developed in five stages:

(1) The occupation of the Rhineland in 1793 and the end of ecclesiastical rule in the territories on the left bank of the Rhine, primarily in the electorates of Cologne, Trier and Mainz, as sanctioned by the Treaty of Basel, 1795.

(2) The sanction under the imperial law of the annexation of these territories by France, and the sequestration of all temporal possessions and properties of the ecclesiastical dominions, as also of all monasteries and other Church institutions. This was accomplished through the Treaties of Campo Formio, 1797, and Lunéville, 1801, which in the Diet at Re-

gensburg in 1803 were confirmed by the Enactment of the Delegates of the Empire (Reichsdeputationshauptschluss, R.D.-H.S.). This Act of Secularization, furthermore, gave the secular governments the right to acquire all ecclesiastical sovereignties, institutions and properties on the right bank of the Rhine, as idemnity for their losses of territory left of the River. By this Act, the initial sequestrations of church properties by revolutionary France were turned into a comprehensive measure of Empire policy. Thus, the Secularization Act of the R.D.H.S. became the foundation under both civil and international law of all future German policies with regard to the Church.

(3) The final dissolution of the Old Empire through the founding of the Rhine League and its sanction under international law in the Paris Treaty of 1806. When Francis I of Austria laid down the Imperial crown of the old German Empire on August 6, 1806, he ended with all legal formality the last remnants of the imperial guarantees upon which the ecclesiastical princes and imperial estates might have fallen back in their protest against the sequestration of their possessions and the voiding of their rights. In the same way, the rights of the secular imperial estates were largely nullified by the Acts of Mediation of the Treaty of Paris.

(4) The Congress of Vienna, 1814 to 1815, finally ratifying the secularization of the ecclesiastical states and church properties, and the mediation of the secular imperial estates. This completed the German revolution in ecclesiastical and secular government which had been set in motion by the French Revolution. The foundations were now laid on which the subsequent history of the thirty-nine post-Napoleonic states of the German Confederation developed.

(5) At the Congress of Vienna the mighty organizational unity of the Catholic Church in the Old Empire was finally dissolved. Apart from the losses of the bishoprics in the old imperial territories, such as Liège, Metz and Strasbourg, the Church had to undergo the dissolution of the old metropolitan order in the mighty archbishoprics of Cologne, Trier, Mainz and Salzburg. Even the exertions of the last Elector of Mainz, Karl Theodore von Dalberg, problematical as they were for a "German" church dignitary, could not hold up the total loss of the Church's political prerogatives. By the grace of Napoleon and the Rhine League, Dalberg first obtained a special dispensation from the secularization rules. As indemnity for Mainz he received in 1803 the principalities of Aschaffenburg, Regensburg and Wetzlar and was endowed with the grandilo-

quent titles of "elector, imperial arch-chancellor, metropolitan-archbishop, and primate of Germany in perpetuity." But as early as 1805 he was forced to cede Regensburg to Bavaria in exchange for Frankfurt, Fulda and Hanau. At the same time an agreement stipulated that after Dalberg's death this last ecclesiastical prince and so-called "primate" of Germany should be succeeded by the young Prince Eugene Napoleon in his secular rule, and by the French Cardinal Fesch (who had meanwhile become co-adjutor to Dalberg) in his bishopric. Immediately after Napoleon's downfall Dalberg withdrew to a Regensburg monastery, and in the end the Vienna Congress did away with this last, and perhaps most shameful episode in the abuse of the ecclesiastical office for political aims. If the revolution in German ecclesiastical affairs needed any further justification, this adventure of the last ecclesiastical princes, treacherous against both government and Church, would have amply furnished it. Even before this, the ignominious behavior of the ecclesiastical princes at the outbreak of the Revolution—through their conspiratorial dealings with the French emigration, their flight from their bishoprics and their determined efforts to save as much of their worldly possessions as possible—had put the seal on the disgraceful last chapter of the once glorious millennial history of the German ecclesiastical principalities.

In the course of this revolutionary transformation the Church suffered enormous losses. The secularization of all ecclesiastical principalities struck three electoral states, the archbishopric of Salzburg, twenty bishoprics, and in addition a large number of princely foundations, abbeys and monasteries, eighteen universities and many seminaries. These comprised a territory of 96,700 kilometers with more than three million inhabitants and an annual princely tax revenue of more than twenty-one million florins. Furthermore, the large domains and the immediate ecclesiastical possessions of the bishops and abbots were sequestrated, as were the large benefices of more than nine-hundred aristocratic members of the cathedral chapters and all properties of the chapters and canonries. The ecclesiastical properties acquired by Prussia alone (including the last secularization in Silesia, 1810) have been estimated at a total value of more than one billion marks (250 million dollars). Article 63 of the R.D.H.S. indemnified the Church through the unimpaired right to receive the revenues from the genuine church possessions and local church properties, including the endowments of the parsonages and the school funds. Article 65 also guaranteed the pious foundations as being pri-

vate property of the Church, under the merely formal supervision of the territorial ruler.[36] Articles 36 and 77 of the
R.D.H.S. provided that the territorial rulers as "universal successors" assumed permanent charge of paying the salaries of
the clergy and of maintaining the services and the church
buildings.[37]

In recognition of the manifest historic necessity which forced
the general secularization, Rome quickly drew the wise and
statesmanlike consequence of accepting the results of the ecclesiastical revolution in Germany as valid under secular and
church law. The manner in which this was done corresponded
to the way Rome ratified the outcome of the Revolution in
France through the concordat with Napoleon in 1801. Here
it was the concordat with Bavaria in 1817, the agreements with
Prussia in the Bull "De Salute Animarum" in 1821, and the
later agreements with the other German states. The results of
the secularization can be characterized by three historical facts
which were fundamental to the subsequent history of modern
German Catholicism.

(1) In doing away with ecclesiastical territorial rule, the
French Revolution created the *political* conditions for the
movement toward the national unification of Germany during
the 19th century. "It was an involved political setting, this
world in which the Germans lived at the close of the 18th
century. The prevailing mood was as incomprehensible to
Germans in the second half of the 19th century as it was still
entirely natural for those around 1800. Absolutism had almost
reduced to naught all individual sense of responsibility and
had mostly killed off all awareness that a higher public circle
of duties existed than the purely personal and familial . . . It
was therefore the luckiest thing that could have happened to
the nation that an outside force overthrew and destroyed all
the rubbish of a millennial constitution, all the bric-a-brac
in the showcases and on the altars of numerous territorial
constitutions, thus setting the nation free for a good look at
itself. And before the German had quite had time to find out
whether all this was really and truly happening to him, the
Frenchman had put in an appearance and had toppled over all
his pagodas." [38] "In shattering the medieval feudal world Napoleon rendered Germany a service, without willing it. Flagrant
breach of legality, brutal contempt for their own past and
unpatriotic selfishness are much rather to be laid at the door
of the German princess."[39]

By thus destroying the political anachronism of the ecclesiastical territories, the French *Revolution* became the main

driving force toward the great *reform* of the German governmental organization, also making it at last possible for the Catholics to reconstruct a positive civic ideology and to become active in the 19th century federative association of the several German states on the basis of equal rights.

(2) The *social* consequences of the French Revolution have reacted in a specially positive way on Catholic Germany. After the secularization had swept into discard the entire aristocratic-feudalistic superstructure which encumbered the hierarchy and the church institutions, the path was clear for the building up of a genuinely democratic organziation, for giving a truly popular Church a body of socially-minded priests. The Revolution as an outside force thus set the scene for social *evolution* which gave the organizational and the social system of the Church new deep roots in the hearts of the people and tied the people and this reformed Church closer to one another. The best proof how painfully alienated from the broad masses of the people, but also from the thin layer of bourgeois intellectuals, this whole feudalistic framework of German Catholicism had become, lies in the immense enthusiasm with which the approach of the revolutionary armies was greeted precisely in the Rhenish electorates. Even in the first onrush of sincere joy at the "advent of freedom," the deeply religious spirit of the Rhenish population kept them from resorting to deeds of outright hatred and open violence against the ecclesiastical pillars of the feudal system. Instead, the memories of their prostrate ecclesiastical princes and all the now impecunious aristocratic beneficiaries were only tinged with contempt and unrestrained scorn and disdain.[40] No better witness can be quoted for the revolutionary enthusiasm of the Rhineland than the great national-political apostle of German Catholicism, Joseph von Goerres. The thoughts and sentiments, the actions and changes of heart of this Catholic revolutionary and revolutionary Catholic, are laid down in his writings of the period 1798 to about 1812 which offer the strongest testimonial for the governmental and social justification of secularization. Here are a few samples: "I believe that in our country the time was ripe to replace the despotic form of government with a more appropriate one, and that to hold on to the old forms would have been a misfortune for humanity."[41] "In the early days of my youth the ideas of republicanism, of bettering the political conditions of mankind in their social relationships have been woven into the very fabric of my mind."[42] "It was the destiny of our generation, after thousands of years full of horror and human misery, suddenly to see appear one mighty

nation which tore from the hands of the usurper the Rights of
Man that the rust of ages had rendered unrecognizable and
raised them up transfigured, in their old glory, before the eyes
of amazed Europe." [43]

"As they can now be sized up in total retrospect, the results
of the Revolution are as follows: Hereditary aristocracy was
transformed into elective aristocracy. Instead of the throne
being surrounded by the solid body of the hereditary aristocracy, the executive power is now assisted by representatives
of an elective aristocracy at its side. Clericalism was abolished
and the religious institutions were completely divorced from
the political. Enlightenment and education gained free, open
ground for their journey toward a larger civilization. Our
country, in particular, gained through unification. There is a
growth of industry because of competition and the opening
up of intellectual perspectives. There is multiplying wealth
thanks to the assistance from a more efficient administration
and the freer traffic with a mighty nation in which abilities
and reputation are decisive for property. Finally, there is cultural progress after the local impediments that had everywhere
hampered it have fallen away." [44]

These trains of thought help us to see clearly in what measure
the social consequences of secularization created the foundations and the opportunities for social self-respect and autonomous social organization in modern German Catholicism.

(3) The consequences of secularization were of equally
decisive significance with respect to Catholic *church policies*
and *cultural policies*. First and foremost, the revolution ended
the threat of a "second reformation" through the Febronianism
of the electors, and initiated instead a truly salutary church reform, *caput et membra*. Secondly, it liberated Catholicism
from the spiritual confinement in the ghetto of ecclesiastical
territorialism and obscurantism, and guided it straight out into
the surf of broad German spiritual life and national upswing.
This confronted German Catholicism with probably the most
difficult task in its modern history. It now became its duty to
participate actively in the intellectual pursuits and to collaborate independently and creatively in the growth and broadening of German civilization. To be sure, some severe abuses of
the articles of secularization had done German Catholicism
much harm. This is true first of all of the senseless scattering of the precious art treasures assembled in churches and
monasteries (especially in Bavaria), and of the flagrant rob-
beries and destruction of invaluable libraries. There is also no
excuse for the dissolution of numerous charitable and educa-

tional institutions. To the harm done to these institutions
the inferior quality of the higher education of Catholic youth
must be partly attributed. Even Heinrich von Treitschke had
to admit that in this respect the secularization was a huge
"breach of the law." The material destruction of German
Catholicism's cultural strength is largely responsible for its
much lamented inferiority in the 19th century. The criminal
theft and injury to so many institutional opportunities for
charity and education has heaped on the sorry heritage of the
18th century further heavy burdens to obstruct the progress
of German Catholicism in the 19th century. And yet, even
these regrettable facts cannot obscure the objective truth that
secularization, taken as a historic whole, was a necessity in view
of the Catholic heritage from the 18th century, and proved an
indispensable precondition and a real blessing for the rejuvenation and regeneration of modern German Catholicism.

Even today some Catholic circles tend to give too much
weight to that peculiar apologetic literature which time and
again points to secularization as a general excuse for all the
shortcomings and failures of German Catholicism in the last
150 years. Some of these latter day apologists are overly zealous
converts, some are clerical maximalists. Against them we here
wish to draw attention, in conclusion, to the judgment of
Joseph von Eichendorff. This Romantic, who is possibly the
most genuine and the most Catholic of them all and by this
very fact perhaps the most realistic judge of the circumstances
and consequences of the secularization, wrote in an almost
unknown essay as early as 1818:

"The general torpor that had in all places befallen the
historical shape of hierarchy seemed in particular to enclose
the ecclesiastical forms of government with a coat of ice which
frigidly repulsed the vernal rays of a slowly expanding higher
intelligence. Hence, not so much energetic opposition, but
rather tough insensibility to everything new; hence that going
to sleep upon the traditional. Hence even today the dispropor-
tionate bias for the old institutional aristocracy; hence the
weighty (though not at all generally justified) complaint about
the backwardness of educational institutions and rural schools;
hence this evident laxity in the internal administration and, in
partial consequence, this tyrannical officialdom; the neglect of
agriculture, commerce and industry due in part to the overwhelming number of idle clerics; this confusion in government
finances and in industrial management, and consequently this
lack of funds for the scarce, disreputable soldiery. Indeed, rocks
that obstruct with neutral apathy the tide of a mightily on-

rushing epoch can achieve nothing except break the waters ineffectually. On the other hand, material strength is in itself something desirable and excellent for the state, though not the idolatry some devote to it. In this context, the dissolution of the ecclesiastical states must indeed be regarded as a boon for Germany, and in the first place for its Catholic sector which is today largely liberated from all the evils that had beset this motley collection of sample sovereignties. German Catholicism can be compared to a wealthy heir to a great past who has long held fast anxiously to the snug protection of his proud ancestral home, but has now been given back to his nation to probe his strength in the general struggle for the new age."[45]

CHAPTER III

CATHOLICISM AND GERMAN ROMANTICISM

1. Catholicism and Romanticism

The works of Hippolyte Taine (1820 to 1893) and Rudolf Haym (1821 to 1901) [46] were followed by confusion that frustrated the numerous attempts at finding a valid definition of the essence of Romanticism. In our own treatment of the problem of Romanticism and of its special significance for our theme, we shall have to apply two rigid limitations. First, we must try to define the notion of Romanticism in general with as little ambiguity as possible in order to construct the groundwork for an equally unambiguous description of the relationship between Catholicism and Romanticism. Secondly, in our factual application of these definitions, we must confine ourselves to that phase in German Romantic political and social philosophy which recently has been designated by the somewhat questionable term of "Political Romanticism." [47] In doing so, we must presuppose in our readers some knowledge of the creative literature and the purely philosophical works of the Romantics, as also some acquaintance with the English and French Romanticists. It is also impossible to go into the repercussions the aesthetics and philosophy of history of European Romanticism had on the growth of Political Romanticism in Germany. [48]

To begin with, we should realize that the movement of Romanticism represented an all-European expression of life as it was experienced at the end of the 18th century up to about the first third of the 19th. In this aspect, Romanticism is as much a legitimate "revolution" of the West's spirit and vital mood against the rationalism of the Age of Enlightenment, as the Renaissance was a spiritual revolution against the ivory-tower nominalism of the Age of Late Scholasticism. The basic purpose of these movements was largely identical in both instances. In modern terminology, the purpose was entirely "existential," which means, that the totality of living, "existing" man was to find expression in an intellectual movement. The Renaissance attempted to liberate man from a confinement inside the lifeless doctrines of human "essence" (So-Sein) of the nominalistic late Scholasticism, by staging a renascence of all natural and supra-natural forms of human "existence" (Da-Sein). In a similar way, Romanticism was the attempt to liberate man from a confinement within the rationalistic doctrines of human "essence" of the Enlightenment, by a renascence of man through a reintegration of human life into the totality of the historical life phenomena in the Western past. The most profound programmatic expression of this quest may perhaps be found in Novalis' (Friedrich von Hardenberg, 1772 to 1801) "fragments" and his manifesto "Die Christenheit oder Europe" (Christianity or Europe, 1799).

Renaissance and Romanticism thus have this much in common that they both strove for a renascence of the totality of human existence and a reintegration into the universal amplitude of all spiritual and historical life. But at the same time, there are also fundamental differences between these two movements, in their historical direction and in the intellectual means by which they sought to realize their aims. The Renaissance pressed forward in order to revive and in-gather organically the entire cultural wealth created in the course of Western history; its direction was toward the future, and this in itself sufficed on principle to assure its historical success. Romanticism, on the contrary, tried to repair the damage done by the rationalistic apostasy by partially turning backward to the universal traditions and uniformities of the Middle Ages; its sights were mainly directed toward the past, and this in itself prevented its ever becoming a force capable of shaping the future. By the same token, Romanticism missed its theoretical chance of becoming a creative cultural movement in Catholicism. Despite the deep roots Catholicism has in the traditions and values of the past, it can never confine itself to cultural and political retrospect, and least of all—well-intentioned though such leanings may be—to reaction and restoration with a bias for the past. For Catholicism has one main direction, toward a realistic and existential comprehension of the world at large. Catholicism is thus at the same time rooted in the past and directed toward the future. "Catholicism both binds and unbinds us. Directed against every form of anarchism, it is the most thorough conservative force; directed against every sort of conformism (and traditionalism) it is also the most thorough revolutionary force." (Lubac) [49]

In its direction toward the future, the Renaissance indeed revolutionized and *reformed* the traditional values and was therefore a true revolution in being a creative one. Romanti-

cism, on the other hand, being directed backward in its striving
for renascence and reintegration could find but one expression,
which was to revolutionize existing conditions in order to
restore the past. In this ambiguous position between revolution
and restoration lies the fundamental difference between the
general historical characteristics of Renaissance and Romanticism. It is the difference between the revolutionary principle
driving toward reforms, and the reactionary principle looking
for restoration. Whereas the Renaissance was revolutionary and
reforming at the same time, Romanticism succeeded in being
revolutionary against prevailing conditions while being reactionary and restorative in the face of novel, future-shaping
trends with their sanctions derived from the past.[50] While the
philosophy and political doctrine of the Renaissance had their
legitimate sources in the finest Catholic traditions of an all-
Western universalism, as manifested in the great example of
the inspired Nicolaus Cusanus[51], Romanticism in its retroversion toward the Middle Ages had to denounce many of the
progressive, partly Protestant, traditions that had their origin
in the Renaissance. However, in doing so, Romanticism did
not feel bound to accept the entire Catholic heritage of the
Middle Ages. Thus, especially in the Romantic doctrines of
the state and society, a peculiar syncretism was shaped. Following the selective principle of subjectivism and occasionalism,
the Romanticists made their choice of those special aspects of
the Catholic world concept of the Middle Ages that happened
to fit in with their momentary purposes, one of these aspects
being the theocentric state and the corporative structure of
society. For their self-willed "synthesis" they arrogated a pseudo-
Catholic legitimacy. This formal legitimacy embraced at the
same time both the revolutionary and the anti-revolutionary
theses of the French traditionalists, such as De Bonald, De
Maistre and Chateaubriand, and of their German epigones,
such as Adam Mueller and Karl Ludwig von Haller; and a
simulated justification through Catholic traditions was assumed for all these reactionary and restorative ideologies.

In these peculiar dialectics that govern the Romantic interpretation of history—revolutionary and reactionary, pseudo-
Catholic and anti-Protestant—we find the basic conditions that
fostered the rich confusion in Romantic intellectual attitudes,
as manifested in such *complexio oppositorum* as the Romantic
ideas on religion and history, on church and state, people and
community. On the other hand, however, these dialectical opportunities offered by the occasionalist revolution and reaction
in Romantic thought indeed reveal a certain kinship with the

cultural principles of Catholicism, though only a formal one. Many Romantics, either from purely sentimental motives or for occasionalist reasons and opportunistic considerations, have followed an urge for conversion to Catholicism. And many superficial observers therefore think of Romanticism as of a specifically Catholic movement. However, as a fundamentally subjectivist and occasionalist philosophy, Romanticism is any-thing but a Catholic theory of life and history. The subjectivist and utterly egocentric character of its ideas of man separates Romanticism basically from the objective, theocentric personal-ism of all genuinely Catholic philosophy of history and anthro-pology. We intend to show below that it is precisely this fundamental contrast between Romanticism and real Catholic anthropology and sociology that has made the Romantic doc-trine of state and society, including the so-called neo-Roman-ticism of Othmar Spann,[52] incapable of building the foundations for a genuinely Catholic doctrine of the state and society, or of being expanded into an independent Catholic system.

Carl Schmitt[53] has the merit of having shown that the subjective occasionalism of Romanticism represents a direct secularization of theological occasionalism. For the latter the things of this world constitute but "occasions" for the acts of God—as in the earlier version of this theory in Descartes and its implementation by Malebranche; for the Romanticists all of reality furnishes but the "occasion" for their own subjective imagination and intellectual activity. Romantic subjectivism simply replaces the objective *causa causans* and creativity of God by the individual's own subjective sentimental urge and by the eternal human quest for harmony and "organic" unity. Romanticism is therefore on the one hand a secularized the-ology which often breaks up the objective spiritual verities into sentimentalities. On the other hand, it also theoretically and ideologically breaks up the realities of life which to the Romanticists are primarily but the occasions for their indi-vidual thinking and feeling. It is unfortunate that, perhaps because of his too sharply pointed antitheses, Carl Schmitt failed to follow his incisive analysis through to its last historical and theological consequences which would have led him to a deeper understanding of the inner contradictions between Romanti-cism and Catholicism, most of all in their political thought. Such a thorough-going analysis would have made it quite clear in what characteristics Romantic "realism" differs from genu-ine Catholic existentialism.[54]

The moment this distinction is established, all these seem-ingly close relations between the Romantic anthropology and social philosophy and the Catholic principles of culture are exposed as fallacious, and therewith the entire pseudo-Catholicism of political Romanticism, as expounded by the German Romanticists, comes into focus. The following consequences can at once be stated, on principle: the basic ideas of Romanticism, to be sure, are directed against the rationalistic dissolution of the world concept and of the reality of spirit and life. In this they run parallel to the objectives of Catholic anthropology and sociology based on Christian Natural Law. In its determined direction toward the world of reality, the Catholic doctrine of culture accords unconditional recognition to the dignity of man and to his autonomy in the various fields of culture. But, though the Romantic too has the direction toward the real world, once he has taken it in and assimilated it to his own life, it only affords him the "occasion" for once more dissolving it into the fancies and ideas of his egocentrist subjectivism. *Thus, while the Catholic believer seeks the world in order to dwell and act in it, fortified by his theological security, the Romantic makes use of his encounter with the world mostly in order to pass through its realities in his flight into all the pseudo-theological incertitudes and perplexities of his occasionalist world concept.* This apparent kinship is also seen in the recognition which both Romanticism and Catholicism accord to the real existence and autonomy of personality, of family, church, state, etc. But whereas Catholic realism, especially as formulated by St. Thomas and Suarez, takes this recognition of real existence as the basis on which to found the theological justification of a truly Catholic anthropology and theodicy, the Romanticist proceeds in the opposite way. He does not use this recognition to elevate the existence of the world into a supra-natural sphere, in the sense of the Scholastics' *gratia supponit naturam*,[55] by which he would achieve an over-all theology in analogy with natural theology. On the contrary, the Romanticist goes more or less in reverse by drawing the entire supra-natural world, and therewith all true metaphysics and theology, back into the "real" world, meaning his own subjective existence. This offers all the possibilities and variations of a secularized theology, of a mystical immanentism and aesthetical pantheism, all of which separates fundamentally the so-called Romantic sociology or "theological" political doctrine of the Romanticists from the genuine concepts of the person, the state and society as established by all Catholic schools and factions.

We have thus clarified the fundamental relationship of Catholicism and Romanticism: as against subjectivist Romantic pantheism we have set objective Catholic theism. As against the subjective aestheticism and occasionalism of Romanticism we have the objective ontologism and realism of Catholicism. As against the Romantics' subjectivistic glorification and deification of the Ego, with its concomitant inner incertitudes, we have the ontological definiteness and theological security of the Catholic within an objective order of existence. And finally, as against the idealizing subjectivism of the organic doctrine of sociology and the pseudo-theology of the Romantic political doctrine we have the objective realism of the sociology and the genuinely theological foundations and security of the political doctrine of Catholicism.

2. *Political Romanticism*

To an even higher degree than the general concept of Romanticism, the special concept of Political Romanticism requires a clarification of its relationship with Catholicism. The peculiar recklessness with which theological concepts and categories were drawn upon to construct the ideologies of Political Romanticism has led observers to assume that Political Romanticism was even closer to Catholicism than was Romantic occasionalism in general. It was all the easier to fall into this error in view of the fact that the leading exponents of Political Romanticism, at least formally, professed themselves to be Catholics. This gives us an opportunity for clarifying the notion of Political Romanticism by confronting the contradictory dialectical notions of Political Romanticism and Romantic Politics, together with the second pair, Political Theology, and Theological Politics. The dialectics of these concepts will guide us in our examination whether it is at all possible to justify political and theological Romanticism by means of Catholicism, and also, how far Catholicism can be used to give legitimacy to political theology and theological politics. We shall thus find an objective point of view from which to probe into the much too little discussed Catholic background and Catholic allegiance of the exponents of these ideologies. A scrupulous analysis of the historical problems posed by this complex of thoughts and ideas—which for reasons of space is given its systematic formulation elsewhere[56]—will immediately reveal the following judgments:

(1) In France Political Romanticism has its foundations in Catholicism; in Germany they are only pseudo-Catholic. (2) The French Romanticists, in the first place the leading Traditionalists, such as Louis Gabriel Ambroise de Bonald (1754 to

1840), François René de Chateaubriand (1768 to 1848) and Joseph de Maistre (1754 to 1821), starting from a genuinely Catholic basic attitude (although with an occasionalist leaning), unquestionably attempted to formulate real "theological politics" to justify their Romantic Restoration policies. (3) The German Romanticists, in the first place the Restorationists Friedrich von Schlegel (1772 to 1829), Karl Ludwig von Haller (1768 to 1854) and Adam Mueller (1779 to 1829), largely falsified the Catholic traditions and concepts from their occasionalist points of view in formulating a basically pseudo-Catholic political theology which had to serve them ultimately to justify their pseudo-Catholic Political Romanticism and their reactionary policies.

This fundamental difference in the basic religious attitudes of the French Traditionalists and the German Restorationists, and therefore in the respective ideologies of their religious policies, is decisive for a real understanding of the modern history of political and social thought in French and German Catholicism. To be sure, in both countries the influence of these ideologies did not reach much further than to serve as theoretical groundwork for the conservative concepts of state and society. As shown above, the occasionalist bias directed backward toward the Middle Ages prevented Political Romanticism from discovering vital possibilities of realization in a creative future, which is sufficient reason for the indirectness and transitoriness of its influence on practical politics—in the Restoration of the Bourbons in France, in the reactionary reign of Friedrich Wilhelm IV in Prussia, and in Metternich's Austria. And yet, the influence of these ideologies weighed heavily on Catholicism as a whole, both in France and in Germany, though in strongly differing ways. And precisely this difference is of the greatest significance for our inquiry: we see on the one hand an active process of development in the Catholic traditions of Romantic Traditionalism in France, which led to modern French conservatism and to the nationalistic extremism of Charles Maurras; and on the other hand the passive, largely pseudo-Catholic traditions of Romantic Conservatism in Germany and Austria, down to the Neo-Romanticism of Othmar Spann and the "Vienna Movement." These trends again reveal with clarity how deeply decisive the cultural and social traditions of a given country are for the way in which Catholicism will be able to develop its social and political program.

This poses the question how far Political Romanticism can be said to be a possible expression of Catholic traditions and Catholic thought in that particular era. We shall have to answer this question in the affirmative for the religious and political theories and ideological aspirations of Political Romanticism in France, and definitely in the negative for Germany. To prove this contention, we shall have to limit ourselves to evidence taken from De Bonald and De Maistre for France, from Von Haller and Adam Mueller for Germany. In this we feel justified because the influence of, say, Chateaubriand and Friedrich Schlegel lies much rather in the fields of aesthetics and philosophy than in actual political and social doctrine.

Already in Chapter II, we pointed to the basic differences which at the turn of the 18th century separated the religious cultural and intellectual traditions as well as the political and social structures in French and German Catholicism respectively. We have seen that, despite all its rationalism and revolutionary secularism, France was as rich in genuine Catholic traditions as Germany was poor in them. This is particularly true of French intellectual culture, as proved by the high standards developed in French bourgeois philosophy of a sense of responsibility in social and political affairs, a phenomenon that has been interpreted in masterly fashion by B. Groethuysen.[57] Only from an atmosphere of Catholic traditions, expressed in religious integralism, church-based monarchism and social conservatism, could such men as De Bonald and De Maistre arise to give systematical ideological shape to the actual contemporary trend of Romantic occasionalism. Here it was the living traditions active in French conservative Catholicism which clamored for men capable from their innermost convictions of expressing them and setting them into action in the actual spiritual struggle against the rationalism of Enlightenment and the secularization process of the Revolution. The program resulting from this combination of religious and historical traditions with the necessities of immediate contemporary reality was now formulated by De Bonald and De Maistre in their systems of theological politics and their ideologies of a new theocentric society and theocratic state constitution. Far superior to the backward direction following from the principles of Romantic occasionalism, it was a vital tradition that made them adopt the theocratic principles of the Middle Ages. For them the decisive advantage of the medieval ideas lay in the fact that the theocentric order of medieval church society did not on principle admit of strained relations between Church and State, because in its fundamentally theocratic structure, this "state" had always been drawn into an actual sociological unity of the church-based society and the society-based church. In a truly "Romantic," though by the same token *historically unrealizable* venture, De Bonald and De Maistre attempted to dissolve the secularized state, which had emerged politically and socially powerful from the Age of Enlightenment and the Revolution, into a new theocentric unity in the democratic order of their State. This indeed presupposed that the religious and ecclesiastical organizations of Catholicism would be largely nationalized to prepare them for the new tasks of truly Catholic and "Romantic" politics; and it also presupposed that the State would be largely drawn into theology to prepare it for the tasks of a new, truly Catholic "theological politics." However, in view of the autonomous trend in Western civilization which demanded a progressive divorcement of the realms of religious and of secular culture, these two aims could not be fulfilled. In Germany, on the other hand, as we shall see in detail later on, Political Romanticism went exactly the opposite way, ideologically. Its aim was to secularize all genuine theological orders and categories by formulating a so-called "political theology"[58] which tended to amalgamate both a secularized church and a secularized society into the pseudo-theological, all-powerful and supreme "organic state."

For a judgment on the historical worth of Political Romanticism in France, it is relevant to state that with its aristocratic and theocratic ideologies it was not capable of intervening successfully and of modifying the French political and historical trends. It is equally relevant to note the abundant wealth of Catholic thought in the ideologies of the French Traditionalists, first and foremost of De Bonald and De Maistre. Without this body of thought, the great fecundity and depth of social and political ideas manifested in modern French Catholicism would have been impossible, even though Catholic thought would decisively reject this traditionalism in modern democratic France. Aside from the theocentric exaggerations of De Bonald's aristocratic traditionalism and the theocratic absolutism of De Maistre's secularized *Civitas Dei,* these two original and self-willed thinkers in their basic writings[59] have endowed Catholic France with a heritage of genuine Catholic thought and profound political and social wisdom. A comparison with this performance suffices to show how underprivileged German Catholicism was in the 19th century in this respect, for German Political Romanticism hardly bequeathed any true treasure to Catholic tradition, not to mention any political and social wisdom. On the contrary, even down to our days, German Political Romanticism has proved a severe ideological burden on German Catholicism in general, and a handicap to positive progress in genuinely Catholic social and political movements, so much so that no autonomous Catholic doctrine of state and society could develop from it.

It is by no means accidental that all leading representatives of political and social Romanticism in Germany were converts from Protestantism who turned Catholic at a certain phase of their intellectual development. Adam Mueller became a convert clandestinely in Vienna in 1805 and came out into the open with it only much later. Friedrich Schlegel was converted in Cologne in 1808. Karl Ludwig von Haller, also at first in all secrecy, became a member of the Church in 1820. Among the numerous exponents of Romantic Conservatism, the "Catholic" reactionary courtier of King Frederic William IV, Joseph Maria von Radowitz (1797 to 1853), whom Bismarck characterized pointedly as "the clever keeper of the wardrobe for the medieval fancies" of the Prussian king, was a Northern German convert. The same is true of the Social Romanticist Karl von Vogelsang (1816 to 1890) who was extremely influential in Southern Germany and Vienna.[60]

If the source materials, especially the programmatic writings and personal correspondence of these converts, are analyzed objectively there can be no doubt that the decisive factors in these conversions were ideological, political, or even outright calculations of practical politics. There were few exceptions, those who were actuated by purely personal and religious motives, such as Friedrich Leopold von Stolberg (1750 to 1819). The facts as described confirm our two main conclusions: first, that of itself German Catholicism did not produce the movement of Political Romanticism. Why this was so has been analyzed in Chapter II.[61] There was a lack of living intellectual traditions which could have guided the aristocratic and bourgeois strata in German Catholicism into a determined intellectual opposition against the rationalism of Enlightenment and the secularism of the Revolution. And, also in contrast to France there was a total lack of dedication to the concerns of society and the state which prevented the bourgeois classes of Germany from developing any vital opposition against the absolutistic state, especially against the fact that all autonomous, creative realism of society, such as the Church and the family, fell into the grasp of the state machine.

Secondly, we find that an alien current of historical thought and politcial action inserted itself into this spiritual, political and social vacuum in German Catholicism. It originated with the conservative Protestant sector of the people who had great difficulty in reconciling themselves to the reactionary rather than conservative ideologies, the rationalism and absolutism of the crude police state and to the primitivism and provincialism of the patriarchal military state. At this point the movement of Romantic occasionalism intervened to shape from these oppositional sentiments a German version of Political Romanticism, under influences coming from the Romantic Conservatism of the Englishman Edmund Burke (1729 to 1797) and from the French Traditionalists.

These influences, together with the occasionalist Romantic retroversion toward the Middle Ages, induced the representatives of these sentiments to turn to Catholicism. This did not only mean that they felt a kinship with the historical traditions of Catholicism; they also embraced German Catholicism as they found it, in the actual shape of contemporary political realities. This was again quite different from France where "the living traditions of conservative Catholicism called for the men who from their own innermost experience would have the power to make vivid use of these traditions for an active intellectual struggle against the rationalism of Enlightenment and the secularism of the Revolution." Here in Germany, on the contrary, these men, lacking traditions of their own, looked for such traditions to the Catholic Middle Ages where they hoped to find an ideological basis to carry on the same struggle as the French traditionalists. These men of the German Romantic "occasion" had also to look to the actual contemporary form of German Catholicism for the social platform from which they could fight for their aims, at least without incurring fundamental contradictions. These facts, much too little heeded, explain the enigma of the conversions of the leading political Romanticists in Germany, in the first place of Friedrich Schlegel, Adam Mueller and Carl Ludwig von Haller.

For the French Traditionalists, a genuine, essential kinship with the spirit of the Middle Ages was at the very bottom of their thinking. De Bonald and De Maistre did not approve of the sociological structure of the medieval Church and society for their own sake. To them, they were merely the expression in terms of history of the fundamental Christian principles of a theological and natural-law order for man and society. They attempted to revive those principles of Christian natural law which would sanction their Romantic political program. The German Restorationists, on the contrary, even after their formal conversion, were never able to establish an essential relationship with the spirit of the Middle Ages. All the occasionalist principle of Romantic retroversion did for Haller and Adam Mueller was to lead them back to the historical forms of medieval society, organized in corporations and estates, mainly in the shape of the feudalistic patrimonial state. Utterly devoid of understanding of the essential principles and categories of Christian natural law, they merely grasped the outward sociological characteristics in the medieval *Ordo* of a society-based church and a church-based society, only to misuse them for an apology of their own reactionary ideologies, with the help of a secularized political theology.

The complete lack of essential kinship with the spirit of the medieval *Ordo,* especially the lack of fundamental acceptance of the Christian order of natural law, once and for all separates the Political Romanticism and the political theology of the pseudo-Catholic German Restorationists from the theological and Romantic policies of the French Catholic Traditionalists.

A valid and secure criterion for the Catholic legitimacy of German Political Romanticism and the "Catholicity" of its exponents can therefore be found nowhere except in the principles of Christian natural law. When these principles are applied to the relations of man to his society and further, to all possible Christian variations in the historical shapes and forms of political and social orders, the result strictly contradicts the principles and programs of Restoration as expounded in all the writings of Haller and Adam Mueller.

Despite the outstanding research work that hase been devoted to almost every other aspect of Political Romanticism, a basic definition of this contradiction has never as yet been tried, even on the part of Catholic critics.[62] We propose to attempt such a definition and description in another context.[63] For the purpose of the present inquiry it must suffice to point to this fundamental contradiction between Christian natural law and the Restoration ideologies of Haller and Mueller. A comparative study of the writings of De Bonald and De Maistre will also furnish palpable proof for this contradiction. Although the theocratic and clerical extremism of these French Traditionalists also makes their ideologies quite unpalatable to every practical thinker on the theme of state and society, especially deeply Catholic ones, these authors are at least in harmony with the principles of Christian natural law. This is especially true of De Bonald's *Théorie du pouvoir politique et religieux* and his *Essai analytique sur les lois naturelles de l'ordre social.*[64] and of De Maistre's *Considérations sur la France* and *Essai sur le principe générateur des constitutions politiques.*[65] It is useful to confront these writings with Haller's

Handbuch der allegmeinen Staatenkunde (Manual of General State Lore) and his most important work *Restauration der Staatswissenschaften*,[66] as well as with Adam Mueller's *Elemente der Staatskunst (Elements of the Art of Politics)*.[67] Such comparisons will show, on the one hand, how strongly Haller and Mueller have based their own ideologies on the French statement of the social and political problems, and, on the other hand, how far the genuine theological and natural-law conclusions of the French authors have been watered down or nullified by the German authors' pseudo-scientific and pseudo-theological secularism.

The French authors have used deep scientific devotion, a profound knowledge of the historical source materials and a thorough, systematic groundwork in theology for the ideological apology of their comprehensive system of Catholic integralism in conservative politics. In this, too, the German epigones appear as poor copyists, in their lack of scientific seriousness, in their attempt to use a pseudo-historical, pseudo-theological secularism for the apology of their system of reactionary politics (Haller), and in the unscientific amateurishness of their Political Romanticism which, especially with Adam Mueller, degenerates into the worst reactionary sophisms and catch-phrases. To dispel all doubt as to the justification of this harsh judgment, we recommend perusal also of the lesser works of these same authors, written in further elaboration of their systems of theological politics and political theology. Compare De Bonald's *Recherches philosophiques sur les premiers objets des connaissances morales*[68] and De Maistre's *Soirées de St. Petersbourg* and above all his *chef-d'oeuvre, Du Pape*[69], with the theocratic ideologies of Haller—principally in the fourth volume of his main work which is devoted to the "Church and Priestly States" —and of Adam Mueller's *Theologische Grundlagen der gesamten Staatswissenschaften* (Theological Foundation of all Political Sciences) and *Die innere Staatshaushaltung systematisch dargestellt auf theologischer Grundlage* (The Internal State Management, expounded systematically on the basis of theology) ;[70] the latter present nothing but a flagrant abuse of theological categories to justify the omnipotent State. These pseudo-theological appologies of the all-powerful patrimonial State have since offered classical material to all later efforts to justify the totalitarian state by means of a secularized political theology. Even Carl Schmitt is more indebted to them than he would care to admit.[71]

To corroborate our severe judgment, we must offer at least some source material. We shall therefore quote some of Haller's and Mueller's basic arguments on the problems of natural law, state and people, as they are to be found scattered over almost every page in the works of these questionable "Catholic" Restorationists. "In the Middle Ages all political doctrine was sentiment rather than science." [72] In view of the great Platonic-Augustinian and Aristotelian-Thomistic traditions incorporated in the medieval state theories, as well as of their nominalistic opponents,[73] this nonsensical utterance of Adam Mueller should be sufficient proof of his stark ignorance. The same liberty through ignorance enables him to proclaim: "The chimera of natural law could come up in the world only because never enough breadth and enthusiasm has been devoted to the idea of the State." [74] With such catch-phrases the quack historian Mueller thinks he can dispose of the entire serious historical struggle to found the State on natural law—just as if Plato and Aristotle, the Stoa, their Western traditions as first formulated by Cicero, Scholasticism, and finally the natural law of the Enlightenment and the Renaissance, had never existed. He then delivers himself of the following positivistic platitude: "We may safely deny all natural law that is supposed to exist outside or above or before positive law; we may safely declare all positive law to represent natural law, since all the innumerable localities which originate positive law exist by force of nature. And because it is true that all positive law is at the same time natural law, we are in the future justified to designate with the term of natural law the endeavor to safeguard true nature within positive law." [75] After this there is little wonder that the author's anthropology is on the same level: "Man cannot be conceived as existing outside the State . . . that man lacks everything when he can no longer feel the ties of the State, that the State is the need of needs, of heart, spirit and body; that, everywhere and at all times, man cannot hear, see, think, feel, love without the State; in one word, that he is unthinkable except within the State." [76]

Faced with such Romantic nonsense, a person with genuine concepts of man and the State must indeed be left deaf, dumb and blind. He will then recuperate through the simple verities which the great Pope Leo XIII has formulated as the sum total of all traditions of truly Christian natural law, in these plain words: "Man is older than the State. And prior to the formation of any state he holds by nature the right to provide for the life of his body." [77]

From his unsound and amateurish "foundations," Mueller then proceeds to formulate his concept of the "organic state." His explanation of what he means by "organic" is just as sophistic as his explanation of the state, that is, each concept is explained merely through itself. "The essence of the Organic is that it is infinitely organized, that it consists of organs; just as the State consists in the infinite degree of states." [78] In hundreds of variations and with a rare faculty of mixing up concepts and ruining the language, Mueller expounds over and over again the brutal dogma of his Leviathan State: "The State is the totality of all human concerns, it is their amalgamation in a living whole." "The State is the intimate fusion of all physical and spiritual needs, of all physical and spiritual possessions, of all the inner and outer wealth of a nation, thereby forming a great, energetic, infinitely motile and animated whole." "The State reposes wholly in itself. Independent of human arbitrariness and invention, the State and Man come to life simultaneously, and from the same place: from Nature, from God." [79] When Othmar Spann pronounces this sort of "universalist" state doctrine to be "the greatest achievement of the German intellect in history," and goes so far as to praise its chief exponent, Adam Mueller, as being "the greatest economist of all times," he only furnishes one more proof for the profound mental confusion and intellectual sophistry which characterizes his own pseudo-Catholic "universalism." [80] However, we attach far greater importance to the judgment of a true Universalist thinker, a contemporary of the Romantic Restorationists, who confronted the sophisms of their dubious "organic" state concept with the clear and genuinely Christian distinction between the relative, secular categories of the state and the absolute, supra-natural order of religion.

We mean the young Protestant-Conservative Leopold von Ranke (1795 to 1886) who in 1836, in the last essay of his "Historic-Political Magazine," in direct protest against the growing influence on authoritative circles at the Prussian Court of the ideologies of the "Catholic" reactionaries, Adam Mueller and Heller, wrote down these fundamental sentences which indeed represent a genuinely Christian repudiation of the pseudo-Catholic ideologies of Political Romanticism: "State and Church are eternally divorced. The Church joins Man to the highest, supreme community. The Church, to be sure, establishes unchangeable rules for all actions, the rules of that mysterious community: religion." "The essence of the Church is unconditionally valid for all mankind, it is the common essence. At least, by its very nature every church must aspire to be universal. On the contrary, the very concept of the State would be destroyed were it to embrace the world. It is true that the essence of the State is divine *afflatus,* but it is also human initiative. It is a community of a limited nature, above which looms that higher community which is free of limiting conditions."[81]

Haller, like Mueller, repudiates the Christian concept of natural law when explaining the essence of man and society. Therefore Adam Mueller who deplores "the unfortunate assumption that there is a qualitative difference between public and private law,"[82] gives special praise to Haller for having "torn the veil from the specter of man's equality before the law."[83] Haller, on his part, scorns "the outrageous, unnatural equality of penalties for all classes and estates,"[84] which will not be tolerated in his feudalistic, patrimonial State. In Haller's feudal, corporate order the people are regarded as politically devoid of rights and initiative, as no more than a "collective beast," as an "aggregate of servile, indentured folk,"[85] who, like the state itself, are the absolute property of the ruling prince of the day. The prince himself is no more than "a wealthy, powerful man."[86] His power is unlimited, for it is a gift of "nature and circumstance."[87] The princes and their power are the State's sole existence since "outside of them the State is nothing."[88] According to this doctrine the power of the sovereign, represented and exercised by himself, is "a gift of fortune, and the highest possible one at that, which like other worldly possessions may have been acquired in various ways, sometimes legitimately, at other times perhaps even illegitimately, and may again be lost."[89] In this way the prince has dominion over the people; he even possesses it as a "private living," as a "manorial service association," as a "patrimonium" (Hauswesen).[90] Thus the peoples are but possessions of the sovereign princes, and the forms of their lives in the state and of their relations to the sovereign are "the highest level of natural relationships of service, of association, and of the so-called private rights." The nations differ from one another only "according to the independence or higher power and liberty of their sovereigns."[91]

These few testimonials should make it abundantly clear that these ideologies of Political Romanticism are worlds apart from anything that could duly be termed Christian, or indeed Catholic. Despite their formal acceptance of certain values and orders of life, such as family and the Church, these pseudo-Catholic Restorationists break loose from all basic Christian traditions in their progressive elaboration since the Middle Ages. For Haller and Adam Mueller, together with the group of men the latter gathered around his *Deutscher Staatsanzeiger,* no longer fought only against the principles of the

French Revolution on people's sovereignty and the division of powers. They fought just as determinedly against the actions of Enlightened Absolutism, and against Humanism and Reformation because, as Adam Mueller complained, "the mirage of the artificial bourgeois condition" had already lasted for fully three centuries.[92]

Carl Schmitt has cast some light on the complexion of the personalities of Haller and Adam Mueller, which was anything but truly Catholic. To those who may desire an even deeper insight into the many contradictions especially marked in the character of Adam Mueller, this prototype of Romantic self-induced fancies and pseudo-religious misunderstandings of genuine Catholicity, we recommend a close study of a book that is unfortunately much too little known, the *Correspondence between Friedrich Gentz and Adam Mueller*.[93] There all necessary documentation can be found for the truly devastating judgment which that genuine Catholic Romanticist, Joseph von Eichendorff, a man habitually very mild in his pronouncements, has bequeathed to posterity, summing up the most mature insight of a life dedicated both to Romanticism and to a vibrant Christian faith.

Romanticism, he said, had moved further and further away from its original goal, namely, "to work at freeing the positive element in Christianity, that is, the Church, in order to make it once more active in art, in life, in the sciences. Once this natural ground for them to stand on had shifted, everyone began to carve out his own brand of Catholicism, anarchically, according to his private poetic points of view." "For the heathen mythology they offered a Christian mythology; in short, they propagated a faith in which they themselves did not fundamentally believe." "In Northern Germany from which these Romanticists stemmed they had almost without exception been raised in Protestant ways and in the non-ecclesiastical sciences and habits of life. It was therefore necessary for them first of all, as it were, to translate themselves into the Catholic idiom that was not their mother tongue. They lacked the natural soil for their Catholic sentiment to grow, which alone could have given them the power to express their convictions with poetical creativity. Hence the insecurity of their attitude, this artificial, erratic, forced Catholicism which, eternally dissatisfied, always strives to reach beyond itself." And Eichendorff winds up his critical observations with a warning not to indulge "in the shrill witches sabbath of this unlovely literature which has finally led into such confusion that the Christians think like pagans and the Jews like Christians." He exhorts German

Catholicism to reawaken the live Catholic spirits, not however "by staging a juvenile revival of Romanticism, nor through contrived, problematical and tendentious novels, but alone through the still, homely, all-powerful force of Truth. . . !" [94]

3. Romantic Catholicism

The catch-phrase about a specifically Catholic Romanticism is misleading. We have analyzed above the contradiction in the theological and philosophical principles that underlies the relationship between Catholicism and Romanticism. The immediate consequence of it is that a specifically Catholic Romanticism cannot possibly arise as an independent philosophy and cultural movement. It is, however, true that there exists a certain kinship between the basic psychological structure of the Romantic "vital sentiment" (Lebensgefuehl) and one special phenomenon in the multiform typology of the Catholic personality. It is the tendency, on encounter with the outside world, to withdraw immediately into the world of sentiment and ideas and, from this refuge of the innermost soul, sally forth in order to grasp and experience the many-shaped reality in the unity of the ideal, by means of an immediate awareness of the whole of the "idea" itself. A man of this type is not so much concerned with taking hold on life as it is, in its existential concreteness; his concern is rather to experience like a revelation (Er-leben) life's essential, fundamental, hidden implications and secrets. This type's inclination is toward the Platonic flight from reality into contemplation and pondering of the mystical enigmas of life. A personality of this sort will measure the actualities of the world and Church with the yardstick of his absolute ideas instead of searching in the historical realities of world and Church for the realistic expressions of ideas and ideals and, in doing so, endeavoring to expand the time-bound possibilities for realizing his ideas and ideals. This is the type of the "restless heart," the unquenchable yearnings and wanderings, a type which has presented the Church both with great blessings and great agitation, especially by that constant call for reforms and for integralism which has enlivened the history of the Church from its beginnings and has often proved a boon by keeping the Church from indulging in too complacent a realism.

This "Romantic type," the type of the "existential perturbation" (Unruhe), has always found a true home in Catholicism rather than elsewhere. The visible effects of these spiritual labors can therefore justly be designated by the term of *Ro-*

mantic Catholicism, if this is taken to mean the sort of cultural action originating from the psychological attitudes of a Catholic of the Romantic type. Within the universal scheme of Catholicism this type had at all times a justified existence and a wide field of action. And yet, it always was, and will always be limited by fixed boundaries. As an autonomous philosophy and cultural endeavor, Romanticism can never be entirely at home within Catholicism, for such a philosophy has to set its aims and aspirations to a goal which is identical with the one Catholicism itself must strive for, which is, to embrace man and the world as a whole, with ideas and reality, nation and humanity, God and history, all gathered into the universal oneness and organical wholeness (katholon) of life itself. As a philosophy, Romanticism sought to shape an autonomous movement of its very own within which this "romantic type" felt called upon to be the sole leader. Being in complete command, he would shape absolutes out of every relative value in the historical record of humanity, mainly by dissolving the orders of life into occasionalist, subjectivist moments of living, and by violating the carrying ideas of this order through subjectivist ideologies. Thus we recognize, on the one hand, the irreconcilable contradictions between the principles of Romanticism and Catholicism, and yet, on the other hand, the vital psychological tensions which establish a true relationship between the romantic type and the Catholic attitude toward life and the world. In these tensions and contradictions we discover the field of possibilities and its limitations for the romantic type to become active within Catholicism, and in this sense we may speak of *Romantic Catholicism in the Age of Romanticism.*

After having gone through this analysis, we are prepared to understand why every basic contribution in Romantic Catholicism usually comes from representatives born and bred in the Catholic persuasion (Gesinnung), not from converts who, as Eichendorff expressed it, "first had to translated themselves, as it were, into the Catholic idiom because they lacked the natural soil of Catholic sentiment (Gesinnung)." These converts were drawn toward the sociological forms of Catholicism only technically by the accident of the occasionalist principle. On the contrary, this same principle fortified the Romantic Catholics in their birthright of Catholic sentiment and, above all, it called to life once again all that wealth of Catholic traditions in the social and political sphere, thereby creating a vivid new idea of a social order. The main actions of Romantic Catholicism have therefore always been directed toward a spiritual (gesinnungsmaessig) criticism of the actual order of society, especially of the existential orders of the social spheres of life. And this "existential" criticism was always supplemented and widened by proposals for a "reform of the spirit" (Gesinnungs-Reform), which in this case implies the search for a new religious-philosophical, theological policy, to implement the ideals of a new order. The pseudo-Catholic Romanticists, on the contrary, (Adam Mueller, Haller, and the others), being predominantly concerned with an "essential" apology of the State as such, shaped their Political Theology mainly to justify the ideologies that show the State to be the supreme epitome of all social order. In the light of our analysis, therefore, the so-called French Political Romanticists were shown to be genuine Romantic Catholics, based as they were on persuasion (Gesinnung), that is, on theology. This is particularly true of De Bonald and De Maistre; and in the efforts of late Romanticism, in Lamennais and his circle of co-workers on the magazine "Avenir," among them Lacordaire and Montalembert, this trend was to become signally creative in social affairs. And it was precisely this circle of "Lamennais of the *Avenir*" which exerted a wholesome influence on the ideas of Romantic Catholicism in Germany, especially on Baader.

Before going into more detail about these cross-influences, we must pay due attention to a significant factor. This refers to the peculiar tension which has always existed between the romantic type of the Catholic with his occasionalist subjectivity and the main body of Catholicism with its own approach to life and society. This tension, constituting one of the essential factors in the "existential perturbation" of the romantic type, implies a serious danger even for the genuine Catholic Romanticist, that of straying from the *Kosmos* of the objective orders and categories of Catholic Realism into the subjective world of sentiments and individual experience of Romantic Occasionalism. As shown above, this tension was not yet too strong with the pure theoreticians of French Traditionalism, although, even from the most tolerant Catholic viewpoint, De Maistre's mysticism contains a most dubious element. But soon, with the last great successor in the line of the French Traditionalists, Lamennais, this tension increased to such a dangerous degree that this great Romantic, and genuinely Catholic spirit finally succumbed to the temptation of sacrificing the Catholic idea and reality entirely to a thoroughly secularized social "Christianity." In the same way, some representatives of Romantic Catholicism in Germany, just because they were true Romanticists, were never entirely free from such one-sidedness of subjectivist Romantic Occasionalism, as we shall show by the examples of Goerres and Baader.

In our context we need not go into an analysis of the strictly poetic achievements of Romantic Catholicism in Germany, especially because we possess a detailed appreciation by its most inspired representative, the immortal Eichendorff himself.[95] This very fact, that the chief representative of Catholic Romantic poetry was able to produce such a realistic account and objective evaluation of the very movement and school of thought which filled his being to the core, offers one more characteristic trait of the peculiarities of German Romantic Catholicism.

We can best explain the general sociological significance of this movement and also its special role in the cultural history and social policies of Germany through an analysis of the thoughts and activities of its three leading representatives, Eichendorff, Goerres and Baader. That so far Catholic scholars have neglected to write comprehensive scientific biographies of these three great exponents of Romantic Catholicism, or to publish their works and their literary estate in critical editions[96] must be taken as a sign of the lack of well founded traditions and of an independent sociological interpretation of the history of German Catholicism.

A. *Joseph von Eichendorff,* 1788 *to* 1851

Down to our day the importance of Eichendorff for its cultural history has been entirely overlooked by German Catholicism, although his life and works have much light to shed on the little known genesis of Catholic political and social thought and action at the beginning of the 19th century. The life story of this scion of a noble family from Silesia fully disproves the widely held belief that Catholic thinking at the turn of the 18th and 19th centuries was quite inferior to the task of digesting the historical and political realities of this era. By his descent from Silesian Catholics, Eichendorff was spared that negative heritage of a long ecclesiastical rule that proved so burdensome to the Rhenish and Southern German Catholics. From the Silesian aristocracy Eichendorff inherited a decidedly positive attitude toward state and society. For, in a manner beneficial to both partners, Catholic realism had largely reconciled itself to the bitter political reality of the Prussian State. This very *synthesis of Catholic persuasion with responsible civic dedication* is typified by the way Eichendorff pursued his secular professional training without in the least

harming the ideals of his Catholic philosophy. In full clarity
of purpose he chose the profession of a civil administrator in
the Prussian state services. The non-Catholic character of this
state irritated him as little as he let himself be disturbed by
the purely secular character of the science of jurisprudence to
which he dedicated himself at the Protestant universities of
Halle and Heidelberg. Finally he selected for his academic
dissertation what was perhaps the most controversial theme a
Catholic candidate for the Prussian civil service could tackle,
"On the Consequences of the Termination of the Secular Rule
of the Bishops and Monasteries in Germany." [97] Already in this
thesis Eichendorff showed a maturity of historical insight and a
sense of political responsibility, imbued with genuine Catholic
realism which for that time, 1818, was probably without parallel in German Catholicism. On the force of this dissertation,
Eichendorff was sent in 1820 as "government councilor" (Re-
gierungsrat) to Koenigsberg "to administer the Catholic ecclesiastical affairs in Prussia." From 1831 to 1843 he worked
in the Catholic division of the Ministry of Education in Berlin.
After almost 23 years of service, he resigned voluntarily in
protest against the growing church conflict. His achievements
during this long period of activity are an example of what a
responsible government servant can accomplish while following
the dictates of his conscience. In this period he wrote a large
number of political memoranda, essays and letters which could
have raised the standard of German Catholic political thought
immeasurably, had they been widely publicized and put to
good use in education, which they were not.[98] Eichendorff
also wrote several historical studies, among them in 1843-44
a comprehensive history of "The Restoration of the Castle of
the Teutonic Knights at Marienburg"[99] a typically Romantic
pursuit.

During his Heidelberg student days, Eichendorff came into
close contact with the circle of Romanticists that gathered
around Goerres. "There dwelt in seclusion a sorcerer who
drew into his magic circle heaven and earth, the past and the
future—that was Goerres." Thus Eichendorff describes in his
memoirs "Heidelberg"[100] this great Romanticist magician;
whereupon he proceeds at once to examine critically the "experimental Catholicism" of these Heidelberg Romanticists.
"Catholicism became all the fashion. And in the way of all
fashion, this one passed away; but the tone once struck lin-
gered on—and as the times grew more and more grave, this
brought forth once again a strong Catholic undercurrent which
now is no longer in need of Romanticism." "Romanticism has

left behind some indelible marks: by constantly pointing to the nation's past, it has fostered patriotism, and through its experimental Catholicism it has revived the need for religion. This love of the fatherland, however, was again cut loose from the Middle Ages and thus was bereft of its historic background and deprived of all national coloring; and thus, from the old abstract citizenship of the world was born the equally abstract infatuation with Germanity (Deutschtuemelei.) On the other hand, the newly stimulated religious sentiment could neither find satisfaction in Romantic Catholicizing nor in revived nationalism." [101]

After his Heidelberg experiences with "Romantic Catholicizing," the genuine Romantic Eichendorff developed a growing sense of distance from the subjectivism and occasionalism of Romanticism because, as a politician and historian and also as a true poet, he always and above all found alive within himself the typical mentality and formal principles of Catholicism. Better than any other among his Romanticist contemporaries, he could therefore become the legitimate critic of Romanticism in general and at the same time the one author competent to bring Romantic Catholicism to fruition. He accomplished his function as interpreter and critic of Romanticism in his two basic works of literary history, "Ueber die ethische und religioese Bedeutung der neueren romantischen Poesie in Deutschland" (On the Ethical and Religious Significance of the Recent Romantic Poetry in Germany, 1847), and "Geschichte der poetischen Literatur Deutschlands" (History of Poetical Literature in Germany, 1857). These two studies indeed give more than merely a systematic history of literature from the Catholic aspect. They also represent the first, entirely successful, attempt at a literary and *sociological interpretation* of the problems of Romantic Catholicism in Germany and a religious and sociological account of German Romanticism in general.[102]

A very special place is also due Eichendorff in the cultural history of German Catholicism for his work as a Romantic poet. None but a heaven-inspired genius could combine in immortal poems the most sublime lyrical nuances and poetical forms with the realism of Catholic vital sentiment and thus create with a mastery hardly equalled by any other Romanticist a true poetical art of Romantic Catholicism, German vintage. His Romantic soul, always kept on the alert by the vitality of his genuine Catholic persuasion, discovered the deeply hidden secret of the Catholic vital attitude, that of comprehending nature and the world realistically. In this poetic presentation of the fields and meadows, the flowers and shrubs, and above all the German forest with all the magic of virgin nature, he endowed this world with striking immediacy. But then this heaven-inspired disciple of the Muses rose even above his work of poetical artistry with its magnificent unveiling of nature's secrets. For this same man also seems to have unveiled *the innermost core of Catholicism's insight into human character* and the art of human guidance which, purely and simply, consisted, and will always consist: *of first accepting the living human being as it is in order then, progressing from this insight, to give it the direction and preach the wisdom for man's daily course, as well as for the highest goals available to man in his duty to strive for higher perfection and accomplishment.* This is the homely, but at the same time the unfathomably deep wisdom of the true realism in Catholicism's management of men and of the genuine idealism of Catholic education of men, the wisdom which Eichendorff wished to express in his poetic masterwork, perhaps the ultimate creative fulfillment of the Romantic knowledge of man, his immortal "Memoirs of a Good-for-Nothing." If we contemplate all these gifts of a great poet together with this wealth of social wisdom and political awareness with which Eichendorff followed his mission as a Romantic Catholic and his profession as a Catholic German citizen, we can finally measure of what German Catholicism deprived itself through more than a hundred years of almost criminal negligence. For until today the Germans know hardly more about Eichendorff than the poems and a few novelettes.

B. *Joseph Goerres, 1776 to 1848*

If Eichendorff can be regarded as "the most Catholic among the Romantics" within the problematical complex of Romantic Catholicism, Goerres may on the contrary be characterized as "the most Romantic among the Catholics."[103] With Eichendorff the "existential perturbation" of Romanticism is so firmly anchored in the core of the religious existence of Catholicism that it becomes active as a harmonious loosening up of Catholic realism. Here all positive opportunities of romantically expanding Catholic existence are fully exploited. For Eichendorff, therefore, nature, man, people, the state, even the Church, are immediately comprehensible facts within the orders of creation and history. They are live realities which, in mutual service, appear as an existential "possessing" and "being possessed." With Goerres, on the contrary, the "existential perturbation" first of all reacts on a labile condition of religious existence in a problematical Catholic faith which, as it lacks a secure fund of positive spiritual and historical traditions, rather tends toward an unharmonious disruption of Catholic realism. With him all negative possibilities of Romantic perturbation threaten Catholic existence. For Goerres, therefore, nature, man, the people and the state, even the Church itself present thoroughly problematical complexes within a problematical order of creation and history, whose hidden implications first need to be puzzled out and justified through an essentialist "ought-to-be" or an act of "appropriation." [103a]

In establishing this *polarity of the existential and the essential approach to the historical realities in Romantic Catholicism,* we find in it an exemplary expression of the fundamental tensions which have beset the problems of state, society and economy ever since the era of Romanticism. These tensions have found one of their expressions in the realism of the Prussian Catholicism in Northwest Germany and the Rhineland as against the Romantic conservatism of Southern German and Austrian Catholicism.

In the course of this development Goerres ran through all the phases of these perplexing relationships, as documented by the chaotic and contradictory mass of his voluminous literary production as well as by his extraordinarily restless life. He never managed to decide definitely for or against the existential unrest of the Romantic approach to life, and thus his story is characterized by the "both this and the other" implied in Romantic existence. This indeed is perhaps the chief source of the powerful influence Goerres exerted on his contemporaries. And from the same source flow the deep repercussions which Goerres' eloquent writings had on the later over-all developments in German Catholicism. The *complexio oppositorum* this great "magician" (Eichendorff) achieved in his Romantic existence and in his publicistic and literary production has an exact parallel in the *complexio oppositorum* of the political and social existence of all-German Catholicism. No wonder then that German Catholicism, whether engaged in aggression or defense against the world outside or involved in inner conflicts among opinions and factions, has the habit of referring to Goerres as an *ultima ratio,* often supplementing a non-existent factual argument with the sheer mythological effect of his name. It is possibly for a similar reason that the Catholic journalists in Germany have chosen for their tutelary saint the father of all Christian "wisdom" in the West, the great Augustinus (Augustine Association of the Catholic Press) , while paradoxically the professional Catholic scientists have made this representative Romantic publicist *par excellence* the patron saint of their "Goerres Society for the Advancement of Catholic Science." Historical logic might have recommended an inverse course——!

In his revolutionary period, which lasted about to the year 1800, young Goerres was typical for the lack of secure political allegiance characteristic of that bourgeois strata in the Rhineland which was burdened with the negative heritage of having been ruled by the ecclesiastical states. Brought up at a Coblenz gymnasium in an amosphere of *Enlightenment,* Goerres first saw his spiritual mentor in Rousseau. He welcomed enthusiastically the events of the French Revolution with their sequel of chasing out from his Rhenish homeland "the barking packs of princes and hordes of clerics." With truly Jacobine fanaticism Goerres founded in 1798-99 the revolutionary paper "Das rote Blatt" (The Red Sheet), which, by the way, was the first political magazine of the kind in Germany, and made every effort to eradicate from the Rhineland the last remnants of Christian historical tradition and Christian attitude toward society. He laid down the aims of his revolutionary secularism in his programmatic" Glaubensbekenntnis" (Profession of Faith) and in his sarcastic "Funeral Oration" for the Holy Roman Empire, a profession of faith in the absolute democratic rule of the people. And yet, the religious kernel implanted in this young Jacobine's heart proved strong enough to cause one more occasionalist turn in his political sentiment only one year later, after he had witnessed in person the revolutionary regiment in Paris of 1799 and 1800. In his pamphlet "Results of my Mission to Paris" (1800) he definitely went into opposition against revolutionary secularism. This marked the end of young Goerres' political apostasy, but not of his intellectual homelessness.

And thus the transformed Goerres turned toward a new world which, he hoped, would compensate him for his Catholic homeland's lack of intellectual traditions. Here for this anxious occasionalist soul of a Catholic German began a period of search around the *Kosmos* of German Romanticism which spanned the wide and complex worlds of Fichte and Herder far down to Novalis and Schelling. Each new discovery in every aspect of these intellectual worlds proffered one more "occasion" to this searching Goerres—in his conscious search for the spirit, but already once more in his unconscious search for God—to give his Romantic soul new food for productive efforts. The outcome was a series of essays expressive of pan-

theistic "internalization" (Verinnerlichung), a series which begins with his "Aphorisms on Organomania" (1803) and ends
with "Mysticism and Novalis" (1806). There follows the personal experience of the Heidelberg Romanticism (1806 to 1808)
which, by way of his new awareness of the concepts of "nation"
and "folk," led him back once more to the traditions of
medieval society and the political mysticism which surrounds
the notions of Emperor and Empire. The "Teutsche Volks-
buecher" (Teutonic Folk Literature, 1807) and the "Wachs-
tum der Historie" (Growth of History, 1808) are the literary
expressions of Goerres' Romantic conversion, the occasionalist
dialectics of which held him captive throughout his life. However, it was not long before the realistic elements of his basic
Catholic structure turned this Goerres of the Heidelberg
period back toward contemporary reality. In 1808 he returned
to Coblenz to serve as a mentor to the awakening German liberation movement. This brought his talents to full fruition,
especially after he had given the Germans their first truly
national political journal, the "Rhenish Mercury." [104] From
1814 to 1816 Goerres developed this medium as the greatest
Romantic periodical of his time. As a Romantic political
thinker, Goerres strove in innumerable articles to establish
the concrete shape of a constitutional state and a realistic
program for a national people's culture; and at the same time,
as a political Romanticist he renewed the occasionalist dreams
of a return to a medieval order under the mystical rule of
Pope and Emperor. Nothing has anchored the historic repercussions of Goerres' work more deeply in all sectors of German
Catholicism than this journalistic activity in the *Rhenish Mercury*. Any faction of modern German Catholicism which wishes
to draw strength from the first realistic traditions of national
and state policies can proudly refer to this realistic political
writer of Romantic Catholicism. But with the same right the
opposing Romantic-Conservative faction can refer to Goerres
in his other shape in which to them he is the founder of the
Romantic Catholic traditions of medieval mysticism of society
and Empire.

In sharp contrast to the Romantic realist Eichendorff, the
Catholic Romanticist Goerres was unable to reconcile himself
with the realities of the Prussian state. He turned his back
on Prussia and once more settled down to work in Heidelberg
(1816 to 1819). His "Deutschland und die Revolution" forced
him to move to Strasbourg. Here, primarily in the circle of
collaborators around the "Katholik" of Mainz, Goerres recovered the atmosphere which made his full-hearted return to

Catholicism possible. When later, in 1827, he was called to the chair of history at the University of Munich, he was fully prepared for his role as the most eloquent and embattled church politician in the fight against Prussia. His "Athanasius" (1838), "Die Triarier" (1838), the pamphlets "Kirche und Staat nach Ablauf der Koelner Irrungen" (Church and State at the Ending of the Cologne Differences, 1842) and the essays in the "Historisch-Politische Blaetter" are some of the products of this journalistic activity by which Goerres' influence reaches far beyond the age of Romanticism into the subsequent course of ecclesiastical policies of German Catholicism. It is undeniable that these achievements in publicizing church and cultural policies merit high praise. Even so, in these activities Goerres was misled by the principles of Romantic Occasionalism to indulge in confessional bias which ministered against the best interests of his just cause. The same may be said of the chief literary work of Goerres, the *Romantic Catholic,* "Die christliche Mystik" (1836 to 1842).[105] In this almost eerie structure erected in enthusiastic faith by an inspired Romantic imagination to give an encyclopedic inventory of the enigmatic facts of religious mysticism, we find in motley stratification as many different layers of genuine Christian mysticism and pagan mythology and demonology as the variations of the occasionalist principle of Romantic mentality admit. But even these vagaries do not cut off this great "magician" from his legitimate allegiance to genuine Romantic Catholicism.

C. *Franz von Baader,* 1765 to 1841

If we regard Eichendorff as the poetic genius and religious conscience of Romantic Catholicism, and Goerres as its publicizing genius and political conscience, then surely *Baader was its philosophical genius and social conscience.* The reasons for the utter ignorance with which German Catholicism has until today shrouded its most inspired Romantic son are varied and explainable, but it remains nevertheless inexcusable.[106] The neglect of Baader was partly the fault of contemporary Catholicism, partly caused by some characteristics of Baader himself. We have analyzed above the historical background that explains the ignorance in German Catholicism of its history of thought and the confessional narrow-mindedness against which ever since Baader's day the best exponents of German Catholicism have been fighting constantly, and not without success. But also on the part of Baader there are several features that have so far excluded him from directly influencing the developments in German Catholicism in the last hundred years and from assuming his rightful place in its official literature. First, Baader as a typical Romantic paid a heavy toll to Romantic Occasionalism in his philosophy of religion, chiefly in his theosophical writings. In sentimental exaggeration of the divinatory experiences of a Romantically perturbed soul, the "Theosophy" attempts a superb synthesis of Neo-Platonism and Augustinism on the one hand with the mysterious *Kosmos* of the *Kabbala* and the mystical worlds of Master Eckhart, Paracelsus, Jacob Boehme, Pascal and the French esoteric Claude Saint-Martin.[107] It is only natural that tradition-bound Catholicism could have but little understanding for such theosophist endeavors. Secondly, Baader found himself implicated in a conflict with Rome because of his occasionalism in church policies, as it also happened to his friend Lamennais who in this respect closely resembles him.[108] Although his "Struggle against Rome" was only of short duration (1838 to 1841), Baader had thereby incurred the pronounced enmity of all Catholics whose thoughts ran in closely formalistic channels. It is to be deplored that these clerical and conservative elements were never able even after Baader's death to forgive these anti-Papist escapades of a Romantic temperament, although toward the end of his life (1841) Baader revoked them in every respect and died in the full peace of his Church. Thirdly, Baader never published a systematic work in his lifetime, only laying down his thoughts in an infinite number of pamphlets, essays and magazine articles. In addition, the extraordinary complexity, both linguistically and logically, of his literary expression badly handicapped the public reception of his thoughts. Neither was Baader able to gather a large circle of students during his Munich teaching activity, so that his ideas were not developed and propagated by a "school." At first only two smaller editions of his writings existed, until between 1850 and 1860 a comprehensive edition which included all his works was arranged by his friends through private subscription.[109] This publication never reached a wide public, and consequently by the 1870's, when the first literary interests made themselves felt in German Catholicism, Baader was as good as forgotten and his works were unobtainable. It was only after the First World War that new interest in Baader arose, but not principally in Catholic circles. It is a remarkable fact that in all the decades of its existence the "Goerres Society for the Advancement of Catholic Science" never paid attention to the Munich university colleague of its patron. The mythos that exalted Goerres as the hero of German Catholicism made everyone overlook that not Goerres but *Baader was the first to create the concept of "Christian Socialism" as he was also the true initiator of Catholic sociology and social doctrine in Germany.*

This Catholic silence has not been broken even today, neither through the latter-day interest in Baader the Theosophist,[110] nor through fragmentary and tendentious interpretations of Baader the "Romantic" social philosopher in the neo-Romantic circles around Othmar Spann,[111] nor through the interest in Baader's work and personality from the formalistic point of view of the history of philosophy[112]. And yet, a thorough, objective, critical and systematic study of the fifteen-volume comprehensive edition—which unfortunately has become a rarity for bibliophiles found only in few libraries—reveals this "theosophist" and "Romantic," Baader, in his rank as the first, and surely the *most original philosopher and sociologist of 19th century German Catholicism.* In the context of our inquiry, Baader's Romantic Catholicism therefore merits at the very least a systematic analysis of its threefold significance for the history of thought in modern German Catholicism. First, it has laid the theological and philosophical groundwork for Catholic personalism and *Romantic existentialism;* secondly, it has established the principles of a modern Catholic sociology; and thirdly, it is a manifestation of the social conscience of German Catholicism.[113]

1. *Baader's Romantic Existentialism*

To do justice to the originality of Baader's thinking, one should be careful to apply the dialectics of Romantic thought to the essence of Romantic Catholicism in an existential, not in a formalistic manner. If this is done, the "existential unrest" of the Romantic will not so much appear as an occasionalist cause of ideological disruption of the realistic orders of life; it will rather be expressive of the effort to grasp the ideas by means of a vivid awareness of reality. In this aspect, this unrest, this perturbation by no means involves the disruption of reason through sentiment or, in other words, the dissolution of the rational through the irrational, or of nature through mystical immanence. On the contrary, reason in this process proves its "reasonableness" even in its experience of the sub-rational and super-rational. This implies that reason neither sublimates the concrete experience of good in an all-embracing eudemonistic doctrine of beatitude; nor does it exaggerate evil in a demoniacal pessimism. In the theological shelter of

Christian Personalism, especially the Augustinian-Thomistic Personalism, and of Catholic realism, this "existential unrest" of the Romantic finally achieves repose in the "rational" certitude that, as Baader expresses it, "reason, Ratio, is *Deo data*, an organ created for man at his birth for the perception of God." This knowledge of the whole *rational order as God-given*, and of all cognition as a free unfolding of human understanding in *the organic evolution of man and humanity toward God*, was then formulated by Baader in one sentence which may be the best expression of the principles of his Romantic Existentialism: *Only through true rationalism can you proceed to supra-rationalism, only through true naturalism to supra-naturalism*" (VI 73 ff).[114] Already this formula reveals the difference between Baader's religious ontologism and the theological ontologism of Malebranche for whom cognition through the medium of the senses and reason immediately constitutes the perception of God. For Baader the vision of God is not identical with primary rational knowledge, for man has first to rise above his own level by way of the knowledge of the world to the knowledge of God (I 6,348; XV 283). By the force of this basic principle, in close adherence to the traditions of Augustine's psychological doctrine of the Trinity, Baader has won absolute theological protection against the theological and philosophical irrationalism inherent in Romantic Occasionalism. When later he still had to struggle against these dangers, sometimes almost succumbing to them, it only happened when the occasionalist principles of the "Romantic" tried to crowd out of his mind the realistic Catholic principle: when Baader, the Romantic, in his concern for purely mystical experience of the supra-natural in a vivid act of divination departed from human reality—as in his special Theosophy. And it also happened when in his concern for Faith he slipped away from the historic reality of the Church, as in his conflict with the historical doctrine of the Papacy. But *whenever Baader, the Catholic, was aware of his natural allegiance to the essentially innate principle of Catholic Realism, the existential essence and the existential orders of the world at large always appeared to him in the light of the best traditions of Catholic thinking*, and then he was able to approve or condemn them with secure judgment. This proved to be especially true in his encounters with concrete individuals, the concrete state and concrete society, with historical reality in general. What makes Baader's achievements in social philosophy and sociological criticism all the more remarkable is precisely the fact that they fall into a time when these Catholic traditions had entirely disappeared from the realm of German thought.

Unfortunately, German Catholicism neither gave due credit to these achievements, nor even knew of them. The same applies to Baader's strictly theological-philosophical foundation of his ideas, which is perhaps his greatest success and raises him to the rank of the only creative philosophical thinker in 19th century German Catholicism. *For Baader was the one German thinker of the era who had an entirely original system of religious existentialism and theistic personalism to set against the other influential systems of the day,* namely, against the sensualism and materialism of the English and French philosophers, the rationalism of Enlightenment, the autonomism of Kant, and finally the pantheism and impersonalism of Fichte, Schelling and Hegel. Now we understand why the unique Kierkegaard chose only Baader for the support of his ideas. He declared that Baader "as a matter of course should be known to all those who wish to ponder these matters," i.e., the personalistic problems of Evil and of Liberty.[114a] Baader had more than the purely philosophical system to set against these other thinkers; he developed an *original and practicable system of Christian political thought and social organization* which is animated by the best traditions of Christian natural law and Augustinian-Thomistic realism. *He placed in the center of his Romantic Existentialism his firm trust in living man and in man's personality who through his own insight of will and reason finds the confirmation of his personal faith in God. "Nemo credit nisi volens"* (No one believes unless he wills it). This is Baader's will to believe, and through this belief to win the power of cognition of the orders of faith and life, as he further expresses it: *"Fides debet praecedere intellectum, ut sit intellectus fidei praemium."* (Faith must precede the intellect, so that the intellect may be the prize for faith). And he rounds out this thought with the maxim: "Credam ut intelligam" (I shall believe so that I may understand). (I 325; V 60; VI 139; X 23, 51)

To find a secure theological-philosophical foundation for his philosophy of society, Baader made strenuous efforts to recapture the best scholastic traditions and therefore devoted himself to serious studies of Augustinus, Anselm of Canterbury and Thomas Aquinas. To find the genuine scholastic core of Baader's Catholic realism and the equally genuine Augustinian-Thomistic foundation of his Romantic Existentialism, it suffices to study his "Spekulative Dogmatik" (VII) or the voluminous excerpts and studies from St. Thomas in Volume XIV of the comprehensive edition. He who looks for the systematic application of these theological-philosophical principles to the burning philosophical problems of the time can find it in almost everyone of the essays which Baader devotes to his philosophy of society, but best of all in the thorough critical review of De Bonald's "Recherches philosophiques" (V 43-120) and Lamennais' "Essai sur l'indifférence en matière de religion" (V 221-246).

There is hardly a problem concerning the Christian reform of social and economic life that has not found its proper treatment in principle in Baader's philosophy of Romantic Existentialism. We point especially to the following subjects: Christian Personalism with its philosophical-theological foundations and its concrete application to the life of man in his association with his fellows; Christian natural law in its application to the problems of man and community; Christian society and the problem of the State; Christian Solidarism and the problem of social liberty; and finally, Christian reformism and the social conscience of Catholicism in its concern for positive social reforms and policies. In these studies *Baader established his position as the first inspired social philosopher of German Catholicism, and as the spiritual father of the "Christian Social" movement in Germany.* The very name was formulated by him for the first time in the demand he proclaimed for the "free evolution of the Christian Social principle in sentiment and insight." For "Religion in its supreme commandement says: Love God above all, and thy neighbor as thyself. This is the principle of every truly free community of life and of every commonwealth, of all true liberty and equality—this is the Christian Social principle!" (VI 94).

2. *Baader's doctrine of society*

There is no doubt that Baader was strongly influenced by the French Traditionalists in his basic theological-philosophic criticism of revolutionary secularism and his demand for a fundamental religious revival of life in society. In these respects he welcomed the writings of De Maistre and De Bonald, and even of the early Lamennais with his extreme Ultramontanism. But in doing so, Baader was nevertheless decidedly *opposed* to their teachings of Romantic ideologies, as the proposal for a political restoration in the spirit of a new theocracy (De Maistre), the aristocratism and absolute legitimism of De Bonald, and the ultramontanism recommended by Lamennais.

To Baader's way of thinking, theocracy was justified only "at the inception of the history of mankind" (IX 28-29); he rejected with determination the monarchistic-authoritarian doctrine of the rule "by the grace of God" (V 343; VI 20, 38, 41-42, 86, 720), and also every legitimistic compact between the Church and Monarchy which would "cheapen the Cross as a mere decoration for secular power" (VI 34-35, 42-44, 65). "The notion of theocracy is alien to Christianity, and consequently to Catholicism, as it is based on the concept of the delegation of secular power by the ecclesiastical." "While many regarded it as an evil that in our day the secular power became separated from religion and the Church, 'Avenir' has taught us to recognize that God has given this an unanticipated turn; for we can already see that the separation has caused the emancipation of religion and its resurrection from the dust." "Now that the spiritual power of the Church has renounced all secular power, it is up to the secular power to reciprocate by liberating that part of ecclesiastical power which, ever since the Schism in the Orient and the Reformation in the Occident, it holds in bondage." (VL 29-44). In this thought the strong influence is particularly visible which the democratically metamorphosed Lamennais (it happened in about 1828) and his 'Avenir' (founded 1830) exerted on Baader. In the period 1830 to 1833 Baader cooperated closely with the democratic minds attracted by this courageous magazine, mostly with Lacordaire and Montalembert. On April 16, 1831 he addressed an open letter to Montalembert, (VI 29-44) which in effect presents the entire program of "a free Church in a free State," a program that later received its sanction from wise Pope Leo XIII in many of his encyclicals, above all in the great Encyclical *Sapientiae Christianae* of 1890.[115]

Unfortunately, Baader and the Lamennais of 'Avenir' were far ahead of their times in respect to church policies, as demonstrated by the Encyclical *Mirari Vos* of 1832, and even as late as the *Syllabus* of 1864. It is therefore no surprise that the theologically irreproachable thoughts of Baader met with sharp opposition from German Catholicism, as "inopportune" to church policies. This general lack of understanding among the leading strata of German Catholicism in their philosophical, political and social backwardness had one particularly regrettable feature in that "conspiracy of silence" which deprived 19th century German Catholicism of all potential spiritual and ideological auxiliary forces which would have been so badly needed in the arduous struggle for political and cultural maturity. Before turning to Baader's special role in the awakening of social consciences in German Catholicism, we quote a few more texts unsurpassed in their modernity even as compared to the freest and most democratic opinions in present-day Catholicism.

On the notions of *law and property:*"Right is only that which goes right toward God" (V 152, 219). "No human government can subsist merely on fear without respect, on selfish interest without love, on gain and property without justice" (VI 38).

On the principles *of state power and people's sovereignty:* "The ruler is not what he is by the grace of the people, and the people not by the grace of the ruler; they are truly all there by the grace of God, and together they have been assigned and have taken over their duties in God and before God" VI 41-42). *"It is surely God's will and imposition that there shall be Government, but it is up to men to decide who shall govern and how.* Accordingly, Paul says: *Omnis potestas est a Deo.* Note that 'potestas' here signifies the government or the office of power, not the holder of power, and if this maxim is taken to imply that God has instituted this or that person, this or that constitution, it is *wrongly* interpreted" (V 343). "The state, the constitution, and society, in whatever form and shape, necessarily become onerous and insupportable if they lack the community spirit of religion; for government without religion, which is despotism, can appear in the form of monarchy, aristocracy or democracy" (VI 20).

Against *revolutionary or reactionary government by force:* "As it would be wrong to drop the respect for true kings because there are also kings of spades or clubs, no one should give up true free-thinking because there is bad liberalism. Unfortunately the error is still fairly widespread that you can get rid of Jacobinism only by means of ultra-Royalism, or of the latter through the former, and that consequently the choice lies only as between anarchical and autocratic despotism. But do not the victims of this error know that the insolent and arrogant lust of despots and the cowardly and servile lust of slaves always and under all circumstances appear together like two galley slaves chained to one another, and that they can also disappear only together—which is why the despot has always to fear the rebel and the rebel the despot?" (VI 29-44).

On *freedom of religion and social liberty: ". . . that the world can return to God only through social liberty, but that such liberty can be granted the world only by God* (religion); that in those times and those countries where everything lies in ruin, the priests must turn the total divorcement of secular power from the cult to good use so that religion will never again become a state religion, which would again make it a tool and slave of secular power" (VI 29-44).

3. Social conscience in German Catholicism

The best proof of the deep roots Baader's social and economic criticism in the spirit of Romantic Existentialism had in genuine Catholicism lies in its realism. But we should recognize that, aside from these essential "Catholic" premises, Baader's social realism was also predicated on two significant existential groups of facts. They are partly of a personal character, partly conditioned by contemporary history. It is first relevant to note that Baader was originally a physician by profession, and that he later practiced for thirty years as a mining engineer. This brought him into close touch with the concrete essence of men's physical and social nature, but also with the technical monstrosities of incipient industrialism and capitalistic enslavement of the working population. There is, secondly, the material he was given by the factual social criticism of Lamennais in the period 1829 to 1835, at which time both men were close collaborators. Furthermore, his work as mining engineer had in his early youth taken Baader to England for four years' residence, 1792 to 1796, and there he had the first opportunities to experience in practice how the working people in industry suffered abuse and how the money system held their social existence in bondage. We may assume that Lamennais' influence gave Baader the direct impulse to think over his English experiences and to measure with the yardsticks of Catholic social conscience the slowly increasing distress of the proletarian way of life among the industrial masses and poor country folk in Germany.

Without these two sets of influences Baader might not have been able to endow the formal ethical principles of social justice with the stirring expressions of factual social morality and down-to-earth social criticism which enliven his writings. Even in the 1830's German Catholicism had not yet produced any theoretical concern with social and community matters, and industrial development had not as yet carried far enough to induce the full shock of actual proletarian distress. Without Baader's vivid impressions of social conditions in England and without the direct impact and stimulus exerted on him by the young movement of social criticism around Lamennais and the *Avenir,* his achievements in criticism and the formulation of policies might not have been possible. Merely on the force of

German experiences he would hardly have found his line, as it also happened ten or fifteen years later to Friedrich Engels who could not have written his "The Conditions of the Working Classes in England," or for that matter to Marx with his "Kapital," unless the French social theories and the personal experience of the plight of the English proletariat had served them as theoretical support and factual impulse. These considerations are of importance especially because far into the 1890's German Socialism and German Catholicism proved equally incapable of drawing a genuine theory of society and economy from indigenous German intellectual traditions or from internal social practice. At last an attempt in this direction was made by Heinrich Pesch.[116] All this emphasizes how severely the social movement in German Catholicism was harmed by the silence that surrounded Franz von Baader.

Three of Baader's studies are of special importance for the history of social ideas in Germany: *Ueber den Evolutionismus und Revolutionismus des sozialen Lebens,"* (Evolutionism and Revolutionism in Social Life" 1834); the memorandum prepared for the Bavarian Government *"Ueber die Proletairs,"* 1834; and the strikingly up-to-date study *"Ueber das dermalige Missverhaeltnis der Vermoegenslosen oder Proletairs zu den Vermoegen besitzenden Klassen der Societaet"* (On the Present Faulty Relationship between the Propertyless, or Proletarians, and the Propertied Classes of Society, 1835) . These studies that even today are practically unknown contain perhaps the most incisive formulations of insight and practical suggestions that ever originated in the social conscience of modern Catholicism.[117]

The essay on *"Evolutionism and Revolutionism"* (VI 73-108) gives a complete ideological application of the principle of social justice to a criticism of modern society. In this it anticipates all the future basic programs of positive social criticism and practical social reforms based on Catholic thought. With astonishing clarity Baader sets forth a program of Christian Social reforms, based on his realistic awareness that "only in sentiment *and* insight is the free evolution of the Christian Social principle possible;" that therefore every reform of the Christian sentiment must be accompanied by the practical implementation by a reform of the social conditions the necessity of which has been recognized. To implement the program of Christian Social reform as outlined by Baader, German Catholicism since the days of Ketteler and Pope Leo XIII had to take up a struggle under particularly difficult conditions. We

again quote some of Baader's formulations which might have been written today:

On the problem of *social liberty:* "Where Christianity is allowed to function freely, there it is identical with the principle of civic liberty and of liberation from one man's oppression by the other. Christianity does admit of the power of men *over* men, but it does not admit of one man being *in* the power of another, as his chattel."

On the problem of *property:* "Christianity has also fundamentally reformed all doctrines and notions of acquisition, possession and consumption of property by doing away with the pagan concept of absolute property without, however, barring individual acquisition and possession. But every use and consumption of property that is not social is anti-social. For he who does not live for society lives against it, and every separatist is a fool in theory and a criminal in practice. No Christian may declare: this property, this right, this office are mine, to handle as I please; for in reality these are God's gifts and tasks (*Gaben und Aufgaben*), and a Christian may therefore handle them only as it pleases God, which in a truly Christian community makes of every possession only an *ex officio* possession, of every consumption only an *ex officio* consumption." "Since according to Christ's teachings men, be they the highest or humblest, exist only by the grace of God, by that same token they cannot and must not do and deal with their persons, their powers and their property as in their own selfish way they like and lust, but only as God wills!"

On the problem of the *proletarian existence*: "A Christian, be he king, high priest or the lowliest of proletarians, may not proclaim: *l'état, l'Église, c'est moi,* or, these arms are mine and I have the right to use them freely, for wage labor or to erect barricades." "When recently the extinction of Christian sentiment and the new sanctioning of pagan jurisprudence gave renewed support to egotism and separatism in the dealings of the powerful and propertied with the poor and powerless, this was bound to debase the state of the proletariat more and more and finally—after the abolition of serfdom, the establishment of *argyrokratie* (money power) and the widely praised industrial division of labor which made supreme concentration of consumption possible—to render it quite unbearable when total irreligiosity had prevailed. Is it surprising that these proletarians, after having frequently enough been thrown together, *ex officio,* into a rabble, finally get the idea to foregather in their own interest or, as they call it, to form associations?"

In that same year, 1834, Baader presented to the Bavarian Government a memorandum on the plight of the *"Proletairs"* (XV 505-510) in which he pointed to "the three basic evils of the time" and applied these thoughts to formulating practical proposals for social reforms. "For a long time three evils have been the vexation and the plight of the Christian states, one of which is the fateful *discord between faith and knowledge* that has poisoned our civic intelligence; the second being the *derelict state of the proletariat*, and the third *the traditional system of money usury.*" It is interesting to note that this memorandum is the first continental document to bring the plight of the proletariat to the attention of a government. This it did with drastic outspokenness, and yet with sufficient wisdom and moderation not to demand the revolutionary overthrow of capitalism, but instead to propose dealing with it through practicable reforms, by restricting the absolute liberty of industry and trade. "We should by no means follow the *ultras* in their foolish conclusions that it would be best to set an end to this progress of industry and mechanization; we should, on the contrary, become wise by experience so that we may learn to avoid the cliffs which the states we mentioned were unable to avoid" (XV 506).

Here Baader refers to the economic conditions in England and France which he described so strikingly in his essay on the *Propertyless and Proletarians.* Since the social criticism and social policy program contained in this essay will be fully reproduced in the appendix, we may be brief at this point. It is important above all that the unavoidable reforms of the capitalistic system of society and economy are here formulated by Baader not indeed as a "socialist" ideology, but rather as a duty of conscience to be exercized by means of a viable Christian social reform program of practical social policies. At the center of these demands is the task of raising the proletariat to a social estate and to lodge it securely in the organic whole of society. In this reasoning and in his demands as a social reformer Baader in 1835 was a forerunner of later genuinely social-revolutionary demands raised by utopian and Marxian socialism which in the 1840's were directed at "making men out of proletarians" once more and vindicating their equal social rights. Here we find in unsurpassed breadth and clarity all the demands raised by the bourgeois and the Catholic social theory and policy in the last century. It is useful in this respect to compare the three works of Baader here quoted with an outstanding modern book on the "Proletariat," whose author is the leading Catholic sociologist Goetz

Briefs,[118] a book that unfortunately also fails to take notice of Baader.

In their efforts toward refashioning the proletarian existence, Baader and Lamennais probably exerted deep influences on one another. From Lamennais Baader may have derived the immediate impulse to concern himself with the problems of the proletariat probably at the time of Lamennais' visit to Munich in 1832 when it is likely that he communicated with Baader on his scheme for the mediating services of a socially-minded priesthood, demands which he had formulated in 1831 in his German essay on "Die Not des industriellen Proletariats und des Bauernstandes" (The Plight of the Industrial Proletariat and the Peasantry) in the Muenchener "Kirchenzeitung" [119] On the other hand, Lamennais adopted Baader's most significant social theses on the problem of the proletariat.[120]

The demand Lamennais raised in his Munich article was for a social office (Diakonat) "of the priest who should stand as an uninterested third party between the two parties who form the compact, to serve as a common bond between the rich who provides the money and the soil and the poor who can only contribute his work to the common fund." To this demand Baader then gave so much added weight that it forms the coping stone of his program for a proletarian social reform. "The original function of the Christian priest was to serve as an advocate and aid in the plight of the propertyless among the people, and as arbiter between them and the property owners; it is this that made Christianity rise as a creed of humanism so speedily above paganism turned inhuman. But what at that time was degenerate paganism is today even more degenerate secularism, and thus the function of the priest remains the same: to oppose this man-despising, man-devouring secularism by loudly proclaiming the law of humanity and Christianity" (XV 509). The proletarians "have the right to be represented by an advocate and this right must be guaranteed them unconditionally in our modern constitutionally governed states. This representation must be administered through spokesmen elected by themselves who, however, should not be assisted by counsel who are police servants or civil servants of any kind, nor lawyers in the strict sense, but should be priests whom alone they could completely trust. Society would thereby reap a double benefit. First, these proletarians would be shielded from the influence of demagogues and quarrelsome lawyers; and second, the clerics now debased to social insignificance would recapture that pristine office of deaconry which, as is well known, is concerned with the care and aid for the propertyless' (VI 138 ff).

With this demand for a *social deaconry of the priests*
Baader has perhaps found the deepest expression of the social
conscience of Catholicism. With this he heralded what was
soon to become an extremely beneficial movement and tradition of religious and social organization largely under the
leadership of priests, in the Catholic labor movement and
social program characterized by the names of Ketteler, Kolping,
Franz Hitze, Heinrich Pesch, Heinrich Brauns, and many
others. Thus, by the visible example of his name and work,
Franz von Baader has prophetically raised the banners for the
lofty efforts of the social movement in German Catholicism
whose labors he accompanies with his recondite spirit.

CHAPTER IV

SOCIAL MOVEMENTS AND SOCIAL POLICIES

1. *The Beginnings: Ritter von Buss, (1803 to 1878)*

The first period of Catholic social movements, 1837 to 1848, was overshadowed by the contemporary controversies in general Church policies. Following the secularization, with the changes it wrought in the political scene, a factual revision of Church-State relationships became unavoidable. It began with the "Cologne disturbances" (1837) and reached a real conclusion only when the Prussian Constitution was introduced in 1850.[121] These controversies, known as "the first culture-struggle," resulted in the great initial reforms of German Catholicism in its political and social structure. On the one hand, the Church was forced into better awareness of the realities of the modern State, and on the other, the State was forced to recognize that the Catholic Church system, in contrast to the Protestant state-church system, required autonomous rights in respect to religion and politics. Combined with the general political and social changes this controversy gave the German Catholics their first opportunity to size up their concrete civic rights and duties in the political sphere, and their rights and duties in social and economic life. In 1848 two events of importance revealed the practical effects of this first period of the reformed political and social spirit in German Catholicism. The one was the Frankfurt National Assembly where the Catholic deputies gave expression to the new spirit in respect to politics. The second was the first German Catholic Convention simultaneously assembled in Mainz which expressed the new spirit in momentous social manifestoes.

The main speakers in Mainz, Ritter von Buss and Emmanuel von Ketteler, are characteristic of the stage of development then reached in Catholic social understanding. At that time, Buss was regarded as the chief representative of the period, now coming to an end, which was dedicated primarily to the social interests of the middle classes and to private welfare work in the spirit of Christian *Caritas*. In social policies Buss's sights were accordingly definitely turned backward, guided by the Romantic ideas of medieval corporative organization. Thus he postulated in Mainz: "The State shall be organized in the spirit of Christian democracy. In this framework we must reconstruct large corporations, comparable to the guilds of old, with the old corporate honors, though ordered in free autonomy, without the former compulsion. The journeymen must again sit at table together with their masters so that they will not feel slighted and consequently become merged with a rabble of proletarians."[122] There was a marked contrast between this "social reformer" who, one should think, had many years of practical opportunity in his Baden homeland to study the growing plight of the industrial workers and peasant smallholders, and Emmanuel von Ketteler, the Westphalian peasant pastor of Hopsten, who challenged the Mainz gathering in a number of deeply moving addresses to look more thoroughly into the social plight of the "propertyless." Ketteler thereby initiated the new phase in the Catholic social movement which in its practical efforts of social reform remains tied to his name.[123] Unlike the socially conservative Buss with his middle-class interests, the young social reformer Ketteler called upon the Mainz convention to embark on a determined fight against the distress of the proletariat which he proclaimed as Catholicism's most urgent task. Ketteler's entire program is characterized by the very first words of his second great sermon in the Mainz Cathedral on December 3, 1848:

"No one can say anything about our era or comprehend its shape without referring again and again to the prevailing social conditions and, above all, to the division between the propertied and the property-less classes, to the plight of our destitute brethren, to the means of giving them help. You may accord as much weight as you please to the political questions, to the shaping of state and government—and yet, the real difficulties we face do not lie there. Even under the best possible constitution we would lack work, bread, shelter for our poor. Paradoxically, the closer we carry our political problems toward bearable solutions the clearer it becomes, though many will not see it even now, that this was only the lesser part of the task before us and that now the social question looms larger than ever, demanding solutions more harshly than ever."[124]

In pronouncing these words, Ketteler showed a better insight into the character of this first phase of the Catholic social movement and criticized it more shrewdly than many a latter-day historian of Social Catholicism. Buss, no doubt, defended his program to the best of his personal understanding of the political and social traditions in which he was raised. But his very origin in the impoverished lower middle classes of Baden and his roots in the secularized Catholicism burdened as it was with the dubious heritage of the 18th century were obstacles to a deeper penetration of the true social problems. Buss, like Goerres, in his spiritual development had to wrestle with that whole tragic heritage of religious and cultural homelessness and lack of secure traditions. The son of a poor family, he studied at Heidelberg and Goettingen, and there came into contact with the liberal doctrines of law and government, at first under the exclusive influence of South-German liberalism as represented by Rotteck and Welcker—for at that time, 1825 to 1835, a Catholic doctrine of government or a Catholic political movement simply did not exist. As so many others among his contemporaries, Buss fell victim to anti-religious free-thinking from which he soon freed himself indirectly by joining the Romanticist movement. Supported by this religious conversion, Buss now developed a remarkable activity, in the spirit of Romantic Conservatism. This position induced him to oppose all influences of the social-reformist ideas taught by Lamennais and Baader. He consciously joined forces with the French circles formed by P.J.B. Buchez (1796-1865), Eduard Alletz (1798-1865) and the Munich of Goerres, with its bourgeois tendencies toward social conservatism.

In the genesis of the political and social consciousness in German Catholicism during the second quarter of the 19th century, Buss merits special interest in one respect. He was the first German Catholic to defend through practical parliamentary action, as a professional politician, the political and social interests of the Church and of the Catholic community. In his many years of activity in the Baden Parliament he rendered exemplary service. He was the first German to propose a bill of social reforms in any parliament.[125] Although this bill for a reform of the factory police administration contained no revolutionary traits whatever—there were no special labor privileges as Baader had already demanded in 1835, only a limitation of working hours to "a maximum of 14 hours a day" with no work at all on Sundays—it was the first step toward government interference in labor problems, though of a preventive nature rather than positive labor legislation. In a way it is therefore justified to credit Buss with being the first German "social politician," a distinction which is usually accorded him by Catholic historians.

It is highly significant that Buss could turn for support of his social "reforms" only to the French authors mentioned above, because there simply was no theoretical groundwork nor practical example to be found in German Catholicism, due to the prevailing ignorance of Baader's thought. Since Buss felt that Buchez was too radical, especially in his proposals for state-supported workers' cooperatives, he gave his allegiance to the lower middle class ideologies of Eduard Alletz, Louis Philip's court sociologist, whose main work he translated in 1838 with the title "Die neue Demokratie, oder die Sitten und die Macht der Mittelklassen in Frankreich" (The New Democracy, or the Habits and the Power of the Middle Classes in France.)[126] Nothing is more apt to characterize Buss's ideological backwardness than the fact that even Alletz's tame reform proposals with their leaning toward a bourgeois constitutional monarchy were too radical for his taste. In a long-winded open-letter with which he prefaced Alletz's book, he developed his own ideology in a queer composite of the Hegelian philosophy of history watered down with the medieval Romanticism of the Goerres circle. His conclusion is that popular sovereignty in whatever shape or form, including all constitutional reforms, the universal ballot, and indeed democracy must be rejected. To insure the fulfillment of the "state purpose," it is necessary that political rule be in the hands of the leading strata of society, the "educated" (die Bildung), for "political society has the shape of a pyramid; the government of the masses rests with the elite." (CVI) No wonder that this political Romantic, who later came under the additional influence of the ideas of the Spanish Conservative, Donoso Cortes,[127] was elevated to the rank of a Baden "Hofrat" (court counsellor) and was coopted to the Imperial Knights' Chapter of the House of Habsburg.

Buss's one lasting merit is his untiring activity to revive and organize the Church welfare work of *Caritas* and the social aid efforts that had been particularly badly jeopardized by the secularization. In this Buss also followed the French example closely, as we see in his meritorious translation of the great three-volume book by Gerando, "System of the Comprehensive Services for the Poor" (1843). In the life and work of Buss we thus see combined all the possibilities and limitations which history in the first half of the 19th century set to the awakening interest in state and society in German Catholicism.

2. *The Social Question*: *Emmanuel von Ketteler* (1811-1877)

"In striving for an understanding of our time we must strain every effort to fathom the Social Question. Whoever achieves this has taken firm hold of this present era; those who fail in this will find the present and the future an enigma!"

From the cathedral pulpit of Mainz, Emmanuel von Ketteler appealed in these words to the German Catholics to give realistic and comprehensive attention to "the social question." This was in 1848, and in the following thirty years under his leadership, the imposing groundwork of Christian Social reform was firmly established upon which later the mature movement of "Social Catholicism" was to develop successfully under the auspices of Pope Leo XIII and Franz Hitze. It is customary when assessing the import of Ketteler's work for German social history to give particular prominence to his plans for social self-help of labor through producers' cooperatives and to his opinions on capitalism, in both of which he was strongly influenced by Lassalle and V. A. Huber. For a deeper insight into the origins of Catholic social thinking such studies are surely important, especially in revealing the Bishop of Mainz's changing attitudes toward capitalism. For this change contributed to the ideological dualism which was to persist: on the one hand, the social reformism, introduced into German Catholic thought by Hitze, which granted guarded acceptance to capitalism; on the other hand, the unconditional rejection of capitalism by the Austrian school of Vogelsang. This attitude of Ketteler's and its consequences were aptly characterized by Goetz Briefs: "Capitalism deserves to be condemned; however, the methods first attempted for its overthrow (this refers to the producers' cooperatives) having proved unavailing, we had to submit to making the best of capitalism in striving to mitigate its horrible effects through social measures. This gives rise to two potential attitudes, the one rejecting capitalism in whatever form, the other striving to temper it through social reforms." [128] In order to understand Ketteler's maturing thoughts on capitalism and other still more important facets of his activities, we should examine the eminently realistic structure of his personality by which the entire pastoral and political influence and the social ideology of the Bishop of Mainz was determined.

Ketteler's personality was by no means characterized by theory and contemplation. He was quite averse to diluting his pastoral duties by abstract studies, as also to dissolving the hard facts of history through Romantic political ideologies and social wishful thinking. A scion of the sound, deeply religious landed aristocracy of the Muensterland, Ketteler was firmly rooted in the traditions of Catholic realism which were so characteristic of his Westphalian homeland. He was thus never in danger of being swayed by the fashions of the day in German Catholicism, neither by Romanticism nor by reactionary conservatism both of which emerged as over-compensations of historical and political inferiority complexes; nor by confessional narrow-mindedness which resulted from an understandable reaction against anti-Church politicians and government action; nor by bourgeois self-righteousness and philistinism, concomitants of an uneasy feeling of being deficient in social self-esteem. In all these respects Ketteler represents one of the soundest and most perfect Catholic types of personality, and it was therefore only natural that he emerged as the most outstanding social, political and spiritual leader in 19th century German Catholicism. As if centered in a focal personality, all the best traditions of German Catholicism achieved in Ketteler a full synthesis of its creative potentialities blended with the German national character. This can be traced in Ketteler's descent and education, in his rise to the bishop's office and the twenty-seven years of his meritorious rule. Thus Ketteler represents the pivot not only of contemporary social and political Catholicism, but of integral Catholic Germany of the 19th century.

Like Eichendorff, Ketteler was born into an environment alive with religious and cultural traditions and imbued with a strong sense of social honor and political responsibility. Throughout the 18th century, his Westphalian homeland was able to withstand the adverse influences of the ecclesiastical rule, most successfully under the long and wise government of Franz von Fuerstenberg (1729-1810). As substitute for the Prince-bishops of Muenster who lived continuously outside their diocese, Franz von Fuerstenberg, easily the most outstanding personality among the ecclesiastical statesmen of his time, was the real master of the Cathedral Church of Muenster from 1762 to its incorporation with Prussia in 1803. In this function Fuerstenberg brought to his country all the blessings of a progressive cultural and social life.[129] This divergence between the wealth of cultural and social traditions alive in the Muensterland and the adverse heritage which weighed down almost all the other former ecclesiastical principalities has been much too little noticed. We find here not only the secret of Ketteler's eminent personality but also an explanation of the fact that such a large number of strong, creative men within German Catholicism are of Westphalian origin. To name only a few: Ketteler, Hitze, Brandt, Brauns, Muckermann, Mausbach, Tischleder, Bruening and Cardinal Count Galen.

Again like Eichendorff, Ketteler first embarked on the career of a Prussian civil servant after pursuing studies of history and government at Goettingen (where he was even a member of a student *corps*), Heidelberg, Munich and Berlin. And also in the same pattern, loyal to his Catholic faith he quit the Prussian government service in 1837 at the outbreak of the Church conflict. Under Goerres' influence he then turned to studies of theology at Munich and Muenster, and was consecrated a priest there in 1844. He served as a chaplain in Beckum (1844-1846), as pastor of Hopsten (1846-1849), became a Provost of St. Hedwig in Berlin as early as 1849, to be promoted to the episcopal see of Mainz in the following year.[130]

When in 1848 Ketteler was sent to the Frankfurt National Assembly by the voters of Tecklenburg, this was destined to be an act of truly providential significance for German Catholicism. This first Westphalian parliamentarian by no means typified the average young priest with barely four years of pastoral experience. Neither can he be taken to represent the average politician, representative of that "clergy degenerated into social nonentity" (Baader). And least of all was he a typical partisan of a confessionalism over-charged with the just resentments aroused by the "culture struggle," or of Romantic-reactionary particularism, as represented by Radowitz. We see on the contrary that the sound political instinct of Westphalian peasant-Catholicism had chosen in Ketteler the very best representative of its traditions. These enabled him to apply Catholic realism creatively to the problems awaiting him in Frankfurt, which was all the more important since—as we shall see in the following chapter—reactionary political pressure groups represented primarily by the dubious "Catholic" politician Radowitz threatened to sidetrack the first frail sympathies of the Catholic representatives in social matters. The same dangers marred the transactions of the First Catholic Convention (Katholikentag). Here, too, the predominantly conservative episcopacy and the clerics and citizens with their largely passive dedication to *Caritas* activities (Buss) were reluctant to tackle social problems and had neither sympathy nor ability to deal with them in a truly realistic and progressive way.

In this situation the emergence of Ketteler indeed produced something like a revolution. This comparatively young Westphalian country pastor, so far totally unknown, actually dared to use before the Parliament, as well as before the Catholic Convention, a language of an oustpokenness, a political realism and a social aggressiveness fully expressive of the embattled spirit of the Year of Revolution, but surprising if measured by the conventionality of the assembled Catholic burghers. Ketteler's speeches, to be sure, at first had little practical effect, especially those before the Parliament on the Christian school problems and those before the Catholic Convention on the social question, though the great funeral oration for the victims of the Frankfurt September revolts already caught the attention of the political public at large. Moreover, Ketteler had at least the one success to his credit of having created an uneasy feeling of aroused social conscience among the listeners at the Catholic convention, a feeling which since has never been absent in German Catholicism. In order to channel these pangs of conscience which from Mainz spread over all of Catholic Germany into effective acts of Catholic realism and social responsibility, Ketteler chose the Cathedral pulpit of Mainz to deliver toward the end of the same year his six famous sermons on "The Great Social Questions of our Time." [131]

These sermons, expressions of an aroused social conscience and appeals to the Church to undertake its social deaconry, subsequently became the real foundation of German Catholicism's social movement. In following the text of these sermons we can even today feel the deep reverberations they had in revolutionizing and evoking men's consciences. In these sermons reflecting the social awakening of the Church, worthy of the sermons of the great Ambrose of Milan, who also might be regarded as a social revolutionary,[132] German Catholicism probably made its most positive contribution to the Year of Revolution, 1848. All the later achievements of Ketteler in social criticism and Church programs, significant thought they were, must rank second in their historical consequences and importance to these veritable "social sermons on the mount" of Advent 1848. We can therefore readily understand that contemporary judgments on this "revolutionary" action of Ketteler's were severe. Some dubbed these sermons "socialistic-communistic preachments" and relegated their ecclesiastical author and his following to the fictitious circle of "democratic ecclesiastics who talk as harshly as Westphalian communists." [133] Compared to these critics, the vision of Karl Marx was far more correct when he could not regain his calm with respect to these sermons and their consequences, even in 1869: "Whenever they think fit these dogs (for instance, Bishop Ketteler in Mainz, the clerics at the Duesseldorf Congress, etc.) flirt with the labor question. As it turns out, in 1848 we have toiled for them, only they enjoyed the fruit of the Revolution in the time of reaction." [134] Marx erred only in one thing: it was Bishop Ketteler, not Marx and his friends, who in 1848 toiled toward the true fruit of the Revolution which then ripened to the benefit of the clerical "dogs who flirted with the labor question!"

From his appointment to the Bishopric in Mainz (1850) until his death Ketteler worked untiringly for organizational solutions of the social question. This activity was directed exclusively toward the social deaconry of the Church. In these efforts the great "social Bishop" was, without realizing it, the loyal disciple of Baader with whose writings he was unfortunately not acquainted. [135] The Bishop had neither leisure nor love for theoretical disquisitions, his time being fully taken up with practical Church policies and social reform work. All the more he remained open-minded in his search for correct practical solutions and effective assistance in his social aims from whatever source they might come as proved by his relations with Lassalle and Victor A. Huber. He did not even shrink from using and quoting Friedrich Engels's book on "The Situation of the Working Classes in England" for his own works. [136] Whoever looks to Ketteler's writings for theoretical and ideological originality will be disappointed, but he might overlook the fundamental significance of these writings in the history of social thought. For his works contain such a wealth of basic insight into the essence of the social problems that even today's Christian Social movements ought not to be deprived of their religious-social and social-political wisdom. This is true primarily of the above mentioned Mainz sermons of 1848, of his numerous pastoral letters, his book on "Liberty, Authority and the Church" (1862) and his major writings on social policies, as "The Labor Question and Christianity" (1864), "Sozial-charitative Fuersorge der Kirche fuer die Arbeiterschaft" (Social Charitable Welfare Work of the Church for Labor, 1869) and "Liberalism, Socialism and Christianity" (1871). [137]

It is possible to carry on the argument about the change in Ketteler's attitude toward the capitalist system expressed in his practical social activities. It is, however, indisputable that Ketteler with his profound wisdom as a true leader of a social priesthood had formed a clear judgment on the character of liberalistic capitalism as an enslaver of men. This judgment in its lasting spiritual significance will serve again and again as guidance for the social conscience of Christendom, and more than ever today when the liberty and dignity of the toiling men and women have to be safeguarded in their social values against the unnatural enslavement in an industrial system which tends to deny all moral social ties.

"There can no longer be any doubt that the whole material existence of the working classes, which are by far the majority of all persons in a modern state, the existence of their families, their daily worries about the very bread required for the subsistence of a man, his wife and children, is exposed to every fluctuation on the markets and in market prices. What feelings must this evoke in these poor people who depend with everything they need, everything they love on the daily accidents of the market price! This is the slave market of our liberalistic Europe, cut out according to the pattern set by our humane, enlightened, anti-Christian Liberalism and Free-Masonry!" [138]

How far Ketteler forged ahead of his episcopal colleagues in his pastoral and social work can be gleaned from his great memorandum on "Die Fuersorge der Kirche fuer die Fabrikarbeiter" (The Welfare Work of the Church for the factory workers) which he put before the Fulda Bishops' Conference of 1869.[139] In this the Bishop of Mainz reviewed comprehensively and critically the state of the social questions in Germany, with extensive references to writings of the Protestant Victor A. Huber on "Die oekonomischen Assoziationen" (1849) and "Die Arbeiterkoalitionen" (1865) and to the great work of K. Marlo (Winkelblech), "Die Organisation der Arbeit" (1859).[140] In full accord with Baader's spirit, this memorandum sets forth concrete proposals how to expand the social mediation services of the clergy who are to be "apostles of peace among employers and employed regardless of persons and systems." To implement this *social deaconry* Ketteler then demanded categorically that "the Church must stimulate the interest of the clergy in the fate of the working classes. They have mostly little interest in these matters because they are ignorant of the existence and the impact of the dangers which lurk in these threatening social conditions, because they have failed to size up the character and the breadth of the social question, finally, because they have no conception of possible remedies. The labor problem must therefore no longer be neglected in the education of the clergy, neither in philosophy nor in the pastoral training. It would be most desirable if selected clerics were directed toward the study of economics and given traveling stipends so that they might become acquainted through their own observation with the needs of labor on the one hand, and with existing welfare services on the other, particularly in France where, as it seems, the religious and moral component receives more attention than elsewhere." In view of the widespread lack of social understanding among the German episcopate in 1869, these daring proposals necessarily failed to induce the Bishops' Conference to take action in the few hours set aside for such matters.[141] And yet, Ketteler's strenuous efforts in his own Mainz seminary together with those of the periodicals which cooperated with him—the "Katholik" and the "Mainzer Journal" and particularly the "Christlich-Soziale Blaetter" (Aachen and Neuss, since 1862)—succeeded by and by in assembling a growing group of socially trained priests. These true disciples of Ketteler later expanded the scope of the social reform activities of the Mainz Bishop in the comprehensive German Catholic social movement with its uninterruptedly growing salutary action.

We here wish to mention briefly the work of a fellow-student of Ketteler's and a kindred spirit, Adolf Kolping (1813-1865). The "Katholische Gesellenvereine" (Catholic Journeymen's Associations) which he founded in 1851 have performed a most significant educational function in their one hundred years of existence. Kolping never devoted his efforts to incisive social reforms and he never claimed to serve the working classes as a whole. The program of this pastoral "journeymen's father" in its wise limitation had highly beneficial results. In many lands, as far afield as America, the young journeymen were gathered into a spiritual and vocational community on religious foundations, to strengthen them in their allegiance to the Church and to guide them by lectures to take active interest in the social problems of their time.[142]

3. Social Romanticism: Karl von Vogelsang (1818-1890)

In the person of Karl von Vogelsang, Political Romanticism made its strongest impact on the development of political and social thought in all of German Catholicism. This influence took three shapes. It is first expressed in Vogelsang's personal life in which the problem of Romantic conversion reached its final and tragic form, an occasionalist interpretation of Catholic realism with theology mixed into the political and social spheres. Secondly, the dialectical principle of Political Romanticism found its expression in Vogelsang's ideology and writings, producing a peculiar combination of conservative or even reactionary political thought and forward-looking social reforms. Thirdly, this syncretism of a conservative Social Romanticism gave some circles of Catholic integralism the opportunity to combine, on the one hand, their theological conservatism and maximalism in church policies with the ideologies of Political Romanticism, thus producing the peculiar *complexio oppositorum* of a "neo-Romantic" conservative sociology which since the 1880's was primarily represented by the schools of the so-called "Vienna Orientation" in the Christian Social Movement.

The fundamental difference between the lives and educational background of Ketteler and Vogelsang clarifies by a vivid example the problem of "Romantic conversion"—as previously shown for Adam Mueller and Haller—in its impact on the social and political ideologies in German Catholicism. Vogelsang descended from an old family of the Mecklenburg landed gentry. He studied law and government at Berlin, Bonn and Rostock and after graduation entered the Prussian civil service to which he belonged until 1848. He then took charge of the family estate in Alt-Guthdorf and in this period of several years he was involved in a serious conflict with the ruling prince in defense of his class interests. In the course of this conflict, after intensive studies of the religious and political problems of the time, he decided to leave Mecklenburg and to join the Roman Catholic Church, a step taken under the influence of Ketteler and the Munich circle of Goerres, at Innsbruck in 1850. He lived in Cologne until 1859 and there carried on a stiff fight against Austrian Liberalism, mostly writing for the magazine "Politische Wochenschrift." Recommended by this activity, he became the traveling companion of Prince Johann von Liechtenstein from 1859 to 1864, when he definitely settled in Austria and there took up his activities first in Pressburg (now Bratislava), later in Vienna. In 1875 he joined the editorial board of the conservative paper "Vaterland." In this newspaper and in the monthly "Monatsschrift fuer christliche Sozialreform" founded by him in 1879, Vogelsang, who never found time to write a book, developed his program of neo-Romantic Christian Social reforms, always in heated controversies with the other line of thought in German Catholicism described above.[143]

This brief account of Vogelsang's biography may suffice to show that this emiently controversial figure of Romantic conversion never managed to find his due place of action among the ideas and movements of Catholic Realism although his personal friendly relations with Ketteler might have pointed the way. However, the fundamental differences in the traditions determining the personalities of Ketteler and Vogelsang might have frustrated such a collaboration under all circumstances. First of all, in Ketteler's personality the true traditions of Catholic Realism—in the line Eichendorff, Goerres, Baader—became active and through their expansion led him to create and build up that Realism in the Catholic political doctrines and social ideologies which was then expounded under the leadership of Rhenish-Westphalian Catholicism, in the circles of Lehmkuhl, Cathrein, Mausbach, Tischleder and Hitze, Pesch, Nell-Breuning, Gundlach and others. In Vogelsang's personality, on the contrary, first of all the traditions of Prussian Conservatism and of pseudo-Catholic Romanticism became active, as developed in the line Adam Mueller-Haller-Jarcke-Phillips-Gerlach-Radowitz. Mixed in with these traditions were those coming from the Conservative state socialism of a Rodbertus-Jagetzow (1805-1875) and the social-reformism of Karl Marlo (Winkelblech, 1810-1865), V. A. Huber (1800-1869) and A. F. Schaeffle (1831-1903). After his conversion to Catholicism, Vogelsang then attempted to develop this *complexio oppositorum* of Romantic Conservatism and Protestant social reformism and to draw from it practical conclusions in the spirit of Catholicism—by means of a typically Romantic, "Occasionalist" selection among genuine theological principles, using principally Thomistic integralism in Dominican formulation as propounded by Austrian clericalism. In these endeavors Vogelsang's personal religious integrity and loyalty to the Church are beyond suspicion. And yet, it is hardly possible today to overlook any longer that the Catholic legitimacy of the absolutistic shape which Vogelsang continuously insisted in giving many details of his "Christian Social Program" is most questionable; and the same probably applies to the Catholic legitimacy of the paradoxical system of "Social Romanticism" itself.

Vogelsang is the prototype of a Romantic Occasionalist whose thinking habits are to take *pars pro toto,* that is, to claim ideological absoluteness for relative fields of independent autonomy in the existential orders and disorders of sociological and historical reality. In his thinking Vogelsang never approached the vital complexes of sociological problems by grasping them systematically. He never succeeded in condensing the manifold variations in the critical aspects of these realities into a systematic unity which would have helped him to find really new and creative programmatic formulations. In tragic limitation he remained tied down by the ideological dialectics of Romantic Occasionalism which forced him to transform all individual, existential aspects of the vital orders into essential generalities of ideational orders or, in reverse, to apply—quite generally and often uncritically—essential categories of the theological and spiritual *Ordo* to judgments and measurements in the relatively autonomous fields of the concrete social and political life. Who practices these dialectics of Romantic Oc-

casionalism will find that the extremes tend to meet; more
than this, they tend to condition one another and to enter
into partnerships. We see, for instance, that Vogelsang claims
the revolutionary principle of State Socialism to be a necessary
counterpart to his conservative opposition to Capitalism as
such. Or, he proclaims the monarchical principle for political
government in an authoritarian, conservative, corporate State
as a counterpart to the clerical opposition to the democratic
state founded on popular sovereignty. Or, finally, the theological intergralism of a long bygone medieval ecclesiastical organisation of society is used to oppose the theological
realism of social and political Catholicism which offers autonomous liberties to the Church and the State in a modern
social order. In his writings[144] Vogelsang has made ample use
of all these possible variants, and furthermore allowed himself
to be used by all politically conservative and integralist circles
as a willing instrument in their fight against the democratic
order of society and the capitalist system in general. Vogelsang
thus became the initiator and ideological protector of all the
factions in Austrian Catholicism which—as we shall see below—developed the institutions of the Christian Social Party,
starting from the conservatism of the original Christian Social
Movement, but leading it to the extreme anti-capitalistic position of the circle around Anton Orel.

The opposition against the liberalistic free-enterprise system
and the autonomous capitalistic profit system which Ketteler
had initiated was justified in the spirit of Catholic Realism.
Vogelsang, however, exaggerated it in extreme rejection and
condemnation of the capitalist system in general. To him,
capitalism was not a predominantly social problem which had
arisen in the course of Western industrial development and as
such could be dealt with through reforms. To him, capitalism
is a fundamentally moral problem, the defection from the
Christian order as established in the Middle Ages. Thus, capitalism is the "fall of man" that began with the Reformation
and now needs to be eliminated. Vogelsang also radically
rejected the property rules as established by Roman Law,
without suspecting that this would imply his rejecting the
formulations given to these principles in the Christian Middle
Ages. He attempted to secure exclusive ecclesiastical sanction
for this extreme anti-capitalism which he had derived from
his occasionalist, one-sided interpretation of the canonical prohibition of accepting capital interest and his equally unjustified
generalization of Thomas Aquinas' criticism of the ephemeral
phenomena in the concrete 13th century property rules and

usurious practices. Vogelsang suspected every view contrary to his own of being "liberal," which meant, un-Catholic. The extensive discussion of the interest problem which, ineffectually supported by the ecclesiastical maximalists, he carried on with Augustin Lehmkuhl, revealed the theoretical dilettantism of this arrogant and intolerant Social Romanticism as clearly as it exposed how ineffectual and impotent was extreme conservative theological integralism in the face of the demand for practical solutions to the capitalist problems.[145] The ideological significance of this controversy, which persists among the various schools even today, especially as between the democratic sympathies of the Jesuits and the conservatism of the Dominicans, was aptly characterized by Ernst Karl Winter: "The climax of the interest controversy came with the clash between on the one hand, the conservative Vienna School of Karl von Vogelsang along with the Dominicans Andreas Fruehwirt and Albert Maria Weiss and, on the other hand, the German School in which at that time the Jesuits were dominant, represented by Augustin Lehmkuhl, later by Biederlack and Heinrich Pesch. This controversy centers around three main points, the problem of capitalism, the question of interest and usury, and the relations between capital and labor. With its origin in Central Europe, this discussion reverberated in the international debates and finally found its consciously compromising formulations in the Papal Encyclical 'Rerum Novarum'. . . ." It was the tragic fate of Vogelsang and his school, which also was decisively influenced by the "Union de Fribourg" of Cardinal Mermillod, that they could not free themselves radically from the odious reproach of fighting for nothing but theological doctrines; that they were unable to realize that the Dominican point of view was largely conditioned by past history;and how much inner consistency and logic the Jesuit point of view had to offer, provided that it was not misused to reverse and hamper the trends of the time, but to shape them dynamically."[146] With all this, it remains Vogelsang's lasting merit that by his radicalism in the property controversy and his equally radical rejection of popular sovereignty and democracy he touched off a serious theological discussion of Christian natural law in its concrete application to the contemporary problems of government, economy and society. Unwittingly and without contributing anything really positive and systematic, he was the initiator of this era of modern Catholic political and social doctrine which, in German Catholicism more than anywhere else, took an active development after the Encyclical *Rerum Novarum*. Vogelsang's ideas for a practical reorganization of economic life in a "corporate," authoritarian structure of society within the framework of a "social monarchy" mostly organized according to medieval precepts, are essentially lower-middle-class and politically reactionary. These ideas were highly praised especially by the "Austrian Orientation"; but history passed them by, and Christian efforts to reform industrial society, to contribute some creative ideas to the problems of capitalism and democracy, received no essential contribution from them. And an ultimate damning opinion on these ideologies of Vogelsang was written by history itself when his disciple Dollfuss made the petty and faulty attempt to perpetuate the great sociological and political misunderstanding of his master in the even greater misunderstanding of his "Christian Corporate State" of 1934. The tragic catastrophe which overtook this neo-Romantic Christian Social experiment of a Christian Corporative Constitution seems to have set a definite end to the entire historical lifespan of Political Romanticism, and consequently to the whole "Social Romanticism" which it inaugurated. It seems that even today this is not understood by Othmar Spann and the circles he inspires with his ideologies which in their methods are more deeply indebted to Vogelsang's ideas and example than their author would care to admit.

4. *The Social Movement: Franz Hitze* (1851-1921)

Franz Hitze[147] more than any of the other praiseworthy representatives of social priesthood in Germany has become a true symbol of social realism in modern German Catholicism. In the life and works of this Westphalian workmen's priest the *social deaconry* of the Church, as postulated by Baader and Ketteler, has found its finest expression. Only if the deeper meaning of this social deaconry is understood can Hitze's life work, and with it the achievements of Social Catholicism in Germany, be rendered full justice. Since "deaconry" in the early Christian sense of the word signified the supplementary practical welfare work to be done along with the priestly duties, this deaconry necessarily assumed a "social" character when it was applied to the concrete plight of those in need. This practical work to aid one's neighbor required by the early Church—". . . even so minister the same one to another as good stewards . . ." (I. Peter 4, 10)—is an additional duty which the Church has to discharge in the social life of the community. It is true that this "social concern" of the Church is not within its essential scope as a religious organism and sacral community. And yet, it has always been one of the foremost offices of the historical Church as a social organism and a society of men. And because these two realms of the Church forever meet and merge within the concrete personalities, because in this way the true secret of Catholicism finds expression in the Church-dedicated society and the society-dedicated Church, the sacral office of the priest and his social deaconry stand in a similar relation. And since the Church as organization and society can only exist and function in time and history, forever directed toward concrete man, equally the office of social deaconry superimposed on the sacral office of the priest must always be directed toward man's practical life in his social co-existence with his fellowmen.

The *social deaconry* finds its tasks outside of the supra-natural orders of sacral and religious life proper. Therefore, the priest's social deaconry is not his primary task for its own sake; instead, it is only a temporal and temporary supplementary duty of the Church within concrete society. Under this aspect, the social deaconry is fully exposed to the laws of historical change in the material tasks of practical life. Its first duty is to render material and direct assistance to a specific person faced by a specific situation at a specific location within social and historic reality. The social deaconry is therefore directed toward the present; its tasks arise and change with the requirements of the day and its services always consist in finding factual solutions to situations of material need. In other words, the social deaconry is the expression of the practically active organized Church society. It is "Catholicism in Action," in the truest sense of this slogan, within the social spheres of life. It should be self-evident that such action, closely linked as it is with actual situations, can never attain that degree of perfection that is prescribed by the Church doctrine in the theories of social existence, formulated to implement the ideals of a Christian life.

And yet, the critics of imperfections in the acts of the social deaconry of the Church have repeatedly made the mistake of judging the temporal tasks and achievements of this social deaconry—equivalent to "Social Catholicism in Action"—by standards of the timeless categories of the Catholic religion and the supra-natural values of Catholic priesthood. This attitude taken by certain groups of Church integralists and maximalists in social philosophy is unrealistic and thoroughly questionable from the Catholic point of view. It is not only sinning against the true essence of the social deaconry but at the same time it severely hampers the chances that concrete social policies and progressive social reforms might improve the social conditions of the time by exerting the full blessings of a practicable social movement.

Only after having discovered the real origin of the tensions between the realistic and the conservative orientations in modern Social Catholicism can we hope to understand them. It was indeed their dogmatic adherence to a maximalist social philosophy which prevented the Catholic Conservatives in Southern Germany and Austria from responding to the challenge of social deaconry as creditably as did those German Catholics who followed the leadership of Ketteler in his social realism and of the "Muenchen-Gladbach orientation" of Franz Hitze and Heinrich Brauns.

Franz Hitze's lifework spans the time from 1880 to 1921. It manifests the great change in German Catholicism in which the progressive developments initiated in the era of Ketteler, slowly transforming the social and political spirit of the German Catholics, was carried to full fruition in active state and society policies. This change was also represented by Windthorst who formulated the political aims, and by Victor Cathrein and Heinrich Pesch in the field of political philosophy and social theory. This remarkable originality of the German Catholic movement and its special achievements were based on this tripartite organizational activity and the division of factual objectives within the entire field of its economic and social policies and concerns, namely the division into cultural affairs, political affairs, and the theoretical problems of Christian state philosophy. In effect, this is merely a practical division of function which presupposes mutual interaction in the task of tackling the entire complex of problems; but it enabled those involved in this work to concentrate in wise self-limitation on either the social, the political or the theoretical aspects in erecting a practicable foundation for the theoretical or "ideological superstructure." By these means only could the social and political orientation in German Catholicism develop from its late beginnings that lacked all tradition, from the first organizations in the 1850's and the time of Ketteler, to their definite shape in the early 1880's. And after this, in mutual interplay of theory and practice, the exemplary achievements of Germany's social and political Catholicism in its state and society doctrines developed impressively and uninterruptedly up to their end in 1933.

It is of supreme importance to understand the basic significance of this wise self-restraint in the efforts to discover the realistic possibilities and necessities in implementing the duties of a Christian state and society. Here is the hidden source of all future achievements. For in this factual devotion to the burning social and political problems of the day in their concrete historic configuration, the majority of German Catholics gave the first historic proof of their coming-of-age, which is all the more to be admired if you recall what handicaps history had piled up against this social and political maturing process.

This new orientation made it possible that the German Catholics became integrated organically and creatively into the full complex of German realities. It would surely have been catastrophic for Germany if, because of a lack of a creative leadership, the awakened Catholic sense of social and political duty had chosen the other possible alternative, of entrenching itself in narrow confessionalism and clericalism and thus becoming estranged from the vital realities of Germany as a whole. This was a present danger even in the 1880's since past trends were still potent in the social philosophy and political theory of German Catholicism, in the shape of hide-bound conservative clericalism and of Romantic maximalism. It is all the more surprising that, under the leadership of the Rhenish-Westphalian Catholics realism won the day decisively. This success is attributable first and foremost to the work of Franz Hitze.

When integralist critics again and again inveigh against the inadequacy of many of these efforts from a purely theoretical point of view, this only proves how thoroughly their theorizing habits and their bloodless conservatism have blinded them to the tasks and duties which confronted Catholic realism at that particular time. These groups cared little about the harsh facts of social and political life. In their theological maximalism they adhered to the long defunct categories of medieval society and therefore believed that political life must be subordinated to theology and social life to clericalism. There was a confusion in their minds between the social deaconry of the Church, which can never be anything but a supplementary service devoted to material conditions of life, and the priestly office or even the infallible doctrinal function of the Church itself. Prompted by this misunderstanding, they demanded the utmost clericalization of political and social affairs and the utmost theologization of the theory underlying government and society. Consequently the danger was great even in the 1880's that the young social movement in German Catholicism could be caught in the toils of confessionalism and integralism. Demands were raised for an exclusive "Catholic" labor movement under clerical leadership and exclusive clerical politics run by a strictly confessional party; all this under the assumption that there existed a specifically "Catholic" order for state and society, even a "Catholic" economic system, totally opposed to all relatively autonomous formations within the modern state, economy and society.

Specifically, this was the attitude of the Social-Romanticist circles of Goerres around the "Historisch-Politische Blaetter" in Munich with J. E. Joerg editor. But after the death of the Bishop of Mainz (1877), even the Ketteler group around the "Katholik" of Mainz led by Chr. M. Moufang and the "Christlich-Soziale Blaetter" of J. Schings and N. Schueren in Aachen (Aix-la-Chapelle) came more and more under the influence of theoretical social maximalism as propounded by the Southern German and Austrian conservatives. Even the young Franz Hitze during his student years in Wuerzburg and Rome was most strongly influenced by these ideas, as can be seen in his early writings, "Die Soziale Frage und die Moeglichkeiten ihrer Loesung" (The Social Question and its Possible Solutions, 1877), "Kapital und Arbeit und die Reorganisation der Gesellschaft" (1880) and "Die Quintessenz der Sozialen Frage" (1880). In this last essay Hitze thus formulated the view current among social conservatives: "We demand a corporate order of society instead of the Socialist people's state with its lack of structure; we demand corporative liberty and equality, both legally as against the reactionary attempts of the Junkers and factually as against the wage slavery under liberal capitalism."

With this creed which amounted to a total rejection of the social realities of his time the young Hitze returned from Rome to his Rhenish-Westphalian industrial region. There the Christian Social and Catholic labor associations founded through Ketteler's initiative so far represented only a poorly organized Catholic social movement which around 1878 had a membership of about 20,000 while the Socialist movement spread with great momentum. But when a little later, as a young chaplain in the industrial town of Muenchen-Gladbach, Hitze had the opportunity "to see with his own eyes the wide-spread distress, the hardships and injustice implied in the social conditions,"[148] this young man underwent a change of heart similar to that of his great countryman Ketteler some time before. His innate Westphalian realism led Hitze away further and further from the ideologies of maximalist Social Romanticism and social theories to face the imperative duties of social deaconry which clamored for practicable social reforms. However imperfect the first solutions might be on the whole, yet they promised some measure of achievement under prevailing circumstances. "Now began a new philosophy and a new program for my life with the aim of devoting all my strength to the lifting up of these masses (of the workers) by means of a comprehensive *social reform,* systematic institutions for their education and self-training, to make them economically, morally and mentally capable of *cooperating in state and society* as mature and responsible persons." [149]

Here we find mapped out the program for Hitze's entire life work in his policies for social reform and cultural education. The "Society Reform" now proposed by Hitze was opposed to maximalism in its theoretical foundations principally in that Hitze took his point of departure in the actual social conditions which he found prevalent among the toiling masses of the era. In his demands he was not going to insist on a total reform of spiritual life and a total reconditioning of state, society and economy in the shape of a Christian corporative state; on the contrary, in his reforms he tried above all to exploit every practical opportunity that might arise for specialized organizational and educational self-help in *concrete political action.* In other words, *practical social reforms* were preferred to the ideals of a theoretically total Society Reform. Improving the social conditions progressively by organized self-help, by first of all utilizing the forces dormant within the Catholic population for an active social and political life, and by firmly rooting these actions in the religious and cultural forces alive in German Catholicism as whole—such was the program of a progressive, realistic *"Society Reform through Social Policies"* which Hitze formulated at that time. In a country like Germany where the Catholics were a minority in numbers as well as in political and economic strength and where the philosophial dangers of materialistic socialism threatened the distressed masses of Catholic labor with ever increasing force, making them an easy prey to social and political agitation, Hitze's program was probably the only possible one for a responsible leader of a Catholic social movement.

It is a testimony to *Hitze's social realism* and pedagogical genius that from the beginning it was entirely clear to him that such a comprehensive program could be realized only, first, if all the strength of the Catholic population could be concentrated on it and, second, if the entire field of Christian popular civilization and national vitality in Germany were brought into its scope. This insight had the salutary effect, even from a strictly Catholic viewpoint, that the social movement in German Catholicism under "Muenchen-Gladbach" auspices was free of clericalism in its leadership and of integralism in its programmatic efforts. Under the aspect of Germany as a whole this insight built a dam against the spreading of confessionalism in social and political action and consequently it became possible to make use of all opportunities to activate the Catholic social movement and social reforms within the framework of a comprehensive Christian and national program for state and society.

In the pursuit of this program Hitze's name became the very symbol for the unification of all efforts tending towards social and educational reforms in German Catholicism, as represented by the "Volksverein," and of all efforts in the social policies in Christian Germany centering around the "Christian Trade Unions." In the first formulation of this program in the 1880's, and even more so later in the time up till 1921 when it was being implemented, other leading personalities naturally made their creative contributions in German Catholicism and in the all-German Christian Social movement. And yet, they all fall into their proper places in the history of modern Catholic social movements and policies only in the framework of Hitze's superior over-all vision. To name only a few of these personalities: Windthorst, Hertling, Trimborn and Stegerwald, August Pieper, and Heinrich Brauns. Through all these years Hitze was the original planner and the leading spirit within the above mentioned threefold division of the creative reform activities of German Catholicism in the period of 1880 to 1921.[150]

It is Hitze's outstanding merit to have organized the Catholic labor movement, to have given it a training in social politics, and to have made it decisively active within the entire German Christian labor movement. The Catholic labor movement began with the founding in 1881 of the organization "Arbeiterwohl" (workers' welfare) in cooperation with F. Brandts, in which Hitze served as executive secretary and also as editor of the periodical of the same name. From here came the impetus for the "Christian Social Workmen's Associations" which began to be organized after 1882. Four years later they already counted 20,000 members who then formed the basis for the "Gewerkvereine" (trade associations) organized after 1894. These associations adopted a program of an inter-confessional labor movement at their Mainz convention of 1899, and on this basis a "Gesamtverband der Christlichen Gewerkschaften" (Federation of Christian Trade Unions) was formed in Krefeld in 1901, under the leadership of Hitze's disciple Adam

Stegerwald, its executive secretary until 1929.[151] It is again primarily due to Hitze that, despite the irritating "disputes of orientation" with the confessionally particularistic "Katholische Arbeitervereine," it became possible to gather the overwhelming majority of the Catholic workers and employees into the ranks of the Christian Trade Unions and to set them to work successfully for constructive social policies. Hitze was also one of the founders and a permanently active member of the "Gesellschaft fuer Soziale Reform" founded in 1901, and co-founder and active collaborator on the inter-confessional periodical "Soziale Praxis" and in these capacities was outstandingly active in establishing and bringing to fruition the Catholic social ideas in the entire social movement of Germany.

Among Hitze's merits the greatest probably lies in the founding of the "Volksverein fuer das katholische Deutschland" in 1890, in cooperation with Brandts and Windthorst. In this "Volksverein" Hitze presented German Catholicism with a unique instrument for social organization and education.[152] His comprehensive activity to educate people for social and political work was without parallel in Germany or, for that matter, in the world at large, both in the thorough groundwork and in the scope of activity and success—in training courses, in spreading enlightenment by word of mouth and in publications, through lectures arranged all over Germany, in profound books, periodicals, and popular pamphlets. In these activities, Hitze, with Windthorst as his second from the very beginning, prevailed victoriously over the influences of narrow confessionalism and negativistic apologetics, at the center as well as in the professional branch organizations. Up to its destruction in 1933, the "Volksverein" thus functioned as the most powerful and beneficial instrument of German Catholicism for the education in social and political action. Without the special contribution of the "Volksverein" the truly admirable progressive expansion of the social and political spirit in German Catholicism would not have been possible, from its beginnings in the 1890's until it became widely visible in the constructive political energies and the creative social conscience of the German Catholics in the era of the Weimar Republic. Quite legitimately, Muenchen-Gladbach where this organization had its seat, with its impressive educational machinery, its rich social archives and unique specialized library, together with its branch institution, the adult education institute "Franz Hitze-Haus" in Paderborn, was regarded as the spiritual center of social and political Catholicism. Accordingly the name of "Muenchen-Gladbach" became quasi-synonymous with the social and political realism of the German Catholics.

Hitze realized from the outset that, just because of the confessional, political and social cleavages among the German people, all attempts to translate philosophical principles and ideals of social reform into concrete action could succeed only if well-defined purposes were mapped out to set in motion the potential political energies of sufficient numbers of people among the Catholic, or rather the Christian workers, farmers and bourgeoisie. To this end Hitze proclaimed the principle of *society reform through social policies,* which means that the power of the political parties should be set to practical work in the mutual interplay between the people, the government and the economic factors. He therefore declared himself for the Center Party in which he saw the proper medium, organized especially for the purpose of making the Catholic masses active in social policies. He worked for his aims from 1898 to 1912 as a member of the Prussian Diet, and from 1884 to 1921 as member of the Reichstag. Always the modest workmen's priest, he only rarely participated in the public debates but exerted his influence all the more untiringly and thoroughly in the committees that had to prepare the regulations and legislation for social reforms. *If ever a Catholic priest was beyond suspicion of confessional narrow-mindedness or clerical pressure politics, if ever the political acts of a Catholic priest in Germany were devoted fully to the social interests of the nation as a whole, this was true of Hitze.* To him, priesthood and religious philosophy were nothing but special gifts of God which procured him the necessary ethical basis and supreme assistance in the discharge of his *social deaconry in the service of the common welfare.* The true regard and unlimited confidence in which all political parties and social organizations held this social genius of Muenchen-Gladbach had much greater momentum by far than the petty criticism to which Hitze had to submit throughout his life on the part of the theorists and integralists in his own camp.

5. *The Social Policy: Heinrich Brauns* (1868-1939)

All students who wish to ascertain what part German Catholicism had in establishing the Weimar Republic will—without detracting from the momentous contributions of the non-Catholic forces of society, especially the Social Democrats—arrive at this conclusion: without the practical, creative realism of Social Catholicism as instructed by Hitze and the "Volksverein," and without the social and organizational achievements of the Christian Trade Unions educated in the same school, neither the original founding of the Republic nor the progressive expansion of its generous social constitution as implemented by social reforms would have been possible. In 1919 Hitze, already near his seventies, devoted what was left of his vital energies to the effort of endowing the young Republic with a legal foundation strong and wide enough to allow a progressive policy of social liberty and justice to be built upon it—a foundation formulated in the basic social clauses of the Weimar Constitution, Articles 157 to 165. Thus the Constitution itself replaced the largely negativistic principles of Wilhelminian social policies which were confined to protective measures for the workers, by a positive social charter which could be implemented by further positive legislation and creative social measures. And the Constitution itself gave Social Catholicism in Germany the opportunity, and indeed the necessity, of trying its utmost to infuse active social policies with the Christian principles.

How fundamentally significant for the social program of the Weimar Republic was this opportunity and what basic responsibility it entailed for Social Catholicism becomes clearly visible when we recall the often overlooked fact that the leadership in planning social legislation and in capably executing social administration lay uninterruptedly, from 1920 to 1928, in the hands of a Catholic priest, Heinrich Brauns. And in the following time of crisis, 1930 to 1932, it was again one of the foremost Catholic social reformers, Adam Stegerwald, who served the same aims. In the fourteen years of the Weimar Republic Catholicism thus almost without interruption bore the main responsibility for the creative expansion of social legislation and administration.

As Reich-Minister of Labor from 1920 to 1928, Heinrich Brauns discharged the duty of building up the social legislation with a gift and a devotion which secured him the steady cooperation and regard of all parties of the Weimar Republic. In the midst of all the difficulties of the reconstruction years, despite the continuous changes in the power relations between the parties, expressed in unstable governments and party combinations, it was surely Heinrich Brauns' very own achievement that the Reich-Ministry of Labor was the only government agency— and its legislation and administration, the only government function—which enjoyed unbroken continuity in planning and execution. This "permanent" Reich-Labor Minister in his vestments of a Catholic priest survived all cabinet changes, all fluctuating party coalitions, and formed the strongest link between the many parties in his efforts to create a common platform for their differing social concepts. And it was perhaps an even more arduous task to coordinate the special interests of the many labor and professional organizations, primarily of the trade unions and employers' associations, amóng which Brauns succeeded in safeguarding the unity of German social policies. Finally, Brauns' political genius and educational mastery were seen at work whenever it was a question of preparing legislative measures in the special committees of the various parties and in the branch organizations of the trade unions, when all these groups had to be guided to recognize the basis for final legislative action common to all parties and pressure groups. In this effort Brauns found a potent helper from the ranks of the Center Party and the Christian Trade Unions in Heinrich Bruening, especially while he was Executive Director of the Deutscher Gewerkschafts-Bund (D.G.B., German Trade Union Federation) from 1920 to 1930 and in his function as social expert of the Center Party and member of the Center's Reichstag group since 1924.

In his untiring labors to introduce a workable social program and to expand it through active social measures, Brauns showed himself to be the most devoted disciple of his master and friend of many years, Franz Hitze. He took over the heritage Hitze left him and cultivated it by positive action as far as at all possible against the enormous political and philosophical handicaps of the pluralistic Weimar party system. Through him "German Catholicism in the line which leads from Hitze to Brauns became the staunchest defender of the government as executor of social policies." [153] Taking into full account the given economic and political realities of the Weimar Republic as a whole, among which these social policies had to be executed, we cannot but feel that even a benign critic like Theodor Brauer[154] overlooked too much of this historic background when he reproached this "line from Hitze to Brauns" with having neglected the Christian Social theory of Society Reform in the one-sided practice of their social measures. Neither Hitze nor Heinrich Brauns as Reich-Labor Minister ever pretended that their efforts to bring about practical social reforms had realized the ideals and theory of Christian society reform. On the contrary, Hitze, and even more Brauns, stressed again and again that they regarded it their foremost task to carry out to the best of their abilities the *duties of social deaconry* as posed by the actual plight of men in the prevailing historical situation, according to the requirements of their office and of their consciences as Catholic *and* German social politicians. The elaboration of the theoretical aspects of the ideal Christian society reform they left to others who—as we shall see below— fully complied with this task of expounding the Catholic social theories systematically. Hitze for his part was entirely the practical social reformer by way of specific social measures to be carried out by using the organizational and political forces available in Catholic and Christian Germany, and in this Brauns was his truest disciple. In the many years he headed the organizing section of the "Volksverein" and its economic and professional divisions (1900 to 1913), *Brauns was admirably adapted to the function of putting the social realism and creative social force of German Catholicism to full use in constructing the edifice of the Weimar Republic.*

After his resignation as Reich-Labor Minister, Brauns rendered a sort of factual account of his activity[155] which is one of the most valuable historic documents by which to study the character of the Weimar Republic and especially the achievements of social and political Catholicism.[156] With almost aphoristic brevity and in the impressive form of a personal oration, he thus characterized his social policies: "We produced by no means a new edition of the social policies of pre-war days. We have gone far beyond the old. I can quite easily make this clear by reminding you that before the war social policies were largely confined to the aim of protecting the workers. The new social policy stresses the legal position of the worker and its aim is to safeguard his existence. This is a difference in essence. If you consider that the primary characteristic of the proletariat was that they did not enjoy equal legal rights with the others, and if you give further thought to the fact that the 'proletarian' attribute lay in the insecurity of the workers' existence, you will see the new labor charter and the new legislation on labor exchanges and unemployment insurance in their true light. You will realize that in giving social policy this new direction we are 'solving' a good piece of the social question." [157]

It can be regarded as an outstanding acknowledgment of the creative achievements of German Catholicism that the social legislation and administration of the Weimar Republic enjoyed international recognition as the most advanced and exemplary to be found in any industrial country. Those negativistic Catholic critics of the creative Catholic contribution to the social policy of the Weimar Republic, who show their inability to form a just opinion of the concrete responsibilities and obligations for positive action in their eternal theorizing and applying of nothing but absolute, perfectionist standards, should pay more attention to the judgment of one of the foremost contemporary Catholic theoreticians, Goetz Briefs.[158] This opinion merits special study because Briefs applies his wide experience in social history and his knowledge of social theory to measuring the achievements of the Weimar Republic according to the standards set by the great Pope Leo XIII in his demands for social reforms contained in his Encyclical *Rerum Novarum*: "Looking over the development of social policies up to the present we arrive at the following result: of the proposals made in *Rerum Novarum* one-and-a-half generations ago, the greater part is largely realized or in the process of realization today, through social measures, labor laws, collective negotiations between employers and employed (shop communities) and through shop management policies carried out by the employers. It is a surprise that this Papal program turns out to have been much more in the line of actual developments than anything proposed at that time by liberal employers and by theorists of social policy . . . What then is the upshot of social policy? In historic aspect, it is to outline the burning problems of the proletarian existence of the masses gradually, always keeping concrete last goals in sight. At the end of this process we visualize the shape of an economy entirely reformed by social policies. The capitalist economy will have been set into a system of standards enforced by law and organization. The economy will then be capitalistic only in so far as it remains profitable for private enterprise under this system of social standards. The field in which business is being transacted according to liberal rules will have been narrowed down by social policy."

If we draw a comparison with parallel achievements of Social Catholicism in other countries, the social movement and activitis of German Catholicism deserve to be viewed with special pride in the practical results achieved under the enlightened leadership of Franz Hitze and Heinrich Brauns in their struggle to implement social liberty and justice.

CHAPTER V

POLITICAL CATHOLICISM

1. The Essence of Political Catholicism

Hardly any other feature of the political ideas and movements of modern times has been so badly misrepresented by
observers of history as that of Political Catholicism. In the limited scope of our present study we cannot analyze everyone
of these misunderstandings which partly survive in our day,[159]
especially in the consciously tendentious interpretations originating with anti-Church and anti-religious groups or, on the
contrary, with extreme confessionalists. We hope only that the
following explanations will contribute to an objective historical
understanding of the manner in which the political conscience
of Catholics came into play under the specific conditions in the
political developments in a certain country. But first it is necessary to analyze some of the basic characteristics of Political
Catholicism.

The term Political Catholicism indicates specially organized
activities of the Catholics in a certain country whose aim it is
to establish the principles of the Christian state and social doctrines in that country's total political life. Under modern conditions domestic politics concern primarily the fields of government and party politics, those of society and culture, and of
economic and social affairs. Accordingly, the effects and interests of the Catholic citizenry are primarily directed toward
bringing their organized force to bear on these three fields.
Thus Political Catholicism has very factual interests in *state
politics* proper, and secondarily in certain *cultural and Church
policies,* as also in certain *economic and social policies.* Our
previous discussion of the sociological problem of Catholicism
(Chapt. I) has already made it clear that "politics," meaning
the concrete political activities of the Catholics of a certain
country, may be quite independent from the "Church" itself
and must, on the other hand, depend on the specific governmental and organizational configuration and on the party structure in existence in that country. Political Catholicism is therefore completely determined by the historical facts of the time

and place. It is neither a basic institution of the Catholic Church, nor a religious or cultural movement under Church auspices, nor even a permanent feature of political life valid for all countries.

Pope Leo XIII has authoritatively proclaimed in repeated pronouncements that the movement and activity of Political Catholicism is to be entirely free of Church tutelage, and he has thereby guaranteed the freedom of political organization and action in the framework of the Christian philosophy. This relationship of *Church and political party* was defined on principle in the Pope's epistle of December 8, 1882: "We should keep aloof from the paradoxical opinion of those who confound Religion with allegiance to any one of the political parties, identifying the two matters to a point where they are almost tempted to regard their political opponents as heretics from the Catholic religion. This is tantamount to dragging politics into the venerable sphere of religion, breaking fraternal harmony and opening the door wide to many mischievous nuisances. It is therefore necessary that religious and political matters be kept apart in one's opinions and judgments according to their different character and nature." With equal precision the Pope's Encyclical *Sapientiae Christianae* (1890) explains the relation between *Church and party politics*: "Political domination is totally alien to the Church. It would be in full contradiction to the function and task of the Church were it to participate in party politics and to serve the fluctuating opinions of lay politicians. *The Church does not regard it as one of its duties to decide which form of government is the best or what are to be the institutions appropriate to the government of a Christian policy. The Church rejects none of the various forms of the state, provided only that religion and morality are protected.* To entangle the Church in party politics and to use it to get the better of one's opponents would be an extreme abuse of religion." [160]

Accordingly, whenever "Catholic" political parties were formed as a special effort to organize the political forces of Catholicism for the sake of national cultural and social activities or to defend the lawful rights and privileges of the Church, this always arose from concrete political necessities to protect the Christian principles in state and society. For the Church as such, that is, the Pope, the bishops or even the lower clergy, to enter the political arena immediately on the side of any special interests would be indefensible. On the other hand, bishops and priests in their capacity as citizens may very well regard it as their privilege and duty to participate actively and as leaders in the political life of their countries. When the modern approach to state and government and the pluralistic party systems emerged, the Catholics in many countries found themselves compelled to close their ranks for the political defense of their interests. In doing so they had to draw on their autonomous political and social forces and traditions and to make their own institutions sound instruments in pursuit of the common welfare of their countries. The history of these efforts to develop the political consciences of the Catholic citizens both as to their ideologies and their organizations constitutes the history of Political Catholicism in Germany.[161] The genesis of the social movements and the state and social doctrines in German Catholicism was filled with tensions between, on the one hand, the conservative, integralist traditions and, on the other, the democratic, realistic trends, and these same tensions very specially influenced the origins and history of Political Catholicism. And yet, no error could be greater than to think that a certain political confessionalism and clericalism which appeared in German Political Catholicism was its main expression—though unfortunately this belief is expressed only too often by anti-Catholic historiographers. This would be doing grave injustice to the unique political achievements of Catholic Germany in the past hundred years.

2. The Beginnings: The "Goerres Circle" (1837-1848)

The evolution of political consciousness in German Catholicism in the first half of the 19th century is dominated by the fact that indigenous ideological traditions, for reasons explained above,[162] were entirely absent. Only by becoming aware of the historically determined ambiguity of these developments can we begin to understand them. The leading personalities in German Catholicism, whose awakening political conscience urged them to act, were exposed to the impact of two strongly divergent strains from the state and social doctrines of the time, those of Romanticism and of (pre-March 1848) Liberalism. As far as the influence of Romanticism is concerned, we have already analyzed its consequences.[164] But the ambiguity is introduced by the second trend, the influence of Young Liberalism on the awakening political thinking of some Catholics, a feature which so far has received only scant attention.

We have seen how Goerres and Ritter von Buss found a way of escaping their initial lack of political traditions by joining the Romanticists. Now we shall observe how these men who gave Romanticism their guarded allegiance were thereby drawn toward the early, i.e., the conservative forms of Political Catholicism as manifested by the "Goerres Circles" and, after 1838, by the "Historisch-Politische Blaetter." The examples of Eichendorff, Baader and Ketteler have shown us how the typical, tradition-based Catholics managed to establish an entirely positive relationship with the political realities of their time. Now we see a different alternative in the position taken by Karl von Rotteck, the leader of the Southern German Young Liberal Movement, a typical example of those Catholic contemporaries who, instead of overcoming their lack of ideological traditions by joining the Romanticists, chose their political opposites, the German Young Liberals.

Karl von Rotteck, scion of a Catholic bourgeois family of Freiburg in Breisgau, was raised in strict religious traditons.[165] During his law studies he came under the strong influence of the legal and political ideals of Enlightenment in the line from Montesquieu to Rousseau and Kant,—as it later temporarily happened to his disciple, Ritter von Buss. From 1818 to 1832 he held the chair of Natural Law and Government at the University of Freiburg. In his activity as academic teacher and leading liberal politician, he could not fail to get embroiled in violent conflicts with the pseudo-Catholic state and social doctrines of Political Romanticism as represented by the groups around Haller and Mueller, and later by their reactionary epigones of the "Berliner Politisches Wochenblatt" and the Goerres Circle. Since especially the groups of the Berlin converts, the K. E. Jarcke, G. Phillips, M. Radowitz, et. al., distorted the Catholic traditions more and more in furthering their pseudo-Catholic, Romantic and reactionary ideologies, Rotteck's liberal principles led him into growing opposition. Unfortunately, the majority opinion among Catholics saw in Rotteck's criticism nothing except hostility against Catholicism itself while in reality he was entirely justified in pointing out how this questionable pseudo-Catholicism ran counter to the genuine Catholic traditions. On his part, Rotteck too often erred by identifying these Romantic converts and reactionaries with Catholicism itself. With the increasing influence of the defenders of Political Romanticism in the beginnings of Political Catholicism, as primarily manifested in the Goerres Circle, the original tensions between pseudo-Catholic Romanticism and the "liberal," though certainly not anti-Catholic, democratic tendencies of Rotteck hardened into a much deeper cleavage which ended later in the determined "liberalistic" hostility against Catholicism as a whole.

In reviewing these developments we feel bound to raise the question whether the presence of an ideological disposition favorable to Catholic realism could not have made this early Southern German liberalism at home in the Catholic camp. This might have prevented the tragic pretension of pseudo-Catholic Political Romanticism to be the sole legitimate attitude in matters of state and society, in this time of searching for political means of expression. One is more and more prompted to answer the above question in the affirmative when one reads the "Politische Annalen" (1830-1832) and the first edition of Rotteck's famous "Staatslexikon" (1834-1844) objectively and compares them with the "Berliner Politisches Wochenblatt " (1831-1872) and the entire literary production of Political Romanticism. It appears from such studies that Rotteck's specific "liberalism" was a much more legitimate precursor of the realism of Political Catholicism with its political and social democracy as opposed to reactionary attempts to establish a State Church, than all of Political Romanticism has to its credit, especially in view of the conservative, clerical movements it inaugurated in Southern Germany and Austrian Catholicism. Incidentally, it is worthwhile noting what strong and successful influence the "Liberal" Rotteck exerted in 1817 in defending the Catholic character of the University of Freiburg and in the following years in defense of Catholicism against reactionary church policies. Especially in the "Cologne Disorders" of 1837 he stood by the Church valiantly.[166] When thanks to the events of 1848 Catholicism finally gained more freedom for its political evolution in Germany, an over-all review of developments will show that Rotteck's Young Liberal Movement contributed very markedly to this emancipation.

Political Catholicism in its early developments before 1848 was largely dominated by these controversies as to Church policies and therefore by a negativistic attitude toward other problems of political and social life. These struggles went on mostly within the Church, without any backing from popular Catholic movements or parties. The only conspicuous layman to take part in these Church controversies which culminated in the "Cologne Church Conflict" of 1837, was Joseph Goerres. This conflict centered primarily around school reforms and reforms in marital law, matters that were most controversial between reactionary Prussia, the constitutional monarchies of Southern Germany and the Catholic Church. Some Catholic representatives in Southern German diets did participate in these struggles—as Buss and Andlaw in Baden; Egger, Abt, Magold and Zimmer in Bavaria; Neeb, Lauteren and Kertell in Hesse—but, lacking the backing of a "Catholic" party, their influence remained negligible.[167] In mighty Prussia, on the other hand, where no parliamentary constitution existed the Catholics were unable to exert any organized political opposition whatsoever. Only in the Rhineland and most of all in Westphalia was there a rather remarkable counteraction against Prussia's anti-Catholic absolutistic State-Church Policy, coming directly from the Catholic clergy and the strictly Catholic aristocracy. The first phase in the evolution of Political Catholicism was therefore confined to the efforts of an embattled episcopate to arouse the German Catholics in defense of their rights in Church politics and their religious liberties, to widen their scope and enhance their functions.

In all these struggles the main literary task fell to Goerres' eloquent pen. In this epoch Goerres succeeded in mobilizing the entire public opinion to form an active front of German Catholicism against the reactionary Prussian State which finally had to yield on all important points. This was done in Goerres' numerous essays in the "Katholik" of Mainz and later, 1838-1848, in the "Historisch-Politische Blaetter" and above all in his fighting books "Athanasius" (1838), "Die Triarier" (1838), "Kirche und Staat nach Ablauf der Koelner Irrung" (Church and State after the Cologne dispute, 1842) and "Die Wallfahrt nach Trier" (The Trier pilgrimage, 1845). In these writings, especially in the "Athanasius" which largely contributed in its forcefulness to the quick liquidation of the Cologne Church Conflict, Goerres presented German Catholicism with the methods and literary traditions to carry on political Church controversies. Political Catholicism later made use of these methods whenever it became necessary—as in the great "Culture Struggle" of the 1870's—to defend the just interests of the Catholic Church in its religious and cultural concerns. Unfortunately Goerres is largely responsible for having introduced into these struggles a straight, and partly unjustified, identification of the Young Liberal Movement with "anti-Church liberalism." This enabled certain reactionary and clerical groups within Political Catholicism to continue quoting Goerres in support of their inability, or rather unwillingness, to make the correct distinction between the political attitude of Liberalism and the "liberalistic" hostilities against Church and religion.

The Munich "Historisch-Politische Blaetter," founded in 1838 by Goerres and his collaborators, was characteristic of this mistaken attitude. The chief editors of this periodical from 1838 to 1851 aside from Guido, Goerres' son, were the two reactionary Prussian converts K. E. Jarcke (1801-1851) and G. P.

Phillips (1804-1877) [168] The political past of these two over-zealous "Catholic" journalists, primarily their reactionary activities in the "Berliner Politisches Wochenblatt" and the fact that this same Jarcke was the successor of Gentz as Metternich's aide in Vienna from 1832 to 1848, shows clearly that it was hopeless to expect from such men positive help in a realistic evolution of Political Catholicism in accordance with genuine Catholic traditions.

3.   The Emergence of Catholic Realism (1848-1871)

The events of 1848 have furnished a vivid proof of the close ties that have existed throughout history between the fates of German Catholicism and those of the German nation as a whole. The Revolution of 1789, for instance, exerted perhaps its most momentous influences on the history of Germany precisely in the changes it wrought in Church politics and in the social and cultural structure of German Catholicism.[169] Similarly, the bourgeois Revolution of 1848 inaugurated a new phase in the history of German Catholicism. In the period to follow, 1848 to 1918, the social and political developments in German Catholicism were an expression of the great events in German history which have been characterized as the social and political emancipation of the Germans. And the three subsequent fateful epochs of modern German history (to mention them already here in passing)—the Revolution of 1918 with its reverberations in the Weimar Republic until 1933; the Revolt of 1933 and the National Socialist Dictatorship until 1945; and the catastrophe of 1945 with the following attempts at reconstruction—mark parallel epochs in the modern evolution of German Catholicism as manifestations of all-German historic traits. This makes it clear once again that no understanding of the history of German Catholicism can be gained without a comprehensive knowledge of the history of Germany as a whole.

In setting an end to the anachronism of the ecclesiastical states in Germany, the Revolution of 1789 did away with the foundations of feudalistic Church policies and with the exclusive domination of German Catholicism by an aristocratic hierarchy. Thereby the Revolution liberated all the forces which during the first half of the 19th century went into constructing a truly popular Church for German Catholicism and into giving a positive turn to all social, political and cultural efforts. In 1848 this first phase, during which the autonomous orders in the social and political activities of the Church slowly ripened toward maturity, came to an end. This year of decision marked the transfer of leadership both in ideologies and in organization from the hands of the Romantic Conservatives to those of determined Realists in matters of society and democracy. As in state policies, the "Year of Revolution" also brought the realistic forces to the fore in social and democratic Catholicism, forces which from now on dominated the social movement from Ketteler to Brauns and the political movement of the Center Party. Thus the year 1848 witnessed the birth of the autonomous orders in the organizations of the Church and in the programs for Church and social policies developed under the influence of Christian realism in the Rhenish-Westphalian tradition.

It is characteristic of modern German Catholicism that, because of the lack of independent ideological and practical traditions of politics, especially in the 19th century, the spirit of a specifically Catholic philosophy in social and political matters could search and find expression only after these same matters had become urgent problems in the all-German discussion. Therefore, efforts to find theoretical formulations and solutions were always preceded by the concern with actual political and social questions and the attempts to deal with them realistically in the organizational forms of Social and Political Catholicism. This may help to explain why the ideas of Romantic Catholicism, especially those of Baader, and the ideologies of Political Romanticism remained without significant influence on the realistic forces of Social and Political Catholicism which began to be organized so successfully right after 1848. We can now also understand (as explained more fully in the following chapter) why it took until the 1880's for this realistic Catholicism to form its own political and social doctrines on the basis of the experiences in the period after 1848, entirely parallel with a general German turn toward a theoretical approach to the social and political problems.

The parallelism between general German history and that of German Catholicism after 1848 becomes especially interesting when we observe the influence of the first on the second. Before 1848 the German Catholics had no feeling for German unity in terms of politics and government. Also in its cultural interests German Catholicism knew no comprehensive unity over and above the various state particularisms. Not even the privileges and policies of the Church in the various Lander and Church districts were represented by an over-all organization of the Catholic clergy and episcopate. Before 1848, neither the conservative Reich ideology of Romanticism, nor the sense of unity in Church politics aroused by the "Cologne Dispute" of

1837 and strongly developed subsequently, could achieve any practical results. Only later, when the momentum of the common surge toward liberty swept the German people into the political unity of the German National Assembly in Frankfurt, did the German Catholics succeed in creating such a center of unity for themselves, for their own cultural and religious efforts, in the First Catholic Assembly in Mainz, 1848. And even the bishops were finally able to set up a common center for the defense of their interests in Church affairs, in the imposing Wuerzburg Bishops' Conference of 1848 when, for the first time since the Council of Trent, all the German bishops including the Austrian foregathered on German soil for common deliberations.

The historical significance of the Catholic Assembly of 1848 with the tradition it created of yearly "German Catholic Conventions" is well known. They had a momentous cultural impact on the German political scene.[170] We have also shown how important this Mainz gathering was for the development of Social Catholicism, especially thanks to Ketteler's initiative. On the other hand, the Bishops' Conference in Wuerzburg of 1848 has received much too little attention. Had the plans of J. von Geissel, Archbishop of Cologne (1796-1864),—a man who in his Rhenish realism and far-sightedness clearly recognized the historic possibilities for the Church if the mighty surge toward political unity could be made to serve the Church as well—been adopted at that time, modern Church policies in German Catholicism might have taken a different course. One can sympathize with Rome when it rejected the plan of Geissel and Ignaz Doellinger (1799-1890) to unify the hierarchically divided leadership of German Catholicism by creating a Reich Church Constitution under a German Primate. Rome remembered too clearly the precedent of Febronianism with its attempt to create a separatist national Church, and the disgraceful abuse of the Primacy by its last representative, Archbishop Dalberg of Mainz.[171] And yet, by its veto of November 9, 1848 against a German Reich Church, Rome made it impossible for German Catholicism to achieve the organizational unity of a German episcopate for common action toward common aims, a unity which would have been so badly needed in the struggles to come.[172] Despite this veto, since this first and last Reich Conference of the German Episcopate in 1848 a remarkable spirit of independence from Rome developed among the German bishops in their Church policies. This went into action with full impact in the vehement, though short-lived, resistance of numerous German bishops against Papal centralism, especially against the "Vaticanum" of 1870, and in the ready assistance which many German bishops, ever since the days of Ketteler, gave to the social realism of the Catholic labor movement and the Christian Trade Unions, and also to the political realism of the Center Party, despite all attempts to establish a clerical and ultramontane tutelage.

The emergence of realism in Church and social policies was supplemented by the decisive influences on the organization of German Catholicism exerted by the new state policies inaugurated by the German National Assembly of Frankfurt and the Prussian National Assembly of Berlin. The German Catholics were now given the first opportunities to delegate their own representatives to an all-German parliament where they would look after their political privileges and demands. For the first time a German bishop, Archbishop Geissel of Cologne, exhorted the German Catholics in a special pastoral letter (April 20, 1848) to do their political duty. For the first time a group of Catholics assembled with the object of forming a political party, the "Cologne Catholic Democratic Party" which gave itself a charter in June 1848 and published the first Catholic electoral platform for the Prussian Parliament. For the first time, with the "Mainz Journal" founded in June 1848, a political newspaper addressed itself to the public to carry on the day-by-day political struggles in defense of the social and political tasks and privileges of the Catholics, efforts in which it was joined by powerful allies in this journalistic phalanx of Political Catholicism, in 1860 by the "Koelnische Volkszeitung" and in 1870 by the Berlin "Germania." For the first time a liberal law of public association allowed a far-flung net of Catholic organizations to be spun for the concerted defense of social and Church activities. And for the first time Catholic politicians assembled in Frankfurt and Berlin to join forces in integrating the various traditions and interests of the Catholic electorate in common political and social action.

Over seventy Catholic delegates entered the Frankfurt Parliament, more than sixty the Berlin Parliament, among them many outstanding personalities, bishops and priests, scholars, artists and statesmen. For the first time the shape of German Catholicism in its social and political structure made its appearance. Here could be seen the predominantly conservative representatives from Southern Germany under the embattled leadership of Ignaz Doellinger; Jarcke and Phillips, the reactionary representatives of the Goerres Circle; and a group of Prussian reactionary aristocrats with Radowitz as their leader. Numerous representatives of the moderately conservative aristocracy came with the Westphalian Hermann von Mallinckrodt (1821-1874) in the lead. It was surprising how many names of delegates from the Catholic bourgeoisie were heard for the first time, such as those of the Brothers Reichensperger of Koblenz. And what was even more surprising was *the decidedly democratic, "liberal-Catholic" spirit of these bourgeois people's delegates* whom the sound realistic common sense of the voters, especially in the Rhineland and Westphalia, had chosen to represent their political and social interests in Frankfurt and Berlin. Characteristically, the top leadership in Church affairs in Frankfurt and Berlin lay in the hands of Geissel, Archbishop of Cologne, and the leadership in religious matters in those of the Westphalian aristocrat, Melchior von Diepenbroek (1798-1853) who in 1845 had been raised to the Archiepiscopal See of Breslau. It was also not by chance that the realistic Church politician who was the incumbent of the Cologne bishopric [174] took the immediate initiative of sending the Westphalian peasant priest Ketteler to Frankfurt, a man whose great merit it was to have gotten rid of reactionary influences by promoting social and political realism and democracy.

The practical results of the first cooperation of all these groups of Catholic parliamentarians in Frankfurt and Berlin were quite remarkable. In Frankfurt, the first draft for the "basic law" of the Reich Constitution, which provided for a tutelage of the Church by the State Church and for special legislation against the Catholic orders (Jesuits and Redemptorists) had to be abandoned. A second draft brought constitutional safeguards for the principles of "a free Church in a free State," in the spirit of its earlier advocates, Lamennais and Baader. An even more favorable solution for the Church privileges was enacted in the Berlin Parliament and then found its place in the Prussian Constitution of 1850. By their strenuous efforts, Geissel and Diepenbroek even persuaded the King of Prussia to give up once and for all his right to a "placet" for Church publications. However, Ketteler's efforts to find a Catholic solution of the school problems were unsuccessful both in Frankfurt and Berlin. Taken as a whole, the first parliamentary success of Political Catholicism in 1848 was great and its influence on positive constitutional measures unique, all this thanks to the courageous political Realism that inspired those who did the work.

The influences of the aristocratic-conservative, and even more of the reactionary circles on the future organizational developments in Political Catholicism had by that time been virtually eliminated, particularly in Prussia, Hesse and Baden.

After 1848 the leadership in Hesse devolved definitely on the groups around Ketteler, in Prussia on the Rhenish-Westphalian Catholics. This finally brought about a definite cleavage between the Southern German Conservatives and the Prussian Catholics. The "Association of Catholic Representatives" of the Frankfurt Parliaments of 1848 and 1850 in which Radowitz presided was already dissolved in 1851. While the Southern German politicians at first only founded loose groups of sympathizers in the Land diets and chambers, the Prussian representatives now formed a much closer working unit. After the election of 1852 they created a "Catholic Fraction" in the Prussian Diet with at first 64 members. But already in 1854 the aristocratic-reactionary group influenced by the perennial Radowitz seceded from the "liberal-constitutional" majority of this fraction. After this the leadership lay entirely in the hands of the Brothers Reichensperger who called themselves "Rhenish Liberals." The Fraction emerging from the elections of 1854 changed its name into "Center." This term at first signified no more than the formal fact that the Catholic representatives sat in the center, between the Conservatives at the "right" and the Liberal groups at the "left." Soon the name became synonymous with the political attitude of the Catholic representatives in the sense of Christian-democratic politics of the middle and of social conciliation. This name and this attitude of the "Center"-Fraction in the Prussian Diet (1858-1870) later became the symbol of the entire Center Party, first provisionally and after 1870 permanently.[175]

In summing up we may say that developments from 1848 to the founding of the Reich in 1870 were marked by a slow, yet steady process of constructing and consolidating the organizational framework of Political Catholicism for the purpose of bringing political influence to bear. And parallel, there was a slow, but equally steady process of social and cultural evolution which made German Catholicism capable of dealing with the tasks and struggles that were to fall to its lot after the emergence of Bismarck's Reich.

4. *The Center Party* (1870-1933)

1. *Catholicism and Prussianism.* When Political Catholicism had emerged from its first stages, a spirit of realism became dominant in its leadership which prevented the ideologies of Romantic Conservatism from gaining decisive influence on the programs of the Center Party. And by the same token, the reactionary political forces of Prussianism and the ideologies of

Prusso-German Pan-germanism were barred from shaping the party politics and actions of the Center. These facts were to determine the entire fate and political history of Bismarck's Reich, all the more since the Center Party bore the full responsibility for the actions of Political Catholicism in Germany from 1871 to 1918. And it is first and foremost the Prussian Center Party which stood at the helm, seconded by the Southern German Center Parties. Thus the history of "Political Catholicism in Prussia" is of paramount importance since, after Bismarck had solved the "German question" by force in 1866, Germany's fate was primarily decided by Prussian politics. For all intents and purposes, the evolution of Political Catholicism in Prussia characterizes the fate of this movement in all of Germany.

Ideologically and in its organizations, Prussian Catholicism had fully emancipated itself from reactionary and Romantic conservatism in the period 1848 to 1870. The following period, 1870 to 1882, was filled with the defense of the ecclesiastical and political rights and liberties of Catholicism against the encroachments from Prussian state absolutism and nationalism. From this Kulturkampf, (the name given to the political struggle for the rights and self-government of the Catholic Church in Germany) the Center Party emerged as the victor,[176] holding off all attempts at "Prussianization" which would have spelled the total subservience of the Catholic Church to Prussian state absolutism and a "Gleichschaltung" (bringing into line) of Political Catholicism with neo-Prussian nationalism and Pangermanism. This victory was due first of all to the principles of political realism brought to the fore by the historical evolution of the years 1848 to 1870.

These developments became possible by the fact that Catholicism was prepared to recognize the leadership of Prussia in the unification of Germany. But just as surely were the Center politicians induced by their realism to oppose with all their energies attempts to identify Prussian power politics and neo-Prussian "culture programs" in the "national liberal" spirit with the political fate of Catholicism and of German civilization as a whole. In the decisive ideological struggle in the years 1866 to 1870, again Ketteler, Bishop of Mainz, exerted his leadership. His book "Deutschland nach dem Kriege von 1866" [177] published in 1867, determined the basic attitude Political Catholicism was to take versus Prussianism. Ketteler always drew a clear distinction between the realities of the Prussian State and the ideologies and practices of Prussian power politics. He fully acknowledged Prussia's role in Ger-

man affairs and accordingly regarded it as a moral duty of the
Catholic citizens to participate actively in German politics. But
by this very participation the Catholics assumed the moral duty
of defending themselves uncompromisingly against the methods
of Prussian power politics, as characterized by Bismarck's an-
nexations of the Northern German states and the fratricidal war
he forced on Austria. In this book, Ketteler censured
Bismarck's ruthless methods and expressed even sharper opposition to the opportunists and nationalists in the Liberal and
Conservative parties who gave their sanction to Prussia's annexationist policies. Above all, Ketteler accused the Conservative Party of violating their principles as Christians and Germans by "paying homage to success, by bending their knees to
accomplished facts and crude power and thereby, almost without exception, violating the principles for which they had professed to stand for so many years. The Conservative Party now
did exactly those things for which they had reproached their
enemies in long struggles. This is a bitter moral defeat, for a
party which professes to be Christian must above all have the
courage to defend Truth in the face of Power. Subservience to
power, cowardice before power, are alien to the Christian. The
Conservative Party in Prussia has failed to stand up to this
test."

Ketteler was equally outspoken in opposing the plans to Prussianize Catholicism in a political "Gleichschaltung" of the
Church by making the Catholic cultural programs and Church
policies identical with those of neo-Prussian nationalism. Ketteler condemned the "usurpation of sovereign power by monarchical absolutism" which even attempted to make the Catholic Church dependent on the Prussian monarch by having
him appoint a Catholic "court bishop" in Berlin. "A court
bishop in Berlin, who would care more for outward etiquette
than for holiness, would hurt the Church more than all its
enemies in Prussia put together. We would therefore regard a
Berlin episcopate as a misfortune." Ketteler goes on to warn
the Catholics not to be hasty in granting recognition to the
results of Bismarck's annexationist policies and to the questionable artifact of the "North German Confederation," claiming that these shifts in the internal equilibrium in favor of
Prussia were bound to react on all future cultural developments, and especially on the relations between Church and
State. "Count Bismarck has achieved incredible success; and
yet, an ultimate judgment on the permanent effects of his actions for the good of Prussia will be possible only when his
system of domestic politics has been developed." This "system

of domestic politics" was revealed soon after 1870 as an attempt
to Prussianize Catholicism radically and to make the Catholic
Church entirely subservient to Prussian state absolutism, in
violation of the guarantees of Church rights which had been
written into the Prussian Constitution of 1850.

Before Bismarck fully embarked on this attempt in the initial stages of the Kulturkampf, Ketteler had to bar an action
in his own camp which would have enhanced the danger of
the Prussianization of Catholicism. This attempt was made by
Friedrich Pilgram, another one of these Protestant-Conservative converts, who was influenced by Political Romanticism
and was on friendly terms with the emerging neo-Prussian Pan-
Germanists. In 1870 Pilgram founded in Berlin a Catholic
daily paper with the revealing name of "Germania." In the
sample issue of December 17, 1870 he outlined a "program"
for the future leading journal of the Center Party which, had
it been put into effect, might have annihilated all that Catholic
realism had accomplished in the period 1848-1870. Pilgram
thus defined the aims of Political Catholicism: "The re-emergence of the Germanic Reich; universalism of the idea embodied by the Kaiser; the Kaiser as protector and patron of
Pope and Church; revival of the ancient German Empire, especially in its Church function; the hegemony of Germanism
in Europe; unity of all Germanic peoples, within one unified
system of states." Ketteler at once raised his warning voice
against this pseudo-Catholic sanction offered to a Pan-German
domination of Europe by Bismarck's Reich—whose founding
Pilgram greeted as "one of the happiest moments of German
history in centuries." "I do not think," said Ketteler, "that we
are justified in proclaiming the existence of such Germanism
as is here taken for granted. Above all, in view of the conditions as they exist in Germany today, I doubt that we can
without vain conceit cherish the immediate expectation that
Germanism and Christianity will emerge as great examples for
other nations to live up to, more than ever happened before
in history." [178] Ketteler's warning was a successful contribution
to frustrating this last attempt of Political Romanticism to win
over Political Catholicism and to subordinate it to the Pan-
German ideologies. Pilgram disappeared after three months
into political limbo. His place was taken by a valiant disciple
of Ketteler's, Paul Majunke, who now really made of the "Germania" the worthy foremost fighting organ of German Catholicism throughout the Kulturkampf. [179]

Thus Ketteler taught a spirit of cool-headedness in observing
critically Prussia's growing expansion as a political force, from

the "North-German Confederation" to Bismarck's Reich. The chief concern was what would be the consequences for Catholicism in political and cultural policies. In this spirit the Center Party was finally founded in 1870. In the first elections in which the Center participated, December 14, 1870, it secured for the Prussian Diet the respectable number of 58 representatives, followed by 65 representatives for the Reichstag in the elections of March 21, 1871. This unexpected electoral success was at once taken by Bismarck as an ominous threat to his political plans. It was to counter this threat that he embarked on the ill-fated Kulturkampf alliance with the National Liberals who, as chief representatives of the nationalistically infected bourgeoisie, had moved into the Reichstag with 125 members. In this alliance the genuine traditions of Old Prussian Conservatism and the genuinely freedom-loving traditions of 1848 democratic Liberalism were sacrificed to this hapless combination of neo-Prussian Caesarism, libertarian nationalism and Pan-Germanism, an alliance which in its ultimate consequences led straight into the German catastrophes of 1918 and 1945.

2. *Liberalism and Prussianism.* The relations with Prussianism have been as decisive for the developments in all-German Political Catholicism as for the developments of all-German Political Liberalism. And just as the history of Political Catholicism in Germany is different from that in any other European country, also, to quote Hermann Oncken, "the problem of Liberalism in Germany is different from the same problem in the foremost countries of Western Europe."[180] While Catholicism was saved from the fate of being Prussianized, Liberalism not only suffered defeat under this threat, but even willingly submitted to the power ideologies and hegemony cravings of Prussia. Therefore Oncken, who is probably the most competent historian of German Liberalism, declared Prussia to be the bane of German Liberalism. "German Liberalism always had the misfortune to gain ascendancy only as the ally of a power whose character and origins were entirely uncongenial."[181] No greater mistake could be made than to believe this German Liberalism to be comparable in its ideologies and political action, ill-fated since about 1859, with the intellectual and political movements of classical European Liberalism or indeed with American Liberalism.[182] For since its marriage to Prussianism, German Liberalism has always been ashamed of its origins in the democratic movements of Early Liberalism. It has exchanged the genuinely liberal ideals of a democratic commonwealth under social and political freedom for the Hegelian

ideology of the absolute State and for the social reaction and creed of dictatorship of neo-Prussian nationalism.

Viewed from this angle, the history of German Liberalism is that of Prussianized Liberalism, plus a "liberalistic," or indeed "libertarian" neo-Prussianism. Especially in Bismarck's Reich, Prussianized Liberalism always formed the nucleus of Prussian policies and, at second remove, of the Prussianized policies in the rest of Germany. *Ideologically,* the function of Prussianized Liberalism was in the first place, to get rid of all Old Prussian conservative ideas, primarily Protestant church loyalties and Lutheran orthodoxy, and in the second place to eliminate all democratic ideas of political and spiritual liberties as presented by Early Liberalism. The surviving crippled ideologies—the Prussian concept of power and the police state, the liberalistic hositility against the cultural influences of religion and the Church, the reactionary selfishness of the agrarians and capitalistic free-enterprise in social and economic affairs—all formed combinations with one another resulting in the neo-Prussian conglomerate of National Liberalism which could as little be regarded as genuinely liberal as in a later day National Socialism could be regarded as genuinely socialistic.

As to *party politics* this fusion resulted in the disintegration both of Conservatism and of early-liberal Democracy. In a dialectical process, the ideas of libertarian Prussianism were amalgamated with those of Prussianized Liberalism to form the "national liberal" ideology which was now to remain at the center of all ideological discussions in Bismarck's Reich. And at the same time, in the Conservative and Liberal party camps there was a constant reshuffling among the various political interests and pressure groups who disappeared and reappeared under various names in motley groupings with the object of taking advantage of all opportunistic chances in Parliamentary coalitions, in ephemeral mutual toleration or assistance or in passing periods of party fights. This explains the mechanism of Bismarck's pluralistic party state with its constant necessity of adapting party groupings to political and ideological tasks of the day. Bismarck proved his great gifts in the resourcefulness with which he made constant use of this ideological and political *complexio oppositorum,* Prussianized Liberalism and libertarian neo-Prussianism, to enforce time and again his personal aims of power in government and cultural affairs, aided and abetted by an ever willing Parliamentarian and legislative power instrument.

From the beginning, Political Catholicism, as later the Social Democrats, was forced by its ideological principles and histor-

ical background into fundamental opposition, both in sentiments and in actions, against this Prussianized Liberalism and
libertarian Prussianism. Accordingly, Bismarck and his Parliamentary followers of the day always had to devote their energies to breaking, or at least eliminating, the political influence of the Catholics and Social Democrats. The history of the
Kulturkampf and of the Anti-Socialist Laws has proved that Bismarck, the inspired task master of libertarian Prussianism,
lacked the ability to recognize one historic necessity, namely
that both Political Catholicism and Social Democracy were
bound to develop into political movements and social forces
with equal political rights and aspirations as those of Liberalism. Until today no really comprehensive and objective study
exists to determine how great is the responsibility of Prussianized Political Liberalism for Bismarck's policies of force as exercized all through the Wilhelminian Reich.[183]

The political marriage of Liberalism with Prussian nationalism began in 1858 with the founding of the "Nationalverein"
which under the leadership of von Benningsen promoted a fed-
deral reform to establish the Prussian hegemony. When Bismarck demanded in 1866 that the Reichstag belatedly vote his
indemnity for the expenditures necessitated by his military solutions of the "German question", the majority among prominent members of the "Fortschrittspartei" (Progress Party) seceded and deserted into Bismarck's camp, founding the "National Liberal Party." This soon became Germany's largest
political party, Bismarck's instrument of power which to the
very end of the Kulturkampf kept the German bourgeoisie,
now to become more and more intoxicated with nationalism,
arrayed behind him. It is peculiar that among the founders and
principal exponents of this party not one real Prussian can be
found: Benningsen and Von Miquel were Hanoverians; K.
Twesten stemmed from Schleswig; Eduard Lasker was born in
Poland; and even Heinrich von Treitschke, the chief literary
representative of National Liberalism, was a pure blooded
Saxon. Perhaps this helps to show how little National Liberalism had in common with real Old Prussian Conservatism, and
to what degree libertarian-nationalistic elements had infiltrated
Old Prussianism and its firm Protestant faith, usurping its
military traditions and developing methods of government in
order to establish their own military and political power instrument for the domination of Germany. To justify this enterprise ideologically, Hegel's doctrine of the absolute state was
made to order, and there was accordingly a renascence of the
philosopher of the "Prussian World Soul" in the political ideol-

ogies of National Liberalism which in the 1860's and 1870's went far beyond the principles Julius Stahl (1802-1861) had dared to propound in his Hegelian apologetics of Conservative Prussianism.[184]

Political Hegelianism, as popularized by the National Liberals, combined with Fichte's nationalism and Bismarck's "blood and iron" philosophy produced this monstrous ideology of neo-Prussian Pan-Germanism which, only in its offspring, National Socialism, fully revealed its sinister meaning for the history of humanity. Today, the deep-seated ideological affinity between National Liberalism and National Socialism, the all-inclusive responsibilities of the one for the other, can no longer be doubted.[185] All that is needed to prove this contention is to compare the Parliamentary pronouncements of National Liberalism and its publications, beginning with the Berlin "Nationalzeitung" down to the rich materials contained in the "Preussische Jahrbuecher" under Treitschke's editorship in the 1870's; the bitter hostility of National Liberalism against Catholicism and against any kind of Christian Church, especially inclusive of Protestant orthodoxy and the Lutheran community, with the parallel products and attitudes of National Socialism.

Here are some quotes from the leading official organ of the National Liberal Party: "The German does not intend to tolerate within his own nation any spiritual kinship with Rome; he rejects the ascendancy of priests and all attempts to blunt the people's intelligence; he stands for enlightenment, an honest conscience and work" . . . "To attain a new level of moral freedom, never scaled before, to construct the foundations of popular morality common to all churches and creeds—this is the goal before us in the first epoch of the rejuvenated Reich" . . . "Our German states and our German Reich are a truly moral community, and therefore a religious community of a much higher order then that represented by the ecclesiastical societies, either those misguided by the Ultramontanes or the self-styled Evangelical Orthodox."[186] And in a similar vein Treitsche wrote in the "Preussiche Jahrbuecher": "Our clerical opposition has underrated the firm bone structure of our state, its military education and discipline, its homogeneous administration; this opposition will founder against these elements of a strong order and against the idealistic upsurge of the reunited nation."[187]

If one is not struck on reading such pronouncements by the similarities with the moral attitudes of the Third Reich further cues will be found in a description of the political spirit prevalent in the newly formed Reich of Bismarck which was published in 1873 by the staunch Liberal Democrat, Paul Lindau, by no means an ultramontane, in his courageous magazine "Gegenwart": "What is all this we read in the journals who claim that they alone are national? One of their confirmed articles of faith is that the Latin world is definitely doomed to be submerged; seen from the vantage point of the Germanic world which has inherited the scepter, America appears as a rotten chaos, England as one large trading shop, while the Scandinavian nations lead an inconsequential life of retirement. There remains only Germany, a conviction quite in accord with that reached several years ago from another point of view by the Court Preacher Hoffmann who declared that the German nation is fated to play the same role in the future that the Children of Israel had under the Old Covenant, that is, to be God's chosen people." [188]

This political messianism and this hostility against the Church which National Liberalism and National Socialism had in common perhaps give us the best explanation why a clash between re-awakened Political Catholicism and Prussianized Liberalism became unavoidable.

3. *The Kulturkampf* (1871-1882) . As stated above, the Kulturkampf was more than merely a confessional and political controversy between the Center Party and the Parliamentary groups of Prussian Liberalism, in the era of the main fight led by Bismarck himself. We may follow the explanation which Rudolf von Virchow (1821-1902)—a man of great renown in medicine who compromised his greatness by his activities as a reactionary amateur politician and a rabid Pan-Germanist—gave to the slogan of "Kulturkampf," a word he had coined, when he proclaimed that "we are not dealing simply with the conflict between feudalism and ultramontanism, but rather with the fundamental positions which Prussia and Germany must assume today in the cultural movements of our time." [189] This is a true statement, and therefore the causes, aims and reverberations of the Kulturkampf deserve to be assigned fundamental significance in the evolution of the political ideologies and the constitutional and cultural conditions of Germany as a whole.

We have uncovered the ideological causes of the Kulturkampf in the dialectical developments of Liberalism and Prussianism, and in the antagonism of Catholicism and Prussianism. In respect to the former, the re-emergence of political Hegelianism was the decisive feature, primarily manifested in the constitutional "reforms," namely, in the Kulturkampf legislation and in the cultural program of neo-Prussian

Pan-Germanism. A second feature was the decision whether Political Catholicism would be given a field for successful action as an expression of the free activities of the Catholic citizens in the framework offered by the political organizations and actions of the Center Party. While the first feature decided the material content and objectives of the Kulturkamp, the second had a twofold consequence for Catholicism. First, there was the negative result that Catholicism was able to repel in united resistance the briefly successful attack on its political liberties and cultural independence, in forcing Bismarck after 1882 to repeal at least the most noxious restrictions enacted in the Kulturkampf legislation. Secondly, there was the positive, and decisive, result that henceforth Political Catholicism was able to build up in the Center Party a permanent and essentially stable parliamentary and general political representation of the majority of Catholics, and to keep it well organized and active till 1933.

The main ideological significance of the Kulturkampf is this: the Center Party emerged in 1870 as a new fact in the political arena of Bismarck's Reich, above all as a palpable testimonial to the political maturity which German Catholicism had achieved in the brief period of growth from 1848 to 1870. The performance of the Center Party during the Kulturkampf finally convinced Bismarck that in the future Political Catholicism would have to be reckoned with as an essentially new facet of the German political realities. How incontrovertible was the claim to full recognition appears from the mere record that from 1874 (in which year, in the face of Bismarck's restrictive measures, the Center almost doubled the number of representatives it had in 1872) right on to 1933, the Center Party in unaltered constancy represented more than 60 percent of the Catholic voters, commanding on the average 90 to 100 seats in the Reichstag and the Prussian Diet. It was the only political party in Germany actually independent of the fluctuations in political climate or in political and social politics right up to 1933.[190]

The *constitutional objectives* of the Kulturkamp were primarily determined by Bismarck's wish to restrict the self-determination of the Catholics in their Church policies and thereby to obstruct as much as possible the efforts of Political Catholicism to bring its organized forces into action. Already in the acts of the First Reichstag Bismarck saw to it—with the aid of the National Liberals, and accordingly against the violent opposition of the young Center Party—that the new Reich Constitution did not contain the "Basic Rights" that had been en-

acted in the 1848 Reich Constitution. Thus Bismarck was able
to eliminate the articles which in the Prussian Constitution of
1850 had guaranteed the rights of the Catholic Church. The ill-
famed "May Laws" of 1873 and their implementation in the
Emergency Law of June 18, 1875 wiped out all remaining
guarantees of the Prussian Constitution of 1850 which had safeguarded the Catholic Church according to the principle of "a
free Church in a free State," a principle of the Prussian Constitution of 1850 which Bismarck had always regarded as a mere
"translation from French waste paper." [191] Bismarck also prevailed upon the Reichstag to prohibit in a new Reich Law of
July 4, 1872 all activities of the Jesuit Order, a measure originally planned for the Reich Constitution of 1848 but at that
time abandoned over the protest of the Catholic members of
the Frankfurt Assembly. On May 13, 1873 several additional
orders, such as the Redemptorists and Lazarists, were prohibited. With these fundamental constitutional changes Bismarck
fulfilled an old wish of the absolutistic bureaucracy of neo-
Prussian character, that of being allowed to exercise the Hegelian unlimited power of the State against the Church. This attitude is characterized by the fact that Bismarck entrusted the
task of drafting and codifying his entire Kulturkampf legislation exclusively to Hegelian jurists. Conspicuous among them
was Heinrich Friedberg, author of the German Penal Code and
Prussian Court Counsel, and his nephew Emil A. Friedberg,
who held the chair of Ecclesiastical Law in Leipzig. The latter
became the chief adviser of Adalbert Falk, an extreme Hegelian Prussian jurist whom Bismarck chose for the post of Prussian "Cult Minister" (Minister of Education and Ecclesiastical
Affairs) and who as such was to become the symbol of the
Kulturkampf in the years 1872 to 1879. This peculiar "professional minister" in the Cult Ministry always regarded it as
his foremost duty to "enforce against the Church the inalienable sovereign rights of the State upon which the Church had
encroached since Eichhorn" (that is, through the Constitution
of 1850) [192]

How firm was the allegiance of Bismarck himself to the
Hegelian principles of church law in his fundamental views on
the correct relationship between the Catholic Church and the
Prussian State can be gleaned from one of his last speeches in
the Prussian Diet, April 21, 1887: "By their whole character
the equality of both Churches in the Prussian State is impossible. They are totally incommensurate entities. Should one
wish complete equality, one would have to accord to the head
of the Catholic Church the identical rights given to the su-

preme head of the Evangelical Church. In other words, as long as the head of the Protestant Church disposes of a share amounting to a full third in our legislature and is in full and sole possession of the executive power, or explicitly, as long as the King of Prussia is the head of the Evangelical Church, it is impossible to speak of formal equality between the two Churches." Thus, fully ten years after the end of the Kulturkampf, Bismarck still held fast to his opinion. This proves more conclusively than many learned dissertations that back in 1871 the unconstitutional Kulturkampf was started because Bismarck thought he could succeed by way of the more and more repressive legislation of the period 1871 to 1878 and with the help of Prussianized Liberalism, to get rid of the ecclesiastical and political equal rights guaranteed to Catholicism by the Constitution of 1850. What Bismarck and his Prussianized "Libertarians" really meant by "liberty" for their political and philosophical opponents was expressed at the very beginning of the Kulturkampf by a clear-sighted prophet of things to come, the leader of the Center Party, Windthorst, in his outspoken Reichstag oration of May 14, 1872: "Gentlemen, I am quite aware of the fact that your notion of Liberty is totally different from that held in *North America*. Your understanding of Liberty consists of according the State all sorts of rights, then making every effort to take hold of the State power and finally crushing by this State power those who hold different views. This is your notion of Liberty!" And almost at the same time, January 16, 1873, the leader of the Center in the Prussian Diet, P. Reichensperger, interpreted for the Prussianized Liberals their idea of Liberty: "The principle of National Liberalism is this: Privileges for myself and my friends, none for the others. It is not a fight and a war I see here; all I see is the unilateral suppression of the interests of the Church which is helplessly exposed to a State that is possessed of all means of utmost violence!"

As to *Church and cultural policies,* the Kulturkampf quite evidently was designed to detach the Catholic Church in Germany from Rome and to enforce a "Gleichschaltung" of all Catholic schools and cultural institutions, as also of the training of the Catholic clergy, with the cultural policies of neo-Prussian Pan-Germanism. By means of the cultural measures mentioned above, Bismarck procured the "legal" basis for the entire rat's tail of repressive regulations and special laws against the Church which were enacted after the dissolution of the Catholic Division in the Prussian Cult Ministry in 1871, especially the notorious "Muzzle Act" with an article for the supervision of pronouncements from the pulpit.

An addition to the Reich Penal Code of 1871, the law providing for the expulsion of Catholic priests (1874), and the financial embargo clauses of the so-called "Bread Basket Law" of 1875—all these followed. Simultaneously, a number of special laws were enacted restricting the education and appointment of Catholic clerics, the influence of the Church on the school system and religious instruction, and especially the future activity of members of Catholic Orders in Catholic educational institutions. These measures, above all the "May Laws" of 1873 and 1875, the edict against the educational activities of Orders and the temporary jailing of numerous bishops and priests which Bismarck actually enforced during the Kulturkampf years, constituted an almost lethal threat to the ecclesiastical and cultural existence of the Catholic citizens. The orderly administration in the dioceses was disrupted, thousands of pastorates in the Prussian sees were vacant, the school activities in the educational institutions and the institutes of higher learning were paralyzed. All this painfully crippled for decades the progress, slow as it had been, toward a sound expansion of the cultural activities of Catholicism.

Bismarck also believed that it was possible to reach his main goal, of cutting loose the German Catholics from the Pope in Rome, with the help of a tiny group of "Old Catholics" who had renounced their allegiance to Rome because of their opposition to the "Vaticanum" of 1870. The entire Kulturkampf legislation and the whole widespread public propaganda activity of National Liberalism under the slogan "Los von Rom" was geared primarily to spreading this Old Catholic schism in all of German Catholicism. Treitschke's "Preussische Jahrbuecher" expressed these aims with full clarity in 1874: "The day draws near when our bishops will rue having turned the force of their opposition against the fatherland rather than against Rome. When this comes to pass it will be time to wipe the dust off the *Ems Punctuations* and to restore to our episcopate its independent national position for which it has now, with the connivance of the State, lost all affection." [193]

It was probably Bismarck's bitterest disappointment when he realized that *Febronian separatism,* as practised among the German episcopate under the last ecclesiastical Electors of unhappy memory, could not be renewed and that the idea of a "National Church" independent of Rome could not be spread among the German Catholics. The three leading personalities to whom German Catholicism is deeply indebted for their inspiration in the victorious defense against the Kulturkampf proved their constant loyalty to Rome duringe the entire struggle, although in pursuit of their own Church policies they had objected in 1869 to the planned definition of the dogma of papal infallibility. First and foremost, there is Bishop Ketteler who during the Vatican Council had led the opposition of the German bishops against the proclamation of the dogma. Secondly, there is August Reichensperger, leader of the Prussian Center, who also had declared himself against papal infallibility as inopportune; and finally Ludwig Windthorst who had taken the initiative in 1869 and had signed the Berlin laymen's petition against the proclamation. August Reichensperger later gave what is perhaps the most impressive expression of that spirit of inviolable loyalty to the Mother Church in Rome and of the unswerving security of the German Catholics in their religious and cultural policies against which the ominous designs of Bismarck and his Prussianized Liberals' Kulturkampf had to founder, when he pronounced these simple words, so characteristic of the spirit which moved the leaders of German Political Catholicism: "This above all is the foundation of our strength: the unity of all Catholics loyal to their faith, *ut omnes unum!*" [194]

4. *Political Realism and Social Give-and-Take* (1882-1918)

Even more than the era of the Kulturkampf itself, the period from 1878 to 1887 in which it was liquidated is characterized by steadily growing political Realism. This applies equally to developments in the camp of Political Liberalism under Bismarck's leadership and in that of Political Catholicism under Windthorst. This is made evident by the historical consequences of the Kulturkampf on the development of political ideologies. We shall therefore have to examine carefully what was the relationship between Liberalism and the political party representing it, and between Catholicism and its own political party in Bismarck's Reich between 1871 and 1887.

As it turned out in the course of ideological developments, the political doctrine and cultural ideology of National Liberalism was unable to justify itself against Political Catholicism represented by the Center Party, and therefore failed to assume leadership. Only for a brief transitory period did the syncretism of the absolutistic state doctrine of liberalistic neo-Prussianism and the Pan-German culture ideology of Prussianized Liberalism succeed in furnishing a usable instrument in the fight against the historical reality of German Catholicism. More and more, the realism of the Catholic political doctrine and the positive Christian-German culture ideal of Catholicism proved their mettle, precisely because the Center Party was forced in the ideological struggle with National Liberalism to face political realities and to seek concrete solutions.[195]

In this the ideological evolution of Political Catholicism ran entirely parallel with the prevailing trend of the era, while the general trend led the ideologies of National Liberalism as manifested in the Kulturkampf of 1871-1879 *ad absurdum*. For independently of the security attained in the ideological position of the Center Party, the advent of Leo XIII to the Pontificate (1878) wrought a decisive change in Rome's attitude toward political and social policies which made it easier for Political Catholicism in Germany to anchor and expand its victorious position that had proved its worth in the Kulturkampf. We may thus state that the manifest failure of National Liberal parliamentary representation, forced Bismarck to abandon the Kulturkampf, and that the Pontificate of Leo XIII with the change in Rome's Church policies greatly facilitated the liquidation of these controversies.

It was therefore by historical necessity that Bismarck's Reich eliminated anti-Church National Liberalism more and more from the political scene after 1878. Even more markedly after 1882, this neo-Prussian Liberalism and Pan-Germanism suffered a metamorphosis from an active political party into an academic, professorial doctrine propagated in Bismarckian and Wilhelminian Germany by a certain nationalistic press. In the Catholic camp, on the contrary, the victory of ideological realism brought the Center Party into ever closer touch with the social and political realities. This found its strongest expression in the *modus vivendi* between Bismarck and Rome, established first in 1882 through a Prussian legation at the Vatican and culminating in the Repeal Acts (1887) by which the Kulturkampf was finally liquidated. Those who would see in these acts and in the parliamentary backing which Bismarck received after 1878 by the Center nothing more than an "opportunistic manoeuvre" of the Center in response to the "tactical concession" of Bismarck would fundamentally misinterpret the significant ideological consequences of the Kulturkampf. Future developments in the party policies both of the National Liberals and the Center lend additional stress to this interpretation.

These consequences of the Kulturkampf for party politics are of special importance in studying the sociology of German party life. We learn how much the sociological structure of every political party in a pluralistic parliamentary state depends on the ideals and ideologies which carry the party programs. We also see that the very existence of a party in such a system

depends on whether its political program is backed by a fundamental idea or only by an ephemeral ideology. The fate of the
National Liberal Party, especially between 1871 and 1884,
proves that their program expressed no genuine political idea
and that the ideology they defended did not correspond to any
deeper intellectual conviction, either on the part of the broad
strata of the people or of a significant group in society. The
Party's impressive rise as the strongest governmental party in
1874, with 155 mandates in the Reichstag and 182 in Prussia,
was due merely to the Party's function as an instrument of the
short-lived political opportunity for bourgeois nationalism
which 1870 had made possible. However, National Liberalism had to fail, ideologically and materially, as soon as it was
confronted with the more basic ideas that came to the fore
during the Kulturkampf and with the political realities of Bismarck's relations with the entire nation. This situation emerged
very soon: the voters withdrew their allegiance from the National Liberals, and the "Realpolitiker" (realistic politician),
Bismarck tossed them aside like a tool that had outlived its usefulness. By 1877 their party following was reduced to 128 in
the Reichstag, and in 1878 there was a further decline to 99,
continued in 1881 down to 47 mandates. From then on until
1918 the Party hovered around a modest average of 45 to 50
mandates. The descent in the Prussian Diet was even more
formidable: of the 182 seats during 1873-1876, only 65 remained from 1881 to 1884 and in the following electoral periods
until 1918 only about 40. This protracted flight of the electorate was accompanied by a progressive disintegration of the National Liberal party program which now reflected only special
political and economic interests in a motley variety of groupings assembled haphazardly in that *complexio oppositorum,*
German Political Liberalism. Thus, in the historical test of the
Kulturkampf, National Liberalism was found wanting in that
main characteristic of a genuine political party—to give expression and representation to genuine political ideas.

In contrast, the Center Party proved its worth as a true political party representative of a spiritual ideal. Securely founded
on the unchangeable ideals of the Christian political and social
doctrine, it could work toward the realization of the concrete
political and cultural tasks. As an outward sign of this stead-
fastness of purpose we find a remarkable constancy in its electoral support which, between 1874 and 1933, always sent an
average of 90 to 100 representatives to the Reichstag and the
Prussian Diet.[196] Within the total organizational and political activities of German Catholicism the Kulturkampf had

only expressed one aspect, that of Church politics. But precisely because these controversies were fought out in the field of formal "party politics" and parliamentary actions, their ideological significance for a deeper understanding of the sociology of the Center Party is great, and that under a twofold aspect.

There is first the fact that by its character as a political party the Center was enabled to carry on this struggle within the pluralistic parliamentary system of Bismarck's Reich. The existence of the Center Party and the freedom of political movement it enjoyed were possible only on the basis of the ideals of true liberalism which had established the liberty of political association and the parliamentary representation of ideas. Therefore, the Center Party found in the ideals of political freedom fostered by genuine liberalism powerful allies in its defense against the political encroachments of Prussianized Liberalism that had been attempted during the Kulturkampf. This struggle could be won only on condition that Political Catholicism, as represented by the Center Party, was basically in conformity with the fundamental ideas of democratic-liberal freedom in political and cultural life and, above all, the idea of "a free Church in a free State". Even before the Kulturkampf, these preconditions for a healthy activity of the Center had been realized by the emergence of Realism in Political Catholicism which we have described. Without these preconditions, that is, without the acceptance on principle of the liberal achievements in establishing a free relationship between Church and State on the one hand, and of the free action of political parties and parliamentary representation on the other, the successful fight in the Kulturkampf would not have been possible. And naturally the same applies to the strong influence the Center Party exerted in the German parliaments after the Kulturkampf. With a perfectly good conscience on the force of its principle of Realism, and therefore successfully, the Center Party was entitled to use the freedoms achieved by genuine Liberalism.

After the Kulturkampf the Center Party had the great good fortune of winning supreme official endorsement for the position it had first assumed entirely on its own responsibility—namely the position of accepting the true liberal doctrines on the essence of the state—through the very first encyclicals of Leo XIII, primarily the *Diuturnum Illud* of 1881. Concerning the parliamentary system, the Pope declared: "In certain cases the statesmen may be selected by the will and judgment of the people, without contravention or contradiction of the Catholic doctrine. There is no reason whatsoever why the Church should not give its assent to the rule either of the One or of the Many, provided only that such rule is just and takes the common welfare to heart. If justice is preserved, the people are entirely free to choose the form of State best suited to their character, or more closely in line with the institutions and habits of their ancestors" [197]. Backed by this ideological apology of parliamentary activities implied in Political Catholicism, the *Center Party* emerged from the Kulturkampf doubly braced for the following period, as the true *Party of Political Realism and Social Equity*. Under the determinedly realistic leadership of Windthorst (1872-1891), Lieber (1891-1902), Hertling (1902-1912), Spahn (1912-1917) and Groeber (1917-1919), the Party was able to play this role so successfully in the entire period from 1882 to 1918 only because its unique social structure guaranteed the permanence of its electorate and the continuity of its programs was assured by its ideas of political and social reform. Which leads us to the second aspect of the political consequences of the Kulturkampf, deeply significant for a sociological understanding of German Political Catholiscism. The electorate of the Center Party had its roots in the entire social structure of German Catholicism. At no time, not at its founding, nor during the Kulturkampf, nor in the period 1882-1918, nor during its most glorious era in the Weimar Republic, did the Center Party represent special political or social interests[198]. The historical evolution of modern German Catholicism in its peculiar shape has had the result that Political Catholicism, as crystallized in the forms of the Center Party, took a totally different course from that of all German political parties. All the others either had their origin in the specific conditions of the German past, as for instance the liberal and conservative parties, or in the defense of special social interests of distinctive strata, as the movement of the German Social Democrats for the interests of the workers.

Since, however, the vast majority of the German Catholics, as a tragic heritage from the ecclesiastical states of the 18th century, had no indigenous political and governmental traditions and were therefore forced by the secularization to reorient themselves according to the new, predominantly non-Catholic realities in state and society, German Catholics from the very beginning had to discover paths entirely of their own which finally led them toward maturity in the specifically German forms of Political and Social Catholicism. Expressed in terms of sociology this means that the basic structure in which Political Catholicism was to develop was not founded on autonomous social levels of a *vertical* order, well defined against one another—such as, of workers and peasants; of the bourgeoisie, the bureaucracy, the aristocracy and the agrarians; or of commerce and industry. On the contrary, Political Catholicism replaced the variety of vertical levels in the social structure by a *horizontal* plane that ran across all these social distinctions by means of a homogeneous, ideational unity, a common expression of what is usually referred to as the philosophical unity of the Catholic vital attitude (Lebensgefuehl), practically expressed in the realms of moral and social life.

This autonomous political and social "particularism" of German Catholicism was originally born of the tragic historical fact of political particularism and confessional cleavages in the Old Reich ever since the Reformation. This also determined the early, horizontally stratified shape of Political Catholicism. The evolution of 1848 to 1866 promoted with increasing emphasis a progressive organic readjustment of German Catholicism to conform with the realities of German life as a whole. But the particularistic ascendancy of Prussia toward hegemony and the anti-Catholic excesses during the Kulturkampf put a decisive stop to this process of assimilation, at least in the sentiments and attitudes of German Catholicism. In the same measure as the marked anti-Catholic confessionalism of the National Liberals and the materialistic disintegration of positive Christianity came to prevail, the political unity of Catholicism founded on its philosophy grew all the closer, above all in the organization of the Center Party. This political unity was further enhanced by the strong conformity in the sentiments and feelings of social responsibility in Catholics, as manifested in the movement of Social Catholicism. We may safely say that *in this close mutual interaction of Political and Social Catholicism lies the secret of the Center's political permanency and also of its special characteristic function of being the party of political and social "give-and-take."* In the 1880's this development received its theoretical formulation in the original political and social doctrines of German Catholicism. Since the equalizing of social interests between the propertied and the property-less demanded, or even presupposed, an equalization of the political interests as between the strong and the weak, between the leaders and the lead, it was only logical for the Center Party to be a true *party of the middle.*

The Center thus stood for the principle of social equalization and political mediation in the sense of seeking vitally necessary compromises within the party itself and accordingly between the social and political realities of German Catholicism. By this very fact the Party was predestined for the role of the arbitrator and mediator within the entire social and political reality of German life after the Kulturkampf. Ever since 1878 the Center Party was called upon again and again to play its game as a party of the middle within the parliamentary constellations, in the Reichstag in the period 1878 to 1918, and most of all in the government policies of the Weimar Republic. The traditional strictures concerning the "lack of principles" and the mere confessional "opportunism" in party politics allegedly practiced by the Center thus appear to be born from a thorough misunderstanding of these historically determined German party developments.

In this manner the Center Party made its positive contributions to the Reich legislation from 1878 to 1918 in a realistic conception of its duties and responsibilities. The most important contributions were: protective legislation for the workers and social insurance schemes under the leadership of Franz Hitze; protective trade legislation and fiscal policies attempting to establish an equitable balance between the interests of industry and agriculture. In the protection of minorities the Center always stood for the interests of the Poles and the people of Alsace-Lorraine; in the realm of military and colonial policies its always took a critical position, positive on principle, but always trying to limit militarism and imperialism—which frequently eliminated the Center from parliamentary influence (thus in the cartel era, 1887-1890, and at the time of the Buelow bloc, 1906-1909). A detailed account of Center politics is given in the great work by Karl Bachem[199]. The pursuit of these "politics of the middle" frequently aroused violent tensions within the Party itself, as for instance when a common ground had to be sought with the markedly democratic leanings of the non-Prussian Center (Land Party of Hessen since 1884, of Baden since 1888, Wuerttemberg since 1894), or in the struggle to uphold the confessional character of the Party, but above all in the sometimes strained relationship of the party with the Catholic workers' associations and the Christian Trade Unions. These tensions came particularly to the fore in the vehement "struggle of orientation" (Richtungsstreit) between the confessionalist-integralist sector Trier-Berlin-Breslau and the non-confessional, realistic sector Koeln-Muenchen-Gladbach, which ended with the latter's victory[200]. With the "Peace Resolution" proposed by Matthias Erzberger to the Reichstag on July 19, 1917[201] we stand at the beginning of the Center's fully responsible participation in the over-all Reich policies, including foreign relations. It led in October 1917 to the appointment of the Center leader and Bavarian Prime Minister Georg von Hertling (1843-1919) to be the Imperial "Chancellor of the

German Reich". This appointment of the Southern German Catholic Hertling as Chancellor and of Friedrich von Payer (1848-1913), a Wuerttemberg Democrat, as Vice-Chancellor, in fact amounted to a declaration of bankruptcy of the Wilhelminian Reich.

5. Constructing a Democracy (1918-1929)

When in October 1917 Count Hertling was appointed to the posts of Reich Chancellor and Prussian Prime Minister this had fundamental significance for two reasons. First, entrusting to the Prime Minister of the largest Southern German State the duties of Reich government denoted the end of the Prussian hegemony. And secondly, it was the first time since the founding of the Reich that a prominent leader of Political Catholicism sat in Bismarck's chair. Yet, Hertling's cabinet was no more than an inadequate compromise solution, born of the ineluctable necessity of the historical moment, but satisfactory neither to the monarchical opponents of a parliamentary constitution nor to the democratic majority in the Center Party. The appointments of Payer, the leader of the Wuerttemberg Democrats, to the post of Vice-Chancellor and of Trimborn, leader of the Westphalian Centrists and a realistic social reformer, to that of State Secretary were indeed made to achieve a quasi-parliamentarian representation in the cabinet. On the other hand, Hertling himself with his pronounced conservative, *anti-parliamentarian*, Southern German mentality was by no means representative of the majority opinion in the Center. Therefore he had to resign in October 1918 when it became obvious that a genuine parliamentary system of government had to be built up. Only Hertling's successor, the "red" Prince Max of Baden with his "Parliamentary War Cabinet" was capable of tackling this task without a previous alteration of the Reich Constitution. In this last "Imperial" cabinet all the parties that constituted the Reichstag majority were represented as prescribed by the Reich Act of October 28, 1918 concerning the Parliamentary Responsibility of the Government. The Democrats delegated von Payer and Conrad Hausmann, the Center Party the State Secretaries A. Groeber, M. Erzberger, C. Trimborn and J. Giesberts, and the Social Democrats the State Secretaries Ph. Scheidemann, G. Bauer, E. David, R. Schmidt and A. Mueller. Thus even before the outbreak of the revolution a constitutional coalition cabinet of the three parties existed on whose *sense of responsibility and spirit of cooperation* the origins and progress of the Weimar Republic were principally to depend, as—tragically—also its downfall: Center, Social Democrats and Democrats.

The character of the Weimar Republic was primarily determined by the positive, realistic political actions of these three parties and by the statesmanlike abilities of their foremost representatives. We can therefore size up the total achievement of Weimar parliamentarism and the special contributions made by each party in no other way than by showing how, according to the dialectical principle, political Realism came to dominate these parties and how they came to cooperate with one another in a common effort to realize those principles they all believed in—political democracy and social freedom. Specifically, if we wish to form a just opinion of the achievements of the Center Party, we shall have to keep the facts of this interdependence in mind. We shall have to examine how much the Center Party in its actions in political and social affairs was forced to yield to the position taken toward these matters by the other parties, primarily to the largest party in the Weimar Coalition, the Social Democrats, and conversely, how great was the dependence of the Social Democrats on the position taken by the Center Party.

The Democrats in this respect had a peculiar role of their own. Their philosophical neutrality, dictated by their genuinely liberal principles of respect for the spiritual and social convictions of others, always prevented serious conflicts with the ideals professed by the Center or the Social Democrats as responsible government parties. The Democrats' potent intellectual tradition which spanned the life work of Friedrich Naumann (1860-1919) and Martin Rade (1857-1935), of Conrad Haussmann (1857-1922) and Friedrich von Payer (1847-1931, of Hugo Preuss (1860-1925) and their successors, Hermann Dietrich (1879-   ), Gustav Stolper (1888-1947) and Theodor Heuss (1884-   ), has made such an essential contribution especially to the constitutional framework of the Weimar Republic that they furnished the indispensable connecting link between Center and Social Democrats. Unfortunately, the limited size of their electorate, recruited mostly from the bourgeoisie, never provided the Democrats with sufficient influence in the brisk interplay of power politics as practised between the two larger parties of the coalition, although the Democrats would have merited such influence by the force of their principles and the outstanding political qualities of their leaders[202].

As it befits the history of its origins, the *Social Democratic Party* was the strongest German mass party, and up till the outbreak of the First World War it stood in determined opposition against the realities of the Wilhelminian Reich. During the First World War the party underwent a slow modification of its theoretically revolutionary party program and of its opposition to any government as a matter of principle—a change inaugurated first by the assent the Social Democrats gave to the war credits in 1914 and by their acceptance of the "Burgfrieden" (truce within a beleaguered fortress). At the end of the war this changed attitude enabled them to let their representatives sit in the last Imperial cabinet of Prince Max von Baden. In 1918 this metamorphosis of the Social Democrats from a theoretically intransigent Marxist opposition party into a parliamentary, governmental Socialist Party proved the strongest agent in overcoming the total revolutionary breakdown and in erecting the edifice of the Weimar Republic. This change also produced some negative features which soon came to light in the opposition of the radical left wing of the Party. This led in 1917 to a secession movement and the founding of two new organizations, the Independent Social Democratic Party (USPD) and the "Spartacus League", soon to be transformed into the German Communist Party (KPD, 1918). The consequence for the Social Democratic Party (SPD) was that from the beginning to the end of the Republic it had to fight on two fronts. It was forced to deploy its forces against the opposition wielded by the revolutionary socialists of the KPD; but all its powers were equally needed for the working out of the moderate, "revisionist" program that would offer socialistic policies in political and social matters within the realistic framework of the Weimar Republic, in practical collaboration with the other democratic "people's" parties of the Weimar Coalition, especially with the Catholic mass party of the Center. In these endeavors the Social Democrats relied primarily on the theories worked out by Georg von Vollmar (1859-1922), Eduard Bernstein (1850-1932) and Karl Kautsky (1854-1938). In the practical politics of the SPD these "revisionists" fulfilled approximately the same educational function, that of making an autonomous, typically German, anti-revolutionary, democratic socialism possible, as the orientation of political Realism did with different connotations in the Center Party. Possibly this parallelism was the main reason for the phenomenon that, ever since the first try-out in the cabinet of Prince Max von Baden, the leading realistic politicians of both the Center and the SPD, despite all their differences in principles and in the philosophical and ideological foundations of their respective party programs, always managed to find a common ground on which to work for democratic improvements in the edifice of the Weimar Republic[203].

We shall here briefly register the names of the leading Social Democratic and Center politicians of the Weimar Republic, because the personal histories and the special characteristics and achievements of each of them form the integral content of the totality of the Weimar Republic, in respect to socio-biography, ideology and governmental and social policies. Among the Social Democrats we have the first Reich President, Friedrich Ebert (1871-1925), the Reich Chancellors of the Weimar Coalition Philipp Scheidemann, Gustav Bauer and Hermann Mueller; Otto Braun, for many years Prussian Prime Minister; and among the many ministers active in the Prussian Governments or in the Reich Cabinets between 1919 and 1932, Karl Severing, Gustav Noske, Rudolf Hilferding, Eduard David, Gustav Radbruch, Adolf Koester, Robert Schmidt, Rudolf Wissel. Among the leading Center figures there were the President of the National Assembly and Reich Chancellor Constantin Fehrenbach (1852-1926), the Reich Chancellors Wilhelm Marx (1863-1946) and Joseph Wirth (1879-) and the ministers and state secretaries Matthias Erzberger (1875-1921), Adam Stegerwald (1874-1947), Heinrich Brauns (1868-1939), Adolf Groeber (1854-1919), Carl Trimborn (1854-1921), Heinrich Hiertsiefer and Johann Giesberts.

These men despite their widely differing origins, education and political ideals, were able to meet in a spirit of mutual give-and-take, and worked together understandingly and responsibly to tide over the broken-down Reich during the armistice and peace negotiations and the deliberations of the National Assembly until the Republic was well launched in its democratic framework. Since in the Appendix we print in extenso the report of Heinrich Brauns on the activities of the Center Party during the Weimar Republic until 1929[204], we shall devote the limited space left us to an account of the last phase of the Center's activities until the end in 1933, under the leadership of Prelate Ludwig Kaas and the chancellorship of Heinrich Bruening.

6. Toward the Catastrophe (1929-1933)

At the party conference held in Cologne in December 1928, the Center Party elected Prelate Ludwig Kaas (born 1881, died 1952 in Rome) its chairman. This Cathedral Capitular from Trier, who was a Member of the Reichstag since 1919, owed his election less to his special qualities of leadership, than to the influence of the clerical circles who exerted strong oppositional pressure against the real candidate, Adam Steger-wald, for many years the able and successful leader of the Christian Trade Unions, against whom they also put up a counter-candidate in the Unions, Joseph Joos, leader of the Catholic Workers Associations. With the election of Kaas, the first cleric to head the Center Party, the trend of a realistic, inter-confessional Center policy on a broad front of state and party politics, as represented by Stegerwald, was definitely de-feated. Consequently, the Center from now on was less prepared to follow a practical policy in close collaboration with the Socialist mass party, and thus the only guarantee for the perpet-uation of the parliamentary system of the "Weimar Coalition" was lost. Kaas quickly proved that he was not the man to carry on this role of cooperation. By June 1928 he brought to bear his influence as the chairman of the parliamentary Center rep-resentation to exclude the Reich Labor Minister Brauns from the new cabinet of the Social Democratic Reich Chancellor Hermann Mueller, thus interrupting the continuity in social policies so ably built up by Brauns ever since 1920. When later, in March 1930, the last cabinet of the Great Coalition or, for that matter, the last strictly parliamentary cabinet of the Re-public, once more under the chancellorship of Hermann Mueller, had to resign over differences between the Center and the Social Democrats concerning the unemployment insurance, this breach between the two parties would surely have been avoided if these problems had still been administered by the capable hands of Brauns who ever since 1920 had time and again smoothed out such differences in social policies. Kaas, however, from 1929 onward did not seem to miss such media-tion with the Left; he seemed on the contrary to work con-sciously toward a clear-cut coalition with the Right. This was flaunted before the public by the provocative negotiations into which Kaas entered in Kissingen with the German Nationalist leader Hermann Hugenberg, and by the latter's letter (Nov. 20, 1929) to Kaas calculated to offend the Social Democrats.

This peculiar political prelate, inexperienced in the practice of leading a large political or social organization, who also had never administered a responsible public office, committed the unforgiveable error from the beginning of his disastrous politi-cal career of transferring indiscriminately the practise of in-ternal party intrigue and compromise in which he was well versed to the vastly more complicated field of the inter-party game of the Weimar Republic in the critical years 1929-1933. But he committed a second, even more ominous mistake. In making the customary tactical and exploratory moves in the interplay of party intrigues and combinations in and out of the Parliament, he was never capable of understanding that meanwhile an entirely new situation had arisen which required new methods of dealing with political pressure. This new situation followed from the ascendancy of the Communists and National Socialists and their totalitarian party organizations which were backed by the armed forces of their respective political fighting troops (Wehrverbaende), namely Hitler's SA and the Communist Red Front, as well as the nationalistic armed organizations of the Kyffhaeuserbund and the Stahlhelm. In the face of this new kind of pressure group, the traditional methods of political and parliamentary "pork-barrel" dealing and compromising were bound to fail. Kaas never gave a serious thought to this revolutionary change in the social structure of the political life in the Weimar Republic after 1928, and did not notice that in consequence of this change the constitutional basis of the Weimar party state was becoming narrower and narrower, most of all for the Social Democrats and the Center. Not even in the days when the National Socialists actually seized all power did he ponder these facts. Instead he proceeded with utterly naive confidence to "negotiate" with the "party leader" and "Reich Chancellor" Hitler and exposed his ineptitude in the disgraceful speech with which he declared his party's assent to Hitler's Enabling Act (Ermächtigungs-Gesetz) of March 23, 1933 before the forum of the last Weimar Reichstag. History has long decided that this political dilettante, a prelate relying on obsolete political tactics in these supremely fateful years which demanded of the Center Party the most crucial political decisions, was anything but a political leader, or rather, was a contributor to the catastrophe of 1933 which he helped to bring about. The naive game of politics as played by the responsible top leader of the Center necessarily also involved the political plans of Reich Chancellor Bruening in disaster.

We have to view the failure of Bruening's plans during his Chancellorship, March 1930 to May 1932, under these points of view. This was the decisive phase in the trend of disintegration of the entire constitutional foundation of the Weimar Republic; and accordingly the parliamentary climate in which alone political parties loyal to the constitution of a democratic people's state could be expected to function was thoroughly poisoned. *Bruening's indisputable merits as a Catholic statesman* are not to be found in his domestic activities as a Reich Chancellor, but rather, between 1920 and 1930, in his work as Executive Secretary of the League of German Trade Unions, in the Christian labor movement, and also, between 1924 and 1930, as the exponent of the Center Reichstag representation in social and fiscal affairs. Special tribute must be paid to his efforts to restore good will among nations, primarily in his successful struggle for Germany's rehabilitation to equality of status and for the wiping out of the last remnants of the ruinous Versailles reparations payments—a success painlessly harvested, immediately after Bruening's downfall at the Lausanne Conference which he had so painstakingly prepared, by Bruening's successor, the Catholic Ephialtes Franz von Papen. And tribute must also be paid to the seriousness and devotion with which Bruening throughout his Chancellorship fought for unpopular measures of fiscal reforms and taxation to save the Reich finances, struggles in which he set a fine example of a politician loyally serving an entire nation by his responsible actions.[205]

As against these merits we must, however, keep on record *Bruening's tragic failure in the field of constitutional policies,* caused by his fateful misunderstanding, which he shared with Kaas,[206] of the real political forces in the country. Bruening was surely influenced by motives other than those of the clerical party-tactician Kaas when he embarked on his dangerous attempt to govern by "emergency decrees" of his "President's Cabinet", in total incomprehension of the real conditions under which the Center Party had to plan its party policies and of the ineluctable necessity of activating the political momentum of the Social Democratic mass party and the German labor force organized in the "Free Trade Unions." His mistakes were primarily caused by the admixture of a basically conservative attitude into the traditions of political and social Realism of the Muenchen-Gladbach orientation, a mixture which in Bruening produced an entirely new type in German public affairs, that of the "Social-conservative Catholic politician". Perhaps, in an era in which the autonomous life of each party had been secure and their different traditions had been respected, this new type of a "social-conservative" as represented by Bruening might have been destined to bring forth a new concept of Political Catholicism. It cannot be doubted that the common crisis of traditional party configurations called for such new formations, for we see similar types of politicians emerge within the other parties, primarily in a circle of friends closely allied to Bruening, the so-called "Popular Conservatives", such as Treviranus, Huelser, Lindeiner-Wildau, Schlange-Schoeningen, Lambach. But at a time when, for reasons analyzed above, the traditional parties were involved in a struggle for sheer survival against the novel totalitarian party formations

and fighting associations, Bruening must be held responsible
for granting much too large an influence on the policies of his
"President's Cabinet" to these experimental "popular conservatives", thereby dangerously undermining the constitutional
foundations of party politics and the unity in the Weimar Party
State. Through these manoeuvers of 1930 to 1932 he made
a renewal of the concentration of forces in a "Great Coalition"
impossible, which would have been the only way to stop the
growing conspiracy against the very existence of the Weimar
Party State. Thus the totalitarian parties found encouragement
and the National Socialists especially were put in a position to
form in October 1931, in the so-called "Harzburg Front", the
final coalition with the German Nationalist Party and the anti-
democratic fighting associations.

Bruening very aptly characterized, in his Reichstag speech
of April 3, 1930 at the beginning of his Chancellorship, the
crisis of the party groupment and of the parliamentary form of
government and, perhaps rightly, pointed to the possibility that
he might have to make careful use of Article 48 of the Constitution which allowed government by decree in an emergency.
But already in this speech which had sharp polemical barbs
against the Social Democrats, Bruening rhetorically deduced
from this right to resort to Article 48 in an emergency the fateful theory that this Article gave him and his "President's Cabinet"—thus actually quasi-independent of parliament—the right
of using this Article at will. He declared, "One thing is needed:
not the parties, only the Cabinet must be in the lead." And
from now on Bruening in his policy of emergency decrees was
permanently guided by this principle and abandoned every
serious attempt to limit this dangerous practice by regaining a
parliamentary basis for his "President's Cabinet". On the contrary, in October 1931 he gave his second Cabinet an additional
orientation toward the Right by releasing Joseph Wirth, taking
into the Cabinet the German Nationalist apostate Schlange-
Schoeningen and the reactionary business representative Warm-
bold, and putting the Reich Defense Minister General Groener
in charge of the Ministry of Internal Affairs, thus making a return to the Weimar Coalition *definitely impossible*. With these
practices Bruening had, without ever quite realizing it, created
the pattern of an almost dictatorial rule under the merely nominal responsibility and consent of "Old Man Reich President"
von Hindenburg, a pattern soon to be imitated and perfected
by the final gravediggers of the Republic, Bruening's successors
in the "President's Cabinets", von Papen and Schleicher. Bruening also failed to foresee that the enemies of the Republic

would necessarily regard the changes he made in his Cabinet and the implied insult to the Weimar Coalition parties as a decisive signal for action. Not even the general attack now organized against the Republic in the "Harzburg Front", the open alliance between Hitler, Hugenberg, Schacht and the representative of the Fighting Associations, Franz Seldte, caused Bruening to seek a last minute *rapproachement* with the Social Democrats and Free Labor Unions as the only thinkable defense move. And he felt equally undisturbed by the machinations of his military "well-wisher", General Schleicher, one of whose intrigues at last brought about Bruening's downfall on May 30, 1932.

The outstanding responsibility of Kaas for Bruening's failure in internal affairs, here briefly outlined, must be clear to all, though the details cannot be closely observed because neither Kaas nor Bruening have as yet felt moved to render a public account of their actions, and still less an accounting for their failures. The fact that both Bruening and Kaas opened formal negotiations with the Harzburg Front and with its chief, Hitler, that the latter even continued such negotiations after the dismissal of the former right up to 1933, and the Center's affirmative vote for Hitler's Enabling Act—all these moves give a completely unambiguous picture of the psychology of the responsible leaders of the Weimar majority parties, especially of the Center Party, in this era of the German's Republic's suicide, their *complete blindness to the sociological changes in the political party structure.*

It cannot be denied that the Center Party by its vote for the Enabling Act carries before history the main burden of responsibility for having robbed the German people of their rights in a formal act of legislation, and thus for having delivered it "legally" over to the Hitler terror. And it is a bad blot on the great traditions of Catholicism that through this vote the responsible Center politicians themselves have given the death sentence to Political Catholicism in Germany. On top of everything else, it fell to Bruening's lot to execute this sentence —when by the end of March Kaas had exchanged the uncertain fates of German Catholicism for the safe seclusion of the Vatican. In Kaas's stead, Bruening had to assume the once honorable office of leader of the dying Center Party for the one function of proclaiming on July 15, 1933, at Hitler's bidding, the "self-dissolution" of the once powerful organization of Political Catholicism in Germany— *De mortuis nil nisi bene!*

5. Political Conservatism (1848-1938)

1. The Peoples Party in Bavaria, (BVP)

Conservatism as propounded by the Goerres Circle did not retain substantial influence after 1848, except on developments in Bavaria and Austria. In the Southern German countries Wuerttemberg and Baden, Catholicism took a distinct turn toward democracy and contributed much political strength to the realistic wing of the Center Party in the Reichstag. The Baden Center Party, founded in 1888, had in its leadership markedly democratic personalities, such as Theodor Wacker (1854-1921), Joseph Schofer (1866-1930), Constantin Fehrenbach, President of the Weimar National Assembly and Reich Chancellor, and Joseph Wirth, Reich Chancellor. From the Wuerttemberg Center Party, founded in 1894, several outstanding political figures emerged,—Adolf Groeber, Matthias Erzberger and State President Eugen Bolz, who was to be murdered by the Nazis. On the contrary, from the Bavarian Center Party, founded 1887, came only conservative politicians whose place was at the extreme Right of Political Catholicism,—Georg von Hertling, Georg Heim (1865-1934), Johann Leicht (1868-1936), Heinrich Held (1868-1938) and Hugo von Lerchenfeld (1871-1944).

Bavarian Political Catholicism always remained loyal to the political and social traditions of the Goerres Circle. After Goerres' death (1848) and the resignation of the Political Romantics, G. Phillips and E. J. Jarcke, from the editorial board of the "Historisch Politische Blaetter" (1851), even the Romantic Conservatives of the Goerres Circle moved somewhat closer to a recognition of the political and social problems of the day. However, this changed emphasis remained securely within the framework of conservative ideologies, with their special concern for the ideas of a Catholic monarchy and a corporative order of society. The attitude of Edmund Joerg (1819-1901), a disciple of Doellinger's, is typical. He was editor of the Historisch Politische Blaetter from 1851 to 1901, and exerted a strong influence on the evolution of Political Catholicism in Bavaria and some in Austria. The history of the political ideas of the Bavarian Center and the ideological motivations of their practical policies, as well as of those of its successor party, the Bavarian Peoples Party (Bayerische Volkspartei BVP), can therefore best be studied in the yearly volumes of this magazine up to the year 1923. Other men who have influenced the development of Conservative Political Catholicism are: Franz Xaver Kiefl, Cathedral Deacon of Regensburg (1869-1928),and above all Albert Maria

Weiss, an Upper Bavarian Dominican (1844-1925), who from his residences in Vienna and Freiburg (Switzerland) published his extremely conservative social ideas, especially in his widely known book "Soziale Frage und Soziale Ordnung" (1892). We can briefly characterize the ideological orientation of these men as reactionary in politics, conservative in social matters, markedly "Grossdeutch" (Greater German), anti-Protestant and anti-Prussian, favoring a loose federation of autonomous states within a Greater German Reich under Catholic leadership. In respect to philosophy, their emphasis was on religious integralism and clericalism in Church policies, rejecting on principle the separation of church and state and demanding a strictly "Christian State", and even a "Christian economy".

In reviewing the concrete political variations and motives of party politics, as determined between 1848 and 1934 by the special conditions and various phases in political developments, we recognize that, with some revisions, the ideas of Weiss and Joerg formed the program of Conservative Political Catholicism. As source material we have specifically the numerous articles by Joerg and his famous "Zeitlaeufe" (chronicle of the times) which he published for fifty years in the Historisch Politische Blaetter as well as his two major works "Geschichte des Protestantismus in seiner neuesten Entwicklung" (1858) and "Geschichte der sozialpolitischen Parteien in Deutschland" (1867). In many respects Joerg's ideas impress as quite "modern" and of wide scope if compared with certain party ideologies prominent in the BVP and the Christian Socialist Party in Austria. Joerg's ideologies also seem superior to those of Max Buchner in his "Gelbe Hefte", published since 1924 as successor to the Historisch Politische Blaetter which exerted strong influence on the reactionary, monarchistic wing of the BVP.

The Bavarian Center Party which emerged from the "Partei der Patrioten" founded in 1868, was active in the Reichstag until 1919 in the framework of the Reich Center Party, and in Bavaria as a separate Land Party. With its special devotion to the Catholic dynasty and the bourgeois-peasant composition of its electorate tied to the ideological traditions described above, this party always retained the character of a decidedly monarchistic, clerical, authoritarian group. When in 1919 the Republic was founded, this attitude quite naturally led to a secession of the Bavarians from the Reich Center Party and the founding of the "Bavarian Peoples Party" [207] under Georg Heim and Sebastian Schlittenhuber, who in 1922 formulated the Party's "Bamberg Program". As to Reich politics, they rejected centralism in favor of a strong local particularism and never entirely subscribed to the principles of the Weimar Constitution. This appeared most clearly in the BVP's intransigent cultural poli-- cies which never adopted the separation of church and state as stipulated in the Reich Constitution and therefore bargained for privileges for the Catholic Church in a separate concordat with Rome (1924-25) which made Catholicism the state religion. Another consequence was the rejection in every form of cooper- ation with the Social Democrats who, despite their large elector- ate, remained excluded from the Bavarian government after 1920. The BVP, with a constant group of about twenty Reichs- tag members, always backed the Center Party in the Reichstag without regard to internal differences and this kept the numer- ical strength of Political Catholicism in the Weimar Reichstag at about the same level as under the Monarchy. Normally the BVP had one minister of its own in the Reich Cabinets, usually the Reich Postmaster. Among the leading figures of the BVP we name Prelate Johann Leicht, for many years leader of the Reichstag group, Hugo von Lerchenfeld, Bavarian Prime Minister (1921-22), German Minister in Vienna (1926-1931) and in Brussels (1931-1933), and Heinrich Held, Bavarian Prime Minister (1924-1933).

Although the BVP had always stressed that its aim was to de- fend without compromise the autonomous Bavarian State and all special "Bavarian interests" against the centralism and "socialism" of the Weimar Republic, they followed the sad example given by Prelate Kaas in the Center in voting for Hitler's Enabling Act in 1933. And the Bavarians also imitated the Center Party in voting "voluntarily" for its "self-dissolu- tion" on July 4, 1933, thus dispatching the traditional "Bavar- ian Lion" into the desert without making any attempt at resistance.

2. The Christian Socialists in Austria

The beginnings of party groupings of the Austrian Conserva- tives reach back to the "Kremsier Reichstag" of 1848 and the "Amplified Reichstag" of 1860. On principle the Romantic program of an authoritarian, corporative order for state and so- ciety as formulated in these early days remained the real program of political clericalism in Austria to the very downfall of Dollfuss's "corporative State" in 1938. The program was for "a Christian Monarchy with an Emperor by the Grace of God at its helm; respect for spiritual and temporal authority; the proper stratification of society; respect for tradition, for estab- lished privileges, for nationality and property." [208] In 1887, the groups of predominantly bourgeois character and German nationality seceded from the wing of feudal aristocrats and higher Church dignitaries to found the "Christian Social Party" which from 1888 to 1907 developed its definite shape under the leadership of the widely known Vienna Mayor, Dr. Karl Lueger (1844-1910). The Party's intellectual fathers were primarily Karl von Vogelsang and Franz Martin Schindler (1847-1922) who were followed after the First World War by Othmar Spann (1878-   ) and Ignaz Seipel (1876-1932). The various stages and shapes of the policies in party and government promoted by the Christian Social Party were naturally greatly influenced by the ideological preferences of these leading personalities. Finally, all these varied developments converged in 1934 in the experiment of the "Corporative State" under the leadership of Dollfuss and Schuschnigg, which was nothing but an expansion of the ideologies and party program of the Christian Social Party, raised to the status of the one and only admissible ideological and political foundation of the State and defended by the "Patriotic Front" organized by the Party.

In strong contrast to the Center Party in Germany, the Christian Social Party never became a real mass party, representative of all strata of the Catholic population of Austria. With its origin in the one-sided petit-bourgeois and peasant interests which prevailed at the time of its founding, the Party never managed to attract the main body of Catholic workers, as did the Center Party. Consequently, when social movements developed in Austria they never gained decisive influence on Political Catholicism, in contrast to the developments in Germany in the line Ketteler-Hitze-Brauns-Stegerwald, by means of the social and political momentum of the Catholic workers organized in the Christian Trade Unions. Nor did the Christian Social Party succeed in starting a self-reliant political movement according to the pattern of historical and political realism set by the Center Party with its definitely anti-authoritarian democratic principles and its constructive parliamentary activity. Instead, the Christian Social Party adopted in the main the traditions of Political Romanticism and its anti-democratic authoritarian doctrines with the modifications they experienced in successive periods in the line from Adam Mueller, the Goerres Circle (Jarcke, Phillips, Joerg) and Vogelsang, on to the neo-Romantcism of Othmar Spann and the authoritarian state concept of Ignaz Seipel, Dollfuss and Schuschnigg.

Thus, Social Romanticism and the neo-Romantic ideology of an authoritarian order for state and society formed the principles and content of the Christian Social program and actions. From the Party's early days until the downfall of the Monarchy (1918), the main emphasis was placed under Lueger's leadership on preserving the social stratification. Instead of concentrating on political considerations, stress was laid on Vogelsang's ideologies of Social Romanticism with the later modifications introduced by the influential Viennese moral theologian Franz Martin Schindler[209]. In this tradition, the Christian Social Party became consciously "anti-capitalistic" since the main fighting front was directed against political and economic liberalism and free enterprise in trade and industry. Because the leaders of Austrian industry and banking were in part of Jewish persuasion, this was the source of the strongly anti-semitic attitude of the Christian Social Party. Only later, after the Revolution of 1918, when the political influence of liberalism had largely disappeared and the organizational and political power of labor had been strongly established under the leadership of the Austrian Socialists, were the Christian Socials forced to shift the emphasis in their political ideologies and practice toward stronger involvement in national government affairs. Precisely in this process the authoritarian political and social doctrines of neo-Romanticism gained decisive influence on the Party and its actions in the Republic until 1934. The authoritarian state doctrine of Othmar Spann[210] and the authoritarian constitutional doctrine of Ignaz Seipel[211] now gained ascendancy. This was expressed most visibly in the strong opposition to democracy and parliamentarism and in the field of party ideologies in the uncompromising hostility against the Austrian Social Democrats.

"The Austrian Catholics were not predominantly workers, but peasants and artisans. The Austrian Social Democrats—wrongly dubbed Austro-Bolsheviks—stressed their anti-clerical attitudes more strongly than their German comrades. They gave their backing to democracy only with certain reservations since Otto Bauer's "Linz Program" still declared the Dictatorship of the Proletariat to be their ultimate goal and they expected armed party troops to supplement the power their electoral vote lacked. All this forced the Austrian Catholics into a certain orientation that was widely different from that held by the Center—preference for agrarian and small-business interests, diffidence toward democracy, reluctance in social reforms. Because after 1918 the Catholics organized in the Christian Social Party had a parliamentary majority only in coalition with bourgeois groups, they entered into alliances with the Greater Germans, the Land League and the "Heimatschutz"

(Patriotic Defense), thus forming an anti-Marxist front. Industry obligingly provided the party funds, and the foreign powers who guaranteed the League of Nations loans lent this coalition their support. Accordingly, ever since 1922 Political Catholicism was caught in an alliance which neither followed logically from its doctrines nor was representative of its spirit. In this way in Austria *Political Catholicism consciously destroyed democracy*. By 1929 Seipel had removed all doubts, through his lectures on constitutional reforms, that his goal was the establishment of an authoritarian state on corporative principles. Finally in 1934 a decision became imperative." [212]

This is an account given by Josef Dobretsberger, a Catholic professor of sociology at Graz University who served as Schuschnigg's Minister of Social Affairs until 1936. His book "Katholische Sozialpolitik am Scheidewege" (Catholic Social Policies at the Crossroads), published 1947, is to be regarded as an important and authentic source for an objective evaluation of the failure of Political Catholicism in Austria. The same is true of Federal Chancellor Kurt Schuschnigg's (1897-   ) book "Dreimal Oesterreich" published in Vienna at the end of 1937, and of Guido Zernatto's—(who was the last Federal Minister and Executive Secretary of the Patriotic Front until the end of the Schuschnigg regime in 1938)—book "Die Wahrheit ueber Oesterreich" (The Truth about Austria), published in New York in 1938. The following presentation which relies on the authentic pronouncements of these responsible ministers and leaders in the "Christian Corporative State" can therefore claim to be objectively correct. The narrow space left us can perhaps be put to the best use by letting these men speak as extensively as possible, both in criticism and in apology of the pseudo-Catholic system of a totalitarian constitution they set up. By our brief comment the reader will be helped to form his own critical judgment of the last epoch in the tragic story of failure and error which was Political Catholicism in Austria.

Zernatto states unambiguously that Spann and Seipel are responsible for the authoritarian system of Dollfuss-Schuschnigg. "After the World War, Othmar Spann gave strong support to the partisans of the corporative idea and presented the Heimwehr movement with his ideas as their program. After the Encyclical *Quadragesimo Anno*, Seipel joined him in spreading the ideas of a new corporative order for which Catholic scholars in Austria had endeavored to win supporters for decades. In Dollfuss both lines of propaganda converged; in his mind the creative spark caught fire; he put into action what up till then had been mere theory and ideology." [213] Similarly Schuschnigg explains that "the Heimatschutz (home defense) was the first movement in Austria to grow beyond formal democracy, the first to write on its banner the fight against over-emphasized parliamentarism, the first to stand up for a corporative order of society in imposing strength. In these efforts for reform, the Heimatschutz found an eloquent advocates in Ignaz Seipel." [214]

Schuschnigg, too, confirms that Seipel's is the basic responsibility for the determined fight of the Christian Social Party against the Socialists and that he thereby created the preconditions for "Austria's future"—the one that was to begin in 1934 with destroying the Socialist movement on Dollfuss' provocation, and was to end with the tragic Dollfuss-Schuschnigg regime and the Hitler system for which they had prepared Austria. "He (Seipel) would never have considered entering a political compact with Socialism, which would have meant making concessions in principle for the sake of peace. From the beginning, Seipel in this held fast to his own opinions; they frequently involved him in strong contradictions, primarily with many of the decisive opinions held by the Reich Center." "In order to safeguard Austria and to establish conditions under which its future would be inviolate, Seipel took the decisive departure of rallying all forces for a political defense against the Social Democracy. He had to pay for this effort in a premature consumption of his vitality, his much too early death, but only after having secured the foundations for the liberty and independence of the Fatherland—the developments have vindicated him!" [215] This profession of optimism Schuschnigg still believed to be justified as late as the end of 1937! Not more than three months later, the same man was a prisoner of the Nazis and had time to ponder the historical reality which showed him that Hitler had set a violent end to this "liberty and independence" contrived by the Seipel-Dollfuss-Schuschnigg system—aided and abetted by Schuschnigg's intimate friends and cabinet ministers, and relying on the identical methods Schuschnigg had used to destroy the Austrian Socialist movement. Hitler could even take over the identical concentration camps in which the "Christian Corporative State" had kept the Socialist "enemies of the state" prisoners until March 11, 1938.

The informed Dobretsberger in a shattering criticism thus describes the realities which were built upon the "foundation stone" vaunted by Schuschnigg in this questionable experiment of a Christian Corporative State with its pseudo-Catholic constitution—efforts which as late as 1938 Zernatto naively hailed as a "fine thing half-way between parliamentary democracy and fascism:"[216] "The corporative constitution which was drawn up after the defeat of the Social Democrats set a corporate parliament in the place of a party parliament. Each one of the seven newly formed vocational bodies had the same number of parliamentary mandates. The workers who had disposed of 45 per cent of the mandates through their Socialist party representation now had 15 per cent. It was the objective to break them up altogether as a class and to pour them into one pot with their employers' organizations of the same vocational group. Being autonomous, the vocational corporations shattered all unity of purpose in economic policies. Where each corporation regulates wages, determines prices, disposes of exports, creates labor opportunities in its own way, special interests roam the country at will, monopolies are formed with the constitutional right to exploit everyone. They may establish prices, expand the restrictive licensing system, prohibit strikes at will. The corporations of 1934-1938 regulated their actions as little according to Christian ethics as did the Franconian feudal lords after their conversion. However, they always referred to the Encyclicals to back up their measures. Even the barbers of Vienna did so when they moved to introduce a municipal ordinance against anyone shaving his own whiskers! The political representation of the Catholics was not more firmly established in the Corporative State than in the Democracy. Catholicism had no longer a party to look after its interests, only fractions in every corporation. To win a majority in the Corporative Parliament in favor of the confessional school it had to vote in the Industry Corporation for higher tariffs, in the Trade Corporation for restrictive licensing, in the Farmers Corporation for debt forgiveness. The log rolling methods for which Democracy had been reproached had even a wider birth in the Corporative State. By having to mix politics with economics, politics ran into a bad reputation and economics into bad business." [217]

The responsible ministers, with Schuschnigg in the lead, never kept it a secret that the Dollfuss-Schuschnigg system was based squarely on the anti-democratic power machine of the Vaterlaendische Front. After 1934 the Christian Social Party had been converted into this broad Front by forming an alliance with the Defense Leagues which were imitations of the National Socialist pattern even to the extent of adopting the division in storm troops, front militias and the hierarchy of officers under the supreme dictatorial command of the Federal "Fuehrer" Schuschnigg. Zernatto gives a complete description of these things.[218] Thus, finally, Schuschnigg felt he could declare, even as late as end of 1937: "We were free to replace the written Constitution by a newly written Basic Law. Its objective was to suppress formal democratic parliamentarism which, because of our special circumstances, had proved worthless. Thus the Corporative State under authoritarian leadership was established in Austria." [219] And even on March 9, 1938 Schuschnigg explained to the representative of the Austrian National Socialists with whom he had carried on negotiations on their participation in government for several months and had already conceded it on principle: "The Constitution is based on the idea of authoritarian leadership and, according to Article 93, confers on the Federal Chancellor the right to determine the outlines of his policy. I refuse to tolerate a coalition government. To form a second front besides the Vaterlaendische Front cannot even be discussed!" [220] The very next day, the National Socialist "Front" took over the government offices and from then on followed the identical principles of "authoritarian" government which only the day before Schuschnigg had proudly professed . . .!

One ought to read over quietly, page by page, these books of Schuschnigg's and Zernatto's in order to understand with what cynical openness they praise their system with its totalitarian claims as a "thing half-way between democracy and fascism," and on the other hand always make the attempt to justify their plans sophistically by referring to Christian traditions and the Papal Encyclicals. Schuschnigg's book we quoted above proves beyond the possibility of a doubt that, as the responsible head of this government system, he was never aware how irreconcilable his anti-democratic, totalitarian priciples were with those of the Christian political and social doctrine as formulated above all in the many Encyclicals of Popes Leo XIII and Pius XI. Perhaps the fault lies with the Romantic ideologies in their specific Austrian variant of Conservative Political Catholicism, a body of thought difficult to comprehend as an ideological unity in its *complexio oppositorum*, which made it very hard for this comparatively young, inexperienced politician and heavily overburdened "statesman" Schuschnigg to form an objective picture of these contradictions.

It remains, however, completely inadmissible for a Catholic statesman jealous of his conscience and reputation to act like Schuschnigg who took it upon himself to write down the following irresponsible opinion of Mussolini's and Hitler's totalitarian systems—even at the end of 1937, after all the experiences, including the murder of Dollfuss in 1934, which the entire civilized world had seen as witness of the anti-Christian spirit of both Fascism and National Socialism: "It is quite possible to adopt the maxim: *L'ètat, c'est moi,* in one form or another; in such a case, the "Moi" does not necessarily have to be a single person; it may comprise a multiplicity of persons, a party. This then constitutes *the totalitarian state with its peculiar rhythm of life, its own philosophy. I think it basically wrong either to reject it unconditionally or to accept it unconditionally. Where it exists, as in Italy and Germany, it may be thoroughly right and useful in its fundamental shape.* However, this does not necessarily mean that, were the pattern to be copied, it would prove equally valid everywhere."[221]

These opinions, to which Schuschnigg gave the special authority and effectiveness of the printed word through his *imprimatur* even in December 1937, prove more blatantly than all other features of the tragic history of the neo-Romantic "Christian Corporative State" what an incapable politician this was and how little he could be trusted with leading and organizing a truly Christian defense of Austria against National Socialist totalitarianism. The "unconditional" rejection of the totalitarian state which Schuschnigg declared to be "basically wrong" seems on the contrary to constitute an absolute duty of conscience for every Christian statesman. On this score no doubt would be possible after the Encyclical *Non Abbiamo Bisogno* of June 29, 1931 which was specifically directed against Fascism, and the Encyclical *With Burning Sorrow* of March 14, 1937 specifically directed against National Socialism. More irrefutably than dozens of critical historical dissertations, Schuschnigg's utterances prove how thoroughly disoriented were the ideologists and statesmen who represented Austrian Conservatism and how incapable they were to grasp the true essence and actual political meaning of the great Papal Encyclicals. This tragic misconception also explains the gross abuse of the Encyclical "Quadragesimo Anno" perpetrated by those who dared deduce from it a justification of the pseudo-Catholic "Christian Corporative State" which, it is to be hoped, was the last experiment in history of the equally pseudo-Catholic Political Romanticism. In this connection an evaluation by Josef Dobretsberger merits special attention, especially since as Social Minister in Schuschnigg's Cabinet this Catholic sociologist was personally involved in this experiment:

"Catholic neo-Romanticism fell into the error of speaking about a corporative 'Constitution,' whereas the Pope spoke merely of a corporate 'Order.' It was completely and utterly futile to undertake the corporative experiment in the narrow space of Austria, intellectually insulated from the outside world. It may very well be that *the Corporative State was really nothing but an escape ideology,* thought out to counter the myths rampant in the great neighbor states, Italy and Germany —thus *more in the nature of a perplexity than a program!"* [222]

Finally, Kurt von Schuschnigg himself provided the ultimate vindication for our harsh condemnation of Austrian Fascism in his last book, entitled: *Ein Requiem in Rot-Weiss-Rot* (Zurich 1946). Five hundred small-print pages feature his "statement of accounts and human confession"; anyone having knowledge of German and reading this account will be embarrassed by the personal egotism, the political arrogance, the meta-political confusion plus flagrant abuse of the categories of Christian political thinking. It is the more regrettable that the American edition of it, *Austrian Requiem,* (New York 1946) authorized by Schuschnigg; does not feature even half of the original text; it also avoids sedulously to reveal the title and place of the original publication, and makes no mention of the deletions that have been made!

The reason for this seems evident: the American edition features mainly the purely human experiences and the reflections of the private life of the "man in protective custody," namely Schuschnigg, alias Dr. Auster. The political reflections of the American edition are limited largely to information of political events sufficiently known, since Schuschnigg, even in 1945, after all the terrible events of the years since 1934, estimates to have no need of either explanation or excuse in his capacity as a statesman or politician.

Right in the beginning of the German edition, Schuschnigg declares in connection with the passing of the office of Chancellor to him in 1934: "I could not visualize in what way the enormously difficult task could be mastered" (page 21); in the American edition, however, he goes so far as to maintain a political self-vindication which eliminates any honest *mea culpa* of a Christian statesman. Here he says: "It was a fact that I had undertaken the task of preserving Austria by means of domestic and foreign pacification, and of coming to a peaceful settlement with the German Reich on the basis of our Constitution—that is, without a party system. *That this task was doomed to failure and that I did not see it is an accusation to which I have no answer—no excuse."* (page 73).

In compensation for this "no answer—no excuse" in the matter of the miscarriages of Austrian Clerico-fascism, and in the

effort to shun the responsibility for the annihilation of the Social Democracy, Schuschnigg offers the naive statement: "It remains an open question whether the bloody events of February
1934 and the resultant break with socialism could have been
avoided." (page 187) . However, in the German edition he com-
pensates the above statement in almost half the book by arrogant meditations and equally paltry dissertations on behalf of
the substance and tasks of the State which surpass even the
meta-political meanderings and confusion of his preceding
book, entitled *"Dreimal Oesterreich."* Notably the fourth part
of the German edition shows Schuschnigg's sympathies for the
authoritative state to have been not less strong in 1945 than
they were in 1937. Here are a few examples which testify distinctly that this kind of a highly questionable "Political Catholicism" was not able to learn a lesson even from the shocking
catastrophe of the years 1933-1945.

"A complicated constitutional casuistry is not necessarily an
advantage. Constitutional laws made *ad hoc* are mostly causing
evil." (page 391) "It is surely substantially false to evaluate
"democratic" and "authoritative" as concepts absolutely anti-
thetical." . . . "It is questionable whether democracies which
term themselves such, truly merit the name; whether there are
not, here and there, oligarchies and ochlocracies hidden under
a mask." (page 380) . . . "Arithmetic equation—equality of all
—in every political matter is not substantial." "Nor is the majority decision at all costs essential." *"It follows that from the
shallow banks of democracy a bridgehead can be built, linking
it with the authoritative cliffs. This is entirely conceivable."*
(page 382) .

CHAPTER VI

POLITICAL DOCTRINES AND SOCIAL THEORIES

1. THE BASIC PRINCIPLES

1. *The Social Metaphysics*

In a general survey of the genesis of modern Catholic political and social doctrines, the origins and the evolution of the indigenous German Catholic theories in these fields deserve a very special place. Their principles of moral philosophy and social metaphysics, and the originality of their historical concepts are significant expressions of the indepent character of German Catholicism. Here is one more vivid proof how closely the Catholic philosophy of life (Lebensgefuehl) and the concrete embodiment of Christian fundamental principles in the realities of state and society are tied up with the *facta contingentia* in the manifold variations of historical and sociological realities on which historical Catholicism is based. In the preceding chapters we have analyzed this interrelation in the field of social and political movements. We have shown how in the course of these developments Catholic realism emerged victorious in Germany. Social realism had been achieved in a severe struggle to express the growing feelings of social responsibility under the special circumstances of modern German history—an entirely autonomous struggle which the combatants took care to keep free of the influences of Social Romanticism, an ideology which they thought fundamentally incompatible. Political realism also was the end product of a struggle of social conscience fought in a historical climate which made it possible for Political Catholicism to develop its independent activities under the protection of the constitutional guarantees of parliamentary and party liberties.

It is only natural that, in the fields of social movements and politics, and in those of social philosophy and political theory, the thinking in German Catholicism had to develop in conformity with the social and political realities. In other words, this political doctrine and philosophy of society had to proceed along the same lines of marked realism in all matters social and of definite democratism in matters political and, by the same token, in strict contrast to the authoritarian ideas of theological integralism and social conservatism. This theological realism and social democratism found their foremost representation in the socio-metaphysical traditions of the Jesuit Order, on the part of those of its leaders who interpreted Thomistic Natural Law and social structure with a realistic emphasis. Gustav Gundlach has aptly characterized these traditions. "In the Catholic world of ideas we find a democratic line principally in the doctrine of Natural Law taught by the whole medieval Thomistic philosophy. This line is stressed even more strongly in the specifically Jesuit amplification of this doctrine which gives the individual a prominent place and culminates in the concepts of the social pact and the people's sovereignty. In the doctrine of Natural Law the inalienable rights of the individual are stressed as against feudalism, absolutism and also as against the authority of the Church and the Order. We should never forget that, aside from its natural source, Catholic Democracy has a supra-natural one: the equality of all the saved before God, through Christ. And in general, the role Catholicism reserves for the individual contains elements that are much less hostile to the idea of democracy than is frequently inferred. The supra-national authority of the World Church through all the ages has set a break on any undue expansion of the omnipotent and absolute state. Wherever a limit is set to state omnipotence, a larger role is reserved for the individual, the family, the vocational corporations, in short for all living forces of a democratic state built up from below. The conceptual world of Catholicism with the objective reality implied in the doctrine of Natural Law and Revelation offers indeed the basis for a sound Democracy"[223].

In this sense, the social metaphysics of the Jesuits seemed predestined to serve as theoretical justification for the social and political realism of German Catholicism. Quite logically therefore, the theoretical foundation and systematic elaboration of the Catholic political and social doctrine in Germany was primarily an achievement of the Jesuits. This tradition comprises the work of Theodor Meyer (1821-1913), Augustin Lehmkuhl (1834-1918), Josef Biederlack (1845-1930) and Victor Cathrein (1845-1931), down to Heinrich Pesch (1854-1926), Oswald von Nell-Breuning (1890-   ), Gustav Gundlach (1892-   ) and Ferdinand Frodl (1886-   ). Their efforts received support from a number of other notable theologians and sociologists who, though not members of the Jesuit Order, were in full sympathy with the doctrinal systems of political and social philosophy expounded by the above-named Jesuits, and kept close contact with them. Together they built up the imposing edifice of the social doctrines of modern German Catholicism which, in its systematic completeness, ideological thoroughness and actual significance for political ideologies, is without an equal in the Catholic world.

There is also a parallel political unity and organizational continuity achieved by Social Catholicism in the social realism of the Muenchen-Gladbach orientation and of the Volksverein as well as the unity in Political Catholicism achieved under the realistic leadership of the Center Party. In mutual historical interdependence and implementation this threefold social, political and theoretical expression of living German Catholicism in the epoch 1870 to 1933 led to an admirable unity of purpose which made such a pleasant contrast to the theoretical controversies and organzational conflicts to be found within Catholicism in other countries, especially in the conservatism as practised in Austria. Accordingly the responsibility of the leaders of German Political Catholicism for the ultimate failure seems all the stronger. It resulted in the destruction of this unity and consequently in a severe break in the evolution of Catholic political and social philosophies in Germany. In view of these sad events it seems all the more necessary to establish a clear understanding of the developments and lasting significance of the social philisophy typical of German Catholicism. This we can achieve by examining them under the point of view of their origin and systematic development based on the realistic social metaphysics of the Jesuits.

Modern Catholic philosophy of state and society began to develop about 1879 when Leo XIII's Encyclical *Aeterni Patris* encouraged a revival of the doctrines of Thomas Aquinas. This so-called "neo-Thomism" or neo-scholisticism is, however, of importance for developments in German Catholicism only if related to the simultaneous revival and expansion of the "Thomistic" traditions of Ludwig Molina (1535-1600) and Franz Suarez (1548-1617), the true originators of the Jesuit Order's social metaphysics. When speaking of the epoch of Thomistic revival inaugurated by Leo XIII, we shall always have to keep these older authors in mind. Students all too often overlook the difference between the "neo-Thomistic" political and social doctrines as expounded by some Dominicans in the tradition of theological integralism and conservatism and the spirit of theological realism and democratism in the teachings of the Jesuit tradition. German developments followed this latter tradition while in Austria the conservatism rested on the spirit of Dominican integralism and conservatism, that is, so far as any tradition of Natural Law and social metaphysics can at all be discovered in the Austrian ideologies after Vogel-sang and A. M. Weiss.

We can form a complete and accurate picture of the original developments in the German Jesuits' social metaphysics by studying the numerous essays contained in their most important publication in social philosophy, the "Stimmen aus Maria Laach", founded 1869, which after 1917 changed its title to "Stimmen der Zeit" and after a brief interruption under Hitler continues to appear today. Beside the fundamental works of the Jesuits we named above, the "Staatslexikon", published for the Goerres Society from 1889 to 1933 (five editions of five volumes each), presents a unique ideological history of the developments in Social and Political Catholicism in Germany in their special relation to the social metaphysics of the Jesuits. Likewise, the "Woerterbuch der Politik", recently published under the editorship of H. Sacher and O. Nell-Breuning[224] offers valuable additional material. Its excellent topical articles and biblio-graphical surveys give eloquent proof of the admirable results achieved by the efforts to revive Catholic social science after the downfall of the old order.

2. The Natural Law Ethics

The political and social philosophy of German Catholicism appears as a logical continuation of the evolving Natural Law doctrines on the essence of man, the state and society, as inaug-urated by the system of Thomas Aquinas and later elaborated principally in Molinism and Suarism. In this Molinian-Suarez-ian amplification we are struck by three characteristics: first, the realism in their epistemological foundation; second, the personalism in their sociological concern; and third, the de-mocratism in the ideo-political orientation.

Their basic *realism* implies that they take man as a moral being, in the sense that concrete man in all his activities within historical realty must be given a justification from the point of view of moral philosophy. In so doing, the contingent historical reality, with the autonomous and independent values of social and political life, is accorded full realistic recognition. This kind of moral philosophy with its basic concern for reality, at all times has as its objects concrete personalities themselves in their activities within the concrete state, society, and economic life as they exist within a concrete period. By means of such natural ethics and moral philosophy it becomes possible to con-struct a realistic political doctrine and a realistic philosophy of society and economy in the spirit of political and social existentialism.

The *personalism* in the realm of sociology implies that at all times the concrete, living person, that is, man in his actions and work, stands in the center of all studies concerning the essence and purpose of state, society and economy. In reverse, all political, social and economic activity is always purposefully directed toward the human personality; in other words, a definite teleological personalism is the precondition for a personalistic political and social concept. State and society, therefore, exist through man and for man; all order of state and society, all economic activity derive their sense and natural purpose from the one fact that they serve man who is both their origin and their end.

The *democratic* orientation must determine the role which authority will play in political and social life and yet preserve the personal autonomy of man. Such genuine democratism prevents usurpation of authority by individuals, in the sense of an absolutistic monarchy "by the Grace of God" or of dictatorial autocracy; it also prevents usurpation of authority by a collective, a dictatorship based on mass totalitarianism. Here, too, the Molinian-Suarezian interpretation of the Natural Law autonomy of political and social life proves its worth as it provides a sound basis in moral philosophy and political ideology for a personalistic Christian doctrine of people's sovereignty and a genuinely democratic order of life.

This threefold characterization of the German Catholic political and social doctrines—in respect to their realism, personalism and democratism—was first elaborated in the spirit of Natural Law and moral philosophy in the fundamental works of Theodor Meyer and Victor Cathrein. Meyer may be regarded as the founder of this tradition—in his essay "Die Grundsaetze der Sittlichkeit und des Rechtes" (1868) and in his fundamental work "Institutiones Iuris Naturalis" (1885-1890), although it should be noted that the Austro-Italian Jesuit, Julius Costa-Rossetti (1842-1900 with his great "Philosophia Moralis" Innsbruck, 1883) had exerted a decisive influence on both Meyer and Cathrein. Then Victor Cathrein, in his "Moralphilosophie" (1890-91), contributed the specific application on moral philosophy of the systems of Meyer and Costa-Rossetti. His book has spread far and wide in many editions (6th edition, 1924) and is still regarded as the standard work illustrative of the social metaphysics of German Catholicism. Cathrein developed his ideas on the basis of Molina's systematic distinction between absolute Natural Law as imbedded in the "nature of man" and formulated in the Decalogue, and relative or "contingent" Natural Law which comprises all natural legal matters (persistente lege naturali in se) as dependent on historical circumstance. Elaborating this distinction according to the requirements of his time, Cathrein created a teleological system of autonomous Natural Law ethics dividing up his material systematically in a section on theological ethics and moral theology and a separate section on philosophical ethics and moral philosophy. With this work Cathrein provided incipient Catholic social philosophy in Germany with a positive, systematic, scientific foundation on which to develop a strictly philosophical political and social doctrine, at the same time giving it salutary security against any systematic interference of integralism and maximalism. In an abstract of his doctrine on the essence of an autonomous Natural Law ethics, published in the Catholic Encyclopedia, Cathrein has characterized this principle most tersely:

"Ethics may be defined as the science of the moral rectitude of human acts in accordance with the first principles of natural reason." "The proper method of Ethics is at once speculative and empirical, it draws upon experience and metaphysics. Supernatural Christian Revelation is not a proper source of Ethics. Only those conclusions properly belong to Ethics which can be reached with the help of experience and philosophical principles"[225].

In a similar manner, Augustine Lehmkuhl in his fundamental "Theologia Moralis" (2 volumes, 1883-84; 12th edition 1914) has systematically followed through the distinction between the categories, realms and values of the state, society and economy and those of theology and philosophy. In doing so he achieved a double purpose: to secure the supernatural, theological foundations of all Christian anthropology and theistic philosophy of law and society; and to prevent studies of state, society and economy from undue subjection to theological methods. In this direction Lehmkuhl achieved special merit by proving unequivocally, as early as 1879 in his discussion with Karl Vogelsang and A. M. Weiss, OP, ("Zins und Wucher vor dem Richterstuhl der Kirche und Vernunft")[226], that it is inadmissible from a scientific point of view to mix up basic principles of theology, in the sense of Dominican integralism, with the purely sociological categories of the orders and details of social and economic life in their temporal causations. He was supported by Josef Biederlack who, in his important study "Die soziale

Frage" (1895, 10th edition 1925) gave the most lucid, systematical and impressive definition of the basic theological principles of all Christian philosophy concerning society and economy and the purely philosophical and socio-metaphysical categories of a Christian doctrine of society and economy. Biederlack and Lehmkuhl thus gave German Catholicism the boon of having an irreproachable scientific foundation on which to base and develop its social theories, thus avoiding,—with the help of the lucid methodical distinction of the absolute realms and values of religion, theology, and Church from those of state, society, and economy,—the confusion of theology, social philosophy and sociology which proved such a bad handicap to Austrian Catholicism with its Romanticism and conservatism.

The basic achievements of Meyer, Cathrein, Lehmkuhl and Biederlack in the fields of Natural Law, moral philosophy, moral theology and sociology,—achievements reaped in the surprisingly short period between 1885 and 1900,—provide German Catholicism today with secure foundations for its political and social philosophy. Their most distinguished characteristic seems to be their strong realism which fortified their Christian sense of responsibility and their scientific seriousness in meeting the problems of political and social life. In this attitude they proved themselves the best planters and stewards of the ideas of realism in social metaphysics as taught by Suarez, ideas aptly characterized by Gustav Gundlach: "The aim that is directed toward eternity in a certain sense coincides with the aim of the present. God can also be found in the present, in the momentary condition of the 'world' He created, this world with all its developments that come in part from natural causes and are autonomous, ever changing implementations of the essential content of civilization, relatively independent of the purely religious sphere. Therefore we regard life as a positive value because it is a life derived from God and directed toward God in the permanent interaction of creation and salvation." [227]. Such attitudes produce "a decidedly positive valuation of human labor and, in cooperation with the Divine contributing factor of Grace, it implies a strongly dynamic concept of Work and, consequently, a positive valuation of the life here below, specifically, of the evolution of human civilization" [228]. We find here a profoundly voluntaristic optimism which views the world of history as an outgrowth of the unity of God's will with human action and clearly harks back in its traditions to the personalistic, voluntaristic metaphysics of Suarez and Duns Scotus. "Suarez directs his sights toward the manifold shape of the world. What distinguishes his method is its empirical, positive, historical trait. In thus stressing the contingent character of reality, he shows that not by chance has he always been a diligent reader of Duns Scotus" [229].

This sketchy reference to the ideological connections between Suarez's realism and the doctrines of Meyer, Cathrein, Lehmkuhl and Biederlack may suffice to show how truly representative of the best Catholic traditions was the system of social metaphysics and social ethics of these four Jesuit authors and how capable it was of giving theoretical sanction and depth to the realism of social and political Catholicism in Germany in its ideo-political and historical causation.

Closely tied to this realism we find the feature of *personalism* as expressed in the dynamic concept of social life and work and the *democratic* concept of the state which are characteristic of German Catholicism. Here we may observe distinctly how securely the social and political anthropology which forms the basis of these ideas in a genuinely Christian system rests on theological principles without however themselves being subjected to "theologization". On principle, these concepts of the state and society are markedly anthropocentric, which means that they are always directed immediately toward concrete individual persons and are thus protected against becoming submerged by social materialism and collectivism, and also shielded against political secularism and totalitarianism. This is particularly true because the theological principles of the Molinist doctrine of Grace provides at the same time the foundation for the personalistic epistemology of Suarez. In both instances *it is man in his living individual person who is at the center of all doctrines.* It is therefore necessary to delve somewhat deeper into the significance of the Molinist doctrine of Grace for social anthropology and of the Suarist epistemology for political anthropology. Only then will we be able to achieve a thorough understanding of the feature of personalism in the doctrine of the worker and of democracy as taught in the political and social doctrines of German Catholicism.

The Molinist doctrine of Grace allows a specific analogy to be drawn between the solution it proposes to the theological problem of Divine Grace and human will with the solution of the problems of social philosophy concerning man's historical existence and his will to work. This relationship of analogy between the theological Grace doctrine and social anthropology has fundamental significance for the personalistic concept of work and the whole sociology of German Catholicism. The theological nucleus lies in the religious concept of man's cooperation with God's acts, as systematically expounded in the Molin-

istic Grace doctrine. "Molinism attempts to solve the difficult
problem how Divine Grace can coexist with human liberty, in
a manner which has always been interpreted as strongly emphasizing the autonomy of the human creature" [230]. This excellent characterization provided by Gundlach is tellingly supplemented by the inspired priest-philosopher Peter Lippert
when he demonstrates that Molinism specifically "recognizes
the precious nucleus of the individual, the surpassing importance of human personality" [231]. In this context, man does not
figure as a passively receptive object of Divine Will and as
elected merely by Divine Grace but, on the contrary, as an
actively cooperating subject, as God's creature who from his
own will-power and decision accepts the Will of God and thus
acts as His personalistic instrument. In this manner, man becomes an active "co-worker with God" in the dispensation and
the reception of Grace.

This theological concept leads to a socio-metaphysical concept which lends a strongly emphasized justification to the social
and political autonomy of man in his role as a citizen and a
worker. If it cannot be admitted even in the theological realm
of Grace that man is primarily a passive object of Divine election, how much less is it possible to maintain that in the social
and political realm man is primarily a passive object of the
social order and the political authority. And if even in the realm
of theology "the active cooperation of man with the acts of
God" [232] can be justified, how much more justification is there
for the postulate that men should engage themselves actively in
the fields of social and political action. Man as "God's co-
worker", theologically speaking, in this same relation of analogy
becomes an active "co-worker in state and society", sociologically speaking. And just as this theological theory leads naturally
to a dynamic conception of God and Grace, the analogous sociological theory must lead quite naturally to a dynamic conception of society and labor. Hence *the concept of the working and
the co-working person is the central idea of the social metaphysics of the Jesuits.* From this point it also becomes clear
why the socio-philosophical system of "Solidarism", founded by
Heinrich Pesch, is based on the principle, "Man in his work is
the master of the world within society" [233].

The pronounced *democratism* of the Suarist doctrine of the
social contract and of the people's sovereignty has its primary
basis in the epistemological personalism which Suarez introduced by his amplification of the strict Thomistic concept of the
"object" (Ding). Again Gundlach goes to the heart of the
matter when he says of Suarez, "His sight is directed toward the

variety of the world. His method excels by its empirical, positive, historic trend and the stress he puts on the contingent character of reality. From the same source he derives his understanding of the inherited Aristotelian-scholastic hylomorphism. Hylomorphism explains the 'object', its unity in its diversity, by means of the eternal idea and essence which represents the *entelechy*, the formal cause of the object. Suarez, however, demands in addition to all this a specific modality of unity for the object. This shows that he views the object not so much in its conformity with other objects, or as an instance of the eternal essence become real, but rather in its unique *individuality*." [234]

This concept of the "unique individuality" constitutes the essential difference between the Suarist notion of the person and the strictly Thomistic formal notion of the individual. Viewing the parts as mere component members of the whole, the rigid formalism of integral Thomism is incompatible with a decidedly personalistic social and political anthropology. In it the "organism" is the fountainhead and the dispenser of authority, and its members, the individual men as citizens, are nothing but subjects. Social and political anthropology according to these principles, as typically represented by the social doctrine of rigidly Thomistic Dominicanism, cannot admit any special apology for individual independence and political autonomy for the members of a society. As in the Dominicans' type of Grace the accent lies on human passivity, in their type of society the emphasis is placed on social and political passivity, on the "object" character of man as a citizen. *This theological and socio-metaphysical concept of the passivity and the "object" character of human personality lies at the bottom of all authoritarian and conservative Christian doctrines concerning state and society.* As against them, by demanding a specific "modality" to allow human existence its voluntaristic autonomy, Suarez made it possible to justify individual man in his metaphysical and Natural Law autonomy, precisely through his personal quality as a member of a concrete society and as a citizen of a concrete state. "When Suarez discovered that the unity of an entity was metaphysically not sufficiently established by mere 'essence' or 'idea' as its formal cause and he consequently demanded a specific 'modality' of unity, it necessarily followed that he raised this same demand for the form of the state as being a moral and legal association of free personalities. Consequently, in Suarez's thinking the 'idea' of the state is accompanied by an additional modality, namely the consensus of those concerned, for only then does the state appear, metaphysically, as satisfactorily constituted in the shape of a unity. This requirement of *consensus* to implement the 'idea' of the state from which it derives its moral, normative necessity constitutes the main characteristic of Suarez's construction as against the Natural Law conception of the Enlightenment, and above all against the social theory of Rousseau" [235].

In shaping these theories, Suarez became the real originator of that type of social and political metaphysics which on principle sees in the state and most other forms of human society a "moral and legal association of free personalities." By interpreting the Christian Natural Law metaphysics and ethics in this spirit, German Catholicism in the main proceeded to evolve its philosophy of law and the state.

2. THE POLITICAL DOCTRINES

1. *The Philosophy of Law*

Extraordinary obstacles had to be overcome in Germany before an indigenous Catholic philosophy of law and a doctrine of the State could emerge. As far as Catholicism itself was concerned the obstacle lay primarily in the lack of a tradition—the negative heritage from the Ecclesiastical States of the 18th century[236]. A second adverse factor was the total neglect of Christian Natural Law by Political Romanticism, a feature that suffices to expose the pseudo-Catholic character of these notions on law and the state[237]. In its bitter fight against revolutionary Natural Law, Political Romanticism had also eliminated all categories of the rationalistic and partly secularized Natural Law of the Enlightenment, and by doing so turned Catholic thinking, helplessly and inconsiderately, over to the enemies of Natural Law, to Hegelian state absolutism and to liberalistic positivism in law. This led to the further consequence that in 19th century Germany the doctrines of law and the state were dominated by thinkers opposed to Natural Law even at the universities of Catholic states like Bavaria. It did not make too much difference whether such hostility stemmed from Hegelian traditions, or from the historical school of law (Berlin and Goettingen), or from liberal positivistic law (Munich, Freiburg, Heidelberg). When for decades the Kulturkampf placed an even stricter embargo on all direct influences of Catholic thinking on German scholarship, this added one more major reason why the Christian doctrine of Natural Law and government was not given any official representation in the normal German university activities before the downfall of the monarchy in 1918. Moreover, the founders of the German Catholic philosophy of law and government did their main scientific work in

Jesuit centers outside Germany (Holland, Tyrol, Rome), since because of the so-called "Jesuit Act" the Jesuits were forbidden all teaching activity at German universities until 1917. It is also significant to note that the true founders of the German Catholic doctrines were not native Germans, Theodor Meyer and Victor Cathrein stemming from Switzerland, Costa-Rossetti from Italy,—both countries in which the Christian Natural Law traditions had never become extinct. Furthermore, A. Lehmkuhl and J. Bierderlack who lived and worked outside Germany had their roots in Westphalia which was the one German region where the Catholic traditions had remained alive even in the 18th century. Therefore, parallel with developments in the realms of social and political thought, these scholars represented the best background for the emergence of spiritual realism in German Catholicism.

These antecedents explain the reaction of non-Catholic German thought when in the 1880's the lost tradition of Christian Natural Law began to be revived. They either greeted such attempts of the "suspect Jesuits" to "ultramontanize" science with deadening silence or, in the few instances where scholarly integrity overcame philosophical ignorance, they marveled at them as if they were a new discovery in philosophy of law. Typical of the ignorance which prevailed in 19th century philosophy of law and government concerning the Christian Natural Law doctrines is the case of Rudolf von Ihering (1818-1892). This outstanding Goettingen jurist and philosopher of law, in his "Der Zweck im Recht" (1877-1883) which created a sensation, had attempted to conquer the fashions of the historical and the positivistic concepts of law by means of a doctrine of social aims of law and morality, partly based on Natural Law concepts. When Catholic critics pointed out to him[238] that such a teleological foundation of law and morality had long ago been given in all detail in the system of Thomas Aquinas and was at this very time (1886) staging a revival of the Christian Natural Law traditions, this great savant could not but confess publicly that he had been completely ignorant of these matters. In the 2nd edition of "Zweck im Recht" (1886) he added a long explanation of his previous neglect of Christian Natural Law, in which he said among other things, "With amazement I ask myself how it was possible that such verities, once formulated, could fall into such complete oblivion in our Protestant education. What erroneous and circuitous ways could Protestantism have avoided had it taken these verities to heart! I myself might never have written my book had I been conscious of them!" [239].

But the same reproach has validity for developments in Catholicism itself right down to the 1880's. Particularly it must be leveled against the traditions of Political Romanticism and of Catholic Integralism and Conservatism as taught by the Goerres Circle. These factions deprived themselves of the last opportunity of putting the Christian Natural Law doctrines to creative use by their willful neglect of Franz von Baader's Romantic Existentialism. All the greater is the merit of the non-Germans, Th. Meyer, Costa-Rossetti and V. Cathrein, in having introduced into Germany the supernational world of thought of the social and legal metaphysics of the Jesuits in order to fertilize an autonomous German Catholic philosophy of law and the state which later culminated in the magnificent synthesis between Catholic vital spirit (Lebensgefuehl) and German thought.

In his study "Die Grundsaetze der Sittlichkeit und des Rechtes" published in 1868, Theodor Meyer made the first and the decisive attempt in 19th century German literature to offer a systematic foundation for a Catholic philosophy of law. Since at that time the scene was dominated by a philosophy hostile to metaphysics and a jurisprudence hostile to Natural Law, this study at first remained practically unnoticed. And yet, its publication was an event of fundamental impact on Catholic Germany. It inaugurated the period of an indigenous German Catholic philosophy of law which was to make a creative contribution to a noble system of metaphysical jurisprudence. These achievements in turn contributed materially to the uprooting of positivistic jurisprudence and to turning the general philosophical interest toward an examination of the basic relationship between law and ethics. Meyer began by proving systematically that any genuinely Christian philosophy of law must first of all rely on a "metaphysics of being", must secondly be based on an "ethics of duty" (Ethik des Sollens) derived from the first, if it finally wishes to achieve a true "order of existence". Thus he established that a doctrine of law must depend on a doctrine of morality, as this in turn must be based on a doctrine of existence. In other words, we find the basis for a positive, Natural Law system in the fundamental relationship between the metaphysical order of existence and the moral order of ethics. In the 2nd volume of his "Institutiones Iuris Naturalis" (1900), Meyer then offered a detailed ontological-metaphysical system of his Natural Law philosophy, closely following the thought of Costa-Rossetti and Lehmkuhl; and Cathrein, also in the 2nd volume of his "Moralphilosophie" (1891) formulated the ethical foundations of this philosophy.

Proceeding to build on these foundations, Cathrein then brought this first period in the development of a Catholic philosophy of law to a climax in his "Recht, Naturrecht und positives Recht" (1901), a work which aroused much attention. In this context we should mention Augustin Lehmkuhl's great Natural Law "Commentary on the Civil Code" (1899) and the works of Georg von Hertling, primarily his "Naturrecht und Sozialpolitik" (1893) and the essays collected in the "Kleine Schriften zur Zeitgeschichte" (1897). In a ceaseless effort Cathrein continued his decisive contributions to the systematic elaboration of Catholic philosophy of law with special regard to the concrete aspects of contemporaneous history, in his "Grundbegriffe des Strafrechts" (1905) and the important study on "Die Grundlagen des Voelkerrechts" (1918).

The subsequent development of Catholic philosophy of law was dominated by the works of Joseph Mausbach (1861-1931) which covered a wide field. This eminent moral theologian of Muenster University made a very special contribution to a deeper penetration of the subject and to a more international reputation of German Catholic philosophy of law, both through his own highly important work and through that of his disciples, Rommen, Tischleder, and others. In his "Die Ethik des heiligen Augustinus" (1909), which inaugurated a new epoch, he first proved the importance of the teachings of St. Augustine for the Christian Natural Law doctrine and for a realistic philosophy of law and civilization. Even Ernst Troeltsch had to confess in 1915 that now, after having studied Mausbach's book, he was compelled to "accord much greater significance" to the influence of St. Augustine on the evolution of the Natural Law and social doctrines than he had done in his great book on "The Social Teachings of the Christian Churches" (London and New York, 1931-1948, German publication 1912) "under too strong an influence of the *History of Medieval Political Theory in the West*, by the Brothers Carlyle" [240]. Later Mausbach continued the traditions of Meyer and Cathrein and amplified them according to the needs of his time in his "Systematik der christlich-katholischen Ethik" (1913), his "Naturrecht und Voelkerrecht" (1918) and the 3rd volume of his great "Moraltheologie" (1920). It should be noted with what extraordinary consistency Mausbach followed up the realistic metaphysics and the political doctrine of Suarez, especially with reference to the problems of the people's sovereignty and the revolutionary right to resist, as proved particularly in his article on "Staatsbuergerlichen Gehorsam" in the Staatslexikon[241] and in his essay "Christliche Staatsordnung und

Staatsgesinnung" (1922). Much instructive material is also to be found in Mausbach's fundamental work "Ethik und Recht" (1922) which he contributed in company with other leading authors, such as V. Cathrein, O. Schilling, M. Grabmann, C. Schmitt, to the important symposium on modern "Katholische Rechtsphilosophie" [242].

Among the most important recent contributions, the following deserve special attention: the essay of Wendelin Rauch (1885-   ) "Eine absolute Lebensordnung aus christlicher Metaphysik" [243]; Johann Steffes (1883-   ) "Das Naturrecht im Rahmen einer religionsphilosophischen Betrachtung" [244]; above all others, Dietrich von Hildebrand's (1889-   ) fundamental essay on the phenomenology of law, "Die rechtliche und sittliche Sphaere in ihrem Eigenwert und ihrem Zusammenhang" [245]. Emil Hoelscher (1884-   ) published a comprehensive, more popular presentation of "Die sittliche Rechtslehre" (1929-1930). The most extensive and comprehensive study is Karl Petraschek's (1876-   ) "System der Rechtsphilosophie" (1932) which pays special attention to a realistic evaluation of the relationship between Christian Natural Law and the various concrete orders of historical positive law. Also Petraschek's instructive articles on "Recht", "Naturrecht", Rechtsphilosophie" in the Staatslexikon[246] repay special attention. Equally Otto Schilling's systematic work on "Christliche Sozial-und Rechtsphilosophie" (1933), is an extremely noteworthy textbook full of actuality and penetration.

As indispensable for a thorough understanding of the basic importance that Catholic philosophy of law in its German variant gained for the modern studies of the problems of law and morality we have to mention the two great systematic works of Heinrich Rommen "The Eternal Return of Natural Law (London-St. Louis 1947, first German edition 1936) and of Johannes Messner "Social Ethics," (London-St. Louis 1949, German edition, "Naturrecht", 1948), two books which already may be said to belong among the permanent international standard works of philosophy of law and of Catholic science in general.

2. The Doctrine of the State

It is of the essence of the Christian concepts of Natural Law that on principle the relationship of ethics versus law comprises the relationship of the individual versus the community, in accordance with the essentially social nature of man, his *ens sociale*. The ethics of Natural Law therefore presupposes a social ethics, in the same way as the metaphysics of Natural Law presupposes a social metaphysics. As the social nature of man requires the existence of society, the Natural Law duties and privileges appear as the duties and privileges of every single individual in relation to society. Since the state is "by nature" a necessity as an essential form of social existence, the legal forms of a state community must be determined by virtue of Natural Law. In this sense, the doctrines concerning the origin of the state and of state authority and state power are already contained in principle in the social metaphysics and in Natural Law Ethics. This means in turn that the historical existence and forms of the state and its concrete legal orders are basically already pre-existant in the philosophy of law. It is the task of a special theory of the state to apply the principles of philosophy of law to the historical existence and the historical forms of the state. Because, according to the Christian theory, no law exists of and for itself, but all law has its origin and existence in a nature-given cause and reason, because in other words the divine order of the *lex aeterna* and *jus divinum* are the foundation for the natural order of existence and the *jus naturale,* and these in turn are the foundation of the historical order of life and the *jus positivum*—for all these reasons no autonomous law of the state exists *per se.* For, in accordance with the natural essence and origin of the state, the law of the state is also determined by Natural Law, and equally, in accordance with the historical existence and concrete objectives of the state, the law of the state is also determined by positive law. Consequently, wherever the foundations of Christian Natural Law in social metaphysics and philosophy of law are treated as the essence and the objectives of the "institutiones juris naturalis", the basic principles of the state concept and the political and legal orders of life are already implied.

For our specific task we may infer from these insights that the Catholic doctrines of the state took their entirely natural departure from the developments in philosophy of law that we described. It is therefore not by mere chance that the specific development of the state doctrine followed upon Theodor Meyer's work that we previously cited, "Die Grundsaetze der Sittlichkeit und des Rechtes." On this basis, and specifically conditioned by the events of the Kulturkampf, Cardinal Joseph Hergenroether (1824-1890) wrote his fundamental work "Katholische Kirche und christlicher Staat" (1872-1876), followed soon by Victor Cathrein's "Die Aufgaben der Staatsgewalt und ihre Grenzen" (1882) which was an important amplification of the first. Then came Christian Pesch with his "Christliche

Staatslehre" (1887) and Costa-Rossetti with "Staatslehre der katholischen Philosophie" (1890). After this, Heinrich Pesch in his important book "Der christliche Staatsbegriff" (1900)[247] offered a first survey of this period (1869-1900) in the development of the Catholic political philosophy. This work retains its special significance even today, not only because of the systematic survey of the authors named above but also because it digests the essential thoughts and texts of the Papal Encyclicals and of non-Catholic authors relevant to the same subjects which today are difficult to procure in detail.

In contrast to the fundamental achievements in the period before 1900, the subsequent history of political doctrines up to the outbreak of the first World War (1914) is markedly poor in systematic output and factual penetration. The main reason was that in this period Political Catholicism played a passive role. The Center Party was forced to submit to a policy of conformity with the over-all Reich politics and with the rather negative social reforms confined to a certain protection of the workers. And since for Catholicism no concrete or novel political or constitutional problems were involved, the theoretical interest in state affairs remained confined to a conservation of the scientific achievements garnered before 1900. This situation was further impaired by the negative after-effects of the Kulturkampf which were particularly noticeable in this period. During the Kulturkampf a new generation of good scholars could not be educated and supported, and a severe shortage of young Catholic scholars active in the social and political sciences now ensued. It can be taken as a sign of this situation that the 3rd and 4th editions of the "Staatslexikon", published 1908 to 1912, contained only minor changes in the most important fields as compared with the 2nd edition published 1901-04. In the articles on subjects of political science, Georg von Hertling followed strict conservatism in line with the position taken in previous decades by Southern German Conservatism. To be sure J. Mausbach found it possible to express his opposition to von Hertling's conservative position in this 4th edition, in his article on "the obedience of the citizen" which we quoted above. But he could do this only thanks to a tactical yielding which the Conservatives staged in order to intercept the growing political momentum of Rhenish-Westphalian Catholicism in its pursuit of political and social Realism. This contrast became clearly visible in the controversies between the followers of von Hertling and Franz Hitze on social policies. In the end Hitze's orientation proved strong enough to force a prominent exposition of their opinion in the Staatslexikon.

Hertling's studies in political theory can be found primarily in the "Kleine Schriften zur Zeitgeschichte und Politik" (1897), his book "Recht, Staat und Gesellschaft" (1906) and the articles in the 4th edition of the Staatslexikon on aristocracy, Aristoteles, Augustinus, authority, politics, republic, state and state power. His general line was strictly conservative, monarchistic, anti-democratic. In his theoretical foundations he relied heavily on the conservative Dominican traditions in the interpretation of St. Thomas and therefore held himself aloof from the Jesuit traditions in social metaphysics. This partiality was expressed in Hertling's extremely conservative formulations of the concept of authority, the monarchistic interpretation of the origin and existence of state power in the sense of an authoritarian bearer of this power "by the grace of God", and consequently his strict rejection of the theory of the social contract and the democratic concept of sovereignty according to the teachings of Suarez and Bellarmine. This theoretical conservatism in political theory also induced Hertling to go into opposition against the Realism in social policies expressed under Hitze's influence in the main orientation of Social Catholicism, as can be seen in Hertling's "Aufsaetze und Reden sozialpolitischen Inhalts" (1884) and his later, somewhat more conciliatory book "Naturrecht und Sozialpolitik" (1893). His conservatism also caused Hertling to express himself at all times as strongly opposed to political democracy and the system of parliamentary government, as shown most clearly in his "Erinnerungen aus meinem Leben" (1919-20). It was therefore no more than simple historical logic that, as representative of Southern German Conservatism, Hertling was unable to exert any notable influence on the evolution of a realistic political attitude of social reformism in German Catholicism. The same clear ideological logic implied that the entire literary work of Hertling on conservative political theory failed to make any positive contribution to the creative expansion of the system of democratic political theories by German Catholicism during the Weimar Republic.[248]

After 1919 the strongly positive development of the state theories of German Catholicism was resumed which affords one more proof of the immediate influence of history on the systematic achievements of Catholic ideologies. Thus the ideopolitical development of German Catholicism was visibly dependent on the entire complex of the historical vital movements of the German nation and state as a whole. When all past ideo-political traditions and political formations of Imperial Germany had completely broken down in 1918, and the German nation was confronted with the task of constructing an entirely new order of life, German Catholics were among the first to feel this all-German duty as a challenge to themselves and immediately began to adapt their political traditions and vital political forces. There followed a profound re-thinking which made Catholics aware of the concrete ideological and political implications of Catholic political doctrine and enabled them to activate their forces in support of the effort of the entire German nation to construct a positive democratic order of social and political life.

These efforts persisted during the entire life span of the Weimar Republic and produced a special literature in political philosophy and politics, greatly enriching German political science by its wealth of ideas. This series began with the fundamental works of Heinrich Schroers (1852-1928) on "Katholische Staatsauffassung, Kirche und Staat" (1919) and of J. Mausbach on "Organisches Prinzip im Staats—und Gesellschaftsleben" (1920) and "Christliche Staatsordnung und Staatsgesinnung" (1922); also August Pieper "Der deutsche Volksstaat und die Form-Demokratie" (1920) and Johann P. Steffes "Die Staatsauffassung der Moderne" (1921). These essays devoted to actual politics were amplified by the more systematic writings of Tischleder (1891-1947) on "Ursprung und Traeger der Staatsgewalt nach der Lehre des heiligen Thomas und seiner Schule" (1923), "Staatsidee, Staatsgewalt, Staatszweck und Voelkergemeinschaft" (1926); also the writings of Otto Schilling on "Christliche Staatslehre und Politik" (1927) and A. Pieper on "Der Staatsgedanke der deutschen Nation" (1928). The book by J. P. Steffes on "Religion und Politik" (1929) and the symposium published in behalf of the Goerres Society by Godehard Ebers "Katholische Staatslehre und volksdeutsche Politik" (1929) which contains valuable contributions by leading Catholic philosophers, historians and theologians, attempted to deal with the problems emerging from the confrontation of the Catholic state theories with German political realities.

In a parallel trend, several leading scholars devoted much effort to finding a deeper ideological and historical foundation for a systematic history of philosophical political theories, by a series of fundamental works on the teachings and systems of the great classics of Catholic political thought. The foundations had been laid already before the war in the great systematic works of J. Mausbach "Die Ethik des heiligen Augustinus" (1909) and Otto Schilling "Die Staats-und Soziallehren des heiligen Augustinus" (1910) and "Naturrecht und Staat nach Lehren der alten Kirche" (1914). After them came Peter Tischleder with the "Ursprung und Traeger der Staatsgewalt nach der

Lehre des heiligen Thomas" (1923) and again Otto Schilling
with his "Staats-und Soziallehre des heiligen Thomas" (1923).
Heinrich Rommen in his most important book "Die Staatslehre
des Franz Suarez" (1926) offered a very original apology for the
traditions of realistic political metaphysics in German Catholicism, supplemented somewhat later in the same spirit and with
the same systematic thoroughness by Franz Xaver Arnold's
"Die Staatslehre des Kardinals Bellarmin" (1934). More in the
sense of historic actuality but following the same spiritual line
this series was brought to a conclusion by three fundamental
works, O. Schilling's, "Die Staats—und Soziallehre Leos XIII,"
(1925) the penetrating monograph by Wilhelm Schwer "Leo
XIII" (1923) and the exceedingly influential presentation by
Peter Tischleder, "Die Staatslehre Leos XIII." (1925) Also the
magnificent encyclopedic article on "Leo XIII" by Tischleder
in the Staatslexikon should not be overlooked.[249] The monographs on the history of ideas we mention in this section have
without any exception a just claim to be regarded as top achievements in modern Catholic scholarship, and they belong among
the standard works in international Christian political philosophy.

The special literature which originated from the necessity
of establishing a politico-philosophical justification for the
legitimacy of the Weimar Republic despite its origin in a revolution merits our attention as an actual example of the reconciliation of idea and reality in a modern Democracy that traces
its formative origin to the people's sovereignty. Here we point
primarily to the fundamental works by Tischleder, "Ursprung
und Traeger der Staatsgewalt nach der Lehre des heiligen
Thomas" (1923) and "Staatsgewalt und katholisches Gewissen"
(1926); also Heinrich Rommen's "Staatslehre des Franz Suarez" (1926). Supported by the realistic traditions of the politi-al
metaphysics of Suarez and Bellarmine down to Mausbach, they
pleaded for the theory of the social contract and the transfer
of power by the people as a whole. Ever since Suarez and Bellarmine, this theory had been the subject of violent dispute between the partisans of the formal and conservative interpretation of the doctrine of Thomas Aquinas which found the origin
and the bearer of state power to be in the state community, and
the partisans of a realistic interpretation and its further development in the tradition of Suarez and the others. According
to the first concept, the people in a state are only indirectly
the bearers of political power and all they can do is to designate
(designatio) or elect the immediate bearer of political power
to whom this power is then transferred "by the grace of God."

According to the second concept the people in a state are themselves the bearers of state power which they transfer directly (delegatio) to the organs of the state in the name of the natural rights of the people, whereby they do not by any means dispose of these rights permanently by their contractual act of delegation, but on the contrary remain the perpetual and original possessors of political power. This difference between the so-called "designation theory" and the "translation theory" has significant consequences for the doctrine of the social contract and the active, i.e., revolutionary, right of resistance. Those who hold fast to the designation theory necessarily reject the democratic theory of the social contract and people's sovereignty and, by the same token, deny the existence of a direct right to resist and to make revolutionary constitutional changes. Those who believe in the translation theory, on the contrary, not only defend the Suarist concept of people's sovereignty but also deduce from it the right of active resistance. In this sense Mausbach declared "because the social contract is the immediate cause of state authority . . . the people as a whole or its authorized representatives may resort to resistance in extreme emergency, when the public welfare is in utter disarray and all legal means have been exhausted, and if necessary they may depose the monarch and change the constitution." [250] In the above quoted works, Tischleder and Rommen gave a detailed justification of this position which, for two reasons, was felt to be very necessary. It is a fact that the supreme Church authority, though more favorably inclined toward the designation theory, had never issued a direct pronouncement against the other, and that Leo XIII could legitimately be quoted as a witness for the translation theory, as proved by Tischleder in his book "Die Staatslehre Leos XIII." Besides, in view of the revolutionary origin of the Weimar Republic, it was particularly necessary for German Catholics to find a ground for conscientious approval of its beginning which would enable them to subscribe wholeheartedly to its Constitution. It is the special merit of Mausbach, Tischleder and Rommen to have offered such a profound and unassailable basis for the translation theory and consequently for the theory of the social contract and the right to resist, a justification which may equally be applicable in other countries under similar circumstances. This is all the more true since, at that time and even more in the last decade, the teachings of Mausbach, Tischleder and Rommen have been approved by the supreme Church authority despite the incessant attempts of the integralist circles to appeal to obsolete conservative Catholic traditions in opposition to these views, for instance Franx Xaver Kiefl's book "Die Staatsphilosophie der katholischen Kirche" (1928). In his last book on "The State in Catholic Thought" (London- St. Louis, 1945) Rommen has presented the entire problem in a great system and has explained the general fundamental significance of the Catholic political theories in the present era. For the discussion of the right of resistance the latest study of Max Pribilla "Vom Widerstandsrecht des Volkes" (1950) is of primary importance; it also contains the best up-to-date international bibliography on the subject.[251]

A modern treatment of the problem of the disparate spheres of the specific legal and social orders of the state and a discussion of the socio-metaphysical significance of this problem for the international legal order and for a community of nations has been offered by Dietrich von Hildebrand in his two essays "Zur Begrenzung des Staates" (1930) and "Die sittlichen Grundlagen der Voelkergemeinschaft" (1931).[252] These essays and the fundamental work on the same theme by Ferdinand Frodl in "Staat und Voelkerbund" (1936)[253] belong without doubt among the most important contributions made in our day to the problem of the philosophical distinction between the general purpose of law and the "specific social purpose of the state" (Frodl).

To complete our survey, attention must be drawn to the works of Franz Xaver Arnold "Zur Frage des Naturrechtes bei Martin Luther" (1937) and of Richard Hauser, "Autoritaet und Macht" (1949), because they treat intensively and specifically the problem of political authority according to the Protestant ethics and its relationship with the Catholic doctrines, a problem which so far had been too much neglected in German literature. Also the newest study by Nell-Breuning, "Zur christlichen Staatslehre" (1947) deserves special attention because; in accordance with its character as part of the new "Woerterbuch der Politik," [254] it gives the most concise, and at the same time excellent survey of all the material realms of the Catholic political theories, and in addition a bibliography of the pertinent German literature.

3. THE THEORY OF SOCIETY AND THE SOCIAL THEORIES

1. *The Metaphysics of Community*

For the development of an indigenous social doctrine in German Catholicism, a strictly realistic social metaphysics was of utmost importance. The search for solutions of the social and sociological problems was in the best tradition of the Catholic world concept in that it established a positive vision of the essential unity of the metaphysical (causal) and the natural-practical (teleological) context of the world with all its problems. The decided Realism and initiative with which all natural and social values of the existing social orders under the given historical conditions were granted recognition, fully correspond to the wise and realistic "assent to the world" (Weltbejahung) of the great Augustine. "Because everything that God has created is good, from the rational creature itself down to the simplest living body, therefore every rational soul acts well when it adheres to the order and, distinguishing, selecting and evaluating, subordinates the lesser to the greater, the lower to the higher, the corporal to the spiritual, the temporal to the eternal." [255] In the same manner, teleological activism pointedly oriented toward real life and obligated to practical action corresponds to the profound realistic world wisdom of Thomas Aquinas. "Practical reason, like theoretical, perceives the truth, but it directs the truth it has perceived primarily toward action."[256] And again in the same manner, the optimistic faith in human personality and its natural right to think for itself and to act as "the master of the world by way of society and in the midst of society"[257] fully correspond to the theological principle which underlies the social doctrine of Pope Leo XIII, with its justification of a realistic world concept, as opposed to all one-sided spiritualistic maximalism, because only this concept secures the real *summa summarum* of the social wisdom of the Church: "Gratia praesupponit, non destruit, sed perficit naturam"—"Grace presupposes nature; it does not destroy it but renders it perfect."

These principles have been given a detailed, practical exposition in Leo XIII's encyclicals, especially in the basic social missive, the Encyclical *Rerum Novarum,* which is also a thorough presentation of the Christian Natural Law doctrine. Particularly in the definition of the inviolability of Natural Law (sanctisima naturae lex est) , in that of the natural rights of the single person (naturalibus singulorum juribus) and in the application of these principles in actual natural justice (justitia naturalis) , Leo XIII's intepretations became the practical foundation for the entire modern Catholic theory concerning community and society and for the definitely realistic approach characteristic of Germany. In these interpretations, three problems are central to the searching interest in social philosophy: first, the relation of the *single person,* as constituting a natural and rational *substantial entity* (naturae rationalis subsistentia) , to the essence of *society*, as constituting a spiritual-moral *entity of order;* second and consequently, the relation of the individual good (bonum singulare), constituting the individual welfare of the human person, to the common good (bonum commune) of society; finally and in further consequence, the orders of natural justice (justitia naturalis) which determine the relations of the individual to society, constituting the special categories of social (legal) justice (justitia legalis), distributive justice (justitia distributiva) and commutative, equalizing justice (justitia stricta et commutativa).

Already in the first decisive works of Theodor Meyer and Heinrich Pesch these three problems received such a fundamental and practical elucidation that in the subsequent fifty years until today nothing more was needed but its elaboration and application to the various actualities. These efforts moved along three lines: the metaphysical problem of person versus community, systematically expressed in a *Metaphysics of Community;* second, the philosophical problem of the individual versus society, systematically expressed in a special *Doctrine of Society;* third, the predominantly socio-economic problem of society and economy, systematically expressed in a special theory of *Social and Political Economics.*

Theodor Meyer undertook to formulate a "Metaphysics of Community" in his work "Die Grundsaetze der Sittlichkeit und des Rechtes." Here we find clearly outlined as to their origin and their community-forming action the specific metaphysical forces which by his nature place man within an order as an "ens sociale" (social being) in the midst of a community in general, and as a *zoon physei politikon* (a naturally political creature) in the midst of a specific society and state. "There are these primordial invisible magnets innate in human nature which sympathetically draw man to man, family to family, connecting them with one another not according to a plan arbitrarily set up by men, but in a plan of divine creation. Starting from the simplest natural ties between individuals in a domestic society, progressing to an association of families in a borough, uniting the boroughs of one tribe in the association of a nation, this enigmatic act of sociable nature marches on to the perfect order of the state or, as the ancients better expressed it, to the great civic commonwealth in a *res publica* or *regnum.*" [258] After the Encyclical *Rerum Novarum,* Meyer later expanded this definition in his important study "Die christlich-ethischen Sozialprinzipien und die Arbeiterfrage" (1891).

Meyer began by showing up the metaphysical character of the

community-forming forces of social human nature which lead to a moral "organism" of community without impairing the personal existence and dignity of the individual human "members" who form it and are its permanent bearers. "These ties are real in the sense that they unite man with his equals in the manner of an organic order by which they form viable higher units in a framework within which the single persons can behave somewhat like elementary parts of a whole. But these ties are moral in the sense that they do not impair the personal dignity of a rational being since they limit his individual liberty in favor of the organic whole but without doing him any real harm because for the apparent loss they offer him rich compensation at incomparably higher interest."[259] These explanations achieved great lucidity in the systematic distinction and drawing of the *analogy* between the natural organism of personal human existence and the metaphysical "organism" of society, a lucidity never surpassed by subsequent attempts in this direction. Here the fundamental distinction is clearly defined between the substantial, existential unit of man and the moral, ordered unit of society, and from this distinction an analogy is derived of man's naturalistic order of personal existence as against the moral order of man's community existence in society. *"Thus the social association which follows from man's social nature enters the ranks of natural organisms in an analogous (i.e., similar, yet not identical) manner and affords an eloquent testimonial to the wondrous unity in the divine plan of creation and order. But it remains distinct from all organic beings in the world of the senses, being a moral organism, and as such forming as separate order of its own."* [260]

In this definition the metaphysical principle of a genuine "organic" concept of the state and society is rendered unequivocally secure against any rejection from the viewpoint of the positivistic and materialistic political and social doctrines with their bias against metaphysics. But at the same time this definition refutes all organic, totalitarian political and social doctrines including the so-called "universalism" of Othmar Spann in its Christian camouflage with its attempt to justify the setting up of a questionable mysticism of "wholeness" (Ganzheit) in the place of a genuine "metaphysics of community."

Meyer's fundamental work received an essential supplementation and amplification in the works of Joseph Mausbach by the addition of a more profound ethical understructure for the problem of community in the spirit of *Augustinian Personalism*. Mausbach's works, in their admirable ethical, personalistic optimism for the progress of civilization, have contributed much toward a fruitful religious and philosophical implementation of the social metaphysics in the tradition Thomas-Molina-Suarez down to Meyer, Cathrein and Pesch. *This gave modern German Catholic social philosophy that distinctive note of strong realistic Personalism in the specific doctrine of society, and of equally strong personalistic Realism in the specific socio-philosophical and socio-economical system of Solidarism.* By Mausbach's basic contribution to this theme, primarily in his "Christlich-katholische Ethik" (1906), his great three-volume "Moraltheologie" (1918) and his "Gemeinschaftsgeist der Religion Christi" (1921), Catholic social philosophy has been enabled to grasp in a manner heretofore impossible the fundamental values of the personalistic ethics and philosophy of civilization of the great Augustine. In this effort with its extraordinary seminal influence on the evolution of German Catholic social philosophy we find the true practical manifestation of the still, quiet work of decades devoted by this inspired scholar and servant of God to developing his fundamental presentation of the "Ethik des heiligen Augustinus" (1909). It is primarily thanks to Mausbach's effort to revive Augustinian Personalism that the German contribution to a "metaphysics of community"—in the line from Scheler to Guardini and Przywara down to Steinbuechel and Hildebrand—has such a distinctive personalistic and truly "existential" character, although in several cases, as for instance Scheler's, this source has never been acknowledged.

The works of Max Scheler (1875-1928) during his "Catholic period" have had strong influence on the discussion of the philosophy of society—although this influence was more in the nature of a stimulant than of an original, systematic and profound contribution. This is particularly true of his numerous essays collected in "Krieg und Aufbau" (1916), "Vom Umsturz der Werte" (1919, "Vom Ewigen im Menschen" (1921) and "Schriften zur Soziologie und Weltanschauung" (1923-1924). Further valuable contributions were made by Theodor Steinbuechel in his "Philosophische Grundlegung der katholischen Sittenlehre" (1923); by Erich Przywara: "Gottgeheimnis der Welt" (1923) and "Im Ringen der Gegenwart" (1929); and Romano Guardini "Der Gegensatz, Versuch einer Philosophie des Lebendigen und Konkreten" (1923); while Johannes Haessle in his "Arbeitsethos der Kirche" (1923) continued straight in the tradition of Theodor Meyer.

Special studies were devoted to presenting, according to the source materials, the precise doctrine of St. Thomas concerning the relationship of man with the forms and orders of society. Robert Linhard, in his "Sozialprinzipien des heiligen

Thomas von Aquino" (1932), attempted to give first of all an interpretation of the ontological-metaphysical proofs for the integral Thomist ethics of society. Edelbert Kurz, on the other hand, with his Franciscan spiritual receptivity for the world at large, offered a particularly timely presentation of the problems of "Individuum und Gemeinschaft beim heiligen Thomas" (1933), while Eberhard Welty followed the tradition of Dominican interpretation in formulating the relationship of "Gemeinschaft und Einzelmensch nach den Grundsaetzen des heiligen Thomas" (1925).

The achievement which had the most far-reaching importance in giving this era a philosophical understanding of the modern problems of community and society goes to the credit of Dietrich von Hildebrand and his fundamental "Metaphysik der Gemeinschaft" (1930). Strongly relying on Augustinian Personalism and using the modern methods of a phenomenological approach to the essence of things, Hildebrand unfolded the problem of the personal roots of communities, and also of their peculiar essence and ontological inter-existence. From there he proceeded to build a systematic structure of the scale of values of the various communities whose purposes he oriented primarily toward their specific importance for the personal existence of man as such. For, "when all due consideration is given to the peculiar quality of communities versus individuals and their personal values, the scale of values of the communities among themselves and the primacy of the single person as against all natural communities must also be clearly recognized."[261] In his study, "Die Kirche als Gemeinschaft und Gesellschaft" (1931), Arnold Rademacher gave these problems as they were presented by Hildebrand a religio-sociological implementation in the direction of theology. Most recently Theodor Geppert in his work "Teleologie der menschlichen Gesellschaft" (1948), using all important German works related to this subject, tried to expand the efforts of Hildebrand and Rademacher in two respects. He attempted to penetrate more deeply into the socio-teleological structure of the natural communities and their socio-philosophical foundation in a metaphysics of society in order to give them secure roots by tying them in with the theological structures of supranatural communities. After this he tried to formulate the so-called socio-theological structure of these supra-natural communities in a special system of a "Theology of Community."

Since every effort to formulate a metaphysics of community must of necessity begin by forming a concept of the personal existence of man as such, it follows that philosophical anthropology gives the introduction to all socio-philosophical inquiries into the essence and purpose of the orders of community. It seems therefore natural that in times of vital crisis as today, the basic questions concerning the community must also penetrate down to the even more fundamental questions as to human existence itself. This is the reason why the socio-philosophical concern in Germany today has reverted to the basic questions of the human being, as particularly expressed in the recent works by Catholic authors, such as: Alois Dempf "Christliche Philosophie. Der Mensch zwischen Gott und der Welt" (1938) ; Romano Guardini, "Welt und Person. Versuche zur christlichen Lehre vom Menschen" (1940); Johann P. Steffes, "Christliche Existenz inmitten der Welt" (1947) ; Theodor Steinbuechel, "Religion und Moral im Lichte christlicher Existenz" (1951), and finally the particularly significant work of Hans-Eduard Hengstenberg, "Grundlegung einer Metaphysik der Gemeinschaft" (1949).

2. *The Theory of Society*

It is the task of a special Theory of Society to present the theoretical foundation of the spiritual and moral relationship "person versus community" in a natural ordered system that comprises the real relations of concrete individuals with a concrete society. In other words, the metaphysical justification of the essentially social nature (sociabilitas) of the human *Person* must now be given concreteness within the visible orders of social activities (activitas socialis) of the human *Personality*. In this relation between *sociabilitas* and *activitas socialis,* that other relation between the "organic" essence of the community and the "organizational" essence of society can best be visualized. While the organic order of society guarantees the autonomy of personal human existence—this order and this autonomy being subject and object, respectively, of natural justice (*justitia naturalis*)—it is up to the specific organization of society to realize these guarantees within the practical order of social justice (*justitia socialis*). Only in this relationship can the metaphysical concept of the "Person" be expanded into the social concept of the "Personality," and only in this expansion can the personalistic basis for the theories of society be secured. It is consequently the primary task of society to create the preconditions for the concrete existence of man with all his evolutionary possibilities—as conceived in the concrete notion of Personality, not the abstract idea of the Person—by means of the various orders of *justitia socialis, distributiva* and *commutativa.*

This also explains the relationship of the individual good with its personalistic character to the common good with its social character. It is a relation of mutual rights and duties whose integral observation (in solidum) serves the order of the entire social system and the whole organization of society. On this foundation of the natural mutual obligation for both the individual and the common good, and in consequence of the solidarity *(solidaritas)* of the individual and social interest and the responsibility for safeguarding a correct equilibrium between the individual and the common good, German Catholicism has constructed a specific socio-philosophical and socio-economical system which Heinrich Pesch characteristically named *Solidarismus.*

A theory of society logically begins by describing the various levels of the natural order, proceeding from the individuals by way of the families up to the state. Such a general theory of society already contains basic philosophical elements because it is determined, even down to its foundations, by profoundly religious, socio-metaphysical concepts of the essence of the family, and a philosophy of law concerning the essence of the state. On the other hand, the material circumstances and economic organization of life are of decisive importance for the real mutual relations of the individual and common good. Any theory of society must devote special interest to the order and development of the economic common good *(bonum commune economicum)* and to work out specific systems of social and theoretical economics. Such a purely factual treatment of the autonomous realms of economic life does not, however, admit of the direct introduction of philosophical concerns, and therefore in a strict sense there is no specifically "Christian," or for that matter "Catholic," economic science. In this, economic theory is different from the general theory of society with its basically and distinctly philosophical character by which our theories will necessarily be characterized as "Christian" in contrast to other systems of society based on other philosophies.

Now, the specific theory of society of German Catholicism with its system of "Solidarism" has from the very beginning strictly observed this necessary distinction, although Heinrich Pesch was at the same time the founder of the general, systematic theory of society and of the specific economic system of "Solidarism." To gain a proper understanding of these developments in German Catholicism we shall have to keep this double line well in mind in examining the parallel strains of the general "Theory of Society" and the special "Theory of Economics" of Solidarism.

It is only natural that in practice these two strains mutually determined and supported one another and that the material fields of interest finally merged in a third phenomenon, the special science of society and economy termed "Catholic Sociology."

In his fundamental work "Liberialismus, Sozialismus und christliche Gesellschaftsordnung" (1901), unjustly forgotten today, Heinrich Pesch was the first to offer a systematic and comprehensive presentation of previous incomplete efforts by German Catholics. In this voluminous work which uses all source materials available up to this time, including especially the concepts of his philosophical opponents, Pesch circumscribed the activistic task which devolves on the individual person, both as the subject and object of all social activity. First he strictly defined this task in opposition to the individualistic concepts of the society of liberalism and the collectivistic concepts of socialism. "Thus man is the master of the world, but only by way of society and in the midst of society! This is not to say that society must first grant him the right of mastering the world or the power to use the goods of external nature for the satisfaction of his needs. No, this right is man's by virtue of his nature which raises him above the world and at the same time directs him toward the world. Only in order to accomplish his mastery, for its factual exercise, for the content of his domination, is man indebted in large measure to society. This is reason enough for seeking his satisfaction only at the expense of nature, not at the expense of society. Man will be mindful of the fact that life in society is to be a blessing for all the others, and that in actions in which so many must take part each individual must yield to the higher purposes of society."

Pesch proceeds to give a definition of society which is in the best tradition of the ethical Realism of Catholicism. "By society we understand an organized community, a permanent association of persons who through common aims are obligated to common action and are guided by a legal authority toward the purpose of their society. The association of a number of persons with mutual rights and duties to form an ethical unity, efforts directed toward a common goal with united forces and under a common leadership—these are the essential characteristics of every true society." [262]

Guided by this concern for common (solidaristic) interests and responsibilities, Pesch formulated the specific realms and orders of *justitia legalis, distributiva* and *commutativa* with such detailed and systematic thoroughness that his formulations serve up to this date as the main groundwork for the efforts of German Catholicism in social philosophy. On the basis of his work Pesch wrote in 1905 the "Grundlegung" (Principles) of his social philosophy which later grew into his monumental five-volume "Lehrbuch der Nationaloekonomie." This gives a special apology for the *principle of Solidarity* which still ranks as the classical principle of German Catholic social philosophy. "The idea of Solidarity in its application to a social community, both as to forming and strengthening it, implies the combination of all efforts which have tended to create or have created a social unity oriented toward a morally permissible or morally required common goal. Solidarity which is called upon to establish in state and economy an equilibrium among individuals, groups and larger units of society cannot be reconciled with exclusively utilitarian conceptions like plutocratic individualism, nor with any sort of one-sided class or group egotisms. Solidarity not only implies an enhancement of powers, not only makes it possible to acquire profit, opportunity, advantage; it also demands sacrifices, discipline and subordination in the line of duty to society, yes, even sacrifices whose immediate advantage for the individual cannot at the time be seen. To offer such sacrifice, however, a higher motive is indispensable, and therefore solidarity among the citizens of a state must be firmly rooted in a moral order." [263]

Pesch also lucidly analyzed the distinction between the unconditional character of "Civic Solidarity" under the obligation of Natural Law and the conditional, specific character under positive law of "Vocational and Cooperative Solidarity." "The state, like the family, is a necessary form of society among men; subordination under the purpose of the state is therefore not a freely undertaken obligation, but a duty under Natural Law. This is, however, distinct from the various forms of cooperative and corporate vocational associations. Here Solidarity indeed acts—be it in a community of interests, a similarity of vocations and the sympathies arising therefrom—as a formative, organizing, binding force of society, but only after the association has become operative either by contract (cooperation) or through an institution of positive law (vocational corporation)." [264]

Until his death in 1926, Pesch continued to work out the social doctrine of Solidarism. Among other systematic elaborations the following deserve to be cited: Joseph Mausbach, "Das soziale Prinzip und der Katholizismus" (1918);[265] Goetz Briefs, "Zur Kritik sozialer Grundprinzipien" (1922);[266] Johannes Haessle, "Das Arbeitsethos der Kirche nach Thomas von Aquino und Leo XIII" (1923) and Gustav Gundlach, "Solidarismus, Einzelmensch and Gemeinschaft (1936).[267] These studies are supplemented by those writings whose concern was to apply the Encyclicals of Pope Pius XI to the modern problems of the social theory of Solidarism: Ferdinand Frodl, "Koenigtum Christi" (1926) and J. B. Schuster, "Die Soziallehre nach Leo XIII und Pius XI" (1936). Finally the large symposium "Die soziale Frage und der Katholizismus" (1931) is of very great importance. It was published by the Goerres Society as memorial issue at the occasion of the fortieth anniversary of the Encyclical *Rerum Novarum*, and it contains contributions of twenty-seven Catholic authors to the problems of the Catholic theory of society and social policies, predominantly from the point of view of Solidarism.[267a]

In most recent years three oustanding social scientists have devoted their efforts to constructing a comprehensive system of sociology, thereby following more or less strictly in the lines of Pesch. Otto Schilling published a well-balanced traditional system of "Christliche Gesellschaftslehre" (1926) which he later supplemented by a presentation of "Katholische Sozialethik" (1929). Wilhelm Schwer, in straight continuation of Pesch, wrote his "Catholic Social Theory" (London-St. Louis, 1940, first German publication 1928) which is probably the most authentic presentation and continuation of the social philosophy of Solidarism. Beyond any doubt the most significant and modern presentation was given by Ferdinand Frodl in his "Gesellschaftslehre" (1936). This work combines a profound survey of the history of ideas with a far-reaching socio-philosophical examination of all the important categories and problems of the principles of the relationship between individual and society, inclusive of its contemporary manifestations. He placed at the center of his inquiry the quality of "sociability" (*sociabilitas*) of human nature.[268]

The following modern presentations, most of them however only sketchy, merit to be listed because they express the constructive spirit that enlivened modern Catholic social theory in the midst of the present vital crisis of Germany: Paul Jostock, "Grundzuege der Soziallehre und Sozialpolitik" (1946); Franz Xaver Arnold "Zur christlichen Loesung der sozialen Frage" (1947); Jacob Barion, "Recht, Staat und Gesellschaft" (1948); and Oswald Nell-Breuning "Zur christlichen Gesellschaftslehre" (1947) and "Einzelmensch und Gesellschaft" (1951). In this connection we must once more refer to the comprehensive, exceedingly important work of Johann Messner, "Social Ethics, Natural Law in the Modern World" (London-St. Louis, 1949, German edition "Naturrecht" 1948) which is probably the most important presentation of the philosophical problems of society from the Catholic point of view.

3. Economy and Society

Solidarism is the only Catholic theory of society that proved able to formulate Catholic basic philosophy in a general socio-philosophical system, and then to bring it down to earth in a concrete and specific "system of social work." The general socio-philosophic system placed *Sociabilitas,* i.e., the essentially social character of man as a person, into the center of its presentation of a doctrine of socialized man. Building on this foundation, the socio-economic special theory of Solidarism then described the specific *activitas socialis* of the working person in the realms of "economy and society." Already in the introduction to his "Nationaloekonomie" Heinrich Pesch thus outlined this task: "Solidarism is not a theological system; it is rather a socio-philosophical system, the system of social work, an economic system. It continues and expands the older traditional systems to include realities introduced by industry." To stress in particular that this task, of analyzing realistically the position and duties of economic man within the orders of economic reality constituted an independent system, Pesch added, "While I gave special weight to the import of Christian philosophy on economic life and, in logical consequence, on economic theory, I have always pointed out that no economic system can be gleaned from the Christian Gospel. It is the task of economic science to construct economic systems; and economic programs to correspond to the conditions, needs and possibilities of the times can only be expected to result from practical economic policies." [269]

From this point of view Pesch strictly rejected every theologization of the main socio-economic concepts, those of work and property, as attempted by certain "Catholic" economic ideologies. He defended the scientific freedom for Solidarism to seek an objective "approach to the older traditional systems to establish an up-to-date system of industry." With equal firmness Pesch turned against those who either wish to make an absolute of the property concept, i.e., the liberals; or to deny it, i.e., the socialists; as also those capitalists who overlook the high personal value of human work, and those socialists who wish to make of labor a purely materialistic phenomenon. Thus the special character and philosophical originality of Solidarism lies precisely in this simultaneous opposition to theologizing Catholic economic integralism on the one hand, and to profit capitalism in contempt of work as well as to socialism in contempt of property on the other hand. For Pesch's detailed reasoning in support of his rejection of individualistic Capitalism and Marxian Socialism in favor of Solidarism, we refer to the texts quoted in the Appendix.[270]

However, despite this opposition on the ground of socio-philosophical principles, there is an essential kinship of interests between the socio-economic system of Solidarism and both the capitalistic economy of Liberalism and the socialized economy of Socialism. Solidarism's significance as a theory of economics lies precisely in this position relative to the other ideologies. The special stress on the personalistic character of the *activitas socialis* of man in his work and the high value ascribed on this basis to labor make possible a fair coordination of the economic interests both under the individualistic principle and under the socialist principle; on this basis a proper settlement between the individual and the common good (bonum commune oeconomicum) can be firmly established as the goal.

Since Solidarism thus gives a central position in its thinking to the high value for the social order of man in his work, and of human labor for the common good, special attention is paid to the necessity of securing the working men's existence and of fairly distributing the returns of human labor. Wherever these requirements are given due weight in the systems of Liberalism and Socialism, Solidarism will deem it a duty to accept and defend such "capitalist" or "socialist" principles and measures. Therefore, Solidarism is clearly oriented toward Capitalism where it is a question of safeguarding the basic principles and institutions of private property, as required by Natural Law in defense of the individual existence of man; and equally, where the technical orders of a capitalist economy must be defended to give working men the necessary scope and security in their economic existence. On the other hand, Solidarism is also oriented toward Socialism where it is a question of according human labor recognition on principle as the source of all wealth and, based thereon, of the demand for a just distribution of the fruits of human labor in the sense of a socialized protection of the social existence of man in his work.

Solidarism finds the best approach to these tasks in demanding, parallel with general human solidarity and with civic solidarity, a specific, *socio-economic Solidarity*, and also, parallel with the preferred position to the *bonum commune* before the social good of the single person, without detracting from his personal values and autonomies, the *bonum commune oeconomicum* is given pride of place in general economic life before the interests of individual economic enterprise without detracting from the natural privileges and material safeguards of the individuals. And finally: since the principle of social solidarity can only be realized in a natural, i.e., a fair, order of the relations between the individual and the common good, in other words, only through the medium of the natural ranks in the social order in ascending line from the person to the family to the nation and state, thus also the socio-economic principle of solidarity can only be realized through the medium of an objective, i.e., a fair order and a vocational structure of economic life.

Consequently, the principle of socio-economic Solidarity requires a threefold order, constructed to safeguard the right relation between man and economy, and the just relation between work and earnings through the right order of labor and capital, on the one hand, and of individual economic interests and the *bonum commune oeconomicum* on the other. In the first order, the problem to be solved is to protect human work and the personal dignity and rights of man in his work by a sound social stratification and the humanization of economic life. For a better understanding of this problem we again refer to the pertinent quotations from Pesch in the Appendix. In the second order, it is the task of the state to safeguard the economic common good by establishing the correct relation of the individualistic principle and private economy with the social principle and social economy. In this respect, while unconditionally rejecting a generally socialized state economy, Pesch gave a fine formulation to the conditional principle of state intervention in economic policies, permissible and often necessary as a subsidiary expedient. "When it appears desirable that the interests of society receive stronger support, certain interventions in economic life on the part of public authorities may be necessary to defend the priority of the social will before the individual will, of the social interests before the individual interests. Such interventions may be confined to supervision and regulation. However, they may also, with several intermediary stages, go so far as to replace private by public enterprise, that is, as far as "socialization" in the specific sense of the term." [271] The socio-economic legitimacy, and the economic wisdom of this formulation is proved by the fact that, as Pesch's formulations of vocational corporate Solidarity and stratification of economic life, they received supreme official Church sanction in the Encyclical *Quadragesimo Anno* of 1931, as the specific principles of subsidiarity (subsidiarii officii principium) and of the corporative order.

From the publication of the first volume of Pesch's socio-philosophical "Grundlegung" (1905) until his death, he worked tirelessly at the systematic elaboration of his great "Lehrbuch der Nationaloekonomie" in five volumes (last enlarged edition, Freiburg 1924-25). This monumental work has no parallel in other countries in the entire socio-economic literature of Catholicism. But it must also be counted among the few important standard works of modern economic science thanks to the breadth of its factual range of problems and the admirable comprehensiveness of the socio-economical survey of literature which includes non-Catholic and non-German works. Along with the studies "Privateigentum als soziale Institution" and "Freiwirtschaft oder soziale Wirtschaftsordnung," in Pesch's extensive literary production special attention is due to his manifesto of 1919, "Neuaufbau der Gesellschaft," because it served to a large degree as the basic program for the constructive social policies and reforms for which German Catholicism fought under the Weimar Republic.

In the last generation a large number of Pesch's disciples and fellow thinkers have purposefully continued to expand the socio-economic system of Solidarism. The task was at all times to deal with the special problems posed by the ideological and socio-political role of mediator between Capitalism and Socialism, in the construction of a system of political economy that sought a realistic reconciliation of the individual with the social principle, of private enterprise with socialized economy. "As much liberty as possible, as much direction as necessary!" (Schwer).

Important for the special problems of Capitalism and Solidarism are primarily the studies of Franz Keller, "Unternehmer und Mehrwert" (1912) and "Der moderne Kapitalismus" (1918); Oswald von Nell-Breuning, "Grundzuege der Boersenmoral" (1928), "Aktienreform und Moral" (1930), "Die Eigentumslehre" (1931), and by the same author the rewarding pamphlets, "Wirtschafts-und sozialpolitische Flugschriften" (12 issues, 1929); also Otto Schilling, "Der kirchliche Eigentumsbegriff" (1930) and the systematic works by Paul Jostock, "Der deutsche Katholizismus und die Ueberwindung des Kapitalismus" (1932) and Franz Mueller/Wilhelm Schwer, "Der deutsche Katholizismus in Zeitalter des Kapitalismus" (1932). A continuation of the solidaristic ideology and evaluation of labor was offered by Theodor Brauer, "Produktionsfaktor Arbeit" (1925), August Pieper, "Berufsgedanke and Berufsstand im Wirtschaftsleben" (1925); Heinrich Lechtape, "Die menschliche Arbeit als Objekt der wissenschaftlichen Sozialpolitik" (1929) and Goetz Briefs, "The Proletariat" (New York, 1937).

When in 1931 the Encyclical *Quadragesimo Anno* was published, it not only turned out to be to a large extent an official confirmation by the Church of the teachings of Solidarism; it also inaugurated a more thorough systematic elaboration of the concept of property and the theory of interest, of the subsidiary character of state intervention in economic and social life, and especially of the construct of a "Corporate Order." This gives the solidaristic interpretation of *Quadragesimo Anno* its special significance. Aside from the commentaries by Gustav Gundlach, "Papst Pius XI zur heutigen Wirtschafts- und Gesellschaftsnot" (1932), A. Retzbach, "Die Erneuerung der gesellschaftlichen Ordnung" (1932), Josef Pieper, "Die Neuordnung der menschlichen Gesellschaft" (1932) and Paul Jostock, "Die sozialen Rundschreiben" (1948), fundamental importance belongs primarily to the great systematic commentary by Oswald von Nell-Breuning, "Reorganization of Social Economy" (Milwaukee, 1936, first German edition 1932). This book by Nell-Breuning gives much more than the usual commentary. It adds a positive application of the essential doctrines of Solidarism in respect to social philosophy and economic theory with special regard to the actual problems arising among Catholicism, Liberalism and Socialism and the more recent ideologies of communist and fascist Collectivism.

Also the commentaries pertaining to the corporative concept as outlined in *Quadragesimo Anno* contributed a great deal to clarify the solidaristic ideas about vocation and economy and to develop them constructively. For this, apart from the commentaries already cited, special attention should be given to the great book by Johannes Messner, "Die soziale Frage" (1932) and to his study, "Die berufsstaendische Ordnung" (1936); also the study by Friedrich Dessauer, "Kooperative Wirtschaft" (1929), and the two-volume symposium which Joseph van der Velde published under the title "Die berufsstaendische Ordnung" (1932-33).

A general ideological and systematical presentation of Solidarism is contained in the writings of Heinrich Lechtape, "Der christliche Solidarismus" (1921), P. W. Haurand, "Das national-oekonomische System von Heinrich Pesch" (1922), Johannes Messner, "Um die katholisch-soziale Einheitslinie" (1930), Franz Mueller, "Heinrich Pesch and his Theory of Christian Solidarism" (1941) and Oswald von Nell-Breuning, "Zur sozialen Frage" (1949). Of special interest and lasting value for the history of systems is above all the great solidaristic symposium by M. Meinertz- H. Sacher, "Deutschland und der Katholizismus" (1918) and the memorial volume of the Goerres

Society we mentioned before, "Die soziale Frage und der Katholizismus" (1931).[272]

4. *Catholicism and Socialism*

The position which German Catholicism takes in regard to Socialism can be well understood only if the evolution of the German Social Democratic Party, the legitimate representative of the Marxist ideology and movement in Germany, is kept in mind. This evolution may be divided into two great periods, first the one during which the Social Democratic movement was identified with the revolutionary social movements and atheistic cultural programs of Marxism, which lasted approximately till 1918; second the one in which German Marxism was split up into the revolutionary movement of Communism and the revisionist movement of German Socialism under the leadership of the Social Democratic Party after the Weimar Republic had been founded.

In the first period, despite many common interests, Catholicism remained in irreconcilable opposition to the entire movement of German Socialism. As long as under the leadership of Engels, Bebel and Kautsky, it professed allegiance to Marx's revolutionary program of atheism and hostility to the Church, rejection of private property, revolutionary overthrow of the political order, collectivization of economy and society, etc., Catholicism was forced into uncompromising opposition. Among the literary documents of this period primarily three books are of lasting historical interest, first Emmanuel Ketteler, "Liberalismus, Sozialismus und Christentum" (1871); second, the well-known book by Victor Cathrein, "Socialism" (New York 1904, first German edition 1890) which till 1923 saw 16 printings and was translated into eleven languages. To this Cathrein added a further study in 1929, "Sozialismus und Katholizismus," in which he made the distinction now required between Socialism and Communism and thereby accorded a more positive evaluation to the former. The third book is by Heinrich Pesch, "Der moderne Sozialismus" (1901) with an appendix "Zur Geschichte der sozialistischen Bewegung in Deutschland." This voluminous work (600pp.) with admirable objectivity and scholarship digests at great length the entire source material available in 1900, especially concerning the works of Marx, Engels, Lassalle, Bebel, Bernstein, Kautsky, as well as the most important Catholic and foreign literature, which gives this work permanent historical value.

Of special importance are also primarily the books by Wilhelm Hohoff (1848-1923), "Warenwert und Kapitalprofit" (1902), "Die Bedeutung der Marxschen Kapitalkritik" (1908) and the collection of his essays on "Die wissenschaftliche und kulturhistorische Bedeutung der Marxschen Lehre" (1929) which were mostly published in the 1890's in Vogelsang's journal "Monatsschrift fuer christliche Sozialreform." This Catholic priest who worked under the sponsorship of Wilhelm Schneider, Bishop of Paderborn, devoted an entire sacrificial life to the one task—to initiate Catholicism to the values of the Socialist criticism of economy and society. Even Johannes Messner made the following sincere comment on this achievement: "It is the lasting merit of Hohoff to have at once recognized the importance of the Marxian criticism of the capitalistic economy and society and to have prepared its fructification for the Catholic social doctrine. This should be rated all the higher since with his insight and effort he stood absolutely alone." [273]

The ideological evolution of the Social Democratic Party after 1918 and its change of direction toward policies of democratic political constructiveness, social reform and non-partisan cultural attitudes had the immediate consequence of establishing a new relationship between Catholicism and this new shape of "German Socialism." At the same time, the whole spirit of the era prevailed upon German Catholicism to devote keener attention to the ethos underlying the socialistic ideas and their deeper social values which found their expressions in the contemporary phenomena of the Socialistic movements. This reevaluation took the first definite form in Max Scheler's, "Prophetischer oder marxistischer Sozialismus" (1919), Theodor Steinbuechel, "Zur philosophischen Grundlegung des marxistischen Sozialismus" (1919) and "Zur Ethik des marxistischen Sozialismus" (1919), Theodor Brauer, "Christentum und Sozialismus" (1920), and Goetz Briefs, "Untergang des Abendlandes, Christentum und Sozialismus" (1920) and "Der soziale Volkstaat und der Sozialismus" (1921). These efforts were systematically followed up by the two fundamental books by Theodor Steinbuechel, "Der Sozialismus als sittliche Idee" (1921) and August Pieper, "Kapitalismus und Sozialismus als seelisches Problem" (1924), in which the new positive Catholic approach to the idea of Socialism is well characterized as "the idea of a superior, more perfect community of life and fortune than was ever achieved before, which takes its vital strength from the unselfish loyalty and devotion of one man for another." After this, in his valuable book "Der moderne deutsche Sozialismus" (1928), Theodor Brauer described in detail the entire effort of modern German Catholicism to achieve a deeper understanding of the Socialist ideas and movements. It is Brauer's special merit to have presented with fine objectivity and erudition the whole ideological evolution within Socialism, including the deeply ethical concern in the movement of "Religious Socialism." This makes of Brauer's book an important continuation of the work Pesch did at an earlier stage of this evolution.

This predominantly religious and socio-philosophical concern also brought forth the politico-religious and social-reformatory ideas that were formulated in the Frankfurt Circle, grouped around the "Rhein-Mainische Volkszeitung" and the movement of the "Catholic Socialists." Out of the Frankfurt Circle came the writings of Ernst Michel, "Zur Grundlegung einer katholischen Politik" (1923), "Zwischen Staat und Gesellschaft" (1926), "Politik aus dem Glauben" (1926) and "Industrielle Arbeitsordnung" (1932); also Walter Dirks, "Erbe und Aufgabe" (1931). The closely-knit circle around the "Catholic Socialists" was represented ideologically by the magazine "Das rote Blatt" and the books by Georg Beyer, "Katholizismus und Sozialismus," (1927), Otto Bauer, "Sozialdemokratie, Religion und Kirche" (1927) and Heinrich Mertens, "Katholische Sozialisten" (1930); also in the social radicalism of Vitus Heller and his magazine, "Das neue Volk."

After the catastrophe of 1945, the circle grouped around Eugen Kogon and his "Frankfurter Hefte" searches for an up-to-date synthesis of socialist ethics with the Catholic theories of society in the direction of a "socialism of liberty." Walter Dirks who belongs to this circle has formulated this effort in his book "Die zweite Republik" (1947) as an attempt of a "socialism with Christian responsibility." As against this trend the Tuebingen theologian Franz Xaver Arnold propagates a "personalistic socialism as a requirement of Christian social pedagogics" (1946) which he expounds in detail in his outstandingly factual book, "Zur christlichen Loesung der sozialen Frage" (1947). Finally, Theodor Steinbuechel in his studies "Karl Marx, Gestalt—Werk—Ethos" (1947) and "Die sozialistische Idee 1848" (1948) has offered a profound presentation of his effort of many years to create among Catholics a positive understanding of the socialist ideas and movements, and to the same effort is dedicated the posthumous collection from his writings, "Sozialismus" (1950).

5. Catholic Sociology

The special historic conditions which have determined the evolution of German Catholicism made it impossible up to the Weimar Republic to organize in the framework of impartial scholarly activities an autonomous Catholic sociology in a specific sense, as an independent science of society devoted to the systematic examination of the historical and contemporary problems of general social interest. It is quite natural that in the first efforts, the criteria of Christian ethics and the Catholic concept of law were decisive for the ultimate evaluations and orientations, and it was as natural that the scientific methods used had to conform to the generally valid criteria of sociological research. Under this viewpoint there are only three Catholic scholars to have represented specifically "Catholic Sociology" as full professors at German universities under the Weimar Republic. They were, Goetz Briefs (1889-   ), at present teaching at Georgetown University, Washington, D.C.; Theodor Brauer of Cologne (1880-1943), and Jakob Strieder of Munich (1877-1936). Their work as well as that of their disciples and other scholars connected with their efforts in the spirit of Solidarism produced studies which stand up to the most strict scientific scrutiny and are of lasting value and of broad sociological interest.

An encyclopedic condensation of the sociological research of German Catholics is to be found in the "Staatslexikon" (1926-1932) whose 5th edition was published by Hermann Sacher in behalf of the Goerres Society. In five monumental volumes the concerted efforts of numerous scholars are here assembled, systematically grouped according to the various object materials and presenting all the essential sources and themes of modern political and social science in a comprehensive review of the complete sociological thought of German Catholicism. Quite recently this work has received an up-to-date implementation in Oswald von Nell-Breuning's and Hermann Sacher's "Woerterbuch der Politik" (1947-1952), with its five systematically grouped parts under the headings: Christian theory of society; Christian theory of the state; the social question; the economic order; systems of social order.

A comprehensive presentation of the whole evolution of political and social ideas and movements in German Catholicism, in the sense as it has been attempted in this study, has not before been tried. However, the following valuable special monographs are available: Franz Albert, "Der soziale Katholizismus in Deutschland bis zum Tode Kettelers" (1914); Goetz

Briefs, "Die wirtschafts- und sozialpolitischen Ideen des Katholizismus" (1925) ;[274] Theodor Brauer, "The Catholic Social
Movement in Germany," The Catholic Social Yearbook, Oxford 1932, (first German edition 1930, under the title, "Der
deutsche Katholizismus und die soziale Entwicklung des kapitalistischen Zeitalters");[275] Johann Messner, "Um die katholisch-
soziale Einheitslinie" (1930); Clemens Bauer, "Wandlungen
der sozialpolitischen Ideenwelt im deutschen Katholizismus des
19. Jahrhundersts" (1931);[276] August Knoll, "Der soziale Gedanke in modernen Katholizismus" (1932-1933). These works
are implemented by those of Otto Pfuelf, "Ketteler" (3 vol.
1899); Theodor Brauer, "Ketteler" (1927) and "Kolping"
(1923); and the monographs by Johannes Nattermann, "Kolping als Sozialpaedagoge" (1925) and Franz Mueller, "Franz
Hitze und sein Werk" (1928).

The history of Political Catholicism is written in the monumental source study by Julius Bachem, "Vorgeschichte, Geschichte und Politik der Zentrumspartei" (9 vol. 1927-1932);
in the thoughtful study by Friedrich Dessauer, "Das Zentrum"
(1929), and in the works by Josef Joos, "Die politische Ideenwelt des Zentrums" (1928) and K. A. Schulte, "Das Zentrum
und sein Wirken in der deutschen Republik" (1929).

In view of the special importance which the social metaphysics of the Jesuits had for the development of socio-philosophical
Realism in German Catholicism, the outstanding work of Gustav Gundlach, "Zur Soziologie der katholischen Ideenwelt und
des Jesuitenordens" (1927) cannot be valued too highly. Valuable implementations will be found in Peter Lippert," Zur
Psychologie des Jesuitenordens" (1923) and Klara Maria Fass-
binder, "Der Jesuitenstaat in Paraguay" (1926). Equally valuable are the works by August Knoll, "Der Zins in der
Scholastik" (1933) and Ernst Karl Winter, "Die Sozialmetaphysik der Scholastik" (1929). Unfortunately the study by
Winter, full of thought and significance as it is, is closly tied
to the Viennese Social Romanticism and therefore not in a
position to give a fair and objective presentation of Jesuit
Social Metaphysics and Solidarism.

For a more profound understanding of the sociological problems of modern society several monographs are of special
value which have their origin in the general sociological interest of the present era in its best spirit. In his "Das gewerb-
liche Proletariat" (1926) Goetz Briefs offered a presentation
of the proletarian sociological problems in a breadth of ideological insight and interpretation never before attained. The
expanded American edition, "The Proletariat" (New York

1937) expresses the whole complex of the author's socio-ethical insights in a manifesto, "A Challenge to Western Civilization" which is in the best tradition of the social concern in German Catholicism from Baader to the present day.[277] In the same spirit Paul Jostock wrote "Der Ausgang des Kapitalismus" (1928) and Aloys Hermens treated the problem of "Demokratie und Kapitalismus" (1931). The catholic scholar of research on capitalism, Jakob Strieder of Munich, left us a number of monographs that are of lasting value for the history of sociology, among them, "Die Genesis des modernen Kapitalismus" (1904), "Studien zur Geschichte der kapitalistischen Organisationsformen" (1925) and "Jakob Fugger" (1926). We have to thank Waldemar Gurian for his original presentation of the development of the "Politische und soziale Ideen des franzoesischen Catholizismus 1789-1914" (1928) and the masterly presentation of a sociology of Russian "Bolshevism" (New York 1933, first German edition 1931), later implemented by his "The Development of the Soviet Regime" (1951) and his religio-sociological analysis of National Socialism, "Kampf um die Kirche im Dritten Reich" (1936). Edgar Alexander gave an ideological biography of National Socialism in "Mythus Hitler" (1937) and an interpretation of the ideological and historical background of the basic cultural and political tensions between East and West in "Rome and Moscow. Western Personalism Versus Eastern Collectivism" (1952).

Among other works of general sociological interest the following merit special attention: Goetz Briefs, "Grundlagen der Wirtschaftspolitik" (1923), "Caritas" and "Gewerkschaftswesen" (1926),[278] "Der klassische Liberalismus" (1930),[279] and the articles "Sozialreform und sozialer Geist; Betriebssoziologie; Proletariat" (1931;[280] Theodor Brauer, "Solidarismus" (1926),[281] "Mittelstandpolitik" (1927), "Sozialpolitik und Sozialreform" (1931) and "Thomistic Principles in a Catholic School" 1943); Gustav Gundlach, the articles "Orden" (1931)[282] and "Stand; Staendestaat, Religioeser Sozialismus" (1931).[283] Finally we wish to point to the books by Adolf Weber who, however, is very close to the classical-liberal viewpoint in economics: "Kampf zwischen Kapital und Arbeit" (1922), "Caritaetspolitik" (1927), "Ende des Kapitalismus" (1930), "Volkswirtschaftslehre" (1933) and "Die neue Weltwirtschaft" (1947).

The downfall of the Weimar Republic dealt the extremely creative development of Catholic Sociology a deadly blow since all its best representatives were forced to flee for their lives. Despite the surprising success that the work of reconstruction in the social sciences had in German Catholicism after 1945, we can hardly assume that this generation will be able to repair the harm sustained.

6. The "Vienna Orientations"

In contrast with the compact ideological unity characteristic of the solidaristic theories of society in German Catholicism, modern social philosophy in Austria brought forth a plurality of systems for which the collective term of "Vienna Orientations" has become accepted. Though there is a great variety of ideologies among these systems, two main trends may be isolated as the sharply contending neo-Solidarism and neo-Romanticism.

Neo-Solidarism was developed in close touch, partly even in complete identification with the doctrines of German Solidarism, and therefore the most important writings of its chief representatives—Johannes Messner, Ferdiand Frodl, Joseph Dobretsberger, August Knoll—have already been cited in the preceding chapters. This trend is remarkable primarily for its stressing of the critique of capitalism, especially by Frodl, Dobretsberger and Knoll. The views expressed by August Pieper and Theodore Brauer can be said to have taken a middle position in their criticism between the German and Austrian variant of Solidarism. In addition to the works already named, this group has been publicly represented in Johann Messner's Vienna journal, "Das neue Reich" (1918-1932). There was an organized movement to back them in the "Katholische Aktion" with its periodical "Volkswohl," founded in 1927 in order to expand on the "Richtlinien" (directives) issued by the Austrian episcopate. Commissioned by the Austrian episcopate, the "Katholische Aktion" organized two momentous "Catholic-social Conferences" in 1929 and 1931 with the objective of bridging over the fateful cleavage that divided the Austrian social movement and to clarify the erroneous neo-Romantic interpretation of the social traditions of the Church especially concerning the Encyclicals *Rerum Novarum* and *Quadragesimo Anno*. The papers read at these Conferences, among them those by Messner, G. Gundlach, O. von Nell-Breuning and Dobretsberger, are contained in the symposia, "Die katholisch-soziale Tagung in Wien" (1929) and "Die soziale Botschaft des Papstes" (1931). There as well as in the criticism of these proceedings by Messner in "Um die katholisch-soziale Einheitslinie" (1931), will be found the best contemporaneous discussion between Solidarism and neo-Romanticism and the best solidaristic criticism of the social-Romantic ideologies and socio-philosophical "universalism." Soon further developments within the neo-Romantic orientations and the experiment of the Dollfuss-Schuschnigg "Corporative State" were to prove that this attempt on the part of socio-philosophical Realism and political Democracy inspired by Solidarism to win ascendancy in Austrian politics turned out to be futile—a fact whose historical roots, as we have shown, lay in inveterate Austrian Conservatism and social Romanticism.

The socio-philosophical ideas of neo-Romanticism were publicized in the "Studienrunde katholischer Soziologen" founded in 1927 and in Othmar Spann's and his disciples' "universalism." In the "Studienrunde" the three main currents of neo-Romantic social philosophy were represented by Anton Orel (1881-   ), Karl Lugmayer (1892-   ) and Eugen Kogon (1900-   ). Orel and Lugmayer are the most radical champions of the Romantic criticism of Society and Capitalism. The Romantic rejection of the Roman-Christian-Scholastic Natural Law doctrine in favor of the historical concept of a specific "Christian-German" law was followed up by Orel and Lugmayer (who in this far surpassed even the ideologies of Vogelsang) by a radical rejection of the traditional concepts of property and society based on the scholastic doctrines and the Christian evolution of Western society with their roots in the "individualistic property idea of Roman Law."

From this initial position these authors resorted to a radical simplification—very similar to that of Marxism—of the property concept and the problems of Capitalism, and therefore the total defeat of Capitalism and the "breaking down of interest slavery" occupy the central position in Orel's and Lugmayer's programs. According to Orel, labor alone creates value and therefore has the only legitimate claim to participate in the goods of this earth and to have access to the exchange of goods. Labor alone is entitled to all of the return, and therefore every form of income without labor—interest, rent, and consequently Capitalism as a whole—must be condemned absolutely. According to Lugmayer, "capital" has its origin only in labor and nature, and therefore the endproduct of all production must be ascribed to labor and nature alone. Interest, rent, dividends have no justification since they are derived only from "possession" without labor; in a truly "Christian-Germanic" sense they are all thoroughly illegitimate and unjust: witness the Bible verse, "If any would not work, neither shall he eat." Orel and Lugmayer tried to derive a special justification of their hostility toward Capitalism from a false interpretation of the Thomist property concept and the Papal Encyclicals. As formerly Vogelsang had found theological support with the Dominican Albert Maria Weiss, now Orel and Lugmayer found such support in the "new" exegesis of St. Thomas by the Dominican Alexander Horvath, "Das Eigentumsrecht nach Thomas von Aquino" (1927), in which the author completely overlooks the legitimate Catholic distinction between the basic personal right of property in its stringent foundation in Natural Law and the concrete use of property as determined by the historical time and founded on a relative sanction by positive legislation.

In his magazines, "Das neue Volk" and "Der neue Weg," and in the following books Orel publicized his ideologies: "Kapitalismus, Bodenreform und christlicher Sozialismus" (1909) "Volkstuemliches Handbuch der Gesellschaftslehre" (1920), and "Oeconomia perennis" (1930). Lugmayer propagates his teachings in the journal "Die neue Ordnung" and through the following studies: "Der Gemeinwirtschaft Werden" (1922), "Das Linzer Programm der christlichen Arbeiter Oesterreichs" (1924), "Leos Loesung der Arbeiterfrage" (1925), "Weg mit der Gewinnwirtschaft" (1926), "Lehren und Weisungen der oesterreichischen Bischoefe ueber soziale Fragen" (1926), "Grundriss zur neuen Gesellschaft" (1927) and in the great modern work "Sein und Erscheinung" (1945-1947). Good reviews of the entire tradition of Social Romanticism from Vogelsang to Orel and Lugmayer are given by Anton Lesowsky "Karl von Vogelsang" (1925), Ludwig Wimmer, "Wucher und Eigentumsrecht" (1926) and T. Allmayer-Beck "Vogelsang" (1952).

In his numerous essays in the "Schoenere Zukunft," Eugen Kogon, in full accord with his publisher Joseph Eberle (1884-1947), attempted to take a medium position between the socio-philosophical views of Orel and Lugmayer and Othmar Spann's socio-philosophical "Universalism." Eberle explained his and Kogon's traditionalism by tracing back to "the older tradition of Adam Mueller, Goerres, Ketteler, Vogelsang, Albert Maria Weiss, and others" the neo-Romantic, conservative attitude taken by the "Schoenere Zukunft" which was founded in 1925 in opposition to Messner's "Das neue Reich." The magazines of Orel, Lugmayer and Eberle just mentioned and the "Katholisch-Soziales Manifest" (1932) of the "Studienrunde" are the best guides for an understanding of the socio-political efforts of the neo-Romantic "Vienna Orientations" to reconcile their ideologies and traditions of social and political conservatism with the specific social teachings of the Church.[284]

By far the most significant ideological and philosophical achievement of Viennese neo-Romanticism is to the credit of Ernst Karl Winter (1895-   ) in his books, "Die heilige Strasse" (1926), "Die Sozialmetaphysik der Scholastik" (1929) and "Platon. Das Soziologische in der Ideenlehre" (1930). To be sure, Winter's "dualism of method" and his distinction between "true" and "pastoral" sociology suffer from a thorough incomprehension of scholasticism's world of ideas. And yet, his attempt to outline a new conservative shape of society with the aid of neo-Kantian Platonism (Natorp-Cohen) and the traditions of "Baroque-Romantic sociology" with the paternalistic, authoritarian family structure as its basis must be rated as an important progress if compared with Othmar Spann's questionable "Christian" legitimacy in his socio-philosophical ideologies of "Universalism."

7. Neo-Romanticism and Universalism

Spann's ideas on state and society do not really belong in the legitimate complex of Catholic social doctrines, just as the neo-Romanticism of his immediate disciples has not a legitimate claim of defending the genuine traditions of a Christian philosophy of history. But since Spann and many of his followers maintain over and over again that they represent the sole genuine succession to the traditions of Christian Universalism, we must at least discuss this questionable claim at the end of our study. This is all the more indicated since Spann's ideology had a serious influence on the development of Austrian neo-Romanticism straight on to the unfortunate experiment of their so-called "Christian Corporative State." And finally, the approbation which the "Catholic" Schuschnigg voiced for the totalitarian principle of government, as we have related, is explainable largely on the grounds of this influence.

Spann was able to exert such a strong influence because the overwhelming sophistry of his system of "Wholeness" (Ganzheit) created such a confusion in modern German sociological terminology that even strictly Catholic circles were caught into its spell. In his struggle against "liberalism and socialism, individualism and collectivism (sic)" Spann had a masterly trick of replacing the traditional interpretations of Universalism, Individualism, Rationalism, Personality, Natural Law, Scholasticism, etc. with his own mystagogical terminology, mostly self-created, words as "Ganzheit, Gezweiung, Gliedlichkeit, Ein-, Aus, und Um-Gliederung, Gegensaetzlichkeit, Rueckverbindung" (attempted literal translation: Wholeness, Be-dualization, Articularity, In-Articulation, Ex-Articulation, Trans-Articulation, Contrasticity, retroverted connection), with the result that a normal philosophical mind can only with the utmost self-control master a certain nausea after once having been caught in the conceptual merry-go-round of "wholeness" in Spann's voluminous opus.[285]

Spann's totalitarian Universalism is by no means based on the legitimate tradition of Christian philosophy. He himself clearly defined his location in the history of ideas as late as 1929: "Back to our own Germanic economic and sociological scholars; back to their very own foundations of their science; back to German Idealism and Romanticism which tower far above Western individualism and Utilitarianism. . . Adam Mueller in his 'Elemente der Staatskunst' has given a comprehensive exposition of a theory of the state, of society and of economics which is destined to become the nucleus of a modern universalistic political science. Kleist in his 'Katechismus der Deutschen' has sketched the framework of folk loyalties and duties. Goerres in his political writings has pulled away the mask from the shallowness of the French democratic state ideal and has demanded a state structure dominated by universalistic ideas." [286] "What sounded reasonable enough in Augustine, with Descartes had become mere shadow-boxing."[287] "Through his philosophy of religion Hegel attempted to reinstate Christianity in its ancient rights."[288] "It is a reproach against neo-Scholasticism that it has laid aside all significant thoughts of German idealism from Kant to Hegel, though these thoughts were profoundly akin to their own; neo-Scholasticism itself thus made no effort to carry on these thoughts and therefore missed the connection with the living present, with philosophical progress that is conditional on German idealism."[289] "The Aristotelian trend of St. Thomas with its bias for logic can also not be understood without inward experience, and therefore Thomas today is being interpreted much too rationalistically by the neo-Scholasticists." [290] "Pesch wished to combine individualism and state socialism in the one system of Solidarism, but in formulating the supporting concepts for his system he proceeded individualistically and, because such a mix-up (Klitterung) is impossible, he remained on the whole eclectic." [291] This by the way, is the only reference to Solidarism to be found in Spann's entire work!

Spann is just as slothful with respect to the Christian Natural Law theories. "Aside from individualistic Natural Law there is also supra-individual or divine Natural Law (lex naturalis-lex divina, jus divinum, divine law) which places the divine order of the world, its morals and laws before the morals and rights of the single person, the subject. . . . Divine or supra-individual Natural Law (!) is represented by Plato, Aristotle, Thomas Aquinas, the Romanticists and Hegel." [292] This again is all that Spann has to say about Natural Law! Whoever has pondered our presentation of the Christian Natural Law doctrines and their fundamental significance for Catholic sociology will not require a detailed interpretation of this utterly un-intelligible nonsense of Spann's identification of *jus divinum* with *jus naturale* and, even worse, of Thomas Aquinas' Natural Law doctrine with Romanticism and Hegel. In this very identification of Thomas with Romanticism and Hegel lies the root of the entire basic contrast between the fundamental Christian principles of the legitimate Catholic political and social theories and the pseudo-Christian ideological sophistry of Spann and his "Univeralism." Anyone who desires additional information before arriving at a final judgment concerning Spann's general qualifications in the philosophy of history should peruse his newest book "Religionsphilosophie auf geschichtlicher Grundlage" (1947). Here Spann dares to propound a historical and philosophical interpretation of the "world religions" with-out even by a word mentioning the religion of the Old Testament. Instead, barefacedly he ascribes to his own "Christianism" the introduction of the theistic concept of Creation and of the personalistic concept of God, of the doctrines of the personal love of God and fellow-men as Christianity's most original achievement, totally ignoring the legitimate historical claims of the religion of Judaism for the authorship of these concepts.[293]

Nothing can better characterize the immense distance that separates this pseudo-Christian, completely Hegelian (verhegelt), totalitarian "Universalism" of Spann from the legitimate Catholic political and social doctrine than this omission of the basic principle of Christian Natural Law—on which rests the entire effort of genuine Christian Universalism and Realism to construct a socio-philosophical framework for the vindication of personal liberty and social justice:

Sanctissima Naturae Lex est!

DOCUMENTS

Franz von Baader: *The Proletariat,* its Plight and Misery, (1835)
    "The sole aim of the present essay is to draw the attention of students of law and public affairs to the great problem which confronts society in our day, that of finding the proletariat its rightful place within the community."

"Indeed, whoever takes only one look at the abyss of physical and moral misery and neglect in which the majority of the proletariat is condemned to live in England and France, has to admit that serfdom itself—even in its most oppressive form of physical bondage always matched by spiritual bondage since the one cannot exist without the other—was less cruel and inhuman, and therefore less un-Christian (for to be Christian is to be humane) than the proletariat's present status of unprotected and helpless outlawry. In England and France, reputedly our most cultured and educated nations, more than anywhere else has the development of the industrial system with its money wages intensified the disproportion between the rich and the poor, many public assurances to the contrary notwithstanding. These denials are usually made in the interest of the argyrocrats (the moneyed interests), and only secondly in the interest of the aristocrats (the landed interests.) ."

"This disproportion between the rich and the poor is the symptom for an abnormal situation in trade and industry. It is easy to see that, on the one hand, the unlimited sale of government securities in all countries absorbs money and constantly drains liquid funds away from production. On the other hand, because of the complete disappearance of wage payment in kind, there is a simultaneous increase in the demand for money. As between these contradictory trends, the increase in production does not benefit the working classes although they have a rightful claim to receive their share in the shape of a more abundant and secure livelihood, and although it is undoubtedly as important a goal of good government to pay the workers decent wages as to produce efficiently and cheaply.

"Our governments so far have not allowed themselves to be persuaded by the loose talk of some economists (Adam Smith among them) that the one remedy against usury on the corn markets and the artificial grain shortage consists in letting the corn trade free altogether and at all times, in other words, in giving the corn usurers their sway without let or hindrance. However, as far as money usurers and the money market is concerned, most governments have followed this counsel. Thus, while the proletariat had to suffer their former serfdom to be transformed into the social liberty of outlaws, we see that several governments have exchanged their former dependence on dynasts and nobles for the even more shameful dependence on puny argyrocrats (rulers through money power) ."

"Now it can be said that the people have mostly exchanged their former land servitute which made of them land serfs (as *glebae adscripti*) for the even harsher and more oppressive "plutonic" money servitude which makes of them money serfs."

"Several governments are making praiseworthy efforts to procure increased intellectual wealth to the proletarians by organizing improved educational institutions. Here I wish to point out that this presupposes and implies the rightful claim of the proletarians to better physical health, or at least to an improvement in their present distressed circumstances. It is just as wrong to ignore their claim to the relief of their intellectual as of their physical need. It is clear that the proletarian who cannot safeguard his physical life within his present income also cannot satisfy his intellectual needs with the old type of education, all the more since these needs are growing under the impact of irreligious intellectualism."

"How often have I, for instance, assisted at meetings and gatherings of factory owners in England which regularly ended by establishing maximum wages and minimum sales prices and therefore were no better than conspiracies against the proletarians whose wages always remained far below the natural price for the one commodity they have to sell, i.e., their labor. The worst way to try to remedy this manifest iniquity is through the chambers and parliaments, for here more than anywhere else the factory owners are at the same time contending parties and judges while they exclude the representation of the interests of the poor wage earning masses from these chambers.

"It is said that the principle of freedom of competition does not admit of any monopolies. However in our present case, in the competition between workers and their wage masters, the latter enjoy the most oppressive monopoly as against the former, and I ask whether such disparity and such pressure deserve to be called a freely functioning industrial system. I ask whether these proletarians can be blamed when they on their part and for the identical purpose begin to associate among themselves against their wage masters."

"In order to recognize clearly the present disenfranchised (noncitizen, because non-secured) status of the proletariat under constitutional governments, it is indeed necessary to have a better insight than has prevailed since the beginning of the French Revolution into the relationship between political and social liberty on the one hand, and the corporative system on the other. It is necessary to understand that an individual does not become entirely free merely by the fact that his individual liberty is established versus all other individuals (especially where government agencies are concerned). He needs at the same time to possess some corporate liberties within society. Consequently, this much praised equality before the law[194], where it is misunderstood and misused as being in conflict with the rights of the estates and corporations, only turns us backward to a levelling system or to the slavery of all, be it under several masters or under a single one."

"Briefly and cursorily, I wish to dispose of only two among the possible objections which might be regarded as the most weighty. The first objection contends that such an association and grouping of the proletariat for mutual insurance, (without which no relief can be found to their misery,) since it runs against the precept of *divide et impera,* would only enhance the danger that one seeks to avoid. Against this it should be noted, (a) that such voluntary associations of the proletariat do in fact already exist; (b) that such associations are a threat and a danger only when originating spontaneously, not when called into life by the governments and supervised and guided by them; (c) that on the contrary nothing but the formation of such legal associations and organs can avoid those dangers."

"Whoever is aware—not through police reports only—of the unanimous desires, proclamations and consultations of the proletariat in various countries will admit that a very real danger exists. Unless the discrepancies and antagonisms between the proletariat and the propertied classes which we have here shown up are soon relieved by public declarations and counter-measures, a reaction of the former to the latter classes is impending which is sure to be more general, better planned and more effective, and by this very fact more detrimental to the propertied classes than any previous revolt. For these mostly artificially managed mob riots grew into real revolutions only because of the negligence and weakness of the governments.

"Although, therefore, revolutions which lack the substance of legality demand no further counter-measures on the part of the governments but police action, the matter is entirely different for those revolutions whose underlying cause is just, or which are partly set in motion by legitimate grievances. In these cases it is the duty of the governments to isolate these legitimate roots and to acknowledge them publicly and spontaneously, without waiting to be coerced into such acknowledgment."

"I cannot believe that anyone will think it sufficient to draw these proletarians before the police courts which will constrain them once more under the old, lost servitude." [294]

Goetz Briefs

The Proletariat

A Challenge to Western Civilization, (1937)

"Proletarians may appear as isolated individuals or they may be constituent parts of a large social group. A proletariat exists wherever the prevailing economic order produces on a large scale the typical conditions of proletarian existence, that is, where great masses of the population exercise no self-initiated control over the means of production and have no income worth mentioning other than what they derive from sale of their labor power.

"Western Civilization and the existence of a proletarian mass stratum evidently do not fit together. Proof of this is the proletarian unrest and the rise of a proletarian philosophy which decidedly disagrees with the fundamentals of Western Civilization. A further proof is this, that since the beginning of the capitalistic age the best minds and the keenest spirits have protested against the social and cultural conditions which modern industrialism imposes upon the laboring masses, and have decried the consequences.

"The Western world has not found a way out of this problem, just as the proletariat has not found its place within the Western civilization. Occasionally the Western mind took refuge in developing a philosophy in regard to the problems, as, for instance the attempt to justify the proletarian phenomenon from a biological or naturalistic viewpoint, or, as in the case of Nietzsche, by taking the proletarian masses as the pedestal for the Superman. All these attempts, however, were futile and offered no solution; they were at most only ways to dodge the issue. It was no less a dodging of the issue when certain groups of the proletariat favored solutions which aimed at a total destruction of the Western civilization. Here indeed the danger became imminent that a cleavage of Western consciousness might occur; and, in fact, it has occured to a certain degree. Its sharpest expression has been and still is the antagonism between social reform on the basis of the Western institutions on the one hand, and social revolution aiming at a radical overthrow of these institutions on the other.

"What is the contradiction between the proletariat and Western civilization? What, after all, is the proletarian challenge to the Western world? There are many possible answers to this question, but they may be reduced to one, namely, that the proletarian man faces the danger, or at least thinks he is facing the danger, of being deprived of personality, of his value and rights as a person."

"In these endeavors to reestablish personality right, labor had to fight its way against opposing forces. The state and the representative economic and social groups were antagonistic to them. Slowly and steadily they yielded to the elemental character of the workers' efforts to build up these institutions. While resisting they tried to compromise with labor's demands: hence observe state interference for the most destitute and endangered groups. Social legislation in fact, by protecting the workers' life, rights, and liberty, by lessening his dependence in the critical periods of his existence, implies the acknowledgment of his personality. Every act introducing reduced hours of work, protecting the jobs, providing security is a new means to this end.

"Taking all these endeavors and their success into account we come to the conclusion that *the process of repersonification of the proletarian is well on its way*—so far as his life in public is concerned! He has gained poise and dignity as a member of labor organizations, as a member of political parties and institutions (it means a tremendous lot for the self-evaluation of labor that, since the War, in Central European countries, former workers could reach up into the heights of minister's chairs and even to the presidency) as a member of economic enterprises started by workers' groups, as a member of organizations, of collective units, etc."

"To gain, in the age of individualism, his personal value, he had to collectivize himself. None of all the organizations he built around himself or which were set up for him had a direct approach to those forms and orders of life within which man most of all is a person, to the communitarian forms and orders of life, represented in the form of the "vital community" called family and in the form of the spiritual community called church. Labor has gained in poise and weight wherever it developed powerful organizations and was protected by powerful institutions. It would be a wicked optimism to assume that it gained automatically within those confines which harbor the most valuable kernel of man's person: in community life, be it the life of vital or spiritual communities.

"The challenge to Western civilization will be raised as long as the laboring man can safeguard his personality only by anchoring it in collective organizations and public institutions, without any relation to the truly communitarian orders of his life, to those which, after all, are the essential social forms in which man as a person grows and matures." [295]

Wilhelm Emmanuel von Ketteler

The Problem of Property (1848)

"In its doctrine on the concept of property the Catholic Church has nothing in common with the ideas on property rights that are generally current in the world, according to which man regards himself as the absolute master of the things he owns. Never can the Church allow men the right to deal and traffic with the bounties of this earth guided only by their whims. When speaking of human property and the duty to safeguard it, the Church therefore always refers to a concept that is essentially determined by the following characteristics: (1) Full and genuine property rights are God's only; (2) Man has been merely granted the right of *usufruct;* (3) When making use of his property man has the duty to bow to the God-given order of things."

"The false doctrine that property confers strict rights is a perpetual sin against nature. This doctrine sees no wrong in the use for the satisfaction of boundless avarice or the worst debauches of sensual pleasure of those things that God has intended only to provide for human food and shelter. It sees no wrong in suppressing the sentiments in human hearts in the face of man's plight and putting in their stead a hardness of feeling, or even a lack of it, the like of which it is hard to find even among beasts. It sees no wrong in declaring permanent theft to be permissible under the law; for, as a holy Father of the Church has said, not only he who steals his neighbor's property is a thief but also he who holds for himself what belongs to another.

"The ill-fated dictum that 'property is theft' is not just a lie. Alongside of a great lie it contains a terrible truth. It cannot any longer be shoved aside with mere derision and scorn. We shall have to destroy the truth in it if we want to regain for it the status of a plain lie. As long as there is but a particle of truth left in it, it can blast to pieces law and order in the world. As one abyss leads to the next, thus one sin against nature brings forth another."

"The distorted doctrine of property rights has been the origin of the false doctrine of communism. But this false doctrine itself is a sin against nature. Under the guise of benign humanitarianism it conjures upon mankind the exact opposite, bottomless disaster, by destroying devotion to work, order and peace on earth, by luring men into a struggle of all against all and thus threatening the very foundations of human existence."

"Like a luminous light the truth of the Catholic Church penetrates these two lying concepts. The Church recognizes the separate truths contained in both points of view and reconciles them in its own doctrine. Once and for all the Church repudiates the individual person's unrestricted property rights, only acknowledging the right of using the fruit of property under the order established by God. In this form the Church protects property and declares that the distribution of wealth as it has developed among men must be recognized for the sake of the general welfare and administration and in the interest of order and peace. On the other hand, the Church also sanctifies the idea of communism by rededicating the use of property to the welfare of all." [296]

Victor Cathrein

Socialism or Social Reform? (1903)

"In view of the steady growth of the revolutionary parties are we to fold our arms in mute contemplation or raise them to heaven in sheer despair? Not in the least. There is no reason for giving up hope. God has ordained that also for national calamities remedies may be found. There is every expectation of averting the threatening danger, if we are serious about introducing social reforms and reviving the true spirit of Christianity."

"*Social Reform.* Socialist agitators endeavor to inspire the workingman with the idea that Christians, especially Catholics, wish to retain social conditions exactly as they are at present, and that they console the laborer solely by referring him to a life to come. Nothing can be further from our real intentions. We also demand social reform most energetically. We are, however, not like socialists, who find fault with every social improvement however well meant it may be; we gratefully acknowledge whatever is done to raise the laboring classes; but our demands are not all satisfied, there is much still to be reformed. At the same time we guard against falling into the other extreme of socialists; we do not flatter the workingmen with visions of impossible and unattainable happiness, merely in order to whet their appetite for luxuries far beyond their reach.

"By the social reform which we advocate there may be secured for even the lowest of the laboring classes a family life worthy of a human being. For this end it is necessary not only that he receive sufficient wages, but also that sufficient regard be had for his life and health, and therefore that his strength be not overtaxed by immoderate labor. He must be treated not only with fairness, but also with love and consideration. Finally, he must have the assurance that in case of misfortune or ill health he is not abandoned or cast into the street. And since in our days personal effort and private charity are by no means sufficient, public authority must by suitable legislation take the necessary measures for this end. Social reform should aim at such a state of things that the humblest laborer may entertain a well-founded hope by industry and economy, to better his condition and gradually to rise to a higher social standing.

"Man may be conceived under a two-fold aspect—as a free and independent individual, and as a social being, destined to live in, and form part of, society. Liberalism—at least in former years—considered man only under the first aspect. It regarded only the individual and his independence, and almost entirely disregarded his social relations. From this standpoint Liberalism tended toward dismemberment of society, and proclaimed the maxim of *laissez faire* as the highest political wisdom.

"A reaction against this tendency was justified, and socialism, in as far as it can be viewed as a protest against extreme individualism, is perfectly right. But socialism, for its part, goes to the other extreme, considering only the social aspect of man, and disregarding the freedom and independence of the individual. It deprives the individual of his liberty, by making him the slave of the community—a wheel in the great complicated mechanism of the social production—which is no less absurd.

"As in most cases, here too the truth is midway between both extremes. Both aspects of man—the individual as well as the social—must be taken into consideration and brought into harmony. This is the unshaken principle from which all rational attempts at social reform must proceed. The institution and promotion of corporative associations are, as we have already noticed, the surest and best means to reconcile the claims of the individual with those of society, and thus to bring about harmony between the conflicting elements.

Revival of Christianity. The most important and indispensable factor in the social reform, however, is the revival of Christianity among all classes of society. F. A. Lange, the historian of materialism, confesses that ideas and sacrifices can still save our civilization and change the way of devastating revolution into a way of beneficial reforms. But whence is the spirit of sacrifice to come? Legislative measures may produce the external framework of a new social order; but it is only Christianity that can give it life and efficacy. Only on the ground of Christianity can the hostile social elements be brought to reconciliation."

"This revival of Christianity, however, must not be confined to the laborer: it must also extend to the higher and more influential classes of society. Is it not bitter irony if our so-called 'cultural classes' expect Christian patience and resignation from the laborer, while they themselves disregard the laws of Christianity, and publicly profess the grossest infidelity? It sounds indeed like irony if the rich preach economy and self-denial to the poor, while they themselves indulge in the most extravagant luxury and dissipation.

"The wealthy must begin the social reform at home. They must come to the conviction that they have not only rights but also duties toward the laboring man—duties of justice and duties of charity. They must bear in mind that they have been appointed by God, as it were, the administrators of their earthly possessions, which should in some way serve for the benefit of all. They should remember that the laborer is not a mere chattel, but a rational being, their brother in Christ, who, in the eyes of God, is equal to the richest and most powerful on earth.

"It is only this bond of Christian sentiment—of mutual love and reverence between rich and poor, high and low—that can bring about a reconciliation of the social conflicts of our times. And since the Church is the God-appointed guardian and preserver of the Christian religion, and since she cannot fulfill this task unless she is free to exercise all her power and influence, we must demand for the solution of the social problem the perfect freedom of the Church in all her administrations." [297]

Heinrich Pesch: Christian Solidarism. (1922-1924)
(Principles of a Christian Social and Economic Theory)
"Solidarism is not a theological system,
but a sociological-philosophical one."

I. The Working Man in Society.

1. Man is the master of the world. This dominion is the common endowment of all men, because each man has the common possession of the same human nature. External nature must serve all men in the satisfaction of their needs.

2. The working man is the master of the world, since work is the indispensible means of world dominion. In our society, industrial labor is the necessary means of suppplying the wants of life.

All the material world and all the powers of nature serve the working man. They provide him with the object, the means, and the conditions of his economic activity. Never in such activity is man the mere object or tool. Even the simplest worker shares the role of dominion. He remains in control of the material, and it is for him that all economic activity exists (anthropocentric-teleological principle).

3. Work is a natural necessity. Without work, there is no provision of wants, no progress. Work is also the duty of man, the individual law for each human being. Labor is a human law, based on human nature itself. It is also the right, the honor, and the joy of man. Reasonable labor is the least of all those things which irritate man.

4. Not only is agricultural, industrial and commercial activity the cause of the national welfare, but human labor must be acknowledged as the chief cause of the material well-being of peoples. A nation is economically stable only when it exercises with full vigor all its potentialities for labor. Also human labor is the chief ingredient in the restoration of a nation which has suffered a catastrophe.

II. The Social Structure of Society.

The division of labor is the historical origin of the social structure of society. This structure develops vertically according to the ranks of the various professions and trades, horizontally according to the particular achievement of each class. In its concrete formation, this structure was often influenced by political, social, or economic ratios of power, but is not a mere result of power, but rather a requisite and a consequence of a healthy social development. Certainly, the fundamental pillars of society, the family, the State, and private ownership, are not the mere products of constraint and power.

III. *Natural Law and Social Duty.*

Positive law has an important significance in economic life. It is the broad outer framework within which economic life is unfolded. Positive law is changeable, but it is necessary, even in a Socialist state. But justice will not be achieved unless the positive law recognizes the Natural Law as the higher norm.

At the basis of this Natural Law is the fact that man is a social being, capable of social living, and needing it for his development. No man lives as an isolated person; he is always a part of society, and a part of the whole human race. The law of mutuality and reciprocity runs through every sphere of life. Man's conduct had significance for his fellow man and for all humanity. Therefore, though the individual may fix his gaze on his own interests, he must at the same time always have regard for the community to which he belongs. Solidarity as a social duty is the relationship of the individual to the social whole and his subordination to its welfare.

IV. *The Types of Solidarity in Society.*

1. The general human solidarity. Christianity makes no distinction between races, nations or classes as regards human solidarity. For it, there is no class of pariahs who have no rights, as in Buddhism; there is no privileged class of capitalistic overlords, who combine egotistic striving for wealth with simultaneous expansion of power and progressive domination of man over man; there is no International which proclaims the permanence of class hatred. The all-embracing brotherhood of true humanity, resting on the Christian recognition of one universal family of God, governs through justice and charity all relationships between man and man, between people and people. Where this bond is lacking, it becomes true that "man becomes a wolf to his fellows!" Without God as a social center, without justice and the love of neighbor, the high ideal of a league of nations remains a mere phantom. The oldest International, Christianity, unites a genuine internationalism with an understanding of true nationalism. It does not conceive the State as a mere product of force, even though force may have historically played a great role in the formation of individual States.

2. The solidarity of the members of a State. The State is more than a mass of individual beings. It is a moral-organic unity, a community of people governed by public well-being as its objective. Citizens are morally obligated to assist this objective. They should serve the public welfare with their labor, positively by

their economic achievements, negatively by respecting the rights of others and the public well-being in their striving for income.

3. The solidarity of those engaged in the same vocation or trade. The true organs of society are the vocations or trades who have "quasi-positions of trust" as they place their work in the service of the community. Since persons in the same trade have common interests, they are entitled to be represented in these interests by an organization such as a trade union. But since these organizations are organs of society, and since the whole must take precedence over the parts, the interests of the community is paramount. The actual organization of these representative trade unions is conditioned by history.

4. Solidarity between management and labor. A worker may be subordinate to the manager of the enterprise in his actual work, but he can never be considered as a means of production. Nor can his wages be considered merely as an element in the cost of production, because, for many, wages represent the basis of their existence.

The workers are united with the manager and owner as fellow-members in work and interest. To achieve this outlook of a unifying vocational interest, the old concept of the manager as "over-lord" must be discarded. A measured right to co-management would stimulate the employees to a greater interest in the success of the enterprise, and strengthen the sense of responsibility and joy in their work among employees. All the trade unions and employers' associations should be represented on the National Economic Council, which would give bases and directives to the Parliamentary bodies.

V. *Christian Solidarism.*

Each economic concept is deeply rooted in a "Weltanschauung," a world-philosophy. Ours is based on the inherited social principles of Christianity. We do not assume that the mere adoption of these principles would immediately eliminate all practical difficulties. Nor are we in favor of reviving long-out-moded types of economy, as for instance, those of the Middle Ages. We realize, as well, that Christian Solidarism could not become operative unless its principles are accepted by whole peoples. Short of this, it might enjoy partial realization if its concepts were adopted by rational insight.

We are convinced that the Liberal capitalistic and Socialistic doctrine damaged the natural communities of family and people, and that an essential factor in the social question is the return to a genuine community. Capitalism ruthlessly endangered the family life of the workers, even though the capitalist managed to maintain his own family life. It is entirely indifferent to the people's needs in social life. It begets the social situation of class warfare, and eliminates the idea of vocation, of ideal dedication, of service in the interests of the community, so that all that remains is an instinctive urge toward the acquisition of money.

Socialism, likewise, injured family and people. Equality as Marxism demands it, is irreconcilable with genuine freedom, for it could only become an actuality through force and terrorism. Nor would mere socialization create a genuine community, without which society cannot exist.

Only a return to Christianity can solve the dilemma The national economy must be directed by ethics and observe justice, truth, sacrifice, charity and community spirit; but it also must utilize the skills that are necessary for its development. This combination of Christian ethics and technical capabilities in the economic realm will make for true progress.

While Christian ethics must be the guiding principle, no politico-economic system can be derived directly from the Christian Gospel. National economic science must construct the economic systems and social programs that will meet man's needs and possibilities.

VI. *Solidarism and Social Reform.*

The time of unrestrained, atomistic individualism is now definitely at an end. Our age will no longer tolerate the conditions which arose out of the unrestrained domination of political economy by private capitalistic plutocracy. There must be new forms of economy and a regulation of social life that will correspond to human needs, if we are to realize the necessary increase of productive capacity and obtain an abundance of goods. In this regulation, vocational self-government will play a decisive role. The raising of the national productive power will grow out of a cooperative effort in unity between employers and employees, guided by expert opinion, and enjoying free self-administration.

The possession of capital for private enterprise is often in danger of being misused because of the unrestrained nature of the free economic system based on exaggerated individualism. Hence private capital also leads to the exploitation of workers and consumers and to the oppression of weaker competitors. I am for private property in the means of production, but I refuse to approve unrestrained use of property and the plutocratic developments that derive therefrom, as demonstrated in the period of *laissez-faire*. It was this diseased order of private ownership that was attacked by Socialism, but which could have been cured by other methods.

In principle it is wrong to eliminate from every sector of economic life the functioning of private property and private enterprise, as long as it meets the demands of the common welfare. Restraints on economic liberty can only properly be imposed according to the demands of social justice. The replacement of private economic activity by public enterprise is only justified in those cases where the needs of the public welfare are not being met by the inept or socially harmful operation of the existing system. The growing economic functions of the State are to be increased only as a means to proper social ends in keeping with the higher law of the common welfare of the whole people. Where this higher law is endangered, the private economic sphere must retreat before the public need. This development can even go so far through intermediate stages, until there is full replacement of certain private businesses by public management, i.e. socialization in the strict sense of the word.

In the new economic order which we seek, the objective reason of all economic life must first be the production and distribution of goods for the people, and not personal profit, as it was in the capitalist period. This production and distribution must correspond with the highest cultural level that can be attained by the whole people, therefore satisfying the interests and needs of all strata of society. In this new economic order, labor will regain the high esteem that it lost in the capitalist period and which it previously possessed in the Middle Ages. Work will not only be asserted as a duty, but as a right and an honor of man. Honor will come to every activity of an economic and cultural kind, not only manual work, but intellectual; not only labor in the factory, but also the work of the middle classes which is so important for increasing the standard of living and for the preservation of society.[298]

Heinrich Brauns

Political Catholicism in Action (1929)

(The social and political role of the German "Center"-Party)

1. A Christian Social People's Party

The Center Party has grown straight from the soil of Catholic creativeness, from joyful activity characterized by the desire to share in the duties of society and government, but also from the grave spiritual struggles that filled the decades after the founding of the Reich and during the "culture conflict" (Kulturkampf, i. e. the struggle between Bismarck and the Catholic Church) .

"No doubt, the Center Party was founded by Catholic Reichstag members and was supported by the desires and political needs of the Catholic population. But no sooner had the Center members of the Reichstag given themselves a charter as a "fraction" (i. e., the Reichstag members of each party, constituted as one group) in 1871, than it ceased to regard itself as a representation of the Catholic sector only. The Center has also never limited its activities to matters of Church policies, nor has it ever thought of promoting political aspirations of the Church by defending only the rights of the Catholics; on the contrary, the Center always stood for equal rights for the non-Catholic sectors of the nation and for all religious communities, strictly adhering to the concept of political parity within the state.

"Consequently, the Center can justly claim to be a political, not a religious party. It must not be regarded as a creation of the clergy. Naturally, the clergy took a hand in party activities, though not so much at the time of its foundation as later during the "culture conflict." It is quite understandable that at that time the clergy came somewhat to the fore. Ketteler must be given credit for having stood in the front ranks in this struggle. But any student of Ketteler's personality will find that he was indeed more of a political figure than a bishop and minister. Furthermore, surely the clergy too has political rights which of course they will wish to exercize with the tact proper to their profession.

"The Center Party has not been founded with the object of becoming an "opposition party," nor for that matter a government party, but simply as an independent political party. From the very beginning its paramount aim was to represent *the people*. This is best documented by its defense of the people's rights, the basic constitutional rights. All motions that originated with the Center Party in the first chapters of its history show this clearly. This is further characterized by the fact that in these years the Center was in very close touch with the Liberals. And above all, the Center's continuous and constant devotion to the *social problems* is an eloquent testimonal to this party's character.

"Furthermore, the Center never was, nor ever wished to be, *a class party,* since it is on the contrary one of the basic aims of the Center to abolish class differences, to stress the ideal of the people's community, of the nation's solidarity, of the participation of all classes in one large popular whole.

"Therefore, the Center has always promoted the harmony of interests among the various classes and estates. To be sure, the Center was built from the very beginning on a religious foundation, and specifically on the firm religious principles of positive Christianity and moral law. This was always the basis of its existence, and has never ceased to determine its political actions. These principles defined the Center's attitude toward *the state,* the ideal of the state, the way to strengthen the state and to fulfill man's duties in the state.

2. *Mutual Independence and Cooperation of Church and State*

As to the proper relationship between church and state, the Center has always demanded that they respect one another and cooperate peaceably. We of the Center have always held the conviction that it would be a useless effort to try to define down to the last theoretical details what should be the relations between religion, state and church. This could lead only to conflict, not to practical results. For centuries men have struggled in vain to solve these problems, and they are therefore best left alone. Life is so varied and manifold that it is much better to tackle matters realistically as they present themselves rather than argue about them on theoretical grounds. This does not, however, imply that fundamental principles should be disregarded, neither in one's thoughts nor in one's actions.

"Since its beginnings the Center was never conservative in the sense of the old conservatives, nor was it liberal in the sense of a dogmatic or downright anti-religious Liberalism. It had its own state concept, that of the Christian state. It denied that the state was omnipotent, in the first place in matters of conscience. But it was just as strictly opposed to the liberal state concept that denied the state all functions beyond those of a night watchman. On the other hand, the Center was never hostile to all forms of Liberalism. In our past political history we travelled many a road side by side with the Liberals, and we might do that again any day. Liberalism as such was, however, unacceptable for Catholicism at that time, and many of Liberalism's tenets remain unacceptable today. And more or less the same holds for the relations of the Center with the German Conservatives.

3. *The Center Party and the Weimar Republic*

When in 1919 we assembled in Weimar, the question arose whether to cooperate with the Left in establishing the constitution, or go into opposition. Up to that time, you will recall, the Center had always sided with the Monarchy; it had condemned the revolution of 1918-19 on principle, and had campaigned for the elections to the National Assembly in a severe struggle against the Left. To form a coalition with the Left only a few days later, in the face of the abstention of the Rightist Assembly members, was of course extremely difficult.

In the end, sheer civic conscientiousness demanded that we answer these questions in the affirmative. Thus, despite earlier developments, the Party made the "sacrifice" to enter the government. First of all, we had to do this for the sake of the constitution. We had never taken a political stand for any concrete form of a *constitution*, but I think I may say that before the war the majority of our followers believed in the monarchy also in theory, though indeed only in a constitutional monarchy that stressed the people's rights.

"It was therefore a difficult leap for the Center to take now to get down to the task of working out a *republican constitution* based on the events of 1918. We have done this not simply to protect ourselves from the dangers of the day and to begin the reconstruction of the Reich. It was also done under the conviction that in the given circumstances nothing was at all obtainable except a republican constitution. In recognition of these facts, the Center declared at its convention in Erfurt, 1926, that it regarded itself as a sponsor of the Republic and that it was resolved to act in this spirit.

4. *The Center as a Responsible Government Party*

In another sense also the Center had to learn a new lesson. Now it does not merely assume responsibility for the one or the other law or project of law; now it bears full, integral responsibility for all government actions, and even to a larger degree than any of the other government parties. The Center has held the post of Chancellor in the Weimar Republic longer than any other party. It was for a long time in charge of important cabinet positions, primarily of the finance ministry and especially for eight years of the labor department.

"This did not come about because of the Center's lust for power. From mere party interest, the Center would have been much better off could we have withdrawn into opposition from time to time. We withstood this temptation for patriotic reasons only. Without the Center's participation, frequently even its leadership, it would have proved altogether impossible to form a government. The antagonisms between the Left and the Right were far too acute. None of the parties on either wing would have been strong enough to assume responsibility or were at all in a position to do so. Time and again it was up to us to take the lead and fill the gap, even when there was no majority in the Reichstag to back us. In this situation it was naturally unavoidable that we determined the Reich policies in many matters, and that we arbitrated the differences within the cabinet and among the government parties. We constantly held a straight line in foreign affairs, though not in the sense of "Erfuellungspolitik" (fulfillment policy) as a goal and at any price.

"We had also the duty to solve thorny problems of internal affairs, problems particularly burdensome to our own followers: revaluation (of private debts wiped out by inflation), compensation of the princes! We had to create the conditions for the consolidation of our new industrial setup, to tackle the new social problems, and in all these crucial matters our mission was partly to mediate, partly to lead and to decide.

5. *Social Politics and Social Reforms*

The German Nationalists used three slogans to characterize their program: Christian, national, social. In comparing this with our own attitude, I would have to add one more word: *democratic*. Furthermore, I would have to point out that these three principles which we also defend: the Christian, the national and the social, have been very differently implemented by ourselves and by the Rightists. Above all, we draw a definite line between national and nationalistic!

"Moreover, we go much further in social matters than they do. In the course of the last decades we have carried out a strongly progressive program, and in working out all parts of the social legislation we have never wavered. In these matters there were no dissensions within the Center Party, or at any rate the position that the Party took proved to be uniform in all essentials. I believe that it is due to this position we took that the weakened Germany was able to realize such a large measure of social progress, progress which—and I say this as a labor minister of many years' standing—has been truly fundamental.

"What we produced was not merely a new edition of the pre-war social policies. We surpassed the old standards. You will readily understand what I mean when I point out that the pre-war social policies were concerned basically with protecting the workers.

"The newer social policies, however, stress the worker's legal rights and the security of his livelihood. This marks a difference in the essence. If we consider that the "proletarian" character consisted substantially in this absence of equal rights with the rest of the population, in the wording of the law as well as in reality, and if we also consider that to be "proletarian" signified the insecurity of one's livelihood, the new Labor Charter, the laws introducing labor exchanges and unemployment insurance, will appear in their true light. We can show that, in giving social reform this new direction we went far toward 'solving' the social problem." [299]

Peter Tischleder, (1926), *Joseph Mausbach* (1911)

The Legitimacy of a Peoples' Revolution

"We propose here to deal briefly with the question whether a lawful right exists to fight in self-defense against a usurper who strives for sovereign power through lawlessness and the use of force. According to St. Thomas and all of Scholasticism, this question is to be answered in the affirmative, for the usurper, as an *"invasor,"* an aggressor, should be treated like a foreign enemy, a *hostis extraneus,* who possesses no rightful claim whatever to the government and therefore leaves the state as a whole a perfectly good right to defend itself. Special attention should be given to the fact that in such a case St. Thomas explicity credits each private citizen with the right to render the usurper harmless, even without being authorized beforehand by the judiciary, in the event that such recourse to higher authority is at the time not open to him.

"This is proved by a passage in the "Commentary in the Sentences" (in 2 dist. 44 qu. 2a2 ad 5), where Thomas describes the usurper as an interloper (*invasor*) who either captures sovereign power by force in disregard of the will of the people, or compels the subjects' acquiescence to his reign, (*quando aliquis dominium sibi per violentiam surripit nolentibus subditis vel etiam ad consensum coactis*). He calls such government *principatus usurpatus.* With every definiteness and assurance Thomas declares that the people's active resistance against such a tyrant is legitimate, for as an *invasor* he has no true authority and therefore no claim whatsoever to the citizens' obedience. He is, on the contrary, an illegitimate suppressor of their liberties of which he has robbed them by force and of which he continues to deprive them. As long as the people has not freely recognized his government, or a higher authority has confirmed it, it may be *potentia* and *violentia,* but it is not *iustitia* and *dominium*. And just as every man, if given the opportunity, is entitled to recover possessions unlawfully taken from him, an oppressed people, indeed each individual oppressed citizen, is entitled to recover his embezzled liberties. Nor is this all. Not only may every subject overthrow such a government by force as soon as there is an opportunity to attempt this; he may even kill the tyrant, provided that no recourse is open to higher authority to obtain an indictment. 'Whoever then, for the sake of his country's liberty, kills a tyrant will be praised and rewarded,' just as Tullius praises those who killed Caesar! Such action is not even made conditional on previous explicit authorization by the entire nation, as we would expect in analogy to the usual safeguards against the private recourse to force (S. Th. 2, 2 qu. 64 a. 1). It is as if the violence itself which the people suffers were like a cry for help and like a power of attorney given every citizen as an organ and soldier of the people to execute judgment on the usurper."

*   *   *

"When we recall that Thomas ascribes the dominant role in the life of a state to the common good; that he derives from it all sanction of legitimacy; that he sees in it the one and only goal for state power; that for Thomas the common good is identical with the self-directed, intrinsic purpose of the state as a whole—we shall not be surprised to find Thomas here teaching that a government has no justification for its existence if it deviates from this rightful purpose, not only once in a while but continuously and deliberately. Therefore, the revolt of a people against such a government is on principle not an insurrection. It is rather a legitimate act in self-defense, the liberation from an illegal oppressor. Only on one condition might it be a moral duty to give continued support to the tyrannical government instead of bending every effort for self-liberation: if, because of insufficient preparation or flaundering execution, the attempted resistance would be bound to inflict on the common good just that kind of severe damage which it was meant to prevent. By this proviso Thomas does not, however, revoke his declaration of principle that active resistance is permissible. He only shows the limits set by the very purpose of the state to the right of resistance which this purpose makes legitimate on principle. It is therefore the tyrant himself—by creating factions to safeguard his domination, by playing one faction against the other, by making of the people helpless victims of his tyrannical exploitation —who is the real insurrectionist. 'On the contrary, those who defend the commonwealth against insurrection'—and according to the clear definition of St. Thomas the tyrant is very specially an insurrectionist—'may not justly be considered insurrectionist, as those do not deserve to be called fighting-cocks who defend themselves against hooligans.'

"The authority of St. Thomas may therefore not be quoted by those who maintain that active resistance is forbidden under every circumstance. They do not give proper weight to the necessity of holding the common good supreme, a requirement which Thomas so strongly stresses. Instead, they are willing to sacrifice the common good to secondary aims, e. g. to the principle of legitimacy."

*   *   *

Thanks to his great logical cogency, Joseph Mausbach takes the much stronger position in his concept of legitimacy as compared with his opponent Cathrein. Mausbach writes: "The medieval and latter-day theory which sees in the social contract the immediate root of government authority combined with the second valid principle that the ultimate purpose of society willed by God is its order and welfare, have led the traditional Catholic philosophy of law and ethics to the same almost generally accepted consequence. It is this, that in a dire emergency, when the people's welfare has been grievously impaired and all legal means are exhausted, the people as a whole or their legitimate representatives have the right to resist and if necessary to depose the monarch and to alter the constitution . . . Those who maintain the opposite view so far usually got entangled in a web of contradictions. They admit (1) that resistance and dethronement may be permissible only where the constitution or election compacts or articles of union expressly provide for such a contingency. However, should not actions that are permissible under positive clauses written into documents be regarded as even more legitimate when they originate in the God-given natural right of the people as a whole? They admit (2) that even the individual citizen may actively resist and even kill the tyrant in lawful self-defense if he does so to protect his life or his life's most cherished values. But does not the welfare of the community rank as high, or indeed higher than the life of the individual? According to these same authors, (3) a usurped government may become legitimized by virtue of a sort of statute of limitation by which the rights of the former dynasty lapse . . . However, such a transfer of legal rights cannot be legitimized by the mere lapse of time or by the actual power status, but only by the compelling need of the commonwealth, by authority of the supreme purpose of the state. Why should not this purpose exert its force in our case when the immediate salvation of the people is at stake, instead of the legitimacy of past lawless acts?"

Dietrich von Hildebrand: Organism and Community

What is the nature of the relation existing between the individual person and the entity which we call community? Furthermore, what is the ontological rank of entities such as state, family, nation or humanity, as compared to the individual person who is a part of them?

A comparison has often been made between organism and community. The relations existing between man and community and the one to be found between organs and the organism have been considered as analogous. Yet insofar as the primary ontological aspect is concerned, this analogy does not hold. Community is a type of wholeness which thoroughly differs from the one which the organism entails.

The organism possesses relatively independent subordinate unities as organs and members which can be designated as real parts of the whole. The members and organs are relative unities in themselves. They are not just pieces of the "stuff" out of which the whole is built; rather they are entities constituting unities of their own in virtue of their definite form and function. Each organ and member is clearly distinguished from the other. The liver, for example, is a relatively independent unity and as such it is distinctly separated from the heart; similarly the hand is clearly distinct as distinguished from the foot and so on. But despite their relative independence, these entities are essentially "parts" insofar as their ontological character is concerned. First of all they cannot subsist by themselves; as soon as they are artificially removed from the organism they perish as something living, and lose precisely the character of a true unity.

Secondly they are characterized by their need for completion and dependence upon the whole; they clearly point toward the whole in which and with which they alone can unfold their specific being.

These parts do not build up the whole; they are not the ontological basis supporting the organism; rather the whole supports the parts. Here the whole is really *prior* to the parts, i. e., the unity of the whole organisms is ontologically the presupposition for the relative unity of each member or organ, that is to say, the presupposition for their existence as specific beings. The origin of living beings, especially of higher animals also reveals this fact. The whole organism at its very beginning consists of *one* cell, the fertilized ovum; this whole breaks up into many cells which will form cells and organs. In this sphere an absolute difference exists between the whole and the parts. The genuine organism is in some way an end point; it is truly a whole and cannot fuse with other organisms to form a new whole of the same ontological rank in such a manner that the original single organism would give up its self-sufficient unity and become a mere part.

In the community, we are confronted with a completely different type of whole. It is built up by parts all of which are completely self-sufficient unities. Individual persons are self-sufficient unities. They even represent "a world by itself," as we saw before. They are the true and most typical substances in the realm of finite beings which we know through experience. But on the other hand they can constitute a new real unity in virtue of their being joined together by a potent principle of unity. It is true that they are parts of the community. But this function of being a member of a community does in no way alter their character as independent beings. In contradistinction to the relation existing between limbs and organisms, individuals build up the community, and are in no way dependent upon the community in their being. Here the parts are prior to the whole.

Thus it is impossible to consider communities such as family, state or humanity to be ontologically akin to organisms. They form, on the contrary, a completely different type of a whole than the organism. Here the individual person definitely ranks ontologically higher than the community. This is clearly revealed by the fact that the individual human person is the most perfect substance among the creatures known to us by experience; whereas communities are not real substances. They have thus been called *moral substances.*

The difference between the relation of members of a community and the community itself on the one hand, and the relation between limbs and organs of an organism on the other hand, is thus plainly clear. The relation between part and whole is the very reverse in both cases.

Only in the supernatural community, the mystical Body of Christ, are we confronted with a community which can be rightly compared with an organism, notwithstanding its incomparable superiority in other respects. The supernatural principle of life in the individual faithful depends upon his being a member of the Mystical Body of Christ. His supernatural life is so linked to his being a member of the community of the Holy Church that the individual cannot subsist independently of the Corpus Christi Mysticum, as a "temple" of the Holy Trinity, although they can subsist in their natural life as human persons.

Thus we can rightly say with respect to this community that the whole has the priority with respect to the parts. Thus St. Paul in comparing the Church with an organism precisely throws into relief the unique character of this community which thoroughly differs from all mere natural communities.[301]

Ferdinand Frodl: *The Essence of Society*

The unity of society will be found to be a manifestation of the one psycho-physical Nature which becomes active in two directions: first, within the existing plurality of persons and within actual existence; second, transcending the first, in the increase of the numbers of actual persons by procreation. Although each separate person is in possession of the complete essential, factual content of Nature, yet the spiritual and physical faculties find their actualization now in this, now in another separate personal unit; but through all these various persons drifts the one life of psycho-physical Nature, set in motion by one essential existence common to all. Thus on the soil of essential material contents a growth of separate, but connected and articulated units of life ripens. In this way there is a common ground embracing the more narrowly defined groupings of personages within the total multitude. They constitute the articulated structure of the whole plurality of persons within orders which take their origin from the essential quality of the very Nature of these persons.

Pondering these thoughts we shall learn that the unity of Society ties together and lends inner order to the plurality of persons in two respects: first, there is the distinction between man and woman, a differentiation in personal existence plainly determined by the spirituality of Nature itself; secondly, there is the diversification among the great number of individual persons caused by the contingent character of Nature in its various psycho-physical characteristics. This constitutes a diversification of personalities that is not intrinsic to the essence itself of personality but is derived from the temporal quality pertaining to the stage of perfection reached at a certain moment.

In the personalistic distinction between man and woman the unifying cause is the spiritual existence which, though it presupposes that the one Nature has distinct manifestations, is again tied together by this one Nature in the fact of personality itself. In the second instance, it is the contingent existence, tied to its material, which makes it possible that the one nature has numerous bearers. The unity then lies not in the bearers themselves, rather in the character of that which they bear. This unity that flows from natural existence and is common to all created, contingent beings, animate and inanimate alike, can on its own, divorced from its spiritual essence, never result in the formation of a Society. Whoever would regard this natural unity in itself to be a social unity would also have to see a society in a heap of stones. Only because in the human beings the contingent, physical existence is tied in one with the spiritual existence, the actual individual manifestations of the one Nature can for their bearers become the cause of unity. Society derives its essential, autonomous unity from the spiritual essence of human nature. Human nature itself is the origin of the personal variety and thus is identical both with the unity and the plurality of persons. Therefore, as between the plurality of persons there is complete mutual ownership of Nature and only the use of it is separate. It is not merely a question of "equality in unity" or of "possessing the one thing in an equal manner." The truth is that there is the one Nature in the numerous persons.

This leads to a further peculiarity of the social unity and to another significant characteristic of Society. If it is true that the unity within the plurality of persons has its basic origin in the spiritual essence of Nature, it follows that it must likewise find expression in the essential vital acts of the spirit, i.e., in understanding and volition; all the more since precisely these basic faculties of the spirit are the foundation of the social existence of man and enable the plurality of persons to exist within the one Nature. The unity within the plurality of persons can not, therefore, be confined to mere existence because existence becomes aware of itself only through the spirit and expresses its vital force only in this true self-awareness.

Thus society, on the one hand, always depends on the existence of a plurality of persons in the unity of Nature, but first only as a potentiality, *in actu primo*. In living reality, *in actu secundo,* we can only speak of Society after the matters given as existant have entered the realm of human awareness, i.e., after this unity has become a more or less perfectly realized fact.

*   *   *

If it is at all possible to distinguish among essential factors of Society which are the constituant and the constituted ones, only the plurality of persons might be regarded as the passively constituted factor. In so doing we, however, disregard the personalistic character of the single individual because, being persons, they already essentially form a Society and on this basis can by their free decision form a new one. Were they non-personal, separate beings they could never, despite the unity of Nature, become a Society.

Only a plurality of persons that are thought of merely as separate beings, not already as bearers of a unified Nature, can be parts passively constituting a Society. In the realm of essences and in reality the constituting and the constituted elements are identical because the plurality of persons as bearers of the one Nature are by that very fact a unity.

From the character of Society as here described we must deduce consequences of decisive significance. First, we recognize that for Society unity and plurality are equally essential. Unity does not impair the autonomy of the separate person, plurality does not **impair** the unity of Nature. As a "Person" the individual remains the one and only of its kind, but as possessed of a specific Nature he is a dependent member of a vital unity. All the free expressions of his nature are characterized by personal peculiarities; but as active expressions of Nature they cannot be completely understood in terms of the separate person, only in terms of the entirety of Nature. A person's actions must be viewed as a whole, not individualistically. From the essence of Society as here explained we can now determine the true object (*objectum formale*) of sociology, and we can draw definite lines of distinction between sociology and all other branches of knowledge.

If it is true that Society is the purality of persons within the unity of Nature, it follows that the most perfect Society will be the one that embraces the most complete plurality within the most consummate unity. This condition obtains nowhere else but in the Trinity. Here we have a plurality of persons which in the most perfect manner realizes the infinite creativity of Nature that is manifested in it. There cannot be more, nor can there be less than three persons in God. And this Trinity of persons does not exist simply in one nature or another, but only in the one Nature, which means that the unity of the Three divine persons is not merely a unity of existence but of essence.

It has been shown that Society among human beings is a plurality of persons, but does not exhaust the fullness of the vital potentialities of Nature. It is merely a unity of existence, not of essence. Man, however, is called upon to participate in divine Nature, and this vital community with God is the ultimate goal and reason of all Creation. Here the community among men reaches its last perfection, for it is here that the unity of Nature is transformed into the unity of essence. In his participation in the one divine Nature the person under Grace enters into full possession of Nature. Every natural community is thus but the foundation of the one true Community, that is, with the Father, the Son and the Holy Ghost. This is the society doctrine of Christianity.[302]

NOTES

INTRODUCTION

1 O. von Nell-Breuning, *Reorganisation of Social Economy. The Social Encyclical developed and explained,* Milwaukee 1936, pg 16-17.

This is the most important modern commentary to the Social Encyclicals of the Popes, especially *Quadragesimo Anno,* which at the same time will best introduce English readers to the Realism of modern German Catholic Social Philosophy. The Jesuit social philosopher Nell-Breuning reaffirms the best traditions of *Realism in modern neo-scholastic Social Metaphysics,* when he opposes the integralistic attempts of theologizing the natural categories of social, economical and political life:

"That this (theologizing) is entirely out of the question, is clear if we consider the relationship between nature and supernature. *Elevation to supernature leaves human nature unchanged in principle. Therefore, human nature retains its full value as a source of knowledge for social order.* All principles for the structural plan of human society are impressed upon human nature by God, and remain so; therefore, they can be recognized in and deduced from this human nature with certainty. The natural order is consummated by the supernatural order in such a way that it remains fully unchanged. That is why the natural order, although we can separate it from the actually given supernatural order only by abstract thinking, is not merely a fancy, but a living *reality* whose misappreciation, denial, or debasement at the same time not only misappreciates, denies, and debases supernature, but actualle deprives it of its foundations, thus making it untenable" (op. cit. pg 17)

"The Pope characterizes the economic laws as natural laws based on the nature of material goods, as well as on the dual nature of man, and continues: 'Reason itself clearly deduces from the nature of things and from the individual and social character of man what is the end and object of the whole economic order assigned by God the Creator' (*Quadrages. Anno 42*). In other words, there is such a purpose explicitly denied by the purely formalistic economic concept of Universalism, and less drastically stated by liberalistic economy in saying that this goal cannot be apprehended by human intelligence. The Pope has more confidence in the human intellect than have liberal economists, and according to him knowledge concerning this purpose exists. He says that human intellect is able to conceive the purpose 'clearly', that is, with scientific certainty. The Pope also gives the sources from which the human intellect can gather the knowledge, and these sources are the same for the essential laws of economics; namely 'from the nature of things and from the individual and social character of man' (*Quadrages. Anno 42*)". (ibd. pg 87)

For the same problem concerning the authority of the Church in the social and economic spheres see also J. Messner, *Social Ethics,* 1949, pg 69-73, and P. Jostock, *Die Sozialen Rundschreiben,* Freiburg 1948, pg 108 ff. For the relationship between *jus divinum*—Revelation and *jus naturale*—natural Reason, see chapt. VI, 1; also J. Mausbach, *Christlich-katholische Ethik,* Leipzig 1906, pg 545 ff and H. Pesch, *Staatsozialismus und Privatwirtschaft,* Freiburg 1918, pg 343 ff.

2 Goetz Briefs, *Die wirtschafts- und sozialpolitischen Ideen des Katholizismus.* Festgabe fuer Lujo Brentano, Muenchen 1925, vol. 1, pg 199. Also G. Gundlach, *Zur Soziologie der katholischen Ideenwelt und des Jesuitenordens,* Freiburg 1927,

CHAPTER I

The Sociological Problem of Catholicism

[1] In the following study it is of course impossible to give more than a systematic outline of the entire complex of problems. A full representation will be contained in my forthcoming monography, *Catholicism and Society in Germany 1789-1950 (Kirche und Gesellschaft. Die sozialen und politischen Ideen und Bewegungen im deutschen Katholizismus der Neuzeit)*. There I intend to correct inevitable shortcomings in the discussion of special problems and in respect to sources, theories and achievements of Catholic movements, thinkers and writers which here partly were given too short shrift or neglected entirely.

[2] As practiced by the exponents of neo-liberalistic secularism; thus recently by Paul Blanchard, *American Freedom and Catholic Power*, Boston 1949; A Bruegmann, *Sozialer Katholizismus im 19. Jahrhundert*, 1939; E. Schmidt, *Bismarcks Kampf mit dem politischen Katholizismus*, 1942; P. Schmidt—Ammann, *Der politische Katholizismus*, Bern 1945. See also G. Mensching's comprehensive essay of a systematic *Soziologie der Religion*, Bonn 1947 which also suffers badly from such misleading generalizations.

[3] For the sacramental notion of the Church and the theological notion of Catholicism, see Karl Adam, *The Essence of Catholicism*, New York 1937; Romano Guardini, *Vom Sinn der Kirche*, Mainz 1923, and Henry de Lubac, *Catholicism*. Paris 1937.

[4] See my Introduction, *Lebendiger Katholizismus*, to my German translation and edition of Cardinal J. Verdier, *Die Kirche und die soziale Frage*, Zuerich 1940

[5] Allocution to the Lenten Preachers of Rome, February 28, 1927

[6] See especially the important book by Lubac, *Catholicism*. The German edition, edited by Hans-Urs Balthasar, *Katholizismus und Gemeinschaft*, Einsiedeln 1943, contains valuable notes with many additions from German sources.

[7] The best modern presentation of these problems is given by Ferdinand Frodl, *Gesellschaftslehre*, Vienna 1936. For the English reader the presentation of the same subject in outline, by Victor Cathrein, *Ethics*, and Augustin Lehmkuhl, *Moral Theology*, both in the *Catholic Encyclopedia V*, 556 ff. and XIV, 601 ff., remains unsurpassed. Also Victor Cathrein, *Moralphilosophie*, 2 vols. Freiburg 1924; J. Mausbach, *Moraltheologie*, 3 vols, 1926, and *Christlich-katholische Ethik* (in: Die Kultur der Gegenwart, Teil I, iv) Leipzig 1906.

[8] H. Pesch, *Lehrbuch der Nationaloekonomie*, vol. II, pg vii, Freiburg 1920, and, *Ethik und Volkswirtschaft*, Freiburg 1918.

[9] For a contemporary evaluation of these problems, see the pertinent passages by Don Luigi Sturzo, *Inner Laws of Society*, New York 1944; and *Nationalism and Internationalism*, New York 1946. Also Alfred Mendizabal, *Catholicism and Politics*, in: European Ideologies, edit. by Felix Gross, New York 1948, and the book by Melvin J. Williams, *Catholic Social Thought*, New York 1950.

[10] Carl Schmitt's, *Politische Theologie*, 1922, is a sad example for the grotesque misunderstanding of the autonomous character of the genuine categories of politics to which the raising of the State to the dignity of a pseudo-theological absolute must necessarily give rise. In his attempt to see Political Catholicism as an absolute, the same Carl Schmitt most clearly demonstrates the spiritual nuisance of any politization of Catholic Universalism. Schmitt goes even so far as to maintain that "when once the eternal light of the Catholic altars will be fed by the same power stations which served the theatre and the dance hall of the town, then Catholicism will have become an understandable, self-evident

matter also sentimentally to the economic thinking of the contemporaries . . . ";
see, *Roemischer Katholizismus und politische Form,* Muenchen 1925; also *Der Begriff des Politischen,* 1933. See note 54

11 Lubac, *Catholicism,* 4th edition, Paris 1947, pg 320

12 See chapter V, *The Essence of Political Catholicism,* and chapter VI, *The Social Metaphsics*

CHAPTER II

German Catholicism in the 18th Century

13 Here, and later in our presentation we use only the *sociological* concept of the "Church" as an organization and a society, and of Catholicism as a historically determinated cultural phenomenon, particularly in the realm of social and political life.

14 Franz Schnabel, *Deutsche Geschichte im Neunzehnten Jahrhundert,* vol 1, pg 83, Freiburg 1937.

15 Unfortunately, Schnabel's and Treitschke's great presentations of German 19th century history are preceded by too sketchy introductions to that era which do not consider adequately the implications for modern German history of the fateful German developments from the outbreak of the Reformation to that of the French Revolution. For a clearer understanding of this complex of problems, I refer to the literature quoted in notes 19 to 22. The English reader will find the best introduction in G. P. Gooch, *Germany and the French Revolution,* London 1920, and the same author's, *Germany,* New York 1925; also in the valuable books by Chr. Atkinson, *A History of Germany 1715-1815,* London 1908, and W. H. Bruford, *Germany in the Eighteenth Century,* Cambridge, England 1935. We also recommend, though with some cautioning, A. J. P. Taylor's spirited introduction to, *The Course of German History,* London 1945.

16 Joseph Lortz, *Die Reformation in Deutschland,* 2 vols., Freiburg 1939-40; Franz Schnabel, *Deutsche Geschichte im Neunzehnten Jahrhundert,* 4 vols., Freiburg 1937 to 1951

17 To this point, see the important work by Joseph Lortz, cited under 16; furthermore, the same author's, *Geschichte der Kirche in ideengeschichtlicher Betrachtung,* Muenster 1950. There is also important source material in J. Schmidlin, *Die kirchlichen Zustaende in Deutschland vor dem dreissigjaehrigen Kriege,* Freiburg 1908-1910, and, *Die kirchlichen Zustaende waehrend des dreissigjaehrigen Krieges,* Freiburg 1940. The most comprehensive presentation and sources are given by K. Eder, *Geschichte der Kirche im Zeitalter des konfessionellen Absolutismus 1555-1648,* Freiburg 1950; and L. A. Veit, *Die Kirche im Zeitalter des Individualismus, 1648 bis zur Gegenwart,* Freiburg 1931-33. Especially valuable are also the official reports of the investigations of the papal *nuncios* Joseph Garampi and Bartholommeo Pacca. See J. Ph. Dengel, *Die politische und kirchliche Taetigkeit des Msgr. J. Garampi in Deutschland 1761-1763,* (1905) ; B. Pacca, *Memorie storiche sul soggiorno del Cardinale Pacca in Germania 1785-1794,* (Roma 1832) , and A. Sleumer, *Kardinal B. Pacca's Denkwürdigkeiten ueber seinen Aufenthalt in Deutschland,* 2 vols. (1908-1909) .

18 See chapters IV and V.

19 Besides the general presentations (see note 17) a good number of valuable monographs on Church history exists; there are in the first place the special articles, difficult to procure, in the Encyclopedias of Hauck-Hertzog; Wetzer und Welte; Buchberger, *Lexicon fuer Theologie und Kirche;* and, *Die Religion in Geschichte und Gegenwart.* Specially important are A. Hauck, *Die Entstehung der bischoeflichen Fuerstenmacht,* 1891; and, *Die Entstehung der geistlichen*

Territorien, 1909. For the Rhenish Electorats, see M. Beer, *Buecherkunde zur Geschichte der Rheinlande*, 1920; and the bibliography in the most recent works by E. Zenz, *Die Trierer Universitaet*, 1949; M. Braubach, *Die erste Bonner Universitaet*, 1947; also F. H. Mering, *Geschichte der letzten vier Kurfuersten von Koeln*, 1842; J. Marx, *Geschichte des Erzstiftes Trier*, 1858-64; and A. L. Veit, *Der Zusammenbruch des Mainzer Erzstuhles infolge der franzoesischen Revolution*, 1927.

20 The works by L. Haeusser, *Deutsche Geschichte vom Tode Friedrichs des Grossen bis zur Gruendung des Deutschen Bundes*, 4 vols., 1859-1860, and Theodor v. Heigel, *Deutsche Geschichte vom Tode Friedrichs des Grossen bis zur Aufloesung des Alten Reiches*, 2 vols. 1893- 1911, are still the best presentations of the history of the last epochs of the Ecclesiastical Principalities. Equally indispensable are B. Erdmannsdoerffer, *Deutsche Geschichte vom Westfälischen Frieden bis zum Regierungsantritt Friedrichs des Grossen*, Berlin 1890-1893; and F. C. Schlosser, *Geschichte des 18. Jahrhunderts und des 19. bis zum Sturz des franzoesischen Kaiserreiches*, 8 vols., 1864-1866. A comprehensive modern discussion of the problems here of special interest to us will be found in the various contributions to the symposium, edited by J. Hansen, *Geschichte der Rheinlande von den aeltesten Zeiten bis zur Gegenwart*, 2 vols. 1922. Furthermore, the Book by Gooch, *Germany and the French Revolution*, mentioned above, and Seb. Merkle, *Die Bedeutung der Geistlichen Staaten im Alten Reich*, 1930, are indispensable.

21 See the paragraph on *Secularisation* and chapter III on *Romanticism*.

22 My large study (cf. note 1) will also contain a detailed discussion. From older sources there exist incisive presentations in the first place in the works by Haeusser and Heigel, vols. I; in K. Th. Perthes, *Das deutsche Staatsleben vor der Revolution*, 1845; and, *Politische Zustaende und Personen in Deutschland zur Zeit der franzoesischen Revolution*, 1856-1869. Furthermore J. von Sartori, *Geistliches und weltliches Staatsrecht der deutschen katholischen Erz-,Hoch-und Ritterstifte*, Nuernberg 1788-1791; and M. Braubach, *Die vier letzten Kurfuersten von Köln, 1931*.

23 I refer principally to L. Eunen, *Frankreich und der Niederrhein oder Geschichte von Stadt und Kurstaat Koeln seit dem Dreissigjaehrigen Krieg bis zur franzoesischen Okkupation*, 2 vols., 1855-1856; F. E. Mering, *Clemens August, Kurfuerst von Koeln*, 1851; E. Renard, *Clemens August, Kurfuerst von Koeln*, 1927; and K. Th. v. Heigel, *Neue geschichtliche Essays*, Muenchen 1902.

24 Heinrich Brueck, Bishop of Mainz, (1899-1901) in his strong criticism of the Rhenish Electors in his essay, unsurpassed even today on the *Emser Kongress*, in Wetzer und Welte's Kirchenlexikon, vol. IV, pg. 484 ff; also the very important literature of notes 30, 32 and 35.

25 The list of art treasures is to be found in Renard, *Clemens August*. There also the enumeration of the great jewelery collection from the estate of this most questionable "servant of God."

26 L. Haeusser, op. cit. vol. I, pg 106

27 ibid., vol. I, pg 98-101

28 We are referring to the shameful expulsion of the Protestants from Salzburg by Leopold Anton von Firmian (1727 to 1744), an act which runs counter to all Christian sentiment, and in addition to the formal clauses of the laws of the Empire. This peculiar type of an "Archbishop" expelled about 32,000 Protestants in 1731-32 from their Salzburg homes which they had occupied for centuries, by force and with the use of methods which in their inhumanity can compare with the totalitarian expulsion methods of our era. Many of these

unfortunates were offered a more worthy homeland by the North American State of Georgia.

29 L. Haeusser, op. cit. pg 101

30 The great Matthias J. Scheeben characterizes this lamentable development of Catholic science in the 18th century Germany as an "epoch of desintegration" (Epoche des Verfalls) and the famous historian Hugo Hurter, S. J. speaks of an *"tristissima theologiae scienciae epocha"*; see J. M. Scheeben, *Handbuch der katholischen Dogmatik,* Freiburg 1925, vol. I, pg 457, and H. Hurter, *Nomenclator literarius theologiae,* Oeniponte 1912, vol. V, pg 853. See also M. Grabmann, *Geschichte der katholischen Theologie,* Freiburg 1933, pg 226, ff, and R. Haass, *Die geistige Haltung der katholischen Universitaeten Deutschlands im 18. Jahrhundert,* Freiburg 1952. Further information is to be found in Fr. Paulsen, *Geschichte des Gelehrten Unterrichtes auf den deutschen Schulen und Universitaeten,* 2 vols., 1896-1899; B. Duhr, *Geschichte der Jesuiten in den Laendern deutscher Zunge* 1907-1913, W. Fink, *Beitraege zur Geschichte der bayrischen Benediktinerkongregation.* Eine Jubilaeumsschrift 1648-1934. (1934); Ph. Funk; *Von der Aufklaerung zur Romantik,* 1925. See also note 32

31 In addition to the French works on this subject, the book by B. Groethuysen, *Die Entstehung der buergerlichen Welt-und Lebensanschauung in Frankreich,* merits special attention, especially volume 2, *Die Soziallchren der katholischen Kirche und das Buergertum,* Halle 1930. The basic difference between the socio-religious preconditions for the development of French and German Catholicism here becomes especially clarified.

32 See H. Brueck, *Die rationalistischen Bestrebungen im katholischen Deutschland, besonders in den drei rheinischen Erzbistümern, in der zweiten Haelfte des 18. Jahrundert,* 1865. Furthermore the valuable essay on *Hontheim* and on the *Emser Kongress* in Wetzer und Weltes Kirchenlexikon. The newest presentation is by F. Vigener, *Gallikanismus und episkopalische Stroemungen im deutschen Katholizismus zwischen Tridentinum and Vatikanum,* Muenchen 1913. In my larger study (note 1) special attention will be given to the problem of the influence of the Ideas of Enlightenment, especially for the development of *Josephinism* in Austrian Catholicism and its dialectic relationship to Political Romanticism.

33 For the influence of *Febronianism* on Ecclesiastical Law at the German Universities of the 18th century, compare E. Zenz, *Die Trierer Universitaet,* 1949; also, aside of the general text books of Ecclesiastical Law, E. Landsberg, *Geschichte der deutschen Rechtswissenschaft,* 1898, vol. III, first part, pg 363-386.

34 The text of the *Ems Punctation* can be found in every source book of Church history. To have read it is indispensable for an intimate knowledge and objective judgment of the degeneration of Church spirit of the last Ecclesiastical Electors.

35 Compare G. P. Gooch, *Germany and the French Revolution,* 1920, and his essay by the same name in *Studies in Modern History,* 1932. Also Alfred Stern, *Der Einfluss der franzoesischen Revolution auf das deutsche Geistleben,* 1926; and Theodor Bitterauf, *Geschichte des Rheinbundes,* vol. I, 1905. For the special consequences for Church history, compare principally Heinrich Brueck, *Geschichte der katholischen Kirche in Deutschland im 19. Jahrhundert,* 5 vols., 1887-1905; and Heinrich Schmid, *Geschichte der katholischen Kirche Deutschlands von der Mitte des 18. Jahrhunderts bis in die Gegenwart,* 3 parts, 1872-1874.

36 The text of the *Reichsdeputationshauptschluss* (RDHS) of 1803 and of the *Rheinbundakte* of 1806 with the pertaining official papers has been re-

published in *Quellen zur Neueren Geschichte,* Heft 10, edidet by E. Walder, Bern 1948.

[37] A critical survey of the consequences of the Secularization for the Catholic Church in. Germany in respect to State and Church politics will be found in G. Ebers article, *Saekularisation,* in *Handwoerterbuch der Rechtswissenschaften,* vol. V, pg 244 ff; and by Gescher-Ebers, *Saekularisation* in *Staatslexikon der Goerresgesellschaft,* 5th edit., vol. IV, pg 1161 ff; in the same place also further bibliographical notes.

[38] Karl Lamprecht, *Deutsche Geschichte,* vol. IX, pg. 146-148, Berlin 1907.

[39] E. Knupfer, *Staatslexikon,* 1926, vol. I, pg. 1362.

[40] Characteristic of this way of thinking is the scurrilous *Funeral Oration* which in 1798 Goerres devoted to the dying "Holy Roman Empire of ponderous memory." The text will be found in J. Baxa, *Gesellschaft und Staat im Spiegel deutscher Romantik,* 1924, pg. 252-266.

[41] Goerres, *Mein Glaubensbekenntnis,* Baxa, pg. 269.

[42] Goerres, *Ausgewaehlte Werke und Briefe;* herausg. von W. Schellberg, Muenchen 1911, vol. I, pg. 50.

[43] Ibd., pg. 51.

[44] Goerres, *Resultate meiner Sendung nach Paris,* 1800. Baxa pg. 354 ff.

[45] Eichendorff, *Ueber die Folgen von der Aufhebung der Landeshoheit der Bischoefe und Kloester in Deutschland,* 1818. Saemtliche Werke des Freiherrn von Eichendorff, vol. 10, Regensburg 1912, pg. 166-167.

CHAPTER III

Catholicism and German Romanticism

[46] H. Taine, *Histoire de la litterature Anglaise,* 1863; *Origines de la France contemporaine,* 1876-1894; G. Haym, *Die romantische Schule,* 1870, 6. Auflage, erweiterte Bearbeitung von Oskar Walzel, edit. von Edwin Redslob, Berlin 1949; also K. Murray, *Taine und die englische Romantik,* 1924; and Fr. Braune, *Edmund Burke in Deutschland,* 1917.

[47] Carl Schmitt, *Politische Romantik,* 1919, 2. edit. 1925; W. Metzger, *Gesellschaft, Recht und Staat in der Ethik des deutschen Idealismus,* 1917; S. Rubinstein, *Romantischer Sozialismus,* 1920; Jakob Baxa, *Einfuehrung in die romantische Staatswissenschaft* 1923, 2 edit. 1931; Peter Viereck, *Metapolitics. From the Romantics to Hitler.* New York 1941.

[48] Compare A. Poetzsch, *Studien zur Fruehromantischen Politik und Geschichtsauffassung,* 1908; A. Mueller, *Die Auseinandersetzung der Romantik mit den Ideen der Revolution,* 1929; Arthur O. Lovejoy, *The Meaning of Romantic in Early German Romanticism—On the Discrimination of Romanticism;* both in *Essays in the History of Ideas,* Baltimore 1948; Gottfried Salomon, *Das Mittelalter als Ideal der Romantik,* 1921; M. A. Viatte, *Le Catholicisme chez les Romantiques,* 1922; Paul Kluckhohn, *Persoenlichkeit und Gemeinschaft. Studien zur Staatsauffassung der deutschen Romantik,* 1925; E. Ruprecht, *Der Aufbruch der Romantischen Bewegung,* 1948. For English readers of special importance is the, *Symposion on Romanticism,* Journal of the History of Ideas, vol. II, i, New York 1941 with contributions by A. O. Lovejoy, G. Briefs, E. N. Anderson, J. Barzun, H. N. Fairchield and others.

[49] Compare the execellent characterization of *Catholicism* by Lubac. note 11.

[50] Compare our characterization of Goerres in the section on *Romantic Catholicism.*

[51] Compare my essay on *German Philosophy,* in *Encyclopedia Americana,* 1952-edition, vol. 12, g. 603 ff.

[52] Compare my criticism of Vogelsang in chapter IV and also chapter VI, *Neo-Romanticism and Universalism.*

[53] *Politische Romantik,* chapter II, 2, *Die occasionalistische Struktur der Romantik,* pg. 115-152.

[54] Carl Schmitt has proved himself to be a prototype of Romantic Occasionalism, in his entire development, from his *Politische Theologie* (1922), his *Roemischer Katholizismus und politische Form* (1925), to his *Begriff des Politischen* (1933) and his questionable activity as crown jurist for National Socialism, in the first place in his *Der Fuehrer schuetzt das Recht, Deutsche Juristenzeitung,* Heft 15, 1934. Hence his deep understanding for the occasionalist type of German Political Romanticism principally with authors like Adam Mueller and K. L. v. Haller. Compare also G. Salomon, *Staatsrecht* in *Deutschland,* in Freie Wissenschaft, Paris 1938. As great as is Carl Schmitt's contribution on principle to the analysis of Romantic Occassionalism, he was unable to "jump over his own shadow", in other words, to draw a distinction based on genuine theological thinking between the pseudo-Catholic Political Theology of Romantcism and an original Catholic Theological Politics. Nevertheless, future attempts in this direction will have to build up gratefully in many respects on Carl Schmitt's insights in his *Politische Romantik.*

[55] See Erich Przywara, *Religionsphilosophie katholischer Theologie,* Munich 1937; and, *Das katholische Kirchenprinzip,* in: Zwischen den Zeiten, 1930, vol. VII, Heft 3.

[56] The present chapter will be elaborated and will be published under the title, *Katholizismus und Romantik, Romantischer Existentialismus oder occasionalistische Romantik?*

[57] Bernhard Groethuysen, *Die Entstehung der buergerlichen Welt und Lebensanschauung in Frankreich.* vol. I, *Das Buergertum und die katholische Weltanschauung;* vol. II, *Die Soziallehren der katholischen Kirche und das Buergertum.* Halle 1927-1930.

[58] Compare note 54. In this respect a straight ideo-historical relationship exists between the pseudo-theological attempt of Adam Mueller, *Von der Notwendigkeit einer theologischen Grundlage der gesamten Staatswissenschaften und der Staatswirtschaft insbesondere,* 1819, and Carl Schmitt's attempt to secularize completely the categories of *jus divinum* in order to find a pseudo-theological justification of Hitler's absolute command over the Law, principally in, *Der Fuehrer schuetzt das Recht* (sic!) 1934. To this compare also my book, *Der Mythus Hitler,* Zuerich 1937. pg 240 ff.

[59] Compare notes 64, 65, 68, 69; also E. Faguet, *Politiques et Moralistes,* 3 vols. Paris 1890-1899; M. Souriau, *Histoire du Romantisme.* 2 vols., Paris 1922; G. Boas, *French Philosophies of the Romantic Period,* Baltimore 1925; S. Merkle, *Die Anfaenge der franzoesischen Laientheologie im 19. Jahrhundert.* In, *Wiederbegegnung von Kirche und Kultur in Deutschland.* Festgabe fuer Karl Muth, Muenchen 1927; W. Gurian, *Die politischen und sozialen Ideen der franzoesischen Katholizismus 1789-1914,* M-Gladbach 1928; L. Ahrens, *Lamennais und Deutschland. Studien zur Geschichte der Franzoesischen Revolution,* Muenster 1931.

[60] A detailed characterization of the numerous converts among the representatives of Political Romanticism and of Southern German and Austrian Romantic Conservatism will be found in D. A. Rosenthal, *Convertitenbilder aus dem neunzehnten Jahrhundert,* Schaffhausen 1866-1870.

[61] Chapter II, 2, *The Heritage of the Ecclesiastical Territories.*

[62] Even Carl Schmitt avoids confronting Political Romanticism with the principles of Christian Natural Law, which makes it impossible for him to

draw an ultimate distinction between Political Theology and Theological Politics (cf. note 54). In general, the entire modern German literature on Romanticism, from Metzger and Baxa to Kluckhohn (notes 47-48) suffers from this lack of knowledge and application of the principles of Christian Natural Law to a criticism of the Romantic State and Society doctrines.

63 Compare note 56.

64 Louis Gabriel Ambroise de Bonald, *Oeuvres completes*, 3 vols. (Migne), Paris 1859.

65 Joseph de Maistre, *Oeuvres completes*, 14 vols. Lyon 1884-1885. English readers will find some of the characteristic ideo-political textes of de Bonald and de Maistre in the new, but very questionable Anthology, *Catholic Political Thought, 1789-1848*, edit. by Bela Menczer, Westminster, Md. 1952.

66 Karl Ludwig von Haller, *Handbuch der allgemeinen Staatenkunde*, 1808; *Restauration der Staatswissenschaften*, 6 vols., 1816-1834.

67 Adam Mueller, *Elemente der Staatskunst*, 3 Teile, Berlin 1809. New Edition accordings to which we quote, *Die Elemente der Staatskunst*. Mit einer Einfuehrung, erklaerenden Anmerkungen und ungedruckten Dokumenten versehen von Jakob Baxa, 2 vols., Jena 1922.

68 Baader, *Rezensionen von Monsieur Bonalds Recherches philosophiques sur les premiers objets de connaissance morale*, 1825. Saemtliche Werke, V, 43-120.

69 See the excellent introduction by Joseph Bernhart to the German edition prepared by M. Lieber, *Vom Papst*, 2 vols. Munich 1923. See also the important study by S. Merkle, mentioned in note 59.

70 The two treatises of 1819-1820 by Mueller are reprinted in Adam Mueller, *Schriften zur Staatsphilosophie*, herausg. von R. Kohler, Muenchen 1923.

71 See notes 54 and 58.

72 *Elemente der Staatskunst*, I, pg. 60.

73 Compare H. Rommen, *The State in Catholic Thought*, London 1945; and, Carlyle, R. W. and A. J., *A History of Mediaeval Political Theory in the West*, 6 vols. New York 1903-1936; J. Bowle, *Western Political Thought*, New York 1949; also, P. Honigsheim, *Zur Soziologie der mittelalterlichen Scholastik*. In: Erinnerungsgabe fuer Max Weber, vol. II, Muenchen 1923.

74 *Elemente der Staatskunst*, I, pg. 40.

75 ibd. pg. 53.

76 ibd. pg. 29, 31.

77 Leo XIII, *Rerum Novarum*, 6.

78 *Von der Notwendigkeit einer theologischen Grundlage der gesamten Staatswissenschaften*. Ausgabe der oesterreichischen Leo-Gesellschaft, Wein 1897, pg. 18.

79 *Elemente der Staatskunst*, I, pg. 48, 36, 45.

80 O. Spann, *Fundamente der Volkswirtschaftslehre*, 1923, pg. 361; *Haupttheorien der Volkswirtschaftslehre*, 1922, pg. 100.

81 Leopold von Ranke, *Politisches Gespräch;* Saemtliche Werke, vol. 49-50, pg. 314 ff.

82 *Von der Notwendigkeit einer theologischen Grundlage der gesamten Staatswissenschaften*, pg 18.

83 *Deutsche Staatsanzeigen*, vol. 2, pg. 510.

84 *Restauration der Staatswissenschaften*, I, 198.

85 ibd. I, XLVI.

86 ibd. I, 459.

87 ibd. I, 467.

88 ibd. I, 496.

89 ibd. I, 467-474

90 ibd. I, 500.

91 ibd. I, 449.

92 *Deutsche Staatsanzeigen*, vol. 2, pg 157. See also H. O. Meissner, Die Lehre *vom monarchischen Prinzip im Zeitalter der Restauration und des Deutschen Bundes, Breslau* 1913; Fr. Meinecke, *Weltbuergertum und Nationalstaat*, Muenchen 1928; W. H. Sonntag, *Die Staatsauffassung Karl Ludwig von Hallers*, 1929; R. Aris, *Die Staatslehre Adam Muellers in ihrem Verhaeltnis zur deutschen Romantik*, 1929.

93 *Briefwechsel zwischen Friedrich Gentz und Adam Heinrich Mueller, 1800-1829*, Stuttgart 1857; *Briefe von und an Friedrich Gentz, vol. 2, Brinkmann und Adam Mueller*, edit. by F. K. Wittichen, Muenchen 1909-1913.

94 Eichendorff, *Ueber die ethische und religioese Bedeutung der neueren romantischen Poesie in Deutschland*, Leipzig 1847.

95 Eichendorff, *Geschichte der poetischen Literatur Deutschlands*, 2 vols. Paderborn 1857.

96 Although Wilhelm Kosch and Heinrich Sauer began as early as 1908 to publish a historical and critical comprehensive edition *"Saemtliche Werke des Freiherrn Joseph von Eichendorff*, Habbel-Regensburg, the general interest in this enterprise was so slight that today, more than forty years later, of the planned 24 volumes only volumes I-III, X-XIII, XXII exist. Similarly, of the publication of a historical and critical comprehensive edition of the works of *Goerres* (Bachem-Koeln) undertaken by the Goerres Society only in 1926, so far only several volumes exist. Neither the Goerres Society nor any German Catholic has up to now undertaken to publish the works of *Baader*.

97 Now available in the Gesamt Ausgabe (GA), vol. X, *Historische, Politische und Biographische Schriften*, Regensburg 1912.

98 These have been collected principally in GA X, quoted above; also the *Tagebuecher* (vol. XI) and the, *Briefwechsel* (vol. XII, XIII), Regensburg 1908-1912.

99 GA, vol. X

100 *Erlebtes. Halle und Heidelberg. Aus dem literarischen Nachlass Eichendorffs*, Paderborn 1866; GA vol. X.

101 ibd., quoted according to GA, vol. X, 336 ff.

102 The definitive ideo-historical and biographical evaluation of Eichendorff has not yet been made. The otherwise well-oriented general biography by Hans Brandenburg, *Joseph von Eichendorff*, Muenchen 1922, and the summary about, *Ein Jahrhundert Eichendorff-Literatur*, by Karl v. Eichendorff in GA, vol. XXII, Regensburg 1914, are in this respect quite insufficient. On the other hand, the attempt at an ideological and socio-political evaluation made by Jakob Baxa in, *Gesellschaft und Staat im Spiegel deutscher Romantik*, 1924, and, *Einfuehrung in die romantische Staatswissenschaft*, 1931, are outright misleading. Hugo Haeusle's introduction to Eichendorff's *Incognito*, Regensburg 1910, and Ilse Heyer's, *Eichendorffs dramatische Satiren im Zusammenhang mit dem geistigen und kulturellen Leben ihrer Zeit*, Halle 1931, as also the study by Rene Wehrli, *Eichendorffs Erlebnis und Gestaltung der Sinnenwelt*, Frauenfeld 1938, offer some very valuable preparatory efforts.

103 German Catholicism has not yet produced a comprehensive biographical evaluation of Goerres, which would be commensurate with his outstanding ideo-historical significance. However, numerous ideo-biographical special studies are recorded in the generally instructive biography by Wilhelm Schellberg, *Goerres*, 1926. Furthermore, we should mention here the, *Goerresfestschrift, Aufsaetze und Abhandlungen zum 150. Geburtstag von J. Goerres*, edit. by Karl Hoeber, Koeln

1926. Best bibliography by Karl d'Ester, *Goerres,* in *Handbuch der Zeitungswissenschaft,* vol. I, pg 1318-1351, Leipzig 1940.

103a With our concept of *Romantic Existentialism* we believe to have indicated an entirely new approach to the explanation of the relationship between Catholicism and Romanticism, in the first place in respect to the religious problem of Romanticism. This is why we make a special effort to show, exemplified by Eichendorff, Goerres and Baader, that it is inadmissible in writing intellectual and socio-political history to identify the ideo-historical content of Catholicism and Romanticism or even to postulate a so called, *Catholic Romanticism.*

In saying this we have made clear our difference with the Catholic apologists of Romanticism, such as: Christoph Flaskamp, *Die deutsche Romantik,* 1924, 1948; *Goethe, Romantik und Katholizitaet,* 1921; *Erneuerung und Verkuemmerung des katholischen Universalismus im 19, Jahrhundert,* 1923. Also Werner Thormann, *Prophetische Romantik,* 1924, Fanny Imle, *Friedrich von Schlegels Entwicklung von Kant zum Katholizismus,* 1927, and K. A. Horst, *Ich und Gnade, Studie ueber Friedrich Schlegels Bekehrung,* 1951. The same opinion justifies our rejection of such outright misleading Anthologies of Political Romanticism, such as, *Katholisch-Konservatives Erbgut,* edit. by E. Ritter, 1933, and, *Catholic Political Thought 1789-1848,* edit. by B. Menczer, 1952.

On the other hand the following studies may well be quoted as in many respects giving a factual confirmation to our new interpretation: A. v. Martin, *Das Wesen der romantischen Religioesitaet,* 1924, and, *Romantische Conversionen,* Logos XVII, 2; also B. v. Wiese, *Novalis und die romantischen Convertiten,* 1929. We propose to give a detailed foundation to our concept of *Romantic Existentialism* and of its special significance for the Catholic Philosophy of History and Society in the book designated in note 56.

104 *Rheinischer Merkur.* Coblenz 1814-1816. Neudruck der Goerresgesellschaft, Koeln 1926; also, *Rheinischer Merkur,* Ausgewaehlt und eingeleitet von Arno Duch, Muenchen 1921, and, *Joseph Goerres' Reden gegen Napoleon. Aufsaetze und Berichte des Rheinischen Merkur 1814-1815;* herausg. von B. Ihringer, Muenchen 1914.

105 *Die Christliche Mystik.* 4 vols. Regensburg 1836-1842. An excellent selection from this voluminous work was made by J. Bernhart, *Mystik, Magie and Daemonie. Die Christliche Mystik in Auswahl,* Muenchen 1927. I should like to point especially to the outstanding introduction by Joseph Bernhart.

106 The causes and consequences will become clear in the respective analyses in chapters IV-VI. The actual "conspiracy of silence" against Baader has been exposed critically according to the sources by David Baumgardt in the introductory chapter, *Die bisherige Baader-Literatur und das Unrecht gegen Baader,* to his book, *Franz von Baader und die philosophische Romantik,* Halle 1927. Thus we need only point it out in general manner. Among the very scarce Catholic literatur about Baader only the summary surveys by Haffner in *Wetzer und Welte's Kirchenlexikon,* 1882, vol. I, 1781-1791 are worth mentioning; also Schmid-Ettlinger in, *Staatslexikon,* 3rd and 4th edition, 1911; also the presentation by Max Ettlinger in his, *Geschichte der Philosophie von der Romantik bis zur Gegenwart,* 1924, pg 109 ff. Special mention should be made of the articles by F. P. Siegfried in the *Catholic Encyclopedia,* New York 1907, vol. II pg. 173-175, and of Menginot in *Dictionnaire de Theologie Catholique,* Vol. II, i, pg. 2. Compared with these older presentations from abroad, the articles of recent times of L. Baur in the *Staatslexikon,* 5th edit. 1926, and in, *Lexikon fuer Theologie und Kirche,* 1930, appear to be disappointingly brief and very poor of content.

107 *Baader's theosophical writings* are collected primarily in vols. IV, XII and XIII of the *Saemtliche Werke*. There is an excellent selection in the publication by Johannes Classen, *Franz von Baaders Leben und theosophische Werke im Auszug*, 2 vols., Stuttgart 1886-1887.

108 *Baaders anti-Rome writings* belong to the years 1838-1840. The titles are, *Rueckblick auf de Lamennais*, 1838 (Sw V. 385 ff); *Ueber das Kirchenvorsteheramt*, 1838 (SW V, 375 ff); *Tunlichkeit oder Nichttunlichkeit einer Emanzipation des Katholizismus von der roemischen Diktatur*, 1839, (SW X, 75 ff); *Der Morgenlaendische und Abendlaendische Katholizismus*, 1840, (SW X, 148 ff). Compare for the retraction of these writings and Baader's reconciliation with the Church in 1841, the documents in SW, XV, 135 ff.

109 *Baaders gesammelte philosophische Schriften*, 2 vols., Muenster 1831-32; *Franz von Baaders kleine Schriften*, Gesammelt und herausgegeben von Franz Hoffmann, Wuerzburg 1847, 2nd edit., Leipzig 1850; *Baaders Grundzuege der Societaetsphilosophie*. Herausg. von Franz Hoffmann, Wuerzburg 1837, 2nd edit. Leipzig 1850. A new edition of this work was published by Alexander Schmid in the *Summa-Schriften*, vol. II, Hellerau 1917. *Franz von Baaders Saemtliche Werke* (SW), vols. I-XVI, heraugegeben von Franz Hoffmann im Verein mit Hamberger, Lutterbeck and others. Leipzig 1850-1860. This is quoted in our text as SW or only the Latin number of volumes.

110 Baader, *Ausgewaehlte Schriften*, Herausgegeben von Max Pulver. Sammlung *Der Dom*, Leipzig 1921; Max Pulver, *Baaders religioese Philosophie*, in: *Das Reich*, I-IV, 1916; Eugene Susini, *Franz von Baader et le Romantisme Mystique. La Philosophie de Franz von Baader*, 2 vols., Paris 1942.

111 Baader, *Schriften zur Gesellschaftsphilosophie*, Herausgegeben, eingeleitet und erlaeutert von Johannes Sauter, Jena 1925; J. Sauter, *Die Grundlegung der deutschen Volkswirtschaftslehre durch Franz von Baader*, Jena 1925; J. Sauter, *Baader und Kant*, 1928; Jakob Baxa, *Einfuehrung in die Romantische Staatswissenschaft*, 1931.

112 *Baader und sein Kreis*, Ein Briefwechsel. Herausgegeben von Fritz Werle, 1924; *Seele und Welt. Franz von Baaders Jugendtagebuecher 1786-1792*. Herausgegeben von D. Baumgardt, 1928; Fritz Lieb, *Franz von Baaders Jugendgeschichte* 1926; David Baumgardt, *Franz von Baader und die Philosophie der Romantik*, 1927; *Lettres Inedites de Franz von Baader*. Edit. de Eugene Susini, vol. I, Paris 1942; vols. II-III, Vienna 1951.

113 Compare note 117

114 Quotations according to SW, *Saemtliche Werke*.

114a Kierkegaard, *Der Begriff der Angst*, translated by Chr. Schrempf, Jena 1922, pg 23, 35.

115 Compare to this point, Ch. Calippe, *L'Attitude sociale des Catholiques Francais au 19ème Siécle*, Paris 1911; L. Fonk, *Lamennais*, Dictionnaire de Theologie Catholique, vol. VIII, 2473 ff, Paris 1925; J. Poisson, *Le Romantisme social de Lamennais*, Paris 1938; *Lamennais*, Catholic Encyclopedia, vol. VIII, 762 ff, New York 1910; W. Gurian, *Lamennais*, Staatslexikon, 5th edit., vol. III, 762 ff, Freiburg 1929; Gurian, *Die politischen und sozialen Ideen des franzoesischen Katholizismus*, 1928; L. Ahrens, *Lamennais und Deutschland*, 1931.

116 See chapter VI.

117 Baader, *Die Kirche und das Proletariat*. Under this title an edition of the original text of these three essays will soon appear with a detailed introduction by Edgar Alexander, *Baader und die christliche Soziallehre*.

118 G. Briefs, *The Proletariat, A challenge to Western Civilization*, New York 1937.

119 *Kirchenzeitung fuer das katholische Deutschland,* Muenchen 1831.

120 Although in the years up to 1835 Baader and Lamennais were friends and stimulated one another in their common socio-philosophical ideas, their paths parted after the latter, a typical victim of Romantic Occasionalism, became a full convert to the ideologies of secularized social Christianity, ideologies which Baader opposed unconditionally (see SW V, 407; VI, 109; XV, 485).

CHAPTER IV

The Social Movements and Social Policy

121 See chapter V.

122 *Rede in der Versammlung vom 5. Oktober 1848. Verhandlungen der Generalversammlung der katholischen Vereine Deutschlands. Amtlicher Bericht,* Mainz 1848.

123 See the following paragraph on Ketteler.

124 Ketteler, *Die grossen sozialen Fragen der Gegenwart, Sechs Predigten gehalten im hohen Dom zu Mainz;* Mainz 1849. Reprinted in Mumbauer, *Kettelers Schriften,* vol. II, pg 210-320.

125 Session of April 25, 1837. See Geck-Bebel, *Zur Geschichte der deutschen Fabrikgesetzgebung, Erste sozialpolitische Rede in einem deutschen Parlament in 1837 von J. Ritter von Buss,* Offenburg 1904; F. Dor, *J. Ritter von Buss,* Freiburg 1911; Franz Schnabel, *Der Zusammenschluss des politischen Katholizismus in Deutschland im Jahre 1848,* Heidelberg 1910; Albert Franz, *Der Soziale Katholizismus in Deutschland bis zum Tode Kettelers,* Muenchen-Gladbach 1914.

126 Eduard Alletz, *Die neue Demokratie oder die Sitten und die Macht der Mittelklassen in Frankreich.* Im Auszug bearbeitet, uebersetzt und mit einem Sendschreiben von F. J. Buss, Karlsruhe 1838.

127 Ritter von Buss und Donoso Cortes, *Zur Katholischen Politik der Gegenwart.* Paderborn 1850.

128 Goetz Briefs, *Die wirtschaftlichen und sozialpolitischen Ideen des Katholizismus.* Festgabe fuer Lujo Brentano, Muenchen 1925, vol. I, pg. 211.

129 W. Esser, *Franz von Fuerstenberg,* 1842; J. Esch, *F. von Fuerstenberg,* 1891; Galland, *Fuerstenberg,* Historisch-Politische Blaetter, Jhrg. 82, 349 ff; 83, 190 ff., Muenchen 1878-1879; A. Eitel, *F. F. W. v. Fuerstenberg,* Lexikon fuer Theologie und Kirche, IV, 244 ff, 1932; M. Braubach, *Max Franz von Oesterreich, letzter Kurfuerst von Koeln und Fuerstbischof von Muenster,* 1924.

130 Fritz Vigener, *Ketteler, Ein deutsches Bischofsleben des 19. Jahrhunderts.* Muenchen 1924; This monumental monograph of this early deceased disciple of Meinecke's is in every way superior to the presentation from the camp of specifically Catholic research. Indispensable is also Otto Pfuelf, *Bischof Ketteler,* 3 vols., Main 1899. See also Theodor Brauer, *Ketteler,* Leipzig 1927; W. Koeth, *Ketteler,* M-Gladbach 1927; E. de Girard, *Ketteler et la Question ouvière avec une introduction historique sur le movement social catholique,* Berne 1896; and D. Walterscheid, *Der soziale Bischof Ketteler und der soziale Papst,* Duesseldorf 1924.

131 See note 124. Reprinted also in, *Predigten,* herausg. von E. Raich, 2 vols., Mainz 1878, and, *Wilhelm Emanuel von Kettelers Schriften,* herausg. von Johannes Mumbauer, 3 vols., Muenchen 1911.

132 Principally in the sermons of social criticism, *De Nabuthae,* and, *De Tobia.* Latin and English text in *Patristic Studies,* vols. XV, XXXV, Catholic University of America Press, Washington D.C. 1927, 1933. See also H. v. Camphausen,

Ambrosius von Mailand als Kirchenpolitiker, Berlin 1929, and F. H. Dudden, *Life and Times of St. Ambrose,* Oxford 1935.

133 Th. Steinbuechel, *Sozialismus.* Tuebingen 1950, pg 262

134 Marx to Engels, September 25, 1869; Karl Marx-Friedrich Engels, *Briefwechsel,* Gesamtausgabe, Dritte Abteilung, Band 4, pg 227, Berlin 1931.

135 Vigener, *Ketteler,* pg 43

136 Ketteler, *Die Arbeiterfrage und das Christentum,* Mainz 1864, pg 207

137 See the list of Kettelers writings in Pfuelf, *Ketteler, vol. 3.* The most important will be found in the edition by Mumbauer quoted in note 131.

138 *Die Arbeiterfrage und das Christentum.* pg 20

139 Text by Mumbauer, vol. III, pg 145-166

140 See Vigener, op. cit. pg 557 ff.

141 ibd. pg 561

142 W. Schwer, *Kolping und seine Zeit,* Koeln 1922; Th. Brauer, *Adolf Kolping,* Freiburg 1923; J. Nattermann, *Adolf Kolping als Sozialpaedagoge,* Leipzig 1925; A. Wothe, *Adolf Kolping,* Recklinghausen, 1950; *Adolf Kolping spricht,* herausg. von A. Stiefvater, Heidelberg 1947.

143 Detailed reports on Vogelsangs life and ideas by Wiard Klopp, *Leben und Wirken des Sozialpolitikers Karl von Vogelsang,* Wien 1930; Anton Orel, *Vogelsangs Leben und Lehren,* Wien 1922, and J. Chr. Allmayer-Beck, *Vogelsang,* Wien 1952; The best critical evaluation presents August Knoll, *Karl von Vogelsang als Nachfahre der Romantik,* Dissertation, Wien 1924; and *Karl von Vogelsang und der Staendegedanke,* in: *Die soziale Frage und der Katholizismus,* Paderborn 1931, pg 64 ff.

144 See to this point the detailed bibliographies in the last study by A. Knoll, and the work by J. Chr. Allmayer-Beck, quoted in note 143.

145 Vogelsang, *Zins und Wucher,* Wien 1884. See also Augustin Lehmkuhl, *Zins und Wucher vor dem Richterstuhl der Kirche und Vernunft,* and, *Deutung oder Missdeutung der kirchlichen Vorschriften ueber Zins und Wucher;* in: *Stimmen aus Maria Laach,* vols. XVI and XXVIII, 1879 and 1885.

146 E. K. Winter, *Die Sozialmetaphysik der Scholastik,* Wien 1929, pg 57-58

147 *Soziale Arbeit im neuen Deutschland. Festschrift fuer Franz Hitze zum 70. Geburtstag.* M-Gladbach 1921; A. Pieper, *Franz Hitze zum Gedaechtnis,* M-Gladbach 1921; J. Kraneburg, *Hitze's sozialpolitische Forderungen und ihre Verwirklichung in der Gesetzgebung,* M-Gladbach 1922; Franz Mueller, *Franz Hitze und sein Werk,* Hamburg 1928; Karl Gosebruch, *Franz Hitze und die Gemeinschaftsidee,* Muenchen 1927; A. Pieper, *Hitze,* Staatslexikon, 5th edit., vol. II, 1215 ff, 1927.

148 Hitze, *Kapital und Arbeit und die Reorganisation der Gesellschaft,* 1880, pg 50

149 ibd. pg 50

150 See the various bibliographies in the works quoted in note 147.

151 O. Mueller, *Die christliche Gewerkschaftsbewegung Deutschlands,* 1905; H. Brauns, *Die Christlichen Gewerkschaften,* 1907; Th. Brauer: *Die moderne Gewerkschaftsbewegung,* 1922; *25 Jahre Christliche Gewerkschaftsbewegung, Festschrift 1899-1924,* Berlin 1924; R. Gres, *Die Entwicklung der christlichen Gewerkschaftsidee,* 1931; R. E. Bowen, *German Theories of the Corporative State,* New York 1947; George Marshall Dill, *The Christian Trade Unions and Catholic Corporatism in Germany,* Dissertation, Harvard University, April 1949; this study by Dill is very important for English readers.

152 *Der Volksverein.* Programmschrift. M-Gladbach 1890; August Pieper, *Sinn und Aufgabe des Volksvereins,* M-Gladbach 1926; Joseph Lins, *Volksverein,* Cath-

olic Encyclopedia, Vol. XV, 502 ff. See also the very important essay by Philipp Funk, *Der Gang des geistigen Lebens im katholischen Deutschland unserer Generation.* In: *Wiederbegegnung von Kirche und Kultur.* Festgabe fuer Karl Muth. Muenchen 1927, pg 77-126.

153 Theodor Brauer, *Der deutsche Katholizismus und die soziale Entwicklung des kapitalistischen Zeitalters.* Archiv fuer Rechts-und *Wirtschaftsphilosophie,* vol. XXIV, Heft ½, pg 240 ff, Berlin 1930.

154 ibd.; the same study was also published under the title, *The Catholic Social Movement in Germany.* Catholic Social Yearbook, Oxford 1932.

155 Heinrich Brauns, *Das Zentrum.* In, *Volk und Reich der Deutschen;* edit. by B. Harms, vol. II, pg 62-88, Berlin 1929. Compare also, *Deutsche Sozialpolitik 1918-1928,* edit. by the Reichsarbeitsministerium, Berlin 1929; and, *Politisches Jahrbuch der Zentrumspartei,* Jhrg. 1925, 1926, 1927-28, edit. by Georg Schreiber, M-Gladbach, 1925-1928.

156 See appendix, *Documents;* H. Brauns, *Political Catholicism in Action.*

157 Brauns, *Das Zentrum,* pg 84; Brauns, *Wirtschaftskrise und Sozialpolitik,* 1924; Brauns, *Die Sozialpolitik vor und nach dem Kriege,* 1927; Heinrich Bruening, *Finanz und Steuerpolitik,* 1927; Adam Stegerwald, *Der deutsche Arbeiter und der deutsche Staat,* 1927; Otto Gehrig, *Zentrum und Sozialpolitik,* 1929.

158 Goetz Briefs, *Wirtschaft, Staat und Gesellschaft im System des Kapitalismus.* In, *Die Soziale Frage und der Katholizismus.* Festschrift zum vierzigjaehrigen Jubilaeum der Enzyklika Rerum Novarum, 1931, pg 256-261.

CHAPTER V

Political Catholicism

159 See chapter I, note 2.

160 Leo XIII, *Sapientiae Christianae,* January 10, 1890.

161 The principal sources to this point are contained in, *Der Politische Catholizismus 1815-1914,* 2 vols., edit. by L. Bergstraesser, Muenchen 1922-1923; *Der Politische Katholizismus von den Anfaengen bis 1918,* edit, by W. Mommsen and G. Franz, Leipzig 1931; V. Kramer, *Buecherkunde zur Geschichte der katholischen Bewegung in Deutschland im 19. Jahrhundert,* M-Gladbach 1914; Karl Bachem, *Vorgeschichte, Geschichte und Politik der Deutschen Zentrumspartei,* vols. I-VIII, Koeln 1927-1932; Georg Schreiber, *Politisches Jahrbuch der Zentrumspartei,* M-Gladbach 1925-1928; *Nationale Arbeit. Das Zentrum und sein Wirken in der deutschen Republik,* edit. by K. A. Schulte, Berlin 1929; M. Meinertz-H. Sacher, *Deutschland und der Katholizismus,* 2 vols., Freiburg 1918; *Katholische Staatslehre und Volksdeutsche Politik,* edit. by G. Ebers, Freiburg 1929; E. Ritter, *Der Weg des Politischen Katholizismus,* Breslau 1934; Justinus, *Katholizismus und Politik. Der politische Katholizismus in katholischer Sicht.* Luzern 1946.

162 See chapter II, 2, *The Heritage of the Ecclesiastical Territories*

164 See chapter III, 3, *Romantic Catholicism*

165 Karl v. Rotteck, *Gesammelte und nachgelassne Schriften mit Biographie und Briefen,* edit. by H. Rotteck, Freiburg 1841-1843; Herman Gerlach; *Die politische Taetigkeit Rottecks,* Jena 1919; Hans Zehnter, *Das Staatslexikon von Rotteck und Welter,* Jena 1929

166 Rotteck, *Die Koelnische Sache, behandelt vom Standpunkt des allgemeinen Rechtes,* 1838. For Rottecks Relations with the Catholicism of the Enlightenment and the Catholic publishers Bartholomae and Benjamin Herder, see, A. M. Weiss-E. Krebs, *Im Dienst am Buch,* Freiburg 1951, and, *Der Katholizismus*

in Deutschland und der Herder Verlag 1801-1951, Freiburg 1952; also H. Schroers, *Die Koelner Wirren*, 1927.

[167] L. Bergstraesser, *Studien zur Vorgeschichte der Zentrumspartei*, 1910; *Der Goerreskreis im Bayrischen Landtag*, Oberbayrisches Archiv, vol. 56; Franz Schnabel, *Der Zusammenschluss des politischen Katholizismus in Deutschland im Jahre 1848*, 1910; Clemens, Bauer, *Der politische Katholizismus in Wuerttemberg bis 1848*, 1929.

[168] Karl E. Jarcke, *Vermischte Schriften*, 4 vols., 1839-1854; Georg Phillips, *Vermischte Schriften*, 3 vols., 1856-1860; Frieda Peters, *K. E. Jarckes Staatsanschauungen in ihren geistigen Quellen*, 1926; A. Dock, *Revolution und Restauration ueber die Souveraenitaet*, 1900; F. Meinecke, *Weltbuergertum und Nationalstaat*, 1928; A. v. Martin, *Der preussische Altkonservativismus und der politische Katholizismus in ihren gegenseitigen Beziehungen*, Halle 1929; Siegmund Neumann, *Die Stufen des preussischen Konservatismus*, Berlin 1930; F. Schnabel, *Deutsche Geschichte im neunzehnten Jahrhundert*, Band 4, 1936.

[169] See chapter II, 3; III, 3; IV, 1.

[170] T. Palatinus, *Entstehung der Generalversammlungen der Katholiken Deutschlands und die erste grundlegende zu Mainz 1848*, Wuerzburg 1893; J. May, *Geschichte der Generalversammlungen der Katholiken Deutschlands*, Freiburg 1904; J. B. Kissling, *Geschichte der deutschen Katholikentage*, 2 vols., Freiburg 1920-1923

[171] See chapter II, 3

[172] Really only after 1933, under pressure from the growing National Socialist persecution of the Church, did the Fulda Bishops' Conference of Prussian and upper-Rhenish bishops and the Munich-Freising Bishop's Conference meet for common deliberations.

[174] Vigener, *Ketteler;* the same, *Drei Gestalten aus dem modernen deutschen Katholizismus Moehler, Diepenbrock, Doellinger*, Muenchen 1926; O. Pfuelf, *Bischof von Ketteler;* the same; *Kardinal von Geissel*, 2 vols. Freiburg 1895-1896; L. v. Pastor, *August Reichensperger*, 2 vols. Freiburg 1899; O. Pfuelf, *Mallinckrodt*, Freiburg 1901; J. Friedrich, *Ignaz von Doellinger*, 3 vols. Muenchen 1899-1901; F. Meinecke, *Radowitz und die deutsche Revolution*, Berlin 1913; E. Ritter, *Radowitz*, Koeln 1948.

[175] Karl Bachem, *Vorgeschichte, Geschichte und Politik der Zentrumspartei*, Vols. I-III, 1927-1928; H. Donner, *Die katholische Fraktion in Preussen 1852-1858;* 1909; H. Wendorf, *Die Fraktion des Zentrums im Preussischen Abgeordnetenhaus 1859-1867*, 1916.

[176] J. B. Kissling, *Geschichte des Kulturkampfes im Deutschen Reich*, 3 vols. Freiburg 1911-1916; Georges Goyau, *Bismarck et l'Eglise. Le Culturkampf*, 4 vols. Paris 1911-1913; further sources in, V. Cramer, *Buecherkunde zur Geschichte der katholischen Bewegung in Deutschland im 19. Jahrhundert;* A. Boethlingk, *Bismarck und das paepstliche Rom*, Berlin 1911; H. Bornkamm, *Die Staatsidee im Kulturkampf*, Muenchen 1950; A. Schnuetgen, *Kulturkampf*, Staatslexikon III, 1929, pg 673 ff; Martin Spahn, *Kulturkampf*, Catholic Encyclopedia, vol. VIII, pg 703 ff., New York 1910.

[177] Also the brief study by Ketteler, *Stellung und Pflicht der Katholiken im Kampf der Gegenwart*, Freiburg 1868

[178] Klemens Loeffler, *Geschichte der katholischen Presse Deutschlands*, M-Gladbach 1924.

[179] ibd.

[180] Hermann Oncken, *Bennigsen und die Epochen des parlamentarischen Liberalismus in Deutschland und Preussen*, Historische Zeitschrift, Muenchen

1910, Band 104, pg 53

[181] ibd. pg 56

[182] Compare to this point principally the vivacious criticism which A. J. P. Taylor devotes to the development of German Liberalism, in *The Course of German History*, London-New York 1946, pg 65 ff.

[183] The best, but onesided presentation is given by Hermann Oncken in his great biography of the founder and leader of National Liberalism, *Rudolf von Bennigsen*, 2 vols., Stuttgart 1910. How little justification there was, however, even for Oncken to attempt an objective description of the development of German Liberalism, especially of the relationship between National Liberalism and Catholicism, can be sufficiently illustrated by one passage from his study, *Politik, Geschichtsschreibung und oeffentliche Meinung*, 1904,: "For all those historians who regard as binding the belief in the God-given Papal Church as custodian of the pure and eternally immutable dogma—and we are thinking of the outward form not only of religious, but also of political obligation—a free movement of historical thinking is impossible right from the beginning." (*Historisch-Politische Aufsaetze und Reden*, Muenchen 1914, vol. I, pg 221-222).

For a general orientation the following works are of special interest: Friedrich Naumann's disciple, Oskar Klein-Hattingen's, *Geschichte des deutschen Liberalismus*, 2 vols., Berlin 1911-1912; O. Stillich, *Der Liberalismus*, Berlin 1911; P. Wentzke-J. Heyderhoff, *Deutscher Liberalismus im Zeitalter Bismarcks*, 2 vols., 1925-1927; O. Westphal; *Welt-und Staatsauffassung des deutschen Liberalismus*, Muenchen 1919. Indispensable for an orientation in the history of ideologies and political ideas are two more recent presentations by Walter Nigg, *Geschichte des religioesen Liberalismus*, Zuerich 1937, and Frederico Frederici, *Der deutsche Liberalismus*, Zuerich 1946.

[184] Compare here the literature quoted in note 183. Furthermore, Otto Volz, *Christentum und Positivismus. Die Grundlagen der Rechts—und Staatsauffassung Friedrich Julius Stahl's*, Tuebingen 1951; Franz Rosenzweig, *Hegel und der Staat*, Muenchen 1920; J. Loewenstein, *Hegels Staatsidee*, Berlin 1927; A. Huebscher, *Die Nachfolge Hegels*, Muenchen 1948; Ernst Troeltsch, *The Social Teachings of the Christian Churches*, New York 1948.

[185] See my essay on, *German Philosophy*, Encyclopedia Americana, 1952-edition vol. 12, pg. 603 ff; Fr. Wilhelm Foerster, *Europa und die deutsche Frage*, Luzern 1936; Edgar Alexander, *Der Mythus Hitler*, Zuerich 1937; W. Gurian, *Der Kampf um die Kirche im Dritten Reich*, Luzern 1936; Peter Viereck, *Metapolitics*, New York 1941.

[186] *Nationalzeitung*, Berlin, February 25, 1872

[187] *Preussische Jahrbuecher*, 1874, I, 523 ff.

[188] *Gegenwart*, Berlin, June 21, 1873

[189] Speech in the Prussian Diet, January 7, 1873

[190] Johannes Schauff, *Die Katholiken und die Zentrumspartei. Eine politisch-statistische Untersuchung der Reichstagswahlen seit 1871*, Koeln, 1928

[191] Hermann Sacher, *Bismarck*, Staatslexikon, vol. I, 937, (1926)

[192] E. Friedberg, *Die Graenzen zwischen Staat und Kirche und die Garantien gegen deren Verletzung*, 2 vols. Berlin 1872; Adalbert Falk, *Reden 1872-1879*, Berlin 1880; E. v. Ketteler, *Die Anschauungen des Kultusministers Dr. Falk ueber die katholische Kirche*, Mainz 1874; E. Foerster, *Adalbert Falk. Sein Leben und Wirken als preussischer Kultusminister*, 1927; David Friedrich Strauss, *Der alte und der neue Glaube*, Leipzig 1872; Eduard von Hartmann, *Die Selbstzersetzung des Christentums*, Berlin 1874; *Die preussisch-deutsch Kirchengesetzebung seit 1871 bis 1877. Vollstaendige Sammlung der auf den Kirchenkonflict in*

Preussen und Deutschland bezueglichen Staatsgesetze und ministeriellen Erlasse, Muenster, 1877.

193 *Preussische Jahrbuecher,* 1874, I, 523 ff; see also chapter II, notes 32 to 34

194 Speech on the Catholic Convention in Cologne 1894; see also P. Reichensperger, *Kulturkampf oder Friede in Staat und Kirche,* 1876; and E. Huesgen, *Windthorst,* 1911.

195 See chapter VI, i

196 See note 190

197 Leo XIII, Encyclical *Diuturnum Illud,* June 29, 1881

198 See the special literature refering to the social and political world of thought of the *Center Party:* Georg Schreiber, *Grundfragen der Zentrumspolitik,* 1925; A. Reeder, *Der Weg des Zentrums,* 1925; A. Stegerwald, *Arbeiterschaft, Volk und Staat,* 1925; K. Grobbel-H. Broermann, *Unterm Zentrumsbanner. Dokumente zur Zeitgeschichte,* 1927; J. Joos, *Die politische Ideenwelt des Zentrums,* 1928; K. A. Schulte, *Nationale Arbeit. Das Zentrum und sein Wirken,* 1929; Fr. Dessauer, *Das Zentrum,* 1931.

199 Karl Bachem, *Vorgeschichte, Geschichte und Politik der deutschen Zentrumspartei,* 1927-1931; Georg Schreiber, *Politisches Jahrbuch der Zentrumspartei,* 1925-1928; G. Schreiber, *Zentrum und Reichspolitik,* 1930.

200 Karl Hoeber, *Der Streit um den Zentrumscharakter,* Koeln 1912; Hermann Roeren, *Zentrum und Koelner Richtung,* Trier 1913; Ernst Thrasolt, *Carl Sonnenschein,* Muenchen 1930; R. v. Nostitz-Rieneck, *Integralismus,* Staatslexikon, vol. II, 1496 ff. (1927)

201 Mathias Erzberger, *Der Voelkerbund. Der Weg zum Weltfrieden,* 1919; *Erlebnisse im Weltkrieg,* 1920. Also Georg v. Hertling, *Erinnerungen aus meinem Leben,* 1919-1921; *Ein Jahr in der Reichskanzlei,* 1929

202 Detailed bibliographies relating to the history and actions of the *Democratic Party* will be found in, Georg Schreiber, *Jahrbuch der Zentrumspartei,* 1926, 1927-28; Anton Erkelenz, *Zehn Jahre deutsche Republik,* Berlin 1928; F. S. Neumann, *Die deutschen Parteien,* Berlin 1932. General material to this subject, Fr. Naumann, *Die politischen Parteien, 1913;* L. Bergstraesser, *Geschichte der politischen Parteien in Deutschland, 1928;* Theodor Heuss, *Staat und Volk,* 1926; same, *Die deutsche Demokratische Partei,* in, *Volk und Reich der Deutschen,* edit. by B. Harms, Berlin 1928, vol. II pg. 104-122; Gustav Stolper, *Die wirtschaftlich-soziale Weltanschauung der Demokratie,* Mannheim 1929.

203 Detailed bibliographies relating to the literature of the *Social Democratic Party* and movement are to be found in the studies by Bergstraesser and S. Neumann quoted in note 202. For the relationship of the SPD with the Center Party, see also Alwin Saenger, *Sozialismus,* in, *Volk und Reich der Deutschen,* vol. II, pg 122-142

204 Heinrich Brauns, *Das Zentrum,* in, Volk und Reich der Deutschen, vol. II, pg 62-68

205 From the time of Bruening's chancellorship there exist three condensed biographical presentations from the circle of his journalistic friends: Ruediger Beer *Heinrich Bruening,* Berlin 1931; Eduard Stadtler, *Schafft es Bruening,* Berlin 1931; Alphons Nobel, *Bruening,* Leipzig 1932. Neither Bruening nor Kaas have so far thought it appropriate to render to the public an account of their political actions.

206 Since, following the example set by Bruening and Kaas, also all the other responsible Center politicians have until today not seen fit to account to the public for the tragic Center policies of the years 1928 to 1933, it is most difficult for an outsider to find an objective point of view. Ohne of the most thoroughly

oriented objective sources from the time of Bruening's Chancellorship is offered by Gustav Stolper's weekly magazine, *Der Deutsche Volkswirt*, Berlin 1926-1933, especially in Stolper's weekly commentaries and, most important, in his essay, *Staatskrise*, 6th year, Nr. 36, June 3, 1932.

207 Georg Schreiber lists the, *Literatur ueber die Bayrische Volkspartei*, in a detailed report in the, *Politisches Jahrbuch der Zentrumspartei*, 1926. Also A. Scharnagl, *Bayrische Volkspartei*, and Hugo Lerchenfeld, *Bayern und das Reich;* both in the *Staatslexikon*, vol. I, 667 ff, (1926). See also A. Ringelmann, *Die Bayrische Volkspartei*, 1920; R. Pfeiffer, *Gedankenwelt und Taetigkeit der Bayrischen Volkspartei*, 1922; Konrad Beyerle, *Foederalistische Reichspolitik*, 1924; and the monthly magazine, *Gelbe Hefte*, edit. by Max Buchner, Muenchen 1925-1933.

208 Friedrich Funder, *Konservative Bewegung in Oesterreich*, Staatslexicon, vol. III, 551 ff, (1929), there also the older literature. Albert Fuchs, *Geistige Stroemungen in Oesterreich 1867-1918*, Wien 1949; furthermore the various essays in, *Katholischer Glaube und Deutsches Volkstum, in Oesterreich*, edit. by Anton Boehm a. others, Salzburg 1933, and, *Oesterreich, Erbe und Sendung im deutschen Raum*, edit. by J. Nadler and H. v. Srbik, Salzburg 1936. See also the excellent bibliography in R. Till, *Pax Austriaca, Sinn und Geschichte der oestrreichischen Staatsidee*, Wien 1948.

209 J. Hollnsteiner, *Franz Schindler (1847-1922)*, in, Staatslexikon, vol. IV, 1250 ff. (1931); here also a bibliography of Schindler's writings. Furthermore, J. Scheicher, *Sebastian Brunner, Wien 1890; R. Kuppe, Karl Lueger und seine Zeit*, 1933, and R. v. Kralik, *Karl Lueger und der christliche Sozialismus*, 1923

210 See chapter VI, *Neo-Romantism and Universalism*

211 Ignaz Seipel (1876-1932), *Nation und Staat*, 1916; *Gedanken zur oesterreichischen Verfassungsreform*, 1918; *Reden in Oesterreich und anderwaerts*, 1926 *Der Kampf um die oesterreichische Verfassung*, 1930. See also, B. Birk, *Dr. Ignaz Seipel*, 1932; R. Bluemel, *Praelat Dr. Ignaz Seipel*, 1933, F. Riedl, *Kanzler Seipel* 1935; A. Knoll, *Von Seipel zu Dollfuss*, 1934; D. v. Hildebrand, *Dollfuss*, 1935 and, *Dollfuss an Oesterreich*, edit. by E. Weber, 1935.

212 Josef Dobretsberger, *Katholische Sozialpolitik am Scheidewege*. Graz 1947, p. 78. This judgment is supplemented by an other one, coming from the well known Italian priest and social reformer, the venerable Don Luigi Sturzo: "Seipel during the second period of his public life, turned to the side of reaction and began to trust in repression and methods of force. Dollfuss, his pupil, went further; he bound himself to Starhemberg who had already organized an armed militia on the Fascist pattern. When Dollfuss became chancellor he came to an understanding with Mussolini; he introduced an authoritarian system when the opportunity was offered him by the Socialist attempt at revolt. The repression of February 1934 was a very sad page in the annals of Austria. Many of the Social Christians were alarmed at the turn their policy had taken; others, such as Dr. Funder, Director of the Reichspost, and Dr. Schmitz, the new Burgermaster of Vienna, approved it". *Nationalism and Internationalism*, New York 1946, pg. 117 ff.

213 Guido Zernatto, Die Wahrheit ueber Oesterreich, New York 1938, pg. 117. See also *Dollfuss an Oesterreich, 1935; Schuschnigg, Oesterreichs Erneuerung*, 1935-1937; R. Schmitz, *Das neue Wien und seine Buergerschaft*, 1936, E. K. Winter, *Monarchie und Arbeiterschaft*, 1936.

214 Kurt Schuschnigg, *Dreimal Oesterreich*, Wien 1937, pg 151-152.

215 ibd. pg. 88-89.

216 Zernatto, op. cit. pg. 82. Similarly, Eugen Lanske in his propaganda book

for the "universal", i.e. totalitarian state, published in behalf of Dollfuss' "Federal Commissariat for Propaganda" in June 1934: "The corporate state in Austria organizes the people from below to the top and orders in an authoritarian (!) fashion the activities of the small community, that is, the family, the borough and the corporations. Here there are some analogies with Italy (corporative system) and with Germany (Reich estates) - - -. Within the Patriotic Front the Fuehrer-principle is completely realized. We can therefore speak for Austria of a limited totality'. Politische *Gesellschaftslehre* Wien 1934, pg. 73-74.

In this conceptual nonsense of a 'limited totality' we notice once more the disastrous influence of Spann's word sophistry and debasement of the language, for a 'totality' naturally demands a whole entity and does not admit of a limitation!

217 Dobretsberger, op. cit., pg. 78, 81. The bad conscience of the Dollfuss regime in relation to Austrian labor was expressed unmistakably in a propaganda book which Alfred Maleta published in June 1936 under the title, *The Socialist in Dollfuss-Austria,* This book, dedicated 'in loyalty to the Fuehrer of the country's Patriotic Front', admits more than two years after the smashing of the Austrian trade Unions and other labor organizations: "Among the most important domestic problems which press for a solution is the one, how to integrate definitively the labor force which formerly was organized mostly in the Socialdemocratic framework, into the new state", *Der Sozialist in Dollfuss-Oesterreich, Linz 1936,* pg. 5 ff. See to this point also the very indicative collection of essays by Ernst Karl Winter, *Monarchie und Arbeiterschaft,* Wien 1936. Furthermore, Pertinax, *Oesterreich 1934,* Zuerich 1935, and Robert Ingrim, *Der Griff nach Oesterreich,* Zuerich 1938.

218 Zernatto, op. cit. pg. 79 ff, 98 ff.

219 Schuschnigg, op. cit. pg 292.

220 Schuschnigg's letter addressed to the National Socialist negotiator Seiss-Inquart, March 10, 1938. Original in Zernatto, pg. 290-293.

221 Schuschnigg, op. cit. pg. 291.

222 *Katholische Sozialpolitik am Scheidewege,* pg. 82. In addition to this book by Dobretsberger, special attention should be paid to the extensive presentation of the general development of Socialism and Political Catholicism in Austria by Charles A. Gulick, *Austria. From Habsburg to Hitler,* 2 vols., Univ. of California Press, Berkeley 1948. This monumental sources-study by an American sociologist is indispensable for a thorough knowledge and fair judgment of the antagonistic developments of Austro-Marxism and Austro-Fascism during the period from 1918 to 1938. The special importance of this work must be acknowledged also from a Catholic point of view, this despite the fact that its author did not take into consideration adequately the very special ideo-political conditioning of Austrian Conservativism and Clericalism by the metapolitical confusion of Social and Political Romanticism.

CHAPTER VI

The State Doctrine and the Social Theories

223 Gustav Gundlach, *Zur Soziologie der katholischen Ideenwelt und des Jesuitenordens,* Freiburg 1927, pg. 73-74; J. Broderick, *The Economic Morals of the Jesuits,* Oxford 1934. For more incisive knowledge concerning the special significance and "modernity" of the Social Metaphysics of the Jesuits we make special reference to the following literature:

Francisco Suarez, *Selections from three works. De Legibus, ac Deo legislatore: Defensio Fidei Catholicae; Fide, Spe et Caritate. In the original texts and an English version* edited by James Brown Scott, *The Classics of International Law.* Edit. by the Carnegie Endowment for International Peace, 2 vols., Oxford 1944. *Political Theories of Robert Bellarmin, Francisco Suarez, Luis Molina, and others.* A selection of texts, translated and edited by George Albert Moore, The Country Dollar Press, Chevy Chase, Maryland, USA, 1949-1950.

John F. McCormick, *The significance of Suarez for a Revival of Scholasticism.* in, *Aspects of the New Scholastic Philosophy,* edit. by Ch. A. Hart, New York 1932. *Suarez, Modernité traditionelle de sa philosophie;* Archives de Philosophie, vol. XVIII, Paris 1949. Karl Werner, *Franz Suarez und die Scholastik der letzten drei Jahrhunderte,* Regensburg 1861. Heinrich Rommen, *Die Staatslehre des Franz Suarez,* M-Gladbach 1927. Franz X. Arnold, *Die Staatslehre des Kardinals Bellarmin,* Muenchen 1934. J. Broderick, *Life and Work of Cardinal Bellarmin,* London 1928. James Brown Scott, *Spanish Origin of International Law,* Oxford 1933. Alois Dempf, *Christliche Staatsphilosophie in Spanien,* Salzburg 1937.

The English reader may find the most timely and beneficial introduction into the Natural Law Theories of the Spanish Scholastics—from Vittoria to Bellarmine—and its special significance for the *democratic* conception of modern Catholic Political and Social Philosophy, in the very outstanding lecture by Heinrich Rommen, *The Natural Law in the Renaissance Period;* in: *University of Notre Dame Natural Law Institute Proceedings* (1948), vol. II, pg. 89 ff; Univ. of Notre Dame Press, Notre Dame, Indiana 1949.

Furthermore, the following Encyclopedia articles with bibliographies *Catholic Encyclopedia, Suarez-Suarism,* vol. XIV, 314 ff; *Molina-Molinism,* vol. X, 436 ff; *Congruism,* vol. IV, 251 ff. *Dictionnaire de Theologie Catholique, Suarez,* vol. XIV/2,2668-2727; *Molina,* vol. X/2,2094-2178; *Congruisme,* vol. III/1,1130 ff. *Wetzer und Weltes Kirchenlexikon, Suarez,* vol. XI, 923 ff; *MolinaMolinismus,* vol. VIII, 1734 ff. *Staatslexikon, 5th edition, Suarez,* vol. V, 207 ff; *Molina,* vol. III, 1377 ff; *Bellarmin,* vol. I, 769 ff

224 *Woerterbuch der Politik,* edit. by Hermann Sacher and O. v. Nell-Breuning, Heft I-VI, Freiburg 1947-1951.

225 Victor Cathrein, *Ethics, Catholic Encyclopedia,* vol. V, 556-565. See also in the same Encyclopedia the following essays by Cathrein, *Law and Natural Law,* vol. IX, 53 ff; *Property,* vol. XII, 462 ff; *Right,* vol. XIII, 55 ff; Augustin Lehmkuhl deals in the same spirit with the fundamental problem of *Moral Theology,* in vol. XIV, 601 ff. See also V. Cathrein, *Moralphilosophie,* 2 vols. Leipzig 1924, and A. Lehmkuhl, *Theologia Moralis,* 2 vols., 1883-1914.

226 Augustin Lehmkuhl, *Zins und Wucher vor dem Richterstuhl der Kirche und Vernunft, Stimmen aus Maria Laach,* 1879, XVI, 225-470; also *Deutung oder Missdeutung der kirchlichen Vorschriften ueber Zins und Wucher,* ibd. 1885, XXVIII, 1 ff. Furthermore in the collection, *Die soziale Frage, beleuchtet durch die Stimmen aus Maria Laach,* the following studies, *Arbeitsvertrag und Streik,* 1889; *Die soziale Not und der kirchliche Einfluss,* 1892; *Die soziale Frage und die Staatsgewalt,* 1892; *Internationale Regelung der sozialen Frage,* 1939.

227 Gundlach, op. cit. pg. 39

228 ibd. pg. 40

229 ibd. pg. 61

230 ibd. pg. 96

231 Peter Lippert, *Zur Psychologie des Jesuitenordens,* Freiburg 1923

232 Gundlach, op. cit. pg. 96

233 Heinrich Pesch, *Lehrbuch der Nationaloekonomie*, vol. IV, Freiburg 1922, pg. 2

234 Gundlach, op. cit. pg. 61

235 ibd. pg. 64

236 See chapter II, *The Heritage of the Ecclesisatical Territories*

237 See chapter III, *Political Romanticism*, especially the attitudes of Adam Mueller and Haller versus Natural Law.

238 Wilhelm Hohoff in, *Literarischer Handweiser fuer das katholische Deutschland, Jahrgang* 23, 1884, pg. 41 ff

239 Rudolf von Jhering, *Der Zweck im Recht*, 2nd edition, part II, pg. 161, Leipzig 1886. In later editions, after Jherings death, the editors have removed this footnote.

240 Ernst Troeltsch, *Augustin, die christliche Antike und das Mittelalter*, Muenchen 1915, pg. 4

241 Joseph Mausbach, *Gehorsam, staatsbuergerlicher;* Staatslexikon 1911 vol. II, pg. 433-438. It is a testimonial to the ideological breadth of the politico-philosophical thinking in German Catholicism that this essay which was in defense of the right, under peoples sovereignty, to make a revolution could be published without hindrance along with the state-authoritarian, monarchistic articles by Georg von Hertling—and this in the Wilhelminian Empire! This article was reproduced essentially unchanged in the 5th edition of 1927, vol. II, 401-407.

242 *Katholische Rechtsphilosophie. Archiv fuer Rechts- und Wirtschaftsphilosophie,* vol. XVI, Heft I, Berlin 1922.

243 *Philosophia Perennis*. Festgabe fuer Joseph Geyser, Regenburg 1930, vol. II, pg. 1111-1131

244 ibd., pg. 1017-1041

245 Hildebrand, *Zeitliches im Lichte des Ewigen*. Gesammelte Vortraege, Regensburg 1932

246 Petraschek, *Recht*, Staatslexikon, 5th edit., vol. IV, 564-582; *Rechtsphilosophie*, ibd., 620-639

247 Pesch, *Liberalismus, Sozialismus und christliche Gesellschaftsordnung*, I. Teil, *Der christliche Staatsbegriff*, Freiburg 1896-1901

248 Hertling, *Kleine Schriften zur Zeitgeschichte*, 1897; *Naturrecht und Sozialpolitik*, 1893; *Recht, Staat und Gesellschaft*, 1906; Articles in Staatslexikon, 3/4th edition, 1911, *Autoritaet, Staat, Staatsgewalt, Monarchie*. Critical presentations by Wilhelm Polle, *Reichskanzler Graf Georg von Hertling als Sozialphilosoph*, Wuerzburg 1933; and Josef Urbanowski, *Georg von Hertlings Gesellschaftslehre*, Bottrop 1936.

250 Mausbach, op. cit., note 241

251 Max Pribilla, *Deutsche Schicksalsfragen*, 2nd edit., chapter V, *Vom Widerstandsrecht des Volkes*, Frankfurt 1950

249 Tischleder, *Leo XIII*, Staatslexikon, 1929, vol. III, 926-960

252 Hildebrand, op. cit., note 245

253 Frodl, *Gesellschaftslehre*, pg 355-400, Wien 1936

254 See note 241

255 Augustinus, *Epist. 140 3-4*

256 Thomas Aquinas, *Sum. Theol. qu. 97 a 11 ad 2*

257 Pesch, *Liberalismus, Sozialismus und christliche Gesellschaftslehre*, Teil I, pg. 48, Freiburg 1901

258 Theodor Meyer, *Grundsaetze der Sittlichkeit und des Rechtes*, Freiburg 1868, pg. 256. See also the very important essay on, *Naturrecht und Rechts-*

philosophie, Staatslexikon, first edit. 1894, vol. III, 1423-1443. This, even today unsurpassed essay was revised for the 3-4th edition by Victor Cathrein, vol. III, 1911, 1292-1314.

259 Meyer, *Die christlichen Sozialprinzipien und die Arbeiterfrage,* Freiburg 1891, pg. 44

260 ibd. pg. 44

261 Hildebrand, *Metaphysik der Gemeinschaft,* Augsburg 1930, pg. 496

262 Pesch, op. cit., pg. 48

263 Pesch, *Lehrbuch der Nationaloekonomie,* Vol. I, pg. 414, Freiburg 1924

264 ibd. pg. 414, see also, Pesch, *Ethik und Volkswirtschaftslehre,* 1918

265 In, *Deutschland und der Katholizismus,* edit. by M. Meinertz and H. Sacher, 2 vols., Freiburg 1918

266 Goetz Briefs, *Zur Kritik sozialer Grundprinzipien, Archiv fuer Sozialwissenschaft und Soizalpolitik,* vol. 49/50, Tuebingen 1922

267 Gundlach, *Solidarismus, Einzelmensch und Gemeinschaft;* in, *Gregorianum,* vol. XVII, pg. 292 ff, Rome 1936

267a *Die soziale Frage und der Katholizismus.* Festschrift zum vierzigjaehrigen Jubilaeum der Enzyklika *Rerum Novarum,* edit. by J. Strieder, Paderborn 1931

268 Frodl, *Gesellschaftlehre,* pg 225-300, chapter, *Das Geselligsein der Menschennatur;* as Frodl informed me, a considerably expanded edition of this most important work will be published during the coming year; the first edition was largely destroyed by the Nazis.

269 Pesch, *Nationaloekonomie,* Vol. II, 1920, pg VI-VII

270 See appendix, texts, 5, *Christian Solidarism*

271 Pesch, op. cit. vol. IV, pg. 208, *Der Begriff der Sozialisierung;* see also his study, *Staatssozialismus und Privatwirtschaft,* in, *Deutschland und der Katholizismus,* Freiburg 1918, vol. II, pg. 331 ff.

272 The most fundamental achievements of Heinrich Pesch and his School in the field of sociology and economics unfortunately are almost unknown outside Germany. None of the basic works of Pesch has as yet been translated into any foreign language, although at the very least the introductory volume of his great masterwork in Economics, the *"Gundlegung"* (3/4 edit. 1924) absolutely merits a translation into the main European tongues. This lack of knowledge of the sources and the leadings ideas of the doctrines of Heinrich Pesch in Social Philosophy and Economics has had especially ill effects in America.

Typical of the lack of understanding in wide circles of non-Catholic sociology in America is the study by Abram L. Harris, *The Scholastic Revival: The Economics of Heinrich Pesch,* in, *The Journal of Political Economy,* vol. LIV, num. 1, Chicago, February 1946, pg. 38-60. Harris with his ignorance of even the basic principles of the Catholic Social Doctrines, is also a typical victim of the disastrous generalizations and misinterpretations of the whole complex of the sociological problems of Catholicism. He thinks he can deal with the fundamental achievements of Pesch with the following naive remarks: "Pesch's economic views are more confusing than enlightening. His chief concern was social reform designed to change the capitalistic economic structure and policies along lines sanctioned by Catholic canons of social morality and theology. His approach to problems of socio-economic organization is a variety of "institutionalism" whose underlying postulates and preconceptions are derived from a refurbished economic ethics of the high Middle Ages" (pg. 40). "He was mainly concerned with questions of social reform. His thinking on these was controlled by scholastic conceptions of man's place in the social order and in the universe. It is as an exponent of neo-scholastic ideology that Pesch is significant. This ideology has much in common with Marxism, its rival" (pg. 59).

It is to be hoped that at least our present work will contribute to clear up such misunderstandings also in the circles of American Sociology. Moreover, Harris might have found in the works which, evidently, he only quoted by their titles sufficient material for a better knowledge of the ideas and achievements of Heinrich Pesch, namely in Schwer, *Catholic Social Theory,* Nell-Breuning, *The Reorganization of Social Economy,* and, Mueller, *Heinrich Pesch and his Theory of Solidarism.*

Recently appeared an excellent *Symposium on Heinrich Pesch,* in commemoration of the 25th anniversary of his death, in the April-issue of *Social Order* (1951) with contributions by Nell-Breuning, Gundlach, Briefs, Mulcahy and J. Yenni. Just before these notes went into print, R. H. Mulcahy, Univ. of San Francisco, published an excellent presentation of, *The Economics of Heinrich Pesch,* (Henry Holt, New York 1952) with a complete list of the writings by Pesch.

273 Messner, *Hohoff,* Staatslexikon, vol. II, 1927, pg. 1324 ff; see also, Messner, *Hohoffs Marxismus. Eine Studie zur Erkenntnislehre der sozialoekonomischen Theorien,* Dissertation, Muenchen 1924

274 See introduction, note 2

275 See chapter IV, note 153

276 See chapter VI, note 267a

277 Briefs, *The Proletariat,* New York 1937; see also appendix of texts, 2

278 Briefs, *Caritas; Gewerkschaftswesen;* in, *Handwoerterbuch der Staatswissenschaften,* 4th edit., vol. III, pg. 135 ff; vol. IV, pg. 1108 ff

279 Briefs, *Der klassische Liberalismus, Archiv fuer Rechts- und Wirtschaftsphilosophie,* vol. XXIV, Heft 1/2, Berlin 1930

280 Briefs, *Betriebssoziologie; Proletariat; Sozialreform und Sozialgeist;* in, *Handwoerterbuch der Soziologie,* edit. by A. Vierkandt, Stuttgart 1931

281 Brauer, *Solidarismus;* in, *Handwoerterbuch der Staatswissenschaften,* 4th edit., vol. VII(pg. 305 ff

282 Gundlach, *Orden;* in, *Handwoerterbuch der Soziologie,* pg. 399 ff

283 Gundlach, *Religioeser Sozialismus; Sozialismus; Stand; Staendestaat;* in, Staatslexikon, 5th edit., vol. IV, pg. 834 ff, 1688 ff; vol. V, pg. 45 ff, 67 fl

284 See, August M. Knoll, *Der Soziale Gedanke im modernen Katholizismus,* Wien 1932-1933; Franz Arnold, *Wiener Richtungen,* in, Staatslexikon, 5th edit., vol. V, 1932, pg. 1295 ff

285 A detailed list of the writings by Othmar Spann, *Schrifttum von und ueber Othmar Spann,* is given by Hans Riehl in the symposium he edited, *Das philosophische Gesamtwerk von Othmar Spann im Auszug,* Wien 1950. The main works by Spann are, *Haupttheorien der Volkswirtschaftslehre,* English edition, *History of Economic Thought,* New York 1929; *Gesellschaftslehre; Kategorienlehre; Der wahre Staat; Philosophenspiegel; Religionsphilosophie; Der Schoepfungsgang des Geistes.*

286 *Vom Wesen des Volkstums, Was ist Deutsch?,* Berlin 1929, pg. 58-60

287 *Philosophenspiegel,* Leipzig 1933, pg. 228

288 *Religionsphilosophie,* Wien 1947, pg. 371

289 *Kategorienlehre,* Jena 1924, pg. 39

290 *Philosophenspiegel,* pg. 152

291 *Haupttheorien der Volkswirtschaftslehre,* Leipzig, 1933 pg. 174

292 ibd. pg. 25

293 For a sociological understanding of the importance of the personalistic Religion of the Old Testament for the development of the Judeo-Roman-Christian Natural Law concept and the socio-religious foundation of Western Personalism, in contrast to Eastern Collectivism, see my *Rome and Western Christianity*, and, *Byzantium and Eastern Christianity*, in, *Background of the Middle East*, Cornell Univ. Press, Ithaca, N. Y. 1952; also Edgar Alexander, *Christianity and the Middle East*, Ithaca, 1953.

DOCUMENTS

294 Baader, *Saemtliche Werke* VI, pg. 125-144, Leipzig 1850.

295 Briefs, *The Proletariat*. McGraw Hill, New York 1937; pg. 25, 268-269, 282-284.

296 Ketteler, *Die grossen sozialen Fragen der Gegenwart*. Mainz 1848. In, *Kettelers Schriften;* edit. by J. Mumbauer, Muenchen 1924; vol. 2, pg. 210 ff.

297 Cathrein, *Socialism*. New York 1904, pg. 363-367.

298 Pesch, *Lehrbuch der Nationaloekonomie;* vol. IV (1922) pg. 2-11; 298; from, *Neubau der Gesellschaft* (1919) pg. 10 ff vol II (1920) pg. vi-ix; vol IV (1922) pg. 208; last paragraph.

299 Brauns, *Das Zentrum* (The Center Party). In, *Volk und Reich der Deutschen;* edit. by B. Harms, Berlin 1929; vol. II, pg. 68-71, 81-84.

300 Tischleder, *Staatsgewalt und katholisches Gewissen;* Frankfurt 1927. Mausbach, *Staatsbuergerlicher Gehorsam; Staatslexikon,* 4th. edit. 1911, vol. II, pg. 433 ff.

301 Hildebrand, *Metaphysik der Gemeinschaft;* Augsburg 1930; pg. 172, 180.

302 Frodl, *Gesellschaftslehre;* Wien 1936; pg. 211-212, 214-215.

PART V:

SOCIAL and POLITICAL CATHOLICISM
in
POLAND, CZECHOSLOVAKIA
and HUNGARY

by

ADAM ZOLTOWSKI - ZBIGNIEW M. OSSOWSKI

J. PECHACEK - W. JUHASZ

CHAPTER I

CATHOLICISM AND CHRISTIAN DEMOCRACY IN POLISH CATHOLICISM

The outbreak of the French Revolution (1789) marked the beginning of a new period in most countries of Europe, and Poland had reasons of her own for remembering approximately the same date as the opening of a new unhappy chapter in her history. The 3rd of May, 1791, witnessed the triumphant enactment of a new Constitution, an event which crowned long endeavors for political and social reform; in 1795, the three despotic neighbors of Poland, always opposed to this country's regeneration, finally partitioned her territory among them.

The impact of Catholicism on what can be called the Polish *ancien regime* was very pronounced. The period of the Reformation had passed almost without leaving a scar; the Church's position was unchallenged, her influence very far reaching, her wealth imposing. She could be considered as strongly welded with the old order of things, while the new order would be the work of secular forces. And yet the Constitution was by no means anti-religious. It proclaimed tolerance for all creeds, but declared "the Holy Roman Catholic faith with all its rights" as the "prevalent national religion." This was at least partly due to the fact that the clergy had by no means been opposed to the reformist currents. On the contrary if any one man had, before the middle of the century, done much to inaugurate the campaign in favor of educational and political improvement it was Fr. Stanislas Konerski (1700-1773), the provincial of the Order of the Piarists and author of a memorable work entitled *Effective Counsels* (1761-4).

Thus the nation on finding itself deprived of its liberty and torn into three parts, at least was not at the same time alienated from is faith. On the contrary it is safe to state that through the Partitions a new bond was forged between the nation and the Church, and the Poles were taught to cherish Catholicism as the one great tradition and inheritance of the past which political calamities were not able to destroy. Such a way of thinking avowedly had its dangers, but it was a safeguard against secularism gaining complete mastery as it had, since the French Revolution, largely penetrated the atmosphere of Europe. It had its repercussion also in Poland, for in the days of the "Duchy of Warsaw" (1807-15) and of the "Congress Kingdom" (1815-31) religious concerns were not in the forefront and many leading personalities were known to be indifferent or even adverse to religion. Yet we have conclusive evidence that this trend had not been instilled into the depth of the nation's soul.

The works of Adam Mickiewicz, the greatest and most popular poet in Poland (1798-1855), who began to write at this very time, show the dominant position that Catholicism occupied in the mind of this man of genius. His great epic *Pan Tadeusz* begins with an invocation of the Blessed Virgin which is more than a literary ornament as it is immediately followed by an allusion to the poet's miraculous recovery in childhood from a mortal illness. The true hero of the poem is no other than a penitent assassin who now a Franciscan friar, is seeking to expiate his sin. In another masterpiece of Mikiewicz, *Dziady* (Forefather's Eve), two priests are among the important characters. One of them is evidently a Uniate, as he has lost his wife, and receives the hero in his house where he is living with his children. This detail, introduced by the author as something entirely natural, also shows how completely the Church Union was merged in the life of Poland's eastern provinces. The other priest, Fr. Peter, plays a more momentous part in the poem. It is he who through his prayers saves the hero from the sin of blasphemy and of revolt against the decrees of Providence. Mickiewicz inaugurated romanticism in Poland, a literary current which in the whole of Europe marked the end of XVIII century rationalistic "enlightenment" and a general tendency to return to religious belief.

In the period which followed the ill-fated insurrectionary war of 1830-31 that was to become the heroic period of Polish letters and thought, the influence of religion was very powerful. Three attitudes towards belief can be distinguished among the representative personalities of the time. A traditionalist and mainly conservative attitude prevailed in the country, as is natural at a time when a nation feels that its religion is attacked and desires to defend it as one of the cherished treasures handed down to it from the past. And at this time precisely, hostile measures against the Church were taken both in the new Prussian and Russian provinces of Poland. In Prussia the "secularization" of most of the convents was enforced, accompanied by confiscation of their property. In the east, Nicholas I carried out more sweeping measures. In 1839, the Uniate Church was suppressed at one stroke, and in 1841 the Latin Church was deprived of all its still very extensive estates. Not only did the Church thus become the pensioner of the Russian Government, but its traditional and concrete influence on social conditions in the countryside met with a sudden end. Soon a conflict also broke out with the Prussian Government over mixed marriages, which led to the imprisonment of Archbishop Martin Dunin (1839), an event bound to make a deep impression on the country at large.

The activity of one of Poland's most renowned preachers' Fr. Charles Antoniewicz S. J., began about the same time. In 1846 he faced a social problem under specially dramatic circumstances. In February of that year the peasantry of western Galicia, at the instigtion of the Austrian authorities, turned against an incipient Polish insurrectionary movement, represented to them as hostile to their emancipation, and carried out a horrible massacre of the landed gentry in which about 2000 persons perished. Fr. Antoniewicz undertook a truly missionary tour of the most troubled districts and obtained astonishing results. Yet Poland in those days was not free to produce any bold initiative or new idea in its homeland, controlled as it was by despotic and suspicious governments. It is abroad, among the refugee communities that the most important developments took place. Here about 1840, a strong religious revival occurred, and in 1842, a significant step was taken in Rome to provide for the needs of the Polish Church and face the new problems of the nation; a group of former Army officers among which Peter Semenenko (1813-86) Jerome Kajsiewicz (1812-73) and Alexander Jelowicki (1808-77) were the best known, founded a religious order known as the Resurrectionists.

The difficulties with which the Resurrectionists had to cope were a function of the general European situation. Political reaction was in its hey-day at this time and the three monarchies which had partitioned Poland, with rare unanimity, stood guard over the existing order. At the same time, however, those revolutionary trends which had been driven underground since Napoleon's rise to power, had by no means become extinct. As the years elapsed, they bestirred themselves with ever greater energy. The July revolution of 1830, in France, gave them their first encouragement, that of 1848 was their achievement, the Paris Commune of 1870-71 their repercussion. They were political in the first place, pursuing the overthrow of absolutism and the establishment of national independence and unity, as was more specially in the case of the Italian *carbonaria*. Even there, however, the appeal to drastic measures of social upheaval were by no means rejected. In France the movement carried a heavy charge of social theories mostly descended from the doctrines of the communist Babeuf, and aiming at the destruction not only of absolutism but of the existing order of society, a venture considered as the necessary condition for any possible progress. The manifold varieties of revolutionary programs were also united in their hostility to the Church, which in the pontificate of Gregory XVI (1836-46) opposed them with justified determination, but did not proceed to develop any views or decisions of its own on the most urgent problems of the times. Thus the Church in those years could have appeared to many as one of the components of the established order which had thrown in its lot entirely with the forces of the past.

The position of the Poles was especially paradoxical; on the one hand the past stood for everything they had lost and was their chief mainstay; on the other, the existing order was their country's doom, and its defenders their implacable enemies. It was understandable that many patriots believed the cause of revolution and Poland's cause to be one and the same, and a universal upheaval their unique opportunity. This was on the whole the attitude of the left or "democratic" wing of the great body of political refugees from Poland after 1831, with the historian Lelewel, and a talented publicist, Maurycy Mochnacki, at their head. The chief social problem of the time in Poland was the position of the peasants who, with the exception of the now Prussian provinces, were still under an antiquated system of serfdom. The democratic party cherished the most sanguine hopes in connection with its plan of raising the peasant question in the whole country in a revolutionary fashion and at whatever cost.

This attitude of impatient endeavor found its expression also in the religious field. Many men who had endorsed the revolutionary program naturally became alienated from the Church and soon repeated the anti-religious slogans which they had learned in their new environment. But radicals were not always prone to irreligion. Some of them had a deep feeling for the traditions of their country and a correct view of the immense possibilities inherent in belief, and were subject to control by the Church. But for that reason precisely they revolted against "the official Church's" apparent indifference to the crimes perpetrated upon Poland. These ideas and reactions present in many minds were to crystalize through the agency of a personality capable of giving them forceful utterance. Andrew Towianski (1799-1878), a country gentleman from Lithania, who arived in Paris in 1841, soon convinced many Polish refugees there that he was the bearer of a religious message of great importance. He formed a "circle" for the service of the "cause of God" and gained an extraordinary ascendency over those who came under his influence. He is and probably will always remain a mysterious and controversial historical figure. The three bulky volumes filled with his interviews and conversations, mostly with men of some importance, make poor reading although they are alluded to as *Symposia*. The ideas are propounded in a monotonous form and have the tendency to become vague and obscure. And yet the extraordinary attraction exercised by this man over many of his contemporaries including many non-Poles is unquestionable.

The Church authorities naturally were soon keeping a vigilant eye on this movement. Certain theses attributed to Towianski were condemned, and the Resurrectionists opposed it whereever it cropped up. Yet Towianski personally does not seem to have incurred ecclesiastical rigors. In spite of the deep impression produced by him on many, his influence would have remained necessarily limited had it not been for the fact that Mickiewicz, by this time at the height of celebrity, was among the first victims of the "master's" extraordinary gift for gaining power over human minds. The poet had entered upon the second phase of his life when his genius appeared to succumb under the burden of public and private misfortune and to burn itself out in a devouring and spasmodic struggle against destiny But Mickiewicz was in a position in which he could effectively propagate ideas, as he was called to a chair of Slavonic literature at the College de France in Paris where the teaching is given not only to students but to the general public as well.

Mickiewicz in his much commented lectures developed his views on "Messianism". This word had first been applied to a philosophy attempting to lay down the laws of future human progress by the Polish philosopher Hoene-Wronski (1778-1853). One definition given by Mickiewicz was the following: "The best developed soul is chosen as an instrument of the Godhead. That is the principal dogma of *Messianism*." The poet thought he had discovered a chosen soul of this sort in no other than Towianski. Yet he also cherished and expounded broader views. All the Slavonic nations appeared to him as gifted with the prerequisites of a higher spirituality and were on the point of developing it for the benefit of the entire human race. Yet the actual birthplace of the new spirit was in one Slavonic nation only,—the one which had suffered the most, which was closest to Europe and which had served Europe most faithfully. And this was no other than the Polish nation. The faith in such a historical mission of the nation is precisely what was to be known as "Polish Messianism" and was the core of the teaching of Mickiewicz at this time. The founding of a religious, political and social unity among all the nations was the goal. Not only tyranny, but materialism and soulless routine in all its many forms, were the chief obstacles to its attainment. The poet at times bitterly denounced the "official Church" for neglecting the great traditions of Christianity and failing to impart to the European body those heroic and inspired impulses of which it stood in such dire need.

The attitude of Mickiewicz and his occasional outbursts were deprecated and criticized by many, yet he was never, personally the object of any ecclesiastical censures. His lectures with those of two other professors, Quinet and Michelet, were suspended by the French Government on purely secular grounds. The restraint observed by the Church authorities proved beneficial. Only three years later when Pius IX showed understanding and good-will towards the Italian national aspirations, conceded a certain liberty of the press, convened a consultive assembly in the Papal States and appointed a civil government, he was acclaimed with enthusiasm by the Poles who saw in these decisions the expression of the longed—for unity of political and religious aspirations. In the spring of 1848 Mickiewicz who was in Rome, made his submission to the Church and received absolution.

This act of humility did not bring peace to the poet's vehement and tormented spirit. Having failed to carry the Pope with him on a crusade of the free peoples against tyranny, he led a small body of men known as the "Polish Legion" from Rome to Milan where it was absorbed in the Piedmontese armies. Though the direct movement inspired by "Polish Messianism" ended in frustration, it had stirred up other intellectual forces, and powerful minds were already seeking for more correct solutions of the problems brought up in the "messianistic circles".

At the present time when throughout a great part of the globe Karl Marx is quoted as a paramount authority, it seems doubly desirable to remember what some contemporaries of his, with no meaner talent and the very highest philosophical culture, thought of the future of the human race. In the same year 1848 in which Marx issued the *Communist Manifesto*, August Cieszkowski (1814-94) anonymously published a volume entitled *Our Father*, which contained his version of the philosophy of history. The author's approach to the great questions of the time was neither traditionalistic nor revolutionary. He was vividly aware that the world was nearing a great crisis, that an entire epoch of human history had come to a close and a new age was beginning, that the inevitable transition to a new order of things could bring into the world felicity or untold woe, that in order to accomplish it safely humanity must abide by the teaching of Christ, and make His Gospel its guide. Endeavors and undertakings in the social and political sphere, if divorced from religion, would always end in disappointment. For holy ends, holy means must be devised, as unholy means necessarily lead to catastrophe. As for revolution, it was sterile and never to be conceived as essential to the attainment of social and political ends. The paramount role and dignity of freedom, were among Cieszkowski's conceptions on which he most eloquently commented. He argued that religious standards applied to the affairs of the world were not only desirable but alone adequate; that the social question was at bottom a religious one and the entire history of mankind the unfolding of a religious theme, the relation between humanity and God.

After the middle of the century, the atmosphere of Europe began to change rapidly. The great expectations of 1848 faded, postivism raised its head, utilitarianism set the tone, and in Poland the unfortunate insurrection of 1863 sounded the knell of romantcisim, the protagonists of which had by this time passed away. But it was of great significance for the future that in Poland, faith had left its lasting imprint on the highest sphere of artistic and intellectual achievement. Although events once more forced Catholic thought back to a mainly traditionalist and defensive position yet its continuity was never broken. It was partly secured by individuals such as Stanislas Kozmian (1811-85) who was Krasinski's schoolfellow and his intimate friend, and who after 1831, spend twelve years largely devoted to political activities in England. His brother Fr. Jan Kozmian was founder of the periodical *Przeglad Poznanski* (Poznan Review) and the inspirer of a definitely Catholic group in Prussian Poland headed by General Desire Chlapowski (1788-1879) who introduced new methods in agriculture, originated a popular press and vocational education of the small farmers. In that province which, since 1840 had been under a relatively liberal government, some other ventures of social character brought excellent results. One of them was the Society of Educational Assistance founded by Dr. Karol Marcinkowski (1800-46). The society collected funds and distributed them among needy youths exclusively in the form of repayable scholarships. In a century of stable currency the scheme proved a great success. The clergy were among the chief beneficiaries and in due course among the most active supporters of an institution which in part compensated the church for the loss of her ancient affluence.

Since 1848, after 17 years of complete absence of parliamentary institutions on Polish soil, the Poles under Prussian sovereignty were called upon to elect representatives to the Prussian Diet. Here the clergy immediately occupied a conscpicuous place and helped to develop those political principles which were destined, for more that half a century, to guide Poles in the legislative bodies of the three partitioning Powers. Among the first to be elected was Fr. John Chrysostomus Janiszewski (1818-91), later to be bishop coadjutor of Gniezno. He sat not only in the Prussian Diet, but also in the German National Assembly of 1848-9 at Frankfurt where he voiced the protest of the Poles against the plan of including the Polish provinces of Prussia in a German Empire. He was also a member of the Polish League, convened in 1849 on the initiative of Cieszkowski, as a sort of National Council of Poland, but soon suppressed by the Prussian authorities. Bishop Janiszeski was a brilliant preacher and gained special renown by his funeral orations which often had a political background.

Another priest, Fr. Alexius Prusinowski (1819-72) was also for many years a deputy to the Prussian Diet where in 1852 he, in collaboration with Cieszkowski, raised the demand for the foundation of a University of Poznan and proved that the amount of estates and funds which had served public education before the Partitions and had been confiscated by Prussia, amply justified such a demand. He also devoted much labor to the editorship of several popular periodicals thus contributing to the gradual rise of general culture in the Polish provinces of Prussia.

Even before the insurrection of 1863, another event symbolized the change of the times. Prince Adam Czartoryski died in 1861 at the age of 91, after having been for many years responsible for most Polish endeavors in the international field. Czartoryski who in his youth had known eighteenth century aloofness from religion, passed through many phases. By the time he became the most influential Polish political leader, he had no doubts about the need of religion for the survival of the nation. By this time it had become a subject of constant Polish concern that the Holy See be adequately informed of conditions in Polish lands and duly prepared to counter the diplomatic manoeuvres of the Partitioning Powers, especially of Russia. But Czartoryski pursued much bolder aims. In order to oppose Russian penetration of the Balkans he endeavored to bring about the Union with Rome of the National Churches there, more especially in Bulgaria. As early as 1827 he had written a book entitled *Essai sur la diplomatie* in which he put forward the idea that the world could not exist without peace and that peace could only be based on a league among the nations and the restoration to them of their full rights. Just before he died he wrote an aphorism which expressed his deep and mature views: "Catholicism should not be founded on the love of country, but patriotism on the love of God."

The events, attendant on and following the insurrection of 1863, destroyed every possibility of a detached and peaceful development of Catholic thought as far as the Polish provinces under Russia were concerned. A storm broke out over the Church. The newly appointed archbishop of Warsaw, Mgr. Felinski, was deported, the same fate was reserved to the bishop of Plock, Mgr. Popiel, and the bishop of Sejny, Mgr. Lubienski, who died on the way into exile. The deportations of the bishops of Wilno, of Samogitia and of Luck were soon to follow. The imprisonment of priests, the closing of churches, the dispersion of religious communities were the order of the day. The attribution of the "Catholic College", a government department for Church affairs, were extended to the point of placing all relations of the Church with the Holy See under its direct control. Two dioceses, those of Podlasie and of Luck, were supressed by a unilateral decision of the Russian Government. The most cruel attack of all was directed against Catholicism by the violent abolition of the Uniate Church within the boundaries of the Congress Kingdom where it had still been allowed. The only conclusion that could be drawn from these loathsome events was that in Poland, for better or for worse, the destinies of Church and nation were interlocked. The courageous language held by Pius IX in his famous allocution of April 24, 1864 and in his Encyclical of July 30 of the same year, showed that the Church was still, as of old, a mainstay of freedom.

These developments were far from having spent themselves when a conflict between Church and State broke out in another quarter. The origin of the so-called "Kulturkampf" in Prussia was Bismarck's desire to subdue the Catholic Church to a similar control by the State authorities as that exercised in relation to the Protestant Churches. By a series of laws enacted in May 1873, the education of the clergy, appointments to ecclesiastical positions and benefices, ecclesiastical jurisdiction and certain other items were made dependent on the secular power. When opposition against this interference with the life of the Church proved determined and unanimous, all payments from the Treasury for religious needs were stopped and almost all the religious orders expelled. (1875).

The purpose pursued by Bismarck in relation to the Church

was in fact very similar to the aims of the Russian administration, yet his action was limited by a Constitution while the possibilities of his opponents were correspondingly increased. The Church in the Polish provinces suffered considerable losses, probably most of all through the expulsion of the religious orders. On the other hand the Catholic community was consolidated by the struggle, the position of the clergy raised and many desirable developments prepared for the future. The Archbishop of Gniezno and Poznan, Mgr. Miechislas Ledochowski, who was imprisoned for his unyielding attitude, gained immense popularity and universal veneration which reached its peak when, on March 15, 1875, he received the Cardinal's purple while in jail at Ostrowo. The Polish people resolutely ranged themselves on the side of the Church, the Polish Party in the Prussian Diet stood beside the Catholic Centre in the forefront of the parliamentary battle and a number of ecclesiastical members such as Mgs. Floria Stablewski (1841-1906), later to be Archibshop of Gniezno, Mgr. Louis Jazdzewski (1838-1908) and some others took rank among the political leaders of the nation.

Again, circumstances were not favorable for theoretical investigation, but practical solutions and developments in a Catholic spirit made visible headway. The Catholic press was one of the greatest needs in such a crisis and found a talended promoter in the person of Fr. Kantecki editor of *Kuryer Poznanski* while popular periodicals and publications multipled rapidly. The need for defense of the Church braced men in all fields of social activity and the final capitulation of Bismarck's government (1880-7), even if only gradual and partial, heartened the Poles in their struggle for their nationality.

When political liberty was attained by the Poles in Galicia, in 1867, a group of men headed by Joseph Szujski (1835-83), Count Stanislas Tarnowski (1837-1917), both university professors, and Paul Popiel (1807-91), formed a conservative party with the ideas of countering the irresponsible dealings of politicians who might have plunged the country into new disaster. If this program, after a time, proved wanting in some respects, its authors nevertheless did not use Catholicism as only a pawn in the political game, but truly felt that without religion, the world would relapse into barbarism. As scholars they perceived that historically Catholicism had been one of the elements of Poland's greatness, and they gave expression to that belief in their teachings at the University of Cracow. It was a priest, the Resurrectionist Fr. Valerian Kalinka (1826-77) who traced in an influential book, a picture of Austrian rule in Galicia and thus revealed its many shortcomings. His confrere,

Fr. Stefan Pawlicki (1839-1916), a classical scholar and historian of philosophy, advocated the application of philosophical thought to social problems. The Jesuit, Fr. Jan Badeni (1858-99) developed a special talent for the direct study of social conditions and having become the Provincial of his order, directed its efforts to the social sphere, giving every encouragement to Catholic workers' organizations and a popular press.

At Lwow where another conservative group had its center, Count Albert Dzieduszycki (1848-1909) taught philosophy and aesthetics in the University, but he was equally well known in Vienna as a leader of the Polish party in the *Reichsrat* and a man of fascinating personality. He lectured and wrote on numerous subjects with great versatility, but in his last works he pointed out, with astonishing perspicacity, the perils threatening modern society and recommended "integral Christianity" as the only true remedy.

Rerum Novarum, described by Cieskowski on his deathbed as a document of great significance, thus found Poland deprived of many possibilities by the fact of its dismemberment, but not unprepared for its reception. Esepcially in western Poland where social and economic conditions were the most favorable, the decades following the issue of this famous encyclical witnessed a most active initiative in social organization. Workers' Unions, small-holders associations, popular reading rooms and parish assembly halls sprang up everywhere. A cooperative model organization for savings and credit acquired great importance and a high reputation. Three priests in particular deserved well of this branch of social service, Fathers Augustin Szamerzewski (1832-91), Peter Wawrzyniak (1840-1910) and Stanislas Adamski (b. 1875) now bishop of Katowice. An entirely original undertaking was the founding in 1886, on a social basis, of a banking institution, *Bank Ziemski,* to help peasants acquire land. It proved a complete success. The atmosphere peculiar to western Poland at this time was a result of the unrelenting oppression the Poles were suffering at the hands of the Prussian State. That produced the fundamental solidarity among them which is so precious an asset in social development.

The same conditions did not exist in Galicia which, till approximately the turn of the century, still labored under the consequences of past neglect. Yet the possibilities offered by political freedom were put to good use. The personality of Countess Hedvige Zamoyska (1831-1923) will long be remembered. When expelled from Prussia, she transferred her school of domestic economy to Zakopane in Galicia. Here she continued for years to inculcate into her numerous pupils principles of Catholic piety and the great traditions of Polish public spirit of which she was the living personification. Near her school stood a house of the Third Order of S. Francis founded by Brother Albert, in his former life Adam Chmielowski (1846-1916), a painter of good standing, who devoted his life to the service of the poor and renewed the most severe traditions of the mendicant orders. Mother Marcelline Darowska (1827-1911), the foundress in 1863 of the order of the Immaculate Conception, belonged to the same generation as the preceding two, and her aim was to give the young generation a firm basis of religious education but also to prepare it for its social duties. The four large educational houses which she established in her lifetime, later to be followed by many others, largely contributed to give Galicia that position of preponderance in education which it enjoyed up to 1914. A significant fact in those years was also the creation in 1914, of a chair of Christian Social Sciences in the University of Cracow. It was filled by Fr. Casimir Zimmerman (1874-1925), a priest who had made a name for himself in Poznan.

The developments and reactions in the Polish provinces of Russia were necessarily inhibited by the rigid political system to which they were subjected. The Church was actually placed in such a position that the most it could achieve was to endure. And when the revolutionary movement of 1905-6 set in, the rapidity and violence of events was again unfavorable to mature and fruitful progress. Yet in the Congress Kingdom a campaign against Tzarist Government schools and in favor of free education was brought to a favorable issue. Free schools sprang up everywhere, in which the teaching was in Polish. Religious education gained much by the change. Mother Darowska established a house at Szymanow near Warsaw (1907), another in secret at Slonim, and Fr. Jan Gralewski (1868-1924) founded a well-known boarding school for boys. Such individual achievements were characteristic of these times of transition.

The restoration of the Polish State after the first World War brought back to the entire Polish people opportunities missing for more than a century. This great change was nowhere more distinctly to be felt that in Church affairs. On large territories where the Church for nearly a century had barely been tolerated every initiative could now be realized if only the necessary means could be found. For the intellectual needs of the Church the Catholic University of Lublin was founded and maintained from private funds, while four State universities had theological faculties. In addition there were thirteen Institutes of Religious Culture in various parts of Poland. Monastic life could again flourish freely and some new establishments attained great importance. The Catholic proess attained a circulation greatly in excess of pre-war times. However, the center of Catholic thought was undoubtedly the University of Lublin of which the Dominican Fr. Hyacinthe Woroniecki, was one of the founders. Besides being a philosopher and theologian he studied many contemporary problems such as that of nationalism. Here Fr. Anthony Szymanski lectured and wrote on social problems and Fr. Stefan Wyzynski, at the present time Primate of Poland, devoted much attention to social needs and developments. A pleiad of students not only propounded the theories concerning social questions current among Catholics of other countries and mostly relating to the life of an industrial population, but took up the rural and agricultural aspects of these questions which were of paramount importance for Poland. These were studied with exactness and perspicacity, and some sociological books of a high intellectual level were produced. In Wilno Fr. Alexander Wojcicki became the historian of the working class in Poland, while in Cracow Fr. Jan Piwowarczyk, a publicist of considerable talent, belied the suggestion of Catholic subservience to the propertied classes, at the same time stressing the divergence of Catholicism and socialism. At Poznan there existed a Catholic School of Social Science with a strong substratum of sociology. On the whole these schools of Catholic Social thought were decidedly reformist, distributionist and progressive. Some of their followers advocated social transformation with so much insistence that they were accused of neglecting stability and economic exigencies. In any case this intellectual movement had not said its final word when the catastrophe of the second world war cut it short and withered many promising prospects.

Its endeavors were supported by the highest ecclesiastical authority in the land. Cardinal Hlond formed the Social Council of the Primate of Poland, established to prepare opinions and pronouncements on current social questions. The Cardinal himself had not waited for this important body to be convened before he addressed his people as a teacher. Of his personal letters none was more important than that of 23 April 1932, on *Christian Principles of Political Life.* Having to deal with an government inclined to exaggerate the role and powers of the State, the Primate reminded his flock that the individual and the family had inalienable rights, that the liberty of the Church and its teaching could claim unqualified respect, that the Church never could be used as a means to any ends foreign to her and that Catholics in public life could not under any pretence betray their principles.

These exhortations did not fall on deaf ears. The vigorous religious revival among the youth of Poland was a striking fact and this religious current made its way into political circles as well. There were the Christian Democrats who advocated the direct application of papal doctrines in social life. There were political groups which considered that Christian principles should necessarily figure in a political program. There were individual politicians who stood for the age-old Catholic traditions of the country. Among these Mgr. Joseph Teodorowicz, Armenian Uniate Archbishop of Lwow, was the most conspicuous figure.

There were also political schools whose ideas were unconnected with religious thought. The influential National-Democratic party was a case in point. Founded in the age of positivism it still bore that mark. It was therefore no mean event when Mr. Roman Dmowski the actual leader of the party, in a much-remarked essay, *Church, Nation and State,* declared that in his opinion good patriots owed unreserved allegiance to the Catholic Church. Dmowski was accused of want of sincerity and of making the Church an object of party manoeuvre, but the impression produced, especially on the younger generation, was profound and the consequences far-reaching. The ageing statesman personally showed how much he was in earnest.

At the present time any outline of Polish political thought would be incomplete without mention of a personage who by universal consent is considered as one of the most forceful figures ever produced by the Church in Poland. In one of his Paris lectures Mickiewicz said: "A nation is educated in religion, in politics and in morals by great examples alone". That remark would best seem to explain the ascendancy of the late Cardinal Sapieha over his countrymen. He was venerated and beloved not for what he thought, said or wrote, but for his inexhaustible charity, for his courage that never faltered and for his determined stand for the dignity of man, of his country and of the Church. His life is in itself a page of political thought that will guide and educate many generations.

ADAM ZOLTOWSKI

2. MODERN FEATURES OF POLISH
CHRISTIAN DEMOCRACY

THE SOCIAL PHILOSOPHY OF POLISH
CHRISTIAN DEMOCRACY

I. *Introduction*

The dynamism of Catholic forces which was inherent in all the resistance movements of World War II resulted in the emergence of strong political parties which were formed in Europe on the basis of Christian Democratic principles. These political parties were to become a familiar feature on the continent.

Catholicism, during the interval between the two World Wars, was, in much of Europe, barred from the social field by Socialism. Catholic activity was often confined to those areas left free by the more or less "liberal" capitalistic systems of the various national states. The prevailing social emphasis at that time was on the notions of the individual and of mercy as a means of alleviating misery rather than on a system of justice for correcting and improving social relations.

Pre-war Catholic thought, as it appeared in the Polish perspective, was static. Moreover, the dynamism left in Catholic action seemed handicapped by the atheistic notions arising out of XIXth century Socialism and attributed to the word "social." Consequently, the lower social classes could easily be persuaded that Catholicism was allied to the prevailing social and political systems permeated by liberal-capitalism. As a matter of fact, this very argument, skilfully applied by the Socialists, was instrumental in driving the French working class into atheism. The situation had became so acute that the French Hierarchy declared France a missionary country.

The social dynamism of Catholicism was recovered during the resistance movements. It was obvious to everyone that Nazi aggression had to be resisted on the level of respective nationalities. This national foundation for action, however, was gradually transcended by the idea of federal unity. No Catholic resistance movement refused to include in its program federal concepts of some sort. Thus the universality of economic and social problems coupled with a need for universal solutions was recognized.

*   *   *

In this introduction, an attempt is being made to explain how Polish Christian Democrats regarded the rest of Europe at the time when Russian occupation had already sealed the doors of Poland but when a few windows facing the West still remained slightly open.

The difficult political position of Poles made them, more than any other Europeans, determined to draw practical conclusions from their past experiences. Already in 1939, immediately following the cessation of hostilities in Poland, studies were started in order to work out a proper evaluation of the past. These studies combined with the new experiences of terror and misery suffered during the German occupation resulted in the introduction of new values in our concepts of Christian Democratic principles. And, for these reasons, Poles were not surprised by the Christian Democratic revival. In fact, Poland although forcibly isolated during the war years by the Germans, again affirmed her ties with Western Christian culture by experiencing the same revival of Catholic social and political thought as was occurring throughout free Europe and achieving it all through her own efforts. Moreover, Polish Christian Democrats, new and old members alike, proved themselves to be fully prepared to accept changes. So was the Polish nation. It will be necessary, of course, to comment upon Polish Christian Democratic traditions which preceded these changes. However, it must be stressed that any approach to the roots of Polish Christian Democracy in this article will be made from an ideological point only recently reached.

The new appreciation of the past became a helpful rallying factor. The great Polish Underground, however, was primarily directed towards the future. The past enabled the Christian Democrats to recapture the Vision—the vision, in turn, stimulated a program.

The opportunity for applying this program in democratic and free circumstances has never occurred. But modern Polish Christian Democrats feel confident that they can put their program into effect as soon as such circumstances are offered to the Polish people.

II. *Ideological Vision*

The HUMAN PERSON, which endured terrible pressure from totalitarianism rampant in Poland from 1939 on, became the focal point of modern Polish Christian Social thought. Viewed in all its metaphysical implications, as exposed by St. Thomas Aquinas, man's personality must be considered in terms of its own development and expansion. Progress, therefore, constitutes the main theme: it must be conceived, explained to the less initiated, approached in actual engagement and, last but not least, planned.

A. The Relation: Its Components.

1. The Notion of the Individual.

Personality is essentially individual. No human is entirely devoid of personality and thus personality is common to all.

Personality may be augmented but may also decline. No one is deprived of a chance to augment his personality, just as no one can avoid God's grace. Personality, when augmented, draws man upwards towards God, Man's last end; personality when diminished, degrades men to their animal nature.

Man can certainly refuse to act to increase his personality just as he can refuse to cooperate with God's Grace. But men can also be acted upon, such as in the case of any kind of totalitarian oppression. When this happens, not only the common, but also the individual personalist values are narrowed. People treated like a herd eventually learn to feel like animals themselves. The fact that man can be acted upon, therefore, puts a tremendous, but seldom realized, responsibility on any kind of government.

Personality is closely connected with LIBERTY: personal values must be achieved in free and deliberate action. REASON and WILL become thus the chief instruments in making man free and increasing his personality.

The individual human person accomplishes its internal liberty as far as reason is able to discover the right balance between the pressure of the natural exigencies of the body and the limitations which must be imposed on the instincts and passions by its will. In religious terms, liberty means freedom from sin, not freedom to sin.

In the material order, reason and will as man's creative powers, are being directed towards the conquest of natural forces inherent in man's earthly environment. Reason and will are gradually liberating him from external natural limitations and expanding his field of action almost into astral space. Hence comes a dynamic notion of science and economics, which, in its full scope, is expanding in society.

2. The Notion of the Social.

Apart from and above the "natural" environment, man is "limited" by a "social" environment of his fellow individuals. This social environment constitutes the proper field where progress can be made.

Man's progress is affected by the "social" in two spheres: the supernatural and the natural.

The Mystical Community of the Church is the supernatural "social" reality. It is essentially independent but reflects strongly on the "social" in its contingent and temporary earthly dimensions.

The "natural" human society, or rather the relations of the individual to the social, still remains the crucial issue of modern times. Some consider this relationship in terms of tension, rising even to the state of class war. This, however, makes hatred an essential component of the relationship. Tension cannot be dismissed, but personalist creativeness requires positive and constructive components, of which love is the most important. It makes "creative tension" possible. Nobody is entirely devoid of fraternal love. As an effect of Grace, love is being increased in its volume by God's direct activity. Nevertheless, it depends, much more than anything else, on the cooperation of the human reason. In its spontaneous form, it is most dynamic but it can be augmented by learning too.

Liberty, in its individual aspect, appears as a considerable negative force accompanying the activity of will in its specialized task of checking instincts and passions. It is love which provides the positive sense to liberty by releasing man's dynamic activity towards the society of his fellowmen. Liberty, enriched by love, does not eliminate, but transcends all mercy, even in its forms exalted in the past by men like St. Vincent de Paul. Thus the focal point of the new Christian approach to the social becomes visible. In this way, Christian Democracy transcends all kinds of charitable organizations.

In the light of love, social values appear above individual ones.

The individual human person is situated at a point where the personal values of his individual self are augmented in society and reflect back on his individual supernatural end. It is in a supernatural society where he achieves finally and irrevocably this end or loses it, but he can accomplish it only as an individual. No social value can equal the value of this individual supernatural end and no society can challenge the individual to abandon it. This remains true on any social level and is the source of the inalienable dignity of each human being. *The progress of the individual depends on the society, but, in turn, social progress is an organic function of the multiplicity and volume of particular achieved personalities.*

Thus the great problem of the MORAL ORDER, which transforms the "social" from an aggregate of individuals into an organic unity, has been posed. This problem will be discussed later.

3. The Notion of the National and of the International.

Included in the many existing social groups are the family, the various professional associations, the state, the nation, the Church and humanity. The individual augments his personality by uniting with still higher sociological groups. In primitive times, the first of these groups was limited by the clearing which man hewed out of the forest with his axe and where he settled with his family and defended against any intruder. Later, under the influence of a common language, a kind of solidarity crystallized among the inhabitants of the different neighboring clearings. Hostility gradually decreased and finally was replaced by national cohesion. This evolution left the family intact but the clearing was never able to recover its position as a unit of social differentiation.

Poland, was already a fully developed nation, when it accepted Christianity. The Church never interfered with the Polish state, recognizing in the nation and in its state, the highest forms of achieved personalization. The Polish nation actually proved its ability for personanlist expansion: the union with Lithuania in the 15th century was a result of a mutual agreement, not of conquest. Thus, one more nation was gained for Christianity.

Personalist values during the 17th and 18th centuries, which animated the extremely numerous Polish nobility and characterized its democratic way of life, were more frequently mistaken for unbounded individual freedom. This resulted in a critical disregard for social values. Consequently, the weakened state of Poland was unable to resist the concerted pressure of neighboring great powers.

After partitioning by Austria, Prussia and Russia, the Polish nation lost the support of the state organization but never lost some degree of personalization. This remained true in spite of all social and moral deficiencies affecting the nation at that time, as well as before.

Polish poets of the romantic period went even farther by asserting that the Polish nation even became a person herself.

Polish Messianism cannot be upheld, but the modern nations certainly acquired some characteristics, analogous to those found in individual human persons. A personalism of nations is manifested whenever some kind of unification of nations is contemplated. Democratic effort aimed at union among nations requires a considerable amount of personalist dynamism diffused in all nations in question; whereas, there was no apparent need for such personalist expansion at the time when nations were being exchanged as a result of dynastic bargaining. There can be no doubt that federal ideas make a nation appear as a unit capable in itself of personalist expansion.

The great concept of the MORAL ORDER reappears here on the international level. Machiavelli and Nietzsche, by justifying the idea of sovereign states clashing with each other in the pursuit of "egoistic" particular interests, invaded the concept of "international." The practical implications of this theory meant that every moral consideration was banned from public and international activity. The federal idea is essentially a reaction against this state of international anarchy. It reinstates the MORAL ORDER on the international level.

One set of moral principles must therefore bind human relations, no matter whether the problem to which the moral principle is to be applied at a given time is a private, public, or international one.

B. The Notion of the Active and of the Engaged.

Dynamism is latent in a social relation. It becomes explicit in social activity. Activity means engagement: man has to engage his spiritual powers of reason and will against the material components of his self. By attaining some degree of liberty over his body, man asserts his individuality and his personality. The conquest of internal liberty is a necessary step towards the conquest of external liberty, *i.e.,* of limitations of the material environment. Thus, LABOR emerges as the determining factor in man's action in acquiring liberty over the material. The labor of man reflects back on himself causing an expansion of his personality.

TOIL is a necessary component of labor. It can be lessened but never eliminated. It is the result of effort needed to overcome material resistance. As the consequence of primordial sin, toil is located at the point where the supernatural converges with the natural and material as well as with the spiritual and human. Man is no longer a perfect creature. He has been left by God to perfect himself. Toil inherent in labor makes this task difficult and painful.

The life of primitive man was thoroughly permeated with toil. He had to rely entirely on his physical strength and endurance. Then, he was little aided by his spiritual forces and the natural elements were all against him. Thus, his whole life's toil was barely sufficient to keep him alive. Consequently, he was pinned down to an animal, rather than a human, way of life. This primitive state, to some extent, still exists in modern society: the unskilled manual laborer is situated at the very bottom of the social pyramid. In most modern societies, below this limit death from starvation threatens him.

Aided by his reason, man soon discovered that, by a joint effort of several individuals, values can be achieved which are unattainable in individual isolation. Once man's "social" nature was asserted, he was able to discover the power of joint spiritual effort in finding the means of lessening toil. In turn, he realized the importance of conserving and saving physical energy and employing the residue in spiritual effort. He became cognizant that, in spite of the toil required by a task, pain is eliminated by the feeling of satisfaction which emerges at the moment of its final achievement. Finally, this satisfaction may stimulate endeavors towards the creation and contemplation of perfect works of art.

All this cultural progress was made possible by labor as well as the peculiar ability of the human mind to record past experiences and transmit them to the next generation. Thus, *technical progress* is made possible. With the chief aim of producing the *maximum* of consumptive goods available to society with the *minimum* of human effort spent and the maximum of natural forces employed, labor aided by reason appears as *productive in character*.

The problem remains as to how to use energy saved from decreased human toil. It should be transferred to a higher kind of labor, *creative in character*. The chief aim of this labor is thoroughly personalist: to elevate humanity from sheer animal existence to a life essentially active and creative.

It has already been said that internal liberty is the first conquest over animal existence. The next step is the external conquest as embodied by technical progress tending to differentiate goods and their consumption. Uncontrolled, technical progress may considerably dehumanize society by making wealth the end in itself. Whereas, the main objective of technical progress consists of the liberation of the maximum amount of people from a bulk of the effort necessary to satisfy the indispensable natural desires of life which were so absorbing in the primitive era.

These liberated efforts must become creative. On this highest level, man engages in labor all his spiritual powers, which will be reflected on technical progress when he discovers further means of freedom from toil and effort.

Labor becomes purely creative when it organizes moral order in society as well as when it directs itself towards the achievement of artistic values. Labor is indirectly creative when it promotes understanding and the contemplation of its moral or artistic achievements, these standing as the highest peak of human utilization.

Cyprian Norwid, the great 19th century Polish poet, in his "Prometidjon," anticipated a still higher zenith: in that one day all labor will be directly connected with BEAUTY and that BEAUTY will reflect LABOR. It is a distant vision but already raises the problem of all the gloomy and depressing interiors of industrial buildings and districts which need not nor should not be.

*   *   *

When mentioning the moral order in connection with labor, an additional point should be emphasized: apart from its role in the moral order of society, love casts a special light on labor. which forms the basis of the sometimes dreaded and often admired solidarity of the conscious working class. This solidarity, moreover, has accompanied labor movements all the way through strikes, the assault on labor organizers, sometimes through bloody clashes and prisons up to the present position of organized labor. Those many instances when able labor organizers refused to take tempting promotions because they would become separated from the living conditions of their fellow workers belong to the same sphere of love.

*   *   *

It is noted that both internal and external liberty have constantly interacted on each other and, consequently, have increased the volume of each. As a matter of fact, the amount of increased liberty is considerable if compared with man's primitive state.

It is, however, understood that modern humanity has been mired on the level of technical progress. The danger of mistaking the wealth of accumulated goods and a comfortable life as the end in society has unfortunately become a reality. This conception of society has further been perverted into individual anarchy on one side and social oppression on the other. Tension developed between these two points, confusing the real issues. On the one hand, individual freedom, often couched in the idea of private enterprise, tends to justify those who are strong enough to gather goods for their own profit, even at the expense and misery of others. On the other hand, extreme socialization tends to destroy any notion of the individual and to dissolve it in the social. Both extremes argue in economic terms derived from technical development and refuse to attempt to transcend technocracy. Both extremes invoke justice to support their tendencies, without attempting to realize that justice becomes thus biased and unfit to dissolve tension.

It is only when human labor establishes the creative level of personalist expansion that the tension between the social and the individual can be broken and the task of liberating humanity from the oppression of technocratic economics can be accomplished. To reach this creative level, a great deal of educational effort is required.

Only a few persons have realized the creative effort of labor and they were never able to go beyond what J. Maritain calls a prophetic "shock minority." If, however, the technical implications of the discovery of nuclear energy are not projected to the creative level soon, it can only be concluded that humanity is heading towards the destruction of its culture and that man will be forced back into the primitive existence of the Dark Ages.

C. The Notion of Ownership.

Ownership is an effect of labor, which constitutes the link between man and all the material objects he owns.

The concept of the human person reflects strongly on ownership.

Ownership is affected by the notion of the individual since it is some one or some unity which owns.

Ownership, viewed as the basis of expansion for the human person, should lose much of its egotistic quality. Individual ownership acquired according to conditions of labor through technical progress augments the personalist potential of the individual. Much depends on the resistance of the individual to the temptations of excessive material wealth. In any event, ownership never ceases to be, in principle, the stepping stone to the creative level. Once the owner has reached this level, ownership becomes integrated into the moral order. Thus new social values are acquired in addition to the individual values. It may therefore be concluded that *a diffusion of private ownership is an essential social exigency.*

Material values which surpass the sphere of direct private ownership are socially important. Thus, the problem of public ownership is posed.

Public ownership cannot be conceived as a concentration of state ownership along Marxist lines.

Public ownership derives its justification from the peculiar ability of the human mind, which enables man to accumulate past experiences for future utilization. This peculiar ability is the source of values which overpass anything individual and private and should be entrusted to society for efficient control. The human person should profit from them through society.

D. The Notion of the Cultural.

If perspectives of Revelation and the supernatural remained closed to the human mind, culture would justly be recognized as the highest achievement of human activity.

The human person is essentially the object and the subject of culture. Man has to start from an active and creative attitude. This attitude prompts him to absorb, according to his mental capacity, the greatest amount of human achievements. Then he endeavors to progress further by his own achievements and to incorporate them into the common current. Finally, he is able to contemplate the goodness and beauty of the most perfect achievements.

Accordingly, several spheres of creative activity are apparent: EDUCATION which forms human souls into personalities; SPECULATIVE SCIENCE which serves TRUTH; and ART which is situated nearest to God's creation.

Thus CULTURE as embodied in the highest activity of the human person means to learn, to contribute to, and to utilize progress. In this way, man receives the highest degree of satisfaction possible in the natural order.

All these values which are sublimated in culture and are surpassed only by religious experience are not necessary nor sufficient to keep the human body alive. Without these values, however, man could not rise above animal existence to achieve human personality.

The hierarchy of values clearly indicates the superiority of the spiritual over the material: it is the spiritual power of the sculptor which causes the transformation of a stone into a work of art.

* * *

The CULTURAL is closely related to the ACTIVE. It may be said, without doing any harm to the spiritual components of culture, that the CULTURAL is the materialized ACTIVE. Much, therefore, of what was written on the ACTIVE can be applied to the CULTURAL, especially with regard to the cultural components of technical progress.

It may be safely assumed that a special sphere of material and technical "civilization" actually exists, opposed to "spiritual culture." There is nothing wrong with this sphere provided it does not hamper the achievement of higher cultural values.

As to the creative level of contemporary culture, it extends

too high above the average level of appreciation and is consequently understood by only a few specialists. It may also
result in a growing feeling of contempt for the average. There is
obviously nothing wrong in seeking Truth and Beauty on their
highest levels. But a gap between the plans of perfection accessible to the average man and those accessible to the exception-
ally gifted should not be maintained long enough to foster an
elite of cultural producers and consumers separated from the
average man by their privileged social position. In this event,
the individual is apt to take the upper hand over the social with
the resulting social failure of the CULTURAL.

Diffusion of CULTURES, quite analogous to the diffusion of
ownership, appears to be another social exigency. An educational effort must endeavor to transcend the technical level of
human activity in order to cultivate a widespread understanding of genuine culture. On the other hand, genuine culture
must devote at least part of its creative powers to the common
man.

Labor is the natural means for securing cultural success in
society. Labor is essentially ordained to liberate man from the
despotism of natural forces. However, it cannot be halted on the
level of the technical process nor be forced below it as, for example, when the capitalist principle of supply and demand tries
to degrade labor to a mere material component of production.

It has already been said that much of the technical level is
permeated by cultural components but, nevertheless, the two
levels are essentially distinct. Only labor can bridge the gap
and level the contradictions, without destroying the distinctions.
Because technical progress is a necessary stepping stone to
higher expansion, it cannot be used to dissolve higher values.

A world transformed by labor appears at the far end of the
vision. This vision, however, is not essential in itself, at least
not in its full perfection, which is unattainable in the temporal order. What is essential is the effort which is being expended in labor towards still higher perfection of the human
person.

E. The Notion of Authority.

What is the origin of authority? This is a most disputed
question since the time of J. J. Rousseau. Absolute monarchy
claimed the origin of its authority directly from God. As soon
as the "social" problem began to assert itself, the theory of the
people as the source of authority was advanced. These two theories became two opposite poles between which tension grew,
until the first theory eventually became the focal point of conservatism and the second theory was advanced by the socially

progressive camp. The latter was a reaction to the idea of Eternal Law regarded as essentially incorporated into the structure of absolutism.

As long as the atheistic approach to the "social" is still opposed to the "theistic" approach to the absolute and the individual, the tension between these theories cannot be dissolved. Obviously, Eternal Law which is God's plan for the world must be realized in natural law, which in turn strongly reflects on positive law. Authority, as closely connected with every kind of law, certainly derives its justification from God. On the other hand, positive law, as it regulates the rights and duties of the citizen in the exclusive field of temporal society, derives its justification from the people. Thus, authority is located at a point on which both natural and positive law converge. This convergence excludes any antinomy, in spite of centuries of friction between these two unfounded assumptions regarding the origin of power.

The much contested problem of Church and State relations follows. Both the idea of a church-state and of the laicised state, (a type of which developed in France in the 19th century) must be rejected in the present historical circumstances. Government over social groups, moreover, is not a direct end of the visible Church nor can the state remain aloof from religious experience, which transcends the highest achievements of the human spirit.

Political authority relies on REASON AND WILL as they are the creative powers of the HUMAN PERSON and capable of planning, constructing and governing those social structures most suited for personal expansion.

Political Authority aims to condition the development of the human person in the temporal society. It is not concerned with supra-temporal ends towards which every human being is essentially directed, no matter how much personality he is able to acquire during his life. The role of the Church is to point to man his destiny and the liberty granted to him by Grace in the temporal order and to remind man of the transcendence of his destiny over any temporal structure. Thus, the unchangeable teaching which is being kept in trusteeship by the temporal Church becomes the backbone of the moral order and a safeguard against perverting authority.

The Church, as clothed in a temporal structure, has to govern itself. The men of the Church, being human, can easily become more interested in governing society than in spreading the supratemporal teaching of the Church. History should make us wary of a Church-state or a state religion.

The laicized state, on the other hand, has destructive effects which forces the Church into an attitude of defending its position first and leaving its teaching duties behind.

The Church, however, must reckon with temporal society which is essentially changeable. Social circumstances during a given historical period may be of great aid to the Church's position. Its associations with temporal and changing social forms must be kept flexible enough to foster Christian inspiration in new currents. For example, the Church proved itself unable to penetrate the working class from any bourgeois position.

The present era, with its extreme decomposition of MORAL ORDER, demands a new synthesis of Church and State. Both should be made complementary in the temporal order of human life without infringing on the sphere of activity of each and with the utmost mutual respect.

It is easy to determine the role of the Church or the State starting from a social *tabula rasa*. The Christian Social Movement, however, had its impetus from given conditions which had developed previously. These conditions were essentially characterized by social injustice. It was this negative situation which ushered the concept of social justice to the fore.

Theoretically, it is against the background of social justice that authority should be analyzed. An abstract picture of authority would show it located above all the dynamic components of society. But the more the balance in the moral order is disturbed, the greater the tension which develops. Contesting forces strive for authority and all advantages inherent in authority are exploited by those who succeed in seizing it.

Christian moral principles appear to be the most suitable ones to attempt to restore the balance in moral order through a Church-State synthesis, centered on the human person. Thus, authority will be above all social dynamism which should be coordinated rather than governed.

*　　　*　　　*

Ideology has a two-fold meaning: regarded as static, it is a conception of TRUTH with ample reservations to allow for human fallibility; regarded as dynamic, it is a VISION reaching far out into the future.

As a vision, it may tend towards a utopia. There are beautiful utopias on record which never became history. A vision ceases to be utopian if it is able to inspire the practical realization of a movement.

Christian Democracy most certainly moves in the practical

order. Aided by Christian principles, it may contain more truth than any other movement. It cannot, however, reach too far into the future nor refrain from reckoning with actual social, economic, and political developments which condition the living generation. Thus, it becomes a political movement.

The Christian Democratic vision therefore must be translated into terms of a social, economic, and political program of a group which will set out to influence the immediate future. This program is necessary in order to prove the ideological dynamism in a practical order.

III. The Program

There are six principles at the base of the program, derived from the vision, directed into the future, but to be applied for the profit of the living generation.

1. *The Christian Principle* determines the character of the moral order. Accordingly, the social, economic, and political structures, the legislative and the educational efforts will be based on Christian philosophy. Private, public and international life will be founded on one ethical basis and on natural law.

2. *The National Principle* points to the past life of the Polish nation, viewed as a spiritual, historical, and cultural community in its highest level of achieved personalization.

3. *The Social Principle* limits the realization of particular ends at a certain point, after which the common good must be considered. Individuals, as well as groups, are equally liable to such limitations. Here love plays an essential role by clearing the way for any kind of positive unification on a higher social level.

4. *Democratic Principle.* Democracy is not an absolute value so that a criminal action would be justified, even if an overwhelming majority would vote for it.

Democracy, in order to achieve its full vital and dynamic value, must be supplemented by moral principles. Then it can move within the moral order where it becomes the most important means of practical, i.e., political, action.

In the case of Christian Democracy, it is obvious that Christian principles are to determine democratic action. As a means of political action, therefore, democracy must serve the human person in keeping the right balance in political forces, in safeguarding individual rights, and in promoting social welfare.

Political forces are too often far from being Christian in principle. Consequently, Christian forces are handicapped by a concerted action against the Christian components of their democratic dynamism.

Christian Democracy asserted itself, not in a thoroughly Christian society, but against anti-Christian and anti-social pressure combined. It proved its efficiency by its origin in an established constellation of political forces mostly hostile to it. It even had to reckon with the forces of Catholic conservatism.

By accepting the principle of democracy, Christian Democratic forces recognize the right of the majority to choose the way by which world problems are to be approached as well as to select a form of government.

On the other hand, the democratic principle justifies Christian Democrats' claim for free action, which they undertake in the name of Truth. This is their minimum claim. If it is denied, it means that society ceases to be democratic.

The frame of democracy offers an opportunity, not only for developing political tension, which often proves to be fruitful, but also for joining forces to achieve ends essentially personalist.

The Polish Christian Democratic program approaches the democratic principle on a field of cooperation between those who know the truth and those who do not yet command the whole truth.

5. *Principle of Authority of Law.* Positive law is the result of democratic action: the substance of law depends on the spirit by which Democracy moves within the moral order. Consequently, law and respect for law are essential for society. Christian Democracy recognizes this fully and strives to bring positive law in line with natural law reflected in Christian moral principles.

6. *Principle of Social Justice* considers influences tending to destroy personalist values of large masses of human beings, which have been especially apparent since the beginning of the industrial revolution. Socialism did much to expose social injustice of the 19th century. It was, however, Leo XIII and all those contributing to the first great social encyclical who determined social justice precisely and defined it in its Christian context.

The notion of social justice underwent a substantial evolution. Ketteler still conceived it as legislative action *for* the workers, originating in the upper enlightened layers of society. Leo XIII authorized direct action undertaken by the workers themselves in order to achieve both improved working conditions from their employers and preventive legislation against human exploitation from the state. Pius XI accomplished the notion of the social by stressing the role of Charity within the moral order which gives meaning to social justice in empirical social conditions. Finally, Pius XII is now putting the finishing touches on the concept of cooperation between management and labor with the state arbitrating from above.

SOCIAL JUSTICE acts as a searchlight focused on whatever is going wrong in society. It justifies change. But the positive action taken to accomplish the change derives its justification from other principles.

*   *   *

Against this background of principles emerges the program, as the link between the far-reaching Vision and practical application.

It opens with a restatement of the basic freedoms promoting the development of the individual as he serves society.

The family, as the intermediate social form linking the individual to society, should be especially cared for.

The concept of self-government is next presented, holding that the state should limit its functions and leave decentralized social groups in a position to govern themselves as far as possible.

The domains of economics and culture should be especially decentralized and freed from unnecessary state interference.

In the domain of economics, self-regulation should be universal, public in character, based on equal representation of management (industrial association) and labor (trade unions), on free elections of governing bodies by majority vote and should embrace all levels of economic and technical progress.

A Supreme Economical Council should be instituted which would comment on all legislative projects designed to affect the country's economy. The Council would also initiate this type of legislation thus enabling it to influence all economic planning. Furthermore, the Council would regulate management and labor relations, control all professional education, and care for the spiritual and cultural needs of workers and their families.

All who directly contribute to and assist in the cultural process of science, art, and education should have their own organizational forms of self-government. These forms should be based on associations of the cultural and educational character and their respective delegates would take part in the Supreme Cultural Council.

With the establishment of these Economic and Cultural Councils, it is thereby hoped that a system of "social" democracy can be made to work parallel to the system of political democracy. Through the mutual cooperation of both systems, the democratic principle will attain its complete fulfillment and the greatest possible diffusion of cultural values will gradually be achieved.

Economic and cultural self-government is the goal, but before it can be reached the whole economic and social structure must be changed. It is not known to what extent changes installed by the present Communist domination will affect the country. Nor can it be known to what extent these changes may impede or facilitate the implementation of the program. Nevertheless, it is felt that some points of the program must be insisted upon in any event.

One of the points which must not be compromised is that of ownership. Ownership, indispensable for the foundations of any social and economic structure, must be diffused extensively. Everyone should be assisted in acquiring something of his own: an apartment, a house with a garden, a farm, a business.

Both labor and ownership must be protected against any infringement from the "individual" as well as from the "social." Labor and capital must be made essentially equal. Intellectual and physical opportunities must be sufficient to guarantee security for the worker, that is, security comparable to that achieveable in the capitalistic system by those who owned property and capital.

Unlimited economic rivalry must be abolished. Healthy competition based on private enterprise coupled with planning from above (state and economic self-government) should be introduced. In larger industrial enterprises, the responsibility of management must be shared with the representatives of workers, not only regarding labor-management relations but the full scope of production. Worker representation may originate from either elections to the boards of particular enterprises or in co-ownership. Worker representatives may be selected by trade unions or directly elected by workers. Co-ownership, in turn, may be direct or shares can be made available to the workers. As a result of such a plan, workers are given an opportunity to learn to assume a new domain of responsibility. It is this domain which has been closed to them by both the capitalistic and Communist systems. Active responsibility of workers with management will, in the long run, transform class war into dynamic cooperation.

Labor, as the chief aspect of human activity, must be profitable enough to secure a decent existence. This problem was treated above, when private ownership was discussed. Profit, however, is of social importance. Excess profits should, therefore, be controlled, and the owner must be prevented from consuming them, above a certain limit, for his private ends. He will be free, of course, to reinvest any amount of profit wherever he deems it advisable and thus a free outlet for his creative potentialities will be retained.

To control adequately key industries, all mining and heavy industries, as well as big financial organizations, will be socialized, but not state-controlled. They should be within the sphere of economic self-government. State ownership should be limited to railways and communication services such as the mails, telegraph and radio.

Agriculturally, the economy should be based on small and medium-sized farms. A restricted number of large farms should be retained to secure seeds and to promote adequate breeding standards. On the other hand, farms which are too small should be given additional lands. A widespread educational system will be essential to raise the living and professional standards of the rural population.

In the cultural sector of society, the creation of an educational system is imperative immediately if a proper expansion of the HUMAN PERSON is to result in the long run. School years should invest the new generations not only with knowledge but especially with all the moral values of character: personal and social responsibility, strength of will, a democratic attitude, a feeling of solidarity with the masses of the population and, last but not least, understanding and appreciation of team work.

Stemming from the most important conclusion derived from the Vision, *that spiritual ends extend over and above any material ends,* young people must be persuaded to believe in all the values of the HUMAN PERSON. They must bear the conviction that it is in the power of the HUMAN PERSON to consciously transform nature and himself and thus to influence history.

The educational system, largely based on Christian moral principles, will be open to the teaching mission of the Catholic Church.

Further, as the most important part of the cultural effort, the educational system should be autonomous. As a segment of the cultural self-government, the autonomy of education should influence all other cultural components.

Needless, to say, no social inequalities of the various members of a learning generation can interfere with the quality of their education. This, it is hoped, will lead to the abolition of social prejudice and to the eventual unification of the intelligentsia with the mass of rural and industrial workers. Such unity is indispensable if a new personalistically-minded Polish nation is to enter history.

In the political field, a balance must be adjusted between liberty and authority and reflected by the governmental system. A balance of this nature is difficult to accomplish. In spite of a democratic system, we have already had experiences with a preponderance of political parties so that no efficient government could be formed and have had to undergo supremacy exercised first by Pilsudski and after his death by an ambitious clique.

It is felt that a parliamentarian type democracy is most adaptable for restoring and maintaining the balance between liberty and authority disturbed by totalitarian tendencies of the prewar regime.

It must also be stressed that the program demands an army which is united to the people. Social differentiation as existed before the war should be minimized by preventing the military's assumption of superiority. Military authority must be fully controlled by the civil government and may never be permitted to influence the civil order of the state.

As it projects into international relations, the program is in full accord with the personalist line of higher international integration. A regional union of Central and East-European nations is visualized.

This Union is not solely a deduction from the 1939 defeat by the Germans but is based on the Vision. However, with regard to Germany and to Russia, a functional plan for collective security embracing roughly the area of eastern Europe cannot be completely dismissed. It is anticipated that the United States and all other powers will assist in creating a situation allowing all the inhabitants of territories located between Russia and Germany to pool their resources to build a bulwark for peace. It is finally hoped that all the burdens placed on society for the sake of international security will be made unnecessary.

B. THE MOVEMENT OF MODERN POLISH CHRISTIAN DEMOCRACY

IV. The Tradition

The turning point in Polish CHRISTIAN DEMOCRACY is found somewhere between November 1939 and June 1940. The decisive events are unknown because they were too common to be pinpointed for separate description. Moreover, they occured outside the organized groups of the political current manifested by the Polish Christian Labor Party and outside the Christian Trade Unions.

At the war's end in 1939, the Christian Democratic political and labor movements went underground. Only a few months previous to this situation, the chairman of the Polish Christian Labor Party, Wojciech Korfanty, had died. He had been forced into exile in 1935 by the pre-war government. He had returned at the first signs of danger in Poland, only to be arrested upon crossing the border and was jailed. After a few weeks in prison, his health broke. Although he was released shortly thereafter, he died within a week on August 17, 1939.

Before Poland became overrun by the Germans, the acting chairman of the Labor Party, Mr. K. Popiel, was able to go abroad, where he became active in the Polish Government in France and later that which was established in London. The working circles remaining in Poland rallied around the prominent personality, Mr. Tempka, vice-president of the Labor Party. The Party received a severe blow when Mr. Tempka (in 1940) and Mr. Kwiecinski, another vice-president and a most remarkable personality in the movement, and three hundred Party members were arrested. (1942) Many of them, including both Mr. Tempka and Mr. Kwiecinski, were executed in concentration camps. It required time for the Party to recover from this assault.

In the meantime, under the impact of German oppression, a considerable number of people started to think along the lines of Christian Democracy, although they did not realize the similarity of their thinking with the Christian Democratic ideology. They began to gather in small circles. In time, they formed regular organizations working in an atmosphere of conspiratorial exigencies. Later, a spontaneous force to unite brought most of them together into one strong movement. The people did not think of political action at first. Unconsciously they gave what was most needed in the Christian Social movement, a cultural current which took its place beside the already existing political and trade union currents.

The fact that so many prominent men from all walks of life became active in this movement is chiefly explained by the impact of Christianity on society as it regained its weakened grip on the Polish mind.

The problem of *radicalism* had to be solved first: could Christianity become reconciled with social radicalism which was still identified with socialist theory? *Radicalism* consists of a negative attitude toward some existing order and a positive tendency to change that order.

Christianity in Poland is identical with Catholicism. The preliminary question to be answered was whether Catholicism approved of the order existing in Poland before 1939. As background for this question Catholicism in Poland was spread over all cross-sections of the nation. Even Socialists were overwhelmingly Catholic on the lower rungs of the party. Though many elements in the Polish population were in favor of radical changes and simultaneously faithful to Catholicism, many others remained opposed or indifferent. The Hierarchy never expressed its official attitude toward radical changes, which no one expected. The only exception was a pronouncement of the late Cardinal Hlond when speaking in 1932 from the Tomb of St. Adalbert in Gniezno. He expressed his acceptance of Christian Democratic principles in social life. On the whole however, Polish Catholicism seemed to share the weakness of its counterparts in other European nations. Except for a few bishops like Sapieha, who later became Cardinal, Lukomski, Przezdziecki, and Kubina, all of them since deceased, the Hierarchy was rather a static force, tending to conservative stability rather than to dynamic change.

In the absence of clear guidance a conclusion concerning the approval of Catholicism of the order in Poland before 1939 had to be reached speculatively.

Two alternative conclusions could be made. First that the social order which had existed before 1939 was considered good enough to exclude need for any radical action from any Catholic source and that Catholicism was consequently linked with this order (although not necessarily with the existing political order) ; or, secondly, that Catholicism as it appeared in Poland in its contingent traditional, if not historical forms, should be reconsidered in relation to the "social" and all confusion in respect to political and social activities of Catholics should be removed.

The second conclusion was finally affirmed. A great deal of intellectual work was done. This effort followed radical lines which before 1939 would not have appealed to the Polish mind but proved to be surprisingly attractive to the Polish mind of 1940, apparently changed by experience of war and terror.

This radical change in general outlook roughly coincided with a similar trend taken up by the clergy. It was headed by the two admirable Jesuit Fathers Kosibowicz, Rostworowski and Father Lewandowicz in Warsaw and by the learned Dominican Father Woroniecki in Krakow. All of these men have since deceased. Several of the professors of the Catholic University of Lublin, which had a distinguished tradition of studying the "social" and promoting its Christian notions through University teaching and arranging "social weeks", also had leading parts in this movement.

Both laymen and the clergy working in this re-evaluation agreed that not enough had been done against the resistance of the existing order to implement the social Encyclicals.

The attitude towards these Papal documents therefore had to be re-examined. All Christian-Social tradition in the political, trade union, educational, scientific, and clerical fields was founded on and derived all its authority from the Encyclicals. An exegesis did not seem to be sufficient any longer. It is obvious that the Encyclicals were retained as a basis on which an elaborated conception of the HUMAN PERSON was built: Social Justice, emphasized in the Papal documents, was applied to protect the human person; Pius XI's idea of charity, only sketched in the "Quadragesimo Anno", was used to strengthen and dynamize the human person.

When reflecting on all the studies, discussions, and considerations leading to the conclusions of the Vision, it was often said that the Christian sense of Polish liberty has been hardened and proved itself against the "furor teutonicus". For nothing could be achieved more freely than what was achieved during the Great Underground. This realization of freedom asserted against the raging terror revealed the human person in its full social liberty and thus completed the final picture of its perfection.

The theoretical achievement was soon followed by a practical one: the political, trade unionist, and cultural currents of Christian Democracy pooled their resources in the underground with each current remaining formally independent. Membership in each was open to all, but no one was compelled to join all three if he happened to be interested in only one aspect of the movement.

The unity of the Vision overwhelmed all three independent currents and a consequent interchange of members resulted on all organizational levels. Following this merging in the underground which was rather complicated and which required time to consummate, the work of translating the Vision into a program was begun. The direction of the program had to be politically geared as it was hoped at that time that the end of German oppression would be the end of all oppression and that political independence would be restored in Poland.

Preparations for political activity following the liberation of the country had to be made. These had been already initiated in the forms of an underground government including a four-party underground Parliament embodied in the Council of National Unity and underground courts of justice. All those who shared in the responsibility of the Great Underground's activities and were fortunate enough to survive the dangers of German terror have repeatedly asserted that they have never felt a greater sense of liberty than when they defied despotism by clandestine liberty.

The splendid tradition of the underground coalition of four main political currents is revered by Poles. These parties were the Nationalist Party, the Polish Peasant Party, the Christian Democratic Party, and the Polish Socialist Party. This coalition included in the Council of National Unity offers an inspiring idea for a new start. All the parties with the exception of the Nationalist Party, are still clearly visible beneath the red taint of the Communist regime. Only the Nationalist Party will have to reassert the political actuality of its program, supplemented by new socially progressive and federalist planks, when renewed political activity is possible in Poland.

The Polish Christian Labor Party took an active part in the Underground state. Three of its most prominent men were elected to head the underground government. The underground Parliament owed much of its success to the dynamism and high standards which the members of the Polish Christian Labor Party contributed to discussions and decisions.

A strong military detachment was trained, equipped and commanded entirely by the efforts of the movement. The detachment was of course incorporated into the Home Army and distinguished itself during the two-month-long Warsaw Uprising.

After the fall and destruction of Warsaw, most of the leading members of the movement gathered in Krakow where the finishing touches to the program were added.

January 1945 brought to Poland only a change of occupation, rather than the anticipated lifting of oppression. And a most trying time began.

The Christian Democratic forces participated actively in all the fateful decisions which followed. Three of its most eminent leaders together with thirteen other representatives of the underground government were lured into a secret police trap, kidnapped to Moscow, tried and duly condemned. When it finally was clear that Poland had been abandoned to its fate, the tragic conclusion was reached to dissolve the Underground State and its Army, and the Testament of the Great Underground was drafted.

The Christian Democratic movement resisted despair and decided to take the only course open to it: to step out into the open, to inspire local party organizations with Christian principles and to thus oppose Communism wherever possible. Consequently, Mr. Popiel, the acting chairman of the Polish Christian Labor Party since 1937, returned to Warsaw from London in June, shortly after Mr. Mikolajczyk's return to Poland. Mr. Popiel immediately joined the home organization.

As all the local organizations of the Party had been renewed and were in good working order, the Polish Christian Labor Party organized in Warsaw a congress on July 15, 1945, its first one since 1937. Only the day before this Congress, the Communist regime which previously had not objected to party activities banned the assembly. This decree was ignored and the location of the congress was moved to the deserted cellar of a ruined factory. 768 delegates had arrived from every section of the country, about half of whom attended the illegal meeting. It was opened by Mr. Popiel in the presence of 360 representatives from local party organizations. The new program was presented and unanimously adopted. Mr. Popiel was re-elected Chairman and Mr. Sieniewicz, Secretary General. Both men are heading the party's exiled organization and have been joined by other members of the Party's Executive who have escaped, such as Mr. B. Biega, Mr. S. Kaczorowski and Mr. J. Starszak.

Thus, backed by a genuinely democratic vote of support, the new Executive Committee increased the activities of the "Church-going people's party" to use Mr. Averell Harriman's expression. Mr. Harriman was at that time the American ambassador to Russia and he used this term during diplomatic discussions at the Kremlin which resulted in Mr. Mikolajczyk's yielding to allied pressure, especially that of Mr. Churchill, and accepting the compromise of a Communist-dominated Polish government. It was apparently Mr. Harriman's intention in employing this phrase to clear the way for Mr. Popiel to enter the government. However, this was never granted. Party activity was tolerated, but the leaders were unceasingly harrassed by the police.

Seven seats were allotted to Mr. Popiel's party in the throughly Communist-dominated National Council of 400-odd seats supposedly serving as a Parliament, and the role of opposition was assigned to the P.C.L.P. as well as to Mr. Mikolajczyk's Polish Peasant Party with 40 seats.

In spite of all handicaps, the Polish Christian Labor Party expanded and soon surpassed the number of 120,000 regular card-carrying and paying members, spread throughout the country.

This situation prompted Communist action and top pressure was used to install a handful of Communist opportunists into the Executive Committee of the party. At the same time, elections were begun in all levels of the local party organizations. No Communist followers had a remote chance for election in any party organization. As time drew near to hold the second party congress, the opportunists in the Executive Committee realized that they had slight chance to keep their positions. The second congress was therefore banned. A wave of terror and arrests began against legitimate party members. Almost no political activity was possible. The decision was taken, in agreement with departmental party organizational leaders, on July 18, 1946 to bring the party's activities to a standstill until a democratic atmosphere was installed in Poland.

At the next session of the National Council, 20 Sept. 1946, Mr. Popiel, before all the state dignitaries and diplomatic corps, went to the rostrum to announce the decision taken by his party and the events leading up to it. At the end of his speech, he threw his councillor's card at the feet of the Council's president. Followed by the other Christian Democratic members of the Council, he left the chamber.

To recall an example of the difficulties encountered at that time, the following incident is cited: on 13 July 1946, Mr. Popiel was summond by Schwalbe, a prominent member of the Polish Politburo, who was deputising for Prime Minister Osobka-Morawski, who is now in jail. Popiel was frankly informed that the congress planned for 1946 could not be permitted as the activities of the Polish Christian Labor Party had become increasingly dangerous especially because it had as its basis the ideology of Polish Catholicism.

This declaration can in itself be justly regarded as evidence of ultimate Christian triumph. It certainly was an appreciation of potential strength, if not an expression of esteem. Materialism, menaced by spiritual revival, could only resort to force which is why the Christian Democratic triumph was destined to tragedy.

When on September 8th, 1946 the Polish Catholic Hierarchy gathered at the shrine of the miraculous picture of Our Lady in Czestochowa for its annual conference, it was officially stated that the Catholics of Poland, amounting to 95 per cent of the population, now had been left without any political representatation. It was the first time in its history that the Polish Catholic Hierarchy official issued a statement of this kind. It was interpreted everywhere as a gesture toward the suppressed Christian Democrats.

A few month's later, Mr. Popiel managed to leave Poland for France. He now directs the work of the exiled organization of the Polish Christian Labor party in Washington, D. C. where he remains in close contact with Mr. S. Mikolajczyk and the Polish Peasant Party.

Soon after Mr. Popiel and Mr. Sieniewicz arrived in the United States, the Christian Democratic Union of Central Europe was formed, with the help of their efforts. The Christian Democratic parties from Czechoslovakia, Hungary, Latvia, Lithuania, Poland, and Yugoslavia are represented in this Union. It is chairmaned by Msgr. Joseph Kozi-Horvath of the Hungarian Christian Democratic People's Movement with Mr. Popiel as Vice Chairman and Mr. Konrad Sieniewicz as Secretary General.

The C.D.U.C.E. aims to foster mutual understanding between the parties represented in it, to widen the sphere of Christian Democratic influence, and to fight Communism from a foundation offered by the free world. The Union directs its work toward the program for a unified central European region to become an integral part of a United Europe.

The C.D.U.C.E., as well as its member parties, is in close cooperation with the *Nouvelles Equipes Internationales,* which is the so-called "Christian International" where all Christian Democratic parties of Western Europe are represented. The Polish Christian Labor Party is also a member of the N.E.I. Prof. S. Glaser, of Brussels, member of the Party's Executive Committee in exile, is its representative on the N.E.I.'s Executive Committee.

Members of the Christian Trade Union Movement who succeeded in escaping from Poland are also organized in exile. Mr. Wladyslaw Michalak, a very active member of the railway branch of the Christian Trade Unions and of the Railway Workers Cooperative Movement, is now living in Ottawa and was elected chairman of the foreign delegation of the Polish Christian Trade Unions. Mr. K. Balon, now living in Hamilton, Canada, was elected secretary general. Mr. Jan Starszak, now in Chicago, who was a prominent organizer of the Christian Workers and Artisans Union, is another outstanding Christian Trade Union member.

These men, together with all the trade unionists who escaped from Poland, strive to maintain the traditions of pre-war Trade Unionism which are illustrated by the official Polish statistics of 1938: total membership numbered 229,000 (as compared with 284,000 in Socialist trade unions) of which 144,000 were paying dues and paying to their trade organizations a yearly total of ZL. 4,142,000 (as compared with 137,000 dues-paying Socialist members paying a yearly total of 2,844,000 ZL). The development of Polish Christian Trade Unions was not closed but only interrupted. The problem facing the exiled organization is to hasten to effect conditions which will permit a new start.

On March 1, 1952 an organizational assembly was held in New York. Trade Unionists from Czechoslovakia, Lithuania, Poland, Slovenia, and Hungary gathered to form the Central European Federation of Christian Trade Unions under the chairmanship of Czechoslovakia's Joseph Podlena. "The aim of the C.E.F.C.T.U.", as written in their program, "is to work out a common program for a social and economic structure of the Central European countries which would guarantee the people of those countries a better and free life in the future." Mr. Balon was elected the secretary general of this organization.

Thus, the first step towards mutual understanding and a joint effort of trade unionism was taken, certainly to be succeeded by other initiatives in the future.

*   *   *

In tracing the course of Polish Christian Democracy from its turning point during the first year of the war, the earlier tradition was not discussed. Although time and new experiences brought many changes, all antecedents are fully recognized as the roots of the Movement.

Father S. Stojalowski was the first to appeal to the aid of Christian principles to better the miserable conditions of the rural population in the Austrian-held part of Polish territory in the last decade of the 19th century. The first Encyclical influenced him to a great extent. He immediately, however, faced the stubborn opposition of the nobility, which resulted in his excommunication from the church. The Holy Father himself had to intervene to clear him from this humiliation. Father Stojalowski was extremely popular with the peasants. He founded a political party which even succeeded in electing a few representatives to the Austrian Parliament. But the party did not survive its founder's death in 1911.

The achievements of Mr. W. Korfanty are also notable. Mr.

Korfanty became a great leader of the Christian Democratic movement in German-held Silesia and in 1937, was elected chairman of the Polish Christian Labor Party. Around 1900 every Catholic in Silesia was expected to vote for the German "Catholic Centrum", which, incidentally, claimed Ketteler himself as inspirer. Korfanty, the son of a miner, was the first to dare oppose the Germanization of the "Catholic Centrum". He was able to get himself and several other Polish miners and workers elected to the all-German Parliament in Berlin. He waged his struggle until finally most of Silesia became incorporated into Poland at the end of World War I.

Other groups and movements, receiving more or less direct inspiration from the Encyclical *Rerum Novarum,* were born and carried their work with varying degrees of success. Some disappeared, others merged. The group, which in 1908 founded the monthly publication *Prad* (the Current) in Warsaw, should especially be mentioned as the first intellectual group to consider social problems from the point of view of Christianity.

Labor movements had begun to spring up in those areas undergoing industrialization. One of them, the Polish Trade Association (Zjednoczenie Zawodowe Polskie) originated in Silesia and later spread to Westphalia in Western Germany where over 500,000 Polish workers had emigrated, attracted by the expanding German industry. This Association became very strong and transferred its power back to Poland after World War I.

One of the first Christian dailies, *Narodowiec,* was founded in Westphalia (1909) and later moved to Lens in the mining area of France. It is still being published there by its original founder, Mr. Kwiatkowski, who, is one of the oldest members of the Polish Christian Labor Party.

Many of these endeavors were disrupted by the World War I. When it ended, a new situation was presented by the rebirth of the Polish nation. Two Christian political parties, the Christian Democratic Party and the National Workers Party entered the decisive elections of 1922. Together they won a total of 61 seats or 14 percent of the 444 seats available.

A similar dualism occured in the labor movement where two trade unions, the Association of Christian Workers and the Polish Trades Federation, were working. The first was closely connected with the Christian Democratic party and it was especially strong in Silesia where the authority of Korfanty was extended to both the political as well as the trade union groups. The other trade union was linked with the National Worker's Party which was more to the left than the other.

In 1926 the coup d'état of Pilsudski was executed and all democratic political groups, including both Christian Democratic parties were forced into opposition. Their leaders were persecuted. Mr. Popiel, then chairman of the National Workers Party, and Mr. Korfanty, together with the great peasant leader Wincenty Witos and the leading socialists were imprisoned and mistreated in the fortress of Brzesc. They were finally released pending a trial. Many of them, Mr. Korfanty among them, had to go in exile.

Under the influence of Paderewski, the great Polish statesman and artist, who was closely associated with the movement, even when living in Switzerland as if in exile, and of General Sikorski, the Polish premier of World War II in exile, the merging of the two parties was decided and finally achieved at the 1937 congress in Warsaw. Mr. Korfanty, who was regarded as the most distinguished personality of the Christian Democratic movement, was elected chairman of the united parties. From that time on, they were known as the Polish Christian Labor Party. The governmental action against Mr. Korfanty was thus condemned and defied. He still had to remain in exile. Mr. Popiel was designated acting chairman. The rest of the history is known.

* * *

When looking back upon the Polish Christian Democratic tradition, it is clearly understood and properly appreciated that the dominating issue up to World War I was Polish independence. The struggle for it overshadowed any other consideration. There is no room to doubt that national feeling deeply penetrated the social structures of the Polish nation. This is best illustrated by the attitude of the 19th century Polish peasant masses to the Catholic Church. Polish peasants were noted for their attachment to Catholicism. The Church and the splendor of the Catholic liturgy, however, acquired during the 19th century a strong national significance and were being opposed universally to German Protestantism and Russian Orthodoxy.

But the predominance of national feelings does not mean that social problems were not present in the historical scene. The lower classes complained of their conditions, although they may have been too impassive to complain loud enough to effect any change. Their silent protest was expressed by an urge to emigrate to foreign lands such as Western Germany, France, Brazil and the United States. It is only partly true that the emigration stemmed from the conditions of national oppression, although this fact may have affected many, especially those young people facing military service. Nevertheless, the chief motivation behind the emigration was the search for a better living. It was not that they were in quest of something better than they had but the fact that not enough remained in each family for each person's livelihood. The Polish novelists, Boleslaw Prus and H. Sienkiewicz as well as S. Reymont in his Nobel-Prize winning novel, *"The Peasants,"* have painted a very realistic picture of peasant life prior to World War I.

The first Christian Democrats, while joining in the peasants' protest, were at the same time accusing the "social" hostility or at least the "social" indifference of the upper classes. It should be remembered that cultural leadership was never restricted to the upper classes. Their claim to such leadership during the 19th century and up to World War I may be justified to the extent which a privileged economic position facilitates cultural activity. The upper classes would have ignored the cultural receptiveness of the masses if it had not been for men like Kulerski, Karol Miarka and others who were editing Polish books in popular form. These books were diffused in astonishing quantities throughout the country.

At the point when the crystallization of Polish Christian Democracy culminated in 1939, it was necessarily assumed that the social aspects of the national effort had been neglected and that the upper classes were in a large part guilty of this negligence.

In 1918 an additional side to the problem appeared and took precedence. A section of those people who had been most involved in the struggle for independence assumed, once that political independence was gained, that the basic social problem had thereby shifted from the nation to the state. With the inherent weakness of the first governments which emerged and fell according to the fluctuations of the struggles between various political parties, Pilsudski's coup d'etat in 1926 was facilitated. Every democratic political party was ruthlessly brushed aside and permitted only a limited oppositional role. Those who dared to go beyond this limitation were mistreated and, in some instances, forced into exile. Pilsudski, with all power concentrated in his hands, built a state, hostile not only to those who were being directed by consciousness of "social justice," but also to the Polish Nationalist Party. Actually, the idea of the nation could not stand when confronted with the idea of the state supported by power. Later, after Pilsudki's death, his successors went even further by proclaiming officially the doctrine of the "elite" and it was put into practice by the ruling circles. This elite, in its pursuit of authoritarian ends, was ironically enough met and crushed by German Nazism.

* * * * *

As stated previously, Christian Democracy asserted itself against social injustice. It gained its social consciousness first against nationalism and later, during the twenties and thirties in Poland, against the concept of the elite. Social justice prove to be incompatible with either situation although both aided in the crystallization process of Chritsian Democracy.

Modern Polish Christian Democrats, after their hardening by the experiences of the German and Russian occupations, now hold two firm convictions. They believe that both nationalism and the concept of the elite have definitely been surpassed by the personalist ideas of international and social Moral Order. Secondly, they are confident that all the perverted effects of the Communist approach to social injustice can be overcome. Moreover, they are certain that social justice will be applied at its best within the democratic system.

Zbigniew M. Ossowski.

CATHOLIC SOCIAL AND POLITICAL MOVEMENTS IN CZECHOSLOVAKIA

1. Historical Background of Czechoslovakian Catholicism

Hardly another nation's history and evolution has been affected by religion so fatefully as that of the Czechs. Palacký,[1] the eminent Czech historian, put it best in his *History of the Czech People*, thus: "Religion", he said, "was and remains the prime postulate in which the Czech spirit excelled from the very outset, while it determined Czech aspirations eminently and permanently: religion was the source from which Czech spiritual activity chiefly stemmed." And Thomas Masaryk, intensely engrossed in Czech religious problematics, wrote in 1904 that "the Czech question is a religious question." [2]

Indeed, the religious problem is frought with fate for the Czech people. Thanks to its farseeing Princes, the Czech nation resolved to adhere to Western Christianity; it adopted eagerly Christ's Gospels, preached in Slavic by the brothers Cyril and Methodius, the monks of Saloniki, and thereby saved not only its national existence, but became, as early as in the 9th century, a definite part of the west European social, cultural, and political commonwealth. Ever since that time, the Bohemian lands responded to every spiritual trend in Western Europe; conversely, no social structural change, emanating from West European countries, came to a halt at the Bohemian border, but rather developed to full fruition in the Czech nation. Repeatedly, these spiritual movements returned to the West from the Czech sphere, having gained in intensity and clarification, as in times of Bishop Adalbert, during the reign of Charles IV, and later during the Hussite wars.

Though paradoxical, it is a fact that however intensely the Czech nation had absorbed religious ideas, its adherence to Christianity—and concretely to Catholicism—never became immutable, nor lasting. The history of the Czech nation is simultaneously the history of a thousand-year struggle of Christianity and Catholicism, vying for the mass of the people, especially for the strata of the small people. Again and again, when it seemed the Czech man had lastingly won for Catholicism, a new rebellion and a new fight set in.

In the 14th century, during the splendid reign of Charles IV, (1346-1378), who planted the best seeds of Catholic Europeanism in Bohemia, the fusion of the Czech nation with Catholicism seemed conclusive. That ruler, his education overshadowing that of other men of his time, founded the University of Prague in 1348—one of the first—and his Court became the gathering-place of the most enlightened humanists, poets, architects, painters, sculptors, scientists and preachers. He strengthened Bohemia's Church, raising the Bishopric of Prague to an Archbishopric, thereby freeing it from the dependency upon the Archbishopric of Mainz. The Archbishops of Prague were noted for their outstanding ethical standards and exceptional erudition. The example of the Bishoprics and monasteries was equally satisfactory. The King himself, devoted to the Papal See, holding the Church in high esteem, was his people's best model. Religious life was so potent then that Aeneas Silvius, the Papal Legate, and later Pope Pius II, gave expression to his amazement, finding so extraordinary knowledge of the Scriptures even among the simple people.[3]

Yet, only a few years after the death of Charles IV, the larger part of the nation stood up against the Catholic Church and against the existing universal order. The Hussite wars rent asunder the bond with the Church for more than two centuries. The causes of this astonishing phenomenon were manifold. First, Hus himself, the Bohemian religious reformer, (1369-1415) greatly influenced the situation by his ability to combine his reformatory efforts with political, social and national movements, extant in the widest masses of the people. The peasants, the cities, and the minor yeomanry strove for an improvement of their social standing and saw in the holdings, the power and the influence of high prelates obstacles preventing their achieving that end.

The forceful national awareness also influenced this evolution, and Hus used this consciousness in his position as Rector of Prague's university. In 1410, he issued his Decree of Kutná Hora, whereby the Czechs were accorded three votes at that university as against one vote they had theretofore, while the foreigners, who up to then had three votes, henceforth were accorded only one vote. The Decree secured a majority for Hus at the university, both among the Professors and among the students, the more so since at that time many foreigners, students and teachers alike, left for the newly founded university in Leipzig. Thus Czech nationlism clashed with the universalism of the Church, and religious individualism and sectarianism struggled against dogmatic unity. The dissensions within the Church hierarchy, in particular the Great Schism, only induced Hus and his followers to clamour for reforms and their demands subsequently degenerated into Christian anarchy. Hus' death sentence, meted out by the Council of Constance, and his burning at the stake, did not stifle the defection of the Czech nation from Rome; on the contrary, it then waxed into open resistance, lasting for almost twenty years. Its protagonists were the Hussite armies, led by Jan Žižka and Prokop Holý. Following several defeats and the subsequent disintegration of the Hussites, culminating in the military defeat of the radical faction in the battle of Lipany, the Church and the Czech Calixtines (the name derives from the chalice and the Communion of both Sacraments) settled their discords at the Church Council in Basle, in 1433. Under its provision, the Church of Bohemia was granted a certain administrative autonomy including several deviating elements, as the Holy Communion "of both kinds".

The Compacts of Basle, however, achieved no reconciliation with, nor produced tighter bonds with the Church. The chasm was too deep. More and more discords cropped up, and when German Protestantism penetrated the Bohemian lands, the majority of Calixtines adopted the new religion, while a minority joined the national Church of the so-called Czech Brethren. The remainder dissolved in various other sects.

The religious upheavals and discords, having begun in Bohemia in the beginning of the 14th century, persisted during all of the 16th century; they reached their peak in the uprising against the traditionally Catholic ruling House of the Hapsburgs, in 1618. This rebellion, ending, in the Bohemian lands, with the defeat of the White Mountain near Prague in 1620, gave the signal to the thirty-year long, all-European religious struggle which in turn ended in the Peace of Westphalia in 1648.[4] Under its terms, Europe was divided in two spheres of influence, the ruling principle being *Cuius regio, eius religio*. The Bohemian lands remained under Hapsburg rule which brought a re-Catholicizing of the Czech people in its wake. Nor was that re-Catholicizing easily achieved. In keeping with the then prevalent trend, forcible means were often used and secular power intervened, for political reasons, more often than spiritual power. The re-Catholicizing was accompanied by Germanization which, having begun with the influx of Protestantism, a century earlier, now continued to slice up confiscated lands and property and to allocate them to foreign aristocracy, in recognition of its aid to the Emperor. This era of confiscation, of merciless punishments, comprising death sentences and forfeiture of property, of retaliation, of expulsions from the country, of Germanization and centralism, was not propitious for the Catholicizing of the Czech people. The Czechs loathed decreed, compulsory religion; a large part went into exile or recanted only on the surface.

However, the unfathomable ways of Providence in human actions asserted themselves: just at the moment when Catholicism seemed an alien graft incapable of implantation on the Czech trunk, the roots of Czech Catholicism proved much deeper than suspected and revealed themselves firmly established among the little Czech people. An ostensibly paradoxical phenomenon occured: Catholicism, spread and dictated by a foreign government, inimical to the Czech language, in the end became the protector and the helper of the Czech nation in the preservation of the native tongue and its bare national existence.

The 17th and 18th centuries were the period of Hapsburg exertions for absolutist centralism and the completion of forcible Germanization. By the so-called Pragmatic Sanction of 1726 the Bohemian lands lost the right to elect a King and became a hereditary part of the Hapsburg Monarchy. Empress Maria Theresa (1726-1789), and her son, Joseph II (1789-1792), completed the centralization of administration, the monarchist absolutism, and the Germanization of the Bohemian lands.[5]

The Czech language as good as disappeared from all official dealings. The upper classes in cities and country side conversed in German. In schools, especially in higher learning, German and Latin prevailed. Only the lowest classes, the peasant bondman, the artisan and the servant in the cities, spoke Czech. National awareness was as good as dead. There were no Czech schools, no Czech literature, no Czech books, theatres or publications, nor any other vestige of national culture. But when the hour was darkest, the Czech nation was rescued by Catholic priests. Names like Plachý, Dobrovsky, Dobner, Voigt, Vydra and others, appeared on the national scene.

Step by step, they began to rebuild the new edifice of national culture. They began by science, by research in local literature and history, in literary history and philology. They went on to reawakening and perfecting. They founded patriotic societies, reading societies, arranged editions of Czech books, sacrificing their savings for the purpose; they themselves distributed them clandestinely in the Bohemian lands, penetrating to the most remote hamlets. (Hanykur, Smidinger, Doucha and others). They founded periodicals, taught Czech and Czech history in schools without pay. On St. John Nepomuk Day, thousands and thousands of pilgrims came to the Saint's tomb in Prague from every corner of the Czech lands and these gatherings were the meetings of all Czech patriots; from them they drew strength and counsel for more revivalist activity. Patriotic and religious feelings blended in perfect harmony. Josef Pekař, the great Czech historian, calls this merger the true *Missa Solemnis* of the Czech nation.

Hand in hand with this national reawakening, the political renaissance unfolded. The great French Revolution did not affect the Czech evolution directly, since at that time national awareness had been at its lowest ebb and political aspirations non-existent. But the revolutionary waves of 1830 and particularly that of 1848, elicited a strong response in the Czech lands. The nation, its self-assurance increasing, conceived a longing for determining its own fate. And again we find priests at the helm of political activity. In the revolutionary actions of 1848, culminating in the Prague uprising which represented the first effort of the Czech nation to take the management of its affairs in the new era into its own hands, many priests were in the first ranks and several atoned for the abortive Prague uprising in prisons.

"In no calling or profession" so writes the historian of the Czech renascence, "had the Czech national movement so many adherents and protagonists as in the clergy. Czech priests not only were the most arduous writers, the most effective apostles of love of the fatherland and nation. It is no exaggeration to assert that barring the Czech clergy, the Czech revival would never have achieved the swift progress it did." The influence of priests gave ideological content to the nation's efforts to achieve national and political emancipation. Patriotism then was representative of humanism, of nobility, soldarity and national brotherhood—not of chauvinism. It stood for an ethical bond, linked by love to the nation, without regard to standing or class.[6]

However, the history of a nation is no tranquil and straight flow of a river. Historic workings of God's plan in a nation present unexpected reverses, conflicts and antitheses. Hard and strenuous is the struggle for the soul of the individual—harder and still more strenuous is the struggle for the soul of the nation. No sooner had the Czech nation recovered from its well-nigh deathly inertia—in the second half of the 19th century —when the spirit of the hidden rebellion against order broke through once more. The anti-religious and anti-Catholic movement, the heritage of the French Revolution, seized the Europe of the 19th century, and influenced the Czech nation profoundly. Upon examining the causes of this phenomenon we shall not fail to notice its great similarity and coherence with the causes of the dramatic religious events in Bohemia in the 15th century, although the recent deviation of the Czech nation from Rome was not accompanied by that passionate pathos which then led to great religious wars. The 19th century deviation of the Czech nation resulted rather in religious decline and indifference, despite some sincere efforts toward reform and some surviving enthusiasms.

The specific Czech element is nationalism, both in the 15th and the 19th century. Vienna policies directed against Czech national and historic-legalistic aspirations, its promises of 1848, never honoured, and in particular the Austro-Hungarian settlement of 1867, caused the Czech nation to swerve away from the Austrian monarchy and the ruling dynasty of the Hapsburgs, conclusively.[7] Since the ruling house always emphasized its close relations to the Church—despite the fact that the policies of the Vienna government have often been inimical to the Church, the resistance of broad masses of the Czech people shifted from a uniquely anti-Hapsburg attitude to one anti-Church as an official institution and main support of the hostile regime. Historic recollections fortified this attitude.

The unfortunate allocation of Bishoprics and other more consequential Church positions tended to reinforce this enmity. Vacated positions were invariably filled by aristocrats, who more often than not were foreigners. For a Czech candidate of the people to get nominated to a Bishopric was the great exception.

The national element, playing an eminent part in the estrangement of the Czech people from the Church, yet was not a specifically Czech phenomenon. At that period, the national movements in Italy and Germany also were sharply anti-Catholic.

However, the longer the Czech nation had to wait for its national rights to be consummated, the deeper became the discord. To be a patriot was synonymous with being against Vienna and against Rome. Associations and national organizations founded in that period, the political parties not excepted, based their programs on Hussitism and the Reformation. The cult of Hus was revived and in the historic Old City Square in Prague, an impressive monument was erected to him, right opposite the column of the Virgin which had been erected in the years 1650-1652. The Reformation was termed the acme of Czech history.

These specifically Czech causes were blended with the then

modern philosophical trends, especially with rationalism, affecting the Czech people more profoundly than other nations. Rationalism found ready access to the intelligentsia, becoming fashionable in both secular and ecclesiastical circles. Already the revivalist generation (Dobrovsky, Smetana) had been swept off its feet by these ideas. Bolzanism[8] became the leading trend at Prague's university. It penetrated into official circles — and even into Church organisations. Many Bishops were in sympathy with Bolzanism. How potent these traditions were, was shown at the Vatican Council: the majority of Austrian Bishops voted against the dogma of the Pope's infallibility and against the prescription of Gallicanism[9], Josephinism[10] and Febronianism[11]. Rationalism penetrated into Seminaries and into Austrian schools.

Czech intelligentsia, beginning with Havlíček, the great journalist of the middle of 19th century, up to Massaryk, followed liberalist tendencies and arrived at an attitude leading to an unequivocal anti-Catholic fight. They deemed a secession from the Catholic anti-Reformation tradition imperative in the interest of the people.

While the inteligentsia was influenced by philosophical rationalism, the Czech working masses were under the spell of atheistic socialism. The Bohemian lands were the most industrialized part of the Austro-Hungarian monarchy and the workers a potent national component. Socialism, coming to Bohemia and Moravia from Germany, and highly anti-Catholic in its manifestations, seized large numbers of the Czech workers.

The German movement "Away from Rome" also exercised some, if limited, influence upon the religious evolution of the Czech people, especialy in nationally diversified regions.

The university of Prague became the focus of the anti-Catholic effort. Philosophical positivism gained ground. Its chief protagonist became Professor Masaryk and he was reinforced by his collaborators, the so-called "realists." In his booklet "In the Struggle for Religion" written in 1904, you may best see his irreconcileable attitude and activity against Catholicism, assumed in that period. Here are a few quotations:[12]

"The Churches are subservient to the old absolutist social order. The Churches, beside being totally monarchist, are plutocratic and aristocratic to boot. They throw a philanthropic bone to the destitute and the weak, yet only that they should wait upon the mighty and the rich."

"The anti-humanitarian and anti-social structure of the Churches. Marx pointed out that there was a religion for slaves. There is much truth in that."

"Nowadays, the Church is entirely siding with violence."

"I wish to say that nothing may be expected from reformed Catholicism."

"For us, ecclesiastic religion, and in particular Catholicism, is a thing surpassed."

Masaryk's attitude toward Catholicism was, for the Czech intelligentsia, authoritative. Catholic college-educated intelligentsia was almost non-existent. High schools and undergraduate teaching were characterised by an inept religious education, owing to the deficiency of the majority of catechists.

Anti-Catholic tendencies penetrated into art, and prevalently into literature.

While these spiritual conditions lasted, World War I broke out. After the Central Powers have been defeated, the Czechs and Slovaks were liberated from the domination of Vienna and Budapest and the Czechoslovak state emerged.[13]

During that war, the secession from Catholicism became even more complete. During the first days of the liberated state the dam of the anti-Catholic torrent broke, threatening to sweep away everything that had been bound up with the nation for centuries. The national resistance, led by Masaryk, had incorporated these tendencies in the fight for liberation and in the basic program of the new state. The Washington Declaration of October 18, 1918, devised by Masaryk for President Wilson, stipulating the ethical and constitutional principles on which the Czechoslovak state was to be based, stated as one of its chief aims the separation of the Church from the State, which in practice meant: elimination of the Church from influencing public life and complete subordination of its organization to state laws.

"The new state was born out of a revolution, if not bloody," as Peroutka says in his "Building of a State," "and revolution longs to hate, to break and to humble somebody. Moreover, there were enough reasons for hating the Catholics." [14]

The reasons intimated by the above author were, among others, the pro-Austrian attitude of some conservative Catholic representatives during World War I. They were not forgiven, while the conduct and pro-Austrian utterances of marxist and liberal leaders were quietly forgotten. It is, however, a matter of public record that some Czech socialist leaders would have viewed the continuance of the Austro-Hungarian empire with favor, if Vienna could eventualy become a capital of a socialist empire instead of that of Catholic Hapsburgs. The marxist international doctrine often made them more than soft-pedal their opposition against the German language which was imposed not only by the Imperial Palace, but also by the Socialist headquarters in Vienna.

Another subject of anti-Catholic propaganda during the war was the attitude of the Papal See, about which the Czech people had been seriously misinformed.

Masaryk, the newly elected President of the State, encouraged the anti-Catholic trend. His mottoes: "Hussitism is our program" or "The Catholics will have as many rights as they will have contrived," were used by anti-Catholic agitators and were even transmitted into the battle-cry: "Rome must be judged and sentenced" or "After Vienna—Rome" (meaning: a fight against Rome must follow the fight against Vienna).

The result of this campaign was a wave of apostasy. 1,388,000 Czechs abandoned the Catholic faith in a little less than three years of post-revolutionary tumults.

The campaign, although patently supported by non-Catholic Churches, namely the Protestant and the newly founded national Czechoslovak Church, was led in the name of historic maxims rather than in that of religious regeneration.

Yet the hope of these Churches that they would divert the seceding stream within their banks, did not materialize, particularly where the Lutherans were concerned. All in all, their gains amounted to 3.7%.

2. *Social and Political Catholicism in Bohemia, Moravia and Slovakia*

Following World War I the Czech nation found itself at the crossroads. For centuries two traditions had been at war with each other in that part of Europe. The tradition of St. Wenceslas and of Cyril and Methodius opposed the tradition of Hus, Žižka and Comenius; Catholicism and Reformation; Christian universalism and spiritual and social union of the Christian West, against national individualism and Christian anarchism. The Czech nation has often purported to be a Hussite nation. Catholicism was said to be not firmly rooted in the Czech mind. Membership in the Catholic Church was termed mere formal relation, lacking deeper significance, being allegedly a residue of historic events and the consequence of the forcible re-Catholicizing of the Bohemian lands. It was opined that once the Czech nation would have become independent, culturally and politically, and so able to unfold its true character in every respect, it would discard Catholicism as outdated.

In the regenerated state, the Czech people, while enjoying its full share of national independence, made its choice. With

post-war nationalism at its peak and revolutionary embroil-
ments rampant, all was conducive to a parting ways with Catholicism. The door to anti-Catholic agitation stood wide open.
No obstacle prevented the Czech nation from turning away
from the Catholic past which, according to liberal historians,
was enforced upon it, having been added to the national body
as an alien graft.

And yet, the Czech people did not part ways with Catholicism. On the contrary: the past mass-apostasy rather regenerated and strengthened Catholicism. Like a tree, freed from
dessicated branches, Czech Catholicism flowered in new splen-
dour, rid of both formal members and the layer of conservatism
and officiousness of a foreign regime. It knew a profound inner
rebirth, a true regeneration. Catholic tradition proved an inherent part of the national character. The amazing strength of
Catholicism, capable of coping with the problems of modern
times and burning social issues, became manifest.

Czech Catholicism was able to muster a modern fighting
front, for defense and conquest. Catholic societies, cultural organizations, physical training groups and trade unions, and
most of all the political movement, assumed an all-important
role. The democratic form of government makes a competition
of all viable forces possible, and compelled the Catholics to
strive in the political arena—be it on the basis of creed or yet
on a wider basis—for a Christian trend in government policies.

The modern Catholic political movement in the Czech
lands grew out of an ancient tradition. Already in the fifties of
the past century, numerous Catholic priests laid the foundations of Political Catholic movements that later were organized. In Bohemia, Canonicus Stulc of Vyšehrad, and in Moravia
Canonicus Sušil, became the forerunners of these endeavours.
Canonicus Stulc participated zealously in public life. He was
jailed for his activity. He opened the Slavic Convention in
Prague, in 1848, founded the Catholic Union, and in the six-
ties started to publish a political tabloid. Bishop Brynych of
Hradec Kralové also did splendid pioneer work—he was a patriotic Church dignitary, hailing from poor people. His motto,
coined for his priests, ran: "Against an association, another association; against the press, another press." He eagerly organized Catholic societies, wrote articles and espoused every effort
of priests or laymen for erecting defense positions designed to
stem the pressure of anti-Catholic advance.

Workers' organizations were of great significance. As early as
in the fifties of the past century, the first Catholic Workers'
organizations, opposing socialist materialism, were set up. Here

the example of German artisan associations, created following the efforts of the Bishops Ketteler, Adolf Kolping and others, was vital.

Also at that time, the first Catholic gymnastic associations sprang into being; at the beginning of our century, they grew into a unified athletic organization, called the OREL.

All these Catholics, building up defense organizations and associations, be they political or non-political, and particularly creating Workers' organizations, drew a mighty incentive and encouragement from the Encyclical of Pope Leo XIII, in particular from the Workers' Encyclical, *Rerum Novarum,* of 1891. Shortly afterward, in 1894, the first convention of Catholic workers was held in Litomysl, Bohemia, and the Christian-Social political movement of Bohemia was inaugurated under the leadership of J. Horský, D.D., editor Jiroušek and Václav Myslivec, later Deputy in Parliament.

In Moravia, the young Catholic chaplain Jan Šrámek, formed and founded the Christian-Social party, having been very active in organizing Christian Workers Trade Unions before. At that time, a strong national Catholic party already has been in existence in Moravia, led by Dr. Hruban, an attorney. However, it was very conservative, based on the past, and loyal to the Austrian regime.

The results of the ardent organizational work of Czech Catholics became especially apparent following the introduction of the general and equal suffrage in Austrian lands, in 1907. The Catholic parties of the Czech lands won 17 mandates to the Reichs Parliament in Vienna. Later, however, in the 1911 elections, they lost this representation to the joint socialist-agrarian coalition, despite the fact that they preserved their number of votes. That experience inaugurated the uncompromising standpoint henceforth assumed by the Czech Catholics of the political movement, in favor of the system of proportionate representation instead of the plurality system.

Lack of leaders of stature, lack of lay inteligentsia, and most of all the deep party splits, affected the political movement of the Czech Catholics adversely in that period. In 1912, for instance, there were in existence, besides the two aforementioned Moravian parties, five different Catholic parties in Bohemia alone. An atmosphere of futile bickering and quarrels pervaded all issues. At last, in 1916, a young priest, named Bohumil Stašek, having made a supreme effort succeeded in uniting these Czech parties in fact, and in 1919 they were formally united under the name of the People's Party.

A parallel process toward concentration took place in Moravia, following the year 1918, Hruban's National Catholic party uniting with Šrámek's Christian-Social party. Šrámek won the leadership in the unified Moravian party. Czechoslovak post-war political Catholicism found in him the sorely needed leader. Henceforth, the evolution of Czechoslovak political Catholicism of that period was firmly linked to his name. Jan Šrámek was born on August 5, 1870, in the tiny Moravian village of Grygov. While a young theologian and priest, he subscribed to the so-called Catholic Literary Modern Movement; later, he embraced a scientific career. He was the first Professor to teach Christian sociology in Austria-Hungary, at the Seminary of Brno. Under the influence of the *Rerum Novarum,* he turned his interest toward organising Christian workers in trade unions and in the political movement. He was only 29, when he founded his Christian-Social party. Šrámek's mental make-up predestined him for his future role in the democratic state. He sought a rapprochement of Catholicism with the democratic and social aims of his time.

Working as a priest in a nationally mixed Czecho-German region influenced deeply his potent nationalism. His patriotic feeling and his efforts to bring about social reforms, caused his secession from Vienna. This culminated at the Party Convention of May 1918, where he made his movement join the unilateral front, opposing Vienna to make common cause with the other Czech parties.

When the overthrow came, Šrámek became a member of the National Committee which took the administration of the nations's affairs into its hands. When, in 1919, the Czech and Moravian People's Party merged, Šrámek was elected chairman of this all-state political party. The deputies of that party founded a common Parliamentary group with those of the Slovak Catholic People's Party (the Hlinka Party). This unified political movement of Czechoslovak Catholicism faced a tremendous task: to stem the onrush of post-revolutionary anti-Catholic pressure and to steer the mass of Czech and Slovak Catholics into new political and social conditions.

Czechoslovak political Catholicism acquitted itself admirably of the task, and the purposeful, self-restrained tactics of its leader contributed very largely to the success. These tactics were entirely in keeping with Šrámek's character. The sturdy priest and politician never was an ostentatious fighter, much rather a man of shrewd and considered strategy. He repudiated pomp and the loud acclaim of the masses. He is not a people's tribune, nor a rousing orator. He was rather laconic, but persevering and stubborn. He was calm and patient, knew how to bide his time, to wait for the propitious moment which would warrant intervention. He knew he could not be hazardous with his forces, could not stake his cause on a single card.

Many wrongs were inflicted on Sramek. In the revolutionary National Assembly, his party was accorded a much smaller number of mandates than were owed to it. Both government and Parliament were at once hostile and scornful toward him. He knew personal slights. He had to witness attacks upon the Church and unjustified accusations of priests and laymen.

Yet, his patience and his calm weathered everything, until he achieved satisfaction. Maneuvering deftly, he repulsed the initial pressure, and during the subsequent development of the Republic, he was able to ensure unquestioned successes for Czechoslovak Catholicism. He achieved a maximum with a minimum of forces.

It is Šrámek's indisputable merit that Czech Catholicism was capable of adapting itself to the republican and democratic regime. He was devoted to the cause of democracy and republic. He provided the Catholic leadership in discovering a creative policy in novel political conditions that were potentially very dangerous.

Šrámek succeeded in preventing the enactment of the law of Separation of Church from State, despite it having been one of the aims of the resistance movement in exile, and the program of almost every Czechoslovak socialist and liberal party. He succeeded in maintaining the equivalence of Church matrimony and civilian matrimony; owing to him, school reforms were put through with much greater restraint than originally intended. Catholic interest was largely heeded upon stipulation of Holidays and Commemorative days.

All anti-Catholic attacks, every pressure in Parliament, press or in discussions, were met by the Catholics with enhanced efforts in organization and work. The dismantling of the column of the Virgin at Prague's Old City Square had repercuussions in the remotest hamlets, in that hundreds of new chapters of the People's Party were established. The first elections to the National Assembly in 1920, marked a significant success for the Catholic political movement. The united ticket of the Czechoslovak People's Party (Sramek) and the Slovak People's Party (Hlinka), brought the election of 33 deputies.

Gradually, the Catholics became a decisive component of the nation, an indispensable partner in almost all coalition governments of the independent state.[15]

The combined organizational successes of the party and the outstanding leadership of Sramek were helped by concurrent circumstances, notably by the regard for Slovakia and the international standing of the Republic. In Slovakia, Catholicism developed in a substantially different way than that in the Czech lands. By the Austro-Hungarian settlement of 1867, establishing legalistic dualism, Slovakia fell to Hungary, while the Bohemian lands remaind in the Austrian domain. The Budapest government exercised stiff Magyarization of all non-Magyar nations, and Slovakia, in particular, suffered at the hands of this ruthless policy. The national oppression went concomitantly with an anti-Catholic policy assumed by the Hungarian government. In consequence, there was no discrepancy between religious conviction and national endeavors in Slovakia. In the fight against Magyar oppression, the Catholic priest Andrei Hlinka distinguished himself greatly. His patriotic activity led to his imprisonment; later, even prior to the liberation, he became the leader of Catholic Slovaks. After Austria-Hungary had disintegrated, Hlinka declared himself for the common state of Czechs and Slovaks, considering it the best mode for satisfying Slovak national aspirations. Unfortunately, difficulties soon arose. The policy of the Prague government was very often at variance with Slovak religious feelings; discords multiplied owing to the tactless demeanor of Czechs, who had come to Slovakia in official capacity. At first, close cooperation was maintained between Hlinka's People's Party and the Czech People's Party; it was manifested by the common Club of deputies and the join candidacy ticket for the elections in the year 1920. Later, however, the government having not adhered to its promise of erecting several Catholic Colleges in Slovakia, Hlinka's Party left the Club in protest and Hlinka's and Sramek's parties parted ways—to the detriment of the common Catholic cause and that of the state. Subsequently, many attempts were made to restore the cooperation, especially following the pressure exercised by the Czech wing of the Party, led by Msgr. Stasek, but the abyss dividing the parties was never again bridged. The reasons were manifold. As mentioned above, Slovak Catholicism had other problems to contend with than Czech Catholicism. The Slovak People's Party was more a national party than it was Catholic. Its main political goal was the widest possible autonomy for Slovakia. The Party sought to attain that goal in joining the opposition and in the end even some of its leaders cooperated with unreliable elements, hostile to the Czechoslovak state.

The Slovak Catholic party was not solely responsible for this state of affairs. The shortsighted attitude of some political parties, which dreaded the combined strength of the allied

Catholic forces, contributed substantially. The Czechoslovak Social Democratic Party for instance, following the elections of 1929, stipulated as its condition that it would join the government coalition only after the Slovak People's Party would have left the preceding non-socialist government. That was the only time when the People's Party had joined the government coalition.

Once more, on occasion of President Benes' election in 1935, the Slovak People's Party, led by Dr. Tiso, joined the ranks of Czechoslovak parties, yet again, the promises made to it having not been honored, it decided conclusively to follow opposition tactics.[16]

The third leading personality in the Czechoslovak political Catholic movement was Monsignor Bohumil Stašek. Even as a young Chaplain he worked in politics and was elected Secretary General and later Chairman of the Czechoslovak People's Party in Bohemia. Stašek combined Šrámek's deliberation and Hlinka's ability to influence the masses. He was a rousing orator and an untiring organizer. His efforts toward achievement of closest cooperation between the Czech and Slovak People's Partiers were sincere. In 1935, at the time of the all-state Catholic convention, his endeavors seemed successful. But the international situation, influenced by the neighboring Hitler Germany, intervened adversely even in Czechoslovak internal matters and Stašek's exertions remained vain. It is characteristic for Stašek to have sought a new, modern action program for the Catholic political movement. Particularly following the issuance of the Encyclical *Quadragesimo Anno,* did Stasek realize the imperative need for a new attitude to be assumed by both Catholics and the Catholic parties toward social and economic problems. He felt that defensive tactics of pre-war Christian-Social European parties, including the Czechoslovak People's Party, would never do the trick permanently. These tactics, being a natural outcome of the missions and positions of Catholic political movements in the first decades following *Rerum Novarum,* were no longer valid in Czechoslovakia after the Czechoslovak state had been established. Even before the war, Stasek and the Czech wing of the People's Party had arrived at a postulate which, now termed Christian Democracy, is characteristic of European post-war Christian parties: it entails the necessity to "de-doctrinise" the Party and endow it with a new social and economic action program, emanating from the new problematics, introducing simultaneously new organizational methods and assuming new tactics, self-relying and aggressive. Monsignor Stašek was one of the great figures of the Czechoslovak pre-World War II Parliament. Following Czechoslovakia's occupation by the Nazis he was arrested for his immutable patriotism and brought to Dachau concentration camp, where he spent almost six years. He returned, his health broken and one eye gone. He avoided post-war political life and died shortly after the Communist putsch, in August 1948, in Prague.

The vicissitudes of other leading personalities of the Czechoslovak political Catholicism were also interesting. Monsignor Andrej Hlinka, the undisputed leader of Slovak Catholics, did not live to see the years of 1938 and 1939 when his successors first obtained an autonomy for Slovakia—as a consequence of Munich, and then the separate existence for Slovakia as a consequence of the Nazi dismemberment of the Czechoslovak State, in March 1939. It is and will remain a matter of lively debate what would have been the reaction of Monsignor Hlinka toward a Slovak State which was created in his name but with the help of Adolph Hitler and Herman Goering. Today the work and memory of Hlinka are claimed by opposing factions in the Slovak Catholic camp. Some claim that Monsignor Hlinka was in favor of the Slovak National independence whatever its cost and whoever its sponsor. Others claim, however, that Monsignor Hlinka who died in 1937, advised from his deathbed his associates to strive for autonomous status of Slovakia within the framework of the Czechoslovak State and prevent at the same time the Czechoslovak State from being dismembered.

Monsignor Jan Šrámek succeeded in the Summer of 1939 in escaping from Nazi occupied Czechoslovakia via Poland to France and later to England. The escape of the 69 year old prelate became almost a legend. In disguise, hidden under the coal of a freight car, Jan Šrámek succeeded in slipping through the Gestapo on the Czech-Polish border. Together with his close associate, Father Frantisek Hála, Secretary General of the People's Party in Moravia, he succeeded in reaching Cracow. Msgr. Šrámek participated actively in the organization of the Czechoslovak Liberation Movement abroad as soon as he had reached Paris. In France he was greatly assisted in his efforts by Cardinal Verdier, Archbishop of Paris, who was familiar with all aspects of the Czechoslovak political life. Another help came from the traditionally pro-Czechoslovak French Catholics grouped mainly around the Catholic daily "L'Aube." Among them figured two intimate friends of Jan Šrámek's: Georges Bidault, then a young Catholic journalist; and Francisque Gay, who became in 1945 Vice-Premier of France and later Ambassador of France in Canada.

Monsignor Šrámek finally succeeded in obtaining a formal recognition for the Czechoslovak National Committee in Paris (he was its acting vice chairman) during his negotiations with the Under-Secretary of State, M. Champetier de Ribes, another prominent French Christian Democratic leader. Šrámek's diplomatic triumph, however, did not last long. In June 1940 France collapsed. Msgr. Šrámek barely escaped with his life. On a British destroyer he made his way out of the already besieged Bordeaux to England. The British Government recognized Sramek's National Committee as a Provisional Government of Czechoslovakia. Msgr. Šrámek became its Prime Minister and remained in this position for five consecutive years. One can only express regret that partly under Soviet and Communist pressure and partly under the spell cast over the Czechoslovaks by the victories of the Red Army, many Czechoslovak socialist and liberal leaders found it more appropriate to have the Czechoslovak Government on the liberated territory led by a fellow traveller and socialist Zdeněk Fierlinger, rather than by a Catholic priest and a great Czech patriot.

The five years of Šrámek's premiership offer, however, a striking contrast to the situation in the first World War. The first Czechoslovak Liberation Movement in 1914 started with Hussite slogans. The liberation of Czechoslovakia in 1918 was marked by an anti-Catholic manifestation which culminated in the overthrow of the Column of the Virgin on the Old Town square in Prague. Twenty years later when the exiled Czechs and Slovaks obtained an official recognition of their liberation efforts by Great Britain and later by all United Nations, they chose Msgr. Šrámek to lead their Government in exile. The contrast between the anti-Catholic trend of the Liberation movement in 1914-1918 and Monsignor Šrámek's premiership in 1939 to 1945 illustrate the distance which the Czechs and Slovaks covered in those 20 years.

A socialist speaker at the 75th birthday of Šrámek made the following significant comment concerning Šrámek's role in these 20 years of his country's history: "Šrámek has not only reconciled his nation with the Church but also he made it again an inseparable part of the Czech life. Figuratively speaking Šrámek *renationalized* the Church."

Msgr. Sramek remained the leader of the Party and the vice-premier of Czechoslovakia until the Communist Putsch of 1948. Three weeks after the Putsch this great political leader of Czechoslovakia made another attempt to escape the totalitarian domination of his country and to continue abroad the fight for its liberation. Šrámek, who succeeded in escaping from the Nazi dominated Czechoslovakia to Poland in 1939 and again in 1940 to make his way out of the Nazi-besieged Bordeaux to England, failed this time to deceive the totalitarian police. In March 1948 a French airplane appeared above an abandoned airstrip in Western Bohemia to pick up the 78 year old Msgr. Šrámek and bring him into safety. The plane was supposed to repeat an operation which was made many times during the Second World War over ocupied France in connection with the underground activities of the "Maquis." The Communist police intervened in the last moment and prevented Msgr. Šrámek from boarding the plane. The old man was put in prison and later, because of his age, he was transferred to a prison-monastery.

*   *   *

Let us go back again. We have said that the tenacious struggle of the People's Party for preservation of Catholic positions in the new state achieved success not only in Parliament and government, also in the field of organization. The elections of 1920 were a victory for the Party and those of 1925, even more so; the Party then was third among Czechoslovak political parties.[17] During the Coalition of non-Socialist Parties—1925-1929 —Msgr. Šrámek served as Vice Prime Minister and during Svehla's illness, lasting two years, as acting Vice Premier. The internal political situation was far from serene: postwar cultural struggles then had not been overcome, when, in 1925, a serious crisis with the Vatican intervened. The Czechoslovak government assumed the sponsorship of the celebrations for Jan Hus. They then had an ostensibly anti-Catholic character. The current Papal Nunzio Marmaggi left Prague in protest and a breaking-off of diplomatic relations with the Vatican threatened. Šrámek, assisted by Dr. Beneš, then Foreign Minister, succeeded in averting the breach and shortly afterward, in 1927, an important agreement, a kind of Concordat, the so-called *modus vivendi,* was concluded between Czechoslovakia and the Vatican. This *modus vivendi* solved all controversial questions, in particular the right of nominating Bishops, the boundaries of the dioceses and others. After that, the relations between the Czechoslovak state and the Vatican remained correct and even friendly. When, in 1935, a grandiose Catholic convention was held in Prague, assembling vast numbers of Czech, Slovak, Ukranian, German, Polish and Hungarian Catholics, the Vatican sent its Legate to Prague, in the person of

Cardinal Verdier, thus manifesting the conclusive reconciliation between the Holy See and the Czechoslovak state. The Convention, co-sponsored by the Czechoslovak government, demonstrated outwardly the fact that religious evolution had brought to an end the cultural anti-Catholic fight but also led to the ever greater participation of Catholics and Catholicism in the life of the nation. The Convention was an eminent testimony of the growing national consolidation, evidenced by the participation of hundreds of thousands of persons from every national minority of pre-war Czechoslovakia.

The spiritual life of Catholicism also deepened and waxed. In some religious Orders, notably the Jesuit and Dominican, significant activity in the field of publishing and studies was concentrated. More and more Catholic intelligentsia graduated from Czechoslovak Grammar schools, Colleges and Universities and acquitted itself excellently in all walks of national life: politics, science, the arts and economy.

It is worth noting that the spiritual and marked successes of Czechoslovak Catholicism brought a decline of its political movement. The 1929 and the 1935 elections marked considerable losses of votes, the causes being both internal and external. Internally, the causes lay in that the Party as a whole, persevered in the tactics, methods and organizational practice as were proven and unavoidable in post-war years (World War I) but had become obsolete in the thirties. Externally, the decline of votes lay partly in that the Catholics no longer felt the imperative necessity of casting their votes uniquely for the People's Party, since the danger of cultural conflict had vanished almost entirely. Moreover, some other parties abandoned, in theory and practice, the former liberal and incidentally anti-Catholic course.

Undoubtedly this trend would have forced, sooner or later, the People's Party to revise its program and tactics; but the racing impact of international affairs preceding World War II, in which Czechoslovakia was the focus, precluded its evolution.

It may be stressed, however, that the program of the Christian Democracy in Czechoslovakia followed the socially progressive trend of its French and Belgian counterparts rather than the conservative aims of other political European movements inspired by Christian ideology. Msgr. Šrámek addressing the Youth congress of his Party on Whitsun in 1947 used the following slogan: "Freedom without bread cannot satisfy us any more than bread with shackles." This slogan—not sufficiently expressive—indicates, however, the basic attitude of the Czechoslovak Christian Democracy which attacks both extreme in-

dividualism and totalitarian Marxism. This refusal to choose
between freedom without economic justice on one hand and
economic equality without liberty on the other, significantly
characterizes the program of the Czechoslovak People's Party.
It makes a parallel movement to that of the French Christian
Democrats whose Secretary General, Albert Gortais, once remarked: "Mankind refuses to let itself be confronted by a false
dilemma, because if capitalistic liberalism has only given us a
caricature of liberty, communism represents only a false liberation." The dictatorship of money was in Gortais' words succeeded by the less hypocritical but more absolute dictatorship of
the Marxist state.

The Czechoslovak Christian Democrats aimed clearly at a
balance between the Western emphasis on political freedom
and Eastern stress on social and economic equality.

When the National Assembly met for the first time in liberated Czechoslovakia—in November 1945—a curious attempt to
link the motto of the French Revolution with the Christian
Democratic program appeared in the first speech delivered by a
Catholic deputy on the floor: "The slogan of the French revolution 'Freedom, Equality and Fraternity' still expresses the unfulfilled human desires and aims of today. While the West,
stressing the ideal of liberty, has often neglected the ideal of
economic equality, the East places its emphasis on material
equality at the expense of liberty. This seeming conflict between freedom and equality could and should be overcome
by putting into practice the often forgotten third part of the
French revolutionary motto 'Fraternity.' Without the Christian
concept of neighborly love—which prevents a man from denying his brother the free exercise of his civil and economic rights
—the concepts of freedom and equality may remain resounding
terms emptied of their contents."

The Christian ideas of social solidarity shaped the Party's
program with respect to private and collective property.
Staunch advocates of private property, the Czechoslovak Christian Democrats developed, however, a positive attitude toward
a collective ownership in those cases in which the continuance
of private ownership of means of production would be at variance with the common good. In accordance with the Christian
democratic doctrine which claims a protection for social groups,
such as family, municipality, trade unions and cooperatives,
intellectual groups within the Czechoslovak People's Party
started several economic and social studies on the subject of the
pluralistic conception of collective property: they advocated
municipal, cooperative and regional ownership of certain means

of production (gas, electricity, hydroelectric plants, sugar factories, breweries, etc.) and in a very few cases State ownership. It opposed radically the *total* transfer of the means of production to the state. This program not unlike certain aspects of the program of the English Fabian socialists was, however, in line with the Christian democratic pluralistic conception of life and recognition of freedom in political, educational, religious as well as in the economic sphere.

When in 1946 the Youth of the Christian Democratic Party published the first number of its new weekly, it expressed its agreement with the French interpretation of the rise of European Christian Democracy by quoting in its editorial Albert Gortais' statement: "The Christian Democratic Movement was born of the conjunction of two decisive factors of our national life—on the one hand an old spiritual current attached to the values issuing from Christian civilization, freedom, justice, fraternity, and respect for the individual; on the other hand, the intense longing for liberation and renovation felt by a people struggling against an inhuman regime imposed by force".

The Czecholslovak Christian Democratic leaders were often inspired by the work and thinking of their French political counterparts, the MRP. This was partly the result of the continued friendship and cooperation between the leaders of the French and Czechoslovak Movements, Prime Minister of France and Minister of Foreign Affairs Georges Bidault on one hand and Vice-Premier of Czechoslovakia Msgr. Jan Šrámek on the other. To some extent it was also a byproduct of the Czechoslovak People's Party conception of international policy of Czechoslovakia. The Czechoslovak Christian Democratic Party endeavored since 1945 to balance the one-track pro-Soviet orientation of the Czecholslovak foreign policy as based on the Czechoslovak-Soviet Alliance Treaty of 1943 by a possible link with the European West, i.e. France. These efforts failed, however, although the Christian Democratic leaders made a last minute effort in the fall of 1947 and went to Paris on a goodwill mission to ask Georges Bidault, then French Foreign Minister, to make a new effort to bridge all differences as to the contents of a new Alliance Treaty between France and Czechoslovakia. The Soviet and Communist opposition to the Treaty —combined with a lack of understanding for the Czechoslovak need of balance manifested in some right wing as well as left wing quarters in France—frustrated this effort of the Czechoslovak People's Party in the field of foreign policy.

The brief period of the People's Party life in the years 1945-

1948, viz. until the Communist putsch, did not conclusively disclose whether the Party had reached the level of other modern West European Christian Democratic movements; however, within the Party, the rebirth was on the march, particular owing to the pressure of the young elements. The events of 1948 forestalled the maturing of these new trends. However, the circumstance that the Party did have and still has outstanding groups of new leaders and an excellent cadre of youth—as was demonstrated at the convention of young Catholics at Whitsun of 1947—prove that the Christian Democratic Movement in Czechoslovakia may expect, following the liberation from the Communist regime, a great expansion and important place in the Nation's political life.

The subsequent conflict between the Communist state and the Catholic Church adds, however, a new element to our analysis as to the future possibilities of the Christian Democratic Political Party in Czechoslovakia. In the person of the heroic archbishop of Prague and Primate of Bohemia, Dr. Josef Beran, not only all Catholics but even religiously indifferent Czechoslovak democrats found a symbol of their fight for human dignity and against the communist totalitarianism.

While in 1918 the Czechoslovak fight against a foreign oppressor was often waged under the banner of Protestant revolt against German-speaking Catholic Vienna, the present struggle against the Soviet and Czechoslovak Communism develops under the impact of the most inspiring example which the Catholic Church and its hierarchy gave to the Czech and Slovak peoples. Under this impact many formerly indifferent Czech and Slovak Catholics experienced a rebirth and deepening of their faith. Non-Catholic democrats saw their fight against Communism closely allied with that of the Catholic bishops. The fight for national, individual and religious freedom became one. It is possible that some Czechs and Slovaks will return to religious indifference if and when the present pressure is gone. We cannot be blind to the fact that many people think of God only when in a desperate need of divine protection.

Nevertheless it can be safely assumed that the Catholic example, and thus also the idea itself, will have a profound impact on all Czechs and Slovaks who strived for national and individual freedom. The question, however, must be asked whether it will mean an added vigor only to a reborn Christian Democratic Political Party; or will it mean rather a strong urge to place the program of the Christian Renovation above the political parties and their struggles and entrust the Catholics in *all* political parties with the defense and execution of such a noble program.

Whatever will be the future development of the respective roles of the Church and the Christian Political Movement, Catholicism in Czechoslovakia may anticipate a glorious future.

At the beginning of our chapter we quoted a historian of the Czech renascence. His words "barring the Czech clergy, the Czech revival would never have achieved the swift progress it. . . ." apply in our opinion to the new situation in Czechoslovakia today. The stand of the Church and its bishops in the darkest hours of the Czech and Slovak peoples has been and will remain an inspiration to courage and a source of hope. This guiding role and example of the Church could have hardly been expressed in more moving words than in the last pastoral letter of Archbishop Beran. It is a letter issued by the Archbishop and all bishops of Bohemia, Moravia and Slovakia on June 26, 1949. This letter which reviewed the conflict between Christianity and freedom on one hand and atheistic Communism and dictatorship on the other, went beyond the confines of a pastoral letter. It defined the position of spiritual leadership of the Church in the present struggle against the totalitarian State by its dignity, by its firmness toward Communism, by great humility in sight of God and deep love for the Czechoslovak people. The pastoral letter which follows immediately and which concludes this chapter represents, we are sure, a document which will be quoted again and again when a new and brighter chapter is opened in the history of Christian Czechoslovakia.

"In these overwhelmingly serious times of our religious and national life we turn to you with this letter of the right-teaching church.

"Love for the nation and for the people of Czechoslovakia leads us to speak in these decisive days, in which we have become witnesses to attacks on the unity and leadership of the Catholic Church here. To know where the truth and right and your place in the church and nation are, hear the voice of your pastors who, being conscious of responsibility before God and the conscience of the whole world, after deliberate consideration cannot remain quiet.

"Having no other possibility of presenting our case, we are endeavoring to do so, as our conscience bids us, by this pastoral letter, imploring God that the voice of the pastors reaches your hearing and that it be heard with credence, and be rightly comprehended.

"We know well how many rights you have been deprived of, just as you are acquainted with the adversities that the church has had to go through lately.

"We have always been aware of the burden of responsibility for the saving of our souls before God. We have always endeavored and we still endeavor today, even if only with small hopes of success, to defend and ensure the sacred rights of you Christians as free citizens of the state, as is naturally demanded by God's order.

"To these humanitarian and commonly recognized rights of man belong not only the freedom of privately held religious convictions and the freedom to execute religious rites, but also the free realization of the principles of this faith as the norm of life of individuals and society—and this without fear of losing personal freedom, civic equality and the endangering of the rights of existence.

"Look around you. Follow what is happening and you will easily come to the conclusion that the Catholic Church in Czechoslovakia has received a very bitter reward for its hundreds of years of service to the nation, for its cultural and charitable activity, for its loyalty to the people, for its fearlessness and suffering during the (German) occupation.

"It stands here today—robbed, deprived of the majority of its freedoms and rights, dishonored, soiled, persecuted secretly and openly.

"Ask yourselves this question, dear Catholics:

"Could we Bishops be satisfied with all this and accept every demand that is in defiance of the laws of God and humanity?

"Could we approve, before our faithful people and before the whole world, every development, even if it was not in accordance with the spirit of the teachings of Jesus Christ?

"Indeed, with gladness we shall render unto Caesar the things which are Caesar's but it would not be possible to sacrifice to him that which is God's *because it behooves us better to obey God than man.*"

J. Pecháček

NOTES

[1] Palacký, Frantisek: Dějiny národu českého v Čechách a na Moravě (History of the Czech nation in Bohemia and Moravia), Prague, 1876-1878 Tempski, 1941, Kvasnička a Hampl.

[2] Masaryk, Thomas G.: Česká otázka (The Czech Question), Prague, 1895, Cas. Capek, Karel: President Masaryk Tells His Story, London, 1934, Allen and Unwin.

[3] Aeneas Silvius, Piccolomini (Pius II.) Historia Bohemica.

[4] Novotný, Václav: Nábozenské hnutí české ve 14. a 15. stoleti. The Czech religious movements in the 14th and 15th centuries, Prague, 1915, J. Otto.

[5] Luetzow, Franz Heinrich: Bohemia—An Historical Sketch, London, 1909, Dent & Sons.

[6] Pekař, Josef: Dějiny československé, (The History of Czechoslovakia), Prague, 1921. Smysl českých dějin, (The idea of the Czech history) Prague, 1929.

Thomson, Samuel Harrison: Czechoslovakia in European History, Princeton, 1943, University Press.

Seton-Watson, Robert William: A History of the Czechs and Slovaks, London, 1943, Hutchinson.

[7] Čapek, Thomas: Bohemia under Hapsburg Misrule, New York, 1915, F. X. Revel Co.

[8] Named after Berhard Bolzano (1781-1848), a priest and a distinguished mathematician, who became professor of the philosophy of religion in the University of Prague in 1805. Though he remained a loyal Catholic, Bolzano was accused of treating theological subjects in a rationalist spirit and was dismissed from the University in 1820.

[9] Gallicanism—Theory maintaining that both the church and the state in France had ecclesiastical rights of their own, independent and exclusive of the Pope (second half of the 17th century).

[10] Josephinism—Anti-Church Policy of the Austrian Emperor Joseph II (1741-1790), the eldest son of Maria Theresa. This policy opposing the authority of the Pope within the Church of Austria and seeking to submit the clergy to lay authority led to secularization of church property and abolishment of several religious orders.

[11] Febronianism—Movement similar to Gallicanism, within the Catholic Church of Germany in the latter part of the 18th century. It aimed at a "nationalization" of the Church and advocated reunion of dissident churches with Catholic Christendom. The name is derived from the pseudonym of "Justinus Febronius", adopted by Johann Nikolaus von Hontheim, bishop of Trier and author of a book containing the basis of that doctrine.

[12] Masaryk, Thomas, G.: Modern Man and Religion, London, 1938, Allen & Unwin.

[13] Opočenský, Jan: The Collapse of the Austro-Hungarian Monarchy and the Rise of the Czechoslovak State, Prague, 1928, Orbis.

[14] Peroutka, Ferdinand: Budování státu I-IV, (The Making of a State), 1934-1936, Fr. Borový, Prague.

[15] Borovička, Josef: Ten Years of Czechoslovak Politics, Prague, 1929, Orbis.

[16] Seton-Watson, Robert, William: Slovakia then and now, London, 1931, Allen & Unwin.

[17] Chmelař, Josef: Political Parties in Czechoslovakia, Prague, 1926, Orbis.

CHAPTER III

THE DEVELOPMENT OF CATHOLICISM IN HUNGARY IN MODERN TIMES

In 1000 A.D., the first Christian sovereign of Hungary, Stephen (István) , received the Crown—emblem of the kingdom of Hungary—from Pope Sylvester II. By the fact that her first King asked the crown from the Pope, Hungary determined the future course of her development. She joined the Western Christian civilization and separated from the Eastern nomadic and half-nomadic form of life, which she still had followed in her new territory in the Danube Valley. The adoption of Christianity and of the Christian civilization was not so difficult for the Hungarians settled in the Danube Basin as the journalism and literature of the last decades, inclined to neo-paganism, liked to represent. The patriarchal monotheism and its form of cult, the shamanism, proved fertile soil to the *anima naturaliter christiana*. Besides, the Hungarians even before the conquest of their present country had contacts with Byzantine Christianity and in their new country, through the conquered Slavs, with Western Christianity. Their connections with the Byzantine Church remained strong until the end of the twelfth century and stopped, most probably, as a consequence of the new religious wave in the thirteenth century. But not for a moment since the foundation of the Hungarian kingdom by Saint Stephen was the Byzantine Church a serious rival to the Roman Church.

From the political point of view, the union with Christendom did not meet with any particular difficulty. The heavy defeats in the second half of the tenth century encountered by the Hungarians venturing into western territories, had made Saint Stephen's heathen father, Prince Géza, recognize that the nomadic way of life had become untenable. This view was supported by the first Christian King himself, and by the other leaders of the Hungarian people who lived in a tribal organization loosely controlled by the power of the sovereign. The Hungarians came to know the institutions of a stable State and social organization through the Germans and the Slavs. In the East the dignity of a prince had always been of a high-priestly, charismatic character, which made it easier for Saint Stephen to establish the idea of government in the name of King Christ, an idea which received strong impulses through direct contacts with the saintly leaders of the Reform of Cluny.

The adoption of Western civilization, of its social and political order, was facilitated by the fact that already Saint Stephen succeeded in thwarting the attempts coming from the west to subjugate Hungary. The real propagators of Western Christian civilization were not so much the western magnates, knights, craftsmen, and merchants taken in by Saint Stephen and his successors, but the German, Slav, and Italian priests and missionaries. Important as was the role of Otto III, German-Roman Emperor, the dreamer of a Catholic world-empire, in the sending of the Crown, the very fact that the Hungarians have ignored it from the beginning proves that to Hungary the Crown has always been the symbol of her independence from every foreign power and, at the same time, of the deep connection between the secular power and the Church. It has become such a sacred symbol as has never been paralleled by crown or coronation in any country. To express it succintly, the Crown embodies to the Hungarian nation the idea of "Christian freedom," an idea of such rich and manifold historical implications as cannot be discussed within the scope of this paper.

The initial act of the foundation of the kingdom united the State-power with the Church. The close connection between the two powers which in Hungary was more intense than in the West and survived, to a certain extent, the Ages of Enlightenment and of Liberalism, brought about many happy results, though, especially in the most recent period of history, became as well the source of grave problems.

Hungary, owing to her geographical position, was the axis of collision not only between the Western and Eastern forms of life, between heathen nomadism (which later on was to make repeated and terrible aggressions on the country) and Christian culture, political and social organization, but also was the most western territory exposed to the influence of the Orthodox Church on the one hand, and of the Greek Catholic and United Greek Oriental Churches (which acknowledged the supremacy of the Holy See) on the other. By the same token, she became the farthest eastern territory affected by Protestantism. These three great groups of Christendom met on her soil.

In the sixteenth century when another terrible heathen power, the Osmanli Turks, invaded the country with longer lasting effects than had any of the nomadic invasions, the majority of the Hungarian people became Protestant. Protestantism gained an important majority in the independent principality of Transylvania which, however, could not entirely escape the feudal supremacy of the Turks, as well as in the part of Hungary occupied by the Turks. But Protestantism spread strongly also in the northern and western part of the country ruled by the Habsburg German-Roman emperors. Due to the influence of the trend particular to Hungarian history which brought into close relationship the power of the State with that of the Church, the Habsburgs, main support of the Catholic Church in Central Europe, became the defenders of the Catholic faith and the adversaries of Protestantism in Hungary. The protection of the Catholic faith was so closely associated with the royal power that the nationalist opposition to the foreign power, which was organized in the counties, proclaimed itself the defender and representative of Protestantism. Consequently, the anti-Habsburg nationalist movements were always more or less Protestant in character, although both among their leaders and adherents a great many Catholics were to be found.

In the seventeenth century the division of Catholics and Protestants was about equal. This proportion however, due to the support of the ruling power, increased in favor of the Catholics, though without diminishing the importance of the Protestant minority. Nor did the Orthodox Church ever cease to exercise a strong influence on the alien nationality groups living in Hungary, namely the Rumanians, Serbs, etc., although conversion to the United Greek Oriental and Greek Catholic Churches, that acknowledged the supremacy of the Holy See, made great progress under the protection of the Habsburg monarchs.

With the triumph of Renaissance the Churches gradually lost their cultural leadership in the Western world. Civilization became more and more secular. This tendency had less strength in Hungary. Cultural leadership was, in the eighteenth century, in the hands of the Churches, especially in that of the Catholic Church. Education in schools of every grade, to the first decades of the nineteenth century, was almost exclusively ecclesiastic. The growth of the lay schools, in which religious instruction was obligatory till 1948, really began only after the defeat in the War of Liberty of 1848-49; and not until 1948, when Hungary has been completely taken over by the Communists, could laic schools occupy the exclusive position in education.

The influence of the Enlightenment made itself felt with growing strength since the middle of the eighteenth century. However, the conflict between the forces of the Enlightenment and the Churches never became quite as violent as it did in most of the Western European countries. On the contrary, the Catholic clergy, particularly the teaching orders, played a role in the propagation of the ideas of the Enlightenment. The most active was the Piarist order which occupied a leading position in the field of Catholic education in high schools and junior colleges during the eighteenth and nineteenth centuries, after the Jesuits had been weakened by the absolutist attack. There are several reasons which made the Piarists, and an important part of the clergy in general, adherents and propagators of the Enlightenment: the new interpretation of the natural sciences that established a close relationship between the idea of organism and the divine planning; the growing national consciousness, the contribution of which to the laicization of the ensemble of European views has been greater than is generally acknowledged; finally, the new appreciation of human dignity and an awakening criticism against the established order. The Piarists were the first to introduce in Hungary the doctrines of Newton, Leibnitz, and Wolff. In their new syllabus set up in 1757, they gave primary importance to the teaching of the natural sciences and of the national history. True to the new humanitarian spirit, they founded the first agricultural school in Hungary. The spirit of Enlightenment won in the only university (at that time) of the country, the University of Nagyszombat, under the direction of the Jesuits, which soon was to move to the cultural center of the country: Pest-Buda.

At the same time there was a growing hostility to religion in the ruling class, the aristocracy. The causes of this phenomenon are also manifold: the growing strength of nationalism as an active and militant philosophy was a determining factor (and we leave open the question whether the decline of religious faith strengthened the development of nationalism, or vice versa?). Another factor was the widening gulf between the leading nobility and the still deeply religious lower classes. Continuous intercourse with Protestants also facilitated indifference toward religious practice, which never had the same importance to Protestants as to Catholics.

Blasphemy became fashionable in the salons of the aristocracy as well as collecting anticlerical, atheistic, or deistic books. Freemasonry became a society and culture-forming power in the centers of the Hungarian country life. As the Church, especially the higher clergy, was one of the pillars of the existing conservative social system, the new humanism became more and more hostile to the Churches. The faith was shaken and in its place nationalism grew into religion. This development was indirectly strengthened by the close relationship between the Habsburgs and the Catholic Church which added an anticlerical tone to the anti-Habsburg nobility.

With the reign of Joseph II, the Enlightenment conquered the Throne. The law of nature was to turn, on the level of the principal power, against its own source: the Catholic Church. In 1785, Joseph II ordered the Hungarian Crown to be transported to Vienna justifying his act of breaking with the traditions of history by the law of nature. His attitude served only to inflame the national consciousness.

The new enlightened despotism claimed the right to extend its rule over the religious sphere, to subordinate or to make it part of the mechanism of the State. The secular power did not intend to annihilate the Churches or the religious faith; it only subordinated them to its worldly ends and viewpoints, the *raison d'état*, and tried to incorporate the clerical system into its own bureaucracy. While thus supporting the Church, it undermined her internally. Josephinism, named after Joseph II, while protecting the Church, cut off her from her supernatural roots. This tendency became manifest in the effort to separate entirely the Hungarian Church from the Pope. Joseph II abolished the majority of the religious orders, which in their very existence proclaim the unity and autonomy of the Church and confiscated their immense properties. His task was partly caused, partly facilitated, by the moral decline of monastic life.

Joseph II's measures had as consequence the union of the forces of the nationalist and religious resistance. At length, this resistance organized by the nobility proved victorious and Joseph II, on his death-bed, withdrew all his decress, with the exception of those guaranteeing complete freedom to the Protestant sects, improving the situation of the clergymen, and alleviating the lot of the serfs.

The surrender of Joseph II, however, did not mean the defeat of Josephinism. Both the nationalist movement and the reigning absolutism subordinated religion to nationalism and to the interest of the State respectively. The influence of Josephinism in its essentials prevailed in fact up to the end of World War I, actually even beyond that, so as to be made use of even by Bolshevism. The Josephinist spirit has continued its effect not only in the outward position of the Church, but in her inner laicization, in the weakness of the spiritual and the transcendental which has characterized the religious life of the nineteenth and twentieth centuries. This was the price then of the intimate relationship with the secular power at a time when that power has become already entirely self-sufficient.

Frightened by the events of the French Revolution, the privileged ruling classes of the nation continued to cling to the Josephinist spirit and turned away from the liberal ideas which were conquering the Western world. The social humanism fell into oblivion and all that remained was Enlightenment centered on their own class interest abhorring all social changes of national inspiration, coupled with a Josephinist ecclesiastical spirit. The Prince Primate, the archbishops and bishops of Hungary mantained their outstanding civil importance, a result of the close relationship between the State power and the Church. However, their civil role was used more in the interest of the existing order than that of religion. This Josephinist atmosphere was favorable to the primitive materialism which was spread by the revolutionary propaganda.

Act XXVI of 1790, guaranteed the free exercise of religion and granted freedom to the serfs. But the leading classes were opposed to all social reforms, thus forcing the reform movements underground.

Another manifestation of the Josephinist spirit was the willingness of the monarchs to employ priests in their service for espionage. Such services were performed, for a certain period, by the Abbot Ignác Martinovics, a former Franciscan monk. Later, this restless man with a tormented soul became the leader of an underground movement which set for itself the task to propagate the ideas of the French Revolution. On May 20, 1795, he was·executed together with several of his companions. The disclosure of his movement caused the monarch, the privileged classes, and the representatives of the Church to be even more afraid of the liberal ideas. This fear of the revolutionary ideas finally led the ruling classes to turn away from the West. This was the first appearance of the ideology of the "guilty West" which since has turned up every now and then in the doctrines of groups otherwise diametrically opposed. The idealized concept of the high morality of the Hungarian ancestors was opposed to the pretended Western depravation. The emient monk-historians of the time, the Jesuit György Pray and István Katona, and the Benedictine Benedek Virág, played an outstanding part in the idealization and glorification of the virtues and morals of the Hungarian past. This fitted into the pattern of withdrawal from the Western ideas and from reforms in general and with the religious indifference which gained even among the clergy.

The education of the clergy was directed by the State, and the supernatural ends were supplanted by the goal of making good citizens. Up to the middle of the nineteenth century the Pope and the Holy See had hardly any contact with the Hungarian Church which became, in a sense, aulic-autonomous, or a national institution to the detriment of her Catholic characteristics. Two types of priest developed: the country priest, or on higher rank the dean or canon, who shared the worries, interests, and patriotic endeavors of the gentry and the priest-teacher who saw his duty as the training of the young generation of the ruling classes with factual knowledge and gentleman-like behavior but hardly occupied himself with the formation of their religious life. Not much was gained, from this point of view, when Emperor and King Francis, in 1802, restored the Benedictine, Cistercian, and Premonstrant orders which had been abolished by Joseph II.

The main reason for this sad state of affairs was that the entirely laicized State authority considered the Church as in the service of its own ends, as an integral part of its own organization. The State assigned to the Church some kind of a supervisory function over society and accordingly, it regulated all the phases of her activities, as it did any other office of its huge organization. The Hungarian Governing Council prescribed even the length of the sermons; prohibited the publication of the resolutions adopted by the national synod assembled in Esztergom, residence of the Primates of Hungary, in 1822. Religious orders were forbidden to keep in contact with their superiors in Rome. The Emperor-King designated bishops without consulting the Pope. The reception of the sacraments became rare among the nobility. The religious practice of an average individual—especially in the case of a man who occupied a position in public life—usually consisted of his being baptised, married in church, the baptism of his children, and his funeral according to the church ceremony. He would go to Mass only on feasts and on the occasion of State festivities. Serious, practicing faith—which existed in spite of all—was looked upon as some kind of abnormality. To think of religion and of final things and especially to talk or write of them was a lack of good manners. This attitude found its expression in the literature of the time.

The cult of the sacraments became rare also in the lower classes of the population including the serfs. The cause was not the lack of piety of the people, but the lack of interest of the majority of the clergy in the spiritual needs of the lower classes. There was a trend manifest among the clergy to abandon its spiritual mission, which had produced such happy results in the seventeenth century and in the first decades of the eighteenth. The strong belief, which remained Catholic in its form, of the simple people did not waver but it became like a pond with rich vegetation, around which the mud rose so high as to cut it off from the vital stream of the spiritual life of the Church.

As the Church did not give sufficient attention to the serfs, the much wronged section of the nation, they created for themselves an independent religious life: to them the supernatural life meant consolation for their sufferings in this world but their priests failed to give them this comfort. The people's piety centered on shrines before which the oppressed and humiliated serfs felt themselves transported into a purer and happier sphere of existence.

The *bourgeoisie* of the towns led a truly intense religious life. This section of the nation had hardly any influence, political or cultural, as yet, the less so because its majority consisted of alien nationalities, mostly German. The strongly emotional religiousness with *biedermeyer* and romantic touches of the Catholic *bourgeoisie* had its great merit in maintaining the cultural role of religion at a time when the other classes of society did not, or could not, care for it. In this atmosphere religion lost much of its cultural and intellectual importance.

Probably under the impact of this spiritual and social vacuum, some exceptional personalities found the way back to the true mission and fundamental meaning of the Church. These men were imbued with the ideals of Catholic humanism which took its inspiration from the example of the saints. One of them was a descendant of an old aristocratic family, which in the course of the centuries gave many a prelate to the Church, Count Fereno Széchenyi. He was the first in the aristocratic circles to break away from the social convention that it did not become a magnate to be a practicing Catholic. His son, István Széchenyi—the most outstanding figure of the modern history of Hungary who has been rightly named "the greatest Hungarian"—led from his early youth a religious life of sincere devotion. In his thinking, in his works, literary and practical, the Christian ethics occupy a central position. From his Catholic mentality grew his basic conviction: the people has to be liberated first culturally, socially, and economically in order to make good use of political freedom. He opposed the nationalism of the nobility, which identified the interest of its own class with that of the nation and which considered patriotism their only obligation in this world and the next. Széchenyi's Catholic humanism recognized the supreme test of religion and patriotism in the right solution of the condition of the serfs. He was the advocate of a Catholicism truly universal, and his liberalism meant that each individual was chosen for redemption by Christ. He believed in the obligation of society and its leaders to every human person. The nation raised Széchenyi to a pedestal, but failed to follow his universal Catholic humanism.

In the 'thirties of the last century, the reformers resumed
their fight with renewed strength for the liberation of the serfs
and for the introduction of the rights of liberty. The young
generation of the nobility firmly believed in the necessity of the
reforms and their opposition to the absolutist authority exercised by the State was growing.

The liberalism of the reformers was in no conflict with a
positive supernatural interpretation in the Catholic spirit. The
Catholic and romantic liberalism which fights for the rights of
liberty and for the oppressed, had a deep influence on the young
aristocrats, and it became the creed of the two great geniuses of
the time: the poet Mihály Vörösmarty; the novelist, thinker,
and statesman József Eötvös. The romantic Catholicism of
this generation remained indifferent to the Catholic ultra-
conservatism of a De Maistre and to other similar philosophies
which had great appeal abroad. The influence of the revolutionary Catholicism of Lamennais was far stronger. *Christian
liberty*—this idea became full of deep significance for them.

The revolutions in Paris and Vienna in 1848, filled the young
reform generation with enthusiasm. The liberal movement in
Hungary set itself the task to realize both the rights of liberty
and the nationalist goals. They also believed that these could
be attained by parliamentary procedure.

In this crisis the liberation of the serfs was accomplished. The
ruling class displayed wise moderation when, in order to prevent the aggravation of the conflict, it voluntarily resigned its
privileges. No doubt, the Christian humanism which held in its
spell many of the reform generation had a great part in the
attitude they adopted. But the selfishness of the great majority
prevented this great achievement, the liberation of the serfs, to
be carried out in the spirit of Christian humanity through the
concession of the minimum land which would have assured the
livelihood of the liberated peasant. Still, for the first time and
in a critical period, all the social classes were united in the
nation.

The clergy renounced without compensation the tithes which
were due to the Church from serfdom. But, the immense
landed property of the Church, the estates of the bishop, chapters, and religious orders, remained intact.

The Constitution of April 1848 did not terminate the close
relation between the Church and the State. Led by the peculiar
logic of history, liberalism, especially its antireligious or indifferent wing, thought it advisable for the new liberal and nationalist State to retain its control over the Catholic Church to
which adhered the majority of the Hungarian people. The

maintenance of the prerogatives of lay patronage assured a free scope of action to the State.

According to the Acts of April 1848, ecclesiastical and educational institutions of the acknowledged religions were to be provided for by the civil authority. This was logical since the Church as the most important cultural and welfare organization, maintained the great majority of schools and a good part of the charitable institutions. The provisions of the law also show that the overwhelming majority of the reform generation, which was looking for a solution through peaceful agreements and reforms, wished to preserve intact the leading role of the Churches—and especially of the Catholic Church—in the field of education and of culture in general.

The suppression of the Vienna revolution, the rebellion of the nationality groups, secretly encouraged by the Court of Vienna itself and directed by the high clergy of the Orthodox Church, decided the Court of Vienna to break with the reform policy, to refuse the recognition of the nationalist efforts. Rather it decided to suppress the Hungarian liberal movement. The result was that the reform movement assumed more and more the character of a revolution under the leadership of Lajos Kossuth. This great popular leader and other partisans of the revolution showed less understanding toward the Catholic Church than the adherents of the peaceful solution.

The War of Liberty broke out under the leadership of Kossuth. The Catholic clergy found itself in a difficult position. The lower clergy in great number joined the war with enthusiasm. The high clergy hesitated: they saw in the continuance of the reign of the Habsburg dynasty a guaranty of the Catholic character of Hungary; also they had to consider that with the outbreak of the revolution the elements intolerant and hostile to the Church had become preponderant. But beyond and above contemporary considerations, those men who were imbued with Catholic culture and whose mentality was determined by their Catholic faith have always been partisans of evolution, moderation, and restraint. That is why István Széchenyi, the great leader of the reform generation, was plunged into a deep and insurmountable spiritual crisis by the outbreak of the War of Liberty. Nor was it by accident that after the Age of Absolutism which had followed the defeat of the War of Liberty, until absolutism in its turn was defeated by world events, it was the devoted Catholic Ferenc Deák who concluded the *Ausgleich* between Hungary and the Habsburg dynasty.

Many a Catholic priest fell victim to the reign of terror which followed the defeat—due to the armed intervention of Czar

Nicholas I—of the War of Liberty. However, the position of the Catholic Church underwent no substantial change during the two decades of absolutism. The Hapsburgs, while oppressing the nationalist idea and the rights of liberty, nevertheless recognized certain achievements of the reform movement, namely the liberation of the serfs and the reform of education.

The Catholic Ferenc Deák, who has become to the nation the symbol of wise moderation ("the Sage of the Nation") obtained the recognition of the Acts of 1848, though at the sacrifice—to a certain extent—of the national independence. The *Ausgleich* of 1867 became the new foundation of the existence of Hungary. The fundamental principles of liberalism were realized. But the basic social problems of the population remained unsolved in the period following the agreement. The big landowners retained their dominant position in politics and economics. More than half of the agricultural population was reduced to live on 5.7% of the country's total arable area.

On June 8, 1867, Emperor Francis-Joseph received the Crown from the Archbishop of Esztergom, Prince Primate János Simor of humble origin, the holder of the nation's highest civil dignity, and the Prime Minister, Count Gyula Andrássy. This act demonstrated the unchanged civil importance of the Catholic Church. The great Minister of Education of the "age of agreement," József Eötvös, was an outstanding figure of that romantic and liberal Catholicism which united in harmony the demands of universal humanity with the belief in the supernatural mission of man. On the other hand, the country gentry, Protestant in majority, began to acquire dominating influence in the government of the country. Kálman Tisza was a characteristic leader from among their ranks. The gentry became the directing political force in the liberal era, which lasted until the outbreak of World War. I. They endeavored to lessen the political and cultural influence of the Catholic Church. Their fight to legalize civil marriage, that is to bring marriage under State control, became a symbol of their laicizing efforts. Essentially it was a fight against the privileged position of the Catholic Church. This hostility was a combination of Protestant and liberal components .These politically influential factors saw in the Church "a State within the State." They demanded the expropriation of the ecclesiastical lands and protested against the pedagogic influence of the Church. They attacked with especial vehemence clerical celibacy which they recognized as a source of the independence of the Church. For similar reason they objected strongly to the dogma of the papal infallibility. (The latter was actually opposed by some of the spiritual leaders of Hungarian

Catholicism, but they submitted unconditionally when the dogma had been promulgated.) Their particular enemies were the Jesuits, whom they termed the enemies of all culture, "the knights of darkness." Thus the tolerance of the great liberal generations was supplanted by open anticlericalism.

If we want to analyze the anti-Church attitude of that sector of the nation which was active in politics, the social factors should not be overlooked. As one of the reasons of the great anticlerical fight in France at the turn of the century was the reluctance of the ruling middle class to grant social reforms and its consequent intention to keep alive the fight against the Church, likewise in Hungary the anticlerical attitude was based on profound opposition to social reforms and the effort to ease the tension through the channel of anticlericalism.

In the Francis-Joseph era the Church was both the prisoner and the privileged ward of the State. The enemies of the Church, more or less unconsciously and in spite of their preference, did not wish to end the exceptional position enjoyed by the Church, because they feared that it would lead to the collapse of the existing social and economic structure. But the new State authority which spread the privileges of the Church out of self-interest, was entirely lay, basically anticlerical, mostly in the hands of men who had no understanding of the supernatural.

Already around the 'seventies, an aristocrat of the Conservative Party, György Apponyi, attempted the foundation of a Catholic Party and started a Catholic periodical in the German language. The higher clergy did not approve of his efforts; not without reason, they feared that the creation of a Catholic party would draw the Church into the whirlpool of daily politics and that secular elements would gain direct influence over the affairs of the Church.

In 1894-95, after bitter fights, the so-called Church policy bills were codified, which made civil marriage obligatory and regulated the religion of children from a mixed marriage on a parity basis. This was the last step needed to make freedom of religion complete. As it has often happened in the history of the Church, the Catholic spirit emerged from this political defeat stronger than before. Catholic consciousness developed a new intensity. The deep sympathy for the defense of the Catholic cause created an atmosphere of reconciliation among the social classes. On the initiative of Count Nándor Zichy opportunity was sought for the Catholic public opinion to express itself on a social scale. In 1894, the first Catholic congress was held in Budapest.

In 1895, Nándor Zichy founded the Catholic Popular Party,

This was the first appearance of a Catholic party in the political arena and for the first time a Catholic body openly included social objectives in its platform. Also it was the first political party seated in the Parliament of the liberal era to give a prominent place to social issues in its programm. The Catholic Popular Party demanded the fixing of minimum wages, the regulation by law of the relationship between labor and employer and the creation of cooperatives in defense of the small consumers. The Popular Party was soon to relax its social program. Its energy—like that of the other political parties—was used up in the so-called struggle for civil rights, that is for certain nationalist achievements in opposition to the all-Monarchy government. But it maintained its popular character and consequently was exposed to electoral terrorism from the side of the successive governments and leading political parties. The father of the future Cardinal Mindszenty, a village farmer, proved his courage against such intimidation.

During the years between the *Ausgleich* and World War I, in an atmosphere of peaceful evolution Hungarian society preserved its liberal character which ensured to the well-to-do a carefree living comparable only to that enjoyed in England. Capitalists founded banks, built factories, created important industrial concerns, and developed the communication system of the country, in complete freedom from the ranking social classes, essentially the four thousand big landowner families. The necessity for social reforms was ignored by most of them and there was no interest in the problems of the peasantry, representing 60% of the country's total population. The *bourgeoisie,* which had a mosaic-like structure and did not yet develop into a strong and uniform social sector, was impressed by the mode of living of the middle landowners and regarded it as its ideal. Interest in politics dominated the intellectuals to the detriment of religion.

The Catholic Church in Hungary succeeded in reestablishing her connections with Rome. It can be stated as a fact that all the reform endeavors within the Church—the search for a more sincere devotion to religious ideas, the recognition of the Christian character of the obligations toward society,—took their inspiration from contacts with, or experience, in Rome. It can be said without exaggeration that the Hungarian Catholic Church grew in devotion and renewed herself—after a long period of slackness and indifference—in proportion to the intensity of her relations with the Holy See.

The monarch continued to exercise his patronage which gave him almost sovereign influence on the selection of the prelates.

The Catholic religion ceased to be the official religion but was under the direction of the State, a basically non-Catholic State. The leaders of the Hungarian Church were selected, in the name of the King, often by an anti-Catholic government or ministry, the main object being that the candidate should not be openly "clerical," "pro-Roman," but sympathetic with the existing ideal of society. Episcopal appointments were often given in compensation for political merits. The patriotic and freely-spending bishop was the prelatial ideal and the majority of the high dignitaries lived up to it. They were hardly in the position to influence the religious multitudes. The government used its influence in school affairs to prevent Catholic education from becoming "clerical" in spirit. It was mainly due to this influence that the moral education suffered while stress was laid on academic instruction. In 1867, the year of the *Ausgleich*, 95.4% of the students attended ecclesiastical schools; in 1908, only 75.2%. Primary schools remained almost exclusively in the hands of ecclesiastics and only after World War I did the state or public schools become serious rivals. Education on high-school and university level was gradually lost to the Church.

The intellectuals (in whose ranks beside the gentry and the scanty *bourgeoisie* of Hungarian origin, Jews and Germans assumed growing importance) regarded practicing religion as a manifestation of "the people's ignorant bigotry" and could not fathom that religious faith may have central importance to an individual belonging to the middle classes. In the literature, prose, drama, or poetry, of the years around 1900 the treatment of religion as a problem of life is completely eliminated.

Before the nineteenth century was over, due to the gradual loosening of the patriarchal system and the lack of new social measures, the conditions of the peasantry grew worse and the first peasant movements began to take shape. Another consequence was emigration on a large scale. In 1898, 270,000 emigrant left the country. Land reform was envisaged only from one aspect: some political groups demanded the dissolution of the ecclesiastical landed estates and they did not stop to consider that while the Church estates contributed to many a public task neglected by the State, similar contribution by the secular big landowners was minimal.

Religious literature was very small in volume in this period. The activity of the Catholic clergy was more important in the field of worldly sciences; in history and related doctrines their work has been essential (György Fejér, Nándor Knauz Vilmos Fraknói, János Karácsony, Remig Békefi, Antal Pór, etc.). The tranquility of their conditions of life enabled scholars in the clergy to pursue their researches undisturbed. On the other hand, the principles of the historical appreciation of the Hungarian past were laid down by lay scholars often strangers to religion. It is characteristic that researches on the old Hungarian heathen practices were mostly done by members of the Catholic clergy. The work of Bishop Arnold Ipolyi was fundamental in this field.

Beside literature of instructive character, serious religious literature of high level was practically non-existant. Catholic fiction written for the large groups of the population was produced in a kind of "Catholic Ghetto" cut off from the live stream of literature. Good Catholic popular writers like István Domonkos, depicter of village life, were practically ignored by literary circles.

József Eötvös, the great organizer of the Hungarian public education, alone elaborated a deep philosophical view. His great historico-philosophical work based on the principles of Catholic humanism foretold the collapse of the liberal era and the coming of inhuman terrorism—but it found no echo in its time.

Baron József Eötvös was the first eminent political personality who demanded autonomy for the Catholic Church and the abolishment of the control of the State. In 1875, a congress on Catholic autonomy convened. Its task, however, was so little in keeping with the prevailing public feeling that it was doomed to failure. Even the majority of the bishops refused to support its aims unwilling to jeopardize their economic resources by displeasing the secular power.

The first anti-Semitic movements were simultaneous with the growth of capitalism and that of the small *bourgeoisie*. The affair of Tiszaeszlár in 1883, raised a scandal which was commented on abroad. An anti-Semitic party was founded but it failed to rally public opinion or the liberal leaders of the political life, and even less the peasantry which has always opposed anti-Semitism.

In the years around 1900, factory labor had begun to assume importance. Before World War I they represented, together with their dependents, 5% of the population. Labor leaders at that time were vehemently antireligious. They looked upon the Church as the obstacle to all social progress and they were unable to differentiate between religion and the position of the Church in the contemporary society. The great majority of labor, which lived without the traditions of the peasantry, became irreligious. Labor missions had not yet been considered.

The highest tension in the country was created by the issue

of the national minorities. The law on the nationalities—work of the two great Catholic statesmen: Ferenc Deák and József Eötvös—promulgated after 1867, was the most tolerant of its kind in Europe. It was inspired by the principles of Christian-liberal humanism and constituted a break with imperialistic policy. The gravity of the question lay in the fact that about half of the population consisted of different nationalities. The intellectuals of the national minorities with growing self-consciousness claimed either the transformation of the Monarchy into a federation of the various nationalities, or wanted to join foreign countries of related nationality. The aggravation of the situation was caused by the abuses of the local authorities which disregarded the humanistic laws. On the whole the peasant masses belonging to minority nationalities were neither better off, nor worse than the Hungarian peasantry.

Minority Church and educational affairs were entirely autonomous and it would seem, they suffered less State interference than the Hungarian Church.

In that time, the Catholic clergy of the minorities maintained closer contacts with the lower social classes than did a good portion of the Hungarian Catholic clergy. This followed, to a certain extent, from their attitude of opposition to the Hungarians and to their leading strata. Both the United Greek Oriental and the Orthodox Greek Churches became the center of those cultural endeavors of the minorities which exercised a strong influence on their movements for political independence. Thus the parish priest Hlinka among the Slovaks, and Stadler, Archbishop of Zagreb, among the Croats were the leaders of the anti-Hungarian independence movements. The Rumanian independence movement was in close connection with Lueger, Mayor of Vienna and the popular leader of the Austrian Catholics, to whom Hungarians were but "Protestant rebels."

In the years preceding World War I, the tension created by the rapid progress of capitalism, the decline of the gentry, and the unsolved social problems, found an outlet in an anti-monarchical Hungarian independence movement. An important portion of the Catholic clergy supported the movement. Under the coalition government, the program of which contained the realization of certain nationalist claims against the interest of the Habsburg dynasty, there were several priest-members of Parliament. The political fight which absorbed all his energies prevented an Albert Apponyi, a statesman so consciously Catholic, to concentrate his efforts on the realization of an ideological program.

If we take into consideration the inherent rules which seem

to govern the Catholic Church and her life, it is not strange to see the first signs of an intense Catholic renewal at a time when seemingly carefree, life-enjoying materialism, metaphysical indifference, and lack of interest in social progress created an atmosphere so unfavorable to the Catholic idea. An extraordinarily gifted young priest of ascetic life, studying in Rome, Ottokár Prohászka, realized the human and social gulf which lay beneath the smooth surface of the era and he saw the only way out in the fulfilment of the Christian command in its ultimate consequences. Just as József Eötvos a generation earlier, Ottokar Prohászka discovered that the liberal optimism which reigned on the surface did not solve the tormenting problems of the human mind and of society. Prohászka, imbued with the spirit of Christ, understood both the individual and collective suffering and his knowledge made him an ardent, restless apostle; he even had to see a couple of his early, searching literary works placed on the *Index Prohibitorum*.

This apostolic restlesness made of Prohászka the initiator of a spiritual Catholicism which aimed at the liberation of the souls from their worldy bondage, the first true genius, since the Counter-Reformation, of Hungarian Catholic literature and theology, and the advocate of a radical solution, in a Christ-like spirit, of the social problems. Spiritualist, creative writer, and social reformer: these basic elements of his personality were united in perfect harmony. On June 10, 1882, the young priest on his way back to his native country, made a vow at the tomb of Saint Francis of Assisi never to forget the poor and the small.

A few quotations from his writings will throw light at the importance of his apostolic initiative, but also the distance which separated him from his contemporaries.

"These poor of the modern age are bitter, dissatisfied people. And the one who has to sink into the bitter worries of livelihood can hardly save strength in his soul for something else, or nerve in his heart for something different. Let us try to speak to such a man of the love of God and the value of the soul; he does not even react to our words. Consider the poor craftsmen with big families who often earn not more than 30 *krajcár** a day, and take these people to the Sunday sermons. The priest may speak from the depth of his heart, and yet will not he see them leave at the most moving part of his speech? Why? Because their soul was not present even while they were there.

"The souls are in the grip of the terrible struggle for life! We must not be surprised that everything disturbs him, everything is nauseating and insufferable that does not speak to him of his great interest, the burden of which almost makes him lose his mind. The Gospel with its resignation and themes of suffering seems an empty shadow which helps the miserable in no way, and merely wastes his time and adds to the confusion in his poor head. Let us try to put ourselves in their position, and then there will descend before our eyes the thick veil of anxiety, which obscures all that the Church preaches of faith and salvation.

"But if under such circumstances the clergy indulges in apathetic idleness, is not this a proof of their not understanding the age and of having no interest in the misery of the people? And when this social disturbance will take on such proportions as to sweep away ethics and theology, faith and religion, and all this before the eyes of society, will the clergy have any business, interest, or task more important than to prove with all its strength and love, influence and power that it is the truest friend and the safest protector of the people? Should it fail to accomplish this, its very right to existence will be at stake before the society of the future.

"These are severe words, but I would that they hit where men are asleep, dreaming of old times." (January 1, 1900)

"The church should descend from her civil summits, from the safety of her traditional prosperity to the people struggling in the economic and social tides of the age, the people struggling at the very bottom. The people, this great body of the nation, must feel: 'They love me!' The people do not find the practical connection between its want, troubles and struggle for life—and religion. The preachers speak to it of things which do not touch its crown of thorns; they do not speak of what is on its mind: of how much injustice, how much oppression it has to suffer. Do we move this millstone of burden? Faith and words do not seem to feel these troubles and therefore the people do not understand either this faith or these words and their eyes are cast down. The peasant strives, suffocates,—the people carries the burden and suffers: has Christianity no paragraph for the protection of the poor? What does not protect it, what does not even heed its miserable situation, what does not even mention its struggles and worries, the people will never pay attention to that." (1895)

"But when speaking of Christian view of life, of Christian social order, of the Will of God, of the right then above all and always it has to be emphasized—this modern poverty is crime and injustice, it is unlawful, and not the Will of God.

"Give us priests who identify themselves with the people, the poor; whose interests lie with those of the poor; who through their apostolic life leave no room for doubt in the heart of the poor so that they can exclaim unanimously: 'These men are for us!' " (1897)

"What is the task that falls to the Church in this democratic progress of the nations? Her task is to stand by the rising mutitude wholeheartedly. The Church, as a spiritual power, is the partisan of progress; the direction of the progress lies in the democratization of culture, of political and economic development. She must not cast away anybody; but she has to understand history, she must be able to read the signs of the times." (October 9, 1898)

And decades later, nearing his death, he wrote:

"We profess the sanctity of private property, but not of all: we reject the frightful usurpation of the plutocracy, the right to accumulation endangering public welfare. Private ownership in capitalism assumed such proportions as to stifle life and to concentrate the wealth of the world in the hands of a few. There is no right, no sanctity to this; the sanctity of private property does not cover such action. It is out of question to cast away the principle; the question is that of limits within which the principle can be carried out so as not to jeopardize the even higher principle, the existence of millions." (1926)

These quotations are one-sided and do not reflect Prohászka's personality and work in all their richness. The spiritual and literary picture of Prohászka is not complete without those purely spiritual workes of his in which the religious experience is revealed in the Hungarian language, for the first time after a very long period, clearly yet intimately, without following sterile patterns.

Prohászka, the writer, the preacher, the theologue, has been placed on a pedestal by the veneration which surrounded him from the beginning of his career. But often, the high esteem which is given to a person in his lifetime makes it easier for his contemporaries who so honor him to pass over the qualities which are disturbing to them. Thus the admiration for the living Prohászka as a writer and a theologian tried to ignore Prohászka, the friend of the weak, the social apostle. His contemporaries in the leading strata, ecclesiastical as well, tried with remarkable eagerness to pass this incomplete evaluation as the true picture of him.

In 1916, at the congress of the OMGE (National Hungarian Economic Association) the organism of the big and middle landowners, Prohászka demanded the expropriation of portions above 10,000 acres of the landed estates for distribution among veterans and returning emigrants. He stressed that he considered this measure as the first step only. His proposal had no effect, not even in the form of angry reaction, because the high esteem of which he was the object protected him from attacks.

The influence of an exceptional genius on his time is always complex. The world around Prohászka did not change, not even the life of the Hungarian Catholic Church. But it is not true either that his activity had a serious effect only on later generations and none on his contemporaries. He was truly a missionary within the Hungarian Catholic Church (the first since the saintly Minorite friar, Didák Kelemen, who lived at the beginning of the eighteenth century) and he had innumerable followers among the modest, anonymous priests of apostolic inspiration who worked hidden from publicity, and in their own restricted fields began to fill with spiritualism the life of their parish and built up gradually the spiritual and bodily care of the poor and unfortunate.

Parallel to the appearance of Prohászka, of great significance were the efforts made in the direction of an internal renewal of the religious orders. In this age of indifference when immanent optimism and nationalism seemed to take the place of religion, the monastic discipline lost much of its severity. This applied equally to the teaching orders (Benedictines, Cistercians, Premonstrants, Piarists) who possessed big lands, and the mendicant orders (Franciscans, Capuchins, Minorites, Dominicans, Servites, Carmelites). The teaching orders—in Hungary, the Jesuits had high schools, generally called gymnasia—were the educators of the sons of the leading social strata of the wealthy peasantry. Boys of peasant origin were encouraged to enter the clerical profession which along with the teacher's profession, offered the only chance to their elevation to the middle classes. The teaching orders obtained excellent results in the pedagogic field and they have outstanding merits in the education of Hungarian talent. Education of girls was in the hands of female religious orders throughout the country with the exception of Budapest. These orders assumed almost exclusive responsibilities also in the field of nursing.

The mendicant orders, especially the three Franciscan orders, had the most frequent contacts with the lower social classes. In the mind of the Hungarian people the concept of "monk" is identified with the Franciscans, who were surnamed "brethren." However, even among the mendicant orders the view was held that a monk should live in the style of the "good" middle classes. This view was obviously contrary to the monastic ideals and necessarily led to the slackening of discipline. On the initiative of a few truly great personalities and encouraged by Rome, a monastic reform movement started in the years preceding World War I. The fight, silent but persevering, between the partisans of the existing conditions and those of the monastic reform went on for more than two decades and ended with the latter's victory. The monastic orders, renewed in spirit, found resources of spiritual and social inspiration to undertake the care of the multitude as their Christian assignment. They founded Tertiary orders and pious societies which opened a new spiritual and social life to those living in abandonment, poverty, and unhappiness. They edited religious periodicals and books; organized home missions and retreats, kept up the shrines, etc.

The Jesuits played an exceptional part in developing a more devoted and more intense religious life and especially a Catholice self-consciousness which occasionally asserted itself in the political field. They were particularly popular with the middle class and small bourgeoisie of Budapest, the importance of which lay in the culturally, economically, and politically centralized position of this city as compared to the rest of the country. The Jesuits filled Catholicism with militant spirit in order to obtain victory for the Catholic cause over the hostile camp of a large leading cultural stratum mainly composed of Protestants, Jews, and Freemasons. A member of great talents of the Jesuit order, Béla Bangha, founded a Catholic press concern, created Catholic scientific periodicals and undertook the organization of the Catholic intellectuals through the creation of various societies. He became the leader of the successful missionary work aiming the conversion of the metropolitan Jews.

Also during the years preceding World War I, the first attempts were made to lead back to the Church the urban proletariat, the factory labor, whose political representation and social protection were exclusively in the hands of the then intensely anti-Church Social Democratic Party and its Trade-Unions.

The initiator of these endeavors were Sándor Giesswein, a priest of great culture and profound religiosity. Giesswein, in accordance with the principles of Prohászka, considered the return of the proletariat to the Church an action not just pious but calling for sacrifice. His social program, in which there was no room for resentment, went in its concrete demands even further than the Social Democrats. Giesswein's efforts failed because he was not backed by a dynamic organization which would have identified itself with, and fought for his ideas. No support was given by the Christian socialist movement which continued to exist and after World War I, when it became "fashionable" to be Christian, attained a certain influence. Unfortunately, instead of practical fight for spiritual and social achievements, it contented itself with echoing the popular slogans and was looked upon by labor as an organism instituted by the ruling classes to betray the objectives of labor. It became more and more shallow and could not establish itself as a serious factor in political life.

Sándor Giesswein, contrary to the current views, was led by the conviction that the Catholic Church was to lend her assistance to any movement which fought for the realization of humanitarian and social ideals even if those movements were hostile to the Church. He believed in the ultimate power of the Christian idea to conquer, by the universality of love, those opponents who unconsciously, in spite of their own views, were fighting actually for the Christian cause. But he was misunderstood by his adversaries as well as by his own side. The orthodox materialism and anti-Christianism of the leaders of the labor of his time prevented these leaders from considering an approach to personalities of Giesswein's type. The same applies to the contemporary *bourgeois* radicalism, the influence of which was confined to a relatively small group of intellectuals. There were among their ranks men of rich mind and of metaphysical responsiveness who felt the attraction of the Catholic idea, but the polarization caused by the antagonism of this group to the Church made understanding and cooperation impossible.

The endeavors to intensify religious life and to bring the Church and the broad strata of the people closer to each other, originating—under Roman influence—with the religious orders and the lower clergy, could not fail to have their effect on the leaders of the Church. The Prince Primates Kolos Vaszary and his successor, János Czernoch, apart from the civil attributes of their dignity, stood up for the issues affecting the Church with greater firmness than did their predecessors. Their authority which had sprung from civil and ecclesiastico-political sources, had begun to assume importance on a purely religious basis. Beside the current type of prelate a new one appeared, able to establish closer contacts with the lower clergy and the various strata of society, and to represent and propagate both the supernatural mission and the cultural functions of the Church in a more effective way. Agoston Fischer Colbrie, Bishop of Kassa, Gustáv Majláth, Bishop of Transylvania, and Gyula Glattfelder, Bishop of Csanád, are representative of this new prelatial type.

World War I made an end to the self-satisfied tranquility of the Francis Joseph era and with it disappeared the carefree materialism which held under its spell especially the ruling classes and a good portion of the intellectuals. Life has become, in every sense, insecure individually and collectively, and the ultimate questions, which had been banished by every possible means, took hold of minds with urgency. Religious and trans-

cendental problems for which there had been no room in literature, were treated by the elder and younger generations of
writers. Men and the young no longer considered going to
church as a sign of sentimental deficiency, though the intellectuals continued to oppose the actual practicing of a religion. In
a strange way, however, intellectual circles antagonistic to the
Church began, in their restlessness, to occupy themselves with
the problems of religion. This wave of religious interest met
with the greatest resistance from the leading political and economic stratum of society, which tried to ignore the social problems of growing urgency.

In 1918, the end of World War I brought about the collapse
of the Habsburg monarchy. Hungary once more became an
independent State. But she has paid a tremendous price for her
independence. She was allowed to retain out of her territory of
320,000 km only 93,000 km; out of her population of 21 million
souls only 7,620,000. Out of 9,900,000 Hungarians 3,603,333
fell under the authority of the foreign States which shared former Hungarian territory. In Hungary, within her new boundaries, only one important nationality group remained, the
Germans, who became a major issue to the Hungarian State
fifteen years later, when Hitler won in Germany.

The revolution of 1918, after an easy victory in the chaos
that followed the lost war, introduced the form of republic. As
no strong and united *bourgeoisie* existed, there was no social
sector capable of leadership to take the place of the former
ruling class which had disappeared, and to undertake the reorganization of the country and the solution of the grave political, economic, and social problems. In this chaos there was
but one well organized though small group: the underground
movement of the Communists formed in their majority of war
prisoners returning from Russia. This chain of events was similar to some extent to that which, after the collapse of National
Socialism, gave such power into the hands of the Communists
in France and Italy. In Hungary at that time, however, the lost
war and the following chaos made easier the Communist seizure
of power. Geographical proximity to militant Bolshevism also
helped. Other factors in favor of the Communists were the lack
of understanding toward Hungary on the part of the Western
Powers and the hostility of the neighbor States which had acquired Hungarian territories.

The Communists seized power in Hungary in March, 1919.
In accordance with their well-known formula, they first forced
into alliance, then annihilated the progressive elements of the

Social Democratic Party. Communism appeared as the terror of a small group under the name of "Proletarian Dictatorship"; its terrorism struck the masses of peasantry with even greater vehemence than it did the middle classes. A few weeks were sufficient for the new regime to provoke the unanimous hatred of the whole population. This first Proletarian Dictatorship was in power only for about five months, and yet it had fatal consequences on the social and spiritual development of Hungary.

The relatively great number of those of Jewish origin among the leaders of the first Proletarian Dictatorship was one of the causes of the anti-Semitic wave in Hungary after the defeat of Communism by the forces of the counter-revolution. The horrors of the Communist regime gave a public legalization to anti-Semitism which up to that time, apart from short-lived outbreaks confined to small groups, had existed only in a hidden form, almost ashamed of itself. Since Bolshevism asserted itself under the pretext of the dictatorship of the proletariat, after its suppression public life was dominated by a strong feeling against the proletariat, which of course made it very difficult for the problems of the industrial labor and of the poor peasantry to be treated in an Evangelical spirit. Many people, under the impact of their experience of the revolution of October and of the Bolshevist regime which followed, confused in their minds democracy, socialism, and Bolshevism and rejected them all as "destructive ideas." The terroristic actions committed by the Bolshevists called for similar reactions, and never since that time could the nation be entirely free from the atmosphere of hatred. Finally, as a result of the hostility to the Church of the Proletarian Dictatorship, the clergy seemed unable to approach the social ideas and needs of the time and the spirit of democracy with the necessary understanding. It has to be stated, however, that for this lack of understanding the new regime, rather than the clergy, was responsible, for while it called itself Christian, it tried to extend its more or less anti-social and anti-democratic influence over the Church. In 1919, the bishops were ready to make voluntarily heavy sacrifices in the interest of a land reform and again, in 1923, they offered a portion of the ecclesiastical landed estates for the same purpose. In both cases it was the government which prevented the proposals of the Church from being carried out, as it had previously opposed the initiative of Ottokár Prohászka, Bishop of Székesfehérvár, who following the Christian principle "to start with ourselves," wanted to begin the land reform on his own lands.

The "white terror," which defeated the "red terror," executed hundreds of innocent victims. If we want to understand the position of Catholicism in the new Hungary, we have to point out certain facts which determined the place of the Church in Hungary between the two world wars.

The doctrine of the counter-revolution was not anti-Christian as that of nazism or fascism. On the contrary, it started out as a Christian movement and emphasized its Christian character in every respect. Thus it followed that the Catholic Church remained a civil, political power. The new counter-revolutionary regime was more than willing to borrow legality from the authority of the Church. However, as an important portion of the governmental elements were Protestant and did they happen to be Catholic, their mentality and attitude were in most of the cases, remote from the Church,—it was actually the leading political social stratum which forestalled the success of Catholic principles in public life. It has to be borne in mind that the Catholic clergy formed that intellectual sector of the nation which almost in its entirety rose from the humble condition of the people. The three Prince Primates of the period, for instance, were Kolozs Vaszary, son of a tailor, János Csernoch, son of peasants of Slovak origin, Jusztinián Serédi, son of a tiler. On the other hand, the ecclesiastical landed estates, approximately 900,000 acres, were intact. The privileges pertaining to civil rights of the Church were maintained. Both of these circumstances necessarily raised the Church above the great mass of the people. The Prince Primate remained the holder of the first civil dignity in the country. The Catholic bishops, the provincials of the teaching orders, the provosts of the chapters, along with the high dignitaries of the other religions, were members of the Upper House of Parliament. Since Miklós Horthy, the Protestant head of the State, was not entitled to lay patronage, the Church, within her own domain, enjoyed greater liberty than in the time of the old Hungary. It was due to this circumstance that the connection between the Hungarian Catholic Church and the Holy See became closer and the intentions of Rome were more or less carried out.

With regard to the social position of the Catholics, a peculiarity arose from the structure of Hungarian society. The owners of the twenty biggest landed estates were Catholic. At the same time, the ratio of Catholics to the poor social strata, the smallfarmers, agricultural and industrial labor, casual laborers, was much higher than in the total population.

Another determining factor in the further development of Catholicism derived from the confluence of two tendencies springing from sources essentially different. One was the counter-revolutionary idea called forth by the anti-Bolshevism and taking shape in the period of the "white terror" that used Catholicism for a sign and standard; the other, the internal renewal of the Hungarian Catholic Church started by the endeavors of Proházka and his associates, who meant to transpose the Christian principles into the reality of life. The coincidence of these two ideas caused a great deal of confusion.

The curious, recurring paradox of the history of Catholicism by which persecution and oppression proved beneficial to the deepening and purification of religious life, prevailed once more in the church-life of the Hungarians detached from their mother-country. In states where the majority and, to a certain extent, the government itself were hostile or, at any rate, strangers to both Catholicism and the Hungarians, the common lot of minority status brought together the social classes and the clergy with the broad strata of the people. As in the past the cultural and social life of the minorities in Hungary had been organized by the Churches, so the Hungarians in minority status relied on the Churches for their cultural and social needs. Thus especially in the Upperlands under Czechoslovakian rule, where a significant portion of the annexed Hungarians was Catholic while the government was definitely laic, the profession and practice of the Catholic faith became intimately linked with the consciousness and open admission of their Hungarian origin—a modification, in the framework of minority status, of the historical relationship between the State and the Church. In the Upperlands and Transylvania, a great many Hungarians reduced to misery were provided for mainly by the ecclesiastic organizations. The task of developing a more spiritual and more social Church was undertaken in the territories annexed to Czechoslovakia by an enthusiastic group of young men, who inscribed the name of Proházka on their standard. Their excellent review, the "New Life," revealed with courage the mistakes of both the new State and the old Hungary. Miklós Pfeifer, Canon of Kassa, was the spiritual leader of the movement; Sára Salkház—her martyrdom will be discussed at a later point—and Luja Esterházy worked in the social field with self-sacrificing devotion. In Transylvania, annexed to Rumania, the bishops Gusztáv Majláth and, after him, Aron Marton were untiring apostles of the social care of the poor and of the defense of the liberty of the Church. Bishop Marton, unswerving before the terror, eventually became one of the martyrs of the Bolshevist religious persecution. The local Franciscans played an important part in the preservation of the Transylvanian Catholic life of the people. Their shrine of the Virgin at Csiksomlyo was the center of the religious life of the Hungarian Catholic peasantry.

In the spiritual and bodily care of the minority Hungarians both in Czechoslovakia and Rumania outstanding contributions were made by the Social Sisters, a religious order of Hungarian foundation, to which reference will be made.

The mutilated, independent Hungarian State was also called the Hungary of Trianon in view of the peace trety of Trianon, that fixed her new boundaries. Trianon meant to the Hungarians both the tearing away of Hungarian territories and population, and devision—the miraculous hope to regain them— became a symbol permeating the Hungarian life. The attitude of the leading social classes was determined by this peculiar "optimism of Trianon" which left no doubt as to the imminent realization of the revision but, simultaneously, did little in the interest of the detached Hungarians decreasing in number and reduced to poverty. In the past, their civil optimism prevented them from facing the cultural and social needs, and now this other kind of optimism exerted a similar effect. An important portion of society entertained no doubt as to the immediate end of all the troubles once revision became a reality and the old way of Hungarian life could be resumed where it had been interrupted.

The first Act of 1920, setting up the new constitution, provided the interruption and not the cessation of the royal power. On this basis Admiral Miklos Horthy was elected head of the State with the title of Regent. After the failure of Charles IV's return, however, the throne was declared vacant on November 5, 1921. This move was enforced under foreign pressure, but the Protestant elements of growing significance in the political life had also an important part in it. From this time on, the idea of the monarchy was pushed into the background. Its supporters were mostly the big landowner aristocrats and the movement was characterized by lack of social concern.

Summing up what was said above, there are two main factors which determined the position of Catholicism in the period following the "white terror":

The counter-revolutionary tendency covered up its racist and antidemocratic endeavors with Christian coloring.

Democracy became odious or, at least, suspicious to the entire leading stratum of society as a result of their confusing Communism with democracy.

These are the two reasons why the ideas of the Christian democracy, which in the beginning had a profound impact though confined to an *élite*, gradually lost their vigor.

Nothing is more characteristic of the situation than the fact that at the general elections the Canon Sándor Giesswein, pioneer of the Catholic labor movement and one of the fervent leaders of the Church reform endeavors, was defeated by the candidate of the official Christian party.

The internal contradictions resulting from the above situation explains why the Christian political power taking over after the collapse of the leftist movements was unable to make the best of its possibilities. Its positive achievements were relatively few.

After the first storms of the counter-revolution subsided, the Party of Christian Union emerged as the most powerful. Its first president was Ottokár Prohászka. In the confusion of political life, the saintly bishop and great apostle of the Hungarian Catholic renewal, was unable to vindicate his high principles, or to prevent the Christian policy from abandoning these principles one by one. The aging bishop did not succeed in making those pure principles, which he never failed to follow in his own life, the pivot of national policy. Shortly afterwards, he withdrew from political life.

The efforts of the new leading sector brought about the formation of one powerful party through the union of the majority of the Christian party with the prosperous farmers' Small Holders' Party of a strong Protestant coloring. This really meant the sterilization of both parties' original ideologies. In substance, Hungary was ruled by this unified party—under varying names—until the victory of nazism.

The unified party, similar to the governing parties before Trianon, became the bulwark of the existing conditions. Men who sustained the reform endeavors founded opposition parties. Thus came into being the Christian Social and Economic Party, and the new Small Holders' Party. In the activities of both an important part was played by Catholic priests and laymen of strong Catholic convictions. Although the opposition parties had a positive stimulating effect on the conduct of the country's affairs, gradually they underwent the same process of ideological sterilization as had the governmental party against which they fought.

This was true especially of the Christian Social and Economic Party. Prominent Catholic men of public life joined its ranks; among them two significant personalities of the ecclesiastic social movement, Sándor Ernszt and Miklós Griger, should be mentioned. The letter was an apostle of the people, in his country-town parish. Miklós Griger founded, later on, a new party under the name of Christian People's Party that—as a result of its decidedly social and legitimist tendencies—found itself confronted by the powerful machinery of the governmental party and had the greatest difficulties to maintain itself.

What was left of the original Christian Party was able to exert almost exclusive power in Budapest, where its activity was confined. Budapest had a more centralized position culturally and economically then capitals of any other country. The Christian Party, which governed the City-Hall of Budapest, was, on the one hand, more retrograde than the Christian Social and Economic Party and, on the other, maintained excellent relations with the country-ruling governmental party. It helped to dress the official policy with Christian slogans and became the hotbed of intentionally antidemocratic endeavors. The leader of this urban Christian policy was Károly Wolf, whose activity typified the self-interested official policy operating under the cover of Christian slogans.

It would be partial, however, to insist only on this aspect. The Christian Party gave proof of a certain receptiveness to social responsibilities and much good was achieved in the field of the care of the poor and children. It built churches and gave financial support to church-life creating thus the outward conditions of a Catholic renewal. In a tragic way, the influence it exerted prevented, to a certain extent, the filling of this framework with spiritual content.

As a result of the prevailing tendencies, the structure of society remained unchanged. As a matter of fact, due to the powerful capitalism and to the economic policy of the big landed estates, the conditions of labor and of the poor peasantry worsened rather than improved as compared to the Francis Joseph era. In consequence, the difference of classes instead of decreasing grew more acute, and the social problem became primarily a matter for the police. The gentry style of life was still the generally admired, obligatory pattern to be followed, the only new element in it being a certain "Christian" coloring, which manifested itself mostly under the form of unrestricted and uncritical respect for authority. Modern historians rightly surnamed this era *neo-baroque*.

The recruiting of intellectuals was even more restricted than in the Francis Joseph era. A portion of the Jewish intellectuals, under the effect of the racist tendency, settled abroad. The rise from the broad strata of labor and peasantry was minimal. In spite of the official anti-semitic tendency, the big and middle landowners and the politicians maintained close economic connections with the leading industrial, commercial, and financial sector. The professional groups of judges and pedagogues remained most homogeneous in character.

The practicing of the Catholic faith and ethics became again a sort of oddity, just as in the pre-war years. The difference, as compared to the liberal period, was the introduction of a "Christian social" code, which meant, among others, an intensive "Christian club-life," attending the late-morning mass—the so-called "perfumed mass"—on Sundays, at which Holy Communion was seldom received, wearing ostentatiously the cross, specification of "Christian" in advertisements, etc.

In this atmosphere, those who belonged to the leading stratum of society had, more or less, to hide their *bourgeois* or peasant origin and give up the characteristics pertaining to it. Thus a tension was created between the outward devotion and a hidden resentment that was altogether favorable to movements of a fascist character.

The land reform put in force in 1920, did not bring much change to the situation of the peasant mass. The social, economic, and cultural conditions of about one third of the population consisting of small farmers, landless agricultural laborers, etc., did not correspond at all to the Christian postulates. The same applied to industrial labor.

The consequence of the internal antagonism, to which we have repeatedly referred, was that, on the one hand, the retrograde tendencies tried to find refuge under the cover of "Catholicism" and, on the other, a portion of the young generation took seriously, and tried to carry out, the implications of the Catholic renewal.

We have already spoken of the Catholic reform endeavors between the two world wars, a few aspects of it, however, concerning primarily the youth, should be still pointed out.

The boy scouts' movement developed from the Catholic schools among the Catholic youth. The leaders of this and related movements were predominantly priests, eminent among them Sándor Sik, a Piarist father, and Tihamér Tóth, the spiritual guide of the university students.

Within the religious orders the young monks, under the guidance of their ascetic elders, consecrated themselves to permeate the lay life with a Christ-like spirit. New religious orders were founded in Hungary for the achievement of this goal. Mention should be made of the Social Mission Society, founded by Ottokár Prohászka, and of the order of the Social Sisters, detached from the former and founded by Margit Slachta, who obtained remarkable results in the field of the social care of girls of the poorer classes. This new religious order for women was in fact, even from an international point of view, one of the first realisations of the new monastic ideal, which aimed at "the acceptance of the world." A saintly village schoolmistress, Sister Scholastica, performed splendid work in child care in the most neglected and illiterate peasant district of the country, the so-called Tiszazug. The School Sisters of Kalocsa made a great contribution to female elementary education of the people. The assumption of active solidarity in the life of the needy was the characteristic feature of the Norma of Eger, a religious society created under the guidance of the Franciscans for the social care of the poor.

New severe communities were created within the religious orders that became the envigorating source of a spiritual-ascetic mentality. Such was the case for the Cistercian order and both female and male branches of the Carmelites.

A considerable portion of the intellectual youth—in a similar way to the followers of Prohászka in Czechslovakaia—advocated a Catholic idea with more spiritual content. Led by this spirit, young Catholic writers and scientists, along with generous supporters of the cause, founded the reviews titled *The Word of our Age* (Korunk Szava), *New Era* (Uj Kor), *Vigil* (Vigilia). The same ideas permeated the yearbook *Priestly Spirit,* prepared for members of the clergy.

The movements of the young generation were accompanied by a breach between the individual life and the principles professed. An even greater portion of the youth, drifting away from the transcendental, gave up religious faith and especially its practice, and ceased to approach the cultural and social problems in a religious spirit. They became attached to a "social racism" and professed the so-called "profound Hungarian" idea, searching for the permanent essentials of Hungariandom as more or less opposed to Western culture. In contrast to them the Catholic and Protestant reform youth entertained intensive connections with the Western—French and English, respectively—tendencies similar in spirit.

Analyzing the interwar period from a Christian viewpoint, we are bound to note that this policy, with its Christian slogans, served to consolidate the country once the earlier convulsive manifestations were over. In this atmosphere, Hungarian culture made great contributions in religion, literature, music and the arts and sciences.

Consolidation, but simultaneously an insistence on the established order to a degree far beyond mere conservatism—these were the two dominant phenomena that left their stamp on the cultural development of this era. Hungarians beyond the frontiers progressed in a decidedly social spirit. In the neighboring states, by which they had been annexed, neither communism nor counter-revolution had as yet achieved successes, and thus political and social life did not become polarized. A more democratic atmosphere, and the difficult lot of a minority, were basic concomitants that colored Hungarian Catholic life in these territories. The early thirties saw the founding of the *Actio Catholica*. Catholic laity till then had played a lesser role in Hungary than in modern Western states. A significant portion of the clergy, certain prelates in particular, looked askance when laymen concerned themselves with Catholic matters; and this was understandable to some extent in view of the close connection between ecclesiastical affairs and temporal power. The existence of the *Actio Catholica*—led by the saintly Zsigmond Milhalovics so dear to the simple men who made up his parish on the outskirts of Budapest—could not overcome the fact that laymen were still afforded no real participation in church life.

In considering the cultural efflorescence of the era of consolidation we should not forget that this interwar period marked the first era in centuries that produced truly original and independent Hungarian scholastic and religious literature. We noted the ground-breaking significance of Ottokar Prohaszka's scholarly and popular works so inspired by a personal experience whose style gave new expression to the transcendental.

In those years evolved an original and creative Catholic theological literature, among whose independent spirits were Antal Schütz, Sándor Kecskés, Joseph Trikal, Joseph Sanasi, Joseph Sipes and Justinian Serédi, Prince Primate and Archbishop of Esztergom. In considering the popularizers, we should mention Tihamér Tóth and Bála Bangha. At Saint Stephen's Academy were gathered the elite of Catholic scholarship. Numerous Catholic journals concerned themselves intelligently and sympathetically — though perhaps not always in proper perspective — with the illumination of world problems from a Catholic angle. The largest Catholic publishing house, the Saint Stephen Society, along with its stricly scholary endeavors and the customary inspirational literature, also devoted attention to popular literature on a serious plane.

With the approach of World War II pre-eminent creative spirits—writers, artists, musicians, scientists, philosophers and sociologists—were attracted more and more to the supra-natural world, towards the "Christ-like solution" of the ultimate. This was also true of free creators outside the sphere of official church literature or scholarship. Mihály Babits, one of the greatest figures in modern Hungarian poetry, turning from an estheticism rooted in antiquity, found the road to Catholicism. His splendid translation of Dante, his anthology of medieval hymns and his history of European literature represent a new, positive evaluation of the long misunderstood literature of primitive Christianity and the middle ages; his "Jonah" is an epos of devotion to God. Among poets far distant from all religious problems, like the highly gifted Dezsö Kosztolányi, this note rings forth: "Still, I was the servant of a great Master." Our greatest modern prose writer, Alexander Márai, even if not active in the church, wrestled not merely with questions of religion and morals, but with those of the Catholic form of life *per se*.

While lay literature became more receptive to eternal values, Catholic poetry, in the strict sense of the word, began to divest itself of the rigid unctuous formalism of "Catholic ghetto-literature." The Piarist Sándor Sík, the Promontrean Lászlo Mécs, Lajos Harsányi the rural dean, as well as a gifted group of lay Catholic poets—among whom Béla Horváth and György Rónai were especially distinguished—did not recoil from the frank and courageous revelation of personal experience.

From the middle thirties on, new storm clouds gathered in the peaceful skies of consolidation. In Germany, National Socialism gained ascendancy. For reasons mentioned, Hungary did not develop a strong democratic public opinion capable of purposefully resisting the advance of fascist ideology; such a prospect was all the less likely, because the counter-revolution that followed Bolshevism avowed ideas with a Christian coloring. The advance of National Socialism was also fostered by the deep gulf between classes, and by the fact that social questions remained unsolved. Since Communism, and to a certain extent even Socialism, endangered active religious adherents, the bitterness and resentment of unprivileged strata often found an outlet in the diseased manifestations of fascism. The spread of such notions was favored by increasing unemployment among educated strata, and the bleak prospects of young intellectuals. These circles espoused the "Turanian" doctrines according to which the root of all evil was a corrupt Western civilization, with emphasis on Christianity and, above all, Catholicism. The Hungarian people, they said, will only prosper if they join forces with their "Eastern cousins" supposedly meaning related Turcic and Mongol tribes, the Japanese, Manchurians, etc.—to destroy the West.

So far these ideas had been confined to a very narrow circle. Now however, their victory in Central Europe could not remain without effect. The lower strata of intellectuals, the middle class and particularly a portion of the German minority in

Hungary, reacted strongly. The trend was fostered by a neo-baroque spirit that clothed in pseudo-Christian garb even doctrines trampling upon the teachings of Christ. And an approach was sought to both the Catholic and Protestant Churches. When for example the leader of the movement, Ferenc Szálasi, was incarcerated, his followers arranged to have masses said throughout the country for his release.

However, there are two reasons why the great mass of Hungarians proved immune to fascist contamination, favored though it was by general conditions: one was the abhorrence of the vast majority of the Catholic clergy—a factor of immense weight at a time when the Church was so dominant in society and in a position to mobilize great masses. Here it was shown that the so-called Christian Trend prevailing in the interwar period was able, for all its defeats, to exert a strong influence over broad strata of society. In 1937 the *Actio Catholica* issued an anti-Nazi brochure titled "Pseudo-Patriotic Paganism."

The other reason which helped decisively in thwarting the triumph of Nazism was the peasantry's instinctive and elemental opposition. This was the more amazing, because the poorer peasantry were the most underprivileged of all social strata. The peasantry, in its traditional sobriety and moral complexion, deep-rooted in faith, plus its instinctive historical perspective, remained as unaffected by National Socialist promises and incitements to hatred, as later by the so similar tactics of Bolshevism. The peasantry constituting more than fifty per cent of the populace, was the social stratum most completely unaffected by Nazism.

In practice National Socialism was expressed through the ever-growing and semi-officially acknowledged anti-Semitism of the leading class and subservient middle class elements. When, on the threshhold of World War II, German influence evoked the so-called Jewish Laws, a sector of the educated classes took over well-paid posts in business—sometimes merely for the use of their names. The poisonous atmosphere of economic conflict blinded a great portion of Hungarian society to the actual nature of what was transpiring.

Certain it is, that both the leaders and the led were spiritually prepared for World War II and the whirlwinds of National Socialism, then Communism. The glorification of pleasure and crass materialism, made even more blatant by assumed religiosity, gained complete acendancy over men in the years preceding world conflagration.

Even in circles unreceptive to racist and anti-Christian propaganda the violence and brutal anti-humanism of Nazi concepts were not without influence. The idolizing of selfishness, generally with nationalistic overtones, even penetrated Christian communities and institutions. At Commencement in one Catholic high school a leading politician known to be a Catholic held forth to the young people on "The Philosophy of Success."

Simultaneously, however, the religious convictions of the peasantry and part of the urban working class strengthened and deepened. The less the reform movement permeated society's leading circles, the more fruitful was its influence among the great masses whose social condition had worsened, rather than improved, since the days of Francis Joseph. The resurgence of religion among the people during the chaotic reform movement made possible their amazing stand in defense of faith and Church after the Communists seized power. In this field the achievements of the Jesuit Order deserve special praise. Its missions reached the most abandoned villages. The *Sacred Heart Journal,* the Sacred Heart Association and other similar endeavors that it sponsored, made weighty concessions to the slogans of the day, but when it came to the religious organization of the masses in the sign of the Sacred Heart of Jesus, its achievements are indisputable.

The greatest creations of Jesuit home missions were KALOT, the Catholic Young Men's Peasant Federation, and KALASZ its complement, the Catholic Young Women's Peasant Federation. Their founder and apostle was the Jesuit Father Jenö Kerkai—now languishing in jail—whose incomparable organizational abilities were reinforced by exceptional moral courage and a lively interest in social problems.

KALOT united the idea of radical social reform with services envisaging the cultural emancipation and moral instruction of the peasantry. It established twenty colleges accommodating 35,000 students of peasant origin. For graduates of its school for settlers it established a modest village at Egeg. KALOT also trained peasant youth for business, a field from which they had been almost completely barred. It demanded land reform. Its 1937 proposal suggested 500 acres as the maximum limit for landed estates. Nor was it afraid even to help organize an agrarian strike. No wonder local authorities hounded the organization. KALOT from the very start was emphatically anti-Nazi. In 1944, when the Germans occupied Hungary they disbanded the organization and put many of its leaders into concentration camps.

Mass pilgrimages to shrines of the Virgin Mary—for the most part organized spontaneously among the peasants—called forth greater and greater crowds. Here and there, amazing revelations occurred; and it is a sad commentary on the times that, just as under the bolshevist regime, police used coercive measures to curb these manifestations or hush them up.

World War II found Hungarian society and Hungarian Catholicism in a situation where the nation, against the will of the great majority, had been dragged into conflict with the Soviet Union and the Western Powers on the side of the Fascist bloc. Though outer, and to a lesser extent, inner pressures forced the government into a German-Italian alliance, it sought to restrict Hungarian participation to a minimum. Leaders of the Catholic Church, headed by Prince Primate Justinián Serédi—who truly epitomized Rome's policy of moderation, conceived in terms of centuries,—regarded with the greatest anxiety Hungary's wartime association with the dictatorships. Jusztininán Serédi adjudged the declaration of war on Russia unconstitutional and, through the Vatican, did all in his power to dissuade the Western Powers from declaring war on Hungary. His endeavors had no prospect of success under the given circumstances.

As far as the nation's future was concerned, public opinion was greatly muddled by the so-called Vienna Decisions, at which Nazi Germany and Fascist Italy, in the capacity of judges, restored to Hungary some of the Hungarian-inhabited territories of which she had been deprived by the Treaty of Trianon. The prelates of the Church, and lay leaders too, were quite aware of the dubious worth of seeming advantages resulting from Hungary's close collaboration with the so-called Axis powers. Their position was rendered more difficult by the circumstance that though Fascism did not meet with much sympathy, it did succeed in fostering anti-Semitism in Catholic public life, the schools, and not seldom even in the circle of the clergy. The Catholic press generally rejected these ideas, but a non-Catholic press, which called itself Christian, eagerly adopted the slogans of Nazidom.

In the summer of 1943 was held a conference at the manse of Baron Vilmos Apor, bishop of Györ, who, despite his station as a member of the ancient high aristocracy, was a zealous advocate of rapprochement between Church and people in the cause of social progress. At this conference were present, among other leaders of the Church, Joseph Mindszenty, Primate-to-be, at that time Dean in Zalaegerszeg, Zsigmond Mihalovics, director of the *Actio Catholica,* Canon and parliamentary representative Joseph Közi Horváth, Catholic spokesman for social betterment, Dean Béla Varga, leader of the opposition Smallholders Party, Jenö Kerkai, Jesuit Father and head of KALOT, Szaléz Kiss, Franciscan Father and organizer of home missions, and certain prominent Catholic laymen. The conference ascertained that "Germany has lost the war, a historic turning point is at hand. The social reconstruction of the nation must be undertaken at the earliest possible moment. The Church does not intend to hinder this process; indeed, she means to foster it in every way, following the precepts of Christ."

In March 1944 Nazi troops putsch-like fashion occupied Hungary. Since a cornerstone of Hitlerian ideology was the extermination of the Jews, in Hungary, too, began the tragedy which became alike fatal to the victims, the guilty and the bystanders. In Hungary, where a very considerable sector of Jews in business and the professions had been converted, Jewish persecution also affected many thousands of Christians. These converts of Jewish origin were between 40 and 50 thousand in number, about two-thirds of them Catholics.

When German influence produced the first signs of a fresh Jewish persecution in the form of the so-called Jewish Laws, the Church set up an organization for the spiritual, economic and personal defense and succor of Catholic converts. The organization was headed by Joseph Almássy, a gifted young standard-bearer of the Catholic reform movement, then, after his early death, by Father Joseph Jánosy, the eminent Jesuit scholar. Taking an active role, and simultaneously representing the Prince Primate, was its chief patron, Count Gyula Zichy, Archbishop of Kalocsa, as well as Baron Vilmos Apor, Bishop of Györ, both openly opposed to National Socialist influences and the persecution of the Jews. Jusztinián Serédi himself, as Prince Primate, played an energetic part.

At the start of Jewish deportations, Jusztinián Serédi protested in a pastoral letter which was to be read in churches throughout the land. However, on government orders, the post office seized every copy. Then, to prevent the Church from taking a more outspoken stand, the government falsely promised that deportations would cease. Subsequently, a statement drafted by Jusztinián Serédi for the Board of Bishops was read in the churches, but by then this could have no practical effect.

Descriptions of the course of genocide, also involving many Catholics and Protestants of Jewish origin, fall outside the scope of this study. For the most part, the upper and middle classes were horrified witnesses to this dreadful concatenation of events. Many felt malicious satisfaction; very many more, deep shame—but very few deduced the consequences. We must not forget the exceptions however among them a very great number of practicing Catholics, mainly little men, who at the risk of their lives rescued persecutees, women and children especially. The working class and peasantry had little opportunity for giving active aid, but did everything possible. The vast majority openly voiced their condemnation. In the capital, many lives were saved by underground organizations composed mainly of young people from the upper classes.

However there was one segment of Hungarian society which fully mobilized itself to aid the victims and this was the Christian religious community including both the Catholic and the Protestant Churches. Mass rescue operations were restricted exclusively to the Churches. The quarters of Catholic religious organizations, cloisters, monasteries, manses and Bishops' residences offered asylum to refugees. Not only Christians of Jewish origin were saved, but also Orthodox Jews and other refugees from political or racial persecution, democratic spokesmen, anti-Nazi statesmen, socialists and communists.

Outstanding in the field of rescue and defense was Papal Nuncio Angelo Rotta, who directed a whole institution made up of young priests and nuns who distributed papal letters of safe conduct and helped victims in other ways; also outstanding was the order of Charitable Sisters, which, under the guidance of Margit Slachta, hid hundreds of refugees even while its chief herself had to flee because of her opposition to the Nazis. The religious orders practically all participated, among them the Jesuits, the Carmelites, the Servitians and the nuns of the Sacré Coeur; pre-eminent among prelates were Endre Hamvas, Bishop of Csanád, Vilmos Apor, Bishop of Györ, Joseph Mindszenty, Bishop of Veszprém, and Chief Abbots Krizosztom Kelemen of the Benedictine Order and Vendel Endrédy of the Cistercians; all these, and many more ecclesiastics risked their lives defending the oppressed. The Holy Cross Society, mentioned above, likewise joined in the work of relief.

The chief mode of rescue naturally was the concealment of refugees. In addition, the Church sent priests to houses denominated as ghettos in order to feed and console the distressed; it secured letters of safety and facilitated conversion in every way possible. Many clerics suffered martyrdom in heroic defense of these victims, for example Sára Salkház of the Order of Charitable Sisters, who died the saintly death of a martyr after consecrating her life to serving victims of oppression. It is not too much to say that Budapest's Jewry in no small degree owe their mass deliverance to the churches.

No matter how much certain depraved elements protested, then and later, against these activities, we are bound to note that this unique and uncompromising stand lent the Church incomparable prestige. The Nazis not only jailed clerics who harbored victims, but also those who testified on their behalf, or who were known anti-Nazis. This was especially true after Nicholas Horthy's belated and fruitless attempt to bolt the Nazi alliance, when, with the approval of the Germans, Ferenc Szálasi, leader of the Hungarian Arrow-Cross, seized the government in concert with a clique of malefactors.

On November 2, 1944, Father Joseph Közi Horváth, a member of the Parliament, on protesting Nazi atrocities, was dispatched to the front by way of punishment. The Nazi dragged off to Dachau many Budapest pastors who had actively worked for the social betterment of the workers. On November 17, 1944 they imprisoned Joseph Mindszenty, Bishop of Veszprém, who was accompanied voluntarily by 266 candidates for the priesthood. The chief crime of the arrested Bishop of Vesprém, besides rescuing Jews and courageously outfacing Nazi authorities, was that jointly with Jajos Schvoy, Bishop of Székesfehérvár, Vilmos Apor, Bishop of Györ and Kriszosztom Kelemen, Chief Abbot of Pannonhalma, he had sent Ferenc Szálasi, the Arrow-Crossist head of the state, an appeal condemning the senseless and criminal prolongation of the war. This is the sole such declaration of which we have any knowledge. For the same reason, Bishop Schvoy was simultaneously incarcerated, and Bishop Apor only escaped arrest by accident.

From the fall of 1944 on, the Nazis and their Hungarian hirelings had to retreat before the Red Army, which surrounded the capital by Christmas and captured it on February 13. The Arrow Crossist hordes fled to Austria and Germany, forcing military organizations and civilians, and particularly the recently inducted youth formations, to leave the country with them. A considerable portion of the middle class also fled westward before the Red Army, some of them returning later. Again the clergy alone held out. Village priests shared the cares and dangers of the abandoned peasantry and defended, this time at the risk of their lives, a populace completely at the mercy of the Red hordes. Of 1005 priests stationed West of the Danube only 11 fled the country. Again the Church gained tremendously in prestige, during the first dreadful months of Russian occupation, by being once more the sole defense of the persecuted populace. The clergy was blessedly active, particularly in protecting women. Vilmos Apor, Bishop of Györ, on Good Friday 1945 was martyred by the bullets of Soviet soldiers seeking to rape women who had found sanctuary in the Bishop's residence. Many a woman in those days died in defense of her honor.

Though the invading Red Army looted the churches, generally it left their pastors alone, and indeed often looked upon them with a sort of superstitious awe. This made possible the clergy's successful rescue operations. At first Soviet Russia spared the Church to some degree in the occupied territories. Persecutions only began after Communist rule was consolidated and there was no longer need to fear either Western intervention or internal resistance. The new system of government was made up of a coalition of democratic parties. Within the coalition Russian bayonets assured the dominance of the Communist Party. Despite intimidation, at the 1945 elections the Smallholders Party, uniting the peasant and the middle classes, received an absolute majority. The greater part of the populace did not doubt that the Communists could be held down to a minority, in view of the general expectation that Western intervention would end the Russian occupation. To the helm of government came leaders of the Smallholders Party, among whom Béla Varga, a clerical representative, became President of the Parliament.

After Jusztinián Serédi's death on Shrove Thursday 1945, the Pope appointed Joseph Mindszenty, Bishop of Vesprém as Prince Primate of Hungary, shortly afterwards raising him to the rank of Cardinal.

Joseph Mindszenty was one of a numerous peasant family. As a gifted theological student he gave up an opportunity to study abroad, in order to devote himself to the spiritual needs of the village people. He became the young abbot at Zalaegerszeg, the county seat of Zala Megye. By virtue of his forthrightness and fearless stand in the face of temporal power, plus his splendid organizing abilities, he became a real force in the county. During the first Soviet Terror (1919), he was arrested. Like so many clerics of his day, he showed a certain reserve towards democratic ideas, this being motivated by his experience in 1919. But always he was the pastor of the poor eminently social-minded and possessing a deep sense of responsibility. It was not so much his logical mind, as rather his exceptional moral conviction, abhorring lies and underhandedness, that led him at once to adopt the sharpest stand against Fascist ideology. Not only in his church district but throughout the whole county, he fought it uncompromisingly. In 1944, just before the collapse, he became Bishop of Veszprém, largest bishopric west of the Danube. From the very beginning, at meetings of the Board of Bishops, he espoused the view that the Church should make voluntary sacrifices in the interest of social reform—an approach that had a decisive effect on Church policies in Hungary, especially after 1945. Leaders of Catholic social movements asked him in the summer of 1944 to persuade the Board of Bishops of the necessity for land reform. Of his trials in the Nazi era we have already spoken.

Prince Primate Mindszenty's past and personality, combined with the extraordinary growth of the Church's prestige, destined him to lead the people in their stand against the new wave of terror. Mindszenty, however, was as much opposed to catastrophic open resistance, as he was to compromise.

The new Prince Primate beheld a nation economically, socially and spiritually ruined; a Church whose financial support was in doubt; a broken leading class and fragments of a decimated middle class, one portion of which had left the country in successive waves, while yet another had been dragged off by the Russians, the remainder having lost all security, material and spiritual. Then there was the destitute peasantry and working class, among them many hundreds of thousands of families whose breadwinner had not returned from prisoner-of-war camps, or had been abducted by the Red Army, leaving the women a prey to its excesses. On top of recent harrowing experiences, came a fresh invasion of terror that made the country relive pagan horrors of bygone Mongolian and Turkish invasions. This new invasion from the East was anti-European and anti-Christian; it glorified violence and respected no human righs. The Russian troops of occupation appeared to be not merely uncivilized, but hostile to civilization itself—at least to the civilization of which Hungary till then had been a part.

Communsm, not just in the first militant phase of the occupation, but progressively as the regime was consolidated, took on the aspect of a grotesque caricature of Christianity. It had its own fanatic dogma and its special dialectics to reconcile the constantly changing "line" with holy writ; there were the massed processions, the adoration of Stalin, the absolute submission to authority, plus so-called self-criticism and false confession, tapped by the hateful farce of the "peace fight." Aspects which caused the faithful to reject Communism's practice and theory lent it dynamism. Outside the Christian Churches, the Communist Party was the sole organization with an elaborated and mandatory ideology—in this case backed by 12 million bayonets.

None the less—apart from a small minority of the deposed leading class which could not reconcile itself with the situation of 1945,—the people as a whole trusted that with Western help the nation's freedom could be secured, and hoped that the aftermath of war's fearful storm might bring rejuvenation to society. This faith in the future declined in proportion to the throttling influence of Communism. For the Reds made no concessions, save those of a purely tactical nature. Their aim, among other things, was the uprooting of all religion and the destruction of the Church as a cultural factor. This endeavor was directed in the first place against the Catholic Church, for the Bolshevists soon realized that the Catholic Church represented the sole organized ideology with which they really had to reckon.

How could the Church subsist and effectuate her teachings, how defend the Christian flock without temporal resources, when faced by so powerful and unscrupulous an enemy? This was the Church's basic problem in Hungary and elsewhere behind the slowly but inexorably descending Iron Curtain. In practice there were two alternatives: uncompromising opposition to a Godless regime inimical to freedom, or an attempt at superficial compromise without surrendering principle. A certain fusion of the two was also feasible, though this, alas, did not develop sufficiently as a conscious policy for reasons to be mentioned. Yet, in essence, the nation's life instinct and the Church's inner cohesion did effect this third solution.

Yet a fourth possibility existed, which we may not call an alternative, because those very few who chose it could no longer exercise their own will. This fourth possibility was complete collaboration with the Bolshevists, involving the double self-deception that such a procedure was a postulate of social rejuvenation, and secondly that it was the only way of saving what still could be saved. Obviously, whatever their intentions, the latter became slaves of the regime and, spiritually speaking, cannot be regarded members of the Church any longer.

In practice, these developments were complicated by the heritage of the past. A significant portion of intellectual leaders opined that the upheaval would allow of reforms which otherwise never could have taken place. We must remember that till 1948 a non-Communist majority ran the government, curbing the Russion-sponsored Communist minority. The trouble was that Moscow ordered reforms only with a view to serving Bolshevist aims. Thus land reform too, desirable in itself, was carried out in the interests of bolshevization.

On the other hand, one also found a goodly number of reactionaries who were opposed to all reform and wanted to turn back the clock to the days preceding the Nazi collapse. The latter thought to utilize the Church and the Cardinal in defense of the past and their own special interests. The Prince Primate felt the compulsion of historic responsibility; and this unavoidably provoked the sharpest reactions from the Bolshevists. At this point we should like to touch briefly upon a key trait of the most dominant personality in the Hungarian Catholic Church. From the earliest days of his career, he had regarded all ques- tions as being of a moral nature. He would not recognize spheres beyond the pale of moral law. This resulted in an in- tense concern with public affairs, which in a Bolshevist era could only end in martyrdom. It was *germane* to his real great- ness that he knew this from the start yet did not depart from his chosen path.

Soviet-sponsored land reform left former owners 200 acres apiece—owners of more than 1000 acres being deprived of all their property. The Church lost nearly 900,000 catastral acres of land; each bishopric, chapter and landed order being allowed to keep but 100 acres. This expropriation involved no compen- sation whatsoever. Two-thirds of the confiscated Church lands were forests which the state did not give to the peasantry, but retained for itself, organizing them into state farms and sof- hozes. The Prince Primate in his first apostolic circular thus referred to land reform as it affected the Church: "God grant that the betterment of the new owners may console the Church for her loss and burdens." Neither the Prince Primate, nor any other Catholic representative ever condemned land reform; they merely criticized injustices committed in its implementation.

A key phase of the Church persecution purposefully effectu- ated by the Communists was the destruction of the Church's financial resources. The expropriation of Church lands, together with the concomitant cessation or modification of advowson were crippling blows. And the general abolition of extensive land tenure, though not without benefits, meant the loss of con- sequential donations. The state, over which the Bolshevists were gaining control, continued to contribute to the maintenance of the clergy, while envisaging the annihilation of the Church. The idea was to keep the clergy subservient to totalitarian power, thus eliminating a focus of resistance. On the other hand, the state ceased to collect Church taxes.

Owing to the interrelationship of Church and state, the Hun- garian people were not accustomed providing for the upkeep of Church and clergy. In the post-war impoverishment that par- ticularly afflicted the faithful, it was difficult to transfer respon- sibility for Church maintenance to the parishioners. Neverthe- less, Church members made far reaching sacrifices. Hundreds of gutted churches were rebuilt, not with the help of state and Party as Communists claimed, but by the parishioners, them- selves, who in addition to making donations, labored without remuneration. There was a veritable flood of donations which the Communist administration sought to discourage in every way. We shall outline below the successive steps taken to undermine the material foundations of the Church.

Here we should like to sketch briefly the relationship between the Church and political power factors in the 1945-1948 interim period leading to Hungary's bolshevization. Mindszenty never concealed his view that the monarchy would have been the best warranty for historic progress and a stable order, and he demanded that no parliament, but a plebiscite, determine the form of state. After Law 1 of 1946 established the republic, he made no further pronouncements on this score.

At the 1945 election the Smallholders Party, supported by middle-class and peasants, received 56% of the total vote. The Social Democratic Party and the Communist Party each got about 16%, while the National Peasant Party, comprising the poorer peasantry, and also receiving many votes from the Reform Party and from anti-Communist intellectuals, polled 8%. Splinter parties may be disregarded. The main Parties joined in a coalition. A fundamental aim of the Communists was to disrupt the coalition Parties; this they effected by branding their leaders and most of their parliamentary members as reactionaries, thus forcing them out of politics and shifting Party control to hand-picked fellow travelers. Mátyás Rákosi, head of the Hungarian Communist Party, aptly referred to these successful efforts of attrition as "salami tactics." These maneuvers primarily demoralized the Smallholders, who were the majority Party. Prominent leaders of this group were constrained to form splinter Parties, which then were swiftly liquidated. Some were forced intto exile; others such as Béla Kovács, its popular Secretary General, were abducted by the Russians.

István Balogh, a rural priest who chose the above indicated fourth course of action, in 1947 was told to organize an opposition Party intended to mislead the mass of Catholics, but had scant success.

These salami tactics culminated in the absorption of the Social Democratic Party by the Communist Party in 1948. Social Democratic leaders who proved recalcitrant were killed, jailed or forced to flee.

The Prince Primate and many on the Board of Bishops looked askance at the close relationship between the Smallholders Party and the Communists within the government coalition. The Prince Primate, strictly moral in his viewpoint, looked upon this with particular disfavor. Consequently he inclined towards the founding of an independent Catholic, or at least expressly Christian, Party. Margit Slachta, head of the Order of Charitable Sisiters, was particularly courageous in espousing the cause of religion and morals on the floor of Parliament. Her Christian Women's party, which fused with a middle class Party during the elections, attained only local success. Hungarian Bolshevists and Soviet occupiers taking advantage of the difficulties attendant on forming a Christian Party, prevented its inception for years. In 1947, at the second parliamentary elections, as the Democratic People's Party led by István Barankovics, such a Christian, and essentially Catholic, Party finally could enter the lists. The Party was thoroughly anti-Bolshevist, but at the same time sought the radical solution of social problems. István Barankovics already had played a significant role in the nation's intellectual life as a publicist of Christian and democratic convictions. In organizing the Party and recruiting mass support, a prominent role was played by two Jesuit Fathers whom we have already mentioned: Joseph Jánosi, a religious scholar, and particularly Jenö Kerkai, founder of KALOT. It was primarily owing to the latter's efforts, and those of enthusiastic young priests, that a majority of the Bishops supported the Party at the 1947 parliamentary elections; and the Church's stand had a decisive influence on the populace, particularly among the peasantry. This support assured victory in the elections, despite Communist frauds and intimidation. The Prince Primate, however, maintained a cool reserve towards the Party, since he felt that its mere launching and entry into politics was something of a compromise. However, in 1947-48 when, in the whole Iron Curtain world outside Hungary, no Christian political Party could exist, the active presentation of Christian viewpoints in politics could only occur through certain compromises. We shall consider the further fate of the Party a little later.

From the beginning, the Communists' main purpose was to disrupt the Church and nullify its cultural influence. As adherents of Moscow's totalitarian centralism, they saw clearly that a crucial force strengthening the freedom and the firm stand of the Church was Rome's centrally directive role of global unity. So they did all they could to restrict the relationship of the Hungarian Catholic Church with Rome. As early as the spring of 1945 they expelled from Budapest the Papal Nuncio, Angelo Rotta, who had accomplished so much in defense of the oppressed.

Still, the decisive step in paralyzing the cultural mission of the Church was the disbanding of Catholic organizations, which commenced in the summer of 1946. Previously, all Christian Socialist workers' groups had been disbanded. Immediately after the change of regime, the parish workers' groups [EMSZO] and

Vocational Societies and their leaders had been deprived of voting rights. Since the Communists wanted to fashion the workers into the militant stratum of the so-called dictatorship of the proletariat, they primarily sought to gain control of this group. They liquidated Catholic social movements first, because the workers now sought the road to religious faith with an irrepressible urgency that did not exclude even Communist Party members.

But the Bolshevists showed even greater hostility to KALOT, the Peasant Youth Federation led by Jenö Kerkai, S.J. The KALOT could not be accused of collaboration with the Socialists, nor of a reactionary attitude, for the Nazis had banned it and some Church authorities accused it of a social radicalism too much in harmony with Bolshevist teachings.

In the summer of 1946 two drunken Soviet soldiers picked a fight on Teréz Körut. A shot rang out and one lay lifeless on the sidewalk. According to the police, the "assailant" was found dead on the roof of a neighboring house. Police claimed they had found a KALOT membership card in his pocket, and said he had been wearing a KALOT uniform. The KALOT never had a uniform.. It was later ascertained that the alleged assailant had never been a KALOT member and on the contrary, had been active in a Bolshevist youth organization. On this pretext Catholic organizations were accused of training youth for murder. Thousands of Catholic organizations were disbanded, their quarters and funds expropriated. Only a scattering of strictly religious groups such as the Jesuit-led Mária Kongregácio could sustain the incessant attacks and persecutions. Early in 1949 the latter also were disbanded.

The "unmasking" of alleged plots afforded a handy excuse for discrediting the Church's influence on youth. In Catholic high schools weapons were found which detectives had smuggled in. May 1946 marked the "unmasking" of the "conspiracy at Gyöngyös." Szaléz Kiss, Franciscan monk and outstanding missionary, was alleged to have had advance knowledge of attacks against Soviet soldiers. They transported him to Siberia. Between the lines, the Bolshevist press already was accusing the Cardinal of indirect incitation to these attacks.

Bolshevist power struck a similarly grievous blow by throttling the Catholic press. It suppressed nearly 200 Catholic journals, published for the most part by the religious orders and not even dealing with politics. The publication of the Catholic Central Press's two dailies was stopped and the founding of a new Catholic daily prohibited. Only two Catholic weeklies and a monthly journal were allowed to apper. Of these, *Uj Ember* [The New Man] became the country's most popular publication. Not even the Bolshevists could impugn its democratic spirit. The *Uj Ember* still continues publication, but advance censorship bans countless articles and forbids discussion of current questions. The journal's tremendous influence on public opinion was muffled by allowing only a small number or copies to appear and by banning its open sale. Identical methods were used to choke off the two other tolerated Catholic journals, the weekly, *Sziv Ujság* [Sacred Heart Journal], which was banned in the course of the anti-Jesuit campaign of 1949, and the monthly *Vigilia,* which still is being published as a scientific, literary and political monthly reminiscent of the French spirit.

An even more grievous step was the strangling of book publishing and book circulation. In 1945-46 was issued a "list of fascist books" including, for purposes of confiscation, innumerable significant Catholic scholarly, literary and inspirational books, among them Ottokár Prohaska's works, the writings of Tihamér Toth, apostle of youth, and many treatises on dogma. Further Catholic book publishing was strangled by advance censorship. Books of a religious nature cannot appear in Hungary since 1949 except for the Bible, of which only limited editions may be printed. This violence to freedom of the spirit far outdoes even the Nazi book burnings. Not even unconfiscated old religious books may be kept in bookshops or libraries, and so cannot reach the faithful. Priests face serious charges if they organize reading clubs or set up parish libraries.

In 1948 the Saint Stephen Society, main Catholic publishing concern, was expropriated together with its subsidiary, the Stephanaeum Press. Then in 1949 came the turn of all the other Catholic publishing and printing establishments.

However, the key phrase of the anti-Church campaign was the fight for the schools.

We have noted that in Hungary the Churches retained their dominant role in elementary instruction as well as their significant role in the middle schools. In 1946-47, of 2908 six-grade elementary schools 1912 were denominational. Of 4018 eight-grade general schools 2386 were denominational. Three out of four schools for kindergarden teachers, 48 out of 58 schools for teachers, 88 out of 175 high schools and 12 out of 25 industrial schools were denominational.

More than two-thirds of the denominational schools, and over half of all schools, were Catholic. As of February 1, 1947 the following schools were in Catholic hands: 2911 six-grade elementary schools and eight-grade general schools, 52 high schools, 87 junior high schools, 32 teachers' training schools, 3 schools for kindergarten teachers, 27 intermediate schools for workers and 36 other types of general and special schools.

The 1946 school reforms brought radical changes in primary and secondary instruction. Following the American example, immediately after World War II a system of eight years' compulsory education was theoretically inaugurated, though not carried into practice. Then, in the following two years, the elementary schools were swiftly expanded to eight grades. Another significant reform was the setting up of various types of workers' schools. This too, was an essentially beneficial and necessary step, because relatively few children of small farmers, landless peasantry and low-income working class had been able to attend high school and college. Therefore the Church gladly undertook both reforms. With the greatest rapidity her elementary schools were turned into general schools. The teaching orders set up workers' secondary schools one after another. Their desire to create a great many more was frustrated by the Bolshevists, who for example would not allow the Benedictines and the Piarists to establish workers' secondary schools in two key Trans-Danubian mining towns, Tata and Dorog. For the most part, the workers themselves approached the teaching orders with such requests. Again provoking the bitter wrath of the Communists, the Cardinal enthusiastically supported these efforts and himself often visited such workers' secondary schools.

Hungary's center of heavy industry, Csepel, with its population of 40,000 had had no high school at all. A delegation of its workers called on Benedictine head abbot Krizosztom Kelemen, asking that the Order establish a high school at Csepel, a request to which the very social-minded abbot—who soon was forced into exile and died in the U.S.A.—readily acceded. The great historic teaching order, began to instruct the youth of this industrial center. It is worth mentioning that Csepel, which the Communists consecrated as the symbol of the new régime, became the center of the workers' new religious trend until totalitarian Bolshevist terror suppressed these endeavors—at least in their outward forms.

While considering the Church's pedagogical role, we should not forget that it was almost the sole forum concerned with the social and moral care of young apprentices, that is those who from childhood were constrained to work in factories and shops. In 1902 the Catholic Church established the first apprentice homes. The Catholic Young Men's Associations, so often derided in the anti-Catholic press, also were concerned with safeguarding the morals of young factory workers and craftsmen. In 1946 the Bolshevists by unilateral action took over all the apprentice homes in the country.

The above school reforms were accompanied by a third: the mass establishment of people's boarding schools. In truth, the secondary and college education of poorer students was hindered mainly by their parents' inability to pay for their room and board. The few existing boarding schools chiefly admitted children of the middle class.

But all three reforms, desirable *per se,* were used by the Communists to further despotic aims. From the start, they had rightly surmised that they never would be able to win over the vast majority of adults. The régime's basis of operations could only be the ever broadening stratum of those they could train from early childhood. A basic premise fo such complete reorientation was the all-embracing indoctrination of the whole populace; and that was why such importance was attached to the immediate introduction of the general schools. For another thing, Communist technocracy, in its drive for swift industrialization, had urgent need of specialized robots. The workers' schools were expanded mainly with this in mind. And the aim of people's boarding schools was to subject youth to perpetual indoctrination even outside school hours. The Bolshevists at once expropriated all such institutions, transforming them into hothouses for raising bolshevist Janissaries. The same end was even more broadly served by the Pioneer Movement among younger children, known in Hungary as the Komsomol; in secondary schools and colleges by the Federation of Working Youth (DISZ). So that nothing might contravene these designs, the Bolshevists early dissolved Catholic and Protestant student organizations and the Social Democratic Youth Federation. The Pioneer Movement, the Federation of Working Youth and the People's Boarding Schools became foci of the purposeful sexual and moral corruption of youth. The idea was to destroy "bourgeois morals," as the Communists called them. They rightly opined that perverted youth would prove more pliable. Catholic authorities, particularly the Cardinal and Margit Slachta, head of the Order of Charitable Sisters, gathered such data and at every opportunity called it to the attention of Bolshevists leaders, naturally to no avail. The Bolshevists always demanded the names of informants, who, if revealed, would have been subject to internment at the very least.

The moral corruption of youth corresponded to the first phase of Soviet sexual pedagogy, which in the Soviet Union ceased ten years ago, yielding to a strict but entirely mechanistic sexual ethics. The second phase prescribed that the worker devote his energies solely to his work. In Hungary, this second phase, begun in 1951-52, is still very far from completely effectuated.

At colleges and universities Bolshevist penetration took several forms. "Undesirable" teachers were fired. Between 1945-48 college and university posts had been assigned to many fine scholars unaffiliated with Communism, but who had been barred from advancement for religious or other reasons. But after 1948, appointments went mostly to fellow-travellers or Communists. Enrollment in universities was dependent on an ideological examination; and, in principle, middle class students were rejected. Most university students were assigned to the people's boarding schools. As a final step, universities and colleges were completely bolshevized. Since the strongly Catholic universities of Budapest and Szeged had been not only laicized, but harnessed to Bolshevist ideology, the Church requested permission to establish a Catholic university at the seat of one or another of the Archbishoprics. The request was not so much as acknowledged.

From the start, the Bolshevists set up a network of tens of thousands of party seminars, lectures, schools and colleges. Only the Catholic Church seriously opposed this pervasive penetration. In Budapest and many rural towns free universites were founded. In Budapest alone, six such universities functioned. The journals *Uj Ember* and *Vigilia* arranged for political lectures throughout the country. The religious orders likewise inaugurated academies of theology and political science, and also sponsored lecture series. Thus in Debrecen, a center of Hungarian Presbyterianism with a population of 100,000, more than 1,500 persons—half of them Presbyterians—would gather to hear such lectures at the Catholic Free University. In 1948-49 these Catholic institutions were banned one and all.

If we seek a clear picture of education in Iron Curtain countries, it is well to take account of a key characteristic of Bolshevist pedagogy: it is based on absolute ideological exclusiveness. Not only does it refuse to tolerate any other viewpoint in the classroom, but it will not even endure political indifference or any objective approach to the facts. Moreover, it demands absolute control in order to mold youth in its image. Against these inroads only the church schools and the assurance of religious instruction could afford a defense.

It was to Cardinal Mindszenty's everlasting credit that he recognized the vital significance of the battle for the free instruction of youth and that he fought it out to the bitter end, successfully mobilizing the broadest strata of the Hungarian people. And this was a prime cause of his martyrdom.

The Cardinal's uncompromising resistance, which we indicated above as the first possible path for the Church, increased in proportion as the nation's Bolshevization progressed. This resistance sprang from two sources: from the consciousness that the Cardinal was the nation's highest-ranking civil dignitary and from his exclusively moral view of events and obligations.

Generally accredited exponents of the second path—accomodation without surrendering principle—were László Banas, Bishop of Veszprém, Gyula Czapik, Archbishop of Eger, Kálman Papp, Bishop of Györ and Endre Hamvas, Bishop of Csanád. Essentially in harmony with this approach were several leading figures of the religious orders, as well as leaders of the largest Christian-spirited opposition Party, the Democratic People's Party.

Certain insufficiently informed ecclesiastics particularly accused Bishoy László Banas (died 1948) of "backing Communist goals" and of being "Cardinal Mindszenty's enemy." This charge was utterly baseless. László Banas, scion of a distinguished family of generals, studied in Rome, acquiring a universal culture that was an amazing synthesis of aristocracy and humility—characteristically, no one ever succeeded in anticipating the prelate's greeting. A great portion of his career was spent in Hungarian territories annexed to Rumania, amid the unending compromise called forth by the lot of a minority. These experiences continued to color his attitude. The Bolshevik press fabricated a fierce battle between the Cardinal and the Bishop of Veszprém, putting faked pronouncements in the mouth of the grievously ill Bishop.

The Cardinal, in his first circular to the Bishops of Hungary —the text of which was written by Bishop Bánas.—excoriated the moral laxness encouraged by the politicians in power, land reform frauds, Party dictatorship, political tyranny and organized persecution. From this time forth, in pastoral letters and personal statements, he protested without ceasing against all forms of terroristic and immoral acts: against infringement of the rights of freedom, against Party despotism, internment and imprisonment, mass expulsion of the German minority on grounds of collective responsibility, persecution of Hungarians in Czechoslovakia, excesses of the administration and police, and the election frauds. These pronouncements far exceeded the strictly religious jurisdiction of the Church, but were in line with her social, moral and cultural role. Each such pronouncement provoked the wild wrath of the Bolshevists.

In the early years, the Cardinal stated: "If our hurts find relief and we may freely continue our work of spiritual care, then we are ready for sincere collaboration."

The Cardinal opined that the Church as a free institution could set conditions for collaboration with temporal power.

At this point, where we consider the inner renascence and outward resistance of the persecuted Church, we must say a word about those who in the period preceding total Bolshevization, chose the fourth path indicated above: that is, willingness to subject the Church completely to the whims of Bolshevism.

This was a very small group, just as it is still a small group today, four years after total Bolshevization. For the most part, a small faction within the anti-Bolshevist coalition played a role in these endeavors. They were joined by a number of publicists and scholars, as well as by some clerics who, practically without exception, had come into moral conflict with the authorities of the Church. Both the lay and ecclesiastic members of this group suffered from unquenched ambition and pride. These men, of whom the Communists gained control by virtue of the fact that they already were compromised, were dropped after a time, as soon as they proved of no further use from the standpoint of propaganda.

The fact that the Cardinal was the sole leader in Hungary who always clearly expressed the will of the people in the face of Communist despots, gave unexampled authority to his every utterance. The Cardinal, on August 15, 1947 proclaimed the Year of the Holy Virgin, placing the suffering land of Hungary under the defense of Mary, Hungary's patron Saint for a thousand years. From the day of his proclamation, until May 31, 1948, countless religious festivities took place at shrines of the Virgin Mary. Despite pressure and threats on the part of the Communist authorities, more than 4 million worshipers took part in these festivities, generally held in the presence of the Cardinal. In spite of strenuous efforts, the Bolshevists could not herd to their own meetings anywhere near the number of people who, despite all terror and many times traveling for days on foot, gathered at these "Mindszenty Days." The religious enthusiasm of the peasantry affected others too. On October 4, 1947 more than 100,000 workers took part in a candlelight procession and sacred convocation that took place during the days of the Maria Congress.

The focal point of Church persecutions became the battle for the schools. First the Bolshevists attacked compulsory religious instruction, since in this they already had some support from coalition parties. Many believed that the compulsory religious education was not easily defensible. After all, most free countries did not have it. But they failed to consider that in a state where power falls into the hands of anti-Church terrorists, optional religious instruction ultimately means no religious instruction at all. The Bolshevists cleverly allowed a faction of the Smallholders Party to broach the problem. In the face of violent popular protest, backed by the first stand of the Cardinal and the Board of Bishops, the régime had to retreat, and the proposal was withdrawn. Mátyas Rakosi, leader of the Communist Party, himself spoke against optional religious education, making a scapegoat of the Smallholders Party.

Nearly a million citizens signed appeals protesting the introduction of optional religious instruction. The issue of the first phase of the battle for the schools resulted in 50% more applications for admission to Catholic schools than could be accomodated. 1200 students applied for admission to the Piarist high schools first-year class which could take care of a maximum of 180 students. The membership of the Catholic Parents' Federation, founded in 1946, rose to a million and a half.

It was a vast surprise both to Communists and the free world that at the August 1947 Parliamentary elections, despite intimidation, fraud and the banning of certain opposition groups, an expressly Christian party, the Democratic People's Party led by István Barankovics, and the Independence Party led by Zoltán Pfeiffer, achieved tremendous victories. The Bolshevists rightly attributed these victories to the Chuch's stand. Their attitude was summed up by Mátyas Rakosi's threatening speech of January 10, 1948: "The Church gives asylum to prominent reactionaries, the majority of the clergy opposes democracy, land reform, the Three Year Plan and peace."

The Bolshevists claimed that the Church was unwilling even to discuss current questions, such as "its place in the people's democracy." Actually, since early 1948, the Board of Bishops had always expressed its readiness to enter into discussions, but the régime always torpedoed them. There were several unofficial meetings between Communist leaders and Gyula Czapik, Archbishop of Eger, Kálman Papp, Bishop of Györ and Istvan Barankovics, leader of the Democratic People's Party, but Bolshevist tactics made progress impossible. After the Communists had carried out successive purges in the coalition parties, and had absorbed and destroyed the Social Democratic Party, in the late spring of 1948 they again took up the battle for the schools, calling for nationalization,

The Cardinal, supported by the Board of Bishops, led the fight in defense of the schools despite the violent Communist campaign against his person. The Board of Bishops protested in a series of pastoral letters, demanding a "free and secret plebiscite." Since the Communists had just seized absoute power, these couragous protests, enjoying the support of millions, could avail nothing. On June 16, 1948 the rubber-stamp parliament voted to nationalize Church schools. Since other opposition parties had been destroyed, only István Barankovics' Democratic People's Party and Margit Slachta's Christian Women's Party voted against the measure. The Catholic Church lost its 3148 schools and could not establish others. The Bolshevists had gained complete control over the education of youth.

The situation of the Catholic Church was aggravated by the fact that the Protestant Churches by then had been forced into an understanding with the régime. Some months previously, the Communists had jailed Evangelical Bishop Lajos Ordass and a number of deacons because of their brave defense of the freedom of the Church. Most lay leaders were forced out so that they could be replaced by fellow-travelers, and a handful of Protestant clerics favoring submission were used to replace deposed Bishops. The Protestant Churches in October and December 1948 made a compact with the régime whereby the salaries of pastors were to be assured for a certain period, but of 1524 protestant schols only 10 secondary schools were retained.

An incident in the battle for the schools provided a characteristic glimpse of Bolshevist terror. On June 3, 1948 Miklos Asztalos, village priest at Pocspetri, was arrested, charged with incitement to murder. This occurred after more than 90% of the villagers had signed protests against the nationalization of the schools. The police were searching for the priest whom the people hid, and he was not even present when a policeman, who had been coarsely reviling religion, was shot and killed in a scuffle. The priest was found by the police, beaten and dragged through the streets, then made to "confess" Moscow-style. Everyone knew this was also meant as a threat against the Cardinal, who was now the target of a flood of calumniation in the Bolshevist press, which accused him of plotting war against the Soviet Union. Father Asztalos was sentenced to life imprisonment; his fellow defendent, who allegedly shot the blaspheming policeman, was executed.

On June 30, 1948 a Budapest crowd was awaiting the arrival of the Cardinal at Mount Gellért Chapel, where he was to lead devotions in honor of the Virgin of Fatima. Police attacked the worshippers and dispersed them.

Then in August 1948 Communist authorities for the first time banned the procession on St. Stephen's Day, one of the most revered holidays of the Hungarian Roman Catholic Church. This was re-named the Feast of Bread, and from 1950 on became the Bolshevist Constitution Day.

Simultaneously the régime attacked the *Actio Catholica*. Under the leadership of Zsigmond Mihalovics, the *Actio Catholica* had united the populace during this period of Church persecution. Zsigmond Mihalovics, who managed to flee to the free world, was sentenced *in absentia* to ten years in prison. And early in 1950 the *Actio Catholica* was put under strict state surveillance.

No longer did the Bolshevists need the support of non-Communist parties. They had trampled into the dust all opposition with the exception of the Catholic Church, whose influence, as a symbol of resistance, grew in exact proportion to the success of Bolshevist penetration. Repercussions in the free world could now be discounted, since the Soviet Union was resolved to break with the West in any case. That was when the Iron Curtain rolled down. It was then that the Bolshevists decided on a showdown with Cardinal Mindszenty, since they felt that their rule of terror could not be consolidated so long as the Church exerted such unquestioned influence on the mass of peasantry and workers. This was the era of complete Bolshevization, when industry and commerce were expropriated and nationalized, when peasant holdings were liquidated and merged into kolkhozes.

The leaders of the Church realized that in the face of ruthless terror they would be forced to make certain concessions. But the Board of Bishops and the Cardinal refused to compromise the freedom of the Church and her spiritual mission. The Bolshevists of course wanted an agreement for tactical reasons only having no intention of adhering to it. Cardinal Mindszenty and his Bishop colleagues wished to negotiate as heads of a free Church, but the Bolshevists would acknowledge no such status. After ostensibly agreeing to a proposal of mediation by the Vatican, they refused to issue the Apostolic Visitor's passport.

The régime already had received Moscow's orders to liquidate Cardinal Mindszenty, who had become a rallying point and universal symbol of resistance to Soviet terror. In November 1948 it sought to force young and old to sign mass petitions for the Cardinal's arrest. Actually it only succeeded in persuading those absolutely dependent on the régime, and even among these there were many who refused. On November 4 the Board of Bishops issued a declaration of absolute solidarity with the

persecuted Cardinal, and this was read in all churches. The
Primate himself sent a message to the people saying that he
realized the duress employed and freely forgave anyone who
signed.

Late in November "Catholic Youth Delegations" made up of
young Bolshevists called on the Bishops to issue an anti-Mindszenty declaration. Simultaneously a small group of laymen,
mainly fellow-travelers, sent Mndszenty a memorandum urgng
him to give up his "reactionary" attitude.

A communique of the December 16 session of the Board of
Bishops at Esztergom, the last over which the Cardinal presided, made it clear that the Board of Bishops always had been
amenable to discussions, though never to unconditional surrender. The régime already had tried vainly to persuade the
dying Lászlo Banas to sign a declaration urging the immediate
resumption of deliberations between Church and state.

On December 20 an official pronouncement of the Church
made these points:

The Board of Bishops and the Cardinal had accepted democracy.

They had never commented on economic nationalization.

The condemned not land reform but faults in its administration.

They have always clung to the rights of freedom.

The Church, in principle, does not oppose the republican
form of government.

The Board of Bishops and Prince Primate did all they could
to re-establish contact between Hungary and the Vatican, but
their efforts proved fruitless.

Cardinal Mindszenty knew that his arrest was at hand, and
that he would have to suffer torture worse than death. Yet he
would not think of leaving the country. It is still a moot question whether the Bolshevists would have allowed him to do so.

On Dec. 26th, the day after Christmas, political police surrounded the Prince Primate's palace at Esztergom and arrested
the Cardinal. Next day the regime issued a communique on the
arrest, accusing the Cardinal of "disloyalty and the crimes of
subversion, spying and currency manipulation." Each Bishop on
that day received the Cardinal's last message saying: "I shall
neither confess nor resign. If I should, that could only be the
result of torture beyond human endurance, and consequently
should be regarded as null and void."

That same day the Bolshevist Minister of the Interior issued
an ultimatum demanding the immediate resignations of Arch-

bishop József Grösz of Kalocsa, head of the Board of Bishops since the Cardinal's arrest, of Bishop Lajos Showy of Szekesfehervar, the Cardinal's intimate friend, of Jozsef Petery, Bishop of Vac, and of Miklos Dudas, Greek-Catholic of Hajdudorog. The reason given was that the Cardinal had made damaging admissions regarding them. Archbishop Grosz and the three bishops emphatically refused to accede.

Again began the process of collecting signatures for anti-Mindszenty petitions, which now demanded that the Cardinal receive the severest possible sentence. But 99% of the workers refusal to sign. Perhaps for the first time in modern history, the whole country joined in prayer and mourning for the Prince Primate.

The period after Cardinal Mindszenty's arrest may be described as that of the most grievous church persecution. Indubitably it was the Board of Bishops' unanimous front, combined with a universal reaction that gave even the Communists pause, which saved the situation. On January 3 the Board of Bishops was invited to the Prime Ministry, where Archbishop Grosz issued a declaration in its name:

"It is not true that the Board of Bishops opposes a republic.

"It is not true that the Board of Bishops agitated against land reform.

"It is not true that the Board of Bishops was unwilling to enter into deliberations.

"On the other hand, no discussions can be initiated so long as the head of the Board of Bishops, the Prince Primate of Hungary, is under arrest."

From every member of the Board of Bishops Matyas Rakosi demanded an anti-legitimist declaration condemning the restoration of the Habsburg Monarchy. Gyula Czapik, Archbishop of Eger, who at the side of the more passive Grosz had an ever greater role in church affairs, refused the demand as contravening the right of free opinion.

January 6 marked the return of the Jesuit Father Mocsy, whom Church authorities, with Bolshevist concurrence, had sent to Rome to consult the Vatican. Father Mocsy brought the Board of Bishops a message from His Holiness. He was arrested at once and is still in jail. In this atmosphere the regime sought in every way, but vainly, to force the Board of Bishops to undertake consultations.

In January 1949 the Bolshevists made another attempt to merge the sole surviving opposition party, the People's Democratic Party into the Communist-dominated coalition. Istvan

Barankovics, head of the party, foiled this attempt by fleeing the country and dissolving his party from abroad. Thus the Bolshevist hegemony prevailed completely.

To many in the free world it seemed incomprehensible why Moscow should have staged such a show-trial for the Cardinal, when the confession drawn up by his executioners was nullified in advance by his message to the Board of Bishops. Moscow and her hirelings should have known that the Calvary of the sainted heroic prelate would be universally regarded as the most dastardly assault on freedom and the dignity of man, and that it would shock the free world from its complacence. Moscow might have realized that she could indulge in no greater anti-propaganda and self-revelation. Plainly it would be a mistake to credit Communists with unfailing purposefulness in wooing the masses. Where dogma is involved, they are capable of the blindest irrationality.

A "people's court" condemned the Cardinal to death on February 8th, but his sentence later was commuted to life imprisonment. In their accustomed manner, the Bolshevists also implicated other ecclesiastic and lay figures at the Mindszenty trial, and these too were given severe prison sentences.

The Mindszenty trial occasioned deep repercussions in the free world. His Holiness on several occasions denounced with moving force this unexampled assault against liberty and the Church.

Soon after the Mindszenty trial, Communists began a persecution directed against an entire religious order. It involved the mass arrest of Jesuit leaders plus expropriation of Jesuit property, funds, Churches and institutions.

Meanwhile the summer of 1949 saw the end of the battle for the schools. Optional religious education was adopted. The law now prescribed that only those children could have religious instruction, whose parents officially requested this before the local soviet, an act automatically taken as a sign of hostility to the regime. In the year 1949-50, 90% of Catholic parents still insisted on religious instruction for their children, but by now only 25% dare face this intimidation.

The nation's new Soviet constitution went into effect on August 20, 1949, and for the first time in Hungarian history Church and state were completely separated. Paradoxically, however, the law would have practical effect only with the fall of the Bolshevist regime in Hungry. At present, there is no prospect of a separation, but only of the tightening of the shackles wherewith totalitarianism holds the Church captive.

A Moscow-sanctioned "Government Church Bureau" has

been set up over the churches with a view to disrupting them from within. Its first act was to expropriate the churches libraries and art treasures.

So much did the Church grow in prestige under persecution, that mass conversions from other faiths occurred for the first time since the Counter-Reformation. Characteristic are the statistics of a large parish in Budapest with a membership of 112,000. In 1938, the year of the Eucharistic World Congress in Budapest, 763,000 persons took Holy Communion, in 1948 1,270,000, in 1949 1,472,000, in 1950 1,693,000.

As we know the so-called peace fight is one of the Soviet Union's most militantly effective tools intended to entice groups in Bolshevized countries and elsewhere, which otherwise would reject Communism. From 1949 on the "peace fight" was used as a means of inducing various compromised clerics to join the "Ecclesiastical Peace Committee," the aim being to organize a "counter-clergy" for the subversion of the Church. This ended in a fiasco, with only 3 to 4% of the recruits playing an active role, though ultimately about thirty per cent of the clergy was pressured into joining. Within the framework of the "peace fight" the Board of Bishops also was required to make a number of peace declarations, but the latter contained nothing that a Catholic priest could not sign in good conscience.

Till the summer of 1952 the regime failed to force the Board of Bishops to sign any dictate. The Board of Bishops maintained its resolve not to enter into any agreement so long as Hungary's Prince Primate was held prisoner. The Communists thereupon seized some ten thousand monks and nuns—comprising the great majority of those in Hungary—and interned them, hoping thereby to snap the last ties with the Vatican.

The persecution of the religious orders actually had begun early in 1950, but the Board of Bishops at that time did not divine their true scope and significance. Now, however, when the Communists resorted to open violence, the Bishops did all in their power to lighten the trials of the internees. Meanwhile the regime threatened to send every single monk and nun to the Soviet Union, and also to initiate the mass internment of priests, unless the bishops acceded to its terms. Under duress the Board of Bishops was forced to abandon the principle that it would only sign agreements as a free agent.

Upon this agreement, members of the religious orders were released from custody, but all religious orders were disbanded except for units of the Franciscans, Benedictines, Piarists and women's orders. These were spared in order that, in a limited way, they might run the six boys' high schools and two girls' high schools that were restored to the Church. A very few members of the religious orders thereafter were able to function as priests; most could find employment only as manual laborers.

The regime's dictate was finally signed on August 30, 1952. Its provisions in brief were:

"The Board of Bishops recognizes and supports the Hungarian People's Republic, and will discipline clerics who foster dissent.

"The Board of Bishops condemns all subversive activities against the Hungarian People's Republic and will not allow religion and the Church to be mobilized against the state.

"The Board of Bishops will urge Catholics to give full support to the Five-Year Plan and will call upon the clergy not to foster opposition to the kolkhoz movement.

"The government of the Hungarian People's Republic guarantees complete religious freedom, and will restore to the Church six boys' high schools and two girls' high schools. It is willing to provide for the material needs of the Catholic Church over an 18-year period on a gradually diminishing basis."

The Board of Bishops knew that the regime would not keep its word, and so never recognized this agreement contracted under duress, emphasizing that its acceptance or rejection depended on the Holy See. The only further development was that the regime, for its part, persistently violated the agreement.

The regime next demanded loyalty oaths of the clergy, as pensioners of the state. The Board of Bishops refused, but allowed others to take the oaths. A year later, however, after staging another mock trial, the regime also forced the Board of Bishops to swear fealty.

Recognizing the continuing great influence of the Church, the regime resolved to abase it still further. The new victim was the head of the Board of Bishops, Jozsef Grosz, Archbishop of Kalocsa. Archbishop Grosz was arrested on May 18, 1951 and sentenced to death on June 18, the sentence later being commuted to life imprisonment. Other clerics whom the regime found unmalleable were also implicated: thus, certain members of the Hungarian-founded Palos Order, and Vendel Endredy, chief abbot of the Cistercian Order, an eminent pillar of the Church. A father of the Palos Order was executed, the other defendants received long prison sentences on charges completely at variance with the facts.

The Grosz trial was aimed to break the will of the Church once and for all. Bishops and heads of religious orders were made to take loyalty oaths in Budapest before Parliament. Using the testimony of the Grosz trial as a pretext, the Government

Church Bureau reorganized the Church, naming "peace priests" to act as vicars alongside each bishop and filling executive posts with its own men. The bishops themselves were placed under the surveillance of the political police.

Despite all persecution, however, the vocation of the priesthood was never more highly esteemed, nor were there ever so many enrollments in theological seminaries. The regime, opining that seminaries had assumed the role of the religious orders and had become nests of "clerical resistance," forced the disbandment of all but four seminaries and the Academy of Theology, which had been separated from the University of Budapest. The leadership of the surviving seminaries likewise was infiltrated with "peace priests." Bolshevist indoctrination was made part of the curriculum, which is now kept under strict surveillance to assure control over the education of youth.

"Salami tactics" had likewise become the rule in the present phase of Church persecution. Priests unwilling to join the "peace movement" are removed from their posts. The greatest crime of all is care for the spiritual needs of youth. Priests so engaged are branded as "corrupters of youth" and put out of the way.

The Bolshevists, as everywhere behind the Curtain, are waging a battle to the death. The Church is isolated from the outside world with the ultimate aim of establishing "National Churches" due to be merged with the pan-Russian Orthodox Church. Yet the churches are more crowded than ever and millions worship morning and evening, even on week days, despite all fulminations of the Party. Believers try to escape surveillance by visiting churches far from their own districts. In villages naturally this is not feasible, but there the innate cohesion and religious feeling of the villagers renders Bolshevists more or less impotent. Miracles and manifestations are of frequent occurrence. Though the Bolshevist authorities have removed wayside crosses and chapels and other characteristic religious landmarks, the people through persecution have become all the more aware of the inner meaning and mystery of these outward forms, and now reveal depths of devotion not unlike those of the first centuries of Christianity. Never in the course of centuries has the Church found so direct a way to the hearts of the people; never has it been so much the Church of the nation. The vast majority of Catholics, comprising almost 70% of the population, are fused in a spiritual community that has dissolved all class differences.

WILLIAM JUHASZ.

PART VI:

CATHOLIC DEVELOPMENTS
in
SPAIN and LATIN AMERICA

by

J. N. Moody - E. Castaneda
Carlos D. Hamilton

CHAPTER I

THE SOCIO-RELIGIOUS PROBLEMATIC OF SPAIN

It was the original intention of the editor to include a treatment of the social and political developments of Spanish Catholicism in this volume. It was soon discovered that a non-partisan analysis of the complex socio-religious situation in Spain was difficult to achieve and that an adequate discussion would exceed the modest limitations of space that were available in a volume of this type. Reluctantly it was decided to confine the treatment of Spain to a few general points with the hope that students might be stimulated to explore the fundamental issues in the Spanish situation in an objective manner.

The editor is in full sympathy with the editorial in the London *Tablet* of 28 July 1951,[1] which asked the Historical Association of Great Britain to join with other professional bodies to study the roots of the Spanish Civil War. Pointing out the abundant material now available, it added:

> "It is a great reproach to the intellectual life of our time that the salient characteristics of such an important event should be left, fifteen years afterward, so much in the world of political propaganda."

Fundamentally, Spain is an integral part of Western Europe. As such, it has been affected by all the major currents of European thought. At the same time, the Spanish historical experience has been developed in partial isolation, with the result that it has characteristics and overtones which are quite distinct from those of the rest of the Continent. The Pyrenees may be compared to a prism which refracts the streams of light coming from the north. The result is that the terms ordinarily used in European historiography have different connotations when applied to the Peninsula. Besides, the Iberian peoples have strong ties with North Africa, and through it, with the cultural centers of the Middle East. And they have been profoundly stamped by influences coming from beyond the seas.

An illustration is available in the case of Liberalism. An attempt has been made, in the essays on France and Italy, to indicate the origins and general directions of this very comprehensive movement. The intellectual currents and economic

changes that produced these modifications in European life in
the eighteenth and nineteenth centuries did not leave Spain
unaffected, but they did take on a distinctive Hispanic colora-
tion. Spanish Liberalism was even more basically anti-clerical
than its counterpart elsewhere; its major preoccupation might
be said to be its struggle with the Church. Sociologically, it
followed the familiar pattern of a bourgeois effort to gain
political power. But the slower pace of Spanish economic
change intensified resistance, the middle class was never strong
enough to win decisive victories, and regional and religious
conflicts complicated the picture. As a consequence, even when
Liberal political institutions were set up, they operated quite
differently from elsewhere in Western Europe. Moreover, Spanish Liberals were as intensely resistant to social concessions
as were their Italian counterparts, and their activities so worsened an already bad agrarian situation that it has remained a
major cancer in Spanish life.

No sketch of Spanish life is complete without emphasis on the
enduring local, provincial, and regional influences. The Spaniards achieved national unity relatively early, but the national
consciousness has never been strong enough to dominate effectively the powerful regional loyalties. So while the other
European states present a more or less consistent picture of a
steadily increasing national sentiment at the expense of provincial allegiances, Spanish history is an oscillation between cen-
tripetal and centrifugal forces, with the latter remaining a
constant threat to national stability.

The struggle for regional autonomy was embittered by the
character of the major agent in unification. Castile played the
role of a Spanish Prussia or Piedmont. Geographically and
historically, it was destined to be the unifier and the dominant
area; yet it lacked adequate resources, and its less commercially-
minded population never won the respect of the more favored
Catalonians or more enterprising Basques. Resistance to Castilian control not only affected Spanish politics. It is evident
in the religious and social conflicts as well.

Catholicism has played a unique role in Spanish history. The
outstanding historical memory of Spaniards is the Reconquest,
which became the nodal concept in the formation of their
national consciousness. This effort to rid the Peninsula of
Moorish control, which flamed intermittently over many centuries, became inseparably attached to loyalty to Catholicism.
It was undertaken, at least ostensibly, in the interest of the
faith. Its success required strong ecclesiastical support. Its progress deepened the association of Catholicism with the most

fundamental aspirations of a people. Even more strongly than in the roughly analogous cases of Ireland and Poland, religion in Spain became inseparable from the realization of the national objectives.[2]

As a consequence, Spanish history emphasized religious orthodoxy even more strongly than did the other emergent national states of Europe. The conviction that a single religious creed was essential for national homogeneity was shared by all in the early modern period, and the acceptance of religious pluralism in a political unit is relatively recent. Spain felt this apparent need for religious unity more keenly because of her historical experience, while the persistence of local and regional loyalties appeared to justify its retention when other peoples moved toward tolerance. Thus, when the suppression of religious minorities was common in all the nascent national states, Spain showed a special rigidity and stronger emphasis on crushing dissent. The brutal persecution of the Moorish and Jewish minorities on the morrow of the successful Reconquest was the consequence of the mood that had inspired this crusading movement. Hence, while deplorable, the Inquisition and its concomitants won powerful popular support.

The relation of Catholicism to this central historical experience also permanently influenced the relations of Church and State in Spain. All the monarchies of the Old Regime succeeded in gaining control of the dominant religious bodies in their territories. But nowhere was this curbing of religious independence more complete than in the Iberian Peninsula. The essay on Latin America in this volume has high-lighted the importance of the *Patronato Real* in the Spanish lands in the New World. It was equally primary in the religious history of the mother country, and it had the same general effects. This Spanish instrument for the control of religion was forged during the Reconquest when the Papacy granted extensive concessions to the Kings who led the attack on the Moors. With the consolidation of the various kingdoms into a single unit, the royal influence in ecclesiastical affairs was broadened. The clergy managed to retain a measure of independence during the Golden Age, but the eighteenth century drift toward Bourbon absolutism completed the process of State control and made the Church increasingly dependent on political forces.

The variety of governments, some of them anti-clerical, which have ruled and misruled Spain in the nineteenth and twentieth centuries have shown no disposition to relax this stranglehold. At the present moment, the Spanish Church is still governed by the Concordat of 1851, whch is basically that of 1753 and which is highly prejudicial to the free functioning of religion.[3] By these arrangements, not only are all important positions in the Church nominated by the civil authorities, but the government maintains strict control over clerical training in the Seminaries and all other aspects of Catholic activity. Under such conditions, vigorous religious reform is nearly impossible. Worse still, while the Church may have gained temporary advantages from this connection in the days of Spanish expansion, she has suffered seriously from the political incompetence and maladministration that has marked the politics of the Peninsula in the recent centuries. As an integral part of Spanish culture, the Church in Spain would have ordinarily reflected the vicissitudes of the national history, which has passed from the intense exuberance and creativeness of the early modern period to the creeping paralysis of the last two centuries or more. But the strict control of the *structure* of the Church has heightened this trend. It has also associated religion with the successive political failures.

It must be noted that this situation did not evolve without serious opposition. Throughout the sixteenth and seventeenth centuries, Spanish Catholicism displayed a vigor and zeal that is still largely unappreciated in English-speaking lands. The work of the religious orders in protecting the Indians and developing a law for their preservation is generally known.[4] But less attention is paid to the long clerical resistance to absolutism in Spain, with concomitant support of provincial autonomy. This period, which marked the greatest rigor against non-conformism, also was a time of the most complete social equality, with the vigorous defense of personal and local liberties by churchmen.[5] The Church was generally on the side of the workers and peasants against the powerful. Advanced social theories were proposed by distinguished clerical scholars who had been impressed by the collectivist civilization of the Incas. Some of these advocated the abolition of private property in land as a solution to Spain's economic woes.

The vitality of Spanish Catholicism had already seriously declined by the beginning of the nineteenth century. It had suffered from the anti-Papal ecclesiastical policy of the eighteenth century Bourbons, from the expulsion of the Jesuits, and from other crippling interventions of the Crown. During the resistance to Napoleon, however, clerics had been particularly active, and the relationship between clergy and people never seemed so close as it was during this national crisis. But the Restoration Monarchy embarked on a stupid, reactionary policy which the clergy in general supported.[6] This period was decisive in modern Spanish history, for the failure to achieve a balance between new and old, to find a compromise that would win general support, poisoned subsequent Spanish development. Since ecclesiastics were involved, Spanish Liberalism was strengthened in its original anti-clericalism. It was the vehemence of the Restoration that insured the hostility toward religion evidenced in the revolts of 1821 and in all subsequent revolutionary movements.

In the second quarter of the nineteenth century, the Church lost the great landed wealth that had been her major support. With the changed political and economic climate, it was inevitable that she would be stripped of the immense holdings which had been accumulated during her great days. But, as in France, the effect of this sudden deprival of her means of support had serious consequences. It further reduced the independence of the clergy vis-a-vis the government, on which they now relied for their meager stipends. It also marks the begining of the divorce of the Spanish clergy from the greater part of the Spanish poor because the dependence on the contributions of the wealthy for the maintenance of religious activities was an increasingly important factor. The tragic result was the failure of churchmen generally to take the leadership in pressing for social reform. Spain certainly belonged to that area which Pius XI described when he deplored the loss of the working class to religion during the course of the nineteenth century.

The fate of the Church is intimately bound up with the most serious social malady in Spain—the agrarian problem. The Liberal governments which expropriated the Church properties sold them in large lots to the highest bidder. At the same time, they encouraged the appropriation of the common land by individual owners. As a result, the great estates, particularly in the south, were built up during this period, often in the hands of *nouveaux riches* who were more ruthless and efficient than the older landed gentry. The lot of the landless and the peasant sharply declined into that chronic misery that is their lot in much of Spain. There is a clear correlation between this process and the religious situation in rural Spain: in the region of the *latifundia* and poverty-stricken agricultural workers, the decline of religious practice has been most complete; in the area of small peasant proprietors, largely the north, Catholicism has maintained its traditional hold.

By the first quarter of the twentieth century, Spanish society was in a state of growing instability, verging on dissolution.

The evolution toward a secular commercial society had been incomplete and had left serious tensions. Into this social disequilibrium came industrialism. Necessary as it was to meet the needs of a growing population on an inadequate agrarian base, industrialism brought a new series of problems. The inability to offer the urban proletariat any reasonable hope of betterment led ultimately to its espousal of revolutionary, and anti-religious solutions.[7]

These conditions have been reflected in the successive Spanish governments of the past one hundred years. It became increasingly difficult to find a basis for stable government; the essential element of a fund of common values or ideas was harder to discover. Spain was not favored with the opportunity to face successively a series of fundamental issues, as more fortunate countries have been. Her problems have piled up to the point where a number of new worlds were simultaneously striving to be born.[8] All modern countries have faced similarly serious problems, but in Spain they have been concentrated in a single framework and intensified by mutual contact. Consequently, there was lacking a consensus on basic questions that alone can insure sound government.

It is this deep cleavage that explains the failure of constitutional government in Spain's recent past. Democracy requires more than institutional forms, such as Parliaments and elections. It demands a fundamental agreement in a majority of the citizens on the objectives and rules of political life. The absence of such basic agreement makes a democratic system unworkable. Allegiance to a common body of political principles is weak in many contemporary European countries; it is nearly non-existent in present-day Spain.

But while Spain conspicuously lacks that minimum of agreement on political fundamentals which is the chief strength of peoples of the English tradition, she has elements of inner strength that come to the surface in times of crisis. These are mobilized when dissolution threatens, and work for the establishment of a new, uneasy equilibrium that while unsatisfactory to many, is temporarily accepted by most. Thus, Spain has had more than her share of revolutionary explosions, and her basic tensions are yet unresolved. Yet she regains some sort of balance after each explosion, like an inebriate who, in his staggering, retains an unconscious impulse to continue toward his objective. Spanish society has not as yet reached that state of dissolution that marked Russia at the close of World War I, or China and Burma more recently. Spanish outbreaks of violence have been followed by periods of relative calm.

The contemporary Spanish attitude toward Catholicism seems to follow this cycle. Large sections of Hispanic society are permanently alienated from the Church, largely for the sociological reasons which have been briefly sketched above. During revolutionary periods, much larger sections of the population have indulged in arson and in the slaughter of religious. Despite the defections and the anti-clericalism, religion still exercises more popular influence in Spain than in most of her neighbors.

The difficulty in establishing stable government in Spain has been aggravated in the present century. There were thirty-two changes of government in the twenty years before the establishment of the dictatorship in 1923. During this period, existing political institutions lost most of their appeal: the prestige of the monarchy dwindled precipitously; parliamentary forms were discredited by fraudulent elections, maladministration, the absence of a positive program by the political parties, and the indifference of the ruling groups of all sorts to social reform. The dictatorship of Primo de Rivera did nothing to repair these basic fissures. The Republic took over easily in an atmosphere of political bankruptcy. But it failed to gain the positive support that was necessary for success: one segment of the population remained fundamentally devoted to the older institutions; another, concentrated in the rural and urban proletariat, was pledged to varying degrees of extremism. Within a month, serious violence from a variety of sources plagued the new regime.

The first year of the Republic was given over to the elaboration of a new Constitution that had marked anti-clerical features. The majority of the Constituent Cortes justified these measures on the ground that the bulk of the clergy and of practising Catholics were supporters of the Old Regime. The claim was correct. Yet in the opinion of most who have sought a balanced judgment, this identification of Republicanism and anti-clericalism was a mistake.[9] While a majority of clerics were wedded to the monarchy, a considerable body of the parish clergy had voted for the Republic,[10] which was also supported by outstanding Catholic intellectuals and some members of religious orders. These might have expanded their influence, had not the payment of old scores against the Church been given high priority. The result was that the enemies of the Republic could claim the label of defenders of the Faith.

The short history of the Republic was one of the polarization of extremes, leading to an explosion. This occurred on both the Right and the Left, with force appearing as the only possible solution to the activists of both sides. As so often happens in similar circumstances, the moderates who wished for a peaceful settlement, and who may have formed a majority of the population, found it more and more impossible to maintain themselves in an atmosphere of increasing conflict. It is significant that the reformist Socialists were meeting with violence at the hands of the Left Wing of their party, while the latter were harassed by the Anarcho-Syndicalists who had become more vigorously revolutionary since the imposition of the dictatorship in the twenties; at the same time, the CEDA, the moderate Catholic groups at least nominally loyal to the Republic, were being violently assaulted by the Falangists!

The will to violence and its increasing employment in the stormy years of the Republic led directly to the Civil War. In the existing international antagonisms, Spaniards were not permitted to write their bloody epitaphs in isolation. Fascist Italy had pledged its support to the revolt beforehand, and it fulfilled its bond with strong German assistance. The increasing intervention of the Soviet Union and of the International Brigades intensified the polarization within Spain and made more complex the issues at stake. The fiction of non-intervention prevented an immediate extension of the Spanish Civil War into a world war, but it also guaranteed the victory of the anti-Republicans.

In this exhausting struggle, the overwhelming majority of the hierarchy and clergy supported the armed attack upon the Republic. Yet even here there were complications: two of the most Catholic provinces of the country fought vigorously with the Loyalists, and isolated Catholics in other areas remained faithful to the Republic.

Catholics outside Spain have passed, as is their right, varied judgments on the dictatorship now ruling in the Peninsula. While all Catholics deplore the violence against religious persons and property that marked the Republican period, divergence of Catholic opinion on the Franco regime has been sharp. The editor of this volume accepts the unfavorable verdict of Don Luigi Sturzo,[11] who sees the present government of Spain as a blend of the old *ideology* of the authoritarianism and conservatism of the early nineteenth century with the Fascist *techniques* elaborated by Mussolini. Accepting this evaluation, it is difficult to see how the existing regime can be defended theoretically in the light of traditional Catholic principles of human liberty and the dignity of the human person. That these principles were once vigorously asserted in Spain by priests such as Vitoria, Mariana, and Suarez merely points up the fact that the present government in Spain is the end-product of an historical accumulation of unsolved problems rather than any genuine flowering of the Catholic tradition in politics.

In the disturbed background of nineteenth and twentieth century Spain, one finds considerable concentration on existing political questions but few significant contributions to Catholic political thought. The same is generally true in the field of social thought. Here the climate was more favorable, as economic Liberalism took very little root in Spain. Catholics, like Spaniards generally, still give allegiance to the pre-capitalistic attitudes toward wealth and economic activity. The *ethos* of capitalism, with its emphasis on thrift, industry, chance-taking, and the possession of wealth as an index of human value, has made little appeal. The thread of anti-capitalist thinking, inherited from the Middle Ages, was never completely broken in Spanish Catholic thought and recurs frequently in Catholic writing on social questions.

Efforts to translate this approach into effective social action in the nineteenth century were spasmodic and generally unsucessful. The early workingmen's mutual aid societies were generally begun under Catholic auspices, but with the growing social conflict they usually disappeared or came under the more aggressive direction of the Anarchists or Socialists. The most promising of the early trade unions was organized in Valencia in 1861 by the Jesuit, Father Vincent,[13] but his movement petered out in 1874 in the face of ecclesiastical and managerial opposition.

Only in the north did Catholics succeed in building a permanent working class movement that could hold its own against the rapidly expanding organizations of the Left. *The Federación Nacional de Sindicatos Cathólicos Libres* was founded by the Dominicans in 1912. It was a genuine labor organization that participated actively in strikes and did not scruple to join with the Socialist unions for common objectives. It was an energetic unit of the Christian Trade Union International, and it published effective studies of working class problems in Spain. Like its rivals, this Christian federation in the Basque and other northern provinces, expanding greatly under the dictatorship of Rivera and under the Republic, maintained its labor support till the tragedy of the Civil War. With the victory of Franco, it has been banned, along with all other forms of free trade unionism.

Papal thought has insisted on the *natural* right of men to form labor unions. Experience has shown that the character of a regime is revealed in its attitude to the free organization of workingmen. Franco's prohibition of genuine trade unionism, and his establishment of state-controlled associations of the Fascist type, is a clear index of the nature of the regime.

Much the same pattern is found in the Catholic agrarian associations or *syndicates* which operated credit banks and other mutual aid activities. They were federated in León and Old Castile in 1912, and, while strongest in the north, had branches in most sections, united in a *Confederacion Nacional Catholico-Agraria*.[14] This movement, too, expanded rapidly in the 20's but was fatally weakened in the Civil War and extinguished by the present regime, which is jealous of any social action that is not strictly State-directed.

There is some evidence of the revival of Catholic social action in Spain in the past few years. The efforts of Bishop Angel Herrera of Málaga have received particularly favorable notice in the world press. This founder of the journal *El Debate* and former president of Catholic Action retired in 1935 to Fribourg to study for the priesthood. Consecrated bishop in 1947, he has interested himself in all aspects of the social problem and has founded the *Escuela Social Sacerdotal* for the social training of the clergy.[15] This initiative has been followed in other dioceses, and a considerable awakening has been reported by visitors who have studied the development at first hand.

Whether these movements can vitally heal the deep scars that were further inflamed in the Civil War, and whether they can mitigate the effect of the present regime's ostentatious avowals of devotion to Catholicism is highly problematical.[16] Spain today, as so frequently before, is in a transitional period. The abnormal political condition has none of the characteristics of permanence. Change will come, and nearly all depends on whether that change will come peacefully as a result of wise concessions or new violence will further embitter Spanish minds. Linked with this, there is another question: will the Church emerge from the trials of the past twenty years with a new vigor and with a capacity to lead Spain toward social peace, or will it become again the target of another cycle of revolutionary disturbances prompted by an adverse judgment on its present course? The evidence is conflicting, the portents are not too encouraging.

J. N. MOODY

CHAPTER II

SOCIAL DEVELOPMENTS AND MOVEMENTS IN LATIN AMERICA

The transitional crisis through which the world is passing has evoked tremendous conflicts in our day and has given rise to complex problems that constitute a serious menace to humanity. Mankind finds itself placed between two materialistic issues: Capitalism and Communism. Some prefer to designate the two camps Democracy and Totalitarianism. Before this dilemma, Catholic social thought has an undeniable right of being heard. The social doctrine of the Church, is, as any other doctrine, a part of universal thought and needs be taken into account in the frantic search for a satisfactory solution of the world crisis. It has been said that the world hungers and thirsts today not only for justice, but for truth and understanding. Through its social doctrine Christianity alone perhaps can bring the desired truth, justice and understanding.[17]

We stand divided between two philosophies of life, two ways of living. The fruit of secularism, materialism, utilitarianism has proved bitter fruit and brought serious social problems. Latin America has not been able to escape the gigantic struggle of the conflicting ideologies of our day. The western world clamors for a return to moral values as the means of saving the basic principles of western civilization, while everybody searches for the root of the evils that confront us today. Some blame the machine, others hold Socialism and Communism responsible, and both socialists and communists alike blame the liberal economic individualism of the XIX century and organized religion, particularly the Roman Catholic Church. "The social conflict which economic liberalism provoked is related to the atheistic revolution. The leaders of every atheistic drive utilize the present economic crisis," said Pope Pius XI in 1933, "to prove to the masses with fiendish logic that God and Religion are the cause of the present universal misery." [18]

Such is in broad outline the situation we face today. It has its roots in the distant past of our modern era. Some find them in our own brave New World. The discovery of America, they claim, was more than a geographic accident that proved

the sphericity of the earth. Economists point out that this
event was a powerful factor in the integration of a capitalistic
society. If we stop to reflect upon the matter, it seems a strange
coincidence that the XVI century, which saw thousands of
zealous missionaries driven by religious fervor come to the
New World to preach the brotherhood of man and carry the
teachings of Christianity to the savage heathens, and thousands
of earnest dissenters to search for religious freedom, witnessed
likewise a revival of the institution of slavery in all its degrad-
ing aspects in both Catholic and non-Catholic America. The
inescapable and harsh reality of the need for labor to develop
a virgin continent and make it bloom appears to have drowned
the religious sentiments and moral considerations of all but
a few stout defenders of the inalienable right to liberty of all
human beings, such as the immortal Las Casas.

That the efforts of the devoted missionaries to protect the
native races were not entirely in vain is proved by the fact
that in the lands settled by Spain there was a lower proportional ratio of legally constituted slaves than in the English
colonies. The temptation of making the native races out and
out slaves was restrained to a considerable extent by the heroic
defense of the missionaries.

Before sketching the role of the Church in the Spanish
colonial empire, necessary to the understanding of the social
problems of Latin America today, it is important to keep in
mind that Spanish colonization differed fundamentally from
English colonization in North America. The Spanish conquest
and settlement assumed, as was to be expected in the XVI
century, a feudal character, whereas the English plan put in
effect a century later was capitalistic from its very inception.
The English colonies were founded by trading companies to
expand trade and commerce with the capital of stockholding
companies. They were, in fact, a business venture. It was the
Spanish Crown on the other hand that first undertook the
great enterprise itself in the XV century, urged by the sacred
charge given their Most Catholic Majesties by Pope Alexander
VI to propagate the faith among the peoples of the new
lands.[19]

So profound was the influence of the Church in the establishment and development of Spain's colonial empire, and so
successful were its efforts in Christianizing and civilizing the
native races that a knowledge of the story of the Church is
indispensable to an understanding of the many problems that
face the countries and people of Latin America today. The
subject is too often ignored, or purposely avoided by writers

and students because of the strong passions it invariably arouses. Many find it much more easy to dismiss the subject with a knowing wink or a shrug of the shoulders, explaining the backwardness of Spanish America by attributing it to the strangling influence of the Church and the lack of political sense of the Spaniard without going into details. Too frequently, it is asserted blandly and without proof that the fanaticism of the Spaniard, a result of the Church's intolerance, is responsible for the prevalent illiteracy, the abject poverty, the deplorable health and sanitary conditions, the inadequacy of the transportation facilities, the inefficiency of the system of communications, the apparently endless revolutions, the dirt, the filth, and the general absence of a social consciousness in Latin America.[20] The fact that Spain developed a colonial system of government more than a century before the first English settlement was founded, that it lasted for three hundred years with minor changes, and that a monumental code of laws for the Indies was devised and compiled is forgotten, as well as the immense educational program of the Church and its constant watchfulness to protect the helpless natives.[21]

Meaning and Consequences of Patronato Real

Contrary to general belief, the Spanish colonies were not Church-ridden, rather the Church in the Spanish colonies was king-ridden. To this encroachment of the Crown are traceable many of the abuses that developed as a result of the subjection of the Church to civil authority. What was the basis for the authority exercised by the Crown over the Church? The basis was the *Patronato Real*. The literal translation of the term "Royal Patronage" does not fully explain all its implications. Under this term are included the various privileges granted from time to time by the Pope to the kings of Spain prior to the discovery of the New World, privileges which in the course of time came to be considered inalienable rights of the Crown, declared by the regalists to be inherent in the exercise of sovereignty. This conception became the basic issue in the reestablishment of relations between the governments of the Latin American countries and the papacy after the attainment of independence. The contention that the royal patronage exercised by Spain's rulers in Amerca was an attribute of sovereignty, stoutly defended by the Spanish ambassadors in Rome, delayed the restoration of normal relations between the faithful in Spanish America and the Vatican for almost a quarter of a century. During this period, a breach appeared which has not been bridged completely.

Alfonso the Wise of Spain dedicated a portion of the *Siete Partidas,* perhaps the first codification of modern law, to a discussion of *Real Patronato,* explaining that the kings of Spain enjoyed these privileges granted by the Pope as a recognition of the services they had rendered in the propagation of the faith, the sustained crusade against the Moors, the care exercised in erecting and founding new churches in the conquered lands, and the faithfulness with which they had endowed and supported them. *Patronato Real,* even as early as the XIII century, included the right of presentation of candidates for appointment to the hierarchy, and to all benefices and honors, the right to a portion of the tithes to help their Most Catholic Majesties propagate the faith and maintain the churches, and, after the discovery of America, the right of *placet,* without which no ecclesiastical decree or communication from the Vatican could be promulgated in the colonies. This last right is generally referred to in Spanish as *Pase Real,* literally "Royal Pass," permission to be allowed to pass and be promulgated in the colonies. Covarrubias, a regalist, in his *Opera omnia,* comes to the conclusion by the XVI century that the right of presentation is not a privilege but an inherent right of the Crown, an assertion that was firmly maintained by the kings of Spain.[22]

In the discussion of the right of Spain to undertake the conquest and settlement of the New World, the Papal Bull of Demarcation of Alexander VI has been the cause of heated argument, but little if any attention has been paid to his bull of February, 1492, issued before the Capitulation of Santa Fe with Columbus. Here is a document dealing with the Christianization of lands taken from the infidels in Africa, given before the New World was discovered. Pope Alexander VI granted the kings of Spain the exercise of *Patronato Real* in all the lands it might wrench from the infidels in Africa. Spain, like Portugal, was expanding into Africa and wished to obtain papal permission to Christianize the conquered peoples. The grant of the rights of *Patronato Real* meant authority for the Spanish Crown to propagate the faith in the lands brought under its jurisdiction, the right to erect churches, and to instruct the infidels in the teachings of Christianity. By implication, it gave a moral basis for jurisdiction over the new lands acquired and authorized the Spanish monarchs to undertake their penetration and occupation.

On what grounds could the Pope give title to new lands? This question, said to have been raised by Francis I of France in questioning the exclusive right granted to the Spanish monarchs by the establishment of the line of demarcation, has its answer in the generally accepted principle of the supremacy of the spiritual over the temporal which prevailed during the middle ages. It was firmly believed that the Pope, as the Vicar of Christ on earth, could give or assign lands occupied by barbarians, a term charitably applied to those ignorant of Christianity, to Christian princes on the basis that temporal jurisdiction was subordinate to spiritual. This is not strange in an age in which the moral authority of the Pope was solicited by secular princes as a guarantee against unscrupulous rivals. The Bull of Alexander VI of February, 1942, was directed to the definition of the jurisdiction within which the rival Christian kings of Portugal and Spain, engaged then in the exploration, conquest, settlement, and Christianization of the dark continent, might find legitimate exercise.

Immediately upon the return of Columbus, King Ferdinand and Queen Isabel of Spain appealed to Pope Alexander VI for identical reasons to legitimatize areas of activity in the lands just discovered, or that might be discovered in the future.

The Papal Bull of Demarcation of May 5, 1493 attempted to designate in a general way the portions of the world not occupied by Christians in which the two great Christianizing and exploring kingdoms of Portugal and Spain might exercise their zeal. It did not, in fact, give title to the lands in the generally accepted juridical sense, rather it gave the Spanish Crown spiritual jurisdiction, the authority to undertake the evangelization of the lands discovered and to be discovered west of the imaginary line drawn to delimit the respective fields of activity, leaving the lands to the east for Portuguese enterprise. It did not impose temporal penalties for violations, but enjoined all Christian princes "under ecclesiastical censure" to abide by the assignment made.

This pronouncement may be said to be the origin of *Patronato Real* in America. To remove whatever doubt might exist on this point, Pope Julius II, by his Bull *Universalis Ecclesiae* of July 28, 1508, given in the fifth year of his pontificate, specifically made all the rights and privileges enjoyed by the Spanish kings under the designation of *Real Patronato* in Spain, Granada, and the other kindoms extend to the Church in the Indies. King Ferdinand and Queen Juana, sole heir to the Kingdoms of Castile and Leon had solicited a clarication of the matter.

"We, after mature deliberation with our brethern, the Cardinals of the Holy Roman Catholic Church, and with their ad-

vice, accede to the request and do grant, through the present
document, by Apostolic authority to the said King Ferdinand
and Queen Juana, and to the kings of Castile and Leon, that
no one may, without their consent, construct or erect or constitute churches in the islands conquered, or that may be conquered in the future, in the lands beyond the sea; and because
it is to the interest of the said sovereigns we further grant to
them the right of *Patronato* in those lands to present worthy
persons for appointment to cathedrals, and all other metropolitan churches, monasteries, dignities in the said cathedrals,
and even metropolitan churches and shrines, and to all other
ecclesiastical benefices, said right to be exercised in filling
within a year all vacancies, subject to canonical confirmation.

"The right of instituting to minor benefices belongs to the
ordinaries, but if they should fail to make provision within ten
days without legitimate cause, than the bishop concerned, or
any other ecclesiastic authority may do so at the request of King
Ferdinand, or Queen Juana, or whoever might be the king." [23]

The vast power in religious matters thus granted to the
Spanish sovereigns, which in truth subjected the Church to the
Crown, were jealously guarded and insisted upon by the kings
of Spain. Pope Paul III reaffirmed the privileges of *Real Patronato* granted to Spain in his Bull of December 18, 1534, by
which the Diocese of Guatemala was created; Pope Sixtus V
repeated the confirmation to Philip III and Philip IV in the
seventeenth century; Benedict XIV, in the Spanish concordat of
January 11, 1753, again recognized the rights of *Patronato Real*
in the Indies, stating "there never has been any question over
the nomination of archbishops, bishops, and candidates to benefices by the Catholic kings whenever vacancies occur in the
Indies."

A great Mexican scholar has summarized the significance of
Real Patronato in the Indies in the following words:

By virtue of it (the Bull of Julius the II), of other concessions obtained later, and somewhat by custom and corruption, the kings of Spain came to acquire such a hand
in the ecclesiastical government of America, that with the
exception of the purely spiritual, they exercised an authority which appeared to be pontifical. Without their permission no churches, monasteries or hospitals could be
erected; nor even could a bishopric or parish be founded.
Clerics and religious could not go to America without expressed license. The kings named bishops and without
awaiting confirmation they sent them to administer their
dioceses. They determined the limits of bishoprics and

changed them as they wished. They had the right of presentation or nomination to all benefices or employments, even to that of sacristan, if they wished. They reprimanded severely, calling to Spain or exiling any ecclesiastic, including bishops who repeatedly acted contrary to orders of the governors, pretending not to hear the voice of the king. They administered and collected the *diezmos,* deciding who ought to pay and how, without making use of bulls and exemptions. They fixed the rents of the benefices and increased them or decreased them as they judged to be convenient . . . Finally, no disposition of the Holy Pontiff could be executed without the approval or *pase* of the king . . . To the king, not directly to the pope, the bishops presented their doubts, and we are surprised to see that those relating to baptism are sent to the council. Always the civil power interposed itself between our Church and the Supreme Pastor.[24]

Fortunately for the Church, the kings of Spain, whatever else may be said about them, remained steadfast and loyal Catholics, who prided themselves in being the champions of the Church in the old world and the new. The religious fervor of the devoted missionaries that carried the teachings of Christianity to the remotest confines of the unchartered lands of America and across the South Sea to the Philippines, China, and Japan received the unstinted support of all royal officials. As a matter of fact the propagation of the faith was from the beginning a powerful motivating force in the exploration and penetration of the New World.

It is not strange, therefore, that the Church and its apostolic mission in America left deep-rooted and inseparable moral traits that have affected the public and private institutions of the colonies. It came to envelop the whole life of the settlers and the natives as well. It gave the Spanish colonial society, says one of the contemporary distinguished scholars of Latin America, "a confused and perplexing mysticism that was the essence of the fusion of two civilizations." [24a]

In the development of culture in the New World, it was the Church, through its zealous missionaries, its learned and saintly men, that performed the miracle of the transformation of a virgin contient and its native races into a civilized Christian community. From the very beginning of the conquest and settlement, the Church sponsored a program of general education for all classes. Pedro de Gante and his little band transmitted the fire of their burning enthusiasm, their love for learning, and their sensitive appreciation for art to the Indian youth. There is no other explanation for the incredible progress made during the early years in the Christianization and civilization of the native races. Thus the secret informer of His Majesty could truthfully report in 1542 that in visiting the school for boys at San Juan de Tlatelolco, he had noted that they spoke Latin "better than Cicero himself." Less than a quarter of a century later Valeriano, a pure blooded Indian, was teaching the beauties of the Greek and Latin classics to the sons of the conquistadors in the Franciscan monastery.[25] The talented missionaries of that glorious century literally breathed new life into the budding colonial art and literature. They evolved a new philosophy of life, as it were, with strange pagan reminiscences, but firmly grounded on the concept of the brotherhood of man, which made all human beings members of the universal family. The influence of the Christian spirit extended beyond literature and art. The new political institutions were based on Christian principles.[26] The *Recopilacion de las Leyes de las Indias* is inpregnated with a sense of human justice not found in any other body of law.

An impartial reexamination of the history of the conquest reveals that it was not a military accomplishment alone, but a spiritual conquest as well, won in many instances by the moral fortitude of the missionary. The Cross in many cases preceded the sword and succeeded in bringing under the influence of Christianity areas that had resisted all efforts to subdue them by force. The figure of the missionary in the history of the Americas is unique, a heroic mystic, a curious mixture of pious innocence and blind credulity, influenced by ethnic, geographic, and economic factors.

The desire to convert the heathen of the New World became an obsession. The same religious fervor that electrified Europe at the time of the first crusades swept over Spain in the first half of the XVI century. Suddenly Europe grew too narrow and inadequate, unworthy of their efforts to expand the kingdom of God on earth. The soldiers of the Cross abandoned it cheerfully for the unexplored wilds of America and the untried privations and sufferings of the new lands.

To work among the heathen, to spread the teachings of the Master among the natives, became a passion. The ecstasy experienced by those who succeeded in coming is vividly portrayed in the account of Fray Francisco Solano, who accompanied Hurtado de Mendoza. Upon his arrival in Santo Domingo, he could not wait to touch the shores of the land where his ardent desire would be fulfilled. Jumping overboard, he waded ashore and cried out with unrestrained joy as he ran up and down the beach "Let me die a martyr, if I fail in my efforts to win new souls." Two hundred years later the same spirit burned as brightly and passionately in the bosom of Fray Junipero Serra, the last of the great empire builders in America. When told in 1749 that he had been chosen to go to New Spain, he cheerfully exclaimed, "The office of apostolic missionary . . . is so high an honor that I could wish for nothing more. . . . There is my life and there, with the help of God, I hope to die." [27] As the pioneers of the early years of the conquest, he gave no thought to the abandonment of friends and dear ones, of comfort and security, of honor and fame. Such was the spirit that animated the planters of civilization in the New World.

As the years of the colonial period lengthened, the inevitable consequences of *Real Patronato* became more and more evident. Although there were devoted ministers of the Gospel who continued to work through three centuries with and for the poor, whose fervent love gave them no rest in the endless task of saving souls and helping the needy, of comforting the sick and making life more bearable for the down-trodden, there were others who became negligent and lax in their duties. Generally speaking, a wide breach developed between the lower and the upper clergy, the unselfish and suffering missionaries and village pastors on the one hand, and the hierarchy on the other. Preferment came through the king and his officials. It could not escape the stultifying effect of political interest and selfish passions. Worldliness crept into the high places and corroded the moral fiber of those on whom the responsibility for leadership rested. This does not mean that every member of the hierarchy, nor every holder of a benefice, was unmindful of his duty. There were among the hierarchy exemplary men, who lived holy lives and contributed richly to the culture of colonial society, but they became the exception.

With the years, those in the administrative positions of the Church had become more and more detached from the humdrum life of the poor. They grew lax in morals, forgot humility, loved luxury and wordly comfort, and became more and more attached to the interests of the Spanish monarchs than to the welfare of the faithful. To visit scattered flocks required traveling over thousands of miles through which there were no roads. This implied a sacrifice they were not equal to and a devotion to the poor they no longer felt.

Under such circumstances the humble parish priests lacked the incentive and the encouragement of the shepherd, the example of his superiors. Public opinion in the remote areas

was practically non-existent. Who was there to help the struggling curate in his fight against human weakness in an environment permeated with pagan customs, among a people who were
little more than half-instructed neophytes? Here are to be
found the roots for the deplorable moral conditions that have
been constantly held up to ridicule by the enemies of the
Church as typical of the clergy in the Spanish colonies.[28]

These were not characteristic, nor were they inherent in the
colonial clergy; rather they were the inevitable outgrowth of
Real Patronato that made the Church in the colonies subservient to the State. The amazing reality is that, though the increasing worldliness threatened to engulf the Church and its workers,
there are found so many who lived exemplary lives and successfully resisted all temptations to follow the easy road of least
resistance. Medical doctors, successful military leaders, and men
who are in close contact with human weaknesses all agree that
there is an indescribable force in the heart of the individual
that can impose itself over all weaknesses: the will to live, the
determination to conquer obstacles, the moral urge of the spirit
to rise above human frailties. This is the force of the spirit, the
hidden resources of the soul that enables a man to fight disease
when medical science has done all that is humanly possible, that
makes a soldier face death with a smile, that turns human weak-
lings into heroes. This type of moral courage remained vibrant
throughout a large section of the clergy in spite of corruption
and worldliness.

The vast wealth of the colonial clergy, somewhat exaggerated,
found expression in the ornate ecclesiastical buildings, the luxurious furnishings, the gorgeous jewels and candelabra of
churches and chapels, in the large amount of productive lands,
and in the capital loaned at interest to small land owners and
property holders. It has been asserted that in Peru at the close
of the colonial period there was not an estate of any size which
did not belong in whole or in part to the clerics. In Lima, out
of 2,806 houses, 1,135 belonged to religious communities,
secular ecclesiastics, or pious endowments.[29]

It is claimed that the Church in New Spain was even richer
than in South America. Lucas Alamán, a staunch defender of
the Catholic Church, estimates that the value of the property
held by the Catholic Church in Mexico at the close of the
colonial period was probably equivalent to one-half that of all
productive real estate. A recent student of the agrarian problem
in Mexico declares that the clergy was an economically priviledged class from the beginning; that the Church received
large grants of land from the Crown; that many monasteries,

cathedrals and individual prelates were given *encomiendas;* that ecclesiastical capital was free from taxation; that the clergy collected tithes and first fruits, in addition to fees, dowries, gifts, bequests, alms, and perpetual trust funds. She concludes that with the immense prestige of the Church, it is not surprising that the clergy came to dominate the colonial era economically as well as politically.[30] While these generalizations are not altogether accurate, it cannot be denied that the value of Church property in colonial Mexico was great.

This accumulation of wealth was not entirely due to a predetermined policy on the part of the Church. In part, it was the result of the genuine religious fervor of the faithful who consistently made bequests to the Church for the maintenance of schools, hospitals and other charitable institutions; and in part, it was due to the investment of revenues derived from tithes, fees, and gifts in real estate and in real estate mortgages. The mortgages were not sought by the Church, but it was only natural that small property holders and farmers should seek to borrow money from the Church, which, because of its condemnation of usury, loaned at lower rates and on maturity was more inclined to extend the note. Back of the whole process that placed the Church in a priviledged position was, as in the case of its moral degeneration, the *Patronato Real.* The vast amount of real esate held in mortmain was the result of the nature of the bequests left by pious souls through the centuries.

A more transcendental consequence of *Real Patronato* was the discrimination practiced in the appointment to the hierarchy. The king and the Council of the Indies felt an instinctive distrust of both the Spaniards born in America and the mestizos. Preference was given, therefore, to peninsular Spaniards for appointment to all positions of trust in civil and church offices. The creoles and the mestizos in the ranks of the clergy were painfully aware of the practice and nursed through the long years of the colonial period a deep resentment which only helped to widen the breach between the upper and the lower clergy.

When the movement for separation from Spain came, it was the lower clergy that led the aroused masses in the seemingly blind struggle for social justice. In Mexico, in Central America, and in South America humble parish priests, who had shared the privations of the common people and knew from personal experience the justice of their cause, did not hesitate to lead them in the fight for freedom, for equal opportunities, and for social justice.

It needs to be kept in mind that religion itself, however,

did not constitute an issue in the revolt from Spanish authority that ultimately resulted in independence. The fact that the lower clergy generally supported the Revolution and that the hierarchy remained loyal to the Spanish cause is significant. According to Dr. J. Lloyd Mecham "It meant that the clericals participated in the movement for social, political, and economic, but not for religious reasons. . . .The American-born whites or creoles resented Spanish favortism and this resentment was as bitterly harbored by the parish priest as by the sergeant in the army or the *regidor* in the municipality." He points out that among the clergy there existed the rivalry of birth; that there were marked economic inequalities between the upper and the lower clergy; and that these two factors combined to throw the lower clergy into the ranks of the revolution.[37]

At the outbreak of the Revolution the rebellion was neither against the king nor the Church as such, rather it was a spontaneous outburst of resentment against bad government and the unbearable preference given to the *gachupines,* the peninsular born Spaniards, in political, military, economic and ecclesiastical offices. The cry of Father Hidalgo on that momentous night of September 15, 1810 gave expression simply and concretely to the spirit that animated his followers, "Down with bad government! Death to the *gachupines!* Long live religion! Long live Ferdinand VII! Long live our most holy Virgin of Guadalupe"

Once the struggle for independence was launched, both the royalists and the revolutionists, fully aware of the all-powerful influence of the Church, evoked the name of religion to justify their respective causes. "Who would believe," exclaimed Father Hidalgo, "that the shamelessness of the Spaniards would go so far as to profane the most sacred things in order to perpetuate their intolerable domination . . . to make use of excommunications against the very spirit of the Church, to launch them when there is no religious issue whatever involved?"[32] It was thus that religion and the Church were brought into the war for independence to serve "as the instrument of one and the other party" until the people became confused and did not know whom to believe.[33]

The Catholic Church had its critics among the revolutionaries, yet these cannot be accused of being atheistic or irreligious. Such criticism as appeared was directed almost exclusively against the Inquisition and the wealth of the Church. The positive stand taken by the Tribunal of the Holy Office against the rebellion evoked angry protests from the clergy itself. The words of Father Hidalgo previously cited are indicative of the just resentment felt against this institution that had become a subservient tool of intolerant Spaniards. No one will maintain that the denunciation of the Inquisition was a denunciation of the Church or Religion, for the Church cannot be held responsible for the questionable activities displayed by the Tribunal during the wars for independence. Father Mariano Cuevas, a well known Jesulit historian of the Catholic Church in Mexico, in speaking on this subject says: "That tribunal, after 1808, did not have in Mexico a personnel which could function validly or licitly; its excommunications were null and they and all the acts of the judges were outside the responsibilities of the Church." [34]

It is not surprising that in view of the implacable condemnation of the Revolution and its intolerant regalism, the revolutionary governments should abolish the Inquisition as one of their first acts. The Junta of Caracas suppressed the Holy Office in 1810; the General Constituent Assembly of Buenos Aires took similar action in March 1813; and later in the same year, when the liberal *Cortes* of Cadiz abolished the Tribunal in Spain, in all the colonies the decision was hailed with genuine enthusiasm by all classes.

The respite afforded from the hated institution by this measure, however, was short lived. Upon the return of Ferdinand VII to Spain in 1814, the Inquisition was reestablished throughout the Spanish dominions with the exception of La Plata. Fortunately, the days of the Spanish king and of the Inquisition itself in America were numbered. The attainment of independence was soon to bring about its permanent abolition. "It had spread a blight over the intellectual life of the colonists; it had smothered the spirit of inquiry; it had silenced the voice of reason; and under its malign influence Christian charity had disappeared. . . . It is to the credit of the political reformers," says Moses, "that they saw in the complete destruction of the Inquisition the first essential step towards individual liberty and social progress." [35]

The excommunications and fulminations of the Inquisition against the Revolution were not the only means employed by members of the Hierarchy in fighting for the king. The considerable contributions in money and supplies of various and sundry nature made to the Royalist cause were as significant in a material way as the former were psychologically. It was for this reason that the revolutionists cried out against the great wealth of the Church being put at the service of

the king's forces. An objective study of the facts reveals that
the financial aid given by the Hierarchy to the Royalist cause
was far in excess of the contributions made by lay Spaniards.[36]

Independence and Patronato Nacional

The success of the Revolution and the attainment of independence brought new problems in the relations with the
papacy. The whole question of the rights of the kings of Spain
over the Church in America under *Patronato Real* had to be
impugned and eventually rejected. The strained relations with
Spain during the wars of independence precluded the appointment of members of the hierarchy to fill the numerous vacancies created by death and voluntary exile. Inevitably, there
developed a serious situation. The decline in the number of
the hierarchy was keenly felt by the faithful and a feeling of
discontent rapidly spread which was a grave menace to the
success of the movement for independence. The ephemeral governments of the early days of the Revolution tried desperately
from the very beginning to establish direct communication
with the Holy Father to reach a satisfactory agreement that
would remedy the situation, but they met the impenetrable
wall of *Patronato Real*. One needs to bear in mind that the
Holy Pontiff was both a temporal and a spiritual ruler to
appreciate the difficulties involved.

The leaders of the Revolution in America fully realized the
significance of the situation. The anxiety felt for the reestablishment of normal relations with the papacy is expressed in the
resolution adopted by the first government of New Granada in
1811. "The proper authority shall attempt as soon as possible
by diplomatic negotiations to establish direct correspondence
with the Holy See for the purpose of negotiating a concordat
and [to obtain] a confirmation of the patronage which the
government exercises over the churches in these dominions in
order that a schism and its dire consequences be avoided. [37]
Similar action was taken by the Congress of Tunja in 1813, and
by the Congress of Tucuman in 1817, but to no avail.

Pope Pius VII was faced with a difficult and perplexing
question. The establishment of direct relations with the revolutionary governments for ecclesiastical purposes seemed inseparable from the political implication of recognition. Spain protested, stoutly maintaining that any official relations between
the papacy and the colonies was injurious to Spanish interests
because it would be interpreted as political recognition of their
yet unattained independence and would constitute a flagrant

violation of the ancient rights of *Real Patronato*. To these two poignant considerations was added a third. The papacy saw in the situation that had arisen an opportunity to reassert its legitimate authority over the Church in America. Clinging to the ultramontane theory, it could claim that the *Real Patronato de Indias* orignated in a concession and was not an inherent attribute of sovereignty. To this both Spain and the new governments objected, Spain because it saw in *Real Patronato* a great moral force in the hopeless task of bringing the colonies under its control again, and the independent governments because they sincerely felt that the rights of *Real Patronato* enjoyed by the Spanish Crown of right now belonged to them. This desire was clearly stated in the resolution first adopted by New Granada in 1811, in which it was declared that the purpose of establishing direct communication with the Holy See was to obtain "confirmation of the patronage which the government exercises over the churches in these dominions." It was their firm determination to have *Real Patronato* become *Patronato Nacional*.[38]

Little progress could be made in the years between 1810 and 1814 in establishing direct communication with the papacy because Pius VII was a virtual prisoner of Napoleon during this time. Furthermore, the question of recognition was premature. The next four or five years saw a pronounced royalist reaction that almost wiped out the rebel governments, with the exception of La Plata. Ferdinand VII, who had returned to Spain after Napoleon's defeat, was able to secure confirmation from the Pope for the candidates proposed to fill the vacancies in America. After the Congress of Vienna the theory of legitimacy had become too firmly entrenched for the Pope to do otherwise. It would have been imprudent to ignore the royal rights of patronage at this time. Pius VII was constrained to issue an encyclical to the hierarchy of America on January 30, 1816 enjoining them to plead with the faithful for a suppression of disorders and sedition.[39] Such action served to widen the breach between the State and the Church in independent Latin America and was to be long remembered by the advocates of a national church.

The capture of Lima by San Martín, the victories of Bolivar in his sweep south from Colombia, and the success of the Plan de Iguala in Mexico, that ended with the conclusion of the Treay of Cordova, changed the picture in America. The liberal revolution of 1820 in Spain that forced Ferdinand VII to restore the constitution of 1812 and the *Cortes* ultimately to expel the *nuncio* from Madrid in January 1823, filled the

Pope with apprehension for the Church not only in Spain but also in America. "He began to question why he should now lend his moral support to a government, which, if its authority were reestablished in America, would cause irreparable damage to the Church in the New World." [40]

Pope Pius VII had begun to realize during the last two years of his pontificate that the spiritual needs of America could not be indefinitely subordinated to the political theory of legitimacy. By 1823 the Spanish colonies had atained *de facto* independence. Continued non-communication with Rome might result in a serious schism or the breakup of the Catholic Church in America. Cardinal Consalvi frankly warned Leo XII, the new pope, that a continuance of the policy observed would bring indifference and "exposure to Methodists, Presbyterians, and even sun worshippers." [41] In 1824 Ignacio de Tejada, minister plenipotentiary to the Vatican for Columbia, Bolivia and Mexico, after being refused admission to Rome, remonstrated in a humble memorial that his mission was not political, but purely spiritual; that his purpose in soliciting an audience with His Holiness was to convey to him the lamentable condition of the Church in Colombia after fourteen years of abandonment. He pointed out that there were 11 bishoprics vacant, and that only 2 bishops were left to care for 3,000,000 faithful souls. "The English, the Dutch, the Swiss, and merchants from the Hanseatic cities," he concluded, "are making their way to America. The English Bible Society spreads its doctrine profusely and we are left without shepherds." [42] Worst conditions existed in La Plata, and they were equally bad in Chile and most of the other former colonies.

Leo XII was faced with a dilemma. The faithful in America should no longer be denied their request for spiritual leaders, but to supply them with candidates nominated by the Spanish monarch would constitute an intolerable affront. On the other hand to permit them to present their own candidates would be recognition of *Patronato Nacional,* national patronage, and an insult to Spain. It would mean the political and spiritual recognition of the independence of the former Spanish colonies. For some unexplainable reason, in spite of the sound warning of Cardinal Consalvi and the increasing evidence of the loyalty of Catholics to the Church in the independent nations of Spanish America, Leo XII issued his debatable encyclical of September 24, 1824, pleading for a return of allegiance to Ferdinand VII. The reaction was a thunderous roar of protest. "The encyclical," declares a prominent and able Mexican historian, "by praising the virtues of Ferdinand VII and advocating a return to the colonial system, alienated many loyal Catholics in America." [43] The confidence won by Pius VII was lost; the determination of laymen and clergy to defend independence, notwithstanding the position of the Church, was strengthened; and the advocates of a national church, compatible with independence, were confirmed in their animosity against a Roman Catholic Church subservient to the interests of Spain.

The uproar had its good effects. Within a year Leo XII, in spite of Spanish pressure, announced a new policy in regard to the Church in America. Agents sent to discuss purely ecclesiastical matters would be received by the papacy. The next two years a number of representatives from different Spanish American countries, who wisely chose clerics to represent them, had audiences with the Pope. The need for action became evident. In the consistory celebrated on May 21, 1827, Leo XII preconized as proprietary bishops six candidates presented by the government of Colombia for as many vacancies. At long last the papacy had decided to disregard the right of *Real Patronato* granted to the kings of Spain. Bolívar hailed the act with enthusiasm and, grasping its full significance, proudly proclaimed the assumption of the right of patronage by the government of Great Colombia.[44] To the violent protests of Ferdinand VII, Leo XII explained that when solicited "for purely spiritual purposes to remedy an unhappy religious situation which threatened to destroy the Church completely," he had no other choice than to act as he had done.[45]

But in ignoring the right of patronage of the Spanish kings, Leo XII had tacitly recognized the contention of the Latin American countries that with the attainment of independence they had inherited the rights of the king of Spain in all matters pertaining to the Church. Such was not the intention of Pius VIII, who succeeded Leo XII in 1829. During his short pontificate, he consistently refused to take any action that might strengthen the implication that the new governments had an inherent right to patronage. The Vatican has since that time adhered without deviation to this view, maintaining at all times that church patronage is not an inherent right of sovereignty.[46]

By the time Gregory XVI succeeded Pius VIII in 1831, no one admitted there was the slightest possibility of restoring Spanish sovereignty over the independent countries of America. It is not surprising, therefore, that the cardinals should point out to the new pope that there was no reason for delaying longer the restoration of normal ecclesiastical relations with the new countries. The new policy that was to determine ecclesiastical relations with America during his long pontificate was defined soon after in the Bull *Sollicitudo Ecclesiarum* of August, 1831, issued in connection with the situation existing then in Portugal. The principles laid down in this important document were equally applicable to Spanish America. The Bull asserted the right of the Pope to exercise freely his authority in spiritual matters. It declared that the discussion of ecclesiastical affairs with temporal governments should not, and could not, be regarded as political recognition, except in so far as recognition of the existence of a government capable of maintaining order was concerned. The Pope would henceforth establish relations with *de facto* governments when sufficient evidence of stability was furnished.[47]

Before the end of 1831 proprietary bishops were preconized for seven existing vacancies in Mexico; in 1832, vacancies in Argentina and Chile were filled; and in 1833, bishops were appointed for New Granada. In each and every instance Gregory XVI was careful not to give formal recognition to the right of presentation by the several governments, although he was not adverse to suggestions without any implied obligation in the final choice. To remove all possible doubt on this important point, however, he addressed an encyclical to the bishops of Spanish America specifically instructing them not to accept national patronage under any circumstances. In the prescribed oath of obedience taken by the bishops, the denial of national patronage was frankly implied.[48]

The reestablishment of normal ecclesiastic relations between the papacy and the countries of Spanish America, it must be borne in mind, was not a political act and, therefore, did not carry with it politcal recognition of the independence of the former Spanish colonies. Gregory XVI had been careful to make clear in his Bull *Sollicitudo Ecclesiarum* that no such interpretation was to be placed upon his providing for the episcopal vacancies in America. The time was ripe, however, for out and out recognition. The death of Ferdinand VII in 1833 and the ensuing civil war in Spain removed the last obstacle. On November 26, 1835, formal recognition was extended to the Republic of New Granada and the patient and tactful Ignacio de Tejada was officially received as the *Chargé* of the young republic on December 14, 1835.

The recognition of New Granada marked the end of the American problem as far as political recognition, the reestablishment of ecclesiastic relations, and Spanish opposition were concerned. "Thereafter the pope's dealings with Spanish America were direct and unhampered by consideration for Spanish susceptibilities. When Rome became satisfied as to the political stability of the new governments set up in America, and, as to their friendliness toward the principles of papal supremacy, recognition was bestowed. The problem of the patronage, however, remained to complicate and strain Papal-American relations for many years to come." [49]

Having traced the relations between the independent governments of Spanish America and the papacy to their political recognition, we will now take up the relations after the attainment of independence in Mexico, space not permitting a discussion of the subject in each and every one of the countries of Latin America.

The Plan de Iguala of February 24, 1821, rightly called the plan of the three guaranties, clearly and emphatically proclaimed that the Roman Catholic Church would be the religion of the state and that the clergy would be protected in all its rights and privileges. Iturbide, who became the president of the provisional *Junta Gubernativa,* was duly installed with full religious ceremonies, and was then chosen president of the Regency. Anxious to keep the good grace of the Church, he requested Archbishop Fonte of Mexico City on October 19, 1821, to outline the policy which the provisional government should assume in regard to the filling of the numerous vacancies that existed, since "the cure of souls" did not admit delay. The archbishop was unwilling to assume the responsibility alone in so grave a matter, so he called a *Junta* of bishops. The unanimous advice given to Iturbide by the meeting of the bishops and the cathedral chapter was that with the attainment of independence the patronage conceded to the kings of Spain had ended; that the exercise of patronage was a concession which could not be exercised by the Mexican government without a grant from the pope; and that pending a settlement of the matter the provision of ecclesiastical vacancies belonged by right of devolution in each diocese to the respective ordinary acting with the canons. The provision of bishops belonged exclusively to the pope.[50] The level-headed archbishop and his advisors had clearly stated the point of view of the Church in the matter of patronage. It is evident that the hierarchy had no intention of exchanging the tutelage of the king, which they had come to dislike intensely, for that of the independent government.

The new government was equally determined, however, to

seize by any means the right of patronage, alleging that it was an inherent right of sovereignty. When the report of the ecclesiastical *junta* was submitted a few months later to the Minister of Justice and Ecclesiastical Affairs, he promptly replied that the right of patronage had passed to the Mexican nation as the successor to the sovereign rights of the Spanish kings. He was supported in this opinion by the report of a congressional committee appointed to consider the matter. The overthrow of Emperor Iturbide postponed action until 1824, when the same question was submitted to a second congressional committee. In its report made on March 8, 1824, it declared that the right of patronage belonged to the nation and should be exercised without further delay in the case of the lesser ecclesiastical offices. As regarded archbishops and bishops, the committee prudently advised that no action be taken until a concordat was negotiated with the papacy.[51]

The question of *patronato nacional* thus became another source of irritation and misunderstanding between the independent nation and the Church.

When after three years of independence the first constitutional law was adopted on January 31, 1824, it was provided in Article 4 that the "religion of the Mexican nation is and shall be forever the Roman Catholic Apostolic" which the nation would "protect by wise and just laws," prohibiting the exercise of any other. The debates on the adoption of this article disclose that it met with little opposition. The absence of strong anticlerical feeling continued. In October, the Federal Constitution adopted retained Article 4 with practically no change, except for some additions. It was declared that the State had the right to conclude concordats, to exercise the right of *placet* in regard to pontifical documents, and to regulate the exercise of patronage. Archbishops, bishops, provisors, and vicars general, although enjoying equal political rights' could not be elected senators or deputies. The ecclesiastical *fueros*, privileges of the clergy, were guaranteed by the nation.[52] Definitely the Church was in no danger. The people were still ardent Catholics who were opposed to the toleration of any other sect. But there could be no doubt that the government took *patronato nacional* for granted, as an inseparable attribute of sovereignty. This assumption by the liberal leaders of independent Mexico, coupled with the great power which the not inconsiderable wealth of the Church gave to the clerical party was soon to bring open attack and to precipitate a century long contest between Church and state.

The Politico-Economic-Religious Struggle

The great wealth of the Church in Mexico did not consist in ready cash. Rather it was in its vast land holdings and income-bearing real estate property. It has been estimated that the amount of real property of the Church almost doubled during the time of the war for independence. Although the number of the clergy declined during the period, the amount of its property increased. That a large portion of the land estates were endowments held in mortmain for the maintenance of hopsitals, charity institutions, schools, and scholarships for the training of young priests is frequently forgotten. Regardless of the humanitarian purposes for which the income of its large real estate holdings was used, the fact remains that it constituted a considerable portion of the national wealth and gave great political power to those who held it.

The breaking up of the population into political parties brought the matter to a head. The conservatives recruited their members from the landed aristocracy, the military, and the clergy. The liberal leaders made capital of the association of the Church with the other two groups. The liberals were the small business men, the professional group, the intellectuals who had little of this world's goods. They naturally identified themselves as the champions of equal rights for all, of democracy, and of federalism, which in those early days was taken to be synonymous with individual freedom. To these incendiary ingredients was added the explosive element of the secret masonic societies: the Scotch Rite and the York Rite.

The first had been introduced into New Spain by the Spaniards at the turn of the century. After the Treaty of Cordova they had looked forward to a constitutional monarchy under a Bourbon. When Iturbide proclaimed himself emperor they had opposed him, but after his overthrow, reconciled to the inevitable, they had come to advocate a centralized republic as their choice.

The second, or York Rite, was born, one might say, with the Constitution of 1824 and the establishment of the first Federal Republic. The amusing thing is that it owed its origin in part to two clerics, José María Alpuche and Ramos Arizpe, who decided to organize York Rite lodges to counteract the influence of the Scotch Rite in national politics. The American Minister Joel Poinsett shortly afterward obtained a charter for the grand lodge of Mexico from the lodge in Philadelphia. The Church became the target of the liberal Yorkino lodges, which began in 1828 to adopt measures when in power to despoil the Church of its temporalities as the first step in weaakening the political influence of the conservatives.

A well known historian of our day puts it this way: "Slowly the work of reform continued against the clerical privileges. The Law of February 7, 1828, gave to the State of Chihuahua the buildings of the College of the Jesuits located in its territory. On April 18 of the same year the Desierto de los Carmelitas was given to San Bartolo, Santa Rosa, and San Bernabé, towns of the Federal District. On May 10, 1829, the sale of the temporalities was ordered. This, together with the property of monastic orders, the Hospitallers of Saint John, the Jesuits, and the Inquisition, which had been declared the property of the nation, were estimated to be worth 8,880,604 pesos." [53] But if its wealth was the object of attack by the liberals, it is of interest to note that the government gracefully abandoned in 1831 its claim to *patronato nacional*.

The insistence on the right of *Patronato Nacional* had practically left Mexico without prelates. By the close of 1821 there were only five bishops residing in Mexico, but six years later not a single one remained.[54] Congress was set, however, on defending the right of *Patronato Nacional* in spite of the urgent situation that had developed and in the instructions finally drawn up in 1827, for the Mexican diplomatic agent to the papacy, this was made a *sine qua non*. Not until 1831 did Pope Gregory XVI preconize *motu propio* proprietary bishops for six vacant Sees in Mexico. President Anastacio Bustamante, friendly to the Church, admitted the action and his government, by the law of May 16, 1831, formally gave up its pretentions to *Patronato Nacional* by granting to the clergy the right to elect canons freely.[55]

There is little to be gained by continuing the historical sketch of the struggle between the Church and the State in Mexico, because in the final analysis it was primarily a phase of a greater struggle, the desire for social justice in the full meaning of the word. A contemporary Mexican student of the social problems of labor very appropriately says: "Three years that followed the Constitution of 1857 must be regarded as the era of liberal capitalism. The ideas of this school of economic liberalism were contained in our Magna Carta and the Government of Juárez gave them systematic application, particularly through the Laws of the Reform. On the other hand, it should be noted, the chaos that reigned in the country since its separation from Spain was beginning to subside; Mexico was getting ready to become a nation. One of the processes that needed modification was the economic order. The capitalistic system of production already implanted in the mines was becoming general; the guilds had disappeared; and the proletariat class, although slowly and in a limited proportion, was beginning to increase. But social inequality was also growing and precipitated the first social clashes. Mexico did not know how to follow the methods of the peoples of Europe and America; its capital continued to grow, but the Government never learned how to improve the condition of the laborers . . ." [56] Economically Mexico continued to be a colony.

After the *Reforma*, in spite of the secularization of all Church property and the complete separation with a vengeance of the Church and the State, the condition grew worse. The large landed estates of the colonial period were now larger; there was no other industry than the extractive one of mining, except for the infant textile mills largely owned by foreign capital. The agrarian problem, resulting from the accumulation of real estate in the hands of the few, was made worse by a series of laws intended to remedy the situation. They began with the Law of disamortization of June 25, 1856; then followed Article 27 of the Constitution of 1857; the Nationalization Law of ecclesiastical properties in which were included many that were not; the Public Lands Laws of 1863 and 1864; the Laws of Colonization of 1875 and of 1883 that brought into being the fatal Land Survey Companies. The result of these measures was the increase of the large land estates, the despoliation of the common lands of the Indian *pueblos*, the depreciation of land values, and the sale of ecclesiastical estates, which went largely to foreigners. "The agrarian policy of the Díaz regime had neither rhyme nor reason. Hardly justifiable in the time of the Spanish domination, when the land was given to Spanish subjects, men of enterprise who had established residence in the country and raised families that were Mexican . . . , the Government of the Republic, that prided itself on its popular origin and its liberalism, granted them to foreigners, mainly Englishmen and Americans, overlooking the danger it represented to the nation . . ." [57] The sale began in the days of Juárez.

In this economic background are the roots of the seemingly endless revolutions and civil strife that characterize the history of Mexico. From the beginning, it was the Church property that excited the greed of the liberal leaders, who became obsessed with the idea that therein lay its strength. In attaining their end, the liberals effected the complete separation of Church and State, adopting legislation that in many instances went beyond the jurisdiction of civil law, such as matters of internal administration of the Church.

Beginning with the relatively mild anticlerical reforms of Gómez Farías in 1833, the movement gained bitterness and reached its climax in the Constitution of 1857. The provisions of this document wrested from the Church all educational activities and the right to hold property. It even legalized the breaking of religious vows. The War of the Reform that followed was a violent reaction to the drastic policy thus instituted and resulted in the promulgation of the Laws of the Reform which went much further. Then came the fatal French intervention and the tragedy of Emperor Maximilian and the mad Carlota.

When the bloody episode ended, the restrictions and the Laws of the Reform continued in force and were for a while applied with all rigor. By 1874 the separation of Church and State was an accomplished and unquestioned fact. From that date until the Revolution of 1910 these laws remained suspended over the head of every Catholic like the sword of Damocles. During his long regime, President Porfirio Díaz did not modify a single provision of the Laws of Reform. The juridical basis of the reform was left unchanged, notwithstanding the conciliatory policy of the Government.

Spiritually, however, the prolonged presidency of Díaz proved a great blessing to the Church; twenty-three new dioceses were established and seven new provinces erected; the number of parishes increased to over 1400; the clergy reached a high of about 5000; and the new fervor was revealed in the founding of several Mexican religious orders. National Catholic Congresses were held in 1903 at Puebla, in 1904 in Mérida, in 1906 in Guadalajara, and in Oaxaca in 1909. The encyclical of Leo XIII, *Rerum novarum,* of May, 1891, on the condition of workers, received wide acclaim and led to the first Agricultural Catholic Congress of Tulancingo in 1904, followed by a second congress in the same city the following year. A third agricultural congress was held in 1906 in the city of Zamora in which a program of social action to improve the condition of the farmers and the peasants was discussed and adopted. It included such matters as a living family wage for the wage earner, low cost housing, and agricultural banks to aid the small farmers with indispensable loans at reasonable rates. Three years after the Revolution of 1910 started, when social problems began to occupy national thinking, a Catholic Congress held at Zamora in 1913 offered the nation a program which was presented by

Father Alfredo Méndez Medina, as advanced, if not more so, than that included in the Constitution of 1917.[58]

The Revolution of 1910 that ended the long regime of Díaz and which started as a movement for free elections, soon assumed a socio-economic character. Neither the Church as such, nor the Catholics as a group were the object of the fury of the revolution in its beginning, but by 1913, under the leadership of Carranza, the old anticlerical liberals had become fully aroused and hurled tirade after tirade against the Church, the clergy, and the Catholics in general. The old Laws of the Reform were revived and applied with grim sternness, new decrees to despoil the Church and weaken her political power were adopted, and the Constitution of 1917 gathered all the venom and made it the fundamental law of the land. Article III emphatically declared that education was to be laical and that no religious body could establish, maintain, or direct primary schools. The evident purpose of the framers was to prevent members of religious orders and of the secular clergy from engaging in teaching. "From this constitution dates the rigid restriction of acts of worship to the churches, although many of these manifestations of faith had long been regulated during the century before. Article 27 incorporated many details regarding church property and made all such the property of the nation. Charitable activity was restricted and the Church reduced strictly to the administration of the sacraments. Article 130 included a number of further provisions regarding the restriction of the number of the clergy, the authority of the states in Church matters, and limitations on the clergy in political life.[59]

Although no concerted effort was made to enforce all the new provisions rigidly, as had been the evident intention of the members of the Convention of Querétaro that framed the new constitution, the situation grew steadily more tense. During the first presidency of Alvaro Obregón open conflict was narrowly avoided. Several of the states, taking advantage of the powers granted to them by Article 130, adopted legislation limiting the number of clergy within their jurisdiction. This was the method adopted to destroy the Church and its influence. If there were no priests, the number of parishes would be reduced and the faith would dry up, and the Church slowly perish for lack of workers.

Things came to a crisis during the presidency of Plutarco Elías Calles. The excuse for the persecution that followed was an innocent statement made by Archbishop Mora y del Rio

of Mexico City during a newspaper interview. His statement
that the hierarchy favored a change in the laws concerning
religion was wantonly interpreted as a desire to overthrow the
government and put a stop to its social reform movement. The
truth is that the Church was in complete accord with the social
program of the Revolution, although it could not approve its
methods in many instances. This simple expression of opinion
was interpreted by the Government as treason to the State. Such
a reaction is explainable when the prevalence of the theory of
the superiority of the state of those days is taken into account.

During the next three years the Church was attacked with a
viciousness never before experienced in Mexico. Foreign priests
were expelled, bishops forced into exile, religious services suspended, and the Catholics left without priests. The hierarchy
declared it was impossible to operate under the existing laws
and Calles replied that it was not a matter of religious liberty
but of open rebellion against the government. The situation
aroused the indignation of Catholics outside of Mexico, particularly in the United States, but was fortunately finally settled
by a temporary arrangement which recognized the right of the
bishops to designate the priests and religious who were to
register as provided by the law. Although no formal arrangement was made, it was tacitly agreed by President Portes Gil
that violent persecution would cease and that the laws would
be more reasonably administered.

Again the conflagration flared in 1931, when the State of
Veracruz reduced legally the number of priests to 1 for each
100,000 Catholics. Tabasco, unwilling to be outdone, passed a
law that barred all priests from its soil. A wave of legislation
to reduce the number of the clergy swept the country. In
Mexico City the number was reduced from 90 to 24; in Chiapas,
to 4 in the entire state; in Guanajuato, 1 to 9,000 faithful. In
October, 1932, Archbishop Ruiz y Flores was deported. The
Presidency of Cárdenas saw a continuation of the attack on the
Church and the Catholics.

In the midst of the persecution there was a religious revival.
The churches were filled at all services and there were many
more masses said than before. In 1936 the Mexican hierarchy
issued a joint pastoral to make clear the position of the Church
in regard to the social program of the Revolution. The position
of the Church in social matters was repeated in clear and emphatic terms. It was affirmed that the Church stood for a just
wage, the dignity of labor, the material welfare of the individual, the right of labor to organize, and for every other principle
of Christian democracy.

The anticlerical atmosphere has steadily cooled since the administration of President Cárdenas. One of the unexpected favorable trends was the voluntary announcement by President Manuel Avila Camacho, upon assuming office, that he was a "Creyente" (Believer), an unprecedented declaration that no president had dared to make in over a century. What is puzzling to the outsider in Mexico and the larger portion of Spanish America is the apparently widespread anti-Catholic feeling in countries predominantly Catholic. The truth of the matter is that anti-clericalism is skin deep and that generally speaking the most radical anti-clerical leaders are not anti-religious. Gómez Farías, the initiator of the Church reform laws, earnestly entreated his children to attend Mass regularly and never neglect their prayers; and Cárdenas, known for his violent anti-clericalism is said to have tipped his hat every time he passed a church because "one always raises his hat before a Church."

Catholicism in Mexico and a large portion of Latin America is much more than a religion. It is a social force, a basic unifying bond of nationality, inseparably associated with the national concept. It is the one thing common to the vast majority of the people. There is no traditional loyalty to the government as such, as is the case in the British attachment to the institution of kingship, or in France to the old French monarchy, or the cabildo in Spain. A priest is declared to have said, "The Catholic Church has possessed such overwhelming power, such intense popular support, and such blind devotion, that it is the State that one may say has been persecuted." Although the statement is an obvious exaggeration, there is a certain element of truth in it and one might say that the anti-clerical laws adopted at different times have been inspired by abject fear, a sense of inferiority on the part of the liberal leaders. Here is to be found the explanation for the fact that at the height of the persecution in the days from Calles to Cárdenas, religious schools continued in operation, religious services never were completely suspended, and the Church was able to carry on its work of charity and to exert itself for the welfare of the poor and the suffering, surreptitiously though it were, and to come out of the holocaust stronger than before, purified and strengthened by the ordeal of fire and blood.

Out of the intense struggle for survival, in which some of the faithful, forgetting the injunction of the Master to the disciple that cut off the high priest's servant's ear, took up arms in the Cristero uprising, a new type of Catholic has arisen. Pope Pius XI, in his Apostolic Letter on the *Condition of Mexico*, issued in March, 1937, firmly told the bishops they must continue to remind their people that the Church promotes peace and order and condemns every violent, unjust insurrection against established authority; that neither the laity nor the clergy should engage in the defense of their rights by violent means; that the restoration of rights illegally appropriated by the State should be sought in the normal and legal exercise of civic rights by the faithful. In other words, relief should be sought in the courts and in the exercise of the ballot.

"Fortunately there has risen up in the ranks of Catholic laity and clergy [in Mexico] a new element which is much more conscious of the times and the conditions. This group does not assume that the Revolution was merely a nightmare and can be wished out of existence. It takes the Revolution for what is is, with the good and the bad; with its virtues and its evils, with its civic accomplishments and its banditry. It does not decry the past; it does not think that a return to the days of Don Porfirio would settle everything. It knows that the Revolution is a tremendous fact which must be taken into account and that over thirty years of experimentation have not left Mexico as it was. It does not deny that there are merits in some of the things that the Revolution has carried out. It is not, in a word, an attitude of blind partisanship, bent on perpetuating a state of friction and warfare which can only redound to the disadvantage of the Church. It accepts the indications of the Holy See on seeking to work out relations with the state and refuses to sanction open, avowed, and unabated hostility. Catholic Action, [the organization of the laity working with and under the bishops] has taken the latter position and its influence as a result has been wide and deep." [60]

But the situation remains always tense because the Government and the Revolutionaries, the professional liberal leaders, are exceedingly sensitive to all criticism and react impulsively to the slightest hint that they have relaxed their vigilance in regard to the violation of the anti-Church legislation. The Communist element knows it, and continuously needles avowed reformers into periods of violent denunciation of the Church for violations of either the new legislation or the old. For instance in November, 1943, the Government suddenly issued a strict order prohibiting the military to attend any religious function whatsoever in uniform, all because of public criticism that army men were falling under the all-enveloping dominion of the Church through laxity of the Federal authorities. The Federal Department of Education, which has been infiltrated by Communist elements more than the other departments of government, is the center of constant agitation that convulses certain sections of public opinion. Every attempt to enforce the provisions of Article III with rigor and to take advantage of it to impose the teachings of Marxism through official textbooks naturally arouses loud protests in the press. The denunciation of the existence of numerous schools under religious direction in violation of Article III is protested with equal vehemence by the pink liberals. The furor dies down and the undemocratic and unfair Article which denies freedom in education is again ignored in a country which is over 95 percent Catholic.

There has been a give and take, however. Catholic schools, as all other private schools, conform outwardly with the government regulations of the Ministry of Education. The official curriculum does not include Christian doctrine, but this is taught at hours off the schedule; the members of the religious orders engaged in teaching do not wear their habits in the schools, the crucifix is not displayed on the walls, Catholic books are not conspicuous, and every reasonable effort is made to avoid antagonizing the sensibilities of the government inspectors. The number of Catholic schools has increased greatly in the last few years, and although the officials of the government know it, they assume an indifferent attitude as long as the outward formalities of the law are observed. Even Mexican seminaries have come back and the Seminary at Montesuma, New Mexico, sustained largely by the Mexican hieararchy, for young Mexican priests to prepare themselves for the ministry, sent its last Mexican seminarian to Mexico this year (1951). For several years it published an official review called *Montezuma,* which had a wide circulation in Mexico among the clergy and laity alike.

The need for Catholic institutions of higher learning for the youth of the land was felt during the days when the persecution of the Church reached its height. It is significant that the first to be established during those tragic days was the *Instituto Superior de Cultura Femenina,* Feminine Institute of Culture, which has continued in operation since that day and has just celebrated its silver jubilee. Founded by Sofía del Valle under the kindly inspiration of Bishop Darío Miranda of Tulancingo, it has a remarkable record of achievement. Its purpose was to bring together a select group of Catholic young women to give them a thorough grounding in Catholic philosophy, apologetics, and action for the better fulfillment of their family and social duties. Hundreds and hundreds of young women have been trained in such institutes during the last quarter of a century, and have become a lay apostolate of great importance throughout Mexico in disseminating Catholic thought and teachings. After the first was established in Mexico City, similar ones were opened in Puebla, Guanajuato, Durango and many other cities. The idea soon spread beyond the confines of Mexico. Its graduates took it into Guatemala and Colombia. Sisters from the United States attended the Mexican institutes for young Catholic women leaders and, impressed by the work, introduced the new idea and methods in this country. The movement crossed the ocean to distant Warsaw, where an institute was founded a few years ago by alumnae from Mexico, which has had to go underground. Sofía del Valle, the founder, and Bishop Darío Miranda were both present at the jubilee celebration held in Mexico City on June 26, 1951.[61]

Eight young women founded another youth organization in the midst of the most bitter days of persecution and have just celebrated their jubilee also, counting in their membership over 125,000 young Mexican women today. The *Juventud Catolica Femenina Mexicana* is an association of Catholic women that has for its purpose the Apostolate of Truth, whose patron is the Virgin of Guadalupe, in whose memorial shrine they celebrated the Silver Jubilee on May 18, 1951. Theirs is a program of Catholic Action, to teach by word and example the basic principles of Christianity. It is the Mexican legion of innocence and decency. In their consecration to the spread of Truth, they prayed: "Grant that we become apostles of Christ that we may more easily attain the spiritual reconquest of the womanhood of our country." Their motto is: The Eucharist, the Apostolate, and Heroism. They are the voluntary catechists of Mexico.[62]

Another institution for women, founded in Mexico City about the same time, was the *Instituto Familiar y Social de Mexico,* (Family and Social Institute of Mexico). This was an educational institution on a different level. It was devised to give a two year course in homemaking to prospective housewives. Its curriculum includes the domestic sciences, training in the fundamentals of religion and the Catholic concept of marriage with all its responsibilities. In its own sphere it has proved very popular and successful. Countless young women have been given the basic training necessary to found successful Christian homes and to raise Christian families.

The Society of Jesus has founded the *Centro Cultural Universitaro* for the purpose of providing instruction for young men at the university level. Since its opening many Catholic student organizations have made it their headquarters and it has become one of the most important Catholic Action centers in Mexico, its alumni furnishing the trained leadership so much needed in the country. It offers a complete program in the fields of history, philosophy, and letters and its work is recognized by the National University of Mexico.

Solemnly advised by Pius XI in his Bull *Paterna sane sollicitudo* of February 2, 1926, that "in the light of the unfavorable conditions prevailing . . . it is necessary that the clergy and the Catholic organizations remain as far removed as possible from the passions of political party" the Catholics in general adopted the policy of not identifying themselves as such with any faction. It was realized, however, that this did not mean that Catholics could not join as private citizens political parties that condemned some of the policies put in practice by the Revolution and offer as the basis for action some of the Catholic social teachings. The thing to avoid was the organization of a Catholic party as such.

Several years elapsed, however, before an attempt was made to form a national organization representative of Catholic social teachings for the purpose of influencing public opinion. In 1939 a courageous young lawyer, Manuel Gómez Morin, decided to bring together a group of able and talented young men to create or arouse a national conscience along traditional lines. This was the beginning of *Accion Nacional*. The founder had attained distinction as an expert in fiscal and monetary matters and had established a solid reputation as a young man of character and integrity. While a very young man, he had served as Under Secretary of Finance during the first administration of President Obregón. Besides being responsible for many important reforms in national finance, he was largely instrumental in the establishment of the *Banco de Mexico,* an indispensable measure for the economic stability of the country. In 1933, as a member of the teaching staff of the Law School, he took a positive and decided stand against Socialist infiltration in the University of Mexico and found himself promoted to the presidency of the institution when it was declared autonomous and given ten million pesos to shift for itself. During his short term of office he had to fight to save the autonomous university from falling under the influence of the extreme left.

It was during these stormy years that Gómez Morin conceived the idea of establishing some sort of an organization to help mold public opinion along Christian lines. Some of his friends advised joining forces with the government to fight Communist infiltration from within, but Gómez Morin felt that a permanent organization that would make its constant goal the desire to develop the national civic consciousness among all classes was preferable. The *Partido de Acción Nacional* was organized in 1939-1940 with young professional men, many of them former students of Gómez Morin, who were joined by outstanding Catholic leaders, such as Efraín González Luna and others.

It aimed to become a national independent party, open and above board. Regional committees were set up, local organizations perfected, leaders chosen, and an earnest effort made to sink its roots deep in the soil and in the hearts of the people of Mexico. There was no hesitancy in frankly admitting that it was an opposition party that sought through constitutional means and by the unhampered exercise of the right of suffrage to try to improve the general condition of the people of Mexico. Intrigue, subversive activities, and conspiracy were scorned and uncompromisingly denounced. It pleaded with its membership and urged sincerely that all activities be carried out within the framework of the law. "In terms of Mexico politics, *Acción Nacional* represents the modern, up-to-date attitude of how to go about things. It is not rooted in the past, nor does it conceive of Mexico's future as a return to Porfirio Díaz. It is not a party that is endorsed by the hierarchy, nor does it have any connection with it. It seeks to prevent anything that runs counter to Catholic teaching but does not maintain any affiliation with, nor direct submission to, the Church. It is in large measure an intellectual movement . . . . Its leadership represents the best in Mexican life, both professionally and spiritually." [63]

It began as a middle class organization of business men, professionals, and intellectuals but it has steadily tried to bring into its ranks and its program the workers and the farmers for whose interests it has labored consistently. Its official organ is *La Nación,* one of the best edited Mexican weeklies today, which represents an objective picture of the life of the nation and fearlessly points out the abuses of the Government and its failings, urges the citizens to stand up for their rights, and expounds the social teachings of the Church. In a recent public lecture sponsored by *Acción Nacional* in June of this year, Rafael Preciado Hernañdez vigorously demanded a more effective represenation of all classes in government as a result of the free exercise of the suffrage. "*Acción Nacional,*" he declared, " is fighting for a democracy founded on the Gospel when it demands the subordination of the State to the people, of the Government to the majority; when it demands a radical reform of the electoral law that will insure the authenticity of the public will, the effective and free exercise of the suffrage, as proclaimed by the true revolutionists of 1910." He then argued that the Constitution of 1917 and the subsequent legislation that has deprived the Mexican people of freedom of education and freedom of religion were largely due to the disfranchisement of the great bulk of the electorate through the application of the electoral laws.

"If there be need of proof of the consequences of the negation of the suffrage, here it is," he concluded. "It is a self evident truth that the general welfare of the Mexican nation depends largely on strengthening the basic bonds that bind its people. Chief among these is the religious. In that case the persecution laws against the Church, including first among them the constitutional provisions of articles 3, 5, 24, 27, and 130, which seriously restrict religious freedom, are contrary to the general welfare of Mexico. Nevertheless they were promulgated and continue in force thanks to the falsification of the public will." [64]

Year in and year out, throughout the nation the members of *Acción Nacional* speak out in their tireless compaign to arouse public opinion and awaken civic consciousness. In April 1951, *Acción National* sponsored a three day Diocesan Peasant Convention, its first, in Guadalajara, which was attended by representatives from 80 parishes and missions. Father Rafael Regalado proposed to the Convention a three-point program to improve the moral condition of the peasant: the development of a consciousness of the dignity of man that personal conduct may reflect his common parentage; the eradication of the deep rooted vices of drunkenness, wastefulness, and indifference; and the introduction of modern methods of cultivation that will enable the peasants to live more like human beings and come to love the land more. The rural housing problem was ably discussed by a young agricultural engineer who explained how inexpensive, but comfortable and hygienic, houses could be built by utilizing local materials that could be made ready for construction by the peasants themselves during the slack seasons. Soil conservation and the measures which the peasants could take individually to prevent erosion were explained. The problem of short term financing for the small farmer was discussed and the importance of fulfilling their civic duties was stressed. "There are two poses that ennoble man," said one of the speakers, "one on bended knees, giving thanks to God for the gifts received from His bounty; the other, standing erect, with chin set, in fearless defense of one's inalienable rights."

It is work like this that has made *Acción Nacional* a real power in Mexico and that augurs well for the future solution of

the many social problems that face the nation today in the light
of Catholic social teachings.

Writers like Alfonso Caso, Mariano Alcocer, Eduardo Enrique Ríos, and older men like Alberto María Carreño and
Rafael García Granados, to menton a few, are regular contributors to *El Universal, Excelsior, Novedades* and *La Nación*,
besides numerous provincial papers that reproduce their columns. They are having a wide influence in molding Catholic
thinking. They write on literary, historical, economic, social,
and political questions and present generally the Catholic
point of view and the social doctrine of the Church.

Catholic Action is a power today in Mexico. The papacy
had recommended it to the Mexican hierarchy and the Mexican
people repeatedly. In an address of the pope to the Mexican
pilgrims, made on June 2, 1931, he pointed out that although
the principal criticism made against it was that it engaged in
politics, nevertheless, it should be organized in Mexico without
devoting any attention to politics as such. "Its mission is
spiritual," the pope declared. "It concerns itself with the formation of Christian consciences."

As soon as a *modus vivendi* had been worked out for the
strained relations between the Church and the Government in
June, 1929, a commission consisting of Father Miranda, Msgrs.
Manuel Fulcheri y Pietra Santa, Bishop of Zamora, Father
Ramón Martínez Silva, S. J., and Father Rafael Dávila Vilches
was named to work on the organization of Catholic Action.
When the plan was completed, it was presented to Archbishop
Pascual Díaz, who submitted it to the hierarchy of Mexico for
approval and suggestions. The statutes adopted are in perfect
accord with the broad outline of Catholic Action as defined
in the various encyclicals of the papacy. It differs in Mexico
in one respect. It is organized along national and not diocesan
lines. Permission for this innovation was obtained by the hierarchy from Rome.

Although it functions on the basis of diocesan and parish
subdivisions, Catholic Action in Mexico is not a diocesan
matter. Its direction is placed in the hands of a national board
of directors who are above diocesan jurisdiction to a large extent. By this means friction between dioceses is avoided, attention is centered on the national character of the various problems, sharp differences between territories enjoying more favorable conditions are obviated, and uniform orientation of great
importance to the movement is attained. The four basic organizations of Mexican Catholic Action are the *Unión de
Católicos Mexicanos* for older men; *the Asociación Catolica de*

Juventud Mexicana for unmarried men under 35 years; *Unión Femenina Católica Mexicana* for older women; and *Junventud Católica Femenina Mexicana* for younger women. In addition to these four, all the other associations whose purpose is some form of lay apostolate are considered federated bodies, such as the *Congregaciones Marianas*, with 25,000 members in 1944. The Boys and Girls Scouts and similar groups are auxiliaries.

Beginning with a few hundred members in 1929, the organization has spread throughout the nation and today includes among its members over half a million. It was officially inaugurated on Christmas Eve in 1929. Intense study groups of both clergy and laymen were given training in Christian leadership. The trained leaders then went into every parish in the archdiocese of Mexico to launch the work of Catholic Action and from there into the other dioceses. In one year the *Juventud Católica Femenina* alone spread to 22 dioceses, organized 133 parish groups, 124 study circles, and enrolled 8,605 young women as members. By 1942 the membership of the entire organization had reached 102,000 and by 1944 more than 400,000. The four basic associations have spread to every diocese, and its affiliated and auxiliary organizations extend to practically every city, town, and village. "Catholic Action is today," said Pattee in 1944, "one of the main forces in Catholic life in Mexico. The influence it is exerting is a source of enormous strength to the Church. Its national organizations and complete integration avoids friction and gives it a power which no similar organization has ever had in Mexican Catholic life." [65]

In spite of differences of opinion among the Catholics in Mexico on various national questions, when the United States declared war on the Axis Powers after Pearl Harbor and Mexico joined the embattled nations of the New World in the gigantic struggle between totalitarianism and democracy, the hierarchy lost no time in expressing is full support of the Government. Catholic leaders like Gómez Morín urged all citizens to lend their aid to the Government in the common cause for the dignity of man. He pointed out that since Pearl Harbor the time for neutrality had passed.

As has been already pointed out, Catholic public opinion had been steadily gaining in importance. In 1942 the Committee on Civilian Defense organized a series of lectures by persons representative of diverse views to determine the attitude of different sectors. It invited Mariano Olcocer, a recognized Catholic leader, to speak on the position of the Church on the war situation. He chose for his subject "The Church and Totalitarianism." Alcocer, a brilliant speaker and clear thinker, realized that his words would be taken as the official attitude of the Church. He consequently had his address approved first by the ecclesiastical censors. One night in October, 1942, in a brilliantly presented address, in the Palace of Fine Arts, he traced the consistent condemnation of nazism, facism, racism, and all manifestations of totalitarianism by the Vatican and the sincere and heroic efforts of the pope and the great Catholic leaders of Europe to maintain peace. He then concluded by repeating the statement of the Archbishop of Mexico of May 30, 1942, in which the ranking prelate had pointed out in discussing Mexico's entry in the war that it was the responsibility of the civil authority to determine the international position of a nation in any given world crisis; and that it was the duty of Catholics, as well as of all patriotic citizens to support the civil power, unless it be evidently contrary to conscience. The Archbishop, Alcocer emphasized, had made it clear that in case of doubt, however, the Government was to be supported in its position. The significance of the incident lies in the fact that Catholic opinion had become an important element that could not be ignored. The unequivocal position of the Church in Mexico as officially presented left no room for doubt.

Since the war, Catholics in Mexico have taken greater interest in the basic problems of the Revolution, such as the distribution of lands and the position of the farm laborer and small land owner, capital-labor relations, freedom of education, and social welfare. Responsible Catholic thinking today does not reject the idea of land distribution or the breaking up of the large estates to make land available for the indigent peasant. There are a few who still consider such a program unacceptable but fortunately they are in the minority. The younger element, formed under the intense activity of Catholic Action, has accepted the precepts of Catholic social teachings. *Accion Nacional* through its public lecture program, designed to educate the public, and, through the columns of *La Nacion,* has constantly kept before the people the fundamental importance of land reform and the improvement of the condition of the rural sector of the population.

In discussing the great emphasis which of late has been placed on industrialization in Mexico, Manuel Castillo, an economist and Catholic leader, points out in an excellent article entitled "The Soil Comes First," that one needs to keep in mind that 70 percent of the population of Mexico lives in rural areas; that it exists under the most miserable social, economic, and political conditions, in many instances as bad, if not worse, than in 1910 at the outbreak of the Revolution.

Taking the Government to task for its indifferent attitude with regard to the peasant and farm laborer, he declared, "To describe rural life and labor in Mexico is to speak of unbelievable and criminal ineptitude, of blind and obstinate partiality, of selfish and unscrupulous exploitation of labor and of man as a productive worker." After a remarkable presentation of Mexican rural life, its misery, its sufferings, and its importance as the economic basis of national prosperity, he warns that all plans and efforts to industrialize the country will prove useless if the welfare of the agricultural worker is neglected and ignored.[66]

To commemorate the sixtieth anniversary of the Encyclical of Leo XIII, *Rerum novarum,* the hierarchy of Mexico issued a pastoral letter of great significance. Quoting from the Christmas message of Pope Pius XII of 1942, they reminded the people of Mexico that "Today, more than ever, the Church must live its role; it must repudiate more firmly than ever, the false and narrow concept of spiritual and internal life that would confine it, blind and mute, to the solitude of the sanctuary. The Church cannot isolate itself in the solitude of its temples and neglect the mission entrusted to it by Divine Providence to help form a whole well-rounded man, collaborating in this manner in laying down the solid foundations of society. The Church . . . cannot renounce its duty to proclaim before its children and the whole universe the fundamental and immutable norms on which society must rest and on which in the final analysis the stability of any new order, national or international, so ardently desired by all the peoples of the world, must rest." They explained that the solution of many of the social problems facing Mexico is to be found in the wise application of the "social Christian doctrine" of the Church, based strictly on moral and spiritual principles.

Speaking of the problems of the proletariat, the worker of our industrial era, they stated that the Mexican industrial worker was not in the same position as in the more highly industrialized nations of the world. The solution of his problems, they agreed, concerned the Government, the industrialist, and the Church. It is the concern of Government to pass the economic and administrative laws necessary for a realistic solution of the temporal well-being of the workers. It is the concern of the employers, as well as the workers, to work out together their respective services to society and to establish the organizations best suited for the improvement of the general welfare and the elevation of the standards of living. It is the concern of the Church to bring men of all classes together that they might work out the solution of this important problem in the light of the Christian teachings of justice and of love for each other. They reminded the faithful that "the Church has never preached social revolution" but from the days of St. Paul to the present it has "exerted itself always to obtain a realization of the fact that man is far more important than economic and technical advantages in the life of human beings struggling to live in accord with Christian principles."

They quoted the Holy Father's address to the workers of June, 1941 in which he said "You are duty bound to fight for a more just distribution of wealth. This has been, and continues to be, the central point of Catholic social doctrine. . . . The Church is opposed to the accumulation of wealth in the hands of a relatively few while the great masses of the people are condemned to starve and live in economic conditions unfit for human beings." The right to a living wage, that this implies, and the evil consequences of its denial were outlined. What road should Mexico follow? "The Church points out to man the conduct that is most conducive to the better safeguard of human dignity, civilization, and a Christian life. Never was such guidance more appropriate or opportune for a country than for ours, now on the road to an unavoidable and beneficial industrialization, that it might avoid the errors of a capitalistic economy built on rugged individualism, preserving that sound equilibrium that should exist between private interests and the Common Good . . ." [67]

The previous week, *La Nacion* had published an interesting interview with Father Pedro Velázquez, Director of the Mexican Catholic Social Bureau, in which the quiet but affable sociologist had emphasized that social justice is not a theory, that it is a duty and an obligation which is not the responsibility of the Church as such, but of the individual citizen. When asked why this social doctrine that was so clearly set forth by Pope Leo XIII in his *Rerum Novarum* in 1890 was not implemented in Mexico, he replied that it is true not only of the Catholics in Mexico, but of Catholics all over the world that the wise precepts proclaimed by the great leader of Christianity have remained largely unknown and exercised little or no influence in developing a conscience on this subject. This general indifference on the part of the Catholic public cannot be attributed to lack of interest among the leaders, nor to the failure of an effort to bring it to the attention of the people. He reminded the interviewer that in Mexico, Bishop Francisco Venegas Galván of Querétaro called attention to its teachings in 1896, prophetically warning the large *hacendados* (land owners), "Wealthy Gentlemen, there is no other way; you either open your hearts to charity and tear it apart from worldly riches as the Catholic Church commands you, and learn to consider your servants as brothers and children of God, lightening their burdens, shortening their hours of work, and raising their pay in accord with the precepts of Leo XIII or you will reap in a not-too-distant day the fruits of accumulated hatred and venom, when the stormy winds of socialism sweep over Mexico raising mighty waves that will bury your wealth and yourselves."

Father Velazquez explained that charity in the Christian sense is not limited to alms; that in its broader and truer meaning it implies social justice. In Catholic social doctrine "alms never excuse one from obligations of justice." In a rapid review of what has been done in Mexico as a result of the social doctrine of *Rerum Novarum,* since its promulgation, he recalled that the Catholic Congress held in Puebla in 1903 had proposed for the first time in the history of Mexico the establishment of agricultural credit institutions, greatly needed even then; that in the fifth session of the said Congress the organization of labor "circles" had been discussed, being the only admissible form of organization for labor in those days; and that in the closing session agricultural labor problems and the need for vocational schools in arts and crafts were subjects for study.

Again in 1904 the second Catholic Congress held in Puebla dedicated the larger portion of its time to a thorough consideration of the various problems related to labor and capital relations. In 1906 the third Catholic Congress celebrated in Guadalajara gave its entire attention to social problems and the question of social justice. In 1909 the fourth Catholic Congress in Oaxaca took up for discussion and recommendations the Indian problem in Mexico, offering realistic suggestions for its solution.

In addition to the national Catholic congresses enumerated, there were several agricultural congresses held under Catholic auspices in Tulancingo, Zamora, and León. The first and second of these, held in 1904 and 1905 respectively, dealt with a number of questions related to the life of the peasant and agricultural worker, the raising of their wage, the control of drunkenness, the protection of children, and the improvement of the "peon" class. "Not a few propagandists toured the country long before the Madero Revolution, disseminating sound ideas on the function of the soil and the evils of large landed estates."

The record of the Church in this respect is more imposing than the average person realizes. In 1913 the *Segunda Gran*

*Dieta Obrera de la Confederacion Nacional de los Círculos Cat-
ólicos Obreros* (Second Congress of Workers of the National
Confederation of Catholic Workers Circles) was held and the
following program, which compares well with Article 123, was
adopted.

"1. The preservation of the home and of family life, which
require:

" (a) The fixing in each industry by a professional council
of a minimum wage for normal adult laborers under normal
conditions.

"(b) Appropriate regulations for the work of women and
children, directed to the suppression of work by married
women and children under twelve years of age, that guarantee
the hygiene, morality and safety of young unmarried women.

" (c) The acquisition of a non-transferable or undividable
homestead, whether it be rural or urban.

"2. Institutions that will insure the worker against involun-
tary stoppage, industrial accidents, sickness and want in old age.

"3. Permanent compulsory arbitration councils for the peaceful settlement of conflicts between capital and labor.

"4. The right to participate as far as possible in the benefits
of production by means of shares or some other means of easy
application.

"5. Protection against fluctuations in monetary values and
manifest or disguised speculations which in various ways cause
national wealth to be concentrated in the hands of the few
by taking advantage of the inexperienced.

"6. Facilities for the organization and protection of the
middle class by means of independent associations of private
and state employees, as well as those of small industries and
trading companies, etc.

"7. Effective protection for domestic labor, particularly that
of women and young seamstresses, organizing for this purpose
the agencies that may be necessary.

"8. Legal representation before public functionaries charged
with the interests of workers." [68]

Here was a program that incorporated all of the provisions
of Article 123 of the Constitution of 1917, offered by the first
nationally organized confederation of labor units in Mexico
four years before they were included in the new constitution.
They represented the influence of the Catholic Social Doctrine.
The first labor organization in Mexico was the *Círculo Católico
de Obreros*. Since the beginning of the century the *Organiza-
ción Nacional de Operarios Guadalupanos,* a group of Catholic
leaders whose purpose was to spread among the laboring classes

the Catholic doctrine of social justice as set forth by Leo XIII, had worked diligently to develop a conscience of social responsibility.

In summing up the role of the Church in Mexico today and its labor in developing a Christian conscience essential to the peaceful solution of its many national social problems we can do no better than to use the words of Father Veláquez: "Let no Catholic in our country think that he has no responsibility in this task, in making the social doctrine of the Church become a living force. If we fail to do so, we do not deserve to call ourselves Catholics, and we will have to suffer the consequences for having contributed to create the same problems which today have brought the world to the brink of an appalling catastrophe. Above all, before God and Country, we will have to render an account of the failure to perform our duty as Christians, free men, engaged in the creation of a world more just and more brotherly, capable of accepting the message of Christ in its entirety." [69]

Carlos E. Castañeda.

CHAPTER III

CONTEMPORARY SOCIAL DEVELOPMENTS IN LATIN AMERICA

Latin America is presently in a state of flux and social tension, with a great variety of social ideas and organizations struggling for popular support. In this short essay, the accent will be upon Chile both because the author has taken some part in the developments in that country, and because Chile is representative of dynamic social advance as well as powerful opposition to every social improvement. Chile also has one of the most advanced programs of social legislation in the contemporary world (Medicina Preventiva, Seguro Obrero, Prevision de Empleados, etc.) . Finally, Chile has influenced developments in other neighboring contries through youth trained in Chilean universities. This has been a primary channel for the spread of Christian social doctrine from the centers of Catholic University youth groups.

Every generalization in regard to Latin America, such as those which foreigners and Americans are prone to make, can easily be false and unjust. It is 10,000 kilometers from the Rio Grande to Antartica, and half as much from Guayaquil to Pernambuco. Within this huge space there are the most complex and varied conditions, with every degree of wealth and poverty, with a climate from tropical to temperate, with a terrain from mountain to costal plain, and with a social development from primitive community to urban industrialization. The population of 150 million is divided among white, Indian, negro, and mestizo, in very different proportions in the various countries. Latin America covers 16% of the world's surface, yet it contains only 6% of its population.

These differences among the twenty-one nations in climate, georaphy, population and cultural development are complicated by historical factors which stretch from the early relations of Spanish colonizers with the indigenous Indians to the present-day divergencies in political evolution. But there are some profound traits in common. Among these language and the Catholic religion are the most fundamental basis for unity.

The stage of economic development of the various countries can be roughly appreciated from the levels of per capita income as determined by Point IV statisticians. Recalling that the index is more than $900 in the United States, this table is significant:

Less than $50 a year:	Ecuador and Haiti.
$ 50—$100:	Bolivia, Paraguay, El Salvador.
$100—$200:	Brazil, Chile, Colombia, Peru.
$300—$400:	Argentine, Uruguay, Venezuela.

These wide divergencies in income, plus equally noteworthy differences in the evolution of labor law and economic organization, should warn all against easy generalization.

The present social condition has been influenced by history. In the pre-European period, the Incas had the most developed social and economic arrangements. They had specialization of labor, economic rationalization, laws regulating the work of children and the aged, retirement provisions, social security, medical assistance for the poor and aged, and land division under central control. Louis Baudin has called the Tiahuantisuyu (the Inca Empire) a "socialist" state. But the term with its Marxist associations is confusing when applied to the Incas, for they based their entire economic, social and political organization on the natural nucleus of the family. Each newly married couple was donated a "tupu"—an elastic amount of land depending on its value—but they could not cultivate it until they had done their share of work on the community land (ayllu), the land of the poor (tierra de los incapaces), and the land of the gods (tierras del Sol).

In the colonial period, missionaries and Castilian kings were conscious of their social obligations and were particularly concerned with the well-being of the Indians. Names such as Las Casas, Vasco de Ouiroga, Montesinos and Luis de Valdivia are sufficient testimony of this fact. The *Leyes de Indias* included social laws on such items as wages, hours of work (8 per day for ordinary workers, only 7 for miners), housing, clothing, food, rest, medical care, Christian instruction, and religious feasts. It has been customary to say that this progressive legislation, which dates from Las Casas's victory over the Chancellor Gines de Sepulveda in the presence of Charles V (1542), was good, but was never applied. Recent research by the department of legal history of the University of Chile on the proceedings of the Royal Audiences has demonstrated that these laws were enforced in the interest of the native worker.

The great exception in the colonial administration's treatment of the Indian was the *servicio personal* which was equivalent to slavery. The first governor to suppress it in Chile was Ambrosio O'Higgins, the father of the hero of Chilean independence. His son, who became Supreme Director of independent Chile, suppressed all forms of slavery in 1811, making his country the second (after Denmark) to take this step. The French Revolution had given the impetus in this direction, but its various governments were tardy in applying the principle to its colonial areas.

In the colonial period the Municipal Councils (Cabildos) also took some initiatives in favor of the native workers, and in addition gave the colonials some experience in self-government. It was the last Cabildo of colonial times which proclaimed Chilean independence on September 18, 1810, following the precedent of the Council of Buenos Aires.

It was the Republican era (nineteenth century) which gave to the Latin American states the *individualistic* classical juridical organization which was derived from the principles of ratonalistic romanticism and the Napoleonic Code. The Civil Code of Chile, the first in Latin America (1855), was the work of the Venezuelan Andrés Bello. It was imitated elsewhere on the continent and in the Spanish Civil Code of 1890. None of these codes recognized the legal rights of the worker. Article 548 of the Chilean Code gave the President the right to create or destroy any labor organization. The *cofradía* or *hermandad*—medieval-type guilds of shoemakers, typesetters, etc., which flourished in the colonial period—lost their juridical status. Only in the Commercial Code, which was influenced more by Spanish than by French precedents, was more attention given to the *ius consuetudinarium* which could be interpreted in favor of workingman's organiations.

In South America, the beginnings of Social Catholicism can be found at the turn of the present century in the Argentine and Chile. In 1899, only 8 years after *Rerum Novarum*, Juan Enrique Concha Subercaseaux, a notable Catholic Chilean leader, presented this thesis in the Faculty of Law on *Cuestiones oberas* (*Labor problems*). Carlos Walker Martínez, another Catholic leader in the anti-presidential revolution of 1891, spoke in 1901 on labor subjects and presented the principles of a Christian social order. By 1900 the sociologist Enrique Concha had already organized one of the first Labor Unions in Latin America by combining 43 workers' associations which he had established in Chile. Many of these were mutualist in character rather than syndicalist, but the new federation included 50,000 workers.

These early Catholic steps at labor organization were to be superseded by more radical efforts from abroad. By 1909 European anarchists had gained control of the labor movement and had a Federation of Anarchist Unions (IWW). Later the Socialists organized the Federation Obrera de Chile. The Catholics did not abandon the field. Concha Subercaseux presented to the Chilean Congress in 1917 the first Latin-American project for a Labor Code and gave a course of lectures in the Catholic University of Santiago on the subject. Another Catholic, Francisco Huneeus Gana, presented a legislative proposal on workers' housing and wrote a booklet *Por el orden social* (1921).

Catholics have been responible for most of the social legislation in Chile from the first law on housing (1906) to the Law on Preventative Medicine (1939) and the recent (1952) reform of the law on workers' social security (Seguro Obrero Obligatorio, Number 4054). Dr. Jorge Mardones, Minister of Public Health and former President of Catholic Action, inspired this last important welfare project.

The first Labor Code in Latin America was the Chilean *Codigo del Trabajo* prepared by President Alesandri in 1924 and published by President Carlos Ibánez in 1931. It was reformed again by Alesandri when president in 1932 and 1938 and by President Gonzalez Videla in 1949. Ibánez was recently reelected president of Chile by a great majority in a free and democratic election, and has announced several social improvement as part of his program. Catholics have declared themselves ready to collaborate in them.

These progressive steps should not obscure the fact that "the condition of poverty in Chile is still the normal status"—to use the words of a radical revolutionary of 1840. The same condition prevails throughout all the continent, with the situation at its worst in Bolivia and Ecuador, and least evident in the Argentine.

Throughout all Latin America the standard of living is very low and the difference in income of the social classes terribly striking. Nutritional diseases afflict 25-30% of the population, principally among the workers. The division of property, especially land ownership, is extremely unjust. Argentina, Chile, Uruguay and Mexico have made some social adjustments, but even in these relatively favored regions, poverty is oppressive, especially among the landless peasants and in the urban slums, Among the poor illegitimacy is a great problem. Alcoholism, and cocainism in Bolivia, Peru and Colombia, makes poverty more oppressive. These conditions have encouraged conservatives, including Catholic capitalists, to argue that it is useless to raise wages until the workers can be taught to expend their income more rationally. But the Catholic scientist, Dr. Mardones Restat of the University of Chile, has demonstrated that the lack of the N element in the B Vitamin Complex predisposes the organism to alcohol, not only in rats which have no psychological problems, but also in humans. In some countries as Chile, wine is cheaper than food rich in vitamins such as milk, meat and eggs.

A Chilean priest, Mons. Guillermo Viviani Contreras has prepared the following table of landownership in Chile from figures drawn from official sources. The book containing the analysis was published by the Vatican Press to forestall criticism by his fellow Catholics.

Acres	No. of properties	Total size m	Value $/m Ch.
Up to 10	32,342	72,559.5	145,584,784
From 10 to 40	30,242	33,759.1	310,884,123
40 to 100	17,846	582,649.1	361,504,999
100 to 200	9,853	691,630	402,769,563
200 to 400	6,473	900,760.5	551,526,895
400 to 1000	5,043	1.592,200.5	980,203,069
1000 to 2000	2,112	1,451,590.3	656,394,436
2000 to 4000	1,268	1,723,857.6	624,797,750
4000 to 10000	779	2,372,398.5	565,884,898
10000 or more	558	13,005,337.7	1,044,141,826

In brief, 500 families control a fifth of all the land of the country. The unequal distribution is even worse in Argentina and Brazil. The poorest of all conditions are to be found among the Bolivian miners who work some of the richest mines on the continent, and among the Central American peasants who labor for wealthy foreign companies.

It is this concentration of landed and industrial wealth that has caused intense opposition to social reform in Latin America. Every proposal for social amelioration, from Catholic or any other source, has been branded as *revolutionary;* and the most vigorous condemnation has been reserved for any kind of workers' association. Catholic landowners and industrialists have been in the forefront of this struggle and have branded all such efforts as "Communistic"—thus defining Communism as the unique defender of the poor. This is the greatest possible service that could be done to the radical cause and partly explains why the union organizations in most Latin American countries has fallen under Communist control. A good deal of the material for the extremists' propaganda has been provided by those who had every reason to prevent its spread.

Thus Latin American capitalists, Catholic and non-Catholic, have shown a singular lack of vision of their own interest and of the general economic welfare. They justify their position by arguments drawn from the individualistic spirit, which is a legacy of the liberalism of the eighteenth cenutry. They dismiss the social doctrines of the Church as an impossible ideal, and deny that they represent a practical moral law. They fail to see that it is impossible to "put back the clock" and to maintain positions that are no longer tenable. Finally, their political fear of Communism hardens them in their conservatism and inhibits a realistic appraisal of contemporary conditions.

This opposition of the ruling class to all legitimate social reform has created a most unfavorable climate for the work of socially-minded Catholics. In 1918, Monsignor Guillermo Viviani, a Chilean priest who is still writing on social subjects, founded a paper called *El Sindicalista* (The Trade Unionist) and established *La Casa del Pueblo,* a federation of 15 Catholic labor unions numbering about 5,000 workers. He immediately found himself involved in a struggle not only with the radicals, but with reactionary Catholic laymen and some of the bishops. Both of his foundations were suppressed by the Archbishop of Santiago after the social apostle had given eight years of arduous and successful work. The priest submitted; but the common people lost their "home" and their hope. Other priests such as Clovis Montero, Samuel Diaz Ossa, and a bishop who was a military chaplain, Monsignor Rafael Edwards, ran into similar conservative opposition. The result was that the workers began to distrust the clergy and lost confidence in their capacity to give social leadership.

Much the same happened in other parts of Latin America. Social movements initiated by Catholic laymen or priests had to develop in isolation, and rarely were backed by the hierarchy as a whole. Thus strength was lost, energies dispersed, and the working class largely abandoned the Church. European anarchists and Socialists, and later native and foreign Communists gained control of the majority of workers' organizations in all of Latin America. In 1934, Communists replaced Socialists in control of the miner's unions in Brazil, Chile, Colombia, Cuba and Mexico. At the very time when the unions were gaining in political power (1930-40) , they were falling under communist leadership in Chile, Colombia, Guatemala, Panama and Uruguay. The Communists are still dominant in most of the unions in these countries. In another group of countries—Bolivia, Ecuador, Venezuela, Brazil, Paraguay and Mexico—the Communists are not in control, but they exercise great influence. Finally, in Argentina, Brazil, Bolivia and Peru, the strong men—Peron, Vargas, Paz Estenssoro and Odria—have exercised official control over the unions and have entered into more or less disguised alliances with pro-fascist elements. In Peru, this was achieved by banning and persecuting the indigenous Socialist Party, Apra.

What is at stake in this situation can be gleaned from the following table. It must be remembered that the trade union movement in Latin America is necessarily of rather recent origin. The first modern workers' organizations, chiefly mutualist, were organized in Argentina and Chile around 1880, and involved drivers, mechanics, railroadmen, printers and bakers. The first labor unions in the strict technical sense of the word were established in Argentina in 1915. They have grown rapidly and exercise an influence beyond their numerical strength. The best figures for contemporary union membership, excluding those in agricultural work are:

Nation	Poulation in millions.	T. U. membership.
Argentina	16.	600,000
Bolivia	3.6	70,000
Brazil	45.	500,000
Chile	5.5	350,000
Colombia	10	250,000
Costa Rica	0.75	50,000
Cuba	5.	300,000
Dominican Rep.	1.2	25,000
Ecuador	3.	125,000
Guatemala	3.	50,000
Haiti	3.	15,000
Mexico	20.	1,000,000
Nicaragua	1.	25,000
Panama	0.75	25,000
Paraguay	1.	25,000
Peru	7.	350,000
Uruguay	2.25	75,000
Venezuela	4.	200,000

Those of the above which are Socialist are federated continentally under the Rightist Socialist Bernardo Ibanez of Chile. The Communists have a Latin American organization under Lombardo Toledano of Mexico. But the existing Christian trade unions have no united continental organization. Here is the contemporary status of the Christian trade unions:

Argentina: The government sponsored GGT unites all the Peronistas *descamisados* except for one non-official organization, the *Confederación de Empleadas* with some 25,0000 members. This was founded by Monsignor Miguel de Andrea, the most conspicuous social and democratic leader in Argentina and one of the outstanding clergymen of all the Americas. It is an independent labor union for women.

Colombia: Until recently the law permitted only one type of official union. Though this law has been reformed, Catholics developed much more social dynamism when they were not legally free to work. JOC, *Juventud Obrera Católica* was established as a specialized branch of Catholic Action only in 1942. Its purpose is to form youth for social leadership. The folowing unions are headed by Catholics in Colombia: *Union de Trabajadores Católicos* in the state of Antioquia; *Federación Minera Católica* at Cundinamarca; *Unión de Trabajadores de Santander; Unión de Trabajadores de Boyacá* (with mutualistic and cooperative emphasis); and one national organization, *Federación Agrícola Nacional,* for workers on the land.

Costa Rica: This small country has given good example to the rest. The late Archbishop Victor Sanabria and the Jesuit Padre Níñez founded some years ago a Catholic labor union called proudly *Sindicato Rerum Novarum.* In the revolution of 1948 their action was decisive against the Marxists and their influence is constantly increasing in an atmosphere of public approval.

Venezuela: No Christian unions. There is a new Christian Social Democratic party working slowly in a very difficult ambient.

Ecuador: Catholic confessional unions can legally exist, but factually Liberal and Socialist politicians strongly oppose them. Everything remains to be done.

Peru: All unions which were led by *Apristas* have been outlawed, but the dictator has a curious tolerance toward Communists. There are no Catholic unions, but there is a Catholic university group that maintains Christian social objectives.

Mexico: The trade union movement is widely discussed among Catholics. CTAL, *Confederación de Trabajadores de América Latina,* is headed by Toledano and is Communist orientated. There are no Christian unions, but Catholic Action works vigorously within the unions and among the peasants. A quarter million Catholic workers have been organized in an annual pilgrimage to Our Lady of Guadalupe.

Puerto Rico: There is only one Catholic union, *Confederación Libre de Trabajadores.*

Chile: After the suppression of the *Casa del Pueblo* in 1926 and the decadence of the *Federación de Obras Católicas,* founded a half-century ago by the Rev. Julio Restat, there have been no Catholic unions until recently. For some years the JOC has given special courses for labor leaders and more recently the late Jesuit Padre Alberto Hurtado Cruchaga, an alumnus of the University of Louvain, founded *El Hogar de Cristo* (for poor children and the aged) and ASICH, *Asociación Sindical Chilena* (for industrial workers). Backed personally by the General of the Jesuit Order and the Holy See, Padre Hurtado won the confidence of the proletariat. At his death in September, 1952, he received the greatest homage ever paid to a priest in Latin America when he was buried from the parish church of "Jesus the Worker." The popular acclaim tended to obscure the intense opposition he received from some Catholic circles and from some of the bishops. His work is now being carried on by young Chilean Jesuits.

Chilean law admits of two types of unions, industrial and professional, according as the workers are organized according to plant or skill. Both types are flourishing and their political importance is steadily on the increase. There is a project of law being considered that would make trade union membership compulsory for every worker in all categories over 18 years of age, leavng to the individual the right to choose his union. The biggest challenge to socially-minded Catholics is to diminish the distrust felt toward Catholics in the non-confessional unions and thus to diminish Communist control. Under such men as Mons. Manuel Larraín Errázuriz, bishop of Talca, some progress is being made in this direction.

*   *   *

It is not easy for North Americans to comprehend this complex Latin American world, especially since there have been misunderstandings on both sides. Anti-American feeling in Latin America is not necessarily of Communist origin, but stems from real or fancied insults they have endured in the past and from a lack of appreciation of their nationalist sentiments and their pride in their ancient culture. North Americans have often been contemptuous of Latin laziness, and have been particularly unfair to the Indian. They forget that the Indian built the monuments of Yucatan, carved the small plots of arable land on the slopes of the Andes, and built the magnificent "Roman" highways of the Incas. They forget, too, that some of this survives in the Indian art and in their skill in silver and wool work. Americans have also been derogatory toward the great achievement of the Spaniards in the conquest and colonization. Such prejudices continue and have impeded understanding, though some progress has been made in recent years. Finally,

Americans have not been adequately appreciative of the constructive work of the Church in this vast area.

The Christian faith is not lost, nor is it sterile, in Latin America. Checked by the sudden emergence of new economic and political forces, it is fighting back all over the continent, from Mexico to Chile, and from Brazil to Ecuador. Small elites of socially-inspired Christian democrats are present and at work in all parts of the hemisphere. The task is hard, the workers are few, and the problems are gigantic. Most serious of all is the resistance of the individualist tradition among the wealthy of all countries. This tradition is hostile to any Catholic social action and to all social legislation. At the same time social Catholics must face the opposition of the radicals, who are often entrenched in government and in union leadership, and who are sometimes favored by legislation. Finally, there is the difficulty that in Latin America everything, even one's daily bread, is mixed with politics. The bishops, following the Pope's directives, are attempting to separate Catholic social action from the political, and some progress is being made in this direction in Chile and Uruguay.

Conditions have sometimes forced Christian social democrats to form their own political party, not as representatives of the Church, but as citizens inspired by Catholic social doctrine. *Falanje* in Chile and *Unión Cívica* in Uruguay are the most outstanding, and they have met twice in Montevideo with similar groups from Colombia (*Testimonio*) and Cuba (*Acción democrática*) in order to plan the vanguard of a vast social Christian movement throughout all the continent. In the new Ibáñez administration in Chile, *Falanje* may hold the balance that may prevent a shift either to rightist or leftist totalitarianism. The chances are good since the new President is neither a Fascist nor a Communist, but is committed to social advance. If so, they will fulfill the traditional role of Christian Democracy in Europe.

The young Christian social movements in Latin America are badly in need of help and inspiration from Europe and America. But they have great native assets: faith in God, in the future and in their cause.

CARLOS D. HAMILTON

DOCUMENTS

Sermon of Friar Antonio de Montesinos, Advent 1511.[70]

"In order to make your sins against the Indians known to you I have come up on this pulpit, I who am a voice of Christ crying in the wilderness of this island, and therefore it behoves you to listen, not with careless attention, but with all your heart and senses, so that you may hear it; for this is going to be the strangest voice that ever you heard, the harshest and hardest and most awful and most dangerous that ever you expected to hear. . . This voice says that you are in mortal sin, that you live and die in it, for the cruelty and tyranny you use in dealing with these innocent people. Tell me, by what right of justice do you keep these Indians in such a cruel and horrible servitude? On what authority have you waged a detestable war against these people, who dwelt quietly and peacefully on their own land?. . . Why do you keep them so oppressed and weary, not giving them enough to eat nor taking care of them in their illness? For with the excessive work you demand of them they fall ill and die, or rather you kill them with your desire to extract and acquire gold every day. And what care do you take that they should be instructed in religion? . . .*Are not these men? Have they not rational souls?* Are you not bound to love them as you love yourselves?. . Be certain that, in such a state as this, you can no more be saved than the Moors or the Turks."

Friar Bartolome de Las Casa on the Indians, 1537.[71]

"The sublime God so loved the human race that He not only created man in such a wise that he might participate in the good which other creatures enjoy, but also endowed him with capacity to attain to the inaccessible and invisible Supreme Good and behold it face to face. . . .All are capable of receiving the doctrines of the faith.

"The enemy of the human race, who opposes all good deeds in order to bring men to destruction, beholding and envying this, invented a means never before heard of, by which he might hinder the preaching of God's word of salvation to the people: he inspired his satellites who, to please him, have not hesitated to publish abroad that the Indians of the West and the South, and other people of whom we have recent knowledge should be treated as dumb brutes created for our service pretending that they are incapable of receiving the Catholic faith.

"We. . . .consider however, that the Indians are truly men and that they are not only capable of understanding the Catholic faith, but, according to our information, they desire exceedingly to receive it. Desiring to provide ample remedy for these evils, we declare. . . .that notwithstanding whatever may have been or may be said to the contrary, the said Indians and all other people who may later be discovered by Christians, are by no means to be deprived of their liberty or the posession of their property, even though they may be outside the faith of Jesus Christ; and that they may and should, freely and legitimately enjoy their liberty and the posession of their property; nor should they be in any way enslaved; should the contrary happen, it shall be null and of no effect.

"By virtue of our apostolic authority, we declare. . .that the said Indians and other peoples should be converted to the faith of Jesus Christ by preaching the word of God, and by the example of good and holy living."

Francisco Suárez, S. J.: *No Unjust Human Law is Binding (1612)*[72]

"Our second inference from the first assertion, above set forth, is: a law not characterized by this justice or righteousness is not a law, nor does it possess any binding force; indeed, on the contrary, it cannot be obeyed.

"This is clearly true, because justice that is opposed to this quality of righteousness in law, is in opposition to God Himself, since it involves guilt, and offence against Him; and therefore, it cannot licitly be obeyed, because it is not posible licitly to offend God. . ."

Suárez: *Legislative Power Resides in the Community as a Whole (1612)*[73]

"It is customary to refer, in connection with its question, to the opinions of certain canonists who assert that by the very nature of the case this legislative power resides in some supreme prince upon whom it has been divinely conferred and that it must always, through a process of succession, continue to reside in a specific individual. . . .The said opinion, then, is neither supported by authority nor by a rational basis, as will become more evident from what follows.

"Therefore we must say that this power to make human laws, resides not in any individual but rather in the whole body of mankind. The conclusion is commonly accepted and certainly true. It is to be deduced from the words of St. Thomas in so far as he holds that the prince has the power to make laws, and that the power was transferred to him by the community. The civil laws set forth and accept the same conclusion. . ."

"The basic reason in support of the first part of the conclusion is evident, and was touched upon at the beginning of our discussion, namely, the fact that *in the nature of things all men are born free; so that, consequently, no person has political jurisdiction over another person, as no person has dominion over another* nor is there any reason why such power should, simply in the nature of things, be attributed to certain persons over certain other persons, rather than *vice versa*. . . . Political power, however, did not make its appearance until many families began to congregate into one perfect community. Accordingly, since this community had its beginning, not in the creation of Adam, nor solely by his will, but by the will of all who were assembled therein, we are unable to make any well-founded statement to the effect that Adam, in the very nature of things, held a political primacy in the said community. . ."

"Therefore, *the power of political dominion or rule over men has not been granted directly by God to any particular individual.*

"From the foregoing it is easy to deduce the second part of the assertion, namely, that the power in question resides, by the sole force of natural law, in the whole body of mankind, collectively regarded. . . ."

"The multitude of mankind should, then, be viewed from another standpoint, that is, with regard to the special volition, *or common consent,* by which they are gathered together into one political body through one bond of fellowship and for the purpose of aiding one another in the attainment of a single political end. Thus viewed, they form a single mystical body which, morally speaking, may be termed essentially a unity; and that body accordingly needs a common head. . . .It is, therefore, repugnant to natural reason to assume the existence of a group of human beings united in the form of a single political body, without postulating the existence of some common power which the individual members of the community are bound to obey; therefore, *if this power does not reside in any specific individual, it must necessarily exist in the community as a whole.*

Suárez: Civil Power Comes from the Community (1612) [74]

The second inference is as follows: Civil power, whenever it resides—in the right and ordinary sense of law—in the person of one individual, or prince, *has flowed from the people as a community,* either directly or indirectly; nor could it otherwise be justly held. . . ."

"A reason for this view, supplied by what we have said above, is the fact that such power, in the nature of things, resides immediately in the community; and therefore, in order that it may justly come to reside in a single individual, as in a sovereign prince, *it must necessarily be bestowed upon him by the consent of the Community."*

Suárez: When Regicide is Justified (1613) [75]

"On the other hand, if one acts in the defense of his very life, which the king is attempting to take violently from him, then to be sure, it will ordinarily be permissible for the subject to defend himself even though the death of the prince result from such defence. For the right to preserve one's own life is the greatest right; nor does the prince, in the situation described, labour under any need that obliges the subject to sacrifice his life for his sovereign's sake, since, on the contrary, the prince himself has voluntarily and by his unjust behaviour placed himself in the perilous postion. I say 'ordinarily', however, for if the state would be thrown into confusion by the death of the king, or would suffer from some other grave injury detrimental to the common welfare, then the charitable love of one's country and a charitable regard for that common welfare, would bind one—even at the peril of his own life—to refrain from slaying the king. But this obligation falls within the order of *charity,* and with that order we are not at present dealing."

Suárez: Forced Conversion. (1621)[76]

"We hold, first, that it is essentially wrong to force unbelievers who are not subjects, to embrace the faith.

"The proof of this proposition is that such coercion cannot occur without lawful power, as is self-evident, since otherwise all wars and all acts of violence could be called just; but the Church does not possess this lawful power with respect to such unbelievers . . ."

"The minor premise of this argument may be proved as follows: the power in question has not been given by Christ, nor does it reside in the princes of the Church from the very nature of the case. . . . ."

"Secondly, this minor premise may be proved by a negative argument, since, in the tradition of the Church, there is no trace of such power, either in its practice, or in Scrpiture; for the words of Christ, 'Compel them to come in' have a very different meaning from this, as I shall show below.

"Thirdly, the same premise is established affirmatively by the words of Paul. . . .This was the opinion expressed by Innocent III . . . and enunciated by the Council of Trent . . . ; and it is the common opinion of Chrysostom, Theophylact, Ambrose, St. Thomas . . .and of Augustine. . .and Jerome. . . ."

"Fourthly, the same premise is proved by the canon law, for this coercion is prohibited therein. . . ."

"Finally, an argument may be derived from the end in view; for such a coercive method of drawing men to the faith would not benefit the Church; on the contrary, it would be much more expedient that the first acceptance and profession of the faith should be absolutely and entirely spontaneous. . . ."

"The same spontaneous element is desirable, secondly, because the coercive method in question would involve many disadvantages, since it would, as a general rule, be followed by feigned conversions and innumerable acts of sacrilege. The unbelievers also would be much scandalized and would blaspheme the Christian religion if, by any human power, they were forced to embrace that religion, which is entirely supernatural. Therefore, the special supernatural power of which we are speaking has not been given to the Church."

Suárez: Unbelievers should be Allowed to Practice their Religion. (1621) [77]

"As to the rites of unbelievers, those which are opposed only to the faith, but not to natural reason, it is a certainty that unbelievers even though subjects, should not be compelled to abandon them; on the contrary, such rites should be tolerated by the Church. So St. Gregory teaches, especially with respect to the Jews, when he forbids that the latter should be deprived of their synogogues, and urges that they be permitted to engage in their ceremonies therein. He likewise teaches that the Jews should be permitted to celebrate their solemn rites.

"The reason for this view is that these rites are not intrinsically evil according to the natural law, and that therefore, the temporal power of the prince does not *per se* include the power to prohibit them; since no reason for the prohibition can be given, save that the rites in question are contrary to the faith, and this is not a sufficient reason in the case of those who are not spiritually subject to the power of the Church.

"The confirmation of this argument is the fact that such a prohibition would be, so to speak, a coercion to the acceptance of the faith; and this coercion, as we have said, is not permissible. The foregoing argument applies in general to the Saracens and to other unbelievers who know and worship the one true God, in so far as pertains to those rites which are not contrary to natural reason.

"However, the Church has always considered that this tolerance is especially advisable in dealing with the Jews, because the errors of the latter furnish a testimony to the faith in many particulars. . . . .Finally, Augustine has said that the Jews should be preserved and allowed to live in their own sects, in order that they in turn may preserve a testimony to the Scriptures such as the Church received, even from her enemies. . . ."

Francesco de Vitoria: Defense of the Indians, (1604). [78]

". . .I ask first whether the aborigines in question (the American Indians) were the true owners in both public and private law before the arrival of the Spaniards; that is, whether they were true owners of private property and posessions and also whether they were among them any who were the true princes and overlords of others. . . ."

". . .the people in question were in peaceful posession of their goods, both publicly and privately. Therefore, unless the contrary is shown, they must be treated as owners and not be disturbed in their possession unless cause be shown."

"Some have maintained that grace is the title to dominion and consequently that sinners, at any rate those in mortal sin, have no dominion over anything. This was the error of the poor folk of Lyons, or Waldenses, and afterwards of John Wycliffe. One error of his, namely, that no one is a civil owner while he is in mortal sin, was condemned by the Council of Constance. . ."

"But against this doctrine, I advance the proposition that mortal sin does not hinder civil dominion. . ."

"Thirdly, I employ against the opposing party their own argument: dominion is founded on the image of God; but man is in God's image by nature, that is, by his reasoning powers; therefore, dominion is not lost by mortal sin. . . ."

". . . .And in the same way that God makes His sun to rise on the good and on the bad and sends His rain on the just and on the unjust, so also He has given temporal goods alike to good and to bad. . . ."

"Now it remains to consider whether at any rate dominion may be lost by reason of unbelief. . . My answer is in the following proposition:. . . .unbelief does not prevent anyone from being a true owner. This is the conclusion of St. Thomas Aquinas. . . .Hence it is manifest that it is not justifiable to take anything that they possess either from the Saracens or Jews or other unbelievers as such, that is, because they are unbelievers; but the act would be theft or robbery no less than if it were done to Christians.

"But because heresy presents peculiar difficulties, let a second proposition be: from the standpoint of the divine law a heretic does not lose the ownership of his property. .. .For since loss of property is a penalty and no penalty is ordained by divine law for that condition, it is clear that from the standpoint of the divine law property is not forfeited on the ground of heresy . . ."

"From all this the conclusion follows that the barbarians in question (the American Indians) cannot be barred from being true owners alike in public and private law, by the reason of the sin of unbelief or any other mortal sin, nor does such sin entitle Christians to seize their goods and lands, as Cajetan proves at some length and neatly."

". . . The Indian aborigines are not barred on this ground (mental incapacity from the exercise of true dominion). This is proved from the fact that the true state of the case is that they are not of unsound mind, but have, according to their kind, the use of reason. This is clear, because there is a certain method in their affairs, for they have politics which are orderly arranged and they have definite marriage and magistrates, overlords, laws, and workshops, and a system of exchange, all of which call for the use of reason; they also have a kind of religion. . . . Now the most conspicuous feature of man is reason, and power is useless which is not reducible to action. Also, it is through no fault of theirs that these aborigines have for many centuries been outside the pale of salvation. . . ."

"The upshot of all the preceeding is, then, that the aborigines undoubtedly have true dominion in both public and private matters, just like Christians, and that neither their princes or private persons could be despoiled of their property on the ground of their not being true owners. . . ."

(Vitoria then examines all of the justifications for the Spanish conquest and rejects them as invalid)

"Let our first conclusion, then, be: The Emperor is not the lord of the whole earth (and never was). . . ."

"Granted that the Emperor were the lord of the world, still that would not entitle him to seize the provinces of the Indian aborigines and erect new lords there and put down the former ones, or take taxes. . . ."

"A second alleged title to the lawful possession of these lands, and one which is vehemently aserted, is traced through the Supreme Pontiff. For it is claimed that the Pope is temporal monarch, too, over all the world and that he could consequently make the Kings of Spain sovereign over the aborigines in question, and that so it has been done.'"

"First: The Pope is not civil or temporal lord of the whole world in the proper sense of the words 'lordship' and 'civil power'. . . ." [70]

"Second: Even assuming that the Supreme Pontiff had this secular power the whole world, he could not give it to secular princes.

"Third: The Pope has temporal power only so far as it is in subservience to matters spiritual, that is, as far as it is necessary for the administration of spiritual affairs. . . ."

"Fourth: The Pope has no temporal power over the Indian aborigines or over other unbelievers. . . ."

"The corollary follows that even if barbarians refuse to recognize the lordship of the Pope, that furnishes no ground for making war on them and seizing their property. This is clear because he has no such lordship. And it receives manifest confirmation from the fact . . . that, even if the barbarians refuse to accept Christ as their lord, this does not justify making war on them or doing them any hurt. . . ." [80]

"Accordingly, there is another title which can be set up, namely, by right of discovery; . . ."

"Not much need be said about this third title of ours, because, as proved above, the barbarians were true owners, both from the public and the private standpoint. . . . And so, as the object in question was not without an owner, it does not fall under the title we are discussing. Although, then, this title when conjoined with another, can produce some effect here (as will be said below,) yet in and by itself it gives no support to a seizure of the aborigines *than if it had been they who had discovered us.*"

"Accordingly, a fourth title is set up, namely that they refuse to accept the faith of Christ, although it is set before them and though they have been adjured and advised to accept it. . . ."

"From this proposition it follows that if the faith be presented to the Indians in the way named only (without adequate proof in reason and example), the Spaniards cannot make this a reason for waging war on them or proceeding against them under the law of war. . . ."

". . . It is not sufficiently clear to me that the Christian faith has yet been so put before the aborigines and announced to them that they are bound to believe it or commit fresh sin. I say this because . . . they are not bound to believe the faith unless the faith be put before them with persuasive demonstration. Now, I hear of no miracles or signs or religious patterns of life; nay, on the other hand, I hear of many scandals and cruel crimes and acts of impiety. Hence it does not appear that the Christian religion has been preached to them with sufficient propriety and piety that they are bound to acquiesce in it, although many religious and other ecclesiastics seem both by their lives and example and their diligent preaching to have bestowed sufficient pains and industry in this business, had they not been hindered therein by others who had other matters in their charge.

"Although the Christian faith may have been announced to the Indians with adequate demonstration and they have refused to receive it, yet this is not a reason which justifies making war on them and depriving them of their property. . . ."

(Vitoria then ennumerates the lawful titles of the Spaniards in the Indies according to international law: to travel and trade peacefully, if they do not harm the Indians; to participate in activities common to natives and strangers; to have their children who may be born there enjoy the right of citizenship; to preach the Gospel whether the natives accept it or not; to accept rule over the natives if they truly offer it voluntarily; to form alliances and friendships by mutual consent. He refuses to pass judgment on the question: could the Indians who subdued for their own good?)

Vitoria: The Binding Power of International Law, 1604.[81]

". . . International law has not only the force of a pact and agreement among men, but also the force of law; for the world as a whole, being in a way one single state, has the power to create laws that are just and fitting for all persons, as are the rules of international law. Consequently it is clear that they who violate these international rules, whether in peace or in war, commit a mortal sin; moreover, in the gravest matters, such as the inviolability of ambassadors, it is not permissible for one country to refuse to be bound by international law, the latter having been established by the authority of the whole world (by general consensus)."

Juan de Mariana, S. J.: Taxation, 1599.[82]

"But another means also can be thought out for alleviating the poverty of provincials. The articles which the people need for existence, such as wine, grain, meat, wool and linen clothing, should be sold, especially if no extreme elegance is involved, with only a small tax; what is missed on account of these things can be made up on the luxury merchandise, such as the spices that Spain would have been able to do without, sugar, silk, strong wine, flesh of fowl and game, and many other articles, without which life is tolerable, and which rather have a great influence on weakening the body and corrupting the mind. Thus indeed will counsel be taken for the needy, of whom we have a great number, and a rein will be placed on the indulgence of the powerful, to keep them from easily pouring out their resources in toadying to their mouth and stomach. . . ."

"At the same time the result will be that neither will the poor be entirely impoverished, from which fresh and serious disorders may arise, nor will the wealthy, who alone use the almost unnecessary merchandise, because of the increased price of it wax too rich in power and possessions. . . ."

"Lastly, in the expenses of the court and in giving rewards, the Prince ought not to be prodigal, lest he exhaust the public treasury. . . . And also he should be convinced that it is not suitable for Spain to be burdened by heavy taxes. . . . Nothing is more oppressive for the provincials than daily to think up new means of diminishing the resources of the wretched. And they do not even take sufficiently into consideration the deep difficulties into which the French have fallen, especially since the royal taxes have grown enormously and since *they have been increased without consent of the citizens by the kings through their dictatorial power."*

Mariana: The Dictator.[83]

"Tyranny, which is the most evil and disadvantageous type of government, as compared with the kingly, exercises an oppressive power over its subjects, and is built up generally by force . . . on the contrary the tyrant establishes maximum power on himself . . . thinks no crime to be a disgrace to him, no villany so great that he may not attempt it; through force he brings blemish to the chaste, he ruins the resources of the powerful, violently snatches life from the good, and there is no kind of infamous deed that he does not undertake during the course of his life."

"In the first place, he (the tyrant) *seizes on his own initiative and by force the supreme power in the nation,* which has not been given him on account of merit, but because of wealth, bribery, and armed power. . . ."

". . . after getting firmly in the saddle, he changes into the exact opposite, not being able to conceal for long his inborn monstrousness; like an untamed and frightful beast he rages against every level of society. He seizes and wastes the possessions of private individuals. . . ."

"This is the doctrine of the tyrant: whatever is lofty in the realm, let it be cast down. This they accomplish either by open force, or by working on it through secret calumnies. They exhaust all the other people, lest they be able to bother them, by ordering new taxes daily, by planting discord among the citizens, by weaving wars out of wars. . . ."

"Consequently he forbids citizens to congregate, *to come together in political meetings and societies, and to talk at all about public business;* this he accomplishes by secret inquisitions, and *by taking away the means of speaking and hearing freely, which is the height of servitude. He does not even allow them the freedom of complaint in such bad conditions.*

"Thus since he distrusts the citizens, he seeks support in intrigue; he deliberately cultivates friendship with foreign princes, so that he may be prepared for any eventuality; he calls in foreigners, who are just about barbarians, but he puts his trust in them. He supports a mercenary army, in his mistrust of his citizens, which is great calamity."

"Finally, he ruins the whole state; he considers it as his spoil in his wretched methods with no respect for the laws, from which he thinks himself exempt;[84] and though he professes to be planning for the public safety, he carries on in such a way that the citizens are crushed by every kind of evil and lead a most unhappy existence. . . . The common people are deprived of all their benefits, and no evil can possibly be imagined which is not a part of the misfortune of the citizens." [85]

Mariana: *Public Relief of the Poor.*[86]

"The work of perfect justice and piety is to relieve the need of the weak and needy, to feed the orphans, and to succor those who lack help. Especially is this a part of the duties of the Prince. This is the greatest and truest enjoyment of wealth—not to use it for one's own pleasure, but for the succor of the many; not for one's present enjoyment, but for justice, which alone does not die. The real duty of human kindness is to open the resources generously to all, which God willed to be common to all. For in fact, He gave the earth to all, to pour forth all its fruits and foods without distinction. Savage and mad greed interfered with the divine gifts, and laid claim for itself; and *it made its own the nourishment and resources that belong to all.* . . . Never does the earth produce so badly of crops and necessities that there would not be enough for all, if the heaps of grain and money, gathered together by the more powerful, are put to common use and used for feeding the poor. For God wills, and it is laid down by His law, that when human nature has become corrupt, a dividing up of goods is necessarily brought about, lest a few possess everything. . . ."

". . . what is pleasing to God ought to be suggested to the Prince, that he does not permit in the Commonwealth certain ones to grow unrestrictedly wealthy and powerful, and others, as is necessary from this fact, be poor beyond measure. For both are the rich corrupted by power, since there would be few that would be able to stand prosperity and bear good fortune, and *there must be as many enemies in a state as there are needy, especially if the hope is gone of emerging from their condition.* . . . Also I like the way Plato puts it—that the arts are neglected both in affluence and want, since neither does the rich man want to pursure them further, being content with the wealth and ease of his condition, nor can the needy, since the faculty for getting the means has been taken away on account of penury. Thus in the Commonwealth he thinks it appropriate that it is considered wrong that some abound in goods while others are in want; and that it should be arranged that there is a limit and a certain moderation in this respect. . . ."

". . . the next best thing to do (since the poor are not being relieved for religious reasons) is that *diligent care be taken that the poor are supported from the public funds.* . ."

I clearly would never be of the opinion that I should think it to be for the public benefit that the property handed over by our ancestors should be taken away from the priests. Yet I contend that it would be very beneficial, if the priests themselves paid attention as administrators that this wealth should be put to better uses and more in consonance with the ancient ones. And who doubts that it would be with much greater profit to the commonwealth and to the churchmen than now is the case, if it was allotted to the support of the poor and, as it were, *again restored to its true owner.* Also in truth as a great number of poor could be supported by these revenues, the people would be relieved of this very heavy burden, which they now carry with difficulty, while many of the clergy give themselves up to a life of luxury, with the result that great hordes live in penury. Therefore, there would be no need for any other public hospices for feeding, caring for, and receiving the poor and the strangers, if this wealth would be turned to salutary purposes."

". . . (where this source is inadequate, public funds must be spent for relief): Thus would come the caravansary for the reception of strangers, the poor-house for feeding the paupers, the hospital for looking after the sick, the orphanages for training the orphans . . . A house would be designated for caring for old people without means. Finally, a foundling hospital would be provided, where exposed infants are nursed and cared for to a fitting age. . . ."

Spanish Bishops: Warning against Revolution, 1931.[87]

"The Church, as custodian of the most exact and noble conception of political sovereignty, derived from God, *never* fails to inculcate due respect and obedience to the legal government, even in times when its officials and representatives abuse and misuse their power to the injury of the Church itself.

"A good Catholic, by reason of the very religion which he professes, should be the best of citizens, faithful to his country, loyally submissive, within the sphere of its jursidiction, to the legally established civil authority, whatever be the form of government. With that loyalty, therefore, the Spanish Catholics will support the civil power in the form in which it actually exists (the Republic).

"And however afflicting may be those conditions by which we see the Church surrounded, you should have no fear, nor presume to arrogate to yourselves the right of judgment, which belongs to the Lord alone; remember that the Church overcomes evil with good, that it replies to inquity with justice, to injury with meekness, to unkindness with blessings, and that in the final event the Christian virtue of suffering is a weapon of victory.

"To assist by our own action in the destruction of the social order, in the hope that out of such a catastrophe might be born a better condition of things, would be a blameworthy attitude, and one whose fatal consequences would make it almost treason both to our Religion and to our native land.

"It is not by seditions and by violent actions that Christians conquer the evils that afflict them; it is by belief in the supremacy and fecudity of the Spirit, in the power of active faith and charity, that victory, by the Lord's help, is attained.

"Our adorable Savior, who affirmed His divine right over mankind by saying 'He who is not with Me is against Me!' did not permit His disciples to call down fire from heaven upon the city which refused them admittance."

Spanish Bishops: *Attitude toward the Revolution, 1937.*[88]

". . . And what hurts us most is that an important part of the foreign Catholic press should have contributed to this mental deviation (misunderstanding the nature of the civil war), which might prove fatal to the most sacred interests that are being contested in our country."

"Before everything else let it be recorded—in view of the fact that the war could have been foreseen, since the national spirit was attacked rudely and inconsiderately—that the Spanish Episcopate has given since the year 1931 the highest example of Apostolic and civil moderation. Adapting itself to the tradition of the Church and to the guidance of the Holy See, it placed itself resolutely on the side of the constituted powers, exerting itself in order to collaborate with them for the common good. And in spite of the continual offenses to the persons, things and rights of the Church, it did not change its purpose of not altering the system of harmony long since established with the civil power. *Etiam dyscolis:* to vexation we always answered with the example of loyal submission in all that we could; with grave, reasoned and apostolic protest when we were obliged to use it; with the sincere exhortation that we have repeatedly made to our Catholic people for lawful submission, for prayer, for patience and for peace. And the Catholic people followed us, our intervention being a valuable factor of national concord in a time of deep social and political commotion.

"When the war broke out we lamented more than anyone the painful fact, because it is always a most grave evil which often enough is not compensated by problematic advantages: *Et in terra pax*. Since its beginnings we have had our hands raised to Heaven that it might cease. And in these moments we repeat the words of Pius XI, spoken when the mutual suspicion of the great Powers was on the verge of bringing war over Europe: "We implore peace, we bless peace, and we pray for peace." God is witness to the efforts that we have made in order to lessen the ravages that always form its train.

"To our desires for peace we join our generous pardon for our persecutors and our feelings of charity for all. And on the battle-fields we say to our sons of the one and other party the words of the Apostle: 'God is my witness how I long after you all in the bowels of Jesusu Christ.' "

". . . The Church has never wished this war nor provoked it, and we do not think that it is necessary to vindicate her from the charge of belligerency with which the Spanish Church has been censored in foreign newspapers. It is true that thousands of her sons, obeying the promptings of their conscience and of their patriotism, and under their own responsibility, revolted in arms in order to safeguard the principles of religion and Christian justice which have for ages formed the nation's life. But whoever accuses her of having provoked this war, or having conspired for it, or even of not having done all that lay in her power to avoid it, does not know or falsifies the reality.

"This is the position of the Spanish Episcopate, of the Spanish Church, in respect to the present war. She was vexed and perse-cuted before it broke out; she has been the chief victim of the fury of one of the litigant parties; and she has not ceased to work with her prayers, with her exhortations, with her influence, in order to lessen its damages and to cut short the days of trial.

"And if today, collectively, we formulate our verdict on this most complex question, the war in Spain, it is first because, even if the war were of a political and a social character, its repercussions in the religious order have been so grave, and because it appeared so clear from its beginnings that one of the belligerent parties was aiming directly at the abolition of the Catholic religion in Spain. We, Spanish Bishops, could not remain silent without aban-doning the interests of Our Lord Jesus Christ and without incur-ring the terrible appellation of *Canes muti,* with which the prophet blames those who, being obliged morally to speak, keep silence in the face of injustice. We speak also because the position of the Spanish Church, that is of the Spanish episcopate, with respect to the struggle, has been tortuously interpreted abroad. A well-known politician in a foreign Catholic magazine imputes it to little less than the mental decadence of the Spanish Archbishops, whom he

qualifies as men stricken in years who owe all that they are now
to the monarchical regime, and who have dragged along the other
bishops for reason of discipline and obedience in a sense favorable
to the Nationalist Movement. Others incriminate us for rashness
in exposing to the contingencies of an absorbing and tyrannical
regime the spiritual order of the Church whose liberty we are
obliged to defend.

"No; above all we claim this liberty for the exercise of our
ministry. From it take rise all the liberties that we vindicate for
the Church, and therefore we have not tied ourselves to anybody—
persons, powers or institutions—even though we thank for their
protection those who have been able to preserve us from the enemy
who wished to ruin us, and although we are ready to collaborate,
as Bishops and Spaniards, with those who are making efforts to
restore in Spain a regime of peace and justice. No political power
will ever be able to say that we have departed for one moment
from this line of conduct.

"We affirm, first of all, that this war has been occasioned by the
rashness, the mistakes, perhaps the malice and the cowardice of
those who could have avoided it by governing the nation with
justice."

"Let it remain, therefore, established as the first assertion of this
document, that five years of continuous insults to Spanish subjects
in the religious and social order put the very existence of the
commonwealth in the greatest danger and produced enormous
tension in the spirit of the Spanish people; that the national conscience felt that, once the lawful legal means were exhausted, there
was no other recourse left but that of violence for maintaining
order and peace; that powers other than the authority considered
as legitimate determined to subvert the constituted order by the
violent implantation of Communism; and finally, that through the
fatal logic of the facts Spain had no other alternative but this:
either to perish in the definite assault of destructive Communism.
already prepared and decreed, as has occurred in those parts where
the Nationalist Movement has not triumphed, or to attempt a ti-
tanic effort of resistance, in order to escape from the terrible enemy
and to save the fundamental principles of her social life and of her
national characteristics."

"We have traced an historical sketch, from which derives this
assertion: the civic-military revolt was in its origin a national
movement of defense of the fundamental principles of every civilized society; in its development it has been one of defense against
anarchy bound up with the forces at the service of a government
which could not or would not guard those principles.

"Consequent on this assertion are the following conclusions:

"First, that the Church, in spite of her spirit of peace and of the
fact that she neither desired the war nor collaborated in it,
would not be indifferent to the struggle. Her doctrine and her spirit,
the sense of self-preservation, and the experience of Russia made this

impossible. On the one side God was suppressed, Whose work must be realized by the Church in the world, and there was caused to the latter an immense harm in persons, things and rights such as, perhaps, has never been suffered by any institution in history; on the other side, whatever might be the human defect, there was the effort to preserve the old spirit, Spanish and Christian.

"Secondly, the Church, with all that, has not been able to identify herself with the conduct, tendencies or intentions which in the present time or in the future might be able to distort the character of the Nationalist Movement, its origin, manifestations and ends.

"Thirdly, we affirm that the civic-military rising has taken a double grip on the depths of the popular conscience—that patriotic sense, which has seen in it the only means of raising up Spain and avoiding her definite ruin; and the religious sense, which considered it as a force necessary to reduce to impotence the enemies of God, and as a warrant of continuity for her faith and the practice of her religion.

"Fouthly, for the moment there is no hope in Spain for the reconquering of justice and peace and the blessings that derive from them, other than the triumph of the Nationalist Movement. Perhaps this is more true today than in the beginning of the war, because the other side, in spite of all efforts on the part of its leaders, offers no guarantee of political and social stability."

"A very eloquent proof that the destruction of churches and the slaughter of priests in a comprehensive manner was a premeditated thing is its frightful number. Although the figures are premature, we calculate that about 20,000 churches and chapels have been destroyed or totally plundered. The murdered priests, counting on an average forty percent in the devastated dioceses—in some they reach eighty percent—will sum up, of the secular clergy alone, about 6,000. They were hunted with dogs; they were pursued across the mountains; they were searched for with eagerness in every hiding-place. They were killed without trial, usually on the spot, for no other reason than that of their function in society."

"As regards the future, we cannot tell what will happen at the end of the struggle. Nevertheless, we affirm that the war has not been undertaken to build up an autocratic State over a humiliated nation, but simply that the national spirit should arise with the strength and the Christian liberty of older times. We trust in the prudence of the men of government, that they will not accept foreign models for the structure of the future Spanish State, but that they will consider the requirements of the national life from within and the course marked by past centuries. Every well-ordered society is based on deep principles and it lives on them, and not on imported and foreign accretions which might do violence to the national spirit. Life is stronger than programs, and a wise leader will not impose a program which may do violence to the inner resources of the nation. *We would be the first to regret that the*

irresponsible autocracy of a Parliament should be replaced by the
yet more terrible one of a dictatorship without roots in the nation.
We nourish the legitimate hope that it will not be so . . ." (Italics
supplied)

Memorandum of Some of the Basque Clergy to Pope Pius XII, 1944.[89]

"On the western side of the Pyrenees there is a people—Euzkadi,
of the ancient community of the Basque States—which has preserved its racial peculiarities and its traditional culture since the
most remote times."

"To its ancient religious beliefs is due, without doubt, the formation of a kind of humanism in the Basque people, that is, a
state of society which respected the individual and served him,
in which he could freely develop and express himself.

"Christianity has become so deeply rooted and is so kept alive
among the Basques, that it has rightly been said that they are
today one of the most Christian races in South-west Europe."

"In recent centuries, particularly in the nineteenth, the Spanish
Monarchs and Governments have deprived the western Basques
of their autonomous regime to such a point that there remain
only a few vestiges of their old liberties in two of their four regions.
In vain the Basques attempted to regain them on several occasions.
But, above all, they made their protest and put up a tenacious
resistance each time the neighboring States made an attack upon
their rights. Their armed resistance against the totalitarian and
centralist 'Movement' of General Franco eight years ago, was an
episode in their age-old fight."

"On the outbreak of the war, the insurgents announced over
their radios that they had taken up arms 'in the name of God
the All-powerful.' In their political program, disputed in some
aspects, reprehensible in others, they incorporated the defense of
Religion, and they called their war 'a holy war' and a 'crusade.'

"From then on, not only those who opposed Franco, but also
those who wished to remain neutral in the conflict, were treated
as enemies of God and of Religion.

"Not to join the 'Movement' because one's conscience would not
allow one to be an accomplice in the crimes of a total war, was
to be regarded as a 'Red' or a bad Christian.

"Whoever fought against the insurgents in defense of the regional
rights and liberties which they were trampling down, attacked God
and collaborated with Communism, according to the mentors of
the insurrection.

"Whoever absented himself from the theater of war or did not
join in the chorus of toadies of Franco, not being in agreement
with those systematic and well-premeditated murders, imprison-
ments, dismissals, exiles, etc., inflicted upon thousands of peaceful
persons, took the part of the enemies of God.

"That is, in order to be a good Christian, to be a Catholic, it was a necessary condition to approve injustice and to practice iniquity.

"But this propaganda did not succeed in every country, nor among all sections of Catholics. Many Basques, who saw how Franco's army practised total war at the front and behind the lines, and opposed Basque autonomy, closed Basque schools, declared Basque political, social and cultural institutions illegal, imprisoned, fined and even shot many of their compatriots for having sympathized with the defenders of their people and their own rights, did not believe in the 'crusade.' This attitude was natural from their point of view: where there was neither justice nor charity, there was no God.

"A great number of the inhabitants of our diocese regarded as reprehensible the conduct of those who, under the banner of Religion, hid such discredited ideas as totalitarianism (point 6 of the falangist program), the suppression of trade union freedom, the opposition to Basque liberties, etc., and tried to justify, in the name of Christ, such reprehensible proceedings as the bombing of open cities, the shooting of innumerable people for the sole reason that they had belonged to political groups opposed to the 'crusade,' confiscations of property, sackings of houses and dismissals from office and employment, which were the punishments inflicted upon their political adversaries by the insurgents."

"Bands of Red gangsters looted and killed in the Government zone; but they did not do it in the name of Christ.

"Franco's supporters, fulfilling orders from their leaders, committed the same crimes to the cry of 'Hail Christ the King'.

"The Basques, who condemned the conduct of the former could not approve that of the latter."

"As the Franco elements were victorious in one part of the diocese of Vitoria from the first day of the revolt, they began the persecution of part of its clergy, in accordance with the anticipated plan (which we all knew), shooting some, imprisoning others, and exiling many. At the beginning of 1938 more than 300 priests of our diocese had been persecuted by Franco and his followers.

"Franco deprived the Church of Vitoria of canonical liberty. He exiled its Bishop. And after more than eight years of exile, he is still not allowed to return home to spend the last years of his life with his family."

"The above, Your Holiness, are some of our complaints and anxieties.

"While being opposed to commenting upon them and even to expressing them in non-competent circles, we believed that we ought to present them to our Father and supreme Pastor in the language which, in our opinion, best expresses the crude reality of the events of which we were the witness and victims."

Appeal to General Franco, 1952[90]

"Faithful to its traditions, the International Federation of Christian Trade Unions, which, from its founding more than thirty years ago, has consistently defended the economic and social interests of workers, has always borne witness of its unswerving attachment to the principle of trade unionism. It has opposed every authoritarian tendency, whether from the left or right, and has not hesitated to sacrifice the most cherished friendships to the principle of freedom. Very often it has found itself alone in the fight, while others, for reasons of political expediency, were denying 'their' principles.

"Freedom of association is an inalienable natural right. By this very nature, man is not sufficient to himself. He is obliged to join with others because he needs them, and because his nature urges him to seek their aid. Society is born of this inherent propensity of human nature, and so are lesser societies which have a more limited goal.

"The right of these latter to exist is not conferred by the State. In this matter the State can only recognize a natural right which it has no power to suppress.

"It is in the name of these same principles that on several occasions the International Federation of Christian Trade Unions has protested against the system of trade unionism now prevailing in Spain. That system is based on a single trade-union organization which is subordinated to a political party and incorporated into the governmental regime. In this system of State trade unions the worker is deprived of the natural and efficacious protection provided by free trade unionism and is delivered over to the uncontrolled forces of capitalistic or political speculations. The living standards of workers today in Spain offer a striking, though distressing proof of this assertion.

"Bearing this in mind the Christian trade unions of various countries, as well as the International Federation of Christian Trade Unions, expressed their solidarity with the workers of the Basque provinces and other regions of Spain when they went on strike, spontaneously and 'en masse,' to show their dissatisfaction with present living conditions. That was a legitimate defense of their rights and it should not have been met by the Government, as happened in Spain, with repressive measures.

"The IFCTU believes that the time has come in Spain to put trade-union life on a sound foundation of healthy freedom. Free association will give to workers a powerful guarantee against all the ups and downs of which they can be, under present conditions, the helpless victims.

"Besides, at this precise moment in history the restoration of one of the essential liberties would have tremendous repercussions far beyond the border of Spain. We are firmly convinced that such a measure would evoke favorable echoes in every country, especially in working class circles. It would, consequently, facilitate the integration of Spain into the community of free peoples, with all the obligations, of course, which that implies, but with all the honor and advantages, too.

"That is why the IFCTU, in the name of all its affiliates, wishes to join its voice to the voice of the bishops and priests of Spain in praying to abolish the trade-union regime now in effect, and to restore in this domain that liberty which is a natural right of man and the essential condition of free and harmonious social life.

"In so appealing to you, IFCTU is convinced that it is interpreting the deepest and most ardent desires of millions of Spanish workers, who are today living under a regime of depressing restraint and who, nevertheless love their country and are ready to sacrifice everything to safeguard its integrity. This love of their fatherland will be powerfully strengthened the day when, in an atmosphere of liberty, they find the means of obtaining through their work a decent livelihood."

NOTES

1 Vol. 198, No. 5801, p. 53.

2 The circumstances and the uneven pace of the Reconquest also intensified regional differences. Spain is like a beach from which the waters have receded at different periods, leaving marks which vary according to the length of time the terrain has been submerged and the circumstances of the recession. Cf. *España en su historia,* Américo Castro, Losada, 1948.

3 There have been minor rectifications. Now the Pope can suggest three names for a bishopric, the government three. But the government makes the choice.

4 Cf. the excellent monograph published under the auspices of the American Historical Association: Lewis Hanke, *The Spanish Struggle for Justice in the Conquest of America,* Philadelphia, Univ. of Penn. Press, 1949. Also, Salvador de Madariaga, *The Rise of the Spanish American Empire,* N. Y., Macmillan, 1947.

5 Gerald Brenan, *The Spanish Labyrinth,* N. Y., Macmillan, 1943, pp. 40-41 and 45-46.

6 In fairness, it must be added that the clergy was partly acting in the heated nationalist atmosphere induced by the struggle against Napoleon since the reforms introduced during the occupation could be rejected as foreign and French. They were also impressed by the anti-clerical measures of the Liberal Cortes of 1812. Granted all this, the Restoration policy was a disaster. It could not possibly have been successful and only prepared the way for retaliation. It is one indication, among many, of the inability of Spaniards of all groups to compromise in political matters.

7 Superficially, the situation in Spain compared with that in Russia: Industrialism, largely stimulated by foreign capital and not necessarily related to local needs, coming into an area where the agrarian problem was unresolved.

8 Thus, while Britain and the U.S. have achieved organic unity and have solved major constitutional questions before having to bear the full weight of the problems arising from industrialization, Spain is still struggling with an incomplete national unity, with wretched land distribution and utilization in a large part of her area, with deep disagreement on the form of government, and with all the bitterness of a neglected and exploited urban proletariat. As

in Germany, the proletarian revolution began before the Liberal revolution had succeeded.

[9] Brenan, in this as in other matters, is objective. Cf. *op. cit,* pp. 235 239.

[10] The parish clergy in the modern period are overwhelmingly of peasant origin and ordinarily extremely poor.

[11] *Nationalism and Internationalism,* N. Y., Roy, 1946, pp. 83-95. For a similar view in greater detail, cf. Jacques Maritain's introduction to Alfred Mendizabal, *The Martyrdom of Spain,* N. Y., Scribners, 1938.

[12] Even the Fascist-minded Falange emphatically rejected Racism during the 30's when the Falangist tie with totalitarian dictatorships was very close. At the same time, it has adopted most of the *methods* of the dictatorial parties abroad.

[13] *Centros Catholicos de Obreros.*

[14] Salvador de Madariaga, *Spain,* London, Jonathan Cape, 1943, pp. 116-117. This federation had 2726 local branches.

[15] Pope Pius XII sent his special blessing to this work on 18 June 1948. He has also encouraged similar efforts whenever found, with strong endorsement of any implementation of Catholic social principles.

[16] There is no suggestion here that these avowals are not sincere. They are, undoubtedly. The question is whether there is being repeated a situation comparable to that in France under Louis Napoleon (cf. above, pp. 135-41). As for the character of the present government—all defenders of the regime declare it is only a passing phase.

[17] Berta Luna Villanueva, *Catolicismo Social y Reformas de Estructura.* (Mexico, 1949) x.

[18] Pope Pius XI, *Caritate Christi Compulsi,* May 3, 1933. See also *op. cit.,* 3-4.

[19] Villanueva, *op. cit.,* 169.

[20] Mary P. Holleran, *Church and State in Guatemala,* (New York, 1949), pp. 8-9.

[21] Felix Osores, *Historia de todos los Colegios de Mexico,* Annotated and edited by Carlos E. Castañeda. Mexico, 1929.

[22] See also Lucas Ayarragary, *La Iglesia en America y la Dominacion Española* (segunda edición) 149-151. Buenos Aires, 1935.

[23] The text of this important and significant Bull is translated from the Spanish translation of the original, printed in full in Ayarragaray, *La Iglesia en America y la Dominicón Española,* 159-161.

[24] Joaquín García Y Icazbalceta, *Biografia de don Fr. Juan de Zumarraga* (Mexico, 1881) p. 127.

[24a] Ayarragaray, *op. cit.,* 9-10.

[25] Carlos E. Castañeda, "The Beginnings of University Life in America," Preliminary Studies of the Texas Catholic Historical Society, III, No. 4, (Austin, July, 1938).

[26] Ayarragaray, *op. cit.,* 10.

[27] Carlos E. Castañeda, "Fray Junipero Serra Pioneer and Saint," *The Serran,* May, 1950 (Supplement).

[28] Charles S. Braden, *Religious Aspects of the Conquest of Mexico;* Juan and Ulloa, *Noticias Secretas,* Chapter VIII; Lucas Alaman, *Historia de Mexico,* Vol. I.

[29] Sebastián Lorente, *Historia del Peru bajo los Bourbones,* (Lima, 1871), 270-271.

[30] Helen Phipps, *Some Aspects of the Agrarian Question in Mexico* (University of Texas Bulletin No. 2515), 45.

[31] J. Lloyd Mecham, *Church and State in Latin America* (University of North Carolina Press, 1934), 50.

[32] Genaro Garica, *El Clero de México y la Guerra de Independencia* (Mexico, 1906) 45-47.

[33] Lucas Alamán, *op. cit.*, II, 31.

[34] Mariano Cuevas, *Historia de la Iglesia en México*, Vol. IV.

[35] A good account and discussion of this institution are found in Jose Toribio Medina, *Historia del Tribunal del Santo Oficio de la Inquisición* en México and Bernard Moses, *Spain's Declining Power in South America.*

[36] Mecham, *op. cit.*, 67.

[37] Ayarragaray, *op. cit.*, 234.

[38] Faustino J. Legón, *Doctrina y Ejercicio del Patronato Nacional*, (Buenos Aires, 1920), 490-494.

[39] P. Pedro Leturia, *La Acción Diplomática de Bolívar ante Pio VII*, (Madrid 1925) 281-282.

[40] Mecham, *op. cit.*, 79.

[41] For the full text of the remarkable summary of the Latin American situation, Spain's obstinacy, and the embarrassing position of the Vatican made by the aged Cardinal see Artaud de Montor, *Histoire du Pape Leon, XII*, I, 166.

[42] Ayarragaray, *op. cit.*, 224.

[43] Vicente Riva Palacio, *Mexico a Través de los Siglos*, IV, 139.

[44] Simón Bolívar, *Cartas del Libertador*, VIII, 105-106.

[45] Ayarragaray, *op. cit.*, 259-268.

[46] In his allocution *numquam fore* of December 15, 1856, Pius IX denied there were any grounds for the legitimacy of national patronage as a right inherited from the kings of Spain. The right of secular presentation was condemned as an error in the *Syllabus*. See Matías Gómez Zamora, *Regio Patronato Español e Indiano*, (Madrid, 1897) 245-246.

[47] Ayarragaray, *op. cit.*, 209-310. The author gives an excellent presentation of the whole problem.

[48] Pedro A. Zubieta, *Apuntaciones sobre las Primeras Misiones Diplomáticas de Colombia*, (Bogotá, 1924), 598.

[49] Mecham, *op. cit.*, 106.

[50] Dictamen de la Comisión de Patronato, June 21, 1823, (Mexico, 1823), 3-5.

[51] *Ibid.*, 5-6, 11-8.

[52] Juan A. Mateos, *Historia Parliamentaria de los Congresos Mexicanos*, II, 806-814, 855-877.

[53] Francisco Bulnes, *Juárez y las Revoluciones de Ayutla y de la Reforma*, (Mexico, 1905), 83-84.

[54] Col. Vázquez Media to Guadalupe Victoria, July 16, 1828. *Riva Palacio Papers*, Univ. of Texas.

[55] Riva Palacio, *op. cit.*, IV, 284.

[56] M. de la Cueva, *Derecho Mexicano del Trabajo*, (Mexico, 1949), II, 263.

[57] P. Rouaix, *Génesis de los Artículos 27 y 123 de la Constitucion de 1917*, (Puebla, Gobierno del Estado, 1945), 22-23; L. Mendieta y Nuñez, *El Problema Agrario en México*, (Mexico, 1946), 139-142.

[58] José Bravo Ugarte, *Breve Historia de México*, Mexico, 1949.

[59] Richard M. Pattee, *The Catholic Revival in Mexico*, (Confidential Report to Catholic Assn. for International Peace, Washington, July, 1944.)

[60] Pattee, *op. cit.*, 14-15.

[61] *La Nación*, July 2, 1951, (Año X, Num. 507) 22.

[62] *La Nación*, May 28, 1951, (Año X, Num. 502) 21.

[63] Pattee, *op. cit.*, 36.

[64] *La Nación,* June 11, 1951 (Año X, Num. 504) p. 12.

[65] Pattee, *op. cit.,* 49.

[66] Manuel Castillo, "Lo Primero es el Campo," *La Nacion,* April 9, 1951. (Año X, Num. 495) p. 7.

[67] "Carta Pastoral Colectiva del Venerable Episcopado Mexicano, en el 60 Aniversario de la Enciclica *Rerum Novarum,*" *La Nacion,* May 21, 1951 (Año X Num. 501.)

[68] Pedro Velazquez, "La Justicia Social no es una Teoria," *La Nacion,* May 14, 1951 (Año X, Num. 500).

[69] *Ibid.,* 9.

[70] Las Casas, *Historia de las Indias,* Lib 3, cap. 4. Cited in Lewis Hanke, *The Spanish Struggle for Justice in the Conquest of America,* Philadelphia, Univ. of Penna. Press, 1949, p. 17. The Dominican preached this serman on the island of Hispaniola. Italics supplied.

[71] *Idem,* pp. 72-73. Las Casas spent his life-time in the defense of the natives He had been encouraged by the Bull *Sublimis Deus* of Pope Paul III, and had been appointed "Protector of the Indians" by Cardinal Jiménez de Cisneros in 1516 as a recognition of his efforts. The result, as stated by Frank Tannenbaum in *Peace by Revolution, An Interpretation of Mexico,* N. Y., 1933, p. 37: "A community, a church, a law, a body of rights—all these were given to him (the Indian) largely because he was considered a human being possessed of a soul and capable of redemption . . . men like Las Casas, Quiroga, Zumarraga, and Fuenleal labored, fought, and defended the Indian against the rapacity of the white man, and in that defense initiated a series of curernts, ideals, ideas, laws, and practices, within which the Indian has more easily saved his race from extermination, and by saving his race, has saved his genius for the world."

[72] *De Legibus, ac Deo Legislatore,* Bk. I, chap. IX; translated by Gwladys Williams, et al., in *Selections from Three Works of Francisco Suarex, S. J.,* Oxford, Clarendon Press, 1944, p. 113. (Carnegie Endowment for International Peace (N. Y.), copyright) In these selections from Suarez references in parentheses and other brackets are eliminated for smoother reading.

[73] *Idem,* pp. 373-376. While these citations do not belong chronologically to the scope of this volume, they are essential for illustrating the points made in the text. They also give substance to the general theme of this study. Italics supplied.

[74] *Idem,* p. 383. Italics supplied

[75] *Defensio Fidei Catholicae, et Apostolicae adversus Anglicanae Sectae Errores, Idem,* p. 709. This Jesuit opinion caused great resentment in the courts of the absolute monarchs.

[76] *De Triplici Virtute Theologica, Fide, Spe, et Charitate, Idem,* pp. 760-762. Though this passage concerns only those unbelievers who are not subjects of Catholic princes, the author then proceeds to show that the essentially the same reasons apply to unbelievers who are subjects, and concludes that these also cannot be coerced to bring them into the Church.

[77] *Idem,* p. 775. Suarez does justify limiting conditions in the practice of these ceremonies.

[78] *De Indis,* from *Relectiones XII Theologicae in duo libros distinctae,* English text in J. B. Scott, *The Spanish Origin of International Law,* Oxford, the Clarendon Press, 1934, pp. i-xlvi. This Dominican has been called the Father of International Law, and Scott terms him a "liberal," pp. 287-288.

[79] Vitoria devotes one of his tracts, *De Protestate Ecclesiae,* to proving that the Pope possesses no strictly temporal power, except as deriving from his spiritual power, cf *Idem* pp. xciii-cix.

80 In *De Jure Belli,* idem p. lii, he affirms that he knows no authority who would declare that differences of religion is a just cause of war.

81 From *De Potestate Civili,* Idem, p. xc.

82 *De Rege et Regis Institutione,* Toledo, 1599. Trans. from the Latin with commentary by George Albert Moore, *The King and the Education of the King,* Washington, D. C., The Country Dollar Press, 1948, Bk, III, Ch. VII, *Revenues,* p. 305. The volume, written for the young Philip III, contains the Jesuit's political principles, plus rules for the education of the prince. The author argues for constitutional government of the monarchical type, with a separation of powers, the supremacy of law, and strict regard for the liberties of the people. Italics added.

83 *Idem,* Bk. I, Ch. V, *Differences between a King and a Tyrant,* pp. 135-141 Cf also, John Laures, *The Political Economy of Juan de Mariana,* N. Y., Fordham Univ. Press, 1928. Italics added.

84 Mariana answers the famous question: Are princes bound by the laws? in the affirmative, *Idem,* Bk. I, Chap. IX, pp. 164.

85 In two following chapters, *idem,* Chap. VI and VII of Bk. I, pp. 142-155, Mariana declares that if the tyrant violates the laws of the land, e.g., *by forbidding or preventing the meetings of the Cortes,* he should be eliminated, by killing if necessary, once there has been an implicit or explicit decision of the people to this effect. These passages caused a storm in France, and the book was publically burnt by order of the Parliament of Paris in 1610.

86 *Idem,* Bk. III, Chap. XIII, *The Poor,* pp. 338-341. Italics supplied.

87 *Pastoral Letter of the Spanish Episcopate,* 20 December 1931, urging loyalty to the Republic, in *The Case of the Basque Catholics,* N. Y., The Basque Archives, 1939, pp. 5-6. On 25 May 1933, long after the Constitution was adopted the Bishops issued a similar appeal, though listing its objections to the anticlerical legislation.

88 *Pastoral Letter of the Spanish Episcopate,* 1 July 1937; text in *The War in Spain,* N. Y., Paulist Press. For obvious reasons, the Basque bishops and the bishops in exile did not sign this document.

89 25 November 1944, in Xavier D'Iramuno, *The Basque Clergy,* London, 1946, pp. 11-26.

90 *The Catholic Mind,* April 1952, vol. I, No. 1072, pp. 247-248.

PART VII:

SOCIAL EVOLUTION
in
MODERN ENGLISH CATHOLICISM

by

CHRISTOPHER HOLLIS

THE SECOND SPRING IN ENGLISH CATHOLICISM

When the smoke of the Reformation's battle cleared away, it was found that England, alone of the countries that had been within the Roman Empire, had declared herself Protestant. Yet the defeat of Catholicism in England was not sudden and complete. All through the latter half of the sixteenth and the seventeenth centuries there was in England, still, a considerable, though ever dwindling minority of Catholics, subject to various forms of disability. The establishment of a Protestant succession to the throne in 1688 brought in a Government that pursued an actively anti-Catholic policy, and this policy was intensified after the defeat of the rebellion of 1715. As the only reason why George I sat on the throne of England instead of the Stuart James III was that James was debarred because of his Catholicism, it was not unintelligible that the supporters of the Hanoverian succession should argue that for the security of their dynasty all regular Catholic organisation must be destroyed. It was to these years immediately after 1715 that the most extensive of the penal laws belong. They were substantially successful. Deprived of any possibility of Catholic education, the new generation that grew up between 1715 and 1745 almost entirely abandoned its Catholicism. Persecution was successful, and by 1745 the Catholics in England had been reduced to a tiny minority—a few old families, a small handful of the faithful in distant Lancashire and Cheshire—of perhaps one in a hundred of the population.

It was the war of American Independence that brought the first sensible Catholic relief. The Irish made it quite clear that, if no relief was granted to Catholics, Ireland would certainly throw her force to the American side. The Jacobite cause was by then dead and the Catholics in England so few that there could be no serious political argument against relief in England. In 1778 the first Catholic Relief Act was passed, by which Catholics could legally purchase and inherit land and the Catholic priest was no longer subject to delation by the common informer simply for being a priest. The practice of the Catholic religion was now legal for the first time for a hundred years, though, of course, the Catholics were still quite without political rights.

Yet even so small a reform as this was far ahead of public opinion, and in 1780 London was disgraced by the savage and destructive anti-Catholic Gordon riots. But the French Revolution, with its persecution of the Church in France, brought a reaction in favour of Catholicism in England. Expelled from the Continent, both French emigré priests and English priests, with their pupils, who had conducted on the Continent English Catholic schools which they had hitherto not been allowed to conduct at home, found a refuge and welcome in England. In 1791 a further Catholic Relief Act was passed which made the building of a Catholic chapel legal on registration, although it might still not possess either a bell or a steeple. The French Catholic emigrés, clerical and lay, made a certain impression on the English mind throughout the years of the French War. There were six thousand of such French lay Catholics in England in 1797 according to a report given to the Duke of Portland, the Home Secretary of the day. They tended on the one hand to create a certain sympathy for Catholicism, as the enemy of the country's enemy, and on the other hand, of course, the Catholicism for which sympathy was aroused was a very Conservative Catholicism—a Catholicism of throne and altar.

With the turn of the century the growing popularity of Catholicism gave vigor to a movement for full Catholic Emancipation. Pitt promised such Emancipation to the Irish bishops as a condition of their support for the Act of Union between Great Britain and Ireland in 1800. Pitt's promise came up against the unshakable conviction of George III that to assent to Emancipation would be to violate his Coronation Oath, and George's opposition forced Pitt to resign in 1801. But Pitt's embarrassment only led his Whig opponents to take up Emancipation with yet greater vigour. A Coalition Government, in which they were included, commonly known as the Ministry of All the Talents, tried to raise the question again in 1807 but was again thwarted by the King's obstinacy.

Thus the Napoleonic Wars ended with Catholic Emancipation still unaccomplished. Yet it was fairly clear that the spirit of the age was such that its accomplishment sooner or later was almost inevitable. As a result of the French Revolution, the early nineteenth century was afraid of dogmatic atheism, whereas the late eighteenth century had so often thought it merely amusing. Sir Walter Scott, though himself far from a Catholic— indeed, he was an opponent of Emancipation who thought Catholicism "a mean and depraving superstition"—had yet, along with other writers of the Romantic Movement, destroyed the eighteenth century's arrogant and facile contempt of the past and brought the picture of Catholic England vividly before the public mind in a way in which it had never been presented since Shakespeare's death.

The Government that ruled Great Britain in the years after 1815 was a Government, under Lord Liverpool, of repression and reaction. Though it contained individual members who were personally favourable to emancipation, there was little chance that the issue would be raised so long as George III was King and Lord Liverpool Prime Minister. Nor was the Catholic cause helped by the divisions among the Catholics themselves. There was little love lost between the Irish and the English Catholics—and Ireland was then a country which contained, not as today, one-tenth of the population of Great Britain, but something more like two-thirds. Even among the English Catholics the most prominent of the laity were willing to accept the formula of what was known as Cisalpinism—that is, a formula, similar to that of Gallicanism in France, by which the power of Rome over the Church should be restricted as narrowly as possible and wide powers of veto and patronage granted to the State. Bishop Milner, the leading English Vicar Apostolic of the day, joined with the Irish in vigorously rejecting any such solution.

As a result, when Catholic Emancipation finally came in 1829, it came not as a concession from the Whigs to the English Catholics, but as a concession of the Tories to the Irish Catholics. George IV, the new King, who succeeded his father in 1820, had in his youth been a companion of the Whigs and had sometimes professed liberal principles with no very deep appearance of sincerity. He habitually mocked at his father's deep old-fashioned Protestantism. But liberal principles had left him long before he reached the throne. In 1829 he commisioned the Duke of Wellington to form a Tory anti-Emancipation Government. In Ireland, as opposed to England, Grattan in the days before the Act of Union had won for the Catholics the right to vote for Parliament, though not to sit in it. Daniel O'Connell, the Catholic leader, conceived the idea that he would exploit this situation by himself standing for an Irish constituency, even though, as the law then was, he would not be able to take his seat when elected. He put himself forward at a by-election in County Clare and was returned by a triumphant majority. The Duke of Wellington and Sir Robert Peel, his first lieutenant in his government, thought that any further resistance to the Catholic claims would inevitably mean civil war. To avoid it, they brought in a bill to give Catholics the right not only to vote for but to sit in

Parliament and to hold all but a very few of the offices of state. But the bill was an ungracious bill, brought in by those who admittedly detested the Catholics, as the only remedy against violence, and the concession was hedged about with ungracious reservations which went far to destroy any appeasing effect that it might have had. Catholic bishops were forbidden to adopt the titles of any sees which at present had Anglican bishops. Religious celebrations were forbidden outside churches and private houses. Restrictions were placed on the growth of religious orders. The property qualification for the franchise was raised in Ireland and thus a number of Catholics who had previously had the vote were disenfranchised. Above all, O'Connel was meanly required to submit himself to another election in County Clare before being allowed to take his seat.

The Tories were opposed to Catholic Emancipation because they were the party of the Church of England and thus automatically reacted against any threat to its privileges. The Whig leaders, on the other hand, tended rather to religious scepticism, which led them to offer toleration to the Catholics not because they had in them any sympathy with or understanding of Catholic things but because it seemed to them a failure in taste to betray excitement about these trivial differences of which no one could know the truth and of which none seemed to have any vital relation to reality. The fears of atheism as a cause of revolutionary violence which the French Revolution had aroused had largely abated in cultured circles by the 1830's. In Whig eyes Bishops had again become ridiculous, and, if they had also become to some extent odious, that was because of the consistent opposition of the Anglican Bishops in the House of Lords to the Reform Act of 1832 for the reform of the franchise and to all other Whig projects of reform.

Throughout the 1830's Great Britain was under the Whig rule of Lord Melbourne. Lord Melbourne was a cultivated and indolent sceptic, who found a certain purely intellectual fascination in theology. He had no prejudice against Catholicism except the primary prejudice that it never occurred to him that it could possibly be true, and he thought it wholly a good thing that advantage should be taken of Catholic Emancipation in order to associate Catholics with the general national life—and naturally, if it should be possible, to associate them on the Whig side. Public opinion was not at that time such that it would have tolerated Catholics in positions of major influence, and the English Catholics were indeed so few in numbers and so lacking in experience that there could be no question of their immediately aspiring to any such posts. Even when it was legal for a Catholic to be elected to Parliament, it was not save on rare occasions possible to find a constituency in Great Britain which would elect him, and the Catholics who had political careers were generally Members of the House of Lords. Yet Melbourne gave minor political office to a couple of Catholics in his administration, and Catholics from the first began to play, as they have ever since continued to play, a certain part in the diplomatic service.

The Continent in these early years of the 19th century was filled with the controversy to what extent it was wise for the Church to lean upon the support of the State. English Catholics inhabitants of a land where there was a State Church which was not the Catholic Church and which was indeed bitterly hostile to the Catholic Church, stood of necessity outside that controversy, and the fact that their problems were so different from those of Continental Catholics caused them in these years very strongly to emphasize their "Englishness," to proclaim loudly that they were not foreigners nor committed to foreign ways, and, as in the case of the greatest English Catholic of those days, Dr. Lingard, the historian, to show a great suspicion of foreign habits of devotion.

On the whole the 1830's was a tranquil decade for English Catholics. They were probably holding their own in numbers without making any spectacular increase. The great new Jesuit school of Stonyhurst, transferred to Lancashire when the French Revolution expelled it from the Continent, was establishing itself as the first of the English Catholic public schools—as the English quaintly call the most rigidly private and expensive of their schools—and was offering a sound, old-fashioned education to the children of the Catholic aristocracy and middle-class, the only classes which in those days before general schooling as a rule received education, whether among Catholics or Protestant. There was for the moment no special challenge which Catholic authority was throwing down and which English society resented. In the irreligious, easy-going society of the later Whigs, it was fashionable to speak of Catholicism with tolerance, if not with understanding. The agnostic tolerance of Catholic things which we find in the Greville Memoirs is a perfect example of the Whig attitude of the day. The main theological controversy of the day in England—the assertion of the supporters of the Oxford Movement that the Church of England was one of the branches of the Catholic Church and that its bishops possessed the Apostolic Succession—did not at that date seem greatly to concern the Catholics one way or the other. Indeed, there were many Protestants who would be heard lightheartedly to say that, if men must concern themselves with these high-church antics, it would be better to have the "genuine article" than to undermine the Establishment by treachery from within. In the realm of scholarship, the influence of Lingard, a Catholic priest, who was the first man to write a scientifically documented history of England, was considerable, and pamphleteers like Cobbett, and novelists like Disraeli in his "Sybil," quarried in Lingard in order to find the material for a slightly overdrawn contrast between the fraternal relations and tranquillity of Catholic England and the horrors of "the dark, Satanic mills," which Protestantism and the new industrialism had fastened on the country. Sir Mark Brunel, the great railway builder and engineer, was the only English Catholic name among the masters of the new industrialism.

But that tolerance, such as it was, was not strong enough to withstand a shock. Catholicism was spoken of with kindliness because it was thought to be dead. English opinion was not yet ready to tolerate it, if it should be found to be alive.

With the 1840's things took a turn for the worse from the Catholic point of view. In 1839 the young Queen Victoria had married Prince Albert of Saxe-Coburg-Gotha, and, doing so had imported into English life a new influence intensely unsympathetic to Catholicism. The Reform Act of 1832, as so often in politics, did not have the immediate effect on English life that many had foretold. The same aristocratic families who had governed England up till then, still continued to govern it in the 1830's. But, as so often, such effects worked through a delayed action. Sir Robert Peel, the Tory leader, saw that his party had no chance of getting back into power save as a middle-class party. He reorganized it throughout the 1830's and his reorganization was rewarded in 1841. Yet many of the new middle-class Tory leaders were of a very different tone in religion as in other matters from the aristocratic leaders of the previous generation. In 1842, Mr. Gladstone joined the first of those many Cabinets in which he was to continue to serve off and on, first as a Tory and then as a Liberal for the rest of the century. He brought into English public life a new attitude towards Catholicism—the attitude of the middle-class. Intensely sincere in his acceptance of Christianity and in his acceptance of the Church of England as the representative of Christianity in this country, he disliked almost pathologically the Catholic Church as a foreign institution, and it was perhaps due to him as much as to any other single man that, whereas in the first half of the century Catholics had appeared to Englishmen as weak people, asking for, and on the whole receiving step by step an increased tolerance, in the latter half of the century Englishmen were taught to look on Catholics as dangerous and offensive people and the air was to ring with cries of "Papal Aggression."

There were, of course, other influences than Mr. Gladstone's personality at work in bringing about this change of public opinion. Three years after Mr. Gladstone entered the Cabinet, there occurred another event of momentous importance—the reception into the Catholic Church of the man who was afterwards to be Cardinal Newman. Newman was the first English theologian and thinker of the first rank to join the Catholic Church in the 19th century. Hitherto the English aristocracy had rested solid in their conviction that the intellectual case for Protestantism was superior to that for Catholicism. No one, it was supposed, could become a Catholic for intellectual reasons. If anyone turned it must be because of some sentimental appeal. "Your partiality to the pagentry of Popery, I do approve," Horace Walpole had written three quarters of a century before Newman's reception, "and I doubt whether the world would not be a loser (in its visionary enjoyments) by the extinction of that religion, as it was by the decay of chivalry and the proscription of the heathen deities." It was the perfect expression of the aesthetic tolerance of that sceptical world. What a shock it was to that world when the leading thinker of the day, having deliberately and explicitly set out to furnish an apologetic for the Church of England, after thirteen years reached the conclusion that such a case could not be sustained by reason and that on intellectual grounds truth lay with the Catholic Church in the traditional sense of that phrase!

Dismay was rife. Tolerance collapsed into panic. There were fears in Church and University circles that the entire company of the Oxford Movement might follow their leader to Rome. These fears were, of course, not fully realized. Neither Keble nor Pusey, the Movement's two most famous leaders after Newman, ever became Catholics. But, on the other hand, there was a steady stream of Tractarian converts, of whom by far the most famous was the man who was afterwards to be Cardinal Manning, who was received into the Church in 1851. The general effect of the conversion of Newman and his followers was to bring home to the English people—what they had hitherto almost forgotten—that there was an intellectual case for Catholicism. It was a lesson that they did not at all like to learn, and it greatly increased Catholicism's unpopularity.

If the reception of Newman increased the unpopularity of the Catholics among the intellectuals, the Irish famine a year later increased that unpopularity among the working-classes. Industrialism had already brought an influx of Irish immigrants. In 1821 there were said to be 12,000 Catholics in Liverpool. In 1832, 60,000, and in 1840, 80,000. In 1841 the Irish-born population in England was 224,128; in 1851, 419,256. The Irish immigrants were unpopular, not so much for any theological reasons, as because in an age of unorganized labor their desperation led them to accept low wages and thus to under-cut their Protestant fellow-workers. There had been anti-Irish riots in Lincolnshire as early as 1831 and there was a good deal of chronic discontent on the railways.

But after the famine there was Irish immigration into Britain—and also incidentally into other English-speaking countries—on a far greater scale. The Catholic population of Great Britain took a large and sudden jump forward and for the first time the greater number of Catholics in Britain were of Irish origin. It was easy to arouse prejudice against these Irish Catholics among their fellow-workers because of their low wages, and in the nation at large because a number of them associated themselves with the Chartist Movement, which was at that time putting forward what was then thought to be the revolutionary demand for universal suffrage.

It was into this world that there broke the controversies about the restoration of the hierarchy in 1851. As can be seen, the restoration was somewhat unfortunate in its moment. "While everything else is in a constant state of change," the sceptical Greville had written in 1848, "Protestant bigotry and anti-Catholic rancor continue to flourish with undiminished intensity, and all the more from being founded on nothing but prejudice and ignorance, without a particle of sense and reason." Had the Restoration taken place twelve years before, when Melbourne was still Prime Minister and before Newman had joined the Church or before the Irish famine, it might well have passed off with a great deal less excitement.

England, when she was still a missionary country, had been governed by Vicars Apostolic. Of these Vicars Apostolic, some were, like the majority of the English Catholic themselves, profoundly national types. There was never a character more redolent of the soil than Bernard Ullathorne, a product of Yorkshire yeoman stock, who had begun his working life as a cabin-boy at sea and his priestly life as a missionary among the convicts of Australia. Ullathorne was consecrated a Bishop in 1846 and lived on until 1884, the last of the Vicars Apostolic. Had the Holy See seen fit to make the experiment of the restoration of the hiearchy through Ullathorne, whatever else Englishmen might have said of it, they could hardly have accused it of being an act of foreign aggression. But it was not Ullathorne whom the Holy Father selected. His choice fell on Nicholas Wiseman, a man of great sanctity, of great energy and of great ability, a master of languages and of much curious learning, but essentially a cosmopolitan figure, more at home in Rome than in England. It was he whom the Pope selected to be the first Cardinal-Archbishop of Westminster and to shape the policy of the redivision of England into its regular dioceses. Wiseman had not the instinctive understanding of English reaction which Ullathorne possessed. He was filled with what experience was to show was a hopelessly optimistic belief that the total return of England to Catholicism was to be expected in the very near future.

On September 29th, 1850, Pius IX in his Letters Apostolic 'Universalis Ecclesia' announced the division of England into twelve suffragan sees, over which Nicholas Wiseman was to preside as Cardinal and metropolitan. In an eloquent but flamboyant letter from the Flaminian Gate, Wiseman announced his appointment to the English people, and then set out on a splendid and leisured progress from Rome to London. Footmen met him on the outskirts of Florence and escorted him through that city with lighted toches. Thence, straying from the direct route, he made a detour to Vienna, and it was Vienna that he learnt of the storm of obloquy with which British public opinion and the British press, headed by the *Times,* had greeted his pronouncement.

"Shall it be tolerated in England in the middle of the nineteenth century," wrote the Times' leading article, "that Roman Catholic priests should slink about the country, insinuating themselves into a dying room, and taking advantage of a credulous girl, with the single and palpable object of securing large sums of money for the aggrandisement of their church?" The irrelevance of the scurrility as a comment on the restoration of the hierarchy is sufficient evidence of the excitement of public opinion. It is not very clear why it should be any easier for a clergyman to "insinuate himself into a dying room" because he called himself the Bishop of Leeds rather than the Bishop of Cambysopolis. Wiseman attempted from Vienna to assuage the excitement by a letter of Appeal to the English People in which in more conciliatory language he tried to show how his appointment could not possibly carry with it any threat to the liberties of Englishmen. "Close under the Abbey of Westminster," he wrote, "there lie concealed labyrinths of lanes and courts, and alleys and slums, nests of ignorance, vice, depravity, and crime, as well as squalor, wretchedness, and disease, whose atmosphere is typhus, whose ventilation is cholera, in which swarms a hugh and almost countless population, in great measure, nominally at least, Catholic; haunts of filth which no sewage committee can reach—dark corners, which no lighting board can brighten. This is the part of Westminster which alone I covet and which I shall be glad to claim and to visit, as a blessed pasture in which sheep of Holy Church are to be tended."

But it was too late. The storm indeed was not indeed quite universal. There were from the first some private sceptics, such as Greville, of the *Memoirs,* who sneered at the excitement as one of those ridiculous fits of hypocritical moral indignation in which British public opinion finds it necessary from time to time to indulge itself and thought that it was all an absurd fuss about nothing. The Non-conformists, with memories of their own trials too recent in their minds, remained honourably aloof. "In the North of England," said John Bright, "the Dissenters have unanimously held aloof from the war that has been got up in reference to this question." But the politicians, at any rate, judged that the overwhelming body of public opinion was on the side of the storm and that the positive course was to ride with it. Indeed, even English Catholic opinion was far from unanimous in support of the Papal action. A Catholic peer opposed it in the House of Lords. Lord John Russell was at that time Prime Minister at the head of a Whig Government, and traditionally the Whigs had been more favourable to the Catholics than the Tories. Yet, as often in British politics, the Whigs were for that very reason the more anxious to take up the cry in order to prevent the Tories from using it against them. The Government brought in and passed the Ecclesiastical Titles Act, by which bishops of any Church other than the Church of England were forbidden, subject to a fine of £100, to take their titles from any place within the United Kingdom. Had any attempt been made to enforce the Act, it would, of course, have been necessary to arrest Cardinal Wiseman and his twelve suffragans, but, though the British people are liable to these fits of explosive moral indignation in which they clamor for ridiculous legislation of this sort, yet they easily repent of their abusrdities at leisure and, when they repent, turn and revenge themselves on those who have led them in their excitement. The Govern-

ment saw that if in fact the bishops were arrested, public opinion with its easy sentimental streak would turn to the victims
of persecution and sympathy would be on the Catholic side.
No attempt was made to enforce the Act and it was quietly
repealed twenty years later in 1871.

The restoration of the hierarchy in fact made no great difference to the fortunes of English Catholicism one way or the
other. It marked a change in a method of organization, but it
made little difference to the mentality of Catholics or Protestants, to the arguments for or against the Catholic claims, to
the challenge of the Church to the new problems of the age,
whether England was ruled by Vicars Apostolic or by diocesan
bishops. Much more important in the long run than the restoration of the hierarchy was the Gotham Judgement, by
which a lay court took upon itself to decide the doctrine of the
Church of England on baptismal regeneration and which drove
into the Catholic Church a steady stream of converts to follow
Newman of whom Manning was by far the most important.
The converts who had moved into the Church with Newman-
Oakley, Ward, Faber—had been, like Newman himself, men
who were primarily interested in the questions of pure theology.
Social and political problems meant little to them. With
Manning a new influence came into the Catholic community.
Manning belonged by origin to the official and administrative
world. The son of a distinguished civil servant, the friend of
Gladstone, he brought to the Catholic body an experience of
a side of life in which that body was inevitably deficient from
its peculiar history. An Englishman himself, he had none of
that jealously of the Irish invasion from which so many English Catholics suffered. He threw himself with keen interest
and sympathy into the problems of the Irish laborers in the
docks and elsewhere. Wiseman soon accepted him as his chief
adviser. Archbishop Errington, who had previously been nominated as coadjutor was sent into retirement, and Manning was
destined to be Wiseman's successor.

For substantially the rest of the century English Catholic
life was, all the world knows, dominated by the two gigantic
figures of Newman and Manning. Sympathy between them was
unfortunately lacking. Newman was doubtless to the world and
to posterity the greater figure and has left behind him contributions to Catholic thought which are quite certain to be
of a permanent value. But in the passing politics, whether of
the State or of the Church, he took little interest; and in the
day to day affairs of English Catholicism it was Manning
who played the greater role. The first half of the nineteenth

century had not been a deeply creative period in Catholic social thinking. Catholic thought had been predominantly concerned with the defense of the regimes restored on the Continent after 1815 and with the problem what should be the attitude of Catholics should those regimes be forcibly changed as they were in France in 1830 and 1848. But, since by an accident there had up till that time been no development of industrialism in the countries of Southern Europe, few Catholic minds had given themselves to the consideration of the probems of the Catholic attitude to the new industrial civilization.

As England was at that date par excellence the country of industrialism, it was obvious that here was a field upon which English Catholics had a very especial contribution to make, and it is for his contribution in that field that Cardinal Manning has his especial importance in English Catholic history, and indeed in English history in general. His close relations with Cardinal Gibbons, particularly in their joint support of the American Knights of Labor, brought about a closeness of relation between British and American Catholics which had not previously existed. He was able to play in the great dock strike of 1889 a part of mediator of an outstanding importance both in itself and because of the lesson that it taught to an English people that up till then little understood it, that the Catholic Church had a teaching upon—indeed a deep interest in—social questions. All too many Englishmen of that day had derived, from a too facile interpretation of Pius IX's *Syllabus Errorum,* a belief that the Catholic Church's only attitude was one of unqualified opposition to all proposals for reform of whatever sort.

Yet it would be a great exaggeration to pretend that Manning was in any way typical of the English Catholics of his day. On the contrary, he was much more nearly an unique figure. It was only in 1891, in the last year of Manning's life, that Leo XIII's "Rerum Novarum," was issued. Manning had been the Pope's constant advisor on social questions and the Cardinal's activities in England confirmed the Pope's impression that active sympathy for working class aspirations produced a climate in which workers could pursue their guest for Social Justice with the moral encouragement of the Church and thus within its active ranks. Manning's contribution was unique, for the majority of the older English Catholics were remote from the Social Struggle and unsympathetic with the Irish laborers in factory and mine. In fact, when the Encyclical, was published, it certainly found among English Catholics very man fewer readers than it finds today. Cardinal Vaughan, Manning's successor, took little interest in social questions. The English Catholics of the nineteenth century still had among them the memory of the catacombs. It was not a generation since they had emerged from persecution, and the storm of the Ecclesiastical Titles Act was a reminder to them how easily a spirit of persecution might again be aroused against them. Most of them, it is safe to say, did not know that the Church had any special teaching upon social questions, and many of them did not wish to know it. They preferred to say that, since England was an overwhelmingly Protestant country, it was not possible to solve these problems upon Catholic lines, and to give their mild support to one or other of the regular political parties, without making any attempt to influence its policy.

The nineteenth century in England was, of course, predominantly the century of laissez-faire capitalism. The Liberal theory had arisen in protest against the system of privileges of the *ancien régime* The Liberals thought of the state as essentially an aristocratic state and thought of its interferences with free competition as interferences to guarantee to some favoured class a monopoly or privilege to which it had no right and which it exercised in opposition to the general good. "Get rid of such interferences," argued the Liberal thinkers through such mouths as those of Adam Smith and Ricardo, "and in conditions of freedom and competition society will so greatly increase its volume of production that everyone must necessarily be far better off." To this argument Marx and the Socialists answered that capitalism might indeed succeed in increasing the sum total of the product but that it provided no means of fairly distributing it. On the contrary, by its insistence that the worker could look for no more than a basic wage it made it certain that the product would not be fairly distributed, made it certain that the only result of increased productivity would be an increasingly wide gap between worker and capitalist—what Marx called "the increasing misery of the poor."

Had Britain allowed herself to be restrained throughout the whole of the nineteenth century within the rigid formulae of laissez-faire, Marx's prophecies might have proved true. But throughout the second half of the century empirical reformers in both political parties saw that a number of social reforms were necesary. By strengthening the Trade Unions and by introducing a limited amount of positive state action, they were able to set up such a balance against capitalist power as to ensure that the workers got, if not a fair share of the nation's wealth, at least substantial benefits out of industrialism's in-

creased production. The latter half of the century was a period
of steadily rising living standards for the working classes. These
reforms may, to some extent, have been reforms of which Catholic teaching would have approved. There may have been a
certain correspondence between some of the actions of British
Governments and the teaching on social questions which Leo
XIII was giving "orbi et urbi" at the same time. But, if so, the
correspondence was, it must be confessed, largely accidental. It
would be surprising to find evidence that any of the politicians
of that day had ever heard of the Papal Encyclicals. Nor did
many Catholics other than Manning play any large part in introducing the knowledge of these teachings into England. More
than that, whatever the correspondences, there was one great
difference between Papal policy and Government policy during
those years. Government policy, while it was alive to the desirability of the workers having higher standard of living, was
quite dead to the desirability of a wider distribution of property. The years were years of a rising standard of living but of a
steady decline in ownership.

When the Liberal Government of 1906 adopted its program of social reform, in which the first foundations of the
modern welfare state were laid, it was a Government composed
without exception of men wholly untouched by any Catholic
influence. There has never been in England any suggestion that
either the one political party or the other was the Catholic
party. Catholics always have been free to belong, and always
have belonged, to both of the political parties. Nor have the
greater number of English Catholics been enormously fervent
members of the political party to which they gave their adherence. The English Catholic has on the whole not been a very
political animal. It is perhaps inevitable that it should be so.
For all its practical convenience, there is a certain degree of
absurdity about a two-party parliamentary system. In order to
retain public attention, the party leaders have to pretend to
enormous differences from one another. But everyone knows
that in fact, if society is to survive, the continuity of its life
must be preserved and that the one party cannot in fact, if it
should come into office, change more than a little of what was
done under its predecessors. The two-party system only works
when both parties have common fundamental principles.

This imposes an inevitable unreality upon Parliamentary life
which makes it distasteful to the critical intellect. No Catholic
can ever take it really seriously, and it is notable that, even in
modern times, when Catholics have been a little more prominent in political life than heretofore, those Catholics, to which-

ever party they belong, have without exception sat more lightly
to their party allegiances than has the average member of Parliament. But the Parliament of 1906 was notable for the first
formal criticism of the party system from a Catholic pen.
Hilaire Belloc was elected to that Parliament as a Liberal, but
he soon quarrelled with his party, and in collaboration with
Cecil Chesterton, he wrote "The Party System." He also wrote
"The Servile State," in which he argued that the whole drift of
modern society with its gigantic units of production, private or
nationalised, was inevitably a drift towards slavery, and that
the only remedy lay in the Distributist State and the distribution of personal property as widely as possible throughout society. Mr. Belloc's theories, which are, of course, based on Catholic tradition and the teaching of Leo XIII, received no
acknowledgement from the regular politicians at the time, but
it is notable that in our own days there is an increasing recognition both among Socialists that nationalisation and Liberals
that capitalism by itself is not sufficient. In all parties men of
goodwill are trying to find through schemes of co-partnership,
profit-sharing, workers' cooperation in management, joint consultation, and the like, means of giving to the workers something of the responsibilities of property-ownership within the
industrial system. The politicians are today, thanks partly to
Mr. Belloc's teaching and though little understanding what it
is that they are doing, are, in some way, attempting to fill
with the remedies of Leo XIII some of those hiatuses which the
insufficiencies of their own remedies have left yawning.

Catholic politics in Great Britain, in so far as they were not
merely Irish politics, have been very largely concerned with the
very important but subsidiary problems of education. Up till
the 1830's the State in Great Britain had not concerned itself
with education at all. Such education as had been provided for
the poor, had been provided entirely by voluntary societies, and
these voluntary societies had been almost always societies of one
or other of the religious denominations, providing education in
accordance with the tenets of that denomination. It goes without saying that in such provision the Church of England, in the
circumstances of the early years of the 19th century, was at an
enormous advantage over other denominations—whether Catholic or Nonconformist—and it had the further advantage that
what were at that date the only two Universities, Oxford and
Cambridge, were also then the exclusive prerogative of the
Church of England and not even undergraduates could be admitted to them until they had subscribed to the Thirty-Nine
Articles, the profession of faith of the Church of England.

"Robbed, oppressed and thrust aside," wrote Newman in his "Idea of a University" in 1852, "Catholics in these islands have not been in a condition for centuries to attempt the sort of education which is necessary for the man of the world, the statesman, the landholder or the opulent gentleman." This was "a moral disability" because "a youth who ends his education at seventeen is no match (caeteris paribus) for one who ends it at twenty-two." "The time is come," he added, "when this moral disability must be removed."

In 1833 the State for the first time adopted the policy of giving grants to these voluntary schools, but the Nonconformists at that time were strongly opposed to such grants, foreseeing that the Anglicans, since they had the greater number of schools, would be the people who would chiefly benefit from them. They argued that the State had no business to concern itself with education at all and that all provision of schools should be left to unassisted voluntary enterprise. But, as industrialism developed, it soon became clear that, if only for purely secular and economic reasons, it was essential that the State should establish and endow some system of general education sufficient to give the nation at least a literate population. The Nonconformists were terrified that the Government would follow a line of least resistance and give their subvention to the existing Angelican schools, which were to be found in most of the towns and villages of the country. Had they done so, it seemed that the solution of the educational problem might lead to a great extension of the privileges of the State religion.

Therefore in the 1860's Joseph Chamberlain, afterwards to become the great Imperialist and Unionist leader but at the time a young Radical and reputed Republican, propounded on behalf of the Nonconformists their new demands that education should be "free, universal and non-sectarian." In 1870 universal education was introduced by the Liberal Government of Mr. Gladstone. The Nonconformists pressed that their formula be adopted, but they were faced with the obstinate fact that the Church of England schools already existed. It was only a minority who carried their sectarian prejudices so far as to demand that the State, by withdrawing the grants from the Church schools, drive them out of business and then quite unnecessarily duplicate the whole system by building new non-sectarian schools by their side in every village of the land. Nor would the temper of the times towards private property have made possible a confiscation of the Church schools. Therefore the problem was solved by a compromise, which, in spite of detailed changes, has basically subsisted to this day. The basis of that compromise is that, if a religious denomination wishes to have a school, it must build it itself, but then, having built it, it can call on public funds for a proportion of the cost of its upkeep. In such schools, of course, denominational instruction may be given. On the other hand, the public authority builds directly and entirely out of public funds "provided" schools in which there may be general non-denominational instruction, but in which no tenet peculiar to any particular denomination may be taught.

The varying details by which these formulae have been applied are beyond the interest of this essay. What is of interest to the Catholic reader is this: before 1870 the Catholic community was still a small and a poor community. The Catholics had very few schools at that time, and they were in no way protagonists in the controversy, on the one side or the other. The controversy was essentially a controversy between the Anglicans and the Nonconformists. It was in the first place only, as it were, accidentally that the law, which was primarily intended to restrict the Anglicans, did in fact also restrict the Catholics. But, as time went on, it became increasingly clear that it restricted the Catholics far more straightly than it restricted the Anglicans. It restricted the Catholics more straightly than the Anglicans, because the Anglicans were on the whole a static body. It is true that they were opening up new parishes in the growing industrial towns and often wished to attach schools to those parishes. Nevertheless, through a very large part of the country—throughout almost all the rural areas—they had their schools already. Their only anxiety was to maintain them and in their maintenance the State was ready to help. The Catholics on the other hand were a growing body, possessed of few schools and anxious to cover the country with as many more as possible. In this task they could look for no assistance from the State.

Nevertheless on this schools issue the Catholics and the Anglicans made common cause for more than half a century. Indeed, the political alignment on the schools question was peculiar. Whereas on other matters the Nationalists supported the Liberals, who were the friends of Home Rule, on the schools questions they acted with the Conservatives in support of Church schools. While the Conservatives denounced Home Rule as "Rome Rule," the Liberals raised their Nonconformist cry against "Rome on the rates." But on this question the standpoint of the religious denominations are more important than those of the political parties. Gradually Anglican opinion, or at any rate the opinion of the official leaders of the Anglican

Church, came to change. Whereas in the nineteenth century Anglican opinion had laid enormous stress on the importance of the inculcation of a specifically Anglican faith, in the years between the wars it began to think of this as of less importance. the negotiations which led up to the Butler Act of 1944 found the leaders of the Anglican Church ready to accept for their schools what is called a "controlled" status, by which they are willing to teach in these schools an "agreed syllabus" of religious doctrine, agreed between the different religious denominations and imposed by the Local Education Authority. If they accept this "controlled" status then they can get full maintenance from public funds. By the peculiar constitution of the Church of England, the Bishops are appointed, nominally by the Crown, in fact by the Prime Ministers, purely secular politicians, very often innocent of any religious affiliation. It therefore naturally follows that in the Church of England, unlike other religious bodies, the Bishops tend to be more latitudinarian than their flocks. There has therefore been a certain volume of protest in some Anglican circles against this surrender by the Bishops and voices have been raised which denounced the controlled status for their schools as insufficient. But on the whole the Catholics have been left to stand alone in their rejection of controlled status and of the financial advantages which go with it. Such isolation is by no means an unmixed calamity.

As England moved on towards the end of the century, the patriotic objections to the Catholic Church as a foreign institution came to have less and less weight. With the weakening of dogmatic Protestantism, it came in educated circles to be rather an advantage than a disadvantage in the Catholic teaching that it challenged some of the ancient dogmas of traditional Protestantism. Agnostics were fond of pointing out how Catholicism had kept itself free from what seemed to them on this or that point to be a folly into which Protestantism had fallen. On the other hand, the closing years of the nineteenth century saw the first evident appearance of what was in the twentieth century to prove itself by far the most formidable obstacle to Catholicism—the obstacle of the Church's teaching on marriage.

In spite of the contribution which Henry VIII's matrimonial problems made to the English Reformation, what was substantially a Catholic view of sex and marriage survived throughout the whole English nation even after the religious schism. For three hundred years after the Reformation there was no regular divorce law in England. A divorce could only be obtained

by a special Act of Parliament, and such Acts were rare in
the extreme. Whatever private acts may have been committed
in prevention of birth were committed in secret. No one ever
dreamed of arguing that such acts were compatible with a
Christian obedience, and it was beyond question only a tiny
minority which ever indulged in such acts at all. Then in 1857
Parliament passed its first Divorce Act and soon after for the
first time birth-control propagandists, such as Bradlaugh, began
to conduct their propaganda openly. Yet still throughout the
nineteenth century divorce was extremely rare, and a very
deep stigma of disgrace was held to attach to anyone who took
advantage of it. Both Parnell and Sir Charles Dilke, for instance,
were driven out of public life because of their appearances in
the divorce courts. Those who advocated the use of contraceptives both were considered and considered themselves enemies of Christianity. The notion that there could be any terms
between contraception and any form of Christianity was unheard of.

The first Papal annulment case which came strongly to public
notice was that in 1880 of the marriage between the Prince of
Monaco and Lady Mary Douglas Hamilton, and it is probably
fair to say that the greater part of the outcry came from
perfectly honest but ill-instructed people, who, ignorant of the
facts of the case and the distinction between divorce and annulment, thought that the Catholic Church was countenancing
divorce and condemned her because she was not upholding
so strict a view of matrimony as that of the Protestants. In
any event, up till the 1914 war, divorce was still extremely
rare in England—much rarer than in many of the states of the
United States—and it was generally understood that it carried
with it a stigma that must gravely handicap the divorced person in social, political or even business life. It is only since the
First, and even more since the Second World War, that with
extended legal facilities and with a greater social tolerance,
divorce has become extremely common and the indulgence
in it is looked upon as a person's private affair which need in
no way effect, say, a political career. Many Protestant clergymen
have gone far to accept this new state of affairs. As a result,
the Catholic stands in a much greater isolation in this question
than he did in the last century.

Even greater is his isolation on birth-control. Whereas the
practices of contraception were very generally condemned in
nineteenth century England, today it is only a small minority
outside the Catholic Church who would be prepared to argue
that there were no circumstances under which contraceptives

should be used. It is common to find many, even among those who call themselves Christians, who take their use quite complacently for granted. Up till the present the use of contraceptives in England, as in other countries, has been most common among the upper and middle classes. The consequence of the falling birthrate has been masked from many people, because, in spite of a steady decrease in the average size of families, the total population of the country has continued to increase since, owing to the fecundity of the past, there has been an ever increasing number of families to have children. But that, of course, is a temporary phenomenon, and we are faced with the prospect at a date in the near future of a population, declining in total numbers and with every year including a greater number of the aged and a smaller number of the young. This discovery has caused a certain reaction against indiscriminate birth-control propaganda, even among people of secularist philosophy, and it is common to hear the argument, advanced, for instance, by the Royal Commission on Population, that means must be found to increase the birth-rate among the educated classes. But, on the other hand, there is among such people a growing concern at the rapid increase of population among non-Europeans with low standards of living—East Indians, for instance, and West Indians—and prophecies are common that, if some means are not found to induce such people to restrict their births, then further international explosions are inevitable. Here again the Catholic stands isolated, to an extent enormously greater than he did in the nineteenth century, in his protest against such practices on the ground that they are wrong, whatever may be the apparent convenience or inconvenience of them in particular cases.

In politics, in mid-Victorian England, it was almost impossible for a Catholic to have a career of any importance unless he happened to be a peer. There were few British constituencies which were willing to elect Catholics as their members. Only three Catholics attained Cabinet rank in the nineteenth century. They were Lord Ripon, Lord Llandaff and the Duke of Norfolk. Lord Ripon had been a prominent Freemason who declared his conversion to Catholicism in 1870. He served in various Liberal Cabinets during the years between 1870 and 1909 and also was for a time Viceroy of India. Lord Llandaff was appointed as Home Secretary in the Conservative Government of Lord Salisbury in 1886, and the Duke of Norfolk was Postmaster-General in Lord Salisbury's Government of 1895.

But the greater number of Catholics in British politics in these years were, of course, Irish. While it was difficult for a

Catholic to get elected for a British constituency, naturally
there was no such difficulty about an Irish constituency, and
indeed English Catholics sometimes found seats in Irish constituencies. Lord Acton, the famous historian, who sat for some
years for Carlow, was a case in point, and Lord Llandaff, when
still a commoner, sat for Dungarvan. But naturally enough the
Irish constituencies predominantly returned Irish Members,
and increasingly so as Parnell persuaded the Irish to take Home
Rule seriously and as, after the Third Reform Act of 1885,
there was an extension of the franchise which enabled the
Nationalists to return a solid block of members from all the
constituencies south of the Boyne. Thus the Catholic voter in
Ireland and a very large proportion of the Catholic voters in
England, who were themselves of Irish origin and of recent
immigration, cast their votes simply on the Irish issue.

The consequence of the obstacles in the way of a political
career for a Catholic was that Catholics of intellectual capacity
found their careers often in law or diplomacy, but even more
often in scholarship, the arts or letters. Lord Acton, Baron von
Hugel, Coventry Patmore, Mrs. Meynell, Francis Thompson,
Gerald Manley Hopkins, Wilfrid Ward, Lionel Johnson, Baron
Corvo make only a selection—the list of Catholic writers in
the second half of the nineteenth century is a long, various and
distinguished one. But the overwhelming majority of the Catholics in England were simple working-folk to whom the great
problem of life was the problem of the struggle to get a living
and to whom education could mean no more than the painful
acquisition of the so-called "three R's." Between them and the
literary Catholics there was a distance that was pathetically
wide.

As has been said, the events of the 1840's increased the
unpopularity of Catholics in England. In the 1850's came the
explosion of the Ecclesiastical Titles Act, and the sympathy
to which Palmerston, in his long domination in the 1850's and
1860's led English opinion with the liberal and nationalist
movements on the Continent, particularly in Italy, increased
anti-Catholic feeling. "I should like to see the Pope reduced
to the condition of the Greek patriarch of Constantinople and
Romagna made into a Republic," wrote Palmerston to his
Foreign Secretary, Lord Clarendon.

Pope Pius IX's *Syllabus*, issued in 1864, seemed to confirm
those elements of British opinion, that were interested in the
subject, in their preconceived opinion that the Vatican was
irrevocably opposed to all progress and all reform. Public
opinion, which had been clamorously excited by Garibaldi's

attack on Rome, was delighted by the Italian entry into Rome in 1870. The coincidence of the Pope's loss of his temporal power with the proclamation of infallibility was greeted with jeers. Educated Englishmen professed to see in the latter claim a childish attempt by the Papacy to compensate itself by the empty assertion of unreal powers for the loss of its real power. There was much absurdly exaggerated talk in English Protestant circles about the volume of discontent among Catholics at the Papal action. The influence of Doellinger and the Old Catholics on the Continent was exaggerated, and much was made of rumors of opposition to the new definition from distinguished English Catholics such as Newman and Acton. Many Englishmen—notably Mr. Gladstone—professed to see in the new Papal claim a reason why the civic loyalty of a Catholic could no longer be relied upon. Only a very small minority had any understanding of the long train of history which led to the definition. The vast majority looked on it as a mere bolt from the blue. It was unfortunate that the reign of Leo XIII was not cast in the same mould of drama as that of Pius IX and consequently public opinion in England at the time never heard of the Encyclicals, a study of which must inevitably have caused a modification of the more glaring of nineteenth century English prejudice about the Vatican.

The first years of the twentieth century saw the end of the long reign of Queen Victoria and the succession of her son, Edward VII, to the throne. This had its importance on Catholic fortunes. For Edward VII was the first soveneign of Great Britain since the expulsion of the Stuarts who was not personally prejudiced against Catholicism. A cosmopolitan, he knew the world as none of his predecessors had known it, and it was on his personal insistence that the very offensive anti-Catholic clauses of the coronation oath were omitted. This omission was of a more than passing importance. Edward's predecessors had been rulers of a United Kingdom, in which the larger island was overwhelmingly and fanatically Protestant, and the smaller island, though indeed predominantly Catholic, quite frankly subject. The overseas dominions were of subsidiary importance. The nineteenth century had changed all that. During the course of it new nations had grown up overseas—nations which had received or were about to receive full rights of Dominion self-government within the Empire. At the same time, the emigration from Ireland, owing to the famine and the general economic distress, had been much heavier than that from Great Britain. As a consequence, while during the course of the century the proportionate population between

Great Britain and Ireland at home changed completely, so that Ireland, which at the beginning of the century had more than half Great Britain's population, had by the end of it less than a tenth, on the other hand, the Irish—and by consequence the Catholics—made a much larger contribution to the populations of the new Dominions than is generally understood. Whereas England remained a Catholic country, the British Empire was a joint Catholic and Protestant enterprise. Indeed, in the Empire at large there were more Catholics than Protestants. The Empire clearly could not have survived had it not been for Edward VII's statesmanship in insisting on an amendment of the coronation oath.

When the 1914 War came, English opinion was bitterly divided on the Irish question. Indeed the international war had only come just in time to prevent civil war in Ireland, and naturally the rising of 1916 had the consequence of keeping Irish matters well before English eyes throughout the war. After it there was the unsavory episode of the Black and Tans, but with the signing of the Treaty most Englishmen hailed with relief the end of a period in which English politics were dominated by Irish issues. Ever since then it has been difficult to get people in Great Britain to take any interest in Irish affairs one way or the other, and this is true not merely of the English in England. Equally the Irish in Great Britain, who had hitherto cast their votes predominantly on the Irish issue, now took their sides in one or other of the English political parties in accordance with their opinions on the English issues. With the decline of the Liberal party and the establishment of the Irish Free State, the greater number of them, being workers and Trade Unionists, moved over into the Socialist ranks. As a result, when in the late War Eire declared her neutrality, there was very little interest in the declaration in Great Britain one way or the other. Irish affairs had become Irish affairs, and English affairs had become English affairs. The two were no longer intermixed—a much healthier condition for both countries.

Catholics, as was to be expected, fought with at least their fair share of gallantry and distinction in both wars. But undoubtedly the second World War was most notable in English Catholic history in that the Catholic body produced in Cardinal Hinsley a national leader who was able to speak to the whole English nation irrespective of creed as no other Catholic had been able to speak to it in modern times. He won for himself as a national spokesman a position second only to that of Mr. Churchill himself. "Probably the best loved Cardinal that

England has ever had," as the Daily Mail wrote of him in an obituary notice.

Since the war Mr. Attlee has been much more generous than any Prime Minister before him in bestowing political office on Catholics. There are two Catholic Ministers, Mr. Stokes and Lord Pakenham, in the present Government and four more Under-Secretaries, but there is no Catholic in any position of major influence over policy and it is not probable than any Catholic will occupy such a position within any foreseeable future.

CHRISTOPHER HOLLS, M. P.

DOCUMENTS

Notes

HENRY CARDINAL MANNING:

The Dignity and Rights of Labour.[1]

"Labour has a right not only to its freedom, but it has a right to protect itself . . ."

"In all the history of civilization, if you go back to the Greeks or the Romans, you find that trades and professions always had their societies and fellowships by which they were united together. It seems to me that this is a sound and legitimate social law. I can conceive nothing more entirely in accordance with natural right and with the higher jurisprudence, than that those who have one common interest should unite together for the protection of that interest.

"From this it would seem to me to follow that the protection of labour and of industry has at all times been a recognized right of those who profess the same craft: that they have united together; that those unions have been recognized by the legislature; that whether they be employers or employed, whether they possess the money—all have the same rights . . ."[2]

". . . I find political economists denouncing all interference, as they call it, of Parliament with the supply or demand of any article whatsoever. . . . I am one of those . . . who are of opinion that the hours of labour must be further regulated by law. . ."

"If the great end of life were to multiply yards of cloth and cotton twist, and if the glory of England consisted in multiplying, without stint or limit, these articles and the like at the lowest possible price, so as to undersell all the nations of the world, well, then, let us go on. But if the domestic life of the people be vital above all; if the peace, the purity of the homes, the education of children, the duties of wives and mothers, the duties of husbands and fathers, be written in the natural law of mankind, and if these things be sacred, far beyond anything that can be sold in the market—then, I say, if the hours of labour resulting from the unregulated sale of man's strength and skill shall lead to the destruction of domestic life, to the neglect of children, to turning wives and mothers into living machines, and of father and husbands into—what shall I say?— creatures of burden—I will not use any other word—who rise up before the sun, and come back when it is set, wearied and able only to take food and to lie down to rest —the domestic life of man exists no longer, and we dare not go on in this path . . ."

"I know that I am treading upon a very difficult subject, but I feel confident of this, that we must face it, and that we must face it calmly, justly and with willingness to put labour and the profits of labour second—and the moral state and the domestic life of the working population first . . ."

Relief of Distress in Winter.[3]

". . . No one denies that present distress demands present relief, nor that the normal condition of society requires that such relief should be provided on principle and in ways sanctioned by a wise political economy and by an official and responsible administration. But when all such public and responsible agencies are inadequate, what is to be done? Men, women, and children are starving or suffering bitterly by cold and hunger . . . Is nothing to be done because the existing agencies are inadequate, inapplicable, or inefficient? This is surely unreasonable and heartless. It is rather a preemptory call to do something, and that in the way which is least exposed to the objections of the scientific and the unwilling. . . .

"I have a true and reasoned respect for political economy within its legitimate sphere but it is circumscribed by higher moral laws to which, if it comes in collision with them, it must at least for a time give way. If on sound and strict principles of political economy poverty and sickness could be remedied by thrift and provident dispensaries, I should rejoice; but knowing, as we all must, that thrift and providence as yet made but little impression upon the multitudes who are poor, hungary, sick, and dying, we are compelled to relieve human suffering for which no sounder or more disciplined relief as yet exists. The Good Samaritan did not delay to pour oil and wine into the wounds of the man half dead until he had ascertained whether he was responsible for his own distress. *Necessity has no law, nor has present distress, except a claim to prompt relief.*" (Italics added)

". . . We have thousands who would work if they could find it, in all conditions and classes, reaching even into the lower middle class. The competition for work is so fierce that multitudes are toiling day and night for starvation wages. In our most thriving trades as in our wealthiest commercial enterprises, men and women by hundreds of thousands are compelled to work for a number of hours beyond human endurance. The hunger and nakedness, disease and death, evolved from our 'healthy social activities' are little known except to those who are familiar with the homes of our poor and with the wards of our hospitals. . ."

Letter to M. Decurtins, Conseiller National of the Grisons.[4]

"My dear M. Decurtins:
I can hardly express to you the satisfaction with which I have read your book, *La Protection ouvrière internationale*. If I am not mistaken, you are the first who has revealed to the public conscience of Europe the condition of the millions whose whole life

is nothing but labour. All political and diplomatic questions must give precedence to those you have treated—the question of the employment of children and women, of Sunday labour, and of hours of work. Until now these things have been decided by the profits of the capitalist and by the cheapness of production.

"Some years ago I was reproached with bad political economy because I said that married women and mothers, who by the contract of marriage had engaged themselves to found a family and to bring up their children, had neither the right nor the duty to bind themselves for such and such a number of hours a day, in violation of their previous engagement as mothers and wives. Such a bond is *ipso facto* illegal and null. You have well set forth this great moral law, without which we should have been a horde and not a nation. Without domestic life, there is no nation. It is the same with men. So long as the hours of labor have no other limit than the gain of the employer, no workman can live a life worthy of a human being. The humblest workman, no less than the man who is rich and literate, has need of certain hours wherein to cultivate his mind and soul; and if such hours are not permitted him, he is lowered to the state of a machine, or to that of a beast of burden. What manner of nation will be formed by men living in such conditions? What must be the domestic, social of politic life of such men? Yet it is to this that the individualism of the last fifty years is leading us.

"A truer political economy would include all that concerns the general wealth of the people. It would rule and limit all the interests and actions of mankind formed into a society; and it would rule them by the higher moral law which is the law of nature and of God. First of all are to be maintained the principles governing the life of man and human society. Buying in the cheapest market and selling in the dearest are secondary matters. . ."

Letter to Count de Mun[5]

"The coming age will belong neither to the capitalists nor to the commercial classes, but to the People. The people are yielding to the guidance of reason, even to the guidance of religion. If we can gain their confidence, we can counsel them; if we show them a blind opposition, they will have power to destroy all that is good. But I hope much from the action of the Church which all Governments are despoiling and rejecting. Her true home is with the People; they will hear her voice. . ."

Christopher Dawson: The Sword of the Spirit.

"We have seen that the Christian view of man and society is far from being a static traditionalism, as its rationalist critics have so often supposed. What distinguishes the Christian view of history from that of secular philosophy is above all the belief in the divine government of the world and the intervention of the Spirit in history and in the power of man to resist or co-operate with this divine action. These conceptions are most clearly expressed in the prophets of Israel, who are in a special sense the bearers of the Sword of the Spirit. For the Prophets not only gave an interpretation of history in terms of the Kingdom of God and the divine judgment, they also show the power of God manifesting itself above all in the prophetic Word. . ."

"The attempt of the mind to dispense with the Spirit, to build a world that should be entirely in man's power and should find its end in him, is no new thing. It is, as St. Augustine showed, a universal tendency that runs through the whole of history and takes on different forms in different ages. But never has it revealed itself so explicitly as it does today in the totalitarian state, which has almost succeeded in constructing a world completely closed to the Spirit and leaving no loophole or corner for spiritual freedom. But the result is so oppressive of human nature, so ultimately self-destructive, that it must inevitably produce a reaction of resistance and revolt, in which the Christian elements in Western civilization will once more make themselves felt. It may seem utopian at this time to speak of the coming of a new Christian order— a new Christendom. But the more we recognize our distance from the goal and the immensity of the difficulties to be overcome, the more hope there is of ultimate success.

"For what we must look for is not the alliance of the temporal power, as in the old Christendom, and an external conformity to Christian standards, but a reordering of all the elements of human life and civilization by the power of the Spirit; the birth of a true community which is neither an inorganic mass of individuals nor a mechanzed organization of power, but a living spiritual order.

"The ideals of such a community was the dream that inspired the political reformers and revolutionaries of the last two centuries, but since they rejected the power of the Spirit their ideals proved unreal and utopian, and they achieved either freedom without order, or order without freedom.

"Today, we are fighting against the totalitarian order, which is the most radical and systematic denial of freedom that the world has seen. But we must recognize that, while we fight for freedom, that freedom alone will not save the world. A true peace can only be secured by the restoration of the spiritual order, for it is only in the Spirit that power and freedom are reconciled and united, so that the Sword of the Spirit is both the power that can deliver us from the hand of the enemy and the force that awakens and sets free the dormant sources of energy is human nature itself."

Cardinal Hinsley:

Religion, the Foundation of Social Life.

The Cardinal Archbishop's Pastoral Letter for Trinity Sunday, 1940.

"Dearly beloved brethren and dear children in Jesus Christ:

"You have read the many plans and suggestions for the reconstruction of Europe after the war. Some of these remain on the natural plane of politics and trade; others insist on the necessity of a spiritual basis for a new and sound order of society. There is a very general if only implied admission that 'modern progress,' through dreams of earthly perfection, is a failure. A civilisation founded on purely material principles must end in final breakdown.

"We have proof positive in the present state of the world that systems of secularist or materialist idealism are built on sand, and great is the fall thereof when the storms and floods rush down. Such collapse is inevitable, unless, as Pius XI declared (Quadragesimo Anno), all men's activities unite to imitate and, as far as is humanly possible, carry out the unity of the Divine Plan which places God as the first and supreme end of all created activities, and treats all created goods as instruments under God to be used in so far as they help towards the attainment of the one supreme end.

"God, first above all and His rational beings obedient to His law written in their consciences—that is the only firm ground on which reconstruction can give promise of stability.

"Without a solid foundation in the recognition of our utter dependence on the Almighty Giver of all good gifts and the answering response of men's wills to the obligations which flow from such knowledge, there can be no fixed standard of right and wrong. Enlightened self-interest, which often in practice becomes sordid selfishness, remains the chief motive power in industrial and social life, regulating the production, the acquisition, and distribution of wealth. Thence follow unchecked competition, national unrest through poverty and unemployment, international trade rivalry and unstable equilibrium between war and peace. Religion alone can create harmony in the multitude of fickle discordant minds and wills; only religion gives to authority its sphere of action and saves submission or obedience from slavery.

"But religion must teach clearly and definitely. Confused and vague views cannot direct the wayward hearts of mankind into the sure paths of peace. Therefore, many are those who have been 'tossed about by every wind of doctrine,' but now seek steadfast conviction and fixed principles. More and more the Holy See is recognized as the trustworthy impartial guide. . ."

"You know well that material conditions affect our moral and spiritual welfare. The hungry and the homeless and the naked must first be cared for as to their bodily miseries before they can attend to spiritual ministrations. Hence the solicitude of the Church is not confined to the spiritual needs of her children so as to neglect their temporal and earthly interests. The Pope and the pastors of the Church regard it as their duty in due season and measure to work for the material welfare of their flock. And Catholics are surely bound to listen to their recommendations and to support their efforts to remedy social evils or physical suffering. Benedict XV in the last war not only strove to bring about a true peace founded on justice and charity, but he spent his energies and means to relieve the famine-stricken people of Russia, to release or comfort prisoners everywhere, to assist the wounded and the sick. Our present Holy Father is acting in the same spirit in this war.

"You know how he had striven with all his strength to preserve peace, and how he is alert to every chance that may arise to stem the bloodshed and to bring about true peace with reparation for wrong done. But shall we not give him our loyal support as far as lies in us? We will at least heed his pleading for our prayers . . ."

"You will have noticed also that our Holy Father rests his hope for the renewal of society, as Pius XI before him, on the Christian education of youth. We cannot suppose that the harm done to the children by the Nazi system, which seizes on the little ones and keeps hold of them from the cradle to the grave, will be counteracted all at once nor that the youth of Russia and Mexico and Spain can forthwith be made immune to the poison with which they have been impregnated by Communist influence. Can we expect that our own National Education will be immediately purged of the secularist leaven which, according to the recent articles and correspondence in The Times, is rearing too many of our citizens of the future to become pagans? . . ."

"We pray that a striking lesson of this war may be learned by our Leaders and by all who love the inheritance of British liberty, by all who have respect for the rights of conscience whether of minorities or of majorities. The youth do not belong to the State simply to be trained, as among the Nazis and Bolshevists, in order to serve the material and military glory of the government in power.

"Our traditional English education demands that the children of a Christian people have by Divine Law a right to full Christian education; that Christian parents have a twofold right and duty, both natural and supernatural, to preserve this priceless inheritance; that Christian children are in no sense the property of a State which has no religion or which is pagan and atheist; that secular instruction is not of such supreme moment as the formation of citizens to be Christians; that parents have an inalienable right to decide on the selection of teachers to whom their children will be entrusted; that the poor as well as the rich in all justice must have this same right and liberty. So wrote Cardinal Manning fifty years ago."

"If European society is to be restored from the wreckage which seems to threaten, those who seek to rebuild it would be wise to begin reconstruction on the principles from which our civilization sprang. The Church of Jesus Christ teaches the true social principles on which a new and better order, national and international, may be built. From the Church may be learned, with authority and with definite consistency, the moral law which regulates social life and our relations with our Creator and with our fellow-men. The Church teaches the obligations of religion, the duties of justice, the dignity of man's personality, the mutual rights and duties of rulers and subjects, the need of self-sacrifice, the call of charity, of filial love, and of patriotism. Her teaching and enforcement of these principles rest on reason and are confirmed by the revelation and example of Christ Our Lord. These truths and principles the Vicar of Christ, our Holy Father, has clearly proposed to the world as the remedy for the evils that ruin the peace and happiness of the world. For us remains the task of applying them with knowledge and discernment in the complex conditions of social, industrial, and political activities as well as in our home circle.

"To our children and to our youth we must impart the truths which will make them value the freedom of the Christian faith and love the sound order of a Christian life. We owe to them that thorough Christian education which may in some degree compensate for the heritage of unhappiness we are bequeathing them. 'But prove all things; hold fast that which is good.' (Thess. v, 21.) May Almighty God abundantly bless you all."

Notes

1 Lecture delivered at the Mechanics' Institute, Leeds, 28 January 1874. Text in: *The Dignity and Rights of Labour and other Writings on Social Questions,* London, Burns, Oates and Washbourne, 1934, pp. 1-34.

2 The Cardinal has explained that "live money" and "live capital" is human labor: 'Labor is, true property, true capital."

3 Letter to the Editor of the *Times,* November 1868, in favor of a project to give cash relief to unemployed during winter period. He is attacking the objections which the'Editor has raised against the project. This letter occasioned a storm of protest, which filled the columes of The *Times* for some time and brought sharp editorial rebuke. Text in *Ibid,* pg. 35-42.

4 *Ibid,* pp. 61-63

5 25 January 1891, *ibid.,* p. 68. In this letter he refers to the irritation his social pronouncements have caused and the charge of Socialism that has been used against him. He remarks: in England, "Socialism is little studied; it is a kind of party cry."

6 Dawson, *Judgment of the Nations.* pp. 151, 159-160. New York, Sheed & Ward, 1942. Permission for quotations granted.

PART VIII:

AMERICAN CATHOLICISM
and the
SOCIO - ECONOMIC EVOLUTION in U.S.A.

by

FRANCIS DOWNING

CATHOLIC CONTRIBUTIONS TO THE
AMERICAN LABOR MOVEMENT

Europe had just discovered, through bloody and long wars, that force would not coerce the religious beliefs in man, when Catholics of Colonial Maryland wrote their Toleration Act. Today it strikes us as incomplete. But it contained the ideal of later Americans and defined the basic problem:

> ". . . that noe person or persons whatsoever within this province . . . professing to believe in Jesus Christ, shall henceforth bee any waies troubled, molested, or discountenanced for, or in respect of, his or her religion, nor in the free exercise thereof." [1]

The ideal is reaffirmed in the First Amendment to the Constitution:

> "Congress shall make no law respecting an establishment of religion or prohibiting the free exercise thereof. . ."

Whatever else the Constitutional phrase meant—and it is currently being disputed—it declared that the Catholic Church would compete, in respect to the State, on equal terms with all other Churches. It meant that no one would be debarred from any public educational facility, and that if Catholics wished to establish their own educational system, they were free to do so. It meant that they could speak freely, have their own press, participate in public life, and win office if they could. Like Napoleon's soldier, each carried a baton in his knapsack. This is not to say that religious persecution did not mar our history; but it would not have the assistance of the State. Under the Constitution, the United States would never know an official religion.

It was the opinion of de Tocqueville that in the United States the spirit of freedom and the spirit of religion were "intimately united." The Catholic priests he met "mainly attributed the peaceful dominion of religion in their country to the separation of Church and State. I do not hesitate to affirm that during my stay in America I did not meet with a single individual of the clergy or the laity who was not of the same opinion on this point." [2]

Tocqueville was writing in 1835, and the abstinence of the American clergy was not so great as he observed. Yet his judgment stands, with minor corrections, and we listen with respect when he says:

> "If the Americans who change the head of government once in four years, who elect new legislators every two years, and

renew the provincial officers every twelve month; if the Americans, who have abandoned the political world to attempts of innovators, had not placed religion beyond their reach, where could it abide in the ebb and flow of human opinions? Where would the respect which belongs to it be paid, amid the struggles of faction? And what would become of its immortality, in the midst of perpetual decay? The American clergy were the first to perceive this truth, and to act in conformity with it. They saw that they must renounce their religious influence if they were to strive for political power; and they chose to give up the support of the State rather than to share its vicissitudes." [3]

In the United States, no religion was fondly allowed to become the State's favorite child. The State was kept free from the domination of the child grown to ruling manhood.[4] Civil liberty, we discovered, was the condition of religious liberty. It was this that Jefferson was talking about when, in 1799, he wrote to Elbridge Gerry: "I am for freedom of religion, and against all manoeuvres to bring about a legal ascendancy of one sect over another." [5]

Obviously to Catholics who held, and still hold, a minority position in this country, freedom of religion and equality of all religions was an enormous advantage. The Catholic Church was to grow, on its own, in an atmosphere of democracy. It was, indeed, a new and rich experiment "in a new nation, conceived in Liberty, and dedicated to the proposition 'that all men are created equal',"

Cardinal Gibbons summed up the attitude of his confreres when he wrote: "The separation of Church and State in this country seems to them (American Catholics) the natural, inevitable and best conceived plan, the one that would work best among us, both for the good of religion and of the State. Any change in their relations they would contemplate with dread. They are well aware, indeed, that the Church here enjoys a larger liberty and a more secure position than in any country today where Church and State are united."

The minority position of Catholics in the infant Republic is abundantly evident. While Catholic explorers and missionaries had opened up large areas of the territory that was to become the United States, and had been the earliest pioneers in much of New England, the Lake region, the far South, and a good part of the territory beyond the Mississippi, these enormous efforts brought little lasting results. Numbers of the Indians were converted and the reports of the missionaries attracted the attention of Europe to the new lands, but the future lay with English settlements along the Atlantic coast. In these colonies, Catholicism was only a fragment, nearly everywhere faced with legal disabilities. Only with the Revolution, in which they played a role of some importance in view of their numbers, did the Catholics gain political and religious freedom.

When the Peace of Paris granted independence in 1783, it is estimated that there were 15,800 Catholics in Maryland, 7,000 in Pennsylvania, 1,500 in New York, and 200 in Virginia—approximately 25,000 out of a population of perhaps four million. They were served by twenty-four priests, all of them in Maryland and Pennsylvania. These clerics had all been Jesuits before the suppression of the Society and eleven were native Marylanders.[6]

The Revolution, which had created the conditions for survival, also solved some of the problems of this tiny minority. The English ecclesiastical authorities quietly yielded their claim to jurisdiction. The efforts of Tallyrand to have American priests trained at Bordeaux and to place American Catholics under a French Vicar floundered when Pius VI appointed Father John Carroll as Prefect Apostolic with authority over all Catholics in the newly liberated land (1784). Five years later he was made bishop of Baltimore and of all the United States. The new appointee came from a distinguished Maryland family. He had served during the Revolution and was known and respected by many of the Founding Fathers. Carroll was a sincere democrat who believed that Religion could flourish best in an atmosphere of freedom. Symbolically, he insisted on an election by his fellow priests before accepting the nomination to the episcopate. His cousin, Charles Carroll, a signer of the Declaration of Independence, was active in the formulation of the Bill of Rights, and the new Bishop hailed the document as a charter of liberty.

The favorable political climate in the new nation was used by Carroll to organize his scattered flocks, and to provide for the new immigration which expanded the Catholic body both numerically and geographically. Even in his time it was necessary to found new dioceses along the seaboard and beyond the Appalachians. The Catholic immigration, which was a steady flow in the first decades of the nation's history,[7] became a wave after 1830. The relations between the older Catholic body and the larger number of newly arrived fixed the destiny of the Church in America. While there are many evidences of friction, the mingling was generally successful. The older generation provided the early leadership and set the general cultural tone of the Catholic body. They insisted on acceptance of American traditions and customs, loyalty to American institutions, the use of English in preaching and instruction, and other assimilationist practices. The new immigrants, who provided the bulk of the Catholic group, also contributed a greater assertiveness in its defense. Generally victims of political or religious oppression in their areas of origin, they accepted the political conditions of their new home with enthusiasm. Their preference, especially that of the Irish, for the more democratic political groupings, first that of Jefferson and later of Jackson, was in part a reflection of their appreciation of the advantages of liberty.

The expansion of Catholicism reawakened latent prejudices and led to the serious crisis of nativism in the second quarter of the

nineteenth century. The burning of the Ursuline convent in
Charlestown in 1834[8] set off a whole series of acts of violence
against persons and property. It is difficult to separate the economic
motive from the religious, but the cry of "No Popery" gave cohesion
to the assailants. In Philadelphia, the request of Bishop Kenrick
that the Douay Version be used by Catholics in public school
reading of the Bible, and that Catholic children be excused from
compulsory Protestant services, elicited the slogan: "The Bible is
in danger. Save it from the Papists." The slogan did not remain
vocal: it quickly led to riotious consequences.

This aggressive nativism left permanent psychological scars in the
Catholic minority, but it did not diminish loyalty to American
institutions. Nor did it lead to the direct intervention of clergymen
into politics. While Catholic groups did involve themselves covertly
or overtly in political issues, and although David Riesman's estimate of the American Church is intriguing,[9] the position of the
Church as a whole is expressed in the resolution of the Third
Provincial Council of Cincinnati in 1861. Faced with the Civil
War, the bishops wrote:

> "It is not for us to enquire into the causes which have led to
> the present unhappy condition of affairs. This enquiry belongs
> more appropriately to those who are directly concerned in
> managing the affairs of the Republic. The spirit of the Cath-
> olic Church is eminently conservative, and while her ministers
> rightly feel a deep and abiding interest in all that concerns
> the welfare of the country, they do not think it their province
> to enter into the political arena. . . The Catholic Church has
> carefully preserved her unity of spirit in the bond of peace,
> knowing no North, no South, no East, no West." [10]

The predominantly immigrant character of the Church in America limited the cultural influence of Catholicism. It also raised
important problems because of the low economic status of the
Catholic group as a whole. Some efforts to ameliorate the lot of
the Catholic immigrant were made in the first half of the century.
But in the decades after the Civil War, the growing industrialization raised the social question in an acute form. An overwhelming
proportion of the Catholic population were workers and their
plight was a challenge to Catholic leadership. In meeting this problem, the Catholic clergy in America were in an enviable position
vis-a-vis their European confreres, for their task was uncomplicated
by political issues. They were not the heirs of any aristocratic tradition, nor was their response hobbled by hostility to the existing
political system. They enjoyed civil liberty, freedom from State
control, and an extraordinary degree of corporate legal protection.
They could write and speak freely. Obvious self-interest indicated
a defense of their own against exploitation. Such restraint as existed
was psychological: the timidity of an unpopular minority and the

influence of the dominant cultural pattern. How American Catholics reacted to these varying motivations forms the substance of this essay.

In a now famous letter, whose contents were disclosed by Father J. J. Curran, a railroad magnate maintained that "the rights and interests of the laboring man will be protected and cared for, not by the labor agitators, but by the Christian men to whom God in his infinite wisdom has given control of the property interests of the country." [11] What was startling about this letter was not what it betrayed, but the conception of rights so long held by conservatives in the United States, and the use to which they put religion and the church in respect of this conception.

Protestant America, in theory and in fact, identified whatever is with what is right, and the social and political and economic protestant as being possessed by "ye ould deluder, Satan." Thus religion, and the clergy was politically regarded as helpful instruments of the State. The "wall of separation" lately made so much of had no perceived existence. In this respect, at least the rich, the well-born and the few did not subscribe to the Yankee belief that "good fences make good neighbors". Arthur M. Schlesinger, Jr. has put the facts succinctly:

> "Federalism had valued the clergy, as well as the judiciary, as a great stabilizing influence in society, hoping thus to identify the malcontent as the foe both of God and the law. Hamilton's curious project, in 1802, of a 'Christian Constitutional Society' disclosed the fervor with which conservatism, where defeated at the polls, was turning to religion and the law for salvation. In the next quarter-century conservatism, in collaboration with the pulpit, worked out a systematic view of America as essentially and legally a religious nation in which the church should assist the state in preserving the existing social order. Jacksonian democracy ran sharply up against these conceptions both of religion and of government." [12]

While it is true that the Catholic laity at this period were little more than half a million, struggling in a hostile atmosphere and that they were not part of this political alliance, their attitude, to social and economic evil was never more than indignation. The statement of Orestes Brownson that through his conversion to Catholicism his interest in labor was merely baptized is more rhetorical than meaningful. Mostly the clergy were more concerned with the mystery of symbol and ceremonial in societies rather than with the mystery of life in the United States.

Even in 1878 the first American Cardinal, McCloskey, seemed to be more impressed by the part of the encyclical which attacked Socialism than by its suggestion that the bishops encourage "societies of artisans and workmen constituted under the guardianship of religion". Even though the latter suggestion was related to the attack the new Cardinal found that:

"We have the elements of revolution and communism among us. It (sic) is threatening. Mischief is brewing on this side of the Atlantic, and it needs all our power to stop the iniquity that is sweeping all before it." [13]

If this expression of fear and caution seems, in retrospect, as unrelated to reality as the rhetoric of the Liberty League, a reformulation of "pie in the sky bye and bye"—it is exactly that. Indeed if it were all, it is possible that the relations of the 19th century Church in the United States to the working men would have been a reflection of its European counterpart with the consequent great loss of workers to the Church. It was not all—even in its own day.

Even if such language as that used by the Cardinal and others[14] sounds like that of Republican *yahoos* in 1950, two things, at least, can be said about it. The first is that it reflected a hostility toward the anti-religious character of contemporary socialism, as well as a kind of parochialism, on the social side, stemming, perhaps, from a peculiar sense of insecurity felt by Catholics in the United States, which impelled them to almost strident declarations of patriotism. And the second is that such language did not reflect either Catholicism or the Church, since the silence of many social-envisioned Catholics was more eloquent and more enduring than that which found fearful voice.

In respect of the first it must be put down that, despite Tocqueville's remarks about the equable atmosphere in which religion and the churches moved in the United States, there was a Protestant attitude of hostility towards Catholics which, like a fever chart, went up and down, but was never quite at rest.

Henry Ward Beecher's father was such a professional fever-raiser who, among his other reasons, left Boston to fight the Catholic Church in the West. However true it was that part of this anti-Catholicism reflected an instinctive dislike for foreigners, Beecher touched religious as well as racial animosity when he said that immigrants "through the medium of their religion and priesthood (were) as entirely accessible to the control of their potentates as if they were an army".[15]

That Lyman Beecher was not mere sound without significance is testified to by Harriet Martineau:

"The removal to Cincinnati of Dr. Beecher, the ostentatious and virulent foe of the Catholics, has much quickened the spirit of alarm in that region. It is to be hoped that Dr. Beecher and the people of Cincinnati will remember what has been the invariable consequence in America of public denunciations of assumed offenscs which the law does not reach; namely mobbing. It is to be hoped that all parties will remember that Dr. Beecher preached in Boston three sermons vituperative of the Catholics the Sunday before the burning of the Charlestown convent by a Boston mob." [16]

It was true, as Bishop John B. Purcell, in a Cincinnati debate on Catholicism with the Rev. Alexander Campell, said: "the abuse of the Catholics . . . is a regular trade, and the compilation of anti-Catholic books . . . has become a part of the regular industry of the Country, as much as the making of nutmegs, or the construction of clocks".[17] Know-nothingism, ritualistic, secret, disciplined, preaching "St. Simon, if not St. Mary", was never quite sober and often quite drunk.

What was not fully recognized by the hierarchy was the compulsion to secrecy in workingman's societies, in an atmosphere where the stature of man was decreased and depressed, and where an exalted freedom to workers was construed to deny the conditions of freedom—equality through unions. Terence Powderly may have set up a false choice in finding the religion of Christ opposed by that of Pinkerton.[18] But, however true was it that the activities of the Molly Maguires were murderous, the reasons for their activities were not reached by their ruthless suppression.

In a world characterized by mismanagement and waste which was baptized by the audacious smugness of our George F. Baers, in which violence was provoked and violence then repressed, in which "the courts began to see a riot in every strike, and a Molly Maguire in every trade unionist," [19] more than a concern for secrecy in human associations was required, or the course and meaning of the secrecy looked into before justice could even be fought for, and before men could lift up their backs, be dazzled by the clean sun and believe liberty lived beneath the lidless stars.

If it is a fair rule of thumb that a society is free whose trade unions are free then the Knights of Labor mark and illustrate a measure of our freedom and our meaning of it in the America of the 19th century. If "the elements of revolution and communism" were actually present, as Cardinal McCloskey maintained, they were not to be revoked by rhetoric. The

avowed purpose of the Knights of Labor was as much a valid
criticism of our society as a hope for amelioration of its evils:

> "To secure to the toilers a proper share of the wealth that they
> create; more of the leisure that rightfully belongs to them; more
> societary advantages; more of the benefits, privileges and emolu-
> ments of the world; in a word, all those rights and privileges
> necessary to make them capable of enjoying, appreciating, de-
> fending and perpetuating the blessings of good government." [20]

Founded, in 1869, by Uriah S. Stephens, it had a membership
of under fifty thousand when in 1878, Terence V. Powderly, a
Catholic, became its Grand Master. Despite its idealism about
the solution of industrial conflict, it was not through arbitration
but by the Southwest railroad strike of 1884, that capital was
compelled for the first time to meet with labor on equal terms.
Jay Gould's compelled response to the strike—collective bargaining—gave the Knights a membership, in 1885, of some
seven hundred thousand. This new strength and new meaning
was shown in the ability of the Knights to help in the acceptance, by Congress, of the Chinese Exclusion Act, in 1882, and in
their large influence in the legislative prohibition on the im-
portation of contract labor in 1885.

What effect the action of Cardinal Gibbons had on the
Knights of Labor, whose effect, in turn, on American society,
on the democratic contest, was great, is disputable. The ruin
of the Knights seems related to other things. The blessing, if it
was that, given the Knights by the Catholic hierachy may have
even been a thread in the unravelling spool of its undoing. But
the position taken by Gibbons has an importance and an en-
chantment aside from all that. The continued appeal to religion
as an ally against labor, its identification with wealth, the regarding of the strike as an exercise in treason, were rebuked
by the Catholic church in America. The New York banker,
Henry Clews, could say in 1886, that "strikes may have been
justifiable in other nations, but they are not justifiable in our
country. The Almighty has made this country for the oppressed
of other nations and therefore this is a land of refuge . . . and
the hand of the laboring man should not be raised against it".[21]

If Terence Powderly put too sharply the opposition of the
religion of Pinkerton to the religion of Christ, it was, nonetheless, an expression of the depth to which anger could run
in a man who felt that he and his institution were enmeshed,
hostilely surrounded, that all eyes of all other institutions—
including those of his own church—looked on with no compre-

hension, and that he and the Knights were pinned and bayoneted about by all of society's available violence.

If in this period railways were the pulsating heart of industry and steel, and iron the essence of railroads and much of manufacturing, some idea of the protected and dominant industry is got from Abraham Hewitt, one of our great iron masters:

> "Steel . . . rails were subject to a duty of $28.00 a ton. The price of foreign rails had advanced to a point where it would have paid (the manufacturer) to make rails without any duty, but to the duty of $28.00 a ton he added $27.00 to his price and transferred from the great mass of the people $50,000,000 in a few years to the pockets of a few owners who thus indemnified themselves in a very short time, nearly twice over, for the total outlay which they had made in the establishment of their business." [22]

Even farmers, as distinguished from farm laborers, had some kind of protection by and representation in a government which was largely an industrial state. In 1862 the Department of Agriculture had been created.

But as the great violence of the railway strikes, an angered response to a ten per cent wage cut of 1877, showed, strikes and even poorly organized unions were regarded as objects of rebellion meriting use of state militia and federal troops. Society seemed to be a highly stratified instrument, whose upper classes were protected and fattened by government—which took sovereignty and the swift use of force to be the same thing.

In no modern country has the attempts of what might be called "the masses" to advance met such rigorous, fierce and, in many areas, religiously sanctioned violence as in America. But trade unions are, and were, disciplined and unviolent attempts to right obvious wrong—necessary, organized exercises in quest of justice.

If Catholics in the American Catholic Church took righteous heed of these facts, they did not shout their protest from the housetops. Until Cardinal Gibbons the attitude of the Catholic hierarchy remained dialectical exercises uncaught by either vision or appreciation of the facts. The notice of Father Augustus J. Thebaud is as refreshing as it is rare: This Jesuit, pastor of St. Joseph's Church in Troy, New York, from 1852 to 1860, observed:

> "But apart from religion (the rich were mostly Presbyterians) what were the relations between employers and employees? They were strictly a matter of business, of wages and work. For every day's labor I will pay you so much, and this done we are quits.

Should you fall sick, it is your affair, even in case you have given me satisfaction for years. Nay, more, should you be incapacitated in working for me, without any fault of yours or mine, I owe you nothing, and it is not to me that you have to apply for relief, but to your personal friends—*I am not one of them.* (italics supplied) Whenever any of my poor parishoners fell sick or met with an accident, if they had not previously been able to lay something by for a 'rainy day'—which was indeed seldom the case—they were forced to apply to their fellow workmen, who never failed to respond. And I did not hear that the rich factory owner ever headed the list of subscribers."

This was one end of the scale in a political and economic world called *laissez faire,* a world becoming increasingly caught in the vise of corporate monopoly in respect of which legislatures seemed to be merely the pliant tool of executives. "It is futile for the public press", wrote George D. Wolff, in the *Catholic Quarterly Review,* of April, 1886, "to be constantly preaching platitudes respecting patience and respect for law, whilst evasions and defiant violations, constantly practiced by mammoth capitalists and corporations, are ignored, condoned and tacitly approved.[24]

Chicago, whose housing facilities were better than those of other cities, was found, following careful investigation in 1883-1884, by the Citizens' Association of Chicago, to reveal "the wretched conditions of the tenements into which thousands of workingmen are huddled, the wholesale violation of all rules for drainage, plumbing, light, ventilation and safety in case of fire or accident, the neglect of all laws of health, the horrible conditions of sewers and outhouses, the filthy dingy rooms into which they are crowded, the unwholesome character of their food, and the equally filthy nature of the neighboring streets, alleys and back lots filled with decaying matter and stagnant pools." [25]

The 1890 census disclosed that about five and one half million of the twelve million families in the country, could be said to be propertyless.[26]

Given the fact that money wages stayed at a fixed point from 1883 to 1886, and that there was an almost fixed pool of about one million unemployed, and given the ironclad oath workers had to take that they were not now, and never would be, members of a union, it was clear that America might be the land of the brave, but its passport to freedom was wealth. The wonder is not that there were signs of revolution, but that there were not more.

According to Powderly, the Knights of Labor was almost two-thirds Catholic. If that be true the Church had a great psychological investment in this union. It had a choice, whether it knew it wholly or not, of following the Canadian hierarchy, and condemning the Knights as a secret organization, or not condemning it. It did not condemn; it approved.

To have condemned it, the Church might irretrievably have put itself on the side of naked, imperiling capitalism; it might have left bitterness and anger, deep, unhealable wounds in the psychic soul of the only organized opposition to social injustice. It might—no one can tell—have meant that the words of Pius XI would have application for us too: "The great scandal of the 19th century was that the Church lost the working class".

Labor priests in the 20th century did not become important and articulate because the Church's record through the 19th century and early 20th century shines like a bright, unbroken beam of light through the encircled gloom. Nonetheless the work of Cardinal Gibbons in preventing the ban deserves continued appreciation. This is as much a tribute to Powderly as to Gibbons—but it was not Powderly who was the cleric.

In his now famous letter to Cardinal Simeoni, Gibbons wrote:

"It can hardly be doubted that for the attainment of any public end, association—the organization of all interested persons—is the most efficacious means, a means altogether natural and just. This is so evident, and besides so conformable to the genius of our country, of our essentially popular social conditions, that it is unnecessary to insist upon it. It is almost the only means to invite public attention, to give force to the most legitimate resistance, to add weight to the most just demands." [27]

Gibbons, too, had more immediate insight into what he was recommending to the Holy See, into its meaning, its consequences, than many of his colleagues. For example:

"In order to preserve so desirable a state of things (general prosperity through the means of sound principles and good social order) it is absolutely necessary that religion should continue to hold the affections and thus rule the conduct of the multitudes. As Cardinal Manning has so well written, 'In the future era the Church has no longer to deal with princes and parliaments, but with masses, with the people' . . . To lose influence over the people would be to lose the future altogether . . ." [28]

There is never any way, with certainty, to evaluate units of history. Yet it seems clear that in this conservative document the anti-clericalism, known to Europeans, was here muted. The organized way of resisting the evils of capitalism, of civilizing the system, was not offended. Gibbons' was a recommendation of great practicality, but it caught, and for a moment held, a vision. *Rerum Novarum* would not come to an America wholly unprepared for it. It would have the advantage of threading itself into a pattern. It would not look like a pragmatic change of front, something to be suspiciously regarded which had come too late.

Nonetheless, it can hardly be maintained that the encyclical of Leo XIII was shouted from the housetops. Nor can it be shown that much serious attention was given—in the training of priests—to its practical implications. It was not, for example, until he was out of the seminary that, in 1894, the future Msgr. John Ryan read his first textbook in economics. This lack of social education was, it would seem, typical. "Social studies as such", writes Richard J. Purcell, *"even the history of the United States,* were long neglected in the seminaries, whose curriculum was European in happy oblivion that the trainees would serve in the small towns and urban centers whose inhabitans were preponderantly Protestant." [29]

One may say, at this point, two things: the promulgation of *Rerum Novarum* put Catholics in the United States into the conflict between capital and labor, and put them in, at least theoretically, on the side of labor. It was impossible in the social conflict any longer to be neutral. The second thing is this: it was going to take some time before *Rerum Novarum* was enthusiastically taught, overtly believed in, and acted upon. In any institution there are always great gaps between teaching and practice. Writing on the sixtieth anniversary of *Rerum Novarum,* John Cort says:

> "As far as doctrine goes there should be no doubt where the Church stands, at least among those who take the trouble to read. But the terrible part of it is that doctrine lives, or dies, or is betrayed, or is perverted by the actions of every man who stands before the world bearing the name of Catholic." [30]

Notorious, and now well known, malpractices of our Big

Business led to the writing of the Sherman Anti-Trust Act, four years before *Rerum Novarum* was written. But in 1895 the C. C. Knight Company held a practical monopoly on all of our sugar refining. The Supreme Court of the United States refused to void this obvious monopoly on the ground that trade was merely accidental to manufacture. Of this and prior and similar rulings, the Attorney General, Richard Olney wrote: "You will observe that the government has been defeated in the Supreme

Court on the trust question. I always supposed it would be, and have taken the responsibility of not prosecuting under a law I believed to be no good." [31] This needs no comment.

It is important to note that in dissenting from his court brethren, in the above case, Justice Harlan wrote:

> "Interstate traffic . . . may pass under the absolute control of overshadowing combinations having financial resources without limit and audacity in the accomplishment of their objects, that recognizes none of the restraints of moral obligations controlling the actions of individuals; combinations governed entirely by the law of greed and selfishness—so powerful that no single State is able to overthrow them and give the required protection to the whole country, and so all pervading that they threaten the integrity of our institutions." [32]

Money, skill, ruthlessness, audacity and immorality made possible the advancement of Big Business. But it exploited men, working men, ordinary men. "If the question should be asked", said Carrol Wright, the U. S. Commissioner of Labor, in 1886, "has the wage-earner received his equitable share of the benefits derived from the introduction of machinery, the answer must be, no." [33] It is debatable, at the very least, if the answer is a different one today.

Two ways occurred to men to rectify this inequity. One way was to form trade unions; the other was through legislation. Between 1890 and Woodrow Wilson's day, no legislation was passed seriously curtailing the power of Big Business. Did it exist, the Courts emasculated it, as we have seen.

But industries, dominated by the corporation, could hardly be successfully unionized. The rise of the C. I. O. alone changed all this. The government actually used troops to break the Pullman strike, in the year of *Rerum Novarum*.. The single remaining instrument of changing American economic and social conditions—the trade union—operated only in the skilled trades. This is an accurate, though brief description of conditions as we opened the 20th century.

It is difficult to find evidence which equates the social influence of the Catholic Church with its possible power. Her possible power was stated by Father Herman Heuser in 1906:

> "No careful observer of things can have a doubt that the Catholic Church possesses an organization which can secure unequal order of action or that she possesses a unique power to control mind, heart and external conduct of that proportionately large majority of religious believers in our country, who claim her name. Her unity of doctrine and the stability of her hierarchical govern-

ment, with a chief pontiff who not only teaches and rules, but also advises with an absolutely directing and restraining effect, are recognized on all sides. It is equally clear that her authority reaches through the closely bound lines of pastoral administration, every individual member of the Church." [34]

It was stated by Cardinal Gibbons that unions needed leaders who would not infringe "on the rights of their employers".[35] What he was talking about, as all of the hierarchy were doing at this time, was Socialism. Gibbons went so far as to oppose boycotts of any kind.

The threat of Socialism in the United States seems, at least in retrospect, to have been without force. It was used, indeed, as Communism often is today, to inspire fear and preserve the status quo. Yet it is not idle to observe—since the Church spent so much time fighting its real or fancied influence—that the well-known Daniel de Leon said in a speech at New Bedford, on February 11, 1898, that: "a trade organization (union) must be clear upon the fact that, not until it has overthrown the capitalist system of private ownership in the machinery of production, and made this the joint property of the people, thereby compelling everyone to work if he wants to live, is it at all possible for the workers to be safe".[36]

Obviously the Socialists were trying to capture the trade unions, and obviously Cardinal Gibbons and the rest of the clergy opposed them. No American priest so effectively carried on this practical opposition as Father Peter E. Dietz. It is the work of Dietz, and others, that has produced the judgment that the American Federation of Labor in the early part of the 20th century was "conservative". Of Dietz, Father Henry J. Browne writes: "In November, 1910, during the St. Louis convention of the American Federation of Labor, he was instrumental in bringing together, with the support and approval of Archbishop John J. Glennon, a group of Catholic labor leaders in an organization called the Militia of Christ for Social Service." [37] He was, of course, engaged in espousing, advancing, and filling with life "Leo XIII's famous encyclical".

The object of the Militia was "the defense of the Christian order of Society and its progressive development." They were ambitious to forward "the economic, ethical, sociological and political doctrine of Christian philosophy as developed in the course of history—the legacy of tradition, interpreted in modern times in the letters of Leo XIII and Pius X". Explicating all this, Father Browne adds that, "It had elaborate (and in some respects still unfulfilled) hopes of promoting social education among Catholics, and ideas for the 'compelling of social action', which included advocacy of Christian principles in trade-unions, interest in labor and reform legislation, yearly conventions conjointly with the A. F. of L., a Catholic celebration of Labor Day, a policy of conciliation, trade-agreements and arbitration".[38]

With John Mitchell, president of the United Mine Workers, Dietz worked very closely. Mitchell, surely one of our most reasonable and conservative of labor leaders, approved the Dietz program, observing, "I believe that the Catholic people should be in the vanguard in the movement for constructive social and industrial reform, and whether there be any justification for the charge, there is a widespread impression that our church is just a little over-conservative in matters of this kind; therefore, it seems to me that our people should adopt and pursue a systematic program for social betterment; that we should identify ourselves with the movement to promote legislation, that is, constructive legislation, for the protection of the great part of the people in our country who are least able to protect themselves".[39]

It is not unworthy of notice that 1911 was the year in which Father John A. Ryan had drawn up a minimum wage bill for the State of Minnesota. Nor, in this whole atmosphere of alleged "socialism", it is without interest to observe that of Ryan's advocacy of the Living Wage, it has been noted that, "outside of New Zealand and New South Wales, the principle of the minimum wage, even at $600.00 a year was revolutionary; in the United States it was socialistic".[40]

Since Father Dietz has been spoken of as "the organizer of the movement of which Ryan has been credited as the academician",[41] it is important to note that one of the things claiming the attention of Dietz and the Militia was:

"Intelligent and active interest in the problems of labor legislation; Municipal reform, civil service and general administration, industrial education, prevention of industrial accidents and diseases, workmen's compensation, workshop factory and mine inspection, and uniform state legislation." [42]

It is the character and content of the work of Dietz which makes Father Browne say that he helped "to make the word of Leo XIII's *Rerum Novarum* come alive." [43]

To return to his trade union activities—and given his own conception of his main task as being the organization of "Catholic trade unionists as such into sodalities under the aegis of the

Church" [44]—Father Dietz was able to get seven prominent Catholic trade union leaders on the Board of Directors of the Militia. Among them was John Mitchell.[45] Five other Catholic union leaders were officers of the Militia. These men obviously met the qualification for executive membership set up by Dietz —"practical Catholics who accept as an axiom, the principle of trade unionism, uncommitted, however, to every special application of the theory." [46]

This last phrase refers to the idea of Socialists to achieve their ends, in part, by direct political action. That trade unions should eschew politics, save, perhaps, in the Gomper's sense, is indicated by what may be called the Kress catechism. At the request of Archbishop Messmer, of Milwaukee, Father William S. Kress prepared, in 1908, a book called *Questions of Socialists and Their Answers*.[47] The point of view is thus disclosed:

> Question: Can the working class secure protection without giving into politics.
> Answer: The law knows no distinction of rich and poor; its protection can be invoked by the one as well as by the other. Labor unions have gained many notable concessions from employers and have secured a considerable amount of legislation without going directly into politics, or what is the same thing, forming a distinct political party.
> Question: What political principles would you advise the working class to adhere to?
> Answer: To vote for capable and honest men, whom no amount of money can corrupt.

It is odd, given Samuel Gompers' absolute opposition to Socialism, that the Jesuit, Marshall Boarman, approving the A. F. of L for its "sane and conservative principles," and "its independence of political parties," should find it necessary to add that for the A. F. of L to support Socialism would cause it to "immediately burst asunder. The great majority of the A. F. of L are Christians and Catholics, and President Gompers, the English Hebrew, knows it." [48] Whatever else this quaint remark indicates, it gives evidence of the preoccupation of the Catholic clergy with "socialism." Mr. Karson quotes Father Charles Bruehl, Professor of Sociology in St. Charles Seminary, Philadelphia, as speaking, to the Catholic delegates at the A. F. of L convention there in 1914, of their being "conservative pillars of order, and a bulwark against revolution." Revolution was hardly a large black cloud on the horizon in 1914. The "Catholic element" in the unions, Bruehl went on, would "overcome the contagion of socialism." [49] The vague use of the word "socialism" is still apparent.

It does not seem to be a mere cavil to note that what Bruehl actually said was that *"without* the Catholic element the trade unions cannot overcome the contagion of socialism; it acts like the salt which preserves from disintegration." [50]

Before we return to Peter Dietz, it may help to understand what a Catholic priest, in the early 20th century, had in mind when he spoke of "conservative pillars of order," etc. In the same address Father Bruehl noted that "unspeakable crimes have been committed in the name of property rights, for greed is as merciless as the grave and as blind as fate." [51] Observing that "no stronger lever for the economic and social uplift of the laboring classes than labor organization has yet been discovered," he went on to take the position that "the hostility and offensive attitude of the unions towards the employers is mostly nothing but the echo of the intolerance and the contempt of the employers who have repulsed the well-meant advances of their employees." And to hold that "to crush labor unions means to open the flood gates of the revolutionary spirit."

One final quotation:
"In cases where the strike is just and necessary for the attainment of just ends, the government may not prevent the exercise of this right neither by *injunction nor force,* unless of course it is unwilling to see to it that justice be done to the workmen. Undoubtedly the State has a right to suppress disorder, violence, and bloodshed which arise in the course of a strike, whether they proceed from the employers or the employees. A strike is not war. It implies neither destruction of property nor violence; it is not aggression, but rather an organized *passive resistance."* [52]

One may argue that the relation of the clergy to trade unions was, to steal a phrase from F. Scott Fitzgerald, "less a romance than a categorical imperative." But the flabby use of the word "conservative," against the Bruehl statement, stands exposed. Woodrow Wilson would have gone no further than that—and in his own time, at least, he was not regarded as conservative. The difficulty about words, as Lewis Carrol's Alice knew, is that they can mean what you want them to mean.

This is not to say that the Church, lay and clerical,—the "better Catholics"—spent more time fighting for social reform than it spent resisting Socialism. We are a long way yet from the Bishop's program of 1919.

Nothing in the record denies the unhappy summation of one of our most careful scholars:

"to the very end of the pre-war (1917) era, despite efforts to strike a positive and constructive note, warring upon Socialism seemed to most people, perhaps, the main social interest of American Catholics." [53]

To return to Father Dietz. In 1911, with the approval of his bishop, John F. Farrelly of Cleveland, he was allowed to give full time to his special work. In his own words, "my resignation takes effect next week, that is as Pastor of Oberlin—and I am going on the road. The Ohio K. of C. and the two branches of the federation will help me get up a lecture circuit."[54] It is proof of his relations with John Mitchell that Mitchell participated in getting Father Dietz released from his parish, and, at the request of Dietz, both Mitchell and John Alpine, a Vice President of the A. F. of L, and a member of the Directors of the Militia, wrote to the Bishop, thus:

"We, the undersigned, interested in the work outlined by the Militia of Christ, see in it a promise of good both for the Church and country, and are desirous of its growth and extension.

"Father Peter E. Dietz would be able to devote himself to this work more effectively if given a larger opportunity, and we ask your Lordship to make it possible for him to give more of his time and effort to the extension of the Militia of Christ until such a time when the progress of the work hold the promise of self-support." [55]

The least that can be said of this extraordinary letter is that it indicates a relation between a Catholic priest and top labor leaders which is hardly characteristic. As shall be seen later the relations—and influence—on the part of the one is as unusual as on the part of the other. Yet Mr. Karson quotes from a letter which, in 1940, Dietz sent to Sister Joan de Lourdes, of Brooklyn's St. Joseph College for Women. In it Father Dietz states that he led a minority of defeated delegates out of the Ohio Federation of Labor convention in 1909 when "the socialists carried the convention." [56] He claims that he helped to bring about the defeat of the socialist-controlled Ohio Federation. He was a fraternal delegate to all A. F. of L national conventions from 1909 to 1917. He gave the opening prayer at the 1912 convention of the Federation in Cincinnati, Ohio.

Dietz, in the same letter, said that Samuel Gompers, president of the A. F. of L, told him that he had "the unique distinction of having secured a reversal of decisions by the Executive Board of the A. F. of L." He championed the Encyclical of Leo in the A. F. of L, and said that he could not recall the "friendships made, the enemies disarmed, the reconciliations effected, the policies considered and reconsidered, conflicts avoided or tempered." [57]

For this unusual record of accomplishment, and, by the way, of social understanding, Dietz, it is needless to say, had the support of the Archbishop of St. Louis, John J. Glennon, who met with Dietz and trade union leaders in 1910.

One of the most enlightened of Dietz's ideas was that of establishing a "school of Social Science" which would train workers to continue what he was doing. Not the least imaginative thing about it was his idea of modelling it on the Rand School of Social Science, and the belief that such a school would, as he put it "make possible a community of priests who will make Social Service their prime object, just as the Jesuits and other orders specialize according to the needs of the times." To this he pathetically adds: "Two priests have already told me that they would be ready to give up their parishes and devote themselves to social work, but I could not give them the word." [58] It is tantalizing to think what a difference would have been made by the development of such an educational project. It is still tantalizing, even in 1951.

Dietz set up a draft constitution for the Social Service Commission of the American Federation of Catholic Societies, in 1913. This document received the rebuke of John Mitchell because it did not specifically advocate "a more equitable distribution of wealth, wage and hour legislation, abolition of child labor." "If," Mitchell wrote to him:

> "upon principles of this kind Catholic men and women can unite, then they can be of real service to society. Unless the Militia of Christ (and by the way, I believe the name should be changed in order to remove misunderstanding) can declare for the above or something substantially like it, I doubt that any real good can be accomplished through it." [59]

Such clothing with definiteness by Mitchell did not argue that Dietz rejected any of these ideas: it argues that Dietz was more conscious of timing, and of the character of his own group.

It is this kind of thing that makes difficult judgments on the Church. In 1913 neither Dietz nor Ryan shied from accepting these things as the objects of necessary legislation. As early as 1905, William Stang, Bishop of Fall River, Massachusetts, advocated social insurance, workmen's compensation laws, and a "limited amount of state ownership." [60] This last was opposed by Archbishop Ireland. With the exception, of course, of state ownership, the Progressive Party Platform of 1912, accepted by Theodore Roosevelt, approved most of the things mentioned by Mitchell in his letter to Dietz. But Dietz properly could reply to Mitchell that "the Federation (of Catholic Societies) is slow." [61]

There seemed to be little advancement beyond the situation described by Father Ryan, four years earlier, when he observed that, of social legislation and teaching "the bishops who have made any pronouncements . . . could probably be counted on the fingers of one hand, while the priests who have done so are not more numerous proportionately." [62] What Republican schismatics approved was not loudly proclaimed by the generality of Catholics. The Methodist Episcopal Church approved the things, asked for by Mitchell, as early as 1908.[63] The Catholics were still fighting something called "socialism." If Dietz despaired there is no record of it. There is only "you are aware that for years I have been trying to influence Catholic Federation in this field. The Militia of Christ was organized largely as a lever to this body. The Federation is heavy and slow. All great bodies are." [64]

As late as 1912, Catholic labor leaders requested from Cardinal Gibbons a document of more explicit support for their movement. This, despite the existence of Leo's Encyclical seemed necessary because "the neutrality especially on the part of many of the clergy is a positive obstacle to progress and a ready weapon to the enemy." It went on to assert that "Catholic laymen in the ranks and as leaders of labor, are oftentimes discouraged because of the lack of moral support by the Church in their struggles for the betterment of human conditions." [65]

When one notes the work of Dietz and others[66] he feels that he is reaching out for and meeting what is unrepresentative. This, in part, arose from the fact that, as Father Ryan observed, in 1908, the "great majority of our clergy in the United States has not yet begun to study systematically or take more than a superficial interest in the important social problems of their age and country." [67]

In part it is true because of the relationship of, at least, some of the hierarchy to men of wealth, and to naivete and ignorance. While for example, giving high praise to Bishop Spalding for his social intelligence and knowledge, Msgr. John Ryan notes this of Archbishop Ireland: "The Archbishop's associations were with the pillars of the contemporary economic order, men like James J. Hill, president of the Great Northern Railway and with William McKinley . . .[68] The Archbishop, for instance, had written an essay called *Personal Liberty and Labor Strikes* in 1901. While supporting unions, he opposed workers who sought to prevent, by force, other workers from taking their jobs.[69] No one praises the use of force, but only naivete could explain Ireland's position—given the normal pattern of police, deputies, sheriffs, the National Guard—the availability to corporations of all the organized violence of the community in all the major strikes of this period.[70] In the textile strike in Lawrence, Mass. for example, dynamite was planted by an undertaker in parts of the city. This little trick was a management plot. Yet when the dynamite was found, the *New York Times,* expressed normal conservative opinion by saying "When the strikers use or prepare dynamite, they display a fiendish lack of humanity which ought to place them beyond the comfort of religion until they have repented."[71]

Yet Ireland could write:
"I have no fear of capital. I have no fear of vast fortunes in the hands of individuals, nor of the vast aggregations of capital in the hands of companies." [72]

It is true that Ireland said this in 1903, but Msgr. Ryan, writing in 1914, could say of him:

"He did not believe that the great industrialists, whose personal friendship he possessed, and who seemed to be 'good men' in all their relations with him and with their neighbors, could stoop to economic oppression of the laborer, the farmer, or the consumer. His judgment was mistaken because he was not in possession of the relevant facts." [73]

It is not without interest to note that Cardinal O'Connell wrote a Pastoral Letter in 1912, in which he said that:

"The living wage . . . is the one which will maintain this (the worker's family) in decent and frugal comfort. The man who accepts less through necessity or fear of harder considerations is the victim of force and injustice." [54]

But he wrote it after the strike was over. Priests, two especially, supported the strikers, and Father Milanese raised money for them. Nonetheless, the above is true.

The Catholic Fortnightly Review noted, in 1909, that Catholic newspapers "not infrequently" supported the "rubber trusts," and "suppressed" "the really salient passages" in Leo's Encyclical "for fear of offending their capitalistic readers and advertisers." [75] And Mr. Abell concludes that "the struggles

of the newcomers for a greater measure of economic justice
were often confused with Socialism by the more well-to-do
Catholics, 'Catholics of the better sort.' " [76]

All this must account for the fact that workers—Catholic
workers—were, indeed, turning to Socialism. In 1902, Bishop
Quigley, of Buffalo, told the Buffalo *Evening News* that:

> "The spread of socialistic principles among the workingmen has
> convinced the clergy and thinking men among the laity that the
> time has come for an organization under the auspices of the
> Church for the insistence upon the settlement of social ques-
> tions." [77]

Mr. Abell notes that by 1909, Catholic workers were "acquies-
cing in Socialist propaganda in trade unions." [78] And he cites
the existence, in Chicago, at this time, of a Catholic Socialist
Society. [79]

In St. Louis, Catholics formed a workingman's Welfare Association partly in response to a peculiar condition in the brewing
industry. "It seems that everyone who joined the brewers union
had to buy the *Arbeiter-Zeitung,* a Socialist newspaper." [80] Sister Joan de Lourdes Leonard quotes a letter from F. P. Kenkel,
director of the Central Verein, saying, "In fact, the subscription had to be paid together with the dues." [81] Obviously the
Workingmen's Association was able to reply to the Socialist
paper in one of its own.

Yet whatever concrete attraction the plans and promises held
out by Socialist propaganda, the favorable reaction to it marked
and illustrated a deficiency in the churchmen—a lack of response on their part, to the economic program of Pope Leo,
and a preoccupation with the rebuke to Socialism. Even in
respect of concrete social reform, Msgr. Ryan noted this peculiarity, between 1907-1915, at least:

> "Intellectual and competent Catholics were willing to work for
> laudable objectives in a Catholic organization, but seemed to be
> timid or fearful of association with non-Catholics for similar
> purposes." [82]

Msgr. Ryan points out that "not in 1893"—Ireland used the
term "social justice" in a sermon in that year—"nor for many
years thereafter, was this phrase in common use by American
priests or bishops." [83] He says that Archbishop Ireland was
surprised at Spalding's remarks on John P. Altgeld, in 1902.
Spalding said of that just man who, during the Pullman strike
opposed President Cleveland's notorious use of troops to break
the strike:

"He had a fine scorn of mere wealth, title, and position, and would have taken delight in a beggar who might have had power to make him wiser or better. He abhorred cant, pretense, hypocrisy and lies . . . With all his heart he loved truth and hated liars; loved justice and hated iniquity . . . (he was) the truest servant of the people and the most disinterested politician whom Illinois had known since Lincoln died." [84]

It is hardly a matter of wonder that Msgr. Ryan praised Archbishop Spalding for his "complete acquaintance with the fundamental facts of our industrial practices, persons, and institutions; (which) enabled him to see through the aura of 'respectability' surrounding these and to perceive a good deal of the underlying plutocratic maneuvering and social injustice." [85]

The relation of unions to the inhuman and malevolent situation created by monopoly capital, and the existence of, and insistence on Socialism became, it would seem, unduly complicated by some Catholic reaction to the Encyclical of Pope Pius X, *Singulari Quodem*—September 24 1912. By it German Catholics were allowed to belong to non-Catholic trade unions. To divide an already weak American unionism by gratuitous religious considerations would seem harmful and sterilizing. But some Catholics now raised the question in the United States of what came to be called "parallel association of Catholic workers."

Writing in the year 1950, Father John F. Cronin says that "some among the clergy take the position that general Catholic associations, such as the Holy Name Society, adequately meet the need of Catholic workers." [86] He, himself, is doubtful about this,[87] and holds that "where Catholics join non-religious organizations, the Church has a duty to provide some parallel associations for the religious training of Catholic workers." [88]

This is noted here because the Catholic Central Verein used the Encyclical *Singulari Quodem* as a springboard to note two things—each of which reveals, and speaks for itself.

First in its *Central Blatt and Social Justice,* an editorial said:
"Practical reasons may force Rome to tolerate interdenomination of unions . . . but 'the ecclesiastical authorities must watch over them closely, and through Catholic Labor Societies they must warn their subjects and make sure of their loyal obedience.'
The second editorial held the Pope's statement:
"Would exclude from the ranks of unions to which Catholics might belong all organizations influenced by and fostering socialism . . . In short, in socialistic organizations we must behold a

danger to society, morality and faith. Catholics, therefore, cannot
be members of organizations founded by Socialists or for Socialistic purposes as e.g. The Industrial Workers of The World, the
American Railway Union, The Western Federation of Miners,
the Socialistic Trades and Labor Unions, the Knights of Labor
etc., *if they are what they are said to be.*[90]

The editorial continued:

"Similarly, to give briefly an example of another kind, the
Farmers Educational and Co-operative Union of America is not
in conformity with the above teaching. From the *America* of
November 26, 1912, we learn that this union is interdenomina-
tional; advocates—these are the objectionable points—religious
interdenominationalism and puts aside the true standards of morality by declaring its aim and purposes to be 'to secure equity,
establish justice and apply the Golden Rule.' These objectionable features make it fall under the unions censured by the
Pope." [91]

Given the fact that the same editor held that if a minority
of the A. F. of L favoring such things as free public school
text books and woman suffrage should have their way, then
the Catholics' only alternative would be to leave it, then the
above raises no surprise.

Otherwise one would have thought that the aims objected
to above would have been approved, rather than subjected to
such theologizing. This is no place in which to write our
economic history. But join the above criticism to these facts:

"The farmer received 30% of the national income in 1869, 19%
in 1890, 18% in 1910, 13% in 1920, and, after the collapse of
the early thirties, 7% in 1933. Farm mortgages and tenancy increased correspondingly: 27% of the farms operated by their
owners were mortgaged in 1890; by 1910 the number had increased to 33% and by 1930 to 42% . . . Even more alarming
were the mounting figures of farm tenancy. In 1880 one-fourth of
all American farmers were tenants; by the turn of the century
one-third of all farmers were tenants; thirty years later almost
half the farmers of the nation were cultivating land which they
did not own." [92]

One is reminded by all this of Msgr. Ryan's stricture about
Catholics not working with other people. One is reminded, too,
of his own surgical judgment on the experience of his own
father. Msgr. Ryan thus comments:

"Until long after I went to college, that is, until about the year
1896, both (of his father's) farms were encumbered by mortgages. For about twenty years, the rate of interest on one of the

two mortgages was 12% annually; on the other the rate was 10% for about twelve years. In the early nineties, the rate was reduced to 6% . . . at that time there was no Federal Loan Law. Nevertheless, the economic situation presented no good reason for the absence of such legislation. To be sure, any attempt to enact it would have been stigmatized as "socialistic" "revolutionary"—or something worse. The dominant economic opinion and policies of the United States in those days were still those of *laissez faire*.[93]

Some men carry the facts of their background with them always in their moral wallets. Such a man was John A. Ryan. Partly in consequence of this memory he became one of the chief seminal contributors to the New Deal, which must fairly be credited with rescuing American capitalism.[94] Sister Joan de Lourdes says that when Father Ryan proposed a course in economics in the Seminary at St. Paul, in 1902, it was "a very unheard of thing."[95] One of his students proposed the Wisconsin minimum Wage Law, and another, Father Vincent O'Hara, defended a minimum wage law for women before the Supreme Court.[96]

It has occurred to all readers of the labor movement that the interest of any religious organization in it contains the possibility of schism. In its desire to protect its own, the temptation is great to form purely religious unions: Europe is filled with the faults and consequences of this fatal error. From that temptation the Catholic Central Verein remained free. And for this intelligence, the ultimate recognition that we were not Europe and owed ourselves the courage to act on that premise, Father Ryan thus praised the Verein for suggesting:

"that Catholic workingmen take an active part in the regular trade union instead of forming separate organizations. In this way the Catholic workers will be able most effectively to combat Socialism, unwise radicalism and every other tendency or method that is hostile to genuine reform."

The Catholic Verein at its Newark convention, in 1910, urged "Catholic workingmen to join the Trade Unions wherever possible (and) to combat the propaganda of Socialism in the Unions."[98] The driving motive of Catholics to get involved with Labor, gets clearer and clearer. This is not to say that their motives were more impure than those belonging to, or leading, other institutions. It is merely to record the pragmatic character of the fact. Socialism brooded over them, and they were as preoccupied with it as was Marvell with Time's "hurrying chariot."

The work of teaching, of propaganda, of spreading the social principles engaged in by the Catholic Verin is rightly famous. Its *Central Blatt and Social Justice* was widely circulated and carried influence. One hundred Catholic newspapers received its weekly press bulletins in English and German.[99] "For us," said its President, "the words 'To Restore all things in Christ' mean the promotion and defense of Christian order in society, against the dangers of Socialism and Anarchy in any form." [100]

Under its sponsorship Workingmen's Societies were formed in Buffalo and St. Louis.[101] There sprung from it Summer Schools for Social Study—one at Spring Bank, Wisconsin; the other (in 1912) at Fordham University.[102] The Journal of the Verein gave space to Peter Collins, of the Electrical Brotherhood. Collins and the convert, David Goldstein, lectured for the Militia of Christ.[103] Collins, among other things, wrote this:

"We advocate Catholic workingmen's societies to be founded in each parish, whose members shall be instructed as to their social duties to church and society according to precepts laid down by Leo XIII . . . only when so instructed and fortified will Catholic laboringmen be able to do their full share in preventing the insiduous enemy from capturing the Trade Union Movement and turning it into a recruiting ground for Socialism, into an appendix of the Socialist Party of the United States." [104]

The overt recognition of class warfare implied in the labor movement, and asserted, of course, by Socialists was stated by Peter Foy, at the Chicago Catholic Congress, in 1902:

"To restore a just and fair balance between the two classes is the chief problem in political science in this our day and generation." [105]

Given the mild strictures Msgr. Ryan made on Archbishop Ireland, the Archbishop, nonetheless, gave some quiet evidence of recognizing the true natures of the social conflict. In what labor writers call "the honeymoon period between capital and labor"—1894-1904—the Archbishop was a member of the well-known National Civic Federation. With Mark Hanna, Charles Schwab, Eliot, of Harvard, August Belmont and John D. Rockefeller, John Mitchell and others campaigned to preserve industrial peace. Accepting unions and trade agreements, the Federation offered itself as an instrument "in establishing right relations between employers and workers." [106] Of course, the animosity was too deep, the powers of the corporations too greedily held, as the broken steel strike of 1901, and the coal strike of 1902 were to prove. Even John Mitchell who opposed the strike was to learn that bitter fact. To his side in this exposure of class fission, Mitchell was able to win over Bishop Hoban of Scranton, Pa. The work of Father J. J. Curran of Wilkes Barre, and of Father Phillips, of Hazelton, Pa. is well known. "These three men had great influence not only with the miners, but with the operators." [107] Not very much is known about him, but John Mitchell got whatever early education he had from a Father Power. Mitchell was only 19 when he emerged from the mine strike of 1889, in Spring Valley, Illinois, beaten—as were all his fellow workers in what has been called—by Henry Demarest Lloyd—"a strike of millionaires against miners."

Looking about for understanding of the forces of his bewildered society, he wanted education, and was given the run of Father Power's library. Oddly enough one of the books Father Power gave to young Mitchell was Edward Bellamy's *Looking Backward*.[108] When one remembers that it is of this book that Norman Thomas has said, "The first I ever read which could be called Socialist . . . and it made a deep impression on me," [109] the difficulty of censorship is apparent, for Mitchell was hardly a "revolutionary" labor leader. One cannot but recall the incisive remark of Cardinal Newman: "In Metaphysics, again, Butler's *Analogy of Religion,* which had so much to do with the conversion to the Catholic faith of members of the University of Oxford, appeared to Pitt and others, who had received a different training, to operate only in the direction of infidelity." [110]

There can be no doubt that up to 1919, the Catholic Bishops had what Sister Joan accurately calls "at least an academic interest in the social problems of their age." [111] Nor could one disagree with her evidential judgment that "there was some social activity on the part of the priests in the period under discussion." [112] Of the laity, she incontrovertibly writes: "From what has been said about the Catholic laity between 1884 and 1919, it would seem that as a whole, there was no keen realization of the pressures of the social question and of the Catholic laymen's obligation to help solve it." [113]

Nonetheless, even given the natural conservatism of our country, it seems patent that, as Selig Perlman put it in 1928, in his classic book, for our labor movement "to make socialism or communism the official 'ism' of the movement, would mean, even if the other conditions permitted it, deliberately driving the Catholics, who are perhaps in the majority in the American Federation of Labor, out of the labor movement, since with them an irreconcilable opposition to socialism is a matter of religious principle." [114] As Father Dietz put it, Catholicism erected a "bridge between the Church in America and the labor movement" enabling it to "take hold of the labor movement." [115]

Given the total judgment of Sister Joan, it would seem in one way to have been a negative victory. That the work of Msgr. Ryan is conspicuous, that he kept making a distinction between the economics of Socialism and its philosophy, makes the truth of this clear. Yet it is clear that, no matter how socially purblind were Catholic leaders up to 1919, the labor movement would, in the absence of this victory, have been a different thing. Like the European labor movement it might have spent its days and nights in bed drunk with ideology. Yet, given the enormous possibilities inhering like gems in *Rerum Novarum*,[116] it seems a shame that its vital forces were not more fiercely seized, expounded and broadcast. The failure so to do enhances the work of those Catholic leaders in the ranks of the labor movement who went on strike in the face the whole physical and legal force of the organized community; and of the handful of bishops and priests who opposed the exploitation of men.

It is true, moreover, that a more enthusiastic response to the labor movement, on the part of Church leaders, could have taken place if they were not so obviously without knowledge of the facts, close to men of wealth, obsessed with fear of "revolutionary elements"—if they had realized that it was always true, as Professor Frank Tannenbaum now puts it that "Trade-unionism is the conservative movement of our time." As he says:

> "The socialists and communists operate with general ideas, and are given over to large plans for the establishment of social 'harmony,' but the trade-union movement seemed to have no rational basis. It lacked a doctrinal foundation. It had no theory, and it offered no explanation of the beginning and the end of things. It was as perplexing and as self-renewing as life itself, and it was internally contradictory. It had no sense of direction. Its arguments—if so they could be called—were sentimental and emotional. It appealed to values the revolutionists repudiated, and, worst of all, it merely sought to improve the position of the workers here and now." [117]

It was the purpose of the Socialists, of course, to capture the labor movement for political purposes, i.e. to produce a political labor party. Catholics can, if they wish, share credit for the failure of such evolution. But—as no one knew better than Msgr. Ryan—when Catholic trade unionists were turning, in the first decade of the 20th century, to socialism, or its propaganda, they were criticising their ecclesiastical leaders, not for the absence of a program,—Leo gave them that,—but for the absence of its meaningful vigorous application.

If one can properly say, as Frank Tannenbaum does, that "trade-uionism has returned the worker to a sense of identity within a moral universe," [118] it is important to make some notes about social legislation. Morrison and Commager assert that "more has been accomplished by labor through social legislation than through strikes and other violent methods." [119]

Three things are involved in social legislation—getting it passed, getting the courts to uphold it, getting it enforced. The ten hour day for women and children in Massachusetts was "the first labor law to be adequately enforced." [120] This law was passed in 1874. This was the year in which the Archbishop of Baltimore, James Roosevelt Bayley was approving charity, rather than legislation or labor unions. Of the Irish Catholic Benevolent Union, he said:

"It extends itself and exerts a proper influence guarding . . . from what is worse than secret societies—that it, the miserable associations called labor organizations. Their idea is Communistic, and no Catholic with any idea of the spirit of religion will encourage them.'" [121]

A fiercely unreluctant regard for property made our courts— even in the earlier part of the New Deal—wholly immune to the demands of life. Much legislation went down before the hammers of this bias. Socialism, too, sincerely feared, or falsely raised, was referred to by judges who lived in comfortable aloofnes from reality. Justice Holmes wrote in 1913 that "when twenty years ago a vague terror went over the earth and the word socialism began to be heard, I thought and still think that fear was translated into doctrines that had no proper place in the Constitution or the Common Law."

Such was the atmosphere in which Father Ryan was working, and in which he was charged both with radicalism and ignorance of the law. About the time Ryan was preparing his book, *The Living Wage*, the court in Illinois struck down a statute limiting the hours of sweatshop labor for women. It was the feeling of the court that women had the same "liberty" to contract for their labor as men. Of this the Chicago *Evening Post* wrote: "when Dora Windeguth, her employer at her elbow, says that she cannot earn enough in ten hours to live, our whole chivalry rises to her defense; let her work twelve hours then. We have always contended that nobody need starve in America." [122]

For a few years—from 1916 to 1923—the establishment of minimum wage legislation was made safe. But in 1923—much to Msgr. Ryan's shared disgust—the Supreme Court wrecked the whole principle. When the Court reversed itself in the West Coast Hotel Case[123] in 1937, welfare was advanced. It was, in a sense, no minor victory for Ryan.[124]

"The ending of the Great War has brought peace. But the only safeguard of peace is social justice and a contented people." [125] With these words from the foreword of their *Social Program* the Bishops, in 1919, brought the Catholic Church into a united and wholly new and envisioned relationship with social action, with labor and with itself. There were, of course, those who regarded the program as "radical." Marc Karson notes a similarity between it and the *Reconstruction Program* of the A. F. of L and writes that it "was more than a coincidence. It was to some degree the result of the intensive efforts made by the Catholic Church to permeate the A. F. of L with social principles." [126] In any event, "the Bishops and the clergy regarded the Program as a moderate application of Catholic moral principles to social and industrial life." [127]

With this Program the Catholic Church, at long last, was home again where it belonged. Yesterday's radicalism is today's conservatism. Thus of the eleven principal recommendations in the Program of 1919, ten "have been either wholly or partially translated into fact." [128] The principal proposals were:

1. Minimum wage legislation; 2. insurance against unemployment, sickness, invalidity, and old age; 3. a sixteen year minimum age limit for working children; 4. the legal enforcement of the right of labor to organize; 5. continuation of the National War Labor Board, for this and other purposes affecting the relations of employers and employees; 6. a national employment service; 7. public housing for the working classes; 8. no general reduction of war time wages and a long distance program of increasing them not only for the benefit of labor but in order to bring about that general prosperity which cannot be maintained without a wide distribution of purchasing power among the masses; 9. prevention of excessive profits and incomes through a regulation of rates which allows the owners of public utilities only a fair rate of return on their actual investment[129] and through progressive taxes on inheritance and income, and excess profits; 10. participation of labor in management and a wider distribution of ownership in the stock of corporations;[130] 11. effective control of mon-

opolies, even by the method of government competition if that should prove necessary.[131]

By any standard the Bishop's Program was, and is, a remarkable document. But the language, it would seem, of the proposed XXII amendment (1924) to the Constitution of the United States moderated the approval of the abolition of child labor the Program contained. Most of the hierarchy, notably Archbishop Curley, of Baltimore, and Cardinal O'Connell[132] saw hidden in it the possibility of Federal Control of education. Many found this opposition difficult to understand.[133] The language is:

"The Congress shall have power to limit, regulate, and prohibit the labor of persons under eighteen years of age." [134]

Later Supreme Court rulings reduced the urgency of ratification.[135] But it is doubtful if the record set down, so brilliantly, in the Bishop's Program was burnished by this opposition. Even after the passage, in 1937, of the Fair Labor Standards Act, Bishop Lucey wrote as follows:

"The writer recently visited a grammar school in our diocese maintained for Spanish speaking children. There were 125 students enrolled. On the day of my visit 5 children were present— 120 were miles away picking cotton. And then I read in a religious weekly: 'Child labor is no longer a problem in this country.' " [136]

It might be said here that the Child Labor controversy is significant if only because it indicates that, unlike Europeans,[137] American Catholic authorities usually stay directly out of politics. Here, as in State Amendments providing for birth control information—e.g. Connecticut and Massachusetts—it was held that a moral right was being, or could be, invaded.[138]

Msgr. Ryan was close to the A. F. of L and to others who favored the Amendment. Ryan quoted Senator Walsh of Montana, who wrote that the Amendment was subjected to "selfish and pernicious propaganda" and Ryan wrote, "under its influence, these Catholics and these other Americans have come to look upon the Child Labor Amendment as the result of a clever and diabolical plot to transfer the control of children from the family to the federal government." [139]

He observed too, that much of the attack on the proposed Amendment derived from "the National Association of Manufacturers, whose very able General Counsel, James E. Emery, wrote one of the earliest pamphlets against the Amendment. Mr. Emery is a Catholic, but for a quarter of a century or more he had appeared before congressional committees in opposition to every important measure of social justice introduced in Congress in that period." [140]

Whatever else be said about this episode it is hardly necessary to record that political disagreement was—as it is—part of the history of our Church in the United States.[141] Unity implies doctrine, not politics or economics.

A set of ideas which contributed, in some measure, it would seem, to Alfred E. Smith's defeat in 1928, was given currency in April of 1927. Charles C. Marshall, an *Open Letter to the Honorable Alfred E. Smith* expressed the feelings of many non-Catholics "as to certain conceptions which your fellow citizens attribute to you as a loyal and conscientious Roman Catholic, which in their minds are irreconcilable with that Constitution which as President you must support and defend, and with the principles of civil and religious liberty on which American institutions are based." [142]

Smith gave "a disclaimer of the convictions" imputed to him, and to all Catholics, in respect of loyalty to the United States: "without mental reservation I can and do make that disclaimer. These convictions are held neither by me nor by any other American Catholic, so far as I know." Smith went on to observe that:

"The Syllabus of Pope Pius IX which you (Marshall) quote on the possible conflict between Church and State, is declared by Cardinal Newman to have 'no dogmatic force.' You seem to think that Catholics must be all alike, in mind and in heart, as though they had been poured into and taken out of the same mold. You have no more right to ask me to defend as part of my faith every statement coming from a prelate than I should have to ask you to accept as an article of your religious faith every statement of an Episcopal bishop, or of your political faith every statement of a President of the United States." [143]

After quoting members of the American clergy on the question of Church and State, and the obedience of Catholics, Smith wrote:

"You claim that the Roman Catholic Church holds that, if conflict arises, the Church must prevail over the State. You write as if there were some Catholic authority or tribunal to decide with respect to such conflict. Of course there is no such thing. As Dr. Ryan writes: 'The Catholic doctrine concedes, nay maintains, that the State is coordinate with the Church and equally independent and supreme in its own distinct sphere.' " [144]

Finally, Smith states:

"But in the wildest dreams of your imagination you cannot conjure up a possible conflict between religious principle and political duty in the United States, except on the unthinkable hypothesis that some law were to be passed which violated the common morality of God-fearing men. And if you can conjure up such a conflict, how would a Protestant resolve it? Obviously by the dictates of his conscience. That is exactly what a Protestant would do. There is no ecclesiastcal tribunal which would have the slightest claim upon the obedience of Catholic communicants in the resolution of such a conflict." [145]

Obviously there were many who remained unconvinced by Smith's reply. There are many reasons for Smith's loss of the Presidency in 1928. But it is clear that among them was the revived nativist fear that were he in the White House the Pope of Rome would be there too. Crosses burning, like frenzy, in the hooded nights of the campaign were frightening illuminations of a fear, deep-rooted and exploited. The event cannot be among the happiest of America's memories.

Nonetheless, some difficulty about the political belief of Catholics was raised again by Msgr. Ryan and Francis J. Boland. In 1941 they published *Catholic Principles of Politics*. They state that "every state in a soundly organized world ought to profess the Catholic religion. The world however, is not soundly organized, for it is not formed of Catholic states . . . Consequently the obligation to profess the Catholic religion stands in abeyance in respect of all modern states. Specifically in 1941 it is inoperative in respect of the United States of America." [146]

Monsignor Ryan says that the unbaptized and those born into a non-Catholic sect can never be coerced into the Catholic Church. Existence of their errors is to be permitted. They are also to be allowed to practice their several forms of worship if they do this 'within the family' or in such an inconspicuous manner as to be an occasion neither of scandal nor of perversion to the faithful. And what of propaganda in favor of their several species of untruths: 'This,' says Monsignor Ryan, 'could become a source of injury and a positive menace to the religious welfare of true believers. Against such an evil they have a right of protection by the Catholic state. On the one hand, this propaganda is harmful to the citizens and contrary to public welfare; on the other hand, it is not among the natural rights of propagandists. Rights are

merely means to rational ends. Since no rational end is promoted
by the dissemination of false doctrine, there exists no right to
indulge in the practice." [147]

There are Catholics in the United States who find this
doctrine frightening. They draw away from it as from a drug.
For the doctrine implies that non-Catholics are here on suf-
ferance, pending the population-triumph of Catholics. As Mr.
Vaughan puts it, "The object of intolerance, Monsignor Ryan
has said, is to prevent perversion of the faithful. We may add
that the best of men—and the worst—have defended this notion.
Intolerance is a kind of policeman for authority . . . It makes
for unity, order and monotony . . .In a benign mood it takes
doubters, critics, dissenters, debaters and agitators into protective custody. When irritated it is more at home with whip,
rack, galolws, guillotine and the stake." [148]

Mr. Vaughan quotes from the opinion of Mr. Justice Frankfurter in the well-known Gobitis' case,[149] "a society which is
dedicated to the preservation of these ultimate values . . . may
in self-protection utilize the educational process for indicating
those almost unconscious feelings which bind men together in
a comprehending loyalty"—and then observes:

> "with little transposition these words of Mr. Justice Frankfurter
> could be easily used by Monsignor Ryan. They are words which
> remind one of Lunacharsky's program for Soviet education. 'In-
> struction is not enough' he said. 'Taken by itself it cannot form
> communists. Many men know Marx perfectly and nevertheless
> remain our worst enemies. It is necessary to educate sentiment
> and will in the communist direction.' Is the Nazi or Fascist
> theory any different?" [150]

It is fair to note that contemporary American Catholic
political writing supports Vaughan's refusal to qualify the
foundations on which the American system of civil liberty has
been based. With the appearance of Maritain's *Man and the
State,* this opinion has been given a firm philosophical base.

Hostility to American Catholics was also fanned by their
attitude to the Spanish issue. To all who have the advantage
of retrospection, the Spanish Civil War was not an isolated
event involving the people of one country. Though the official position of the United States expressed itself in a Congressional resolution forbidding munitions to be exported "for
the use of either of the opposing forces in Spain," [151] most
people in the United States seemed to be indifferent to the
war or to its outcome.[152]

But by 1938 a good many people had taken sides. Some of the choosing reflected national origins; some was affected by religion. Our foreign policy has always had to calculate its effect on people of varying national backgrounds.[153] In any event the *Commonweal* ran a statement on Spain on June 24, 1938. Among other things, it said:

"In this country there has been violent partizanship either for the Spanish Nationalists or for the Madrid-Barcelona government. We feel that violent American partisanship on either side with regard to the Spanish question is bad, not only because the facts are obscure, but chiefly because both sides include elements that no American wants imported into this country. Neither has begun to enforce or even propound anything comparable to the bill of rights, which protects an individual from unbearable abuse of authority.

"We are quite frankly wholehearted partisans of the personalist, Christian state. The seeds of both fascism and communism will germinate only, in the soil of injustice, and then must be fertilized by a general public conviction that the leaders of the non-totalitarian states are deficient in moral strength and do not deserve the confidence of their people.

"It is for these reasons that we believe that the wisest, as also the most charitable and perhaps the most difficult course is to maintain that 'positive impartiality' *a sanity of judgment toward both sides in Spain, expressing a preference for specific ideas and actions when they are certainly known, but being an uncritical partisan of neither.*" [154]

This position was paralleled in the same month, in *The New World,* official organ of the archdiocese of Chicago. It suggested that "everyone in the United States keep fingers crossed pending developments." [155]

America, the Jesuit weekly, on July 2, said:
"This review has judicially examined the Loyalists and finds that they have attempted to destroy Spain socially, economically, culturally and spiritually. It is unalterably opposed to them.

In like manner, this review has judicially examined Franco and the Nationalists. It finds that, despite their faults and mistakes, are Christian, truly Spanish, and are eager to build a new social order founded on justice and charity. It asserts, finally, its freedom and its intention to criticize and to condemn, if justice and charity be violated." [157]

For its editorial position, as given here, the *Commonweal* paid heavily. From one-fifth to one-fourth of its subscriptions were almost instantly cancelled—among those cancelling was a fairly large number of priests. There was, it is manifest, some civil war among Catholics in the United States, over this still debated political issue.

In 1913, Father Vincent O'Hara complained that the "real radicalism" . . . is the "radicalism of unregulated greed, with contemptible and picayunish policies, especially toward employees who are unorganized; greed with its cry for dividends and its contempt for humanity." [158]

To that greed and contempt the C. I. O. was hardly one of the less meaningful responses. Yet during its early years, and while some of its major battles had still to be won, Bishop Lucey could discern the old timidity among Catholic leaders. In the presence of "isms" and supposed "revolutionaries" enough of the clergy were refrigerated in inaction, though petulantly critical, for him to declare:

"Too many of us confuse Communism with labor unions organized by industries. Too many of our orators and writers are discussing the modern labor movement without studying it." [159]

A trained economist, he could afford to say that:

"Since comparatively few of our speakers and writers have ever attended a school of social science or taken a course in economics, we can understand why their opinions on the labor movement are not always reliable." [160]

The sit-down strike gave many unnecessary alarm, and the Association of Catholic Trade Unionists were regarded by many Catholic clergymen as bordering on radicalism.[161]

But Bishop Lucey could say, in 1938, of Catholic leaders:

"Our attitude toward labor appears at times to be aloof and detached. As organized labor marches down the highway of its destiny we seem to stand by the roadside offering comment and criticism." [162]

It can hardly be said that that judgment could still stand. But it can hardly be said, either, that there has been enthusiastic and unanimous assent to the Bishop's injunction:

"I think we ought to get into the parade and go down the road with labor. We should be with them, for them and of them. They belong to us and we belong to them." [163]

To a Catholic nothing startling is said when he reads:

"Man is not an isolated individual living in a social vacuum, but a social being destined to live and work out his salvation in association with his fellow beings. He is a member of a community, and he has, in consequence, duties of commutative justice and duties of social justice and duties of charity which emerge from this relationship. On no other foundation can man build a right social order or create that good society which is desired so ardently by the great mass of mankind." [164]

The test is whether the words are applied to life; how they are applied; and whether one can lisp them prettily and still be untouched by such charges—in 1938 or in 1951—as Bishop Lucey made. The chapter in Malcolm Johnson's book *Priests on the Waterfront*[165]—gives testimony to the fact that words are filled with life when men get close to life. The frenzied priest in F. Scott Fitzegrald's *Absolution* makes a remark which too many have taken literally: "But don't get up close," he warned Rudolph, "because if you do you'll only feel the heat and the sweat and the life." [166]

> "It is an unfortunate fact that large numbers of workingmen have become alienated from religion. This is true of Catholics in some of the older countries. In the words of the Supreme Pontiff it has become the great scandal of the modern world. No matter how we explain the defection, the fact remains that Christian truth and principles of conduct have become greatly obscured 'so that we are confronted with a world which in large measure has almost fallen back into paganism.' " [167]

It is easier, as Bishop Lucey pointed out, to be aloof and detached and to criticize than to feel the heat and the sweat of life. Catholic oratory and writing is no less free of purely rhetorical assault on Communism than is other, more secular, oratory. But that is not enough to deal with evil, or with the reason for alienation from religion.

Mr. Ray Wescott, one of the young Catholic New York Transport Workers who helped break C.P. power in that union, gives, in his reported thoughts, the answer to rhetoric and argument—as opposed to action. After the victory:

> "I was thinking how little Harry Sacher, our ex-counsel, who's never been accused of being unfriendly to the commies, would always bait me about communism. When we'd be at a negotiating session, in between talks, he used to get a kick out of asking me, 'Hey, Ray, let's talk. What're you really against communism for? What've you get against it?' I couldn't argue with him. He could tie me up in knots about economics. The only thing I could say to stop him was that I believed in God and communism was atheistic. It was the only thing that would stump him. But I begin to think you don't have to argue." [168]

Arguments must be made, of course. The fact that, in our age of disenchantment men grow impervious to argument, increases the need for it. All that is meant here is that word must pursue deed, and not remain—having spoken—aloof from marriage. The Catholic Church is one of the chief, one of the most vigorous institutions in the United States containing and teaching a set of moral values. Those values are at constant, salutary war with the secularism which "is threatening the religious foundations of our national life and preparing the way for the advent of the omnipotent state." [169]

Man does not live by bread alone, and cannot live without it. That he eat, and preserve his spiritual freedom, is the special difficulty of man in the 20th century. To its reconciliation the Church in the United States has contributed since, especially, the breadth and precision of social thought was made manifest in the program of 1919.

Yet there are Catholic churchmen who go so far as to call the Church secularized. For example, Father Daniel M. Cantwell, of Chicago, writes: "Secularism has fashioned our idea of the Church. We still think and talk of it as a bureau, as an organization. We see its strength in numbers and in Catholics in high places—political and economic—rather than in the Holy Spirit moulding individuals and institutions." [170]

He goes on to say, "Secularism confuses morality with social respectability. In my experience girls came from our schools more convinced about the 'evil' of smoking than about the evil of signing racial restrictive covenants to keep negroes out of our neighborhoods. After all, suppose every girl in our schools smoked would it be comparable to the genuine evil of having one of them leave unconvinced about the sin of racial segregation, of refusing to join a labor union, of paying their domestic help less than a living wage?" [171]

He then writes tersely, "And granted that there is always need for delicately trained consciences, surely there is no longer place for remarks like: "Would Our Blessed Lady smoke?" or "Would she chew gum in public?" It is much more important that we ask "Would she sign a restrictive covenant?" or "Would she refuse to join a labor union?"

Father George Dunne, S.J. of California, speaks, too of the sin of segregation. "The racist mind," he says, "has contrived an almost limitless number of evasive analogies to justify the unjustifiable." [173] He ends a surgically incisive essay by noting that, "It has been sufficiently proved that racial segregation violates strict justice. But the point here being made is that, even if justice were not violated, no one would pretend that charity is not grievously wounded. Racial segregation is certainly a sin against charity, and, in the Christian dispensation, is certainly immoral and not to be tolerated. We can go to hell for sins of charity as easily as for sins against justice, perhaps more easily." [174] In the archdioceses of St. Louis, New Orleans, and Washington, D.C., segregation has been excluded from the Catholic schools. Doctrine has, at long last, made intimate friends with practice. But there are places where, as yet, they do not speak to each other. Like a New England lady, they wait for formal introduction.

It was the opinion of Msgr. Ryan that "in present day conditions the state should be regarded as by far the most important agent and instrument of social justice." [175]

With reference to that judgment, it is merely recorded here that Pope Pius XII has said that "a system of socialized medicine that would prevent the application of 'materialistic and atheist theories' and aid in improving the physical health of nations," was supported by him.[176]

Writing, on the Pontiff's behalf, to Charles Flory, president of the French Catholic *Semaines Sociales* Msgr. Montini was quoted as saying:

> "Just laws for hygiene, prophylaxis or healthy housing, the concern for placing within everybody's reach medical care of high standards and for stamping out social scourges such as tuberculosis and cancer, a legitimate preoccupation for health of young generations and many other iniatives that favor the health of the body and spirit within the framework of healthy, social relations —all this contributes happily to the prosperity of a people and to its internal peace."

Warning against what is called "Malthusian pronouncements" violative of "the rights of a human person or at least their practice of even the right to marriage and procreation," the letter ends, with reference to the meeting in Montpellier, France, of the *Semaines Sociales:*

> "To deepen Catholic doctrine and if need be to define new applications of it, to react against trends of thought widely diffused yet permeated by materialist and atheist theories, to exercise a positive influence on public opinion and on the responsible organisms: such is the task for which the present session at Montpellier must prepare militant Christians with the aim of promoting a true health policy inspired by the social doctrine of the Church." [177]

What effect this will have in the United States, one cannot

say. But it is manifest that the social teachings of the Popes
are talked of and more loudly taught than they were in 1891.
Voices critical of many unjust practices are being heard. They
are now more than voices crying in the wilderness, though
there are wildernesses, even fine places in which if they are
heard, they are not listened to. The number of social illiterates
are still in excess of the allowed quota. But the new wind is
rising, and the rivers flow.

Although the evidence is hardly overwhelming on this
point,[179] it is more than likely that more Catholic priests will
die in the United States of whom it can be rightly said what
so an acute and knowledgeable a man as John L. Lewis said,
of Msgr. Ryan:

> "The hosts of American labor have lost a tried and true friend
> in the death of Msgr. Ryan. Labor today is enjoying greater
> success than ever before in its history, thanks to the wisdom and
> courage of such men as the monsignor who, in the dark days of
> the past decade, never lost an opportunity to raise his voice in
> defense of labor's rights or in furtherance of economic security
> and social justice in America." [180]

FRANCIS DOWNING

DOCUMENTS

Alexis de Tocqueville: Democracy in America[181]

"About fifty years ago Ireland began to pour a Catholic population into the United States; on the other hand, the Catholics of America made proselytes, and at the present moment more than a million of Christians professing the truths of the Church of Rome are to be met with in the Union. The Catholics are faithful to the observances of their religion; they are fervent and zealous in the support and belief of their doctrines. Nevertheless, they constitute the most republican and democratic class of citizens which exists in the United States; and although this fact may surprise the observer at first, the causes by which it is occasioned may easily be discovered upon reflection.

"I think that the Catholic religion has been erroneously been looked upon as the natural enemy of democracy. Among the various sects of Christians, Catholicism seems to me, on the contrary, to be one of those which are most favorable to the equality of conditions. In the Catholic Church, the religious community is composed of only two elements, the priest and the people. The priest alone rises above the rank of his flock, and all below him are equal.

"On doctrinal points the Catholic faith places all human capacities upon the same level; it subjects the wise and the ignorant, the man of genius and the vulgar crowd, to the details of the same creed; it imposes the same observances upon the rich and the needy, it inflicts the same austerities upon the strong and the weak, it listens to no compromise with mortal man, but, reducing all the human race to the same standard, it confounds all the distinctions of society at the foot of the same altar, even as they are confounded in the sight of God. If Catholicism predisposes the faithful to obedience, it certainly does not prepare them for inequality; but the contrary may be said of Prostestantism, which generally tends to make men independent, more than to render them equal. . . ."

"But no sooner is the priesthood entirely separated from the government, as in the case of the United States, than it is found that no class of men are more naturally disposed than the Catholics to transfuse the doctrine of equality of conditions into the political world. If, then, the Catholic citizens of the United States are not forcibly led by the nature of their tenets to adopt democratic and republican principles, at least they are not necessarily opposed to them; and their social position, as well as their limited number, obliges them to adopt these opinions. Most of the Catholics are poor, and they have no chance of taking part in the government unless it be open to all the citizens. They constitute a minority, and all rights must be respected in order to insure to them the free exercise of their own privileges. These two causes induce them, unconsciously, to adopt political doctrines which they would perhaps support with less zeal if they were rich and preponderant.

"The Catholic clergy of the United States has never attempted to oppose this political tendency, but it seeks rather to justify its results. The priests in America have divided the intellectual world into two parts: in the one they place the doctrines of revealed religion, which command their assent; in the other they leave those truths which they believe to have been freely left open to the researches of political inquiry. Thus the Catholics of the United States are at the same time the most faithful believers and the most zealous citizens.

"It may be asserted that in the United States no religious doctrine displays the slightest hostility to democratic and republican institutions. The clergy of all the different sects hold the same language, their opinions are consonant to the laws, and the human intellect flows onward in one sole current. . . . "

Archbishop John Ireland: No Barrier against Color[182]

"We hold today an anniversary, most glorious in its memories, which it behoves the whole people of America to commemorate and to honor. On the first day of January, in the year of grace, 1863, by proclamation of President Abraham Lincoln, the chains of slavery, in the eye of the law of the land, fell from the limbs of three million or more men, brothers of citizens of America, and citizens of America as their brothers, and their legal emancipation logically and swiftly led to the total and practical blotting out of slavery on American soil.

"Slavery was horrid. We cannot recall it without sorrow and shame. Well may the head of the Catholic Church, Leo XIII, say in a recent letter than 'slavery is opposed to religion and to the dignity of man. . .'

"In the concrete, as practised and defended, slavery was the ownership of the human being, whose manhood was ignored, who was made to be the chattel. And how come it, I could ask in the name of justice, that the unborn child, whose father ever was a freeman, was shorn without his own fault or act, of the right to the free use of the powers of soul and body? Certain stages of civilization, it has been said, rendered slavery a social necessity. Certain stages of barbarism they should be called, and Americans should not have lowered themselves to barbarism.

"Slavery is inhuman. It is unchristian. 'There was scarcely anything,' writes Leo XIII, 'dearer to the Church from the beginning than to see slavery which oppressed so many human beings by its miserable yoke, removed and entirely destroyed.'

"The Christian religion emphasized the brotherhood of man, the value of the soul, charity to the weak and the oppressed. Slavery was the denial of Christian principles and Christian virtues. It was the denial of the freedom of the Gospel, which found access to the soul of the slave, only as the master permitted or ordained. Let us on this emancipation day thank God for the blessings of Christianity. The spirit of Christian freedom is today poured out upon the nations of the earth. The mighty social wave which is now lifting upward upon its crest the masses of the people of all lands, is but another manifestation of the same heavenly spirit.

"Let us do our full duty. There is work for us. I have said that slavery has been abolished in America; the trail of the serpent, however, still marks the ground. We do not accord to our black brothers all the rights and privilegs of freedom and of a common humanity. They are the victims of an unreasoning and unjustifiable ostracism. They may live, provided they live away from us, as a separate and inferior race, with whom close contact is pollution. It looks as if we had grudgingly granted them emancipation, as if we fain still would be the masters, and hold them in servitude.

"What do I claim for the black man? That which I claim for the white man, neither more nor less. I would blot out the color line. White men have their estrangements. They separate on lines of wealth, or intelligence, of culture, of ancestry . . . But let there be no barrier against mere color.

"Why a barrier of this kind? Where can we find a reason for it? Not in color. Color is the merest accident in man, the result of climatic changes. The colors of the human skin are of many different kinds, the shadings of the so-called white race are not easily numbered. Why visit with the ire of our exclusive pride the black, even into its lightest shadings, scarcely discernible to the eye from the olive dark, a shading most admired in the white family of nations?

"Not in race. Men are all of the same race, sprung from the one father and the one mother. Ethnology and Holy Writ give the same testimony. The subdivisions of race are but the accidental deviations from the parent stock, which revert to the same model as easily with the length of years as they diverted from it. The notion that God by special interposition marked off the subdivisions of the human family, and set upon each one an indelible seal of permanence is the dream of ignorance or bigotry.

"The objection is made that Negroes are of inferior intellectual part to the whites. I reply, that there are white men inferior on those lines to other white men, and still no wall of separation is built up by the latter against the former. Treat Negroes who are intellectually inferior to us, as we treat inferior whites, and I shall not complain. And as to a radical inferiority in the Negro as compared to his white brother, we can afford to deny it, in the presence of his achievements in the short years which have elapsed since restitution was made to him of his freedom, and any inferiority which exists, we may attribute to his unfortunate condition of long centuries whether in America, or his native Africa.

"We are the victims of foolish prejudice, and the sooner we free ourselves from it, the sooner shall we grow to true manhood. Is it to our honor that we persecute men because of the social conditions of their fathers? It is not so long ago since the proudest peoples of Europe were immersed in barbarism. It is not to our honor that we punish men for the satisfaction of our own pride.

Why, the fact that the Negro was once our slave should compel us to treat him with liberality extraordinary, to compensate him if possible for wrong done, and obliterate in mutual forebearance and favor the sad memories of years gone by.

"The Negro problem is upon us, and there is no solution for it, peaceful and permanent, than to grant to our fellow citizens practical and effective equality with white citizens. It is not possible to keep up a wall of separation between whites and blacks, and the attempt to do this is a declaration of continuous war. Simple common sense dictates the solution. The Negroes are among us to the number of eight millions; they will here remain: we must accept the situation and abide by the consequences, whatever pride or taste may dictate.

"I would break down all barriers. Let the Negro be our equal before the law. There are States where the violation in the Negro of the most sacred personal right secured impunity before the law. In many states the law forbids marriage between white and black— in this manner fomenting immorality and putting injury no less upon the white whom it pretends to elevate as upon the black for whose degredation it has no care.

"Let the Negro be our equal in the enjoyment of all the political rights of the citizen. The Constitution grants him those rights: let us be loyal to the Constitution. If the education of the Negro does not fit him to be a voter, and an office holder, let us for his sake and our own, hurry to enlighten him.

"I would open to the Negro all industrial and professional avenues—the test for his advance being his ability, but never his color. I would in all public gatherings, and in all public resorts, in halls and hotels, treat the back man as I treat the white. I might shun the vulgar man, whatever his color, but the gentleman, whatever his color, I would not dare push away from me.

"Shall the homes of the whites be opened to the blacks, shall all meet in the parlor in perfect social equality? My answer is, that one's home is one's castle, the privileged place where each one follows his own likes and his own tastes, and no one, white or black, rich or poor, can pass the door without an invitation from the owner, and no one can pass censure upon the owner's act.

"I claim the right I grant to others—and my door is open to men of all colors, and no one should blame me. Social equality is a matter of taste; the granting of it largely depends on our elevation above the prejudice, and the identification of minds and hearts with the precepts and the counsels of the Gospel."

Bishops' Program of Social Reconstruction, 12 February 1919.

Housing for Working Classes[183]

"Housing projects for war workers which have been completed, or almost completed by the government of the United States, have cost some forty million dollars, and are found in eleven cities.

While the Federal Government cannot continue this work in time of peace, the example and precedent it has set, and the knowledge that it has developed, should not be forthwith neglected and lost. The great cities in which congestion and other forms of bad housing are disgracefully apparent ought to take up and continue the work, at least to such an extent as will remove the worst features of a social condition that is a menace at once to industrial efficiency, civic health, good morals and religion."

Social Insurance.[184]

"Until this level of legal minimum wages is reached the worker stands in need of the device of insurance. The State should make comprehensive provision for insurance against illness, invalidity, unemployment, and old age. So far as possible the insurance fund should be raised by a levy on industry, as is now done in the case of accident compensation. The industry in which a man is employed should provide him with all that is necessary to meet all the needs of his entire life. Therefore, any contribution to the insurance fund from the general revenues of the State should only be slight and temporary. For the same reason no contribution should be exacted from any worker who is not getting a higher wage than is required to meet the present needs of himself and family. Those who are below that level can make such a contribution only at the expense of their present welfare. Finally, the administration of the insurance laws should be such as to interfere as little as possible with the individual freedom of the worker and his family. Any insurance scheme, or any administrative method, that tends to separate the workers into a distinct and dependent class, that offends against their domestic privacy and independence, or that threatens individual self-reliance or self-respect, should not be tolerated. The ideal to be kept in mind is a condition in which all the workers would themselves have the income and responsibility of providing for all the needs and contingencies of life, both present and future. Hence all the forms of State insurance should be regarded as merely a lesser evil, and should be so organized and administered as to hasten the coming of the normal condition.

"The life insurance offered to soldiers and sailors during the war should be continued, so far as the enlisted men are concerned. It is very doubtful whether the time has yet arrived when public opinion would sanction the extension of general life insurance by the Government to all classes of the community.

"The establishment and maintenance of municipal health inspection in all schools, public and private, is now pretty generally recognized as of great importance and benefit. Municipal clinics where the poorer classes could obtain the advantage of medical treatment by specialists at a reasonable cost would likewise seem to have become a necessity. A vast amount of unnecessary sickness and suffering exists among the poor and the lower middle classes because they cannot afford the advantages of any other treatment except that provided by the general practitioner. Every effort should be made to supply wage-earners and their families with specialized medical care through development of group medicine. Free medical care should be given only to those who cannot pay."

Labor Participation in Industrial Management.[185]

"The right of labor to organize and to deal with employers through representatives has been asserted above in connection with the discussion of the War Labor Board. It is hoped that this right will never again be called in question by any considerable number of employers. In addition to this, labor ought gradually to receive greater representation in what the English group of Quaker employers have called the 'industrial' part of business management— 'the control of processes and machinery; nature of product; engagement and dismissal of employees; hours of work, rates of pay, bonuses, etc.; welfare work; shop discipline; relations with trade unions.' The establishment of shop committees, working wherever possible with the trade union, is the method suggested by this group of employers for giving the employees the proper share of industrial management. There can be no doubt that a frank adoption of these means and ends by employers would not only promote the welfare of the workers, but vastly improve the relations between them and their employees, and increase the efficiency and productiveness of each establishment."

Main Defects of Present System[186]

"Nevertheless, the present system (industrial capitalism) stands in grievous need of considerable modifications and improvement. Its main defects are three: enormous inefficiency and waste in the production and distribution of commodities; insufficient incomes for the great majority of wage-earners, and unnecessarily large incomes for a small minority of privileged capitalists, Inefficiency in the production and distribution of goods would be in great measure abolished by the reforms that have been outlined in the foregoing pages. Production would be greatly increased by universal living wages, by adequate industrial education, and by harmonious relations between labor and capital on the basis of adequate participation by the former in all the industrial aspects of business management. The wastes of commodity distribution could be practically all eliminated by co-operative mercantile establishments, and co-operative selling and marketing associations."

Co-operation and Co-partnership.[187]

"Nevertheless, the full possibilities of increased production will not be realized so long as the majority of the workers remain mere wage-earners. The majority must somehow become owners, at least in part, of the instruments of production. They can be enabled to reach this stage gradually through co-operative productive societies and co-partnership arrangements. In the former, the workers own and manage the industries themelves; in the latter they own a substantial part of the corporate stock and exercise a reasonable share in the management. However slow the attainments of these ends, *they will have to be reached before we can have a thoroughly efficient system of production,* or an industrial and social order that will be secure from the danger of Revolution. *It is to be noted that this particular modification of the existing order, though far-reaching and involving to a great extent the abolition of the wage system,* would not mean the abolition of private ownership. The instruments of production would still be owned by individuals, not by the State."

Abolition and Control of Monopolies[188]

"For the third evil mentioned above, excessive gains by a small minority of privileged capitalists, the main remedies are the prevention of monopolistic control of commodities, adequate governmental regulation of such public service monopolies as will remain under private operation, and heavy taxation on incomes, excess profits and inheritances. The precise methods by which genuine competition may be restored and maintained among businesses that are naturally competitive, cannot be discussed here; but the principle is clear that human beings cannot be entrusted with the immense opportunities for oppression and extortion that go with the possession of monopoly power. That the owners of public service monopolies should be restricted by law to a fair or average return on their actual investment, has long been a recognized principle of the courts, the legislatures, and public opinion. It is a principle that should be applied to competitive enterprises likewise, with the qualification that something more than the average rate of return should be allowed to men who exhibit exceptional efficiency. However, good public policy, as well as equity, demands that these exceptional business men share the fruits of their efficiency with the consumer in the form of lower prices. The man who utilizes his ability to produce cheaper than his competitors for the purpose of exacting from the public as high a price for his product as is necessary for the least efficient business man, is a menace rather than a benefit to industry and society.

"Our immense war debt constitutes a particular reason why incomes and excess profits should continue to be heavily taxed. In this way two important ends will be attained: the poor will be relieved of injurious tax burdens, and the small class of specially privileged capitalists will be compelled to return a part of their unearned gains to society."

Pope Pius XII: Progress and Problems of the American Church[189]

"We confess that we feel a special paternal affection, which is certainly inspired of Heaven, for the Negro people dwelling among you; for in the field of religion and education, We know that they need special care and comfort and are very deserving of it. We therefore invoke an abundance of heavenly blessing and We pray fruitful success for those whose generous zeal is devoted to their welfare."

The Christian in Action. Statement of the Bishops of the U.S. 1948
Religion and Citizenship.[190]

"The inroads of secularism in civil life are a challenge to the Christian citizen—and indeed to every citizen with definite religious convictions. The essential connection between religion and good citizenship is deep in our American tradition. Those who took the lead in establishing our independence and framing our Constitution were firm and explicit in the conviction that religion and morality are the strong supports of well-being, that national morality can not long prevail in absence of religious principle, and that impartial encouragement of religious influence on its citizens is a proper and practical function of good government. This American tradition clearly envisioned the school as the meeting place of these helpful interacting influences. The third article of the Northwest Ordinance passed by Congress in 1787, re-enacted in 1790, and included in the Constitutions of many States enjoins: 'Religion, morality and knowledge being necessary to good citizenship and the happiness of mankind, schools and the means of education shall forever be encouraged.' This is our authentic American tradition on the philosophy of education for citizenship.

"In the field of law our history reveals the same fundamental connection between religion and citizenship. It is through law that government exercises control over its citizens for the common good and establishes a balance between their rights and duties. The American concepts of government and law started with the recognition that man's inalienable rights—which it is the function of government to protect—derive from God, his Creator. It thus bases human law, which deals with man's rights and their correlative duties in society, on foundations that are definitely religious, on principles that emerge from the definite view of man as a creature of God. This view of man anchors human law to the natural law, which is the moral law of God made clear to us through the judgment of human reason and the dictates of conscience. The natural law, as an outstanding modern legal commentator has written, 'is binding over all the globe, in all countries and in all times; no human laws are of any validity if contrary to this.' Thus human law is essentially an ordinance of reason, not merely a dictate of will on the part of the State. In our authentic American tradition this is the accepted philosophy of law."

Jacques Maritain: Church and State[191]

"I would therefore say, summing up quite briefly what would require a long historical analysis; there was a *sacral age*, the age of medieval Christendom, mainly characterized on the one hand by the fact that the unity of faith was a prerequisite for political unity, and that the basic frame of reference was the unity of that social body, religio-political in nature, which was the *respublica Christiana*, on the other hand by the dominant dynamic idea ot strength or fortitude at the service of justice. In that sacral era, the principles that we are considering were therefore applied principally in terms of the social power of the Church . . . ;and as a consequence the political power of the Holy Empire and the kings was an instrument for the spiritual aims of the Church. In this way the Church was to assert the freedom of the spirit in the face of the ruthlessness of the temporal power, and to impose on it such restraints as the truce of God. Let us not forget, moreover, that in the Middle Ages not only the differentiation of the body politic as such was not completely achieved, but the Church had, as a matter of fact, to make up for a number of deficiencies in the civil order, and to take upon herself, because she was shaping civilization in her own womb, many functions and responsibilities pertaining of themselves to political society. In post-medieval centuries—a period which can be called the baroque age—sacral civilization disintergrated, while in the political order the notion and reality of the State was gradually arising, yet the tenets of sacral civilization were more or less preserved—in forms which were hardening, since they became more legal than vital—so that the notion of State-religion, for instance, came to the fore.

"The modern age is not a sacral, but a secular age. The order of terrestial civilization and of temporal society has gained complete differentiation and full autonomy, which is something normal in itself required by the Gospel's very distinction between God's and Caesar's domains. But that normal process was accompanied—and spoiled—by a most aggressive and stupid process of insulation from, and final rejection of, God and the Gospel in the sphere of social and political life. The fruit of this we can contemplate today in the theocratic atheism of the Communist State.

"Well, those Christians who are turned toward the future and who hope—be it a long range hope—for a new Christendom, a new heavenly inspired civilization, know that 'the world has done with neutrality. Willingly or unwillingly, States will be obliged to make a choice for or against the Gospel. They will be shaped either by the totalitarian spirit or by the Christian spirit.' They know that a new Christianly inspired civilization, if and when it evolves in history, will by no means be a return to the Middle Ages, but a typically different attempt to make the leaven of the Gospel quicken the depths of temporal existence. They feel that such a new age will aim at rehabilitating man in God and through

God, not apart from God, and will be an age of sanctification of
secular life. But along what lines can this be imagined? This means
that the Christians of whom I am speaking have to establish and
develop a sound philosophy of modern history, as well as to
separate from the genuine growth of time, from the genuine
progress of human consciousness and civilization, the deadly errors
which have preyed upon them, and the tares which are also growing
among the wheat and which foster the wickedness of the time. In
order to conceive our own concrete historical image of what is to
be hoped for in our time, we have to determine and take into
account, as an existential frame of reference, the basic typical
features which characterize the structure of our age, in other
words the historical climate or the historical constellation by which
the existence and activity of the human community is conditioned
today.

"As I have just put it, the historical climate of modern civilization, in contradistinction to medieval civilization, is characterized
by the fact that it is a 'lay' or 'secular,' not a 'sacral' society. On
the one hand the dominant dynamic idea is not the idea of strength
or fortitude in the service of justice, but rather of the conquest
of freedom and the realization of human dignity. On the other
hand the root requirement for a sound mutual cooperation between
Church and the body politic is not the unity of a religio-political
body, as the *respublica Christiana* of the Middle Ages was, but
the very unity of the human person, simultaneously a member of
the body politic and the Church, if he freely adheres to her. The
unity of religion is not a prerequisite for political unity, and men
subscribing to diverse religious or non-religious creeds have to share
in and work for the same political and temporal common good.
Whereas 'mediaeval man,' as Father Courtney Murray puts it,
entered the State (what state there was) to become a 'citizen,'
through the Church and his membership in the Church, *modern
man is a citizen with full civic rights whether he is a member of
the Church or not."* (Italics supplied).

"Hence many consequences derive. First, the political power is
autonomous and independent within its own sphere. Second, the
equality of all members of the body politic has been recognized
as a basic tenet. Third, the importance of the inner forces at work
in the human person, in contradistinction to the external forces
of coercion; the freedom of individual conscience in regard to the
State; the axiom—always taught by the Catholic Church, but disregarded as a rule by the Princes and Kings of old—that faith
cannot be imposed by constraint—all these assertions have become,
more explicitly than before, crucial assets to civilization, and are
to be especially emphasized if we are to escape the worst dangers
of perversion of the social body and of state totalitarianism. Fourth,
a reasoned-out awareness has developed, at least in those parts of
the civilized world where love of freedom is still cherished . . .
with regard to the fact that nothing more imperils both the

common good of the earthly city and the supra-temporal interests of truth in human minds than a weakening and breaking down of the internal springs of conscience. Common consciousness has also become aware of the fact that *freedom of inquiry, even at the risk of error, is the normal condition for men to get access to the truth,* so that freedom to search for God in their own way, for those who have been brought up in ignorance or semi-ignorance of Him, is the normal condition in which to listen to the message of the Gospel and the teachings of the Church, when grace will illumine their hearts." (Italics supplied).

"On the other hand, we see that statements like Cardinal Manning's famous reply to Gladstone are unquestionably true. 'If Catholics were in power in England tomorrow,' Cardinal Manning wrote, 'not a penal law would be proposed, not a shadow of constraint put upon the faith of any man. We would that all men fully believed the truth; but a forced faith is a hypocrisy hateful to God and man . . . If the Catholics were tomorrow the 'Imperial race' in these kingdoms they would not use political power to molest the divided and hereditary religious state of the people. We would not shut one of their Churches, or Colleges, or Schools. They would have the same liberties we enjoy as a minority.' *Such a statement is valid, not only for England, but for every freedom loving country. It does not refer to the requirements of an hypothesis reluctantly accepted, but to the requirements of the very principles soundly applied in the existential framework of the modern historical climate. Even if one single citizen dissented from the religious faith of all the people, his right to dissent could be by no means be infringed upon by the State in a Christianly inspired modern democratic society.* Even if, by the grace of God, religious unity were to return, no return to the sacral regime in which the civil power was the instrument of the secular arm of the spiritual power could be conceivable in a Christianly inspired democratic society. The Catholics who are ready to give their lives for freedom do not cling to these assertions as a matter of expediency, but as a matter of moral obligation or of justice . . . (Italics supplied).

NOTES

[1] H. S. Commanger, *Documents of American History,* N. Y., 1945, p. 31.

[2] Alexis de Tocqueville, *Democracy in America,* ed. by Henry Steele Commanger, Oxford, 1927, p. 203.

[3] *Ibid,* p. 204.

[4] I am using the world "State" here in the European sense. For what is meant by the First Amendment is that no "national religion" may be established by the Federal Government.

[5] Cited in Saul K. Padover, ed, *Thomas Jefferson on Democracy, Mentor* Books, 1949, p. 31.

[6] Of the others, five were from England, five were from England, five from the Germanies, and three from other European countries. Scattered individuals or groups of Catholic origin existed in the other colonies, but without eccles-

iastical organization, they were absorbed into the dominant religions of their environment.

7 In 1807, there were 70,000 Catholics, with 70 priests and 80 Churches in the country; by 1830, there were 14,000 with 16 churches in New England alone. In 1816, there was no Catholic organization in Ohio; in 1830, there were 24 priests, 22 churches, a newspaper, a college and a seminary. Cf, Ray Allen Billington, *The Protestant Crusade,* N. Y., Macmillan, 1938, p. 37.

8 *Ibid,* Chapter III.

9 *The Lonely Crowd,* Yale, 1950, pp. 247-248: "The American Catholic Church possesses immense veto-group power because it combines a certain amount of centralized command—and a public picture of a still greater amount —with a highly decentralized priesthood and a membership organization of wide-ranging ethnic, social and political loyalties; this structure permits great flexibility in bargaining."

10 John Francis Maguire, *The Irish in America,* N. Y., Sadlier, 1868, p. 461.

11 Dulles, Foster, Rhea, *Labor in America* (New York 1949, P. 191.) Thomas G. Crowell Co.

12 *The Age of Jackson,* Boston, 1945, P. 350. Little Brown and Co. Boston.

13 Cited in Browne, Henry J. *The Catholic Church and the Knights of Labor* Washington, 1949, P. 27. Catholic University of America Press.

14 Cf. Browne, Chap. I

15 Paxton Hibben, *Henry Ward Beecher,* New York, 1942, P. 52. Heritage Press. N. Y.

16 Cited ibid, P. 51.

17 Ibid; P. 64.

18 Cf. Browne, op. cit. P. 53.

19 Ware, Norman J. *The Labor Movement in the United States,* New York, 1929, P. 49. Appleton-Century-Crofts, Inc.

20 Henry Steele Commager, *Documents of American History* (N.Y. 1948) II, P. 7. Appleton-Century-Crofts, Inc.

21 Morison & Commager, *The Growth of the American Republic,* New York, 1950, cited, vol. II P. 152. Oxford University Press.

22 Ibid; vol. II, P. 134.

23 Browne, ibid; cited at P. 5.

24 David, Henry, *The History of the Haymarket Affair,* New York, 1936. cited at P. 12. In this year Catholics were advised by the Synod of Cincinnatti in the Provincial Council of Milwaukee, to abandon unions because of their alleged violent, socialistic character. Cf. Aaron Abel, Rev. of Politics, Oct. 1945, P. 468. Rinehart and Co., Inc.

25 David, ibid; at P. 15

26 David, ibid; at P. 14.

27 Browne, ibid; P. 368-69.

28 Ibid; P. 372.

29 Studies, No. XXX, June, 1946, P. 156, italics ours.

30 The Commonweal, May 11, 1951, P. 115.

31 Morrison and Commager, ibid; Vol. II, P. 145.

32 Ibid; PP. 144, 45.

33 Ibid, P. 147.

34 *Catholicizing the United States,* Ecclesiastical Rev. March 1906, P. 35.

35 Cited by Marc Karson, The *Catholic Church and Unionism,* Industrial and Labor Relations Rev. July, 1951. P. 529. Cornell University, Ithaca, N. Y.

36 *What means This Strike,* in *Capital and Labor,* N. Y. Public Library P. 19.

[37] Henry J. Browne, *Peter E. Dietz, Pioneer Planner of Catholic Social-Action,* The Catholic Historical Rev. Jan. 1948, P. 448. Washington, D. C.

[38] Browne, ibid; P. 448.

[39] Letter to Dietz, June 1, 1911, cited by Browne, ibid; P. 450.

[40] Purcell, ibid; P. 158.

[41] Cf. Browne, op. cit; and note 2—P. 448.

[42] Cited in Karson, op. cit. P. 534.

[43] Browne, op. cit. P. 454.

[44] Karson, ibid; P. 533. The words are those of Dietz.

[45] Cf. Karson, ibid; P. 543. The names, and the affiliations of these leaders are listed.

[46] Karson; quoted, ibid; P. 535.

[47] Karson, ibid; P. 531.

[48] Cited in Karson, ibid; at p. 531.

[49] Ibid; P. 531.

[50] Rev. Charles Bruehl, *The Conditions of Labor,* in *Addresses at Patriotic and Civic Occasions by Catholic Orators,* New York 1915, P. 51, italics supplied.

[51] Bruehl, op. cit. P. 79.

[52] Bruehl, ibid; PP. 65-79, italics supplied. The reader does not need to be reminded that from the time of the Pullman strike until the passage of the Clayton Act (1914) the use of the injunction to break strikes was a favored and successful device. The Supreme Court in the Duplex Printing Press case emasculated the provisions of the Clayton Act regarding injunctions (1921) Cf. Commager, *Documents of American History.* No. 403, 445. Appleton-Century-Crofts, Inc.

[53] Aaron I. Abell, *the Reception of Leo XIII's Labor Encyclical in America, 1891-1919,* The Review of Politics, VIII, Oct. 1945, P. 493. Notre Dame, Ind.

[54] Dietz to John Mitchell, Aug. 30, 1911, cited in Karson, ibid; P. 537.

[55] Karson, ibid; cited P. 536.

[56] Karson, ibid; P. 533.

[57] Karson, ibid; P. 533.

[58] Dietz to Mitchell, Dec. 30, 1911, quoted in Browne ibid; P. 452.

[59] Quoted by Browne, ibid; P. 453.

[60] Abell, ibid; P. 453.

[61] Ibid; P. 454.

[62] Abell, ibid; P. 485.

[63] Commager, Documents (1948) 2, P. 232.

[64] Browne, ibid; 454.

[65] Browne, ibid; P. 455.

[66] Cf. Sister Joan De Lourdes Leonard, *Catholic Attitude toward American Labor—1884—1919.* Columbia Univ. 1946, P. 62-74.

[67] Ryan, quoted in Leonard, ibid; P. 56.

[68] Ryan, *Social Doctrine in Action,* New York, 1941, P. 21. Harper & Bros.

[69] Leonard, ibid; P. 32.

[70] Cf. Ware, *Labor in Modern Industrial Society,* or Dulles, *Labor in America,* or Yellen, *American Labor Struggles.*

[71] Dulles; op. cit. P. 216, (N. Y. 1949).

[72] Ryan, ibid; P. 27.

[73] Ryan ibid; P. 27.

[74] Leonard, ibid; P. 40.

[75] Abell, *Rev. of Politics,* Oct. 1945, P. 482.

[76] Abell, ibid; P. 480. "Even the better sort seemed to have little idea of

anything that reaches beyond parish charity." Archbishop Ireland, cf. Leonard. ibid; P. 86.

77 Leonard; ibid; P. 50.

78 Abell, ibid; P. 482.

79 Abell, ibid; P. 482.

80 Leonard, ibid; P. 95.

81 Leonard, ibid; P. 95.

82 Ryan, *Social Doctrine,* etc. P. 124.

83 Ryan, ibid; P. 43, He notes the use of the term 8 times in the Bishop's "*The Church and Social Order,*" of 1940.

84 Ryan, ibid; P. 31-32. It was this last sentence which seems to have elicited Ireland's surprise. Altgeld had pardoned the three imprisoned men condemned on no evidence—for their alleged part in the Haymarket bombing. cf. David, op. cit. For this, "Altgeld was assailed throughout the country for what since has been universally recognized as simple justice." Dulles, op. cit. P. 125.

85 Ryan, ibid; P. 31.

86 Cronin, *Catholic Social Principles,* Milwaukee, 1950. P. 425. Bruce Publishing Company.

87 Cronin, ibid; "Such a position does not seem consonant with the directions of the popes or the needs of modern times." P. 425.

88 Cronin, ibid; P. 425. As examples, he gives the A.C.T.U. labor schools, etc.

89 Karson, op. cit. P. 531. editorial written in Jan. 1913. Given the brutal episode conducted by the coal operators against the Western Federation of Miners at the notorious Cripple Creek, the I.W.A. was formed in Chicago in 1905. One of the delegates was Father T. J. Hagerty, a labor editor, and early friend of industrial unionism. Cf. Dulles P. 210-11.

90 Karson, ibid; P. 531-32. Italics supplied. Most of this is merely amusing, especially the references to the Knights, and the American Railway Union, which had been opposed and feared by the Brotherhood of Locomotive Firemen and other as containing the principle of industrial unionism. The origin of the Socialism of its erstwhile leader, Eugene V. Debs, is instructive cf. Dulles, ibid; P. 172, ff.

91 Karson, ibid; P. 532, cf. Murray Lincoln's remark "Strictly speaking, a Socialist cooperative is as impossible as a Catholic bicycle or a Republican grapefruit . . . In a country where a majority of the people is Socialist, the cooperatives obviously will reflect Socialist views to some extent, and where, as in the United States, the majority is conservative coops will be conservative. Nevertheless a coop is not a chameleon; by its very nature it makes certain demands on its environment . . . This implies an environment friendly, in some degree, to democracy" cf. Dimock, *Business and Government* (N. Y. 1949) P. 775. Henry Holt & Co.

92 Morrison and Commager, ibid; II P. 204.

93 Ryan, ibid; P. 6.

94 For an attempt by a Republican, Catholic politician to use the Vatican unfairly in an attempt to discredit Ryan politically among Catholics, see Ryan, ibid; P. 116. He calls it "probably the most extreme instance of unfriendly and unfair criticism of my writings." P. 115.

95 Leonard, P. 55.

96 Ibid; P. 56-62.

97 Karson, ibid; P. 540.

98 Ibid, Pfl 538, But see, especially, Leonard ibid P. 91. ff.

99 The Verein operated a day nursery in St. Louis, for the children of the poor and of working families since 1915 cf. Leonard op. cit. P. 91 n.

[100] Karson, ibid; P. 538.

[101] Cf. Leonard, ibid; P. 45, P. 95, passim.

[102] Cf. Abell, *Rev. of Politics,* Oct. 1945, P. 487.

[103] Abell, op. cit. P. 489.

[104] Karson, op. cit. P. 539-40. For a reaction of socialists to the work of Catholics cf. Browne, op. cit. P. 454, also Karson, ibid; P. 535.

[105] Abell, op. cit. P. 475.

[106] Cf. Dulles, op. cit. P. 186.

[107] Elsie Gluck, *John Mitchell,* (N. Y. 1929) P. 73.

[108] McAlister Coleman, *Pioneers of Freedom* (S. Y. 1929) P. 180. cf. Gluck, ibid.

[109] Quoted by Arthur E. Morgan, *Edward Bellamy,* (N. Y. 1944) P. XII. Columbia University Press.

[110] Leo L. Ward, ed. *The Uses of Knowledge,* Croft's Classics, P. 9. Columbia University Press.

[111] Leonard, op. cit. P. 50.

[112] Leonard, ibid, P. 76.

[113] Leonard, ibid; P. 105.

[114] Selig Perlman, *A Theory of the Labor Movement,* (N. Y. 1928) P. 169. Macmillan Company Permission to quote granted.

[115] Karson, op. cit. cited P. 542.

[116]. A Protestant minister once said to Father Ryan: "You have a very great advantage over men in my position. We have to guard against offending the members of many different denominations, while you can hang your 'radical' utterances on a Papal Encyclical." Purcell, op. cit. P. 158.

[117] Cf. Francis Downing, *Labor: the Counterrevolution,* The Commonweal, May 18, 1951. The quotation from Tannenbaum, Frank, *A Philosophy of the Labor Movement,* (N. Y. 1950) appears at P. 138. Alfred A. Knopf, Inc.

[118] Cf. Downing, ibid; P. 138.

[119] Morison and Commager, op. cit. II P. 169. This is, at least, arguable. It presumes that strikes per se are "violent". Moreover, it forgets that without strikes, often,—e.g. the General Motor's strike in 1935—"labor" might not exist.

[120] Morison and Commager, ibid; P. 169. cf. the opening chapters of Frances Perkins' *"The Roosevelt I Knew."* The Viking Press, N. Y.

[121] Abell, op. cit. P. 468. They were, he said, not only in "opposition to capital, but to government itself." Fortunately many Catholics were encouraged to belong to them, in disagreement, obviously, with Bayley's idea of the "spirit of religion." This was the year of the Tompkins Square riot in New York. The N. Y. Times wrote of them: "The persons arrested yesterday seem all to have been foreigners—cheifly Germans or Irishmen. Communism is not a weed of native growth." Dulles, op. cit. P. 116.

[122] Morison and Commager, op. cit. II 171.

[123] Cf. Walter F. Dodd, *Cases on Constitutional Law,* (St. Paul, 1950) P. 709 ff. The West Publishing Co.

[124] When *Quadrigesimo Anno* was published, the rector of Catholic University declared it a "Vindication of John Ryan." Ryan, op. cit. P. 242.

[125] *Bishops' Program of Social Reconstruction,* foreword. National Catholic Welfare Conference. Wash. D. C. 1939, 20th Anniversary Edition, P. 2.

[126] Karson, op. cit. P. 542.

[127] Bishops' Program, P. 4.

[128] Bishops' Program P. 5. To the National Conference of Catholic Charities in 1938, Robert Jackson said: "What suffering might have been spared to me, had the voice of Bishops been heeded by those who came to power in 1920,

instead of having to wait for the disaster-born administration of 1933," Ryan, op. cit. P. 151.

129 Cf. Commager, Documents, No. 438, 439, 440, for "fair return" ideas of that time. Also Dodd, ibid; P. 681 ff.

130 Cf. Chamberlain, Neil, W. *The Union Challenge to Management Control*. (N. Y. 1948) This is an original contribution to labor relations. Harper & Bros.

131 Cf. David E. Lilienthal *T. V. A. Democracy on the March*, (Pocket Books, N. Y. 1944).

132 No reference is made to this by Cardinal O'Connell in his *Recollections of Seventy years*, (Boston, 1934). The book is seldom visited by the realities of the social struggle. Houghton Mifflin Co.

133 For a quiet and later explanation of it, cf. Bishop Robert E. Lucey, *Should We Hurt the Church?* The Commonweal.

134 Commager, Documents, P. 149.

135 Cf. Dodd, ibid; P. 399-410.

136 Lucey, op. cit. P. 490.

137 Cf. G. E. R. Gedye, *Betrayal in Central Europe*.

138 Cf. Commager, Documents, P. 377-78, for the case of Pierce vs. Society of The Sisters, 1925. The court held that Oregon's Compulsory Education Act (1922) "unreasonably interferes with the liberty of parents and guardians to direct the upbringing and education of children under their control." Msgr. Ryan relied on the courts for similar rulings if the Child Labor Amendment were used to move into education.

139 Ryan, The Commonweal, May 25, 1934, P. 105. This is from a letter to Commonweal. It contains acid judgments and is worth reading.

140 Ryan, *Social Doctrine* etc. P. 225.

141 Archibishop Curley and Msgr. Ryan argued their different sides before the same Catholic audience on the same day. Ryan, ibid; P. 233.

142 Albert E. Chandler, *The Clash of Political Ideals*, (New York, 1949, P. 275). Appleton-Century-Crofts, Inc.

143 Albert E. Chandler, ibid; P. 276 Smith's reply to Marshall appeared in the *Atlantic Monthly* for May, 1927. From Progressive Democracy: *Addresses and State Papers of Alfred E. Smith*, with an Introdduction by Henry Moskowitz, Copyright, 1928, by Harcourt, Brace & Company, Inc.

144 Chandler, ibid; P. 278.

145 Chandler, ibid; P. 278.

146 James N. Vaughan, *On Modern Intolerance*, The Commonweal Reader (N. Y. 1950) P. 95.

147 Vaughan, ibid; P. 96.

148 Vaughan, ibid, P. 97.

149 Cf. Commager, op. cit. P. 641-45. This opinion was reversed in the Barnette case in 1943. cf. Commager, ibid; P. 645-49. For a fuller report see Dodd, op. cit.; page 540-48. The opinion of Justice Jackson is, by now, a classic.

150 Vaughan, ibid; P. 99. "God made man," Vaughan concludes, "to be free; else men are only animals. Freedom is manhood. The area of human freedom should never be so narrowed as to make the fear of man's force and ostracism the substitute for self-responsonsibility and the fear of God which are along the beginnings of all wisdom." P. 103. Cf. Emmett John Hughes, *Report From Spain*.

151 Thomas A. Bailey, *A Diplomatic History of the American People*, (New York, 1946) P. 741. Appleton-Century-Crofts, Inc.

152 Ibid, Bailey. Results of Gallup Poll, n. 741.

153 Cf. Bailey, ibid; P. 667 ff.

154 The Commonweal, June 24, 1938, excerpted P. 230. italics supplied.

155 Cited in Commonweal July 15, 1938, P. 327.

156 Cited in Commonweal, ibid; P. 327. Teachers at Fordham University, a Jesuit school, were not hampered in any way by the then President, Rev. Robert I. Gannon, from taking positions differing from the above. There were those who did.

157 Some of the criticism sent to the editors of the Commonweal is given here: "Freedom of the Church to do her divine work is above and beyond all other liberty whether political or economic." Another: "If your combination statement on Spain is the best you can do, better pull down the blinds and turn the key." Another: "But the Spanish war, Mr. Editor, is a revolt of the God-loving people against a diabolical plot against a government of oppression inspired and financed by Moscow and its Arch Devil Stalin." Selected from printed letters appearing in Commonweal, July 15, 1938, P. 325.

158 Leonard, op. cit. P. 64. 1913 was the year of the famous Pujo investigation of control of money and credit. See Commager, Documents II, P. 258, for excerpts from that report.

159 Lucey, op. cit. P. 491. In case the phrase "by industries" is unclear, presumption dares to point out that the reference is to industrial unionism.

160 Lucey, ibid, P. 491.

161 The A.C.T.U. was founded in New York City, in 1937. Its Chaplain, Father John Monaghan, is one of the leading "labor priests of the country". Malcolm Johnson—Crime on the Labor Front, P. 218 (McGraw-Hill Book Co.) calls him a fighter with a whiplash tongue and a fiery eloquence." Johnson quotes him, P. 220, as saying "When the Church and the community cease to be interested in the men that labor, both the Church and the community die."

162 Lucey, ibid, P. 523.

163 Lucey, ibid; P. 523. Hardly prejudicial in its favor, Widick and Howe say of the A.C.T.U.: "One of the A.C.T.U.'s big triumphs has been in the Transport Workers' Union where its specially trained followers helped defeat a Stalinist machine that had run the union for fourteen years." They also make this astounding claim: "At present, there are 100 Catholic labor schools, from which 7500 (sic) students graduate each year into the labor movement." As Churchill once remarked "Some chicken, some neck." B. J. Widick and Irving Howes the U.A.W. and Walter Reuther (N.Y. 1949) n at P. 156. The A.C.T.U. deserves an historian and a history.

164 The Church and Social Order. A statement of the Archbishops and Bishops of the ADM. Board of the N.C.W.C. 1940. P. 1.

165 Johnson, ibid; P. 214-226. "There is little union democracy in the I.L.A. (International Longshoreman's Association (Union) —A few West Side union leaders, aided by a group of courageous Catholic priests from Xavier Labor School and the nearby parishes, have tried to run clean locals." Daniel Bell, Fortune, June, 1951, P. 196.

166 The Portable F. Scott Fitzgerald, New York, 1945, P. 565. The Viking Press.

167 Church and Social Order, P. 1. By S. L. Greensdale, The Macmillan Company, N. Y.

168 Jules Weinberg. Priests, Workers and Communists, Harpers Magazine, Nov. 1948, cited at P. 56. Permission to quote granted by Pritchett-Brandt, author's representatives.

169 The Christian In Action, Statement of the Bishops of the United States, 1948, N.C.W.C. P. 4.

170 Cantwell, Secularism in Church, The Commonweal Reader, P. 180. italics supplied Harpers, N. Y., 1950 (Copyright, The Commonweal). See the speech

of Bishop Bernard J. Sheil before the Chicago C.I.O. convention in 1945. It appears, with an introduction by Francis Downing, in Commonweal, January 5, 1945, PP. 294-96. The C.I.O. later distributed it in pamphlet form.

171 Cantwell, ibid; P. 181, italics supplied.

172 Cantwell, ibid; P. 181. Given Cicero, Illinois, in 1951—a negro prevented by physical force from occupying a home for which he had paid rent, we have not all been touched by the pregnancy of Father Cantwell's questions. It is fair to presume some Catholics in the Cicero destructive mob.

173 Dunne, The Commonweal Reader, P. 156.

174 Dunne, ibid; P. 165. It is possible that there are Catholics who are wholly unaffected by the Cantwell-Dunne, et. al. argument. Perhaps more than argument—example—is required. Father John La Farge, S. J. has been arguing and acting in the Catholic Interracial Council, for years; as yet it whispers.

175 Ryan, *Social Justice and The State,* the Commonweal Reader, P. 177.

176 *New York Times,* July 18, 1951, P. 31C.

177 *N. Y. Times* for a declaration on the need for increased interest in the religious and moral needs of rural communities, as stated, in Rome, by the first International Congress on Rural Problems, see *N. Y. Times,* August 12, 1951, P. 80.

179 That the Catholic Press Association, at its convention in Rochester, N. Y. invited Senator McCarthy to be its guest speaker, hardly makes it a candidate for a Nobel Prize.

180 Purcell, op. cit. P. 171.

181 Trans. by Henry Reeve, edited by Henry S. Commanger, NY., Oxford Univ. Press, 1947, pp. 195-197. This selection is drawn from the first part of *De la démocratie en Amerique,* published in 1835.

182 Delivered I January 1891. Reprinted by the Catholic Interracial Council, 20 Vesey Street, N. Y.

183 NCWC, Washington, D.C., 1939 ed., pp. 19-20.

184 *Ibid,* pp. 22-23.

185 *Ibid,* pp. 23-24.

186 *Ibid,* p. 26.

187 *Ibid,* pp. 26-27. Italics in this section supplied. When one recalls the date (1919) and the high authority of this document (the bishops of the Administrative Council of the National Catholic War Council) one is not surprised by the designation "radical" given to it by many contemporary commentators.

188 *Ibid,* pp. 27-28

189 *Sertum Laetitiae,* Catholic Mind, Vol XXXVII, No. 886, 22 November 1939, p. 927. In this connection, the note in *Civil Liberties,* the organ of the American Civil Liberties Union, No. 91, April 1951 is worth quoting: 'Louisiana: Archbishop Joseph F. Rommel of New Orleans told clergy and parishoners that segregation must end in Catholic churches and activities and efforts were made to end the practice in social and civic functions.' Several northern dioceses have been officially and effectively interracial for a long time. Today, one Archdiocese in the deep South, New Orleans, and two border archdioceses, Washington, D. C., and St. Louis, are non-segregated in churches, schools, seminaries, religious houses, hospitals, welfare activities, etc. . . . The movement is spreading elsewhere. The overcoming of internal resistance to these changes has been sufficiently aired in the press". For details, cf. The *Catholic Interracial Review,* 20 Vesey Street, N. Y.

190 NCWC, Washington, D. C., 1948.

191 *Man and the State,* Univ. of Chicago Press, 1951 pp. 157-162 and pp. 181-182. The entire must be read to get the whole scope of the argument. The

volume also contained a justification of democracy as the sole reasonable evolution of Christian principles, and brilliant chapters on human rights and world government. The references will bring the student into contact with most contemporary Catholic political thought.

192 The same author has done this in his *True Humanism*, N. Y., Charles Scribner's Sons, 1938, chap. iv.

ACKNOWLEDGMENTS

Our indebtedness for permission to quote is gratefully acknowledged to the following publishers, individuals and authors' representatives:

America, Carnegie Endowment for International Peace, Catholic Historical Review, Catholic Truth Society, The Clarendon Press, Librarie Armand Colin, Columbia University, The Commonweal, Country Dollar Press, Thomas Y. Crowell Company, Mr. Mario de la Cueva, Duke University Press, Harper & Brothers, Harper's Magazine, Alfred A. Knopf, Inc., Little Brown & Company, Sister Joan de Lourdes, McGraw-Hill Book Company, Inc., The Macmillan Company, National Catholic Welfare Conference, The New York Times, Oxford University Press, Pellegrini & Cudahy Publishers, Princeton University Press, Mary Pritchett-Barbara Brandt, The Review of Politics, Rinehart & Company, Inc., Sheed & Ward, The Society of Authors, Thought, The University of Chicago Press, The University of North Carolina Press, University of Pennsylvania Press.

CONTRIBUTING AUTHORS

Alexander, Edgar, New York; former German Center Party; member of the Cultural Policy Committee of the Reichstag; author of *Mythus Hitler, Deutsches Brevier, Lebendiger Catholizismus, German Philosophy, Christianity and the Middle East, European Unity;* editor of, *Die Kirche und die Soziale Frage;* contributor to the *Encyclopedia Americana;* at present working on *Rome and Moscow* (Carnegie Grant).

Castañeda, Carlos E., Professor of Latin American History, University of Texas; member of the Mexican Academy of History; author of *The Mexican Side of the Texan Revolution, Our Catholic Heritage in Texas* (VII vols.), etc.

Downing, Francis, Professor of Political Science, Brooklyn College; formerly assistant educational director, United Automobile Workers; associate editor of *Commonweal*.

Haag, Henri, Docteur en Philosophie et Lettres; Maitre des Conferences, Université de Louvain; author, *Les Origines du Catholicisme Libéral en Beligiqué,* etc.; member of the Comité de Rédaction, *Revue generale Belge*.

Hamilton, Carlos D., Professor in the Faculty of Law in the State University of Chile and of Spanish and Hsipanic American Literature at Hunter College, New York; author of *Introduccion a la Filosofia Social, Filosofia juridica de Francisco Vitoria, Comunidad de Pueblos Hispanicos,* etc.

Hollis, Christopher, Member of Parliament; one of the editors of the *London Tablet;* author of The *Monstrous Regiment, The American Heresy,* etc.

Juhasz, William; formerly of the Faculty of History of Religion and Culture, Szeged University, Hungary, and editor of *Vigilia,* Catholic scientific monthly. Author of *History of Religion, The Culture of the Incas, Technical Civilization and Christendom,* etc.; Research in the National Committee for a Free Europe.

Micaud, Charles, Professor of International Relations, University of Virginia; author of *The French Right and Nazi Germany, 1933-1939,* etc.

Moody, Joseph, N. editor; Professor of Modern European History, Cathedral College and Notre Dame College.

Ossowski, Zbigniew M., Master in Law, Poznan University, editor of resistance journal *Polska Abrodzona.*

Pechacek J., editor of Radio Free Europe in Munich, Germany; leading personality in Czechoslovak Catholic Youth Movement. Previously to the Communist Coup he was secretary to the Czech Vice-Premier, Jan Sramek.

Vignaux, Paul, Directeur d'études a l'École des Hautes Etudes de Paris; Secretary-General, Syndicat Général de l'Education Nationale (CFTC) ; author of *Traditionalisme et Syndicalisme, Nominalisme au XIIe Siècle,* etc.

Zoltowski, Adam, Director of the Polish Research Center, Ltd., London; formerly Professor at the University of Vilna; author of *The Border of Europe,* etc.

INDEX